The Advertising Age

Encyclopedia of Advertising

THE AdvertisingAge

Encyclopedia of Advertising

Volume 3

P–Z

Editors
JOHN MCDONOUGH AND THE MUSEUM OF
BROADCAST COMMUNICATIONS

KAREN EGOLF, ADVERTISING AGE

Illustration Editor
JACQUELINE V. REID
HARTMAN CENTER FOR SALES, ADVERTISING, AND
MARKETING HISTORY OF DUKE UNIVERSITY

FITZROY DEARBORN
An Imprint of the Taylor & Francis Group
New York · London

Published in 2003 by
Fitzroy Dearborn
An imprint of the Taylor and Francis Group
29 West 35th Street
New York, NY 10001

Published in Great Britain by
Fitzroy Dearborn
An imprint of the Taylor and Francis Group
11 New Fetter Lane
London EC4P 4EE

10 9 8 7 6 5 4 3 2 1

British Library and Library of Congress Cataloguing-in-Publication Data are available.

ISBN 1-57958-172-2

First published in the USA and UK 2003

Typeset by Andrea Rosenberg
Printed by Edwards Brothers, Ann Arbor, Michigan
Cover design by Peter Aristedes, Chicago Advertising and Design, Chicago, Illinois

Front cover illustrations: *Pepperidge Farm Goldfish,* courtesy of Campbell Soup Company. *Reggie!* candy bar. *Packard Motor Car Company,* used with permission of Studebaker National Museum Archives. *Carbolic Smoke Ball. Close-Up Toothpaste;* the CLOSE-UP print ad was reproduced courtesy of Chesebrough-Pond's USA Co. *Truth* antismoking campaign, courtesy of the American Legacy Foundation. *Absolut Vodka* (Absolut Warhol), under permission by V&S Vin & Sprit AB, Absolut Country of Sweden Vodka & Logo; Absolut, Absolut Bottle Design and Absolut Calligraphy are trademarks owned by V&S Vin & Sprit AB, © 2001 V&S Vin & Sprit AB. *Tio Pepe,* courtesy of Gonzalez Byass. *Chocolates Matias López.*

Back cover illustrations: WOOK radio station, Washington, D.C. *Corn Nuts,* courtesy of Kraft Foods Holdings, Inc. *Wheaties,* courtesy of Michelle Akers and the General Mills Archives. *Rock the Vote,* courtesy of Rock the Vote Education Fund. *Dial Soap,* courtesy of the Dial Corporation. *War Production Board. Harness' Electropathic Belt.*

CONTENTS

LIST OF ENTRIES

P

Package Design

The package has become a symbol of everything that advertising and experience have established in the consumer's mind about a product. Without its package, a brand is nothing more than a commodity. The notion of the package as a unique signature element is so powerful that it helped displace the storekeeper as adviser and counselor to the consumer. The combination of branding and packaging made possible the self-service revolution in the marketplace, a change many retailers did not welcome at first, as it came at the expense of their control over portions and prices.

Beyond its function as a container and preserver, the package is the manufacturer's last defense against losing the sale and works in partnership with advertising—"a silent salesman," the *Wall Street Journal* has called it. If the job of advertising is to stimulate demand, the purpose of the package is to close the sale, to make a bold statement of character at the point of purchase that either beckons with the promise of something new or comforts with the reassurance of something familiar. Either way, the package is a statement of standardization, a nullification of spontaneity, surprise, and irregularity.

Because of the latter role, the term *packaging* is disparaging in some contexts—the packaging of vacations, for example, or of a presidential candidate—even though the purpose of any package is to provide the consumer with a sense of certified purity. It is the prefabricated unreality of such purity that disturbs the social critics, who have argued that some things should be allowed to proceed with a natural spontaneity. The problem for the consumer, however, is that spontaneity offers no guarantee of satisfaction. The packaged "environment" or "experience" as something safe reached its peak in the success of Disneyland and other theme parks, not to mention the Carnival cruise and the Club Med vacation.

The importance of the package to the sale is so crucial that often more time is spent on designing the package than the product. A package's impact, however, is often nullified on the store shelf when it is placed beside a package of equal impact, and together they contribute to the intense design clutter created when perhaps 30,000 products in a store are calling out simultaneously for attention. The ambient "clutter" of advertising on television and in magazines can be ignored far more easily than the actual clutter of competing packages in a retail supermarket.

Early Packaging

Among the first products to adopt distinctive packaging were the patent medicines marketed in England and America as early as the 18th century. But package and label were not yet a guarantee of content. In 1754 an American-made preparation was passed off as Stoughton's Drops, an English elixir, using a shipment of Stoughton bottles and labels, despite the fact that such trademark piracy was already illegal. As early as 1623 King James I of England offered patent protection not only to a soap product but also to its labeling or "trade dress," which was distinguished by a rose and crown. Although counterfeiting and substitutions would always represent problems in trademark law, the notion that a package had some legal protection traces back at least to the earliest colonial times and continues today in most copyright codes, though it does not extend to certain structural features that flow naturally from a package's function, such as handles or an attached top.

Although the underlying technologies required for package making, such as paper and cardboard production and multicolored lithography, progressed from the late 1700s through the 19th century (the first paper bag–making machine was built in Bethlehem, Pennsylvania, in 1852), packaging as a mass commercial marketing function began to achieve momentum only at the threshold of the 20th century. It came with the development of three things: first, folding boxes and the machinery to assemble and stock them; second, the technology of canning, which was first developed in France in 1795 and took a big leap forward in the 1850s when Gail Borden managed to safely package condensed milk in a vacuum-packed can; and third, bottle-making technology that introduced the first screw-top bottle in 1872 and the first automatic glass-blowing machine in 1903.

Among the first products to utilize the transformational power of packaging was oatmeal, which from the 1870s through the turn of the century was promoted up the food chain from horse feed to a "delicacy for the epicure" and "a delight to the children." Branding and packaging gave the product that soon became famous as Quaker Oats a perceived personality that could be promoted and sold anywhere. In his book *The Total Package* (1995), design critic Thomas Hine called it "alchemy through packaging." Packaging gradually became the third of marketing's power tools, joining advertising and branding; any one of these might make for a marketing success, but all three together could virtually guarantee a triumph. Recognition of the power of the package did not come instantly, however. As late as 1900, only 7 percent of print advertising carried any photo or artwork of the box or container, according to the 1928 book *Packages That Sell*.

Its relative anonymity began to change as packaging opened vast opportunities for all marketers, not just perishable commodity producers such as J.A. Wilson Meatpacking Company and Libby, McNeill & Libby. It provided manufacturers in all categories the opportunity to reposition and expand their selling and pricing strategies. The same Walworth hammer or wrench once offered in bulk in the hardware store could be packaged in an attractive box and sold at a premium as an item of gift merchandise. This development of course was not lost on any marketer's competition, which typically responded in kind, setting off a type of "arms race" in packaging design.

The "Science" of Packaging

As the importance of package design grew, so did the sense of specialization surrounding it. After World War I, a large-scale manufacturer would think twice before trusting his own instincts to create a package. Psychological factors came into play as increasingly sophisticated marketers recognized the emotional overtones of a package's visual elements: shape, color, graphics, and imagery. They all became "a battle ground of theory and argument," according to *Fortune* magazine in 1931. Advertising people tended to favor food packages that prominently pictured their contents in appetizing ways, while a new breed of professional design specialists favored "purity of physical form," or abstracted representations free of the detail reality imposes. Some manufacturers continued to regard the package as a container with little selling power, although that view was in decline by the 1920s. In May 1931 the American Management Association held a four-day symposium in New York City devoted exclusively to packaging science. While some companies clung sentimentally to outdated designs created by a deceased founder, Procter & Gamble Company President Richard Deupree regularly revised and updated the graphics of his company's classic Ivory Soap brand.

As design specialists entered the packaging field in the early 1930s, they brought with them a strong sense of German modernism that was often at odds with the conservatism of many advertisers, whose attitude was summed up by Henry Ford when he said, "I wouldn't give a nickel for all the art in the world." Ford's cars reflected his indifference to design and packaging, which would become one of the reasons General Motors Corporation would overtake Ford Motor Company in the early 1930s using a strategy of annual design changes that put a high value on visual appeal and styling.

The same was true in the packaged-goods field. In the 1920s designer Arthur S. Allen became a prominent exponent of color and simplicity, designing or supervising the packaging for Graham crackers, Lifebuoy soap, Lux soap, Eveready dry cells, Kleenex tissues, Baker's chocolate, and the Dixie Cup, itself a container. Joseph Sinel was among the major U.S. designers most influenced by the German design ethos. He believed that a package was a three-dimensional cube, cylinder, or rectangle and that its label should make the most of such possibilities. His design for the Van Camp soup can was dominated by a deep V cradled in the curve of a sideways C against a cool, steel blue background.

A few package designers worked for ad agencies. Rene Clarke, for example, created the Snowdrift cooking fat can and cosmetics marketer Richard Hudnut's Le Debut powders box while at the Calkins & Holden ad agency. But most worked in their own studios and believed that packaging was part of the larger scheme of industrial design. They saw the package as a combination of structure and graphics in a way that the average advertising craftsman who worked with flat graphics did not. These designers included Norman Bel Geddes, whose streamlined work included the General Motors Futurama pavilion at the 1939 New York World's Fair and the boardroom of advertising agency J. Walter Thompson Company in New York City; Walter Dorwin Teague, who designed the Ford Pavilion at the 1939 World's Fair and a number of Eastman Kodak Company cameras; Donald Deskey, whose work spanned the furniture creations produced for New York's Radio City Music Hall to the orange and blue target design he created for the first package for P&G's Tide detergent in 1947; and, most well known of all, Raymond Loewy, creator of the Pennsylvania K4S streamlined steam locomotive, the 1938 Studebaker Champion, and the Coldspot refrigerator for Sears, Roebuck & Company.

While many of these designs were architectural in nature, and a long way from the package goods sold in grocery stores, they were nonetheless packages; as such, they provided the inspiration for a generation of purely graphic designers who turned to packaging. By the end of the 1930s the concept of packaging had expanded to include everything from the simple toothpaste tube (first introduced by the Colgate-Palmolive-Peet Company) to the retail environment in which it was sold. Functional machines such as radios, vacuum cleaners, kitchen appliances, cars, and steam engines were created with a sense of form and glamour that hid their working components without affecting their function.

Stores as Packages

Another area of marketing that felt the impact of packaging was retailing. By the end of the 20th century retail stores were as much "packages" as were the thousands of packages they contained. In

1916 Clarence Sanders, responding to the increased volume of package goods, organized the shelf space of his Memphis, Tennessee, Piggly Wiggly food store as a series of aisles through which customers could pass, making shopping something close to a self-directed production line process. By allowing the package to speak for itself, Sanders expanded his chain to 1,200 stores within six years and established the blueprint for modern self-service systems.

Restaurants also saw the possibilities of speeding and standardizing casual eating long before the McDonald's Corporation arrived on the scene. Although a restaurant did not package the food early in the century, it organized and systematized the process of having a meal, thus lowering prices by removing such time- and labor-consuming elements as table service. The Horn & Hardart Automat, which first packaged the fast-food dining experience as a business, opened in 1908 in Philadelphia, Pennsylvania. In 1921 White Castle became the first freestanding restaurant of standard design, providing a standardized menu that offered reliable uniformity without an overabundance of choices. Howard Johnson's followed in 1925, starting as an ice cream parlor, then expanding to package the dining experience for motorists. At the same time, gas stations were undergoing a revolution in packaging, as companies such as Shell Oil Company, Gulf Refining Company, Texaco, and Standard Oil Company began to impose an architectural cohesion and a single identity onto their empires. Teague was commissioned to design the classic Texaco A-frame service station.

By the mid-20th century, package design fell into certain expected graphic and color patterns that had been dictated by previous experience and successes. The bull's-eye graphic of P&G's Oxydol laundry detergent was varied and carried forward in the concentric circles used for the Tide package. These designs and their colors were not arbitrary. The dominant orange and yellow used for the Tide box were intended to alarm and convey a sense of heavy-duty power. (Those colors distinguished the brand from P&G's milder Dreft.) The bold lettering of the word "Tide" was in blue and intended to offset the possible dangers implied in the orange and yellow with a safer, reassuring emotional message. P&G was aware of the similarities between its Tide and Oxydol designs and took care to distinguish the two. Oxydol was plainly a target design centered on the "O." Tide, on the other hand, used concentric circles of bright colors behind the brand. "They are less likely to be perceived as a target," Thomas Hine suggested, "and more as waves . . . of force. Both [designs] reinforce the name of the product, which speaks of something both wet and inexorable." Not surprisingly, the correlation between color and emotions is not consistent from culture to culture. In Japan soft pastels express the traditional social contract of mutual accommodation and respect, and dominate much of packaging design. In the United States bold color contrasts have been attributed to the country's history of individualism. American brand names in the packaged soaps category typically are single-syllable words printed on a 10 degree to 20 degree angle ascending upward from left to right, suggesting all the positive implications of progress.

"Hidden Persuaders"

At the same time, design elements also became more subtle, evoking notions of "hidden persuaders" at work. As far back as the 1930s, psychologist Louis Cheskin asked a sample of 1,000 consumers to evaluate two different products. In fact, the products were identical, except that one was packaged with a graphic design that featured triangles, the other, circles. Eighty percent preferred the product with circles incorporated in its packaging. Exactly why people preferred circles to triangles is less important than the consistency of the preference. Cheskin consulted with P&G on the design of both the Oxydol and Tide packages.

As packaging technology grew, marketers were quick to discover the opportunities presented to prepackage ingredients that once were sold separately, setting off a whole new category of "convenience" products. In 1954 Swanson, a unit of the Campbell Soup Company, introduced one of the breakthrough products of the post–World War II era: the frozen TV dinner. Sold in aluminum trays compartmentalized to contain separate foods (meat, potato, vegetable, and later dessert), it required only reheating and could be served straight out of the package. Infinite variations on and extensions of TV dinner cuisine followed, from simple to gourmet, from generous portions to low-calorie, low-fat offerings.

The era of general prosperity that followed World War II saw the launch of an enormous number of new products, some of which introduced fresh package design concepts. Secret and Ban deodorants were applied with a large ball that transferred the product from inside the bottle to the skin in a constant rolling motion. The repositioning of Marlboro cigarettes by the Philip Morris Companies from a woman's brand to a man's was accompanied by a package redesign that turned the flimsy cigarette pack into a more rigid cardboard container that became one of the three main selling points in the advertising tag line, "Filter, flavor, flip-top box." It was one of the first campaigns created for the brand by the Leo Burnett Company, which won the account in November 1954 from the Biow Agency. Deodorants, cleaners, paints, and insecticides began appearing in aerosol spray cans that expelled an even, cloudlike plume at the touch of a tab.

Changing Sizes and Materials

By the late 1950s packages were offering consumers an ever-proliferating choice among portion sizes. Coca-Cola went from its six-ounce bottle, to 12 ounces, then 16, and on to one liter and two liter sizes; from the six-pack to the eight-pack; from returnable glass bottles to disposable cans and glass and plastic bottles; from cans requiring a "church key" to self-opening snap-top rings in 1963 (rings that consumers soon discovered worked in parking meters, adding unanticipated value to a Coke or Pepsi); from the six-pack as the standard unit of sale to the 24-can case. The switch from glass to cans was, like most packaging breakthroughs, as much a product of technology as design. The all-aluminum beer can first appeared in 1958 and eventually replaced the more expensive tin-and-steel can with its awkward vertical seam on the side.

The change in packaging materials affected all product categories. Milk went from glass to cardboard to that most universal of materials, plastic. The trend in packaging was inevitably toward larger-sized containers as marketers found that bigger portions were an inexpensive way to justify higher prices while at the same time giving the consumer extra value, at least on a unit basis (i.e., buying 64 ounces of a product would cost less per ounce than buying 12 ounces). But when Campbell introduced its "soup for one" can in the 1980s, it promptly flopped. Campbell thought it saw a packaging opportunity for the young single person that was not there.

Package redesign generally is not undertaken lightly or even preemptively. Typically it comes when there is evidence of a slip in market share or a shift in the competitive environment. By the end of the 20th century, a redesign was considered important enough to call in one of the many consulting agencies that specialized in packaging, such as Landon & Associates or DC Worldwide. Less quantifiable but just as necessary is the need to keep the product graphics in step with the spirit of the times. This often requires walking a fine line between ignoring fads while recognizing fundamental change. In the late 1960s psychedelic imagery was everywhere, but few marketers of major brands embraced it in their packaging, partly because of its controversial association with drug use but mainly because it was seen as a passing trend. Packaging design, like a logo, is a fundamental aspect of an established brand's identity and usually changes only incrementally. Advertising instead can become the outlet for a marketer's urge to generate brand excitement because it is far more flexible and can easily accommodate the most ephemeral fad, then quickly move on to something else; it is far enough removed from the most basic elements of product identity to insulate the brand from mistakes. Most packaging changes are subtle and driven more by improvements in technology than by image tinkering—such as the switch from metal toothpaste tubes to plastic ones. Other packaging changes retain their familiar structure while at the same time incorporating more obvious improvements. When shampoo marketers abandoned glass bottles for plastic ones in the 1960s and 1970s, all that was lost was the occasional hazard of broken glass on the shower floor. Such improvements may be briefly promoted but usually are adopted quickly by competitors, removing any special competitive advantage.

Concern for security and safety has become an issue in package design in recent years, particularly for medications and food products that lend themselves to invasive tampering and deliberate contamination. While a secure container can be a useful marketing point, it would seldom be the central one. Like auto safety features, it is something people are not inclined to pay for. The incentive lies more with the marketer, which must take measures to protect itself from product liability lawsuits.

Transcending Containment

In certain rare preserves of luxury commerce, the product is so defined by the package that the power of the package becomes more precious than the goods inside. In other words, some packages become so compelling as sheer works of art that they alone become the object of desire. Such is often called "experiential packaging" in the industry. The music business has produced some intriguing examples of such packaging in opulent boxed sets of recordings that embody two of the most important functions of packaging at its highest level: that it stir an uncontrollable impulse to acquire the item and that the buyers be able to boldly showcase their ownership in a way that evokes esteem in themselves and admiration in their friends. The statement is not in the music, which the owner perhaps already has in other forms, but in the box itself as a work of visual splendor.

But in packaging a product to be consumed, the designers of these CD boxed sets have achieved a rare distinction. Such packaging—which also characterizes expensive liquors (Absolut vodka), perfumes, and elegantly bound book collections—transcends the function of containment. The product sits forever on exhibit as an ornament or item of furniture, so invested in its own design that its owners dare not open it, as if to do so would be to defile it.

JOHN MCDONOUGH

Further Reading

Arthur D. Little, Inc., *The Role of Packaging in the U.S. Economy: Report to the American Foundation for Management Research, Inc.*, Cambridge, Massachusetts: American Foundation for Management Research, 1966

Bender, May, *Package Design and Social Change*, New York: AMACOM, 1975

Franken, Richard B., and Carroll Burton Larabee, *Packages That Sell*, New York and London: Harper, 1928

Gobé, Marc, *Emotional Branding: The New Paradigm for Connecting Brands to People*, New York: Allworth Press, 2001

Hine, Thomas, *The Total Package: The Evolution and Secret Meanings of Boxes, Bottles, Cans, and Tubes*, Boston: Little Brown, 1995

"The Package As Merchandiser," *Fortune* 3, no. 5 (May 1931)

Sook, Kim Queena, "The Potion's Power Is in Its Packaging," *Wall Street Journal* (21 December 2000)

Stern, Walter, editor, *Handbook of Package Design Research*, New York: Wiley, 1981

Wilson, Richard Guy, Dianne H. Pilgrim, and Dickran Tashjian, *The Machine Age in America, 1918–1941*, New York: Brooklyn Museum, 1986

Packard, Vance 1914–1996

U.S. Writer and Social Critic

Vance Packard, born in 1914 in Granville Summit, Pennsylvania, was one of the more controversial figures in advertising during the 1950s and 1960s. Packard, who earned his bachelor's degree from Pennsylvania State University in 1936 and his master's degree from Columbia University in 1937, worked as a reporter, columnist, and editor for various newspapers and the Associated Press until 1942. Over 15 years, he wrote for various national magazines, primarily pieces on economics and the behavioral sciences. He also taught courses in reporting and writing at New York University and Columbia.

Packard made his primary contribution to advertising in his role as a social critic. He was thrust into prominence with the publication of his first book, *The Hidden Persuaders,* in 1957. It quickly climbed the best-seller charts and was soon translated into several languages. Although the book reached a very wide audience in a very short time, it did not win universal acclaim. In fact, accounts of the time reveal a deep dichotomy: consumers loved the book; advertisers loathed it.

The Hidden Persuaders, whose title itself played to cold war fears of wide-ranging conspiracies, was written for an audience of postwar consumers who had seen the supply of available goods expand exponentially and whose incomes had also risen. Packard posited that advertisers were guilty of mass manipulation by using knowledge gleaned from psychologically based interviews, or "depth probing," to sell their goods. Marketers had used—or, as he contended, abused—psychology to discover new ways of selling by appealing to consumers' anxieties and aspirations without their conscious knowledge. The book, advertised as a study of "the way most of us are being manipulated—far more than we realize—in the patterns of our everyday lives," was the first published book-length history of motivation research.

The Hidden Persuaders recounted many of the "depth probing" studies being done at that time to determine consumer attitudes toward various products, and focused on the methods Packard believed were being used to manipulate consumers. While he stopped short of calling for a ban on such practices, Packard did ask for restraint in their use. He was disturbed by the "Orwellian configurations of the world toward which the 'persuaders' seem to be nudging us," and was concerned that some of the "persuaders" seemed to "fall unwittingly into the attitude that man exists to be manipulated." The book was a call to morality and ethics on the part of advertisers, and to awareness on the part of consumers. Conceding that "some pushing and hauling of the citizenry is probably necessary to make our $400 billion-a-year economy work," Packard noted that people can "choose not to be persuaded," so long as they are aware of what is going on.

Consumers hailed the new work; advertisers, on the other hand, were not so complimentary. It was discussed in advertising circles, but rarely in glowing terms. *Advertising Age* ran several items about the book; before it was published, one headline said,

"Packard book is searching probe of motivationists"; after it had reached popularity, this changed to: "'The Hidden Persuaders' is a disservice to advertising." Three years later, prior to the publication of Packard's *The Waste Makers,* the headline was a testy "That man's here again." (Still, when *Advertising Age* selected its top 100 advertising influencers of the century in 1999, Packard was cited as number 99.)

Reviewers discredited Packard on the basis of a lack of scientific evidence for his claims and for his use of generalizations and anecdotal evidence; he was called a "morality huckster" who seemed to make advertisers "unnecessarily sinister."

One critic, ad consultant James D. Woolf, wrote, "This book, as I say, cannot possibly increase public respect for advertising and the advertising business, and it will certainly do nothing to heighten your pride and my pride in our means of making a living." However, the book had no such intent; it was, simply, a study of motivational research into the psychological buying habits of the public. It was written to highlight some of the perceived abuses of advertising and to increase public awareness of advertisers' tactics.

Packard himself—along with his publisher, which had to quickly order reprints—was surprised at how popular the book became. He posited that shoppers are constantly led astray by advertisers' attempts to seek out their innermost needs and fears, to overcome any resistance to their messages, and to form the minds of consumers. He cited examples of efforts to subtly persuade consumers by playing on their subconscious habits and thought processes so that the appeals are, in a real sense, "hidden." He identified these target areas as the need for emotional

Vance Packard.
Courtesy of Vance P. Packard.

security, reassurance of worth, ego gratification, creative outlets, love object, sense of power, sense of roots, and immortality.

Although his other books were not as successful as *The Hidden Persuaders,* each was well received, and several did become best-sellers in their own right. Each concerned some aspect of American life, from Packard's views on social stratification and American behavior (*The Status Seekers*) to planned obsolescence (*The Waste Makers*) to early "Big Brother" concerns (*The Naked Society*) and on to sexuality, the rootlessness of the American people, and the impact of our changing society on children's lives (*The Sexual Wilderness, A Nation of Strangers,* and *Our Endangered Children*). Packard died at the age of 82, having popularized through his writing his social ideas based on America's postwar prosperity and the rise of consumerism.

BARBARA KNOLL

Biography

Born in Granville Summit, Pennsylvania, in 1914; earned bachelor's degree from Pennsylvania State University, 1936; earned master's degree from Columbia University, 1937; worked as a reporter, columnist, and editor for various newspapers and the Associated Press until 1942; wrote *The Hidden Persuaders,* 1957; wrote *The Waste Makers,* 1960; taught courses in reporting and writing at New York University and Columbia; died 12 December 1996.

Selected Publications

The Hidden Persuaders, 1957; revised edition, 1980
The Status Seekers: An Exploration of Class Behavior in America and the Hidden Barriers That Affect You, Your Community, Your Future, 1959
The Waste Makers, 1960
The Pyramid Climbers, 1962
The Naked Society, 1964
The Sexual Wilderness: The Contemporary Upheaval in Male-Female Relationships, 1968
A Nation of Strangers, 1972
The People Shapers, 1977
Our Endangered Children: Growing Up in a Changing World, 1983
The Ultra Rich: How Much Is Too Much? 1989

Further Reading

Horowitz, Daniel, *Vance Packard and American Social Criticism,* Chapel Hill: University of North Carolina Press, 1994
"Packard Book Is Searching Probe of Motivationists," *Advertising Age* (29 April 1957)
"That Man's Here Again," *Advertising Age* (8 August 1960)
Woolf, James D., "'The Hidden Persuaders' Is a Disservice to Advertising," *Advertising Age* (1 July 1957)

Packard Motor Car Company

Principal Agencies

Young & Rubicam, Inc.
Maxon, Inc.
Ruthrauff & Ryan, Inc.
D'Arcy Advertising Company, Inc.
Benton & Bowles, Inc.

The first great advertising slogan in the automotive industry was also one of the most enduring. It was introduced by J.W. Packard around 1901 in response to a potential customer's letter requesting sales literature. Having no brochures, Packard's secretary asked him how to respond, and Packard said to tell the customer to "Ask the man who owns one." By 1902 the slogan had begun to appear in ads and promotional literature. It was used for more than 50 years, nearly the entire life of the company.

The Packard Motor Car Company had its origins in the New York and Ohio Company, an electrical manufacturing operation owned by brothers J.W. and W.D. Packard, of Warren, Ohio. In 1898 J.W. Packard purchased a Winton automobile that was so plagued with problems he complained directly to Alexander Win-

ton, who apparently told Packard to build a better car if he thought he could. Packard took that advice to heart, and the brothers produced their first automobile in November 1899. In September 1900 Packard's car business, by then called the Ohio Automobile Company, exhibited and sold three of its cars at the first U.S. auto show in New York City.

In 1902 Henry B. Joy, a wealthy resident of Detroit, Michigan, purchased one of Packard's cars. He was so pleased with the vehicle that he traveled to Ohio to meet J.W. Packard and invested $25,000 in the company, which soon was renamed the Packard Motor Car Company. Packard and Joy agreed that a new manufacturing facility would be needed to meet their goal of producing 200 cars per year, and Joy soon secured additional capital and a production site in Detroit. When the company moved to its new factory and headquarters in 1903, Joy took over general management. Although he stayed in Warren, Packard retained the title of president until 1909, when he became chairman of the board. Packard died in 1928.

With the Detroit-built 1904 Model L, Packard automobiles began achieving recognition for breaking speed and endurance records. The new car bore an upright, yoke-shaped radiator and

The Packard in the Austrian Tyrol   *From the etching by E. Horter*

This 1914 ad for Packard automobiles was an early example of "lifestyle" advertising.
Used with permission of Studebaker National Museum Archives.

hexagonal wheel hub indentations, both of which would become Packard trademarks through the 1950s. In 1904 the company sold 272 cars in the United States, exceeding its earlier goal, though failing to turn a profit.

The introduction of the Packard Thirty in 1907 established Packard's reputation as a marketer of luxury cars. More than 1,400 units were sold that year. Packard soon entered the light-truck market, only to exit in 1923 to refocus on its car business. The Packard Twin Six—the first U.S. production car with a V-12 engine—was introduced in 1915, and sales in 1916 exceeded 10,000 units. Joy, the man largely responsible for building the company, became chairman of the board that year, relinquishing the title of president. The engineering expertise the company had developed with its powerful engines led Packard into the field of aviation. The company began producing the Liberty aircraft engine in 1917 and was a supplier to the Allied forces during World War I.

The 1920s saw Packard sales steadily increase, along with the size of the total automobile market. By the second half of the decade, Packard was far outselling other luxury cars such as Pierce-Arrow, Peerless, and Cadillac. The company touted its cars' reputation for quality and durability in its ad campaigns.

As the Great Depression hit, the demand for luxury cars decreased sharply. Packard offered a reduced-price model in 1932 backed by a newspaper ad blitz, but it did not truly enter the mid-priced field until 1935. A new, less-expensive model called the One-Twenty (and later an even cheaper One-Ten) was successful in dramatically increasing the company's U.S. unit sales, which soared from around 6,500 in 1933 to more than 95,000 in 1937. In 1932 Young & Rubicam (Y&R) was awarded the Packard advertising account, which it would hold for 19 years.

In April 1941 Packard introduced the Clipper, a new line of sleekly styled models, but in early 1942 the company switched to wartime production as the United States entered World War II. Packard again was a supplier for the Allied military forces, producing both marine and airplane engines, including the Rolls-Royce Merlin aircraft engine.

Despite coming through the war in good financial condition, Packard struggled to reconvert to civilian production. The first postwar model was the 1946 Clipper, essentially the same model that had been produced before the war. A series of labor problems and difficulties with steel suppliers hampered the company's efforts and contributed to financial losses. The first completely new postwar Packards were not introduced until August 1947. Production and sales began to improve in 1948, and Packard's best U.S. sales year came in 1949, when the company sold nearly 100,000 units.

Packard launched a completely redesigned lineup for 1951 with its biggest ad campaign ever, encompassing newspapers, magazines, and TV sponsorship on the ABC network, but these measures were not enough to overcome a downturn in the domestic auto market. Another big ad push for the introduction of the 1952 Packards would be Y&R's last for the company. Maxon, Inc., was appointed Packard's new agency in July 1951, moving the campaigns away from targeting traditional luxury car buyers and aiming instead at buyers stepping up from mid-market cars.

In May 1952 James J. Nance became president and general manager of Packard. Nance came from outside the auto industry, having been with General Electric's Hotpoint division. Under his direction Packard offered an extended model range for 1953, reviving the old Clipper name for a line of mid-priced cars. A shake-up in the marketing staff was accompanied by a huge ad push, with $8 million being budgeted for 1953, up from $4.5 million in 1952.

Packard's 1953 sales fell short of target and worsened in 1954, despite another huge outlay in ad spending. It was becoming more difficult for independent carmakers to turn a profit. Nance and leaders of other independents began considering mergers. Studebaker Corporation, which manufactured mass-market cars and trucks, was experiencing a sales slide and financial losses of its own. Despite the weak positions of both companies, Nance saw a merger with Studebaker as a way to cover the broader auto market and compete with the "Big Three" U.S. automakers and the recently formed American Motors Corporation. Packard bought Studebaker in October 1954, creating the Studebaker-Packard Corporation. Shortly after, Ruthrauff & Ryan was appointed the new ad agency for the Packard division.

A hot U.S. auto market and redesigned cars helped Packard's sales increase in 1955 to slightly more than 52,000 units, but Studebaker-Packard's losses totaled $29 million that year. Packard ad spending was initially sustained for the 1956 models, despite additional corporate losses. In January 1956 the company awarded the Packard account to the D'Arcy Advertising Company, but by late summer a decision had been made to cease production of Packards and close the venerable Detroit plant.

Studebaker-Packard needed an infusion of capital, and in August 1956 the Curtiss-Wright Corporation agreed to invest $35 million and assume management of the company under its chairman and president, Roy T. Hurley. Production and marketing were consolidated at the Studebaker facilities in South Bend, Indiana. D'Arcy resigned the Packard account in October, citing the consolidation as the reason. Benton & Bowles, then Studebaker's agency, was assigned the Packard account.

In early 1957 Studebaker-Packard began producing models in South Bend designated Packard Clippers. The new Packards were little more than rebadged Studebakers, however, and were poorly received, selling just more than 5,000 units. In April, Benton & Bowles resigned the Studebaker-Packard account, charging Curtiss-Wright with a "complete lack of understanding of the agency's role." Burke, Dowling and Adams, Inc., then took over the account, but tumultuous agency-client relationships continued as D'Arcy, which had held the Packard account for nine months in 1956, was again appointed the Studebaker-Packard agency. By that time, however, production of Packard-badged cars had ceased for good. The Packard name, which for decades had stood for premium luxury cars, was dropped from Studebaker-Packard's corporate moniker in 1962.

SCOTT MACDONALD

See also color plate in this volume

Further Reading

Brown, Arch, and Richard Langworth, *Great Cars of the 20th Century,* New York: Smithmark, 1991

Denison, Merrill, *The Power to Go: The Story of the Automotive Industry,* Garden City, New York: Doubleday, 1956

Longstreet, Stephen, *A Century on Wheels: The Story of Studebaker: A History, 1852–1952,* New York: Holt, 1952

National Packard Museum <www.packardmuseum.org>

Rae, John Bell, *The American Automobile: A Brief History,* Chicago: University of Chicago Press, 1965

Rubenstein, James, *The Changing US Auto Industry: A Geographical Analysis,* New York and London: Routledge, 1992

"The Sales Statistics in *The-100 Year Almanac and 1996 Market Data Book,*" *Automotive News* (24 April 1996)

Paley, William 1901–1990

U.S. Broadcasting Pioneer

William Paley, founder of the Columbia Broadcasting System (CBS), spent most of his career building the company's reputation, only to watch it be compromised and transformed in his waning years. Paley was born in Chicago, Illinois, on 28 September 1901 to Ukrainian Jewish immigrants. He attended Western Military Academy in Alton, Illinois. After attending the University of Chicago, Paley completed his studies at the University of Pennsylvania, where he received a bachelor of science degree in 1922.

At age 27 Paley left his father's successful Congress Cigar Company. Intrigued with radio's potential as a medium for advertising the company's products, he acquired a 41 percent stake in CBS in September 1928 for the sum of $417,000. The 16-station network had been formed in February of the previous year as United Independent Broadcasters but changed its name a few months later when the Columbia Phonograph Company provided financing. Columbia sold its interests back in December, leaving the way open for Paley to move in and assume control. He would turn CBS into a $5 billion broadcast empire by the time of his death in 1990.

His 41 percent ownership of the company assured him the presidency and the opportunity to make some revolutionary moves that shaped the future of broadcasting. In 1931 CBS began broadcasting over experimental TV station WRXAB in New York City while continuing to buy formidable radio stations such as WBBM-AM in Chicago, KMOX-AM in St. Louis, Missouri, and WJSV in Washington, D.C. (among whose assets was Robert Trout, who became the voice of Columbia world news as World War II approached).

In 1933 Paley formed the Columbia News Service, the world's first radio network news operation, and launched the first international daily news summary, *The CBS News World Round Up,* five years later. By 1937 CBS listed its stock on the New York Stock Exchange and entered the recorded music business by acquiring the American Record Corporation.

In the early years of the network Paley took an active part in attracting advertisers, including Creamo Cigars, a product of the American Tobacco Company. American's president, George Washington Hill, was dissatisfied with the restrictions the National Broadcasting Company (NBC) imposed on his often aggressive and somewhat crude advertising messages ("There is no spit in Creamo"). In a face-to-face meeting, Paley offered Hill a much more accommodating opportunity at CBS, including an order waving the network's policy against quoting prices. Even as Paley relaxed standards for Hill, however, he stiffened them on other fronts. He banned the advertising of such products as laxatives and deodorants and limited the time allotted to commercials, setting standards later adopted industrywide. Also, after bitter experiences in the early 1930s with corporate sponsors that used network time to broadcast political opinions and attack New Deal policies (Ford Motor Company was particularly harsh in pressing its views on listeners), he declared a policy of no opinions or personal comments in news broadcasts, a move that discouraged advertisers from using news as a platform for political opinion making.

His service as a colonel in North Africa and Italy during World War II, working in psychological warfare, prepared Paley for the rough-and-tumble process of bringing television into its prime. He returned from the service determined to seize control of his network's program content and talent from advertisers by establishing an in-house entertainment production unit and limiting advertisers to buying 30-second blocks of time.

As chairman of CBS, presiding over 30 TV affiliates in 1948, Paley launched a series of television news hallmarks, including *The CBS Morning News* (1957) and *60 Minutes* (1968). CBS challenged and overcame NBC program dominance with *I Love Lucy, The Ed Sullivan Show,* and *All in the Family.* The CBS "eye" corporate logo was synonymous with class and quality during CBS's heyday. Paley nurtured such personalities as newsmen Edward R.

William Paley.
© *CBS Photo Archive.*

ration, who became CBS's primary shareholder and business leader. After a five-year, self-imposed sabbatical, Paley deposed Thomas Wyman, who had been named CBS's chairman in 1983 and mandated much of the financially ravaging change. Even then, Paley watched with dismay as Tisch downsized staff, sold nonbroadcasting assets such as the recorded music and toys divisions, and drastically reduced the scope of the legendary media empire.

Although confined to a wheelchair, Paley spent time almost daily in his 35th-floor executive suite in CBS's "Black Rock" headquarters in Manhattan. He called his long tenure at CBS "accidental." "I was always going upward, but it wasn't really a path I laid out for myself to follow. It just happened."

An avid patron of art and theater, Paley was chairman of the Museum of Modern Art in New York City and founded the Museum of Broadcasting, to which he donated $12 million. He died on 26 October 1990 from a pneumonia-related heart attack.

DIANE MERMIGAS

Biography

Born in Chicago, Illinois, 28 September 1901; graduated from the University of Pennsylvania's Wharton School, 1922; acquired Columbia Phonographics Broadcasting System, a network of 16 radio stations, 1928, and renamed it the Columbia Broadcasting System, 1929; started experimental television broadcasts, 1931; formed the world's first radio network news operation, the Columbia News Service, 1933; launched a series of television news hallmarks, including *The CBS Morning News* (1957) and *60 Minutes* (1968); died in New York City on 26 October 1990.

Selected Publication

As It Happened: A Memoir, 1979

Further Reading

Buckman, Adam, "CBS Mobilized to Pay Tribute to Its Founder," *Electronic Media* (6 November 1990)

Christopher, Maurine, "Paley Leaves Broadcast Legacy," *Advertising Age* (8 November 1990)

Dillion, Susan J., and Don West, "Farewell to the Man in the CBS Eye," *Broadcasting and Cable Magazine* (5 November 1990)

Fox, Stephen R., *The Mirror Makers: A History of American Advertising and Its Creators,* New York: Morrow, 1984

Smith, Sally Bedell, *In All His Glory: The Life of William S. Paley, the Legendary Tycoon and His Brilliant Circle,* New York: Simon and Schuster, 1990

Murrow, John Daly, and Robert Trout and entertainers Lucille Ball, Carroll O'Connor, Jack Benny, George Burns, and Gracie Allen. Walter Cronkite, who for two decades anchored *The CBS Evening News* under Paley's tutelage, aptly observed, "The pioneer era in the history of broadcasting died with William Paley."

For more than two decades Frank Stanton handled daily management of CBS, freeing Paley to exercise his programming genius, which Stanton described as a combination of "skill, inspiration, and luck." But in later years, after fending off takeover attempts by Ted Turner, Paley often found himself overruled by CBS executives whose primary interests were financial and who felt that news and other programming should pay their own way.

Despite illness and depression, Paley made a surprising comeback in tandem with Laurence Tisch, chairman of Loews Corpo-

Papert, Koenig, Lois, Inc.

Formed in 1959 as Papert & Free; reorganized as Papert, Koenig, Lois, 1960; became first agency since 1929 to go public, 1962; Lois departed 1967; agency closed, 1969.

Major Clients

Clark Oil & Refining Corporation
National Airlines, Inc.
New York Herald Tribune
Pharmacraft Laboratories
Quaker Oats Company
Xerox Corporation

Papert, Koenig, Lois, Inc. (PKL), began in September 1959 as Papert & Free, a rare partnership whose principals consisted of two husband-and-wife teams. Frederic Papert came out of Kenyon & Eckhardt, where he had been a creative supervisor on the Pepsi-Cola and Equitable Life accounts. His wife, Diane Papert, had been a copy group head on the Revlon account at Warwick & Legler. William Free was a veteran of McCann-Erickson, where he had been an art group chief for Coca-Cola, Dorothy Gray cosmetics, and Nabisco. His wife, Marcella Free, resigned from Lennen & Newell as copy group head on Lorillard to help found the new agency.

Starting with a staff of 15, the agency set up offices in the Seagram Building in New York City. Its stated mission was to offer major agency talent in a small agency setting. Charter clients included Guards Club, Ltd., and the Courtland Line Company, makers of men's colognes and sporting goods, respectively.

In January 1960 Free returned to McCann to become executive art director. His wife also left to form a copy consulting business. In their place two new principals joined the agency: Julian Koenig and George Lois, both from the creative department of Doyle Dane Bernbach (DDB), which was then among the most admired agencies in advertising.

Koenig had already achieved legendary status in the agency business as the creator (along with art director Helmut Krone) of the "Think Small" campaign for Volkswagen. Lois had started his career at CBS, moved to Lennen & Newell and later to Sudler & Hennessey before going to DDB, where he won three gold medals from the New York Art Directors Club. He was said to be streetwise, often ill-tempered, and brilliant.

The reorganized agency, called Papert, Koenig, Lois, Inc., began a period of steady growth based on the DDB model of creative excitement. Its print work combined elements of advertising with *New Yorker*–style cartoons. Xerox assigned the advertising for its office copiers to PKL in May 1961, and the agency demonstrated the copier's simplicity by showing a chimpanzee operating the machine. Pharmacraft Laboratories picked PKL for its Fresh deodorant brand, and Clark Oil & Refining Corporation switched to PKL from Tatham-Laird, which had created the "Fizbee and the Chief" radio campaign.

PKL became a seminal agency of its time. As early as 1962 it was spinning off fresh talent that would help shape 1960s advertising, the most prominent being Carl Ally, who left PKL in July to form an agency with partner Amil Gargano. Two years later another future agency star, Marvin Sloves, moved into PKL from Ted Bates & Company; in 1967 he would become a founder of Scali, McCabe, Sloves. That same year six other executives left to form two other shops. In 1962 PKL stated that its billings had surpassed $17 million, impressive growth considering that its previous fiscal year ended with billings of $5.9 million. Ultimately, 1962 proved less profitable than stated, though still very good.

On 14 May 1962 the agency made the move that would ultimately change the financial structure of the industry. It filed with the U.S. Securities & Exchange Commission to sell 100,000 shares of class A common stock. The announcement startled the industry for several reasons. First, no ad agency since Albert Frank-Guenther Law in 1929 had made a public offering, and in that case the outstanding equity was only about 2 percent. Second, although stock offerings were being discussed in the industry, most observers assumed that the first to make the move would be a major agency. Third, the lack of hard capital in the service-oriented ad business seemed to make it an unlikely enterprise in which to sell stock. Finally, the traditional nature of the business had always favored confidentiality in deference to clients; for an agency to offer stock would require it to disclose much specific financial information.

Nevertheless, 100,000 shares, or 20 percent of PKL stock, hit the market on 20 September 1962 at $6 a share, reflecting book value of the agency. This meant a price-earnings ratio of 25, which was considered high at the time. The price quickly increased to $8, but then, like many other stocks, it was hurt during the Cuban Missile Crisis in October. By the end of the year it had stabilized at around $6. Billings for the year rose dramatically, however, from $5.9 million in 1961 to $14.7 in 1962. Other agencies also went public, including Foote, Cone & Belding (in 1963) and DDB (in 1964). In the early days of advertising initial public offerings, the move was widely regarded more as a strategy to attract and hold talent than as an attempt to raise capital, although DDB saw its price rise sharply. Other early agency equities were inclined to languish, however.

In 1964 the agency opened a London, England, office, and in June 1965 it picked up its first business from the Procter & Gamble Company, the $1.5 million Salvo detergent tablet account. It also won a $5 million assignment from National Airlines, Inc., a client it had served briefly in 1963. In an effort to diversify into hard goods, the agency acquired Century Cycle Corporation, an importer of French motorbikes, in 1966; within two years it was seeking to sell the asset.

Along with DDB the agency became a significant player in political races. It used spontaneous footage of Jacob Javits in his 1962 race to become a U.S. senator from New York. That technique led Steven Smith, husband of Jeanne Kennedy Smith and an

"If Vodka has no taste, how come I can tell which one is WOLFSCHMIDT?"

GENERAL WINE AND SPIRITS CO., NEW YORK 22. MADE FROM GRAIN, 80 OR 100 PROOF. PRODUCT OF U.S.A.

In the 1960s Papert, Koenig, Lois, Inc., distinguished itself from other ad agencies with advertising such as this work for Wolfschmidt vodka.
Courtesy Jim Beams Brands Co. All rights reserved.

influential adviser to the Kennedy family, to recommend the agency to Robert Kennedy in his 1964 Senate campaign against Kenneth Keating. PKL won the account, and Kennedy won the subsequent election.

In May 1967 PKL, then the 17th-ranked U.S. agency with billings of $40 million, underwent another reorganization. Norman Grulich replaced Koenig, who became chairman of a newly formed PKL executive committee. The reorganization came amid growing reports of an atmosphere of mayhem within the agency. In April former PKL Vice President William Casey sued to void a five-year employment contract on the grounds that he had been physically attacked by Lois and another coworker. In another confirmed incident three executives got into a fight that resulted in a production executive being knocked unconscious. "It took an hour to mop up the blood," one witness told the *Wall Street Journal.* Casey testified that he was "afraid" of Lois.

Then in September Lois, who was reportedly preparing to head a PKL special projects subsidiary, announced he was leaving the agency with two other executives, J. Ronald Holland and James Callaway, to set up a new shop, Lois Holland Callaway (LHC). PKL's billings dropped by 25 percent in the next 18 months, while LHC's rose to $22 million in 15 months. The loss of Xerox was particularly hard for PKL.

Papert took over the presidency in 1969, and three former partners from Jack Tinker & Partners joined the agency. But PKL fortunes continued to fall, and by the end of 1969, a decade after its founding, PKL faded away. LHC lasted until 1977. Lois went on to launch Lois Pitts Gershon in 1978, which evolved into Lois/USA. Louis/USA filed for bankruptcy in 1999.

JOHN McDONOUGH

Further Reading

Fox, Stephen, *The Mirror Makers: A History of American Advertising and Its Creators,* New York: Morrow, 1984

"Lois Hits Critics of Shops That Go Public," *Advertising Age* (1 June 1964)

"PKL Goes Public with 20% of Its Stock," *Advertising Age* (14 May 1962)

Prial, Frank J., "Papert-Koenig, Which Had Fast Growth As a Small Shop, Hopes Its Slump Is Ending," *Wall Street Journal* (23 May 1968)

"Two Husband-Wife Teams Form New 'Compact' Agency—Papert & Free," *Advertising Age* (21 September 1959)

"'Vicious Vitality' Is Basis of Good Ad, Says Koenig," *Advertising Age* (25 April 1966)

Paradiset

Founded by Björn Rietz, Stefan Öström, and Joakim Jonasson, in Stockholm, Sweden, 1990; majority stake acquired by DDB Needham, 1993; with the departure of Jonasson, employees were preparing to acquire the shares held by the three founders, 2001.

Major Clients
Diesel
Hennes & Mauritz
Ikea
Mandarina Duck
Thomson Travel

Paradiset, the highly creative and nonconformist Stockholm, Sweden–based advertising agency, was opened in 1990 by three college friends, Björn Rietz, Stefan Öström, and Joakim Jonasson. All three had attended Stockholm's IHR School of Marketing prior to working with various Swedish ad agencies.

Before forming Paradiset, both Öström and Jonasson had worked their way up the corporate ladder at two of Sweden's best known consumer brand marketers, Öström at global furnishings group Ikea and Jonasson at fashion and accessories retailer Hennes & Mauritz. Both left their previous employers after highly successful periods as directors of marketing.

Rietz, Öström, and Jonasson set about building an advertising agency according to three main principles. First, they believed that creative advertising sells and that it saves money because of its success in sales; second, they knew that creative advertising needs a strategic platform; and third, they resolved that their agency would offer a high-quality service to clients.

From the very beginning, however, a fourth principle came into play: the foundation on which the agency would be built should not be assembled around a few creative superstars but around a company of equals. The agency's name, Paradiset, came from this fourth principle—the creation of a horizontal organization where all employees would feel equally important, producing an advertising agency that strove to be "a paradise" for employees and clients alike.

In its first year, Paradiset won the Diesel global jeans and fashion account. This was pivotal both to building a long-standing close client relationship and to strengthening Paradiset's status as a full-service, quality agency that was not merely another new kid on the block. It proved a challenging and rewarding test for Paradiset, as the fledgling agency found itself, straight out of the blocks, handling Diesel's advertising in 89 countries where the company's products were sold. The awards for the agency's work for Diesel have been many and distinguished, including the Grand Prix at the International Advertising Festival in Cannes, France, in 1997.

As the 1990s progressed, Paradiset's client list grew to include Helly Hansen (yachting and outdoor clothes and equipment), Björn Borg (brand marketing), Mandarina Duck, OLW snacks, Cloetta candy and chocolate, the Aftonbladet newspaper group, Telia Mobile, Spendrups breweries, Seriously Vodka, Lastminute.com, and Thomson Travel, for which in 1998 Paradiset won a Silver Egg Award, the Swedish counterpart of the Clio in the U.S.

Campaigns and clients may differ, yet Paradiset has maintained a consistent approach to its creative and production work: "Do the opposite!" In a world where consumers are bombarded with messages and seemingly endless choices, Paradiset philosophy is that ads must make an impression if they are to be noticed. "Every now and then you have to cause a commotion if you want to make your mark. . . . Down with the mundane," Paradiset's Managing Director Helena Westin has said.

Paradiset added the U.K.-based travel agency Thomson to its client list in January 1997. The next year, Thomson acquired Swedish travel agency Fritidsresegruppen. Paradiset set about

Paradiset DDB created this humorous ad for travel-package marketer Thomson Sverige, a subsidiary of the U.K.-based Thomson Travel Group. *Courtesy of Fritidsresor AB.*

adding a new element of vitality and excitement to its advertising. A traditionalist shop would have created campaigns featuring all the basic ingredients expected from Scandinavian-based vacation advertising: sun, beaches, palm trees, beautiful tanned bodies all having a wonderful time in exotic places. Instead, Paradiset's campaign for Thomson highlighted the main reasons Swedes so desperately want to travel to the sun and the beaches: Sweden's miserable weather—the rain, the cold, and, of course, the snow. Reaction to Paradiset's first campaign for Thomson was as swift as it was positive: 100,000 phone calls and 10,000 vacations booked in the first two days of the campaign, topped off with an increase in overall awareness of the Thomson brand name in Sweden from zero to 77 percent within one month.

It was only a question of time before Paradiset caught the eye of a worthy global suitor. In January 1993 DDB Needham acquired 51 percent of Paradiset. Rietz, Öström, and Jonasson retained the other 49 percent personally. Starting in the mid-1990s, Paradiset gave birth to a number of sibling companies in Sweden that today form the DDB Sweden Group.

At the outset of the 21st century, the existing management structure viewed Öström as chief executive officer of DDB Sweden Group and Westin, who joined the agency in November 1996, as managing director and account director of Paradiset. In 2000 Paradiset had gross income of $9.8 million, up 3.7 percent over 1999, on billings of $55.9 million. In January 2001, employees of Paradiset were preparing to acquire the shares held by the three founders. Jonasson left the agency in 1999, while Rietz and Öström remained at Paradiset.

GERARD O'DWYER

Pepperidge Farm, Inc.

Principal Agencies
Ogilvy, Benson & Mather, Inc.
Saatchi & Saatchi Advertising
Young & Rubicam, Inc.

Pepperidge Farm, Inc., was founded in 1937 by Margaret Rudkin, a Connecticut woman who began baking bread in a search for healthful recipes for her asthmatic son. Rudkin's use of top-quality ingredients and her preference for a low-key approach to advertising, one that created an "all-natural," wholesome image for the product, produced the company's signature style. Historically, Pepperidge Farm tended to depend more on in-store demonstrations and on advertising inserted into packaging than on newspaper or broadcast ads. Nonetheless, the company came increasingly to rely on television to revitalize its image.

In the first quarter-century of its operations, Rudkin dominated all aspects of the company, including its advertising efforts. Pepperidge Farm, named after the pepperidge, or sour gum, trees on the homestead in Fairfield, Connecticut, owned by Rudkin and her husband, got its start when she shared some of her homemade bread with her doctor. In turn, her doctor sparked local interest by touting the bread's benefits to his patients. Rudkin began selling the bread to a local grocer at a premium price, a quarter per loaf, at a time when most loaves cost a dime. Despite the economic pressures of the Depression, the business quickly grew to include mail-order distribution and sales through an outlet in Grand Central Station in New York City. A 1939 *Reader's Digest* article, "Bread DeLuxe," helped make the company a household name, and as business increased tenfold over the following decade, its operations were moved from Rudkin's home to a plant in Norwalk, Connecticut.

Advertising and promotion efforts from 1937 through the early 1950s were minimal and consisted principally of in-store demonstrations by Rudkin herself. But in 1953 Rudkin took the demonstrations to television, starring in minute-long spots that showed her in a kitchen discussing the bread and extolling its health benefits. The spots, created by Kenyon & Eckhardt, Inc., proved so successful that the entire 1954 advertising budget of $100,000 was devoted to television, and the medium has remained a substantial, if not the primary, vehicle for the company's promotional efforts since.

After directing Pepperidge Farm's modest advertising campaigns for more than two decades, Rudkin retained Ogilvy, Benson & Mather, Inc., in 1960. Shortly after Pepperidge Farm hired the ad agency, print and broadcast advertisements began featuring a stereotypical New England character named the "Old Man," also known as Titus. He was played by actor Parker Fennelly and was patterned after Fennelly's crusty Titus Moody character on the Fred Allen radio program. The first of these ads showed Titus sitting in a haystack, wearing a string tie and overalls while plugging the health benefits of Pepperidge Farm breads. For more than three decades this iconic Yankee, played by Charlie Welch after Fennelly's retirement in the 1970s, embodied nostalgia for "old-time" values and integrity, dropping his R's as he peered out from under his straw hat to remind consumers that "Pepperidge Fahm remembahs" what they want in baked goods.

When the Campbell Soup Company acquired Pepperidge Farm in late 1960 in a stock swap valued at approximately $28.2 million, Rudkin slowly began to extricate herself from the company's daily operations. Although Pepperidge Farm continued to roll out new products, the advertising approach remained remarkably consistent from the 1960s through the early 1980s, stressing "homemade" quality and family tradition in appealing to wealthier and more mature consumers, particularly those 45 and older.

In the mid-1980s company President Richard A. Shea sought to capture a national constituency by creating the American Collection line, naming each product after a specific U.S. location. Cookies such as Nantucket Chocolate Chunk, Chesapeake Chocolate Pecan, and Sausalito Chocolate Macadamia helped establish the company's image as more than just a regional bakery. The Titus character remained Pepperidge Farm's primary pitchman, with his New England accent evoking a sense of history and classic excellence for the new products in the American Collection lines. The American Marketing Association thought so highly of the efforts supporting the American Collection lines that it awarded Pepperidge Farm two Edison Awards for Best New Product (one for the American Collection cookie line and one for the American Collection frozen dessert line) in the late 1980s, and

"Real bread should have character. It should be firm and satisfying, with a rich, creamy color. This is our standard for Pepperidge Farm White Bread"

— says Margaret Rudkin

"You can be homesick for real bread even if you've never tasted it," says Mrs. Rudkin— who started the bakery at Pepperidge Farm.

"Real bread should have the color of rich cream, with a good substantial texture, and a tender golden crust.

"The flour should be *hard* wheat flour, high in natural proteins. Milk adds nourishment as well as honest flavor. And I personally prefer old-fashioned *cake* yeast. It seems to give a homey taste, like the bread my grandmother used to bake."

Mrs. Rudkin's standards are strictly adhered to at Pepperidge Farm today. This is why Pepperidge Farm White Bread has *character*. How long has it been since *you* tasted real bread?

A 1965 ad for Pepperidge Farm bread emphasized the brand's wholesome ingredients, recalling the homemade bread of an earlier era.
Provided courtesy of Campbell Soup Company.

named Pepperidge Farm "Marketer of the Year for Best New Products" in 1990. Despite the marketing accolades and the success of these new products, Pepperidge Farm slashed its advertising budget by 55 percent, to $8 million, for the fiscal year beginning on 1 August 1990. The company changed its approach the following year, however, and devoted $12 million to an advertising campaign that emphasized the indulgent, decadent character of its luxury cookie lines on the one hand and the wholesome, healthy ingredients in its Family Request and Light Style bakery products on the other.

Under new President Dale F. Morrison, Pepperidge Farm began a campaign in 1995 to double its sales, substantially increasing its advertising budget in the process. Advertisements continued to stress the high quality of Pepperidge Farm's lines, but in revamping the company's image, they moved away from the Titus character. Part of the overhaul included a revitalization of the Goldfish crackers brand, which received its first national advertising campaign; in the new ads, the previously sedate goldfish grew larger, sported sunglasses, and wore a bright smile. Television commercials continued to stress the product's healthy ingredients and noted that Goldfish were baked rather than fried, but also featured children singing, "I love the fishes 'cause they're so delicious," adding a youthful energy to the company's staid image. The efforts proved successful, as Goldfish sales jumped 25 percent, from approximately 6.8 million to 8.5 million bags, in the first year of the campaign.

Citing a conflict of interest because of an account with another baker, Ogilvy, Benson & Mather resigned as Pepperidge Farm's advertising agency, and the company selected Saatchi & Saatchi Advertising to determine the best use of its $10 million to $15 million advertising budget. The new agency helped produce a distinctive series of spots titled "Suspicions," featuring a mother trying to determine who had eaten her beloved Milano cookies and introducing the tag line, "Treasure was meant to be discovered." The emphasis on adult indulgence was extended to the American Collection line, which was rechristened the Chocolate Chunk Cookie Classic line and supported by television advertisements promising that "Satisfaction is just one bite away."

Using a design created by Marketing and Design Communications, Pepperidge Farm unveiled a new logo in December 1998, marking the first alterations to the brand's signature in 35 years. The logo retained the classic lettering but made the farmhouse more visible and colorful in an attempt to suggest comfort, fresh-baked quality, and vitality while retaining vestiges of nostalgic appeal. The redesign was accompanied by a switch in ad agencies from Saatchi & Saatchi to Young & Rubicam in January 1999, heralding yet more changes for a company whose advertising had shifted from an emphasis on the past—"Pepperidge Fahm remembahs"—to an emphasis on the future.

DOUG BATTEMA

See also color plate in this volume

Further Reading

Dougherty, Philip H., "Pepperidge Farm Line of Desserts," *New York Times* (2 December 1987)

"Fishing for Kids: Pepperidge Farm, Inc.'s Goldfish Cookies," *Food and Beverage Marketing* 12, no. 9 (September 1993)

Hays, Constance, "Will Goldfish Tactics Help Campbell's Soups?" *New York Times* (18 October 1998)

Pollack, Judann, "Goldfish Hook Kareem to Help Push Snack Brand," *Advertising Age* (11 November 1996)

"Total Freshness and Rapid Response," *Bakery Production and Marketing* 27, no. 10 (September 1992)

PepsiCo, Inc.

(Pepsi-Cola Company)

Principal Agencies
Newell-Emmett Company
Biow Company, Inc. (later Biow-Beirn-Toigo, Inc.)
Kenyon & Eckhardt, Inc.
Batten Barton Durstine & Osborn

The Pepsi-Cola Company traces its origins to August 1898 in New Bern, North Carolina, when Caleb D. Bradham first devised and named the formula that would launch one of the world's most famous soft drinks. For more than a century, the Pepsi brand has fought to overtake sales of its archrival Coca-Cola.

The "cola wars," as the competition has been called, have had little to do with the drinks themselves, which, apart from technical reformulations, have remained essentially unchanged for generations. Rather, they have been wars of marketing and advertising. Because Pepsi was introduced 12 years after Coca-Cola, for years it defined itself in relation to the market leader through slogans, jingles, advertising campaigns, and a succession of four major advertising agencies. Even after a century of competition, however, Pepsi still likes to view itself as the "feisty newcomer" struggling in the shadow of tradition cast by "the competitor."

Pepsi and its competitor share essentially common origins. Both were born in the rural American South after Reconstruction, both were concocted by drugstore operators, and both were first marketed as "medicines." The name Pepsi-Cola was supposed to connote the digestive enzyme pepsin and suggest a cure for peptic ulcers. Bradham patented his formula, registered the Pepsi trademark, and incorporated in 1902.

It was a crisis of manufacturing, not marketing, that would engulf Pepsi in the first of a series of bankruptcies. A sharp drop in sugar prices after World War I left the company buried under a stockpile of overpriced sugar and debt. In 1923, after taking on Wall Street investor Roy Megargel as a partner in the hopes of financial rescue, Bradham was forced to sell out for $35,000 to Megargel's Craven Holding Company. He returned to the drugstore business and died 11 years later. Craven moved Pepsi to Richmond, Virginia, while Megargel, now the company's largest stockholder, sat on the board and watched the company eke out modest growth through the 1920s. It was reorganized again in 1928 as the National Pepsi-Cola Company. In May 1931, during the Great Depression, Pepsi experienced its second bankruptcy and the departure of Megargel. Charles Guth, president of the Loft Candy Store company, then purchased Pepsi for $150,000 and moved the company from Richmond to Long Island City, New York. With few bottlers, the company's future was bleak. Advertising consisted of small newspaper ads, billboards, and standard point-of-purchase materials, all created by the company. The Standard Directory of Advertisers lists no advertising agency of record for Pepsi through most of the early 1930s.

One marketing idea quickly reversed Pepsi's fortunes. In March 1934 something astonishing began appearing in Baltimore, Maryland, grocery stores—12-ounce bottles of Pepsi selling for five cents each. Without raising the price, Guth had taken Pepsi off the gold standard of the soft-drink business, the six-ounce sales unit. In the midst of the Depression, he offered customers what they wanted most—a bargain. Sales grew, bottlers materialized, and the race was on to meet a new demand. By 1936 Pepsi had a $500,000 advertising budget and retained the Brown Agency, a small shop in the Baltimore Times Building, to create advertising materials such as enamel signs and to handle local newspaper promotions. Pepsi had no money for network radio, which was the glamour end of the business. However, ad spending doubled by 1938, and Pepsi moved its account to the Metropolitan Advertising Agency in New York City.

In the midst of the Pepsi renaissance, though, the company changed hands once again. In July 1939 Phoenix Securities, Philadelphia, Pennsylvania, which owned 29 percent of Loft, took over Pepsi. Walter Mack, a vice president of Phoenix, now headed Pepsi. In June 1940 Phoenix sold off the last of its Loft stock, cutting Loft's last link to Pepsi.

With manufacturing and distribution on sound footing, Mack knew that marketing would drive Pepsi's future. He fired Metropolitan and in the summer of 1939 heard presentations from several major advertising agencies. It was during this agency search that one of the most famous and enduring advertising jingles in history was created by Lord & Thomas (L&T), one of the agencies soliciting the account. The tune was based on the old English ballad, "John Peel": "Pepsi-Cola hits the spot, / Two full glasses,

In 1939 the comic-strip characters Pepsi and Pete helped popularize Pepsi-Cola soft drink's 12-ounce bottle, offered for the same 5-cent price as competitors' 6-ounce bottles.
Pepsi-Cola Company.

that's a lot. / Twice as much for a nickel, too. / Pepsi-Cola is the drink for you."

But the dictatorial Mack believed that a client should always know more about advertising than its agency. He rejected L&T and chose Newell-Emmett Company, an agency he felt he could control more easily. According to a 1955 account in *Advertising Age,* he kept the jingle L&T had commissioned and told Newell-Emmett to run it on as many local stations as possible in 15-second time slots, where brevity would buy frequency. The campaign broke in September 1939 on WOR, New York City, between news bulletins of Adolph Hitler's invasion of Poland. Soon everybody was humming it. Mack envisioned the jingle on jukeboxes as well as radio, so band leader and trumpet virtuoso Bunny Berigan was brought in to record a full big-band version with the Pepsi lyrics sung by Fredda

Pepsi's 1961 slogan "For those who think young" helped define a
generation of Pepsi advertising.
Pepsi-Cola Company.

Gibson, who would become a well-known pop singer in the 1950s
using the name Georgia Gibbs.

Pepsi advertising bought 300,000 spot plays of the jingle at 15
seconds each in the first year and more after that. There was no
escaping it. Clock chimes installed in Pepsi's Long Island City,
New York, plant banged out the tune every 30 minutes. During
World War II, as the company managed to ingeniously dodge the
constraints of government sugar rationing by importing the commodity from Mexico in the form of syrup, the jingle sold war
bonds: "Uncle Sam is calling you / to fight this war and see it
through. / By buying bonds and stamps today, / you can help protect the U.S.A." By the time it was replaced after more than a
decade, the jingle had given Pepsi a permanent place among the
cultural bric-a-brac of American civilization.

Newell-Emmett also developed a comic strip campaign using
characters called Sarge and Large. Mack changed their names to
Pepsi and Pete and began running the campaign in Sunday comics
sections (ten times a year in 187 newspapers in 1941). They were
also used in an animated short film for movie theaters.

In May 1942 Newell-Emmett took Pepsi advertising to network radio for the first time in a weekly five-minute slot on the

NBC Blue network (soon to become ABC). But the effort was too
small to make an impact. A second try in February 1946 with a
15-minute Sunday evening commentary program by journalist
Quentin Reynolds was also brief, as was a third network attempt
sponsoring a program called *Counterspy* from January 1949 to
June 1950.

After World War II Pepsi's advertising budget was nearly $4
million. The company had surpassed Royal Crown Cola and Dr
Pepper. Pepsi's prosperity was characteristic of the times. The
New Deal and the war had transformed the American working
class into a postwar middle class that could now afford television
sets, new cars, and houses in the suburbs. But such prosperity was
increasingly at odds with Pepsi's thrift message. "Twice as much
for a nickel" made the product look cheap in a time when consumption was finally acceptable. The agency tried to shift the message to quality, but more than ten years of positioning was
becoming obsolete.

In 1948, with sales dropping $10 million in one year, Mack
took steps to separate the old Pepsi from the new. He moved company headquarters from Long Island City to Fifth Avenue and
57th Street in Manhattan, and he fired his ad agency. (Young &
Rubicam, which handled Everess, Pepsi's sparkling water introduced in 1946, was not affected.) As of 15 May 1948, the Biow
Company, Inc., replaced Newell-Emmett. Milton Biow had given
America "Call for Philip Morris" and "B-U-L-O-V-A—Bulova
watch time." In 1949, with a $3 million budget in hand, he
intended to give it "Twice as much for a penny more."

Despite the new advertising campaign, Pepsi's sales continued
to decline. In October 1950, with Pepsi sales down $16 million
from 1947, Mack resigned. Alfred Steel, whom Mack had
recruited from Coca-Cola in April 1949, succeeded him. "More
bounce to the ounce" became the Pepsi mantra as Steel took
over. The old "John Peel" jingle was phased out, and a stylish
movie actress, Polly Bergen, personified Pepsi's modern image as
she talked about "the light refreshment that refreshes without
filling." "Reduced calories" became a Pepsi theme years before
RC invented Diet-Rite and the whole diet beverage product category, as slender women in Dior suits set the new upscale Pepsi
look. Even the Pepsi logo was lightened from two hyphens to
one.

The only thing to put on weight was the ad budget, which was
approximately $8 million by 1955. Rumors of an agency change
began after D'Arcy lost the Coca-Cola account to McCann-
Erickson. John Toigo, speaking for Biow-Beirn-Toigo (BBT; formerly the Biow Company, Inc.), said he knew nothing about a
Pepsi agency switch and that in any case he was loyal to BBT.
When an *Advertising Age* reporter queried Steel about this, he
played dumb: "The whole thing is news to me, pal." Nonetheless, two weeks later, in December 1955, Pepsi fired BBT and
hired Kenyon & Eckhardt (K&E). What Steel had not said, but
what had angered Pepsi for several months, was that BBT's high-
fashion Philip Morris campaign was very similar in art design
and type style to its campaign for Pepsi. In Pepsi's view, it was
plagiarism, as the Pepsi Company credited Steel with inventing
its glamour look. *Advertising Age* called it "one of the most bit-

ter advertising wrangles in history." BBT, which had been the nation's 11th-largest agency in 1944, folded in June 1956.

K&E officially took over in April 1956 and raised the stakes of elegance and good taste still higher. "Say 'Pepsi, please'" became the slogan, and the sales gap between Coke and Pepsi closed to 2 to 1 (from 5 to 1 in 1950). At the same time, international growth surged, a fact that led Pepsi international chief Don Kendall to instruct K&E to hire a young TV director named Alan Pottasch to run the overseas account. That September the aura of refinement climbed to new heights as K&E introduced, "Be sociable, look smart." Pepsi was now being served from champagne coolers as "young and fair and debonair" men in tuxes and women in cocktail dresses toasted each other to George Shearing-style jazz. In trying to tell a quality story, the advertising emphasis drifted from product qualities to an association with a quality-conscious lifestyle. The principle was good; the problem was that for a soft drink, the lifestyle lacked any sense of reality.

On 21 April 1959, Steel, the man who had made Pepsi the nation's 57th-largest advertiser, died at age 57. Steel's demise coincided with important change. There would soon be Pepsi in new pop-top cans, a new nonscript logo, new Manhattan offices at 500 Park Avenue, new brands such as Teem and Patio, the first Diet Pepsi-Cola, and, of course, a new agency. On 3 March 1960, after hiring a number of K&E's top executives, including Pottasch, who became director of marketing, Pepsi invited 11 top agencies to make presentations. On 11 April Batten Barton Durstine & Osborn (BBDO) won the account; the Coke machines were hauled out of its offices and new Pepsi coolers were hauled in.

Don Kendall, who had joined Pepsi in 1947 as a syrup salesman and later ran its international division, secured control of the company in 1963 and began the acquisition spree that would turn Pepsi into a multinational conglomerate. First came the Tip Corporation, maker of Mountain Dew, in September 1964. Then in 1965, Pepsi acquired Frito-Lay and created PepsiCo, Inc., as a holding company for its acquisitions.

Kendall confronted a major international lead by Coca-Cola, which had been working the world market since 1926. Pepsi had not even begun to go international until 1934, when it began producing in Canada. Soon its focus shifted to the Caribbean and Latin America, but progress was slow. Steel began the penetration of Brazil in 1952, yet as late as 1967 Coca-Cola retained a virtual monopoly on Rio de Janeiro. Under Kendall, the number of bottlers outside the United States grew from 70 to 278 between 1957 and 1962. In the 1960s, working with Schweppes, Perrier, and other bottlers in Europe, the company made huge strides. Pepsi also set up franchises in China and Japan in the mid-1960s. And in September 1973 Kendall traveled to the Soviet Union to finalize the deal that would make Pepsi a symbol of Cold War détente.

With Kendall absorbed in making Pepsi a multinational empire, BBDO assumed an authority over advertising content and style earlier Pepsi agencies had not enjoyed. BBDO appreciated K&E's efforts to fit Pepsi into a lifestyle context, but it also recognized it was the wrong lifestyle. Under the direction of creative director Phil Dusenberry and Pepsi marketing chief Pottasch, cocktail dresses were replaced with surfing gear. Pepsi zeroed in

In the 1980s Pepsi updated its classic 1960s slogan to target the children of the original "Pepsi generation." It also ran ads that appealed to the African-American market.
Pepsi-Cola Company

on a young population that saw itself as distinct from its parents in ways earlier generations had not.

Three weeks after John F. Kennedy was inaugurated as president of the United States, Pepsi set out to take that generation for its own. To the tune of "Makin' Whoopie," Joannie Sommers sang the message that would define the Pepsi personality for the rest of the century: "For those who think young." The phrase became a colloquialism. The campaign symbolized a fierce new aggressiveness against Coke. Four years later BBDO launched the "Come alive. . . . You're in the Pepsi generation" campaign, also with Joannie Sommers, and the phrase "Pepsi Generation" became virtually interchangeable with the later term *baby boomer*. While the music remained important and memorable, the visuals also carried strong messages: sports, active recreation, and a sense of challenge and reward. Even when the emphasis moved back to a specific product claim—"Taste that beats the others cold, Pepsi pours it on"—the images stayed focused on high-energy outdoor play.

The 1960s would be a difficult time for advertisers placing their bets on youth and lifestyle. For Pepsi, it made the company's

In 1991 singer Ray Charles and the Uh-Huh Girls' "You got the right one baby" made a series of memorable TV spots for Diet Pepsi.
Pepsi-Cola Company

commercials a kind of social commentary in a period of cultural conflict and controversy. Like any advertiser, Pepsi saw what it wished to see. Rock music, with it associations of drugs and sex, was virtually ignored until the 1980s, when Pepsi embraced "bubble-gum" rockers such as the young Michael Jackson, as well as veterans Lionel Richie and Tina Turner. In the 1970s the folk sound seemed safer. While Coke hit the charts in 1972 with the Seekers' ballad "I'd Like to Teach the World to Sing," Pepsi used a different folk style in "You've got a lot to live, and Pepsi's got a lot to give." As for the pop music charts, Pepsi had charted five years before with its own music for Diet Pepsi, "Music to Watch Girls By." At a time when the record industry was starting its dissolution into smaller and smaller niches, advertising jingles began to replace pop tunes as the music everybody knew.

It was also at this time that Pepsi commercials became multiracial. For the first time viewers saw black and white consumers, not only in the same commercial but actually socializing together. A sanitized counterculture sensibility pervaded even the most traditional visuals of swimming holes and farm life, as lines such as "you be you, I'll be me" blended a nonjudgmental open-mindedness with red-white-and-blue patriotism. The appearance of a motorcyclist in the commercial "This Happy Land" even acknowledged the subversive impact of the movie *Easy Rider*. In an interview with *Advertising Age* in 1998, Ted Sann, chief creative officer of BBDO, said, "The notion behind 'A Lot to Give' was that there was a lot of turmoil going on around the country and there was a sense of showing what people in the country were really like and what was going on. There was one spot in that campaign called 'Hippie Wedding.' I think Woodstock was the dividing line."

But BBDO knew that the United States was not a happy land. In the wake of the Watergate scandal Pepsi canceled a mid-1970s campaign called the "Smilin' Majority" in favor of "Join the Pepsi People, Feelin' Free." With the company moving into Communist countries, Pepsi executives wondered whether the "Feelin' free" theme would antagonize the local regimes. Translations carrying the meaning "carefree" proved a diplomatic solution. Except for minor adjustments of that kind, Pepsi's advertising campaigns were created to play around the world.

BBDO rarely shifted the advertising back to Pepsi as a product. When it did, the impact on Pepsi's traditional competitor, Coca-Cola, was significant. Beginning in 1975, Pepsi began using filmed taste tests in a subordinate campaign that showed consumers tasting unidentified samples of two colas and picking their favorite. When a body of data began to accumulate that showed Pepsi leading Coke, Coca-Cola decided it had to act. It chose to reformulate its most basic brand into a sweeter tasting beverage, akin to Pepsi. Coke customers rejected it while Pepsi drinkers ignored it. The Pepsi taste test campaign, which concluded in 1982, is one of the few advertising campaigns ever to have provoked a market leader to remake its flagship brand in the likeness of its second-place rival.

Whereas the first 60 years of Pepsi history sorted conveniently into neat chapters divided by bankruptcies and marked by CEO strongmen, the decades since have assumed a remarkably seamless flow. Not even the acquisition and subsequent divestiture of the company's restaurant interests (KFC, Taco Bell, and Pizza Hut) or the acquisition of Quaker Oats Company (2000) and South Beach Beverage Company (2001) have disturbed the larger vitality of the basic Pepsi brand. Its acquisition in 2000 of Quaker brought Foote, Cone & Belding (FCB)—which handled Quaker's Aquafina water, Gator Aide sports drinks, and Tropicana juices—into Pepsi's family of agencies.

In the 1990s the company increased it spending to reach Spanish-speaking consumers in the United States. It retained Dieste & Partners, a minority market agency in Dallas, Texas, and one of BBDO's sibling shops within the Omnicom Group. One Dieste commercial ("Go-o-al") became the first Spanish-language Pepsi commercial to win a gold Lion award at the International Advertising Festival in Cannes, France.

Pepsi remains the number-two cola behind Coca-Cola, it believes, because of Coke's "monopoly" on the fountain market, which includes fast-food franchises and other institutional customers and which represents much of Pepsi's future growth potential. On 7 May 1998, PepsiCo, Inc., filed suit in Federal District Court claiming that Coca-Cola had used threats against independent distributors to prevent them from handling Pepsi. Although Pepsi has allocated a portion of its consumer advertising to encourage buyers to ask for Pepsi at the fountain, this is a battle that will be fought in the courts before it has a major impact on consumer advertising.

In 2001 FCB and its parent company, True North Communications, was acquired by the Interpublic Group of Companies, parent of McCann-Erickson, which had handled Coca-Cola since 1955. Though FCB and McCann-Erickson were separate agency groups within Interpublic, Pepsi was very sensitive to the conflict with Coca-Cola. Pepsi not only cut its ties to FCB but sued to prevent several FCB employees from working on competing Coca-Cola brands (Dasani water, Powerade sports drinks, and Minute Maid juices) for two years. The case was settled out of court with a compromise arrangement. Nevertheless, the case was closely watched because it seemed to challenge the freedom of agencies to replace lost business in a timely manner with a new account in the same field.

In 2000 Pepsi-Cola Company had sales of $20.44 billion, an increase of 3 percent over 1999 sales; earnings were $2.18 billion, up 6.5 percent over the previous year. Its parent PepsiCo spent $2.10 billion in measured media, up 4.5 percent over the year earlier. PepsiCo's most heavily supported brands included Pepsi and Diet Pepsi, Quaker foods, Gatorade sports drinks, Tropicana juices, and Mountain Dew beverages.

JOHN McDONOUGH

Further Reading

Dara, Rajendar, *The Real Pepsi, the Real Story*, New Delhi: Dara, 1991

Dietz, Lawrence, *Soda Pop: The History, Advertising, Art, and Memorabilia of Soft Drinks in America*, New York: Simon and Schuster, 1973

Enrico, Roger, and Jesse Kornbluth, *The Other Guy Blinked: How Pepsi Won the Cola Wars,* New York and London: Bantam, 1986

Louis, J.C., and Harvey Yazijian, *The Cola Wars,* New York: Everest House, 1980

Mack, Walter, and Peter Buckley, *No Time Lost,* New York: Atheneum, 1982

Martin, Milward W., *Twelve Full Ounces,* New York: Holt Rinehart and Winston, 1962; 2nd edition, 1969

Stoddard, Bob, *Pepsi: 100 Years,* Los Angeles: General, 1997

Perfume

While the use of perfumes and scented oils goes back centuries, the advertising of perfume did not become widespread until the early 1900s. A century later, fragrance sales in the United States alone exceeded $5.4 billion, and an estimated $243 million per year was being spent on advertising in this category.

The modern perfume industry was born in France, coinciding with the rise of French couture and the discovery of particularly fragrant flowers growing in the Provence countryside around such villages as Grasse. Paris became the center of the industry, and one of its pioneers, Gabrielle "Coco" Chanel, introduced her Chanel No. 5 fragrance in 1921. It was the first synthetic scent to be mass-produced and remained a best-seller into the next century.

The marketing of scents intensified in 1927 when French couturier Jeanne Lanvin created a perfume called Arpege. The in-house-developed advertising slogan, "Promise her anything, but give her Arpege," became an advertising classic as memorable as the scent. Most fragrances at the time were produced in France. (An exception was the California Perfume Company, which was founded in 1886 and eventually became Avon.) In 1932 the English designer Worth introduced Je Reviens.

The next big launch came in 1935, when the French designer Jean Patou introduced Joy. Although he was advised to delay the launch because of the Depression, Patou went ahead, hoping people would buy the fragrance to take their minds off the harsh economic times. Other popular scents of the day included Jicky and Shalimar, marketed by Guerlain; Tabu by Dana; and Narcisse Noir by Caron. All were French. These perfumes, mostly oriental in tone, were positioned as a way to escape to exotic places at a time when most people could not afford to travel.

In 1934 William Schultz introduced a line of soaps, toiletries, and perfume oils he called Old Spice. Although the original Old Spice was for women, a men's version was also introduced, and Schultz formed Shulton to market his products and retained Wesley Associates, New York City, to handle advertising. By 1935 sales of Old Spice totaled $982,000. While business was hampered during the war years, Old Spice became one of the first successful men's fragrances, followed by Canoe and Dunhill for men in the late 1930s. Shulton sold Old Spice to American Cyanamid in 1970, which in turn sold it to Procter & Gamble Company (P&G) in 1990.

But perfume advertising itself remained relatively static, with advertisements showing bottles or women applying scents. The prevailing attitude was that advertising could not really push something that consumers had to smell to experience. During World War II, chronic shortages of perfume halted growth of the business.

Fragrance marketing sprang back to life in 1947 with Christian Dior's release of his first fragrance, Miss Dior. Advertised by the Albert Woodley Company, New York City, the fragrance was marketed as the ultimate in femininity—a counterpoint to the jobs many women had assumed during the war. Miss Dior advertisements showed women engaged in traditional feminine roles, suggesting that men were in charge of buying perfume for their wives. It was even deemed improper for women to buy their own fragrances; they were accepted as gifts of love.

Chanel No. 5, marketed by Bourjois, Inc., and advertised by Lord & Thomas, New York City, grew in popularity in the United States in the early 1940s, although World War II affected perfume production. The marketer was one of the first to use celebrity "faces" such as Catherine Deneuve to represent the brand.

In 1979 Doyle Dane Bernbach launched the most famous of all Chanel campaigns, "Share the fantasy." The TV commercials, directed by Ridley Scott (who went on to make such feature films as *Thelma and Louise* and *Gladiator*), featured strikingly surreal images of romance against imaginative musical backgrounds such as "I Don't Want to Set the World on Fire" done in the style of the Ink Spots. The campaign was ranked by *Advertising Age* as 36th among the 100 best of the century and was the only perfume campaign to make the list.

In 1953 Estee Lauder Companies introduced Youth Dew, which did double duty as a perfume and bath oil. Lauder also used celebrities to promote its brands; Youth Dew was endorsed by Hollywood screen legends Gloria Swanson and Joan Crawford. Fragrances, however, were still considered to be a male purchase. Galbraith-Hoffmann Advertising, New York City, was Lauder's agency of the period.

In 1969 designer Paco Rabanne influenced the fragrance business with a scent called Calandre that was notable for its melding of fine fragrance with artistic packaging. Rabanne brought his artistic flair to the creative aspects of the bottle and the scent. He wanted a fragrance so avant-garde that it would shock people. Fragrance notes were reminiscent of the forest and the ocean and,

Fragrances such as Jean Patou's Joy, introduced in 1935 and seen here in a 1938 print ad, offered consumers a touch of luxury and escapism during a time of harsh economic reality.
Copyright Jean Patou, Inc.

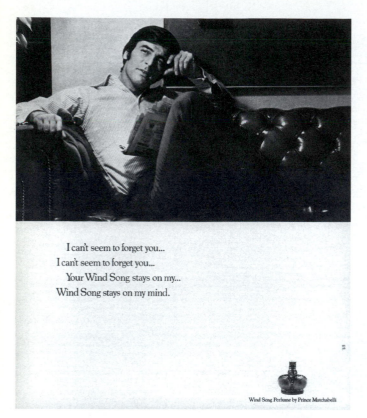

I can't seem to forget you...
I can't seem to forget you...
    Your Wind Song stays on my...
Wind Song stays on my mind.

Wind Song Perfume by Prince Matchabelli

The J. Walter Thompson Company created this romantic campaign for Prince Matchabelli's Wind Song perfume in the late 1960s. *Courtesy of Prince Matchabelli.*

rather than being square, Rabanne's bottles resembled sculptures. The advertising by Ogilvy & Mather was equally bold. In one sophisticated ad, the risqué dialogue between a man and a woman on the phone suggests a casual sleepover the night before.

Despite the radical social changes of the 1960s, the prevailing attitude in the perfume industry during those years was largely conservative; it was still widely held that scents should be reserved for special occasions and that men selected fragrances for women.

All that ended in the 1970s when Revlon, Inc., revolutionized fragrance advertising with the launch of a new fragrance, Charlie, named after company founder Charles Revson. Although Charlie was a knee-jerk reaction to a new scent from archrival Lauder, the Charlie ad campaign shook up the fragrance market. The first ads, from Grey Advertising, hinted that women should be free to make their own choices—including the purchase of perfume. Revlon's in-house Creative Workshop in 1973 created the best-known campaign, featuring model Shelley Hack as the "Charlie girl," an independent—perhaps even employed—female who selected her own scent. The final kicker to the campaign came via fashion: the model wore a pantsuit, an uncommon image for the time. In its first year on the market, Charlie racked up more than $10 million in sales, according to *Advertising Age*. Charlie advertising became an empowering message for women across the United States; it convinced women not only to buy the scent for themselves but also to wear fragrance daily rather than just for special events.

Charlie was not the only success story of the 1970s. In response to the hippie counterculture revolt and the back-to-nature ethos of the times, American perfumers were looking for alternative scents. Jovan, Inc. found just that in musk oil. The 1970s have even been dubbed "the musk years." Jovan used a unique marketing approach for its musk: it touted the scent as appropriate to be worn by either men or women.

The success of Charlie and musk opened the floodgates to glitzy perfume marketing. Creative campaigns came at a rapid pace from companies such as Prince Matchabelli, which offered up the notable "I can't seem to forget you, your Wind Song stays on my mind" from agency J. Walter Thompson Company for its Wind Song fragrance. William Esty Company worked on other Prince Matchabelli campaigns, such as Cachet's "As individual as you are." Aviance Night Musk's "It's going to be an Aviance night," was penned by Lois Geraci Ernst, the founder of the agency Advertising to Women.

Independence gave way to sexuality in the 1980s, as companies backed sexy, heavy perfumes with heavy ad budgets. At the same time, fragrance sales started to shift from mass retailers such as drugstores to department stores, where beauty consultants spritzed shoppers and pushed sales. The popular practice of gifts-with-purchase or purchase-with-purchase mushroomed, fueled by promotions from Lauder.

The biggest marketing advance of the decade was made by Giorgio Beverly Hills in 1982. Giorgio was the first fragrance to be advertised with a new tool: scent samples inserted into magazines. The samples offered a way for marketers to get customers to smell the fragrance without going to a store. Giorgio locked up perfume advertising in *Vogue* for an entire year with scent strips. Eventually, magazines sported several scent samples in each issue, causing some subscribers to complain. In 1990 the industry faced lawsuits from consumers claiming they suffered allergic reactions to the scented pages. By 1995 the samples were encapsulated so they had to be activated to be smelled, and most magazines started limiting the number of samples per issue while some just refused them. But the practice worked: Giorgio sales swelled to $100 million after only five years on the market. Other heavy-hitting scents, such as Yves St. Laurent's Opium, Dior's Poison, and Drakkar for Men from Guy Laroche followed in Giorgio's wake. Most successful scents were launched in department stores at premium prices.

In the 1980s marketers began to approach celebrities to lend their names to their own signature scents. Parfums International, a unit of Unilever Group, introduced a series of scents tied to the glamour surrounding Elizabeth Taylor. The first was called Passion. In 1987 Unilever sent Taylor to department stores in nine cities to sign perfume bottles and have tea with select shoppers. Television spots in the $10 million marketing effort showed Taylor, wearing a low-cut evening dress, reading poems about passion. A decade later, in February 1996, Taylor appeared in a promotional stunt as guest star in four CBS Monday-night series, all the same night. Series writers developed plot lines around her Black Pearls fragrance for each show, allowing her to appear as herself while promoting the scent.

The designer craze spread to the men's segment, too, with scents such as Geoffrey Beene's Grey Flannel (1975), Halston Z-14 (1976), and Polo by Ralph Lauren (1978) hitting the shelves. With designer products in demand, Calvin Klein entered the fray, spending in 1985 more than $17 million on Obsession, which the marketer licensed to Chesebrough-Pond's. The campaign shook up the world of scent advertising with shots of nude men and women. The shock effect worked for Klein: Obsession hit first-year sales of $30 million. To boost sales after three years, Klein launched another campaign starring model Kate Moss in TV spots created by in-house agency CRK; again, the campaign drew criticism, targeted at its use of the waif-thin Moss. Obsession was followed by other brands such as Eternity, Truth, and CK One, which was marketed to both men and women as a "unisex" product, as Jovan's musk had been earlier. The campaign, by Wieden & Kennedy, New York City, in collaboration with CRK, sought to reach young customers who had turned away from fragrance purchasing. A later campaign for CK One, introduced in 1999, incorporated e-mail; it introduced three characters, Tia, Robert, and Anna, who could be reached by e-mail.

After the sexual overtones of fragrance advertising in the 1980s, the scents launched during the 1990s reflected a shift to romance, with introductions such as Chanel's Allure, Dolce Vita from Dior, and Pleasures by Estee Lauder. A 1994 spot from the Arnell Group, New York City, for Chanel No. 5 took a new tack on romance, showing a model sitting in a packed theater, watching a movie. As the action progressed, the model morphed into Marilyn Monroe, then changed back to herself, hugging a huge bottle of the marketer's signature fragrance.

To launch Pleasures, Lauder in 1995 tapped the Lowe Group, a break from its longtime relationship with Saatchi & Saatchi. Their $15 million to $20 million network television spots featured actress Elizabeth Hurley, Lauder's new face at that time. Bates USA handled media.

As ad budgets continued to balloon, the stakes for entry into the fragrance market started getting too high for mass-market brands. Marketers claimed they needed to spend at least $30 million for a successful new-product introduction and at least $10 million to maintain a brand. P&G—which had been marketing such brands as Navy and California—exited the business, leaving Coty, Inc., as the only major fragrance supplier in the U.S. mass market. The company decided to introduce only new scents based on existing strong franchises. Revlon maintained its existing scents, such as Charlie, Fire & Ice, and Jontue, but no longer developed new products. The move had a dramatic impact on the mass-market fragrance business, which saw sales decline through the late 1990s.

Many retailers started adding their own scents in the late 1990s, including Tiffany & Company, The Gap, Victoria's Secret, and Ann Taylor. Victoria's Secret even spun off separate stores from its lingerie units to sell fragrances such as Dream Angels and Heavenly. In 2001 Victoria's Secret introduced a new scent called Pink in ads starring model Gisele sitting in a dresser drawer; ads were handled in-house. Avon, although best known for color cos-metics, remains a factor in fragrance, too. With a push from its newest scent—Women of Earth—Avon's fragrance business topped $1 billion in sales in 2000.

The late 1990s also saw efforts to get men to move beyond using the perennial favorite Old Spice. Launches included a men's Obsession formulation and a Tommy Hilfiger scent notable because it marked the first licensing deal between Lauder and a designer. Sports stars also got into the fragrance world. In 1996 Michael Jordan The Fragrance was launched. It won the Fragrance Foundation's FiFi award for Star of the Year in 1997.

Sensing that interest in traditional fragrance products was declining, marketers started touting aromatherapy products such as scented candles and bath additives. One of the most successful such lines, with U.S. sales exceeding $70 million, according to Information Resources, Inc., was Coty's Healing Garden, a collection of products with ingredients designed to evoke a particular feeling—lavender, for example, for relaxation. A print campaign was handled in-house.

Custom blends also began to increase in popularity thanks to companies such as Jo Malone and Reflect.com. At Jo Malone, patrons "play" with oils to create a scent. Reflect.com, owned by P&G, allows customers to order a customized scent on-line. New York City–based Deutsch handled advertising for Reflect.com. Although P&G no longer is a player in the traditional marketing of scents, it maintains a presence in perfumes via Reflect.com. In addition, the Internet has opened a way for consumers to buy favorite scents on-line via sites such as Sephora.com.

Despite a fragmentation in the market, the major houses continue to stick with tried-and-true formulas of using famous faces and designers. Lancôme, for example, introduced a new scent called Miracle in 2001 with ads starring actress Uma Thurman.

FAYE BROOKMAN

Further Reading

Brookman, Faye, "Coty Plants New Fields," *Women's Wear Daily* (20 November 1998)

"Calvin Klein Cosmetics Company Introduces New Obsession Fragrance Advertising," *PR Newswire* (29 July 1993)

"Fine Fragrance Update," *Happi* (November 2000)

The Fragrance Foundation, "Expanding the Appreciation, Use, and Sales of Fragrance Globally" <www.fragrance.org/main.html>

The History of Perfume <www.perfume2000.com/history/history.asp>

Hughes, Kathleen A., "Perfume Firms Go All Out in Effort to Lure Buyers," *Wall Street Journal* (10 December 1987)

Informationist (August 1985)

Informationist (January 1990)

"Marketing: The Great Perfume Wars," *Newsday* (23 February 1986)

"NPD Beauty*Trends* Reports the Women's Fragrance Industry Is Poised for a Brighter Year: Fragrance Gifts Are Welcome This Holiday Season" <www.npd.com/corp/content/news/releases/press_001205.htm>

Perrier

Principal Agencies
Mathieu, Gerfen & Bresner, Inc.
Waring & LaRosa, Inc.
Hal Riney & Partners
Publicis/Bloom
Ogilvy & Mather Worldwide

Historical data indicate that Caesar's troops probably drank from the original source of Perrier, a spring once called Les Bouillens (French for boiling waters). The spring was first commercialized in 1863. In 1888 it was owned by a farmer named Rouviere, who, in 1898, gave the site to a local organization whose senior director was a prominent physician named Perrier. In 1903 Sir St. John Harmsworth, an Englishman, acquired control of the spring. Harmsworth renamed it Source Perrier. The spring was thereafter under English management, and the company, known as the Compagnie de la Source Perrier, was formed in 1906.

Output from the spring increased, reaching more than 1.2 million bottles during World War I. During the 1930s the business began to decline, and Harmsworth's heirs took control of the company after his death. In 1945 the French controlled the Compagnie de la Source Perrier. Business started to build for Source Perrier during the 1950s, with over 130 million bottles sold. Source Perrier exported approximately 25 million bottles toward the middle of the 1950s, and, based on demand, Perrier built a new factory. During 1954 Perrier expanded into the soft drink and soda market with two new products, Pschitt and Gini.

Perrier has held a presence in the United States since the beginning of the 20th century, but demand for its bottled water began to increase only during the mid-1970s, when health-conscious Americans began switching from soft drinks to mineral and other bottled waters. In 1981 Perrier began to use the tag line "Earth's first soft drink." During the late 1970s and early 1980s, the company began to sponsor various events, such as the Olympic Games in 1984. In 1985 the company introduced Perrier with a Twist (a lemon-and-lime drink).

Waring & LaRosa, Inc. (W&L), was awarded the Perrier account in 1981 after Perrier dropped the Mathieu, Gerfen & Bresner advertising agency. In 1983 Batten Barton Durstine & Osborn (BBDO) acquired W&L. BBDO allowed W&L to operate independently, and W&L retained the Perrier account. In 1986 Hal Riney & Partners, then a new agency, was awarded the Perrier account.

Perrier continued to grow in sales until February 1990, when the company voluntarily recalled its bottles off U.S. shelves because of benzene contamination, eliminating Perrier from the market for four months. The U.S. Food and Drug Administration (FDA) ruled the benzene content harmless, but Perrier did not want to appear negative to the consumers—benzene was a suspected carcinogen. There were no other waters recalled. The cost

A 1917 ad showed the distinctive Perrier bottle and label.
Courtesy The Perrier Group of America.

to Source Perrier was estimated to be around $200 million, plus losses to the brand's equity and market share. In an attempt to regain consumer confidence and market share, Perrier developed an art contest, inviting amateur artists to create a new package design. In conjunction with this promotion, Perrier began an advertising campaign with the theme "The art of refreshment." At this time Perrier changed agencies from Riney back to W&L.

In July 1990 Perrier faced another setback when the FDA made the company drop the words "naturally sparkling" from its labels, because this term was misleading.

In 1992 W&L again lost the mineral water account (although W&L retained other brands marketed by the Perrier Group), this time to Publicis/Bloom, then newly formed by Publicis. Publicis/Bloom created a new campaign that supported the "art bottles" marketing approach. Then in 1997 Perrier awarded its global account to Ogilvy & Mather Worldwide, whose Paris, France, office had won the grand prize at the 1991 International Advertising Festival in Cannes for a French ad for Perrier. The agency was given an estimated $40 million to $50 million for the international campaign and was placed in charge of creative and media duties. OgilvyOne (the direct and interactive arm of Ogilvy & Mather) was brought in to help bring Perrier into the 21st century; OgilvyInteractive, a division of OgilvyOne, was the on-line agency of record. Perrier developed and launched its Internet site during 1999. The site was designed to link the company's many brands without a loss of brand equity to any one.

Nestlé S.A. purchased Source Perrier in 1992 for a sum equivalent to approximately $2.8 billion. Nestlé formed Nestlé Source International and later renamed it Perrier Vittel S.A.

In 2000 Source Perrier was the leading supplier of bottled water in France. Perrier was also one of the best-selling imported sparkling waters in the United States. The Perrier Group of America, a division of Nestlé created in 1992, had numerous brands in addition to Perrier, including Arrowhead, Calistoga, Deer Park, Ozarka, Vittel, and Zephyrills. It had the largest market share in North America, almost three times that of its closest competitor, Suntory.

JAMES R. OGDEN

Further Reading

Dougherty, P., "Waring and LaRosa Gets Perrier Account," *New York Times* (5 November 1981)

Dougherty, P., "BBDO Will Buy Waring," *New York Times* (15 November 1983)

Lubove, Seth, "Perched between Perrier and Tap," *Forbes* (14 May 1990)

McCarthy, M., and N. O'Leary, "Ogilvy Wins $40–50 Mil. Perrier Account," *Adweek* 38, no. 39 (29 September 1997)

Personal Care Products

When surveyed, 90 percent of middle-class Americans claim to have had a bath or shower within the last 24 hours. It is impossible to determine whether this is true, but it is a fact that most people would have others believe that it is. Although deeply entrenched, this cultural preference for washing and bathing—some call it an obsession—is a relatively recent development that is by no means shared by people in other countries.

Before the mid-1800s, soap was not the highly refined commodity it is today, and the technological innovations that facilitate frequent soap consumption by all Americans had yet to be introduced. Implicit in the 18th-century clergyman John Wesley's admonition that "Cleanliness is indeed next to godliness" was the suggestion that the condition was both uncommon and difficult to attain. Soap in those days was made from animal fats, and the greasy lye-based substance spoiled so quickly that people did not wish to apply it to their bodies too often. Rather than washing, for example, Benjamin Franklin recommended a bit of dry cleaning: he sat naked in front of an open window to air himself. Many of the grooming practices considered natural and/or inevitable in the United States at the beginning of the 21st century are neither; they are culturally constructed habits that had been inculcated—largely through advertising—over the past 100 years.

The Selling of Soap

"Modern" soap appeared in the middle of the 19th century, around the time that magazines supported by advertising began to address national audiences. By substituting vegetable oils for animal fats, soap makers were able to eliminate the problem of perishability; moreover, by molding the product into cakes, they enhanced its marketability. Having improved their manufacturing processes and made their product more desirable, soap makers began to develop brand names to distinguish their lines of soap from those of their competitors. The high profit margin in soap manufacturing encouraged firms to experiment with advertising to develop regional and then national markets. The soap industry was among the first to employ advertising as a regular part of doing business, and it has remained at the forefront of innovation in techniques of mass persuasion.

In 1879 the Procter & Gamble Company learned the significance of an effective trademark when the company renamed its White Soap, calling it Ivory. Employing simple slogans such as "It floats," and meaningless but marketable assertions such as "99 and 44/100 percent pure," the firm was selling 30 million cakes a year by 1890. During the 1880s, although public discussion of such personal matters as cleanliness was still considered a questionable commercial practice, Pears' Soap began running page ads, using arresting illustrations and provocative copy ("Good morning, have you used Pears' Soap?"). The use of the pronoun *you* made toiletry ads seem personal in the otherwise anonymous impersonal world of the mass marketplace. A few years later, the same firm discovered the effectiveness of testimonial endorsements by well-known people, introducing another advertising technique that was soon widely copied.

During the 1880s and 1890s, the firm of Enoch Morgan's Sons, working with the American humorist Artemus Ward, marketed Sapolio soap with jingles that made the brand synonymous with "Spotless Town." By the late 1890s, Dr. Woodbury's, Cuticura, Wool, and Fairy soaps had joined in the clamor urging Americans to buy soap. Woodbury created the "Facial Purity League," offering buttons to all of its "members." B.T. Babbitt pioneered the sales device of the premium by ascribing value to wrappers of Babbitt's Best Soap; 25 wrappers entitled the purchaser to a picture. Rebates and fund-raising, introduced by Wool Soap in 1898, earned a penny per remitted wrapper for the Women's Christian Temperance Union. As advertising techniques advanced, the soap industry began to reshape American attitudes regarding both personal hygiene in general and the importance of the regular use of soap in particular.

Manipulating Odors

Soap manufacturers were not alone in their efforts to influence the everyday grooming behaviors of Americans. By the 1920s toiletries were among the most-promoted category of commodities sold in the United States, second only to food in advertising revenue. Lambert Pharmacal brought into vogue the practice of gargling by introducing and alerting consumers to the ostensibly debilitating effects of the "disease" of halitosis, which seemed to strike unwitting victims in epidemic proportions after it debuted in ads in 1921. The promised cure was Listerine.

Originally marketed as a disinfectant intended for hospital use, Listerine was transformed into an everyday necessity by advertising created by the company's house agency, Lambert & Feasley, Inc. Milton J. Feasley masterminded the campaign, which presented Listerine as a panacea for the socially self-conscious, first by alarming Americans about the dire consequences of offending others with hygienic slights, then by offering immediate though temporary relief from the social anxieties that the ads were designed to generate. Bad breath was a silent and secret crippler, the ads insisted, destroying relationships and ruining lives. A 1923 ad summed up the tragedy in its headline, "Always a bridesmaid, but never a bride." Seventy-six years later, *Advertising Age* ranked it among the century's top 100 ads. According to the ads, bad breath and its consequences were unmentionable—except in the ads themselves. Not even husbands and wives could discuss this delicate subject unless and until, as the ad copy warned, halitosis had been cited as grounds for divorce. The only defense against the problem was gargling.

When halitosis first assaulted the public consciousness in the Listerine ads of 1921, Lambert Pharmacal's annual earnings amounted to $115,000, and the firm did not rank among the nation's 100 largest national advertisers. By the last years of the decade, however, its annual expenditures on magazine space kept the company between fourth and sixth place among national advertisers. Meanwhile, its earnings skyrocketed from $115,000 to more than $8 million. Yet neither the product, the price, nor the package had altered significantly. Instead, consistent promotion of the negative appeal, reiterated on page after page, month after month, year after year, convinced millions of Americans to incorporate the mouthwash habit into their daily routine. Other firms were quick to realize the significance of effective mass persuasion, triggering what sociologist Robert Lynd described as "a ceaseless quest for 'million dollar merchandising ideas.'" Imitators and their ads soon abounded in the mouthwash market.

Bad breath was not the only advertised grounds for ostracism. Shortly after Lambert Pharamacal set out to make Americans worry about the alleged impact of their breath on others, Lever Brothers' ad agency Ruthrauff & Ryan introduced the term *B.O.*, or *body odor,* in its campaigns for Lifebuoy soap. The idea that perspiration might offend was not new, however; tiny ads for underarm Mum and Odorono had appeared in the back pages of women's magazines since the turn of the 20th century. But beginning in the 1920s, as magazines stuffed with ads began to inundate Americans with news of merchandise for sale, it became commonplace to find full-page testaments to "The Most Humiliating Moment in My Life." Because one never knew when disaster might strike, the ads enjoined, social acceptability required the perpetual use of products designed to mask, remove, neutralize, or otherwise adulterate the body's natural smells. Through continual repetition of the supposed social costs of going without deodorant, advertisers succeeded in reframing human odors as offensive and socially unacceptable.

The "negative appeal" of these advertising approaches may have had much to do with the meteoric rise of toiletry consumption. Advertisers claimed to know the message that one's scent could unwittingly telegraph, and it was not pretty. People who neglected hygiene risked the loss of their jobs, their chance at romance, the respect of their colleagues, their reputations, and the love of their offspring. The necessity for deodorizing was hammered into American culture over the course of decades. Deodorant soaps, sprays, antiperspirants, mouthwashes, foot powders, breath fresheners, scented shampoos, and douches came to play a prominent role in the everyday determination of Americans to win friends and influence people.

Specialty formulas soon found their niche. Lysol ads of the 1920s, for instance, warned women not to experiment with such a delicate matter as feminine hygiene, but to rely on Lysol, a product of Lehn & Fink Corporation, and advertised by the Lennen & Mitchell Agency. By the last decades of the century, aggregate expenditures on the purchase of products designed to alter body aromas were in excess of $3.5 billion per annum.

There isn't a girl who can't have the irresistible, appealing loveliness of perfect daintiness

Within the Curve of a Woman's Arm
A frank discussion of a subject too often avoided

A woman's arm! Poets have sung of its grace; artists have painted its beauty.

It should be the daintiest, sweetest thing in the world. And yet, unfortunately, it isn't, always.

There's an old offender in this quest for perfect daintiness—an offender of which we ourselves may be ever so unconscious, but which is just as truly present.

Shall we discuss it frankly?

Many a woman who says, "No, I am never annoyed by perspiration." does not know the facts—does not realize how much sweeter and daintier she would be if she were *entirely* free from it.

Of course, we aren't to blame because nature has so made us that the perspiration glands under the arms are more active than anywhere else. Nor are we to blame because the perspiration which occurs under the arm does not evaporate as readily as from other parts of the body. The curve of the arm and the constant wearing of clothing have made normal evaporation there impossible.

Would you be absolutely sure of your daintiness?

It is the chemicals of the body, not uncleanliness, that cause odor. And even though there is no active perspiration—no apparent moisture—there may be under the arms an odor unnoticed by ourselves, but distinctly noticeable to

others. For it is a physiological fact that persons troubled with perspiration odor seldom can detect it themselves.

Fastidious women who want to be absolutely sure of their daintiness have found that they could not trust to their own consciousness; they have felt the need of a toilet water which would insure them against any of this kind of underarm unpleasantness, either moisture or odor.

To meet this need, a physician formulated Odorono—a perfectly harmless and delightful toilet water. With particular women Odorono has become a toilet necessity which they use regularly two or three times a week.

So simple, so easy, so sure

No matter how much the perspiration glands may be excited by exertion, nervousness, or weather conditions, Odorono will keep your underarms always sweet and naturally dry. You then can dismiss all anxiety as to your freshness, your perfect daintiness.

The right time to use Odorono is at night before retiring. Pat it on the underarms with a bit of absorbent cotton, only two or three times a

week. Then a little talcum dusted on and you can forget all about that worst of all embarrassments—perspiration odor or moisture. Daily baths do not lessen the effect of Odorono at all.

Does excessive perspiration ruin your prettiest dresses?

Are you one of the many women who are troubled with excessive perspiration, which ruins all your prettiest blouses and dresses? To endure this condition is so unnecessary! Why, you need *never* spoil a dress with perspiration! For this severer trouble Odorono is just as effective as it is for the more subtle form of perspiration annoyance. Try it to-night and notice how exquisitely fresh and sweet you will feel.

If you are troubled in any unusual way or have had any difficulty in finding relief, let us help you solve your problem. We shall be so glad to do so. Address Ruth Miller, The Odorono Co., 719 Blair Avenue, Cincinnati, Ohio.

At all toilet counters in the United States and Canada, 60c and $1.00. Trial size, 30c. By mail postpaid if your dealer hasn't it.

Dr. Lewis B. Allyn, head of the famous Westfield Laboratories, Westfield, Massachusetts, says:

"*Experimental and practical tests show that Odorono is harmless, economical and effective when employed as directed, and will injure neither the skin nor the health.*"

Address mail orders or requests as follows:
For Canada to The Arthur Sales Co., 61 Adelaide St., East, Toronto, Ont. For France to The Agencie Américaine, 38 Avenue de l'Opéra, Paris. For Switzerland to The Agencie Américaine, 17 Boulevard Helvetique, Geneve. For England to The American Drug Supply Co., 6 Northumberland Ave., London, W. C. 2. For Mexico to H. E. Gerber & Cia, 2a Gante, 19, Mexico City. For U. S. A. to The Odorono Co., 719 Blair Avenue, Cincinnati, Ohio.

This 1919 ad for Odorono deodorant openly addressed a previously taboo subject.
The ODORONO print ad was reproduced courtesy of Chesebrough-Pond's USA Co.

Whiter Teeth

It was not until after World War I that Americans began to adopt the habit of regularly brushing their teeth. Before then, a mass market for toothbrushes did not exist. Tooth powders and creams, or dentifrices, had been sold for decades. They had been advertised to some degree since the Civil War, when the producer of Sozodont painted its product's name in such large letters on Maiden's Rock, Minnesota, that it was visible for miles to steamboat passengers on the Mississippi River. The first commercial dentifrices were marketed and consumed mainly to cure pyorrhea (inflammation of the gums) rather than to beautify the teeth. Between 1914 and 1931, however, the volume of advertising for toothpastes and powders increased 30-fold in America. In his classic study *The Economic Effects of Advertising*, Neil Borden noted that this outpouring of pronouncements on oral hygiene from firms such as Pepsodent (Lord & Thomas), Kolynos (Blackett-Sample-Hummert), Colgate (Benton and Bowles, Ted Bates & Company), Ipana (Pedler & Ryan), Pebeco (Lennen & Mitchell), and Squibb (Geyer-Cornell-Newell) "quite clearly must have been an important factor in bringing about the marked growth in primary demand for dentifrices." Using brush and paste every day to whiten, brighten, freshen, and clean one's teeth became not only fashionable but a part of normal oral dental hygiene. The positive impact of advertising on the growth of dentifrice use during the 1920s seemed obvious.

Toothpaste promotion was especially intriguing to Borden because, despite the many brands on the market, 90 percent of this increased demand involved only a dozen of the most heavily advertised brands. He compared brand preferences of consumers with advertisers' outlays for specific trade names and discovered an extraordinarily close correspondence. In 1938 Scripps-Howard Newspapers undertook an inventory of cupboards in 53,000 homes in 16 cities, in which homemakers identified the specific products on their shelves. Toothpastes or powders were reported in almost 90 percent of the homes surveyed (although only 69 percent of respondents reported that they owned toothbrushes). When Borden then compared the specific brands of paste and powder identified by housewives with the amount spent to promote those brand names in the national magazines, newspapers, farm journals, and on radio broadcasts, the correlation was virtually one to one.

Controversies

The advertising of toiletries was not without controversy. The American consumer movement can be considered at least in part a reaction to the unverifiable and frequently outrageous claims made by promoters of personal care products. During the 1920s, for example, Pebeco toothpaste was a best-selling brand that enticed purchasers by offering, through its ads, to cure "acid mouth," described as a potentially debilitating condition. The campaigns promised scientific proof of the effectiveness of Pebeco toothpaste against "acid mouth" and provided a packet of litmus paper with every tube purchased. The "acid test" was not a mere

metaphor in the 1920s but the promotional technique of a toothpaste manufacturer. Yet toxic ingredients in Pebeco, if ingested, could prove fatal. Such threats to the health and safety of consumers were brought to light in a series of exposes, among them the influential 1932 book *100,000,000 Guinea Pigs*. The potential health hazards of personal-care products and cosmetics continued to be an issue for consumers throughout the 20th century as specific ingredients (dyes, antibacterial substances) were revealed to pose health threats.

The Business of Cleanliness

One of the more significant reactions against claims made by toiletry promoters came in the form of an unprecedented cooperative advertising campaign launched by soap manufacturers in the 1920s and 1930s. The Cleanliness Institute, established by soap manufacturers in 1927, was created specifically to counter the potential threat to soap consumption posed by the surging sales of deodorants and various cosmetics. Those products masked rather than removed scents, blemishes, and other deficiencies of hygiene, and the soap makers feared that ads for those other products could make bathing seem unnecessary. The booming market for make-up—and especially the growing sales of the cold creams recommended for removing it—threatened to make soap seem redundant or obsolete. The soap industry did not stand idly by.

The mission of the Cleanliness Institute was to promote the importance of regular and frequent washing with soap. The *New York Times* immediately heralded what it described as a "new public welfare organization of national scope." The print ads and radio commercials produced by the institute resembled the individual firms' efforts to sell their specific brands, but the overall message—the importance of soap and water as the basis of personal hygiene—took precedence over the citing of brand names. The campaign infiltrated classrooms across America with textbooks, posters, fliers, and other materials designed to instruct teachers how to instill in every schoolchild the desire to be washed. The institute produced so-called news releases, expert advice on hygiene, scripts for radio spots, and prewritten speeches to be delivered to community groups, corporate interests, state and local public health agencies, medical societies, and nursing and education associations. It published the *Cleanliness Journal*, which was sent free of charge to social workers, health officials, and civic leaders.

Between July 1930 and November 1931 the advertising agency Newell-Emmett Company, Inc., coordinated a massive experiment on the effectiveness of a variety of magazine advertising appeals in promoting this message, using coupon returns as the measure of readers' responsiveness to 21 tested pitches. In the findings it published, Newell-Emmett concluded, "Surely here are differences worth the study of many advertisers." Acting in concert, the soap industry envisioned the day when the habit of washing and the consumption of soap might be so ingrained in Americans that it would take on the appearance of a biological function. As Roscoe C. Edlund, the director of the institute, observed in 1930, "The business of cleanliness is big business." Its trade association, renamed the Soap and Detergent Association, has continued to represent the soap interests to the present day.

VINCENT VINIKAS

See also Bristol-Myers Squibb Company; Colgate-Palmolive Company; Crest; Feminine Hygiene and Intimacy Products; Lever Brothers Company/Unilever; Procter & Gamble Company; *and color plate in this volume*

Further Reading

Borden, Neil Hopper, "The Effect of Advertising on the Demand for Dentifrices," in *The Economic Effects of Advertising*, by Borden, Chicago: Irwin, 1942

Coupon Returns: One Advertiser's Experience, New York: Newell-Emmett, 1932

Hoy, Suellen M., *Chasing Dirt: The American Pursuit of Cleanliness*, New York: Oxford University Press, 1995

Kallet, Arthur, and Frederick John Schlink, *100,000,000 Guinea Pigs: Dangers in Everyday Foods, Drugs, and Cosmetics*, New York: Vanguard, 1932

Lambert, Gerard B., "How I Sold Listerine," in *The Amazing Advertising Business*, New York: Simon and Schuster, 1957

Lynd, Robert S., and Alice C. Hanson [Jones], "The People as Consumers," in *Recent Social Trends in the United States: Report of the President's Research Committee on Social Trends*, New York and London: McGraw-Hill, 1933

Miner, Horace, "Body Ritual among the Nacerima," *American Anthropologist* 58 (1956)

Vinikas, Vincent, "Lustrum of the Cleanliness Institute, 1927–1932," *Journal of Social History* 22 (Summer 1989)

Vinikas, Vincent, *Soft Soap, Hard Sell: American Hygiene in an Age of Advertisement*, Ames: Iowa State University Press, 1992

Persuasion Theory

Persuasion theory is the set of precepts and tenets that attempt to explain, predict, and manipulate the impact of communications of various kinds, including advertising and public relations. In advertising, in particular, persuasion theory concerns the attempt to influence people to do something they otherwise would not consider had they not been exposed to the message or feelings conveyed by the advertisement.

Advertising is considered to be a tool of persuasion, as it usually attempts to influence its audience and "win them over." Like other tools of persuasion, advertising seeks to create, change, or shape the attitudes and behavior of receivers. Such change does generally occur, even though receivers tend to recognize the conflict that exists between their own goals and those of the advertiser. For example, buyers of goods typically want lower prices and better selections. Manufacturers and retailers, on the other hand, typically seek to increase profit margins by raising prices and offering fewer options. Persuasion attempts to reduce the natural condition of estrangement separating advertisers from the public, while at the same time moving the public to the position advocated by advertisers. These ideas lead to the widely held belief that advertisers and audiences alike participate in the process of persuasion.

Persuasion theory in advertising consists of both state-of-the-art knowledge and classic perspectives concerning the models, methods, thoughts, and relationships among advertising variables. It advances and tests models that attempt to position and clarify advertising variables. Perhaps most important, it permits researchers to undertake systematic and contingent studies so that advertising can be better understood.

Beyond the theoretical realm, persuasion theory has value at the practical level as well. Advertisers use it when making decisions about creative message strategies, media plans, and research projects. It helps agency personnel and advertisers better understand all phases and aspects of advertising campaigns, shedding light on such critical functions as researching the situation, planning, creating, executing, coordinating, scheduling, and controlling the campaign. Persuasion theory also aids advertising strategists in making informed decisions about such factors as claims and basic appeals, formats, executional elements, and copy.

Advertising's Effects

Understanding the effect of advertising—whether positive or negative—on its audience is the focal point of persuasion theory. Positive effects include such variables as extent of audience exposure and attention to a message, extent of audience interest in the message, degree to which the audience recognizes and remembers the sponsor's name and experiences warm feelings for the sponsor or brand, and the like. Favorable results also include effects that lead toward further purchases or that are deemed important to advertisers (e.g., providing word-of-mouth endorsements, visiting a Web site, voting for a candidate, requesting additional information, or scheduling a product demonstration). When an ad has a positive impact on its audience, those who receive the message may bolster its "executional cues." For example, receivers who hold positive attitudes toward the source of the message—say, a popular cartoon character or a star athlete—may associate those positive feelings with the brand, thus reinforcing an already strongly favorable attitude toward the brand. When their reactions to executional elements are positive, readers, viewers, and listeners tend to like and value the advertisement as well as the brand or the company.

Conversely, audiences can react negatively to advertisements, judging a message to be irrelevant, difficult to understand, or unworthy of their attention. Research has found that audiences at the turn of the 21st century were well versed in these negative reactions, as indicated by the ease with which most use the remote control to change channels during television commercials. Likewise, research has shown that ads based on fear appeals are often ignored by the public, who simply conclude that the negative consequences dramatized in the message would never actually befall them. Audiences may respond negatively to the source of the ad message or any other executional element.

Negative reactions to advertising campaigns have led to public outcries, boycotts, and regulatory action. In 1997 R.J. Reynolds Tobacco Company, the marketer of Camel cigarettes, agreed to phase out Joe Camel, a popular cartoon spokes-character, under pressure from the antitobacco lobby, which contended that Joe Camel was too powerful an influence on teenagers. Earlier the National Organization for Women successfully opposed the motherly Mrs. Olson, a fictitious spokeswoman for Procter & Gamble Company's Folgers coffee, arguing that commercials featuring her unfairly stereotyped young women as being incapable of making a cup of coffee without the assistance of an older woman. The threat of negative effects, such as a campaign's failure, can provide advertisers with the impetus to advance persuasion theory and unearth better explanations for why advertising succeeds or fails.

Because persuasion theory investigates both how advertising influences people and how they resist it, it helps advertisers predict how best to deal with an audience's possible reactions. It is also helpful in designing media plans that are concerned with the dissemination of the message rather than with message creation.

Message Learning Theory

Early interest in building a body of knowledge about persuasion theory can be traced to Yale University, in New Haven, Connecticut, and psychologist Carl I. Hovland, who conducted studies there during the 1940s and 1950s. Hovland was credited with undertaking the first systematic research projects on learning and attitude change. He and his peers, Icek Ajzen, Martin Fishbein, Milton Rosenberg, and Wilbur Schramm, are credited with creating the discipline of persuasion theory.

Hovland's work, *Message Learning Theory,* posits that the more people learn and remember from an advertisement, the more persuasive the advertisement will be. His research focused on a range of factors linked to learning and memory. Research designs were built around the step-by-step process through which people were persuaded: attention, comprehension, yielding, and retention of the message. Message learning theory can be divided into several areas of study. Message repetition, for example, seeks

to discover the ideal number of times an audience needs to be exposed to a message to trigger desirable effects. Message repetition studies attempt to isolate the number of repetitions that precede "wear-out," a threshold beyond which the audience becomes satiated with and tunes out the message.

Many practical guidelines for developing advertising strategy were posited by message learning theory. Guidelines suggest, for example, that repetition of the message increases learning; commercials wear out faster among serious TV users; and commercials that employ brand users as the message source wear out more slowly than do those that use only straightforward claims and basic support. Message learning theory also investigates the temporal order of messages, with the goal of identifying where best to place strong arguments within the advertisement.

Research into "source characteristics" is another major track within message learning theory. Hovland and his colleagues argued that the source of the message had a huge persuasive impact on audiences. They posited that audiences evaluate the source using two independent characteristics—the degree to which the speaker is perceived to be an expert on the topic and the degree to which the speaker is perceived to be trustworthy. Message learning theorists also investigated characteristics of the receivers. They sought to determine if certain audience segments, once separated from the general population on the basis of personality traits or demographic characteristics, are more readily persuaded by advertising than other groups.

Finally, the characteristics of communication channels—television, radio, newspapers, magazines, and billboards, among others—were studied, and a number of conclusions were drawn. For example, evidence suggested that radio was a poor choice for an advertiser conveying a message that is difficult to comprehend. The core of message learning theory resides in the belief that the degree of persuasion is associated with the degree to which the audience learns and retains the message. The greater the learning and retention, the greater the persuasion.

Self-Persuasion Theory

In sharp contrast to message learning theory, self-persuasion theory argues that advertisers can learn a great deal about advertising effectiveness if they explore how people persuade themselves after being exposed to an advertisement. In self-persuasion theory, the degree of persuasion is linked to the way receivers become involved with and react to the message. Those following this school of thought contend that learning is not the only factor triggering persuasion; the audience does more with an advertisement than simply remember its arguments. Receivers become involved with the advertisement, and elaborate on the message. They take an active role in establishing the advertisement's meaning and persuading themselves to bolster, accept, distort, derogate, or reject the advice contained in the message.

The elaboration-likelihood model proposed by Richard E. Petty and John T. Cacioppo in 1986 demonstrates the self-persuasion theory. It posits three forces that cause receivers to elaborate in one of two ways when processing an advertisement.

Here the term "elaboration" implies issue-relevant thinking about such aspects of the advertisement as its topics, arguments, implications, consequences, promises, and executional elements. The three forces are motivation (i.e., the need for information about brand-based benefits), the ability or expertise to grasp the arguments, and the opportunity to process benefit-based claims. The two routes that receivers can elaborate on are the central and the peripheral routes. If receivers have the motivation, ability, and opportunity to process information, they will follow the central route in processing the information, elaborating rationally on such direct benefit-based claims as gas mileage or trunk space when dealing with the purchase of a car, for example. Conversely, receivers will elaborate on the peripheral cues (e.g., the setting, originality, humor, and feelings conveyed) contained in the advertisement when they lack the motivation, ability, and opportunity to judge rational, benefit-based appeals. This model highlights the central premise of self-persuasion theory; persuasion depends on the involvement that receivers attach to the message.

Three Learning Theories

Persuasion theory has borrowed much of its foundation from other academic fields, especially the behavioral sciences. Three widely used learning theories borrowed from the behavioral sciences are classical conditioning, instrumental learning, and social learning theory. Common to these theories is the view that learning is a process by which human behavior is acquired or changed through events in one's environment. Moreover, an explicable or predictable relationship exists between stimuli and responses. Learning theory produced several implications for advertising strategists:

- Individuals differ in their ability, readiness, and motivation to deal with a persuasive message.
- Reinforcement is helpful in establishing response.
- Active participation is better than passive participation.
- Meaningful responses to messages are learned more easily than meaningless ones.

Classical Conditioning

Classical conditioning learning theory, in particular, concerns passive learning; certain conditioning over time triggers specific learned behavioral responses. The effects of the classical conditioning approach have been applied in studies investigating the persuasive effects of advertising. Here the research question centers on how best to design advertising to condition an audience's attitude so receivers respond in a way favorable to the advertiser. Most importantly, advertising messages that draw on the classical conditioning approach are without direct, benefit-based brand claims; that is, they lack rational claims using facts and evidence that support them—such as gas mileage, trade-in value, number of seats, and trunk space when purchasing a car. The goal is to associate positive feelings with the brand through such execu-

Yale University psychologist Carl Hovland, shown in 1940, was one of several pioneering social scientists credited with creating the concept of persuasion theory.
Yale Picture Collection, Manuscripts and Archives, Yale University Library.

tional elements as pleasant or compelling music, lifestyle associations, desirable moods, and humorous messages.

Perhaps transformational advertising best explains the effective role of classical conditioning in persuasive advertising. In transformational advertising, the brand or offering is paired with pleasant feelings, humor, or warmth in such a way that the pairing changes, in a highly favorable direction, the experience of buying and using a product. For example, experts believe that the experience of smoking a Marlboro cigarette, due to its masculine, cowboy image, is different from that of smoking a Virginia Slims cigarette, which is geared toward women. Similarly, advertising has been credited with transforming the image of Levi Strauss and Company's 501 jeans far beyond the generic level of basic utilitarian attributes.

Transformational advertising is expensive, requires frequent and consistent exposure, and has long-term results, which may make its use inappropriate for products related to drudgery or unpleasant but necessary experiences, such as oven cleaners and car waxes. In addition, to be accepted by an audience, transformational advertising must be consistent since the message is abstract rather than factual or concrete.

Transformational advertising has demonstrated the persuasive power to turn around negative attitudes toward brands and services. State Farm Insurance Companies' campaign themed "Like a good neighbor, State Farm is there!" helped people see the positive side of an insurance company. Preliminary findings from research employing classical conditioning suggest that it works best for products that are neutral or unfamiliar to the receivers, and in addition, forward conditioning tends to be more effective. Forward conditioning occurs when the conditioned stimulus (i.e., the product, service, or political figure) is presented for a few seconds before it is paired with the unconditioned stimulus (e.g., the pleasant music or humor).

Instrumental Learning

Instrumental learning, a second learning theory also called operant conditioning, concerns the manipulation of behavior through reward and punishment. Given a desired or "correct" response, a reward of value to the receiver is given in an attempt to fix or strengthen that person's behavior. Conversely punishments can be given for unacceptable behavior. People wish to maximize rewards and minimize punishments in operant conditioning. Research indicates that receivers have accepted verbal messages as rewards for specific behaviors. Verbal messages can communicate acceptance of a response or can play to the receiver's ego, for example, building rapport with an audience and serving as rewards. In addition, many advertisers are concerned with demonstrating the direct or higher-order rewards accrued from using their offerings. Research has shown that promises suggesting benefits and rewards should be perceived as trustworthy and credible. Findings also suggest that powerful support for claims are needed to maximize their persuasive impact.

Social Learning

Social learning theory was developed as researchers sought a theory of learning that did not rely on passive learning. They believed that people reward themselves intrinsically, planning actions around self-learned satisfactions. Reinforcement is defined as knowledge of the probable and imagined positive and negative consequences of future behavior. Reinforcement, according to social learning theory, serves two functions. It conveys the information people use to distinguish favorable and unfavorable outcomes, and it also is viewed as motivational in that it directs future behavior.

Social learning theory appeals to advertisers because it suggests that people tend to observe others, learn from that observation, and model their behavior after others. Advertising provides receivers the opportunity to learn how to behave by allowing them to observe others as they encounter situations commonly facing the audience; thus, people or characters depicted in advertisements serve as models, and the audience can elect to follow or avoid their behaviors. According to social learning theory, audiences are most likely to copy a person or character who is similar to themselves, appears to be competent, and has high status. For example, Bill Cosby is an effective source in Jell-O advertising. He is seen as having ideologies, experiences, and values that are similar to the audience, especially regarding children. Moreover, he is recognized as being very successful in his career.

Other Insights

Advertisers have also benefited from insights unearthed by attribution theory and the theory of reasoned action. Attribution theory underscores the importance of causal inference, or a person's "perception of why things occur"; the chain of events and consequences are important. Causal meaning is essential in advertising for several reasons. Source credibility is strongly influenced by the type of causal inference receivers make concerning why the speaker is advocating a particular position. Causal attribution strives to explain why and how people make inferences about their own attitudes and reasons for their behavior. The types of causes that receivers see underlying events have a significant impact on how customers react to a company. Attribution theory was used to better understand the effectiveness of positive and negative claims in advertising. (Positive claims attempt to establish the superior benefit of a brand over its competition; conversely, negative claims indicate lack of brand superiority on one or more attributes.) Findings have shown that the believability of some product claims and the credibility of a message are increased by disclaiming superiority across brand attributes, especially when disclaiming superiority on criteria of little importance to buyers.

In a different vein, attitude theory was applied to advertising because experts originally believed that attitudes precede and influence purchase. Attitude theorists sought to uncover directives on the best ways to create, shape, and reinforce attitudes, believing that if positive attitudes could be created, actions desired by advertisers likely would follow.

The theory of reasoned action contends that behavior is rational and rarely caused by only one or two beliefs. This theory views attitude, defined as a predisposition to respond either positively or negatively to an object, as an overall factor that includes multiple beliefs about several salient and deterministic attributes. In contrast to the feelings-based behavior noted in the elaboration-likelihood model, reasoned action posits that an intention to behave is purposeful, goal-oriented, and unaffected by feelings and emotions. Choice is reasoned and based on sound judgment; it may be influenced by one intention to comply with the norms of others.

Attitude research findings, when combined with the directives uncovered from research into information processing, provide advertisers with food for thought as they create their messages. Because not all attributes are equally important to an audience, advertisers are urged to emphasize deterministic attributes and mention salient benefits of their products or services. Audiences will often reject objects that fail to offer salient attributes, although these attributes are not always strong enough to cause choice. Choice, instead, tends to depend on the evaluation of deterministic attributes since they are most highly sought by the audience.

Many other theories exist that are useful in advertising, such as cognitive consistency theory, information integration, the selectivity model, and price perception theory, each providing valuable perspectives on advertising. Persuasion theory tells advertisers how best to research, design, and disseminate advertisements to increase the persuasive effectiveness of their campaigns.

ALLEN E. SMITH

Further Reading
Aaker, David A., V. Kumar, and George S. Day, *Marketing Research,* New York: Wiley, 1980
Aaker, David A., and John G. Meyers, *Advertising Management,* Englewood Cliffs, New Jersey: Prentice-Hall, 1975; 5th edition, by Rajeev Batra, Meyers, and Aaker, Upper Saddle River, New Jersey: Prentice Hall, 1996
Ajzen, I., and M. Fishbein, "Attitude-Behavior Relations: A Theoretical Analysis and Review of Empirical Research," *Psychological Bulletin* 84 (1997)
Bettinghaus, Erwin P., and Michael J. Cody, *Persuasive Communication,* New York: Holt Rinehart and Winston, 1968
Davis, Joel J., *Advertising Research: Theory and Practice,* Upper Saddle River, New Jersey: Prentice Hall, 1997
Dunn, S. Watson, *Advertising: Its Role in Modern Marketing,* New York: Holt Rinehart Winston, 1961
Keller, Kevin Lane, *Strategic Brand Management: Building, Measuring, and Managing Brand Equity,* Upper Saddle River, New Jersey: Prentice Hall, 1998

Kleppner, Otto, *Advertising Procedure,* New York: Prentice-Hall, 1925; 14th edition, as *Kleppner's Advertising Procedure,* by J. Thomas Russell and W. Ronald Lane, Upper Saddle River, New Jersey: Prentice Hall, 1999
McGann, Anthony F., and J. Thomas Russell, *Advertising Media,* Homewood, Illinois: Irwin, 1981
O'Guinn, Thomas C., Chris T. Allen, and Richard J. Semenik, *Advertising,* Cincinnati, Ohio: South-Western College, 1998; 2nd edition, 2000
Petty, Richard E., and John T. Cacioppo, *Communication and Persuasion: Central and Peripheral Routes to Attitude Change,* New York: Springer-Verlag, 1986
Rosenberg, Milton J., et al., editors, *Attitude, Organization, and Change,* New Haven, Connecticut: Yale University Press, 1960
Sheth, Jagdish N., and Dennis E. Garrett, *Marketing Theory: Classic and Contemporary Readings,* Cincinnati, Ohio: South-Western, 1986
Solomon, Michael R., *Consumer Behavior,* Upper Saddle River, New Jersey: Prentice Hall, 1991
Vakratsas, Demetrios, and Tim Ambler, "How Advertising Works: What Do We Really Know?" *Journal of Marketing* 63, no. 1 (1999)

Pet Care Products

In the early years of the 20th century the U.S. pet supply industry consisted of small, largely regional manufacturers, distributors, and retailers. Hartz Mountain, incorporated in 1926, became one of the first national companies in the business. It began importing and selling canaries from Germany and by the 1950s had achieved annual sales of $18 million from items such as bird food, aquariums, and fish food.

Although other pet supply brands—including Tetra Fish Food, Ralston-Purina's Kitty Litter (eventually discontinued after its name became generic), and Kaytee, the largest supplier of bird and small animal food—established themselves in niches, Hartz Mountain grew to dominate the pet supply industry as a whole, ultimately offering 1,200 products, including everything from pet toys and shampoos to its best-selling flea collars. Hartz often was the only brand available in a pet store.

The company chose not to enter the dog and cat food market, however, where there were strong existing companies selling through supermarkets. Since the 1930s several food processors had marketed dog food. Armour had Dash, advertised by Foote, Cone & Belding; Swift sold Pard, advertised by J. Walter Thompson Company; and General Foods had Gaines, handled by Benton

and Bowles. In the late 1950s the dog and cat food market began to grow rapidly, with regional companies expanding nationally and new companies entering the market. In the late 1950s and early 1960s the pet food industry's average annual growth topped 10 percent, up from 5 percent per year since World War II, thanks to new product introductions and increasing pet ownership.

Purina introduced Dog Chow in 1957. Within 16 months it became the market leader in dry dog food, with a share of more than 15 percent. The company put $3 million into advertising the launch, using the theme "Is your dog an eager eater?" and distributing 18 million coupons, including 3 million free samples. Dog Chow's growth came at the expense of Gaines and its Gravy Train brand—which recovered somewhat through heavy advertising—and its Gainesburger line extension, as well as Alpo and Ken-L-Ration.

In the cat food segment, Purina added Cat Chow in 1962, again backing the product with advertising, including coupons as part of a campaign by Gardner Advertising Company. It earned a 17 percent market share within the year, mostly taken from Quaker Oats Company's Puss 'n Boots, which had a 70 percent pre-Cat Chow share and had been the market leader since 1950. Meow Mix and 9-Lives were other leading brands.

A 1976 campaign for Ralston Purina's Meow Mix used the slogan "Tastes so good cats ask for it by name."

Despite the existence of these dominant companies, the pet food segment, like the pet supply market, was fragmented; some 3,000 brands were available across the United States by the early 1960s. One supermarket chain reported it carried 32 different brands of pet food. In addition, fewer than 50 percent of U.S. pets at the end of the decade were fed prepared foods, many eating family leftovers instead.

Development of the Premium Sector

The pet care industry came into its own in the 1970s. In the pet supply segment, Hartz had more than a 75 percent share by the end of the 1970s. In the dog and cat food sector, growth came from the introduction of both new brands and extensions of existing lines.

In the face of this product proliferation, marketers relied on advertising more than ever. In 1972 Purina launched a comparative newspaper campaign directed against Alpo, emphasizing the relatively high nutrition and low price of Purina High Protein Dog Meal, and in 1979 it coordinated the coupons for its entire pet line into a single "Circus of Savings" promotion.

Despite rising industry sales and successful new-product introductions, the 1970s was a difficult period. Costs were increasing, but national wage and price controls kept manufacturers from raising retail prices. Still, one sector of the industry—premium pet foods—began to shine. Introduced in the mid-1970s, these higher-fat, higher-protein, low-mineral, no-additive foods were sold only in pet stores and veterinarians' offices. They included Science Diet, which has been the market leader since its 1977 introduction and in 2000 was a $1 billion-plus brand, and its primary competitor, Iams.

By 1982 there were 48 million dogs and 44 million cats in the United States, compared with 25 million and 22 million, respectively, in 1960. The premium sector continued to drive category growth through the 1980s. Premium brands started to appear in grocery stores, with Kal Kan's Pedigree (introduced in 1987) and Purina's O.N.E. (1988) among the leaders. More than 70 other superpremium pet foods were introduced since the 1980s.

Meanwhile the mid-priced supermarket brands were caught between the premium trend and supermarket customers' propensity to choose lower-priced private-label products—including proprietary premium offerings—over national brands. High advertising spending continued, with much of it aimed at making the products seem delicious to pet owners; for example, Purina's Butcher's Blend relaunch in 1987 resulted in the first pet food-related scratch 'n' sniff ad.

A major battle between leading advertisers developed in 1985, when Alpo filed suit against Purina, accusing its Puppy Chow advertising, which promoted the product as able to prevent or heal joint disease, of being deceptive. After years of suits and countersuits, Purina ended up paying $12 million in damages and running corrective informational ads. Although Alpo won the battle, it had to spend far more than anticipated defending its own puppy food line against unsubstantiated counterclaims.

Arrival of Superstores

In 1987 John Doughty changed the pet care industry by opening the first pet supply superstore, PetSmart, in Phoenix, Arizona. As of early 2001 there were more than 1,300 pet superstores in the United States, generating an estimated 75 percent of pet-related sales. PetSmart was the largest of these chains worldwide as of 2000, with 558 stores, followed by Petco with 485, and Pet Value International with 398, mostly outside the United States. The top two held a combined 15 percent of the U.S. market.

Whether national or regional, all of the superstores advertised heavily during the 1990s. The ten-unit Pet Supply Depot in Massachusetts ran a campaign that included print, in-store marketing, direct marketing, and broadcast ads. PetSmart aired consumer TV spots from the EvansGroup with the tag line, "PetSmart. Where pets are family," and spent an additional $1 million (as of 1995) on newspaper advertising targeting animal adoption centers, training schools, and veterinary services.

By the early 1990s the specialty market accounted for $1 billion of the $6.7 billion pet food market, with Hill's Pet Nutrition—then the owner of Science Diet—claiming 40 percent of that and Iams, 35 percent. Iams tried to lure customers away from supermarkets by offering a free bag of Iams if the pet owner brought an empty bag of a supermarket brand to a pet store, but this effort was unsuccessful since the two sales venues attracted different customers. Iams turned to direct mail, increasing brand loyalty by sending new pet owners a letter about nutrition that was addressed to the pet and referred to its owners as parents. Colgate-Palmolive Company emphasized veterinarian endorsements in its advertising for Science Diet.

Increasing competition from specialty retailers, superstores, and discounters prompted grocery chains to emphasize their private-label brands. Kroger, for example, repositioned its Pet Pride dog food and Cat's Choice cat food as upscale and supported them with in-store displays, coupons, color ads, and price promotions.

The importance of advertising in the pet food category during the 1990s was illustrated by Alpo's situation. It was fighting Kal Kan's Pedigree and Carnation's Mighty Dog for the top spot in the dog food market. But its parent company, Grand Metropolitan, cut its advertising budget by 64 percent, and Alpo lost the number-one position to Pedigree.

Dot-com Marketers

At the end of the 20th century, when consumer spending on dogs and cats was growing at 15 percent annually, the Internet became a high-profile distribution channel for pet supplies, although Web-based sales represented less than 1 percent of the total market. The leader was PetSmart.com, launched in 1999 as an independent company owned by the superstore chain. Its site attracted an estimated 1.2 million visitors per month, more than twice as many as its closest rival, Petopia.com, which was 20 percent owned by the superstore retail chain Petco. The most publicized competitor was Pets.com, launched in 1998, which carried more than 13,000 items and reportedly generated an average sale of $100.

These "dot-coms" did a considerable amount of advertising, spending between $5 million and $20 million per campaign. Petsmart.com ran ads on broadcast and cable networks and Internet portals such as Excite and Lycos, as well as print efforts; it also piggybacked on its brick-and-mortar partner's newspaper inserts to 40 million households. Rival Petopia tagged onto in-store and online advertising by its partner Petco and sponsored live events such as dog walks. Another Web site operation, Petstore.com, aired TV and radio spots in New York City and San Francisco, California, and bought banners on Ask Jeeves and Yahoo!; Allpets.com ran radio and classified ads in selected markets; and Petplanet.com enlisted spokespersons such as actress Susan Sarandon.

The most visible of all, Pets.com, placed ads on Thanksgiving Day football games and during Super Bowl XXXIV in January 2000 (a $2 million effort), had signage in 1,500 Safeway outlets, and mailed a print magazine to 1 million computer-using pet owners, veterinarian offices, and humane societies. It had revenue of $600,000 in the quarter before it started advertising; the following quarter's revenue jumped to $5 million. Pets.com's sarcastic spokes-character, a sock-puppet dog, created by TBWA/Chiat/Day, became the first ad icon from the dot-com world; after appearing in 13 TV spots, it became a pop-culture phenomenon. Still, the puppet's popularity did not prevent the company from folding in late 2000, unable to cover expenses that included nearly $15 million in advertising expenditures.

Morris and Friends

The sock puppet canine was just one of many well-known pet-related trade characters. Morris the Cat, the spokes-character for 9-Lives created by the Leo Burnett Company, is a case in point. Introduced in 1969, Morris was still active (in the form of a lookalike) more than 30 years later. The character's job was to convince brand-switching owners to select 9-Lives brand for their "finicky" cats. Morris ran for U.S. president in 1988, and more than 34 members of the media attended the press conference announcing the campaign. "The Morris Report," a 52-page color publication, was published in 1986 and had a circulation of 35,000.

Purina used a canine named Ike, the Lucky Dog, to promote its Dog Chow, while other companies associated themselves with already famous dogs and cats including Rin Tin Tin (Gaines), Benji (Purina's Moist 'n Chunky), Snoopy (Ibco), and Sylvester (9-Lives). Alpo opted for human celebrities, including actor Lorne Greene (*Bonanza*) in the 1970s and animal author and TV personality Joan Embery in the 1980s. Meanwhile notable pet industry jingles included Purina Cat Chow's Cha-Cha-like "Chow Chow Chow" and Meow Mix's "Meow, Meow, Meow, Meow" song, sung by special effects–enhanced cats. Avrett, Free & Ginsberg created the "Chow-Chow-Chow-ing" cat; Della Femina, Travisano & Partners was behind Meow Mix's singing feline.

Pet care brands have also been active in social causes. Purina sponsored Pets for People, which provides senior citizens with free pets from shelters, and the Big Cat Survival Fund, which finances the breeding of endangered species in zoos. 9-Lives was associated with the Animal Humane Association, National Adopt-a-Cat Month, and National Cat Health Month; Iams sponsored a Pet Adoptathon; PetPlanet.com worked to combat the plight of homeless pets; and Petsmart has Humane Society adoption centers in its stores.

As the industry moved into the 21st century, 58 million pet-owning households in the United States purchased food and supplies to the tune of $23 billion, according to the American Pet Products Manufacturers Association. As throughout the industry's history, growth—forecast at 10 percent to 15 percent per year—will likely be supported through significant advertising expenditures by pet supply manufacturers and retailers.

KAREN RAUGUST

Further Reading

Farrell, Dennis J., "Pet Business Silver Anniversary: 25-Year Retrospective," *Pet Business Magazine* (8 January 1999)

Freeman, Laurie, "Pets.com Socks It to Competitors," *Advertising Age* (29 November 1999)

Gallanis, Peter J., "Pet Supplies: Pure-Plays Teach Old Dogs New Tricks," *Discount Store News* (13 December 1999)

Murray, Barbara, "Iams to Expand to Grocery Chains," *Supermarket News* (17 January 2000)

Waggoner, Judy, "Chilton, Wis.-Based Bird Food Maker Continues to Spread Its Wings in Business," *Post-Crescent* (31 December 2000)

Pfizer, Inc.

Principal Agencies
William Douglas McAdams
Leo Burnett Company
Bates North America

Cline, Davis & Mann
Merkley, Newman, Harty
Deutsch, Inc.
Bates USA

In the past 150 years Pfizer has gone from a small Brooklyn, New York, chemical manufacturer to one of the largest and most-respected pharmaceutical companies in the world. Although the company was founded in 1849 and has a distinguished history, only recently has it become a household name, thanks largely to two notable achievements. In 1998 the company launched Viagra, a novel erectile dysfunction drug that has become a $1 billion-plus a year blockbuster and is often viewed as one of the most shrewdly marketed drugs of all time. Two years later, Pfizer initiated a hostile takeover of the Warner-Lambert Company that resulted in a $90 billion merger of the two companies and gave Pfizer control of Lipitor, a cholesterol-lowering drug, and blue-chip brands ranging from Listerine to Rolaids.

Two cousins, Charles Pfizer and Charles Erhart, formed Pfizer in 1849 after they arrived in Brooklyn from Germany. At first, the venture was a small chemical manufacturer, but it achieved early success after developing a way to improve the palatability of a treatment for parasitic worms. Through the latter half of the 19th century, citric acid—made from lemons, limes, and oranges and used in soft drinks and cleaning fluids—became Pfizer's central product. But raw material shortfalls left the company struggling to survive on the eve of World War I. Then in 1917 a government food chemist joined the company and pioneered a way to produce citric acid from a by-product of the cheese-making process.

While Pfizer was making scientific advances, the company offered a harbinger of the marketing prowess that it would come to be known for in the late 20th century. In December 1929 the company held a summit of its scientific and sales staffs, the first of a what was to become a twice-a-year event, giving each staff a chance to hear about the other's work.

Mass production of citric acid laid the groundwork for one of Pfizer's next great successes: mass production of penicillin. Since the discovery of the germ-killer by British scientist Alexander Fleming in 1928, production of the apparent miracle drug had been limited. As World War II unfolded, a race was on to develop a way to increase production. Using a fermentation method similar to that used to produce citric acid, the company felt it had the potential to become a mass distributor. First, however, it made the critical financial decision to invest heavily in new equipment and other infrastructure to put it in position to do so. The U.S. government turned to a number of companies to produce penicillin needed for the war effort using Pfizer's technology. But thanks to its equipment investments, Pfizer claimed it produced the bulk of the penicillin used by the Allies through the remainder of the war. Pfizer touted its "outstanding service as the world's largest producer of penicillin" in a print ad that included photos shot inside its factories. It was Pfizer's success with penicillin that launched the company on a trajectory from a local chemical manufacturer to a pharmaceutical behemoth and prompted it to go public in 1942.

At the end of the 20th century, Pfizer became as well known for its marketing wizardry as it was for its expertise in research and development. But early on, Pfizer was content to develop drugs and allow other companies to market them and attach brand names. Then in late 1950 Pfizer began to do both. When a new antibiotic, Terramycin, received government clearance, the company launched its own marketing initiative behind the drug and began building its now well-respected, large sales force. The ad agency William Douglas McAdams handled the Terramycin account and, with the help of a medical ad legend, physician Arthur Sackler, revolutionized drug promotion. With the advent of "miracle drugs" came aggressive spending and higher-quality creative work; Pfizer's campaign for Terramycin served as a bellwether. The product became the first in a long line of antibiotics Pfizer would develop, including Diflucan and Zithromax, which the company promoted via direct-to-consumer advertising in the 1990s. In 1959 William Steere, who would lead the company through its 1990s glory days, joined as a sales representative.

In the 1950s and early 1960s, Pfizer, by now using the Leo Burnett Company for its advertising, went on an acquisition binge that saw the company move into new areas and diversify. Among the acquisitions were the Coty cosmetic line (which was sold in 1992 after 29 years), Desitin anti-itch ointment, and Barbasol shaving cream—all sold over the counter through different channels than prescription drugs. (Other over-the-counter brands Pfizer continues to market include Ben-Gay and Visine.)

In 1970, as Pfizer accelerated its emphasis on developing a pharmaceutical pipeline, the company changed its name from Charles Pfizer & Company to Pfizer, Inc., and released a new logo, now widely recognized, that featured the Pfizer name inside a blue oval. Research conducted in the 1970s led to three extremely successful Pfizer drugs, all launched in 1992, that helped boost the company's fortunes: Zithromax, via an estimated $15 million campaign from Campbell Mithun Esty, Minneapolis, Minnesota, that was notable for being the first direct-to-consumer ads for an antibiotic; anti-hypertensive Norvasc; and antidepressant Zoloft.

In the 1990s Pfizer cemented its role as a world-class marketer. In late 1996, the company underwent a restructuring that unified the domestic and international sales and marketing operations, an example of how the pharmaceutical business was becoming increasingly global in scope. Pfizer achieved success not only by marketing drugs it developed but also by engaging in comarketing deals with other companies to help promote drugs it developed. Prominent examples include the 1997 launch of Lipitor with Warner-Lambert Company and the 1999 launch of an anti-arthritis drug, Celebrex, with what was then Monsanto Company. Both became almost overnight blockbusters with moderate help early on from direct-to-consumer advertising. Bates North America handled the Lipitor account until 2000, while the Leo Burnett Company had the Celebrex business. The Lipitor account was valued at about $55 million, while Celebrex eclipsed $70 million in 2000, according to Competitive Media Reporting. The Celebrex campaign was notable because the U.S. Food & Drug Administration asked the marketers to alter the TV spots in late 2000 since the federal agency felt the marketer was out of bounds in promoting the efficacy of the drug.

But Pfizer is perhaps best known for marketing a drug it discovered itself, largely by luck: Viagra. In 1992 clinical trials on a

Because our best friends have diabetes, too.

At Pfizer, we're determined to find the cures of the future. A cure for your father's Alzheimer's, your sister's heart disease, your best friend's diabetes. A cure for the ailments that touch all our families. To help create this better world, we decided to create an even better company. At the newly expanded Pfizer we have the largest pharmaceutical research team in the world, with a scientific staff of 12,000 dedicated people looking for solutions to age-old problems. This year we're spending approximately $4.5 billion searching for new cures and in the coming years we'll invest even more. We're now poised to do more for human health than any other pharmaceutical company in history. At Pfizer, our company has changed, but our mission hasn't.

Life is our life's work.

www.pfizer.com

TOMORROW'S CURES

A corporate ad for Pfizer, Inc., promoted the company as a humanitarian institution.
Creative by Botham, Inc. Couresty of Pfizer, Inc.

drug designed to improve blood flow to the heart of angina patients failed to produce a major breakthrough; however, some men reported that the drug had an intriguing, unintended side effect: it led to erections. Six years later, Pfizer launched Viagra. The new drug quickly posted huge sales figures and became part of the cultural vernacular. Partly with the help of an ad campaign by Cline, Davis & Mann, Inc., featuring former U.S. Senate majority leader and one-time presidential candidate Bob Dole, Pfizer was able to redefine the alarming term *impotence* as "erectile dysfunction," or E.D, for short. Dole did not plug Viagra directly but encouraged men suffering silently from E.D. to seek medical help. Subsequent ads emphasized Viagra's ability to resuscitate romance. Still later, Pfizer used the theme "Love life again."

In 1999, on the heels of Viagra's success in the consumer marketing arena, Pfizer began to look beyond its roster of agencies specializing in ads targeted at physicians. Seeking shops to handle some of its prominent prescription drugs, the company considered several established Madison Avenue agencies. The account for Zyrtec (an anti-allergy drug second in sales to Schering-

Plough's Claritin) went to New York City's Deutsch, Inc.; D'Arcy Masius, Benton & Bowles won the migraine remedy Relpax; the antidepressant Zoloft went to Deutsch; and following the Warner-Lambert takeover, the Lipitor business was shifted to Merkley, Newman, Harty. In a new approach to allergy remedies, a category typically filled with ads containing green (grass) and blue (sky) colors, Deutsch opted to use largely black-and-white images when it launched its first Zyrtec campaign in 2000.

The desire to gain full control of Lipitor revenue perhaps above all drove Pfizer's 1999 hostile takeover of Warner-Lambert. Pfizer, which had made some unsuccessful advances to Warner-Lambert, launched the process in stunning fashion. On 4 November 1999, an hour after Warner-Lambert and American Home Products (AHP) executives gleefully announced their intention to merge, Pfizer jumped in with a higher, hostile offer for shareholders. At first, Warner-Lambert rejected Pfizer and maintained its interest in merging with AHP, but the company finally relented and opted to go with the higher offer. The merger became official in mid-2000; the addition of Warner-Lambert brands such as Benadryl, Certs, Neosporin, Schick, Sudafed, and Trident gave

Pfizer a much stronger presence in over-the-counter products. In 2001 Bates USA, the flagship agency of Bates Worldwide, handled all but the Schick and Trident accounts, which were at the J. Walter Thompson Company.

DAVID GOETZL

Further Reading

Carlson, Peter, "Potent Medicine: A Year Ago, Viagra Hit the Shelves and the Earth Moved: Well, Sort Of," *The Washington Post* (26 March 1999)

Langreth, Robert, Gardiner Harris, and Steven Lipin, "Warner-Lambert Concedes Pfizer Bid May Be Better Than an AHP Merger," *Wall Street Journal* (14 January 2000)

Lipin, Steven, et al., "Mixing It Up: In Biggest Hostile Bid, Pfizer Offers $80 Billion for Warner-Lambert; It Acts As Target Confirms Its Own Plan to Merge with American Home; Coveting a Hot Heart Drug," *Wall Street Journal* (5 November 1999)

Rodengen, Jeffrey L., *The Legend of Pfizer,* Fort Lauderdale, Florida: Write Stuff Syndicate, 1999

Pharmaceuticals

Pharmaceuticals advertising in the United States entered a revolutionary growth period in the late 1990s as drug companies began to advertise prescription drugs directly to consumers at unprecedented levels. For decades, starting at the beginning of the 20th century, drug companies had promoted prescription medications solely to physicians, who determined which drugs their patients took. But a mix of factors in the century's last decade altered the landscape and led to the arrival of the pharmaceuticals category as one of the most important to TV, magazines, and other ad outlets.

Pharmaceuticals advertising dates to the 19th century, when itinerant peddlers—the proverbial "snake-oil" salesmen—sold patent medicines directly to consumers with no intervention from the government. Print advertising, too, was unregulated. Newspaper ads for patent medicines often used hyperbolic language, promising to cure everything from pimples to cancer. The marketers of these dubious remedies also tried to create doubt about the legitimacy of trained medical practitioners, positioning their products as a substitute for professional medical care.

Shrewd advertising allowed one marketer to turn a homemade concoction into a fortune. Lydia E. Pinkham began marketing her Vegetable Compound in print ads after she launched it in 1875 at age 56. Because the product allegedly treated an array of "female" problems, including "the change of life," Pinkham used a made-by-women-for-women appeal, billing the product as "invented by a woman [and] prepared by a woman." The product became a huge seller by the turn of the century. Ad scholar James B. Twitchell included the advertising for Lydia Pinkham's Vegetable Compound in his book *Twenty Ads That Shook the World* (2000).

In the 1800s both patent medicines and "ethical drugs"—what are now referred to as prescription drugs—were advertised to physicians. Patent medicines were also advertised to consumers, fueling their widespread use. This did not sit well with the medical profession, in part because patent medicine marketing cast aspersions on physicians. The American Medical Association (AMA) decided to fight back. In 1905 the AMA formed a Council on Pharmacy and Chemistry, which served as an oversight body, judging what qualified as a legitimate drug. The council in turn developed a directory for physicians of drugs in use at the time. Medical publications consulted the directory when weighing whether to run ads promoting certain drugs, according to *Medicine Ave.: The Story of Medical Advertising in America* (1999).

In the late 1990s, with direct-to-consumer (DTC) pharmaceuticals advertising experiencing huge growth each year, some physicians objected to the swell of ads, believing that consumers requests for specific drugs were exerting undue influence on decisions that should be made only by medical practitioners. And many doctors wished DTC would just go away. In the early years of the 20th century, physicians had prevented such advertising by means of the AMA Council's directory. Medical journals would not accept ads for drugs that were not listed in the directory, and the council would not clear any drug that was supported by ads directly aimed at the public. In 1906 the federal government formed the Food and Drug Administration (FDA), which took over supervision of drug promotions. Pharmaceuticals companies cooperated with the AMA and FDA and advertised ethical drugs to physicians only. Over time, a specialty developed that continues to be prominent: medical professional advertising.

In the 1920s, as mass advertising for consumer products took root, some pharmaceuticals companies dabbled in advertising for over-the-counter products. In keeping with the trend at the time, these ads were heavy with text about product benefits. And advertisers were careful not to arouse the anger of the medical profession. In 1921 E.R. Squibb & Sons sought to create a print campaign that would give the company a corporate brand identity as well as plugging individual products such as sodium phosphate, magnesia dental cream, and cold cream. Squibb, which had never before targeted the public, turned to N.W. Ayer's Raymond Rubicam to perform the difficult balancing act of promoting the products without provoking doctors. The result, which would prove to be a prototype of later pharmaceuticals advertising, was a campaign that was careful to portray Squibb as an altruistic company

CARBOLIC SMOKE BALL

WILL POSITIVELY CURE

COUGHS Cured in 1 week	CATARRH Cured in 1 to 3 months.	HOARSENESS Cured in 12 hours.	THROAT DEAFNESS Cured in 1 to 3 months.	INFLUENZA Cured in 24 hours.	CROUP Relieved in 5 minutes.
COLD IN THE HEAD Cured in 12 hours.	ASTHMA Relieved in 10 minutes.	LOSS OF VOICE Fully restored.	SNORING Cured in 1 week.	HAY FEVER Cured in every case.	WHOOPING COUGH Relieved the first application.
COLD ON THE CHEST Cured in 12 hours.	BRONCHITIS Cured in every case.	SORE THROAT Cured in 12 hours.	SORE EYES Cured in 2 weeks.	HEADACHE Cured in 10 minutes.	NEURALGIA Cured in 10 minutes.

As all the Diseases mentioned above proceed from one cause, they can be Cured by this Remedy.

£100 REWARD

WILL BE PAID BY THE

CARBOLIC SMOKE BALL CO.

to any Person who contracts the Increasing Epidemic,

INFLUENZA,

Colds, or any Diseases caused by taking Cold, after having used the **CARBOLIC SMOKE BALL** according to the printed directions supplied with each Ball.

£1000 IS DEPOSITED

with the ALLIANCE BANK, Regent Street, showing our sincerity in the matter.

During the last epidemic of **INFLUENZA** many thousand **CARBOLIC SMOKE BALLS** were sold as preventives against this disease, and in no ascertained case was the disease contracted by those using the **CARBOLIC SMOKE BALL**.

THE CARBOLIC SMOKE BALL,

TESTIMONIALS.

The DUKE OF PORTLAND writes: "I am much obliged for the Carbolic Smoke Ball which you have sent me, and which I find most efficacious."

SIR FREDERICK MILNER, Bart, M.P., writes from Nur. March 7, 1890: "Lady Milner and my children have derived much benefit from the Carbolic Smoke Ball."

Lady MOSTYN writes from Carbalton, Cary Crescent Torquay, Jan. 10, 1890: "Lady Mostyn believes the Carbolic Smoke Ball to be a certain check and a cure for a cold, and will have great pleasure in recommending it to her friends. Lady Mostyn hopes the Carbolic Smoke Ball will have all the success its merits deserve."

Lady ERSKINE writes from Spratton Hall, Northampton, Jan. 1, 1890: "Lady Erskine is pleased to say that the Carbolic Smoke Ball has given every satisfaction; she considers it a very good invention."

Mrs. GLADSTONE writes: "She finds the Carbolic Smoke Ball has done her a great deal of good."

Madame ADELINA PATTI writes: "Madame Patti has found the Carbolic Smoke Ball very beneficial, and the only thing that would enable her to rest well at night when having a severe cold."

AS PRESCRIBED BY

SIR MORELL MACKENZIE, M.D.,

HAS BEEN SUPPLIED TO

H.I.M. THE GERMAN EMPRESS.

H.R.H. The Duke of Edinburgh, K.G.
H.R.H. The Duke of Connaught, K.G.
The Duke of Fife, K.T.
The Marquis of Salisbury, K.G.
The Duke of Argyll, K.T.
The Duke of Westminster, K.G.
The Duke of Richmond and Gordon, K.G.
The Duke of Manchester.
The Duke of Newcastle.
The Duke of Norfolk.
The Duke of Rutland, K.G.
The Duke of Wellington.
The Marquis of Ripon, K.G.
The Earl of Derby, K.G.
Earl Spencer, K.G.
The Lord Chancellor.
The Lord Chief Justice.
Lord Tennyson.

TESTIMONIALS.

The BISHOP OF LONDON writes: "The Carbolic Smoke Ball has benefited me greatly."

The MARCHIONESS DE SAIN writes from Padworth House, Reading, Jan. 13, 1890: "The Marchioness de Sain has daily used the Smoke Ball since the commencement of the epidemic of Influenza, and has not taken the Influenza, although surrounded by those suffering from it."

Dr. J. RUSSELL HARRIS, M.D., writes from 6, Adam Street, Adelphi, Sept. 24, 1891: "Many obstinate cases of post-nasal catarrh, which have resisted other treatment, have yielded to your Carbolic Smoke Ball."

A. GIBBONS, Esq., Editor of the *Lady's Pictorial*, writes from 172, Strand, W.C., Feb. 14, 1890: "During a recent sharp attack of the prevailing epidemic I had none of the unpleasant and dangerous catarrh and bronchial symptoms. I attribute this entirely to the use of the Carbolic Smoke Ball."

The Rev. Dr. CHICHESTER A. W. READE, LL.D., D.C.L., writes from Bunstead Downs, Surrey, May 1890: "My duties in a large public institution have brought me daily, during the recent epidemic of influenza, in close contact with the disease. I have been perfectly free from any symptom by having the Smoke Ball always handy. It has also wonderfully improved my voice for speaking and singing."

The Originals of these Testimonials may be seen at our Consulting Rooms, with hundreds of others.

One CARBOLIC SMOKE BALL will last a family several months, making it the cheapest remedy in the world at the price—10s., post free.

The CARBOLIC SMOKE BALL can be refilled, when empty, at a cost of 5s., post free. Address:

CARBOLIC SMOKE BALL CO., 27, PRINCES ST., HANOVER SQ., LONDON, W.

The improbable list of cures touted by patent medicines of the 19th century led to the first efforts to regulate pharmaceutical advertising.

working to benefit people—not just to sell products. The ad told a brief, self-serving history of Squibb, referring to its physician-founder Edward R. Squibb as "inspired not by hope of financial gain [for he had money enough for all his needs], but by professional duty and personal honor." The ad also told the story of a sagacious man in Baghdad who, when asked by a younger man what makes a "Priceless Ingredient," gave the answer that would become a long-standing tag line for Squibb: "The 'Priceless Ingredient' of every product is the honor and integrity of its maker."

As the century progressed and television became increasingly popular, the marketers of over-the-counter (OTC) medicines began to use the medium as an important ad vehicle. Some found that a well-devised ad could build a brand nearly overnight, especially if it contained a clever tag and pithy message. Rosser Reeves of Ted Bates & Company was particularly skilled at crafting such ads. Reeves applied his theory of the unique selling point, or USP—a central differentiating theme including a tangible benefit of the product—to the marketing of nonprescription drugs. An ad in 1952 for Whitehall Laboratories' Anacin brought home the agony of a headache by depicting a hammer clanging inside the outline of a human head. A mother who had a headache asked her children, "Can't you play somewhere else?" The USP tag line followed: "Fast, fast, fast relief." Reeves also devised the famed "How do you spell relief? R-O-L-A-I-D-S" for Warner-Lambert—a message that has continued to be employed in TV ads for that product, later marketed by Pfizer.

Television provided a prime medium for another OTC heartburn treatment, Miles Laboratories' Alka-Seltzer, which used humor to deliver its message. In the 1960s and 1970s, a trio of agencies—Jack Tinker & Partners; Doyle Dane Bernbach (DDB); and Wells, Rich, Greene (WRG)—created memorable ads that established the brand through images such as two tablets fizzing in a glass of water and rhymes such as "Plop, plop, fizz, fizz, oh what a relief it is." After Tinker, DDB held the account for only a short period but created the "Spicy Meatball" and "Wedding Night" ads. The account then went to WRG in 1970, which offered two classics of advertising—"I Can't Believe I Ate the Whole Thing" and "No Matter What Shape Your Stomach's In." In the tradition of the Anacin and Alka-Seltzer work, nonprescription headache and heartburn remedies continued to be heavily promoted in TV ads.

By the 1990s, much of the focus of pharmaceuticals advertising had changed from its mid-century emphasis on OTCs to the burgeoning arena of direct-to-consumer ads. On a certain level, DTC ads presented agencies with a challenge unlike any other: no matter how well an ad worked with a consumer, another entity—the physician—served as the gatekeeper, determining whether a product sold. On the other hand, many of today's common OTC drugs began as prescription products. For instance, Chlor-Trimeton, a medicine for hay fever, was a prescription drug until 1976, when it became OTC. Lotrimin, Tagamet, Motrin, Naproxyn, Benadryl, and many other common OTC medicines available today once required a doctor's prescription. The transition to OTC status may or may not come after a prescription's basic 17-year patent has expired and the drug can be manufactured as a generic by any

Over 65?

Under Medicare, you are now eligible for protection against a potentially serious health hazard.

The hazard— pneumococcal pneumonia

In spite of modern antibiotics, *pneumococcal pneumonia* remains a leading cause of serious illness, hospitalization, and death among people 65 and over—especially when certain chronic ailments are present, such as diabetes or lung, kidney, or heart disease. *Pneumococcal pneumonia* is a year-round threat to health. It is not the same as a cold or flu—but it can follow as a complication in patients weakened by these illnesses.

How modern science can help protect you

A vaccine called PNEUMOVAX® (Pneumococcal Vaccine, Polyvalent, MSD) is now available that may provide protection for as long as five years against the most common causes of *pneumococcal pneumonia* in the United States. PNEUMOVAX is not a cure or a treatment, so it's important to remember that you must receive the vaccine well before such an infection develops.

What you can do

Ask your doctor how PNEUMOVAX can help you. If your physician decides you should be protected against *pneumococcal pneumonia* and you are given this vaccine, you will not need to be revaccinated for at least five years.

And now, Medicare coverage

Both the cost of PNEUMOVAX® (Pneumococcal Vaccine Polyvalent, MSD) and its administration are now covered by Medicare. Why has the government decided to pay for this vaccine? The answer is simple and sensible: *Preventing* a disease is much less costly than having to treat it. So, helping to prevent *pneumococcal pneumonia* is in the public interest—and certainly in *your* interest. Be sure to ask your doctor about PNEUMOVAX on your next visit.

 A message from Merck Sharp & Dohme— leader in vaccine research

Copyright © 1981 by Merck & Co., Inc.

Tear out this coupon and show it to your physician

Dear Doctor:
Please inform this patient whether or not he or she is an appropriate candidate for vaccination with PNEUMOVAX® (Pneumococcal Vaccine, Polyvalent, MSD) under Medicare coverage.

Although in format they resembled public service health advisories, Merck & Company's 1981 ads for Pneumovax pneumonia vaccine were the first to use direct-to-consumer appeals to create brand awareness for a prescription drug.
Courtesy of Merck & Co., Inc.

qualified company; contrary to the perceptions of many, patent life actually has no relation to OTC status. Many out-of-patent drugs continue to be sold by prescription only. The FDA makes this decision. But because of the time pressure companies are under to maximize return on a product before its patent expires and exclusivity is lost, there is a great incentive to establish a strong brand-name image during the period of exclusivity.

Drug companies first began to test the FDA's tolerance for DTC advertising in the 1980s. The initial direct ad ran in 1981; it was for Pneumovax, a pneumonia vaccine manufactured by Merck & Company. The creative work was handled by the medical advertising agency Kallir, Philips, Ross. The ad was seen as a "special public health situation," according to the authors of *Medicine Ave.*, and not as a watershed. In 1983 Boots Pharmaceuticals provoked an outcry when it ran TV and print ads in test markets comparing the cost of Motrin—which was licensed by Upjohn for the U.S. market—to the company's Rufen brand. The FDA objected and required that the marketer include specific medical information (for example, the side effects of the drug) in the ads, thus bringing this information into the realm of the

Rolaids controls
the drip of excess acid
in your stomach

consumes 47 times its weight in excess stomach acid. Each Rolaids tablet protects your stomach with thousands of medicated particles that control the steady drip of excess acid, give relief that lasts for hours.

When your stomach drips excess acid, you can suffer indigestion, that burning sensation.

Rolaids, with its exclusive buffering action, breaks into thousands of absorbent particles.

Each particle consumes 47 times its weight in excess stomach acid to bring fast, soothing relief.

In this 1965 print ad for Rolaids Antacid tablets, the discomfort of acid indigestion and the means of achieving relief were graphically illustrated.

advertising copywriter. As DTC advertising progressed, agencies often found themselves at odds with the FDA over the ways in which possible side effects should be presented. The government agency frequently insisted that ads be revised when it felt a marketer or agency had not been thorough enough. After only a short time, Boots discontinued its campaign, but its legacy had a longer shelf life. In a speech, FDA Commissioner Arthur Hull Hayes referred to DTC as a legal marketing option, a viewpoint that created controversy among physicians and others. Hayes then declared a two-year moratorium on direct-to-consumer appeals in which actual brand names were mentioned; however, "seek-help" ads, which simply encouraged people to see their doctor for a particular problem, continued to be allowed.

Over time, both approaches would prove to be useful, depending on the marketplace. Marketers that were the dominant force in a particular category often resorted to the "seek-help" or "unbranded" ad, assuming that people who went to the doctor's office would likely emerge with a prescription for their product anyway. By the same token, conventional wisdom held that a second- or third-ranked brand should employ only branded ads, thus avoiding an inadvertent contribution to a competitor's revenue.

DTC advertising continued to gain ground in the late 1980s and into the 1990s. Notable campaigns included one in 1988 by Upjohn for its new baldness inhibitor, Rogaine. Smoking cessation products such as Habitrol from Ciba, Nicoderm from Marion Merrell Dow, and ProStep from Lederle were also supported by DTC initiatives. Later, Rogaine and Nicoderm would become OTC products and receive heavy ad support by marketer Pharmacia Corporation. Jordan McGrath Case & Partners/Euro RSCG, New York City, handled both OTC accounts.

In 1997 marketers and agencies received a boost when the FDA loosened its tight reins on broadcast DTC ads, requiring them to list only the major side effects. The new FDA guidance also stated that TV or radio ads must direct consumers to "your doctor," and provide toll-free numbers, Web sites, and accompanying print ads for additional information. The FDA's move was viewed as a landmark in pharmaceuticals ad history and unleashed a boom in DTC ads. TV ad spending in the category jumped from $309 million in 1997 to $1.1 billion in 1999, according to consultancy IMS Health.

By far the most aggressive was the Schering-Plough campaign for Claritin, a non-sedative antihistamine, first patented in August 1981 and approved for prescription sale in April 1993, by which time 12 years of the patent monopoly had been consumed in the approval process without any sales. (Through various legal and legislative methods, however, the patent was later extended to December 2002.) When the FDA relaxed restrictions on DTC advertising, Schering moved quickly to pump $322 million into the marketing of Claritin. The ad agency Messner Vetere Berger McNamee Schmetterer/Euro RSCG launched a print and television campaign that was without precedent. Because FDA rules still placed firm restrictions on content, these early DTC commercials were vague. If a marketer named a brand, it could not explain what the medication did; if it offered an explanation, it could not name the brand. Schering chose to establish the brand without explaining benefits. The commercial showed the profile of a woman's face against a blue sky with puffs of clouds. Viewers found the spots frustrating at first. Judging by the drug's name, many viewers assumed it was an acne remedy. There was no way to tell without further investigation. In time, however, the FDA further relaxed restrictions, permitting greater specificity. The impact of the Claritin campaign, combined with the sales of erectile dysfunction treatment Viagra (Pfizer) and several other drugs of high public interest, changed the rules for DTC advertising forever.

Also contributing to the growth of DTC were the establishment by managed care companies of drug formularies (lists of brand-name drugs doctors in the plan could prescribe) and the resulting desire of drug companies to create consumer demand to force the health plans to expand their offerings; an increased interest among consumers in maintaining their own health; and a shift in attitude in the pharmaceuticals industry in which marketing became a major focus of companies that had previously emphasized research and development.

DTC ads made household names out of several brand-name prescription drugs, including the heavily promoted allergy drug Claritin and Viagra (which hardly needed advertising to draw attention). Both brands were noticeable for using celebrities to create consumer interest: Claritin with former *Good Morning America* host Joan Lunden in ads from CommonHealth's Quantum Group (part of the WPP Group); and Viagra with unbranded ads using former senator and presidential candidate Bob Dole in ads from Omnicom's Cline, Davis & Mann. Yet despite the Claritin and Viagra examples, in which companies spent heavily and the products produced healthy sales figures, DTC advertising was not always a surefire investment. In 1999 Hoffmann-La Roche launched a campaign behind the newly introduced weight-loss drug Xenical, from Lowe Consumer Healthcare, New York City, and the brand failed to take off. Merck, enlisting the aid of Young & Rubicam Advertising, spent an estimated $175 million on Propecia, a drug to stop hair loss, from 1998 through 2000 before halting its efforts.

As DTC advertising grew, it created a seismic shift in the agency world. Medical agencies specializing in professional ads were at the forefront of the boom, but as the genre developed, marketers began to turn to Madison Avenue's blue-chip shops to handle growing DTC accounts, where spending sometimes topped $100 million a year. Particularly successful was Deutsch, New York, which won Pfizer's Zyrtec (an allergy drug) and Zoloft (an antidepressant) accounts in a competition that included an array of creative shops. By 2001 some Madison Avenue executives were looking to hire people with experience working on accounts such as Vioxx and Celebrex (arthritis drugs from Merck and Pharmacia/Pfizer, respectively) as much as those with experience on Coke and Pepsi. At the outset of the 21st century, virtually all of the major ad networks and holding companies had acquired agencies that specialized in medical advertising.

DAVID GOETZL

See also Alka-Seltzer; American Home Products Corporation; Anacin; Bristol-Myers Squibb Company; Geritol; Ipana

Ads suggesting that consumers ask for professional advice, such as this 1982 example from Schering Corporation, have been widely used by pharmaceutical marketers.

Toothpaste/Sal Hepatica; Johnson & Johnson; Lambert Pharmaceutical; Medicine Show; Pfizer, Inc.; Warner-Lambert; *and color plate in this volume*

Further Reading

Alperstein, Neil, and Mark Peyrot, "Consumer Awareness of Prescription Drug Advertising," *Journal of Advertising Research* 33, no. 4 (July 1993)

Hall, Stephen S., "Prescription for Profit," *New York Times Magazine* (11 March 2001)

Med Ad News (1981–)

Medicine Ave.: The Story of Medical Advertising in America, Huntington, New York: Medical Advertising Hall of Fame, 1999

Pharmaceutical Executive (1981–)

Twitchell, James B., *Twenty Ads that Shook the World: The Century's Most Groundbreaking Advertising and How it Changed Us All*, New York: Crown, 2000

Philip Morris Companies

Principal Agencies
Picard, Bradner, and Brown
Biow Company, Inc.
Leo Burnett Company

The Philip Morris Companies traces its roots to a small London, England, tobacconist—a man who never saw North America and did not anticipate or attempt to found a tobacco empire. Philip Morris's first shop opened in the middle of the 19th century and originally specialized in Havana cigars and pipe tobacco—the "respectable" forms of tobacco consumption for English gentlemen of the day. In the wake of the Crimean War (1854–56), Morris noted the prevalence of cigarette use among British officers and soldiers who had developed in the field a taste for the cigarettes rolled by their Turkish allies out of sweet, aromatic Turkish tobacco. These English soldiers made cigarettes the latest vogue and more or less respectable. Determined to supply their demand, Morris began to roll and sell high-quality cigarettes in his establishment. In 1870 Morris opened a fashionable shop in Bond Street that catered not just to soldiers but diplomats and members of Parliament. In 1896 the firm of Philip Morris and Company (by then under the management of Morris's widow and brother) even received a warrant of appointment as tobacconist to the Prince of Wales, an illustrious devotee of cigarettes.

The Morris family lost control of the company in 1894, but the name Philip Morris had cachet and so was retained first by William Thomson in England and later by an American, George Whelan, who in 1919 made the Philip Morris Company of England part of his conglomerate Tobacco Products Corporation by creating the new American firm Philip Morris & Company, Ltd. Both the British and American owners positioned the company's cigarettes—including Cambridge (commonly called Philip Morris), Players, Oxford Blues, and English Ovals—as premium or luxury cigarettes.

The Luxury Smoke

Presented to the public as luxury items, and priced accordingly, Philip Morris brands did not capture much of the American market. The "Big Four" in the tobacco industry during the first decade of the 20th century (after the breakup of American Tobacco, of which, rather remarkably, Philip Morris had not been a part) through the 1950s were American Tobacco Company (Lucky Strike), R.J. Reynolds Tobacco Company (Camel), Liggett & Myers (Chesterfield), and P. Lorillard Company (Old Gold). Brown & Williamson (Kool, Raleigh) overtook Liggett & Myers for the number-three position in the 1960s.

Philip Morris made progress in the market, however, creating a comfortable, elitist niche for itself. In the mid-1920s the company tried to expand its niche and market share when it took the lead in marketing to women. Reuben Ellis, a former salesman for the

tobacco trust and then for Melachrino cigarettes, was named president of Philip Morris & Company in 1924. In January 1925 he created a new brand, Marlboro, as a cigarette for women. This was a daring move, despite the fact that women had been smoking for decades; that hotels and department stores in New York City, Chicago, Illinois, and elsewhere had long provided women's smoking rooms; and that college campuses nationwide were confronting the issue of "co-ed" smoking and beginning to relax restrictions. Women represented between 10 percent and 15 percent of the cigarette market in 1925, yet vocal and organized critics of women's "cigarette habit" persisted, and the large marketers feared a public backlash should they openly acknowledge and appeal to the feminine market.

National advertising for Marlboro, created by the New York City agency Picard, Bradner, and Brown, appeared in tony publications such as *Bon Ton* and *Vogue* in 1926 and received a glowing review in *Advertising and Selling* in March 1927. As with its other brands, Philip Morris positioned and priced Marlboro as a luxury cigarette, but with unmistakably feminine appeal. The delicate-looking white package featured a royal crest under the brand name, and the company name overlaid the crest in a florid script. Early advertisements showed an obviously female hand holding a cigarette; copy described Marlboro as "Mild as May." Later, the message became even more explicit. The ads running in the spring of 1927 often showed women in the act of smoking: "Women—when they smoke at all—quickly develop discerning taste." They took women's smoking for granted yet diffused potential opposition by targeting the elite rather than the middle class.

Philip Morris was well ahead of the industry leaders in marketing to women but failed to capture the female market. Liggett & Myers (L&M) made an indirect appeal to women in 1926 with the "Blow some my way" ads for Chesterfield cigarettes but did not continue the campaign. American Tobacco took the plunge in 1928 on behalf of its flagship Lucky Strike brand. Through celebrity endorsements from well-known women such as Amelia Earhart and Helen Hayes, American made a broad-based appeal to women by urging them to "Reach for a Lucky instead of a sweet" when "tempted to indulge." The Lucky Strike campaign took American Tobacco from a distant third in the market in 1925 (with a 16 percent share of the market) to a strong first in 1931 (with more than 33 percent), surpassing both R.J. Reynolds (RJR) and L&M. In that same period, sales of Marlboro increased but, with only a few hundred million units annually, represented a fraction of 1 percent of the U.S. cigarette market.

The People's Cigarette

Philip Morris found itself in trouble in the early years of the Great Depression. Marlboro's premium price of 20 cents per package was too steep for the average person, even though the company had been advertising it as affordable. Likewise, the eponymous

Philip Morris brand—an import from Great Britain made solely of Turkish tobacco and sold in a faux-cedar box for 25 cents—was priced above the mainstream market. The company's now-forgotten Paul Jones brand sold well at 10 cents per package, but did not generate much in the way of profit at that price. In January 1933 company President Ellis, who died later that year, decided to rename and reformulate the namesake Philip Morris cigarette as Philip Morris English Blend at 15 cents a pack and signed the Biow Company, Inc., to advertise the new brand in 1932. It was Philip Morris's first entry into the 15-cent sector, where 90 percent of the cigarette market lay. Biow's efforts propelled Philip Morris English Blend to the number-four position—behind Lucky Strike, Camel, and Chesterfield—by 1938; Philip Morris was now a real contender in the marketplace, a concern for the "Big Three." (The "Big Four" became the "Big Three" when Lorillard faded as a leading power in the cigarette market by the early 1920s, although it still had a niche among fans of Turkish and Turkish blend cigarettes; American, Liggett & Myers, and Reynolds formed the "Big Three" by the early 1920s, Reynolds having secured its place during WWI.) At the heart of Biow's campaign was the diminutive bellhop Johnny Roventini singing out "Call for Philip Morris" on the company's weekly radio programs. Roventini also appeared in print ads and store window cardboard cutouts. The campaign was the creation of Milton Biow and Kenneth Goode, Philip Morris's ad consultant since 1924. Although a bellhop and the "Call for" slogan had first appeared in a 1919 poster, Philip Morris had dropped the theme after a short time. Also, the new Philip Morris was less expensive than its all-Turkish predecessor—15 cents, rather than a quarter, for a package of 20 cigarettes—and a good value in the hard times of the Depression. Roventini became so fundamental to Philip Morris's advertising that he was taken off the weekly talent billing for radio expenses and made an employee of Philip Morris.

World War II helped lift the nation out of the Great Depression and was a particular boon for the tobacco industry. Philip Morris—the brand and the company—made tremendous gains in the early 1940s: company sales overall were up one-third by 1941, almost another quarter by 1942, and another quarter by 1943. The company, a distant but solid fourth in the domestic cigarette industry, suffered a dramatic slump in sales immediately after the war ended, but revived late in the decade. The advertising budget increased dramatically, with a considerable proportion going into radio advertising and, later, television. Among the radio programs sponsored were *Heart's Desire, Queen for a Day,* and *One Man's Opinion.* In 1951 company Chairman Al Lyon foretold a "hit" in the new sitcom genre on television and signed up *I Love Lucy.* By 1953 the show was in first place, but its sponsor remained mired in fourth position—going just so far (it had 11 percent of the domestic cigarette market) and no farther.

Philip Morris was stagnant and even in decline by 1954. American Tobacco's Pall Mall edged the Philip Morris brand out of fourth place. Even within the company it was acknowledged that the flagship brand had become stale and dreary. The stuffy brown package was uninspiring and in need of a makeover; Roventini was losing his charm for the public. The company entered the market for king-size cigarettes in 1940 with Dunhill—an old filterless brand to which Philip Morris added a cork tip and on which Executive Vice President Alfred Lyon lavished a great deal of money and attention. Marlboro, "America's luxury cigarette," had little appeal to either men or women and in 1954 still claimed less than 1 percent of the market.

Compounding the problem of waning public interest in Philip Morris was the rising public anxiety about smoking. For years the industry had tacitly acknowledged minor risks associated with smoking—such as coughing and throat irritation—in various advertising slogans and campaigns. Some of the ads created for Philip Morris by the Biow Agency claimed, "You're safer smoking Philip Morris"; Dunhill was touted as the king that "screens out irritants." With the exception of RJR, whose national advertising emphasized only pleasure, not safety, each of the other major companies publicized the health benefits that accrued from smoking their products.

Early in the 1950s, however, scientific studies asserting the dangers of cigarette smoking began to be taken seriously. One study in particular, by physicians Ernst Wynder and Evarts Graham of the Sloan Kettering Institute, published in the December 1953 issue of *Cancer Research,* made the front pages of the nation's newspapers and induced a measure of panic in the tobacco industry. Wynder and Graham reported on a more serious issue than minor cough and throat irritation: their paper described experiments with tobacco smoke condensate that had produced cancerous tumors on the skin of lab mice. Their conclusions suggested a link between smoking and cancer.

Within weeks of the article's appearance, the chief executives of the leading cigarette makers, including Oliver McComas of Philip Morris, met at the Plaza Hotel in New York City to discuss the best means of dealing with a potential crisis of public faith. Their response was two-pronged, paradoxically both hopeful and cynical. To begin with, they set up the Tobacco Industry Research Committee (TIRC), an organization devoted to issues of smoking and health, jointly funded by 14 tobacco marketers and associated groups of growers and warehouse concerns. Underlying the establishment of TIRC was the hope that further research would prove that cigarette smoking was not dangerous. Failing that, the industry leaders hoped their research would produce safe cigarettes without significant difficulty or additional cost.

In the meantime, however, they decided at that very same meeting to follow the advice of John Hill (of the new public relations firm Hill & Knowlton) and launch a public relations offensive that, while affirming their commitment to their customers' health, openly questioned the validity of the charges leveled against them. The evidence, they claimed, was inconclusive at best and allegedly tainted by the researchers' determination to attract publicity and money for their laboratories. The industry line for the next 40 years had been established. The industry set its own scientists to work to disprove a link between smoking and cancer and told the public not to worry.

The public did worry, though, and per capita cigarette consumption declined 10 percent in the early 1950s. In response, the industry expanded production of filter-tip cigarettes and marketed filtered brands as safer, milder, smarter smokes, even as it denied any danger associated with its other products. Filtered cigarettes were not new: Benson & Hedges (B&H) had been selling Parliament filter-tip cigarettes since the 1920s; Brown & Williamson introduced Viceroy in 1936 and quickly outsold Parliament, becoming (and remaining for nearly 20 years) the leader in the filter segment. Before the 1950s, however, filtered cigarettes were a small portion of the market and the "Big Three" did not pay much attention to developing their own entries. But as science took aim at tobacco, the public craved the reassurance apparently offered by filter brands such as Viceroy. Industry leaders took notice and, albeit unenthusiastically at first, rolled out their own filter brands. The small P. Lorillard Company launched Kent filters in 1952; Liggett & Myers debuted L&M filter cigarettes in 1953; and RJR introduced Winston in 1954—addressing in its advertising the fears and complaints about lost taste and smoking satisfaction that had earlier kept the industry leaders at a distance from the filter fray. Winston ran ads tagged "tastes good—like a cigarette should," produced by William Esty & Company. By the end of 1954 filtered brands accounted for a tenth of cigarette sales. That same year Philip Morris moved decisively to revive its bottom line by joining the filter wars.

George Weissman had much to do with the re-creation and revival of Philip Morris in the 1950s and 1960s. He worked in Ben Sonnenberg's public relations (PR) company until Philip Morris's McComas—in a drive to breathe life into his faltering company by hiring sales, finance, and PR managers away from top companies—made Weissman his executive assistant. Weissman identified a variety of problems with Philip Morris—including the absence of organized departments for marketing, sales, and product research and development—and in 1952 generated an internal memo on the subject that spurred the company's executives to action. Weissman also urged a quick entry into the filter field. Impressed, McComas promoted Weissman to vice president, with responsibility for marketing, packaging, and new products.

By 1954 the company was preparing to launch its "new" brand—Marlboro. An in-depth, 18-month survey conducted at Weissman's directive had revealed several facts about the customers the company hoped to bring into the Philip Morris fold. First, 61 percent of the (mostly male) 10,000 respondents had tried and abandoned filtered cigarettes, deeming the flavor inferior or the image weak. Second, Marlboro had considerable positive name recognition. Finally, although attached to a "women's cigarette," the name Marlboro nonetheless had a masculine ring. The company thus determined simultaneously to effect a sex change on the brand and to create a filtered cigarette that delivered all the flavor smokers associated with unfiltered cigarettes.

Philip Morris in 1954 made an equally momentous decision in the history of advertising: it signed with the Leo Burnett Company, Chicago. Burnett was a young company, founded by its namesake in 1935, with a handful of staff. In 1950 its billings topped $22 million; in 1954 they topped $50 million. The agency signed with Philip Morris before the launching of the new Marlboro and worked with the company to create a brand and image that brought not merely quick results and temporary popularity but enduring appeal for, and recognition by, generations of smokers. This partnership has endured for almost half a century and is in no small measure responsible for Philip Morris's climb to industry dominance.

The Marlboro Man

Burnett and Philip Morris weighed carefully what ought to be emphasized about the new product. "Filter, flavor, flip-top box" summed up the "new" qualities of Marlboro cigarettes. Marlboro's tobacco blend had been reworked to produce a strong, flavorful smoking experience, rather than one that was as "Mild as May" (as the old Marlboro ads claimed) or "off" (as disappointed consumers perceived other filtered blends to be); and its packaging—a bold red-and-white graphic design with up-to-date lettering on a unique, crush-proof, flip-top box—was entirely new and distinct from any other brand's. More important in the Marlboro marketing scheme than the tangibles of "Filter, flavor, flip-top box," however, was the "regendering" of the product. Whereas before Marlboro's personality had been elitist and feminine, it was recast as down-to-earth and ruggedly masculine. The image pegged to the new brand when rolled out in late 1954 and early 1955 was the now-iconic "Marlboro Man"; the tag line was "You get a lot to like."

Everything was riding on this effort for Philip Morris. The company had purchased B&H early in 1954 for $22.4 million, but the investment had not yet paid off. Indeed B&H's Parliament cigarette, the pioneer of the filter market, had lost 10 percent in sales under the new ownership. Philip Morris had slipped to number five in the industry.

Advertising for Marlboro was everywhere—from newspapers and billboards to radio and television—and consumers responded. The rugged Marlboro Man (at first portrayed in a range of roles—gardener, construction worker, pilot, and outdoorsman—but ultimately a cowboy) appealed to men and women, young and old. Burnett succeeded in re-creating Marlboro's image without sacrificing the female segment of the market. RJR's Winston filter was the runaway best-seller among filters, but by 1957—after just two full years on the market—Marlboro was closing in on the runners-up, Viceroy and L&M. In 1960, with Marlboro still well behind Winston and struggling to break out and ahead, Burnett launched the "Marlboro Country" campaign, creating an enduring image in American popular and consumer culture. As Richard Kluger explained in his monumental history *Ashes to Ashes*, this campaign sold the idea that "Marlboro Country" was "unpolluted [and] free of hazards to one's moral and physical health—precisely the opposite of what science and the government were saying about smoking cigarettes."

"Marlboro Country" was well populated, but in the mid-1960s science and the federal government began to suggest that it was also unsafe. U.S. Surgeon General Luther Terry issued a damning report in 1964, specifically linking cigarette smoking with disease—especially lung cancer. In the months following the Surgeon General's Report, the Federal Trade Commission (FTC) moved to restrict cigarette advertising and mandated strong health warnings on packaging. The industry, united behind the front of the Tobacco Institute, hired Earle Clements, a former senator from Kentucky, to lobby Congress to prevent FTC regulation. The mission of the Tobacco Institute, opened in Washington, D.C., in 1958 with support from the industry, was to represent the interests of the tobacco companies, growers, wholesalers, and advertisers, and remind lawmakers and the general public of the contributions made by tobacco to America's economic well-being and to the individual American's pleasure and mental health. Clements's lobby—including the Advertising Federation of America and the National Association of Broadcasters, both of which profited enormously from unregulated cigarette advertising—persuaded Congress to make an end run around the FTC. The Cigarette Labeling and Advertising Act of 1965 required mild health warnings on packaging but blocked state and local action against the industry, while preventing the FTC and other federal agencies (such as the Federal Communications Commissions [FCC]) from taking action to regulate tobacco advertising.

Success despite Regulation

In 1969, however, antismoking advocates thought they had hit on a strategy to combat the tobacco industry's advertising and public relations successes when the FCC put a novel interpretation of the "Fairness Doctrine" into effect to counter cigarette advertising by mandating equal airtime for the antismoking forces. (The Fairness Doctrine required broadcasters, as a condition of receiving an FTC license, to provide balanced coverage of controversial issues.) The antismoking ads began to air to considerable effect. One particularly wrenching commercial featured actor William Talman (of *Perry Mason* fame), who was dying of lung cancer, encouraging others not to lose out on life as he was because of cigarette smoking. Tobacco companies were nervous and so were broadcasters, which began to contemplate a plan to gradually phase out all kinds of tobacco advertising to avoid stringent regulation by Congress or the FCC. Once again, however, the tobacco companies dodged the intended bullet when they agreed to withdraw voluntarily from radio and television advertising by January 1971. The industry shrugged off both regulation and the pressure of antismoking ads that had been forced on it by the Fairness Doctrine as it shifted its multimillion-dollar advertising spending away from the broadcast media (which had accounted for 80 percent of the industry's ad spending in 1970) to print media and outdoor advertising. Expenditures on outdoor ads increased by 1,000 percent between 1970 and 1971.

Philip Morris performed superbly under the pressure applied to the tobacco industry after the 1964 report. From the 1960s to the 1980s, in the face of potentially lethal charges that cigarettes were themselves deadly, Philip Morris nonetheless managed to win over new and old smokers; the company won the reputation of being one of the smartest-run and most sophisticated companies in the United States; and its stockholders were vastly enriched.

Philip Morris—the first tobacco company large or small to appeal to women nationally when it introduced the original Marlboro brand in the 1920s—renewed its address to the female market with the introduction of Virginia Slims in 1967. Virginia Slims and other "feminine" cigarettes were never more than niche brands, none representing more than 3 percent to 5 percent of the overall market, but they boasted some creative, influential advertising. American Tobacco actually beat Philip Morris's Virginia Slims to the punch with its Silva Thins brand, but Philip Morris and Burnett crafted a sassy and humorous campaign to appeal to the women who comprised roughly 35 percent of the adult domestic market in 1967. With its congratulatory tag line "You've come a long way, baby," which capitalized on the women's movement and emphasized liberation and independence, Virginia Slims quickly passed Silva Thins in market share. That initial campaign remained memorable more than 30 years after it was unveiled in clever, but short-lived, television spots. A more recent campaign—inaugurated in December 1999—continued to push the liberationist theme with copy that urged women (now drawn from every race, class, and ethnic background) to "Find your voice."

After securing its place in the women's cigarettes niche, Philip Morris turned to marketing a low-tar, low-nicotine cigarette that would allay any potential health concerns entertained by the masses of smokers or would-be smokers. Already more than 90 percent of the company's brands were filtered by 1970; Virginia Slims offered 100s; and Marlboro Lights appeared in the 1970s. But company President Joseph Cullman needed a new brand to enter in the growing field of low-tar contenders such as RJR's Vantage and Lorillard's True. The Merit brand debuted at the end of 1975 in a blizzard of advertising: Philip Morris set aside an unprecedented $40 million for advertising in the brand's first year. Burnett created a winning campaign touting the notion that, unlike its low-tar competitors, Merit also delivered rich taste. By 1977 Merit had captured 2.4 percent of the domestic market; in 1979 the brand accounted for one out of every five cigarettes sold by Philip Morris.

In its Merit campaign, Burnett portrayed Philip Morris as the vendor of a sensible, healthful product. More commonly, however, the company positioned its products as part of a youthful, "cool," and vibrant lifestyle. In 1956 Marlboro became the first national sponsor of the National Football League (NFL) telecasts, linking cigarette smoking with sports, vigor, and masculinity. Sports sponsorship continued to keep Philip Morris on television even after the tobacco industry's self-imposed ban on broadcast advertising was put in place in 1971. In addition to the NFL, Philip Morris underwrote NASCAR racing in the United States, Le Mans racing in Europe, and, best known of all, the Virginia Slims Tennis Tournament—all of which elevated public awareness of the company throughout the 1980s.

Beyond these successful efforts to build image and keep its products in America's living rooms on the small screen, Philip Morris also began appearing on the big screen in the 1970s and 1980s, as product placement in motion pictures became an effective—and for a time unchallenged—means of indirect promotion. Tobacco companies paid hundreds of thousands of dollars to ensure notice by the movie-going public. In 1979, for example,

Philip Morris paid $42,500 to have Marlboro cigarettes and the Marlboro logo featured prominently in the film *Superman II*. In 1988 the company paid $350,000 to have its Lark cigarettes appear on screen with James Bond in *License to Kill*. In addition to those overt placements, Philip Morris also acknowledged to Congress that in 1987 and 1988 it gave away cigarettes as well as various products and props for 56 films.

By the end of the 1980s Philip Morris led the cigarette market, having finally pulled ahead of RJR on the strength of its Marlboro brand. In the 1990s, however, Philip Morris, like the rest of the tobacco industry, watched its public image erode before a wave of litigation, investigation, and regulation. By the end of the decade, cigarette advertising had been cut by more than half and the companies' options for publicizing their products were rigidly circumscribed

In the 1990s loopholes that had permitted tobacco companies to get their names on-screen by sponsoring various sporting and other events were closed, and the ban on televised cigarette advertising was finally and fully enforced. The Virginia Slims Tournament was one of the first casualties of the new and ongoing tobacco wars when the Women's Tennis Association (WTA) dissolved its decades-old relationship with Philip Morris. The WTA was responding to women and antismoking groups that protested the irony and deception inherent in linking an athletic event with a product that posed so many risks to the health of smokers and those forced to become "second-hand" smokers. (Kraft Foods, a subsidiary of Philip Morris acquired in 1988 as a result of ongoing efforts to diversify the company's holdings, stepped in briefly to sponsor the tournament but withdrew in 1993.) By 1995 the Justice Department was involved in negotiations with Philip Morris to remove signs from football stadiums, baseball parks, and basketball and hockey arenas, thus ending this form of free, indirect TV advertising.

The settlement reached by the tobacco industry and a majority of states' attorneys general in 1998 further limited the means by which Philip Morris and others could market their products. The Marlboro man no longer rides the range and Marlboro country can no longer be glimpsed just off the highway since billboards across the nation came down in 1998 and 1999. Marlboro gear—caps, jackets, towels, and duffel bags—that had been available as premiums and allegedly appealed to youthful smokers was discontinued. Moreover, the settlement mandated that Philip Morris, along with its competitors, contribute to a fund for antismoking education and advertising.

The company began to diversify its holdings in the late 1960s, and, over the years, has acquired Miller Brewing (1969), Seven-Up (1978, sold in 1986), and Kraft Foods (1988). These subsidiaries have ensured Philip Morris's continued viability in the marketplace should cigarettes become unprofitable. In 1999, however, cigarettes remained quite profitable, and Philip Morris remained the industry leader. In fact, in 1999 the company exercised its option to purchase outright from the Liggett Group (formerly Liggett & Myers) the Chesterfield, L&M, and Lark cigarette brands.

U.S. cigarette sales declined overall somewhat in the course of the tobacco wars of the 1980s and 1990s, but Marlboro retained its number-one standing and Philip Morris had 42 percent of the domestic market in 1990. The company was an international powerhouse as well—led by Marlboro, with a 17 percent share of the world cigarette market but pushing to reestablish Chesterfield as a favored brand in Europe as well, especially among young men.

After years of controversy, however, the company needed a public makeover. Notably intransigent in the face of apparently solid scientific evidence on the questions of second-hand smoke, tobacco's cancer-causing properties, and the effect of advertising on young smokers, Philip Morris and its Chief Executive Officer Geoffrey C. Bible had to face an American public that overwhelmingly believed Philip Morris, like the rest of the industry leaders, had manipulated and lied to consumers. Philip Morris began in the mid-1990s to distance itself from the youth market, ending all sample giveaways to minors, adding a label reading "Underage sale prohibited," and encouraging the licensing of all cigarette retailers. In the late 1990s, still seeking to enhance its public image, Philip Morris once again turned to Burnett and toward the end of 1999 launched a $100 million multimedia campaign promoting Philip Morris as a concerned citizen. On its Web site (www.philipmorris.com), in television spots, and in magazine ads, Philip Morris highlighted its involvement in addressing and solving the problems of hunger, disaster relief, domestic violence, and youth smoking, using the slogan "Working to make a difference." The Web site even conceded and examined the health risks of tobacco the company had spent years denying. As part of its image campaign, the company in 2002 changed its name to Altria Group, a moniker created by the WPP Group's Landor Associates, San Francisco, California.

NANCY BOWMAN

Further Reading

Cullman, Joseph F., III, *I'm a Lucky Guy*, New York: Philip Morris, 1998

Fairclough, Gordon, "Philip Morris TV Ad Campaign Seeks to Repair Cigarette Maker's Image," *Wall Street Journal* (13 October 1999)

Glantz, Stanton, et al., *The Cigarette Papers*, Berkeley: University of California Press, 1996

Hilts, Philip J., *Smoke Screen: The Truth behind the Tobacco Industry Cover-Up*, Reading, Massachusetts: Addison Wesley, 1996

Kluger, Richard, *Ashes to Ashes: America's Hundred-Year Cigarette War, the Public Health, and the Unabashed Triumph of Philip Morris*, New York: Knopf, 1996

Miles, Robert H., and Kim S. Cameron, *Coffin Nails and Corporate Strategies*, Englewood Cliffs, New Jersey: Prentice Hall, 1982

Myerson, Allen, "Selling Cigarettes: Who Needs Ads?" *New York Times* (3 March 1994)

Pollack, Judann, "Cigarette Advertising in 'New Marketing Era,'" *Advertising Age* (27 September 1997)

Pollack, Judann, "Virginia Slims Translates Theme for Many Cultures," *Advertising Age* (13 September 1999)

"A Smokin' Marlboro Man," *Business Week* (9 September 1994)

Sobel, Robert, *They Satisfy: The Cigarette in American Life,* New York: Anchor/Doubleday, 1978

Teinowitz, Ira, "Philip Morris Hits Youth Smoking," *Advertising Age* (10 July 1995)

Thackray, John, "The Marketing Merlins of Philip Morris," *Dun's Review* (April 1968)

Photography and Photographers

The objective of any advertising campaign is to convey an image or brand message that will motivate people to buy the product or use the service. The process of creating a photo-driven ad campaign begins with information derived from the overall marketing strategy. On the basis of this information, a member of the agency's creative department—usually an art director—determines what is needed pictorially for the campaign. Because advertisers are selective about the values and attitudes associated with their product, the basic photographic image idea is often determined before the photographer is hired. In some cases advertisers may choose thematic or impressionistic pictorial elements that appeal to consumers primarily on an emotional level; conversely, a campaign may call for a very literal visual representation of a product. It is the task of the photographer to translate the art director's pictorial scheme into the actual image (or series of images) that will be used in a campaign.

The style of photography used plays an important part in bringing the theme to life. For example, still-life photography, in which the product is artfully arranged as part of a tabletop display, is often used in ads for liquor brands when a close-up "beauty shot" of the product is needed. (This convention is typically observed even when the photo is not the main focus of the ad.) Portrait photography, shot either in a studio or on location, is often the preferred style when a model or celebrity figure is used to represent the brand. In some cases a specific geographic image, such as an aerial shot in the desert, is mandated by the ad's creative team to suggest a particular mood. Some photographers specialize in photographing food, and they may hire freelance food stylists who understand the artistry (and artifice) necessary to craft a mouthwatering image.

Logistics are discussed well in advance of a photo shoot. These business discussions between photographer and art director will also determine the day rate the photographer will earn (per day of shooting) and set a budget for expenses, which may include the cost of hiring assistants, stylists, and make-up artists, as well as equipment-related expenses (lenses, lighting equipment, etc.), studio rental fees, or fees for location permits.

A Look Back

Early print advertising used drawings or illustrations to convey information about a product. Illustration continued to be the norm in advertising long after the invention of photography, due to the prohibitive costs associated with shooting, developing, and reproducing a photographic image in print. In the 1920s, however, advertisers that had relied solely on illustrations found that swift advances in the technology of photography made it practically and economically feasible to use a mixture of illustration and photography. These advances included the development of a mass-produced, streamlined camera body, cheaper film, and easier-to-print negatives. Printing and production processes became more efficient, making it fairly inexpensive to place quality reproductions of photographs in print ads.

When photographs were first used in advertising, people believed that photography depicted objective "truth." By extension, the photographic likeness of a product was presumed to depict the truth or essence of the brand. Ads using photos, therefore, were perceived as both factual and persuasive, implying authenticity and desirability. Among advertisers it was considered a great coup to illustrate an ad with photos of the actual product, especially when the product itself was an innovative one, such as the latest model of a domestic washing machine, icebox, or automobile.

In Russia and Western Europe, the avant-garde of the art world influenced illustration and design in the first decades of the 20th century. Propaganda posters produced during the Russian Revolution and World War I focused on highly charged patriotic concepts, combining illustration with photography and typography to create a new graphic art form. By the 1930s European advertisers were experimenting with photomontage and photo collage, which juxtapose the three visual elements of photography, illustration, and typography to derive a whole new meaning collectively. European artists such as Man Ray, Piet Zwart, and Laszlo Moholy-Nagy manipulated photographic images to sell chocolate, automobile tires, and radios.

In the United States, however, photographic depictions in advertising were much more literal and idealized, even though—ironically—photographs in ads were so heavily retouched that they resembled illustration. By the 1930s it was finally possible to obtain negatives, positive transparencies, and prints with the capacity to render a seductive range of values and colors in both natural and artificial light. These advances in color reproduction technology dramatically changed advertising, which came to be defined by its use of vibrant colors, and entire print campaigns began to be saturated in color.

In 1936 *Life* magazine was launched, a significant event because the magazine's stories were heavily supplemented by photographs. *Life*'s photojournalistic style was provocative and memorable, and it coincided with the public's insatiable appetite for images from around the world. The print ads that appeared in the magazine soon mimicked its editorial photographic style. In addition to *Life*, *Look* magazine (in the United States), *Picture Post* (Britain), and *Paris Match* (France) all created photojournalistic looks that were adapted for advertising.

In the 1930s many renowned photographers, such as Herbert Bayer, Cecil Beaton, Walker Evans, Paul Outerbridge, Charles Sheeler, Edward Steichen, and Margaret Bourke-White, produced images for commerce. Many of these artists' styles continue to be emulated; for example, Bourke-White's machine aesthetic, the Art Deco style, and Walker Evans's Farm Security Administration work in black and white inspire contemporary commercial and noncommercial photographers alike.

After World War II, a number of photojournalists and photographers with artistic aspirations continued to be involved in advertising. The 1930s, 1940s, and early 1950s are considered by many to be the golden age of photography, and contemporary ad campaigns often employ nostalgic pastiches of photos reminiscent of that era. In a world of color, a black-and-white image can stand out and get noticed.

Marlboro: A Case Study

The Marlboro campaign from Philip Morris has always been photographically driven. Before the 1950s the brand was packaged as a milder women's cigarette, and ads created by the Milton Biow agency featured straightforward photos of sophisticated, well-dressed women using the product. In 1954 Philip Morris decided to switch its target audience for Marlboro from women to men. The new campaign created by Leo Burnett Company, Chicago, Illinois, eventually centered upon a familiar western icon, the cowboy. The early close-up, portrait-style photographs depicted a handsome young man wearing the garb of a rancher and smoking Marlboros; in a bottom corner of the ad, a package of the brand was prominently displayed. The campaign evolved visually through the years, coming to incorporate wider elements of the western environment while maintaining the general character of the established campaign. The changes were due to the ever-increasing public concern (and legal mandates) about cigarette advertising.

By the late 1990s Marlboro print advertising featured only Western landscapes. Not only had the product disappeared; gone too was the lone macho figure of the "Marlboro Man," who had been replaced in some ads by still-life close-ups of ranch gear—horses, saddles, ropes, and fences. Other ads show a recognizable western American landscape, sometimes appearing in soft focus. Because these symbols represent wilderness, nature, masculinity, and death in American culture, they might seem to be surprising choices for an advertiser aiming to appeal to a broad segment of the market. However, the campaign was effective. Marlboro is an extremely popular brand worldwide, smoked by persons of both sexes and of all occupations. Despite the changes in the photo-

graphic campaign, the advertisements have continued to evoke a consistent brand image, serving so effectively as a shorthand reference to the brand that the product itself is no longer even shown. When *Advertising Age* surveyed the 20th century's greatest campaigns, the Marlboro Man was ranked as the top ad icon of the century.

The Picture of Fashion

Richard Avedon, one of the foremost fashion photographers of the 20th century, once said, "All photographs are accurate. None of them is the truth." Avedon's fashion style evolved into a creative way of cropping images to show clothes and fashion accessories as objects of desire, a style that continues to be emulated by others in the industry. Fashion photographers have played a huge role in shaping photography as both an artistic and a commercial medium, often employing the latest technological advances in the field. A successful fashion photo does not simply show clothing or suggest exquisite tailoring; it conveys an attitude, encouraging consumers to buy the clothing in order to instill that image or feeling in their own lives.

Fashion brands compete avidly for the top photographers. In the 1980s and 1990s, Herb Ritts and David LaChappelle were two well-known fashion photographers with their own distinctive styles. Ritts's work invoked Edward Weston and the photographers from the golden age of photography. He used black and white in his advertising photography, as in an image of a woman's nude, tapered back for Norwegian Cruise Lines. In contrast, LaChappelle (who began his career creating fine art images for *Interview* magazine) created photos for such brands as Keds, Estée Lauder, Volvo, Levi's, and Diesel jeans using vivid, sometimes garish color and surrealistic references.

Fashion photography has influenced the look of television commercials, which seek to emulate the power of the still image by appropriating it frame by frame, sometimes lifting imagery directly from an existing print campaign. The fashion photographer Matthew Rolston gained industry fame in the late 1990s with his "Generation X" TV spots for the Gap brand, which featured groups of singing or dancing young people wearing the company's unisex clothing.

Impact of Technological Developments

Advances in photographic technology have greatly affected the process of graphic design. In 1979 the Scitex Company introduced a computer-based system for the production of color separations and montages. This invention all but eliminated the painstaking process of color matching and reduced a sometimes-unknown color quantity as it honed in on the true hues seen with the naked eye.

The advent of the digital still camera was perhaps the most revolutionary development of the late 20th century. The first digital camera was introduced in 1982 by the Sony Corporation, and by the late 1980s such cameras, as well as flatbed scanners, were allowing photographers and graphic artists to store and manipu-

"Oh, Ted, we must never lose this snapshot!"

IT's only a snapshot. A little square of paper. Yet it holds all the sweetness of the world's most precious baby.

Right!—they must never lose it. How important it is that they have it—that they are not letting the days slip by and make their changes, without the picture record.

The record can be a truer one than ever now. With *Kodak Verichrome Film,* your snapshots are more natural and lifelike. Bright light isn't necessary . . . no more squinting at the sun. With Verichrome you take people at their best. Load your camera with Verichrome and see the difference. Eastman Kodak Company, Rochester, New York.

The pictures you will want TOMORROW... you must take TODAY

Accept nothing but the familiar yellow box with the checkered stripe.

KODAK VERICHROME FILM

The photographs in this 1933 Kodak campaign from the J. Walter Thompson Company were taken by the renowned photographer Edward Steichen.

late negatives, prints, and slides on computers. The software program Photoshop, developed by the Adobe Corporation, is widely used by photographers, ad agencies, art directors, and graphic artists worldwide. Such photo software eliminates the need to retouch photos in the darkroom and substitutes digital methods, which can produce astounding results. Digital technology also spawned advances in color reproduction. Whereas certain colors or shades (e.g., lime green) cannot be accurately reproduced with traditional printing techniques, digital prints can match exactly colors that appear in the original. The digital camera is widely used for catalog shoots and for many print ads—especially those produced under tight deadlines. In spite of the digital revolution, however, large format, medium format, and 35 mm photography remained popular with commercial photographers, and the digital and analog techniques continued to coexist.

JAN ARRIGO

See also color plate in this volume

Further Reading

Aaker, David A., and John G. Myers, editors, *Advertising Management,* Englewood Cliffs, New Jersey: Prentice Hall, 1975; 5th edition, edited by Aaker, Rajeev Barta, and John G. Myers, 1996

Avedon, Richard, *Evidence: 1944–1994,* New York: Random House, 1994

Frith, Katherine Toland, *Advertising in Asia: Communication, Culture, and Consumption,* Ames: Iowa State University Press, 1996

Kellner, Douglas, *Media Culture: Cultural Studies, Identity, and Politics between the Modern and the Postmodern,* New York and London: Routlege Press, 1995

Presbrey Frank, *History and Development of Advertising,* Garden City, New York: Doubleday Doran, 1929; reprint, New York: Greenwood Press, 1968

Rosenblum, Naomi, *A World History of Photography,* New York: Abbeville Press, 1984; 3rd edition, 1997

Pillsbury Company

Principal Agencies
Hutchinson Advertising Company
McCann-Erickson, Inc.
Leo Burnett Company, Inc.

Since its beginnings as a flour milling company in 1869, Pillsbury has evolved into a diversified food brand encompassing products ranging from baking mixes and toaster pastries to refrigerated dough. Through acquisitions, it also has expanded into the frozen vegetable market under the Green Giant brand, frozen pizza under the Totino's and Jeno's brands, and easy-to-prepare Mexican foods under the Old El Paso brand. Pillsbury is also the caretaker of some of the best-recognized advertising icons in the food industry, including the Pillsbury Doughboy and the Green Giant. In 2001 this portfolio of brands joined such venerable names as Cheerios and Yoplait when General Mills purchased Pillsbury from its parent company, the U.K.-based Diageo.

Pillsbury originated in 1869 when Charles A. Pillsbury bought a one-third stake in a flour mill in Minneapolis, Minnesota. Later that year, Pillsbury joined neighbor and competitor (and forerunner of General Mills) the Washburn Crosby Company, to form the Minneapolis Millers Association. C.A. Pillsbury and Company was profitable from its first year in operation and, by 1872, was producing 2,000 barrels of flour daily.

The company registered its first trademark, Pillsbury's BEST XXXX, in 1875. Millers of the day used the triple-X mark to identify their best grades of flour, a tradition dating from early Christian times; Pillsbury added the extra X to signify that its flour was the best on the market. The company also has always identified its products with a round blue logo bearing white dots around the perimeter to represent the nails on the head of a flour barrel. From the beginning Pillsbury aggressively pursued those that infringed on its trademarks; in 1885 the company won an injunction against a competitor that used the word *Best* and the symbol XXXX to identify its brands.

During the 1880s, Pillsbury's production tripled; by 1887 it was the world's largest flour milling operation. The company promoted its brands both to the trade and to consumers through newspaper and magazine advertising. In 1883 it became the first milling company to buy space in the trade publication *Northwestern Miller,* where it promoted its wares to flour exporters.

The company's philosophy was that advertising alone could not build the business of a staple product such as flour but that advertising could earn a good return on the investment. "It is up to the flour itself to carry the burden," said Charles Pillsbury (quoted in William Powell's *Pillsbury's Best*). In the 1890s the company increased the frequency of its advertising, placing print ads in the University of Minnesota's *Gopher Yearbook,* among other publications. Most consumer ads spotlighted the company's 196-pound barrel of flour, the standard consumer size at the time, while some promoted 98-pound sacks, known as halves.

The late 1890s marked the introduction of Pillsbury's products other than regular flour. Some of the items included Vitos wheat breakfast food and Germos, a health flour, both brought out in 1897; Flaked Oat Food came out in 1898. Vitos was the most successful of these early products, thanks in part to the company's consumer advertising in publications such as *Cosmopolitan*. Revenue from these new items also enabled Pillsbury to increase its advertising budget for flour. Vitos sales were large enough to lead Pillsbury, as well as its competitors, to introduce a range of breakfast foods.

In 1889 an English financial syndicate purchased several mills and elevators, along with water-power rights, in Minnesota. The purchase included Pillsbury Mills. Charles Pillsbury remained managing director of the new company, which was called Pillsbury Washburn Flour Mills Company, Ltd., and was one of the largest mills in the world. By 1908, however, the merged company was in financial trouble and went into receivership.

For a year or so, the company stopped creating new advertising, although it continued to buy space in consumer and trade publications. Many of its trade ads sought to reassure its loyal customers that Pillsbury Washburn was still in business. Ads featured headlines such as, "Mills in operation, business resumed, all contracts to be filled."

Pillsbury Washburn came out of receivership in 1909 and reorganized as the Pillsbury Flour Mills Company. It had fallen in rank to second among the largest companies in flour milling, then the fifth-largest U.S. industry. Pillsbury began to expand its product line into consumer items such as health bran, pancake flour, and wheat cereal. "Pillsbury's family of foods," as the company's flours and other products were called in its marketing materials, were advertised to housewives through publications such as the *Ladies' Home Journal*.

Pillsbury also launched an in-house flour laboratory during this period, which it publicized to the trade. Ads told commercial bakers, which were growing in number, that Pillsbury used the lab to test its flour in every conceivable commercial use, under true-to-life conditions. This meant, the ads said, that the company's products were sure to be of consistently high quality.

In 1929 Pillsbury introduced cake flour. It began advertising its products on national radio the same year. A proprietary character, Little Nick, was used to introduce Pillsbury-sponsored programming, such as the cooking show *Cooking Close-Ups* and one of the earliest network soap operas, *Today's Children* (1933–37). The latter was popular and spawned ancillary products, such as sheet music under the Today's Children name, which further helped promote Pillsbury.

In the early 1930s Pillsbury introduced more new grain products, along with a yellow cake mix, a pie crust mix, and a hot roll mix. It also acquired companies such as Globe Grain and Milling, which allowed it to diversify into new lines of pancake mixes, biscuit mixes, and pasta. The company, later known as Pillsbury Mills, Inc., stayed within the kitchen staples segment throughout the 1940s, enlarging its scope by focusing on exporting flour and increasing non-U.S. sales, selling items made specifically for food service, and supplying manufactured products—such as dry soup mixes—to U.S. troops fighting in World War II. By the end of the war, it had hired the Leo Burnett Company to work on postwar products with its existing agency, McCann-Erickson; it dropped McCann-Erickson in favor of Burnett in May 1949. During the 1940s, however, McCann-Erickson produced the long-running radio series *Grand Central Station* for the company. In the 1950s Burnett moved Pillsbury into daytime radio and television with long sponsorships of *Arthur Godfrey's Talent Scouts* and *Arthur Godfrey & His Friends* (1949–58), Art Linkletter's *House Party* (1950–54), and *The Edge of Night* (1956–84).

In 1949 Pillsbury started a tradition by sponsoring the Grand National Recipe and Baking Contest—later known as the Pillsbury Bake-Off—at the Waldorf-Astoria Hotel in New York City. Billed as the first national cooking competition, it was planned as a one-time promotion. It was such a success, however, that it became an annual event. The primary purpose of the contest is to generate publicity. But over the years it has also led to the development of new products inspired by contestants' entries. Pillsbury even introduced a Bake-Off line of products.

In 1951 Pillsbury bought Ballard & Ballard, which owned a process for storing refrigerated dough in cardboard tubes. The process was invented by a Louisville, Kentucky, baker in 1930 and refined over the years. The acquisition of Ballard & Ballard marked Pillsbury's entry into the refrigerated dough market, which became a company mainstay. The launch in 1965 of refrigerated crescent rolls coincided with the debut of the Pillsbury Doughboy, as well as the signature tag line, "Nothing says lovin' like something from the oven," both created by Burnett. The Doughboy, also known as "Poppin' Fresh," continued to represent Pillsbury's refrigerated dough products and served as an ambassador for the brand and for the company as a whole.

Pillsbury diversified throughout the 1950s and 1960s; by 1963 the Pillsbury name was on 127 products. The company advertised on both radio and television in the 1960s to support its new and continuing product lines. In fact, Pillsbury was one of the sponsors of *The Ed Sullivan Show* the night the Beatles first performed on U.S. television.

In 1964 Pillsbury opened the first Poppin' Fresh restaurant as part of a joint venture. The chain grew around a fresh-pie concept until Pillsbury sold most of the units in 1983. In 1967 Pillsbury acquired the Burger King fast-food restaurant chain, becoming the first large U.S. food company to make a significant foray into restaurant operations. This acquisition was one of many in the 1960s, some of which took Pillsbury into unrelated businesses, such as life insurance, household cleaners, publications, and computer time-sharing.

Acquisitions accounted for half the company's growth from the mid-1970s through the mid-1980s, with notable purchases including Totino's Finer Foods, a frozen pizza marketer, in 1975; restaurant chain Steak & Ale in 1976; canned and frozen vegetable purveyor Green Giant (also a longtime Burnett client) in 1979; and ice cream maker Häagen-Dazs, frozen fish company Van de Kamp, and another frozen pizza marketer, Jeno's Pizza, all in the 1980s. Pillsbury also acquired several restaurant food suppliers and restaurant operators during the early part of the decade. Internally generated product introductions in the 1980s focused on microwaveable foods, such as popcorn, pancakes, and pizza, marketed to consumers. Both new and acquired products were advertised aggressively.

From 1972 through 1986, Pillsbury broke sales and earnings records each year through acquisitions, strong sales of its 200 products available in 55 countries, and the healthy performance of its restaurant chains. In 1984 the company surpassed General Mills in volume and in 1986 introduced its most successful internally generated product ever, Toaster Strudel.

However, growth started to slow, both in the agricultural products sector and in the restaurant division. In 1988 earnings fell precipitously, and the company announced that it would rid itself of much of its restaurant business, keeping Burger King, Bennigan's, Godfather's Pizza, and Steak & Ale. Burger King, in particular, had proved a magnet for criticism in the late 1980s. Many of its new products had failed, and its advertising was inconsistent and unloved by analysts. A notable example was the notorious "Herb the Nerd" campaign from the J. Walter Thompson Company.

Pillsbury's problems were not limited to restaurants. Company-wide, it had high executive turnover, an inconsistent advertising strategy, new product failures and underperformances, and a lack of in-store promotions. Pillsbury, a pioneer in microwaveable foods, lost its leadership position in that sector. The refrigerated dough market, where Pillsbury maintained a 70 percent share, remained a bright spot; new products such as Grands! biscuits were among the best-selling introductions in the company's history.

Meanwhile, the company was fighting a takeover attempt by U.K.-based Grand Metropolitan (GrandMet, which in 1997 was renamed Diageo after merging with Guinness). Ads portrayed Poppin' Fresh wearing boxing gloves to illustrate the company's antagonism toward the merger. GrandMet succeeded in acquiring the company in 1989 for $5.8 billion, however, at which time it slashed jobs and cut expenses, funneling much of the savings into broader, more consistent advertising campaigns.

Pillsbury divisions outside of refrigerated dough, notably Burger King, required much of GrandMet's early attention. The fast-food chain was taken out of Pillsbury's jurisdiction and placed in a separate GrandMet division. GrandMet sold Pillsbury's other restaurant chains, as well as the food division's Van de Kamp and Bumble Bee operations.

At the same time, Pillsbury continued to purchase additional food companies and brands throughout the 1990s, including McGlynn Bakeries' frozen products division and Roush Products, a bread mix manufacturer for food service and commercial bakeries. In 1995 Pillsbury acquired Pet, Inc., which brought Old El Paso, Pet-Ritz, Downyflake, and Progresso into the Pillsbury fold. A noted advertising campaign premiered almost immediately in support of Old El Paso, a market leader in Mexican foods; the dancing Nacho Man character gained popularity as soon as he was introduced and was revived in many subsequent spots.

Pillsbury focused increasingly on attracting minority consumers as the 1990s proceeded, both through niche marketing campaigns and by adding more diversity to its mainstream advertising efforts. It tried to attract ethnic consumers as Bake-Off contestants; commercials portrayed the Doughboy singing blues tunes and rapping. The company introduced more than 80 new products in 1994 alone, and its international reach extended to 70 countries; its Green Giant and Häagen-Dazs brands became market leaders in Japan. It was also making its first moves into marketing in cyberspace, with a Green Giant/Prodigy tie-in, one of the most successful such promotions up to that time.

By the end of the 1990s, baking-related goods, still the company's core focus, remained strong, but sales for brands such as Progresso, Old El Paso, and Häagen-Dazs were flat or shrinking. In 1999 Pillsbury relaunched the Green Giant as its advertising spokes-character for Green Giant frozen and canned vegetables after an eight-year hiatus, but the 75-year-old brand's sales were flat and profit margins were thin.

In July 2000 General Mills announced it would purchase Pillsbury from Diageo in a $10.2 billion deal, combining Pillsbury's brands with its Betty Crocker, Cheerios, Yoplait, and Big G brands. Despite the parallel histories of Pillsbury and General Mills, there was little overlap between the products of the two $6 billion companies. In fact, baking mixes were the only area where both companies' brands were key players. Diageo announced that it would spin off the Pillsbury baking mixes to avoid antitrust concerns and that it would sell the Green Giant canned vegetable business (retaining the frozen line). Diageo was set to gain a one-third-ownership position in General Mills, which would become the world's third-largest food company. The merger became final in 2001.

KAREN RAUGUST

Further Reading

Gibson, Richard, "Grand Met to Focus on Marketing, Ads of Burger King after Pillsbury Is Bought," *Wall Street Journal* (20 December 1999)

Grant, Tina, editor, *The International Directory of Company Histories*, 33 vols., Chicago and London: St. James Press, 1988–2000; see especially vol. 13, 1996

Hume, Scott, and Julie Liesse Erickson, "What's behind Pillsbury Woes," *Advertising Age* (7 March 1988)

Hume, Scott, and Bob Geiger, "Pillsbury Battles Grand Met," *Advertising Age* (24 October 1988)

"Linda Keene: Making a Stale Business 'Poppin Fresh,'" *Sales and Marketing Management* 144, no. 4 (April 1992)

Merrill, Ann, "General Mills Buys Pillsbury for $10 Billion," *Minneapolis Star Tribune* (17 July 2000)

Powell, William J., *Pillsbury's Best: A Company History from 1869*, Minneapolis, Minnesota: Pillsbury Company, 1985

Pirella Göttsche Lowe

Founded as Pirella Göttsche in Milan, Italy, by Michael Göttsche and Emanuele Pirella, 1981; joined the Lowe Group and changed its name to Pirella Göttsche Lowe, 1985; formed media agency Chorus Media in a joint venture with CIA Medianetwork, Italy's leading media group, 1995; name changed to Lowe Lintas Pirella Göttsche & Partners, 1999.

Major Clients
Arena Swimwear
Avis Rent A Car, Inc.
Axa Insurance
British Telecom
Condé Nast
Cuore and Fini (Chiari & Forti Group)
L'Espresso
Johnson & Johnson
Levissima (San Pellegrino Group)
Max Mara
La Repubblica
Unilever

Pirella Göttsche was founded in 1981 in Milan, Italy, by Emanuele Pirella and Michael Göttsche. Pirella, a copywriter, and Göttsche, an art director, had worked together for more than 15 years at the time. They met in 1965 while working at Young & Rubicam (Y&R) in Milan. Y&R, at that time the agency with the best creative reputation in Italy, had a multinational creative department, with art directors from across Europe routinely teamed with Italian copywriters. Pirella, a junior copywriter, worked with Horst Blachian (from Y&R, Frankfurt, Germany), Tony Carillo (from Y&R, New York City), Paul Arden (art director at Saatchi & Saatchi, London, England, and future creative director of the agency), Kobi Wiesendanger (from Y&R, New York), and Göttsche (from Y&R, Frankfurt), under the creative directorship of Geoffrey Tucker (from Colman Prentiss Varley, London). Of all the pairings, Göttsche and Pirella became the agency's most award-winning team, winning the Golden Rose in 1964, the award for copywriter of the year (Pirella) in 1967, and at the Art Director Club of Italy awards in 1968.

In 1971 Göttsche, then 29 years old, and Pirella, 31, left to form their own agency, Agenzia Italia, which became known for producing the most sophisticated campaigns in Italy. Its creative department, full of young and inexperienced yet talented staff, became a training ground for other agencies' future creative directors.

Göttsche and Pirella sold a minority interest in Agenzia Italia to BBDO International in 1977, but the relationship ended in 1981, when Göttsche and Pirella left Italia/BBDO following a split with the third partner, the chairman of the agency, over creative differences. That same year Pirella and Göttsche started anew with a few other partners holding minority shares; the duo

opened a new shop, Pirella Göttsche, with initial clients such as Zegna, Alessi, Fendi and Krizia perfumes, and Cinzano. In five years the agency reached billings of $80 million, thereby joining the ranks of the top ten Italian advertising agencies.

Pirella Göttsche had an easily identified style—elegant layouts combined with aggressive, ironic headlines. The agency launched several new products in Italy, such as Gatorade from Quaker Oats Company; Pomì, a tomato sauce from Parmalat; Bonduelle vegetables; the daily newspaper *La Repubblica;* perfumes from Valentino, Fiorucci, and Krizia; Superga shoes; the MTV cable television network; and Alessi designer kitchenware.

In 1985 the Lowe Group purchased the agency and changed its name to Pirella Göttsche Lowe. Lowe, a unit of the Interpublic

This K de Krizia perfume ad, "Hymn to a woman," won an Epica award for Pirella Göttsche Lowe in 1990.
Agency: Pirella Göttsche SpA. Concept and Copy: Emanuele Pirella. Art: Enrico Maria Radaelli.

Group of Companies, provided access to the international network that Pirella Göttsche had lacked. Pirella Göttsche Lowe's rapid growth over the years, with billings of $144.4 million in 1999, was the result both of growth in existing accounts and also the acquisition of new business, such as Aprilia motorbikes, Muller yogurt, Intesa bank, and Coop retailers. Pirella Göttesche Lowe has collected a variety of awards, both national and international. It has received honors from the Art Director Club of Italy and the Cannes International Advertising Festival (bronze Lion, Superga shoes, 1997; gold Lion, Volvo, 1999; silver Lion, Artemide lamps, and bronze Lion, Excite.com, 2000), and the Grand Prix from Epica (Superga shoes, 1997).

To offer its clients a greater integration between creative and media cultures, Pirella Göttsche Lowe in 1995 formed media specialist Chorus Media, in a joint venture with CIA Medianetwork. Majority-owned by Pirella Göttsche Lowe, Chorus Media provided planning, buying, and placement and control services.

In fall 1999 the agency was renamed Lowe Lintas Pirella Göttsche & Partners after Interpublic merged the agency's parent, then known as Lowe & Partners Worldwide, with Ammirati Puris Lintas. In 2000 the agency had gross income of $32.4 million on billings of $323.4 million.

EDOARDO T. BRIOSCHI

Planned Obsolescence

Many manufacturers reduce their risk of doing business by intentionally designing products that have short life spans—in other words, they engage in "planned obsolescence." The result is to stimulate continually fresh cycles of demand for the product in question. General Motors designer Charles F. Kettering once described it as "the organized creation of dissatisfaction." Planned obsolescence is practiced largely to increase the frequency of consumers' purchases, although it may in part be a response to consumers' demands for new product designs, added features, and perceived social needs. It is practiced by many manufacturers, including those in the automobile, toy, computer hardware and software, consumer electronic, home appliance, and apparel industries.

According to Michel Kostecki, editor of *The Durable Use of Consumer Products* (1998), the commercial objective of selling larger quantities of products—as opposed to encouraging the optimal use of products—originated in England in the early 17th century, when that country began to appreciate the vital importance of commerce to the national well-being. Kostecki cites four main factors that influence companies to incorporate planned obsolescence into their product designs:

- the public's desire for novelty;
- the high costs of repair and re-manufacturing;
- incompatibility of new parts and technology with old;
- decreasing profits.

After a firm designs a product, advertisers promote the product's features, advantages, and benefits to consumers, accentuating the positive aspects planned obsolescence brings to the new product. Constructive features include technical advances such as faster, more efficient, more reliable, and/or lower-priced goods with additional options the consumer desires. Moreover, novelty in and of itself attracts some buyers simply because they take pleasure in being the first ones to own the latest gadget or technology. Through word of mouth these so-called early adopters then stimulate others to purchase newly introduced goods. It is thus in part because of the customer's demand for newer and better products that manufacturers continue to design products that will shortly be superceded by newer, better, or faster models.

In some cases, consumers make a replacement purchase because it is more cost-effective to buy a new item than to fix the existing one. Often the new model can be bought at a lower cost than the original and offers the consumer additional advantages, such as recently introduced options or features. In addition, new technology may be incompatible with the older technologies or products users currently possess; dissatisfaction with the performance of an existing product is therefore another motivation for consumers to seek out the most up-to-date goods.

Finally, industries incorporate planned obsolescence into their designs because it allows them to sell more products and generate more sales revenue. This is not entirely a selfish act. When a company increases its revenues, it is then able to engage in economies of scale that often result in reduced prices for consumers, increased equity for stockholders, and additional job benefits for employees. In addition, the company can reinvest its earnings to fund research and development projects that will yield more desirable and efficient products that consumers will buy in the future—as the planned obsolescence cycle evolves.

The Strategy of "Cannibalization"

The major effect of planned obsolescence through technical advancements is decreased product life spans. Table 1 compares the length of a product's life span in the late 1940s with that in the early 1990s.

Consumers typically consider new technologies desirable when they are superior to old technologies; however, new technologies

Table 1.   Product Life Spans.

Type of Product	Life Span in Late 1940s (years)	Life Span in Early 1990s (years)
pharmaceuticals	24	8
food	20	5
tools	16	4
games	14	3
cosmetics	12	3

are not always superior. Companies that depend on their reputations for being innovative often incorporate planned obsolescence in order to support the company's image. Intel Corporation, a marketer of microchip processors used in personal computers, practices a strategy that leads to "cannibalization." This is a process whereby a company's new products reduce demand for its older products—and thus eat into existing sales.

Businesses have recently come to accept this practice in order to avoid the risk that competitors will gain market share by presenting an advanced product of their own. For example, Intel purposely introduces new processing chips before the old processing chips become obsolete. In his book *Creating the Digital Future* Albert Yu, senior vice president and general manager of the Microprocessor Products Group at Intel, wrote, "We learned early on that given the pace of technological advances predicted by Moore's Law (that chip capacity doubles every 18–24 months), we must continue to develop better and better products to obsolete our existing products, or someone else will do that for us and leave us behind."

Intel's goal was to create a processing chip that would render obsolete its newly completed 486 chip, which, said Yu, "had made obsolete our own 386 processor, which had obsoleted our 286 earlier." The result was the Pentium processor, launched in 1993. But Intel did not stop with that processor; it continued to create faster chips, releasing the Pentium II processor in May 1997, the Pentium III processor in February 1999, and the Pentium 4 in the fall of 2000. Although two years elapsed between the first two releases, that was not enough time to render the Pentium II chips out-of-date. In fact, numerous consumers continued using Pentium II processors in their computers instead of upgrading to the Pentium III. Therefore, even though the Pentium III chip was technically better than the Pentium II, most consumers viewed the innovations as nonessential and continued using the Pentium II chip.

The marketing strategy of cannibalization is not limited to durable goods but extends over the whole range of product categories. When Miles Laboratories introduced Alka-Seltzer Plus in 1970, it quickly diminished the sales of its flagship brand, Alka-Seltzer. The reasoning was that it was preferable for sales to move to a product extension within the company rather than to a competitor's product. Also in the 1970s, Coca-Cola cannibalized its successful diet cola, Tab, by introducing Diet Coke. The strategy in this case was that the company's main entry in the category

would be strengthened by competition with the powerful Coke brand. Instead, Diet Coke was very successful—but at the expense of Tab.

Firms may think it is necessary to constantly improve their products in order to maintain market share, but customers do not always agree with this logic. Hence it is important to consult with consumers to gauge whether or not they will accept product improvements. Most customers prefer improvements that enable existing products to be upgraded continuously so that they never will become obsolete. Such a policy would also be less wasteful than replacing old items with new and therefore more environmentally friendly. But would this be practical for companies? No, according to David Lascelles, a writer for the *London Financial Times*. Lascelles contends that planned obsolescence is now thoroughly embedded in the process of industrial design. As more product markets become saturated, the only way manufacturers can generate new sales is by introducing a fresh model that lures the consumer back into the store.

Case in Point: Computers

Computers offer an example of a product that can be easily upgraded. They have "slots" for additional memory cards or other features, and the product design is often modular. Still, the pace of change is so fast in the computer industry that even the most flexibly designed machine can be out of date within a few years. Moreover, not all computers are amenable to upgrading. Product life extension is a valid corporate strategy, but it must not detract from manufacturers' more traditional concern for quality and performance. Extending the life span of a product such as a computer is effective only where manufacturers can do so without adversely affecting the product, the producer, or the consumer.

In addition to the longevity of the hardware, the computer user must consider the durability of the software. In 1995 the computer software producer Microsoft Corporation introduced Windows 95, a remarkable improvement over its Windows 3.1 operating system. Consumers around the globe embraced this revolutionary technology, and it quickly became the standard operating system for professional and personal use. Three years later, in 1998, Microsoft launched Windows 98. Although Windows 98 included features not available with Windows 95, many consumers did not see a need to buy the product. Consumers questioned the rationale of spending hundreds of dollars for a new operating system when their existing systems met their needs. In 1999 Microsoft released Windows 2000, which, according to the company, can help organizations to "Internet-enable their business with a reliable, manageable infrastructure that is optimized for existing and emerging hardware." Microsoft introduces new software frequently in order to improve a user's operating system, yet the majority of individuals do not upgrade their systems because they do not see an immediate need to do so.

In an article entitled "Throw Away Those Dated Beliefs on '90s Disposability" (*Columbus Dispatch*, 15 March 1998), Barnet D. Wolf took issue with the idea that computer users are reluctant to buy new, improved products. "Few owners can resist

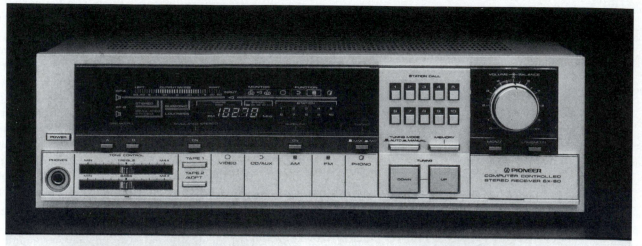

THE LONGER YOU OWN IT, THE LESS OBSOLETE IT WILL BECOME.

A lot of stereo equipment starts becoming outdated as soon as you lift it out of the box.

But not Pioneer's SX-60 Receiver. It's been planned for the future, not for obsolescence.

Because it's not just designed to be a stereo receiver, but the control center for the home entertainment system of the future.

The SX-60 has both the performance and features necessary to interface with the video and digital recording hardware and software you will certainly be buying over the next two decades.

To begin with, the SX-60 has the ability to accurately reproduce the wide dynamic range of digital recordings because of its revolutionary Non-Switching, low distortion amp (80 watts per channel into 8 ohms, 20-20,000 Hz with no more than 0.005% THD). Its incredible 95dB signal-to-noise ratio can easily handle the 90dB digital range.

And when the video/audio marriage is consummated, you'll have a receiver that will remain compatible. A video input in the SX-60 enables you to listen to VCR or video disc programs through your stereo system. And a simulated stereo circuit transforms the mono output of video (and AM) broadcasts to create theatre-quality, stereo-like imaging.

The SX-60 features Quartz-PLL digital synthesized tuning that locks in stations and prevents any drift. Plus there are 10 FM and 10 AM electronic station pre-sets and precise digital readout.

As for ease and accuracy of operation, all of the SX-60's circuits are completely microcomputer controlled.

Finally, a fluorescent pictographic display provides visual reference to the receiver's vital operating mode.

While this display may give the SX-60 a futuristic appearance today, you can rest assured that 10 or 15 years from now, it will fit right in.

⨀ PIONEER®
Because the music matters.

Directly addressing consumer concerns about obsolescence in this 1983 ad, Pioneer Electronics, Inc., characterized its SX-60 receiver as "planned for the future."

Is Volkswagen contemplating a change?

The answer is yes.

Volkswagen changes continually throughout each year. There have been 80 changes in 1959 alone.

But none of these are changes you merely see. We do not believe in planned obsolescence. We don't change a car for the sake of change. Therefore the doughty little Volkswagen shape will still be the same.

The familiar snub nose will still be intact.

Yet, good as our car is, we are constantly finding ways to make it better. For instance, we have put permanent magnets in the drain plugs. This will keep the oil free of tiny metal particles, since the metal adheres to the magnets.

Our shift, we are told, is the best in the world. But we found a way to make it even smoother. We riveted special steel springs into our clutch plate lining.

The Volkswagen has changed completely over the past eleven years, but not its heart or face.

 VW owners keep their cars year after year, secure in the knowledge that their used VW is worth almost as much as a new one.

Denouncing change for its own sake, this 1959 ad emphasized the enduring style and value of Volkswagen.
Courtesy of Volkswagen of America with the cooperation of Arnold Communications.

the temptation to upgrade," he wrote. "It is a foregone conclusion that the computer will be out of date soon after it is purchased." Of course, Wolf pointed out, obsolescence is relative. If the computer user does not install software created long after the machine was built, the computer can last for some time. However, most computer owners continually buy new software, thus turning their fast, powerful machines into slow and weak ones. Eventually, they become so exasperated that a new—and generally more expensive—computer seems to be the only solution.

Yet, one advantage of better technology is a decrease in product price. In the late 1990s many computer manufacturers offered powerful personal computers for less than $1,000. In essence, one could buy a personal computer—once a $1,500 purchase with the expectation that it would be obsolete in a three years—for the price of a television set. At approximately $500 a unit, it would cost the same to upgrade every year, which is a strategy Gateway and PeoplePC decided to adopt. With Gateway's "YourWare" lease, Gateway customers pay for the cost of their computer each month. The leasing system allows them to replace their technology every two years, thus acquiring "obsolescence protection." These two companies were hoping to capitalize on the concern that many consumers experience when buying a computer, namely that an expensive purchase will quickly become out of date. By making computers affordable and upgradeable, Gateway and PeoplePC sought to mitigate consumers' frustration with planned obsolescence.

Boon or Nuisance?

In the mid-1970s marketers began referring to planned obsolescence as "value engineering," defined by Eric Meng in a 1999 article for *PM Network* as "the process of searching for creative alternatives that increase product functionality while reducing costs." Maximizing the product's value to consumers means that consumers may have to replace the products they already own with newer versions. It is the marketer's duty to inform consumers about a product's enhancements and encourage them to purchase the new products. Since the new products are updated models of those currently in use, many consumers will have prior knowledge of them. This familiarity is beneficial to the marketer, especially if current consumer opinion of the product is positive. Once consumers know about the availability of the new item, advertisers must facilitate the actual purchase. This can be a challenging task, particularly if the products are enhanced every two or three years, as is the case within the computer industry and several others, including the music recording industry. Advertisers must convince buyers to purchase newer styles of goods by explaining design improvements and how consumers can make use of them.

Inevitably, there are those individuals who regard product innovation as a nuisance rather than a pleasure. David E. Ross wrote in the *Los Angeles Times* ("Planned Obsolescence–Its Same Old Tune," 1993):

I have an extensive collection of vinyl records, cassettes and compact discs. Already I have difficulty obtaining needles for my record player . . . I do not look forward with joy to developments that will impair my ability to keep my cassette and compact disc players in repair. . . . Now that the market for cassette and compact disc players is saturated, the manufacturers refuse to accept the resulting decline in sales. Instead, they will ask us to abandon music collections accumulated over many years for use with older equipment and buy new, incompatible equipment.

In some cases innovation is seen as more than a nuisance; the strategy of planned obsolescence is especially insidious in the electronic games market, where the advertising is targeted to children. By rolling out product improvements according to a schedule even when the technology is fully developed, the obsolescence factor becomes particularly artificial and—because it is used to manipulate children—ethically dubious.

Toward "Continuous Improvement"

At the turn of the 21st century the movement was away from planned obsolescence toward "continuous improvement" or "product optimization," in which manufacturers strive to produce superior and long-lasting goods that will maintain consumer satisfaction. Kostecki cites three basic approaches toward improving the durability of products:

- a straightforward approach signifying that products are made to last;
- a traditional approach relying on schemes of extended product use such as maintenance services;
- a future-oriented approach implying a global conception and management of optimal-use systems.

The benefits of continuous improvement are competitive advantage through improved consumer loyalty, enhanced image, and improved economic returns. Properly implementing any one of these methods should ensure positive returns for any company whose goal is continuous improvement.

Although some manufacturers regard planned obsolescence as necessary in order to promote product advancement and acceptance, many consumers perceive it as detrimental to the marketplace because it encourages spending on unnecessary goods and produces waste. Yet without planned obsolescence, consumers would not have the opportunity to experiment with and embrace new product designs and technologies. A few industries have attempted to ease the consumer's burden by offering lower-priced models and trade-in offers. Nonetheless, planned obsolescence will continue to be a marketing strategy in many industries.

NOEL MARK NOEL

Further Reading
Curtis, Chris, "Managing Successful Product Development," *Machine Design* 70, no. 1 (December 1999)

Frand, Erwin A., *The Art of Product Development from Concept to Market,* Homewood, Illinois: Dow Jones-Irwin, 1989

Gateway < www.gateway.com/index.shtml>

Hollins, Bill, and Gillian Hollins, *Over the Horizon: Planning Products Today for Success Tomorrow,* Chichester, West Sussex, and New York: Wiley, 1999

Intel <www.intel.com/pressroom/kits/processors/quickref.htm>

Kostecki, Michel, editor, *The Durable Use of Consumer Products: New Options for Business and Consumption,* Dordrecht, The Netherlands, and Boston: Kluwer Academic, 1998

Lascelles, David, "Business and the Environment: A Longer Life for Green Goods," *London Financial Times* (18 October 1995)

Meng, Eric, "The Project Manager's Toolbox," *PM Network* 13, no. 8 (August 1999)

Millier, Paul, *Marketing the Unknown: Developing Marketing Strategies for Technical Innovations,* Chichester, West Sussex, and New York: Wiley, 1999

Nagashima, Hidesuke, "LP Records Seen Disappearing in Coming Years," *Japan Economic Newswire* (15 December 1988)

PeoplePC Toshiba Personal Computer <www.peoplepc.com/about/computerdetails.htm>

Ross, David E., "Planned Obsolescence—Its Same Old Tune," *Los Angeles Times* (10 January 1993)

Webster, Bruce, *The Art of 'Ware,* New York: M and T Books, 1995

Wolf, Barnet D., "Throw away Those Dated Beliefs on '90s Disposability," *The Columbus Dispatch* (15 March 1998)

Yu, Albert, *Creating the Digital Future,* New York: Free Press, 1998

Point-of-Purchase Advertising

Three key promotional tools are used by retailers: coupons, advertised specials, and point-of-purchase (POP) displays. Point-of-purchase displays can range from simple "sale" signs to elaborate interactive displays. However, the objective of the display is generally the same—to prompt unplanned purchases. POP displays stimulate sales by drawing attention to otherwise overlooked products; they also serve as a purchase reminder. They are commonly used for impulse-purchase items such as cookies, crackers, salted snacks, and beverages and for infrequently purchased products such as baking ingredients and condiments.

In recent decades POP promotions have grown in importance because of the burgeoning number of brands and the increasing amount of money spent on unplanned purchases. A family of four spends 61 percent of its grocery dollars on unplanned purchases. Even when shoppers use a shopping list, the specific brand they choose is determined at the store in 73 percent of cases. More than half of these shoppers report that they are frequently influenced by POP displays.

While POP displays are often accompanied by sales promotions or coupons, they also have been shown to increase sales even in the absence of such incentives. Experiments suggest that retailers could generate increases in sales simply by placing a promotion sign (with no price cut) on the shelf. Such signs not only attract attention but also typically signal a "good deal," thereby encouraging purchase. In some circumstances, these displays can produce a "bandwagon effect"—that is, a decision to purchase because it seems everyone else is.

POP displays can reinforce an advertising message and provide a vivid comparison with competing brands. In effect, POP displays provide a brand-building opportunity that can be targeted to both first-time buyers and loyal users. With the rising popularity of "loyalty clubs" and the increased emphasis on building a core brand franchise, advertisers have begun to shift their attention to how POP displays can increase the amount each person buys. Thus, in addition to attracting new customers, POP is being used to increase the purchase volume of loyal, repeat users.

Certain kinds of POP displays tend to make consumers buy more than they otherwise would. Research has shown that nearly any sign with a number in it, suggesting that shoppers buy more than one of something ("Limit 6 per person," "Buy 12 for the weekend," "4 for $4"), is more effective in stimulating sales than signs without numbers. Several studies have documented this effect. In Sioux City, Iowa, signs with high purchase limits ("limit 12 per person") doubled the number of canned goods people bought. Signs suggesting multiple purchases ("Buy 12 for the weekend") stimulated an increase in sales ranging from nearly 50 percent to more than 100 percent in a chain of Philadelphia, Pennsylvania, convenience stores. Multiple-unit pricing—"3 for $3" rather than "$1 each"—increased sales in 12 of 13 categories in Chicago, Illinois, supermarkets by an average of 30 percent.

Research has consistently documented that consumers purchase more of an item when POP displays suggest a high number. While very low or single-unit limits may increase the number of buyers through so-called deal signaling, higher limits may increase the number of units each buyer purchases through anchoring. Anchoring promotions include multiple unit pricing ("2 for $2") and purchase quantity limits ("limit 12 per person"). Therefore, some managers use low limits to stimulate trials of new or low-share brands, and higher limits to stimulate stockpiling of established brands.

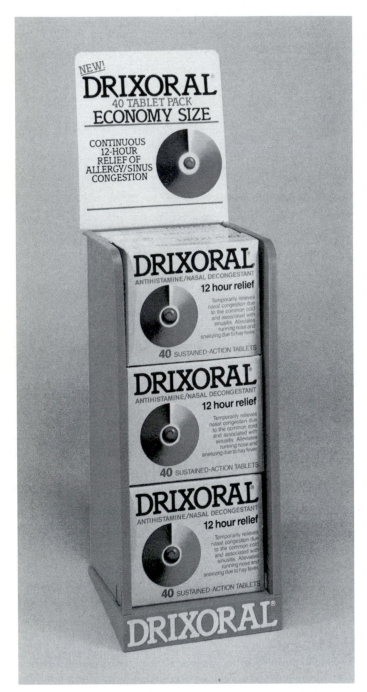

This award-winning 1983 counter display unit effectively attracted attention to the product while taking up only minimal space. *Reprinted with permission of PBC International from Point of Purchase Design by Robert B. Konikow © 1985.*

Even in the absence of a price promotion, signs that suggest an occasion for use of the product (e.g., "Buy some for snacks") showed surprising sales increases in a series of pilot studies done in truck stops across the Midwest. Research is under way to determine the types of POP signage that will have the greatest impact on sales—without offering a price discount. Early findings indicate that the types of signs that are most effective dramatically dif-

fer depending on whether a more hedonic product (such as perfume or candy) is being promoted or a more utilitarian product (such as light bulbs or store brands of soap). For the former, POP signs that focus on nonmonetary promotions are more successful, whereas monetary promotions are more appropriate for the latter.

POP displays take up store space, which becomes increasingly valuable as competition among brands intensifies. The battleground becomes even broader as manufacturers seek to increase the frequency with which people consume their products or the range of other products for which they substitute it. Many store managers are asked to accommodate more displays than they have space for, forcing advertisers to bid against each other for floor and shelf space. Compensation may take the form of a straight payment, special discounts, or other terms that give a retailer sufficient incentive to provide the coveted space.

With the help of cooperative retailers, in-store experiments, and scanner data, experts who study POP are continuing to gener-

This supermarket-aisle display promoted Hefty paper plates in 1985. *Reprinted with permission of PBC International from Point of Purchase Design by Robert B. Konikow © 1985*

ate new insights. At the same time, for both manufacturers and retailers, POP displays are continuing to influence unplanned purchases, build brand equity, and increase purchase quantities.

BRIAN WANSINK

Further Reading

Chandon, Pierre, Brian Wansink, and Gilles Laurent, "A Congruency Framework of Sales Promotion Effectiveness," *Journal of Marketing* 64, no. 4 (October 2000)

Davis, Scott, J. Jeffrey Inman, and Leigh McAlister, "Promotion Has a Negative Effect on Brand Evaluations—Or Does It? Additional Disconfirming Evidence," *Journal of Marketing Research* 29, no. 1 (February 1992)

Inman, J. Jeffrey, and Leigh McAlister, "A Retailer Promotion Policy Model Considering Promotion Signal Sensitivity," *Marketing Science* 12, no. 4 (Fall 1993)

Inman, J. Jeffrey, Anil C. Peter, and Priya Raghubir, "Framing the Deal: The Role of Restrictions in Accentuating Deal Value," *Journal of Consumer Research* 24, no. 1 (June 1997)

Kahn, Barbara E., and Leigh McAlister, *Grocery Revolution: The New Focus on the Consumer,* Reading, Massachusetts: Addison-Wesley, 1997

Wansink, Brian, "Advertising's Impact on Category Substitution," *Journal of Marketing Research* 21, no. 4 (November 1994)

Wansink, Brian, and Kymberli Allen, "Promotions That Influence Trial *and* Quantity," Champaign: Food and Brand Lab, University of Illinois, 1999

Wansink, Brian, and JaeHak Cheong, "What Do Shopping Lists Really Tell Us?" Champaign: Food and Brand Lab, University of Illinois, 1999

Wansink, Brian, Robert J. Kent, and Stephen J. Hoch, "An Anchoring and Adjustment Model of Purchase Quantity Decisions," *Journal of Marketing Research* 35, no. 1 (February 1998)

Wansink, Brian, and Michael L. Ray, "Advertising Strategies to Increase Usage Frequency," *Journal of Marketing* 60, no.1 (January 1996)

Wansink, Brian, and Scott Seed, "Making Brand Loyalty Programs Succeed," *Journal of Brand Management* 8, no.3 (February 2001)

Polaroid

Principal Agencies

Batten Barton Durstine & Osborn
Doyle Dane Bernbach, Inc.
Ally & Gargano, Inc.
BBDO Worldwide
Burrell Communications
Goodby, Silverstein & Partners
Bartle Bogle Hegarty
Leo Burnett Company
Bcom3 Group

Edwin H. Land invented the Polaroid Land Camera in 1947, ten years after he founded the Polaroid Corporation. The inspiration for his invention came in 1943 when he snapped a picture of his daughter, Jennifer, during a family vacation in Santa Fe, New Mexico. Jennifer, three years old at the time, wanted to see the picture right away, and Land began working on ideas that would lead him to develop the world's first instant camera.

The first public demonstration of the instant-print camera occurred on 21 February 1947 at the annual meeting of the Optical Society of America in New York City's Hotel Pennsylvania. At this event Land created a self-portrait, showing how simply and quickly his new invention worked. The next day, the *New York Times* ran a copy of this 8-by-10-inch sepia portrait with a story headlined, "The camera does the rest," a play on Kodak's slogan, "You press the button, we do the rest." The following week, a full-page reproduction of the photograph was printed in *Life* magazine.

Land, who was born in 1909, initially founded Polaroid to produce a variety of specialized lamps and variable density windows based on his work in adapting polarized materials for sunglasses, 3-D movies, and military use. N.W. Ayer & Son handled advertising in the early days, followed, in 1945, by Batten Barton Durstine & Osborn (BBDO), of Boston, Massachusetts, which became Polaroid's agency of record until 1954.

Polaroid introduced the Model 95 Land Camera at Boston's Jordan Marsh department store on 26 November 1948. The camera sold for $89.50. Rolling out its product market by market, Polaroid told dealers that it did not want a display unless it dominated the store; anything less, Polaroid's strategy declared, was unworthy of this new development in photography.

On 9 February 1949, Polaroid launched a test campaign for its Land camera in Florida supported by page ads in newspapers, window displays, radio announcements, posters, and sky signs. Many public demonstrations were given at resort hotels, where people were invited to pose for pictures to see how the camera actually worked. On 25 April 1949, Polaroid introduced the camera in Los Angeles, California, with similar marketing strategies. Polaroid began its first national campaign with a page ad in the

13 June 1949 issue of *Life* magazine. Print ads also appeared in *Holiday, National Geographic, Time,* and *The New Yorker,* as well as in newspapers in every major U.S. market.

During the 1950s Polaroid worked to make its film and cameras extremely popular with consumers. Enthusiasts were attracted to its immediate results and the opportunity to retake pictures if initial results weren't what they had hoped. In the summer of 1952 Polaroid introduced its second consumer product, the Pathfinder Model 110, the basic folding-bellows-style camera with a more sophisticated lens and shutter system, retailing for $249.50. Magazine ads were headlined, "Picture yourself on Christmas with a Polaroid Land Camera." Live television advertising began on NBC's *Today* with host Dave Garroway.

Continuing its consumer assault, Polaroid on 14 June 1954 introduced its Highlander camera with an initial advertising budget of $630,000 for the product's first two months. Also that year, Polaroid 3-D glasses were used to view the first 3-D stereoscopic movie, *Bwana Devil.* Polaroid's 3-D viewing glasses account remained with Cunningham & Walsh, which was appointed in 1953.

In July 1954 Polaroid named Doyle Dane Bernbach, Inc. (DDB), as its agency, replacing BBDO. Polaroid's relationship with DDB continued for the next 30 years. When Jack Paar began hosting *The Tonight Show* in 1957, Polaroid came on board as one of its first sponsors; the camera company had been a frequent advertiser on that late-night show when it had been hosted by Steve Allen and called *The Steve Allen Show.* Polaroid finished the decade with the 1959 introduction of its 3,000-speed film and wink-light, which allowed indoor photography without a flash, spending a record $2.5 million on advertising from the end of September through the Christmas holiday.

Moving into the psychedelic 1960s, Polaroid introduced instant color film to the consumer market with Polacolor film. This film, introduced with the Land Automatic 100 camera in 1963, was sold in film packs rather than rolls. Polaroid used nearly 3,000 outdoor posters in the principal cities of 19 U.S. states to promote its Polacolor film through the summer of 1963.

Polaroid won three Clio awards for commercials from DDB in 1965. This coincided with a dramatic increase in its ad spending from $8.5 million in 1964 to more than $18 million in 1966. Polaroid also brought out its Swinger camera in 1965, targeting a younger photo-taking consumer with the theme, "It's the camera for a whole new generation." Swinger retailed for $19.95.

Its next big introduction came the week of 24 March 1969, when Polaroid spent $2.2 million on a "blitz week" campaign to introduce the Colorpack II camera. The $29.95 Colorpack II produced color pictures in one minute and black-and-white pictures in ten seconds. In October, Polaroid introduced television and magazine advertising that featured singer Perry Como as spokesman.

With the arrival of the 1970s, Polaroid began to focus on minority marketing. In 1970 the company assigned a special project for its Polaroid Land Camera to Zebra Associates, New York City, targeting the African-American consumer market. The campaign included ethnic radio and African-American–oriented newspapers in 26 top markets.

The SX-70 camera and color film were introduced in 1972. The new film eliminated the need to peel the negative from the positive print, and the image developed outside the camera. The SX-70 was also the first folding single-lens reflex camera in history. DDB created a lavish, $20 million advertising campaign with actor Sir Laurence Olivier as the spokesman.

Polaroid also expanded its international focus, spending $49 million in worldwide advertising in 1974, a major hike over the previous year's figure as it rolled out its SX-70 system beyond North America. Land resigned as president of the company in 1975 and passed the title to a longtime associate, William J. McClune, Jr., who had joined the company in 1939 to start a quality-control program. Land continued to hold the titles of chairman, chief executive officer (CEO), and director of research.

Meanwhile, as patents began to expire, Polaroid began facing competition in its instant camera niche. In 1976 Kodak created an instant print camera and film packs of its own. Polaroid responded by filing suit in U.S. District Court in April, alleging that Kodak had infringed on 12 patents for both the camera and film. Kodak countered, stating that the patents were invalid or unenforceable. Five and a half years later, the 75-day trial began in October 1981; the judge deliberated for several years. It wasn't until September 1985 that the ruling was made against Kodak and the company was ordered to stop making and selling instant-print cameras. During this time however, Kodak had sold more than 16 million instant-print cameras. In 1991 Kodak was ordered to pay Polaroid $925 million.

In March 1976 Polaroid began marketing Pronto, Polaroid's fourth and least expensive model in the SX-70 line. Actor Alan Alda was chosen as the spokesman for the $4 million launch of the Pronto camera. He was replaced by actor James Garner, who took over the role as spokesman for Pronto when it debuted on the Academy Awards show with the slogan, "Picture yourself— Pronto."

The association with Garner soon spawned one of the best advertiser-presenter relationships ever. Snappy repartee and a light-hearted battle of the sexes characterized DDB's award-winning commercials for Polaroid from 1977 through 1983, in which Garner was joined by Mariette Hartley. *Advertising Age* spotlighted these popular commercials in its feature "The Best TV Commercials Ever." The Garner-Hartley team also introduced Polaroid's Sun System line of cameras.

In 1980 Edwin H. Land stepped down as CEO but continued as chairman and assumed a new position of consulting director of basic research in Land photography. (McClune added the title of CEO.) In 1982 Land resigned from the board to work full-time with the Rowland Institute for Science, Inc., a privately endowed, nonprofit, basic research organization Land had founded in 1980. He died in 1991 at the age of 81. Meanwhile, McClune was elected chairman of the board in 1982 and continued as president-CEO.

In 1984 Polaroid ended its 30-year relationship with Doyle Dane Bernbach and appointed Ally & Gargano, Inc., as its agency. Ally & Gargano began a national rotation of commercials with a high emotional appeal. In one of the spots, a little boy bids good-bye to his mother on his first day of school. When he gets on the school bus and opens up his lunch box, he finds a Polaroid picture of his mother with a note saying, "I love you." Some of these new spots played on consumers' fears about inept film processing, stressing that Polaroid instant film is never ruined by an outside film developer.

That October, Polaroid offered buyers of Polaroid cameras 25 percent discounts on all round-trip airfares with Trans World Airlines (TWA). The promotion, with its theme "Polaroid's passport—25% off TWA's world," started only weeks after a major airline fare war broke out. Polaroid hoped the promotion would spur spirited gift giving of its products through the holiday season. Ally & Gargano lost the $40 million Polaroid consumer account in October 1985, however, when consumer recall tests showed poor results. BBDO Worldwide became the company's agency of record in December 1985.

Meanwhile, overseas sales continued strong. Saudi Arabia even saw its first photography contest, sponsored jointly by Polaroid and Japanese light truck manufacturer Isuzu in 1985. Polaroid was able to make inroads there where other cameras could not. With instant pictures, the religious taboo against women showing their faces outside the home was not a problem as there was no need to take the pictures to an outside film developer.

On 21 April 1986 Polaroid introduced the Spectra camera as an upscale camera, with British actor Ben Cross as its presenter and the theme, "We take your pictures seriously." Later advertising for Spectra compared the image results with 35mm camera pictures. Spectra sales took off in Europe, Australia, and Japan, where the camera was introduced as the Image System in September 1986 through Ogilvy & Mather, London, England. In August 1989, Polaroid pulled its $20 million pan-European account from Ogilvy and reassigned the business to local agencies on a country-by-country basis.

Polaroid also refocused on the youth market. With the technical supervision of agency Goodby, Berlin & Silverstein, of San Francisco, California, Polaroid rolled out its Cool Cam camera in 1988 with five 30-second spots written, directed, and produced by kids. This was Polaroid's first attempt to advertise to the youth market since the 1960s.

In a 1989 campaign to make people more aware of the multiple uses of instant photography, BBDO Worldwide prepared a series of commercials targeted at instant photography's business, professional, scientific, and consumer uses. In one spot a little boy is shown walking down a street with an empty leash. In a store window he spots a Polaroid picture of his dog and is reunited with his pet. These commercials were themed, "Nothing works like a Polaroid" and "Before it's a memory, it's Polaroid."

The Captiva camera was the most researched consumer product in the company's history. Introduced in 1993, it was based on market research from more than 15,000 consumers. The Captiva featured contemporary styling and a hands-free storage system that allowed users to continuously take pictures, with the pictures stored inside the camera.

THE SWINGER the Polaroid Land camera that gives you a black and white picture in 15 seconds.

In a mid-1960s campaign for its Swinger camera, Polaroid took a cue from the growing prominence of the youth culture. *Couresty of Polaroid Corporation.*

In 1995 BBDO Worldwide abruptly left Polaroid to handle the Eastman Kodak Company's $50 million global branding account. Polaroid spent just $9 million that year, with most of the advertising handled by Burrell Communications, of Chicago, Illinois. Commercials for the Talking OneStep and Captiva cameras featuring comedian Sinbad were the only spots to run through the end of the year. Burrell, which specialized in reaching the African-American market, had worked with Polaroid for two years.

Goodby, Silverstein & Partners took over the account in September 1995. The agency produced commercials with the tag line, "See what develops." A series of these commercials had fun with some of the myths about instant pictures, such as the advice that shaking the picture would help it develop faster. At the same time, the London, England, agency Bartle Bogle Hegarty launched a European campaign using the slogan, "Live for the moment," playing on the need for instant gratification of the current generation.

The Expressions line of cameras, linked to the U.K. musical group the Spice Girls in 1998, was marketed to children 9 to 12 years old, whereas the Wave camera was marketed to the 12-to-17 age group. Goodby, Silverstein & Partners handled this $40 million campaign while targeting the 18-to-34 crowd with a $20 million campaign for PopShots, an instant single-use camera.

Continuing to target youth markets at the turn of the century, Polaroid teamed up with many of the most popular singing groups to market its I-Zone camera. The I-Zone camera produced color photographs or photograph stickers. One commercial featured a young man who stuck instant pictures on his nipples and then wiggled his chest. Teen singing sensation Britney Spears was hired to promote the camera during her 2000 "Oops! . . . I Did It Again" tour. During the concert she would invite a young man from the audience on stage, serenade him, and pose with him for a pocket-snapshot (Britney's idea). The I-Zone camera was also the official camera of the "Sears Presents Backstreet Boys Into the Millennium" tour and the U.S. mall tour of the all-girl pop group Nobody's Angel. The camera was co-promoted with the fashions of designer Todd Oldham's TO2 collection. In 2000 Polaroid worked on the Internet with theglobe.com to build a co-branded microsite to promote the I-Zone Instant Pocket camera. The Web site used the I-Zone's catchy theme, "Where will you stick it?"

In May 2000 Bcom3 Group was appointed to handle Polaroid's $100 million global advertising account. Chicago-based Leo Burnett Worldwide became the lead global agency, replacing Goodby, Silverstein & Partners as the agency of record for the United States. Bartle Bogle Hegarty, a Bcom3 affiliate agency, continued to handle European advertising.

Sales had been poor for some time, however. Polaroid had not responded effectively to the challenges posed by the rise of one-hour film developing shops or advances in digital technology. The company's debt mounted. In October 2001 Polaroid filed for bankruptcy protection.

STEVE CLOVER

Further Reading

Day, Barry, 100 Great Advertisements, London: Times Newspapers, 1978

Fox, Stephen R., The Mirror Makers: A History of American Advertising and Its Creators, New York: Morrow, 1984

Goodrum, Charles A., and Helen Dalrymple, Advertising in America: The First 200 Years, New York: Abrams, 1990

Kanner, Bernice, The 100 Best TV Commercials—And Why They Worked, New York: Times Business, 1999

Levenson, Bob, Bill Bernbach's Book: A History of the Advertising That Changed the History of Advertising, New York: Villard Books, 1987

Political Advertising

Modern political advertising in the United States traces its origins to the elections of 1952, when, for the first time, the political conventions that nominated the presidential candidates—Adlai Stevenson and Dwight D. Eisenhower—were broadcast on television. No longer were candidates selected by deal-makers in smoke-filled rooms. Even before the advent of TV, however, politicians found ways to get their names before the public—rallies, debates, and train trips punctuated by so-called whistle-stop speeches, to name a few.

Among the earliest forms of political advertising were coinlike tokens that could be carried or worn on a coat. Some bore ferrotypes (an early form of tintype photography) portraying the image of a candidate. Sloganeering sometimes caught the electorate's interest; the notions of Manifest Destiny and western expansion created a stir in the election of 1844. The snappy slogan "54–40 or fight!" (a reference to the dispute with Britain over the U.S.-Canada border) boosted James Polk's presidential campaign. Also popular in early political campaigns were colorful embroidered or printed ribbons, which offered the electorate an opportunity to "show their colors" politically, especially at rallies.

In 1896 the New Jersey–based company of Whitehead & Hoag revolutionized political campaigns with the production of the first pinback buttons. "Buttonmania" captured the attention of the electorate, and pinback buttons would make their way as a personal advertising statement in product advertising, in protest movements, and for fans of sports teams.

Nonetheless, the overwhelming amount of money spent on political campaigns in the early days went into the mechanics of campaigning—transportation, lodging, entertainment, and general public relations—not into media advertising. It was not until just after World War I that advertising professionals first began acting as advisers to political candidates, although for many years they remained in the background. Albert Lasker took a leave of absence from Lord & Thomas to assist in the Warren Harding campaign of 1920 and later to serve in his administration.

The first open involvement of an advertising agency in a U.S. presidential race was in 1936, when Hill Blackett of Blackett-Sample-Hummert went to work as a media adviser for the Republican campaign of Alfred Landon. No advertisements were produced, however. The agency functioned mainly as a clearing-house for the purchase of radio time for Landon's campaign speeches. Although radio time was offered free to candidates prior to nomination, party candidates had to pay once nominated. On election eve Blackett arranged for a "debate" broadcast between Michigan Senator Arthur Vandenberg and recorded excerpts of speeches by Landon's opponent, Franklin Roosevelt. The program was routinely cleared by CBS officials, despite a rigid prohibition against the use of any recorded material by the network (a policy NBC maintained as well). When the program went on the air and management realized the Roosevelt portions were pre-recorded, they ordered it cut off immediately. Blackett was enraged and tried to sue CBS, claiming suppression of free speech, but nothing came of it.

Chester LaRoche of Young & Rubicam, Bruce Barton of Batten Barton Durstine & Osborn (BBDO), and other prominent ad executives were active in organizing exposure and support for Wendell Willkie in 1940; his first national exposure was as a guest on the radio panel show *Information Please,* sponsored by Canada Dry and produced by the J.M. Mathes agency. BBDO worked behind the scenes for Republican candidate Thomas Dewey in 1944 and 1948.

Commercials finally would be introduced in the 1952 presidential campaign between Stevenson and Eisenhower. Ben Duffy, president of BBDO, had met General Eisenhower when Eisenhower was serving as president of Columbia University after World War II. Eisenhower became the Republican nominee in the summer of 1952. Dewey, who was an important Eisenhower strategist, pressed for BBDO's involvement after the convention. As a result, BBDO and Kudner Agency, Inc., became co-agencies for the Republicans. The BBDO account executive on the campaign was Jock Elliott, future president of Ogilvy & Mather. As in times past, BBDO managed the candidates' rallies and television appearances. It later bought the 30 minutes of TV time in which Richard Nixon gave his celebrated "Checkers" speech (in which he denied taking political contributions for personal use—with the exception of a dog, "Checkers," given as a gift to his daughters).

There was also the shadow of a third agency involved in the Eisenhower race in the person of Rosser Reeves, who was then the chief creative mind at Ted Bates & Company. (The agency itself had no involvement in the campaign.) Reeves, the leading theoretician of hard-sell advertising of the 1950s and 1960s, believed that the best way to communicate a candidate's views was in short 60-second capsules. He had floated the idea in 1948 to Dewey, who rejected it on the grounds that such presentations would look too much like commercials.

Reeves was asked to work on the 1952 campaign by a group of Eisenhower supporters from Texas. BBDO and Kudner, both competitors of Bates, restricted Reeves's responsibilities to the preparation of a series of short spot announcements. Eisenhower made himself available to Reeves for a single day in September, and Reeves filmed 40 brief statements on a range of issues from inflation to communism; these would become the "Eisenhower Answers America" series. Film of citizens asking the scripted questions was shot separately and edited to supply the appropriate answers. Although they lack production value or elegance, these spots are generally considered the first presidential campaign TV "commercials," and they revolutionized national political campaigning. BBDO (but not Reeves) would return for the 1956 campaign and Richard M. Nixon's run in 1960. The agency was also active in Republican Ronald Reagan's campaigns.

There was no shortage of Republican supporters among the executives of American advertising, but the Democrats were not so fortunate. By 1956 it was clear to both parties that TV would

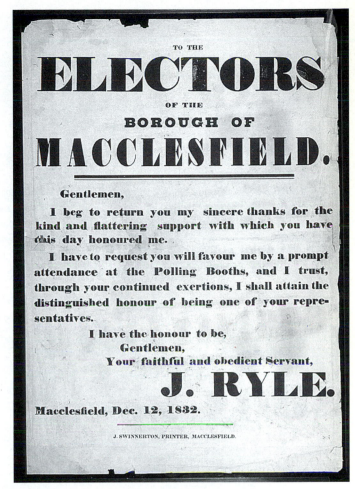

A far cry from today's political ads, this British broadside poster from 1832 sought to remind supporters of candidate J. Ryle to go to the polls and vote.
Courtesy of the Rare Book, Manuscript, and Special Collections Library, Duke University.

be a critical campaign battleground. If many major agencies were unwilling to take on a Democratic candidate for fear of alienating a valued client, Norman, Craig & Kummel went after the Adlai Stevenson candidacy with great fervor, stirred by both political passions and a desire to go head-to-head against BBDO.

Directly in charge of the Stevenson campaign were two of the agency's principals, Eugene Kummel, then vice president and secretary, and Walter Craig. They added touches that were totally new to political conventions. For example, they helped the convention manager in Chicago, Illinois, hire singers, performers, and a color guard. Craig took over most of the work of planning a candidate's arrival and departure—what routes should be followed, what signs should be carried by the crowd in the hall. They also provided the introduction to the keynote speech of the convention, with a script written by the agency prior to the convention. Despite its efforts, Norman, Craig & Kummel lost the fight to BBDO and Dwight D. Eisenhower. After the election, former President Harry S. Truman, referring to the effects of political advertising, commented that 1956 had been "the first time in

Rock the Vote, an organization committed to drawing young adults into the political process, relied on striking graphics and a brief text message in this 2000 print ad.
Rock the Vote Education Fund.

148 years that a president had been elected without carrying Congress with him."

Four years later the close contest between John F. Kennedy and Richard M. Nixon was decided partly on the strength of their televised debates. One TV spot for Democratic candidate Kennedy featured a film clip of then-President Eisenhower responding to questions at an actual press conference. Asked by one reporter if Nixon, during his years as vice president, had put any specific ideas into action for the administration, Eisenhower answered, "If you give me a week, I might think of one. I don't remember." Nixon was forced to defend his record.

In the Cold War atmosphere of the mid-1960s, political advertising played to Americans' fears. In what political pundits believe was the most effective use of TV in a campaign, a commercial for President Lyndon B. Johnson from Doyle Dane Bernbach showed a little girl in a field of flowers. The tranquility of the "Daisy" spot, however, was broken by its ending, an exploding atomic bomb, none too subtly tagging the president's opponent, Barry Goldwater, a staunch hawk in relations with the Soviet Union, as too trigger-happy to be president. Johnson immediately ordered the spot to be pulled, but ensuing media attention helped elect him by a landslide.

The amount spent on broadcast advertising grew steadily during the second half of the 20th century. Less than 5 percent of campaign expenditures in 1952 were devoted to radio and TV time. By 1972, 15 percent of campaign expenditures went to broadcasting, and by 1988 approximately 20 percent of nearly $2 billion went to purchase airtime.

By 1996 the presidential campaign was being fought primarily on the airwaves. This was apparent in the primaries. Advertising expenditures in New Hampshire rose from $851,000 in 1992 to $2.7 million in 1996. Without a competitor, Bill Clinton spent $12 million of his $30.9 million limit on TV commercials in the middle of the primaries, $42.4 million during the postprimary/preconvention period, and $44 million on TV ads in the general election.

Because political advertising, unlike product advertising, must achieve results in a short period of time, political practitioners use specialized types of advertising: image, issue, and negative advertising. Frequently, candidates follow a formula of concentrating on issue or image ads at the beginning of a campaign to put themselves in a positive light. The most skilled practitioner of such advertising was Ronald Reagan, who used it to good effect in the 1984 campaign. "Feel good" spots for the Reagan reelection campaign from the famed Tuesday Team (a group of advertising professionals who took leaves of absence from their regular ad jobs to work on the Reagan election advertising) and written by team member Hal Riney (of Hal Riney & Partners) showed patriotic themes while musing on the theme, "It's morning again in America." Riney himself did the voice-over.

The use of negative ads—often saved for the later stages of a campaign or resorted to only when the image and issue ads have failed—has been increasing in U.S. political campaigns. In 1988 a TV spot (later known as the "Willie Horton" commercial, although neither Horton's name nor image was included)

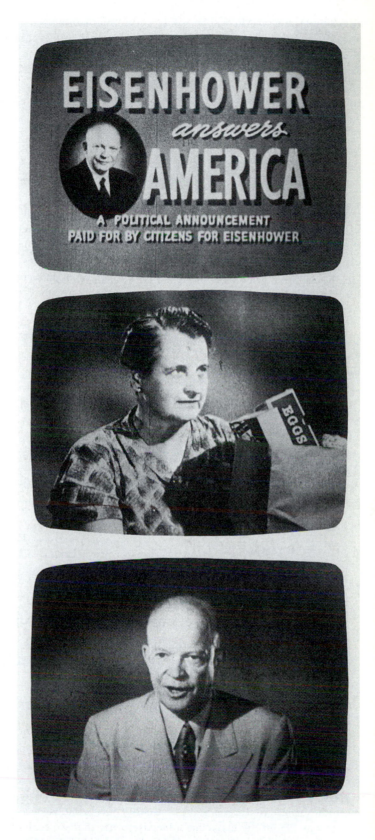

This 1952 series of spots for Republican candidate Dwight D. Eisenhower is considered to be the first American television commercial used in a presidential election campaign.
Couresy MIT Press.

attacking Democrat Michael Dukakis as soft on crime showed a photo of an African-American man; the voice-over said, "A crime quiz. Which candidate gave weekend passes to rapists and murderers who weren't even eligible for parole? Michael Dukakis." (The ad was a reference to a state of Massachusetts furlough program for prison inmates; Horton had committed a murder while out on furlough.) This particularly negative ad was influential in Dukakis's defeat by George Bush. One study contends that at least one-third of all presidential campaign commercials in the 1980s and 1990s were negative. In local elections in the latter decades of the 20th century, fully one-half or more of the spots were negative in tone or substance.

Political advertising was quickly adapted to the Internet. In 1998 Russ Feingold, Democratic senator from Wisconsin, was among several political candidates to take their polished, but grassroots, campaigns directly to individual voters via Web sites. The dialogue created with constituents allowed a level of personalization never seen before, and near-instant feedback became an integral part of these campaigns.

Advocacy groups and political action committees (PACs) have brought an infusion of so-called soft money into the political arena. Whether representing the interests of tobacco companies with specific corporate agendas or local gay rights groups, PACs arose in the late 1980s to wield unprecedented power on the airwaves.

While glitzy multimillion-dollar ad campaigns in support of political candidates were commonplace in the United States by the turn of the 21st century, they remained less utilized around the world. Some countries such as India ban paid television advertising time, instead using a time-voucher system. Similarly, when elections are called for in many democracies, the campaign period remains quite short—30 days in such countries as Canada.

Nonetheless, the value of a carefully selected advertising agency came to the fore internationally in the late 1970s. Indeed, some believe an ad created by Saatchi & Saatchi for Margaret Thatcher in 1978, then the Conservative Party's candidate for prime minister of Britain, won her the campaign. The agency seized upon hard times in Britain and created a print ad showing a long, winding line outside an unemployment office. The ad's headline, "Labour's not working," was a direct attack on the Conservative Party's opposition. The advertising brought Maurice and Charles Saatchi worldwide notice and helped them build an advertising powerhouse.

Seeing the effect of provocative advertising in the United Kingdom and the United States, candidates elsewhere began to expand the role of the advertising adviser. Candidates around the world now routinely turn to consultants, agencies, "spinmeisters," and financial experts to manage their campaigns. In 1999, for example, President Bill Clinton's team of Stanley Greenberg, James Carville, and Robert Shrum aided Ehud Barak in defeating Benjamin Netanyahu for the office of prime minister of Israel.

MIKE RYAN

Further Reading

Colford, Steven W., "Presidential TV Ads Have Addressed Issues, Set Emotional Tones, and Caused Controversy," *Advertising Age* (28 February 1995)

Cresswell, Stephen, "History of Political Collectibles," *Buttons & Ballots* (Summer 2000)

"Milestones in Presidential Campaign Commercials," The Freedom Forum Online: <www.ammi.org.livingroom candidate>

Polykoff, Shirley 1908–1998

U.S. Advertising Copywriter

Shirley Polykoff, the woman who would make hair coloring acceptable to women around the world, was born 18 January 1908, in Brooklyn, New York, the second of three daughters of Hyman and Rose Polykoff, Russian Jews who had immigrated to the United States. Her mother, in particular, pushed her children to become Americanized through education (sending her daughters to Girls' High School in Brooklyn) and reading. But Polykoff, in her 1975 autobiography *Does She . . . or Doesn't She*, acknowledged that it was "from the magazine advertisements that we really learned how to be truly American. How a home should look. How a table should be set. How to dress. How to be well groomed."

One of Polykoff's first full-time jobs was as a secretary at *Harper's Bazaar*, where her first attempt at copywriting got her

fired. The magazine was scheduled to run an ad in *Cosmopolitan*. But when *Cosmopolitan* called right before a holiday weekend saying it had to have the ad copy immediately, almost everyone except Polykoff had already left the office. So she wrote the copy touting an upcoming issue but misspelled the names of several famous writers scheduled to appear in the issue. Instead of the expected pat on the back and possibly a raise, Polykoff was fired—and vowed to get even with the publication by "making it as an ad writer."

Polykoff landed her next job writing copy for a women's fashion and specialty store in Brooklyn, where she wrote advertising with headlines such as, "Rhinestones, a girl's next best friend." Among the department stores she worked for early in her career were J. Bamberger & Company and Kresge Company.

Retail experience helped her land her first job at an advertising agency, Peck Advertising Agency, in New York City, in the early 1930s, where she wrote copy for I.J. Fox, Inc., a retail furrier, and B.T. Babbit, Inc.'s Bab-O cleanser. Like most women at that time, she quit her job when she got married, on 10 May 1933; unlike her peers, however, she was soon back at work at the insistence of her husband, lawyer George P. Halperin, who apparently preferred Shirley Polykoff the career woman to Polly Halperin, as she was known socially, the housewife.

In 1943 Polykoff took a job as a copywriter for Frederick-Clinton Company, where she handled as many as six different shoe accounts at one time. In 1955 she became a copywriter for Foote, Cone & Belding (FCB) working on the Playtex account. Shortly after she started, the agency landed the Clairol, Inc., account. As Polykoff wrote in her autobiography, "The F.C.&B. copy chief came by, tossed some papers on my desk, and said, 'Guess what, Polykoff, we just got the Clairol company. It's yours, honey, on account [sic] you're the only one around here who can write that kind of schmaltz.'"

Polykoff, who had been using chemicals to keep her naturally blonde hair from becoming too dark since she was 15, was sensitive to the issues that kept most women from changing their hair color. At the time, only about 7 percent of women in the United States colored their hair, and those who did were mainly actresses, models, and other women considered "fast." The campaign's well-remembered line, "Does she . . . or doesn't she," was inspired by Polykoff's first meeting with her future mother-in-law, the Old World–style wife of an Orthodox rabbi. Polykoff got along well with Halperin's father and siblings, but as soon as they left his family's home, she asked Halperin what his mother thought of her. According to her autobiography, he was evasive but finally said, "She says you paint your hair. . . . Well, do you?" Embarrassed, Polykoff wrote, "I could hear his mother thinking as she cleared away the dishes: 'Zee paint dos huer? Odder zee paint dos nicht?' Freely translated, that means, 'Does she . . . or doesn't she?' So maybe my mother-in-law wrote the line."

While the double entendre of the headline could be considered risqué, the rest of the ad was not. Polykoff deliberately chose fresh-faced models to show that real women used the product. She added a child to the scene to emphasize that the product would reproduce the same shining, natural softness of the child's hair, along with the line, "Hair color so natural, only your hairdresser knows for sure." (She also added a wedding ring to the model's hand so the product, *Miss* Clairol, wouldn't appear to be promoting unwed motherhood.) The copy was friendly, with sympathetic, caring overtones. Finally, to gain acceptance from the whole family, not just women, she looked beyond the traditional fashion and women's magazines to run the ad and instead targeted a family magazine—*Life*. But that magazine turned down the ad. *Life*'s all-male advertising panel objected to what it saw as an off-color headline. So Polykoff challenged the board to show the ad to the magazine's female employees; she was gambling on the fact that "nice girls" of that era would never acknowledge see-

Shirley Polykoff.
Photo from the American Advertising Federation's 50th Anniversary Advertising Hall of Fame book.

ing a double meaning, especially in mixed company. She was right. *Life*'s female employees all insisted the ad was about hair color, and Clairol's ten color pages were accepted. So was the product: within six years, hair coloring sales were up 413 percent, and more than 50 percent of women in the United States were coloring their hair.

Polykoff's follow-up to that campaign posed the question, "Is it true blondes have more fun?" and another campaign, this time targeted at women 35 and older, declared, "If I've only one life, let me live it as a blonde." For other colors, she wrote, "Every woman should be a redhead at least once in her life!" and "You can be a rich brunette (the kind men marry)."

She followed up her success on Miss Clairol with a campaign in the early 1960s for Clairol Loving Care, a nonpermanent coloring product designed to cover gray hair. The campaign ran with the slogan, "Hate that gray? Wash it away!" and the tag line, "Makes your husband feel younger too, just to look at you!" In 1964 Nice 'N' Easy shampoo-in hair color was introduced with the line, "The closer he gets, the better you look." And in 1974 a jingle for Clairol Kindness Instant Hair Curlers sang out, "Curlers on your head, shame on you!"—and resulted in sales of $25 million the first year and $70 million the second.

Along with her creative success came raises and promotions. By the time Polykoff left FCB, she was senior vice president-creative director, chairman of the creative board, and the first woman on the agency's board of directors. For a while she also was the highest-paid agency employee at FCB. She initially insisted on making no more than $25,000 a year because she believed a wife should never make more than her husband; after Halperin's death from liver cancer in 1961, the agency doubled her salary twice in the ensuing decade.

In February 1973 she retired from FCB and, with longtime coworker Raymond Betuel, launched Shirley Polykoff & Betuel, Inc., in New York City's Drake Hotel. The agency opened with the equivalent of $12 million in media billings, handling the Miss Clairol creative account as well as Kimberly-Clark Corporation's New Freedom sanitary napkin, a new Maybelline cosmetics line from Schering-Plough Corporation, and Houbigant, Inc., fragrance products. Betuel died in 1974 of liver cancer, the same disease that had killed Polykoff's husband. She later changed the name of the shop to Shirley Polykoff Advertising, Inc., and her daughter, Alix Nelson Frick, joined the agency. Polykoff left to become a consultant in September 1981, effectively closing the agency.

In 1967 she was named "Advertising Woman of the Year" by the American Advertising Federation for her contribution to the beauty industry through her Clairol campaigns. In 1973 she was inducted into the Copy Club's Hall of Fame. And in 1980 she became the first living woman inducted into the Advertising Hall of Fame. She died on 4 June 1998 at her home in New York City at the age of 90.

KAREN EGOLF

Biography
Born in Brooklyn, New York, 18 January 1908; hired as copywriter at Foote, Cone & Belding, 1955; wrote "Does She...or Doesn't She" campaign for Clairol, Inc., 1956; retired from FCB and opened own agency 1973; inducted into the Advertising Hall of Fame, 1980; resigned to become a consultant, effectively closing her agency, 1981; died in New York City, 4 June 1998.

Selected Publications
Does She . . . Or Doesn't She? And How She Did It, 1975

"Will You or Won't You . . . Take a Chance," *Advertising Age* (1 February 1982)

Further Reading
"AAF to Honor Fondren, Polykoff," *Advertising Age* (5 June 1967)

"Ad Hall of Fame Adds 3," *Advertising Age* (22 December 1980)

"Carl Ally, Y&R, DDB Top One Show Winners," *Advertising Age* (10 June 1974)

Gladwell, Malcolm, "True Colors, Hair Dye, and the Hidden History of Postwar America," <www.gladwell.com/1999_03_22_a_colors.html>

Maddux, Heather, "Shirley Polykoff: Does She . . . Or Doesn't She?" <www.ciadvertising.org/studies/student/99_fall/theory/maddux/polykoff/polyhome.htm>

Thomas, Robert McG., Jr., "Shirley Polykoff, 90, Ad Writer Whose Query Colored a Nation," *New York Times* (8 June 1999)

Poppe Tyson. *See* Modem Media Poppe Tyson

Popular Culture

If culture is defined as a specific stage of a civilization and the characteristics, features, and artifacts of that stage, there is little doubt that advertising is a significant element of contemporary culture in the developed world and particularly the United States. While advertising often has a controversial impact on art, morals, education, and manners, scholarly research generally regards it—along with food preferences, motion picture trends, fashion fads, and contemporary music—as a facet of popular culture or material culture.

Culture can be viewed as the ways of living built up by a group of human beings, or tangible and intangible concepts that characterize a group of people or a way of life. Culture is transmitted from and advanced by one generation to another. The cultures of groups of people whose values and ways of life differ from those of the overall society of which they are a part are called *subcultures*. To the extent that specific market niches can be identified by their cultural preferences, advertising necessarily becomes a part of that cultural mix, both defining and reflecting it.

Despite attempts to trivialize its impact on culture in general, advertising, with its pervasive nature, clearly reflects and influences the norms, values, rituals, and artifacts of complex cultures. Additionally, techniques of U.S. advertising are increasingly in demand by other countries that seek to increase their standards of living. Advertising is everywhere in American society. To those who see it as a positive element, it is simply pervasive. To its critics, advertising is intrusive, forcing its way into every nook and cranny of life in the United States.

Media Impact on Culture

Advertising's power comes from its relationship with the mass-media system. Newspapers, magazines, radio stations, and commercial television carry advertising to almost every person in the United States. This continual barrage of advertising introduces and reinforces cultural cues as advertisers see them.

The ability of advertisers to communicate cultural cues is a serious concern to many, as is the role of the mass media as a vehicle for carrying advertising messages to the public. The mass media are powerful cultural influencers, so any perceived control over messages transmitted in the media by a second powerful influence—advertising—is a concern.

The editorial or programming content of the print and broadcast media has an exceedingly strong impact on social and cultural change. Television entertainment programming, for example, moved toward a more accurate reflection of U.S. culture in the 1970s, presenting black Americans in the working world in programs such as *Julia*. It also defined business culture as male-dominated, hard drinking, womanizing, and ruthless in early episodes of *Dallas*. In the 1990s television programming began to portray gay characters as sharing most of the same values and behaviors as other Americans.

Until the 1970s, TV and motion pictures depicted a country without brands. Common brand name products were nonexistent, hidden, or replaced with generic or fabricated names in programs of that era. But beginning in 1972, TV and movies more realistically reflected the brand-name landscape of contemporary culture.

The mass media system in the United States is financed primarily by advertising. It is logical then to assume that advertisers can apply pressure in order to control what the public reads in newspapers and magazines, hears on the radio, and watches on television. Given this potential to affect a culture—and given advertisers' influence on the media—advertising has become a cause for concern for social critics of all kinds. Paid print advertisements and commercials pay reporters' and editors' salaries; finance ink, paper, printing presses, radio studios, and television cameras; and, in many cases, create profit for the media enterprise.

Publishers, network executives, and other media managers expend a great deal of effort to keep the advertising and editorial/programming functions separate, so that each is free of the other's control. The refusal of magazines to alter their content—for example, by eschewing articles on the health effects of smoking—or of broadcast networks to refuse to air certain types of programming have caused these media to lose both advertisers and revenue.

Advertisers do attempt to avoid adverse publicity or to generate marketing opportunities, and they occasionally pressure the media to keep negative information out of the news or to tailor program and news content so as to create promotional opportuni-

ties. In addition, the media design special sections or programming or advise advertisers of upcoming content to attract or retain advertising.

The influence of any one advertiser over media content is reduced when a newspaper or television network has many advertisers. While such diversity helps prevent a single advertiser from gaining enough economic power to dictate content or cultural cues, it also results in clutter: too many ads in newspapers and magazines, on radio and television, and on buildings in business areas. Clutter, in turn, reduces the impact of advertising, as overwhelmed consumers increasingly ignore ads with which they are being bombarded.

Advertising is an important informational and educational resource in itself. One other enormous benefit provided by advertiser support of the mass media is free or low-cost access to a remarkable amount of news and information. Detractors who desire a society without advertising may change their positions when reminded that "no advertising" means no weekly grocery-sale inserts or classified ads, which allow readers to learn of money-saving offers or the variety of used goods for sale. Advertising serves other valuable functions—providing solid consumer product information, advising people about the availability of life-enhancing new products, and making known the dates and time of cultural events such as art exhibits and concerts.

Advertising is not as pervasive in other countries as it is in the United States because the range of consumer products and services is not as great, and so there is less reason to advertise to stimulate demand. Although industrialized countries with free-market systems have a fair amount of advertising, developing countries or those with government-controlled media have less. In these countries, advertising's influence as a communicator of cultural norms and its ability to move a society toward a consumer culture are limited.

Cultural Responsibilities

Despite the choices and opportunities that advertising in the United States promotes, critics worry about entrusting the establishment or reflection of cultural norms to advertising. At issue are the social cues that advertising sends to the public in its representation of morals, manners, rituals, and art. If one were to interpret contemporary U.S. culture solely through its advertising, one could conclude that it is primarily young, healthy, active, and Caucasian; that society is primarily made up of upper-middle-class people; that men hold most of the power and make the important decisions; that the family unit is made up of a married male and female who have bright children and much leisure time; that the wise advice of the elderly is universally revered; and that dogs talk.

Many observers contend that too much modern advertising focuses on sexual relationships, for example, or promotes products that enhance opportunities for sexual relationships. They fear that the impact of advertiser-determined sexual cues is harmful because they contribute to a decline in moral standards. The use of gratuitous seminudity in ads also suggests to some a culture

Artist Andy Warhol and Absolut vodka were a natural match for an advertising campaign; each started with advertisements that they converted into icons of American popular culture.
Under permission by V&S Vin & Sprit AB. Absolut Country of Sweden Vodka & Logo, Absolut, Absolut Bottle Design and Absolut Calligraphy are trademarks owned by V&S Vin & Sprit AB. © 2001 V&S Vin & Sprit AB.

obsessed by bodies and sex. Indeed, seminudity or suggested nudity in advertising is used to draw attention to the ad, and it is effective because a nude or seminude figure triggers either moral disapproval or an enthusiastic, sexually centered response.

Contemporary U.S. culture places high value on romantic and sexual relationships, and advertisers have found ways to exploit those values. In the United States, advertisers work in a moderately restrictive environment, where major marketers often cater to the most conservative mainstream values. In contrast, many European countries have more relaxed attitudes about sex, and therefore their advertising is more candid. U.S. advertisers go beyond conservative norms only when their target market is sophisticated enough not to take offense and when the media used can narrowly target the message to a particular segment without leaching into the general marketplace. But as the U.S. population has become more diverse and technology has made it possible to target increasingly narrow audiences, advertisers have less incentive to adhere to traditional restrictions. This trend is likely to continue as mass marketing is replaced by marketing targeted at small "niche" markets.

Cause or Effect?

A long-standing debate concerns whether advertising and the mass media determine social trends, rituals, and behavioral norms or merely reflect already-established trends, rituals, and norms. Contemporary U.S. popular culture is largely focused on social relationships. Most contemporary popular music has lyrics that revolve around love and coupling. Decisions about clothing, hairstyles, and what kinds of car to drive reflect self-image and are often manipulated by advertisers appealing to the desire to attract potential partners.

Alcohol consumption also is a part of American culture, as is the advertising of alcoholic beverages. Adult consumption of alcoholic beverages is legal and, for the most part, encouraged by society. On the other hand, smoking is no longer as prevalent in the United States as it once was, and cigarette advertising is limited to certain media. In the 1940s everyone from movie stars to corporate executives smoked; in the 1990s magazine articles, public-service announcements, and the absence of smokers in media entertainment sent the message that smoking is unhealthy.

Another area of concern has been advertising's representation of women. There is little argument that advertising helps to set standards for female beauty and that those standards often are unobtainable for most. Advertising tells women that they can come closer to the ideal through the purchase of cosmetics, clothing, or weight-loss products. Modern versions of the stereotypes of men as bosses or doctors and women as secretaries or nurses still existed at the start of the 21st century, as well. From laundry detergents to impractical undergarments, women's purchase decisions often are governed by an imperative to please men. And girls, through encouragement to emulate women, are encouraged to grow up quickly. While in the United States such advertisements are in the minority, those that communicate such messages are highly visible. Ads that promote ideal standards of beauty tell females that they are not acceptable to society without enhancement through cosmetics, designer fashions, and jewelry. Such messages negate feelings of individual self-worth. By focusing on particular body parts—such as legs in hosiery advertisements—or portraying women as passive and sexually available, these messages suggest that women are possessions and objects of desire. Some social scientists contend that such dehumanization in advertising and entertainment contributes to violence against women.

In addition to defining individuals' roles within a culture, advertising also creates rituals and sets behavioral norms. Alcoholic beverage advertising, for example, depicts drinking as an accepted element in partnering rituals. Couples depicted in advertisements share drinks to celebrate successful relationships, and young people in scanty swimwear drink beer on moonlit beaches. Yet, it is estimated that than 90 percent of all rapes in the United States involve drinking.

Some advertising seems to promote casual sex as a cultural norm and, as a result, encourages it as a social behavior. At a time when too casual an approach to sex can lead to serious health threats, this message, too, may be irresponsible.

Advertising also communicates norms of responsible behavior. It attempts to show ideals of American culture that are positive, such as stable family life, the rewards of hard work, acceptance of the contributions of all people within society, and the benefits of social diversity. Public-service messages—many created or supported by the advertising industry or corporate advertisers—address social problems and encourage responsible social behavior.

Cultural attitudes, customs, and standards of behavior vary greatly in different parts of the world. Effective advertising reflects the culture of its home country in order to play to that nation's belief system and make the advertising message palatable and welcome. Social taboos are determined, and avoided, and standards of manners observed in media messages. Observers in the United States often cite the relaxed standards toward nudity and sexuality in advertising in other countries. The acceptance or rejection of such themes is based on the culture of the people exposed to the advertising. When debating if U.S. advertising should become as permissive as some in South America or Europe, two questions are relevant: Does a push for more permissive themes set trends rather than reflect them, and are people in countries with these more permissive attitudes better off as a result?

America's Material Culture

While some claim that American society is too consumer-oriented and materialistic, the United States has used its ability to work hard, innovate, and constantly improve the standard of living and the lifestyles of its people to develop a highly advanced material culture. With material wealth have come advancements in health care, nutrition, and safety, which have resulted in longer, more comfortable lives; reduced rates of child and infant mortality; and the virtual elimination of several deadly diseases. Innovative technology has enhanced the accessibility of information, two recent examples being the Internet and e-mail. Electronic

Taco Bell's late-1990s campaign entered into American popular culture with its "Yo quiero Taco Bell" slogan.
Taco Bell Corp. in cooperation with Studio Animal Services, LLC. Photography: Cat Saleeby.

networks connect global businesses and cultures to share resources and solve mutual problems. People support businesses through on-line investing and direct e-commerce purchases. The ability to use advertising to compete in the marketplace has rewarded innovators with profits that translate to jobs, a tax base, and stability for others. For society, this competition has led to better-performing, less-costly products and services.

Critics of consumer culture question the effects of advertising, the cost of consumer goods, the validity of added value via advertising, brand proliferation, and the functional benefits of one brand over another. Some argue that advertising adds to the cost of consumer products and so is harmful in a consumer culture. Further exploration into the workings of a material culture, however, shows that mass manufacturing, marketing, and merchandising result in efficiencies of scale that lower unit costs. Advertising is the tool that stimulates mass sales and thus can reduce the costs of consumer products and services.

A material culture also revolves around the idea that marketing and manufacturing add value to products. Phenomenal growth in the number of product categories, products, services, and brands is the result of the basic idea that adding value in any form to a product or brand results in new or enhanced consumer demand. It is the job of advertising to communicate product and service improvements or introduce new products that make consumers' lives better.

Brand-name advertising links traits such as dependability, quality, cost-efficiency, and particular images to various products, and these traits have value. When choosing a brand of power tool that is nationally advertised, a purchaser may make the decision to buy more quickly and with more confidence than if buying an unknown brand, an added value to a consumer. The advertising tells potential buyers that the brand is successful enough to be able to afford national print and television rates, has demonstrated product expertise as a result of having a line extension, and may focus the improvements and expansion of the brand solely on power tools.

On the other hand, critics of advertising charge that there may be no functional differences between brands except for the higher costs of national advertising passed on to buyers and users. Likewise, they oppose brand proliferation, which offers too many brand choices but little substantial performance differences among brands.

The Significance of Subcultures

Subcultures are segments within society that share values, rituals, and behaviors that may differ from those of the overall culture. Advertisers have long been aware of the differences in buying and using patterns of various subcultures. Religion and race have always been part of studies of modern demographics, as marketers and advertisers recognize their role in choosing food, housing, dress, and personal or health-care products within subcultures.

Advertisers also use their recognition of social diversity in efforts to find advertising media that can effectively reach members of subcultures. There are, for example, Korean, Hispanic, African-American, Catholic, and Jewish media outlets, as well as some that target gays and lesbians.

Niche marketers target subcultures with products that are responsive to their lifestyles, values, beliefs, and dreams. Yet even this targeting has cultural ramifications. To some, it is a symbol of isolation from the overall culture; to others, if a subculture is not targeted with so-called mainstream products such as automobiles or stereos, it represents a failure by a marketer to recognize cultural commonalities.

Still more controversy arises when subcultures are targeted with advertising for controversial products such as cigarettes or alcoholic beverages. Advertisers find themselves faced with subcultures that say both, "Target us, we're major consumers," and also "Don't target us with mainstream products we might consider dangerous or not in our best interest."

Controversies have arisen over advertising of cigarettes and malt liquors targeted at the black community, as well as lottery tickets targeted to low socioeconomic groups. Heileman Brewing Company was forced by public outcry to abandon ads for Colt 45 Powermaster malt liquor that targeted low-income, inner-city blacks in 1991; R.J. Reynolds Tobacco Company's Uptown cigarette suffered a similar fate for similar reasons in 1990. The classic critical exploration of lottery marketing was done as a Harvard case study of the Massachusetts Lottery in 1989, carrying the sub-head, "It's a chance to make your dreams come true." Both the targeting of this group—and the offense taken by its members and others—contribute to yet another set of cultural stereotypes: that the African-American community does not have the disposable income to waste on nonnecessities such as beer and cigarettes or that black people are heavy drinkers who cannot handle their liquor. Likewise, objections to lottery advertising imply that minorities and the economically disadvantaged can be duped into the purchase of a lottery ticket.

In the last decade of the 20th century, black Americans became a central focus of advertising imagery, not just for the purpose of reaching black consumers but also to appeal to the millions of mostly young white consumers who had come to regard the anti-authority behavior described in rap music as something cool and desirable. It is a prime example of the way in which advertising both feeds popular culture and appropriates its language and cultural symbols in order to market goods.

Culture and Creative Messages

Persuasive messages are most effective if they are compatible with their targets' current beliefs, values, and worldviews. As a result, creators of advertising often use contemporary culture as a cue for developing successful advertising messages. Many advertising agencies provide company time for creative supervisors, copywriters, and art directors to go to movies, read novels, surf the Web, and explore museums and shopping malls. The creators of modern advertising need to know if the popular TV game show *Who Wants to Be a Millionaire* is going to be on the lips and in the minds of the American public in the days to come. Keeping up a dynamic culture allows creative staff to write and produce advertisements that exploit familiarity, compare or contrast with other cultural messages, and lampoon or present a serious side to popular thinking or lifestyles.

In return, advertising helps provide colorful additions to language and life. Long after it was heard in the well-known TV ads, the Wendy's International, Inc., tag line "Where's the beef?" remained a part of contemporary language, describing a lack of content and value in political rhetoric; Andy Warhol's Campbell's soup can imagery symbolizes an era in art; and "Takes a lickin' and keeps on tickin'," "Now you're cooking with gas," and "It's not nice to fool Mother Nature" still emerge from the mouths of people too young to remember their origins, to describe tenacity, progress, and major mistakes, respectively.

Advertising often takes a light look at culture—in order to attract attention to commercial messages or make them more palatable—and blends it with creative executions that play to cultural sophistication. In ads for innovative Web-based technology, off-the-wall teenagers show chief executives how to register online stock accounts, and bleary-eyed recluses peering at their computer screens are invited to see the sun again.

Advertising in other countries differs greatly from that in the United States as a result of their different cultural and language cues. Many U.S. advertising professionals view global commercial messages as refreshing and down to earth, because other cultures do not share Americans' super-sensitivity to cultural foibles.

KURT WILDERMUTH

See also African-Americans: Representations in Advertising; Age: Representations in Advertising; Critics of Advertising; Minorities: Representations in Advertising; Sex in Advertising; Women: Representations in Advertising

Further Reading

Fox, Stephen R., *The Mirror Makers: A History of American Advertising and Its Creators*, New York: Morrow, 1984

Hovland, Roxanne, and Gary B. Wilcox, editors, *Advertising in Society: Classic and Contemporary Readings on Advertising's Role in Society*, Lincolnwood, Illinois: NTC Business Books, 1989

Jewler, A. Jerome, *Creative Strategy in Advertising: What the Copywriter Should Know about the Creative Side of the Business*, Belmont, California: Wadsworth, 1981; 7th edition, as *Creative Strategy in Advertising*, by Jewler and Bonnie L. Drewniany, 2001

Kern-Foxworth, Marilyn, *Aunt Jemima, Uncle Ben, and Rastus: Blacks in Advertising, Yesterday, Today, and Tomorrow*, Westport, Connecticut: Greenwood Press and Praeger, 1994

Ogilvy, David, *Ogilvy on Advertising*, New York: Crown, and London: Pan, 1983

Packard, Vance Oakley, *The Hidden Persuaders*, New York: McKay, and London: Longmans, 1957

Pratkanis, Anthony R., and Elliot Aronson, *Age of Propaganda: The Everyday Use and Abuse of Persuasion*, New York: Freeman, 1992

Sivulka, Juliann, *Soap, Sex, and Cigarettes: A Cultural History of American Advertising*, Belmont, California: Wadsworth, 1998

Thorson, Esther, editor, *Advertising Age: The Principles of Advertising at Work*, Lincolnwood, Illinois: NTC Business Books, 1989

Vanden Bergh, Bruce G., and Helen E. Katz, *Advertising Principles: Choice, Challenge, Change*, Lincolnwood, Illinois: NTC Business Books, 1999

Positioning

Brand positioning is an important tool by which advertisers differentiate their products and services in the marketplace. Simply stated, a brand's "position" is an idea or concept that the brand is made to represent in the mind of the consumer. Most product and service categories, ranging from toothpaste to automobiles to computer retailers, are highly competitive, with many brand names fighting for consumer attention. Through positioning, a brand can develop a unique and meaningful image in the mind of the target audience.

The idea that a brand needs to stand for something has been reflected over the years in such concepts as "unique selling proposition" and "brand image." *Positioning* as a distinct term, however, was given wide currency by Al Ries and Jack Trout in their 1981 book *Positioning: The Battle for Your Mind.* Positioning can be accomplished in one of two ways. The first is to make the brand virtually synonymous with the product category, so that it is the brand that comes to mind when consumers think of the product. Examples include Xerox, Kleenex, and Scotch tape. Often the brand that stands for the category is the sales and profit leader in that category. In many cases, such a position is gained by being the first brand to aggressively advertise and promote within the product category.

Once a particular brand becomes synonymous with the category itself, other brands need to compete differently. Hence, the second approach to positioning—make the brand stand for a simple but meaningful concept. In automobiles, Volvo virtually owns the concept of "safety." In toothpaste, Close-Up stands for "sex appeal." Dove soap stands for "soft and gentle," and Maytag is virtually synonymous with "reliability" in appliances. Such positionings are established through years of consistent and single-minded advertising.

Effective positionings should be simple, meaningful, and unique. Simple concepts such as "thickest ketchup" (Heinz), "easy to use" (Macintosh computers), and "tough off-road" (Jeep) are easier than more complex formulations for consumers to process and associate with the brand name. Positioning must also be meaningful to the target audience. Positionings such as "comfortable jeans for women" (Lee jeans), "European driving performance" (BMW automobiles), and "inexpensive air travel" (Southwest Airlines) work well to the extent that these concepts strike a responsive chord with target customers.

Finally, an effective positioning should be unique within the product category. The positioning "reliable," for example, can be used in a number of product categories such as watches (Timex), appliances (Maytag), and automobiles (Honda). But within any single category, it is difficult for two brands to "own" the same concept in consumers' minds.

Advertising is the primary way in which a brand's positioning is established. A powerful and focused campaign can reposition a brand and bring it new life through a new image. Repositioning replaces one set of consumer expectations and associations with another. Pepsi-Cola was first positioned for its value starting in 1934: "Twice as much for a nickel." In the 1950s it became a light and sociable drink. Since 1964 "the Pepsi Generation" has marked it as the beverage of youth. Marlboro languished when advertised as a woman's cigarette but became successful when it targeted men and associated itself with masculine images of the American West. Saab automobiles, once perceived as lacking a distinctive positioning, found new life in positioning its cars as great winter vehicles.

While advertising is the primary tool for communicating a brand's positioning, other elements of the marketing strategy can reinforce the positioning decision. Promotion, while typically viewed as a mechanism for providing price discounts, is an excellent opportunity for communicating brand positioning. For more than 75 years Breitling timepieces have developed an association with the aviation industry, thereby gaining positioning as an aviator's watch. Breitling has sponsored aviation competitions and an attempt to circumnavigate the globe by balloon. Breitling's use of promotion strategically reinforces the positioning the brand has built over the past century. Likewise, Virginia Slims has strengthened its position as a woman's cigarette through its sponsorship of women's professional tennis and other sports.

Product design can also reinforce a brand's positioning. BMW automobiles' position as the epitome of "European driving performance" is reflected in the tag line, "The ultimate driving machine." The design of BMW automobiles embodies this positioning: near-perfect weight balance, rear-wheel drive, award-winning engines, available manual transmissions, and the specially identified high-performance "M series."

Not only can positioning inform elements of the marketing mix for products, it can serve the same function for services. Enterprise Rent-A-Car became the industry sales leader by positioning itself as the rental car company for the insurance replacement market (as opposed to the airport destination market). All of Enterprise's marketing activities focus on that positioning. Its advertising communicates that Enterprise will "pick you up" at the repair facility. In most major cities the company has multiple leasing sites for customer convenience. Company representatives work to build good relationships with local auto body and repair facilities. Enterprise's positioning clearly drives its marketing activities.

In short, then, positioning is a simple, meaningful, and unique concept with which a brand is associated. Effective positioning helps a product or service differentiate itself and compete more effectively. Though ideally an effective positioning should drive many elements of the marketing mix, advertising is the primary vehicle for communicating a brand's positioning to the target audience. Over time, highly focused, single-minded advertising delivers and reinforces a brand's unique positioning, and eventually, that positioning concept becomes closely integrated with the brand in the mind of the consumer.

BRIAN D. TILL

See also color plate in this volume

Further Reading

Hooley, Graham J., and John Saunders, *Competitive Positioning: The Key to Market Success,* New York: Prentice Hall, 1993

Ries, Al, and Jack Trout, *Positioning: The Battle for Your Mind,* New York: Warner, 1981; revised edition, 1986

Ries, Al, and Jack Trout, *The 22 Immutable Laws of Marketing,* New York: HarperBusiness, 1993; London: HarperCollins, 1994

Post-Keyes-Gardner, Inc.

Founded by merger of Post, Morr & Gardner, Inc., Chicago, Illinois, and Keyes, Madden & Jones Advertising, also of Chicago, 1963; forged international partnership with Brunning Group, Ltd., London, England, 1967; merged with Cunningham & Walsh, 1978.

Major Clients

Amana Refrigeration Company
Atchison, Topeka & Santa Fe Railway Company
E.J. Brach & Sons
Brown & Williamson Tobacco Corporation
Jos. Schlitz Brewing Company
W.A. Sheaffer Pen Company

Post-Keyes-Gardner, Inc. (P-K-G), was created in 1963 through the merger of Post, Morr & Gardner, Inc., and Keyes, Madden & Jones Advertising. With roughly $30 million in annual billings, the new agency immediately became one of the five largest advertising agencies in Chicago, Illinois.

In 1960 Carl M. Post, executive vice president at Grant Advertising, left to become president of Gordon Best & Company, in Chicago. A year later Post bought the company from Best with partner Frank F. Morr. The third partner, F. Sewall Gardner, came over from the former Chicago office of Dancer, Fitzgerald, Sample in April 1962 bringing 24 people with him. Shortly thereafter Post began merger discussions with Keyes, Madden & Jones.

If Post and Gardner represented half of P-K-G's heritage, then Freeman Keyes represented the other half. Keyes joined the Russell M. Seeds Company, Inc., of Chicago in the late 1930s, to handle the Brown & Williamson (B&W) tobacco account. B&W's principal agency was Batten Barton Durstine & Osborn (BBDO), which handled the company's major cigarette brands, Raleigh and Kool. But by 1939 B&W had assigned several smaller brands (Avalon and Wings) along with its smoking tobaccos to Seeds, which also handled the W.A. Sheaffer Pen Company and parts of Grove Laboratories. By 1944 Seeds entered into the ranks of major U.S. ad agencies (then considered to be any shop with annual billings of more than $10 million) when it became the agency for the *Raleigh Cigarette Program* with Red Skelton.

Keyes, who produced the program, had signed Skelton to a long-term contract with Seeds when he had first brought the comic into radio in 1939 on *B&W's Avalon Time.* It was a contract that would continue to produce capitalized fees for the agency well into the 1960s, when Skelton was one of the most popular comedians in television. Billings dropped slightly in the mid-1940s until 1948 when BBDO resigned B&W, and Seeds inherited the entire Raleigh account. The agency was billing about $11 million by 1950. In May 1953 Seeds acquired Cruttenden & Eger, which brought agency volume to $16 million. Billings remained flat through the middle of the decade, by which time Keyes had become Seeds chairman.

In September 1957 Keyes set up a separate agency structure with Seeds as the titular parent company. He brought in Edward D. Madden from International Latex as president and Howard A. Jones from Grant Advertising as executive vice president and named the agency Keyes, Madden & Jones (KMJ). In December 1958 the agency undertook an affiliation with Donahue & Coe, of New York City, to service a group of accounts each had in the other agency's city. Although the agency was aggressive in seeking new business, growth was steady to slow. Keyes decided that the only way he could become a major presence was through the merger. Finally, on 1 March 1963 Keyes joined with Post and Morr to form P-K-G, with B&W as the anchor account.

P-K-G continued on the acquisition track. It embarked on a tense set of negotiations in 1963 with Maxon, Inc., of Detroit, Michigan, in a proposed merger said to have the potential to become the third-largest in advertising history, creating an agency with annual billings estimated at $70 million. The talks soured, however, and the deal fell through.

Also in 1963 P-K-G acquired a longtime Leo Burnett Company client, the Atchison, Topeka & Santa Fe Railway Company, a $2 million account. (Santa Fe had severed its 22-year relationship with Burnett on 1 November because of a perceived conflict with United Airlines.) P-K-G opened an office in Honolulu, Hawaii, in 1964 to handle the Primo Beer and Kona Coffee accounts, the former a recent acquisition of the Jos. Schlitz Brewing Company.

In 1965 Gordon Conn, marketing director of Florists' Transworld Delivery Association (FTDA), joined P-K-G as chief of the agency's Detroit office. As a result of Conn's move, FTDA shifted

The smallest refrigerator we make is in the big refrigerators we make.

compartments (set one without affecting the other); adjustable cantilevered shelves*; butter conditioner; porcelain crispers plus Amana's exclusive, non-chip, washable, acrylic-enamel finish. And Free-O'-Frost, too.

Whew!

How come no other make has so many features? No other maker knows refrigeration like Amana. See for yourself at your nearest Amana dealer. Today.

Amana®
Backed by a century-old tradition of fine craftsmanship.

You put meat in it, but that's the only similarity between our meat keeper and everyone else's. Amana's meat keeper is really a "refrigerator within a refrigerator."

Because it refrigerates while it stores. Lets you keep meat without spoiling, twice as long as ordinary meat keepers.

This meat keeper has a special cold control of its own. You can keep temperature as much as 10° colder than the rest of the refrigerator...perfect for fresh meat storage.

A separate jet of cold air surrounds the meat keeper pan, to cradle it in a blanket of cold (but no air blows directly on the meat itself.) This way, your meat stays fresh and flavorful longer.

Our "little refrigerator" is a bonus you get with our big refrigerators. Like the new 16.7 cubic foot freezer-at-the-top model (at right) and 22.3 cubic foot side-by-side (at left).

Just check these features: Fast freeze shelf; independent cold controls for both refrigerator and freezer

Only 35½" wide

Only 32" wide   *Pat. Pending

The "refrigerator within a refrigerator" campaign was created by Post-Keyes-Gardner, Inc., for Amana in 1967 during a period of significant growth for the agency.
Courtesy Amana Company.

its $2 million account to P-K-G. FTDA was no stranger to P-K-G executives, as Grant Advertising, Post's former agency, had handled the account for 15 years. In spite of the FTDA business, P-K-G suffered that year when two of its accounts left the agency. First, the Jos. Schlitz Brewing Company took away the Old Milwaukee beer account, which had an annual ad budget estimated at $3.5 million–$4 million. Next, candy maker E.J. Brach & Company, a P-K-G client that shifted agencies five times in the early 1960s, left for Arthur Meyerhoff Associates in 1965, taking with it more than $1 million in annual billings.

In 1966 P-K-G claimed $40.7 million in billings, roughly $4 million more than in 1965. The Amana Refrigeration Company signed with P-K-G that year in what turned out to be a three-year relationship resulting in about $800,000–$1 million in annual spending. The W.A. Sheaffer Pen Company, an account valued at about $1 million, also signed with P-K-G in 1966. Fifteen employees were hired for the creative department, most from New York City agencies.

P-K-G made its first foray into international advertising in 1967, after forging a partnership with Brunning Group, Ltd., London, England, Britain's seventh-largest ad agency. As part of the expansion, P-K-G brought on board Geoffrey Goodyear, former general manager of Grant Advertising's European operations. At year-end P-K-G had about $360,000 in overseas billings.

The late 1960s were a time of transition for P-K-G. First came its move to two floors in Chicago's new high-rise, the John Hancock Building. Almost two years earlier, P-K-G had been the first commercial tenant to sign a lease for space in the building. Then in 1969, six years after serving as the principal architect of P-K-G, Post retired at 54, having built the agency into an industry powerhouse that claimed $46 million in annual billings.

In 1970 La Choy Food Products, a division of Beatrice Foods Company, signed a contract with P-K-G beginning in January 1971. A former Lennen & Newell (L&N) client, La Choy was said to have product plans that conflicted with those of other L&N clients. The Chinese-American food company announced that it was introducing a line of frozen Chinese foods and would be backing the launch with newspaper and Sunday supplement ads as well as spot television commercials.

By 1973 P-K-G was only one of two agencies founded since 1960 that posted more than $50 million in billings (Wells, Rich, Greene was the other). The Chicago agency also benefited when longtime client B&W Tobacco decided to consolidate all its media buying and planning functions under one roof. As a result, P-K-G became responsible for all media for B&W's Kool, Viceroy, Raleigh, and Belair cigarette brands. In 1972 B&W spent a total of $22 million in print advertising for the four brands.

In 1973 client Alberto-Culver terminated a six-month-long "experiment" under which the Melrose Park, Illinois, beauty products manufacturer allowed two small New York City advertising agencies to handle its account. As a result, P-K-G gained an estimated $4 million–$5 million in billings. Less than a year later, however, the peripatetic Alberto-Culver transferred its products to Arthur & Wheeler, which already handled roughly $20 million in Alberto-Culver billings.

In 1975 the agency lost the $10 million account for Schering-Plough's Maybelline cosmetics division, as well as smaller accounts for Masonite Corporation's hardboard division and Peter Hand Brewing Company's Old Chicago beers. But the following year P-K-G acquired Paterno Imports' Gancia Asti Spumante account, valued at $500,000.

By 1978 P-K-G was billing $80 million annually. In September 1978 Cunningham & Walsh announced it was merging with P-K-G to gain a foothold in the Midwest that would complement its offices in Los Angeles and San Francisco, California.

DEREK DATTNER AND AMY I.S. DATTNER

Further Reading

"Alberto Drops N.Y. Shops; Post-Keyes Added to Roster," *Advertising Age* (17 December 1973)

"Alberto Shifts Accounts, but Keeps P-K-G," *Advertising Age* (16 September 1974)

Curme, Emmett, "Merger of Post, Keyes Is Consummated," *Advertising Age* (4 March 1963)

Curme, Emmett, "Santa Fe Picks Post-Keyes for $2,000,000 Billing," *Advertising Age* (2 August 1965)

"Florist Telegraph Account Shifts As Conn Joins P-K-G," *Advertising Age* (1 February 1965)

Kanner, Bernice, "C&W Finally Finds Midwest Link via Post-Keyes Merger," *Advertising Age* (4 September 1978)

"Post, Keyes Celebrates 10th," *Advertising Age* (18 June 1973)

"Post-Morr Says Merger in Works; 'Not Yet': Maxon," *Advertising Age* (12 August 1963)

"Schlitz Seeks New Agency for Old Milwaukee," *Advertising Age* (15 November 1965)

"Sheaffer Names Post-Keyes for $1,000,000 Account," *Advertising Age* (21 March 1966)

Pouzilhac, Alain de 1945–

French Advertising Executive

Alain de Pouzilhac is chairman and chief executive of Havas Advertising, the world's fourth-largest marketing services group. He was born in Sète, a town in the south of France, which also was home to his favorite poet, Paul Valéry, and the well-known French singer George Brassens.

De Pouzilhac made his debut on the media stage at the age of 11, when he became the host of a daily show called *Europe Jeunesse,* broadcast on Europe 1, one of France's biggest radio stations, under the name "Petit Alain." During his show, which was broadcast for three years from 5 P.M. to 7 P.M., de Pouzilhac initiated a series of on-air chats with listeners of his generation. His precocious media talent was not matched in the classroom; after he repeated the fifth grade twice, de Pouzilhac's parents decided to enroll him in boarding school.

Despite his keen interest in sports, especially rugby and soccer, de Pouzilhac's lead subject at university was philosophy (he left school without formally graduating) and received honors from the French newspaper *Le Figaro* for his reflections on freedom. In 1969 de Pouzilhac secured a job at the ad agency Publicis Conseil as a traffic assistant, a necessary stepping stone at the time for a move into account management. A year later he joined Doyle Dane Bernbach (DDB) as an account executive before being promoted to account director.

De Pouzilhac joined Havas Conseil in 1975 as general manager of a group of clients, including Darty, Panzani, and Fruite, all French brands in the distribution and food sectors. From there, he steadily climbed the corporate ladder until he became chairman and chief executive officer (CEO) of Havas Conseil in 1982. Throughout this period, de Pouzilhac forged strong relationships with all his clients and still personally managed Darty after a quarter of a century.

It was also at this time that de Pouzilhac became aware of the disadvantages for Havas in remaining a heavily French-focused agency group. Two years before he joined Havas, the agency had merged its advertising activities into a subsidiary called Eurocom. In 1982, aware of the increasing need to move into the international arena, de Pouzilhac took Eurocom public, with Havas retaining a minority stake. In 1985 Eurocom and Young & Rubicam (Y&R) entered into a joint venture dubbed Havas Conseil Marsteller (HCM). As European head, de Pouzilhac would go on to win the Peugeot and Philips accounts, thus laying a European foundation for the first Eurocom network. By 1986 Eurocom comprised some three dozen advertising agencies.

The company expanded its presence in the United Kingdom in 1989—the year de Pouzilhac became CEO of Eurocom Advertising—by acquiring a stake in the group. The same year, the Japanese advertising agency Dentsu became a partner in HCM, which was renamed Havas Dentsu Marsteller (HDM). In 1990 Eurocom bought out both Y&R's and Dentsu's interests in HDM's European network of ad agencies.

Already the number-one ad agency in France, Eurocom strengthened its dominance in 1992 through its merger with the number-three agency, Roux, Séguéla, Cayzac & Goudard (RSCG), to become Euro RSCG Worldwide, with de Pouzilhac as chairman and CEO. His main focus was to develop the group's international business, in particular that in the United States, and in time the agency managed to pick up major clients in this market, including Intel Corporation and MCI Worldcom. In 1996, in order to increase the group's competitiveness, de Pouzilhac launched Havas Advertising and restructured the group into four divisions: Euro RSCG Worldwide, Campus (later Arnold Worldwide Partners), Media Planning Group, and Diversified Agencies Group.

In February 2000 Havas Advertising announced the purchase of the U.S. marketing services group Snyder Communications for $2.2 billion. This deal was crucial to de Pouzilhac's dream of turning Havas into a global communications force and improving its profits in the United States. The four Snyder companies acquired—Arnold Communications, Bounty SCA Worldwide, Brann Worldwide, and Circle.com—represented areas in which the group was eager to strengthen its offerings.

Alain de Pouzilhac.
Courtesy of Havas Advertising.

The enlarged Havas Advertising became the fourth-largest advertising communications group in the world, comprising 20,000 employees in 75 countries with annual revenue of $2.2 billion. Havas included the world's largest ad group in interactive services and the world's largest direct-marketing brand. More than half the group's client base was in the most dynamic sectors of the world's economy: telecommunications, technology, financial services, media, and health care.

In December 2000, in a move designed to create one of the world's top five media specialist agencies, de Pouzilhac consolidated the media departments of Havas's U.S. agencies. At the same time, Havas purchased the media department of Jordan, McGrath, Case & Partners in New York City.

Always passionate about advertising, de Pouzilhac is also a fervent advocate of sports and is highly competitive. His father was a professional rugby player at Narbonne, France, and Sète, his hometown, was home of the French league soccer champions in 1936. De Pouzilhac has said that he believes he learned the subtleties of management by participating in school sports, an experience that enabled him to harness the talents of an advertising group full of strong personalities. In 1999 his passion for sports drove him to create Havas Advertising Sports. He was also president of the Narbonne rugby team.

ANNE-MARIE CRAWFORD

Biography
Born in Sète, France, 11 July 1945; hosted his own daily radio show, 1956 to 1959; left university and joined advertising agency Publicis Conseil, 1969; moved to Doyle Dane Bernbach, 1970; joined Havas Conseil, 1975; named chairman and chief executive officer (CEO), 1982; took Eurocom subsidiary public, 1982; named CEO of Eurocom, 1989; named chairman and CEO of Euro RSCG, the agency formed by the merger of Eurocom and Roux, Séguéla, Cayzac & Goudard, 1992.

Selected Publications
L'impératif moral: Retour à la morale ou simple besoin de nouvelles règles du jeu? (with Bernard Cathelat), 1997

Quelles élites pour le XXIe siècle: Après l'âge du management gestionnaire, l'ère du leadership visionnaire? (Bernard Cathelat and Yves Cannac), 1997

Le retour des clans: Après l'ère de l'individualisme, entrons-nous dans l'ère des tribus? (Bernard Cathelat and Claude Bébéar), 1997

L'alternative des valeurs féminines (with Bernard Cathelat), 1998

De l'Homo Sapiens à l'homme interactif (Bernard Cathelat and Michel Brossard), 1998

Du corps machine à la santé harmonique (with Bernard Cathelat), 1999

Les nouveaux horizons de la consommation (with Bernard Cathelat), 1999

La soif d'émotion (with Bertrand Gallé), 1999

Les Screenagers, 2000

Presenters

The use in advertising of celebrity presenters closely associated with a particular product or service is a marketing industry tradition that has stood the test of time. Advertisers and their agencies have long believed that employing a well-known performer or public figure to promote their products or services would lend credibility and allure, helping to distinguish them from the competition. For the most part, this approach has been successful, although some have questioned the use in advertisements of radio and television journalists, questioning whether their roles as presenters may have compromised their professional objectivity.

In 1950 Betty Furness, a former stage actress trying to break into TV, began appearing in commercials for Westinghouse refrigerators and appliances, beginning a relationship that would last 11 years and making her one of the best-known personalities of early commercial TV. Furness helped establish the effectiveness of the presenter in television, and she made it acceptable for a woman to assume the role. Soon General Electric (GE) was being represented by Kathi Norris, Colgate by Candy Jones, Admiral by Murial Williams, Borden by Betty Johnson, Lincoln-Mercury by Julia Meade on *The Ed Sullivan Show*, and Chevrolet by Dinah Shore.

The most successful presenter in early television, however, was probably Arthur Godfrey, who sometimes frightened advertisers with his unwillingness to take their products seriously but who connected with millions of viewers in the process. The folksy broadcaster, who started doing morning radio ad-lib style in the early 1930s at WJSV in Washington, D.C., took a casual but sincere approach that translated to viewers as trustworthy. Although he pitched many products on his various television broadcasts, his most regular brand association was with Lipton Tea, which sponsored his weekly *Talent Scouts* show through Young & Rubicam.

In the 1940s and 1950s it was commonplace for even the most hard-nosed broadcast journalist, such as Edward R. Murrow, to serve as a quasi-representative if not an actual spokesperson for a sponsor's product or service. But as the lines began to blur between objective news efforts and commercial interests—even on popular hybrid programs such as NBC's *Today*—the practice became taboo. Mike Wallace learned the hard way when, after doing commercials for Parliament cigarettes for several years, he decided he wanted to become a full-fledged news reporter. He had to buy out his Parliament contract, then spend several years working in small markets before he was able to go on the network as a reporter for CBS.

Ronald Reagan's big TV break came when he became the host of *General Electric Theater* for CBS on Sunday evenings from 1954 to 1962 and starred in 34 episodes. Reagan's genial talk of progress was synonymous with GE's technological advancements, and American patriotism became a more prominent and memorable part of the program than some of the entertainment components themselves. The GE motto, "Progress is our most important product," remained constant. Over the decades the celebrity spokesperson technique has proven effective. Familiar personalities such as Paul Reiser for AT&T Corporation, Candice Bergen for Sprint, and Whoopi Goldberg for MCI engaged viewers visually and verbally.

The choice of a presenter to represent a brand or product involves many considerations. Although the final choice must lend itself to rational justification in terms of the presenter supporting the positioning of the product, as often as not the selection hinges to some extent on personal taste.

Once a choice has been made, the agency approaches the personality through a talent agency, personal agent, or business manager to begin negotiating terms. There are companies in advertising to assist agencies in making such contacts. Once such a consulting company becomes involved in a negotiation, the agency will pay the presenter through the consultant, which will take an agreed-upon commission before transferring the money to the presenter.

The costs of retaining a famous presenter depend on many factors. The more unique the qualities of the presenter and the more appropriate to the brand, the higher the fee, since the actor knows that the campaign may depend on his or her participation. In other cases, when any number of actors might meet the requirement, the bargaining power of the individual diminishes. Also, the longer the campaign is to run, the greater the commitment of the presenter to the brand. The duration of the use period is spelled out in the contract, usually with options to renew.

Some campaigns require very little of a star, because the individual is secondary to the concept. In the 1970s Ogilvy & Mather developed a campaign for the American Express credit card that suggested the product could give any cardholder instant standing, even though he or she might not be known in a restaurant or store. It used a series of presenters with famous names but not necessarily famous faces, who asked, "Do you know me?" The agency was able to get such figures as author James Michener and bandleader Benny Goodman to make appearances, each for a flat fee of $20,000; ultimately, it became a source of prestige to be asked to participate in the campaign.

An actor must consider many factors in accepting an offer to represent a product. If a major star, for example, is approached to do a campaign for a local or regional advertiser, such as an automobile dealer association, he or she knows that accepting the offer means forfeiting any chance of doing a national campaign for a competing brand in the product category, not only during the run of the campaign but for some period thereafter. Therefore, he or she will likely demand a fee that will not only compensate for work itself but also cover any other lost advertising opportunities. Depending on the star's stature, agencies were once able to exert considerable influence over performers' activities once they committed to a lucrative campaign. Presenters could, for example, be barred from appearing as a guest on any show sponsored by a competitor. But as advertiser relationships with specific programs faded, such issues lost their importance. Today actors who do commercials are under few constraints.

Even chief executives occasionally step into the limelight as spokesmen for their brands. Among the better known and more effective was Lee Iacocca, chief executive officer of Chrysler Corporation. With Chrysler battling a wave of Japanese imports and nearing bankruptcy in the 1980s, Iacocca made a charismatic, personal appeal in TV commercials, resulting in a congressional bailout of the automaker and a rise in car sales.

The physical presence of the presenter in a commercial creates a warmer, more confident feeling on the part of the consumer than if the presenter appears only as a voice, heard but unseen. These pitches are very different from personal endorsements, in which the presenter attaches a personal testimony.

While ad campaigns often use celebrities, marketers have found that presenters need not be recognizable personalities to enhance a brand's performance. Successful unknown presenters have included Maytag's fictitious lonely repairman; the characters Fred Bartles and Ed Jaymes, who pitched E.& J. Gallo's Bartles & Jaymes's wine coolers; and the anonymous fast-talking Federal Express guy from the 1980s. In general, however, presenters, who are surrogates for the advertiser, have been show business personalities or high-profile athletes who bring a human face to a corporate image and who are well compensated for their time.

The two highly publicized commercials Michael Jackson made for Pepsi-Cola Company's Pepsi were the forerunners of the big-budget celebrity ads that dominated much advertising during the 1980s and 1990s. Pepsi paid $5 million for the rights to Jackson's image and $2 million to produce the spots, handled by BBDO Worldwide, New York City.

Other popular celebrity presenters have included Karl Malden and Jerry Seinfeld for American Express Corporation, John Cleese for Philips Electronics' Magnavox, Jim Palmer for Jockey International, Kathie Lee Gifford for Carnival Cruises, Ed McMahon for Budweiser, and Muhammad Ali for Rockport Company's footwear. The 1990s saw Elizabeth Taylor emerge as the spokesperson for Elizabeth Arden's White Diamonds fragrance, and pop singer Whitney Houston represented AT&T. Some advertisers relied on several different personalities. Pepsi rotated Cindy Crawford, Michael J. Fox, Madonna, and Michael Jackson through its advertising. Nike featured athletes such as Michael Jordan and Bo Jackson. Cosmetic companies relied largely on actresses and models—Melanie Griffith and Cindy Crawford for Revlon, Elizabeth

"There's only one way to get confidence like this."

Q: Why will Depend® undergarments give me added confidence?

A: Only Depend Elastic Leg Under-garments offer the Absorb-Loc® leakage protection system.

Q: What is the Absorb-Loc system?

A: It is a unique leakage protection system made up of super absorbent material. Material that quickly locks in 25% more than before. So you'll feel drier. And more comfortable.

Q: Is Depend the only one with the Absorb-Loc system?

A: Yes. That's why there's only one way to get protection and confidence like this.

Q: Where can I get more information?

A: Consult your doctor or pharmacist about bladder control problems. And for a free sample and booklet, call 1-800-4-DEPEND. And get back into life.

Depend
Undergarments

Get back into life with Depend.™

June Allyson

© 1990 Kimberly-Clark Corp.

In this 1990 ad, 1940s motion picture star June Allyson was the presenter for Depend undergarments.
© 1990 Kimberly-Clark Corporation. Used with permission.

Hurley for Estee Lauder Companies, and Cybill Shepherd for L'Oreal Source.

A product often requires just the right personality to make the advertising work. For example, 1940s film star June Allyson added just the right spirit and gracefully aging celebrity needed to sell Kimberly-Clark Corporation's Depend incontinence products. Some presenters have become so closely identified with a product that the two cannot be separated even in death. Years after its founder Colonel Harlan Sanders died, Kentucky Fried Chicken resurrected him in the form of an animated spokes-character. Many of the most beloved presenters have, in fact, been animated characters, such as Tony the Tiger for Kellogg's Sugar-Frosted Flakes and the Snap, Crackle, and Pop characters for Rice Krispies, both from Leo Burnett Company.

Some presenters bring a personal situation or cause to an advertisement that makes it more poignant or effective. For instance, actor Yul Brenner's antismoking messages—filmed just prior to his death from lung cancer and aired soon thereafter—proved courageous and arresting.

The use of presenters can backfire, however, if the celebrity becomes enmeshed in questionable, disgraceful, or even illegal activities. Perhaps the most dramatic example is that of professional athlete-turned-actor O.J. Simpson, onetime spokesman for Hertz Corporation. In 1984 the consumer research company Video Storyboard Tests rated Simpson the most popular athlete-turned-spokesperson. But when he was accused of murdering his ex-wife in 1994 and became the defendant in a highly publicized criminal trial, public perception of him altered radically and his value as a spokesperson was destroyed.

Other professional athletes have caused grief for their sponsoring corporations after agreeing to appear in—or having appeared in—commercials in which they pitched or endorsed products. Often, it was difficult to separate the athlete's reputation from that of the company. Still, Converse signed bad boy basketball star Dennis Rodman to a multiyear deal just weeks after he kicked a photographer in the groin during a National Basketball Association (NBA) game, saying its negotiations with the athlete had begun months before the incident. At the time many in the sports marketing field openly questioned the ethics of the deal. "What are they saying? That this is the right shoe to kick somebody with?" asked Lesa Ukman, executive director of the *IEG Sponsorship Report*, a trade publication that tracks celebrity endorsements, as quoted at the time in the *Boston Globe*. It was not Converse's first brush with a celebrity whose behavior caused embarrassment. Several years earlier, Converse's Boston, Massachusetts, ad agency, then known as Houston Herstek Favat, produced an ad featuring James Brown, the "godfather of soul." Before the highly regarded ad was aired, Brown was accused of beating his wife. The ad never ran.

The 1990s were a particularly difficult period for celebrity image, owing in part to intensified media scrutiny and a rash of arrests and embarrassing incidents. Pepsi had boxer Mike Tyson under contract before he was convicted of rape, and the company featured Michael Jackson in its television commercials before he was accused of child molestation. A subsequently more cautious

Pepsi did background checks on Cindy Crawford and Shaquille O'Neal before using them in commercials.

Nike had invested for promotional reasons in Michael Jordan before his gambling problems became public and contracted with figure skater Tonya Harding before she was convicted of conspiracy in the assault on her rival, Nancy Kerrigan. Nike even contributed $25,000 to Harding's legal defense fund. Kerrigan created her own stir when, after signing a promotional contract with Walt Disney Company, the Olympic silver medalist was overheard making unflattering remarks about a celebratory parade at Walt Disney World while she was actually on the parade float.

Nor have such gaffes been limited to athletes. Actress Meryl Streep told the *New York Times* that her one-time $3 million pitch for American Express was strictly business, declaring, "I don't believe in the company." Actress Cybill Shepherd was spokesperson for the beef industry until she revealed that she did not eat meat. Shepherd's *Moonlighting* TV series costar Bruce Willis was dropped by the Seagram Company as spokesperson for its Golden Wine Cooler after it was learned he had earlier sought help for a drinking problem. Tennis player Jennifer Capriati, who was promoting Prince racquets and Diadoro designer sportswear, was arrested for drug possession. Singer Paul Simon bowed to cries of elitism when fans and the press found out his 1991 concert tour had been underwritten to the tune of $1 million by the American Express Gold Card in exchange for his being a spokesperson for the card and its services.

In some cases, personalities have overshadowed the products or services they were presenting and were quickly dismissed as a result. In the early 1980s, the esteemed actor-producer Orson Welles was fired by Vintners International after he made the line "We will sell no wine before its time" more famous as his own than that of the product. Michael Cliff, chief executive officer of Vintners International, which owned the Paul Masson brand, called Welles a "video vampire" who "stole the show." The phenomenon repeated itself with other high-priced presenters, leaving consumers to wonder which pantyhose football great Joe Namath was selling and which automobile manufacturer's Corinthian leather actor Ricardo Montalban was pitching.

One disturbing celebrity spokesperson effort was Health-Extra's early 2000 ads for disability insurance featuring actor Christopher Reeves, whose acting career came to an abrupt halt after a near-fatal fall from a horse that left him paralyzed from the neck down. Reeves's photo above copy that read, "I've seen too many families destroyed, not from disability but from financial drain," appeared to be overkill to some. "The banner [ad] goes beyond a reasonable celebrity tie-in and winds up just being creepy," *Advertising Age* noted in an April 2000 editorial.

Occasionally, presenter arrangements can border on the absurd. At one point in 1995 Pizza Hut had Rodman, entrepreneur Donald Trump, and conservative talk-show host Rush Limbaugh on its payroll simultaneously, all promoting stuffed-crust pizza in spots created by BBDO Worldwide.

The best presenters over the years have also been the most memorable. Joe DiMaggio was hugely successful representing

Dime Bank and Mr. Coffee. Actors James Garner and Mariette Hartley created a series of advertisements for Polaroid Corporation featuring breezy, humorous exchanges. Polaroid and its agency Doyle Dane Bernbach signed the duo for five years in the late 1970s and early 1980s. Some of the dialogue in these commercials was ad-libbed by the couple, who shared a natural chemistry on camera. In 1979 Garner, a higher-profile actor than Hartley at the time, refused to continue making the commercials unless Polaroid offered her more money to stay onboard. It did.

The Polaroid commercials ended Garner's 25-year absence from TV pitches; he had done a Winston cigarette commercial in 1954 at the outset of his career. Garner professed to exercise a conscience about his work as a presenter, having refused breweries because he did not drink beer and declining a $1 million offer from Ford Motor Corporation for its Maverick, which had the same name as his ABC television series at the time, because he was racing Chevrolets on the weekends when he was off-camera. Demonstrating just how effective celebrity presenters can be, Hartley began sporting T-shirts that read, "I'm not the real Mrs. James Garner," when their good-natured give-and-take had TV fans convinced that the pair were married in real life. Hartley, who at the time was married to commercial producer Patrick Boyriven of Benton & Bowles, acknowledged that the commercials actually revived her lagging career and helped her to develop a natural style of acting that served her well in solo commercials and TV and film performances afterward.

Perhaps the single most popular presenter of the modern television era has been comedian Bill Cosby, who has promoted everything from Jell-O to cameras to Coca-Cola to insurance. The only person ever to beat Cosby during his 14-year reign over the ad industry's public approval index was the Pope. By the time Cosby joined E.F. Hutton's "When E.F. Hutton talks, people listen" campaign, he was probably already overexposed. Cosby's contract was canceled after only nine months, and the 14-year campaign abandoned.

Likewise, veteran actor John Houseman, whose esteemed stage and film career was punctuated by the popular motion picture and TV series *The Paper Chase*, was sublime at attracting new clients to Smith Barney with "We make money the old-fashioned way" but failed miserably to be taken seriously when pitching McDonald's Big Macs, an idea that came from the Leo Burnett Company.

Houseman said that to maintain his credibility, he limited himself to only two simultaneous corporate commercial campaigns. Smith Barney and its agency, Ogilvy & Mather, which were the first to see the presenter potential of Houseman's bow-tied, imperious Professor Kingsfield from *The Paper Chase*, became outraged when the actor began accepting other jobs as spokesperson for such companies as Chrysler-Plymouth and Puritan. At the time other agencies and advertisers began passing over Houseman, complaining that he had lost his credibility, just as football star Namath had a decade earlier.

Serving as a spokesperson has, at times, proven to be tricky business because the role can be so easily confused with product or service endorsements, leading to a situation in which the spokesperson becomes liable for false claims. For instance, singer Pat Boone came under legal scrutiny for his endorsement of the acne product Acne-Statin in 1978. Boone finally agreed to a settlement with the Federal Trade Commission that held him personally accountable, which became the forerunner for new endorsement standards.

DIANE MERMIGAS

Further Reading

Bird, William L., "General Electric Theater" <www.mbcnet.org>

Carmichael, Matt, "Cybercritique: Celebrity Plugs Produce Absurd, Disturbing Ads," *Advertising Age* (17 April 2000)

Conrad, Eric, "Caution: Falling Idols: Ad Firms Growing Wary of Tainted Sports Heroes," *Fort Lauderdale Sun-Sentinel* (8 October 1995)

Forkan, Jim, "Houseman Named '82 Star Presenter," *Advertising Age* (2 August 1982)

Freedman, Alix, "Marriages between Celebrity Spokesmen and Their Firms Can Be Risky Ventures," *The Wall Street Journal* (11 January 1988)

"FTC Says Star Responsible for Endorsement," *Advertising Age* (15 May 1978)

Garfield, Bob, "Pizza Has the Crust to Roll Out 'Incorrect' Celebs," *Advertising Age* (1 May 1995)

"Hertz Hustles Simpson Out of Its Auto Ads," *The Detroit News* (20 June 1994)

Marshall, Christy, "It Seemed Like a Good Idea at the Time," *Forbes* (28 December 1987)

Pendleton, Jennifer, "One Step to a Winning Sales Pitch," *Advertising Age* (30 July 1979)

Pressler, Margaret Webb, "On the Heels of Notoriety," *The Washington Post* (28 January 1997)

Reidy, Chris, "A Questionable Role Model: Converse-Rodman Deal Draws Mixed Reaction from Marketers," *The Boston Globe* (28 January 1997)

Sutherland, Max, *Advertising and the Mind of the Consumer: What Works, What Doesn't, and Why*, St. Leonards, New South Wales: Allen and Unwin, 1993; 2nd edition, by Sutherland and Alice K. Sylvester, St. Leonards, New South Wales: Allen and Unwin, and London: Kogan Page, 2000

Wiggins, D. Joel, "Ronald Reagan" <www.mbcnet.org>

Wyndham, Bill, "Now Cosby Wants to Run the Show," *Sunday Age* (18 July 1993)

Procter & Gamble Company

Principal Agencies
Procter & Collier Company
J. Walter Thompson Company
Blackman Company (later Compton Advertising, Inc.)
Benton & Bowles
Young & Rubicam, Inc.
Saatchi & Saatchi Advertising
N.W. Ayer & Company
Grey Advertising Agency, Inc.
Leo Burnett USA

Martin Van Buren was president of the United States and the last stand at the Alamo was front-page news when two men who married into a Cincinnati, Ohio, family made some minor news of their own in 1837. A 36-year-old candle maker, William Procter, forged his now-famous partnership with 34-year-old soap maker James Gamble, making soap and candles from the animal fats and wood ashes that were abundant by-products from the industrial and hog slaughtering businesses in the Ohio River port.

A Passion for Branding

From those 19th-century roots sprang a company that played a central role in inventing branding. The Procter & Gamble Company (P&G) launched its first magazine advertising in 1881 and pioneered both radio and television advertising. The company's brand management system became the model around which marketing departments throughout the world would be organized in the 20th century. But consumers were the driving force behind branding at P&G from the 19th century onward.

Because many freight handlers were illiterate at the time, in the 1850s dockworkers began marking P&G's candle crates with a cross. The symbol evolved into a star to identify the contents as P&G's star candles. Another version showed the stars surrounded by a circle, with a crescent moon on the right side. P&G inexplicably discontinued use of the "man-in-the-moon" symbol later in the 1850s, until a New Orleans, Louisiana, retailer refused to accept a shipment of unmarked goods, believing they were imitations. By 1875 P&G had begun to take legal steps to protect its trademark and registered it with the U.S. Patent Office in 1882, when federal legislation for the first time provided formal legal protections for trademarks.

Almost from the beginning, P&G was an advertiser. Starting in 1838, the company, like other industrial companies of its era, advertised its Town Talk, Mottled German, Princess Queen, and Duchess brands in small newspaper ads. By 1870 P&G's total annual advertising budget was only $1,500.

The company's advertising did not begin in earnest until it had a unique selling proposition based on laboratory research and inspired by consumer feedback. James Norris Gamble, son of the cofounder, worked in the 1870s to develop a white soap equal in quality to imported castile soaps. He purchased a white-soap formula from another manufacturer and made improvements, ultimately launching P&G's White Soap in 1878. One day, a worker accidentally mixed too much air into his batch of soap, and within weeks P&G began getting orders for more of the "floating soap." Another founder's son, Harley T. Procter, inspired by a Bible reading, changed the name of White Soap, and by 18 July 1879, what would become P&G's first major national brand was trademarked "Ivory."

Procter became a prototype for what would be generations of brand managers who would succeed him, combining consumer insight, product knowledge, laboratory research, and marketing to develop the Ivory brand. He commissioned an independent chemical analysis of Ivory and seized upon a phrase that found the soap "99 and 44-100% pure." He recognized that the floating quality would let consumers easily find the bars of soap in the wash water.

Procter's passion for the brand succeeded in swaying P&G's board in 1882 to allocate what was then a massive media budget of $11,000 to advertise Ivory nationally. The first Ivory ad appeared in a religious weekly, *The Independent,* on 21 December 1882. It was unusual in that it targeted consumers at a time when most ads targeted dealers or retailers: "The Ivory is a laundry soap, with all the fine qualities of a choice toilet soap, and it is 99 and 44-100% pure." Reliance on scientific validation and claims of technological superiority would be a cornerstone of P&G marketing for decades to come, perhaps the most vivid and successful example being the American Dental Association's Seal of Acceptance for Crest toothpaste in 1960.

Procter was convinced that the new national magazines coming on the scene in the late 1800s—*Good Housekeeping, Harper's Monthly,* and *Ladies' Home Journal*—would be the best advertising vehicles for Ivory. His early support for those magazines also established a precedent for P&G, which would become an early supporter of radio, TV, cable TV, and Internet advertising in later generations. P&G also was quick to enter outdoor advertising, with Ivory ads on storefronts, fences, and trolley cars.

Over time, Ivory ads became increasingly sophisticated color productions, with illustrations from some of the best-known illustrators of the time. P&G paid $1,000 for illustrations, and Ivory's ad budget increased to $300,000 by 1897. Joining Ivory in P&G's stable of brands was Lenox, a yellow laundry soap advertised primarily to the grocery trade.

But the turn of the century brought new challenges to P&G, whose business had skyrocketed to $3 million in annual sales. Procter had been acting as P&G's one-man, in-house advertising agency, but in 1900 the company contracted with Procter & Collier Company, a Cincinnati printer that handled advertising as a sideline. About this time, Ivory was challenged by a host of new competitors promising results "as good as P&G's Ivory." P&G responded by improving Ivory and increasing ad spending.

Safe!

IT FLOATS

99 44/100% PURE

⟦Safe for baby's skin. Safe for mother's complexion. Safe for father's early-morning temper, because he never has to *hunt* for it! Ivory is always on top.⟧

Ivory soap's two most enduring slogans, "It floats" and "99 44/100% pure," are both seen in this 1928 print ad.
Courtesy of The Procter & Gamble Company.

Laundry habits were changing, too. A new yellow soap, Fels Naptha, was eliminating much of the scrubbing in laundry work. By 1902 P&G began producing its own White Naptha, backed, like Ivory, with substantial advertising. By 1920 White Naptha became the best-selling soap in the world.

With production booming, P&G expanded, opening new plants in Kansas City, Missouri, and New York City's Staten Island by 1907. P&G acquired soap flake brands and the Schultz Soap Company, a maker of powdered soaps. When P&G's growing demand for cottonseed oil, a key ingredient of its soaps, became harder to meet, the company began processing its own oil. With its new processing capacity, P&G began developing an all-vegetable shortening through a process called hydrogenation, filing for a patent on the new concoction in 1910. In a meeting at the office of then-President and Chief Executive Officer (CEO) William Cooper Procter, the proposed product names Krispo and Cryst were combined to form Crisco—P&G's next brand.

An ad in the *Ladies' Home Journal* in 1912 touted Crisco as "An absolutely new product. A scientific discovery which will affect every kitchen in America." To prove Crisco's superiority, the fledgling advertising department at P&G, which also created the *Ladies' Home Journal* ad, commissioned on-site taste tests at a Cincinnati bakery. P&G also sponsored cooking schools as part of the Crisco introduction.

The J. Walter Thompson Company (JWT) created color ads—the first time P&G had ventured outside its Cincinnati shop, Procter & Collier. JWT later went on to work for P&G archrivals Unilever and Kimberly-Clark Corporation. But in 1922, when it awarded the Crisco and Ivory accounts to Blackman Advertising, of New York City, P&G embarked on what would become its longest-standing agency relationship. Blackman later became Compton Advertising, which itself was later acquired by Saatchi & Saatchi Advertising. Ivory remained with Saatchi until 1997, when it was switched to Grey Advertising in New York City.

By 1923 P&G was making its first entry into radio advertising with Crisco radio shows broadcast on WEAF in New York City. P&G advertised on such programs as Emily Post's etiquette chats. These were product-oriented shows that wove the brand into the programming. But P&G decided that product-oriented programs were not the best way to reach consumers. By 1933 the company made the first of what would be many investments in daytime serial dramas, which were dubbed "soap operas" after their sponsorship by P&G and later its competitors.

Oxydol's Own Ma Perkins was P&G's first soap opera, carrying spots that would become the prototype for P&G advertising for decades to come. Produced by the Blackett-Sample-Hummert Agency, *Ma Perkins*'s success led P&G to develop serials for Crisco, Ivory, and Camay. Oxydol also ushered in what would become a staple of advertising by P&G and other advertisers for decades: the slice-of-life ad.

A typical spot on *Oxydol's Own Ma Perkins* had a husband and wife conversing at the dinner table. "A big meal like this on wash day?" the husband asks, "And we're going to the movies? Say, where's that old backache?" His wife responds, "I've found a new soap called Oxydol, dear. No more backaches for me."

With the Great Depression wracking the U.S. economy in the 1930s, P&G President Richard Deupree resisted pressure from some shareholders to cut back on ad spending, reasoning that people would still need to buy such staples as soap, regardless of the economic conditions. Perhaps because it never let up on advertising, P&G also made it through the Depression without laying off any workers.

P&G was spending $2 million on network radio by 1935 and $4.5 million by 1937, holding newspaper spending stable at approximately $2 million as prices fell during the Great Depression. By 1939 P&G had 21 radio programs on the air and spent $8.8 million on network radio, with only $4.8 million going to magazines and newspapers. The same year, P&G advertised on the first commercial TV broadcast, as sportscaster Red Barber pitched Ivory during a broadcast of a baseball game between the Cincinnati Reds and Brooklyn Dodgers.

Emphasis on Market Research

As P&G's experimentation in new media continued, the company also laid another cornerstone of its marketing approach: market research. In 1923 the company began its first formal consumer research. P&G manufacturing executive Wes Blair, who also had launched the company's first pilot manufacturing plant, followed sales and advertising executives into the field, where he distributed product samples and talked to consumers about them. That early work led to what the company called an economic research department, in which P&G began in-depth studies of consumer habits, probing not only their reactions to products but also the effectiveness of P&G advertising.

P&G began linking special offers to its advertising, such as "Ma Perkins" flower seeds for 10 cents plus an Oxydol box top. By 1934 P&G's market research department had a staff of 34 and was also measuring such variables as ads' cost-per-thousand consumers. P&G began test marketing new products regionally before rolling them out nationally. Promotional contests were common at P&G. In 1936 a Williamsburg, Virginia, woman won a life income of $1,000 a year for writing an essay about Camay soap "in 25 words or less." Between 1933 and 1938, $400,000 was awarded in prizes to people who finished the line "I like Ivory Soap because. . . ."

P&G's product research continued during the Great Depression. German scientists during World War I had developed an alternative to detergents based on soap. These "surface active agents," or surfactants, became a focus of P&G research in the 1920s. By 1933 P&G introduced Dreft, the first synthetic detergent based on surfactants for all-around household use. But Dreft couldn't remove heavy dirt, and P&G focused research on developing a heavy-duty synthetic detergent.

Another offshoot of synthetic detergent research was the development of a liquid shampoo to replace soap. Drene, P&G's first shampoo, was launched in 1934. But it cleaned hair too well, taking away all the oils in the process, so P&G added conditioning agents to overcome the problem. P&G developed its first hair-care research facility in response to the early problems with Drene, offering employees free shampoos and hair waves if they were willing to have different sides of their heads washed with different shampoos. Synthetic detergents also inspired P&G to try its first toothpaste, Teel, which was discontinued when it turned consumers' teeth brown.

Besides championing continued strong advertising support during the Depression, Deupree was also laying some of the other foundations of P&G's distinctive corporate culture. He convinced President Cooper Procter of the need to give salespeople more responsibility, which led to the company's policy of exposing executives to a wide variety of responsibilities. He helped establish the company's promote-from-within policy and insisted executives keep memos to no more than one typewritten page. The one-page memo would become a rigorous P&G writing discipline followed for decades, until the advent of e-mail. It helped remove ego from the decision-making process, former P&G executive Gordon Wade said, because the writer was not around when ideas were discussed. Only the memo's contents were considered. A memo would be adorned with the recommendations or comments from each senior manager as it worked its way up the hierarchy to the ultimate decision-maker.

Brand Management

Deupree's term as president of P&G, which began in 1930, also ushered in the beginning of the brand management system, the brainchild of the man who would ultimately succeed Deupree—Neil McElroy. McElroy joined the company in 1925 as a mail clerk, working his way to manager of the promotion department by 1929. He helped introduce a new soap brand, Camay. And he was among company executives who decided that the new brand was being held back by too much "Ivory thinking," particularly at its ad agency, Blackman Advertising, which also handled Ivory. Camay was moved to Pedlar & Ryan, also in New York City, to allow it to compete against Ivory without restrictions, and McElroy became the brand's supervisor. McElroy's stint on Camay was short. He became the marketing executive running P&G's first overseas subsidiary, Thomas Hedley & Company in England, in 1930. There he studied P&G's top rival, Unilever, at close range.

He returned to Cincinnati a year later determined to reshape the company's management system. In a pivotal three-page memo that defied the one-page norm, McElroy outlined his one-person, one-brand idea, in which a brand manager would oversee an assistant brand manager for each of P&G's brands. The assistant, he wrote, would "follow through on office work laid out by the brand manager; make field studies as directed by the latter; stay in close touch with the advertising and field plans. . . . Finally, he'd be able to step into the shoes of his superior at a moment's notice."

The basic principle of brand management—to operate each brand as a separate business—became a fundamental part of P&G's operations for decades to come. P&G's brands competed fiercely with one another in some cases, despite reservations from P&G executives who thought such internal strife would be sui-

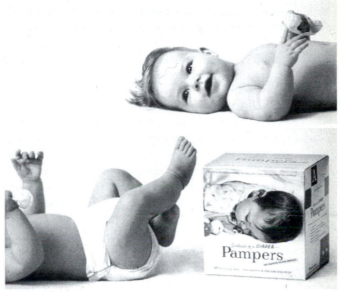

This lucky baby never wore a diaper in his life!

Instead . . . he wears new PAMPERS— the discovery that makes diapers old-fashioned!

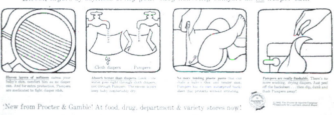

Eleven layers of softness bring your baby heavenly comfort as no diaper can!

'New from Procter & Gamble' At food, drug, department & variety stores now!

Introduced in 1961, Pampers disposable diapers helped simplify the lives of modern mothers.
Courtesy of The Procter & Gamble Company.

cidal. *Time* magazine noted in the 1930s that McElroy won his point by persuading his elders that the best way to keep the fast-growing company from becoming too clumsy was to have its brands compete with one another.

Not until the mid-1980s, when P&G appointed vice presidents and general managers to oversee categories of brands, was the concept of "one-manager, one-brand" significantly modified. The brand management system became the organizing principle for most of P&G's competitors around the world and also found its way into other industries. The brand management system, and its promise of allowing young executives to run their own businesses within five years of joining the company, also became a key recruiting tool for P&G.

While military production became a priority for P&G during World War II, the company continued advertising. By 1945 P&G was spending $15 million on radio, twice as much as for all other media combined. Among the radio shows P&G sponsored during the war, *Perry Mason, Queen for a Day,* and *Professor Quiz* would be converted to TV shows in the postwar era, as P&G turned to consumer marketing—and TV—with a vengeance. P&G turned its national sales force, brand management system, and advertising prowess to work as consumers unleashed demand that had been bottled up by wartime rationing and materials shortages.

Some of the programs sponsored by P&G during the prime years of network radio were: *Against the Storm* (1939–42; Ivory soap), *Beulah* (1947–53; Dreft), *Brighter Day* (1948–55; Dreft), *Brave Tomorrow* (1943–44; Ivory), *Central City* (1938–39; Oxydol), *The Girl Next Door* (1937; Oxydol), *Everyman's Theater* (1940–41; Oxydol), *Dreft Star Playhouse* (1943–45), *Jack Smith Show with Dinah Shore* (1950–52; Oxydol), *FBI in Peace and War* (1944–50; Lava), *The Goldbergs* (1937–41; Oxydol), *The Guiding Light* (1937–41; White Naptha soap; 1947–56; Duz), *I Love a Mystery* (1943–44; Oxydol, Ivory), *Life Can Be Beautiful* (1938–1954; Ivory, Spic and Span), *The Life of Riley* (1945–50; Teel, Prell), *Ma Perkins* (1933–60; Oxydol), and *The Man I Married* (1939–41; Oxydol). Other long-running P&G-sponsored shows included *Pepper Young's Family, Right to Happiness, Red Skelton Show, Truth or Consequences, Road of Life,* and *Young Dr. Malone.*

Washday Miracles

By 1946 P&G researchers had finally developed the heavy-duty synthetic laundry detergent they had worked on for so many years. The new phosphate compound cleaned without leaving harsh mineral deposits. And while P&G executives knew it would cut into sales of its existing Dreft and Duz brands, they also believed they had a revolutionary product on their hands. In what would become typical P&G style, they test-marketed the new brand, Tide, in six cities, trying two different advertising mixes in three sets of cities selected based on the hardness of their water supplies.

Tests showed that Tide was wildly popular. P&G backed the 1947 national rollout with $21 million in advertising and promotion support. Benton & Bowles was assigned the account, which it kept until the business was moved to Compton Advertising in 1961. Ads touted Tide as "a modern washday miracle," and results confirmed the hyperbole. By 1948 synthetic detergents had captured 20 percent of the market for household laundry products, as competitors Lever Brothers and Colgate-Palmolive Company introduced competing products—Surf and Fab, respectively. Aiding the laundry detergent category was the rapid spread of washing machines, whose household penetration grew from 3 percent to 33 percent in the United States in the decade following World War II. By 1949 Tide was the number-one detergent in the United States, outselling P&G's Oxydol and Duz.

But Lever and Colgate-Palmolive were gunning for the top spot. The best defense, P&G decided, was to grab the number-two position for itself. So P&G launched Cheer in test markets in 1950, backed by newspaper, comic supplements, radio, and outdoor advertising. Cheer was assigned to Young & Rubicam, Inc., but sales were sluggish. Then P&G added bluing, which was val-

ued by homemakers who added separate bluing agents to their white wash to give clothes a slight blue tint. "It's new! It's blue!" became the tag line for Cheer in TV advertising for the brand in the mid-1950s. Fifty years later, Cheer was still packaged in a blue box and remained a distant number two to Tide in the United States; Leo Burnett USA, Chicago, Illinois, handled the account.

Cheer was the first of many category segmentation moves in laundry detergent by P&G, whose researchers realized detergents could be formulated to meet very specific laundry requirements. Cheer would later be positioned for superior cleaning in cold water, a positioning that would be transformed into superior color protection and fabric care in the 1990s. Oxydol eventually became a heavy-duty synthetic detergent, too, but with a color-safe oxygen bleach, though the bleach would later be added to other, higher priority brands as well. P&G also launched Dash as a low-sudsing concentrated detergent, Bold with brighteners and fabric softeners, Gain with a strong "fresh" scent, and Era in the late 1970s as P&G's first liquid laundry detergent, aimed at a growing segment then dominated by Unilever's Wisk. P&G also worked to expand the boundaries of laundry care. The company launched Downy fabric softener in 1960, inventing a new category in the process, as well as what would become a $1 billion-a-year brand.

The growing constellation of brands made P&G the leader in laundry care, which remained the company's largest business. By 2000 global sales of Tide and its sibling brand, Ariel, topped $3 billion. Tide remained P&G's flagship laundry detergent and flagship brand, getting most of P&G's improvements in laundry technology first. Key to Tide maintaining that position, however, was the culmination of a lengthy debate within P&G between those who believed that the Tide brand could not be extended into liquid detergents and those who believed that it must.

In 1984 a fast-rising brand manager named A.G. Lafley led the introduction of Liquid Tide, backed by an estimated $100 million in advertising. The detergent contained 12 cleaning ingredients, two to three times the number found in other leading liquids at the time. As liquid detergents continued to grow and ultimately overtook powders as the leading detergent segment in the mid-1990s, the move proved fortuitous. Tide held onto its leadership position. As he worked his way up P&G's laundry business in the 1980s and early 1990s, Lafley would also fortify Tide's leadership with launches of Tide with Bleach and Ultra Tide, a concentrated version of Tide powder.

Health and Beauty Products

As P&G built its laundry detergent business, it also began building its health and beauty business. Following the launch of Drene in the 1930s, P&G launched Prell shampoo in 1946. An early radio spot from Benton & Bowles ended with the somewhat Freudian tag line, "I'm Tallulah the tube, take me home and squeeze me!" Tallulah Bankhead, a well-known actress at the time, was not amused. She sued P&G for $1 million, ultimately settling for $5,000 in a controversy that P&G estimated brought $10 million in free publicity for Prell.

Under Howard Morgens, then vice president of advertising, P&G's "drug products" business included Drene and Prell and was managed separately. Morgens's unit soon delved into home permanents with the Lilt brand and then toothpastes with Gleem, the latter with a launch budget of $19 million in 1953 that had been surpassed only by the original Tide launch. Backed by ads from Compton, Gleem quickly gained on category leader Colgate, getting 20 percent of the $135 million category to Colgate's 37 percent.

Not content to be second, P&G began working on a toothpaste that would prevent cavities. Working with researchers at Indiana University, P&G developed Fluoristan, a trade name for stannous fluoride with a polishing agent. Test marketed under the Crest brand name in 1955 in Columbus, Ohio, the toothpaste got off to a slow start. A brand group led by P&G Associate Advertising Manager John Smale began working to get an endorsement from the American Dental Association (ADA) as early as 1954. By 1960 the efforts had paid off; for the first time, the ADA allowed its name to be used in consumer product advertising. Crest highlighted the endorsement in TV and print ads from Benton & Bowles, which stressed "25 to 49 percent fewer cavities with Crest." Crest sales nearly tripled to more than $380 million to overtake Colgate within a year. Technological advances continued, and in 1985 a Tartar Control Crest helped the brand fend off a surge by Colgate in the early 1980s.

Following in the health and beauty businesses were the introduction of Sure and Secret deodorants, Scope mouthwash, and Head & Shoulders dandruff-control shampoo in the 1960s. These successes set the stage for P&G to move deeper into over-the-counter drugs, with the 1982 acquisition of Norwich-Eaton Pharmaceuticals, marketer of Chloraseptic and Pepto-Bismol, as well as the 1985 acquisitions of Richardson-Vicks, marketer of Vicks cold and cough remedies and a then-little-known shampoo brand called Pantene, and the Metamucil and Dramamine brands from Monsanto Company. Those deals by 1986 made P&G for a time the largest marketer of over-the-counter drugs.

The "Disposables" Business

Another acquisition, the 1957 purchase of Charmin Paper Mills and a regional toilet paper brand, moved P&G into another major category. The company's long-range planning had analyzed trends in nonwoven fabrics and concluded that by the mid-1980s, consumers would be using disposable sheets and shorts, clearly a threat to P&G's laundry business. Although those predictions never quite materialized, Charmin would be the beginning of a large paper and disposables business for P&G. Early on, P&G developed a new way to dry paper pulp that would form the basis of an improved Charmin. It was also used in White Cloud toilet tissue and Puffs facial tissue. P&G also launched Bounty paper towels in the 1960s, which, like Charmin, would become the leader in its category.

By 1961 P&G had followed others, including Johnson & Johnson, into the disposable diaper market. Despite favorable reviews in early consumer tests, Pampers, handled by Benton &

Bowles, was slow to catch on. Pampers spent seven years in test markets before being marketed nationally. It was not that consumers disliked the product. But like other disposable diaper brands, Pampers suffered from an image problem. Mothers felt they were shortchanging their children by putting paper diapers on them. Some also balked at the price of ten cents a diaper. P&G knew it would have to produce Pampers in mass quantities to get the diapers down to six cents each. And to develop a market of that size, it would have to overcome mothers' reservations about the product.

Thus, one of the real innovations behind Pampers was the marketing. Ads from Benton & Bowles focused on the closeness of the mother-child bond in addition to benefit-oriented copy discussing diapers that were "flushable through modern plumbing facilities" and "a highly sanitary diapering method." When Pampers was launched, fewer than 1 percent of diaper changes involved disposables. By 1985, 98 percent of U.S. households with infants were using disposables.

Not every venture into paper products was as successful. Rely superabsorbent tampons, launched in 1974, quickly became a leading brand. But a rising chorus of consumer accusations linked the tampons to a rare but potentially fatal disease: toxic shock syndrome. When a government report concluded that Rely may increase risk of contracting the disease, P&G pulled the product off the market.

Tenacious as always, P&G was not about to give up on the feminine hygiene market. It launched Always sanitary pads in 1983, and the brand captured category leadership from Kimberly-Clark Corporation's longtime leader Kotex by 1996. A year later, P&G reentered the tampon category with the acquisition of Tambrands and its Tampax line.

More Acquisitions

By the late 1950s acquisitions had become a major source of growth for P&G. First as vice president and general manager, later as president, Howard Morgens led P&G on an intense round of acquisitions in the late 1950s and early 1960s. Besides Charmin, Morgens also spearheaded the acquisitions of the peanut-processing business that would spawn Jif Peanut Butter, the Duncan Hines business, the Folgers coffee business, and the Clorox Chemical business in bleach.

P&G's buying binge, however, attracted the notice of antitrust regulators. The Clorox deal was challenged almost immediately, and after ten years of legal wrangling that ended in the U.S. Supreme Court, P&G was forced to spin off Clorox in 1967. P&G was allowed to keep Folgers following a review, though it was forced to clear any additional acquisitions with the Federal Trade Commission through most of the 1970s, essentially putting a halt to any deals.

With two newly acquired brands, however, the 1960s would become the decade of icons for P&G. Actor Dick Wilson, starring as Mr. Whipple, admonished wayward shoppers, "Please don't squeeze the Charmin." In the process, Benton & Bowles had found a way to broach the subject of toilet paper softness without

Demonstrating the absorbent qualities of Bounty towels, Rosie, the down-to-earth waitress, became one of the most recognizable ad spokespersons in the 1970s.
Courtesy of The Procter & Gamble Company.

talking about how it worked. Folgers would soon become the cornerstone of P&G's food and beverage business, backed by the memorable if oft-parodied slice-of-life dramas from Cunningham & Walsh that always ended with actress Virginia Christine's Mrs. Olson declaring, "Mountain-grown Folgers. It's the richest kind." Nancy Walker as Rosie the waitress joined the triumvirate in the 1970s in ads for Bounty, "the quicker picker upper," from Benton & Bowles.

Meanwhile, P&G placed heavy bets on a new food brand of its own, Pringles potato chips. Early test market results pointed to a huge success, and P&G ramped up manufacturing accordingly. Soon, however, consumer "taste fatigue" set in, and cans of perfectly shaped Pringles potato chips lingered on store shelves. P&G stuck with the brand through nearly two decades of slow sales, trying numerous marketing approaches aimed at getting it back on track until it discovered a market segment for which taste fatigue was less of an issue—teens and preteens—targeted by ads from N.W. Ayer & Company and featuring fast-paced music and the slogan "Once you pop, you can't stop." P&G recognized that teens would eventually tire of Pringles. But they would be replaced by a new generation of youths.

Disappointments with Rely and Pringles, combined with overall economic problems in the United States, led P&G in new directions in the 1970s. The company focused increased attention on drug research, hoping to tap one of the few industries growing faster than the general economy. One promising product from the P&G labs was Olestra, a fat substitute that was not absorbed by the body. After nearly two decades of review by the Food and Drug Administration, Olestra was allowed to debut nationally only in 1998. Consumers—already sated with reduced-fat products introduced in the 1990s and, in part, discouraged by reports linking Olestra to digestive problems—greeted it with a lackluster response.

In the 1980s, unfettered by the stricter antitrust enforcement of the 1970s, P&G again turned to aggressive acquisitions. Besides the Norwich-Eaton Pharmaceuticals and Richardson-Vicks deals in 1982 and 1985, P&G further expanded into Europe with the acquisition of Blend-a-Med toothpaste in 1986 and then entered the cosmetics business with the 1989 acquisition of Noxell and its Cover Girl and Noxzema brands. The company continued to round out its brand portfolio with the acquisition of Sunny Delight in 1989, Old Spice in 1990, and Max Factor cosmetics in 1991.

Globalization

Globalization became another priority. P&G launched a joint venture in China in 1988, sowing the seeds of what would become a $1 billion business by the late 1990s. Refusing to give up on Japan despite early problems there, such top executives as Durk Jager, John Pepper, and Lafley focused their efforts on turning the company's business around. By 1993, P&G had opened a new headquarters and technical center in Kobe, Japan, and for the first time, more than half the company's sales (then $30 million) came from outside the United States.

Not all P&G products traveled well, however. A prime example was Tampax tampons, which faced particular religious and cultural barriers in certain societies outside the United States. After P&G bought Tambrands, Inc., in 1997, the company launched a major marketing campaign to introduce the product in Latin America, where only 2 percent of women used tampons (versus 70 percent in the developed world). "Everywhere we go," a P&G marketing director told the *Wall Street Journal* in 2000, "women say 'This is not for señoritas [unmarried women].'" The product tended to encounter resistance in heavily Roman Catholic countries, including Italy, although the church took no position on its use. At the turn of the new century the company was still attempting to formulate a marketing model that it could export globally.

As P&G concentrated on acquiring and consolidating new brands and making old brands global, the company stopped launching new brands of its own. The company that had spawned dozens of brands each decade from the 1930s through the 1970s did not launch a single new consumer brand into national distribution from 1983, when it introduced Always, to 1998, when it launched Febreze fabric refresher.

Indeed, P&G went in the opposite direction, discontinuing or selling many of its brands. Between 1993 and 2000 P&G discontinued White Cloud and sold such brands as Duncan Hines, Fisher Nuts, Hawaiian Punch, Attends, Lava, Oxydol, Biz, Clearasil, Prell, and Coast. Most appeared past their prime. But one, White Cloud, would come back to haunt P&G six years after it was discontinued, when Wal-Mart Stores acquired rights in 1999 to use it as a private label of paper products and diapers from an entrepreneur who staked a claim to the brand after P&G abandoned it.

By the early 1990s, efficiency had become the third leg of P&G's strategy, besides acquisition and globalization. With the help of Jager, Chairman and Chief Executive Officer (CEO) Edwin Artzt launched P&G's "everyday low pricing" or "value pricing" strategy, cutting back on the use of coupons and price promotion with retailers and using the savings to boost advertising and cut prices. After initial resistance, retailers ultimately accepted the idea, though both competitors and P&G would continue to use price promotion, and the package-goods industry's overall reliance on price promotion spending remained steady at about 75 percent of all marketing expenditures.

Through it all P&G continued to be the world's biggest advertiser by far, spending more than $3 billion annually on advertising throughout the 1990s. When the world's biggest advertiser spoke, people listened. In a 1994 speech to the American Association of Advertising Agencies, Artzt created a major commotion in the advertising community when he warned that advertising-supported TV, and indeed advertising itself, was in peril if advertisers and agencies did not take the development of interactive media seriously. The speech, written by Bob Herbold, who would soon leave P&G to make his own mark on interactive media as executive vice president and chief operating officer of Microsoft Corporation, addressed interactive TV. Although the speech was delivered before Netscape had launched the first Web browser, it became a sort of clarion call marking a new era of interactive marketing.

Following some relatively minor manufacturing consolidations under Chairman and CEO John Smale in 1989, P&G undertook a more dramatic restructuring under Artzt in 1993. Layers of management were eliminated, including brand assistants, the bottom rung in the brand management hierarchy, and advertising managers, whose roles were subsumed under the new title of marketing director. A company that had made it through the Depression without layoffs reduced the number of its employees by thousands in the restructuring.

P&G's management was always conservative, disciplined, and, some would say, stodgy. But it had seldom been harsh. That changed under Artzt. Ill will within the ranks of P&G and its recently departed employees ran rampant, culminating in a public relations fiasco that rivaled that of Rely. A report in the *Wall Street Journal* said that P&G was considering selling its food and beverage business. Enraged, Artzt both vehemently denied the report and accused the reporter, Alecia Swasy, of obtaining trade secrets. He convinced Cincinnati police to search Cincinnati Bell telephone records to check for calls to Swasy in an attempt to find the source of the leak. The search proved unsuccessful, but publicity about it led to a reprimand for Artzt from P&G's board and helped spawn Swasy's book *Soap Opera*, an at-times scathing exposé of Artzt and P&G.

But perhaps a bigger change for P&G had come in 1987, under Smale, when P&G restructured its management, giving vice presidents and general managers broad control over categories of products and, in some cases, diminishing the role of brand managers. The fierce competition among P&G brands, in which brand managers refused to share data with peers down the hall, was over. Category managers were now arbiters and ultimate decision-makers on investments for brands. The effect on cost reduction was clear. But some P&G alumni likened category management to the economic planning of socialism, saying it sounded good on paper but led to slow growth in practice. Doug Hall, a former P&G brand manager who later opened an invention and new-product evaluation consulting firm called Richard Saunders International, traced slowing growth throughout the packaged-goods industry in the 1990s to the diminished role of brand managers and the rise of category management.

Based on P&G's results, the criticism appears to hit the mark. After its major acquisition binge ended in 1993, P&G grew only around 4 percent a year, just ahead of inflation, from $30 billion in 1993 to $40 billion in 2000. But there were still bright spots. Two-in-one shampoo and conditioner technology helped turn Pert from a sleepy also-ran to one of the top-selling hair-care brands in the world in the late 1980s and early 1990s. Pantene, a little-known throw-in from the Richardson-Vicks deal, was transformed in 1992 through the addition of Pro-V (vitamin) technology and massive advertising from Grey Advertising into what stands today as a $1 billion-a-year global brand. P&G maintained its leadership in laundry detergents and built its category-leading market shares for Bounty paper towels in the 1990s. But across its entire portfolio of brands, P&G was consistently losing market share to smaller rivals

in the United States, even as it expanded brands overseas in the 1990s. The company lost category leadership to Kimberly-Clark in diapers and Colgate-Palmolive in toothpaste.

Where it counted to Wall Street, however, P&G was winning big. Thanks to efficiency efforts, P&G earnings consistently grew 10 percent to 15 percent annually, two to three times the pace of its sales growth. P&G ranked with Coca-Cola and Gillette as the bluest of the blue chips, outpacing most other major corporations in stock price during the 1990s.

Relying on efficiency, finance, manufacturing, and logistics to deliver the numbers, however, was a big change for a company built on research and marketing. And a gnawing concern grew among both investors and P&G executives that the company could not continue to deliver earnings so far out of pace with sales. That led to another restructuring and a new philosophy by 1999. Having already gravitated toward global management of its categories and brands since the late 1980s, P&G took the final step of naming division presidents, category vice presidents, and even marketing directors and brand managers with global profit-and-loss responsibilities.

New CEO Durk Jager also moved to end P&G's new-brand drought. The launch of Febreze in 1998 was followed by the Dryel home dry cleaning and Swiffer electrostatic duster brands in 1999. P&G launched more than a dozen other new brands into test or limited distribution as it also made a massive expansion of its newly acquired Iams pet food brand from pet specialty stores to supermarkets and mass merchandisers.

Targeted Marketing and New Media

The combination of a massive global restructuring and a frenetic new brand development cycle, however, proved too much for P&G. Its marketing spending rose 15 percent in fiscal year 2000, though media advertising was up only around 4 percent, as P&G invested heavily in sampling and other promotions behind new products. Inventory soared, too, as P&G built up stocks of the new products. Rising energy prices, a Latin American price war with Unilever, and falling sales in European operations affected most severely by restructuring-related management changes, also ate into P&G's profits. After P&G missed Wall Street earnings forecasts for two consecutive quarters in early 2000, Jager stepped down after only 18 months as CEO. In another first for P&G, many insiders and outside observers believed Jager was asked to leave by P&G's board.

John Pepper, who had been chairman and CEO before Jager, returned as chairman, and Lafley became president and CEO in June 2000. Harkening to his days running P&G's flagship Tide brand, Lafley promised to focus marketing and new-product development efforts primarily on P&G's ten brands with $1 billion or more in global sales, which collectively make up nearly half the company's sales. Besides Tide, those brands included Tide's sibling brand, Ariel, along with Pampers, Charmin, Bounty, Always, Downy, Pantene, Folgers, and Pringles. New brands, such as Swiffer and Febreze, and brands nearing the $1 billion threshold, including Iams and Olay, were also to be priorities. But the new-brand launch schedule became less aggressive than under Jager. And Lafley's ongoing review of the bulk of P&G's existing 300 brands could lead to a faster pace of divestitures than even in the 1990s.

Lafley promised fewer "big-bang mass media launches" and more targeted marketing aimed at developing lasting relationships with consumers. P&G changed its agency structure in 2000 from paying commissions on media to commissions on brand sales, paving the way for the movement away from higher-priced mass media. Also, the company began using a host of interactive and off-line direct marketing approaches, such as a Web site for a restaging of Pantene in 2000 called getprofile.com, which, months before the new hair-care products reached store shelves, invited consumers to log on to get personalized product recommendations and samples. Some new-product launches, such as Crest Whitestrips, a home tooth-whitening system, were accomplished via direct-to-consumer sales over the Internet or toll-free phone ordering prior to national retail launch in a process P&G called "diffusion," with the idea of seeding new products among "early adopters" who would talk to their friends about them.

Increasingly P&G conducted its consumer research via the Internet. On-line testing allowed concepts to be tested in one-fourth the time and at a tenth of the cost of conventional testing. The company even revamped its corporate Web site with a new section designed to solicit new product ideas from consumers and get their responses to ideas submitted by others.

Yet despite P&G's skill at building and maintaining brands and the rich rewards and stability that accrue to the agencies it employs, its focus on strategy and consumer research has resulted in a reputation for creative work that is formulaic and unimaginative, a burden that P&G's major agencies often have to carry as a cost of doing business with the world's largest advertiser. That this approach has long characterized household package-goods advertising generally owes much to the fact that P&G has led the field for so long and been such an influence on its competition. Many in the ad industry believe that agencies working for P&G are reluctant to think outside the "P&G style" for fear of not meeting the expectations of a valuable client. The result is that in times when breakthrough creative work is highly valued, agencies with

long package-goods experience generally, and those with P&G experience in particular (especially midsize agencies such as Benton & Bowles, Compton, and Tatham, Laird & Kudner, all of which were once dependent on P&G), may be regarded as old-fashioned and stodgy. P&G itself took note of this and in the late 1990s began encouraging its agencies to provide more nontraditional creative ideas. Nonetheless, over the years it has been the company's very success in marketing and advertising that has been the biggest deterrent to its building a more adventurous and innovative creative reputation.

JACK NEFF

See also Crest; Ivory Soap; *and color plate in this volume*

Further Reading

Decker, Charles L., *Winning with the P&G 99: 99 Principles and Practices of Procter & Gamble's Success,* New York: Pocket Books, 1998

Dumaine, Brian, "P&G Rewrites the Marketing Rules," *Fortune* (6 November 1989)

Johnson, Brad, "Bob Herbold Reflects on 1994 Speech He Wrote," *Advertising Age* (14 August 1997)

Lief, Alfred, *It Floats: The Story of Procter & Gamble,* New York: Rinehart, 1958

Neff, Jack, "P&G Redefines the Brand Manager," *Advertising Age* (13 October 1997)

Neff, Jack, "P&G and Unilever's Giant Headaches," *Advertising Age* (24 May 1999)

Neff, Jack, "Marketers of the Century," *Advertising Age* (13 December 1999)

Neff, Jack, "Does P&G Still Matter?" *Advertising Age* (27 September 2000)

Procter & Gamble: The House that Ivory Built, by the editors of *Advertising Age,* Lincolnwood, Illinois: NTC Business Books, 1988

Schisgall, Oscar, *Eyes on Tomorrow: The Evolution of Procter & Gamble,* New York: Ferguson, 1981

Swasy, Alecia, *Soap Opera: The Inside Story of Procter & Gamble,* New York: Times Books, 1993

Production: Commercials

In the early days of television, both ad agencies and clients viewed the production of a TV commercial as a mysterious process controlled solely by an autonomous director. Agencies and clients awarded the job to one of a limited choice of directors and then sat back and waited for the results. It was an informal process—there were no bid forms, no directing specializations, no conference calls, no committee meetings, no cost consultants, no

computers, and no videocassette recorders. Commercials themselves were more narrative, less effects-driven, and more jingle-oriented.

By the end of the 20th century, a combination of factors—technology, costs, collaboration, globalization, and agency buyouts—had rid the industry of its mystery, and making commercials became one of the most accountable crafts around. Over the years, as the mystique of making commercials diminished, the many roles of the ad agency—as keeper of the creative flame, technical and cost consultant, marketing partner, and quality controller—increased correspondingly.

The commercial's journey through the agency is a well-defined process, much of which was established after the 1972 founding of the Association of Independent Commercial Producers (AICP). There followed the standardization of bid and editing forms, necessitated by increasing costs, a need for better understanding of the procedures, and a desire on the part of clients to monitor what their agencies were doing.

Since about 1980, little has changed in the number of processes and checkpoints required as a commercial is produced by an ad agency. First, the client gives the account team a brief, which includes an on-air deadline and the latest date at which the client needs to approve the final commercial. The account group, the planner, and the creative team—creative director, copywriter, and art director—then research, provide insight into, and generally refine the concept. Next, it is up to the copywriter and art director to come up with ideas and craft the storyboards. Once the creative director and client okay the results, the producer gets involved.

Of those in an ad agency involved in the production of a TV commercial, no one is more influential than the producer. Owing to technological advances and the prevalence of global agency mergers, the producer presides over an increasingly international arena, sharing a wide array of accounts and people. While the creative team may work on two or three projects a year, the producer routinely handles ten to 12. The producer's responsibilities include developing the agency vision, compiling a list of directors, and explaining the brief to the production company and the possibilities to the client. The producer analyzes the bid, suggests alternatives, recruits the best available talent, and regulates the shoot, while also keeping an eye on the bottom line. "The producer is the keeper of the dream, the interpreter, the executor, and the enhancer," said Barbara Mullins, senior vice president–director of TV production/North America for BBDO, an agency responsible for some of television's most expensive commercials, for clients such as PepsiCo, Visa USA, Frito-Lay Company, FedEx Corporation, and General Electric Company. The producer's initial task is to review about 50 sample reels of film in order to assemble a list of possible directors. "In classic Hollywood terms we are the purveyors of talent," said Bob Nelson, executive vice president–director of broadcast production at Lowe Lintas & Partners Worldwide, New York City. "It's our responsibility to know who's out there and what they've done."

With so many production companies and directors to choose from, it is difficult for producers to keep up to date on who has done what. Of the thousands of available directors, only a few tend to get the top jobs. "Agencies tend to aspire to a higher level of director than they really need," said David Perry, executive vice president and director of advertising production at Saatchi & Saatchi, New York City. "We all aspire upward."

Some ad agencies require a particular area of specialization from a director. This high level of selectivity originated in the 1980s, when agencies wanted to know exactly what they were getting in a director. Soon, directors who had once done a variety of projects started to be pigeonholed under headings such as cars, tabletop, fashion, beauty, comedy, or dialogue. During most of the 1990s, MTV directors, with their highly visual styles and flashy editing techniques, dominated the market. By the beginning of the 21st century, an important area of specialization was comedy, largely propelled by the precipitous rise of dot-com companies in late 1999 and 2000. The outrageous comedic style of dot-com advertising became known as "bad boy" advertising. But, according to Nelson, directors with an agency background were back in vogue by 2001.

Some agencies established long-term relationships with directors. Over the decades, the perennially award-winning director Joe Pytka became known as the Pepsi director, which meant that he would not do work for the Coca-Cola Company.

A director usually has a sales representative (rep), or agent. Attached either to a production company or an independent firm, these reps traditionally present their directors and close the deal. As the business has evolved, reps have had to become more marketing- and less personal relationships–oriented. More directing options for agencies have translated into fewer ongoing relationships and less repeat business. "Every shoot is a blind date for both parties," Perry has said. "You can't assume any kind of relationship."

While the production house is rarely a consideration on its own, those with a distinctive specialty sometimes have an advantage. Moreover, the best directors often have the best production companies. Usually, three to five directors are invited to bid on a job. Industry estimates put the director's average day rates in 2001 at $10,000 to $25,000, up from $3,000 to $5,000 a day in the mid-1980s, according to the AICP. Accordingly, the average cost of a commercial also increased, from $180,000 in 1989, to almost $400,000 in 1999, according to the American Association of Advertising Agencies.

Once the director is chosen, the producer sells the proposed job to the client. The agency creative team and the director then discuss such specifics as location, casting specifications, set design, post-production, and budget. The shoot itself can take hours or days and involve a small team or as many as 50 cast and crew members, depending on rigging and whether children or animals are involved, with their attendant social workers and trainers. Athletes and celebrities come with entourages and their own trailers.

As costs began escalating in the 1970s, some agencies started their own in-house production facilities as a means of keeping control and offering a creative outlet for in-house talent. Disappointing creative results and a lack of resources, plus the realization that the best talent lay outside the agency, forced most big agencies to close or scale down in-house production toward the end of the 1980s. For example, although Ogilvy & Mather Worldwide once had one of the largest in-house production facilities, its later in-house facility, Eye-Patch, is used for the bulk of its testing and presentations, as well as some client work. It is not designed to be in competition with outside production houses.

In most cases, once the shoot is over, the director hands his creation over for editing, post-production, and music. (In Europe, with its reputation for excellent post-production facilities, director-auteurs stay much more involved and hands-on.) Editing was revolutionized in 1992 with the invention of the Avid, a digital film-editing system that offered faster, cheaper, more versatile editing and replaced the bulky flatbed, the traditional film-editing machine that had been used for the previous 100 years.

Messner Vetere Berger McNamee Schmetterer/Euro RSCG established its own editing facility, Berwyn Editing, in the mid-1980s. It is independently owned and works exclusively for Messner. With 13 Avids, a Henry post-production console, and a recording studio, it was designed as a full-service editing resource to enhance the agency's work for clients such as MCI Corporation, Volvo, and Intel Corporation. It is also used in new business pitches and sales videos.

Once the rough cut is finished, it moves into post-production, which takes a fraction of the time it originally did, thanks to the introduction of computers such as the Henry and the Flame. Post-production is where special effects, typography, color, sound recording and mixing, casting for voice-over, tape transfer, and blowups occur. Technological advances have resulted in higher-quality commercials than ever before, although some in the industry suggest the whole process has become less enjoyable. Such technological advances also mean that ad agencies' involvement is only likely to increase in the future. Technology, for example, has vastly improved the quality of commercials shot cheaply on video, so much so that many predict agency creative people will be editing and directing more.

After completion of the commercial, the producer's involvement is over and the final digital master is handed over to the agency's broadcast traffic and media departments. It then becomes their responsibility to get the spot on the air.

ANN COOPER

Further Reading

Shoot (November 2000) (special 40th anniversary supplement)

Production: Programming

For the first quarter-century of network broadcasting, advertising agencies representing major advertisers had primary responsibility for assembling and producing the radio and early television programs in which their clients' products were showcased. It is not an exaggeration to say that the major ad agencies were to broadcasting what the movie studios were to the motion-picture business. Behind the scenes, agencies became show business impresarios, employing producers, writers, directors, actors, and musicians. Agencies became both shapers and servants of popular taste and culture. This went on from the late 1920s into the early 1950s, by which time a number of factors began to erode ad agency influence on program production. Today modern ad agencies concentrate their creative resources on making compelling commercials. But in the beginning network broadcasting made many of those same agencies key show business decision makers and the principle patrons of some of the biggest comedy and dramatic stars of all time.

Of the many business models on which a national radio system might have been founded and financed—among them a government-operated service; a private system controlled by schools, churches, the print media, and other institutions; or through the profits of radio sales—the one that finally evolved in the United States, toll broadcasting, owed much to the model of the telephone. The cost of a phone call was routinely based on the number of minutes the caller used. Transmission, not content, was the phone company's only responsibility. The American Telephone & Telegraph Company (AT&T) projected essentially that same model into broadcasting when it established station WEAF in New York City in 1922. "[AT&T] will provide no program of its own," it said in its opening announcement. Instead it would "provide the channels through which anyone with whom it makes a contract can send out their own programs." With that, the foundation was laid for commercial broadcasting in the United States.

The emergence of radio as an advertiser-supported medium fundamentally changed the structure and role of many ad agencies. Traditionally, their creative and production responsibilities had centered on magazine, newspaper, and other print media. But as radio gained in importance during the end of the 1920s, many advertisers interested in using it turned to their agencies to guide them into the new medium. For the most part, it was only the larger agencies whose clients could afford the costs of network radio advertising. Many medium and small agencies continued in their traditional roles, entering radio only occasionally or on a local basis.

The agencies that did enter radio established radio departments, first simply to broker time and later to scout talent from the theater and vaudeville stage and local radio stations. This was how Lord & Thomas, of Chicago, Illinois, came upon *Amos 'n' Andy* and brought it to network radio in 1929 for Pepsodent toothpaste. Batten Barton Durstine & Osborn (BBDO), the J. Walter Thompson Company (JWT), Ted Bates & Company, McCann-Erickson, the William Esty Company, Young & Rubicam (Y&R), Blackett-Sample-Hummert, and Benton & Bowles

In this 1960 ad the J. Walter Thompson Company highlighted the wide range of popular television programming sponsored by its clients. *Courtesy of J. Walter Thompson Company.*

were among the other agencies that became active in radio. As clients increasingly pressured their agencies to get them into the new broadcast medium, the range of agency responsibilities also increased. Radio departments began subcontracting the creation and production of appropriate programs for their clients' advertising, finding competent people where they could and often supervising the work. BBDO recruited William Stuhler on the basis of his staging of the Triangle shows, the annual satirical reviews of the Princeton University Triangle Club. Other production people came from local and regional radio.

The involvement of ad agencies in program production was not always a smooth process. Senior agency executives were sometimes suspicious or indifferent to radio. Raymond Rubicam, who founded Y&R in 1923, had little interest in the new medium. But he was wise enough to stand aside for younger subordinates who did. One of those was Chester LaRoche, who recognized advertising's future in radio but had no experience himself. He hired Bill Stauffer, whose experience working in a bookstore apparently qualified him as a judge of literary content. BBDO's Stuhler moved to Y&R and soon hired Sylvester ("Pat") Weaver

and Hubble Robinson, each of whom would go on to celebrated careers in network television.

By the end of the 1930s agencies had established formidable bureaucracies that produced more than 80 percent of all network commercial radio programming. They oversaw vast staffs of joke writers, dramatists, singers, announcers, actors, comedians, and major stars, all under the supervision of producers, directors, and often writers employed directly by the agency broadcast departments. By 1938 the radio department at Y&R was nearly 40 percent larger than the copy department; the latter was responsible for generating the actual commercial messages read by announcers during a show. Agency account executives became the liaison men overseeing it all. They traveled by train between New York City and Los Angeles, California, negotiating with talent agents, facilitating artist-advertiser relationships, and attending live broadcasts with the client in the "sponsor's booth" (the choice studio seating that networks routinely provided to such VIPs).

The networks themselves reserved the right to review program content to ensure that it conformed to their standards of taste. But on most matters the final authority was the sponsor. When the

Glenn Miller Orchestra's *Moonlight Serenade* series was sponsored by Chesterfield cigarettes, Chesterfield's ad agency, Newell-Emmett Company, would not permit the orchestra to perform an arrangement Miller had recorded called "Sold American" because of its reference to rival Lucky Strike.

The only production handled by the networks was that created to fill unsold time. These "sustaining" shows, in which the performers received union scale fees, ran without sponsors and were paid for by the networks. In August 1938, when the CBS network was unable to sell a weekly hour that was opposite JWT's hugely successful *Chase & Sanborn Hour with Edgar Bergen and Charlie McCarthy,* it decided to invest in its own prestige by bringing the Orson Welles Mercury Theater to the air. When the program achieved great notoriety with its presentation of "The War of the Worlds," the F. Wallis Armstrong Company agency, whose major client was the Campbell Soup Company, quickly bought the show, which became *The Campbell Playhouse.*

Advertiser control of programming represented a major revolution in mass communications. For the first time, advertisers did not have to compete against other advertisers for attention in a common carrier such as a magazine or newspaper. Sponsorship gave each advertiser the ability to gather its own audience on an exclusive basis and not only address it without competitive interference but also profit from the goodwill generated by its association with a popular entertainment. In some cases, a sponsor's support would continue for years, making its brand synonymous with a favorite star. General Foods Corporation and Jack Benny were linked for a decade through Y&R. Bob Hope and Bing Crosby became so closely associated with Pepsodent Company (Lord & Thomas) and Kraft Foods Company (JWT), respectively, that references to the brands even appeared in their movies. The radio program *Fibber McGee and Molly* and its sponsor, S.C. Johnson & Sons, were joined in a legendary association for 15 years by ad agency Needham, Louis & Brorby. And *The Lux Radio Theater,* which featured major movie stars in radio plays, sealed Lux soap and Hollywood glamour in a partnership than ran from 1934 to 1954. JWT, the producer of the program, rented a theater on Sunset Boulevard that became the home of the series for its 20-year run.

The agency controlled not only program production and content but the choice of airtime as well. As long as an agency filled a designated period with acceptable programming, it amounted to a de facto claim that the network was virtually powerless to revoke. The "time franchise," as it was called, was a practice originally offered to advertisers as an inducement long before networks learned the advantages of strategic programming. Once the practice was accepted, however, advertisers fought to keep it. When major shows went on their usual summer hiatus, it became customary for agencies to develop low-cost summer replacement programs primarily to hold the show's time slot. When a sponsor canceled a show, the agency would often hold the time period by offering it to another client. When Texaco walked away from its *Texaco Star Theater* with Milton Berle in 1953, the TV program was picked up by Buick and became the *Buick Berle Show* in the same time period. The Kudner Agency, Inc., handled both advertisers.

The networks, meanwhile, grew increasingly frustrated trying to accommodate this outside control. Coming out of World War II, CBS and NBC took active measures to expand their own production capacity, with a view toward developing and scheduling their own inventory of programming and selling it to advertisers. But the momentum of single sponsorship was still strong, and radio was more powerful than ever after the war. It is significant that the most important and influential new trade publication to appear after the war was called *Sponsor,* launched in 1946.

Some believed the arrival of television would shift the balance of production control toward the networks. But it would be a slow process because the same institutions, and many of the same people who had built radio, were now building television using the same business models. In 1950 the majority of the top-ten television programs were produced by a single agency, Y&R. The extent of advertiser control was dramatically asserted after the publication in 1950 of *Red Channels,* a magazine that purported to expose actors and writers working in television whom the editors alleged to be communists. Y&R, acting on behalf of General Foods, dismissed actors from several prominent TV shows, setting off a wave of backroom blacklisting that persisted for more than a decade.

As radio programming had been before, most television programming was produced live under agency supervision. JWT had a separate casting department to manage the weekly production of the *Kraft Television Theater.* In producing *Man Against Crime* for R.J. Reynolds Tobacco Company's Camel cigarettes, the William Esty Company ran the show directly out of its New York City office through it own production staff, which commissioned scripts from a small army of freelance writers. Among the instructions writers received were: only sympathetic characters should be seen smoking, never criminal types; no cigarette should be smoked in a state of nervousness; no story line could involve arson or a fire, lest viewers be reminded of the fires caused by smoking; and no one should ever cough.

Esty also produced the first important nightly news program, the *Camel News Caravan,* and among the edicts to be observed covering the world news was that no world leader was to be pictured smoking a cigar (Winston Churchill excepted), and "no smoking" signs were not to be seen in any news film.

Because the theater, like the advertising business, was largely centered in New York City, agencies found a wealth of writing and acting talent particularly suited to the rigors of the weekly "television theater" format. Kraft, Philco Corporation, Westinghouse Electric Corporation, Goodyear Tire and Rubber Company, Alcoa Corporation, and U.S. Steel Company all sought prestige as sponsors of live anthology drama series with their name built into the shows' titles. Young writers such as Rod Serling, Paddy Chayefsky, and Reginald Rose found themselves attending regular script conferences at JWT and BBDO. But the anthology format also invited problems. It lacked the defined parameters of character and formula that controlled a regular series. When Rose wrote a play for *Westinghouse Studio One* about a black family moving into a white suburban neighborhood and the vigilante efforts to get the family out (*Thunder on*

Sycamore Street, based on a real incident near Chicago, Illinois), the sponsor, agency, and network were all pleased, but insisted that the story could not present a black family as the moral center of the story. Such a notion would be considered too controversial for segments of the Westinghouse audience, namely the South. (Rose's solution was to withhold any specific information about the family, resulting in what broadcast historian Erik Barnouw later called "an extraordinary social Rorschach test" on a national scale, as viewers projected their own pet prejudice onto the otherwise neutral story.)

Such sponsor restrictions were no more severe than those that had restrained radio, which had rarely addressed the rise of fascism or the struggles of organized labor in the 1930s. In controlling the environments of their selling messages, most sponsors did not wish to associate their brands with provocative content that might antagonize potential buyers, particularly when such brands went into the homes of millions. The goal was to avoid upsetting the consumer. Ultimately, critic Martin Mayer wrote in *Madison Avenue U.S.A.,* sponsors sought "gratitude." But gratitude came in different forms. Thus, makers of inexpensive packaged goods tended to be the most cautious and conservative, since their profits depended on volume sales and frequent repeat purchases. Durable goods manufacturers such as Westinghouse were inclined to allow a bit more latitude because their ad strategies were two-pronged: to build a prestigious image as well as generate sales. At the other end, for advertisers that sold mainly to other corporations and not the general public, building prestige was the sole purpose of their ads. Thus, a marketer such as Alcoa, whose targets were well-educated decision makers in industry and government, was willing to support a relatively low-rated but much-esteemed program such as Edward R. Murrow's *See It Now,* even when it took on highly sensitive social issues.

While advertisers and agencies struggled to hold onto their power over programming, they faced a new force not even they could control: the rising cost of TV production, by some accounts as much as 500 percent each year. In the early 1950s it was among the most frequently discussed issues in the trade press. The situation played into the long-term goals of network executives, who were fighting to displace the advertiser influence that had burdened them since the beginning of radio. To this end, Pat Weaver, then president of NBC, promoted a relatively new broadcast program model called the "magazine" format. *Today, Tonight, Home,* and *Saturday Night Revue* were all launched in the late 1940s and early 1950s as network productions and offered to advertisers in 15-minute segments, thus depriving any one agency of effective control over content. While this made it possible for a number of smaller advertisers to enter TV, major advertisers such as the Procter & Gamble Company, Lever Brothers, and Colgate-Palmolive-Peet Company continued to dominate the air, especially in daytime television, where a number of soap operas were owned outright by advertisers. As late as 1959 NBC reported that 32 companies, or 10 percent of its advertisers, were responsible for 65 percent of its revenue.

But the ability of advertisers and their agencies to support full production of a single program was waning. The first line of

retreat was alternating sponsorship, in which two noncompeting advertisers would trade sponsorship every other week. By the 1955–56 season Stopette deodorant and Remington Rand, Inc., alternated on *What's My Line?* After 21 years Lucky Strike relinquished every other broadcast of *Your Hit Parade* to cosmetics marketer Richard Hudnut. At the same time, agencies began to scale back their broadcast departments. JWT sold its talent and casting office to Talent Associates, an independent production company headed by David Susskind.

As the decade went on, the networks became increasingly assertive in building their own schedules with more highly rated, self-produced shows. In 1956 CBS cleared a 90-minute slot in its Thursday night schedule to create *Playhouse 90.* The sponsors of the three displaced shows (General Foods, Singer Sewing Machine Company, and Bristol-Myers Company) were told that CBS would either bring them in as participating sponsors on *Playhouse 90* or try to find another time period for their existing shows. CBS insisted it was not taking away their time; they had the option of running commercials on *Playhouse 90.* The advertisers saw it as coercion, however, if not outright eviction. "It used to be our function to kick around ideas with our clients," one agency executive told *Sponsor* magazine in 1955. "But no more. Today all we can do is look at the lists of what the networks have to offer. . . ."

The role of the agencies was in transition in the late 1950s, as their influence continued to decline for another decade from what it had been in the heyday of radio. Between 1955 and 1965, the number of single-sponsor network programs on the three networks dropped from 75 to 12, while programs under participating sponsorship grew from ten to 57. The turning point would become the scandal that broke in 1958 in which sponsors and agency producers were accused of rigging the outcomes of big-money quiz shows. With the support of Congress and a reform-minded Federal Communications Commission, the networks moved in and took virtually complete control of their schedules.

As ad agencies retreated from program production, they turned their attention to the main challenge of spot advertising and participating sponsorship: how to make the selling message memorable in the context of an increasingly cluttered ad landscape. Without advertiser control over program content or the ability to integrate messages into a show, the television commercial was on its own when it came to holding viewer attention. Agency resources were redirected from mounting entire shows to the creation and production of commercials that in a sense were 60-second (and later 30-second) programs, capable both of entertaining and selling to the consumer.

JOHN MCDONOUGH

Further Reading

Barnouw, Erik, *A History of Broadcasting in the United States,* 3 vols., New York: Oxford University Press, 1966–70; see especially vol. 2, *The Golden Web, 1933 to 1953,* 1968, and vol. 3, *The Image Empire: From 1953,* 1970
Barnouw, Erik, *The Sponsor: Notes on a Modern Potentate,* New York: Oxford University Press, 1978

Boddy, William, *Fifties Television: The Industry and Its Critics,* Urbana: University of Illinois Press, 1990

Cone, Fairfax M., *With All Its Faults: A Candid Account of Forty Years in Advertising,* Boston: Little Brown, 1969

Smulyan, Susan, *Selling Radio: The Commercialization of American Broadcasting, 1920–1934,* Washington, D.C.: Smithsonian Institution Press, 1994

"What Are Your 'Rights' to a Time Slot?" *Sponsor* (5 April 1954)

Product Placement

Product or brand placement is a form of advertising in which brand-name products, packages, signs, and corporate names are intentionally positioned in motion pictures and television programs. Placement can be in the form of verbal mentions in dialogue, actual use by a character, visual displays such as a corporate logo on a vehicle or billboard, brands used as set decoration, or even snatches of actual radio or television commercials. Commercials may even be specially developed for use in a specific film, as in the case of Ramses condoms in *Lethal Weapon 2.* Product placement has been referred to as stealth advertising, yet not all placements are subtle and unobtrusive; advertisers pay to have their brands noticed.

During the early decades of the film industry, Hollywood largely avoided the appearance of known product names in movies. When products were used, studios were required to obtain legal clearances and perhaps pay a fee for use of a copyrighted brand name, such as the appearance of a *National Geographic* magazine in *It's a Wonderful Life* (1946). Thus, instances of product placement in motion pictures were rare until the 1970s. But by then propmasters and set decorators achieved cost savings and realism by obtaining name-brand props from manufacturers. Before long, the manufacturers came to recognize the promotional value of such exposure. What began as a matter of convenience soon blossomed into a formal industry. Studios created product placement departments and product placement specialists scanned scripts looking for placement opportunities. Companies such as Associated Film Promotions established warehouses of products at the ready for showcasing in films.

Trends

During television's infancy advertisers sponsored entire programs such as *Camel Caravan* and the *Kraft Television Theater.* Agencies also had a hand in the production of many shows. Product appearance and use was often blatant. Prompted by the strong role advertisers had in programming, as well as "under-the-table" payments made in exchange for on-air displays, the Federal Communications Commission (FCC) enacted so-called "payola laws" in the late 1950s. Product placement on television came to be regulated by FCC rules. Paid placements are no longer permitted unless the featured brand is listed as a sponsor. However, brands may appear if they are donated or if they are used for realistic effect. Theatrical films aired on TV are excluded from FCC rules on product placement, as are cable and first-run syndication programs.

Product placement in motion pictures received a boost from the unanticipated success of Reese's Pieces following its appearance in *E.T. the Extra-Terrestrial.* The film, released in 1982, prominently featured Hershey's Reese's Pieces candy. Although the brand was available prior to the film's release, its appearance in the film was credited with stimulating a 65 percent sales increase. M&M/Mars had been approached first about a scene in which the character E.T. is coaxed out of hiding by a trail of candy, but the company declined the opportunity. Ray-Ban sunglasses experienced a 55 percent gain in sales following prominent use by Tom Cruise in the 1983 film *Risky Business.* Similar success stories for other brands firmly established the importance of product placement.

The use of feature films as a strategy for introducing new products has grown increasingly sophisticated. Savvy marketers now build elaborate marketing communication plans cross-promoting films and brands. For example, BMW used *GoldenEye* (1995), a film in the successful James Bond series, as an integrated element for introducing a new model, the BMW 328i. In 1995 BMW was awarded the Super Reggie Award as the best promotion of the year by the Promotional Marketing Association. Apple Computer used a similar strategy with its laptop line in 1996's *Mission: Impossible.* And in 2000 Eastman Kodak Company built a $1 million-plus promotion around the appearance of its digital cameras in the sequel, *Mission: Impossible 2.*

As successful marketing efforts incorporating motion pictures continue to mount, the casual use of brands as props will diminish. While current practice does not require filmmakers to identify brands placed in films, viewers can reasonably assume that prominently featured brands have offered some compensation or other consideration in exchange for the appearance.

Advantages

Brand placement may begin with one of several parties. Studio representatives, aware of script development, may approach brand marketers or their advertising agencies pitching the film and its placement opportunities. Films produced outside the Hollywood studio system might also pursue this route. Alternatively, marketers interested in brand placement might contract with an agent to represent their brands to studios and producers.

What is common among these groups is that scripts are developed, selected for production and then reviewed for placement potential. Scripts may then be forwarded to placement agents or advertising agencies where brand marketers assess the placement in terms of their marketing strategies. Should the marketer wish to proceed, negotiations are undertaken regarding payment, availability, merchandising opportunities, and promotion of the placement and film. Different rates are charged for placement, depending on whether a brand is mentioned in dialogue, is used by a "star," or is used by other characters. An industry trade group, Entertainment Resources & Marketing Association, operates as an information clearinghouse and works to advance the professionalism and growth of the brand placement industry.

Brand placement offers marketers several advantages over other advertising media, especially cost-efficient communication. Over the life of a film, including its theatrical run, premium cable appearances, other televised broadcasts, and home video rental, cost-per-thousand exposures continues to decrease, eventually declining to mere pennies on the dollar. Brands are also featured in a clutter-free environment devoid of competitive messages. Films can be selected that target consumers who may be difficult to reach with more conventional advertising methods. Nearly three-fourths of the audience for theatrical films is between the ages of 16 and 39, a group highly prized by advertisers. Associating brands with particular actors, films, or contexts allows the marketer to associate a brand with congruent lifestyle or usage situations. Tobacco is banned and alcohol brands have voluntarily refrained from advertising in the broadcast media. Films offer these brands the full sight, sound, and motion capabilities they do not have access to in radio and television. Finally, product placements are one means for overcoming the all-too-common problem of advertising avoidance made possible in television by the remote control and other devices for "zipping," "zapping," and muting commercials.

Perhaps most important to the marketer is the captive nature of the audience. In terms of communication potential, the theatrical situation is ideal. Viewers are seated in a dark theater facing the screen with few other distracting stimuli. Brands are featured to fullest effect in naturalistic contexts readily understood by viewers.

Marketers do give up some control in a placement situation. For example, scenes featuring a brand may not appear in the final theatrical version of a film, or scenes may be edited to accommodate television broadcasts. Also, each placement entails some risk. With conventional advertising methods, marketers can demand guarantees regarding audience size (of course, in the case of theatrical films, there are no ratings or other prior estimates of audience size). Should a broadcast or cable program underperform, advertisers can demand make-goods (commercial spots provided free to advertisers when program ratings fall short of projections). If a film fails, there may be no similar opportunity. This last pitfall is potentially disastrous if the marketer has built a comprehensive campaign strategy around the film. Similarly, other placement support strategies in the retail and distribution channels are jeopardized if a film does not open as scheduled.

One matter of concern to commercial television is the potential conflict between a program's advertisers and the brands that appear within a program. Coca-Cola would not, for instance, want to sponsor a movie or show in which a character is shown drinking Pepsi. Moreover, commercial television networks may be averse to selling brand placements for fear that marketers might shy away from more conventional broadcast advertising.

Assessing Effectiveness

The success of brand placement is generally assessed through case studies and anecdotal evidence. There are few academic studies detailing the specific communication effects associated with brand placement strategies. Published research has shown only a marginal increase in brand recall as a result of product placement and little change in attitude toward the brand. While some new brands have been successfully launched via placement strategies, many brands featured in films are already familiar to viewers. In this case, placement may best serve as a means of maintaining visibility and top-of-mind awareness among target markets. Placement may be successful in terms of developing or strengthening brand preference, or viewers might perceive the brand to be endorsed by the star.

Two other important media concepts, reach and frequency, are more difficult to quantify. If many people view a theatrical film through any outlet, reach may be high, especially among specific target groups. Generating frequency may be more difficult, unless a film is viewed several times. If a brand is featured more than once in a single film vehicle, frequency can be generated. Other media strategies may offer better frequency opportunities than brand placement. In the case of a television program, a product featured in multiple episodes of a series will offer an opportunity to generate frequency.

The type of film and its content can affect brand placement possibilities. For example, films depicting earlier historical periods will offer less placement potential than films depicting contemporary times. One area of product placement research has focused on the frequency with which particular branded products are featured in films. Frequently observed product categories include automobiles, fast foods and other snack items, and alcoholic beverages and soft drinks. Tobacco brands are also found to appear regularly in feature films.

Studies of television programming have shown that branded products appear most often in news programming and situation comedies. The most commonly appearing include automobiles, foods, and corporations.

From the perspective of the placement agent, successful placements provide client brands with national exposure opportunities that minimize price while maximizing screen time. Another important concern is film theme or content. Many brands may be reluctant to associate with violent or overly dramatic material. A particularly important consideration is merchandising tie-ins. Many marketers seek to use the film to drive sales and distribution strategies. This is riskier, given the fickle nature of the film audience and the potential for release date delays.

BMW of North America introduced its BMW 328i in the 1995 James Bond film *GoldenEye,* dubbing it "the BMW that made James Bond switch." (Bond previously had driven other automobiles, including an Aston Martin and a Lotus.)
© 2001 BMW of North America, LLC. Used with permission. The BMW name and logo are registered trademarks.

Critics

Brand placement in feature films and other entertainment contexts has been criticized on aesthetic and public policy grounds. Film critics suggest that brand placement compromises the artistic integrity of films. Many contend that films have become little more than elaborate advertising vehicles used by marketers to showcase brands. And, since marketers are more likely to prefer upbeat, positive contexts to promote brands, film exploration of dramatic or controversial material could decline if studios rely more heavily on placement to underwrite film production costs. Product placement professionals readily admit that the most important placement execution characteristic is the portrayal of the product in a favorable light. Product placement agencies carefully distribute their products to studios and production companies with stipulations such as that the product not be shown in a negative way or not be used by a "bad guy."

Public policy critics maintain that brand placement is nothing more than subtle advertising, interjecting a commercial message where no message is expected. These critics suggest that the selling message is more powerful, given the relaxed state of the viewer. If a consumer does not expect to be sold to, mechanisms for evaluating sales messages might not be activated. Some policy groups have suggested that brand placements be banned or identified in opening or closing credits. The Center for the Study of Commercialism proposed petitioning the Federal Trade Commission (FTC)—which is charged with regulating advertising—to force movie producers to run disclaimers acknowledging paid product placements. As of this writing, no identification is required, although filmmakers are free to note placements, if they wish to do so.

Another concern of placement critics is the prevalence of alcohol and tobacco brands in films. Current broadcast regulations deny access to tobacco products; distilled spirits were, prior to 2002, absent from broadcast TV owing to self-regulation, although beer and wine did appear in commercial broadcast channels. (In December 2001 NBC announced that it would begin accepting advertising from distillers that would run after 10 P.M.,

Eastern Standard Time but then reversed that decision in March 2002). Films offered these marketers their only opportunity to portray these brands being fully used. Criticism focuses on imagery portraying smoking and drinking activities as common, powerful, or seductive. Also, when films are broadcast on commercial television outlets, brand placements allow tobacco marketers to circumvent broadcasting regulations, thereby exposing the brand and its use to millions of viewers.

Brand placements also appear in contexts other than film, including music videos and video games. As new technologies allow producers to develop fully interactive environments, brand placement may be added. Virtual reality technologies allowing participants to enter scenarios entirely controlled by designers—an auto racing simulation, for example—could feature brands in realistic settings, such as signage at racetracks or on the dashboard of the vehicle. Designers of video games might begin seeking support for their production efforts, as have filmmakers.

Brand placement as a marketing communication strategy in mediated contexts appears to be firmly entrenched. Unless regulations are implemented to curtail such placements, the practice will likely continue. Brand agents and studio marketing departments in search of revenue will need to avoid creating a new type of advertising clutter. Predicting hits and placing brands will always be risky propositions, but more and more advertisers may find benefits in imbuing their brands with the aura of Hollywood.

LANCE KINNEY AND BARRY SAPOLSKY

Further Reading

Babin, L.A., and S.T. Carder, "Advertising via the Box Office: Is Product Placement Effective?" *Journal of Promotion Management* 3, nos. 1–2 (1996)

Kalinichenko, I.A., "Brand Props in Prime-Time Television Programs: A Content Analysis," Master's thesis, University of Georgia, 1998

McCarthy, Michael, "Studios Place, Show, and Win: Product Placement Grows Up," *Brandweek* (28 March, 1994)

Miller, Mark Crispin, "Hollywood: The Ad," *The Atlantic* 265 (April 1990)

Sapolsky, B.S., and L. Kinney, "You Oughta Be in Pictures: Product Placements in the Top-Grossing Films of 1991," in *The Proceedings of the 1994 Conference of the American Academy of Advertising,* edited by Karen W. King, Athens, Georgia: American Academy of Advertising, 1994

Promotions and Merchandising

Promotions and merchandising are key efforts underlying the success of any retail business. Efforts to convey merchandising and special promotional activities to target audiences account for the bulk of retail advertising expenditures. To achieve maximum success in retailing, merchandising strategies and promotional plans must be highly integrated. Moreover, because promotion and merchandising are interdependent entities, retailers pay a great deal of attention to coordinating, scheduling, and integrating the two activities.

Merchandising encompasses the buying, selling, and control of merchandise and affects every area of the retail operation. It is a retail maxim that to achieve success, a merchandiser must have the right merchandise at the right time in the right quantities with the right presentation and at the right price.

Merchandising consists of the activities involved in acquiring particular goods or services and making them available to targeted consumers through attractive displays and promotional activities under a controlled system so that both the retailer and the shopper reach their goals. Specific merchandising tasks include estimating demand, buying merchandise, planning inventories, designing floor layout, pricing merchandise, supervising merchandising budgets, advertising and promoting merchandise, creating displays and signage, designing window dressings, and establishing external as well as internal store ambience. Promotion supports merchandising, with merchandising strategy conveyed to consumers through promotion. "Retail operations," in contrast to merchandising, typically include such activities as building maintenance, receiving goods, fulfillment and delivery, stocking, and purchasing nonmerchandise goods and services.

Merchandising Strategy

Retailers must make several decisions before merchandising and promotional strategies can be formulated and implemented. Merchandising parameters begin to take shape with the task of identifying and understanding customers. In settling on target markets, retailers examine "trading area" factors that affect merchandising, such as demographics, lifestyles, geographic pull and traffic patterns, consumer trends and shopping habits, and other socioeconomic indicators.

Next, retail store strategy is formulated. Retailers decide on a particular retail store category and select store image or personality and a positioning strategy. All subsequent decisions are made in light of the store image and its positioning strategy. A store's image is a reflection of general attributes, merchandise attributes, price attributes, physical attributes, customer service evaluations, community services, employees, and promotional programs. General attributes include target markets sought, positioning strategy, geographic coverage, reputation, and market standing. Merchandising attributes include assortment, quality, stock on hand, brand names sold, dependability, and innovativeness. The nature, type, and quality of advertisements and special promotions also influence overall store image. Finally, retailers must translate store image goals into store atmosphere, a task that considers merchandise strategies.

Once the retailer's strategic plan is formulated, concerns such as administrative organization, store policies, and merchandising parameters must be addressed. Merchandise strategy is the plan that sets goals and objectives for merchandising activities, determining the types, quality, and other characteristics of goods and services to buy and sell. Merchandise quality must be related to the retailer's desired image.

Critical Choices

The choice of merchandise and suppliers has far-reaching implications for retail operations. The selection of higher-quality goods, for example, generally requires higher levels of customer service, high-quality and expensive advertising, more elaborate and costly visual merchandising, and highly trained sales clerks. Retailers, thus, have to settle on the types and levels of customer service to offer. The choice of merchandise quality and service level helps determine the type of customer attracted to the store and the set of customer expectations the store must match. Low-quality merchandise tends to attract customers who desire functional product benefits. In contrast, such characteristics as status, top-quality service, exclusivity, and style underlie merchandise that attracts upscale customers seeking extended or higher-order benefits, such as prestige, positive social distinction, and outward signs of power and wealth.

Decisions are made regarding width and depth of assortment. Width of assortment refers to the number of different goods and service lines or categories that the retailer elects to offer. Depth of assortment refers to the variety of merchandise in each distinct line of goods and services. Once those types of decisions are ironed out, buyers subsequently evaluate and select merchandise, given established guidelines. They identify and evaluate suppliers, negotiate prices and terms, select suppliers, and purchase merchandise. Negotiations generally focus on delivery date, quantity purchased, regularity of reorders, price and payment terms, discounts, amount and type of promotional assistance and support, discounts and allowances, and point of title transfer.

Next, handling and inventory management policies and procedures are specified before goods are received. In planning for handling, retailers must concern themselves with such important aspects as facilities, handling equipment and technology, inventory methods, storage capacities, the receiving of goods, accounts payable, reordering practices, and the like. During the handling phase, retailers typically undertake such activities as receiving and sorting goods, marking prices and registering inventory, stocking, setting up displays, specifying floor quantities and assortments, fulfilling customer transactions, and delivering goods. Also, retailers deal with returns and damaged or spoiled goods. Pilferage and

This 1935 Colgate-Palmolive ad showed druggists how to set up sales displays as part of a nationwide campaign.
Courtesy of Colgate-Palmolive Company.

inventory control systems are designed and activated. A key component of successful merchandising concerns the reevaluation of service providers, vendors, and suppliers.

Merchandising also involves pricing strategy, price, price adjustments, and consumer deals, a form of sales promotion that tends to attract deal-prone segments through price-based incentives. Merchandisers should price goods and services in a way that recognizes pricing constraints, provides customer value, and increases the retailer's likelihood of achieving the profit goal. Pricing strategy and consumer deals ought to be consistent with the retailer's strategic plan and the competitive situation.

Retailers, after assessing competition, select between market penetration and price-skimming strategies. Market penetration focuses on low price settings in hopes of attracting large numbers of price-conscious shoppers and balancing low margins against high stock turnover. In contrast, price skimming sets price at the high end of the relevant range of prices. It ties to the retail strategy of focusing on branded items, implementing high levels of customer service and the targeting of upscale consumers, who demand higher-order gratification in merchandise and enjoy a store's exclusivity, prestige, and glossy image. Here, margins are

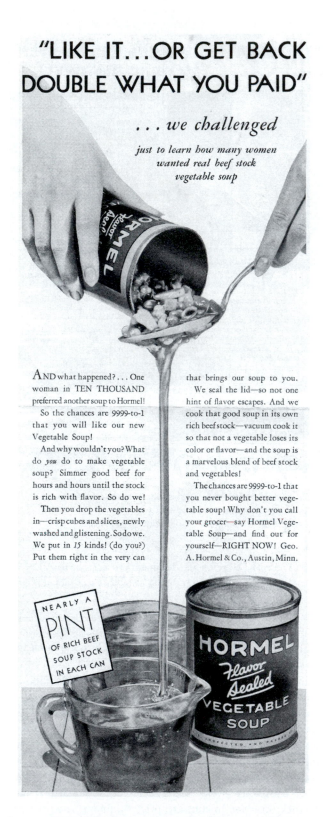

"LIKE IT...OR GET BACK DOUBLE WHAT YOU PAID"

...we challenged

just to learn how many women wanted real beef stock vegetable soup

AND what happened?...One woman in TEN THOUSAND preferred another soup to Hormel!

So the chances are 9999-to-1 that you will like our new Vegetable Soup!

And why wouldn't you? What do *you* do to make vegetable soup? Simmer good beef for hours and hours until the stock is rich with flavor. So do we!

Then you drop the vegetables in—crisp cubes and slices, newly washed and glistening. So do we. We put in 15 kinds! (do you?) Put them right in the very can

that brings our soup to you. We seal the lid—so not one hint of flavor escapes. And we cook that good soup in its own rich beef stock—vacuum cook it so that not a vegetable loses its color or flavor—and the soup is a marvelous blend of beef stock and vegetables!

The chances are 9999-to-1 that you never bought better vegetable soup! Why don't you call your grocer—say Hormel Vegetable Soup—and find out for yourself—RIGHT NOW! Geo. A. Hormel & Co., Austin, Minn.

NEARLY A
PINT
OF RICH BEEF SOUP STOCK IN EACH CAN

HORMEL
Flavor Sealed
VEGETABLE SOUP

In the 1930s Hormel shook up marketing by offering a "double your money back" guarantee of consumer satisfaction for its line of beef-stock-based soups. This follow-up ad reported that only one woman in 10,000 took the company up on its offer.
Ad titled "Like it...or get back double what you paid" reprinted by permission of Hormel Foods Corporation.

usually higher and stock turnover is lower in comparison to retailers adopting the penetration pricing strategy.

A price strategy can be based on demand, cost, competition, or some combination of the three. Demand-oriented pricing attempts to set prices at levels acceptable to patrons and target markets. But demand is often difficult to gauge, and the approach is time-consuming. Cost-oriented pricing is the most widely embraced pricing method. It centers on markups based on either the cost of goods sold or the selling price. Large retailers, lacking time and resources to conduct demand-oriented or competition-oriented pricing research, use simple markup formulas configured around various departments, space allocations, merchandise type, or the like. Competitive pricing strategy is based on observed and tracked pricing practices of close competitors. It entails such research techniques as mystery shopping and content analysis of competitors' price advertising in newspapers. In varying degrees, most retailers use some combination of all three pricing orientations.

One recent trend in retail pricing and merchandising is a movement toward "everyday low prices." Originated by manufacturers, everyday low prices attempted to forestall forward buying by retailers (i.e., the practice of balking at goods sold at regular manufacturer prices, stocking up on goods when manufacturers offer trade sales, holding the acquisitions in inventory, and selling them at full price to patrons at a later date). A number of retailers have embraced the everyday low pricing strategy as a way to stabilize sales at an acceptable level, establish a consistent store image, and manage consumer expectations. Price, merchandising, and promotion are so interrelated that a retailer cannot plan one without considering the other two.

The Store

Just as merchandising is deeply integrated with strategic retail plans, so is visual merchandising, the type of merchandising most readily noticed by customers. Visual merchandising entails such considerations as the store's exterior and interior treatments, displays and window dressings, colors, lighting, textures, flooring, props, signage, store layout, and floor plans.

Visual merchandising concerns the design of the exterior of the store and the layout of its interior. Customers' perceptions of ambience and merchandise derive, in a significant part, from their judgments of the exterior and interior designs. Exterior design communicates at a glance the type and quality of a store. Customers also perceive store personality by interpreting exterior window displays in terms of design acumen and the types of merchandise and moods conveyed. Exteriors must align with the retailer's strategic plan in terms of its focus on either direct, utilitarian product benefits or higher-order hedonistic gratification, such as exclusivity, prestige, and social image.

In turn, interior store layout starts with the allocation of floor space. Selling space is the area allotted to displaying and demonstrating merchandise and conducting transactions. In contrast, merchandise space is the area set aside for holding inventory. Customer space contributes to shoppers' perceptions of store image. It includes public bathroom and lounge facilities, seating arrangements, dressing and waiting room facilities, restaurants, elevators and people-moving devices, gift wrapping and other customer service areas, parking, aisles, and the like. Customer space and selling space are tied to the overall store image strategy and affect merchandising. High-quality retailers allocate much greater space to customer service than do their low-image counterparts, which typically increase selling and inventory space allocations and skimp on customer space.

Selling space and customer space is then subjected to traffic flow analysis. The goals of traffic flow analysis include making shopping efficient and intelligent for customers, encouraging the customer to spend, providing atmosphere, permitting shoppers either to rush or browse, and increasing impulse purchasing. Other goals involve minimizing customer confusion, reducing the need for customer service personnel, reducing pilferage, placing products and services, grouping like and complementary products, and locating display areas.

Once the floor plan is mapped, set, and implemented, retailers' concern focuses on achieving the desired image and sales goals through "atmospherics" or store ambience and merchandise display. Adolph Novak, a recognized store designer, defines ambience as "the general quality of design which expresses the character of the store, resulting in institutional personality immediately recognized by the public."

The internal backdrop for atmospherics and visual merchandising concerns such interior design aspects as flooring, fixtures, lighting, walls and ceilings, textures, and windows. Interiors are carefully designed. Store designers and visual merchandisers consider a basic set of principles in designing interiors and displays. Balance, or symmetrical weighting, results in a pleasing presentation of merchandise. Emphasis refers to the dominant point of a display that conveys the key impression. Harmony implies that all elements fit together. Lifestyle presentations, for example, focus on harmony in that all of the items displayed together pertain to a particular activity or hobby enjoyed by a segment of shoppers. Proportion concerns the ratio of one component to others.

Other elements of design include proximity, which suggests that like items ought to be placed closest together; rhythm, which implies a consideration of the appropriate pace or tempo of movement; and texture, which relates to harmony and emphasis as well as to touch and sight. Texture can be perceived either through touch or sight and generally consists of components that either contrast roughness against smoothness or materials that reflect or absorb light. In the effective use of texture, the designer communicates both harmony and emphasis. In addition, dominance implies that while all of the items in a display relate to one another, only one idea jumps forward to be readily recognized by shoppers. Each display should project only one dominant idea. Like texture, color also permits contrast and emphasis. Color expresses a store's personality, a wide array of moods, and ties merchandise and store ambiance to holidays. Lighting and fixtures are other noteworthy aspects of visual merchandising. The main objectives of lighting are to allow customers to see the merchandise, to attract attention, set a mood and create ambience, and provide a safe environment. The major lighting methods

include pinpointing, spotlighting, floodlighting, emergency lighting, diffused lighting, indirect lighting, and special effects. Fixtures are essentially the skeletons for displaying merchandise. Fixtures include windows, counters, a wide assortment of stands and racks, shelves, and platforms and elevators.

On Display

Merchandise display, a critical facet of visual merchandising, concerns the selection, organization, and arrangement of displays and merchandise. The major function of display is to entice and inform shoppers, leading them toward the purchase decision. Other benefits of effective displays include such things as building and reinforcing the retailer's image or goodwill, increasing probabilities for complementary and future sales, and familiarizing shoppers with the store. Additional benefits derive from conveying trends in merchandise, strengthening shoppers' perceptions of the retailer's sense of style, demonstrating products and services, conveying credence or intangible properties of merchandise that otherwise would dampen sales, and so forth.

A number of errors in displaying merchandising have been identified. These include too much or too little merchandise, too many props, inappropriate use of displays, irrelevant or dated displays, and displays that take too long to create. Other problems are attributed to the lack of attention to an underlying theme or the necessary details to convey the theme in a relevant manner. Misapplied principles of display design also yield ineffective displays.

Several guidelines for planning and arranging merchandise displays have been advanced:

- Develop a powerful, unique selling proposition.
- Use accepted design principles to direct the shopper to the dominant element of the display, thus reinforcing the selling proposition.
- Keep the display as simple as possible.
- Avoid clutter.
- Limit visual tension by reducing the number of competing elements in a display.
- Eliminate any cue or element that distracts from the sales message.
- Use displays that, when visible to the customer, relate to the selling proposition and merchandise being displayed.
- Make the merchandise, not the props and displays themselves, take up the bulk of display space.
- Use lighting, color, movement, and music that is appropriate to the season and selling message.
- Avoid mixing styles unless there is an exceptional justification.
- Consider the "pop culture" surrounding the merchandise when designing a display.

Displays that are relevant to the audience capture attention and build desire. But until promotion draws people into the store, calls their attention to the merchandise, and persuades them to buy, merchandising is an expense, not an asset.

An ad for Chrysler's 2000 holiday sale featured a wide range of promotional sales techniques, including financing discounts, cash allowances, and lease rate reductions.

The 2000 Chrysler advertisement is used with permission from DaimlerChrysler Corporation.

In any discussion of retail advertising and promotion, it is important to note one critical caveat: retail advertising and consumer sales promotion cannot compensate for deficiencies in merchandising. Promotional campaigns and heavy media expenditures cannot overcome merchandising mistakes, such as offering the wrong merchandise, unacceptable prices, the wrong service level, or creating a difficult and confusing shopping environment.

Retail advertising and consumer sales promotions perform three essential communication functions: they create store image; they convey a store's specific product lines and promote certain individual goods; and they communicate a store's special promotions and events, enticing shoppers to visit and purchase.

The Creative Message Strategy

Advertising and promotions have two orientations as well. One concerns the strategic plan of the store. The other orientation is tactical in nature and concerns temporal matters, such as capitalizing on special holidays, events, and other selling apertures that are expected to arise during the short-term planning period. These two orientations comprise the heart of a retailer's creative message strategy and become the focus of promotional efforts.

The strategic orientation concerns the long-term impressions retailers wish to establish in the minds of consumers. The impressions involve store image and personality, store positioning strategy, and customer service quality. Store image is critical: it is the major factor attracting shoppers to a store. It represents shoppers' general perception of, and association with, a store and, once made, is very difficult to change. Image is the central node to which shoppers affix more specific beliefs, and as such, retailers make concerted efforts to shape a desirable store image. Positioning strategy builds on store image, as it attempts to translate the image into a distinctive competitive advantage by setting the store apart from competitors, especially close rivals, in a favorable manner. Retailers attempt to shape customer expectations of service quality through advertising and promotions. Persuasive communications attempt to align consumers' perceptions of the store with desirable levels of specific attributes underlying service quality evaluations.

In contrast to the strategic orientation, promotion assumes a tactical or temporal orientation. The bulk of retail sales promotions target opportunities expected to arise during the current, short-term planning period, generally one year or less. In its *Dictionary of Marketing Terms* (1995), the American Marketing Association defines sales promotions as "the media and non-media marketing pressure applied for a predetermined, limited period of time at the level of consumer, retailer, or wholesaler in order to stimulate trial, increase consumer demand, or improve product availability." Other commonly used sales promotion tools are special events, samples, contests, sweepstakes, continuity programs, product and service literature, premiums, bonus packs, coupons, N-fors (e.g., offering one shirt for $35 and the second shirt for $20), rebates and other consumer price deals, and point-of-purchase materials (POP).

Promotional programs need to be coordinated with financial merchandise strategy and the availability of goods. In addition, managers distinguish between the effective promotional programs that need to be continued and the unsuccessful ones in need of adjustment or deletion. Once merchandisers identify an opportunity to commit promotional dollars, a target audience is identified and analyzed in terms of product usage patterns, preferences for sales promotion, and other relevant behavioral characteristics. Dates and times for implementation of the promotion are identified and scheduled, taking into account the promotional programs of competitors.

Retailers plan and schedule sales promotions using display calendars to highlight dates and times that present significant opportunities to increase sales. The calendar schedules and coordinates points of sales aperture (an opening or a special opportunity to advertise and sell products, such as Valentine's Day for jewelry sales) with appropriate promotional programs and tools. Calendars typically are created for a one-year planning period so that no sales opportunity is overlooked. Budget shortfalls are more easily avoided if resources are allocated according to the calendar. Some retailers make special calendars available to customers on a monthly basis, announcing store events and demonstrations.

Sales Promotion Tools

Savvy merchandisers identify the sales promotion tools best suited to accomplish their varied promotional objectives over the course of the planning period. For example, retailers faced with the task of launching a new product into a category marked by a high degree of brand switching are best served by demonstrations linked to price savings or favorable finance terms, displays offering deals on prices, and other consumer price deals. Conversely, retailers need to consider free samples, trial-size packages, demonstrations, consumer shows, and point-of-purchase literature when their objective is to launch a new family brand into a category characterized by high brand loyalty. When the goal entails the need to explain, magnify, and promote a brand's determinant attribute (the benefit or function of a brand or firm that is most desired by buyers), retailers generally use POP displays, product

This 1990 corporate ad for Sears, Roebuck & Company promoted its specialty stores to real estate developers that were seeking to attract businesses to their shopping centers.
The 1990 "Your Money's Worth and a Whole Lot More" Sears advertisement is reprinted by arrangement with Sears, Roebuck and Co. and is protected under copyright. No duplication is permitted.

literature, demonstrations, contests, or sweepstakes to highlight the attribute. To associate specific feelings with a store or brand, retailers use special events, premiums, and prizes that evoke those feelings. For example, to link a jewelry store to the feeling of "love," a jeweler in Florida ran a Valentine's Day contest asking men to submit love letters written to their wives. The prize for the best letter was a diamond tennis bracelet, which was given to the winner's wife. The goal obviously was to associate Valentine's Day, romance, and gift giving with the retailer.

There are many other promotional goals that are best served by specific sales promotion tools. Retailers may seek to increase sales from existing customers. To reach that objective, retailers might consider such sales promotion tools as a sweepstakes that involves repeated store visits or a continuity program. One hair salon's continuity program, for example, gives one free haircut after every seventh cut. To attract deal-prone consumers (i.e., price-conscious buyers) through promotions, retailers might consider offering consumer deals such as sales, coupons, rebates, and N-fors, among others. Special packaging or displays are effective promotions used to link a retailer with a holiday. To attract specific lifestyle groups to a store, retailers may consider sponsoring events, conducting demonstrations, or using displays to link a brand with special activities associated with the lifestyle.

Retailers specify their degree of commitment to promotion. Some elect to become a promotional store, establishing an aggressive merchandising and promotional orientation, selling low-margin items, and seeking high stock turnover. Conversely, nonpromotional stores emphasize upscale goods and services, exclusive brand availability, image, style, and high customer service levels. Advertising is selective, consumer price deals receive little emphasis, and sales promotions play a small role in the overall promotional plans. However, prestige displays and service displays are featured. Service displays communicate the store's special services, features, and facilities instead of merchandise; prestige displays highlight upscale products whose established image and high market standing make a statement about the image of a retailer that displays them.

In contrast, semipromotional stores fall between promotional and nonpromotional stores in terms of reliance on merchandising and promotion. Semipromotional stores use both prestige and service displays but also use merchandise displays. Image, merchandise, and price promotions receive balanced attention. The semipromotional store identifies both bargain hunters and upscale customers as within its target audience.

Big Business

Sales promotion in the United States is a huge business. It is used heavily by retailers and manufactures alike. Manufacturers aim trade sales promotions at retailers to influence their product selection decisions. Likewise, retailers receive from manufacturers a good deal of assistance with consumer sales promotions as part of their retail support and assistance programs.

Manufacturers and retailers frequently join forces with one another to influence consumers through joint consumer sales promotion. Joint sales promotions entail special deals offered to consumers by two or more brands, manufacturers, or retailers. They combine their resources to capitalize on opportunities for sales growth and profits, or to reach other key marketing objectives. Natural-use complementary relationships among different brands, such as the shared use of peanut butter and jelly, or athletic shoes and socks, present a reason for manufacturers to offer a cross-coupon promotion (e.g., each brand offers a coupon for the other brand on its package). To combat falling seasonal demand, retailers can join together in offering an enticing bundle of goods and services at an attractive price. To attract specific groups to their brands or to establish brand or store personality, different parties come together in sponsoring special events. As the cost of promotions increases, joint sales promotions make sense.

Sales promotions can backfire, however. An overreliance on consumer price deals, for example, may easily condition shoppers to buy only when a brand is on sale or the store is having a special promotion. Except in the case of a promotional store, store image is about persuading buyers to value the store in its own right, not on the basis of its consumer price deals. Experts suggest that promotions be carefully designed so that buyers learn something important about the brand or store in addition to simply enjoying the extra inducement. As retailers spend more and more on sales promotions, competitive pressures are likely to increase. However, it is important to remain mindful of the strategic retail plan, environmental conditions, and the goals of merchandising as resources are allocated to promotion.

ALLEN E. SMITH

Further Reading

Bennett, Peter D., editor, *Dictionary of Marketing Terms*, 2nd edition, Lincolnwood, Illinois: NTC Business Books, 1995

Berman, Barry, and Joel R. Evans, *Retail Management: A Strategic Approach*, New York: Macmillan, 1979

Drew-Bear, Robert, *Mass Merchandising: Revolution and Evolution*, New York: Fairchild, 1970

Engel, James F., Hugo G. Wales, and Martin R. Warshaw, *Promotional Strategy: Managing the Marketing Communication Process*, Homewood, Illinois: Irwin, 1967

Govoni, Norman, Robert Eng, and Morton Galper, *Promotional Management: Issues and Perspectives*, Englewood Cliffs, New Jersey: Prentice Hall, 1988

Hollander, Stanley C., *Multinational Retailing*, East Lansing: Michigan State University, 1970

Lewison, Dale, *Retailing*, Upper Saddle River, New Jersey: Prentice Hall, 1982

Lusch, Robert F., *Management of Retail Enterprises*, Boston: Kent, 1982

Mason, J. Barry, and Morris L. Mayer, *Modern Retailing: Theory and Practice*, Plano, Texas: Business Publications, 1978

Mills, Kenneth H., and Judith E. Paul, *Create Distinctive Displays*, Englewood Cliffs, New Jersey: Prentice Hall, 1974; 3rd edition, as *Applied Visual Merchandising*, by Mils, Paul, and Kay B. Moormann, 1995

Pegler, Martin M., *Visual Merchandising and Display*, New York: Fairchild, 1983

Schultz, Don E., and William A. Robinson, *Sales Promotion Essentials*, Chicago: Crain, 1982; 3rd edition, by Schultz, Robinson, and Lisa Petrison, Lincolnwood, Illinois: NTC Books, 1998

Shipp, Ralph D., Jr., *Retail Merchandising: Principles and Applications*, Boston: Houghton Mifflin, 1985

Varadarajan, P. Rajan, "Joint Sales Promotion: An Emerging Marketing Tool," *Business Horizons* 28, no. 5 (1985)

Wells, William, John Burnett, and Sandra Moriarty, *Advertising Principles and Practice*, Upper Saddle River, New Jersey: Prentice Hall, 1989

Ziccardi, Donald, and David Moin, *Masterminding the Store: Advertising, Sales Promotion, and the New Marketing Reality*, New York: Wiley, 1997

Propaganda

Propaganda, like pornography, is difficult to define, even though most people assume they can recognize its manifestations. The distinction between persuasion and propaganda is a matter of definition, as demonstrated by the fact that the terms are frequently used interchangeably. Whereas all propaganda has elements of persuasion, not all persuasion is propaganda. When the motive of presentation and the accuracy of the message are taken into account, then persuasion and propaganda can be more easily differentiated.

In the case of advertising, which utilizes the mass media with the goal of convincing the consumer to buy a product or use a service, persuasion plays a significant role. It would be simplistic, however, to pronounce all advertising to be propaganda. If a message of persuasion is judged to benefit the source but not the receiver, then it should be recognized as propaganda. To a great extent, advertising does not fall into this category because it benefits society by sharing information, stimulating the economy, creating competition, reducing the cost of goods, and supporting print, broadcast, and cyber media.

Categories of Propaganda

Oliver Thomson, author of *Mass Persuasion in History* (1977), has suggested that there are seven categories of propaganda: political, economic, war (or military), diplomatic, didactic, ideological (or religious), and escapist (or diversionary). Although his scheme classifies consumer advertising as a form of economic propaganda, it is one of the less insidious forms. Even if advertising were proven not to be propaganda, however, there would still be the issue of content. Advertising messages are infused with ideology and myth, shaping the viewer's perceptions. It is not just products that are offered for sale but a way of life and a worldview, though such messages are often subtle. In *Advertising, the Uneasy Persuasion: Its Dubious Impact on American Society* (1984), Michael Schudson pointed out that during the 20th century advertising approaches shifted from the logical to the emotional, which complicates the discussion about propaganda. Modern advertising often transmits a superficial representation rather than a view of reality, what Schudson defines as "capitalist realism." But propaganda, as traditionally understood, is usually more purposeful and direct.

According to Alfred McClung Lee in his book *How to Understand Propaganda* (1952), propaganda is "one of the key instruments of power seekers." Generally speaking, propaganda is a systematic scheme or concerted effort to influence a body of people to accept and act on particular ideas, doctrines, ideologies, myths, and practices. As traditionally understood, propaganda focuses its attention on the political. The most effective propaganda disguises itself as fact or news, whereas it actually is comprised of half-truths purposely constructed to bias the receiver's judgment or opinions. In most cases propaganda is achieved by psychological manipulation, especially by the use of symbols, and it is disseminated by mass communications. The "negative advertisements" frequently broadcasted during U.S. political campaigns could be considered a form of propaganda. Brainwashing is an extreme form of propaganda, a process of using subtle or crude mental and physical pressure and torture to achieve indoctrination. Communistic brainwashing is the theme of the cold war film *The Manchurian Candidate* (1962).

Propaganda in repressive and totalitarian regimes is typically wedded to terror and backed up by force or the threat of force, creating an atmosphere of oppression and a situation in which human rights are violated. Such settings are characterized by managed information and outright censorship, which should not be confused with public relations as practiced in democratic societies. Although public relations managers operating in a free society are advocates for an employer, client, or cause, they have a professional sense of responsibility and accountability to the public. Unlike leaders of repressive regimes, the public relations agent in an open society must strive for credibility by contending with competition from a number of sources of information.

The Early Development of Propaganda

The use of the term *propaganda* can be traced to 22 June 1622, when Pope Gregory XV established the Congregato de Propaganda Fide (Congregation for the Propagation of Faith). The purpose of the organization was "to reconquer by spiritual arms, by prayers and good works, by preaching and catechising, the countries . . . lost to the [Catholic] Church in the debacle of the sixteenth century and to organize into an efficient corps the numerous missionary enterprises for the diffusion of the gospel in pagan lands." A counter to the Protestant Reformation, the group aimed to propagate Roman Catholic doctrines. Hence, the English word *propaganda* was derived from the Latin, literally meaning "propagation." In this sense propaganda was not originally considered sinister or malevolent. If Protestants were displeased with the reassertion of Catholic missions, it was not because they opposed religious proselytizing but rather because they opposed the type of proselytizing being carried out by Catholics.

It was the invention of the printing press that enabled the Reformation leaders to attack Catholic hegemony, for it provided a way for ideas to be widely disseminated. Protestants printed and circulated pamphlets and broadsheets that viciously attacked Catholicism, and Catholics responded in kind. The religious wars of the 17th century were essentially propaganda battles—with political agendas—that utilized technology to influence the masses. Although the concept of propaganda was discussed by Plato and Aristotle and later put into practice by the rulers of ancient Rome (emperor worship, like the cult of Vladimir Lenin, was ritualized propaganda), it was not until the Protestant Reformation that propaganda was linked with mass communications.

It is important to underscore the fact that modern propaganda came out of a European context. The Enlightenment, with its emphasis on knowledge and science, was a contributing factor, for it inspired a sense of will to challenge religious authorities. The Enlightenment also encouraged individualism, which presented new challenges for rulers in both the sacred and secular realms. Because the public now demanded to be reasoned with, maintaining control of the social order would henceforth require new approaches. Such cultural dynamics created a need for persuasion, as tradition alone was not strong enough to control restless individualism.

Propaganda in the 20th Century

The necessity for persuasion gave birth to propaganda at a time when available technology enabled it to have a wide audience. In *Propagandes* (1962; translated as *Propaganda: The Foundation of Men's Attitudes,* 1965), the French philosopher Jacques Ellul noted this link between technology and propaganda and argued that by necessity developed nations exist in an environment of propaganda. If Ellul's thesis is an exaggeration, as some have suggested, it is nonetheless true that many of the propaganda channels—television, radio, the press, cinema, leaflets and flyers, music, literature, and the Internet—are part of the very same communications infrastructure upon which society relies for its existence and identity. The fact that modern propaganda is a European legacy perhaps explains why fears about mass persuasion largely remain a Western concern.

Film is a propaganda channel that has been used extensively in many societies in order to foster certain viewpoints. John Stuart Blackton's *Tearing Down the Spanish Flag* (1898), supporting the U.S. invasion of Cuba during the Spanish-American War, is considered the world's first propaganda film. D. W. Griffith's film *The Birth of a Nation* (1915) is a work of propaganda, portraying the Confederate states as victims of Reconstruction and thus rationalizing Southern policies toward blacks. Likewise, Sergei Eisenstein's *Potemkin* (1925) depicted atrocities under the czars as justification for the Russian Revolution. *The East Is Red* (1965), a musical with a cast of 3,000, honored Mao Zedong as the savior of China. U.S. films addressing social problems associated with drugs, alcoholism, and sexual promiscuity have included the documentaries *Chinese Opium Den* (1894), *Father and Drunkard* (1908), *Whatsoever a Man Soweth* (1917), and *Reefer Madness* (1938). The 1941 Nazi film *Ich klage an* (I Accuse) argued for the right of the state to impose euthanasia. The U.S. pro-life film *The Silent Scream* (1985) graphically argued against abortion by depicting the procedure as an act of murder.

Radio has also served as an important propaganda channel. In 1916 Russia became the first nation to use shortwave radio to transmit propaganda, appealing to German soldiers to desert. The BBC, founded on 1 January 1927, was conceived as a means of uniting the scattered British Empire. When the Nazis came to power in 1933, they launched an aggressive shortwave broadcasting campaign to legitimize their government. During the war that followed, Germany had the highest number of household radios, the result of a policy that provided inexpensive radio receivers in order to better control the populace. In 1933 Japan took steps to seal off foreign broadcasts by banning the ownership of shortwave radios in the home country as well as in occupied territories. The Axis powers attempted to demoralize U.S. servicemen with the radio shows of Berlin Betty and Tokyo Rose. During the cold war, Radio Free Europe and Radio Liberty beamed U.S. programming at Eastern Europe and the Soviet Union, respectively, in an attempt to penetrate the Iron Curtain.

That propaganda has become something negative, particularly in the United States and Europe, is in large measure owing to the legacies of both world wars and the cold war. In fact, the 20th century may well be remembered as a period in which propaganda became a major preoccupation of the developed nations. In less than a hundred years there was a shift from local political and ideological controls to a worldwide struggle for social and cultural dominance. The cold war represented the culmination of what was essentially global propaganda warfare.

It is interesting to note that it was not Winston Churchill but Joseph Goebbels, the Nazi propaganda chief, who was the first to use the term *iron curtain* as a metaphor for Soviet ideological and political control. As Goebbels stated after the 1945 Yalta Conference:

> If the Germans lay down their arms, the whole of eastern and southeastern Europe, together with the Reich, would come under Russian occupation. Behind an iron curtain, mass butchering of people would begin, and all that would remain would be a . . . dull fermenting mass of millions of proletarian and despairing slave animals knowing nothing of the outside world.

Goebbels thus offered a prediction of the postwar period, an analysis that would be adopted by Western statesmen and pundits in the subsequent cold war with the Soviet Union. Considering that the two world wars were interrelated conflicts and that propaganda was a major feature in both, it is not surprising that propaganda came to play a role in later international disputes. If, in the eyes of the victors, Germany was in the wrong twice, it is ironic that Western leaders would come to perpetuate the most gifted Nazi propagandist's analysis of the Soviet Union.

World War I

World War I was marked by the systematic use of propaganda as a tool of warfare. It also was the first time national governments had used massive propaganda campaigns to control public opinion. Four propaganda objectives were apparent: to generate hatred toward the enemy; to maintain alliances; to obtain cooperation of neutral parties; and to intimidate the enemy. Both sides were guilty of exaggerating the events of the battlefield, especially in portraying the enemy as barbaric and cruel, a tactic now known as "atrocity propaganda." Britain, for example, fabricated news accounts that the Germans had established "corpse factories" for producing glycerin. (Consequently, during World War II some people initially disbelieved reports about the Nazi concentration camps, assuming the allegations to be the handiwork of propagandists.)

Propaganda contributed to bringing the United States into World War I and forcing Russia to withdraw. Both Germany and Britain made considerable efforts to manipulate American public thinking, with appeals through art and printed material. Germany targeted German émigrés and Irish-Americans, seeing these groups as possible starting points in gaining a broader influence. One German propaganda effort, *The War Plotters of Wall Street,* actually became an American best-seller. British propaganda aimed at the United States emphasized the traditional and cultural ties between the two countries, while at the same time excluding Germany. England spent considerable sums on propaganda intended to draw the United States into the war. Although Germany failed in its American propaganda, by orchestrating the return of Vladimir Lenin to the czarist capital, it managed to set up events for Russia's withdrawal.

The United States entered the war in 1917 after German U-boats had sunk several American ships. The initial difficulty the U.S. government faced was mobilizing its citizenry, which included a sizable pacifist and isolationist segment as well as large minority groups of Austrians, Germans, Poles, and Russians. On 1 April 1917, President Woodrow Wilson established the Committee on Public Information (CPI), appointing George Creel as its director, to prepare the home front for making war.

Creel initiated a propaganda campaign with the slogan, "The war to end all wars." He persuaded newspapers to print CPI-sponsored articles that explained America's purpose in entering the conflict. CPI cartoons that depicted the German leader, William II, as monstrous and inhumane were also published by national newspaper chains. CPI produced movies, including one that portrayed the kaiser about to rape a woman dressed as the Statue of Liberty. The Four-Minute Men program covered the nation with wartime speeches in the form of pre-approved four-minute scripts that were read throughout the country by 70,000 individuals. War posters—9 million were printed in 1918 alone, among them James Montgomery Flagg's celebrated depiction of a pointing Uncle Sam ("I Want You . . .")—were a ubiquitous reminder of the struggle. The American government, acting as the gatekeeper of information, carefully managed the news of the war in its sanitized *Official Bulletin.*

After World War I, scholarly attention focused on the dangers of propaganda and mass communications. Harold D. Lasswell, in *Propaganda Techniques in the World War* (1927), saw the propagandist as banging a hammer on the anvil of the masses and shaping society as a result. Such ideas exaggerating the effectiveness of propaganda gave rise to the first mass communications theory. Known by different names and variations—"bullet theory," "hypodermic-needle theory," and "stimulus-response theory"—the idea was that most people were extremely naive and received messages passively. It was assumed that if the messages of mass communications hit their targets, the desired results, whether for good or for evil, would be achieved.

The Institute for Propaganda Analysis, established in New York in October 1937, was founded to counter what was perceived as a blind spot among the public. Its stated mission was "to help the intelligent citizen to detect and to analyze propaganda,

by revealing the agencies, techniques, and devices used by propagandists." Ironically, after the Japanese attack on Pearl Harbor the institute suspended its operations. But one of its lasting contributions was the identification of seven basic propaganda devices: name-calling (or labeling), glittering generalities, transference, testimonials, appeals to plain folks, card stacking, and the bandwagon effect.

These devices became the standard for assessing political propaganda as well as advertisements for products. The name-calling tactic labels an idea or object in a negative light. Its opposite is the glittering generality, associating the subject with something virtuous. The technique of transference links the focus of attention with something that people admire, whereas the testimonial links it with a personality. The plain folks device seeks acceptance by appealing to ordinary people. Card stacking presents a one-sided argument. The bandwagon approach attempts to convince the receivers that "everybody is doing it"—i.e., the idea or object is accepted by everyone around them. The effectiveness of these devices has not been convincingly proven, but it seems that they work on some of the people only some of the time. Nonetheless, the seven propaganda devices pervade modern life as they are used in advertising and public relations campaigns.

Use of Propaganda by the Soviets

Certainly another reason for the studied interest in the power of propaganda was the rise of the Soviet Union. At first the Russian Revolution was welcomed by the Western powers, especially the United States, because it was seen as an overthrow of an autocratic and oppressive government. However, the new regime, which called for a worldwide revolution to depose capitalism, also disturbed and alarmed outside observers. Rule by a "dictatorship of the proletariat" (Karl Marx's concept of a dogma-trained elite) crushed dissent and eliminated political opposition, something considered intolerable by Western leaders. As early as 1902 Lenin, the leader of the new regime, had outlined his strategy and propaganda methods in *Shto Dyelat? (What's to Be Done?).* He was considered the first politician to plan political propaganda with care and at the same time to think in terms of disseminating his ideas globally. In addition, he distinguished between propaganda and agitation, the latter involving more of a call to action.

Newspapers were important propaganda tools in the Soviet Union. Often they were pasted on walls and bulletin boards so that every member of the public could read them. The goal was to make a "new Soviet man." The communist leaders strictly controlled the two major newspapers—*Pravda* (Truth) and *Izvestia* (News)—and they provided a daily ritual of political dogma and news presented from a strict ideological perspective. (In time, Soviet citizens circulated the joke that "*Pravda* is not *Izvestia,* and *Izvestia* is not *Pravda,*" an indication that propaganda did not always fool the Soviet proletariat.) Lenin also instituted what would become a tradition of sloganeering. "Bread, peace, and land" was the theme of the revolution, the three-fold promise of ending the food shortage in the cities, withdrawing from the war against Germany, and providing land to the people. "All power to the Soviets" was the principal slogan, which rationalized the dictatorship (the carefully controlled soviets, or councils) that was, according to theory, to usher in a glorious communist society.

After Lenin's death Joseph Stalin took control and ruled the U.S.S.R. from 1924 to 1953. His purges of the 1930s, in which millions were put to death or sent to the gulag, were an example of terror and force wedded to propaganda. Stalin used show trials to purge the Soviet bureaucracy of any potential threats to his absolutism. Such trials, which included scripted confessions, were dramatically broadcasted on the radio and reported in the press. Stalin used the memory of Lenin in a ceremonial and bizarre way, preserving the deceased leader's body and putting it on permanent public display in a mausoleum on Moscow's Red Square. By creating and building on myths, Stalin himself became a myth in his own lifetime. Nikita Khrushchev, his successor, later denounced Stalinism for its "cult of personality."

In Soviet society, commercial advertisements were practically nonexistent. Stores were labeled by their utilitarian purpose: bread, dairy, meat, hardware. The labels on product packages were likewise bland and uniform, merely identifying the contents. The "name brand" concept was not a significant factor in Soviet consumerism, although on the black market certain Western goods were highly coveted. The pomp and pageantry of military parades, such as the annual May Day spectacle in Red Square, were more important for the regime than the advertisement of goods and services.

Hitler and Mussolini

While Lenin and Stalin were attempting to build a new society, Adolf Hitler was remaking Germany. In *Mein Kampf* (1925) Hitler proposed to conquer the world and at the same time "disintegrate the present state of affairs and to infiltrate it with a new doctrine." The Ministry of Public Enlightenment and Propaganda put into operation Nazi social controls. Hitler's propaganda techniques were not characterized by the dissemination of abstract doctrines but instead relied on the repetition of simple phrases, ruthless and violent attacks on critics and enemies, a refusal to allow objectivity, and the singling out of scapegoats (first the so-called Versailles Traitors, then communists, and finally Jews). Goebbels's "big lie" strategy operated under the principle that an outrageous untruth could become conventional wisdom if told repeatedly. Spectacle and ancillary symbols, most notably the black swastika, were also Nazi propaganda tools.

Benito Mussolini, the Italian fascist leader and ally of Hitler, coined the term *totalitario* to describe his regime. "All within the state, none outside the state, none against the state" was his definition of fascism. Americans adopted the term *totalitarianism* to describe both fascism and communism, often referring to one as "brown fascism" and the other as "red fascism." While Hitler justified the aggression of Germany by citing the humiliation the country had received after World War I, Mussolini decreed that it was necessary for Italy to reassert itself and to regain parts of the territory of the Roman Empire. Meanwhile, Japanese propaganda

(or "thought war," as it was called) explained that the militarism of the Rising Sun, that is, of Japan, was an effort to save Asia from colonial subjugation and Western exploitation, including the prevention of a communist takeover of China. After being attacked by Germany, the Soviet Union propagandized that it was fighting a "fatherland war" and cited past examples of thwarted invasions from the West, including Napoleon's 1812 campaign.

World War II

World War II can be seen as a clash of ideologies, a struggle among democracy, fascism, and communism. The conflict was cast in ideological terms when U.S. President Franklin D. Roosevelt and Prime Minister Winston Churchill of Britain signed the Atlantic Charter, a joint declaration issued on 14 August 1941. The Atlantic Charter was essentially a propaganda document that established an ideological basis for the union of the Allies. The manifesto declared a vision of a postwar world, including four freedoms: freedom of speech, freedom of worship, freedom from fear, and freedom from want. Despite the ideological contradictions, both Britain and the United States welcomed the Soviet Union as an ally to help defeat Hitler.

U.S. propaganda during World War II employed two psychological approaches to rally public support, and a different type of poster was used for each strategy. The first appealed to patriotic sensitivities, using the colors red, white, and blue and showing images of strength such as fists and muscles, tools and equipment, and artillery and tanks. Slogans for this group included "United we win," "Man the guns," and "Keep 'em fighting." The second tactic was negative and unromantic, tapping into fear and hatred; it employed posters that showed the realities of war in human costs. These posters featured images of corpses, blood, and gravestones accompanied by words designed to counter complacency: "Warning! Our homes are in danger now," "This is Nazi brutality," "He knew the meaning of sacrifice."

Cinema was an important propaganda channel for all nations fighting in the war. Germany and the United States made films that are now considered classics of propaganda. Although there were similarities between the two, there also were notable differences. Leni Riefenstahl, a film director working for Hitler, actually inspired Frank Capra, who made films as a major in the U.S. Army. Riefenstahl's films were documentaries that romanticized the Nazi Party. Her first film in this vein was *Sieg des Glaubens* (Victory of Faith), which was released in 1933. But the film she is most remembered for is *Triumph des Willens* (Triumph of Will), a celebration of a week-long Nazi Party rally held in Nuremberg in September 1934. Another of her works, also permeated with Nazi ideology, is *Olympia*, a two-part film on the 1936 Berlin Olympic Games.

Triumph des Willens premiered on 28 March 1935. Its purpose was to demonstrate to the German people the solidarity of the Nazis and to introduce the leaders of the party. After its release the film was shown in German cities during a four-week run and probably was viewed by nearly every adult. The rally was an impressive propaganda event, attended by a million and a half people, and the film is powerful and highly artistic, but it has all

In an effort to stir up patriotic sentiment, this 1941 ad described a world where Americans were forced to acknowledge Adolf Hitler as God.

of the appearances of a documentary. It begins with Hitler's plane coming out of the clouds, accompanied by an orchestral version of the Nazi anthem. These words then appear on the screen: "Twenty years after the outbreak of the war, sixteen years after Germany's crucifixion, nineteen months after the commencement of the German renaissance, Adolph Hitler flew to Nuremberg again to review the columns of his faithful adherents." The German viewer, if he or she were not one with the masses, would have had to feel socially isolated.

Ironically, *Triumph des Willens* inspired the American "Why We Fight" series. Produced by Capra, the "Why We Fight" films were designed to foster troop morale and to counter isolationist feelings among the American public. The project had a threefold aim: to show that the United States was in danger and had no choice but to fight; to show in graphic detail the brutality and totalitarianism of the opposition; and to show the fighting spirit and courage of the Allies. *Prelude to War*, the first of the series, was viewed by 9 million soldiers and made available free of charge to commercial theaters across the United States. Six other films followed: *The Nazi Strike, Divide and Conquer, The Battle of Britain, The Battle of Russia, The Battle of China,* and *War Comes to America.*

Capra's wartime films consisted of compilations of footage obtained from other sources, including the enemy's own propaganda films. In addition, new film was shot and spliced in as needed, along with animation provided by Disney Studios. The narration and musical scores were what achieved the intended effect of making the images of the Allies positive and the images of the Axis powers frightening. Strategies for conveying the American ideology included simple, direct narration and the repetition of statements. In addition, praise of Allied determination and courage was contrasted with condemnation of the enemy's brutality and ignorance of freedom. Quotes from enemy leaders "proved" their duplicity, as with Hitler's statement in a 1938 interview: "I am willing to sign anything. I will do anything to facilitate the success of my policy."

Propaganda in Communist China

After World War II China experienced a revolution in which the Marxist leader Mao Zedong achieved power. He borrowed many ideas about propaganda and agitation from the Soviets, and the works of Lenin and Stalin were standard reading fare for Chinese communists. Ideological warfare was considered "the fundamental form of class struggle." The classic Chinese Marxist dictum "thought determines action" equated mass persuasion with the socialization of the people's minds. "Our people are poor and blank," explained Mao, "but the most beautiful poem can be written on a blank sheet of paper." This was similar to Stalin's remark that "the writer is an engineer of the human soul."

In a speech given on 1 February 1942, Mao suggested that propaganda was like medical treatment, as if not having the correct political thinking were a form of illness:

Any person who has committed errors is welcome to treatment until he is cured and becomes a good comrade, so long as he does not conceal his malady for fear of taking medicine or persist in his errors until he becomes incorrigible, but honestly and sincerely wishes to be cured and made better.

In the same speech Mao elaborated on the course of treatment, an example of brainwashing: "In reasoning we must begin by administering a shock and shouting at the patient, 'You are ill!' so that he is frightened into a sweat, and then we tell him gently that he needs treatment."

Not all of the propaganda approaches by Chinese Marxists were of foreign origin. The accumulated political and cultural experience of China could be found in the regime's thinking. For example, Mao's writings were punctuated with Chinese proverbs and maxims, such as "To become a new man" or "Submission by mouth is not nearly as desirable as submission by heart." Likewise, Peng Chen, Mao's propaganda minister, made use of parables based on the theme of good peasants against evil landlords.

What was new to China was the mass spectacle, which was copied from the Soviets and perhaps, indirectly, from Hitler as well. The Long March of 1934 gave a mythical quality to the regime, as did Mao's nine-mile swim in the Yangste River when he was 73 years old. These feats gave Mao an aura of invincibility. The 6,215-mile Long March, a grueling tactical retreat from the forces of Chiang Kai-shek, inspired many Chinese to join the Communist Party. As with Lenin and Stalin, a cult of personality developed around Mao. During the Cultural Revolution, which began in 1966, Chinese citizens carried with them small red books that featured selected statements from their leader. "Mao is the red, red sun in our hearts," crowds chanted in his presence. The Cultural Revolution relied on writers and artists to promote an insular ideology that presented Western values as outside threats.

A Pervasive Technique

If publicity is considered to be a somewhat benign form of propaganda, then propaganda campaigns have been a characteristic of all societies, democratic as well as totalitarian. Many social movements have relied on publicity campaigns to educate and convince the public. For example, both Amnesty International (an advocacy group for political prisoners) and Greenpeace (an environmental organization) have disseminated their messages globally by means of publicity. MADD (Mothers Against Drunk Driving) has campaigned against intoxicated drivers with billboards and slogans, and the American Cancer Society has attacked cigarette smoking with extensive public-service announcements. The nuclear freeze movement of the 1980s was a propaganda effort instigated by the Soviet Union. The plaque left on the Moon by the *Apollo 11* astronauts might be considered a propaganda stunt, for it proclaimed, "We came in peace," at a time when the United States considered space to have practical military uses.

The public domain is filled with discourse that is either propaganda or persuasion, depending on the intent of the sender and the attitude of the receiver. Examples of such potentially ambiguous discourse include such slogans as "Give peace a chance" (Vietnam War protesters), "Just say no!" (National Council on Drugs), "Guns don't kill people. People do" (National Rifle Association), "Right to life" (National Right to Life anti-abortion movement), and "Workers of the world, unite" (Karl Marx and Friedrich Engels). Whether persuasion or propaganda, advertising is often the means of getting out the message.

In 1941 the Advertising Council was formed to produce television spots for "good causes," which was part of a concerted effort to present the advertising industry as do-gooders. The resulting "cause marketing" introduced wholesome cultural icons such as Smokey Bear for the National Forest Service and the "Crying Indian" for the Keep America Beautiful campaign, but any attempt to effect social change cannot escape the propagandistic connotation. The legendary Apple Computer TV commercial "1984," aired only once (during the 1984 Superbowl), did a twist on the theme of propaganda by presenting an Orwellian world and suggesting that its product—the Apple Macintosh computer—offered a way to escape the oppression of IBM as "Big Brother." Marshall McLuhan's aphorism "the medium is the message" presents a dilemma for anyone wishing to distinguish propaganda from advertising (or vice versa), but Michael J. Phillips in *Ethics and Manipulation in Advertising* (1997) argues that despite everything, the human agency of the target audience prevails.

ROGER CHAPMAN

See also color plate in this volume

Further Reading

Berg-Pan, Renata, *Leni Riefenstahl,* Boston: Twayne, 1980

Cole, Robert, editor, *The Encyclopedia of Propaganda,* 3 vols., Armonk, New York: Sharpe Reference, 1998

Earle, Richard, *The Art of Cause Marketing: How to Use Advertising to Change Personal Behavior and Public Policy,* Chicago: NTC Business Books, 2000

Ellul, Jacques, *Propagandes,* Paris: Colin, 1962; as *Propaganda: The Formation of Men's Attitudes,* translated by Konrad Kellen and Jean Lerner, New York: Knopf, 1965

Hunter, Edward, *Brainwashing: The Story of Men Who Defied It,* New York: Farrar Straus and Cudahy, 1956; enlarged edition, as *Brainwashing: From Pavlov to Powers,* New York: Bookmailer, 1960

Jackall, Robert, editor, *Propaganda,* New York: New York University Press, and London: Macmillan, 1995

Jowett, Garth S., and Victoria O'Donnell, *Propaganda and Persuasion,* Newbury Park, California: Sage, 1986; 3rd edition, Thousand Oaks, California, and London: Sage, 1999

Lasswell, Harold D., *Propaganda Technique in the World War,* New York: Knopf, and London: Paul Trench Trubner, 1927; reprint, as *Propaganda Technique in World War I,* Cambridge, Massachusetts: MIT Press, 1971

Lee, Alfred McClung, *How to Understand Propaganda,* New York: Rinehart, 1952

Maland, Charles J., *Frank Capra,* Boston: Twayne, 1980

McLuhan, Marshall, *Understanding Media: The Extensions of Man,* New York: McGraw-Hill, 1964

Packard, Vance, *The Hidden Persuaders,* New York: McKay, and London: Longmans, 1957; revised edition, New York: Pocket, 1980; London: Penguin, 1981

Phillips, Michael J., *Ethics and Manipulation in Advertising: Answering a Flawed Indictment,* Westport, Connecticut: Quorum Books, 1997

Schudson, Michael, *Advertising, the Uneasy Persuasion: Its Dubious Impact on American Society,* New York: Basic Books, 1984

Thomson, Oliver, *Mass Persuasion in History: An Historical Analysis of the Development of Propaganda Techniques,* New York: Crane Russak, and Edinburgh: Harris, 1977

West, Darrell M., *Air Wars: Television Advertising in Elections Campaigns, 1952–2000,* third edition, Washington, D.C.: Congressional Quarterly Press, 2001

Yu, Frederick T.C., *Mass Persuasion in Communist China,* New York: Praeger, and London: Pall Mall, 1964

Prudential Insurance Company

Principal Agencies
J. Walter Thompson Company
Ted Bates Worldwide (later Backer Spielvogel Bates Worldwide)
Lowe & Partners/SMS
Deutsch/Dworin, Inc.
Fallon McElligott

Prudential Insurance Company of America—since 2001 known as Prudential Financial, Inc.—is a global insurance and financial services company with one of the most recognizable trademarks in the world, "The Rock," inspired by the Rock of Gibraltar. In 2002 Prudential had total assets of $564 billion, $22.1 billion in total equity, more than $1 trillion of life insurance in force, and 15 million customers. The company was organized in 1875 as the Prudential Friendly Society by John Dryden in Newark, New Jersey. Dryden, an itinerant insurance agent, took the Prudential part of the name from the Prudential Assurance Company of London, England, and adopted its strategy of offering low-cost "industrial" insurance to the working class. The British company, which raised no objection to the venture, even provided early support.

In 1895, while returning from Europe, Dryden met Charles Austin Bates, an advertising agent. Bates convinced Dryden of the importance of modern advertising methods but was unable to meet Dryden's request to create an emblem that represented the company's principles. Previous advertising simply had associated the company's 11-story Prudential Building in Newark with the phrase "Tower of strength."

After his discussion with Bates, Dryden turned to Mortimer Remington, an account executive with the J. Walter Thompson Company in New York City. Company tradition holds that while riding on a train from Newark to New York City, Remington saw a rocky hill that reminded him of the Rock of Gibraltar—and thus found his metaphor for stability. An alternative story has him copying a picture of Gibraltar from a library book and superimposing on it the slogan, "The Prudential has the strength of Gibraltar." An advertisement bearing the new symbol and slogan first appeared on 20 August 1896 in *Leslie's Weekly*.

Prudential's logo subsequently became the heart of its brand identity. Actual chunks of the Rock of Gibraltar sometimes were incorporated into the structure of Prudential buildings as publicity gimmicks. During the early stages of World War II, the company temporarily deleted the slogan from its advertisements because it feared that Nazi General Erwin Rommel's Afrika Corps might seize Gibraltar. After the war the slogan was restored but was again abandoned in the 1970s when Gibraltar became the source of political tensions between the United Kingdom and Spain. The company's "Own a piece of the Rock" advertising campaign was developed under the direction of Henry E. Arnsdorf, vice president for public relations and advertising, in the home office.

Prudential entered the television market early, sponsoring the *Prudential Family Theater,* a one-hour dramatic anthology series carried by CBS on Tuesday nights from 10 October 1950 to 27 March 1951. Other sponsorships included *Your Show of Shows,* starring Sid Caesar and Imogene Coca, on NBC. The comedy program ran on Saturday nights from 25 February 1950 to 5 June 1954. In the 1970s Prudential also bought advertising time as a participating sponsor from CBS to support its long-running *M*A*S*H* series. But the program with which Prudential was most closely identified was *The Twentieth Century,* a CBS documentary series hosted by Walter Cronkite on Sunday evenings from 1957 to 1969. In 1966 *The Twentieth Century* became *The Twenty-First Century.* Each program began with the series title superimposed over a picture of the Rock, which iconically represented history itself.

Chief Executive Officer Robert Beck became dissatisfied with the symbol in 1978 as the company continued to expand globally and to reposition itself as a financial services conglomerate with subsidiaries in the banking, real estate, and investment industries. Lee & Young Communications, a New York City firm specializing in corporate identities, helped Prudential introduce a new symbol in 1984. The traditional Rock was replaced by a series of diagonal lines of varying widths, suggesting dynamic change while retaining an impression of the original symbol. The new Rock was supported by an advertising and public relations campaign intended to gain acceptance for the implied change of identity. In the 1990s the symbol was again modified, this time to reflect the more traditional design used in the 1970s.

In 1970 Prudential began a 20-year relationship with Ted Bates & Company, Inc. Capitalizing on the popularity of *Heaven Can Wait,* a 1978 film, Prudential began a three-year series of commercials that took a somewhat lighthearted approach to death. A representative ad featured angels escorting a young man up a stairway to heaven as he says, "I thought I'd have more time." An angel replies, "Doesn't everybody?" When the agency's research showed increasing media coverage of so-called near death experiences, Prudential switched to a more somber approach to preparing for mortality. In 1987 Bates merged with Backer & Spielvogel to form Backer Spielvogel Bates Worldwide. After Prudential bought Bache, an investment and brokerage company, in 1981, Backer Spielvogel Bates launched a new campaign, based on the tag line "Rock solid. Market wise," for the new Prudential-Bache Securities. When the stock market crashed in 1987, the agency countered with advertising intended to restore confidence. Print advertising for Prudential-Bache Securities proclaimed, "Rock solid. Now, especially now, you need an investment firm that is rock solid."

In 1990 Prudential surprised Madison Avenue by switching its national advertising account to Lowe Marschalk, Inc., a unit of the Interpublic Group of Companies. However, a restructuring the following year led to the creation of Prudential Securities. Supported by a strong advertising campaign, the firm reported record earnings but had to defend itself against a U.S. Securities and Exchange Commission probe and investor lawsuits claiming

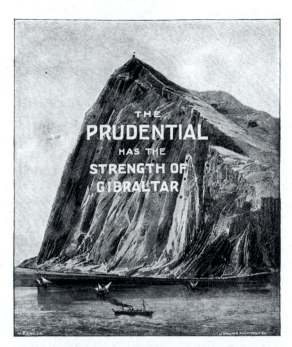

The Prudential Insurance Company of America adopted the Rock of Gibraltar as its symbol in 1896, one year before this ad was created for Prudential by the J. Walter Thompson Company.
Courtesy The Prudential Insurance Company of America.

that Prudential had misled investors. In 1994 Deutsch/Dworin created a defensive campaign based on the message, "Prudential Securities today. It starts with straight talk." However, an investor sued a stockbroker who appeared in a "straight talk" commercial, and Prudential Securities removed the ad.

In 1995 Prudential Insurance replaced Lowe & Partners/SMS (the renamed Lowe Marschalk) and hired Fallon McElligott. The agency devised a campaign intended to move the consumer from anxiety to empowerment with the theme "Live well. Make a plan. Be your own rock." The life-planning, financial responsibility concept, which *Advertising Age* termed "inner 'rock'-ness" and "a path to spiritual solace," featured, for example, a grandfather playing with children at the beach and intoning, "Prepare yourself well, not half well." Older people themselves became the solid "rocks" who replaced the company's institutional Rock. The campaign ran for six months.

In August 1996, however, Prudential moved its media and creative functions in-house. As of 2000 the company had no agency relationship of any kind.

When the Dow Jones Industrial Average plunged in the late summer months of 1998, Prudential placed 43 print ads and 59 television commercials during a two-week period. Print advertisements carried the headline, "In times like these, where can investors find solid ground?" Prudential's challenge in the 21st century will be to maintain a "solid ground" brand image and an advertising strategy that serves its diverse constituencies in a global marketplace. In 2001 Prudential converted from a mutual company to a publicly traded company and adopted the name Prudential Financial, Inc.

PAUL ASHDOWN

Further Reading

Campbell, Bruce, "Chipping Away at THE ROCK," *Working Woman* (November 1985)

Carr, William H.A., *From Three Cents a Week . . . : The Story of the Prudential Insurance Company of America,* Englewood Cliffs, New Jersey: Prentice Hall, 1975

Heed, Thomas J., and Carrie Rothburd, "The Prudential Insurance Company of America," in *International Directory of Company Histories, Volume 30,* edited by Jay P. Pederson, Chicago: St. James Press, 2000

May, Earl Chapin, and Will Oursler, *The Prudential: A Story of Human Security,* Garden City, New York: Doubleday, 1950

Sheehan, Robert, "That Mighty Pump, Prudential," *Fortune 69, no. 1* (January 1964)

Psychographics

The degree of success enjoyed by advertisers depends directly on how well they offer the right thing in the right way to the right audience. Success eludes advertisers that fail to recognize opportunities within a market, neglect to profile and understand their audiences, or fail to correctly translate market knowledge into campaign strategy. Therefore, advertisers routinely use psychographic research methods to profile audiences. A lucid psychographic profile, accurately grasped and integrated with other valuable background information, helps strategists to design effective advertising campaigns and more effectively disseminate their messages.

The audience profile should reveal something about how the audience relates to the offering. The California Milk Processor Board, for example, recognized that the non-Hispanic market could be persuaded to purchase more milk when reminded through humorous messages that running out of milk is an inconvenience. In contrast, audience profiles suggested that appeals claiming either that "milk is good for you" or that "milk makes food taste great" did not inspire them in ways that would boost declining milk sales.

Profiles are also intended to reveal the foundation upon which the advertiser can build empathy with the audience, leading to a more meaningful and relevant dialogue between buyers and sellers. Audiences attend to messages when their arguments and other elements are personally relevant and interesting. During the 1970s Merrill Lynch, a financial services firm, captured the attention of its audience through advertisements that superimposed its slogan "A breed apart" onto scenes of a solitary bull. The strategy was developed on the basis of a customer sketch that showed that persons who invested heavily in the stock market were independent-minded, upwardly mobile achievers.

Accurate profiles are signposts that distinguish valid creative directives from ineffective approaches that are likely to trigger what advertisers call "message derogation." Using a psychographic profile of young affluent people, the retailer Bergdorf Goodman found that this group rejects flashy brand images disseminated by well-known fashion designers. These consumers achieve status by setting trends rather than following them, and they therefore gravitate toward lesser-known specialty designers instead of established brands.

Lifestyle Research

To enrich basic demographic and geographic profiles, advertisers use psychographic methodology, or lifestyle research. Such research aims to understand the current or likely future lifestyles of particular types of consumers for the purposes of profiling, selecting, serving, and/or influencing markets. Although practitioners regularly interchange the terms *psychographics* and *lifestyles*, a distinction between the two concepts is warranted. The term *psychographics* refers to the methods used in lifestyle research to profile markets. The term *lifestyle* refers to the pattern of living that shapes how and why people choose to spend their time, money, and energy. A lifestyle is defined by taking into account the audience's demographics, values, activities and interests, relationships with product categories, tastes and preferences, personality traits, and self-image. Attitudes and opinions, expectations and desires, emotions, positions on issues, fears, and reactions to likely future scenarios have also been factored into psychographic profiles of market segments.

Market segmentation, or the separation of the mass market into more meaningful clusters, is a fundamental marketing task. Within each cluster, audience members share common needs or lifestyles, and those needs or lifestyles trigger particular responses to certain marketing and advertising strategies. The shared traits within one market segment separate its members from those in other clusters displaying different needs, habits, or preferences. By profiling market segments, marketers better understand each cluster, determine if a given group is of interest to the advertiser, and identify how best to serve and persuade the desirable consumers.

In the earliest attempts at market segmentation, demarcations were based on crude demographic and geographic variables (e.g., age, income, gender, occupation, region, climate, zip code, etc.) alone. Marketers began to realize, however, that such demographic and geographic variables failed to explain certain differences in buyer reactions to various marketing mixes. Researchers therefore found additional dimensions useful in profiling audiences, for example, usage rate (e.g., heavy, moderate, or light user of a product category), types of benefits or uses desired, attitudes, and prior commitments (e.g., home ownership defines the market for homeowner's insurance).

William Lazer's seminal 1963 article, "Life Style Concepts and Marketing," introduced the notion of lifestyle patterns as determinants of market behavior. His approach was a welcome addition to standard marketing segmentation methods, and lifestyle research was quickly embraced by advertisers. By the mid-1970s, practitioners had built a sufficient base of experience with psychometrics and lifestyle segmentation to permit synthesis and critical review.

Applications

Lifestyle research is more than a marketing and segmentation tool, however. Knowledge of lifestyles factors into creative advertising strategy and media planning. Such knowledge also helps shape usage stereotyping (recommended situations, conditions, and times when a product/service is especially useful) and other customer strategies. Microsoft, for example, when competing with America Online for Web surfers and advertisers, enhanced customer value by configuring its network to reflect the interests of particular consumers. Thus, Web users were linked quickly to advertisers serving their lifestyles.

In addition, psychographics is often applied by designers when shaping the form, outward appearance, or packaging of products. Lifestyle profiles also influence consumer sales promotions, determining the types of premiums offered and the kinds of prizes given away through contests and sweepstakes. Distribution strategies, affinity and continuity programs, retail store image and ambiance, merchandising tactics, and Web links are all grounded in lifestyle profiles. In general, psychographic analysis assists researchers in tracking shifts in the consumer psyche and assessing the fit between the needs of a market segment and the company's capability to satisfy those demands.

In advertising, psychographic profiles can help identify ways to present particular brands to consumers so those persons will link the products with their lifestyles. Media planners consider lifestyle profiles when selecting the appropriate media for their advertisements. In the 1980s and 1990s, the Television Bureau of

What it means to be a breed apart.

Imagination, instinct, and versatility (not size alone) set Merrill Lynch apart from the herd.
Too many people see only the size of Merrill Lynch; they miss the subtler qualities that truly make us a breed apart.
Imagination. Our investment

bankers came up with a creative way to raise $75 million for an oil exploration company.
Traditional ways of raising the capital would have overly diluted earnings or impaired financial flexibility. So we suggested, developed and placed a public offering of convertible preferred

stock—all within 40 days.
Instinct. One of our corporate clients wanted to buy back 200,000 shares of its own stock—in a week. Getting the best price was a question of market timing ...of knowing when to walk out of the market, when to watch and wait, when to move in and buy

aggressively. That's instinct.
And because of it, we were able to buy back the whole 200,000 shares within ½ point of the starting price.
Versatility. We can also help you reach your personal financial goals, despite changing markets and tough tax laws.

In 1953, a man walked into our St. Louis office and bought $487 worth of stock.
Over the years, he moved up in his company; as his assets grew and his needs changed, his Merrill Lynch Account Executive kept pace—with equities, commodities,

real estate partnerships. Now he's buying tax shelters in $10,000 lots.
How can Merrill Lynch's unmatched resources benefit you? Ask us. Find out what it means to deal with a breed apart.

Merrill Lynch
A breed apart.

Merrill Lynch's imagination, instinct, and versatility were characteristics that made the company "a breed apart," according to this 1979 print ad targeted at consumers who also valued these qualities.
Courtesy of Merrill Lynch.

Advertising, for example, recommended that computer advertisers place less emphasis on demographics and more importance on lifestyles when choosing appropriate television shows for their commercials, and the bureau accordingly suggested that good media buys were *Northern Exposure* and *Meet the Press,* two television programs that attracted "actualizers," a lifestyle segment highly receptive to technology. To influence another attractive technology segment labeled "experiencers," people who use computer technology for entertainment, education, and small business, the bureau suggested *Beverly Hills, 90210* and *Married . . . with Children.*

Lifestyle considerations now permeate the full spectrum of marketing and advertising planning activities, and the classes of variables included under the umbrella of psychographics have also expanded. Psychologists continue to produce a steady stream of creative techniques that probe deeper into the psychology of consumers. William Wells and Doug Tigert were among the pioneers in the field, and in the early 1970s they grouped psychographic variables into three categories: activities, interests, and opinions (AIO). Wells and Tigert used questionnaires (known as AIO

scales) to rank such activities as work, hobbies, entertainment, sports, and shopping; family life, fashion, and recreation were among the wider set of variables included under interests. In the decades since those initial studies were conducted, psychographic research has progressed to collecting opinions concerning social and other issues of the day, future perspectives, self-perceptions, personality traits, politics, business and economic climates, confidence in the economy, personal outlooks on relevant conditions, products, culture, and other factors.

Gathering Data

Psychographic research is based on either general lifestyle dimensions or specific product-market measurements. General lifestyle research uses questionnaires asking a broad cross section of questions that need not be directly related to narrow product-market factors. This type of barometric research permits advertisers to track shifts in psychographic variables over time, identifying the precursors of market change. In addition, general studies can be useful to companies marketing and advertising in foreign countries. General studies are typically considered to be secondary data, since they are fielded first by research firms and later sold to advertisers.

Secondary data on lifestyles are found in books and government documents. For example, *Lifestyle Market Analyst* is a bound reference guide published by Standard Rate and Data Service (SRDS) that provides profiles of audiences defined in terms of lifestyles, demographics, and geography. The first section of the guide consists of a geographical breakdown of the United States by area of dominant influence (ADI). Classifications are based on such factors as occupation, education, ethnicity, age, marital and family status, and credit card usage. Classifications are described in terms of absolute percentages and through an index facilitating a comparison of the local area to the national average. Across each ADI, consumer participation in a host of lifestyle activities is then grouped into five broad categories. The information enables advertisers to fully understand the characteristics of geographically defined target audiences. The second section is arranged by lifestyle activity, with descriptors portraying individuals who participate in specific lifestyle activities, such as Bible reading, physical exercise, and entertainment. The third section, organized by household characteristics, helps advertisers to understand demographically defined target audiences.

Profiles of lifestyles are found in syndicated studies published by marketing research firms and advertising agencies. SRI International in Menlo Park, California, publishes Values and Lifestyle Segmentation 2 (commonly referred to as VALS2), the most widely used psychographic tool for segmenting markets in the United States. VALS2 segments the adult U.S. population into eight groups—actualizers, fulfilleds, believers, achievers, experiencers, strivers, makers, and strugglers—and these profiles are based on differences uncovered in the attitudes, motivations, lifestyles, and resources of the various sectors. Profiles, in turn, are used to predict the receptivity of different segments both to advertising messages and products/services. General studies are commonly criticized as too unreliable, rigid, and simplistic. When developing an advertising campaign, advertisers often find the general findings irrelevant and unusable.

Psychographic profiles are found in syndicated geodemographic studies as well. Typically, geodemographic studies (also known as psychodemographic studies) segment the mass market on such dimensions as geography, demographics, and the media usage, lifestyle choices, possessions, and purchasing behavior of consumers. The *Sourcebook of ZIP Code Demographics,* published by CACI Marketing Systems, contains statistics on all residential zip codes in the United States. It provides information on population, gender, age distributions, ethnicity, households, and families. CACI's ACORN Clustering System provides information on specific populations as small as block groups (250–550 households), blocks (25–59 households), and ZIP+4 groups (6–25 households). The PRIZM system by Claritas, Inc., and Strategic Mapping's Cluster PLUS 2000 divide U.S. neighborhoods into 62 and 60 clusters, respectively. These types of studies are based on the notion that people living within the same local area are more likely to share characteristics and act in similar ways than individuals dispersed across the United States. However, they also uncover real differences within neighborhoods. In addition to analyzing geodemographic data to develop advertising strategy, marketers use geodemographic clusters to locate receptive customers, evaluate locations for special events, assess alternative retail sites, sharpen distribution strategy, target direct mail and sales promotions, and develop new products and services.

Product market–based psychographic instruments are designed to investigate a narrow set of areas directly related to the product market of interest to a particular advertiser. Typically, these studies are considered primary research because they are conducted at the request of an advertiser and are designed around a narrow set of preordained variables specifically related to the product market in question. A product market–based psychographic study is considered most meaningful to advertisers that seek specific insights into how and why a certain product category fits into the lifestyles of selected target audiences. For example, the Cahners In-Stat Group, a digital communications research firm, identified five potential customer groups for wireless telephone services that could not be distinguished on the basis of demographics alone.

Psychographic studies are conducted across the globe. Some advertisers have found success in global advertising (i.e., one message transferred uniformly across countries), but many other advertisers use psychographic research to adapt their messages to the cultural nuances of a country or region. For example, SRG/Nielsen identified several segments within the Chinese market: the "Little emperor" group (one-child families), "Chinese yuppies" (professionals with disposable incomes), "Working women" who use convenience products, and the older, more conservative "Practical minded" sector. A study of more than 3,200 Egyptian consumers by Wafai and Associates profiled four psychographic segments: "Variable traditionalists," "Rebels," "Enlightens," and the "Steeped establishment."

Psychographics will probably remain a mainstay of advertising strategy for the foreseeable future. Advertising planning efforts are enriched when audience profiles include demographic and psychographic descriptions. The utility of psychographics, however, will likely be tested by the desire on the part of advertisers to create uniform global messages. Another challenge facing psychographics may come from increasingly savvy consumers who are swayed only by credible, benefit-based claims of a brand's superiority rather than through abstract images and feelings-based appeals, which are derived mainly from lifestyle profiles.

ALLEN E. SMITH

See also color plate in this volume

Further Reading

Alsop, Ronald, "Advertisers Put Consumers on the Couch," *Wall Street Journal* (13 May 1988)

Bainbridge, Heather, "Beyond Demographics," *Wireless Review* 16, no. 11 (1999)

Crawford, C. Merle, *New Products Management*, Homewood, Illinois: Irwin, 1983; 6th edition, Boston: Irwin/McGraw-Hill, 2000

Cui, Geng, "The Different Faces of the Chinese Consumer," *China Business Review* 24, no. 4 (1997)

Davis, Joel J., *Advertising Research: Theory and Practice,* Upper Saddle River, New Jersey: Prentice Hall, 1997

"Egypt's Psychographics," *Market Africa Mid-East* 1, no. 13 (1996)

Lazer, William, "Life Style Concepts and Marketing," in *Toward Scientific Marketing: Proceedings of the Winter Conference, December 27–28, 1963,* edited by Stephen Greyser, Chicago: American Marketing Association, 1964

Plummer, Joseph T., "The Concept and Application of Life Style Segmentation," *Journal of Marketing* 38, no. 1 (1974)

Wells, William, "Psychographics: A Critical Review," *Journal of Marketing Research,* 12, no. 3 (1975)

Wells, William, John Burnett, and Sandra Moriarty, *Advertising: Principles and Practice,* London: Prentice-Hall International, and Englewood Cliffs, New Jersey: Prentice Hall, 1989; 5th edition, Upper Saddle River, New Jersey: Prentice Hall, 2000

Wells, William, and Doug Tigert, "Activities, Interests, and Opinions," *Journal of Advertising Research* 11 (1971)

Publicis Group

Founded as Publicis by Marcel Bleustein-Blanchet, 1926; purchased Intermarco, 1972; purchased Farner, 1972; engaged in stock swap with Foote, Cone & Belding, 1988; purchased Feldman, Calleux & Associés, 1993; purchased Hal Riney & Partners, 1998; purchased the Evans Group, 1998; name changed to Publicis Group, 2000; merged with Bcom 3, 2002.

Major Clients
Colgate-Palmolive Company
Hewlett-Packard Company
Nestlé
Renault
Shell Oil Company

Publicis was founded in 1926 in Paris, France. With the help of its radio station, Radio-Cité, Publicis became a well-known advertising force in France during the 1930s. It closed during World War II but reopened in 1946 and soon became France's second-largest advertising agency. In the 1940s Publicis was the first French agency to establish a market research department. In 1968 the agency produced France's first television commercial. Publicis and the U.S. advertising agency Foote, Cone & Belding (FCB) exchanged stock in 1988. The relationship soured, however, and by 1996 both companies were seeking to end the alliance, which was formally dissolved the following year. Publicis retained a 10 percent stake in True North Communications (formerly FCB).

Origins

Twenty-year-old Marcel Bleustein-Blanchet, son of Russian-Jewish émigrés, started Publicis in a Parisian working-class neighborhood in 1926. The first office was in a second-floor walkup: its two rooms formerly had been a kitchen. Bleustein-Blanchet had little business experience or formal education, but he possessed considerable charisma and organizational skills. Publicis's first cli-

ents were companies owned by Bleustein-Blanchet's relatives and friends: Levitan Furniture, André Shoes, and Brunswick Furs. By 1929 he was able to hire his first two employees, Roger Godard and Lucille Cazavan, who stayed with the company for the next 30 years.

The 1930s saw Publicis turn to the medium of radio. The print media in France were dominated by Havas, the country's largest advertising agency, press agency and seller of advertising space; Bleustein-Blanchet thus saw radio as an unexplored source of advertising accounts. He traveled the French countryside approaching provincial stations and offering them exclusive contracts to book their advertising space in return for guaranteeing them yearly revenue. With increased advertising revenue, Publicis moved to a more sophisticated office and by 1935 purchased its own radio station, which it renamed Radio-Cité. Radio-Cité became one of Paris's most popular radio stations with live entertainers such as Edith Piaf, Maurice Chevalier, and Josephine Baker. Radio-Cité also popularized radio game shows, the most famous being *Radio Crochet* (Radio Hook), in which amateur performers sang on stage until a hook pulled them off, ending the act. Radio-Cité also revolutionized radio news; its broadcast news staff offered hourly news briefs. By the late 1930s Radio-Cité had the largest advertising revenues of any French radio station with Publicis handling most of the accounts.

Expansion

Publicis turned to cinema advertising as well in the mid-1930s, producing many advertising shorts. Bleustein-Blanchet did more than merely produce commercials; he also established a subsidiary that managed the distribution of cinema advertising. By the time of World War II, Publicis had exclusive distribution rights to more than half of France's movie houses. Havas, Publicis's major competitor, took notice of its vibrant and smaller rival and signed an agreement with Publicis in 1938: the two took over the failing French film company, Gaumont. The venture included not only

Gaumont's production company but also its chain of movie houses.

Despite the success of Publicis in radio and cinema (media that accounted for just 5 percent of total French advertising spending), the company had only a small foothold in print media. Bleustein-Blanchet realized that in order to compete with Havas, which handled ad spending 20 times that of Publicis, his company had to increase its presence in print. As a result, Publicis launched the Régie-Presse in 1938. French advertising agencies usually did not approach a newspaper or magazine directly to buy advertising space but instead turned to an intermediary, a *régie*, to arrange the purchase of space for their clients. The *régie* would receive a commission for service on finding the space. Havas dominated this space-purchasing niche as well, so Publicis found its initial entry in this arena hard going.

Bleustein-Blanchet, always looking to innovate, traveled to the United States for the first time in 1938. While there, he had an extended meeting with David Sarnoff, president of the Radio Corporation of America (RCA) and its subsidiary, the National Broadcasting Company (NBC). Sarnoff introduced Bleustein-Blanchet to the pollster George Gallup. Bleustein-Blanchet later admitted to not understanding the mechanics of polling, but he did recognize the significance of polling for advertising and politics. Most French advertising had been based on intuition, hunches, or tradition. Publicis had little time to put these new techniques into practice, however, as war broke out the following year.

Soon after the German conquest of France in 1940 and under pressure from the Nazi-controlled Vichy government, Publicis closed its doors. Bleustein-Blanchet fled to unoccupied southern France and then Spain, eventually making his way to England where he joined the Free French Forces. At war's end he returned to Paris. His radio station's transmitter destroyed, his office requisitioned by French bureaucrats, his personal possessions few, Bleustein-Blanchet faced an uncertain future. With little to lose, he restarted Publicis in 1946, joined by many returning prewar employees. An important addition was his young nephew, Claude Marcus, who proved vital to the company's postwar professionalization.

Postwar Period

With nationalization of French radio broadcasting following the war, Publicis could no longer rely on radio advertising as its major revenue source. Accordingly, Publicis revived Régie-Presse to broker advertising space. While Publicis had little to work with in ravaged, postwar France, Havas too had experienced problems during the war and was in a state of disorder. The French state had an 80 percent stake in Havas and stripped the company of its news and information agency. By 1953 Régie-Presse brokered space for France's largest newspaper, *France-Soir,* and largest weekly magazine, *Nous Deux,* among many others.

Many of Publicis's old clients returned in the immediate postwar years and the firm was fortunate to land its first international (and American) client, Colgate-Palmolive Company, in 1947.

Publicis benefited from Colgate's technical expertise and applied the experience gained on the Colgate account to the French market. With the cachet of a large multinational marketer as a client, Publicis attracted other French and international enterprises, among them Nestlé, in 1952, Shell Oil Company, in 1954, and Renault, in 1962. Publicis even opened an office in New York City in the late 1950s, although its billings were small and limited mostly to a few French companies that marketed in the United States.

Publicis also helped small French companies grow into much larger businesses. Two such examples are Prénatal (maternity wear) and Boursin (cheese). Prénatal started as a husband-and-wife shop in the late 1940s; with marketing guidance and ads from Publicis, it grew to more than 200 stores throughout France 20 years later. Boursin in 1964 had been a regional cheese maker that did not believe much in advertising. Publicis devised a campaign with the slogan, "Du pain, du vin, et du Boursin" ("Some bread, some wine, and some Boursin"), which was wildly successful; sales increased tenfold over the next five years. In 1968—the year the first commercials appeared on French TV—Publicis ran the first television commercial in France, an ad for Boursin.

Publicis continued to innovate in the 1940s and 1950s. As a result of his meeting with George Gallup, Bleustein-Blanchet established France's first market research department in 1948. Its first important account came in the form of a public opinion poll for France's prime minister, Pierre Mendes-France, in 1954. Other French agencies soon followed suit, opening their own market research departments. To obtain additional new ideas, Publicis sent younger managers to advertising agencies in London and New York.

Publicis gained notoriety in 1958 by opening Le Drugstore in the ground floor of its new Champs-Élysées office (the former Astoria Hotel). Le Drugstore was a not a place to buy pharmaceuticals but a trendy café and retail outlet that sold magazines, electronic gadgets, and gifts. Such a combination was a marketing innovation for 1950s France. Despite opening during a period of growing anti-American political rhetoric in the late 1950s and early 1960s, Le Drugstore was a hit, as the French eagerly sought American goods and imitated American patterns of consumption.

The agency sought other sources of revenue in the early 1960s with the creation of two more internal departments. The first, Information Industrielle, encouraged marketers to place institutional advertisements, something French companies rarely did. The second, Jeunesse-informations ("Youth Information"), specialized in the placement of advertisements targeted at French youth. Its establishment coincided with the peak of France's postwar baby boom. Both departments also created ad campaigns.

Bleustein-Blanchet and Publicis also worked for the French government. Publicis did the advertising for a 1952 government bond issue ("You can bring a needed and decisive contribution to national recovery") that was the most successful issue of its kind up to that time. Publicis also helped reduce an oversupply of French beef in 1961 with its "Suivez le Boeuf" (Follow the Beef) campaign. Such relationships probably helped the agency land the state-controlled Renault account in 1962.

Internationalization

The 1960s witnessed Publicis continuing to modernize as the agency's first-generation employees were retiring. The agency recruited new executives from France's finest universities, something that would have been unheard of 20 years earlier when advertisers had a reputation as snake-oil sellers. Publicis had narrowly surpassed Havas to become France's largest advertising agency in billings by 1962. (Havas, though, would retake the lead in 1966.)

The most significant setback for Publicis came in 1972 when a fire completely gutted the agency's Parisian office. The potentially crippling blow was overcome by cooperation from Publicis's largest clients (Renault, Nestlé, and Colgate-Palmolive), which housed the agency's employees until Publicis could construct new headquarters. Even two competitors, Elvinger and Synergie, provided office space for the agency. By 1973 Publicis was reinstalled in its Champs-Élysées office adjacent to the Arc de Triomphe.

Simultaneously, in 1972, Publicis began to focus on foreign markets. The New York City office had few accounts, and Bleustein-Blanchet saw the U.S. market as too difficult to penetrate. Europe was another matter, however. Publicis's main problem was a shortage of cash. The solution for Bleustein-Blanchet was to sell 20 percent of his stake in the agency (which had been solely owned by the Bleustein-Blanchet family). This placed Publicis for the first time on the Paris Bourse (stock exchange). With new resources, Publicis purchased the Dutch advertising agency Intermarco (which handled the advertising for Philips Electronics) and the Swiss agency Farner, merging them as Intermarco-Farner. In terms of world advertising billings, Publicis ranked 26th and Intermarco-Farner 33rd; the combined billings of the two earned Publicis a place in the ranks of the world's top 20 ad agencies. With Intermarco-Farner, Publicis began to open offices in all Western European countries throughout the 1970s and early 1980s.

Still, Publicis had its eyes on the largest advertising market of all, the United States. Bleustein-Blanchet finally retired in 1988 after leading for more than 60 years. His successor, Maurice Lévy, had risen through the company ranks (he started in the then-small computer information department in the early 1970s) and had an appetite for further expansion, especially to compete with the ever-growing Havas and its subsidiary, Eurocom. Publicis and Lévy reached an agreement in early 1988 with the American agency Foote, Cone & Belding (FCB). Each agency was strong on its home continent but weak abroad; the two had no conflicting accounts. In a stock swap, each received a 20 percent stake in the other.

The alliance soon soured; however, Publicis purchased the French agency Feldman, Calleux & Associés (FCA) in 1993. FCA's American subsidiary, Bloom-FCA!, competed with FCB, which complained to Publicis. Meanwhile, FCB was in the process of a reorganization that would create the holding company True North Communications. In 1997, against Publicis's wishes, True North acquired Bozell, Jacobs, Kenyon & Eckhardt. This reorganization diluted Publicis's holdings in FCB to 11 percent. Publicis responded with an attempted hostile takeover of True North in late 1997, which failed.

By 1998 the two agencies were in a process of divorce. Despite the sour experience with FCB, Publicis felt pressure to seek further globalization but through acquisition rather than merger. Three laws passed by the French government in the 1990s further encouraged Publicis to intensify its extranational operations. The 1991 Evin Law (*Loi Evin*) forbade most tobacco and alcohol advertising; the 1992 Sapin Law (*Loi Sapin*) regulated media brokers and dropped the standard 15% commission for agencies, and the 1994 Toubon Law (*Loi Toubon*) required that all advertising be done in French. As a result of this legislation, combined with the French recession of the early 1990s, all ad agencies saw their profits dip, which made the relatively unregulated United States market all the more attractive.

Publicis continued its push for internationalization. It derived new revenue in 1994 by offering one-third of its stock on the Paris Bourse.

Under Lévy's leadership, Publicis became a true multinational force, acquiring offices in more than 76 countries in Asia and North and South America. After a failed hostile buyout of True North Communications in 1997, Publicis succeeded in making important acquisitions in the United States, purchasing Hal Riney & Partners and the Evans Group in 1998 and Frankel & Company and Fallon McElligot in 2000. Later in 2000 Publicis continued its purchasing spree, acquiring Saatchi & Saatchi for $1.7 billion in stock. Both worldwide and within the United States, Publicis ranked among the top six agencies in billings, with important accounts such as Hewlett-Packard Company, Saturn Corporation, Toyota, and Procter & Gamble Company. In August 2000 the shareholders voted to add the word *Group* to the company name.

In March 2002 Publicis Group and Bcom3 Group agreed to merge, forming the fourth largest communications group in the world. The companies also announced the creation of a long-term partnership between Dentsu, Japan's largest ad agency, and Publicis.

CLARK HULTQUIST

Further Reading

Bleustein-Blanchet, Marcel, *The Rage to Persuade: Memoirs of a French Advertising Man,* translated by Jean Bodewyn, New York: Chelsea House, 1982

Boutelier, Denis, and Dilip Subramanian, *Le grand bluff: Pouvoir et argent dans la publicité,* Paris: Denoël, 1990

Crumley, Bruce, "Maurice Lévy's Style: Low Profile, Big Goals," *Advertising Age* (28 September 1998)

Martin, Marc, *Trois siècles de publicité en France,* Paris: Éditions Odile Jacob, 1992

Melcher, Richard, and Gail Edmundson, "A Marriage Made in Hell," *Business Week* (22 December 1997)

"True North Gives Up Lawsuit As Publicis Wrangle Nears End," *Campaign* (18 December 1998)

Wells, Melanie, "Monsieur Big," *Forbes* (4 September 2000)

Public Relations

Public relations has become an essential management function in governments, companies, and nonprofit organizations throughout the world. Once largely a local practice, public relations (PR) today is carried out on a national and global scale. In 2000 public relations was a $3.4 billion industry in the United States and $4.6 billion worldwide, according to the Council of Public Relations Firms, based in New York City. After the United States, the next most widely developed markets for public relations are Canada and the United Kingdom, followed by the countries of Western Europe and Asia. Emerging public relations markets include Latin America and Eastern Europe.

In 1998 Philip Kotler, professor of international marketing at the J.L. Kellogg Graduate School of Management at Northwestern University, wrote that "of the five major communications tools—advertising, personal selling, sales promotion, direct marketing, and public relations—it is the last two that are receiving the most attention and recording the most growth. Public relations can account for its growth by its great versatility, its aptitude for drama, and its capacity to break through the information clutter and capture attention and interest."

There is no comprehensive industry-wide accounting of public relations budgets, but the 2001 *Thomas L. Harris/Impulse Research Public Relations Client Survey,* the largest annual survey in the field, revealed that the average internal public relations budget of 1,500 major U.S. corporations (with average revenue of $3.5 billion) participating in the survey was almost $1 million. The same companies each spent $1.3 million in public relations fees with their PR firms.

Definition and Purpose

Definitions of public relations are elusive because public relations covers such a broad spectrum of activities. One popular shorthand definition, "Doing good and getting credit for it," has been expanded by Fraser P. Seitel, author of *The Practice of Public Relations,* one of the leading public relations textbooks, as "the practice of doing the right thing—of performing—and communicating the substance of that performance." Another widely used textbook definition, from *Effective Public Relations* by Scott M. Cutlip, Allen Center, and Glen M. Broom, is "the management function that identifies, establishes, and maintains mutually beneficial relationships between an organization and the various publics on whom its success or failure depends." Those diverse publics, now generally referred to as "stakeholders," range from employees, investors, customers, and communities to legislators, regulators, and activists.

A stakeholder-based definition of public relations was formulated by Clarke L. Caywood, chairman of the Department of Integrated Marketing Communications of the Medill School of Journalism at Northwestern University, in his 1997 *Handbook of Strategic Public Relations and Integrated Communications.* Caywood calls public relations "the profitable integration of an organization's new and continuing relationships with stakeholders including customers by managing all communications contacts with the organization that create and protect the brand and reputation of the organization."

Public relations is the sum of many parts and therefore should not be equated exclusively with any of its tools and tactics, particularly publicity. Public relations, by definition, is as much about doing the right thing as saying the right thing. Public relations has often been called "the conscience of the corporation." The term "PR" also has a negative connotation in the minds of some, who believe it is synonymous with "spin," a term borrowed from the lexicon of modern political consultants that implies manipulation, misrepresentation, and distortion of the truth.

Today's practitioners are more likely to see their role in terms of "reputation management." This term was popularized by the magazine of the same name that began publishing in 1996. Editor Paul Holmes defined reputation management as "a counseling discipline that recognizes the importance of reputation as an organizational asset and seeks to insure that management decisions are taken in an environment in which reputational implications are fully understood, evaluated, and considered, so that an organization's behavior earns it a strategically appropriate reputation with important stakeholder groups." The wide range of work done by internal public relations departments and public relations firms can be seen from the results of the 2001 *Harris/Impulse Research* survey. Clients reported that the types of work they do most (internally or with outside firms) are media relations, special events, internal communications, and investor relations.

Origins

While historians trace public relations to ancient origins and its practice in the United States to revolutionaries such as Samuel Adams and Thomas Paine, who used pamphlets and public events to raise public support for the American Revolution, public relations is largely a 20th-century development. When muckraking journalists in the first decade of the century roused the public against alleged abuses of big business, business leaders began to recognize the necessity of telling their side of the story.

A major figure in the development of public relations was Ivy Ledbetter Lee. In direct contrast to the "public be damned" attitude of many business and financial leaders of the day, Lee counseled his clients on open and honest communication. In his famous "Declaration of Principles" to newspaper city editors, Lee pledged to supply the press and the public with prompt and accurate information on behalf of his business clients. The document drew a clear distinction between the role of his "press bureau" (the term *public relations* was not yet in common use) in supplying news and information and the role of advertising agencies in supporting sales. Lee is perhaps best remembered for his longtime work for John D. Rockefeller. Lee represented the Rockefeller family from 1914 until he died in 1934. Rockefeller engaged his

Caterpillar Tractor Company's 1952 public service campaign for road improvement also served to advertise its machinery.
Reprinted with cooperation from Caterpillar, Inc.

services while under fire for strikebreaking activities during a long and bitter strike against the Colorado Fuel and Iron Company. In the wake of a notorious event in which 53 miners were killed, known as the Ludlow Massacre, Lee was credited with restoring the family reputation by extolling Rockefeller's philanthropy in education, science, and medical research. While some argue whether Lee was on the right or the wrong side of that conflict, his role was similar to that of an attorney representing a client before a jury—except that public relations makes its case before the court of public opinion.

Another legendary figure in public relations history was Edward L. Bernays. Bernays, often called "the father of public relations," died in 1995 at the age of 103, his career having spanned three-quarters of a century. During World War I, Bernays was a member of the Committee on Public Information headed by George Creel, which is credited with mobilizing public support for the war. In 1923 he wrote *Crystallizing Public Opinion,* the first book on public relations, and taught the first course on the subject at New York University. He was known in particular for his efforts to humanize President Calvin Coolidge's image. Other accomplishments included making bacon and eggs the American breakfast of choice, promoting Ivory soap through a nationwide school soap sculpture program, and working for such corporate

giants as General Motors Corporation and General Electric Company (GE). For GE, for example, Bernays created the Golden Jubilee of Light to mark the 50th anniversary of Thomas A. Edison's invention of the electric lightbulb, an event that brought together Edison, Henry Ford, Marie Curie, and President Herbert Hoover.

Other notable early public relations pioneers included Benjamin Sonnenberg, John W. Hill, Carl Byoir, and Henry Rogers. Sonnenberg was social arbiter, press agent, and publicity counsel to some of the most important businessmen and famous personalities of his era. He was celebrated not only as the greatest publicist of his time but as a world-famous collector of art, brass, sculpture, and china. In the 1930s and 1940s, his Gramercy Park mansion in New York City served as a gathering place for America's most affluent, talented, and powerful men and women. His signature accomplishment was to convince his client Texaco to sponsor broadcasts of New York's Metropolitan Opera on radio.

John W. Hill cofounded Hill & Knowlton in Cleveland, Ohio, in 1933. When Hill won his first major account, the American Iron and Steel Institute, the agency moved its headquarters to New York City. There Hill built the world's first broad-service public relations counseling firm, adding such services as public affairs and financial relations and establishing agency offices in Europe and Asia. His autobiography, *The Making of a Public Relations Man,* described the evolution of the role of public relations in modern business management.

In 1930 Carl Byoir founded the public relations firm bearing his name initially in Havanna, Cuba, before moving it to New York City. At mid-century Carl Byoir & Associates and Hill & Knowlton were the two dominant public relations firms representing major U.S. corporations. Byoir himself is best known for promoting Cuba and Florida as travel destinations and for creating the "Birthday Ball" for President Franklin D. Roosevelt to raise funds for the Infantile Paralysis Foundation, which led to the creation of the March of Dimes.

Henry C. Rogers and his partner, Warren Cowan, formed Rogers & Cowan, based in Los Angeles, California, which became the largest and most successful public relations firm on the West Coast. Rogers represented such motion picture stars as Rita Hayworth, Joan Crawford, Frank Sinatra, Dean Martin, and Paul Newman. He was, according to a profile in the *New York Times,* "very much a product of the '40s and '50s satisfying the masses as they luxuriated in their popular culture." In his autobiographical *Walking the Tightrope,* Rogers presented a candid account of what it was like to perform a balancing act between high-powered clients and the media.

Perhaps no single figure contributed more to the practice of corporate public relations than Arthur Page, who headed public relations for American Telephone & Telegraph Company from 1927 to 1947. Page did much to establish public relations as a management function. He counseled management that gaining public approval was based on performance in the public interest. His philosophy continues to guide the Arthur Page Society, a New York City–based organization of the chief public relations officers of the largest corporations and public relations firms.

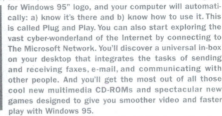

Windows 95 (as represented by these happy squares of color) is incredibly simple. But it is also incredibly substantial, with features and abilities far beyond what you're used to. Since we're using orange type here, we'll start by talking about some of its orangeish qualities. Things like potential. For instance, thanks to the new 32-bit architecture, you can squeeze more speed and capacity out of your computer. "The 32-bit what?" you may be saying. In conversational English, it simply means that Windows 95 can handle much more data at a time than your old 16-bit Windows. You can run many 32-bit applications at once. Print while you play a game. Stuff like that. Plus, as an added bonus, DOS is no longer the bogeyman in the basement of Windows. Yet you can still run your favorite DOS applications whenever you like.

From the serene world of blue, Windows 95 brings you a calming quality called "ease of use." Take installation, for instance—disarmingly easy. And that Start button you see up in the corner of this ad? It accesses the power of Windows 95 and starts up any application. There's also a taskbar at the bottom, the top or the side (your choice) of the screen that tells you what programs are open and allows you to instantly return to them. With new 32-bit programs like Microsoft Office for Windows 95, you'll go from calling your files things like VANYTYLK.doc, to naming them Virtually Anything You Like. Many new multimedia CD-ROMs will automatically play when you put them in the drive. Connecting back to your office network from a laptop is much simpler. To delete something, just drag it to the recycle bin. Easy, easy, easy.

This part of the ad is green because it talks about all the ways Windows 95 will allow both you and your computer to grow. Plug in any new peripheral like a printer, CD-ROM drive, scanner, modem or whatever, that carries the "designed for Windows 95" logo, and your computer will automatically: a) know it's there and b) know how to use it. This is called Plug and Play. You can also start exploring the vast cyber-wonderland of the Internet by connecting to The Microsoft Network. You'll discover a universal in-box on your desktop that integrates the tasks of sending and receiving faxes, e-mail, and communicating with other people. And you'll get the most out of all those cool new multimedia CD-ROMs and spectacular new games designed to give you smoother video and faster play with Windows 95.

To find out more fun stuff, visit Windows 95 on-line now at http://www.windows.microsoft.com, or in stores beginning August 24. A yellow section is just too hard to read.

WHERE DO YOU WANT TO GO TODAY?™

Extensive marketing public relations in the form of prelaunch publicity for Microsoft's Windows 95 software contributed to the success of the product launch in 1995.
Windows and the Windows logo are registered trademarks and Where do you want to go today? and the Windows Start logo are trademarks of Microsoft Corporation. © 1995 Microsoft Corporation. Reprinted with permission from Microsoft Corporation.

The post–World War II period saw the rise of corporate public relations departments (usually called corporate communications) and the rapid growth of newly formed public relations firms, many of them started by returning veterans. In New York City, William Ruder and David Finn started Ruder Finn in 1948, and in 1953 Harold Burson, in partnership with advertising executive William Marsteller, founded Burson-Marsteller. That same year Daniel J. Edelman opened the agency bearing his name in Chicago, Illinois.

From Service to Subsidiary

During the 1950s many of the largest advertising agencies operated public relations units under the agency name. They included Young & Rubicam (Y&R), McCann-Erickson, and Batten Barton Durstine & Osborn (BBDO). Most of these divisions were discontinued because they were unprofitable (big advertising clients expected the agency to provide public relations at low or no cost) and unable to compete with independent public relations firms that clients regarded as PR professionals. The most successful were J. Walter Thompson Company (JWT), later merged with Hill & Knowlton (now owned by JWT parent WPP Group); Bozell Public Relations, then BSMG, which became a division of True North Communications before True North was acquired by Interpublic Group of Companies, which merged BSMG into Weber Shandwick; Ketchum Public Relations, now owned by the Omnicom Group; and Burson-Marsteller, now in the WPP Group.

In the 1970s advertising agencies, including those that had earlier abandoned their own public relations units, recognized that public relations was an important component of a "full-service" agency. They also saw public relations as a contributor to "below the line" profits (i.e., not dependent on media commissions) and a means to gain access to clients at the top management level. The first major public relations firm to be bought by an advertising agency was Carl Byoir & Associates, acquired by Foote, Cone & Belding in 1978; it was subsequently sold in 1989 to Hill & Knowlton. Other major acquisitions included Burson-Marsteller by Y&R, and Hill & Knowlton by JWT. The growth of public relations firms was largely a U.S. phenomenon until the 1970s, when three U.K.-headquartered agencies acquired major PR firms in the United States and elsewhere. Saatchi & Saatchi acquired the Rowland Company; WPP acquired two major U.S. advertising agencies—JWT, with its PR subsidiary Hill & Knowlton, and Ogilvy & Mather, with its PR subsidiary Ogilvy, Adams & Rinehart; and Shandwick PLC, a public relations conglomerate, acquired several public relations firms around the world and a dozen in the United States, including Golin/Harris and Rogers & Cowan, whose brand names are still retained.

By 2000, 12 of the top 15 public relations firms were owned by advertising agencies. Only three independently owned public relations firms remained among the top 15: Edelman Public Relations Worldwide, with fee income of $168.4 million; Ruder Finn, with fee income of $75.6 million; and Waggener Edstrom, with fee income of $56.2 million in 2000, according to the Council of Public Relations Firms. The three top advertising organizations in terms of PR fees in 2000 were the Omnicom Group, with $612.1 million in U.S. fee income and three of the top ten firms: Fleishman-Hillard, Ketchum Public Relations, and Porter Novelli International; WPP Group, $531.1 million and Burson-Marsteller, Hill & Knowlton, and Ogilvy Public Relations; and Interpublic Group of Companies, $371.3 million and Weber Shandwick Worldwide and Golin/Harris International.

The top ten U.S. public relations firms had combined 2000 revenue of $1.68 billion and accounted for 50 percent of the total U.S. PR market. The fastest growing areas of public relations in the 1990s were healthcare, technology, and investor relations. PR firms specializing in these areas grew dramatically, and many were acquired by the largest full-service public relations firms.

PR and Marketing

Marketing public relations (MPR), the use of public relations strategies and techniques to achieve marketing objectives, is only one of the principal functions of public relations, but it represents a significant portion of the work of corporate communications departments and the billings of public relations firms. Among the heaviest users of MPR are companies in high tech, pharmaceuticals, entertainment, travel and tourism, publishing, food and beverage, cosmetics, fashion, toys, books, consumer electronics, and financial services.

The purposes of MPR are to promote awareness of the client's product or services, stimulate sales, facilitate communications, and build relationships between consumers and companies and their brands. The principal functions of MPR are product publicity, event sponsorship, and the support of social causes. Now recognized as a key element in integrated marketing communication campaigns rather than as an isolated function, MPR is best used in integrated marketing to create excitement in the marketplace about new products before the advertising breaks. Prelaunch publicity offers a unique window of opportunity to make headline news. Some of the most successful products of the 1990s—including Windows 95, Nintendo 64, Apple's iMac computer, and the 1998 Volkswagen Beetle—were sold out before the first advertising appeared because of massive publicity.

Marketing public relations is also widely used to revitalize old products, to cultivate a core consumer base, leverage event sponsorship, and influence opinion leaders. Public relations is also used to link brands with causes that people care about, alleviate consumer fears to gain market acceptance, defend products at risk, and give consumers permission to buy. In a classic case, immediate action and open communication enabled Johnson & Johnson (J&J) to rebuild its Tylenol brand after product tampering caused seven deaths in the Chicago area in 1982. J&J began a public relations blitz after the cyanide-laced capsules were discovered. To repair the damage to the Tylenol brand, James Burke, J&J's chairman and CEO, gave interviews and made television spots to explain what the company was doing to control the situation. Overall, the company spent $100 million on the effort, and sales returned to 80 percent of pre-crisis levels within three months.

One of the principal tactics of MPR is product publicity. In contrast to paid advertising, publicity is nonpaid information about products that is used by the media because of its news value. This implied third-party endorsement gives publicity high credibility. Publicity has the unique capability of dramatizing the news and reaching consumers who might avoid ads or sales pitches.

In addition to conducting marketing public relations, both PR firms and in-house client PR departments can perform the following functions:

- Media relations—liaison between the company and the media. Media relations encompasses media planning, media training, release of relevant corporate news, arranging executive interviews and news conferences, responding promptly to media inquiries, and evaluating media coverage.
- Public affairs—counseling management on relationships between the government, community, and society.
- Issues management—an early-warning system that identifies emerging issues and monitors existing issues that could affect the organization and recommends a course of action to avert problems.
- Investor relations, also called financial relations— communication between public companies, their shareholders, and the financial community. IR is responsible for financial analyst meetings, annual and interim reports, other communication with present and potential shareholders, and media relations with the business news media.
- Crisis communications—counseling management on what to say and do to protect the organization's reputation in case of an emergency.
- Community relations—maintaining favorable relations and support in communities where a company has facilities through sponsorship of activities such as local events and open houses that benefit the community.
- Employee relations—facilitating dialogue with employees and keeping them informed about company news through meetings, events, publications, closed circuit television, intranet sites, e-mail, and voice mail.
- Special events—planning and conducting contests, competitions, news events, press conferences, seminars,

speeches, symposia, anniversaries, and celebrations that involve consumers and other important stakeholders. Some of the best-known marketing-related public relations events are the Pillsbury Bake-Off, the Gillette Million Dollar Sports Challenges, and the Coca-Cola Olympic Torch Relay. Other public relations functions include executive speechwriting, handling corporate contributions, administering corporate identity programs, and "lobbying" company and group views to legislators at all government levels.

Organizations

The two major professional organizations serving the field are the Public Relations Society of America (PRSA), headquartered in New York City, and the International Association of Business Communicators (IABC), located in San Francisco, California. Organized in 1947, PRSA is the world's largest organization for public relations professionals. Its nearly 20,000 members represent business and industry, counseling firms, government associations, hospitals, schools, professional service firms, and nonprofit organizations. PRSA publishes *The Strategist,* a quarterly journal, and *Public Relations Tactics,* a monthly newspaper. IABC has 13,700 members and publishes *Communications World.*

Both PRSA and IABC have accreditation programs requiring candidates to pass written and oral examinations. Accredited PRSA members are designated APR (Accredited in Public Relations); accredited IABC members are designated ABC (Accredited Business Communicator). PRSA and IABC each has its own code of ethics. The PRSA Code of Professional Standards for the Practice of Public Relations was adopted in 1950. IABC adopted its first code in 1976. Both encourage their members to be truthful and accurate, and both have the ability to suspend members for violations.

In 1998 the Council of Public Relations Firms, the first trade association to represent the interests of U.S. public relations firms, was formed in New York City by large and midsize agencies.

In addition, several networks of independent public relations firms serve clients worldwide and compete with the large multi-office international public relations firms.

Annual public relations awards competitions honoring the best public relations programs in various categories are sponsored by the Public Relations Society of American (Silver and Bronze Anvils), IABC (Gold Quill Awards), and *PR Week* and the *Holmes Report* (Sabre Awards).

THOMAS L. HARRIS

Further Reading
Barmash, Isadore, *"Always Live Better Than Your Clients": The Fabulous Life and Times of Benjamin Sonnenberg, America's Greatest Publicist,* New York: Dodd Mead, 1983

Caywood, Clarke L., *The Handbook of Strategic Public Relations and Integrated Communications,* New York: McGraw-Hill, 1997

Cutlip, Scott M., and Allen H. Center, *Effective Public Relations,* New York: Prentice-Hall, 1952; 8th edition, by Cutlip, Center, and Glen M. Broom, Upper Saddle River, New Jersey: Prentice Hall, 2000

Gabler, Neal, "The Fathers of PR," *New York Times Magazine* (31 December 1995)

Gross, Sidney, "Bill Moyers Tracks 'The Image Makers,'" *Public Relations Journal* 40, no. 6 (June 1984)

Harris, Thomas L., *The Marketer's Guide to Public Relations: How Today's Top Companies Are Using the New PR to Gain a Competitive Edge,* New York: Wiley, 1991

Harris, Thomas L., *Value-Added Public Relations: The Secret Weapon of Integrated Marketing,* Lincolnwood, Illinois: NTC Business Books, 1998

Hill, John W., *The Making of a Public Relations Man,* New York: McKay, 1963

O'Dwyer's Directory of Public Relations Firms (annual; 1985–)

Rogers, Henry C., *Walking the Tightrope: The Private Confessions of a Public Relations Man,* New York: Morrow, 1980

Seitel, Fraser P., *The Practice of Public Relations,* Columbus, Ohio: Merrill, 1980; 7th edition, Upper Saddle River, New Jersey: Prentice Hall, 1998

Weiner, Richard, *Webster's New World Dictionary of Media and Communications,* New York: Webster's New World, 1990; revised edition, New York: Macmillan, 1996

Wilcox, Dennis L., Phillip H. Ault, and Warren K. Agee, *Public Relations: Strategies and Tactics,* New York: Harper and Row, 1986; 6th edition, New York: Longman, 1999

Public Service Advertising

Although most advertising has as its ultimate goal the sale of a product or service, there are other uses for advertising. Some ads aim to enhance a company's reputation or image (a goal that may indirectly affect sales), while others seek to enlist public or legislative support for causes such as labor laws, antitrust actions, or environmental regulations. Still other ads are created and placed in the media in the interest of the public welfare. All of these fall into the category known as public service advertising.

Ad agencies, working with nonprofit organizations, create public service advertisements, also known as public service announce-

How to Make Cooking Fats Do Double Duty!

OF COURSE YOU CAN! There's no conflict between rationing and saving your used cooking grease to make gunpowder for our men at the front. And the reasons are very simple. First, the government doesn't ask for your fats *until you've got all the cooking good out of them.* And, second, even if you consume a lot of them in using them over, *what you have left* is vitally important. No housewife need think she has too little to turn in! Because just one simple tablespoon of used fat will make *five machine gun bullets.* Save every precious drop. Keep it in a can. When full, rush it to your meat dealer.

Approved by the War Production Board. Paid for by Industry

During World War II newspaper ads such as this 1943 example urged the American public to conserve vital resources in support of the war effort.

ments, or PSAs, designed to persuade consumers to engage in behaviors that actively promote healthy behaviors or good citizenship. Media organizations often donate space and time for the distribution of these messages. To gain control over the distribution of their advertisements, nonprofit organizations and state and national governments sometimes pay for these services.

One of the earliest examples of nongovernmental public service advertising was sponsored in 1906 by an organization known as the American Civic Association. Its members were concerned citizens who feared that electric companies would divert water from Niagara Falls. They purchased ad space in national magazines to solicit contributions and support. The ads raised public awareness, and the electric companies were forced to adopt measures that reduced diversion from the falls.

Early corporate advertising was sometimes portrayed as promoting public service. For example, during the early 20th century, American Telephone & Telegraph (AT&T), by then a legal monopoly, ran advertising that characterized telephone service per se as a "public" service. The ads claimed that the telephone contributed to human progress, banished loneliness, and bound together the fabric of the community. Some ads characterized the company as a "democracy of Bell telephone owners."

Patriotic Appeals

In the United States the federal government is a frequent sponsor of ads designed for public service. During the Civil War, the government sold bonds through newspaper advertising. During World War I, the government created a Federal Committee of Public Information—essentially a propaganda bureau—to inform and persuade the public about the war effort. The committee had a Division of Pictorial Publicity led by the artist Charles Dana Gibson. Gibson called upon the talents of top illustrators of the day, including James Montgomery Flagg (creator of the historic "I Want You" poster). Other artists who contributed to the war effort were J.C. Leyendecker (famous as the illustrator for Arrow shirts) and Howard Chandler Christy (whose illustrations of female figures were known as "Christy Girls"). After the war ended, the government continued to sponsor public service advertising. Ads and posters supported airmail, food conservation, aid for drought victims, and public reclamation projects.

When the United States entered World War II, advertising professionals felt that their talents could be used to promote the war effort. The War Advertising Council was created in 1942 to work with the government's Office of War Information (OWI). The council's first president was Chester LaRoche of Young & Rubicam. Price Gilbert of Coca-Cola headed the Bureau of Graphics and Printing for the OWI. Norman Rockwell was among the many illustrators who contributed art to the effort. Ads encouraged wartime conservation, enlistment in the armed forces, the participation of women in the workforce, and the purchase of war bonds. "Rosie the Riveter," an illustration of a female industrial worker, became a popular icon.

Corporate advertisers joined the effort by promoting their employees as "soldiers of service" or praising consumers for their patriotism. Those who could not go to the front were encouraged to become "home-front heroes" by planting vegetable gardens, salvaging tin and paper, conserving resources, and taking war jobs. Some critics contend that this period represents the birth of "consumer culture." Advertisers used the war effort as an opportunity to promote a pro-business ideology that combined commerce and civic virtue. The reasons that government and business cooperation was so fruitful during World War II go beyond matters of mere expediency. The fact that the appeals came from industry enhanced their credibility, particularly when those messages urged employers to hire women. Because of materials shortages, there were fewer products to advertise. The war effort was a way for advertisers to remain visible. Advertising professionals were known to boast about their efforts during the war, characterizing advertising as "psychological warfare" and an "information weapon."

Serving the Public Good

At the end of World War II the War Advertising Council changed its name to the Ad Council and extended its services to government agencies and nonprofit organizations. Today, the Ad Council continues to coordinate production and distribution of national public service advertising campaigns. Its operating expenses are paid by donations from corporations, foundations, and constituent organizations.

Advertising professionals donate their time to create PSAs. The organization for which the campaign is developed often pays out-of-pocket production costs (which might be as much as $100,000). The Ad Council then distributes the advertisements to publishers and broadcasters, which may choose to donate space or time to publish or broadcast the ads. By the mid-1970s, the Ad Council was acquiring more than $500 million a year in media time and space for public service advertising. The organization claimed to have acquired nearly $1 billion in donated media space/time in 1997.

The council conducts approximately 35 campaigns per year. Selected campaigns must be noncommercial, nondenominational, nonpolitical, and significant to all Americans. Well-known campaigns have included the "Smokey Bear" ads (U.S. Forest Service, from Foote, Cone & Belding), "A Mind is a Terrible Thing to Waste" (United Negro College Fund, from Young & Rubicam), and the National Crime Prevention Council's "Take a Bite Out of Crime" (from Saatchi & Saatchi). Other campaigns have promoted health and safety, environmental preservation, the arts, and other causes.

According to the 1934 Communications Act broadcasters have a mandate to serve the public interest of the communities in which they operate. This act requires the Federal Communications Commission (FCC) to grant and renew broadcast licenses only when broadcasters uphold their obligation to public service. This mandate is not extended to print media because the "spectrum" of print media is not limited as is the spectrum of broadcast media. The roots of the U.S. networks' modern news divisions are in the public affairs departments of the 1930s, which arranged for the broadcasting of the national political conventions, inaugurations, elections, presidential addresses, and other events of general interest, all without sponsor support.

Based on a 1998 survey of local broadcasters, the National Association of Broadcasters estimated that each U.S. television station airs an average of 137 PSAs per week, and radio stations average 122 a week. Based on these figures, the industry group Public Opinion Strategies suggests that television stations are donating airtime worth $1.12 billion annually, while radio stations donate airtime worth $3.14 billion. The "Big Four" national television networks—the American Broadcasting Company, Columbia Broadcasting System, National Broadcasting Company, and Fox network—provide an estimated additional $342 million

The one sure thing the future holds.

We'll be there.

American Red Cross

http://www.redcross.org   1-800-HELP NOW

This 1999 ad emphasized the dependability of the American Red Cross. *Provided courtesy of the American Red Cross*

worth of airtime. Broadcasters also support public service efforts by participating in or sponsoring fund-raising events (e.g., telethons) and by broadcasting public affairs programming.

Some authorities dispute these estimates. Representatives from organizations such as the Center for Media Education, Action for Children's Television, and the Minority Media and Telecommunications Council point out that estimates of donated media time are not provided by an independent source. PSAs are often broadcast during late-night time slots, when other advertising revenue is not available. Critics argue that such airtime is not as valuable as broadcasters claim.

Because they seek to control when and where PSAs appear, organizations promoting social issues are increasingly willing to pay for placement. Various government offices, including the armed services, regularly pay for advertising. In the 1990s the U.S. Congress granted nearly $1 billion to the White House Office of National Drug Control Policy for a five-year antidrug campaign. The Partnership for a Drug-Free America, a nonprofit coalition of advertising professionals, agreed to produce the antidrug messages. Officials hoped that the congressional funds could be used to pay for broadcast airtime and print advertising space and that publishers and broadcasters would be willing to match purchased ad space/time with donated space/time. Similarly, state governments were funding antismoking advertising campaigns with settlement money from lawsuits against cigarette marketers or from excise taxes on cigarettes.

"Social Marketing"

The fact that nonprofit and government agencies have become increasingly willing to pay for ad placement represents a shift in favor of the view that social causes can be "sold" in much the same way as products are. A field of research and practice called "social marketing" adapts marketing principles for the promotion of social causes.

A debate over social marketing has continued since the early 1970s, when the practice first emerged. According to the social marketing perspective, the promotion of social issues can be more successful if promoters use marketing principles such as segmentation and copy testing. On the other hand, social issues differ fundamentally from products; they may, for example, be more closely related to deeply held values or more likely to provoke anxiety among consumers. Frequently, the target audience is opposed to the social issue being promoted or it may be very difficult to reach (e.g., drug abusers). To what extent social causes and products can be promoted in the same ways as commodities and brands remains to be seen.

National television networks sometimes produce and run their own public service messages. These PSAs typically feature actors from popular prime-time series with messages about teacher recruitment, mentoring, staying in school, and other noncontroversial issues. While these network messages benefit from star power, critics contend that they promote the networks as much as any social issues and that the network-produced PSAs are replacing prime-time airing of other PSAs.

Cable networks also produce PSAs. From 1990 to 1992 MTV sponsored the "Rock the Vote" campaign, designed to encourage young adults to vote. In early 1999 the network launched "Fight for Your Rights," a campaign against violence in schools, neighborhoods, and college campuses. Local publishers and broadcasters also produce and distribute advertisements on behalf of local nonprofit organizations.

Corporations continue to produce public service advertising as well. Oil companies have sponsored ads urging consumers to conserve fuel. Beer company advertising urges consumers not to drink and drive. A beer ad that ran during the 1999 Super Bowl encouraged parents to talk to their children about drinking alcoholic beverages.

One well-known cause-related marketing campaign was the result of an alliance between American Express and the foundation overseeing the renovation of Ellis Island and the Statue of Liberty. In 1983 American Express promised to donate one cent from every card transaction to the foundation. The campaign resulted in $1.7 million in donations from American Express. Cause-related corporate ads generally serve both corporate and social objectives. Such ads depict their sponsors as philanthropic, responsible corporate citizens. Consumers feel they are supporting their favorite causes when they purchase a product.

Some observers claim that such alliances can compromise the independent status of the nonprofit organizations. For example, both the Arthritis Foundation and the American Cancer Society serve as important sources of information about diseases. Both organizations have entered into cause-related marketing alliances with pharmaceutical companies. The Arthritis Foundation allowed McNeil Consumer Products to market a line of pain relievers using the foundation's name in exchange for a minimum of $1 million a year in research funding. The American Cancer Society made a similar licensing agreement with SmithKline Beecham, marketer of the NicoDerm CQ nicotine patch for smoking cessation. It remains to be seen whether nonprofit organizations can remain unbiased sources of information when they accept funds from corporations.

New Media

Toward the end of the 20th century public service advertising began to find its way into new media. Nonprofit organizations have been on the Internet since its inception: the ".org" suffix designates a nonprofit organization. Nonprofit organizations first ventured into what might be called, in more narrow terms, on-line advertising when advertisements for Earth Share appeared on the Prodigy on-line service beginning in 1993. The National Fatherhood Initiative ran banner ads distributed on the Alta Vista search engine Web site beginning in 1996.

The Ad Council creates on-line advertising for many of its affiliated nonprofit organizations. The Internet Advertising Bureau, a trade organization for the Internet advertising industry, asks its members to donate 5 percent of their ad space to public service advertising. On-line PSAs usually take the form of banner ads that direct a viewer to the nonprofit organization's Web site. Industry observers claim that few Internet advertising companies sell all of their available ad space, so donating space to PSAs is not a particular sacrifice for the advertising company. Time will tell whether Internet advertisers will continue to donate space after their ad revenues begin to grow. The Ad Council also works to place public service messages in other new media, such as automated teller machines, airport monitors, and videotapes.

TRINA SEGO

Further Reading
Andreasen, Alan R., "Social Marketing: Its Definition and Domain," *Journal of Public Policy and Marketing* 13, no. 1 (Spring 1994)

Andreasen, Alan R., "Profits for Nonprofits: Find a Corporate Partner," *Harvard Business Review* 74, no. 6 (November/December 1996)

Beatty, Sally Goll, "Advertising: Brawl Over Do-Good Advertising," *Wall Street Journal* (29 September 1997)

Fitzgerald, Nora, "A Social Contract," *Adweek* (Eastern edition) (3 November 1997)

Fox, Frank W., *Madison Avenue Goes to War: The Strange Military Career of American Advertising, 1941–1945,* Provo, Utah: Brigham Young University Press, 1975

Goodrum, Charles, and Helen Dalrymple, *Advertising in America: The First 200 Years,* New York: Abrams, 1990

Honey, Maureen, *Creating Rosie the Riveter: Class, Gender, and Propaganda during World War II,* Amherst: University of Massachusetts Press, 1984

Johnson, Greg, "Advertising: Sending Messages: Public Service Announcements Find a Receptive Home on Internet," *Los Angeles Times* (27 August 1998)

Kotler, Philip, and Eduardo L. Roberto, *Social Marketing: Strategies for Changing Public Behavior,* New York: Free Press, and London: Collier Macmillan, 1989

Kotler, Philip, and Gerald Zaltman, "Social Marketing: An Approach to Planned Social Change," *Journal of Marketing* 35, no. 3 (July 1971)

Marchand, Roland, "The Fitful Career of Advocacy Advertising: Political Protection, Client Cultivation, and Corporate Morale," *California Management Review* 29, no. 2 (Winter 1987)

McConnell, Chris, "Adding up the Public Service Dollars," *Broadcasting and Cable* 128, no. 14 (6 April 1998)

McConnell, Chris, and Paige Albiniak, "Putting a Price on Public Service," *Broadcasting and Cable* 128, no. 14 (6 April 1998)

Petrozzello, Donna, "MTV to Launch Anti-Violence Effort," *Broadcasting and Cable* 128, no. 43 (19 October 1998)

Pytka, Joe 1938–

U.S. Director of Commercials

Joe Pytka was born in the Pittsburgh, Pennsylvania, suburb of Braddock in 1938. The son of a machinist, Pytka grew up during difficult times for the steel-making region, and it is to this upbringing that he has attributed his strong work ethic. A perfectionist, Pytka has a reputation for routinely eliciting the best from those with whom he works, and he has earned numerous awards for excellence in his profession.

Pytka first wanted to become an artist; he began studying art at Pittsburgh's Carnegie Museum at the age of eight. Although he was accepted into Carnegie Tech's art program, his father persuaded him to try his hand at something more practical; his brief career at the University of Pittsburgh studying chemical engineering was, he has said, "disastrous." Never earning his college degree, Pytka left school for a job at a film lab in Pittsburgh.

Pytka worked for several years making documentaries for WQED, the Public Broadcasting Service television station in Pittsburgh. Applying documentary techniques to 30- and 60-second TV spots, he began shooting commercials in the late 1960s to supplement his income between the longer projects he was doing in documentary and dramatic television programming.

Pytka did not turn seriously to advertising until the early 1970s. Some of his early work included spots for Iron City Beer, Pittsburgh National Bank, Nationwide Insurance, and Stoney's Beer. He worked primarily with Ketchum, McLeod & Grove in Pittsburgh.

Although Pytka has two feature films to his credit—the critically acclaimed box-office disappointment *Let It Ride* (1989) and the commercially successful *Space Jam* (1996)—he will be best remembered for the more than 25,000 commercials that he has directed.

Pytka's advertising classics include "Thank You for Your Support" for E.&J. Gallo Winery's Bartles & Jaymes wine coolers; "Hare Jordan," featuring the animated Bugs Bunny and basketball superstar Michael Jordan, and "Bo Knows" for Nike; "Nothing but Net," featuring Jordan and Larry Bird for McDonald's; "Uh-huh," sung by Ray Charles, for Diet Pepsi; "Real Life, Real Answers," for John Hancock life insurance; and the mess-making infant for DuPont Stainmaster. Other award-winning spots include those for Hallmark Cards, Infiniti, Apple Computer, AT&T Corporation, Polaroid Corporation, ESPN, and Mars, Inc.

Other major clients have included Eastman Kodak Company, IBM Corporation, American Express Company, United Air Lines, General Electric Company, Federal Express, Walt Disney Company, Anheuser-Busch, Levi Strauss & Company, The Gap, Delta Air Lines, Miller Brewing Company, Adolph Coors Company, Chevrolet Motor Division, Ford Motor Company, Dodge Car/Truck Division, Volvo, Coca-Cola Company, Hershey Foods, the Museum of Contemporary Art (Los Angeles, California), Partnership for a Drug-Free America, the American Indian College Fund, AltaVista, and Microsoft Corporation.

Pytka's brother, John, is also a respected advertising director. Together they launched their production company, Pytka, in Venice, California, in 1984. Revenue for the company was in the $25 million–$30 million range in 1997.

Joe Pytka.
Couresty of Joe Pytka, Director. © 1997 Douglas Kirkland.

Considered by many to be at the top of his field, Pytka's work has earned him numerous awards, among them a Grammy, two Grand Prix awards at the International Advertising Festival at Cannes, seven Palms d'Or at Cannes, three Directors' Guild of America Awards (with 14 nominations), and many Clios.

Pytka was awarded the first prime-time Emmy for a commercial in 1997. The winning commercial, "Chimps," was created by BBDO for cable TV's HBO network. In the spot, chimps are shown reciting famous lines from films featured on HBO while noted ethologist Jane Goodall studies them through her binoculars. Later, we see her in her room with the TV tuned to HBO in the background. In a voice-over, we hear her journal entry: "Their inexplicable behavior continues. Got to go now. *Braveheart* is on." Unnoticed by Goodall, several chimps are watching HBO with her through the window. The 60-second commercial featured chimpanzee footage shot at the Gombe Preserve in Tanzania in Africa, set against several familiar lines of dialogue from classic feature films for HBO.

Pytka has consistently been at the forefront of innovations in visual style. For example, he used the so-called shaky camera technique well before anyone else. And in spots such as those for the "Heartland" campaign for Anheuser-Busch's Bud Light, or in spots for Bartles & Jaymes Wine Coolers, he pioneered the idea of casting "real people"—not actors—in TV commercials.

Pytka is as widely known for his personal style as for the style of his work. He has a reputation as a perfectionist whose ranting aggression on the set is legendary but whose results are worth the process. Although Pytka is known for terrorizing cast, crew, and clients, his commercials show the opposite qualities—humanness, empathy, and humor. According to *Advertising Age*, "Pytka's uses of lighting, warm humor, and emotional relationships won worldwide acclaim and established him as the most consistent master of the best in American TV commercial work." Yet, as Pytka said in an interview with *Forbes*, "I'm an irritator and an agitator—I have no charm." Apparently he does not need it, as he consistently ranks as the top advertising director in the United States.

BARBARA KNOLL

Biography

Born in Braddock, Pennsylvania, 1938; launched Pytka, a Venice, California, production company, with his brother, John, 1984; directed the theatricals *Let It Ride*, 1989, and *Space Jam*, 1996; won the first prime-time Emmy for a commercial, 1997.

Further Reading

Kanner, Bernice, *The 100 Best TV Commercials—And Why They Worked,* New York: Times Business, 1999
Levine, Joshua, "I Have No Charm," *Forbes* (7 December 1992)
Rothenberg, Randall, *Where the Suckers Moon: An Advertising Story,* New York: Knopf, 1994

Q

Quaker Oats Company

Principal Agencies

Lord & Thomas

Ruthrauff & Ryan, Inc.

Needham, Louis & Brorby, Inc.

Adcom (house agency, later Bayer Bess Vanderwarker)

Compton Advertising

J. Walter Thompson Company

Foote, Cone & Belding Communications, Inc.

Omnicom Group, Inc.

By the beginning of the 21st century, Americans had been eating Quaker Oats oatmeal for almost 100 years, and while the company's cereal product lineup had changed minimally over the years, its marketing continued to be dynamic. Much of the credit can be traced to the company's beginnings and one of its cofounders, who is considered the father of modern advertising.

Three millers—Ferdinand Schumacher, Henry Parsons Crowell, and Robert Stuart—founded American Cereal Company before the turn of the 20th century. Each man had his own area of expertise. Schumacher focused on the milling; Stuart, the packaging, production, and shipping; and Crowell, the advertising. In 1901 the company name was changed to Quaker Oats.

Early Ad Efforts

Owing to his painstaking attention to detail and relentless pursuit of brand exposure, Crowell is considered by many to be the father of modern advertising. He pioneered scientific endorsements, customer testimonials, cash-prize contests, sampling, market testing, giveaways, and box-top premiums. He also was the man behind the Quaker icon on all the company's products. Crowell found a picture of a Quaker gentleman in an encyclopedia and decided he looked "earnest, hard-working, and virtuous," just like the hot cereal. It is a symbol that has endured, even surviving an attempt by the Quakers themselves to have laws passed that would bar trademarks with religious connotations.

The company came out with its first cold cereals, Puffed Rice and Wheat Berries, and in 1908 hired advertising agency Lord & Thomas, under Albert D. Lasker, to help promote them. The creative minds of Crowell and Lasker worked well together, and Quaker quickly came to be Lasker's best account. Lasker talked Crowell into changing the name of Wheat Berries to Puffed Berries to simplify the advertising by promoting two puffed cereals, and he convinced him to raise the price of the first cold cereals from ten cents to 15 cents a box and to invest the extra nickel in advertising. Thirty years after its start, however, the relationship soured when Quaker hired a company to judge all its advertising for effectiveness before it was released. Lasker resigned the account in 1938.

By 1940 the business was divided between Ruthrauff & Ryan (Quaker Oats, Puffed Wheat, and Puffed Rice), Sherman & Ellis (Aunt Jemima), Mitchell-Faust Advertising (macaroni products), and Sherman & Marquette (Farina and Ful-O-Pep Feeds). After World War II, Needham, Louis & Brorby replaced Sherman & Ellis. A decade later further agency changes were in place, with Compton Advertising; Clinton E. Frank, Inc.; and the J. Walter Thompson Company taking the major brands.

Second Generation

Creative advertising continued after the founders passed the torch to the next generation. R. Douglas Stuart, son of company cofounder Robert, was a master of promotions whose campaign ideas included featuring the internationally famous Dionne quintuplets in Quaker Oats ads. He also was one of the first corporate advertising executives who believed a company such as Quaker, which was expanding, should have multiple ad agencies.

Quaker repeatedly returned to the basic healthfulness of oats as its central marketing point, but it sought to appeal not just to parents but to their children as well; cereal, according to Quaker, could be nutritious and taste good at the same time. For example, in its first and only ad for Quaker, Doyle Dane Bernbach (DDB) created the "Hey, Mikey," campaign in 1971 in which two boys

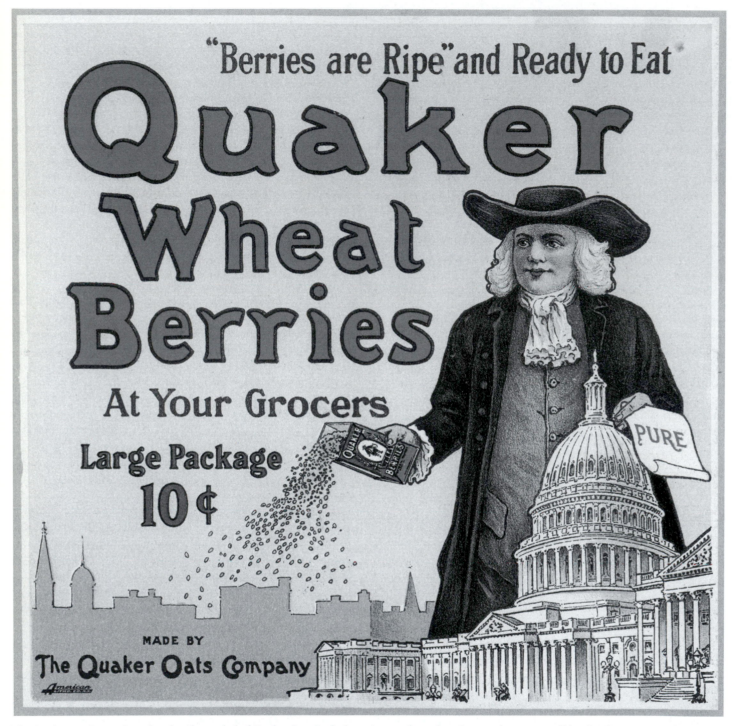

The Quaker gentleman, introduced as the symbol of Quaker Oats in the late 1800s and seen here in an early 1900s rendition, has become an enduring icon for the marketer.
Courtesy of Quaker Oats Co.

discover that their finicky three-year-old brother likes Life cereal. *Advertising Age* ranked it 64th among the 100 greatest ads of the century in 1999. Although that advertising campaign continued, Quaker's relationship with DDB ended in 1972.

Diversification efforts became a company strategy for growth, and by the second half of the 20th century Quaker's corporate portfolio had grown to include chemical products, restaurant chains, and toy companies, most of which were divested by the early 1990s, when Quaker decided to focus on food products. In the 1960s the company decided to take much of its advertising in-house and in 1969 formed an agency called Adcom, which was billing nearly $50 million by 1985. It was spun off shortly thereafter and became an independent shop (although with Quaker business) under the name Bayer Bess Vanderwarker, Inc., whose billings grew to more than $175 million by 1995.

Success with Gatorade

By far the biggest of Quaker's acquisitions was Gatorade, a sports drink acquired with the purchase of Stokely-Van Camp in 1983. Gatorade became Quaker's largest single brand worldwide by the early 21st century, accounting for almost 40 percent of sales and operating income and a more than 80 percent market share in the category. After Gatorade was spun off into a separate division in 1991, division head Peter Vitulli signed a deal to make basketball superstar Michael Jordan the brand's worldwide spokesperson. Gatorade also became a sponsor of the United States' first all-pro Olympic basketball team, led by Jordan. Bayer Bess Vander-warker, Gatorade's agency, created the "Be Like Mike" campaign, and Jordan signed a long-term contract with Quaker. Foote, Cone & Belding (FCB) inherited the prized Gatorade account when its parent True North Communications acquired Bayer Bess in 1996. Jordan's much-publicized, albeit temporary, retirement from basketball caused some tinkering with the long-running campaign, and the brand sought out endorsement deals with other high-profile and up-and-coming athletes.

Misjudging Snapple

After Quaker's tremendous marketing success with Gatorade, analysts were aghast at the marketing debacle of Snapple, a New Age line of fruit juices and iced teas the company acquired in late 1994 for what was immediately perceived as too high a price—$1.7 billion. Prior to Quaker's purchase, Snapple had become a cult favorite, aided by the quirky use of Snapple employee Wendy Kaufman as the "Snapple lady" and of controversial radio personality Howard Stern in its advertising. Quaker's first act after the acquisition was to drop both of them.

Quaker took its marketing and distribution formula for Gatorade and applied it to Snapple with dismal results. By mid-1996 Quaker had fired the New York City ad agency Kirshenbaum Bond & Partners, which sought to position Snapple against soft drinks Coca-Cola and Pepsi-Cola, and switched the account to

FCB. FCB kicked off a $40 million media spending and sampling effort to get people to try Snapple, with the tag line, "Spread the good taste all over the place." The campaign failed, and in 1997 Quaker sold Snapple to Triarc Companies for a fire-sale price of $300 million. Cadbury Schweppes acquired Snapple and several other brands from Triarc in 2000 for $1.45 billion.

Meanwhile, Quaker continued to put a modern-day spin on the health claims of its core cereal products. In early 1997 Quaker received approval from the U.S. Food and Drug Administration to make claims about oatmeal's ability to lower cholesterol and reduce the risk of heart disease. It ran simultaneously with the "Oh, What Those Oats Can Do" campaign from Jordan, McGrath, Case & Taylor, New York City.

In the fall of 1998 Quaker oatmeal's "Warms You, Heart and Soul" campaign highlighted about 100 residents of Lafayette, Colorado, who, by eating Quaker oatmeal every day for 30 days, had succeeded in lowering their cholesterol levels. The seven TV spots and one print ad from FCB were the second effort from the agency since it had won the hot cereal business from Jordan, McGrath in 1997. In 2000 PepsiCo, which was eager to enter the athletic beverage field with the leading brand, Gatorade, acquired Quaker for $13.4 billion, PepsiCo's largest acquisition ever. In September 2001 PepsiCo fired FCB and moved its $300 million-plus account, including Quaker cereals and Gatorade, to Omnicom Group, Inc.

MARY ELLEN PODMOLIK

Further Reading

Dotz, Warren, and Jim Morton, *What a Character! 20th-Century American Advertising Icons*, San Francisco: Chronicle Books, 1996

Goodrum, Charles A., and Helen Dalrymple, *Advertising in America: The First 200 Years*, New York: Abrams, 1990

Lefton, Terry, "The Post-Mike Millennium," *Brandweek* (3 January 2000)

Marquette, Arthur F., *Brands, Trademarks, and Good Will: The Story of the Quaker Oats Company*, New York: McGraw Hill, 1967

Pollack, Judann, "Ordinary People Star in New Fall Quaker Effort," *Advertising Age* (17 August 1998)

Quantitative/Qualitative Research

Advertising and related marketing research can be divided into two categories: quantitative and qualitative. This division is useful in describing and thinking about the various methods available, but it is also arbitrary and can distract from the best possible research. Researchers often view these approaches in complemen-

tary terms and consider the information offered by each since both are often applied together.

Quantitative research constructs marketing issues in terms of numbers and uses these numbers for statistical analysis. Typical sources of such data are surveys with scalable items, experiments with measurable independent and dependent variables, and purchase information obtained from scanner data. The goals of quantitative research may be descriptive (e.g., profiling market indicators in percentages), correlational (e.g., assessing associations between such factors as age and brand purchase), or causal-predictive (e.g., one direct mailing piece tested against another).

Qualitative research is composed of the insights, themes, and basic understanding of a situation. Though numbers may be used in conjunction with qualitative research, it is usually framed in verbal terms. For instance, focus groups, the most widely used form of qualitative research, usually yield transcripts of group discussions about a product or service. These transcripts are then interpreted and key themes identified. Numbers relating to the frequency of particular responses may be used but are not essential.

Comparing Approaches

In comparing the two broad approaches of qualitative and quantitative research, the following issues are important: objectivity versus subjectivity, degree of structure, method of analysis, and final use or disposition.

Objectivity versus Subjectivity

Qualitative research is widely considered to be less objective and scientific than quantitative research. Qualitative research is based on direct interpretation by the analyst and is said to be more of an art than a science. Some qualitative analysts admit to being subjective, and many claim that such subjectivity is inescapable. By contrast, quantitative research is usually considered objective and scientific since it is formulated in terms of numbers and is subject to rigorous statistical analysis. Sometimes these two approaches are framed in terms of being positivistic (objective-scientific) versus post-positivistic (subjective or even anti-scientific). However, since most quantitative research relies on good qualitative research, the argument over scientific validity is for all practical purposes moot. Thus, though we may be informed by exploring these different philosophical perspectives, it is probably more important to view each type of research in its own domain and to consider how the two may be used together to provide the best quality information.

Degree of Structure

Quantitative methods are considered to be structured with definite measures and types of analyses, while qualitative methods are said to be unstructured because their approaches to data collection and interpretation are much less defined and programmatic. Quantitative questions are sometimes referred to as closed-ended questions and qualitative questions as open-ended. For example, a closed-ended question might involve asking a person to rate his feelings about a commercial on a scale of one to seven, with "7" representing "Like very much," "1" representing "Dislike very much," and the in between representing intermediate hedonic or liking categories. An open-ended question might be, "Tell us whether you like or dislike this commercial and why." Such a question leaves room for unexpected answers, though it is harder to quantify.

Qualitative questions may be asked in more or less-structured formats. A structured format refers to a series of questions seeking predetermined types of information. A less-structured format, sometimes referred to as phenomenological or existential-phenomenological, is one in which questions with less direction are posed and the information sought is conceived in open-ended terms. Providing as few biasing cues as possible helps to get closer to the consumer. For example, if the researcher was interested in what consumers derived from automobile advertising, she might ask, "Tell me about some automobile advertising you have seen." The consumer might respond immediately, or might ask, "Where should I begin?" The interviewer might then respond, "Start anywhere you feel like." As the interview progresses, the interviewer provides further prompts when necessary such as, "Tell more about that ad." These prompts move the interview along and are parallel to the series of questions in a structured interview, except that they are less directive.

Method of Analysis

Quantitative methods employ a wide variety of statistical methods that look for statistically significant and behaviorally meaningful differences in predicting behavior. Statistical significance means that a variable has achieved a certain probability level of having an effect. Often that level is 95 percent or more. Behavioral meaningfulness refers to the general size or applicability of that effect. For example, a study of purchase behavior might use a regression analysis method in which a number of predictor variables are examined to see if they forecast such behavior. The predictors (also called independent variables) might include such variables as advertising expenditures, competitor advertising expenditures, marketing expenditures, and sales promotion expenditures. Suppose further that advertising expenditures are found to have a statistically significant effect. The next question might concentrate on whether to increase such expenditures. To answer, the size of the effect and whether it will meaningfully increase purchases should be considered.

The analysis of qualitative research proceeds in different ways, deals with different questions, and provides different answers. Such analysis would be more interpretive than predictive and seeks to provide fuller insight. Analysis involves reading interview or focus group transcripts, listening to audiotapes, and viewing videotapes, all generically referred to as texts. As these texts are reviewed, their meaning is clarified in a circle between reading and interpretation. This is sometimes referred to as a hermeneutic circle process, a term derived from Bible studies in which people go back and forth between the text and their interpretive reading. Part of this process brings in additional perspectives, from other people or from other literature. Based on this process, an interpretation is hammered out that is generally thematic.

An interesting hybrid of quantitative and qualitative research is known as cognitive response analysis. Often used in advertising and other studies, study subjects think aloud while engaging in an activity, including watching commercials. Often such data are coded in terms that can be quantified, such as product-related thoughts concerning the product shown, message-related thoughts concerning the ad itself, source-related thoughts concerning the source of the message, and unrelated thoughts. These thoughts can be scaled in numbers and further analyzed statistically in relation to other variables. For example, two commercials are compared in terms of the frequency of each type of thought they produce. However, because various thematic elements may emerge from the application of the cognitive response technique, its textual data are also susceptible to qualitative analysis and interpretation. Therefore each aspect of a commercial is analyzed in terms of cognitive response data for the themes or meanings that consumers provide.

Final Use or Disposition

The most frequent application of quantitative and qualitative research has been to use qualitative research as an exploratory step leading to eventual quantitative study and confirmation. To study image perception change evoked by a commercial, for example, researchers might conduct focus groups to see what effects are taking place and then use these results to construct a survey to confirm these effects on a larger and more quantified scale.

Qualitative research is sometimes used as the primary research mode. Its findings are then used to answer research questions and formulate advertising strategy without any accompanying quantitative research. Though sometimes a matter of cost and convenience, this approach can also reflect the belief that qualitative methods answer the research need by themselves.

Ultimately the relationship of various modes of research should be one of triangulation. Triangulation means that researchers use different types of research and then compare the results for convergence. This approach is an ideal that often cannot be fully embraced in the everyday world. Many large companies follow this philosophy to varying degrees, using many methods and researchers. If the results of triangulation are convergent then it is likely that the research is pointing in the right direction; if the results are not convergent, this could reflect validity problems with the modes of research, or it could mean that deeper issues exist that have not been addressed. It might indicate, for example, that one research study did not measure what it purported to measure or that the two studies did not really measure the same effects.

Focus Groups

Focus groups are the most commonly used type of qualitative research. They are employed widely not only in marketing and advertising but also in organizational, political, and related areas. In advertising, focus groups have been widely used at all stages of campaigns from creation to recall testing. For instance, in their 1990 book *Focus Groups: Theory and Practice*, David W. Stewart

and Prem N. Shamdasani report that data from focus group studies have prompted such companies as General Electric and AT&T Corporation to cancel commercials before they have been aired. In *The Focus Group: A Strategic Guide to Organizing, Conducting, and Analyzing the Focus Group Interview* (1994), Jane Farley Templeton describes an interesting case study of the use of focus groups to test different "creative materials" and positioning for cocktail mixes. Several different target audiences were used. Though there were specific findings for each target audience, class and reputation issues emerged as a common theme across targets. Other examples of the influence of focus groups on advertising include Hamilton Beach creating an ad campaign that stressed a more youthful appeal for its home appliances; the British Tourist Authority updating its image and developing a new ad campaign; Lucent Technologies developing its name and logo; Carnival Cruise Lines revamping its spokesperson strategy; Screenvision Cinema Networks exploring theater advertising; Cross & Blackwell, a producer of packaged food products, finding it had high prompted awareness relative to spontaneous awareness and setting out to change this; a testing of advertising concepts by Novell, a computer software maker; and the reformulation and glamorization of an industrial product, the insecticide Durban Pro, by DowElamco.

Focus groups vary in size, though 6 to 12 participants are common. Controversy arose over whether focus groups composed of strangers are more effective in terms of idea generation than those composed of people who know one another. The evidence appears to indicate that the two types of groups are about equal in quality.

The main idea of a focus group is to get people to talk in depth about a particular topic. The role of the moderator is to keep the conversation flowing, keep it on topic, and try to involve all participants. The moderator must probe for details when necessary and ensure that the proper degree of depth is achieved. The sessions are usually recorded (audio or video), and often one-way mirrors are used so that the marketing team can observe the group and, in particular, watch the body language of the participants. Incentives are usually given for focus group participation, and these vary depending on the participants. Focus groups involving doctors or professionals often require larger incentives than other kinds of groups. Everyday consumers may be paid as much as $50 to $100, depending on geographic locale and the amount of time spent.

Conducting focus groups is a managerial process that includes planning, execution, analysis, and reporting to the client. Planning includes determining the type of research to conduct, what to ask, where to do it, and who is to do the research. The idea is to conduct targeted, useful research that answers specific questions. The development of a strong focus group interview guide or protocol in which questions are laid out in advance is a critical part of planning. Stewart and Shamdasani reported on a focus group interview guide in which people were asked to discuss the relative importance of several predetermined factors, including advertising, that influenced their car purchase decision. Other topic questions, along with probes (e.g., "why or why not?"), were also mentioned.

Execution depends on the moderator, who is responsible for what happens in the focus group. Often the moderator is an outside consultant who participates throughout most or all of the process and is also responsible for the analysis and interpretation of the groups. The transition from execution to analysis is important because the number of groups to be used is often determined by the moderator's assessment as to whether more groups would produce different or contrary information. When the process of conducting focus groups is finished, the analysis begins. Various forms of analysis can be used. Often a form of coding is employed. For example, statements may be coded in terms of agreement-disagreement among group participants. Thematic analysis, which develops the main points of a focus group, may also be used. Whatever analysis is applied, it is useful for more than one person to assess the results for triangulation purposes because two analysts often interpret the same texts differently. A final report is then written for the client in which the results are summarized and recommendations are made.

Moving Target

Recent developments in both quantitative and qualitative research have followed the trend toward more on-line activity. Focus groups are conducted on-line through the use of focus group software. So-called on-line, or wired, groups operate in a more anonymous environment than do face-to-face focus groups, and participants are thought to be freer to express their opinions. Each person's opinion appears to carry equal weight. Opinions are registered on the computer screen and people can see each other's opinions while they are writing their own. A *Harvard Business Review* study reported, however, that people felt alienated by the experience, perhaps because they did not feel that they were regarded as individuals.

Still the use of on-line focus groups likely will grow for several reasons: they are cost-efficient; they are flexible and allow marketers and advertisers to reach broad audiences both nationally and worldwide from one central location; follow-ups by e-mail are relatively easy; and new technological developments, such as Netcam (video), which allows people to see one another live, and increased bandwidth (Internet capacity), which allows for better and faster communication, may reduce the alienation. The rapid evolution of information technology, especially of the Internet, seems to ensure that on-line focus groups and other forms of on-line qualitative research will develop. Advertisers and their researchers need to fol-

low the strategy that many traditional retailers have followed, to move on-line while continuing their efforts off-line, until at some point an optimum balance is established.

Researchers need to be creative, but this does not mean reinventing—or tampering with—the wheel. Quite the contrary, researchers need to study their field and keep up with developments. Whether the research technology is quantitative or qualitative, the target is moving, and the current research environment neither mimics the research of yesterday nor completely presages the research of tomorrow. Beyond these broad parameters and trends, each research situation has its own unique elements and calls on the investigator to exhibit insight and creativity both in terms of the method employed and the emergent themes uncovered. Knowing when to use which method, triangulating the methods, drawing on one's experiences, and developing a sense of confidence in judgment are all parts of this process.

STEPHEN J. GOULD

Further Reading

Altheide, David L., *Qualitative Media Analysis,* Thousand Oaks, California: Sage, 1996

Denzin, Norman K., and Yvonna S. Lincoln, editors, *Handbook of Qualitative Research,* Thousand Oaks, California: Sage, 1994

Gould, Stephen J., "Protocol and Cognitive Response Analysis," in *The Elgar Companion to Consumer Research and Economic Psychology,* edited by Peter E. Earl and Simon Kemp, Cheltenham, Gloucestershire, and Northampton, Massachusetts: Elgar, 1999

Greenbaum, Thomas L., *The Practical Handbook and Guide to Focus Group Research,* Lexington, Massachusetts: Lexington Books, 1988; as *The Handbook for Focus Group Research,* New York: Macmillan, 1993; 2nd edition revised, Thousand Oaks, California: Sage: 1998

Kiely, Thomas, "Wired Focus Groups," *Harvard Business Review* 76, no. 1 (January/February 1998)

Morgan, David L., and Richard A. Krueger, editors, *Focus Group Kit,* 6 vols., Thousand Oaks, California: Sage, 1998

Stewart, David W., and Prem N. Shamdasani, *Focus Groups: Theory and Practice,* Newbury Park, California: Sage, 1990

Templeton, Jane Farley, *The Focus Group: A Strategic Guide to Organizing, Conducting, and Analyzing the Focus Group Interview,* Chicago: Probus, 1994

R

Radio

Radio began as a wireless communication system employed mainly for ship-to-ship and ship-to-shore communication and as a hobby for wireless enthusiasts. Before World War I, radio hobbyists built send-and-receive transmitters and communicated (first in Morse code, then in voice) with their associates in distant places. Although the ban on amateur broadcasting during the war temporarily slowed the nonmilitary use of radio, wartime training and technical advancements led to a boom in amateur interest in radio. By 1922 a sizable group of radio enthusiasts had developed. It included among its ranks both curious amateurs and individuals who worked for churches, stores, manufacturers—in short, any enterprise that had a message, commercial or otherwise, to deliver to the listening public.

It was not long before radio's unprecedented kind of widespread, unselective, and pervasive communication—in a word, broadcasting—awakened both hopes and anxieties in peoples around the globe. A great debate followed that became a dominant theme of advertising history in the 1920s: who should pay for radio and who should profit from it. In most nations, governments followed Great Britain's example and chose a state-chartered system, supported by a tax on receivers, with no commercial advertising permitted. Radio was too powerful a tool for nation-building and civic control, it was argued in those nations, to allow the medium to fall into the hands of irresponsible merchants. In the United States, however, radio became an element of commerce. The Radio Corporation of America (RCA) was formed by a consortium of companies—consisting of General Electric (GE), United Fruit, American Telephone and Telegraph (AT&T), and Westinghouse—led by the GE general counsel Owen D. Young. Its purpose: to acquire the interests and patents of American Marconi, which had been doing pioneering research in the U.S. since 1899, and to centralize control over radio patents in U.S. hands. Its principal role would be to manufacture radio equipment. On the transmission side, legal restrictions on amateur radio operators and the creation of a new kind of class-B license in 1922 ensured that only stations operated by companies that could afford live talent and a well-rounded schedule would get the best broadcast frequencies and highest power assignments in the United States. These were assigned by the federal government to various individuals and institutions.

Advent of Networks

By the late 1920s, U.S. radio had developed into an advertising medium. Most early stations—such as Gimbel Brothers' WIP, the *Chicago Tribune*'s WGN, and Westinghouse's KDKA—served to advertise their owner's primary business, although most stations also made their transmitters available, either for a fee or simply to fill time on the broadcast schedule, to song publishers, concert arrangers, magazines, newspapers, hotel orchestras, movie theaters, and other parties with businesses to promote. The AT&T station WEAF is frequently credited with pioneering "toll broadcasting," a system by which anyone with something to sell could buy time on the air and put on a show to promote their product.

In 1926 RCA and AT&T (along with its subsidiary Western Electric) were the two largest electrical manufacturing firms in the United States. As long as their business was wireless radio, the radio alliance presented no antitrust problems, as AT&T's principal business was wired telephone service. The problem developed when RCA began to plan a national network of radio stations in which AT&T long-distance lines would become the conduit from city to city. At that point AT&T dropped out of the partnership and sold its stations, which included WEAF, to RCA. In November 1926 RCA formed the National Broadcasting Company (NBC) on the basis of its own New York flagship station, WJZ, and the newly acquired WEAF. This meant that RCA would actually feed each of the two networks of affiliates out of New York City. When the planners sat down to determine which affiliates would be associated with which network, they used a red pencil to link WEAF stations around the country and a blue pencil to link the WJZ affiliates. Thus were born the Red Network and the Blue Network.

The Columbia Broadcasting System (CBS) was established two years later, under the direction of cigar-company scion William S. Paley. With a network system, great economies of scale could be realized for advertisers: a program produced in New York could reach millions of listeners across the nation, at very little additional cost. An industry, and an audience, was born.

Early programs were performed live and ran the gamut from the *Eveready Hour,* which starred "red-headed music maker" Wendell Hall and his ukulele under the sponsorship of the National Carbon Company, to *Amos 'n' Andy,* a comedy based on blackface vaudeville routines and comic strips, which aired on the *Chicago Daily News'* station WMAQ. These shows went national on the NBC network, and many others joined them. At first, stations and networks put together their own programs and then sought out a sponsor to provide support. By the mid-1930s, however, advertising agencies had taken over the production of radio programs, sensing that they could do a better job for their clients if they relied on their own marketing and showmanship skills, rather than following the somewhat "stuffy" and cautious tastes of network executives. Programs of every type—including big-name variety shows, daytime serials, star-studded cinematic adaptations, comedy series, adventure serials, and prime-time dramas—emanated from the newly formed radio production departments of advertising agencies large and small. Some of the largest agencies, such as J. Walter Thompson (JWT), Young & Rubicam (Y&R), and Blackett-Sample-Hummert (B-S-H), pioneered in genres and techniques of production that live on today.

Role of Sponsorship

Thus, during its most vital and, some would argue, most glorious period, U.S. radio broadcasting was the creation, and the creature, of the advertising industry. Advertising agencies and their clients took full advantage of the absence of barriers between commercials and program content. In J. Walter Thompson's *Fleischmann's Yeast Hour,* starring Rudy Vallee, references to the product were worked into the show's script. On the air, Vallee introduced his guests as his own special friends and spoke of his musical selections, but the JWT creative staff behind the scenes acknowledged that Vallee was working from a script that they had written for him. It was deemed unseemly for a star such as Vallee to openly promote the sponsor's product; therefore, during the program, Vallee would be heard wandering among the tables in his fictional nightclub, eavesdropping on conversations, which often concerned that ever-fascinating topic, Fleischmann's Yeast. Another highly successful and influential JWT show, *The Lux Radio Theatre,* featured legendary film director Cecil B. DeMille as putative producer and director, selecting films for adaptation, recruiting stars as guests, and casually chatting with them—frequently about Lux soap products—before and after the production. In fact, the almost equally legendary JWT staff members, including Danny Danker, George Wells, Carroll Carroll, and Sanford Barnett, did the actual writing, production, and direction.

One of radio's best-loved programs and advertising vehicles was the long-running *Jack Benny Show,* produced by Young & Rubicam for General Foods' Jell-O Pudding and Grape Nuts until 1944. The program's plot usually revolved around the production of a radio show. It starred Benny, playing a stingy but good-hearted host, who was also named Jack Benny, and Benny's real-life wife, Mary Livingston, playing his secretary and companion, along with announcer George Wilson; flamboyant band leader Phil Harris; various singers; and Eddie "Rochester" Anderson, who played Benny's butler/valet. Through the "show within a show" format, Benny presented a highly successful program that contained most of the standard elements found in other comedy and music shows while simultaneously parodying radio, popular culture, and the sponsor alike.

Procter & Gamble (P&G) probably sponsored more daytime programs than any other U.S. company, while the pioneering husband-and-wife team of Frank and Anne Hummert (of the Blackett-Sample-Hummert agency) were the most prolific producers of daytime serials, or soap operas. Raymond Stedman, author of *The Serials* (1977), has estimated that 46 percent of the daytime serials aired on network radio between 1932 and 1937, and 30 percent of those introduced between 1927 and 1942, were authored by the Hummerts and their dozens of assistants (see Table 1).

By the late 1930s advertising agencies had moved much radio production to Hollywood, California, in order to be close to the

Table 1.   Programs by Frank and Anne Hummert.

Program (years broadcast)	Selected Sponsor(s)
Arnold Grimm's Daughter (1937–41)	General Mills
Bachelor's Children (1935–59)	Old Dutch Cleanser, Colgate, Wonder bread
Backstage Wife (1935–59)	Sterling Drug, Procter & Gamble
Betty and Bob (1932–40)	General Mills
Central City (1938–39)	Procter & Gamble
David Harum (1935–51)	Babbit Corporation
Guiding Light (1937–)	General Mills, Procter & Gamble
Front Page Farrell (1941–1951)	Whitehall Company
Helpmate (1941–44)	Old Dutch Cleanser
John's Other Wife (1936–40)	Whitehall Company
Judy and Jane (1932–35)	Folger's Coffee
Just Plain Bill (1932–55)	Whitehall Company, Miles Laboratories (Alka-Seltzer)
Lorenzo Jones (1937–55)	Sterling Drugs, Procter & Gamble
Ma Perkins (1933–60)	Procter & Gamble
Mrs. Wiggs of the Cabbage Patch (1935–38)	Hills Cough Drops, Old English Wax
Old Gal Sunday (1937–59)	American Home Products, Procter & Gamble
Rich Man's Darling (1936–37)	Old Gold Cigarettes
Romance of Helen Trent (1933–60)	American Home Products, Procter & Gamble
Second Husband (1937–46)	Sterling Drugs
Stella Dallas (1937–55)	Sterling Drugs
Strange Romance of Evelyn Winters (1944–48)	Sweetheart Soap
Young Widder Brown (1938–56)	Sterling Drugs

ANOTHER YOUNG & RUBICAM RADIO SHOW

The Colgate HOUSE PARTY

IN THE ROLE OF HOST, Brad Brown, with his friendly voice, makes everybody feel right at home ... and ties the show together.

MUSIC FOR THE WHOLE FAMILY is provided by the eminent Don Voorhees and his orchestra.

HOWARD CLANEY puts sincerity into the commercials ... makes them pleasing.

TO ATTRACT WOMEN, Donald Novis was selected. A romantic tenor who has packed theatres wherever he has made personal appearances.

MEN, WOMEN AND CHILDREN like the way the Melody Boys put over a song ... either as a male trio or when harmonizing with the Rhythm Girls.

TO WIN THE CHILDREN, TOO, Arthur Boran was chosen. He is radio's foremost mimic and supplies the comedy with his impersonations of outstanding screen, stage and radio stars.

TO APPEAL TO MEN is the assignment given Frances Langford. And this diminutive singer has the charm and personality to do this job in a big way.

EVERYBODY LIKES HARMONY ... so the Rhythm Girls are spot-lighted on "The Colgate House Party."

THE PRODUCT: Dental cream and dental powder, used alike by men, women and children.

THE PROBLEM: To create a radio program that would appeal to all three groups.

THE SOLUTION: A variety show handled in a fresh, new way. "The Colgate House Party."

THE STRATEGY: Each entertainer was selected because of his or her ability to make a high-spot appeal to a different member of the family, and all are so woven together that they provide sparkling entertainment for everybody.

THE TIME: Every Saturday night at 9:00 P.M. (E.D.S.T.) over N. B. C. red network.

Some other Young & Rubicam Radio Shows now on the air are: The Byrd South Pole Expedition—for Grape-Nuts ... Albert Spalding—for Fletcher's Castoria ... 45 Minutes in Hollywood—for the Borden Company ... The Horton Varieties of 1934—for Horton Ice Cream ... The Dixie Circus—for Dixie Cups ... Beatrice Fairfax—for La France ... General Foods Cooking School—for General Foods Products ... *and* 21 separate local station shows for Fels-Naptha.

YOUNG & RUBICAM, Inc.
advertising

NEW YORK   CHICAGO
PHILADELPHIA   DETROIT

This 1934 print ad promoting the agency's services to marketers cast Young & Rubicam, Inc., as a creator of sponsored radio programming.

film industry, with which radio producers increasingly exchanged stars, scripts, and properties. Daytime serials and a few other programs continued to be produced in New York City and Chicago, Illinois, however.

Radio networks in the United States established continuity acceptance departments in the late 1920s as a way of exerting some control over the material aired on their licensed outlets. By the late 1930s, however, they found themselves in the frustrating position of acting as mere "time brokers" to increasingly headstrong and obstreperous marketers and agencies that seemed to delight in finding new ways of subverting, avoiding, or outright attacking the networks' efforts to air tasteful programs.

Era of Regulation

As the networks ceded creative control in the 1930s, however, their business boomed. Even as the Depression decimated most American economic and social structures, radio networks grew more profitable than ever. Their success could be partially attributed to the passage of the Communications Act of 1934, which defeated a campaign to institute government subsidies for public service broadcasting in the United States and confirmed the dominance of commercial radio, leaving untouched its system of sponsor control. The newly formed Federal Communications Commission (FCC) licensed and regulated broadcasting stations, but the networks themselves were untouchable—except through their owned and operated stations—as they and their sponsors remained protected under the First Amendment of the Constitution from any government interference with radio content. By the late 1930s, NBC was running two highly successful networks, the slightly more commercial Red and the slightly more upscale Blue, while CBS had also grown.

Under their economic arrangement with the networks, affiliate stations received payment from their network for providing "clearance" of certain hours of the day and night for the broadcasting of shows, which the network had sold to its sponsors/clients. This "station compensation" could amount to a sizable proportion of an affiliate's income. Stations could program the remaining time themselves with either local or syndicated productions and sell these shows to local advertisers. However, under the terms of their license agreements with the FCC, stations were also expected to serve the public by airing a certain number of unsponsored, "sustaining" programs, which were thoughtfully sold to the affiliates by the networks.

This arrangement worked well as long as NBC dominated the market; as CBS developed into a powerhouse of programming, however, it eliminated the sustaining fee—and at the same time, much of the sustaining programming. NBC eliminated its charge for sustaining shows in 1935, and most sustaining programs now consisted of entertainment waiting for a sponsor. By the early 1940s, sponsored programs occupied most of radio's broadcasting schedules.

There were several challenges to the network dominance of radio in the 1930s and 1940s. Early regulation had emphasized that radio should function ideally as a live medium, but by the

mid-1930s the FCC had somewhat relaxed its restrictions on recorded, or "transcribed," programs, mandating that stations could air electronic transcriptions as long as they were announced as such. With recording technology still dependent on scratchy pressings or acetate discs, networks continued to enforce a ban on transcription programs. But smaller independent stations came to depend on nationally syndicated recorded shows as well as "spot" advertising, both of which slowly also made inroads into the schedules of network affiliates. In 1934, four powerful independent stations (WOR, Newark, New Jersey; WLW, Cincinnati, Ohio; WXYZ, Detroit, Michigan; and WGN, Chicago) formed the Mutual Broadcasting System (MBS), as an alternate source of network programming and as an alternative outlet for advertisers that did not need or could not afford the complete distribution of the major networks. MBS, which pooled programs produced by its member stations, eventually became a leader in syndication to smaller stations across the country.

In 1943, after an FCC investigation into the market power of the networks produced some government-mandated structural changes designed to increase competition, NBC transferred its Blue network to Lifesaver magnate Edward Noble to form the American Broadcasting Company (ABC). The FCC also forced NBC and CBS to relinquish control of their talent bureaus, through which they had dominated radio production, and to loosen the tight network hold over affiliate relations. Despite these reforms, large advertisers and their agencies continued to produce the bulk of network programming. By 1945, five agencies provided 46 percent of CBS's income and 33 percent of ABC's.

Wartime Changes

World War II brought new challenges to advertising and to radio in the United States. Radio and advertising executives played key roles in the government's campaign to boost morale and spread wartime information and propaganda. Key among these efforts was the creation of the Armed Forces Radio Service (AFRS), which sent transcribed programs (recorded on disc) to hundreds of temporary radio broadcasting stations in troop encampments around the world. Some feared that the advertisement of products would make troops homesick and would send the unappealing message that companies were sponsoring the war; therefore, the programs were carefully "denatured" (the advertising was removed), and public service messages or music were inserted in their stead. Shows such as *Command Performance*—in which U.S. servicemen "commanded" their favorite performers to appear—and *Jubilee*—the AFRS's belated attempt to provide black soldiers in the racially segregated military with black-oriented entertainment from the equally segregated world of U.S. radio—had an impact around the world. In many countries, the experience of hearing American jazz and other elements of American popular culture on radio for the first time inspired postwar efforts to liberalize public broadcasting systems. The most notably affected nation was Great Britain, where advertising was introduced on the new medium of television in the mid-1950s.

On the American homefront, the wartime dominance of women both as talent and as audience swept a generation of female performers, many of them former supporting players in Hollywood, onto prime-time airwaves. Comediennes such as Lucille Ball, Joan Davis, Eve Arden, and Ann Sothern (along with many of their male counterparts) formed their own production companies, often organized through their talent agents, and sold their own shows to sponsors and agencies. Also during World War II, public interest in news brought radio into a new role of national importance. Sponsored news programs became one of the most significant genres of the period, as networks began to establish international news organizations. American radio had reached its finest hour, providing the country with both information and entertainment, offering morale-boosting messages at home and abroad, and realizing an increasingly central role in politics through broadcasts of political conventions and Franklin D. Roosevelt's "fireside chats" (a term first coined by CBS newsman Robert Trout in March 1933).

After the war, the nation's attention turned to television. The new medium grew slowly, hampered by debates over standards and a freeze on television station licenses (1948–52), but by 1953 television had clearly usurped many of the entertainment functions that radio had once fulfilled in national life. As more and more programs, performers, producers, and advertisers switched to television, network radio struggled to survive. Only a few hardy shows remained on the radio airwaves, many of them simulcast versions of television originals, such as *Arthur Godfrey's Talent Scouts* and *You Bet Your Life*. Even *Ma Perkins* said goodbye in 1960, one of the last of the daytime serials to hold on to its aural perch. Programming on the national radio networks dwindled to primarily musical and news shows, which were not enough to fill all the hours of airtime. However, the number of radio stations on the air actually increased after the war, thanks to revised FCC regulations and an increased demand for lower-power stations. Radio became a local medium, featuring local tastes, recorded music, and the talents of a new breed of local radio announcers, soon to be known as disc jockeys, or DJs.

Decline of Networks

One of the first groups to recognize the opportunities that local radio presented was the African-American community. Such entrepreneurs as Jack L. Cooper and Al Benson of Chicago had been producing programs for African-American listeners since the 1930s, but network broadcasters (and other sectors of the entertainment industry) had long neglected black audiences and largely relegated black performers to minstrel-derived "blackface" roles. The desertion of the AM band by the national organizations after World War II meant that stations had to build on their local audiences, which in postwar industrialized cities across the country included sizable African-American populations. In cities such as Memphis, Tennessee; Atlanta, Georgia; Birmingham, Alabama; and New Orleans, Louisiana, station owners (most of whom were white) saw that by airing previously excluded black music and community identity programming, they could sell advertisements

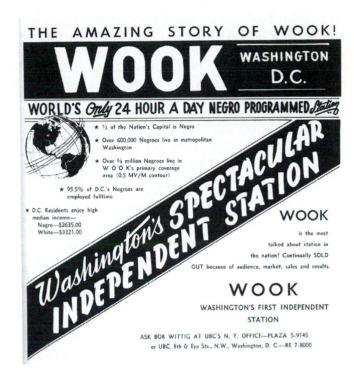

Washington, D.C., radio station WOOK, which appealed to African-American listeners, emphasized the desirable demographic characteristics of its audience in this ca. 1950 ad.

to companies eager to attract African-American consumers. Innovative DJs such as Nat D. Williams and B.B. King spoke a hip dialect taken from the streets of their communities and played rhythm-and-blues records for black audiences—and, increasingly, for a crossover audience of white youth. Rock 'n' roll and soul music would eventually rise from this fertile ground, along with the invention of segmented format radio, a significant innovation in marketing and culture.

One of the first formats to emerge was the "top 40," the invention of which is usually credited to Todd Storz and Gordon McLendon, the owners of a group of stations. In an endeavor that presaged most of the new media trends in the decades to come, Storz and McLendon targeted the youth, or teen, market—a wise move as the nation felt the first impact of the baby boom. Playing the new rhythm-and-blues–inflected rock 'n' roll music and employing DJs such as Alan Freed and Wolfman Jack, who imitated their black counterparts in language and style, top-40 stations translated a long-suppressed black musical tradition into a hybrid form that appealed to American teens of different races.

However, the top-40 format hit a snag in the late 1950s, when the "payola" scandal broke. The music-rights organization American Society of Composers, Authors and Publishers (ASCAP) resented the role that the upstart Broadcast Music Incorporated (BMI) had played in breaking ASCAP's hold on the music business by actively licensing new music, much of it the top-40 sounds played on new format radio. Prompted by ASCAP's objections, as well as by the quiz show scandals in the television industry, the FCC determined to look into the relationship of DJs to the music they promoted on-air. Developing personalized "playlists" of music for their specialized audiences and rotating songs on the new "musical clock" system, DJs exercised great power over which records would reach their audiences. Since each play of a new song title consisted of a form of advertising for the record company that produced it, DJs could profit financially by promoting certain songs. A DJ might accept direct payments from record companies, acquire partial ownership of record companies, or make money from co-songwriting credits. The careers of several prominent DJs were ruined in the FCC investigation.

Format Radio

Not surprisingly, as the youth market continued to prefer rock 'n' roll and advertisers continued to pursue that market, parents and others with more mature preferences sought relief from such youthful exuberance. Other specialized formats targeting older audiences appeared, such as "beautiful music," country-and-western, middle-of-the-road, and all-news. Networks soon adapted news services to fit the different formats, and advertisers, whose reliance on new forms of market research motivated advertising segmentation, found suitable outlets for different lifestyle-related products. The Radio Advertising Bureau, formed in 1951 as the Broadcast Advertising Bureau (it changed its name in 1955) provided centralized marketing, research, and promotional services to help stations survive in the segmented, localized era of format radio. Under the influence of these powerful marketing research methods and newly "discovered" audiences, various forms of programming thrived. Spanish-language radio, which, like black radio, had received a boost in the late 1940s, developed into one of the fastest-growing segments of the market. New networks emerged, such as the National Black Network and Sheridan Broadcasting, that specialized in black-oriented formats and eventually developed the powerful urban contemporary format, and the Spanish International Network, one of the growing number of services oriented to the Latino market.

The process of segmented formatting was accelerated by the liberation of a powerful force that had long been suppressed by competing corporate interests: FM (frequency modulation) radio. FM had been developed and promoted by Edwin H. Armstrong in the 1930s, and the FCC authorized limited FM transmission before World War II, but RCA opposed its development as a competitor against AM. It was not until after the war that the regulatory agency expanded the FM band to 88–106 MHz, setting aside the frequencies between 88 and 92 for public and educational stations. For the first time in U.S. history, educational radio had won a victory in its long battle to survive. In 1970 the National Public Radio network was formed, bringing in-depth news programs and eclectic music and information to nonprofit stations, mostly on the FM band, across the country.

FM also evolved into the preferred setting for stations playing music formats other than rock 'n' roll. Superior in many ways to AM transmission and aided by the development of new stereo audio equipment, FM came into its own in the 1960s. Many classical music FM stations such as WFMT in Chicago restricted the use of pre-recorded commercials and prohibited the use of jingles as incompatible with the seriousness of the programming, and a variety of eclectic and "progressive" formats—including jazz, hard rock, folk, album-oriented rock, alternative, free-form, and underground music—also found audiences on FM. Even though some of these formats were critical of the power of consumer culture, advertising to the youth market via FM continued to be profitable.

Automation

In the 1970s trends in radio programming in the United States changed once again. The rise of automated formats, the proliferation of syndicated programs, and the sheer commercial success of radio in the television age brought a new kind of national concentration to the industry. Computerization allowed many stations to eliminate on-air personnel by programming a limited rotation of a prefabricated playlist, complete with advertising and news slots. A local announcer was needed only to announce occasionally the local time and weather conditions and to slot in local ads when necessary. As programming became automated, standardized, and streamlined, station managers replaced local personalities hosting shows geared to local tastes with nationally syndicated shows of the top music in a particular category, which had been selected to reach a desired target audience. Format radio had become too popular, and too profitable, to leave in the hands of local talent. A host of subformats bloomed within the broader categories. "Progressive" rock, once the home of extended periods of uninterrupted music, whole album sides, offbeat artists, and often openly political messages, now fragmented into such prepackaged formats as adult contemporary, soft rock, oldies, alternative, contemporary hits, and disco. By the late 1970s, satellite distribution had made automated formats even more ubiquitous. A split that had already developed between AM and FM widened: FM became almost exclusively the home of music stations, while AM featured more nonmusic formats such as all-news, talk, nostalgia (big band, blues), and sports.

The trends that began in the 1970s continued into the 1980s and 1990s, although those latter decades were also marked by many major changes. First, talk radio rose to unprecedented heights. National syndication and satellite technologies facilitated interaction between listeners and hosts on call-in shows using toll-free numbers, and the call-in talk show, which had once been regarded as the home of aging cranks, now boasted popular new hosts, such as Larry King and Dr. Ruth Westheimer, and new audiences, including maturing baby boomers, who were increasingly likely to turn to radio less for music and more for information. Advertisers welcomed the upscale, well-educated audiences the hosts of these shows attracted as they moved from local phenomena to syndicated national personalities. Radio syndication itself had undergone fundamental changes.

Deregulation and Consolidation

The popularity of talk radio helped reverse the declining fortunes of AM radio. In 1975, 61 percent of the U.S. audience tuned to the AM dial at some point in the day, but by 1989, that number had declined to 26 percent, and only 22 of the top 100 stations in the United States were AM stations; most of those were in smaller markets. By 1992, however, AM listenership was again on the upswing.

A new generation of controversial "shock jocks" and their stylistic heirs began to emerge. Led by the flamboyant Howard Stern, the influential right-wing talk show host Rush Limbaugh, and self-help specialists such as Dr. Laura Schlessinger, the talk show format spilled over onto FM and even onto television. The congressional election of 1994, in which the Republican Party captured both the House and the Senate for the first time in decades, catapulted a new kind of radio listener into the public eye: the Republican victory was credited to the politically involved white male conservatives who followed Limbaugh and other like-minded radio hosts.

Deregulation of the broadcasting industry, which began in the 1980s under Mark Fowler, chairman of the FCC in the administration of President Ronald Reagan, sparked a wave of mergers and consolidation in the radio industry. With the relaxation of government restrictions on the ownership of radio and television stations, media companies merged in unprecedented numbers. Capital Cities Communications bought ABC radio and television; United Stations purchased RKO Radio Networks; Westwood One, already one of the largest radio networks, purchased both MBS and the NBC radio network, which NBC's new owner, General Electric, did not want. In 1988 the first American radio network, NBC, ceased to exist. In the biggest consolidation of all, Infinity Broadcasting purchased Unistar, itself the merged combination of Transtar and United Stations in 1993. Then Westinghouse, the new owner of CBS, swallowed Infinity in 1995.

The next year, growing media conglomerates, guided by the new concept of "synergy," successfully pressured the federal government to pass the Telecommunications Act of 1996, which contained several deregulatory provisions. Most notably, the law removed restrictions against a company owning multiple stations within a single market. Within a couple of years of the passage of the law, individual radio conglomerates owned half of the local broadcasting stations in many smaller cities.

In early 1999 the proposed merger of Chancellor Media, Clear Channel Communications, and Capstar made that company the single largest owner of radio stations in the world, with over 488 stations across the United States. The company's ownership of five or six stations in large cities such as New York and Los Angeles did not represent an enormous percentage of those markets, but in smaller cities such as Fresno, California, where Chancellor owned nine radio stations, or Spokane, Washington, where it owned 11 stations, the giant conglomerate drowned out almost all other radio voices in the area. Together, the four largest companies (Chancellor, CBS, ABC, and Emmis) controlled over 75

The advantages of radio as an advertising medium were highlighted in this 1992 corporate ad from Arbitron, Inc., a New York City–based company that measures U.S. radio listenership.
Courtesy Arbitron, Inc.

percent of the radio audience in the ten largest U.S. metropolitan areas at the end of the 1990s. Whether this consolidation will result in a decline of radio's local qualities remained to be seen.

Audience Splitting

Networking began to rise once again in the 1990s. Splitting the listening audience into ever finer segments, national syndicated networks of all descriptions emerged and spun off even more highly targeted formats. In 1992 Westwood One offered the long-popular program counting down the week's top songs hosted by Casey Kassem in two versions, one for contemporary hit stations and one for adult contemporary. Westwood One marketed three separate concert programs as well: *In Concert,* for album-oriented stations; *In Concert: New Rock,* for alternative outlets; and *In Concert: High Voltage,* for hard-rock formats. Specialty syndicators, such as the American Comedy Network, created different "hot" and "mild" versions of song parodies and jokes to fit different market tastes. Advertisers could now target ever-finer demographics in a context that provided tailor-made content. However, by the late 1990s, consolidation in the radio/record company relationship had brought back a system very similar to the payola days of the 1950s, with independent promoters paid by the record labels increasingly intervening in the selection of music on station playlists. What is good for advertisers and record promoters does not necessarily create a system that best serves the public interest, or even what the public is interested in.

Stations in the 1990s could choose from a variety of network offerings. They might take the traditional route and subscribe to a comprehensive format, or pick and choose from a variety of syndicated and networked news, sports, music, comedy, and talk options. "Drive time" (6 A.M. to 10 A.M. and 3 P.M. to 7 P.M. on weekdays) remained the most popular and highly rated radio time, but statistics showed that Americans listened to radio throughout the day, at home, in the car, and at work, for a national average of 3 hours and 20 minutes per listener per week. Within these broad outlines, radio listeners were consistent, loyal to just two or three different stations, and programming was extremely specifically targeted. In 1998 the radio industry experienced a record year, with advertising revenue in excess of $13 billion, up from $8.7 billion in 1992.

Radio's Future

Digital delivery of radio by cable, satellite, and Internet will likely change radio programming again in the first decade of the 21st century. These new technologies have yet to converge in a way that makes all three venues simultaneously available to most consumers, but millions of Americans already receive audio channels that are available only via cable or satellite, rendering traditional over-the-air radio irrelevant to those listeners, except during those hours that they spend in their cars. The Internet promises to reshape the whole symbiotic relationship between the music industry and radio that emerged in the 1950s, as the World Wide Web becomes a delivery vehicle allowing individuals to program their own particular preferences in music, sports, talk, and news. Advertising will have to adapt to the new technology, perhaps by embedding ads on Web page interfaces for these new services or by advertising on digital satellite channels.

Even as such technological breakthroughs promise to alter one of the last bastions of mediated localism in the United States, current proposals advocating the revival of low-power (10- to 100-watt) local stations may win approval from the FCC. William E. Kennard, the head of the FCC in the administration of President Bill Clinton, indicated that this new localism may be a logical measure to help counter technological national convergence. If low-power stations become a reality, they may open up new avenues for local business and groups and make coordination through trade organizations more important than ever. More important, low-power stations could preserve for radio one of its most valuable qualities: its adaptability. Despite numerous social and technological challenges, radio was the 20th century's most consistent and intimate medium. As one radio expert commented: "Radio's like an alley cat with nine lives . . . It's a survivor. You can't ever kill it."

MICHELE HILMES

See also Soap Opera

Further Reading

Douglas, Susan, *Inventing American Broadcasting, 1899–1922,* Baltimore, Maryland: Johns Hopkins University Press, 1987

Fornatale, Peter, and Joshua E. Mills, *Radio in the Television Age,* Woodstock, New York: Overlook, 1980

Hilmes, Michele, *Radio Voices: American Broadcasting, 1922–1952,* Minneapolis: University of Minnesota Press, 1997

Keith, Michael C., *Voices in the Purple Haze: Underground Radio and the Sixties,* Westport, Connecticut: Praeger, 1997

MacDonald, J. Fred, *Don't Touch That Dial! Radio Programming in American Life, 1920–1960,* Chicago: Nelson-Hall, 1979

Pease, Edward C., and Everette E. Dennis, *Radio: The Forgotten Medium,* New Brunswick, New Jersey: Transaction, 1995

Putro, Rebecca, "Why Radio Thrives," *American Demographics* 16, no. 5 (May 1994)

Smith, F. Leslie, John W. Wright II, and David H. Ostroff, *Perspectives on Radio and Television: Telecommunication in the United States,* Mahwah, New Jersey: Erlbaum, 1998

Smulyan, Susan, *Selling Radio: The Commercialization of American Broadcasting, 1920–1934,* Washington, D.C.: Smithsonian Institution Press, 1994

Stedman, Raymond, *The Serials: Suspense and Drama by Installment,* Norman: University of Oklahoma Press, 1971; 2nd edition, 1977

Williams, Gilbert A., *Legendary Pioneers of Black Radio,* Westport, Connecticut: Praeger, 1998

Ralston Purina Company

Principal Agencies
Gardner Advertising Company
Checkerboard Advertising Company
Fallon-McElligott
D'Arcy Masius Benton & Bowles
Tatham Euro RSCG
Berlin Cameron & Partners

The Ralston Purina Company was founded in 1894 as the Robinson-Danforth Commission, a horse- and mule-feed business. Using $12,000 in borrowed capital, William H. Danforth, the company's founder, began selling feed near the company's modern-day headquarters on the banks of the Mississippi River in St. Louis, Missouri. In the early 1900s Danforth began selling a whole-wheat breakfast cereal under the Purina label.

The name Purina was adapted from the company slogan, "Where purity is paramount." The cereal was later renamed Ralston Wheat cereal after receiving an endorsement from one Dr. Ralston, a physician and natural foods enthusiast of the day with a large following. In 1902 the Ralston and Purina names were joined to form the Ralston Purina Company. Ralston Purina's famous "checkerboard" logo came about as the result of a marketing decision made by Danforth that was based upon a childhood memory: Danforth recalled a family of farm children who came to town every Saturday in distinctive red-and-white checked outfits. Their mother used the same bolt of red-and-white cloth to dress all her children.

Ralston Purina continued to expand its cereal offerings, and the founder's son, Donald Danforth, introduced new cereals such as Wheat Chex (1937), Rice Chex (1950), and Corn Chex (1958). In the 1930s the company began to rely heavily on advertising and promotions to help it compete for scarce Depression dollars. Ralston mastered the art of celebrity endorsements, sending Dog Chow Checkers dog food to the South Pole with Admiral Richard E. Byrd in 1933.

That same year the company hired the Gardner Advertising Company, with offices in New York City and St. Louis, and went into radio with a children's cowboy show called *The Tom Mix Ralston Straight Shooters*. Based on the career and legend of Tom Mix, a real-life cowboy turned movie star in the silent film era, the series ran from 1933 to 1951. Mix never appeared on the show but was played by a series of actors. The theme song, based on "When the Bloom Is on the Sage," became familiar to two generations of schoolchildren. The program was produced and directed for many years by Charles E. Claggett of the Gardner agency. The ads were laced with frequent promotions for merchandise that could be obtained by sending Ralston box tops to "Checkerboard Square, St. Louis, Mo." Claggett later joined Ralston and set up a house agency that functioned under the name Checkerboard Advertising into the 1970s, with Claggett himself as president.

By the mid-1950s, Ralston Purina had established itself as a consumer-products company with the successful introduction of a new dry dog food, Dog Chow. The product was so successful that production could not keep up with demand, and the supply had to be rationed to consumers.

The 1960s and 1970s were characterized by a series of acquisitions, including the Van Camp Seafood Company (sold in 1988), Foodmaker, and Jack in the Box. Gardner Advertising Company delivered creative advertising and made the "All you add is love" Purina Dog Chow tag line famous during this time. The company also entered the moist cat food category with its Tender Vittles brand and introduced a new brand of children's cereal, Cookie Crisp.

During the 1980s Ralston continued its growth with the acquisitions of Continental Baking, Eveready Batteries, and Beech-Nut Corporation, and it advanced its pet food and cereal operations in Europe and the Far East. One popular TV advertising effort in the 1980s and 1990s was the Eveready "Energizer Bunny" campaign, introduced in October 1989 by Chiat/Day. The drum-playing pink bunny (named by *Advertising Age* as one of the top ten advertising icons of the century) showcased the product's unique selling proposition—long-lived batteries—in an inventive and fresh way. Credit for creating the original campaign goes to DDB Needham, in Chicago, Illinois, which got the account from incumbent William Esty Company, Inc., after Ralston Purina put the Eveready business up for review in 1986. In 1989 the account shifted to Chiat/Day when Eveready disagreed with DDB Needham about the scope of the bunny's use as an advertising vehicle. The resulting, second-generation campaign, which showed the bunny interrupting advertisements for fictional products, was cited by *Advertising Age* as one of television's best campaigns.

The 1990s saw further restructuring. Most notably, in 1994 Ralcorp was created as Ralston Purina spun off its smaller businesses, led by its cereal products and Beech-Nut Nutrition Corporation. The big pet foods and Eveready divisions were thought to be frustrating the needs of these smaller but growing businesses. Ralston Purina's cereals by this time comprised private-label brands (accounting for 60 percent of its sales), the four Chex varieties, and a few smaller brands.

The company decided to consolidate its branded cereal advertising and in October 1994 awarded the business to D'Arcy Masius Benton & Bowles, St. Louis. The agency was charged with the task of broadening the Chex brands' appeal beyond their traditional adult target. Focus-group research had revealed that moms did not think their kids liked the brand, yet 40 percent of Chex sales were to kids. The resulting campaign was designed to get mothers to add Chex to their shopping lists by pointing out that eight out of ten kids liked Chex. Beech-Nut also changed its strategy from the mass appeal of television to a more focused effort that involved ads in parenting magazines, public relations, and a direct-mail program from the Chicago agency Cramer-Krasselt.

The 1990s saw a renewed effort for Ralston Purina's dog and cat foods business from Fallon-McElligott as well as other shops.

The Amateur's Guide to Love.

Everybody knows there are lots of kinds of love.

If you're a dog, love comes in cans, cellophane bags, sacks and boxes.

Because, if you're a dog, food is love.

What nobody ever told you (or your dog) is there's a lot of difference between all those different kinds of food.

We think you ought to know the facts of life. And love.

Love in Cans.

Of all canned dog foods, the most expensive is 95% meat and meat by-products.

Expensive canned dog foods "without a speck of cereal" sound good to you. But they may not be so good for your dog. Because most of them contain a lot of fat. And feeding your dog a lot of fat at every meal can be as bad for his health as it could be for yours.

What about the cheaper canned dog foods, that are only part meat or meat by-products? The fact is they're mostly water. 75% water with a can around it, that you have to pay for and lug home.

Love in Cellophane Bags.

Canned dog foods "without the can" look as human as hamburger, because they're made to look appetizing to people, so people will think they're appetizing to dogs.

Often they are. Not because they look like hamburger, but probably because they contain so much sugar. (As much as 15% sugar.) Sugar helps keep them soft and juicy, without the can.

Love in Sacks and Boxes.

More often than anything else, the dog food vets recommend is dry dog food.

And the one they usually suggest is a sack or box of Purina Dog Chow.

Professionals know that Dog Chow contains protein; in fact nearly twice as much protein, pound for pound, as the leading canned meat product does. And it contains more kinds of protein than just meat or meat by-products can provide.

If you read the ingredients on a box or sack of Dog Chow, you'll see it contains no added sugar, and one of the reasons it's low in cost is because you don't pay for water, in a dry dog food.

What you pay for is concentrated food with 43 nutrients. And these 43 nutrients are what every dog needs, every day.

We've been raising dogs, ourselves, for nearly half a century. We ought to know more about what they need than anybody does.

If you want to know more about your dog, or about dog food, write Purina Dog Chow, Checkerboard Square, St. Louis, Mo. 63188. We answer every letter. And we'll answer yours. We know that nobody would bother to write us a letter, unless they've got a dog they love.

For your pet's health . . . see your veterinarian annually.

PURINA DOG CHOW THE EAGER EATER DOG FOOD

A 1973 ad for Ralston Purina's Purina Dog Chow promoted dry food as the most healthful diet for dogs—and therefore the most appropriate way for dog owners to show how much they love their pets.

In an effort to cut through the multiplicity of ads for cat litter, Berlin Cameron & Partners created a campaign for Tidy Cat that deviated from the traditional approach focused on the embarrassment associated with a smelly litter box. Instead it employed humor and portrayed felines debating the merits of a product strong enough for use in households with multiple cats. Print ads featured the same humorous theme. This was the first ad support for the rebranded Tidy Cat, introduced when the product was repackaged for multiple-cat homes.

The advertising campaign for Purina's flagship brand, Purina Dog Chow, from Fallon-McElligott (*Advertising Age*'s "Agency of the Year" in 1996) won the Grand Effie award in 1995 for its effectiveness in boosting sales (which rose more than 20 percent). The campaign featured dogs that became finicky eaters or developed stomach problems after their owners switched brands. Research by Fallon had shown that pet owners mistakenly assume that their animals need variety in their diets. In 1999 the agency won a Gold Effie for its "Incredible Dog Food, Incredible Dogs" campaign.

In addition to traditional media, Ralston Purina also ventured into newer forms of communication. It developed Web sites, including the highly creative Tidy Cats site from Fallon-McElligott (www.tidycat.com), which won an award in the 1997 *I.D. Magazine* "Interactive Media Design Review." Its other brands (Cat Chow, Kitten Chow, and Meow Mix) also had a presence on the World Wide Web. In addition, the company sponsored its own event in the emerging "extreme games" for dogs. The first Purina Dog Chow Incredible Dog Challenge—with 1,200 canine competitors, an audience of roughly 4,000 spectators, and coverage on cable television's ESPN—was held in St. Louis in 1998.

By December 2001 the company was poised to be acquired by Switzerland-based Nestlé SA in a $10.1 billion deal that required the merged company to divest Meow Mix and Alley Cat dry cat foods to Hartz Mountain Corporation in order to gain U.S. government approval. The new company, based in St. Louis, would operate under the name Nestlé Purina Pet Care. At the time of the proposed merger, Nestlé held 32 percent of the U.S. cat food market and 10 percent of the dog food market with U.S. sales of

$3.7 billion; Ralston Purina had 25 percent of the cat food market and 28 percent of the dog food market with sales of $2.25 billion.

RAJESH V. MANCHANDA

Further Reading

Brody, Barbara, "Ralston, Clorox Bring New Tactic in Pet Market," *Advertising Age* (20 July 1998)

Fitzgerald, Kate, "Dog-Beat-Dog World," *Advertising Age* (22 June 1998)

Liesse, Julie, "How the Bunny Charged Eveready," *Advertising Age* (8 April 1991)

Liesse, Julie, "Ralston Spinoff Happy to Be Small," *Advertising Age* (12 December 1994)

"Research Currents: Trophy and Gold Winners of the 1997 ARF David Ogilvy Research Awards," *Journal of Advertising Research* 37, no. 4 (July/August 1997)

Rapp Collins Worldwide

Founded by Stanley Rapp and Thomas Collins as Rapp & Collins, New York City, the direct-marketing division of Foote, Cone & Belding (FCB), 31 January 1965; parted with FCB to become an independent agency, 1969; merged with Stone & Adler, Chicago, Illinois, to form Rapp, Collins, Stone & Adler, 1971; Rapp & Collins acquired by Doyle Dane Bernbach (DDB), while Stone & Adler remained independent, 1976; became part of Diversified Agency Services division of the Omnicom network, 1986; renamed Rapp Collins Worldwide, 1993.

Major Clients

Capitol Records
Dell Computer Corporation
Doubleday & Company
Encyclopaedia Britannica
Glaxo Wellcome
SBC Communications
Sears, Roebuck & Company
United Parcel Service

In the 1960s, as direct marketing became more cost-effective and general advertising agencies strove to keep clients' direct-mail spending in their own shops, large agencies became interested in establishing their own mail-order specialty units. Following that trend, Rapp & Collins was formed in 1965 as an autonomous division of Foote, Cone & Belding (FCB), New York City, making FCB the first major agency to create a separate office devoted exclusively to mail-order, or direct-response, advertisers.

Before Rapp & Collins even opened its doors on 31 January 1965, the agency signed a sizable first client, Capitol Records, with a $2 million account. Stanley Rapp and Thomas Collins had never met before FCB asked them to lead the new agency. Rapp, previously vice president–creative director at David Altman Advertising, was hired as president, and Collins was named executive vice president/creative director, moving from vice president

in charge of copy at direct-marketing agency Wunderman, Ricotta & Kline.

From the start, Rapp was determined to go after new business rather than serving only FCB's existing client base. He was quoted in the 21 December 1964 issue of *Advertising Age* as saying: "Mail order has reached a point on the American scene where this form of advertising distribution is important to the knowledge boom, the cultural explosion now taking place. People have more time and money to spend for intangibles, and intangibles are best sold by mail order."

By the end of its first six months, Rapp & Collins was operating on a profitable basis, with clients including Britannica Home Library Service, Doubleday & Company, Famous Artists Schools, and Film Corporation of America. But within a few years, the agency realized that its new-business growth was being impeded by potential account conflicts with its parent; as a result, Rapp & Collins split from FCB to become an independent shop in April 1969, taking three accounts with it, including Encyclopaedia Britannica.

Life as an Independent

In its first six months as an independent agency, Rapp & Collins won 11 new assignments from six new clients and suffered only one account loss. It doubled its billings from $3.5 million to $7 million, making it the third-largest direct-marketing agency (trailing Wunderman, Ricotta & Kline and Vos & Reicherg). And Rapp and Collins, two men who did not even know each other five years earlier, became known in some Madison Avenue advertising circles as the "Rodgers and Hammerstein of mail-order advertising."

The 1970s brought an increased interest in direct marketing throughout the United States; the first half of the decade saw an explosive 100 percent growth in the volume of direct marketing, making it a $250 million industry. On 1 October 1971 Rapp & Collins merged with Stone & Adler, of Chicago, Illinois, which had been founded five years earlier by Robert Stone and Aaron Adler. The new agency, with combined billings of $10 million, maintained its status as the third-largest direct-marketing agency in the United States, with a client list peppered with large publishing accounts such as Time-Life Books and Ziff-Davis Publishing.

Despite its success as Rapp, Collins, Stone & Adler, the New York City and Chicago entities parted ways in 1976, when Rapp & Collins joined the billion-dollar, publicly traded Doyle Dane Bernbach (DDB) network of agencies to become the wholly owned direct-marketing subsidiary of one of the world's largest and most-recognized agency families. (Stone & Adler remained independent.) As part of DDB, Rapp & Collins was able to mount a global presence by opening shops in London, England; Paris, France; Hamburg, Germany; Amsterdam, The Netherlands; Sydney, Australia; Tokyo, Japan; and Mexico City, Mexico, establishing an international foundation that it would build on in the decades that followed. Its first move into Europe came in 1983, when DDB acquired London-based McCorkell, Sidaway & Wright and created MSW Rapp & Collins.

Three years later, when DDB joined Batten Barton Durstine & Osborn and Needham Harper Worldwide in the megamerger that formed the Omnicom network, Rapp & Collins became part of the second-largest group of direct-marketing agencies in the world. Omnicom merged Rapp & Collins with another of its shops, the Direct Response Group, Dallas, Texas, to create the $100 million Rapp Collins USA, a unit of Omnicom's Diversified Agency Services group.

In 1987 Rapp and Collins published their first of four books on advertising, *MaxiMarketing: The New Direction in Advertising, Promotion and Marketing Strategy*, which reflected on the changes in the direct-marketing industry. They traced the industry's development from the "mail-order advertising" of the 1960s to an expanded discipline in the 1980s, in which a new generation of marketers communicated with customers one-on-one via telephones and computers. The book created significant publicity for the authors' agency, which signed eight new clients in the year following its publication.

The success of the book led Rapp to resign in 1988, after 23 years with the agency he founded, to devote his time to writing and public speaking. A year later, Rapp Collins USA merged with Marcoa DR Group to snatch the number-three marketing-services agency spot away from Foote, Cone & Belding Communications; it trailed only Ogilvy & Mather Direct and Young & Rubicam's Wunderman Cato Johnson.

Further Expansion

The 1990s were a time of further expansion for the agency—internally through new business and externally via acquisitions, domestic and abroad—helping the shop take the lead as the largest worldwide direct-marketing agency by the middle of the decade. In 1992 and 1993 Rapp Collins became the first direct-marketing agency of record for Pizza Hut and Pepsi-Cola Company, respectively. The firm rounded out its specializations by acquiring a promotions agency, U.S. Communications Company,

Minneapolis, Minnesota, and Hughes Database Marketing, a company based in Texas and Canada. Shortly thereafter, the agency was renamed Rapp Collins Worldwide.

Its 1994 purchase of the London-based direct-marketing firm WWAV created the largest U.K. direct-marketing agency and allowed Rapp Collins to leverage WWAV's resources to help its U.S. clients expand their direct-marketing efforts into Europe. That same year, Rapp Collins acquired teleservices company Optima Direct, Washington, D.C., and direct-response TV specialist Shain Colavito Pensabene Direct, New York City; five years later the latter was merged into the media department of Rapp Collins, New York City, to form SCP/Rapp Collins Media.

By the end of 1995 Rapp Collins was number one in the world, with growth outside the United States surpassing its domestic level. Its non-U.S. revenue in 1995 was $96.4 million, a 33.2 percent increase over the previous year. That year the agency expanded beyond Europe, opening five offices in Latin America and one in Hong Kong. In 1996 Rapp Collins strengthened its Canadian presence with the acquisition of Communicaide Integrated Marketing Services in Mississauga, Ontario, merging it with Hughes Rapp Collins, also in Canada, to create Rapp Collins Communicaide, whose client roster came to include Glaxo Wellcome, Labatt Breweries of Canada, Sears Canada, and United Parcel Service (UPS) Canada.

The agency's international extension helped position it to win global accounts from Adobe, which tapped the shop for its North American, European, and Pacific Rim businesses, and Dell Computer Corporation, which awarded WWAV Rapp Collins its $56 million pan-European direct-marketing account. But the agency did not neglect internal development and in 1995 established its first start-up, InfoWorks, a data analytics consultancy. Two years later it formed its Marketing Technology Center in Dallas to provide additional production and execution services, and in 1998 it established Acuity HealthGroup to specialize in bringing a data-driven marketing approach to the pharmaceutical industry. During Rapp Collins's global expansion, Stanley Rapp returned to agency life after an eight-year respite to become chairman and chief executive officer of McCann-Erickson Worldwide's new global direct unit, now called McCann Relationship Marketing Worldwide.

In time to usher in the 21st century, Rapp Collins formed Rapp Digital in New York City; it then folded into Rapp Digital its 50 percent stake in Internet services company Critical Mass, in Calgary, Alberta, Canada, with offices in Chicago and Stockholm, Sweden, to help clients develop interactive marketing strategies. In 2000 it landed the $200 million consolidated direct-response advertising account of SBC Communications after the latter's acquisition of telecommunications company Ameritech; it also won the $30 million business-to-business account of UPS.

Rapp Collins Worldwide has come a long way from its modest beginnings as a two-man shop within a larger agency. In 2000 the agency existed as its own global network, with more than 2,800 employees in 60 offices in 30 countries around the world. In 1999 its $166.4 million in revenue made it the eighth-largest full-service marketing-services agency and the third-largest direct-marketing shop in the United States. It was ranked third internationally, with $145.6 million in non-U.S. sales.

CARA BEARDI

Further Reading
Hatch, Denny, "How the MaxiMarketing Gurus Go to Market," *Target Marketing* 19, no. 1 (January 1996)
Rapp, Stan, and Thomas L. Collins, *MaxiMarketing: The New Direction in Advertising, Promotion, and Marketing Strategy,* New York: McGraw Hill, 1987
Rapp, Stan, and Thomas L. Collins, *The Great Marketing Turnaround: The Age of the Individual, and How to Profit From It,* Englewood Cliffs, New Jersey: Prentice Hall, 1990
Rapp, Stan, and Thomas L. Collins, *Beyond MaxiMarketing: The New Power of Caring and Daring,* New York: McGraw Hill, 1994
Rapp, Stan, and Thomas L. Collins, *The New MaxiMarketing,* New York: McGraw Hill, 1996
Rose, Matthew A., "Great American Copywriter: Tom Collins," *Direct Marketing* 50, no. 10 (February 1998)

Ratings

Ratings are a measure of a broadcast or cable program's listening or viewing audience. They are expressed as a percentage of a specific target audience. For example, by checking the ratings for a certain television program, an advertiser might discover that 14 percent of U.S. women ages 18–34 watch that program. Advertisers generally seek to target highly specific demographic groups. Ratings thus provide them with information that is useful in choosing one program over another as a vehicle for a particular ad.

Ratings are one of the most powerful forces in broadcasting, capable of determining the success or failure of the network, station, program, producers, advertisers, and salespeople. Networks and stations that offer programs with high ratings gain advertisers, thereby earning the revenue they need to succeed. Television and radio programs with low ratings are quickly canceled. Because advertising prices are determined by demand for the ads, higher ratings generate higher prices, bringing more sales commissions to the sellers of advertising and more money to the program producers, stations, and networks. A single rating point—up or down—can mean thousands of dollars in the selling price of a 30-second spot.

Ratings for radio and TV programs are compiled by market research firms. These firms use sampling techniques such as diaries, telephone surveys, and electronic devices to record consumers' viewing and listening habits. The companies analyze the collected data to estimate viewing and listening ratings by program for the entire population. The data are then sold to the media, advertisers, and advertising agencies. When a potential advertising buyer expresses an interest in a particular station or network, the broadcaster is often willing to provide the ratings for free.

Ratings are percentages, not actual numbers of listeners or viewers, although these numbers are also provided by most audience research companies. As estimates of the "reach"—the percentage of the target audience that sees or hears the ad—ratings provide advertisers and ad agencies with useful information for media planning decisions.

Ratings are usually expressed in terms of households, ages, and genders. This system allows the advertiser to choose the programs that reach the maximum percentage of the target audience. For example, an automobile manufacturer advertising a new vehicle might choose as the target audience all women ages 35 to 54 who live in the United Kingdom. If television is chosen as the medium, the ad agency for the auto company will check the ratings for all television programs in Britain and find those with the highest ratings among women in that age group in order to get the sales message to as many potential buyers as possible. This practice, called target marketing, eliminates waste (defined as purchasing ads that do not reach the target audience) while minimizing the marketing costs of selling the car.

Methodologies

Many methodologies have been used to compile ratings. These include paper diaries, telephone interviews, and electronic devices such as the "people meter" that the ACNielsen Corporation uses to monitor television-viewing households. All methodologies are less than perfect, relying upon the listener or viewer either to list program choices or to remember them after the fact. Even the data collected by the people meter, which automatically records the program being watched, has room for error, as a human researcher adds supplemental information about the demographic characteristics of the viewers.

Owing to the need for technical support and the high cost of equipment, metered ratings are expensive. For that reason, they are used mainly for national viewing ratings. Because the data collection is automatic and continuous, ratings can be produced for viewing from the previous day. Nielsen sells these "overnights" to large advertisers and agencies.

Nielsen's advanced people meters are in only a small percentage of U.S. homes. For local ratings, the printed diary remains the most common survey method. Such diaries are inexpensive and can be easily mailed to households.

Telephone interviews have been used in varying degree since the beginning of ratings. Coincidental surveys ask consumers what they are watching or listening to at the time of the call and are considered reliable because recall is not a factor. Other telephone surveys ask about past media usage.

Worldwide Use

The use of broadcast ratings is most highly developed in nations with extensive, privately owned commercial media. In much of the world, especially in emerging markets, governments or quasi-governmental corporations control the media and have a huge impact on media growth. In India, for example, radio broadcasting is a state monopoly, and only 24 percent of Indian households have a radio. In Italy relaxation of a government monopoly in the 1970s fostered a huge growth in private television stations. By 1991 Italy had more than 1,300 private television stations, one for every 10,000 households, a greater broadcast density than any other country.

The need for ratings grows with the development of communication media. The most complex communication systems tend to have the most sophisticated ratings systems, as advertisers demand data to make their media buys more efficient. In many Third World countries the media are underdeveloped, radio sets and television sets are not widely distributed, and reading levels are not adequate to support much of the print media. In these countries, ratings will not be in demand until the communication systems mature.

Cultural values often determine the value of ratings. In Japan ratings for car radios are not yet being tracked although they represent one-third of all radios in the country. Attempts by ACNielsen and Video Research to use television audience meters met with initial success but then encountered a backlash from the Japanese public, who criticized the stations for emphasizing numbers rather than the quality of their programs. In Indonesia, Survey Research Indonesia is trying to develop consumer segmentation studies but has encountered consumer reluctance to divulge information.

Relationship of Ratings to Shares

The concept of rating is a measure of what advertisers call "net reach." The rating number counts as its base all households that have radios or televisions, whether or not the set is turned on. A rating of 13 for a particular program means that 13 percent of all households with radios listen to that program. Since nearly all U.S. homes have more than one radio (the average is more than four per household), this universe of households is considered to be 100 percent. So advertisers would say that the program "reaches" 13 percent of all households in the market.

Share is a different measure. It counts only those radio or TV households that are listening to or viewing a broadcast. Sets that are not turned on are not counted. For a specific program, therefore, shares are always higher than ratings. Because they represent net reach in the target audience, ratings provide more useful data for the advertiser.

Gross Rating Point (GRP)

Ratings are related to the frequency of ads in the following equation used by advertisers: R x F = GRP. In this equation, R stands for rating or reach, F stands for frequency (number of ads scheduled), and GRP stands for gross rating points. GRP is a way to measure the cumulative effect of numerous ad messages in a single campaign. Target ratings for the programs bought by the advertiser are multiplied by the number of ads scheduled in that program, and then all are added to generate gross rating points for the ad campaign (see Table 1). The total is referred to as "gross" rating points because if an individual sees more than one ad he or she is counted more than once. Hence the totals are not an estimate of "net" reach but are "gross" numbers of advertising impressions.

Brief History

The concept of ratings began in the United States in the 1920s and parallels the growth of radio and television. Only seven years after New York City radio station WEAF aired radio's first commercial (a ten-minute spot) in 1922, Daniel Starch was hired by NBC to produce data on radio listenership. Starch, a Harvard professor, had been providing readership information for the print media, and his pioneering study of radio was based upon more than 17,000 personal interviews conducted in 105 cities and 68 rural counties. His 1929 research showed that radios were in 34.6 percent of households, but the data did not include any information about listening patterns for specific stations and programs. The study's usefulness to advertisers was therefore limited.

Radios were being purchased by U.S. families at a staggering rate in the late 1920s, and advertisers, with no other data available, began using fan letters from listeners as an indication of a program's popularity. NBC received 1 million letters in 1929 and 2 million in 1930. Even so, many advertisers were not sure whether to regard the new medium as a serious outlet for advertising. The Association of National Advertisers (ANA), a dominant trade group, became concerned with the conflicting listenership claims of radio networks and the flimsy data upon which those claims were based. In 1930 it commissioned Archibald Crossley, head of a research firm, to conduct radio research. It was the beginning of a 16-year run for the Cooperative Analysis of Broadcasting (CAB), a joint effort that changed radio broadcasting forever. Crossley enrolled advertisers to pay

Table 1. Sample Calculation of Gross Rating Points (GRPs).

Program	Rating	Number of spots	GRPs
Drama	17	3	51
CBS movie	11	4	44
Soccer game	8	1	8
Total		8	103

for a 12-month study of 50 cities, covering 17,000 radio-listener families. Telephone calls asked about listening during the previous 24 hours. It was not long before publications such as *Variety* and columnists such as Walter Winchell and Ed Sullivan began discussing "Crossley ratings."

In the fall of 1934 the CAB faced its first major competitor, C.E. Hooper, a former Starch researcher, who had started his own firm, Clark-Hooper, with Montgomery Clark, also from Starch. (The two later parted company, and Hooper went into the radio ratings business on his own as C.E. Hooper, Inc.) Hooper was using a new technique for data collection, the coincidental phone survey, in which consumers are asked what they are listening to at the time of the call. These new ratings showed higher numbers for programs, and Hooper claimed the data had greater accuracy because of its immediacy. What eventually became known as "Hooperatings" gained increasing acceptance. Trying to compete, Crossley proposed a new national survey for the CAB, which was turned down because of its expense. Two years later, in 1946, the ANA disbanded the CAB and hired Hooper to serve the subscribers.

When television came on the scene in the late 1940s, Hooper reluctantly met the demand for ratings and produced television's first Hooperatings in 1948, combining more than 1.7 million coincidental phone calls with 4,800 household diaries. Projections were made for all 34 million U.S. television-viewing households. But Hooper's real love was radio, and in 1950 he sold his company to a new research entrepreneur, Arthur C. Nielsen.

Hooper's methodology of telephone calls and diaries was cumbersome and expensive, making it difficult and costly to produce ratings as frequently as advertisers demanded. Nielsen had a solution—the Audimeter, a trademarked name for an electronic device attached to a radio that monitored the listener's choice of programs. Nielsen was a firm believer that the ratings should result from an impartial scientific observer such as the Audimeter rather than from the listener's memory. He was convinced that methodologies such as diaries and telephone surveys were by their very nature unreliable and inaccurate. Ultimately, the fact that his meter system allowed the continual production of ratings data was the decisive factor in the advertiser's choice between Nielsen ratings and Hooperatings. Hooper was producing three rating studies per year. A.C. Nielsen announced in September 1949 that his company was going to supply the astounding number of four rating reports each month. It was the end of the Hooperatings. In March 1950 Nielsen bought out Hooper for between $500,000 and $750,000, and a new era in ratings began. A.C. Nielsen and Company (later ACNielsen Corporation) was to become the largest market research firm in the world, eventually concentrating on the new medium of television and discontinuing local radio ratings in 1963.

As advertiser demand for ratings increased, other companies entered the scene. Eugene Katz, then president of the Katz Station Representative Company, hired Robert Salk and formed Audience Surveys in the late 1940s to provide radio ratings, but the firm never made money and was disbanded after several years. The first Pulse report appeared in 1941 and expanded gradually,

becoming a dominant radio ratings provider. Its success was due to an expansion of the service to include all radio listening around the clock, including automotive and other "out of home" listening. By 1963 Pulse was providing radio ratings for 250 U.S. radio markets and had 150 ad agencies and 650 radio stations as clients. Pulse primarily used telephone interviews to compile its data.

In the 1970s Pulse was challenged by Arbitron, a company that returned to the use of the diary to measure both radio and television usage. Arbitron had strong financial support from its parent company, Control Data Corporation, and used new computer systems to produce speedier ratings that were less expensive than the Pulse ratings. As advertisers and agencies began to support and accept the Arbitron diary information, Pulse suffered a gradual decline in clients and by 1978 was out of business. It had operated successfully for more than 35 years.

Arbitron took over as the king of local radio ratings, and the company retained that position at the start of the 21st century. With Nielsen concentrating on television ratings, Arbitron built its local radio ratings business by returning to the less expensive diary method and moving to replace monthly ratings with four-times-a-year ARB Radio Local Market Service. No major competitor appeared until Thomas Birch founded Radio Marketing Research in the early 1980s. Birch reports used telephone interviews to generate a monthly and quarterly service. Birch provided ratings for some smaller markets not rated by Arbitron and competed with ARB in other markets.

Another successful ratings service began in Seattle, Washington, in 1982. Willhight Research filled a niche left open by Arbitron and Nielsen—small local markets. Willhight used telephone interviews to assess the listening of the previous day. In 1992 Strategic Radio Research in Chicago started providing AccuRatings, a measurement of core radio listeners or stations "listened to most."

Advent of TV

When television arrived in North America in the late 1940s, it was so instantly popular that radio, along with other media, seemed to be finished. Why would one want to listen to a program when one could see it? C.E. Hooper did not fully comprehend the power of the new medium, but two of his employees did. Encouraged by the CBS and NBC television networks, Edward G. Hynes, Jr., and Robert B. Rogers formed Trendex in 1950. Using telephone coincidental research, Trendex reports became supplements to Nielsen reports on national television viewing. Over time, the telephone methodology gave way to the ease and lower cost of Nielsen's metered service for national viewing levels.

In local markets Arbitron moved into television ratings with its successful diary systems. By 1961 ARB was measuring every major U.S. television market and adding to the demographics it provided. Arbitron had been a leader in the field of television ratings, expanding the geographic breakdowns (defining total survey areas, or TSAs) in 1960, the area of dominant influence (ADI) in 1966, and, in later years, the designated market area (DMA) and

Radio station K-NUZ in Houston, Texas, boasted of its number-one ranking from the Hooper, Nielsen, and Pulse ratings services in this 1959 ad.

primary market area (PMA). Innovations introduced by Arbitron include Spanish-language diaries in 1965, sample balancing in 1969, and in the 1980s the PRIZM project, which combines demographic and geographic data. In 1984 Arbitron and Burke Marketing Services formed a joint venture, ScanAmerica, a sophisticated electronic meter system combining viewing patterns with product purchases.

Meanwhile, A.C. Nielsen solidified the company's hold on the national ratings, developing the National Television Index (NTI) in 1950 and reporting ratings on total U.S. television households in 1960. During 1964 NTI began using a new sample base and added the Mountain Standard Time zone. By 1965 electronically monitored homes numbered 1,150, increasing only gradually to 1,250 in 1982. The NTI made its most dramatic change in 1983 when satellite cable networks induced Nielsen to increase the sample size to 1,700 metered households. Nielsen also had its share of innovations, introducing data on national audience composition (NAC) in 1954 and the Nielsen Station Index (NSI), a separate ratings service, the same year. When local radio service was discontinued in 1963, Nielsen completely updated its TV services, changing to four- instead of eight-week reports and increasing sample size. In the fall of 1976 Nielsen introduced the rating of homes with unlisted telephone numbers. (Such homes typically were not represented in ratings surveys, since telephone books were often used as a source of respondents.) Over the years Nielsen has increased the demographics, adding new data as demanded. For network television Nielsen's NSI and NTI remain the dominant ratings systems in the United States.

A new television ratings competitor arrived in 1982, when AGB Research PLC, a U.K. firm with British Broadcasting Corporation (BBC) support, brought people meters to the United States. AGB has had limited success in competing with giant ACNielsen, however.

Other ratings companies that failed to gain wide acceptance in the United States included Videodex, a Chicago, Illinois, company started in 1949 that used panel opinions; Tele-Pulse, the Pulse company's attempt to measure TV ratings in the early 1950s; the Telerad system, which ambitiously attempted to build a national sample of 20,000 households; TPI (Television-Personal Interview), a firm that used teams of interviewers and telephone surveys in 1958; Albert Sindlinger's attempt to sell qualitative data in the late 1950s—an effort that was definitely ahead of its time; and the Tanner Electronic Survey Tabulation (TEST), an innovative service that used panel trucks equipped with rotating antennas and scanning gear that could detect and record all TV set data within 300 yards, while driving between five and 50 miles an hour.

Highly detailed long-term network audience information, combined with data on viewers' buying and lifestyle habits, is now provided by Mediamark Research, Inc. (MRI), and Simmons Market Research Bureau (SMRB). Their extensive volumes offer perhaps the most sophisticated use of consumer research yet developed, covering not only broadcast media but print as well. The television networks and local stations set their published advertising rates based upon audience rating surveys taken during four sample periods during the regular seasons. Each sample period is called a "sweep," and the networks and stations typically program their most attractive shows and specials during a sweeps period in order to score the largest possible audience ratings and thus set rates at a maximum level. Once ad rates are published, however, they are subject to discounts based on the buying power of the advertiser or agency and other factors. Large agencies will sometimes purchase network or spot time slots at a discount and later recommend them to clients in their media plans.

Critics

The use of broadcast ratings has always had its critics. One of the major concerns is the validity of the numbers. Broadcasters and others have suggested that the ratings are based upon samples too small to generate statistically valid results. It is difficult for non-statisticians to understand that small sample sizes can generate accurate projections with small standard deviations, even in very large populations. Once a sample size reaches 1,000, sampling errors are 3.5 percent or less, even in large populations. Most media research firms use generally accepted statistical analysis to project results to the whole market. Of course, the larger the sample, the more valid the results. To the extent that these companies use methodologies and samples that are statistically valid, though, their estimates are reliable.

Typically, broadcasters that criticize the ratings are those with low ratings themselves. Local radio stations with low ratings assure advertisers that ratings do not matter and emphasize their experiences with successful advertisers. Television stations attempt to sell a program with low ratings by emphasizing the loyalty or uniqueness of its viewers. In 1998 the major television networks in the United States considered developing their own ratings systems, since the independent ratings from ACNielsen increasingly showed those networks losing their audiences to cable networks.

Since advertisers in developed countries are increasingly in search of more detailed information about the consumer, and because research companies can readily sell such data if they can compile it, privacy issues are likely to become an ethical problem in the future. The consumer's desire for privacy will threaten the validity of the research. The statistical validity of research may decrease as a result of skewed samples caused when researchers miss homes with unlisted telephone numbers or consumers refuse to respond to interviewers or to fill out diaries. The proliferation of telemarketing in the United States is prompting more and more people to get unlisted phone numbers in order to avoid calls from marketers or to purchase caller identification services that enable them to ignore such calls. The Internet provides yet another way for researchers to breach consumers' defenses. Resistance to such efforts is likely to grow, resulting in fewer responses.

Trends

Long-term ratings for individual programs have been declining for decades as television and radio have become more fragmented. Cable and satellite networks have greatly expanded the number of programs available. When consumers are given more options, they take advantage of them. In the United States in the 1950s there were only three main choices for television viewers. ABC, CBS, and NBC provided all of the television programs for their local affiliates, while Dumont was a weak fourth network until it disappeared in 1955. A popular show with Ed Sullivan or Jack Benny on CBS could reach upward of 30 percent to 40 percent of all households in the country. By 1999 the Fox network, UPN, and WB (the Warner Brothers network) had become viable fourth, fifth, and sixth networks, appealing to young audiences and minorities.

Moreover, cable and satellite channels now provide thousands of programs, many with very specific content related to a wide range of hobbies and interests. The result is lower average ratings for individual programs. At the end of the 20th century the highest rated prime-time television programs in the United States rarely had household ratings around 17 or 18, meaning that less than one-fifth of all potential households were viewers. The remaining 83 percent were either watching other programs or not watching at all. Only special-event broadcasting is capable of garnering the high ratings of the past. Usually the highest-rated television program in the United States each year is the Super Bowl football game, with ratings in the 1990s of about 45 percent each year.

Radio ratings have showed similar patterns of decline as more stations have entered the market. Most midsize cities in the United States now have 30 or more radio stations, each attracting a small proportion—usually less than 2 percent—of listeners at any given time. Like TV networks, radio stations also target specific age groups or genders, making the ratings for individual stations even lower.

With lower ratings for specific programs in both television and radio, broadcasting is becoming less a mass medium and more a narrowly targeted one. This is a long-term trend that is likely to continue as the population becomes more diverse, the media compete more fiercely for ad dollars, and new forms of communication are developed. The Internet, as a new medium, will take more and more of the consumer's time. The ratings of other media will suffer as a result.

As new methodologies are developed and new advertiser needs arise, ratings are likely to become increasingly specific. Today advertisers can find the ratings for women in the 35-to-44-year-old age group who bought a digital camera in the past year. In the future they may also be able to find out how many cameras a woman owns, whether she subscribes to a photo magazine, what brand of camera she prefers, how old her current camera is, and how much she is willing to spend on a new one—and then determine which programs she watches.

MARK MATTHEWS SECRIST

Further Reading

Beville, Hugh Malcolm, Jr., *Audience Ratings: Radio, Television, and Cable*, Hillsdale, New Jersey: Erlbaum, 1985; revised edition, 1988

Donnelly, William J., *Planning Media: Strategy and Imagination*, Upper Saddle River, New Jersey: Prentice Hall, 1996

Frith, Katherine Toland, editor, *Advertising in Asia: Communication, Culture, and Consumption*, Ames: Iowa State University Press, 1996

Head, Sydney W., *World Broadcasting Systems: A Comparative Analysis,* Belmont, California: Wadsworth, 1985

Jones, John Philip, editor, *How Advertising Works: The Role of Research,* Thousand Oaks, California, and London: Sage, 1998

Jugenheimer, Donald W., Arnold M. Barban, and Peter B. Turk, *Advertising Media: Strategy and Tactics,* Dubuque, Iowa: Brown and Benchmark, 1992

Noam, Eli, *Television in Europe,* New York: Oxford University Press, 1991

Sherman, Barry L., *Telecommunications Management,* New York: McGraw-Hill, 1987; 2nd edition, 1995

Sissors, Jack Z., and E. Reynold Petray, *Advertising Media Planning,* Chicago: Crain, 1976; 5th edition, by Sissors and Lincoln Bumba, Lincolnwood, Illinois: NTC Business Books, 1996

Surmanek, Jim, *Media Planning: A Practical Guide,* Lincolnwood, Illinois: NTC Business Books, 1985; 3rd edition, 1996

Surmanek, Jim, *Introduction to Advertising Media: Research, Planning, and Buying,* Lincolnwood, Illinois: NTC Business Books, 1993

Wimmer, Roger D., and Joseph R. Dominick, *Mass Media Research,* Belmont, California: Wadsworth, 1983; 5th edition, 1997

Ratto Agency

(Ratto/BBDO)

Founded by David Ratto in Buenos Aires, Argentina, 1974; won Chrysler business, 1975; became BBDO Worldwide's representation office, 1979; name changed to Ratto/BBDO when BBDO acquired 20 percent interest in the agency, 1987; won PepsiCo business, 1989; David Ratto passed presidency to son Carlos, assuming role of consultant, January 1999.

Major Clients

America Canal 2 (TV channel)
BankBoston
Effem Argentina (Mars candies)
Nike Argentina
Pepsi Cola Argentina
PepsiCo Snacks Argentina
R.J. Reynolds Tobacco Company (Camel cigarettes)
Sancor (dairy products)
Volkswagen Argentina

Few industry figures in the history of Argentina's advertising are regarded with as high esteem as David Ratto, the founder of the highly acclaimed Buenos Aires advertising agency Ratto/BBDO. During a career stretching from the aftermath of World War II, through the legendary rule of General Juan Perón and his first wife, Eva, to the turbulent years of the military junta (1978–1983), and on to the restoration of democracy, Ratto received countless prizes and awards. None perhaps was as special as the trophy that he received during an evening gala held in his honor in April 1998 to commemorate his remarkable 50-year career.

In a ceremony held in the Argentine capital's Luna Park, Ratto was named "Argentine champion of advertising." It was most fitting that the award was handed to him by another venerable industry doyen, Ricardo Pueyrredon, founder of Pueyrredon Propaganda, the agency where Ratto began his career in 1948.

"My father completely changed the way of doing advertising in this country," said Carlos Ratto, who assumed the presidency of Ratto/BBDO in January 1999 when his father stepped down to lead a "more peaceful life," although he continued to lend a hand with the agency as a consultant to the board.

After working in New York City in the early 1960s, David Ratto introduced to Gowland Publicidad, the agency he had cofounded in 1958, the system of bringing together copywriters and art directors under the guidance of a creative director. The system soon became commonplace in Argentina.

Through the late 1960s, Ratto worked to develop the status of the creative department in the Argentine advertising industry by teaching at the Universidad del Salvador and becoming more involved with creative trends around the world. For example, he was named representative for Latin America at the Cannes International Advertising Festival in 1969, when, to his delight, an Argentine shop won the Grand Prix.

But by the turn of the decade, when he was a partner with Ortiz, Scopesi y Ratto/Ogilvy & Mather, David Ratto still believed that the local industry had a long way to go to raise creative standards. "What he's told me most struck him during client meetings," said Carlos Ratto, "was that the focus was almost entirely on the cost of media buying. About five minutes was spent on creative content. That's when he decided to open his own agency."

Named David Ratto, the new shop was launched in 1974, the year General Perón died and the beginning of one of the country's most politically turbulent periods. The agency had fewer than a dozen executives at first, mainly to service leading publisher Editorial Atlantida. It was only after the agency acquired the Chrysler Corporation business a year later that Ratto knew he would have to incorporate media buying into the agency. By 1977 David Ratto was a full-service agency.

With the agency quickly establishing itself as a leading creative shop, it did not take long for BBDO Worldwide, which in the late 1970s was looking for a tactical association in Argentina, to single out the David Ratto agency as an ideal partner. At the time, Argentina's inward-looking and highly protected economy had made it difficult for more than a few multinationals to establish local partnerships in the country, notably Grey Advertising with Casares; McCann-Erickson with Gowland; and Ogilvy & Mather with Ortiz, Scopesi & Ratto.

BBDO flattered the David Ratto agency by offering it the local work on R.J. Reynolds Tobacco Company's Camel cigarette account, the first time the tobacco giant allowed an agency outside the United States to create campaigns for the brand. David Ratto returned the compliment by becoming the U.S. agency's representation office. The ensuing period with Camel produced memorable work. Said Carlos Ratto, "Even when we lost the account in the early '80s, we produced a special campaign just to say good-bye to the camel."

David Ratto managed to resist persistent advances by BBDO for closer ties for several years. He instead launched himself into the fragile restoration of democracy that began with the downfall of the military junta in 1983. For the following four years, Ratto became chief media adviser to the elected government of Raul Alfonsin. It was during this period that Carlos Ratto joined the agency as an account assistant.

In 1987, once it became obvious that Argentina was open to globalization, the agency finally entered into a formal partnership with BBDO, surrendering 20 percent ownership to the holding company.

A defining moment for Carlos Ratto came in 1989 when he was working on several accounts, including Volkswagen (VW), Seagram's, and Reckitt & Colman, all well-established brand names. When the account director for VW suddenly left the agency, VW asked the elder Ratto to let Carlos take over the account. Two years later, Carlos Ratto was promoted to managing director and vice president. The year 1989 was also important for the agency as BBDO took the PepsiCo account from the J. Walter Thompson Company.

For most of the 1990s, the agency consistently won prestigious accounts, in many ways mirroring the upturn of the country's advertising industry, buoyed by a spate of major privatizations and an unprecedented opening of the economy that led to an invasion of international companies and brands into Argentina. Client acquisitions included: PepsiCo Snacks, 1993; Federal Express, 1993; Argencard (MasterCard), 1993, although the account was lost in 1996; Nike, 1994; S.A. Alba (ICI Paints), 1996; Effem (Mars candies), 1999; and local dairy giant Sancor, 2000.

Creative awards also continued for both the agency and its founder, including a bronze Lion for a Volkswagen "New Beetle" ad at Cannes in 2000.

When David Ratto stepped down as agency president in 1999, it could have heralded a period of uncertainty for the agency. But a smooth transition was ensured by his continuing presence as a consultant, the expected choice of his son Carlos as his successor, and the promotion of longtime colleague and General Manager Roberto Ameal to the post of vice president-managing director.

ALI QASSIM

See also color plate in this volume

Further Reading
France, Miranda, "Coke/Pepsi Battle before Court Decision Will Set Comparative Ad Precedent," *Advertising Age* (13 December 1993)

Recall

The extent to which an ad is remembered is a critical component of the effectiveness of any advertising campaign or commercial. Consumers must remember a brand name before they can be persuaded to buy the product. Over the years, a variety of techniques have been designed to measure the impact and effectiveness of advertisements.

Research Tools and Techniques

Methods for assessing the effectiveness of advertising have proliferated since the early days of the profession and continue to do so with the introduction of new media. Inquiry tests, for example, are designed to measure effectiveness on the basis of inquiries generated by ads appearing in various print media.

Recognition and recall tests, also known as readership studies, most associated with Starch INRA/Starch Readership Report, have long been viewed as a fundamental tool for assessing advertising effectiveness in the print media. They generally involve asking a representative sample of respondents whether they saw a given advertisement, read it, and how much of it they remember. Bruzzone Research Corporation of Alameda, California, uses recognition tests to measure brand recognition, testing commercials that have aired on national prime-time television. McCollum/Spielman of Great Neck, New York, on the other hand, uses brand recall tests to measure brand awareness. Respondents in a theater view an hour-long TV pilot in which several commercials are nested. At the end, respondents are asked to list all the brands they remember having seen.

The day-after test of TV commercials was employed by the U.S. ad agency Young & Rubicam. Later it became associated with the Burke Marketing Research Company of Cincinnati, Ohio, and came to be known as the DAR (day-after recall) test or the Burke DAR test. In the DAR test, respondents exposed to the commercial under scrutiny would be interviewed the following day. Both unaided and aided recall were used to measure advertising effectiveness. Once a very popular tool, the DAR has since been largely replaced by other research methods, although these are in many ways often largely variations on the Burke DAR test. Widely used post-testing studies include ASI Recall Plus from Ipsos-ASI, Inc., which uses cable television to show commercials in a test market before going national; the In-View system of Gallup & Robinson, Inc. (G&R), which tends to test only in a single city; and the Mapes & Ross system, which tends to test in three U.S. cities simultaneously.

ASI's Print Plus test and G&R's Impact test are day-after print recall studies. In these tests respondents are given a magazine to read and then are interviewed by phone the following day.

Recall Versus Recognition

There has been much debate over the use of recall versus recognition to test advertising effectiveness. Beginning in the early 1990s, however, researchers began to note that consumer recall of TV commercials was on the decrease. They attributed this trend to the decreasing attention that people give TV—not to smaller audiences, clutter, or poor-quality programming. This does not mean, however, that researchers should forgo the use of recall measures, but rather that they need to be aware that recall and recognition measures have different implications.

G&R, Inc., has developed the advertising response model (ARM). This model shows that an ad must break through the clutter in order to gain attention. ARM uses multiple copy testing measures in order to identify message- and execution-related variables, important in influencing persuasion. This method can help identify how the ad was processed by viewers and whether the message- and execution-related variables were appropriate for the communication objectives set by the company.

The Advertising Research Foundation (ARF), based in New York, designed the Copy Research Validity Project (CRVP) to assess various copy-testing measures, including persuasion, salience, recall, communication, communication reaction (liking), and communication reaction (diagnostics). The ARF study suggests that an ad's likeability is a valid measure of advertising effectiveness and that liked ads are apt to be informative as well as entertaining.

Likability and Humor

Liking an ad has important implications for memory. It has been suggested, in fact, that liking an ad may have less to do with

entertainment and more to do with communication and persuasiveness. A 1992 study found that liking was highly correlated with persuasiveness. The study employed a copy-testing approach called Tele Test. Respondents were questioned 24 hours after being given videocassettes of an unreleased pilot TV show in which several ads were embedded. An earlier study found that people who liked a commercial "a lot" were twice as likely to be persuaded by it as people who simply felt neutral. The authors noted that likeable advertising has an impact on persuasion because a likeable commercial affects the emotional component of consumers' attitudes toward the brand. The same study also found that commercial liking went beyond entertainment. "People like commercials which they feel are relevant and worth remembering," it concluded.

Humor has often been used to increase an ad's likeability, but this effect is not inevitable. Many consumers expect information from ads, and humor will not necessarily cause them to form favorable attitudes toward a product or service. On the other hand, people who want to think only as much as is necessary may look to likeability cues such as humor. The use of humor in advertising should, therefore, be regarded as a tool for segmenting potential purchasers.

Because of their social influence, celebrities have often been used to aid recall and recognition of ads. Nevertheless, there is always risk involved when using celebrities to promote products and services. In the 1990s, for example, the negative publicity surrounding such figures as Michael Jackson and O.J. Simpson made marketers realize that celebrity endorsers could in fact have a deleterious impact on the public's attitudes toward the brand. The risk is potentially greater for new or unfamiliar brands, as celebrity endorsers have a strong influence on how consumers evaluate the brand. Research also suggests that the attractiveness and likeability of a celebrity is not necessarily consistent with consumers' purchase intent. It has been found that celebrity endorsements are better suited to products that have high psychological and social risk. Moreover, attractiveness of a celebrity is most effective with attractiveness-related products.

Developments of the 1990s

Toward the end of the 20th century there was an increase in the use of persuasion measures such as consumer purchase intentions and pre- and postpurchase attitudes as sources of both creative and diagnostic information. A copy-testing method called Sequence (Structural EQUations Estimation of New Copy Effectiveness) extends previous copy-testing research by assessing the strength of linkages in consumers' minds among brand beliefs, brand attitudes, and purchase intention, and it does so without incurring additional costs for data collection.

Another new type of research also emerged in the 1990s: the single-source study, which involves linking a household's advertising exposure to actual household purchasing behavior. Here, tracking studies conducted at regular intervals measure changes over time in advertising awareness, recall, interest in and attitudes toward the ads, and purchase intentions. Techniques used include telephone interviews, mail surveys, and mall intercepts. One drawback of this kind of study, however, is that it fails to establish audience exposure to the advertisement.

BRETT MARTIN

Further Reading

Belch, George Eugene, and Michael A. Belch, *Introduction to Advertising and Promotion Management*, Homewood, Illinois: Irwin, 1990; 5th edition, as *Advertising and Promotion: An Integrated Marketing Communications Perspective*, Boston: Irwin/McGraw Hill, 2001

Biel, Alexander L., and Carol A. Bridgwater, "Attributes of Likable Television Commercials," *Journal of Advertising Research* 30, no. 3 (June/July 1990)

Chow, Simeon, Randall Rose, and Darral G. Clarke, "SEQUENCE: Structural EQUations Estimation of New Copy Effectiveness," *Journal of Advertising Research* 32, no. 4 (July/August 1992)

Dubow, Joel S., "Advertising Recognition and Recall by Age—Including Teens," *Journal of Advertising Research* 35, no. 5 (September/October 1995)

Du Plessis, Erik, "Recognition versus Recall," *Journal of Advertising Research* 34, no. 3 (May/June 1994)

Greene, William F., "Observations: What Drives Commercial Liking? An Exploration of Entertainment vs. Communication," *Journal of Advertising Research* 32, no. 2 (March/April 1992)

Haley, Russell I., and Allan Baldinger, "The ARF Copy Research Validity Project," *Journal of Advertising Research* 31, no. 2 (April/May 1991)

Kamins, Michael A., "An Investigation into the 'Match-Up' Hypothesis in Celebrity Advertising: When Beauty May Be Only Skin Deep," *Journal of Advertising* 19, no. 1 (1990)

Mehta, Abhilasha, "How Advertising Response Modeling (ARM) Can Increase Ad Effectiveness," *Journal of Advertising Research* 34, no. 3 (May/June 1994)

Naccarato, John, "Content Analysis as a Predictive Methodology: Recall, Readership, and Evaluations of Business-to-Business Print Advertising," *Journal of Advertising Research* 38, no. 3 (May/June 1998)

Till, Brian D., and Terence Shimp, "Endorsers in Advertising: The Case of Negative Celebrity Information," *Journal of Advertising* 27, no. 1 (Spring 1998)

Zhang, Yong, "Responses to Humorous Advertising: The Moderating Effect of Need for Cognition," *Journal of Advertising* 25, no. 1 (Spring 1996)

Red Cross. *See* American Red Cross

Reeves, Rosser 1910–1984

U.S. Advertising Executive

To advertising executives three letters have rarely meant as much as USP. "Unique selling proposition," the brainchild of pioneering advertising man Rosser Reeves, is based on the premise that every product, service, or company can be reduced to a single marketing exhortation. For example, Anacin acts fast—hence the slogan, "Fast, fast, fast relief." And Bic ballpoint pens are reliable: "It writes the first time, every time."

Like all advertising rules, USP has limitations. The best way to sell a product differs not only at different times but also under different circumstances. The USP concept endures, however, not least as a selling proposition for the agency with which Reeves was long associated, Ted Bates & Company.

Born in 1910 in Danville, Virginia, Reeves entered advertising more by accident than design. He initially wanted to be a lawyer, then a history teacher, and he enrolled at the University of Virginia in 1928. Faced with economic difficulties in 1929, he had to leave college early to take a job with a bank in Richmond, Virginia, where he eventually entered the advertising department.

After joining Cecil, Warwick & Cecil, Inc., in New York City in 1934, Reeves rapidly became known as a brilliant theoretician of sales techniques. He moved to Ruthrauff & Ryan and then to Blackett-Sample-Hummert before accepting a job with Benton & Bowles. In 1940 he left that agency to join his Benton & Bowles colleague Ted Bates, who was establishing his own agency, Ted Bates, Inc.

It was there that Reeves came up with USP. He began with the basic premise that to sell, a product first has to be good. Quality is not enough, however. A product also has to have its own USP. To

Rosser Reeves.
Bates USA.

Reeves, consumers were not irrational creatures driven by hidden motives even they did not understand. Instead, the problem for consumers was that they received too many messages. Therefore, the challenge to advertisers was to create singular memorable messages that the consumer could easily understand.

The USP must follow three rules. First, the advertiser must present a definite proposition: If you buy X, you will get a specific benefit. Second, the benefit must be unique to the particular product, unavailable in the products offered by competitors. And third, the proposition must be a "selling" one; that is, the benefit must be one that many people will want. (For example, Colgate toothpaste "cleans your breath while it cleans your teeth.")

Reeves took a systematic approach to the formulation of a product's USP, analyzing the product involved and all its qualities. To this end, Reeves and the Bates agency hired scores of specialist consultants. To find a USP for Palmolive soap, for example, tests were set up with Northwestern University to prove that using the soap for one minute a day would improve a person's skin. These findings then became the message, and, like all USP messages, once the Palmolive USP was found, Reeves's policy was to reiterate it. He later said, "If an idea is a good one and applies to the product, it will be good for an indefinite length of time."

According to Reeves, it was the USP idea that was the key element of an advertising campaign. Once the USP had been found, he contended, "any good copywriter can write a good ad." Reeves's concept harked back to the views of the pioneering advertising executive John E. Kennedy, who argued that the essence of an advertisement could be summed up as "salesmanship in print." If the medium was television, Reeves's ads coupled simple themes with crisp demonstration: M&M's candy "melts in your mouth, not in your hands"; "Wonder Bread helps build strong bodies 12 ways."

In 1961 Reeves published *Reality in Advertising,* a work that grew out of a memorandum to new Bates executives. It sold more

than 30,000 copies in six months, was translated into seven languages, and drew more accounts to Reeves's agency. The USP concept brought enormous success to the Bates agency, even though the advertisements produced by that firm in the 1950s and 1960s were often disparaged by other advertising professionals for their lack of creativity. Reeves did not mind that his ads were unpopular with his peers. He argued that what mattered was that the ads were effective.

An advertisement Reeves created for Anacin was typical of his work. It showed three boxes, each symbolizing a different aspect of headache pain, superimposed on a drawing of a human head: one box depicted a jagged bolt of electricity; the next, a pounding hammer; the third, a coiling spring bolt. Beneath the three boxes appeared a trail of little bubbles of medicine making their way up from the Anacin logo at the bottom of the ad. Many creative professionals hated the campaign, but Anacin sales increased in 18 months from $18 million to $54 million.

A "go for the jugular" man, Reeves became known as "the prince of the hard sell" and "the ultimate pragmatist." In *Reality in Advertising*, he asked, "Now what do you want of me? Fine writing? Do you want masterpieces? Do you want glowing things that can be framed by copywriters? Or do you want to see the goddammed sales curve stop moving down and start moving up?" Some regarded his approach as too simplistic. Many, including ad executive David Ogilvy, questioned the effectiveness of advertising based solely on logic and argument.

Critics also pointed out that Reeves sometimes employed ethically questionable tactics, as his advertisements often skirted the truth. Many ads featured actors in white coats, looking and sounding like doctors as they promulgated sometimes dubious USP claims. The Federal Trade Commission forced the agency to drop claims for Carter's Little Liver Pills and issued additional complaints against a string of other advertisements, including a commercial that made it appear as if a shaving cream could work on sandpaper when, in fact, the paper used was not really sandpaper.

In his private life, Reeves was also a pragmatist. He argued that the advertising business was a good one because a person could make money that could then be enjoyed in leisure. He raced yachts, played chess at the national standard, and flew planes. His celebration of leisure was another characteristic that did not endear him to other advertising executives more dedicated to work-oriented lifestyles.

In 1952 Reeves wrote the "Eisenhower Answers America" campaign for Dwight D. Eisenhower's presidential campaign. Using information gathered in Gallup polls, Reeves determined the three most important issues to Americans at that time (the Korean War, economic problems, and political corruption) and designed 30-second spots in which Eisenhower, filmed in an empty TV studio, answered scripted questions from voters. (The questions were actually filmed after Eisenhower's "responses.") The ads were revolutionary because they represented the first time that a presidential candidate bought television airtime for brief commercials rather than for lengthy political speeches. Reeves convinced Eisenhower to take this innovative approach because Reeves's research showed that listeners did not retain information from speeches, whereas short, frequently repeated messages were more likely to stick in the voter's mind. Like Reeves's commercial advertisements, these political ads attracted criticism: they were often described as "vulgar," and even Eisenhower himself deprecated the ads, saying, "To think that an old soldier should come to this." Despite the criticism, "Eisenhower Answers America" was, like so many of Reeves's commercial campaigns, a success.

Reeves left Bates, where he was then serving as chairman, in 1966. He died of a heart attack in 1984. The Rosser Reeves Collection, which contains many photos, writings, and other documents related to Reeves's life and work, is housed in the State Historical Society of Wisconsin in Madison.

ERIC CLARK

Biography

Born in Danville, Virginia, 10 September 1910; attended University of Virginia, 1928–29; became a copywriter with Cecil, Warwick & Cecil, Inc., 1934; joined Ruthrauff & Ryan, 1934; joined Blackett-Sample-Hummert, 1938; moved to Benton & Bowles, 1939; joined Ted Bates, Inc., where he created the concept of "unique selling proposition," or USP, 1940; retired as Bates chairman, 1966; died of a heart attack in Chapel Hill, North Carolina, 24 January 1984.

Selected Publications

Reality in Advertising, 1979

Further Reading

Clark, Eric, *The Want Makers,* London: Hodder and Stoughton, 1988; New York: Viking, 1989

Fox, Stephen, *The Mirror Makers: A History of American Advertising and Its Creators,* New York: Morrow, 1984

Meadows, Ron, "They Consume Advertising Too," *ADMAP* (July/August 1983)

Meyers, William, *The Image-Makers: Power and Persuasion on Madison Avenue,* New York: Times, 1984

Regulation. *See* Government Regulation

Religion, Advertising of

Although nonprofit organizations have embraced marketing practices wholeheartedly for decades, churches have been slower to adopt them, especially in the area of advertising. The propagation of religions for centuries was primarily accomplished through word of mouth—preaching, evangelism, and witnessing.

Traditionally, many houses of worship viewed as sacrilegious the use of money from tithes and offerings to buy space and time in the mass media. Marketing—with its slick Madison Avenue image—was deemed unethical by many religious organizations. Others feared that marketing techniques might be exploitive or irritating.

A 1993 article in *Christianity Today* titled "Will the Great Commission Become the Great Ad Campaign?" condemned frequent reliance on modern marketing methods. "The mass media are secondary to the firsthand witness of individuals and groups of believers," wrote author James Engel.

In the last two decades of the 20th century, however, marketing and advertising were increasingly used as effective tools for houses of worship. George Barna, a leader in the church marketing movement in North America, wrote that "ministry, in essence, has the same objective as marketing: to meet people's needs."

When Barna first advocated the use of modern marketing techniques, however, he was branded a heretic by some.

According to the 1999 *Yearbook of American & Canadian Churches,* the end of the 1990s was a low-growth or no-growth period for most established churches. Yet despite the overall decline in mainstream church attendance, those churches that adopted a marketing orientation experienced steady growth. The marketing-oriented viewpoint involves researching the needs and demographics of the target groups, providing relevant programs, and using a variety of marketing techniques to publicize church services.

Clergy, for the most part, were unexposed to seminary courses, books, or workshops about church marketing until recently. A study by Stephen McDaniel published in 1989 revealed that ministers were actually more receptive to marketing activities conducted by houses of worship than the general public. A follow-up study published in 1995 reported that clergy were willing to advertise events, but not necessarily persuasive messages. Low-profile advertising (such as a sign in front of a church or synagogue) was found to be preferable to billboards or promotional products (such as pens or bumper stickers). Churches that resorted to advertising before the recent surge in its popularity were admired by some and denounced by others.

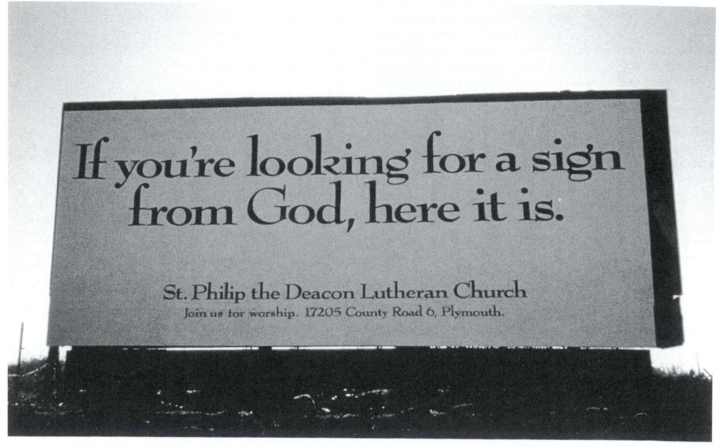

HMS/Ruhr created this billboard in 1996 for St. Philip the Deacon Lutheran Church in Plymouth, Minnesota.
Created by Michael Gustafion.

Methods and Resources

Five main methods of advertising for the religious marketer are outlined in the book *Marketing for Congregations: Choosing to Serve People More Effectively* (1992). These techniques are: paid advertising—permits total control of the message content and selection of the delivery vehicle (what medium and when); public service advertising—lacks control over timing of these free messages by nonprofit groups; sales promotion—encourages short-term use or purchase through incentives of goods and services; publicity—provides credibility through use of nonpaid message in medium, but lacks any control over message content and timing; and personal selling—lacks control of message content but can provide instant feedback on reception of message by designated target.

Churches attempting to reach younger generations in the early part of the 21st century had more tools than did their counterparts a generation before. One of the earlier practical resources was a 1988 book, *Marketing the Church: What They Never Told You About Church Growth,* by Barna, founder and president of the Barna Research Group. His California company provides workshops, publications, and full-service marketing research for organizations and individual churches. Some of his other books include *User Friendly Churches* (1991) and *A Step-by-Step Guide to Church Marketing: Breaking Ground for the Harvest* (1992). Another work, *Advertising the Local Church: A Handbook for Promotion,* was started in 1978 as a small notebook by George H. Martin and expanded with subsequent editions into more than 120 pages. In addition to *Marketing for Congregations,* books on the topic by others have included *Marketing Your Ministry: Ten Critical Principles* (1990), *A Generation Alone: Xers Making a Place in the World* (1994), and *Marketing for Churches and Ministries* (1995).

Likewise, denominational magazines became interested in advertising during the 1990s, featuring articles with titles such as "Promote Your Church on the Church Page," "Direct Mail Tops Ad Survey," "Reach Out With Press Releases," and "Advertise Your Activities For Free." In 1995 Haworth Press published the first volume of its *Journal of Ministry Marketing & Management.* The inaugural issue's preface stated, "The 1990s ushered in an era of increasing emphasis on professional development of church and ministry administrators. . . . *JMM&M* is an applied journal devoted to addressing marketing and management issues in all types of church and ministry settings."

Faith in Advertising

In the summer of 1987, the First Methodist Church of Cleveland, Ohio, hired the advertising agency Robert Carter & Associates to create awareness among college students. Its print ads used such headlines as "Summertime and religion is easy," "Rush at East 30th and Euclid. We don't have a Hell Week," and "Look into our Master's program." Although the previously low attendance among the targeted group was increased, many church members felt the ads were irreverent.

Fallon McElligott, of Minneapolis, Minnesota, started producing creative print ads for the Episcopal Church in the 1980s. After growing in popularity, the Episcopal Ad Project expanded to include slick camera-ready ads that could be purchased for $10 by a variety of churches throughout North America. A 1984 sales brochure noted, "The Episcopal Ad Project has already helped to raise attendance at many churches throughout the country. Isn't it time you put your faith in advertising? You just might help a lot of people put their faith in God." For wider distribution, the company's name changed to Church Ad Project. The black-and-white ads—still popular and available into the 21 century—use artwork or a photograph along with a clever headline to effectively capture readers' attention. The 2000 catalog provided even more selections at $35 per ad, with a one-year license agreement for their use. Some are seasonal, but most of the ads are attempts to invite nonchurchgoers to consider giving the church another chance at meeting their needs. To use the contemporary print ads, a church merely had to add its name and address or other tag line in the space provided. Despite the success of such ads, a few critics have voiced disapproval of using sacred symbols and pictures on the entertainment pages of the daily newspaper, which is a more appropriate location to capture the attention of nonchurchgoers than the typical weekend "church" page.

The Church of Jesus Christ of Latter-day Saints has long been involved in advertising, running public service television spots promoting family values. In 1995 the church celebrated its 50th such advertising campaign.

Broadcast media have also been used by a number of other churches to promote their various programs and services. The Lutheran Church–Missouri Synod kicked off a 1984 evangelism campaign using such advertising channels as radio, television, audiocassette tapes, toll-free telephone lines, and newspapers. Costing close to $100 million, the advertising crusade targeted nonchurchgoers also. "This program will obviously benefit the Lutheran church," said Lutheran radio host Dale Meyer, "but a rising tide raises all ships, and we intend this to be a blessing to all Christendom."

The Cincinnati, Ohio, office of Young & Rubicam developed a public service ad campaign in 1994 for the Ursuline sisters of the United States and Canada, who were having difficulties recruiting new members. The agency did not charge the order for its services for the $70,000 creative project geared for radio and newspapers.

Television commercials are now available from production facilities that allow individual churches to add their names to the professionally edited 30-second and 60-second selections. Similar to the Fallon McElligott series of print ads, these broadcast advertisements are meant to capture the attention of nonchurchgoers.

Impact Productions, based in Tulsa, Oklahoma, has created such ready-to-run, 30-second commercials for churches and church-related institutions since 1991. "We have 61 different commercials currently available, along with related print collateral," said Shane Harwell, vice president of sales and marketing. "About 2,500 churches have license agreements to use our spots, which primarily run on cable."

Christianity is not the only religion that uses marketing techniques to expand its influence. Buddhism has used celebrity endorsements to help establish more than 1,500 Buddhist centers in the United States. Such individuals as actor Richard Gere, singer Tina Turner, L.A. Lakers coach Phil Jackson and the Nobel Prize-winning Dalai Lama have contributed to media coverage of this religion worldwide.

Nor is the trend limited to North America. Metro Manila Bible Community, for example, is a thriving nondenominational church meeting in a renovated theater in downtown Manila in the Philippines. Print ads, direct mail, and fliers have been used effectively to grow a youthful membership that enjoys contemporary drama and music. However, some countries are not as open for churches to advertise or promote their services. Greece, for example, is 98 percent Greek Orthodox, but only 2 percent attend church on a regular basis. The Greek constitution calls for up to four years imprisonment for inducing someone to convert to one's faith.

Assessing Effectiveness

A survey of media use by Texas churches was published in 1986. Conducted by William Moncrief, Charles Lamb, Jr., and Sandra Hart, the limited study found churches listing Yellow Pages (85 percent), newspapers (69 percent), direct mail (61 percent), and signs (52 percent) as media in which they had run ads. The study asked clergy whether they thought churches needed to become more businesslike or less businesslike to grow. Whereas 68 percent indicated that churches needed to become more business-oriented, only 14 percent indicated that they should become less businesslike.

Randall Hines conducted a 1992 survey of the advertising practices of the 100 largest churches in the Southern Baptist Convention. Churches ranked both their frequency of use and perceived effectiveness among ten advertising options: billboards, direct mail (to nonmembers), door-to-door fliers, newspaper church page listings, newspaper display ads, radio, television, transit, Yellow Pages display ads, and Yellow Pages listings. The most-used media within the previous 12 months were newspaper display ads and Yellow Pages listings, both cited by 91.2 percent of the responding churches. Ranked next in frequency of use were Yellow Pages display ads (75 percent), direct mail (69.1 percent), and radio (67.6 percent).

When asked to rate their perceived effectiveness of the same 10 advertising options, 72.3 percent of the Southern Baptist churches using direct mail ranked it as their top choice. Almost as many (71.7 percent) of the churches using radio perceived it as effective.

Ranked next in perceived effectiveness were television (69.4 percent), billboards (63.6 percent), and Yellow Pages display ads (60.8 percent). Direct mail came in fourth in frequency of usage, but first in perceived effectiveness. Although the two most popular forms of advertising by these large churches were newspaper display ads and Yellow Pages listings, both were perceived in the bottom half for effectiveness. This shows how difficult it is for churches—as well as other advertisers—to assess just how effective individual advertising efforts can be.

"Megachurches" and Targeting Generation X

The term *megachurch* was coined in the 1990s to describe a church with a weekly attendance of at least 2,000. Gail Stout, writing in the September 1999 edition of *Church Business,* analyzed the growing trend toward huge congregations:

> There is a growing number of big business megachurches in the United States today serving 2,000 or more parishioners each week. . . . They show more local concern, use marketing techniques, add modern music and multimedia approaches, and tend to the needs of members once fulfilled by social services. These megachurches tend to be nondenominational and more experimental than traditional churches.

Typically, megachurches use a variety of advertisements to attract the nontraditional churchgoer. Statistics show that the young men and women of Generation X are turned off by traditional outreach campaigns but find relevance in contemporary services complete with drama and quality music. Gen-Xers with children expect pristine nursery facilities and extensive children's activities. Unlike previous generations, they may prefer to be contacted by their churches via e-mail and cell phone. As early as 1993 the InterVarsity Christian Fellowship teamed with Leighton Ford

Ministries to cohost a Baby Busters Consultation on how to target Generation X. Several other similar workshops have dealt with marketing concepts for expanding ministry opportunities or targeting certain overlooked publics.

Certainly not the last to embrace Internet advertising, houses of worship and religious organizations in recent years have produced Web sites to reach certain targeted groups. From simple home pages to banner ads and links to other Internet sites, these new methods of advertising are still being developed, expanded, and evaluated.

RANDALL HINES

See also color plate in this volume

Further Reading

Barna, George, *A Step-by-Step Guide to Church Marketing: Breaking Ground for the Harvest,* Ventura, California: Regal, 1992

Hines, Randall W., "Church Advertising Practices and Perceptions," *Journal of Ministry Marketing and Management* 2, no. 1 (1996)

Hisrich, Robert D., and John W. Pearson, *Marketing Your Ministry: Ten Critical Principles,* Brentwood, Tennessee: Wolgemuth and Hyatt, 1990

Martin, George H., *Advertising the Local Church: A Handbook for Promotion,* Minneapolis, Minnesota: Episcopal Ad Project, 1984

Shawchuck, Norman, *Marketing for Congregations: Choosing to Serve People More Effectively,* Nashville, Tennessee: Abingdon, 1992

Stevens, Robert E., and David L. Loudon, *Marketing for Churches and Ministries,* New York: Haworth, 1992

Stevens, Robert E., and David L. Loudon, "Preface and Introduction," *Journal of Ministry Marketing and Management* 1, no. 1 (1995)

Resor, Helen Lansdowne 1886–1964

U.S. Advertising Pioneer

Helen Lansdowne Resor was one of the most influential women in U.S. advertising. Over four decades, she and her husband, Stanley Resor, built the J. Walter Thompson Company (JWT) into an advertising powerhouse. She was lauded by legendary advertising man David Ogilvy as "the greatest copywriter of her generation" and was instrumental in opening the advertising profession to women.

She was born on 20 February 1886 in Grayson, Kentucky, and was the eighth of George and Helen Bayleff Lansdowne's nine children. In 1890 her mother left her father and moved with her children to Covington, Kentucky, where she had family; she eventually became a librarian and sold real estate to support her family. Her mother set an example for Helen of feminism and the need for self-sufficiency. In his history of advertising, *The Mirror*

Makers, Stephen Fox related Helen Bayleff Lansdowne's cautionary words to her daughters: "You're never going to get caught the way I was. You're going to learn how to work."

In 1903 Helen Lansdowne graduated from high school as class valedictorian and took a job with the World Manufacturing Company, a local manufacturer of toilet preparations sold by mail. She next was hired as a bill auditor for Procter & Collier, an advertising agency in nearby Cincinnati, Ohio, that acted as the in-house shop for the Procter & Gamble Company (P&G). A year later, she got a job writing retail ads for a Cincinnati newspaper, the *Commercial Tribune*, and in 1906 she took a copywriting job at the Street Railways Advertising Company, which controlled most U.S. streetcar advertising.

In 1907 Stanley Resor, who had been hired as a salesman at Procter & Collier in 1904, asked Lansdowne to return to the agency as a copywriter. Although her family opposed the move, believing that Resor would expect too much work, Lansdowne accepted. While at Procter & Collier, she wrote copy for Brenlin window shades, Red Cross shoes, and Higgin all-metal screens.

In 1908 Resor was offered a job managing the Chicago, Illinois, office of JWT; after he refused the offer, JWT instead hired him and his brother, Walter, to open an office for the agency in Cincinnati. Resor, in turn, hired Lansdowne to be the branch's copywriter, thereby making her the agency's first female copywriter.

In January 1911 she was promoted and moved to JWT's New York City office, where, among other accounts, she worked on the introductory campaign for a new P&G product, Crisco vegetable shortening. The assignment was out of character for P&G, which had not hired an outside ad agency in 20 years, and it led to another first for the advertiser: Lansdowne made five appearances before the company's board to discuss the campaign, becoming the first woman ever to attend a P&G board meeting.

In 1916 a group headed by Stanley Resor bought the agency from founder James Walter Thompson for $500,000, and Resor, who had earlier moved to New York City, became president. On 6 March 1917 Lansdowne and Resor were married. Together, they ran the agency, Stanley Resor focusing on administration and client services and Helen Resor on the preparation of ads, and both of them working out key decisions and strategies. The *J. Walter Thompson News*, an internal publication, in 1984 described their relationship as "almost mystical." It continued: "They enlarged each other. It was a case of the whole being far greater than the simple sum of the parts."

On the copywriting and creative side, Helen Resor was the first woman to successfully plan and write national advertising rather than just retail efforts. In particular, she is credited with creating a new style of "feature story" advertising that closely resembled its surrounding editorial copy in magazines, using illustrations and text that appealed to the reader's emotions. This type of emotional appeal was best demonstrated in her ad for Andrew Jergens Company's Woodbury facial soap. Another of her innovations was the use of endorsements, which she legitimized in a Pond's cold cream campaign. But perhaps her biggest contribution to copywriting was her firm conviction that "copy must be believable"—an idea that eventually became a fundamental JWT tenet.

Helen Lansdowne Resor.
Photograph by Edward Steichen. Reprinted with permission of Joanna T. Steichen.

While Woodbury facial soap had long been advertised for ridding the skin of blemishes, after the account moved to JWT in 1910 Resor positioned the soap as a beauty product. The ad used a painting of an attractive couple in evening attire accompanied by the headline, "A skin you love to touch." The copy explained how using the product would increase the beauty of one's skin and offered a reproduction of the painting and a week's supply of the soap for 10 cents. While sales of the product increased 1,000 percent as a result of the ad, it was initially considered too risqué and controversial and was banned by some magazines; William Hetherington, at the time a young employee at the agency, later told *Advertising Age* that the phrase "A skin you love to touch" was even scorned by some of the staff at JWT. But time would prove the critics wrong. Ad executive Albert Lasker later said the Woodbury ad, with its use of sex appeal, was one of three great landmarks in advertising history; the ad also was ranked 31st on *Advertising Age*'s list of the top 100 campaigns of the 20th century.

For Pond's cold cream, Resor took endorsement advertising to a new level by persuading well-known and respected women, from socialites to European royalty, to back the product in advertising. The first ad, in 1924, offered an endorsement by Alva Belmont, a New York City society leader and feminist; Belmont agreed to attach her name to the product after JWT offered to donate $1,000 to the National Woman's Party. The ads, which included coupons that readers could mail in for a product sample, later featured such figures as the Queen of Rumania, who drew 9,435 coupons, according to Fox in *The Mirror Makers*; Mrs. Reginald Vanderbilt, 10,325 coupons; and the Duchess de Richelieu, 19,126 coupons.

Other accounts Resor worked on included Cutex, Lux, and Yuban and Maxwell House coffees. She was a pioneer in using artists to work on advertising, and as a result JWT was the first agency to hire illustrator Norman Rockwell. Resor also improved the quality of photography in advertising by signing Edward Steichen, recognized as one of the greatest photographers of the time, to an exclusive contract in 1923; other renowned photographers first hired by JWT included Cecil Beaton and Youseff Karsh.

In addition to her ground-breaking creative work, Resor was actively involved in mentoring young women in advertising, earning JWT a reputation as early as the 1920s as being the "women's agency," where women had a chance to succeed and be promoted. She set up a women's editorial department that was separate from but equal to the men's copy groups to encourage women to share their ideas freely. Among those whose careers she guided were copywriters Aminta Casseres, Margaret King Eddy, Nancy Stephenson, and Ruth Waldo, who became the agency's first woman vice president. Resor extended her feminist beliefs outside the office as well, organizing a group of women from JWT in a suffragette parade in New York City.

She also donated her time and the agency's resources to the support of U.S. efforts in both world wars. During World War I she created ads for the Red Cross and the YMCA. After the war, President Herbert Hoover asked her to put together a campaign to promote food conservation. During World War II, Resor and the JWT creative department created a campaign themed, "Women must work to win the war," using car cards, posters, newspaper ads, and radio spots to persuade 3 million women to take jobs in war factories and related civilian areas by the end of 1943. Other organizations she supported included Radcliffe College, the Planned Parenthood Association, and the Travelers Aid Society, which helped homeless women during the Depression.

Resor, who at one time supervised two-thirds of the business handled by the agency's offices in New York City and Boston, Massachusetts, and was eventually promoted to vice president and director, was active at JWT until September 1958, when she fell in the agency's reception area and injured her head; after that, she made few appearances at work and left when her husband retired in February 1961.

Resor died on 2 January 1964, 14 months after her husband's death on 29 October 1962. Stanley and Helen Resor were inducted into the Advertising Hall of Fame in 1967; she was honored for her copywriting and for her work as vice president and wife of the president of JWT. During their tenure, the agency grew from a handful of U.S. offices and fewer than 100 staff members to a worldwide staff of almost 7,000 with 57 offices in 23 countries and $360 million in billings.

KAREN EGOLF

Biography

Born in Grayson, Kentucky, on 20 February 1886; became a copywriter for Procter & Collier, Cincinnati, Ohio, 1907; became a copywriter for the new Cincinnati office of J. Walter Thompson Company (JWT), 1908; promoted and moved to JWT's New York City office, 1911; married Stanley Resor, 1917; served as vice president of JWT until retirement; died 2 January 1964; inducted into the Advertising Hall of Fame, 1967.

Further Reading

"Artist-Teacher-Oldtime Adman Recalls Ad Pioneers of 1915," *Advertising Age* (15 November 1965)

Fox, Stephen R., *The Mirror Makers: A History of American Advertising and Its Creators*, New York: Morrow, 1984

Helen Lansdowne Resor <www.ciadvertising.org/studies/student/00_spring/theory/asfeezor/public_html/helenresor/helenresor.htm>

"Helen Resor, 77, Famed Copywriter of JWT, Dies," *Advertising Age* (6 January 1964)

J. Walter Thompson Company News (10 January 1964)

J. Walter Thompson Company News (February 1984)

Keding, Ann Maxwell, "Helen Lansdowne Resor," in *The Ad Men and Women*, edited by Edd Applegate, Westport, Connecticut: Greenwood Press, 1994

Mayer, Martin, *Madison Avenue, U.S.A.*, New York: Harper, and London: Bodley Head, 1958; reprint, with a new introduction, Lincolnwood, Illinois: NTC Business Books, 1992

"Quiet, Competent, Helen Resor Helped in Shaping of JWT," *Advertising Age* (5 November 1962)

Resor, Stanley B. 1879–1962

U.S. Advertising Pioneer

Stanley Resor was born in 1879 in Cincinnati, Ohio. He received his undergraduate degree in classics from Yale University, New Haven, Connecticut, in 1901. In 1904 he began working as a salesman at Procter & Collier, the in-house advertising agency for the Procter & Gamble Company. In 1908 he and his brother Walter were hired by the J. Walter Thompson Company (JWT) to open a Cincinnati, Ohio, branch of the agency. In 1916 Resor and a group of associates purchased JWT, and Resor became president of the agency, a position he would retain for 39 years. The following year, 1917, he cofounded the American Association of Advertising Agencies (AAAA) and married coworker Helen Lansdowne, who would become one of the most prolific and prominent copywriters of the time. In 1955, at the age of 76, Resor became chairman of the board of JWT. He retired from JWT in 1961 and died on 29 October 1962.

Under Resor's leadership, JWT became the largest advertising agency in the world, a position it would retain for nearly 50 years. Yet Resor's influence extended beyond the boundaries of his own advertising agency to the profession as a whole. His legacy is best captured in three achievements. First, he pioneered the use of advertising to fuel consumer desire for products and services. Second, he passionately advocated the position that advertising was a science rather than an art. Third, he worked to raise the stature of advertising to professional status.

During Resor's youth his family's financial situation declined. Historian Stephen Fox has argued that this experience, as well as his wife's similar circumstances in her childhood, influenced the couple's development and use of the "emulation style" of advertising, in which goods and services are made desirable through their association with the lifestyles of the upper class. During the 1920s the Resors began to revive the form of advertising known as the testimonial. They solicited endorsements from society doyennes, celebrities, and even royalty for a wide range of beauty products. One series, which used the headline "She's engaged. She's lovely. She uses Pond's," featured debutantes whose engagements (as well as their use of Pond's cold cream) were described in detail. In an article in *Printers' Ink*, Resor observed that consumers, and especially women, would respond to this "spirit of emulation." His assertion appeared to be correct, judging by the fact that JWT's billings increased from $10.7 million in 1922 to more than $37 million by the end of the decade.

Resor's insistence that advertising should be viewed as a science also shaped his business practices. He filled the ranks of JWT with like-minded, college-educated employees at a time when a college degree was still a rarity. Resor began commissioning research studies as early as 1912. By the 1920s his agency was publishing a census of retail trade in the United States that reportedly was used by over 2,300 companies. This census has been heralded as the beginning of the field of market research. Resor's own articles on advertising reflected his belief that human behavior

was governed by "laws" and that advertisers should seek to discover and understand these laws in order to work effectively for their clients.

In 1920, to further his quest to make advertising more scientific, Resor hired John B. Watson, one of the most eminent behavioral psychologists of his day. Watson was ostensibly hired as head of research at JWT. However, his charisma and prominence soon led him to become an unofficial ambassador for the agency. He traveled the country, making speeches about the "science of advertising" and appearing at public gatherings in place of the more reticent Resor. In embracing Watson's beliefs that consumer desires could arise as a result of conditioning, Resor helped legitimize the role of applied psychology in advertising—a role that remains somewhat controversial to this day.

Another of Resor's favorite "scientific" devices was the "Thompson T-square"—five basic questions that had to be addressed before a marketing plan could be formulated for a client. These were similar to the "who, what, when, where, and why" mantra of journalism and were a device to help the agency gather factual information about a brand and its competitors.

Resor's attempt to elevate advertising to the status of a profession influenced not only the internal workings at JWT, but also the ways he interacted with fellow members of the advertising community. Once new employees arrived at JWT, they entered the "University of Advertising"—a rigorous two-and-one-half-year training program that familiarized them with the inner workings of the entire agency. In this program all new hires, including even the illustrious Watson, were required to expand their understanding of marketing and advertising through activities such as delivering Yuban coffee to wholesalers and working as salesclerks at Macy's department stores. Resor's dedication to this program was due to his desire for well-rounded employees.

Also in an effort to "professionalize" advertising Resor refused to present "speculative" (i.e., free) creative work when the agency was involved in a new business presentation. Resor believed speculative pitches were highly unethical and would only harm the reputation of the agencies that participated in them.

Perhaps Resor's most enduring professional activity was his cofounding of the AAAA in 1917. The following year Resor developed its code of ethical standards. He served as president of the organization from 1923 to 1924. Resor was also instrumental in the development of the Audit Bureau of Circulations, the Advertising Research Foundation, and the National Outdoor Advertising Bureau. In addition, he strove to improve the actual image of advertising itself by urging magazines to adopt printing processes that would enable ads to be run in color.

Resor's greatest accomplishments could be viewed as contradictory. For instance, he sought scientific laws regulating human behavior, yet the testimonial approach that his agency made famous appealed to consumers on a clearly emotional level. He

Stanley Resor.
Courtesy of the J. Walter Thomson Company.

argued that speculative campaigns were unethical, but the "rich and famous" whom he contracted for testimonials often did not really use the products they endorsed. Nevertheless, Resor's influence as president of the largest agency in the world during the formative years of the advertising profession remains significant.

CELE C. OTNES

Biography

Born in Cincinnati, Ohio, 30 April 1879; received degree in classics from Yale University, 1901; began working as a salesman at Procter & Collier, 1904; hired by J. Walter Thompson Company (JWT) to open a Cincinnati, Ohio, branch of the

agency, 1908; headed group that bought agency and became president of JWT, 1916; married co-worker Helen Landsdowne, 1917; cofounded the American Association of Advertising Agencies, 1917; became chairman of the board of JWT, 1955; retired, 1961; died 29 October 1962; inducted into the Advertising Hall of Fame, 1967.

Selected Publications

"How One Big Agency Trains Its Staff to High Efficiency," *Associated Advertising* 10 (August 1919)

"Individual Effort Has Its Day," *The Fourth Estate* (5 November 1921)

"Advertising," in *An Outline of Careers*, edited by Edward L. Bernays, New York: n.p., 1927

"What the American Association of Advertising Agencies Does to Make Advertising Scientifically More Effective," *The Annals of the American Academy of Political and Social Science* 115 (September 1924)

Further Reading

Ewen, Stuart, *Captains of Consciousness: Advertising and the Social Roots of Consumer Culture*, New York: McGraw-Hill, 1976

Fox, Stephen, *The Mirror Makers: A History of American Advertising and Its Creators*, New York: Morrow, 1984

Kreshel, Peggy, "The Culture of J. Walter Thompson, 1915–1925," *Public Relations Review* 16 (Fall 1990)

Kreshel, Peggy, "John B. Watson at J. Walter Thompson: The Legitimation of 'Science' in Advertising," *Journal of Advertising* 19, no. 2 (1990)

Pope, Daniel, *The Making of Modern Advertising*, New York: Basic Books, 1983

Restaurants/Fast Food

In the United States, restaurants, and especially purveyors of fast food, have long been among the largest spenders on advertising campaigns. Their television commercials have been the source of some of the best-remembered catchphrases and characters in advertising history, from "Where's the beef?" to "Yo quiero Taco Bell." Restaurant chains have also developed highly publicized tie-ins with licensed entertainment properties, through which they have sought to increase traffic by enticing children with limited-edition collectible toys.

White Castle, founded by Billy Ingram in Wichita, Kansas, in 1921, is credited with being the first hamburger restaurant and the first restaurant to implement a "carryout" style of service. Ingram offered his goods in multiple quantities, using the tag line,

"Buy 'em by the sack." In the summer of 1933 White Castle ran a coupon advertisement in city newspapers in each market where it had a restaurant, offering five hamburgers, carryout only, for just ten cents.

While the chain lost money on each burger sold during the promotion, it increased its customer base. Millions of newspaper readers clipped the coupons during the week of the sale and lined up for blocks to redeem them. Many of these customers had never tried a hamburger before. Shortages were a problem, but the campaign was successful enough that the chain ran it again the following year. In the meantime, White Castle ran a stream of noncoupon ads to keep demand steady. The success of this promotion showed White Castle and its competitors the value of both newspaper advertising and coupons. Advertising in the restaurant category was born.

Bringing in Customers

In the 1950s the number of U.S. households with television sets increased, and many hamburger chains began to test advertising on this new medium. Some of them spent a great deal on TV ads, especially in local markets. White Castle continued to prefer print advertising and coupons to either television or radio, but eventually it allowed its managers to spend some of their advertising budgets on broadcast media.

The company focused on attracting children to its stores; at the time, there were 54 million children in the United States, consuming 40 percent of the nation's food. Eighty-one percent of mothers said they bought at least one item per week at their child's request. The focus on children has remained a mainstay of restaurant advertising strategies. White Castle also played a role during the 1950s in another restaurant strategy that continues today. It gave out premiums, including fold-up castles and collectible trading cards that were redeemable for prizes such as footballs and flash cameras.

McDonald's, which by the late 1950s had already become a much-emulated force in the restaurant industry, did not develop its first television campaign until 1963. Like the White Castle newspaper efforts three decades earlier, the campaign, which cost $180,000 and targeted customers in California, where most of the chain's stores were located, brought many people into McDonald's for the first time. The experience taught the company a lesson on the value of TV advertising, one it never forgot.

Ray Kroc, McDonald's leader during its years of great expansion, believed in advertising and noted that while the return sometimes is not measurable, it can be reflected, he said, in the smiles of children who love Ronald McDonald (the chain's widely known clown icon) and is worth the investment. In his memoir, *Grinding It Out* (1977), Kroc pointed out, "I never hesitate to spend money in this area because I can see it coming back to me with interest."

By 1966 McDonald's had reached $200 million in sales and claimed to have sold 2 million hamburgers; it had also hired its first advertising agency, D'Arcy Advertising. That year the company made its first appearance in the Macy's Thanksgiving Day Parade in New York City with its All-American Band, an annual rite that continued into the 21st century. McDonald's ad icon Ronald McDonald also made his debut in the parade that year.

In 1967 McDonald's started its Operators National Advertising Fund, which asked its franchisees to contribute 1 percent of sales for national advertising. (Each franchisee also contributed a percentage of sales to an advertising cooperative consisting of franchisees in the local markets.) The fund allowed the company to launch a national TV campaign for the first time, making Ronald McDonald and tag lines such as "Two-all-beef-patties-special-sauce-lettuce-cheese-pickles-onions-on-a-sesame-seed-bun" (which introduced the Big Mac) part of the national consciousness in the United States. The advertising fund has become

franchised restaurant chains' standard method of paying for advertising.

In 1970 McDonald's switched agencies, moving its account from D'Arcy to Needham, Harper & Steers. Keith Reinhard, vice president–creative director at Needham, would become the agency's creative director and a major figure in the company's future advertising. The first national television campaign occurred before McDonald's had become the ubiquitous phenomenon it is today. Most of the company's restaurants at the time were located in the suburbs; urban and rural consumers had not yet been exposed to the McDonald's experience. The national campaign created latent demand for McDonald's food, which helped the company expand quickly over the next decade.

Meanwhile, in Texas a Taco Bell franchisee became the first in that chain to try television advertising. Taco Bell founder Glen Bell had started selling tacos at his hamburger stand in San Bernardino, California, McDonald's territory, and had expanded throughout California, relying on newspaper advertising and highly publicized Mexican-themed grand openings to attract business. The Texas franchise was among the chain's first locations outside California and, in the mid-1960s, sponsored the *Bozo the Clown* television show, which was just starting up in Texas. The franchisee offered a free taco during one afternoon hour on a certain day and found itself inundated by 2,000 children.

Much of Taco Bell's advertising, especially in newspapers, listed menu items along with explanations of what they were, a tactic necessary to spur sampling of Mexican food in cities that at the time were unfamiliar with it. Meanwhile, publicity stunts continued; for example, the company took a seven-foot fiberglass sculpture of the Taco Bell boy, the corporate character, placed it on water skis, and towed it through the inland waterways of St. Petersburg, Florida, to publicize the chain there.

By the mid-1960s Kentucky Fried Chicken had expanded to 300 outlets throughout the country and was well advertised, associating itself with the likeness of founder Colonel Harland Sanders and the phrase "finger-lickin' good." Sanders began with a single home cooking–style restaurant in Kentucky in the 1930s and was an early proponent both of printed menus and of advertising. He often boasted that his restaurant sign was the biggest in Kentucky. Sanders was well on his way to becoming a celebrity by the 1960s, especially after the company's first major national television campaign in 1965, in which he starred. Even after Sanders sold his restaurant, he continued as the company's public face, appearing at store openings and on national television programs such as *The Tonight Show*, as well as in national advertising. Many people thought he was a fictional character, such as Aunt Jemima or Betty Crocker.

Although it had been advertising for four decades, White Castle did not create its first systematic advertising strategy until the 1970s, when it developed consumer profiles based on surveys of potential customers. Working with agency Warner Simpson Advertising in the early 1970s, it joined its rivals on national television, running ads with the tag line, "The White Castle hamburger. Without it, all hamburgers would taste the same." The

Onetime chief executive officer Dave Thomas, of Wendy's International, Inc., seen here in a commercial TV spot from 1996, proved an effective spokesman for the company.
Courtesy of Wendy's.

company also tried to differentiate itself by poking fun at its reputation and its small square hamburgers, marking the first time a restaurant chain had undertaken such a comedic tactic.

Advertising played a role in Domino's early development in the late 1960s and early 1970s. The pizza chain's decision to locate its outlets near college campuses and not in residential areas was based largely on advertising efficiency: the company could reach college students effectively and inexpensively through their college newspapers, while targeting the general public required more-expensive and less-targeted, general-interest advertising.

In 1971 one Domino's outlet ran a newspaper promotion offering a dollar pizza on Super Bowl Sunday, which produced an unexpectedly large response and led to subsequent annual promotions. It was the beginning of many sports-related marketing efforts for the company. In the 1980s it began sponsoring a race car called the Domino's Pizza Hot One and later sponsored an entire race, the Domino's 500. In the late 1980s Domino's founder Tom Monaghan bought Major League Baseball's Detroit Tigers, in part because of expected synergies with Domino's.

Entertainment Tie-Ins

Even more prevalent than sports sponsorships by restaurant companies, particularly the leading quick-service restaurants, are entertainment tie-ins. Almost every chain rotates entertainment promotions on a four- to six-week basis; often the central focus of these promotions is a children's-meal toy premium. These entertainment tie-ins attract children and, along with them, their parents into the store. Most of these promotions now involve collectible premiums that change periodically, thus encouraging customers to return to the outlet several times over the course of a monthlong promotion.

McDonald's and Burger King have taken the lead when it comes to high-profile entertainment tie-ins. In 1997 McDonald's shook the industry by linking with the Walt Disney Company in an exclusive ten-year partnership that encompassed all of Disney's entertainment properties and theme parks in 109 countries. In 1997 McDonald's executed 400 tie-in programs in conjunction with Disney films and other properties around the world, including seven in the United States. The U.S. tie-ins reportedly increased sales of McDonald's products 7 percent over the previous year and increased annual purchase frequency from 22 to 24 times. The campaigns were handled by Frankel & Company, McDonald's promotion agency.

Many of McDonald's competitors questioned the deal, as it excluded them from lucrative partnership opportunities with Disney. Some McDonald's franchisees also balked, noting that it could lock them into associations with unsuccessful films or other licensed properties. Overall, however, the two partners seemed to be satisfied with the deal, and McDonald's competitors have sought similar partnerships of their own, many of which have been successful.

Another notable McDonald's initiative was a tie-in with Ty Inc., whose collectible Beanie Babies line was a huge fad in the United States in the mid-1990s. In 1996, the first year of McDonald's promotion, premium shortages proved severe, despite the 120 million "Teenie Beanie Babies" the restaurant distributed. McDonald's doubled its order to 240 million for the second year of the promotion and still sold out. As the fad lost momentum, however, sales figures showed declines.

The year 1998 was a notable one in the history of restaurant/entertainment tie-ins. In June McDonald's launched its first truly global Happy Meal promotion, built around Disney's film *Mulan*. The company offered a single toy premium in all markets, with packaging in 38 languages. In the fourth quarter McDonald's allied with Disney/Pixar's *A Bug's Life*; it was one of the first campaigns to incorporate film footage in its TV spots that had been created specifically for that purpose, rather than integrating movie clips into the ads.

Meanwhile, McDonald's rivals aligned with other films, most of which did not meet box office expectations. Seafood chain Long John Silver's, Inc., developed a tie-in with *Lost in Space* in its biggest such effort ever; Burger King chose *Small Soldiers,* a film considered too violent for young children; and Taco Bell tied in with *Godzilla,* an almost universally panned film that did well at the box office but, owing to too-high expectations, was a disappointment. While all these quick-service restaurants were left with undistributed premiums, they continued to use licensed properties prominently in industry marketing.

Taco Bell's situation was somewhat different in that it linked its Godzilla promotion to its proprietary talking Chihuahua (created by ad agency TBWA/Chiat/Day). The dog, which uttered the tag line, "Yo quiero Taco Bell," had begun as an extra in a commercial but soon was given an expanded role, becoming a pop-culture icon. Sales of a $2.99 plush puppy version of the restaurant's spokes-pooch in Taco Bell outlets represented the company's best promotion ever; it helped drive revenue 9 percent higher for the fourth quarter of 1998. Despite its popularity, the Chihuahua campaign was discontinued in 2000, blamed in part for the chain's flat sales. Many observers believed other factors contributed more to the company's woes.

Icons

The Taco Bell Chihuahua is one of many restaurant icons that have become a part of the social consciousness in the United States. Wendy's hamburger chain spawned a popular fad in 1983 with its "Where's the Beef?" campaign, which featured actress Clara Peller; the phrase even popped up in the presidential debates that year. Ronald McDonald has been a staple of advertising for three and a half decades and popular enough that a video series starring his animated likeness became a surprise hit in 1999 when offered for $3.49 each at McDonald's outlets. Pizza chain Little Caesar's spokes-character is an animated cartoon Caesar, whose vocabulary is limited to "Pizza! Pizza!" Jack in the Box has a long-running campaign featuring Jack's giant head on top of a human body. The ad agency Cliff Freeman & Partners has become a specialist in these types of campaigns, creating Wendy's "Where's the beef" campaign, Little Caesar, Jack in the Box, and an animated Old South colonel for KFC Corporation.

Restaurant executives have also become treasured icons. The first of these was the real "Colonel Sanders," who, in his white suit and whiskers, became the living personification of Southern fried chicken. After his death he was reprised in hip, animated form, accompanied by the tag line, "We do chicken right." Another perfect mating of product and personality was Arthur Treacher's Fish and Chips. In the 1930s Treacher, an actor, became the epitome of the perfect English butler—meticulous, well spoken, and slightly haughty in an amusing way. He made a comeback in the 1964 film *Mary Poppins* and then became Merv Griffin's sidekick on Griffin's late-night TV talk show. In the early 1970s his name and image became the basis for the Arthur Treacher's Fish and Chips chain. The deadpan delivery of Dave Thomas, the founder of Wendy's, made him a favorite in a long-running campaign for the chain until his death in 2002. Sometimes criticized for being funny but not emphasizing the product benefits, all these irreverent characters and live spokespeople represent an attempt by restaurant chains to distinguish their brands from others in a highly competitive market.

The Industry in the 21st Century

The market for restaurant food, and particularly fast food, was not growing rapidly at the end of the century, and one chain's loss was another's gain. Many observers believed that the brands with the greatest ad presence and recall draw the most traffic, which is key, even if only for a short period, such as the four to six weeks of an entertainment tie-in.

A few market share points mean a significant amount of money in the $110 billion quick-service restaurant industry; a 1 percent change in "share of stomach" translates to more than $400 million in sales. These numbers explain why media spending among fast-food restaurants is as high as in any other segment. McDonald's spends more than $500 million each year in measured media on global sales of nearly $40 billion. Burger King spends more than $400 million annually.

Research shows that consumers look for several attributes when choosing a fast-food restaurant, including food quality, prompt service, cleanliness, and premiums that are fun. Each facet gains or loses importance in a chain's advertising on a more or less cyclical basis. For example, in 1998, when most chains were focusing on characters or tie-ins, Burger King's strategy was to promote the superior taste of its products, although it did not totally eschew tie-ins. Subway Restaurants' advertising often stresses the health benefits of its food versus that of its competitors.

Restaurants also turn to advertising to repair their image when something goes wrong. A notable example occurred in the early 1990s, when Denny's was sued for allegedly discriminating against black customers. In the aftermath, its ads, in addition to touting its food, talked about Denny's desire to be inclusive. The commercials were required to be racially diverse—as dictated by a consent decree from the court—with 25 percent of the actors African-American and another 5 percent other nonwhite. Denny's also agreed to spend at least 10 percent of its advertising budget at minority-owned ad agencies. All these actions helped the company extricate itself in a relatively short time from what had seemed to be almost insurmountable trouble.

As the competitive landscape has grown more crowded, the major restaurant chains have intensified their ad efforts. Within the hamburger segment, where, by 2000, McDonald's held more than a 40 percent share of the U.S. market, followed by Burger King, Wendy's, Hardee's, and Jack in the Box, the two leading chains were maintaining or increasing spending; smaller chains such as Carl's Jr. were also increasing media spending and seeking entertainment tie-ins.

The same was true in the pizza segment, where market leaders Pizza Hut, Domino's, Little Caesars, and Papa John's—respectively the category's top four—were waging aggressive campaigns as part of what they referred to as the "pizza wars." Papa John's and Domino's in particular were trading jabs and lawsuits, accusing each other of misleading advertising.

Even the Mexican food segment, where Taco Bell dominated—it had 7,000 units in 2000 compared with number-two Del Taco's 360—has seen an increase in activity. Del Taco started a humorous campaign tweaking Taco Bell in 2000. Meanwhile, the latter was trying to come up with an effective strategy to replace the Chihuahua.

In this competitive market, entertainment tie-ins will continue to make their presence felt. For every failed promotion—such as 1999's *Star Wars* tie-in involving all three Tricon Global Restaurants units, KFC, Pizza Hut and Taco Bell—there are successes. Burger King's 1999 Pokémon promotion, for example, featured 57 toys in 56 days and 151 trading cards and became the chain's best tie-in to date.

Ad messages and slogans continue to evolve—for example, McDonald's "Did somebody say McDonald's?" was replaced with "We love to see you smile" in 2000—as chains strive to stand out. One thing is certain, however: restaurant advertising, particularly in the fast-food segment, will be around for a long time to come. Because of the sheer size of the industry and its advertising budgets, the category's campaigns and characters will remain ubiquitous in popular culture.

KAREN RAUGUST

See also Burger King Corporation; McDonald's Corporation; Wendy's International, Inc.

Further Reading

Adamson, Jim, Robert McNatt, and Rosemary Bray McNatt, *The Denny's Story: How a Company in Crisis Resurrected Its Good Name,* New York: Wiley, 2000

Baldwin, Debra Lee, *Taco Titan: The Glen Bell Story,* Arlington, Texas: Summit, 1999

Elliott, Stuart, "Taco Bell Abruptly Drops the Agency That Created Its Popular Wisecracking Spokesdog," *New York Times* (19 July 2000)

Hogan, David Gerard, *Selling 'Em by the Sack: White Castle and the Creation of American Food,* New York: New York University Press, 1997

Kramer, Louise, "As Sales Flatten, Top Pizza Chains Turn Up the Heat," *Advertising Age* (23 February 1998)

Kramer, Louise, "McD's, Disney: Year-Old Pact Is a Happy Deal," *Advertising Age* (11 May 1998)

Kramer, Louise, "McD's Steals Another Toy from BK," *Advertising Age* (15 November 1999)

Kroc, Ray, and Robert Anderson, *Grinding It Out: The Making of McDonald's,* Chicago: Contemporary Books, 1977; 2nd edition, New York: St. Martin's Press, 1987

Monaghan, Tom, and Robert Anderson, *Pizza Tiger,* New York: Random House, 1986

Pearce, John Ed, *The Colonel: The Captivating Biography of the Dynamic Founder of a Fast-Food Empire,* Garden City, New York: Doubleday, 1982

Results Advertising

Founded by Ogilvy & Mather Asia/Pacific, 1995; won a gold Lion at the International Advertising Festival at Cannes, France, for a poster marketing McIlhenny Company's Tabasco sauce, 2000.

Major Clients

BP Oil
McIlhenny Company
Thai Telephone & Telecommunication (TT&T)
Unilever

Thailand, with its distinctive brand of humor and savvy attention to detail, has long been regarded within Asia as home to the region's best advertising creative people. But it took the Bangkok office of WPP Group's Results Advertising, a regular winner at major advertising festivals, to place the Southeast Asian nation firmly on the global creative advertising map.

Ogilvy & Mather Asia/Pacific opened Results Advertising in Bangkok, Thailand's capital, in 1995, followed by offices in Taiwan and India, primarily to serve local businesses that wanted a smaller, more entrepreneurial agency. But the agency performed extraordinarily well, almost overshadowing its larger sibling agency, Ogilvy's own Bangkok office.

Just one year after it opened, Results gained international attention with its ad promoting Black Cat, a domestic whiskey brand. The spot spoofed B-grade Hollywood mafia movies while positioning the Thai whiskey as an affordable alternative to its more expensive Western competitor, Johnnie Walker Black Label, marketed by U.K.-based United Distillers & Vintners.

Subsequent creative awards and steadily increasing business were marks of the agency's success. Despite a sluggish local economy, a staff of 22 was generating $4 million in capitalized billings by 2000 and predicting 14 percent growth in 2001. The agency is "street smart, young, and has attitude," said Miles Young, Ogilvy & Mather's Asia/Pacific chairman in Hong Kong. Although reluctant to assert that Results appeals to Thai clients that disdain foreign multinational agencies, out of nationalism or personality clashes, Young admits cautiously that many Thai clients "want Ogilvy, but in a different package."

Such clients are also attracted to Results Advertising's strong creative reputation. "That's why I hate to use the words 'second agency' to describe it. It does have reporting lines into Ogilvy, but it was not designed to handle conflicts. It operates independently and often pitches against O&M," Young told *Advertising Age*.

And it often wins in such contests, which has built up Results beyond its creative hot-shop origins into a full-service agency offering both creative and strategic planning services. Other marketing-related disciplines, such as media buying and public relations, are outsourced to WPP Group sibling companies, such as media shop MindShare. In addition to local business, Results has picked up multinational clients, including BP Oil and Unilever. The Thai shop stands out, not only as a leading light among small, locally run ad agencies, but also for taking on some of the biggest names in the industry while retaining the size and soul of a smaller, more entrepreneurial shop.

Its managing director, Rook Soratana, joined Results in 1998 from Euro RSCG, Bangkok, where he was group account director. He worked with creative director Jureeporn Thaidumrong, who joined Results in 1997 following top creative posts at Leo Burnett Company and Dentsu Young & Rubicam in Bangkok. (Thaidumrong left Results in September 2001 to join Saatchi & Saatchi). They took over from the agency's founding executives, Decha Tangpanitansook and Suthisak Sucharittanonta, formerly managing director and creative director, respectively, who got the agency off to an impressive start.

In 1995, the agency's first year in operation, for example, it picked up two gold awards at the prestigious local Top Advertising Contest of Thailand (TACT) festival. Results, Bangkok, made its first appearance at the International Advertising Festival at Cannes, France, in 1996 as a finalist in the TV/Cinema category and won a bronze Lion award the following year for the Black Cat spot, again in the TV/Cinema category.

The agency's strong reputation was put in jeopardy when Tangpanitansook and Sucharittanonta defected to BBDO in 1997. It was a "huge challenge for Jureeporn to maintain the agency's reputation, its equity as a creative powerhouse," said one insider.

But Results continued to perform well. Between 1996 and 2000, it took home 37 more TACT prizes, including 28 gold awards. By 2000 it had won 18 creative awards from the Asia Pacific Advertising Festival since 1998 and 15 Asian Advertising Awards since 1996.

In 2000 the agency clinched a coveted gold Lion at the Cannes International Advertising Festival for a poster for McIlhenny Company's Tabasco sauce, the first time a gold Lion had been awarded to a Thai agency. Results also picked up three Clio awards—a silver for ads for Feldene gel in 1999 and two bronzes for work for Hacks Candy and Toshiba air conditioners in 2000. The agency also won two awards at the London International Advertising awards (for Tabasco and Toshiba), plus 22 finalist certificates.

In New York City it received a Bronze Pencil at the One Show for Black Cat Whiskey and two finalist certificates for Mitsubishi Diesel Engine and Tabasco, and the New York Festival named Results a finalist for a Citroën ZX magazine ad in 1997. Characterized by Soratana as "driven by an attitude to work that could potentially take on the biggest names in the ad agency business while retaining the soul of a small agency," Results has, in a very short time, acquired a name for itself both within Thailand and beyond.

NORMANDY MADDEN

Retail Advertising

Retailers are businesses involved in the sale of goods and services to consumers for personal, family, or household use. Retail advertising is essentially the advertising of such enterprises—supermarkets, department stores, specialty shops, restaurants, service stations, convenience stores, and any other businesses that sell goods or services to the ultimate consumer for personal use.

Because retailing is highly competitive, most retailers find that advertising is necessary if they are to succeed. Consumers rely heavily on retail advertising for information on product availability, prices, features, store hours, store locations, fashion, store credit terms, and discounts. Consumers receive this information on a daily basis from an abundance of retail advertising, and much of their shopping is guided by the ads they see.

Local Advertising

Retailers know that consumers more than a certain geographic distance from their location are not likely to shop with them and therefore aim their advertising messages at potential customers living and working near their store locations. This measure of proximity varies depending on the type of store, products offered,

and population density, but in general consumers shop at locations that are convenient. Because retail advertising is geographically targeted to consumers in the local area, it was historically called local advertising. Local advertising and retail advertising are not synonymous, however, as by the mid- to late 20th century, many retailers had international operations and advertised internationally.

Retail advertising can be divided into two categories: local and national. (Internet advertising, which could possibly be considered to be international retail advertising, is more accurately described as a form of direct marketing.) Local merchants that own a single location in a single market or trade area engage in local retail advertising, using local media to reach customers living and working near their establishment. On the other hand, retail companies that have expanded their store operations to multiple markets across the country engage in national retail advertising. These multistore retailers use broad-reaching national or international media to efficiently communicate with their customers. McDonald's Corporation, for example, is a retailer that utilizes national and international media to reach its customers around the world.

Retail Advertising vs. National Brand Advertising

Retail advertising is distinct from and can be contrasted with national brand advertising based not on the geographic reach of the message but on its appeal. The retail advertiser focuses on bringing customers into the store for their shopping needs, while the message appeal of brand advertisers attempts to build demand for a specific brand or product, which may be available at a variety of retail outlets. The brand advertiser's message says, "Buy the product bearing our brand wherever it is most convenient to you." The retail advertiser's message says, "We don't care which brand you choose, because we carry many great brands, just come and shop at our store."

Another characteristic that makes retail advertising unique is immediacy, both in the advertising appeal and the evaluation of effectiveness. Unlike national brand advertising, which is typically designed to increase awareness and general interest for a brand or product over time, retail advertising is meant to drive store traffic and increase sales immediately. Retail advertising has a sense of immediacy not found in national brand advertising. Products advertised in retail ads are intended to be purchased that day. The tone of much retail advertising is, "Hurry in while supplies last!" Customers can choose from many available products and brands and make their purchases immediately. This sense of immediacy makes retail advertising exciting and dynamic. Sales results can be seen at the cash register within hours after the advertising hits the media, and the effectiveness can be evaluated within days, rather than the weeks or months that national brand advertisers must wait. This quick gauge of advertising effectiveness can be exciting and challenging for retailers, as they must quickly adjust their advertising strategy if short-term sales results are not favorable.

Management Structure

Regardless of the size of the retail organization, someone must be responsible for coordinating the advertising effort. The advertising management structure for retailers is as varied as the stores and the products they carry. Small store owners, although busy with a variety of other managerial duties, typically handle the advertising function themselves. Local media and the manufacturers of products to be advertised frequently assist the store owner in creating and placing advertising. Local newspaper and radio stations often create layouts and write spots based on the information provided by the store owner. Pre-made ads may be provided and partially paid for by the manufacturer, requiring only the addition of the store name and address.

Larger chain stores typically coordinate their advertising through an advertising department made up of advertising professionals who work for the retail company. The advertising department of a large chain may be organized according to a centralized or decentralized advertising management system. A centralized system operates with one corporate advertising department, usually located at the company's headquarters. The corporate advertising department not only prepares ads and buys advertising time and space for the stores, but also serves as a communicator to the stores in the field for overall promotional planning. In the centralized system, all stores promote the same items at the same time. The decentralized advertising management system allows for an advertising department covering a region of the total marketing area or in some cases in each store location. These departments are responsible for creating, coordinating, and placing advertising for their location only. Because a decentralized system has flexibility in items advertised and is physically close to store management and customers, it can often be more effective.

In both the centralized and decentralized systems, the advertising departments for large retailers are headed by an advertising manager who typically reports to the vice president of marketing or merchandising. The advertising manager's staff may consist of copywriters, art directors, graphic artists, and production personnel as well as media buyers. For a retail-advertising department to be effective, it must work closely with merchandise buyers, merchandise managers, and the store's general manager to determine which items and prices to promote. Communication about what will be advertised is essential in a retail operation. Store management must be prepared to serve the increased customer volume that advertising can generate and to process any discounts that may be offered in the ads. Large advertising efforts may require additional personnel to handle increased store traffic or may require that buyers stock up on certain items. Poor communication and coordination among advertising, operations, and buyers can create a disaster that will result in unhappy customers and lost sales and profits. For this reason, many large department stores assign an advertising manager and copywriter to each department in the store, such as home furnishings, clothing, and appliances. They coordinate directly with the merchandising manager and buyers for that department and become specialists in their line of products.

In-House Agencies

Small and intermediate retail organizations often do not use the services of outside advertising agencies but instead utilize in-house advertising agencies. Many retailers set up their corporate advertising departments as in-house agencies for two primary reasons: the job requires a full-time staff that is present daily to handle the volume and detail involved in retail advertising, and newspaper and other local media are usually not agency commissionable, which eliminates the cost advantage and compensation stream of an outside agency. The in-house agency may function in much the same way as an outside advertising agency, with one exception: its only client is the retailer. These in-house agencies not only create advertising but also place media directly on behalf of the retail company. In-house agencies sometimes handle large budgets and operate separately so as to obtain agency discounts from the media on national buys.

It is not unusual for large chain retailers, such as such as Sears, Roebuck & Company, McDonald's, and Wal-Mart Stores, to use both an in-house advertising department and an outside full-service advertising agency. The in-house unit is responsible for the overall advertising budgeting and planning, making daily advertising and promotional decisions, supporting store managers and franchisees with advertising materials to be used at the local level, and acting as a communication line between the stores in the field and the corporate marketing decision-makers. The outside advertising agency is used to establish an overall advertising campaign and brand image; to produce national advertising, particularly television spots; to place national media buys; to assist in research and strategic planning; and to provide specialized creative services that are usually not available in-house.

Some retailers may subdivide the business into marketing areas, each with its own ad manager and perhaps a regional agency that works with the national agency. The automobile industry exists on a unique two-tier basis: the manufacturers' advertising is designed to build the brand image (Ford, Buick, Volkswagen), while members of the dealer network are organized into regional "dealer associations," each with its own ad agency, to develop specific traffic-building promotions and sales events. Usually the national agency for the manufacturer will shoot and distribute a library of footage of the car that can be assembled at the discretion of local agencies. This was also done by Kroger Company in the 1980s; Kroger's agency, Campbell-Mithun, prepared an inventory of high-quality food footage that local marketing areas could use as they saw fit, thus amortizing the cost of production over the entire retail network.

Retail advertising is a dynamic and exciting field that requires people who are able to work quickly. A retail advertising manager must not only be proficient at creating ads and placing media, he or she also must be educated on the nature of the retail business. A retail advertising manager who does not appreciate the time and physical effort required to run a store, who cannot read a retail profit-and-loss statement, or who does not understand the concepts of controlling product and labor costs and optimizing sales per square foot will not succeed. Retail advertising managers must be flexible, aware of the competitive marketplace, and well-informed about consumer trends. They also must know their customers, understanding how they buy and where they get their shopping information.

The Advertising Message

Whether it is created by an in-house advertising department or an outside agency, the advertising message is critical to both the short-term sales and long-term success of the retail business. There are generally two types of retail advertising messages, promotional and institutional. The promotional ad message features a particular product or group of products at a special or discounted price. These ads are coordinated with special store sale events and are designed to drive store traffic and increase store sales in the short term—for example, sales on seasonal merchandise. For promotional ads to be most successful they should feature popular items that customers want. It is important that items be priced competitively and stocked adequately. Retailers should not waste their advertising budgets promoting slow-moving, unpopular, or out-of-season merchandise. An ad for wool cardigan sweaters will produce much better results if run in January

A 1977 print ad for Sears, Roebuck & Company, one of the largest retailers in the United States, used shopper testimonials to emphasize Sears's commitment to customer service.
The 1977 "Where America Shops" Sears advertisement is reprinted by arrangement with Sears, Roebuck and Co. and is protected under copyright. No duplication in permitted.

than it will if it is run in July. Retailers are sometimes tempted to advertise during off-peak sales periods or to feature items that are not selling well. They will realize a much higher return on their advertising investment if they choose to promote popular items during times when customers want them the most.

The effectiveness of promotional advertising can be readily measured by analyzing overall store customer counts, product movement, discounts taken, and overall sales. Because the effects of promotional advertising can be seen immediately, the retailer tends to depend heavily and sometimes exclusively on this type of advertising. However, institutional advertising, though not as easily measured in the short term, can produce stronger business results over time.

Institutional advertising is designed to create a positive brand image for the store. Institutional ads do not focus on particular products and prices but instead attempt to position the store in the minds of consumers and leave a favorable impression. Retailers may emphasize in institutional ads overall quality, customer service, variety, unique merchandise, convenience, dependability, or fashion distinctiveness. Regardless of the specific positioning strategy employed, institutional advertising attempts to influence customers' decisions to shop at that particular retail store for reasons other than discounted prices. Institutional advertising builds loyal customers who will continue to patronize the store whether it has a sale running or not. Loyal customers who will pay full price are the retailer's most valued asset. Institutional advertising over time builds this type of customer base.

In today's retailing environment, most stores will not run purely institutional advertising. They favor promotional ads for their ability to create measurable sales spikes in the short term. However, many advertising scholars and professionals caution against overdependence on promotional advertising at the expense of brand-building institutional ads. In response, some retailers have tried to compromise, using national media such as network television or national consumer magazines to run institutional advertising and local media such as newspapers or radio for promotional advertising. Another compromise strategy is the creation of ads that serve both purposes, such as an image-building institutional commercial tagged with a featured sale item and price. For example, Taco Bell's "Yo Quiero Taco Bell" campaign, featuring the talking Chihuahua, is primarily an image ad but also features a specific menu item at a special price, such as nachos belle grande for $1.99, at the end of the spots to ensure that customers have a reason to visit the restaurant that day.

Retail Advertising Budgets

Although many retailers are small local operations, retail advertising is big business. Based on statistics for 1997, total U.S. advertising spending by retailers such as department and discount stores was estimated at more than $10 billion, up 14 percent over 1996. Restaurants and fast-food purveyors accounted for another $3.1 billion, an increase of 6 percent over 1996. Based on advertising spending statistics for 2000, the top ten largest retailers spent more than $3.8 billion on advertising, up 7 percent from 1999. The top ten fast-food hamburger chains spent an additional $3.4 billion on advertising in 2000, an increase of 7 percent over 1999. Sears was the 12th-largest advertiser in the United States in 2000, spending $1.46 billion. McDonald's was the 17th-largest U.S. advertiser, spending more than $1.2 billion. J.C. Penney Company spent more than $1 billion, as did Federated Department Stores ($1.1 billion). Target Corporation spent $826 million, and Home Depot spent $651 million in 2000.

Research shows that on average retailers spend 3 percent of net sales on advertising. Most retailers forecast sales at the beginning of the year and from that forecast derive an advertising budget. As a retailer adds more locations in a market, the percentage spent on advertising may decrease because media efficiency is realized by adding retail locations to a single media market. The cost of advertising a single location in a market in most media is the same as the cost of advertising several locations. In other words, a local television spot costs the same regardless of the number of retail outlets in that market. As the number of store locations increases and advertising costs remain relatively constant, the percent of sales spent on advertising decreases. Most large chain stores spend much less than 3 percent of sales on advertising. Wal-Mart, the largest retailer in the United States in sales volume, reported spending less than 1 percent of sales on advertising in 1997. Sears, Federated Department Stores, and Circuit City each spent between 1 percent and 2 percent, while some single-store, small retail owners spend as much as 10 percent of sales to adequately promote their shops.

Franchising

The advertising efficiency realized by multiple store locations in a single media market, among other factors, makes franchise ownership attractive to retailers. Franchise chains are groups of retail locations that carry the same name, store design, product lines, trade practices, and advertising message but are owned individually by franchisees. Franchisees generally are bound together by a contract administered by a corporation, the franchisor, which owns the retail concept, product ideas, and trade name. The franchisor allows the franchisees to use the retail name, sell the franchisor's products, and participate in the franchisor's advertising program in exchange for a royalty and advertising fee that the franchisee pays monthly.

Many retail chains are franchised, including fast-food restaurants, auto parts stores, quick copy and printing shops, quick-lube service centers, postal and mailbox service stores, and motels. Franchise ownership of specialty clothing, department stores, and discount or mass merchandise chains is less common. The franchisees pay into an advertising fund managed by the franchisor with input from an advertising committee comprised of franchisees. By pooling their advertising funds, franchise owners can take advantage of economies of scale in advertising production and media buying. For example, it is much less expensive for a franchise retail chain to buy network television advertising than to buy individual spot television advertising in the more than 200 television markets across the country.

Cooperative Advertising

Cooperative advertising is the sharing of advertising costs by a retailer and a manufacturer. Many retailers also include cooperative advertising funds as part of their budgets. It currently represents more than $15 billion per year in advertising support for retailers. Manufacturers will provide "co-op" advertising money to retailers that carry their brands. The ads typically feature the manufacturer's brand along with the retail store name and location. The ad is approved by both parties, and the cost of the advertising is shared. This source of advertising funds from manufacturers helps the retailers extend their often limited advertising budget while providing additional exposure for the manufacturer's brand. Some retailers fail to take advantage of cooperative advertising money available from manufacturers because they are not aware of it or because they believe that it is too difficult to coordinate the shared production and placement of the advertising.

Retail Advertising Media

Most retail advertising spending comes from owners of small shops in hundreds of communities. It is because of retail advertising that newspapers remain the leading medium in terms of advertising revenues (in 2000 newspapers drew the most ad dollars at $18.8 billion, followed by network TV at $18.4 billion). Retailers, both big and small, use newspapers as their primary means of reaching their customers on a weekly and sometimes daily basis. Newspapers provide retail advertisers a geographically targeted, immediate, flexible vehicle in which to promote their merchandise. Because a newspaper is a printed medium with which customers spend time and keep as a reference, it is the ideal place for retailer to feature a variety of items, prices, and details in their ads. Newspapers are printed daily with short lead times, allowing for timely promotions and quick changes in advertising copy, which are essential to the retail advertiser.

Radio is also a popular advertising medium with retailers, especially local retail advertisers. Like newspaper, radio is geographically targeted, has short lead times, and can be extremely adaptable to changing copy needs. Radio used in combination with newspapers for special sale and promotional events can be very effective. Because radio is an out-of-home medium, spots are often heard when customers are already in their cars or out shopping and can prompt them to visit a certain store almost immediately for that special deal.

The disadvantage of radio for retailers is that the message must be limited to a few items or ideas. Complicated details about prices, hours, store addresses, and phone numbers cannot be communicated easily. The retailer is unable to show products or store locations on the radio but must rely on strictly verbal communication.

Another medium frequently used by retailers is outdoor advertising. Outdoor billboards and posters are used to feature specific items, particularly unique or specialty items, and to direct customers to specific locations. Outdoor advertising, like radio, is encountered outside the home and is therefore an effective means for reaching customers who are already in transit, who may be near the store's location, and who are likely to be in the mood to shop. Outdoor advertising has limited space for the message, so retailers must keep their copy short and be simple, direct, and graphically oriented. Outdoor advertising is particularly useful in providing directions for motorists who may be speeding by retail locations on highways and expressways. McDonald's billboards—featuring its trademark Golden Arches and the headline "Stomach on empty?"—direct drivers to the McDonald's location at the next exit.

Television is considered the ultimate medium for many retailers. It combines visuals and audio to create powerful, memorable advertisements. Television reaches large numbers of potential customers quickly, thus driving traffic and sales in the short term. Television has the added advantage of being a prestige medium and can be used to enhance the image of many retailers. Television advertising is primarily used by large chain stores because of its cost and broad geographic reach. Retailers such as Wal-Mart, Sears, Kmart, Home Depot, and Best Buy are major television advertisers. Sears is estimated to have spent $355 million in television advertising in 2000, and Kmart Corporation, $184 million. Fast-food restaurants rely almost exclusively on television to reach a large, geographically dispersed, active, young audience with simple messages about their food products. Tricon Global Restaurants, the parent company of the international fast-food chains Taco Bell, KFC, and Pizza Hut, spent a total of $301 million in U.S. network television in 2000; McDonald's spent $299 million for its single brand. Total television advertising for all these chains is undoubtedly much higher when spot, syndicated, and cable television is included. Television is not reserved for large national chains. Many local retailers such as car dealers, banks, and furniture stores use local, or spot, television, especially during the evening news, to promote their retail locations to a broad audience in the local area.

Other Types of Retail Promotion

In addition to mass media advertising, retailers depend on other communication methods to promote their locations and products. These methods include fashion shows, local store marketing, couponing, publicity, charity events, sweepstakes, contests, premiums, and many other kinds of sales promotions. Point-of-purchase material (POP) is widely used in retail promotion. This category includes posters, counter cards, product displays, window banners, danglers, register toppers, shelf talkers, menu board posters, illuminated displays, neon signs, and any other visual item that promotes products at the retailer's location. POP has been characterized as the "silent salesman" that works the floor every day, all day long without asking for a raise or a vacation. It is an in-store reinforcement of the advertising message appearing in the mass media. POP has been shown to increase sales of specific items 400 percent over broadcast advertising for those items.

Future Trends

Retailers have emerged at the beginning of the 21st century as a primary force behind the marketing of consumer goods. The demand for shelf space by manufacturers and the increased information available via scanner technology has positioned retailers as the leader in the distribution channel. At the same time, the retail industry is changing and growing. Retailers are looking outside the walls of their stores for new ways to reach shoppers. New media and innovative technology, such as the Internet and shopper databases, have created challenges and opportunities for retailers. Nonstore retailing via catalogs, interactive television, infomercials, electronic kiosks, and storefronts on the World Wide Web have expanded the sale of retail goods outside the walls of the stores and into the homes of the customers.

These changes in the world of retailing will undoubtedly create new demands, challenges, and opportunities for the retail advertising professionals of the coming century. As competition increases beyond the stores in the neighborhood to virtual stores on the Internet, communicating with customers will become even more important. Understanding how consumers make shopping decisions in this new retailing world will be critical to positioning and promoting the retailer's location and products. In order to be successful, the retail advertising manager must master advertising media such as the Internet, direct mail, and database marketing while never forgetting the basics of effective retail advertising: to promote popular products at competitive prices during times when customers want them the most.

JAMI A. FULLERTON

See also Ohrbach's; Sears, Roebuck & Company; Wal-Mart Stores, Inc.; Wanamaker, John

Further Reading

Cassell, Dana K., *How to Advertise and Promote Your Retail Store,* New York: American Management Associations, 1983

Drake, Mary Frances, Janice Harrison Spoone, and Herbert Greenwald, *Retail Fashion Promotion and Advertising,* New York: Macmillan, and Toronto, Ontario: Macmillan Canada, 1992

Gentile, Richard Joseph, *Retail Advertising: A Management Approach,* New York: Chain Store, 1976

Hasty, Ronald W., and James Reardon, *Retail Management,* New York: McGraw-Hill, 1997

Quinton, Jack, *Retail Advertising: The How and Why: A Basic Guide for Retail Advertising Using All Media,* Chicago: National Sporting Goods Association, 1979

Ziccardi, Donald, and David Moin, *MasterMinding the Store: Advertising, Sales Promotion, and the New Marketing Reality,* New York: Wiley, 1997

R.J. Reynolds Tobacco Company

Principal Agencies

N.W. Ayer & Son, Inc.

Erwin, Wasey & Company, Inc.

William Esty and Company, Inc.

Long Haymes Carr, Inc.

Leber Katz Partners, Inc.

McCann-Erickson/New York

Young & Rubicam, Inc.

Mezzina/Brown, Inc.

Gyro

Founded by Richard Joshua ("Dick") Reynolds in 1875 as a small manufacturer of plug chewing tobacco, the R.J. Reynolds Tobacco Company (RJR) was the first tobacco company to recognize the importance of professional advertising agencies and the first to engage in a $1 million advertising campaign, which created the first nationally marketed cigarette brand, Camel. Camel quickly became a best-seller and made RJR the industry leader for most of the 1920s. Throughout the 1930s and 1940s, RJR, the American Tobacco Company (ATC), and Liggett & Myers vied for market dominance, but the success of Winston filter cigarettes, introduced in 1954, put RJR back on top for the next 25 years.

Early Years

Dick Reynolds was born in 1850 and grew up in Patrick County, Virginia. His father and grandfather had marketed chewing tobacco since at least 1828, and they trained Dick (and his four brothers who survived into adulthood) in the arts of cultivating, selecting, and blending tobacco and the production of plug tobacco for chewing. In 1874 Dick Reynolds moved to Winston, North Carolina, to take advantage of its proximity to the "Bright belt" of tobacco production (i.e., the area where the mild, pale-leaf tobacco called Bright was grown) and a superior railroad system; a year later he founded the R.J. Reynolds Tobacco Company. By the mid-1880s Reynolds's company was producing more than a dozen popular brands of chewing tobacco. By the early 1890s RJR was the largest employer in North Carolina and the industry leader in the Bright plug category, building a large new factory to meet the expanded demand for its product.

At that time Reynolds himself acted as the guiding force of a new sales department that embraced an aggressive, systematic program of advertising. In 1894 he spent $4,000 on advertising, and after his tobacco production increased by 200,000 pounds that year, he quintupled the advertising budget in 1895, when his sales doubled. Reynolds employed a variety of strategies, some more creative than others, to move RJR brands. He routinely reserved advertising space in both trade journals and local newspapers and placed folksy ads that appealed to the farmers in his rural region.

Like his rivals, Reynolds also distributed circulars, testimonials, and premiums to attract both retailers and consumers to his product. In one series of circulars, Reynolds highlighted his populist sympathies, promising silver in exchange for RJR tobacco tags (essentially the equivalent to modern-day proofs of purchase) should the 1896 presidential election result in the selection of "free silver" candidate William Jennings Bryan. Reynolds's Schnapps

Kicking Machine drew the attention of customers and then delivered a kick to the buyer who made the mistake of choosing anything other than Reynolds's Schnapps brand chewing tobacco.

Turn-of-the-Century Changes

As Reynolds's company expanded, it became a tempting target for the American Tobacco Company trust, created by James "Buck" Duke in 1890. Duke's empire was based on the cheap mass-production of cigarettes, in which he pioneered and excelled. Reynolds fought becoming a casualty of Duke's trust, but in 1899 financial troubles forced Reynolds to sell two-thirds of his business to American Tobacco for $3 million. Under the purchase agreement, Reynolds continued to manage RJR.

Reynolds was the largest plug tobacco producer in North Carolina before his deal with Duke. Once their agreement was implemented, Duke expected Reynolds to work to consolidate control over the plug market in the southeast region of the United States. In the first years of the 20th century, however, chewing tobacco was falling out of favor with the U.S. public, and smoking tobacco for pipes and, to a lesser extent, roll-your-own cigarettes became more popular and profitable. Reynolds recognized this trend, and in 1907 he defied Duke's wishes by debuting Prince Albert, a smoking tobacco blend that would challenge the national leaders, American Tobacco's Bull Durham and Duke's Mixture.

The Prince Albert brand was a departure for RJR. Reynolds consented for the first time to use Kentucky Burley rather than North Carolina Bright tobacco in the blend, and the royal reference in the brand name seemed to indicate Reynolds's desire to sell the product to a more elite class of consumers than those usually targeted by RJR brands. The care lavished on the brand's packaging, launch, and subsequent advertising and distribution revealed Reynolds's commitment to a new focus for his company and his recognition of the importance of advertising. Reynolds participated in every phase of the creation and launch of Prince Albert. He took particular care over the label, which first graced small bags and then two-ounce red tins. The package bore an image of Britain's King Edward VII in the "Prince Albert" coat he had made famous, with the legend "Prince Albert" above the picture and the words "Now king" below—implying that both the prince and his namesake tobacco had triumphed and had become leaders in their respective nations. In the case of Reynolds's smoking tobacco, the declaration was premature, for it was not an immediate best-seller. But sales took off in 1910, the year that Reynolds retained N.W. Ayer & Son, Inc. Prince Albert represented one-third of the company's output by 1912 and claimed 3 percent of the U.S. pipe tobacco market in that year. Prince Albert's share of the U.S. smoking tobacco market continued to grow after 1912—it was the "Joy smoke" and the "Smoke without a sting," according to Ayer's copy.

RJR Enters the Cigarette Market

In 1890 the U.S. tobacco industry, with Duke leading the way, produced 2.2 billion cigarettes. The gains over the next decade were modest, peaking in the mid-1890s at 4 billion and then declining in response to a determined anticigarette crusade that swept the United States. By 1910, however, cigarette consumption was on the rise again: annual production of cigarettes had more than doubled to 8.6 billion. Reynolds wanted to take advantage of Americans' growing acceptance of, and fascination with, cigarettes, and a 1911 federal court order dissolving the American Tobacco trust cleared the way for him to enter this expanding market. Four major companies were spun off in the breakup of the trust and divided the various branches of the tobacco business among them. RJR walked away with its freedom and slightly less than one-fifth of the chewing tobacco market, but the company did not receive any part of the ever-more-lucrative market for cigarettes in the settlement. Nonetheless, Reynolds was determined to tap that market, and cigarettes, not smoking tobacco, represented the bulk of RJR's business after 1913.

RJR's earliest brands—the inexpensive Reyno and the pricey, cork-tipped Red Kamel—failed to entice consumers, despite promotions for those brands that ran the gamut from premiums and Indian totems to gifts of sophisticated cigarette lighters. In 1913 RJR broke every mold and seized a commanding position in the tobacco industry when the company introduced Camel cigarettes to the U.S. public. RJR's rivals—ATC, Lorillard, and Liggett & Myers—had long favored Turkish or Bright tobacco for their cigarettes, but RJR let Burley leaf dominate those strains in the Camel blend. RJR's daring decision to abandon premiums as a means of promotion further distinguished Camel from the rest of the field, as did the brand's low price. Camel cigarettes cost ten cents for a package of 20, a nickel less than the price charged for its rivals, Liggett's Fatima, Lorillard's Zubelda, and American Tobacco's Omar.

More significant, however, was the advertising campaign for Camel created by Ayer—and its $1 million price tag. Account executive William Armistead first encouraged the company to test the product nationally: a few retailers in cities nationwide received single cartons of Camels (but no supporting advertising), which the store managers were instructed to leave open on their counters to determine the initial level of consumer interest in the new brand. When consumers in those markets began to ask for the brand by name, Ayer crafted a campaign that preceded as well as accompanied the product introduction into the entire U.S. market. For weeks before Camels were actually available, newspapers nationwide carried the mysterious promise that "The Camels are coming." The drama was heightened as the copy in new ads foretold that "Tomorrow there'll be more Camels in this town than in all Asia and Africa combined!" Thus, consumers' and retailers' curiosity and appetites were whetted by the time ads announced that "Camels are here!"

Once Camels arrived, Ayer worked to highlight the brand's novel qualities. Its Turkish-domestic blend was allegedly superior to either kind of tobacco smoked alone. The elimination of premiums was presented as a positive virtue: smokers would receive "Quality, not premiums" for their dime because "the cost of the tobaccos prohibits their [premiums'] use." The campaign succeeded brilliantly and made Camel the first national brand of cigarette. By 1916 RJR's share of the cigarette market had passed those of Liggett and Lorillard, and RJR was snapping at the heels of American Tobacco. By 1920 RJR had gone from a distant fourth place to first in the cigarette business.

RJR and Ayer changed the way that cigarettes were marketed in the United States, but the company faced stiff competition as it tried to remain an industry leader. ATC, now under the leadership of George Washington Hill, introduced its own blended cigarette, Lucky Strike, in 1916, and that brand captured 11 percent of the market in its first year. Its ascendancy was interrupted only by World War I: both RJR and ATC went to war, but because the U.S. government contracted to buy cigarettes from the companies at their prewar market shares, far more Camels than Lucky Strikes saw action in Europe.

RJR remained on top of the cigarette market for most of the 1920s. In 1925 Camel held 40 percent of the market, placing the brand far ahead of Liggett & Myers's Chesterfield brand (25 percent) or ATC's Lucky Strike (16 percent). Market dominance was a costly venture, however, and in 1925 RJR spent $10 million on "dealer helps" and various print ads. RJR's advertising budget nearly doubled in 1927—reaching $19 million—but RJR no longer set the industry standard. By 1930 ATC was outspending and outselling RJR (and the rest of the industry).

Marketing Mistakes in the 1920s

One of RJR's marketing mistakes in the 1920s was its initial failure to advertise to female smokers, a rapidly growing sector of the cigarette market. Women in the United States had smoked prior to the 1920s, but the practice was considered socially offensive, and none of the larger tobacco companies advertised directly to female consumers before the late 1920s. RJR was the last of the "Big Three" tobacco companies to address women in advertising, running its first female-friendly campaign in 1929. The first of these magazine and newspaper ads showed two men proffering Camels to an attractive young woman, who wondered whether she should accept the invitation to smoking pleasure and camaraderie. Other ads showed a lone young woman reviving herself by smoking a Camel at the end of a day of fashionable fun. RJR had moved into this market too slowly, however. ATC vaulted from a distant third in the U.S. cigarette market in 1925 to a strong first in 1931 on the strength of its "Reach for a Lucky" campaign, which was aimed directly at women striving for the thin, trim look highlighted by "flapper" fashions but which succeeded in winning over male consumers as well. (The original slogan was "Reach for a Lucky instead of a sweet" but was modified to "Reach for a Lucky when tempted to indulge.") By 1931 Lucky Strike controlled more than 33 percent of the cigarette market.

In general, RJR's advertising in the 1920s stagnated. In addition to neglecting the female market, RJR ads created by Ayer failed to counter ATC's claims that "toasting" made Lucky Strike a superior and more healthful product with "no throat irritation." Ayer also failed to take full advantage of the new medium of radio. Only in 1931 did Ayer begin producing radio spots for RJR's brands, whereas the half-hour *Lucky Strike Dance Orches-*

tra had been on the air since 1928 (the program evolved into the long-running *Your Hit Parade* in 1935). Camel's most memorable tag line of the 1920s—"I'd walk a mile for a Camel"—was not an Ayer creation, although Ayer incorporated the phrase into some print ads later in the decade. The slogan has been variously attributed to an exchange between RJR executive Marcus Reddington and a golf partner, or to an alert billboard artist who heard the pronouncement from a grateful stranger with whom the artist had shared a Camel. In any case, RJR ended its 18-year association with Ayer in 1931 and signed a contract with Erwin, Wasey & Company, whose first ad for Reynolds appeared in February 1931.

Erwin, Wasey turned to a time-honored means of drumming up customer enthusiasm—a $50,000 contest in which consumers were invited to come up with winning ideas about the benefits of Camel's new moisture-proof cellophane wrapper. Contest announcements ran in nearly 4,000 local, national, and college newspapers, and although the promotion generated a huge response from the public, Camel sales continued a downward trend even as advertising costs increased. Erwin, Wasey proved to lack imagination: all of its new ideas for RJR revolved around contests, while some of its ads revived the "Camels are coming" copy from the Ayer campaign of 1913. In November 1932 RJR abandoned Erwin, Wasey and signed William Esty & Company, Inc.

William Cole Esty had worked for the J. Walter Thompson Company for several years, rising to the rank of vice president, before leaving to establish his own ad agency in 1932. Reynolds Tobacco was one of Esty's first clients, and he moved aggressively on all fronts to restore Camel and RJR to industry dominance. The success of his efforts led to a profitable 57-year relationship between Esty and the marketer.

Esty dramatically expanded RJR's presence in network radio. Like its chief rivals of the day, RJR devoted a significant portion of its advertising budget to the sponsorship of musical programs aimed at young adult audiences. American Tobacco had the *Lucky Strike Hit Parade;* Liggett created *Chesterfield Time* with Fred Waring; and RJR was fortunate enough over the years to feature the talents of Glen Gray, Benny Goodman, Bob Crosby, and Johnny Mercer on its long-running *Camel Caravan.* This program, according to popular historian Harris Lewine, helped launch swing music and brought a new generation to the aging Camel brand. During the 1930s and 1940s, Esty kept RJR among the top 20 advertisers in network radio.

The Print Push

The bulk of RJR's advertising budget in the 1930s and 1940s was devoted to print ads. In the depths of the Great Depression, the Esty agency crafted a series of campaigns with clever themes that renewed general public interest in the Camel brand. The first campaign—unveiled in 1933—directly attacked claims about the advantages of Camel's chief rival, Lucky Strike, in a series of ads that revolved around magic tricks and the secrets behind them. In magazine and newspaper ads, comic strips, and an in-house publication titled *The Magician's Handbook of Cigarette Tricks,* the campaign asserted that while it was "fun to be fooled," it was, in fact, more fun to be "in the know"—about the cigarettes one smoked as well as magic tricks. Empty slogans such as Lucky Strike's "It's toasted" were just a marketing sleight of hand, whereas Camel boasted superior quality with "No tricks. Just costlier tobacco and a matter of blend."

The public responded positively to Esty's "Magic" campaign and to those that followed. A "Healthy Nerves" campaign debuting in 1933 relied on the images and endorsements of such athletes as tennis star Bill Tilden and baseball player Mel Ott to persuade smokers that Camel steadied the nerves and made a person more physically and psychologically fit to face life's challenges. In a later campaign shop girls and society mavens touted Camel's healthful properties—the brand reportedly soothed jangled nerves and aided in digestion. A 1934 campaign—"Get a Lift with a Camel"—promised renewed energy. Camels "don't get your wind," claimed a campaign launched in the spring of 1935. By 1936 Camel and RJR were back on top, outselling ATC's Lucky Strike and Liggett's Chesterfield.

The aggressive edge to Esty's campaigns of the 1930s was blunted in the 1940s. The Federal Trade Commission (FTC) investigated the cigarette maker's claims and deemed Esty's health claims for Camel suspect at best, fraudulent at worst. RJR, like others in the industry, became the defendant in several lawsuits. Compounding its legal woes, Reynolds ceded industry and brand dominance once again to ATC and Lucky Strike during World War II, as RJR was hindered by dull advertising and by its lack of a stockpile of tobacco sufficient to compensate for shortages caused by the war. An enormous billboard in New York City's Times Square in 1942 that featured the old slogan "I'd walk a mile for a Camel" and real, 15-foot-high smoke rings emanating from the mouth of an image of a U.S. serviceman caught the attention of passersby; other than that, however, Reynolds's advertising lacked spark. Meanwhile, ATC struck a patriotic note when it repackaged Lucky Strike in clean white—supposedly because there was a wartime shortage of the chromium used to make green ink—and produced the memorable announcement that "Lucky Strike green has gone to war!" The alleged chromium shortage was a fiction, but the brand immediately gained 38 percent in sales.

The decade after World War II was a high-water mark for the U.S. cigarette industry and a turning point for RJR. The war created millions of new smokers as the U.S. government once again made cigarettes part of every soldier's kit, and cigarette sales soared when these new customers returned home from Europe and the Pacific. The FTC suits against the tobacco industry, which had been prolonged for years by industry stonewalling, pronounced Reynolds and the other companies guilty of deception and false claims in their advertising, but these rulings did little to change industry practices and offered no damning evidence of the dangers of smoking. For a few years the U.S. public remained relatively unconcerned about the possibility that cigarette smoking posed health risks, and during that time television became a viable advertising medium that changed the way tobacco—and everything else—was sold.

Early in the 1950s, however, health claims about cigarettes began to trouble the public and the industry's bottom line. The industry for years had tacitly acknowledged minor risks associated with smoking, such as coughing and throat irritation, in various advertising slogans and campaigns, and all of the companies publicized the alleged health benefits of smoking their particular products. P. Lorillard's Old Gold brand debuted in the 1920s with the promise that there was "Not a cough in a carload," and the "toasting" of the tobacco used in Lucky Strikes allegedly offered the smoker's throat protection against irritation and cough. In the mid-1940s RJR publicized an allegedly independent poll of 113,000 physicians, which revealed that a majority of the doctors who smoked preferred Camels to any other brand of cigarette. Moreover, Reynolds's advertising urged smokers to take the "T-Zone Test" to prove to themselves that Camels caused less throat irritation, and a pamphlet sent to doctors' offices and organizations encouraged medical professionals to recommend "slow burning" Camels to those patients needing an adjustment in their "smoking hygiene." Switching to Camels, the pamphlet claimed, would control the "vague, subclinical effects" of too much nicotine and yet offer a pleasurable smoking experience.

Smoking Linked to Lung Cancer

In December 1953, however, two physicians, Ernst Wynder and Evarts Graham, induced a measure of panic in the tobacco industry by publishing an article that suggested a clear link between smoking and lung cancer. Within weeks of the article's appearance, the chief executives of the leading cigarette makers met in New York City to discuss how best to deal with a potential crisis of public faith. Their response was two-pronged. First, they established the jointly funded Tobacco Industry Research Committee (TIRC), which, they hoped, would either prove that cigarette smoking was not dangerous or find ways to produce safe cigarettes without significant difficulty or cost. Second, the industry leaders decided to follow the advice of John Hill, of the newly established public relations (PR) firm Hill and Knowlton, and launch a PR offensive that, while affirming their commitment to the health of their customers, openly questioned the validity of the charges leveled against cigarettes. The evidence, they claimed, was inconclusive at best and tainted by the researchers' determination to attract publicity and more money for their laboratories. Thus, at that meeting the strategy that would be pursued by the industry for the next 40 years was established.

A significant decline in cigarette consumption in the United States following the publication of the Wynder and Graham study indicated that the public was indeed worried about the health effects of smoking. In response, the industry expanded production of filter-tip cigarettes and marketed them as safer and milder smokes, even as the companies denied that their other products posed a risk. In this uncertain environment, RJR staged its comeback. Camel was the best-selling cigarette in the United States, but ATC produced a wider selection of brands and held the lead in overall unit sales. Reynolds finally moved beyond its single-minded devotion to Camel and created Winston filtered cigarettes.

There were already several brands of filtered cigarettes in existence, but none held a significant portion of the market. Winston, however, effectively addressed consumer complaints that filtered cigarettes did not taste good and failed to offer the same satisfaction found in unfiltered brands. Whereas ads for other filtered brands emphasized the alleged health benefits of filters, Winston ran ads proclaiming that Winston "tastes good—like a cigarette should." By the end of 1956, Winston was the top seller among filtered cigarettes.

On the heels of Winston's success, Reynolds released another new offering, Salem menthol cigarettes, in 1956 in a campaign created by Esty that suggested physical well-being and refreshment—but avoided direct references to health. Salem was advertised as being as "Refreshing as springtime itself," and the brand soon outsold its Brown & Williamson rival, Kool. Although not created specifically for women, Salem found a niche among female smokers, many of whom erroneously believed that menthols were less hazardous to one's health than regular cigarettes; in fact, Salem did far better among that constituency than did RJR's Embra brand, which when introduced in the late 1960s as a "women's" brand followed Philip Morris's Virginia Slims but failed to achieve any of that product's success.

In the 1960s advertising for Winston and Camel helped maintain Reynolds's position as industry leader, although the competition changed as Philip Morris's Marlboro man rode onto the scene to challenge the Winston brand. RJR's advertising budgets increased considerably during the decade. In 1962 Reynolds spent a staggering $28.8 million on spot television advertising and sponsorship. The Lorillard company, a distant second among the "Big Six" tobacco companies in television advertising, spent $21.7 million. In 1965 Reynolds sponsored a number of TV programs, including *Today, Wide World of Sports,* and *McHale's Navy.* The company also sponsored radio programming. Print advertising became a secondary medium as television reached maturity in the 1960s.

By the 1970s, however, Reynolds and the rest of the tobacco industry had to reconsider their place in the market and recalculate their advertising strategies in light of increasing political pressure to regulate cigarettes and tobacco advertising. In 1964 U.S. Surgeon General Luther Terry issued a report specifically linking cigarette smoking with disease, especially lung cancer. In the months following the report, a legislative contest pitted the FTC, which moved to restrict cigarette advertising and mandate strong health warnings on packaging, against the tobacco industry (united behind the front of the Tobacco Institute) and the industry's allies, the Advertising Federation of America and the National Association of Broadcasters. The result of the battle was the Cigarette Labeling and Advertising Act of 1965, which required mild health warnings on cigarette packaging but blocked state and local actions against the industry and prevented federal agencies from taking action to regulate tobacco advertising.

The tobacco companies also voluntarily agreed to withdraw all radio and television advertising by January 1971. With this move, the industry avoided both regulation and the pressure of anti-smoking ads that radio and TV stations were forced to air under the Federal Communications Commission's "Fairness Doctrine," which mandated that if one viewpoint on a controversial issue received broadcast time, then opponents must be allowed to respond on air. The industry's advertising campaigns shifted away from broadcast media (which had accounted for 80 percent of the industry's advertising spending during the 1960s) and back to print and outdoor advertising.

Responding to Health Concerns

In the wake of these developments, Reynolds directed a significant portion of its advertising budget to launching brands that supposedly addressed the concerns of consumers who worried about the health effects of smoking but could not bring themselves to quit. A flurry of low- and ultra-low-tar brands were introduced by tobacco companies in the late 1960s and early 1970s; Reynolds's entries into this market were Doral, Vantage, and Now. These brands and their advertising campaigns were somewhat hampered by the fact that they were supposed to respond to health concerns that Reynolds and the rest of the industry elsewhere dismissed as unfounded.

Esty handled the premiere of Doral in 1969, and the ads touting a "Doral Diet"—low in tar and nicotine, high in taste and pleasure—were moderately successful. As a full-price brand, however, Doral never captured more than 1 percent of the total market. Repositioned as a low-price bargain brand and assigned to Long Haymes Carr, Inc., in the 1980s, Doral's prospects improved. Its growth continued through the 1990s as one-time RJR leaders Winston and Salem began to fade.

Leber Katz Partners, Inc., directed the advertising for Vantage and Now, and Vantage in particular achieved early success in the low-tar market. Leber Katz did not strike any kind of a defensive posture or make any health claims for Vantage when the brand was launched in the early 1970s. Instead, the ads met potential consumer concerns with a blunt statement of the situation—people were worried, but people wanted to smoke—and asked the question, "What are you going to do about it?" The ads were reasoned, low-key, and appealed to educated urbanites. By 1975 Vantage had a 3 percent share of the total market and briefly led the low-tar field. When Philip Morris introduced Merit in 1976, however, Vantage all but folded, the brass and creativity of the original Leber Katz campaign no longer evident.

By the mid-1980s Philip Morris had surged ahead of Reynolds on all fronts. Furthermore, Reynolds, like the rest of the tobacco industry, witnessed the erosion of its public image by a wave of litigation, investigation, and regulation in the late 1980s and the 1990s. The claims made by the TIRC in the wake of the first "cancer scare" were no longer tenable by this point in history. It was all too clear to the public that cigarette smoking was harmful and addictive, and evidence was emerging that the tobacco industry leaders' first commitment had always been to their own financial well-being rather than their customers' health. In this environment, the U.S. Congress and the individual states became willing to move against the tobacco industry as they had not done in earlier decades. The industry was forced to settle some lawsuits and required to pay huge damage awards in others. In 1998 the tobacco companies became subject to new regulations that severely limited the manner and media in which cigarettes could be advertised in the United States.

Thus, as Reynolds struggled to redefine itself and stage another comeback in the marketplace, it was stymied. The cartoon character Joe Camel (an updated version of Old Joe, the Barnum & Bailey circus camel that had served as the model for the original package image in 1913) was introduced in the United States in 1987 by the Trone Advertising Agency. RJR stuck with its new "smooth character" for a decade but went through a series of advertising agencies in the process of revitalizing and popularizing the old Camel brand. Leaving Trone in 1988, RJR signed with McCann-Erickson, only to abandon that agency in 1989 in favor of Young & Rubicam, Inc. (Y&R). Reynolds formed a lasting relationship with Y&R executives Bill Brown and John Mezzina, who left Y&R in 1991—with Joe Camel and the Reynolds account—to form their own company, Mezzina/Brown, Inc. Reynolds and Mezzina/Brown consigned Joe Camel to the archives in 1997 after enduring several years of controversy. Antismoking activists argued that the anthropomorphized camel was a means of attracting children and teens to the cigarette habit. The character had, after all, successfully expanded the European youth market when it was first unveiled in France in the early 1970s. Reynolds and its agencies argued in turn that the Joe Camel campaign was intended simply to update the brand and foster loyalty and inspire fun among adults—in much the same way that MetLife used the cartoon character Snoopy to sell insurance to adults. They failed to persuade critics or the general public, and new packaging (featuring a more realistic figure of a camel) and the new Mezzina/Brown tag line, "What you're looking for" replaced the controversial "Smooth Character" campaign.

In the 1980s and 1990s, if not before, RJR gained a reputation among agencies as a difficult client, one that, according to *Advertising Age*, "pitt[ed] shops against one another on a project-by-project basis." As a result, there was tremendous turnover in the agencies handling RJR's brands, and during this period the *Standard Directory of Advertisers* did not always list an agency for RJR brands, even for such mainstays as Camel. The chronology of advertising for these decades is therefore imprecise.

In 1995 *Advertising Age* described RJR brands as "seriously mismanaged" and the company in need of "major marketing revamping." Winston's market share had fallen to less than 10 per-

cent; Camel was seen as appealing to kids (although not as much as Marlboro), but the brand was not gaining much in overall market share among adults; and the 40-year-old Salem brand was faltering. In the late 1990s, however, Reynolds found a voice. Much of the company's advertising of that period was marked by what can only be described as "attitude." Long Haymes Carr took on the Winston account in 1996 and created the confrontational "No Additives, No Bull" campaign. Also in 1996, the Gyro agency of Philadelphia, Pennsylvania, undertook the relaunching of Red Kamel cigarettes, which had been absent from the market for 60 years. An early tag line in the new campaign declared, "Back for no good reason except they taste good." None of these campaigns threatened to topple Philip Morris from its perch, but at the start of the new century RJR remained an industry giant and a profitable subsidiary of the commodities conglomerate RJR Nabisco, which had been created with the merger in 1985 of RJR and Nabisco. The combined companies were valued at $5.25 billion.

NANCY BOWMAN

See also Nabisco, Inc.

Further Reading

Glantz, Stanton, et al., *The Cigarette Papers*, Berkeley: University of California Press, 1996

Hilts, Philip J., *Smoke Screen: The Truth behind the Tobacco Industry Cover-Up*, Reading, Massachusetts: Addison Wesley, 1996

Kluger, Richard, *Ashes to Ashes: America's Hundred-Year Cigarette War, the Public Health, and the Unabashed Triumph of Philip Morris*, New York: Knopf, 1996

Lewine, Harris, *Good-Bye to All That*, New York: McGraw Hill, 1970

Merrill, Cristina, "Nicotine Rush," *Adweek* (Eastern Edition) (11 November 1996)

Miles, Robert H., and Kim S. Cameron, *Coffin Nails and Corporate Strategies*, Englewood Cliffs, New Jersey: Prentice Hall, 1982

Pollack, Judann, and Laura Petrecca, "RJR Suspends Salem Agency Review," *Advertising Age* (3 February 1997)

Sobel, Robert, *They Satisfy: The Cigarette in American Life*, New York: Anchor/Doubleday, 1978

Teinowitz, Ira, "Marketing, Ad Woes Choking RJR Brands," *Advertising Age* (26 June 1995)

Rightford, Searle-Tripp & Makin. *See* Ogilvy & Mather Rightford

Hal Riney & Partners, Inc.

Created from Ogilvy & Mather, Inc., San Francisco, California, by Hal Riney and renamed Hal Riney & Partners, 1986; acquired by Publicis but continued to operate independently, 1998.

Major Clients

Alamo Rent A Car
eToys
First Union Bank
E. & J. Gallo Winery (Bartles & Jaymes wine coolers)
Miller Brewing Company (Henry Weinhard's Private Reserve
    beer)
Saturn Corporation

As a specialist in brand development, Hal Riney & Partners, Inc., has established a reputation as one of the most respected creative agencies in the United States. Its founder, Hal Riney, whose voice often is heard in the agency's work (he is a well-regarded voice-over talent), was trained as an art director but was called "the best copywriter I've ever known" by no less a judge than advertising legend David Ogilvy. Riney has said that he knew early in life that he wanted to be in advertising, and after a stint in the U.S. Army as a news writer he joined Batten Barton Durstine & Osborn, in San Francisco, California, working in the mailroom in 1956. After serving as a junior account executive, he became an art director and later a writer and creative director. In 1972 he became creative director at Botsford-Ketchum, and in 1976 he left to head Ogilvy & Mather, Inc., in San Francisco.

In 1986 Riney bought the office and renamed it Hal Riney & Partners; the new shop had 105 employees and billings of $85 million. By 1998, when the agency was acquired by Paris, France-based Publicis, it was billing $700 million and had established a reputation for memorable, successful campaigns.

One outstanding example of the agency's work was its campaign for E. & J. Gallo Winery's Bartles & Jaymes wine coolers, which ran about 90 ads over a three-and-a-half-year period in the mid-1980s. The idea of using two elderly yokels as spokesmen for a product targeted to hip 20-somethings took some selling on the part of the agency. Each spot ran for about two weeks and featured the two recurring characters, only one of whom ever spoke, and a joke about starting a company. All of the commercials were directed by Joe Pytka. The basic formula was easy to vary, and sometimes as many as 11 different versions were shot in one day. The Gallo name never appeared in the spots, which were condemned by a rival marketer as deceptive in that they hid the fact that the giant Gallo winery was behind the wine coolers—not some homespun, shoestring family vintner. Riney resigned the labor-intensive account in 1988, but not before bringing national attention to his agency and doubling sales of the Gallo cooler in one year.

Earlier work in the late 1970s for Henry Weinhard's Private Reserve beer was similar to the Bartles & Jaymes campaign in that Riney created almost everything from the marketing strategy to the product name and then wrote some humorous commercials. But these commercials were limited to a regional audience in the western United States, where Fred Wessinger, president of Blitz-Weinhard Company, credited the campaign with gaining the beer a 20 percent share of the premium beer market. Riney had the account through 1984, but the succeeding agency, W.B. Doner & Company, in Southfield, Michigan, continued the amusing tone of the ads. The account returned to Riney in 1999, after the Miller Brewing Company bought the brand; a year later, Miller switched the account to the Portland, Oregon, agency Wieden & Kennedy, saying it wanted an agency based in the Northwest.

A major coup for Hal Riney & Partners was the 1988 acquisition of the $90 million General Motors Corporation (GM) Saturn car account. GM's decision to go with Riney surprised many in the industry who thought the agency was too small to service the start-up automaker, which would not even begin building cars until 1990. The agency met the challenge in an unexpected way— by marketing the company and virtually ignoring the car. Riney was able to convince GM that it was the company, not the car, that set Saturn apart. The initial launch campaign was followed by another round of emotional spots featuring the dedication and commitment of the people who made the cars. After pressure from Saturn dealers, the agency created ads focusing on real Saturn owners and what their cars meant to them. The tag line, "A different kind of company. A different kind of car," appealed to some consumers, who developed an almost cultlike devotion to the brand. In 1999 the agency responded to the introduction of the larger "L" series with a new tag line, "The next big thing from Saturn," and a continuation of the usual warm, fuzzy feelings.

The agency had a hugely successful year in 1996, gaining about $200 million in new billings in nine months and increasing its total billings by almost one-third. Added to the agency roster were two technology accounts, Acer Group and Sprint Spectrum.

Tom Henry, director of marketing communications for Acer America Corporation, credited the work of David Verklin, Riney's corporate media director and executive vice president, with Riney's gaining the account. Verklin was part of a new management team that included Scott Marshall, who became president of the agency in 1995. In 1997, however, Acer America cut its ad spending to about $10 million and moved its business from Hal Riney to Kahn/Weber/Harris.

Riney's reputation for branding attracted Subway Sandwiches and Salads to the agency, which developed a two-pronged campaign approach, dubbed the "Smile and bite" ads, in 1996. The "Smile" component was a branding campaign designed to promote long-term sales and build image. "Bite" was an aggressive, promotion-driven campaign. The Subway campaign marked the first time the agency had used cable TV's segmented audiences to great advantage.

Cable television also played a role in Riney's campaign for First Union Bank. Rather than a warm-and-fuzzy approach,

Writers Association of New York's Copywriters Hall of Fame. At the awards ceremony, Bernbach said of Robinson, "She helped make it possible for Doyle Dane Bernbach to have the courage of its convictions, to know the difference between good creative work and mere creative acrobatics." Robinson, he said, helped to "turn advertising from a business into a profession."

In addition to copywriting, Robinson helped mentor many up-and-coming advertising talents at the agency, including Mary Wells and copywriter Paula Green. She was also involved in public-service efforts, was a member of the creative review board of the Media-Advertising Partnership for a Drug-Free America, and a founding member of Ads Against AIDS.

KAREN EGOLF

Phyllis K. Robinson.
Courtesy of DDB New York.

Biography
Born in New York City, 22 October 1921; graduated with bachelor of arts degree, Barnard College, 1942; hired as copywriter, Bresnick & Solomont, Boston, Massachusetts, 1946; joined Grey Advertising Agency, Inc., New York City, 1947; joined launch team of Doyle Dane Bernbach, Inc. (DDB), as copy chief, becoming first female copy chief in U.S. advertising, 1949; promoted to vice president, 1956; inducted into Copywriters Hall of Fame, 1968; retired from DDB, 1982.

another musical, *Cry for Us All,* which ran on Broadway in 1970.

Robinson, who was promoted to vice president in 1956, quit as copy chief when her daughter was born in 1962. She switched to working three days a week and continued working part-time at the agency until she retired to open a consultancy in 1982.

Robinson was honored for her copywriting skills in 1968, when she became the eighth person inducted into the Advertising

Further Reading
"Big Billings Don't Necessarily Constrict Creativity, Doyle Dane's Robinson Declares," *Advertising Age* (20 October 1958)
"Listen to Angry Young Voices in Ad Field, DDB's Phyllis Robinson Says," *Advertising Age* (3 June 1968)
Neuberger-Lucchesi, Roxanne E., "Phyllis K. Robinson," in *The Ad Men and Women: A Biographical Dictionary of Advertising,* edited by Edd Applegate, Westport, Connecticut: Greenwood Press, 1994
Revett, John, "Comments of a Copy Chief," *Advertising Age* (15 July 1968)

Ross Roy, Inc.

Established in Detroit, Michigan, 1926; became full-service agency, 1940; grew through acquisitions in the 1950s–70s; as Ross Roy Group, continued to absorb other agencies during the 1980s; acquired by Omnicom, 1995; changed name to InterOne Marketing Group, 2000.

Major Clients
Chrysler Corporation (later DaimlerChrysler)
Dodge Brothers Corporation

Ross Roy, a successful automobile salesman, founded his own agency in 1926 in Detroit, Michigan. His sales record at a Dodge dealership in Janesville, Wisconsin, had attracted the attention of Dodge Brothers Corporation executives, who were impressed by Roy's use of competitive product information as a sales tool. He persuaded the top brass at Dodge that direct, feature-by-feature comparisons of its cars with competing brands would be of great value to all Dodge salesmen. Previously, auto salesmen had ignored competitors.

Ross Roy, Inc., introduced the "job-rated" theme in 1940 in its first ads for Dodge trucks.
The 1940 Chrysler advertisement is used with permission from Daimler-Chrysler Corporation.

This "comparison selling" approach led to the birth of the agency, and in 1927, when Chrysler Corporation acquired Dodge Brothers, Ross Roy's sales approach was extended to all Chrysler Corporation dealers, including those selling the Plymouth and DeSoto brands. Soon "Ross Roy comparisons" were part of the sales pitch of every salesman representing the Chrysler line. The agency continued to grow with Chrysler, specializing in sales training and merchandising, and during the 1930s the company produced education and training films.

Ross Roy became a full-service advertising agency in 1940 when it acquired the Dodge truck division account, for which it created the successful "job-rated" theme. The agency adopted an "advertising with follow-through" approach, which included sales training, filmstrips for dealers, and direct mail.

The agency had barely begun to hit its stride when the United States entered World War II in December 1941. Ross Roy had 82 people on its payroll at the time of the Japanese attack on Pearl Harbor; a week later, the agency had cut that number in half and was set for a long siege, as commercial auto production stopped. As war orders poured in to the automakers, however, those companies, Chrysler among them, realized they not only had to provide automotive and other products for the war effort but also operational, training, and service manuals. Ross Roy was poised to produce these materials. By the end of the first quarter of 1942, the agency had rehired all those who had been let go, and at the war's end it had 180 employees.

Postwar Progress

The Chrysler Corporation continued to be the agency's largest client in the immediate postwar years. In 1947 it had billings of $5.9 million; by 1950 this had grown to $9.8 million. Ross Roy's work included merchandising and sales training for the Chrysler, Dodge, DeSoto, and Plymouth brands and work for Dodge trucks, the parts division, and Canadian operations. By the mid-1950s the agency also had offices in New York City; Chicago, Illinois; Los Angeles, California; and Windsor, Ontario, Canada. Billings for the decade peaked in 1953 at $18.9 million, when the agency ranked 35th among American shops. In addition to Chrysler, clients included American Steel Wool Manufacturing Company, Dana Perfume, Eljer Company (a marketer of plumbing fixtures), Esquire socks, Lake Central Airlines, and Radio Corporation of America's custom records and recorded program services.

Growth also came through merger. In 1950 Ross Roy absorbed the C.C. Fogarty agency in Chicago and Zeder-Talbot on the West Coast. An even larger and more significant acquisition came a decade later; in July 1960 Ross Roy merged with fellow Detroit agency Brooke, Smith, French & Dorrance (BSF&D), creating an operation known briefly in the early 1960s as Ross Roy-BSF&D.

The combined shop, with annual billings of about $25 million, melded Ross Roy's strengths—merchandising, selling aids, sales training, and direct mail—with BSF&D's long suit, creativity. Roy said, "We will truly be able to offer clients advertising with follow-through, which means creative help at every single step of the selling and distributive function." John S. Pingel, who was executive vice president of BSF&D before the merger, became president of Ross Roy four years later.

Growth continued in the 1970s with the addition of two long-time Detroit agencies, Zimmer, Keller & Calvert (1970) and Gray

& Kilgore (1974). By the middle of the decade, billings had risen to $92 million, ranking it 19th among U.S. agencies. Many Chrysler Corporation divisions and components continued to dominate the agency's client roster, but others on the list included Greyhound Food Management, Inc.; Michigan Tourist Commission; Kelsey-Hayes Company; Owens-Illinois, Inc.'s Libbey Glass Division; Parke, Davis & Company; Storer Broadcasting Company; and Uniroyal, Inc. Separately, the New York City operation, which was billing $9.5 million, handled Bacardi & Company and General Electric Company's Plastics Business Division and Silicone Products Department, among others.

In 1980 daily operations of the agency, now billing $191 million, were turned over to Glen Fortinberry, who resigned as vice chairman of the J. Walter Thompson Company to become president and chief operating officer of Ross Roy. He presided over a decade in which the Ross Roy Group added agencies including Griswold, with offices in Cleveland and Columbus, Ohio, and Calet, Hirsch & Spector, with offices in New York City and Clearwater, Florida.

Roy, the agency's founder, died in August 1983 at the age of 85. Shortly before his death, he was asked to identify the most important factor in the agency's success. His reply: "Doing more for the client than the client asked you to do."

Diversification

Late in the 1980s the agency moved from its longtime headquarters in Detroit to suburban Bloomfield Hills, Michigan. By the end of the decade, billings of the Ross Roy Group, fattened through the absorption of Calet, Hirsch & Spector and other agencies, surpassed $650 million, and its client list, although still dominated by Chrysler accounts, now included Kmart Corporation, Detroit Edison, La-Z-Boy Chair Company, and Michigan Bell Telephone.

Fortinberry, then the agency's chief executive officer (CEO), died of leukemia in August 1993, at the age of 65. At the time of his death, the agency had 1,000 employees and billings of more than $700 million. During his tenure the agency had broadened its national presence and expanded its capabilities in areas such as direct marketing, Yellow Pages, public relations, and franchise marketing. Peter Mills, who assumed the titles of chairman, president, and CEO, succeeded Fortinberry. Mills had most recently been president and chief operating officer of BBDO North America.

In 1995 Omnicom Group, parent company of BBDO, acquired the company; then known as Ross Roy Communications, it had become one of the largest independent shops in the United States. After the acquisition, the agency resigned its other accounts to concentrate on the business of Chrysler Corporation and, later, of DaimlerChrysler.

On 1 January 2000 the agency changed its name to InterOne Marketing Group; moved its headquarters to Troy, Michigan; and reinvented itself as a customer relationship management agency. Timothy Copacia, the president and CEO, defined the renamed agency as "customer-centric, nurturing lifelong relationships." Copacia said that the agency, part of the BBDO Worldwide network, would pursue new business, although during its first year as InterOne, DaimlerChrysler remained its sole client. A restructuring at Chrysler in March 2001 provided an opportunity for InterOne to increase its local direct mail and customer relationship work for the carmaker.

ROBERT GOLDSBOROUGH

Further Reading

Crichton, John, "Agency Develops from Unique Service Setup," *Advertising Age* (24 March 1952)

Halliday, Jean, "Chrysler Group Restructures," *Advertising Age* (26 March 2001)

"Now It's Official—Newly Merged Detroit Agency Is Ross Roy-BSF&D," *Advertising Age* (25 July 1960)

"Ross Roy to Be Renamed," *Advertising Age* (20 December 1999)

Serafin, Raymond, "Ross Roy Builder Fortinberry Dies," *Advertising Age* (23 August 1993)

Russia and the Commonwealth of Independent States

Since the failed coup of August 1991, the subsequent resignation of President Mikhail Gorbachev, and the dissolution of the Union of Soviet Socialist Republics, trade and investment opportunities in the new Commonwealth of Independent States (CIS) have taken something akin to a roller coaster ride. In the early 1990s many companies saw the former Soviet Union as the next marketing frontier. At the time, Bruce MacDonald, general director of marketing for BBDO in Moscow, remarked, "If I were a Western company, I'd get on a plane and come here right now."

A multitude of Western firms did just that. Among those entering the Commonwealth were Johnson & Johnson, Eastman Kodak, Holiday Inns Worldwide, Procter & Gamble, and Kellogg. Philip Morris signed agreements to supply more than 20 billion cigarettes—the largest order in the company's history—but still only about 5 percent of the market for cigarettes in the Commonwealth. In 1991 Visa became the first credit card available to the general public in the former Soviet Union. And in 1992 General Motors' Trinity Motors—a Russian, American, and British joint venture—opened its first dealership in downtown Moscow. The Cadillac Seville ($50,000), the Chevrolet Caprice ($23,500), and the Chevrolet Corsica ($17,500) were among the eight models available.

The inflow of imported products was substantial. By 1994 Russian President Boris Yeltsin complained about the "Snickerization" of the country's economy, referring to the phenomenal success of Mars, Inc., in penetrating the candy market (a newspaper poll at the time revealed that only 15 percent of Russians had never tasted a Snickers bar). By 1997 annual advertising sales crossed the $1 billion mark.

However, in late 1998 political and economic chaos in the region had brought many marketing activities to a slowdown, if not an actual halt. Russia was struggling with the worst economic crisis since the collapse of the Soviet Union. Some companies had suspended sales of their products; General Motors, for example, stopped sales of its Chevy Blazer despite having just introduced a new ad campaign for the vehicle. Other firms fled the market. Uncertainty replaced the rosy glow of optimism regarding marketing opportunities in the Commonwealth.

Fortunately, by the end of 2000 many markets in the CIS had recuperated. According to the *Moscow Times,* annual ad sales for the year were nearly $1.4 billion, representing a 45 percent increase over 1999—a clear signal that foreign companies were returning to the Russian market.

Regional Profile

The population of the Commonwealth of Independent States in the 1990s exceeded 290 million, making it one of the largest markets in the world. The land area is slightly less than 2.5 times the size of the United States. The CIS consists of ten independent republics (Armenia, Belarus, Kazakhstan, Kyrgyzstan, Moldova, Russia, Tajikistan, Turkmenistan, Ukraine, and Uzbekistan). Five other former Soviet republics (Azerbaijan, Estonia, Georgia, Latvia, and Lithuania) are not members of the Commonwealth.

Prior to the dissolution of the Soviet Union, it was common to view the U.S.S.R. as a single cohesive entity, possessing little ethnic or economic diversity among its republics. Since the formation of the Commonwealth, however, it has become apparent that this presumed homogeneity was a fallacy. The resulting new nations differ from one another in size, culture, capacity for reform, available resources, and market potential. Russia, with its nearly 149 million citizens, is by far the largest of the republics. In contrast, Estonia, the smallest, has fewer than 2 million citizens. Similarly, there is a wide range in per capita gross national product (GNP), with a high of more than $5,700 for Belarus and a low of $1,600 for Tajikistan. While the official language is Russian, there are more than 200 languages and dialects (at least 18 with more than 1 million speakers each). Most international marketers perceive Russia, because of its enormous size and extensive resources (the country is one of the world's leaders in the production of oil and natural gas and is fourth in the mining of coal), as offering the greatest potential among the newly emerging markets in the former U.S.S.R.

The influx of Western investment, along with the privatization of state enterprises, served to create a rapidly growing middle class in many republics. While 99 percent of Russians were employed by the government during the final months of communist rule, Russians today are increasingly employed in the private sector. The privatization of factories began in 1992; within 18 months more than 80 percent of Russian industry had been privatized. During the same period, millions of retail stores passed from state ownership into private hands. Market surveys have revealed that as much as 40 percent of the average worker's income is never reported to tax and statistics collectors, which means that the purchasing power of these consumers is as much as two-thirds higher than officially reported.

Not only is the middle class expanding, significant growth appears to be occurring in the upper level of the economic spectrum. This new class of wealthy consumers, called "super-spenders," represents the top 5 percent income bracket; members of this group earn about $1,000 per month (ten times the income of the average Russian). Super-spenders generally own their own businesses or work for international firms. Interviews with business managers revealed that nearly 90 percent of all private-sector production, profits, and sales goes unreported to tax authorities. Given the magnitude of the private sector, it is likely that the true size of Russia's gross domestic product (GDP) is about twice as high as officially reported.

For a significant segment of the Russian population, however, poverty is on the rise, and employment security continues to erode. While unemployment is constant at around 9 percent to 10 percent, many employed workers are not getting paid. Indeed, millions of factory workers, farmers, doctors, civil servants, engineers, and schoolteachers go without pay for months. It is estimated that between 20 percent and 30 percent of Russia's population is living below the poverty level.

Development of Advertising

The traditional Soviet view of commercial advertising considered it a parasitic activity and a drain on the economy. In accordance with Marxist principles, it was associated with "bourgeois decadence." However, following the death of Soviet dictator Joseph Stalin in 1953, Communist Party leaders concluded that advertising, used in great moderation, could be employed to address certain issues. Yet capitalist and socialist advertising were seen as quite distinct. Capitalist advertising was perceived as wasteful because it served a single company in its quest for sales in the face of continual excess supply. In contrast, socialist advertising was not intended to be competitive but instead worked to fulfill the overall economic plan by redirecting demand.

Initially Soviet advertising dealt only with political propaganda or public service announcements. Over time, however, Soviet managers were encouraged to advertise certain goods and services. One common use of advertising was to promote the sale of unacceptably large inventories. Another was to sell obsolete goods. Still another was to promote seasonal goods, especially if perishable.

When Russia was a part of the Soviet Union, advertising there was largely limited to promotions for state-run programs, such as this 1929 poster, "The Development of Transportation under the Five-Year Plan," by Gustav Klutsis.

A 1988 photo showed Mike Adams (left), of Burson-Marsteller, the first Western public relations man in Russia, along with Gary Burandt of Young & Rubicam, the first Western advertising executive in that country. *Photo courtesy of Gary Burandt.*

Communist hostility toward advertising further dissolved during the Nikita Khrushchev years (1958–64). During this period stores were allowed to advertise their locations, and citizens could place classified messages. Vneshtorgreklama (All-Union Foreign Trade Advertising Agency) was established in Moscow in 1964. Vneshtorgreklama, which operated under the Ministry of Foreign Trade, served foreign clients desiring to promote goods in the Soviet Union. This agency created ads for foreign goods for placement in magazines, trade journals, and other media, the vast majority of which were business-to-business messages. Vneshtorgreklama also provided services to foreign trade organizations attempting to promote goods abroad.

For domestic advertising, one organization was intended as a supreme coordinating body—the Mezhduvedomstvennyi Soviet Po Reklame (Inter-Departmental Council on Advertising, or IDCA). The IDCA had four sections, dealing with the advertising of manufactured goods; the advertising of food products; advertising methodology and aesthetics; and the economics and orga-

nization of advertising. Subordinate to IDCA were three major regional advertising organizations: Soyuztorgreklama, Rostorgreklama, and Ukrtorgreklama. The first, the All-Union Trade Advertising Combine, handled domestic advertising throughout the Soviet Union. Rostorgreklama handled advertising for Russia, and Ukrtorgreklama handled advertising for the Ukrainian republic.

Several features of the Soviet system prevented further steps in the evolution of advertising in the late 1960s and 1970s. First, the Soviet economy was centrally planned, and resource allocation was predominantly under administrative control. Central planners were responsible for establishing rational consumption norms so that, according to official doctrine, private consumption would reflect people's true wants rather than the interests of private sellers. In short, consumption was supposed to be regulated so that demand would not be stimulated beyond the point thought to be rational or desirable.

A second brake on the development of advertising was the adherence of the economy to a production orientation, rather than a market orientation. The success of an enterprise was determined mainly by whether it fulfilled production plans, not by whether it met unsatisfied demands. Last, the Soviet economy was characterized by scarcity rather than abundance. Many goods of interest to consumers—from shoes and clothing to automobiles—were simply unavailable, and those that were available were typically of poor quality. Shortages were the norm, and prices were fixed by the state. Because items advertised in the former Soviet Union tended to be surplus or items that the government hoped to dump, advertising was generally perceived as a cue not to purchase the promoted item. These factors could not help but devalue marketing and advertising.

Effects of Perestroika

In the 1980s the first years of perestroika, or economic restructuring, served to undermine the institutions and processes of the former Soviet economy without replacing them with efficiently functioning markets. Prior to 1987 all foreign contracts came through the Ministry of Foreign Trade, which controlled the activity of about 50 specialized foreign trade organizations (FTOs). Each FTO was responsible for the export and import of a specific group of products and services. FTOs coordinated the purchasing from foreign vendors and the selling to foreign buyers. A decree issued in early 1987 stipulated that firms could engage in joint ventures with foreign companies but that the shares of foreign partners in any such ventures could not exceed 49 percent. Less than a year later, foreigners were allowed controlling interests in joint ventures. Russian enterprises were thereafter allowed to conduct business directly and independently with foreign partners.

Despite the increased potential for private enterprise, companies operating in the new Commonwealth, both domestic and foreign, faced a number of factors that complicated business transactions: rapidly changing laws concerning corporate activities, price deregulation, an unstable currency, and high levels of crime and corruption. Existing laws and regulations tended to change frequently, often without sufficient prior notice, or they were subject to arbitrary application. Investors were unsure whether they had legal title to what they purchased, a situation that posed a significant impediment to business activity.

The lifting of price controls resulted in the prices of consumer goods jumping from a minimum of 100 percent to several hundred percent. There was a strong belief, however, that price deregulation would be the right medicine for the economy. Initially, increased prices did not translate into increased availability; many shops remained empty and lines long. Russia's annual rate of inflation declined from 2,300 percent in 1992 to 130 percent by 1995, and dropped to 22 percent in 1996. During the mid-1990s, the ruble stabilized after fluctuating in value considerably during the early years of transition. In 1998, however, the ruble was devalued significantly. Between August and October, the U.S. dollar rapidly increased from six rubles per $1 to 20 rubles per $1. As a result, prices for imported goods increased. Consumption of imported goods such as automobiles, cigarettes, cosmetics, and shampoo declined dramatically because new prices were unreasonable for the average consumer. For example, a bottle of Head & Shoulders shampoo cost about 100 rubles—a steep price when the average annual salary in Moscow was about 1,200 rubles. With the economic upturn in 2000, however, the consumption capacity of the population once again increased.

Increasingly, those doing business in many CIS markets ran the risk of encountering the local version of the Mafia. During the early stages of the transition, the underworld stepped in to fill the vacuum created by the dissipation of state authority and the absence of a codified legal system. Initially, organized crime limited its activities to black marketing, theft, and providing protection previously offered by the police. In Russia, for example, the need for protection was initially limited to the operators of kiosks, restaurants, and nightclubs. Unfortunately the situation grew worse. According to a report commissioned by President Yeltsin, three-quarters of all private enterprises were being forced to pay between 10 percent and 20 percent of their earnings to criminal gangs. Clearly, the cost of protection was not only a drain on the fragile economy but also served to scare off potential investors.

Role of Western Ad Agencies

Advertising agencies followed their clients into the new Commonwealth. Ogilvy & Mather became the first officially registered Western advertising agency in the former Soviet Union when, in February 1989, it formed a three-way joint venture with the Soviet shop Soyuztorgreklama and Hungary's Mahir. In the mid-1990s, independent of its joint venture, Ogilvy saw its business skyrocket to $5 million. Prior to the dismantling of the Soviet Union, an agency team from Young & Rubicam (Y&R) was sent to Moscow to build Young & Rubicam/Sovero—a joint venture between Y&R and Sovero, a Soviet advertising agency. "We are three to five years ahead of the marketplace," noted Gary Burandt, former head of Young & Rubicam's Moscow concern. But a scarcity of goods and competing brands meant that adver-

Pepsi-Cola was the first foreign brand to be widely advertised in Russia, as seen in this outdoor café in Moscow in 1988.
Photo by Gary Burandt.

tising was not yet necessary. Instead Y&R offered a range of other services to its clients, including public relations, consumer testing, management consulting, and simple handholding to help U.S. companies understand the market. By the beginning of 1993, however, Y&R was doing $5 million in billings, boasting a fully staffed creative department that produced advertising messages for Sony, Jacobs Suchard, and Russia's privatization program.

Bozell SMG Moscow was also tied closely to the reform process. The agency worked on behalf of the Russian government in a public education and information program that was credited with helping the cause of economic reform. In addition, the agency took major steps in obtaining desperately needed market information. To measure results of its work, Bozell SMG created an unprecedented nationwide database of every newspaper, TV and radio station, local official, election result, and demographic, including population density and ethnic makeup. This system led to the establishment of a nationwide media and trend monitoring system. Within days the agency could monitor ads and tell clients which products were selling and which were not.

Ogilvy, Y&R, and Bozell SMG were not the only Western advertising/public relations agencies with branches in the former Soviet capital; rival agency D'Arcy Masius Benton & Bowles established a full-service office in Moscow in 1990 in a partnership with the Promstroy Bank. McCann-Erickson and BBDO also opened offices in Moscow. After ending a joint-venture agreement with Novosti in 1992, McCann-Erickson began to operate independently and represented such multinationals as Coca-Cola, General Motors, and Nabisco Foods Group. When BBDO first opened its doors, the agency's three employees spent most of their time on public relations and marketing consulting. By 1998 nearly 30 staffers were devoting at least 60 percent of their time to media and creative projects.

Tailoring the Message

The official Soviet policy regarding the role of advertising in a centrally planned economy affected not only the degree to which advertising was employed but also the content of commercial messages. Traditionally, citizens in this market saw relatively few advertisements, and those they were exposed to usually targeted business people rather than consumers. From a copy standpoint, most advertisements were quite restrained and tended to be informative rather than persuasive. However, consumers experienced a dramatic increase in the exposure to Western-style advertising during the 1990s.

Despite the sudden blitz of commercial messages that took Russia by storm, consumer attitudes toward advertising were surprisingly positive. A study by Gallup International found, for example, that 83 percent of Russian respondents said advertising plays an important role in the health of a modern economy (compared with 72 percent in the United Kingdom and 84 percent in Germany). And 72 percent agreed that if a product is legal to sell, it should be legal to advertise (compared with 71 percent in Britain and 82 percent in Germany). These findings suggest that Russian consumers were rapidly approaching Western attitudes toward advertising in a relatively short time.

International marketers entering the area are faced with deciding whether to use ads that are identical or similar to commercial messages employed in their domestic markets or to adapt their ads for local use. On the one hand, replicating campaigns employed in the West may prove effective. Consumers in the Commonwealth may be somewhat enamored with that which is foreign. When communism collapsed, Russia was flooded with foreign goods that previously had been available only to the privileged few. Suddenly, imported food, drink, and cigarettes were all the rage. Similarly, Western-style advertisements, using glossy visuals and persuasive copy, elicited attention when compared with their Russian counterparts. On the other hand, while the use of standardized messages may be effective for some audiences, it could prove less than effective for others. It appears that there may be a growing rift in Russian society between the "haves," who have embraced the concept of capitalist culture and have the rubles to purchase foreign brands, and the "have-nots," the low-income consumers for whom Western goods are simply out of reach. As one might expect, for the latter group, advertising is little more than a reminder of what they can ill afford. As a result they may be more critical of commercial messages.

In 1998, when the devaluation of the ruble sent the price of imports sky high, many shoppers had no recourse but to return to Russian brands. It was a change many were happy to make: the romance with Western goods was on the wane. In the early years of the 21st century it appeared that Russian was "in," foreign well and truly "out." Western companies were apparently scrambling to adapt to the new patriotism. Nestlé, for example, invested in local manufacturing facilities and created products tailored to the Russian palate. Likewise, its advertising, complete with czars, duels, and balls, borrowed liberally from Russian culture and literature.

Another drawback of U.S.-style campaigns is that they may have scant or condensed product information, designed for Western consumers who are already familiar with a brand or product category. But product information is essential to consumers whose exposure to both product categories and a variety of brands is still comparatively limited. Because consumers in this market are hungry for product information from the West, advertising copy that contains all relevant information, technical and otherwise, is likely to be the most successful. Advertisers would also be wise to highlight the company that stands behind the product, since a well-known firm in the Western world may well be unknown to most consumers in this region.

Given that many consumer goods produced in the former Soviet Union were traditionally of rather poor quality, messages emphasizing product quality over image-oriented advertisements may be especially well received. And because relatively few commercial messages are competing for the audience's attention, it may not be necessary to employ attention-grabbing techniques so common to Western advertising.

The list of international advertising blunders is lengthy. Rather than determining irrelevant or inapplicable approaches via trial and error, international marketers would be well advised to determine how consumers in the various republics will respond to Western models, appeals, and artifacts in commercial messages, as well as when and where a standardized campaign can be employed rather than an adapted message.

No Turning Back

While the economic downturn of the late 1990s frightened some companies, for many firms the CIS remained an attractive market because of the pent-up demand for goods. Some companies actually chose to increase their investment during the period of economic difficulty. Coca-Cola, for example, launched its first television ad campaign using messages specifically tailored for Russian consumers in 1998. Coca-Cola is not unfamiliar with marketing in countries experiencing turmoil. During the Mexican economic crisis in 1994 and 1995, when the peso was devalued by more than 50 percent, Coca-Cola increased its level of marketing activity. Since then the brand has gained ten share points in that country. Since the 1998 collapse, both the economy and consumer spending are experiencing an upswing—and advertisers have responded. The top spender in 2000 was Procter & Gamble Company ($429 million, versus only $255 million in 1999). The Wm. Wrigley Jr. Company, marketer of chewing gum, placed second, virtually tripling its ad budget. Such spending signaled a healthy turnaround.

The road from a state-controlled to a market-driven economy has been anything but an easy one. During the 1990s the republics of the Commonwealth faced political instability, changing legal structures, inflation, unemployment, and increasing levels of crime and corruption. Since the demise of communism, consumers have had a taste of the West and now crave the goods and lifestyle of their former foes. Despite the challenges facing the region at the start of the 21st century, conventional wisdom suggests that Russia has gone too far toward the privatization of its industry and the implementation of free market dynamics to ever return to communism.

BARBARA MUELLER

Further Reading

Chadraba, Petr, *The Central and Eastern European Markets: Guideline for New Business Ventures,* New York: International Business Press, 1995

Church, Nancy, "Advertising in the Eastern Bloc: Current Practices and Anticipated Avenues of Development," *Journal of Global Marketing* 5, no. 3 (1992)

Coplin, William D., and Michael K. O'Leary, "The Commercial Prospects for Eastern Europe and the Former Soviet Republics," *Planning Review* 20, no. 6 (November/December 1992)

Epstein, Gene, "Economic Beat: Don't Believe All You Read about Russia's Economy: They're Doing Better Than They Say," *Barron's* 75, no. 51 (December 1995)

Fellman, Michelle Wirth, "Firms Suspend Distribution, Marketing in Russia," *Marketing News* 32, no. 21 (October 1998)

Gutterman, Steven, "Study: Russians Quick to Embrace Ads As Comrades," *Advertising Age* (20 June 1994)

Klebnikov, Paul, "Russia: The Ultimate Emerging Market," *Forbes* 153, no. 4 (February 1994)

Miller, Russell R., *Selling to Newly Emerging Markets,* Westport, Connecticut: Quorum, 1998

Mueller, Barbara, "From the Cold War to a Hot Marketplace: The Role of Advertising in the Commonwealth of Independent States," in *The Proceedings of the 1993 Conference of the American Academy of Advertising,* edited by Esther Thorson, Montreal, Quebec: American Academy of Advertising, 1993

Mueller, Barbara, "New Marketing and Advertising Frontiers," in *International Advertising: Communicating across Cultures,* by Mueller, Belmont, California: Wadsworth, 1996

Shama, Avraham, "Transforming the Consumer in Russia and Eastern Europe," *International Marketing Review* 9, no. 5 (1992)

Stanat, Ruth, "Central and Eastern Europe: The Last Frontier," in *Global Gold: Panning for Profits in Foreign Markets,* by Stanat, New York: American Management Association, 1998

Wells, Ludmilla Gricenko, "Western Concepts, Russian Perspectives: Meanings of Advertising in the Former Soviet Union," *Journal of Advertising* 23, no. 1 (March 1994)

Ruthrauff & Ryan, Inc.

Opened by Wilbur Ruthrauff and Fritz Ryan, 1912; experienced growth each year for the next 40 years, becoming a major U.S. agency in the 1930s through its work for Lever Brothers and Dodge; suffered sharp billing declines after 1952; merged with Erwin, Wasey & Company, Inc., to form Erwin, Wasey, Ruthrauff & Ryan, 1957; became part of Interpublic, a holding company that also owned McCann-Erickson, 1963; dropped from the agency nameplate and closed, 1964.

Major Clients

American Air Lines, Inc.
Campbell Soup Company (Franco American brand)
Canadian Pacific Railway Company
Dodge Brothers Corporation
Dr Pepper
Gillette Safety Razor Company
B.F. Goodrich Company
Lever Brothers Company (Rinso, Lifebuoy, Spry)
A.H. Lewis Medicine Company (Tums)
Noxzema Chemical Company
Packard Motor Car Company
Pennzoil
Wm. Wrigley Jr. Company

When Ruthrauff & Ryan, Inc. (R&R), was at its peak in the 1930s and 1940s, it had a well-defined profile among top New York City agencies. "Young & Rubicam for the classes," the saying went, "Ruthrauff & Ryan for the masses." It was a reputation the agency readily embraced. Starting around 1932, the Chicago, Illinois, and New York City offices each displayed a huge mural showing a sea of faces—the masses. Above was the agency's credo: "This is your market. To sell them you must know them." R&R saw its greatest success during the Great Depression and World War II but was unable to survive the prosperity of the 1950s. To the extent that there was an R&R style, it was inelegant and hard-selling, both characteristics rooted in the agency's direct-mail and catalog background.

The original partners, both graduates of Yale University, in New Haven, Connecticut, first met during a visit to Cape Cod, Massachusetts, sometime around 1910 or 1911. Neither had an advertising background. Wilbur Ruthrauff made his living as a rent collector, while Fredrick ("Fritz") Ryan was a moderately

successful real estate salesman and freelance author of sales letters. They opened their agency in 1912 on a capital investment of
$2,000 and went after mail-order clients. A coin toss decided who
would occupy the only available private office in their first quarters. Ruthrauff got the office; Ryan got the presidency, although
the agency was run on a 50-50 basis until Ruthrauff's death in
1941 at age 63.

White Space = Money Wasted

Their success was swift. By the 1920s Ruthrauff & Ryan was
established as a force to be reckoned with in direct mail. Serious
students of such advertising still hold a number of R&R campaigns
in high regard: the Roth Memory Course ("Of Course I Remember
You, Mr. Addison Simms of Seattle"); *The Book of Etiquette* from
Doubleday ("Again She Orders—A Chicken Salad, Please"); and
the Arthur Murray Dance School ("How I Became Popular Overnight"). The most famous of the early R&R direct ads was the
work of 25-year-old copywriter John Caples for the U.S. School of
Music: "They Laughed When I Sat down at the Piano, But When I
Started to Play!" In 1976 *Advertising Age* named it one the ten
greatest ads ever created (although the same ad failed to make the
publication's 1999 list of the top 100 of the 20th century).

Out of this early work, R&R developed a reputation for taking on undistinguished products and differentiating them from the
competition with simple, though sometimes detailed, copy written
in a newsy manner. In the late 1930s R&R showed no hesitation
in using direct response techniques in major media when it seemed
appropriate. The agency launched Dale Carnegie's best-seller,
How to Win Friends and Influence People, in a series of densely
packed, editorial-style ads that included two or three sidebars setting out celebrity endorsements and other points of interest. In the
manner of the mail-order style, each ad ended by asking for the
sale and providing a coupon. Payment was made to the postman
on delivery (COD—cash on delivery—was the direct marketer's
most powerful tool, aside from the postal service itself).

Even in conventional media ads, R&R layouts tended to be
segmented and cluttered with a multiplicity of typefaces and photographs of different sizes and shapes competing for attention. A
sequence of individual photos, each captioned and often using
comic strip–style dialogue balloons, resembled the storyboards
that would become familiar a generation later in designing television commercials. The dense look was one that seemed to reflect
the notion of white space as money wasted. While many agencies
adopted the style, not all executed it as ruggedly as R&R. When
B.F. Goodrich moved its account from R&R to Batten Barton
Durstine & Osborn in 1940, the harshness of the R&R look was
softened with a more spacious visual feel. Nevertheless, R&R
took pride in its hard-selling philosophy and spelled it out to leading advertisers in a series of house ads in *Fortune* magazine. One
of these read:

> Many an advertiser has found himself on the wrong side of
> the ledger because, in framing his sales to the mass market,
> he endowed prospects with a refinement and subtlety which

in reality they do not possess. Our choice of advertising
appeals, therefore, must embody concessions to popular
taste. This kind of advertising may seem too down-to-earth
at times, but it sells! It always has sold. And it always will
sell. For today's best advertising is a slice of life itself.

Radio, with its power to reach millions regardless of literacy,
became a perfect medium for R&R in the late 1920s. It brought
Goodrich Silvertown Tires to the air as sponsor of *The Shadow* in
1937–38. The transcribed series, which starred a young Orson
Welles, was produced and directed for the Mutual Network by
Ruthrauff's son, Bourne, who would later head the agency. In
December 1925 R&R won its first Lever Brothers business,
Rinso, and began a 27-year relationship with the company. It
launched Spry, a cooking oil competitive with Procter & Gamble's
Crisco, in 1932 and was soon building Lever brands Lifebuoy and
Rinso to leadership positions on radio through such network
shows as *The Lifebuoy Program with Al Jolson* and soap operas
such as *Big Sister.*

Lifebuoy is a good case study in R&R advertising. Using the
fear of social isolation, a favorite appeal of direct-mail advertisers,
R&R decided to position Lifebuoy as a "health soap" that could
stop body odor. But while the concept was strong, consumers
were offended by the phrase "body odor." So Cal McCarthy, an
account executive who had joined R&R in 1932, created the
euphemism "B.O." for the offending idea. Starting in 1935 and
for the next 20 years, B.O. became part of the American idiom,
always pronounced in R&R commercials in a deep and implicitly
scolding bass voice.

By the mid-1930s R&R had offices in New York City; Chicago,
Illinois; St. Louis and Kansas City, Missouri; Detroit, Michigan;
Los Angeles and San Francisco, California; and Seattle, Washing-
ton. Its basic client roster included, in addition to Lever Brothers,
Cocomalt, Canadian Pacific Railways, Franco-American, Gillette,
Goodrich, Ironized Yeast, Lea & Perrins, Noxzema, Tums, and
Wrigley. Growth over the next 20 years would rest largely on the
growth of these core clients.

Enduring Client Relationships

In 1926 the Lever account more than any other helped turn R&R
from a direct-mail shop to a full-service, media-oriented ad agency.
Dodge became a major growth client in 1934 when Ruthrauff
himself wrote the first ads. One headline—"Powders her nose in
the sand"—set the style for the rough-and-ready Dodge ads to
come. In 1936 R&R put Dodge on the radio sponsoring *Major
Bowes Original Amateur Hour* every Sunday morning and *The
Harry Richman Dodge Program*, a weekly variety show.

Among the most unusual episodes in R&R's history was its 17-
year relationship with American Air Lines. On 1 April 1938, P.P.
("Pete") Willis joined R&R. Willis had recently liquidated his
own Chicago agency, P.P. Willis, Inc., which had served the American account (then called American Airways) from 1930 until it
was sold in 1937. After the sale, Blackett-Sample-Hummert took
over the business until it was suggested at American that Willis

continue handling the work. Rather than form a new agency, Willis chose to bring the business to R&R, which was so eager for the account it agreed to pay him $1,000 a month and a substantial percentage of its American commissions "for life" or until the account moved elsewhere. It was an extraordinary contract, under which Willis became an agency unto himself within R&R. In 1946 Willis left the agency to join American and signed a paper terminating the contract. A year later he was fired by American and returned to R&R to work on other business until 1952. Then in November 1954, shortly before American moved its account from R&R to Lennen & Newell, Willis suddenly claimed he had never terminated his R&R contract and sued the agency for commissions since 1946. In a legal battle widely covered in the business press, R&R was at first held liable for $1 million in back payments. But the decision was reversed in 1956 by Chicago Judge Abraham Lincoln Marovitz.

The hard-selling R&R style was very much to the liking of George Washington Hill of the American Tobacco Company, whose subsidiary, American Cigarette & Cigar, marketed the Pall Mall brand. In 1940 Hill had Pall Mall moved from Compton Advertising to R&R, and when Lucky Strike took over sponsorship of the *Jack Benny Show* from General Foods in the fall of 1944, all production duties for the Benny show were assigned to R&R, even though the brand's principal agency was Foote, Cone & Belding (FCB). But soon two key events changed everything. One was beyond R&R's control: the sudden death of Hill in September 1946. Following a power struggle within American Tobacco, Vincent Riggio became president, and he shifted R&R's Lucky Strike and Pall Mall billings to FCB.

But the other event was of R&R's own making. The agency had become very much a family business by the end of World War II. Fritz Ryan's son Barry was now president. And Bourne Ruthrauff and Quincy Ryan were senior vice presidents. Under family leadership it had become by 1945 the sixth-largest American agency behind J. Walter Thompson Company (JWT), Young & Rubicam, N.W. Ayer & Son, McCann-Erickson, and Batten Barton Durstine & Osborn. Although in 1943 the company's closely held stock was distributed initially among 16 senior R&R executives at $5 a share, the installation of a second generation of Ruthrauffs and Ryans in controlling positions angered several nonfamily stock holders. Feeling double-crossed, Raymond Sullivan left the agency in July 1946, taking with him two key R&R executives, Donald Stauffer and Heagan Bayles. Along with Robert Colwell from JWT, the four men established Sullivan, Stauffer, Colwell & Bayles (SSC&B). It quickly became the first of the "hot" postwar agencies and, using its connections to R&R talent as well as to its clients, began to whittle away at its base. Lever Brothers moved Lifebuoy and Silver Dust from R&R to SSC&B, which saw its billings double to $10 million by the end of 1948. Noxzema followed the same year. SSC&B even picked up Pall Mall, reportedly on the basis of relationships at American Tobacco that Stauffer had built while handling the *Jack Benny Program* at R&R.

R&R still managed to continue its tradition of growth, reaching an estimated record of nearly $50 million at midcentury. In

This 1925 campaign from Ruthrauff & Ryan, Inc., helped sell 2 million copies of Doubleday's *Book of Etiquette.*
Reprinted with cooperation from Bookspan.

February 1952 it celebrated its 40th anniversary in apparent good health by announcing the acquisition of Melamed-Hobbs, a Minneapolis, Minnesota, agency formed in 1931 as the McCord Company, Inc. The purchase brought in additional billings of about $2.1 million. Another agency, Strang & Prosser, was purchased in Seattle. Then a month later R&R began its 12-year slide into extinction.

End of the Line

In March the agency lost its $9 million Dodge account to Grant Advertising after 18 years. The following October, Lever Brothers moved Rinso to Hewitt, Ogilvy, Benson & Mather and Spry to FCB, thus ending a relationship that had made R&R the top Lever agency before the war, outranking even JWT. R&R ended 1952 out of the ranks of the top ten for the first time since agency rankings had been initiated by *Advertising Age* in 1944. The $9 million Motorola account was won in 1952 and lost two years later. In September 1954 R&R thought it had replaced Dodge with Packard. But 13 months later it lost the Packard business to

D'Arcy Advertising. By the end of 1956 R&R had fallen from the industry's sixth-ranked American agency a decade before to the 20th, with $39 million in billings.

In 1957 a new management team headed by Bob Watson and F. Kenneth Beirn took over, ending the Ruthrauff and Ryan dynasties. Surviving founder Fritz Ryan had died two years before in December 1955, just 11 months after his retirement at age 72. His son Barry Ryan moved briefly into the chairmanship and then stepped down for the new management group.

The new bosses turned their attention to locating a merger partner, and they soon found one. On 30 August 1957, R&R joined with Erwin, Wasey & Company, which had been founded in Chicago in 1914 as Wasey & Jefferson. It was the largest agency merger in history to that point. The combined unit was called Erwin, Wasey, Ruthrauff & Ryan (EWR&R) and briefly became the 11th-largest agency in America. There was considerable imbalance in the resources of the two agencies. Erwin, Wasey was more than twice the value of R&R and had a strong international network, which made R&R the weaker of the two partners. Also, all of the R&R founders were deceased, while Louis Wasey was still active and would remain so until his death in 1961. Most important, real authority fell to David Williams from the Erwin, Wasey side, who went on to take full ownership under the banner of the David Williams Company.

EWR&R set no fires. Growth was erratic and failed to keep pace with that of the industry. By 1961 it had fallen to the rank of 20th. Finally in October 1963, in a move that startled the industry, the agency was bought by Interpublic, a holding company created to contain a group of separate agencies while avoiding problems of client conflict. The deal created considerable excitement, though more for its size than for any substantive issues. It was the biggest advertising acquisition in history and made Interpublic the world's largest advertising company.

For R&R, however, it was the end of the line. In December 1964 the names Ruthrauff & Ryan were officially and permanently dropped from the EWR&R agency logo by Interpublic. There was brief talk of reviving the name by starting a separate agency, but nothing came of it. Thus, what had once been among the most powerful names in advertising ceased to exist.

JOHN McDONOUGH

Further Reading

Bart, Peter, "Advertising: Interpublic Creates Anxieties," *New York Times* (9 October 1963)

Bart, Peter, "Advertising: Williams Deal Makes Interpublic No. 1," *New York Times* (18 October 1963)

"Bob Watson Is R&R's New Chairman, as Paul Watson, Barry Ryan Retire," *Advertising Age* (11 March 1957)

"Merger Creates 11th Biggest Agency—EWR&R," *Advertising Age* (2 September 1957)

Redden, Ellis L., "Motorola Ad Chief Strongly Urges Agency Speculative Presentations," *Advertising Age* (26 May 1952)

"Ruthrauff & Ryan, Now 40 Years Old, Has Had Billings Gain Every Year," *Advertising Age* (2 February 1952)

S

Saatchi, Charles (1943–) and Maurice (1946–)

British Advertising Executives

Born in 1946 in Baghdad, Iraq, and raised in London, England, Maurice Nathan Saatchi spent the 1980s taking the advertising world by storm. In September 1970, at age 24, he began what was to become one of the most notorious advertising careers of the late 20th century. His older brother, Charles Nathan, born in 1943, also in Baghdad, led Maurice into the business. (Two other brothers, David and Philip, were not involved in advertising.) Charles had started out in advertising five years earlier, first as a copywriter with the London office of Benton & Bowles and later with Collett Dickenson Pearce. After gaining experience on such notable accounts as Ford Motor Company and Selfridges department store, Charles joined forces with fellow copywriter Ross Cramer to open their own agency, CramerSaatchi.

While Charles was working his way up in the advertising world, Maurice completed his education at the London School of Economics, graduating with first-class honors. From there he went to work for Haymarket Publications, publisher of *Campaign* magazine, Britain's leading advertising trade publication. Maurice proved to be a shrewd negotiator and businessman. When hired at Haymarket, he asked about the starting salary, an uncommon question in that day. When told he would receive the standard £1,000 a year, he declined, explaining he required £2,000 to cover his expenses. He was then hired at twice the normal salary. While at Haymarket, Maurice closely observed the business practices of executive Michael Heseltine, who strived to acquire at least two new magazines each year. Maurice would later show a similar determination for acquiring advertising agencies.

A New Type of Agency

Charles and Maurice joined forces and, on 14 September 1970, opened the doors to Saatchi & Saatchi Advertising. The brothers envisioned a new type of advertising agency. As explained in a teaser ad in London's *Sunday Times*, Saatchi & Saatchi eliminated the account executive in favor of a "coordinator who is not briefed by the client, does not brief the creative people, does not pass judgment on ads, and does not present ads to the clients, but works with the creators as a day-to-day administrator."

Many have speculated as to who represented the power source driving Saatchi & Saatchi. Charles, a brilliant copywriter, shied away from publicity. Maurice, on the other hand, was outgoing and gregarious. He became recognizable by his trademark black suede shoes, Commes des Garçons suits, and owlish glasses. Though he did not hold an official title in the company, Maurice acted as the director, soliciting new business. At a time when advertising agencies generally did not pursue the clients of rival shops, Maurice aggressively targeted new accounts. Kevin Goldman, in *Conflicting Accounts* (1997), wrote:

> His pitch would go along these lines: "Hello, my name is Maurice Saatchi and we have a new advertising agency. Although you are probably very happy with your present advertising agency, I think we have found a way for you to make more money and sell more products."

He then would invite the executive he was targeting to visit Saatchi & Saatchi's office to hear more details.

Saatchi & Saatchi quickly developed a reputation for outstanding and outlandish creative work. Meanwhile, the brothers became known for their outrageous behavior. One story described how Charles reportedly attacked Maurice with a chair. The publicity generated by the agency's advertising and the antics of its creators helped Saatchi & Saatchi accrue billings and earn profits almost immediately.

Party Politics

One of the most important accounts developed by Maurice was that of Conservative Party candidate for prime minister, Margaret Thatcher. In 1978 the Conservative Party, facing strong

Maurice Saatchi.
Courtesy of Lord Saatchi.

Taking on the World

Having conquered the United Kingdom, Maurice turned his sights on the world, particularly on Ted Bates Worldwide. In May 1986 Saatchi acquired the Bates agency for $450 million, making Saatchi & Saatchi the largest advertising holding company in the world. Unfortunately, Maurice's long string of costly acquisitions and lack of attention to daily operations had left the company in financial trouble. Although Charles withdrew from active involvement in the business (he was dropped from the board in 1993 but retained as honorary president at more than $1 million a year), Maurice developed a reputation as a man-about-town, wining and dining clients and spending extravagantly.

In 1990 American fund manager David Herro began investing in the agency. As the company continued to struggle, Herro identified Maurice as the problem, and by the mid-1990s he undertook a plan to have shareholders oust the agency's cofounder. Following an eight-and-one-half hour board meeting on 14 December 1994, Maurice was dismissed from the company he helped build. His brother and several top executives soon followed.

Maurice immediately sprang into action, starting a new agency, originally dubbed the New Saatchi Agency, and began attracting some of his former company's top clients, particularly British Airways (BA). His goal was to ruin the agency he had built. To pitch BA, Maurice created the perfect facade: he rented office space in London's Soho area, hired receptionists, decorated offices with fine furniture and flowers, and covered the walls with fine art from his brother's storied collection. A sign above the entrance buzzer to this location read, "Dress Rehearsal, Ltd." To prepare, he personally toured BA headquarters and interviewed managers. Maurice then produced videos of Andrew Lloyd Webber saying he would write the music for the airline's campaign and of media mogul Rupert Murdoch outlining the discounts Saatchi could get for BA in his media properties. The show sold; British Airways moved its business to the renamed M&C Saatchi. The agency went on to gain accounts such as Mars, Inc., and Pedigree Foods. It was named *Campaign*'s 1999 "Agency of the Year."

In 1996 Prime Minister John Major awarded Maurice the title Lord Saatchi. By the end of the 20th century, Maurice controlled subsidiaries Megalomedia, a media services company, and eMC-Saatchi, a digital communications company.

While Maurice Saatchi's reputation grew, the influence of his brother Charles diminished to the point where his presence in the agency became little more than ceremonial. As Charles's involvement in advertising lessened, he turned to his longtime interest in art collecting. He had bought his first painting in 1969, a minimalist work by Sol LeWitt. By the mid-1980s he had amassed a collection of 800 works worth about $250 million. His tastes and purchases were carefully watched by the art world. If Saatchi became interested in a new artist, the artist's price on the market soared. By the same token, if he sold off multiple works by the same artist, he could depress an artist's price. He became such a powerful force that some believed he

opposition from the reigning Labour Party, decided to take a new approach to its advertising. Rather than relying on volunteers to develop its advertising message, Communications Director Gordon Reece hired Saatchi & Saatchi to develop an edgy campaign attacking the Labour Party. The agency's first ad carried the headline "Labour isn't working" above a photo of an unemployment line. In 1979 Thatcher won the election. Maurice later commented that it was that success that propelled Saatchi & Saatchi to the status of a truly world-renowned agency. According to Goldman, Maurice said, "The victory in 1979 was the basis of our expansion, particularly in the United States. Mrs. Thatcher was respected in America and she made us." Maurice would maintain ties to the Conservative Party, later adding John Major to the client list of his agency (then known as M&C Saatchi). In this respect, Maurice stands as one of the pioneers in political campaigning in England.

By 1973 Maurice already had turned his focus to conquering other agencies. His goal was to make Saatchi & Saatchi the largest advertising agency in the world. Demonstrating the same straightforward approach he used to woo accounts, Maurice sent letters to other agencies stating, "I am sure this will be the last thing on your minds, but I wondered if you felt it would make sense to dispose of your company." In 1975 the agency took over Garland-Compton, giving Saatchi & Saatchi a listing on the London Stock Exchange and vaulting it to number five in the British advertising market. By the end of the 1970s, Saatchi & Saatchi reached number one in Britain. Maurice's aggressive tactics earned the agency the nickname "Snatch-it & Snatch-it."

used his influence to manipulate the market. In addition to his personal collection, he also purchased works for Saatchi & Saatchi PLC.

When Maurice was fired in 1994, Charles joined his brother in launching the New Saatchi Agency in 1995, but his subsequent involvement was once again limited by his outside interests, which now included, in addition to art collecting, go-cart racing. Though there was little in the advertising business that interested him, he remained a loyal supporter of his brother and said on more than one occasion that his main reason for maintaining a role in advertising was to "see Maurice happy."

ANNE CUNNINGHAM

Biography (Charles)

Born 6 June 1943, Baghdad, Iraq; attended Christ College briefly, 1959; joined Benton & Bowles, London, as a copywriter, 1965; joined Collet Dickenson Pearce, 1966; opened CramerSaatchi, 1970; launched M&C Saatchi, 1995.

Biography (Maurice)

Born 21 June 1946, Baghdad, Iraq; raised in London, England; graduated with first-class honors from London School of Economics, 1967; first job at Haymarket Publications, late 1960s; established Saatchi & Saatchi Advertising with brother Charles, September 1970; dismissed from Saatchi & Saatchi, December 1994; started M&C Saatchi, 1995; awarded title Lord Saatchi, 1996.

Further Reading

Goldman, Kevin, *Conflicting Accounts: The Creation and Crash of the Saatchi & Saatchi Advertising Empire*, New York: Simon and Schuster, 1997

"Hubris Redeemed" <www.forbes.com/forbes/97/0113/5901042a.htm>

Kleinman, Philip, *The Saatchi & Saatchi Story*, London: Weidenfeld and Nicolson, 1987; as *Saatchi & Saatchi: The Inside Story*, Lincolnwood, Illinois: NTC Business Books, 1989

Saatchi & Saatchi Advertising

Established by brothers Charles and Maurice Saatchi in London, England, 1970, when partnership of Charles Saatchi and Ross Cramer (CramerSaatchi) dissolved; name changed to Cordiant Communications to disassociate the agency from its founders after resignation of the Saatchis, who left to form their own agency, M&C Saatchi, 1995; Cordiant divided into 2 entities—Saatchi & Saatchi and Cordiant Communications Group, 1997; Saatchi & Saatchi purchased by Publicis Group, 2000.

Major Clients

British Airways
Conservative Party (Margaret Thatcher campaign)
Procter & Gamble Company
Toyota

In 1970 Saatchi & Saatchi Advertising—the agency whose motto was "Nothing is impossible"—launched an aggressive ad campaign to create brand awareness for itself. It also challenged the traditional 15 percent agency commission, increasing it to 22 percent and promising clients that it would get them the cheapest media rates. Charles Saatchi was convinced that promoting his ad agency would set it apart from the rest. He believed that since advertising agencies were supposed to be experts in promoting their clients, there was no reason they could not use these same strategies to promote themselves. Saatchi & Saatchi was profitable from the beginning—$231,300 in its second year, which increased to $257,000 in its third.

Expansion

The Saatchi brothers—Charles and Maurice—created a tradition for their new agency: when it saw something (or someone) that it wanted, it went after its goal at any cost. While that aggressive attitude built an international reputation for the agency, foolish acquisitions would later trouble the brothers.

Among these executives they recruited was Tim Bell, who came from the London, England–based agency Geers Gross in September 1970 as media director. Bell, who soon was referred to as "the ampersand in Saatchi & Saatchi," developed a close-knit relationship with the brothers, but it eventually ended in a vicious dispute.

In 1972 the Saatchis decided that they needed an experienced account executive as well. They called on Bill Muirhead, whose résumé included a stint at Ogilvy & Mather, recruiting him from Dorland Advertising only three days after he had joined that agency.

While Charles held sway in the creative department, Maurice handled the client side. The brothers began breaking with standard agency practice when they decided to go directly after other agencies' clients. In 1973 the acquisitions began. The first was not an advertising agency, however, but a property company, Brogan Developers, to house Charles's ever-increasing art collection.

Some purchases were successful; others were not. First there was E.G. Dawes, an agency in Manchester, England. Then the Public Synthese of Belgium and Optadragon of France were acquired. George G. Smith, a small London agency purchased by the brothers, was found to be virtually bankrupt.

These deals marked the beginning of a series of buyouts, takeovers, and mergers. Adhering to the idea that bigger was better, Saatchi & Saatchi continued to take on other companies at an astonishing rate. Meanwhile, it was making a creative name for itself as well. One effort that helped to establish Saatchi & Saatchi's creative reputation was the "Pregnant Man," an ad for the Health Education Council promoting the use of contraceptives. The ad showed a picture of an apparently pregnant man. The copy posed the question, "Would you be more careful if it was you that got pregnant?" It became the most discussed ad in London and was soon featured in *Time* magazine, affording it major U.S. exposure.

In 1975 Maurice Saatchi decided to take on a business manager. He attempted to recruit Ron Rimmer, then manager-director of the Garland-Compton agency, which handled advertising for Procter & Gamble Company (P&G). Maurice's pursuit of Rimmer led to a merger between Garland and Saatchi. After a dispute about the name, they agreed on Saatchi & Saatchi & Garland-Compton, which people shortened to simply Saatchi & Saatchi.

To assist in the numerous mergers and acquisitions, the brothers hired British businessman Martin Sorrell, whose financial skills helped Saatchi & Saatchi's ongoing expansion. And the company was no longer concentrating on advertising agencies. The brothers now bought research companies, management consulting firms, and other marketing services–oriented companies. They wanted their clients to see Saatchi & Saatchi as a full-service agency, one that made it unnecessary to go elsewhere for any type of service.

In 1978 Saatchi & Saatchi put together one of its most noted campaigns: for the Conservative Party endorsing Margaret Thatcher. The ad displayed a seemingly endless line of unemployed workers; the copy read "Labour isn't working" (a reference to the United Kingdom's Labour Party). With the help of this campaign, Thatcher became prime minister. Maurice later credited the campaign and Thatcher's success as a major spark igniting the success of Saatchi & Saatchi.

In March 1982 the agency undertook transatlantic expansion, beginning with the purchase of Compton Advertising, an agency based in New York City. In June 1983 the brothers also bought McCaffrey and McCall, Inc., and in 1984, after buying Yankelovich, Skelly & White/Clancy Shulman, a market research company, they acquired the Hay Group, a management consultancy with offices throughout the world. In 1985 the brothers purchased the Rutland company, a New York City–based public relations firm.

By then Saatchi & Saatchi was so big that the brothers decided to divide it in two. One half served as the communications division, comprising advertising, sales promotion, corporate promotion marketing, and public relations. The other half housed consulting services for management, research, and recruitment.

This split forced the brothers, for the first time, to look beyond their tight circle for someone to run the communications division. That person was Anthony Simonds-Gooding, chief executive at Whitbread Brewery. (Simonds-Gooding's subsequent resignation in 1987, however, proved an embarrassment to Saatchi & Saatchi, as it publicly exposed the company's extreme financial vulnerability.)

The year 1986 proved to be a significant one for Saatchi & Saatchi, which continued its buying binge. In May the third-largest U.S. agency at the time, Ted Bates Worldwide, which also owned Campbell-Mithun, Minneapolis, Minnesota, and the William Esty Company in New York City, was consumed by the brothers. New York City–based Dancer, Fitzgerald, Sample (DFS), Inc., was the next company absorbed by the Saatchis that same year. The famous Wendy's fast-food restaurant campaign "Where's the Beef?" had been DFS's most recent claim to fame. Maurice was impressed not only with the shop's creativity but also with its client roster, which included such names as P&G, Toyota, General Mills, and Nabisco. Backer & Spielvogel also joined the Saatchi & Saatchi empire in 1986.

Financial Problems

In 1987 Saatchi & Saatchi reported growth for the 17th year in a row. The company now set about to buy Midland Bank, an acquisition requiring a bid of $6.4 billion. The bid was rejected, however, and on 19 October 1987, the stock market crashed. Saatchi & Saatchi stock fell by one-third in just one day. Moreover, Simonds-Gooding's precipitous departure in September had left the company with a less-than-adequate replacement: Victor E. Millar.

David Newlands (who had succeeded Sorrell in 1986) began to warn the brothers of troubled waters ahead. It was becoming evident that they were simply going to run out of money. Indiscriminate acquisitions over the years had left the company in a difficult position. Adding to this concern was a trend among marketers toward reduced ad budgets. In 1991 ad spending declined for only the second time in 50 years, and advertisers began cutting agency commissions to 11 percent. Under this lethal combination of circumstances, the Saatchi & Saatchi empire was beginning to crumble.

Sorrell, in his new home at the WPP Group, was employing the same strategies previously used by the Saatchi brothers: buying up every company in sight. Seeing this made Charles nervous. He attempted to merge with WPP—under the Saatchi & Saatchi name—assuring Sorrell he would still run the business. Sorrell refused the offer.

Focused on the goal of making Saatchi & Saatchi the world's leading advertising agency, Maurice refused to believe that the company was in financial trouble and simply announced that its acquisition phase was over. He considered selling off the consultant side of the business while maintaining a minority stake.

In need of help to guide them through their financial peril, in October 1989 the brothers hired Robert Louis-Dreyfus, a businessman, graduate of Harvard Business School, and scion of one of France's richest families. They coaxed him out of retirement to

This 1978 campaign from Saatchi & Saatchi Advertising for the U.K.'s Conservative Party helped elect Margaret Thatcher prime minister. *Copywriter: Andrew Rutherford, Art Director: Martyn Walsh.*

become chief executive of Saatchi & Saatchi Company PLC. Louis-Dreyfus set out to transform the company, a move that ultimately resulted in some of the Saatchi brothers' closest friends losing their jobs. Louis-Dreyfus also focused his energies on the ongoing sale of the consulting businesses.

With Louis-Dreyfus playing a bigger part in the business, tensions increased. Millar resigned in December 1989, after his hopes of running the consulting side of the business were dashed. His break with Maurice and Charles was not amicable.

In 1990 Saatchi & Saatchi caught the attention of the American investor David Herro. He began investing in Saatchi & Saatchi, despite the company's poor financial condition, believing he could turn it around. Herro began regularly attending management meetings, and his involvement deepened when he challenged Maurice, claiming that the latter's actions as chairman had not been in the best interest of the shareholders. Tension between the two grew, and by May 1990 there was a new board at Saatchi & Saatchi that included Charlie Scott, who had been hand picked by Louis-Dreyfus.

Louis-Dreyfus and Scott began the financial restructuring of Saatchi & Saatchi. Then in 1991 Louis-Dreyfus was accused of insider trading by the U.S. Securities and Exchange Commission (SEC). He admitted no wrongdoing but paid a civil penalty and promised to obey SEC rules in the future. There was no trial. After the case was settled, he began to put his energies back into saving Saatchi & Saatchi.

By this time Maurice and Charles were fading further into the background of their own company. They had given up control for the well-being of the company (the relationship of Maurice, in particular, with Louis-Dreyfus had not always been cordial).

When Louis-Dreyfus first began to talk about resigning at the end of 1991, it was decided that Scott would take over his post. Scott agreed, provided that the brothers acknowledge the importance of restoring the company to financial health. The brothers agreed, and Louis-Dreyfus's resignation became official in June 1992.

Dissention and Dissolution

In December 1993 a board meeting took place. Charles was voted out as a board member with a new, albeit empty title of honorary vice president. Both brothers were asked to leave the Berkeley Square offices. They had now completely lost control of the company. Charles resigned in 1994, although he argued that he had been forced out. Maurice would officially resign in January 1995.

Six days after his resignation from the company, Maurice was followed by three of his most loyal comrades: Muirhead, former chief executive officer (CEO) of Saatchi & Saatchi North America; Jeremy Sinclair, former acting chairman of Saatchi & Saatchi PLC; and David Kershaw, former chairman of Saatchi & Saatchi in the United Kingdom. Combined, this group had more than 60 years with Saatchi & Saatchi. Together with Charles, they embarked on a new venture, the New Saatchi Agency, as soon as legal matters could be straightened out. In May 1995 the new company won a crucial battle for the British Airways account. A mutiny began at Saatchi & Saatchi, as more and more employees came over to the new enterprise.

Saatchi & Saatchi launched a barrage of lawsuits against the new agency and many of its top employees, and changed its name to Cordiant in February 1995. In the acrimonious environment, the newly renamed agency was dropped by several major clients almost instantly. The New Saatchi Agency also changed its name, becoming M&C Saatchi.

For a time, it seemed that the Saatchi brothers had gotten the better part of the deal, nabbing for M&C Saatchi such former Saatchi & Saatchi accounts as Qantas Airways and British Airways in 1995.

But in 1997 Cordiant announced it would "demerge," creating Cordiant Communications Group (with Bates Worldwide as its chief agency) and a new iteration of Saatchi & Saatchi. Each retained a 50 percent share of Zenith Media, the earlier shop's media arm, and New Zealand brewing executive Kevin Roberts was named CEO of Saatchi & Saatchi.

Two years later Saatchi & Saatchi suffered a further blow when its hot creative shop, Cliff Freeman & Partners, New York, bought itself back from its parent. In 2000 the Paris, France–based Publicis Group acquired Saatchi & Saatchi for $2 billion, creating the world's fifth-largest advertising company.

The agency has suffered ups and downs since its acquisition. In 2001 the shop closed its San Francisco office, a victim of the demise of the dot-coms. But in April 2002 P&G consolidated its worldwide Pampers disposable diapers account at Saatchi & Saatchi.

For 2000 Saatchi & Saatchi had consolidated network total gross income of $754.9 million on billings of $6.73 billion; its U.S. gross income was $387.1 million on $3.46 billion in billings.

KARA HUNTER

See also Cordiant Communications Group

Further Reading

Fallon, Ivan, *The Brothers: The Rise and Rise of Saatchi & Saatchi*, London: Hutchinson, 1988; as *The Brothers: The Saatchi & Saatchi Story*, Chicago: Contemporary Books, 1989

Fendley, Alison, *Commercial Break: The Inside Story of Saatchi & Saatchi*, London: Hamish Hamilton, 1995; as *Saatchi & Saatchi: The Inside Story*, New York: Arcade, 1996

Fox, Stephen R., *The Mirror Makers: A History of American Advertising and Its Creators*, New York: Morrow, 1984

Goldman, Kevin, *Conflicting Accounts: The Creation and Crash of the Saatchi & Saatchi Advertising Empire*, New York: Simon and Schuster, 1997

Kleinman, Phillip, *The Saatchi & Saatchi Story*, London: Weidenfeld and Nicolson, 1987; as *Saatchi & Saatchi: The Inside Story*, Lincolnwood, Illinois: NTC Business Books, 1989

Millman, Nancy, *Emperors of Adland: Inside the Advertising Revolution*, New York: Warner, 1988

Sivulka, Juliann, *Soap, Sex, and Cigarettes: A Cultural History of American Advertising*, Belmont, California: Wadsworth, 1998

St. Luke's

Founded by the London, England, office of Chiat/Day after the staff learned its parent company was being sold to Omnicom Group, 1995; won Ikea and Clarks accounts, 1997; opened first overseas office in Stockholm, Sweden, 2000

Major Clients

BT (British Telecom)
Central Office of Information (Working Families Tax Credit, New Deal, Electoral Commission)
Clarks
HSBC (Hong Kong Shanghai Banking Corporation)
Ikea

When the London, England, office of Chiat/Day learned its parent company was being sold to advertising giant Omnicom Group in January 1995, Andy Law, then chairman of the agency, led an employee rebellion that was to create a unique advertising company. Law, the only Chiat/Day employee in London guaranteed a job in a forced merger with Omnicom's TBWA, had the backing of all 35 employees in the subsequent buyout. To show solidarity with him, employees crossed a "quarantine line" Law had drawn in the office after announcing he was going to quit. The buyout was negotiated on a deferred acquisition payment of up to $3 million based on agency income over the following seven years.

Not only did Law and his fellow workers want to create a new company, they also wanted to create new ways of doing business and treating employees. Crucial to that goal were the ideas of making all employees co-owners and giving clients a new way of approaching advertising decisions. In short, St. Luke's claimed to have created the world's first cooperative stake-holding advertising agency.

The original 37 employees—from receptionist to account director—each paid approximately $75 for the right to receive an equal share in the new agency. The remaining 75 percent of the share capital was set aside for yearly distribution to existing and future employees; at the beginning of the 21st century, all 135 employees continued to receive an equal yearly share payout.

Employee ownership, greater participation in decision-making, and cooperative working arrangements may all be reasons why the company claimed a low staff turnover.

Another radical approach—born of Chiat/Day's revolutionary open-plan-office approach to business—manifested itself in the workplace. St. Luke's staff created an office space radically different from those of their industry peers. The company pioneered a hot-desk approach to office work, complete with in-house mobile phones, a communal "hub," a café rather than a dining area, and "chill out" rooms.

Similarly, St. Luke's clients are also treated to a radically different approach to client service. Law and his team were bringing the entire client list (including HSBC and Boots) with them, but he wanted the company to offer them even better service. The company designed its four-story headquarters building, located near London's Kings Cross railway station, to facilitate collaboration with clients and allow interaction with them in a brand-driven environment; thus, St. Luke's clients did not find themselves attending agency meetings in pedestrian boardrooms. Rather, they arrived and found themselves sitting down in their own "Brand Rooms." These rooms—up to ten of them—are designed around a theme that uses elements of a client's individual brand and its associated lifestyle. For instance, the Ikea room is fitted out as a living room using Ikea furniture products, while the room for Clarks is fitted out as a miniature shoe shop complete with foot measurement boards. When St. Luke's held the EuroStar Channel tunnel train service account, it fitted out the dedicated campaign room with the client's train seats and etched-glass sliding doors normally found between the train cars.

At the start of 2000, St. Luke's acquired the building next door to its headquarters, doubling its available space and allowing greater innovation in the working environment. The company, which has been variously tagged with labels such as "flaky" and "weird," soon added to its Chiat/Day client list with some significant wins, including the IKEA and Clarks accounts. The British advertising magazine *Campaign* named St. Luke's "Advertising Agency of the Year" for 1997.

In 1998 St. Luke's continued its growth by winning the British government's Central Office of Information Welfare to Work, or New Deal, campaign. The $27 million campaign aimed to remove 250,000 unemployed youngsters from welfare rolls and get them into jobs. The agency's interest in reality-based advertising is best seen in the New Deal campaign, which features senior executives of companies that have set up jobs for the program.

The ethically focused, emotion-led approach to the advertising business, combined with a propensity for reality advertising, has also cost the company. St. Luke's claims to have walked away from a potential tobacco company account and from a Monsanto Company pitch. The potential client shied away from the agency's pitch, which reportedly sought to encompass an honest, all-inclusive look at genetically modified food issues. Nor has it endeared itself to others in the advertising industry with its decision not to enter campaigns for awards.

St. Luke's has prided itself on its fundamental turnaround approach since the split with Chiat/Day and its policy of open sharing of ideas by the project team. In the past the agency's forte was in work with clients committed to national TV advertising as part of the campaign; however, a recent diversification strategy has led to a variety of alternative activities, such as consulting projects for BSkyB (the satellite channel owned by Rupert Murdoch), BP (the petroleum company), and the Body Shop; the development of a short film program involving a tie-in with Britshorts (an on-line venue for short film development for aspiring film directors); and innovative equity-share deals with successful on-line companies such as Smartgroups (a portal community Web site).

During a sabbatical from the company in 1998, Law penned the book *Open Minds: 21st-Century Business Lessons and Innovations from St. Luke's*. He said he wanted to create a business reference book to instill St. Luke's corporate ethos in students of advertising and marketing and to translate that experience into the business world.

By 1998 the company was pitching only accounts spending at least $7.5 million. However, according to the company, financial focus is only one of four corporate aspirations that also include campaign creativity, client business, and staff welfare.

The approach appears to have paid off. In 1996 profits before tax were $430,500; a year later profits were $1.74 million, and by 1999 the agency reported gross profits of $3.64 million on billings of almost $120 million. In the first three years, share values increased from 1.5 cents at launch to $1.80 in 1998. At the end of 2000 the shares were trading at around $2.65.

The company also made its first overseas expansion in October 2000 when it opened an office in Stockholm, Sweden. Tim Hearn, who had been one of the agency's creative directors in London, led the office; by 2001 it had won three accounts, including Telia (a telecommunications company that is part of Ericsson, Inc.).

Universal share ownership remained a lynchpin of the company's success, even if it did carry, at times, certain administrative burdens. Everyone has a say in the future direction of the company, with strategic decisions being made on 18 October (St. Luke's Day).

SEAN KELLY

Further Reading

Alburty, Steve, "The Ad Agency to End All Ad Agencies," *Fast Company Magazine* 1 (December 1996)

Dearlove, Des, "From Fantasy to Reality—The Changing Business," *The Times* (26 March 1998)

Law, Andy, *Open Minds: 21st-Century Business Lessons and Innovations from St. Luke's*, London: Orion Business, 1998

Leadbeater, Charles, *Living on Thin Air: The New Economy*, London and New York: Viking, 1999

Lewin, Roger, and Birute Regine, *The Soul at Work: Listen, Respond, Let Go: Embracing Complexity Science for Business Success*, New York: Simon and Schuster, 2000

Sal Hepatica. *See* Ipana Toothpaste/Sal Hepatica

Sara Lee Corporation

Principal Agencies

Ivan Hill, Inc.

Cunningham & Walsh, Inc.

Hill, Rogers, Mason & Scott

Foote, Cone & Belding (later FCB Worldwide)

Edward H. Weiss & Company

Doyle Dane Bernbach

Benton and Bowles, Inc.

Lintas: USA (later Ammirati Puris Lintas)

Sara Lee went from humble beginnings delivering fresh cakes in Chicago, Illinois, neighborhoods to become a market-dominating national distributor of frozen desserts. The Kitchens of Sara Lee, as the company was called in 1949, turned out products that became associated with quality. Throughout its history the brand has struggled not with guaranteeing consumers' satisfaction but rather with persuading them to treat themselves more often.

In 1935 Charles Lubin and his brother-in-law bought a small chain of neighborhood bakeries in Chicago called Community Bake Shops. Lubin had been a baker's apprentice since age 14 and worked as a baker at several retailers until he became co-proprietor at age 32. Over the next 14 years he expanded his business while ruminating on the idea of mass marketing a fresh cheesecake or coffee cake to food stores over a large area. In 1949, eager to expand the business, he parted ways with his brother-in-law and named his first product, a cream cheesecake, after his 8-year-old daughter, Sara Lee. Lubin decided to change the name of the business as well, and the Kitchens of Sara Lee began distributing cheesecakes to area restaurants with one delivery truck.

Advertising began in 1951 and was initially handled by Dancer, Fitzgerald, Sample, Inc. That relationship lasted just a few months before the account was transferred to Ivan Hill, Inc., thus beginning a 12-year relationship between Lubin and Ivan Hill. Lubin introduced two products in 1951 that would soon become synonymous with the name Sara Lee: All Butter Pound Cake and All Butter Pecan Coffee Cake. Sales that year reached $400,000, and Lubin put a quarter of that sum into advertising.

In 1952 a buyer from Texas was impressed enough with Sara Lee's cakes to request a shipment be delivered to him in Dallas. This initiated Lubin's interest in perfecting the process of freezing the fresh cakes, thereby freeing him of the inherent geographic restrictions of the bakery market. Working with Ecko Products Company, Sara Lee developed aluminum pans in which the cakes could be baked, frozen, and then shipped. This type of packaging was a first in the food industry. In addition to cakes, entire meals could now be frozen and shipped in a single container, an innovation that soon yielded the TV dinner, introduced by Swanson in 1954.

In 1954 ad spending reached about $250,000, and Sara Lee estimated that it spent three times as much promoting its cakes as its nearest competitor in the Chicago area. Lubin also showed a penchant for the spectacular, setting up a mammoth billboard on Chicago's Michigan Avenue that featured a three-dimensional slice of coffee cake, measuring 27 feet by 14 feet. He also sent 100 frozen cakes to the U.S. Senate during a filibuster. (Publicity stunts in later years included a four-story birthday cake for the bicentennial celebration of the United States in 1976 and a large cake in the form of a book for the Chicago Public Library's 100th anniversary in 1972.) In 1956 Ivan Hill, Inc., became the Chicago office of Cunningham & Walsh Inc. (C&W), which continued to handle the Sara Lee business.

Sara Lee's marketing strategy focused on taste and the quality of its ingredients. In 1955 the company's cakes sold for 79 cents, about twice the price of rival products. Advertising touted the number of pecans on top of a Sara Lee coffee cake or the fact that Sara Lee used only butter as a shortening (a quarter pound in each coffee cake). The company's marketing executives believed that competitors offering an inferior product at a lower price were performing a valuable function—expanding the market for frozen desserts—and that Sara Lee would benefit in the end as consumers gravitated toward the high quality of its products.

Butter, in particular, became an integral part of Sara Lee's image. In 1961 an intensive ad campaign was structured around the tag line, "Sara Lee cakes—they're all better because they're all butter." Sara Lee's use of butter merited a publicity visit from the American Dairy Princess of 1961. This wholesome quality had its appeal in the 1950s and 1960s but became detrimental in the 1980s when consumers began to seek out lighter, low-fat products. Sara Lee's marketing was then undermined by the rich, heavy image of the product that lingered in the minds of its customers, many of whom recalled the baked goods of their childhood in the 1950s and 1960s.

By 1955 Sara Lee had extended its distribution from coast to coast, entering the San Francisco, California, and New York City markets. Consolidated Foods Corporation purchased the Kitchens of Sara Lee in August 1956 for $2.7 million. Sara Lee spent $850,000 on advertising in 1956.

In July 1961 Ivan Hill and three other partners purchased the Chicago office of C&W and opened as Hill, Rogers, Mason & Scott, keeping the $2 million Sara Lee account, which constituted about half of its $5 million business. One of the agency's new tasks in June 1962 was to inform the Chicago area that fresh cakes would no longer be available; Chicago had been the only area in which fresh Sara Lee cakes could still be purchased.

In 1963 Sara Lee's marketing team decided to end the company's relationship with Hill. In June of that year, following a review, it awarded Foote, Cone & Belding (FCB) the account, then valued at $2.5 million. Also added to the agency roster was North Advertising, which would handle frozen dinners, new products, and test market efforts. The company had already broken ground on a state-of-the-art manufacturing plant in Deerfield, Illinois, that would allow production to increase sharply, thus warranting a bigger agency. The plant opened in 1964 and was named one of the top-ten new manufacturing plants in the United States by *Factory* magazine in May 1965. Lubin retired in 1965.

A line of frozen prepared dinners, starting with Chicken Sara Lee in 1959, was assigned to Edward H. Weiss & Company in April 1966, replacing North Advertising. FCB continued to handle the rest of Sara Lee's products, but only until October 1967, when the $3 million account was awarded to Doyle Dane Bernbach (DDB) because, as one company marketing executive said, Sara Lee wanted the "maximum of creative excitement in our advertising."

DDB did provide Sara Lee with its most memorable tag line and jingle. In 1968 "Everybody doesn't like something, but nobody doesn't like Sara Lee" began appearing in print ads and in television and radio spots, as well as on Sara Lee delivery trucks. The simple but grammatically skewed line accompanied advertising that positioned the product as an everyday treat that could help consumers get through their day. The line spoke a degree of truth as well: A 1971 study showed that 90 percent of the people interviewed recognized the Sara Lee name and accepted its image of high quality, but fewer than 25 percent of all consumers were actually buying Sara Lee products. Everyone liked Sara Lee—but apparently not everyone bought Sara Lee. That year the company claimed responsibility for 80 percent of all the frozen baked goods advertising that the public saw, and its share of the frozen baked goods market ran between 70 percent and 80 percent.

Despite the memorable campaign, the Kitchens of Sara Lee decided to move the account to Tatham, Laird & Kudner (TLK) in October 1972. The theme in the following years focused on the ingredients, which were described as "fresh" and "honest." One tag line read, "Why serve anything but the honest best?"

In June 1973 TLK lost the bakery goods account to Benton & Bowles, Inc., but retained the frozen entrée line. A conflict had been cited because Tatham was also the agency for Libby, McNeil & Libby, a company related to Stouffer Foods, a Sara Lee rival. Tatham lost the frozen entrée business in 1975 when Sara Lee pulled the line off the market.

In a move prescient of changing consumer attitudes, Sara Lee introduced Light 'n Luscious frozen cakes in 1977. The product

This 1969 advertisement was created a year after Sara Lee Corporation debuted its "Nobody doesn't like Sara Lee" slogan.
Images provided by Sara Lee Bakery.

claimed to have one-third fewer calories and no artificial sweeteners. Sara Lee spent $4.8 million in measured media in 1978.

Ad spending waned in the late 1970s and dropped precipitously in 1980 to $900,000, as FCB regained the Sara Lee account that year. The frozen baked goods market underwent considerable erosion in the early 1980s owing to competition from fresh baked goods such as Warner-Lambert's Entenmann's products. Sara Lee advertising rose once more to $5 million, and it used testimony from consumers who said they preferred a Sara Lee cake to one in a "generic" package, easily identified as Entenmann's.

Consolidated Foods Corporation decided to change its name in 1985. The holding company owned business concerns in a variety of food and clothing industries but wanted a name that had more consumer recognition. In a testament to the brand recognition and quality associated with the Kitchens of Sara Lee, Consolidated Foods chose to rename itself the Sara Lee Corporation in April 1985.

FCB, believing it was on course for a conflict of interest between Sara Lee and its larger Kraft account, resigned the $5.6 million account in 1986. Chiat/Day picked up the Sara Lee business, which increased that year to $9.4 million, in part to back the

In 1977, in response to consumer demand for lighter desserts, Sara Lee introduced its Light 'n Luscious line of reduced-calorie, cholesterol-free cakes.
Images provided by Sara Lee Bakery.

introduction of Bagel Time frozen bagels. One of Chiat/Day's first assignments was to update the old "Nobody doesn't like Sara Lee" theme. It chose jazz artists Manhattan Transfer and Al Jarreau to contemporize the theme.

Founder Lubin died in July 1988 at the age of 84. His daughter, Sara Lee Schupf, was featured in advertising in late 1989. As part of an overall consolidation of agencies within the Sara Lee Corporation, Lintas: USA took over the advertising for the Sara Lee bakery lines in 1990.

The early 1990s saw consumers swept up in a frenzy for fat-free foods. Increasingly, Sara Lee's products were becoming single-serving desserts, with lower fat and sugar content than their predecessors. The Kellogg Company's Mrs. Smith's Frozen Foods Company surpassed Sara Lee for leadership in the segment (gaining a 15.9 percent share to Sara Lee's 15.7 percent share) in the $1.1 billion frozen baked goods market for the year ended 14 March 1992.

Ammirati Puris Lintas resigned the Sarah Lee bakery account in October 1996. The account landed back at FCB (which had in the meantime become FCB Worldwide). In 1998 Sarah Lee unleashed its first umbrella ad campaign in almost a decade with the theme, "Add some delicious to your life." Sara Lee had slipped to the number-three position in the $380 million frozen desserts market, behind Pillsbury Company and Pepperidge Farm. In 1999 Sara Lee's media ad spending through FCB Worldwide was estimated at $16 million.

The "Nobody doesn't like Sara Lee" tag line was dusted off once again in 2000, supporting the introduction of Calzone Creations frozen entrées and Sara Lee Cake Bites. Although no longer preeminent, the brand continued to retain its image of quality and well-deserved self-indulgence.

MARK SCHUMANN

Further Reading

Levenson, Bob, *Bill Bernbach's Book: A History of the Advertising That Changed the History of Advertising*, New York: Villard Books, 1987

Sarnoff, David 1891–1971

U.S. Media Executive

David Sarnoff, during four decades as a top executive of the Radio Corporation of America (RCA), helped shape two mass media as well as the future of communications. He was one of the early giants of radio and television. A man of contradictions, Sarnoff promoted radio and television as mass entertainment media for the public, though his primary interest was not programming. He would boast of his rank as an army general, though he repeatedly fought with government officials.

Sarnoff made his mark in radio and television not as an engineer or showman but as an industrialist. He saw innovations in programming and operations as a means to an end: sales of RCA radio and TV sets. Nonetheless, Sarnoff was a visionary. He conceived the idea of creating national broadcasts by linking many stations into a network; he played an integral role in creating the first radio network, NBC, in 1926, and the first TV network, again NBC, in 1940.

Other Sarnoff interests in the 1950s and 1960s included satellites, rocketry, and computers. Early on, he envisioned technology that today is omnipresent. Sarnoff said in an address in 1965, "The time will also come when an individual carrying a vest-pocket transmitter-receiver will connect by radio to a nearby switchboard linked to communications satellites and be able to see and speak with any similarly equipped individual anywhere in the world." In his acceptance speech after receiving an Advertis-

ing Council public service award in 1965, Sarnoff spoke of "the coming revolution in communications," saying:

> Today's console and table model furniture may be displaced by an all-purpose television screen mounted on the wall. It would be coupled to a sound system and a high-speed electronic printer for recording any information the viewer wishes to retain. This means that the major channel of news, information, and entertainment in the home will be a single integrated system that combines all of the separate electronic instruments and printed means of communication today—television set, radio, newspaper, magazine, and book.

Sarnoff's first experience with the mass media was through newspapers and wireless telegraphs. He was born 27 February 1891 in Russia and emigrated with his family to the United States in 1900. At age nine, he supported his family by selling Yiddish-language newspapers in New York City. As a teenager, Sarnoff was hired as an office boy at American Marconi Company, which had been established in 1899 to exploit the wireless patents of inventor Guglielmo Marconi. Sarnoff went on to become a wireless telegraph operator there, leading to one of his claims to fame: on the evening of 14 April 1912, the young Sarnoff heard faint

David Sarnoff.
David Sarnoff Library, Princeton, New Jersey.

wireless reports of the sinking of the *Titanic*. He was one of a number of wireless operators who reported details of the tragedy to the newspapers, and Sarnoff would later claim that he was the only operator permitted to remain on the air after U.S. President William Howard Taft ordered others to remain silent (in order to quell conflicting reports sent on overlapping signals).

As early as 1915, he proposed to Marconi the idea for a household fixture called a "radio music box"—at a time when radio was still called "the wireless" and its use was primarily limited to shipping news and the amusement of amateur wireless enthusiasts. The idea was rejected.

RCA was formed after the General Electric Company (GE) absorbed the U.S. assets of Marconi in 1919. Sarnoff was appointed general manager in 1921. On 3 January 1930, the 39-year-old Sarnoff became president of RCA. In 1932 the U.S. Justice Department forced RCA's divestiture from GE on monopoly and restraint of trade grounds.

RCA began manufacturing radios for the home in the 1920s. In 1926 RCA formed the National Broadcasting Company—NBC—as a means to sell radio sets. NBC itself consisted of two networks—the Red and the Blue—each fed from its own New York City flagship station, WJZ and WEAW, respectively, which RCA acquired when it bought the broadcasting assets of AT&T. The two networks launched in simulcast on 15 November 1926.

Although programming was not Sarnoff's primary focus, he had even less interest in advertising. When he first broached the idea of a radio network in 1922, he saw it as a "nonprofit" public service; he found the idea of ad-funded radio to be outrageous and believed that manufacturers of radio sets should own and operate stations. Profits from selling sets, and not advertising, would pay for programming. However, the costs proved too high, and, surprisingly, listeners were receptive to advertising, especially if it saved them from having to pay for broadcast ser-

vices. By the time NBC was launched, it was ready to sell airtime to advertisers.

Even as Sarnoff was building a radio empire, he was looking ahead to the potential of television, and as the 1930s arrived, RCA moved ahead with the development of an electronic TV set. In Great Britain, the London Television Service started up in November 1936 and was a huge success. In the United States, Sarnoff kicked off RCA's TV broadcasting efforts with a flourish on 30 April 1939 by televising the opening of the New York World's Fair. That year NBC began regular service, broadcasting from the top of the Empire State Building.

But there were serious problems facing the fledgling medium. For one, NBC's quality was not on a par with that of the British service. Also, for a nation still struggling to get out of the Depression, the cost of a TV set—as much as $600—was prohibitive. In addition, Sarnoff's radio archrival, William S. Paley, chief of the Columbia Broadcasting System—CBS—had no interest in advancing the new medium since his network did not manufacture television hardware, and TV was seen as a potential threat to radio. Finally, there were no TV broadcast standards; they would not be set by the Federal Communications Commission (FCC) until 1941.

The advent of World War II brought the development of television to a halt. The London Television Service was shuttered, and Sarnoff turned the resources of his company to such wartime areas as radar and sonar. The RCA chief became a communications consultant to General Dwight D. Eisenhower. Sarnoff left the service in 1944 with the rank of brigadier general in the Army Reserve Corps. "The General" would brandish that title with pride for the rest of his years at RCA.

Sarnoff, who was appointed chairman of RCA in 1947, faced the postwar years with a new competitor. Citing antitrust concerns, the FCC in 1941 ordered NBC to divest itself of one of its networks. NBC contested the decision all the way to the U.S. Supreme Court and lost, and in 1943 sold for $8 million the less popular Blue Network to Edward J. Noble, manufacturer of Life Savers candy; the network would become the American Broadcasting Company (ABC).

After the war, with peacetime and prosperity sweeping the land, television boomed. RCA introduced black-and-white, or monochrome, TV on a large scale. But Sarnoff saw monochrome as a transitional phase to color, and this notion set the stage for a great battle between Sarnoff and Paley.

In 1940 CBS Laboratories developed a "mechanical," as opposed to electronic, TV system that achieved excellent color images. CBS applied to the FCC for acceptance of its color system. However, CBS's technology would render all existing electronic, monochrome sets obsolete since they would not be able to receive the color images. Sarnoff urged a hesitant FCC to hold off for six months, by which time RCA would have an electronic color system that could be received by both color and black-and-white sets. But the FCC went ahead and adopted CBS's system in September 1950. In the ensuing struggle, Sarnoff again would fight all the way to the Supreme Court.

War also interfered again that year, with the Korean conflict hurting the introduction of CBS's sets. In 1953 CBS abandoned its color efforts as "economically foolish" in light of 25 million incompatible black-and-white sets in use at the time. On 17 December 1953, the FCC adopted standards along the line of those proposed by RCA. These standards for electronic TV, rather than competing technologies, became the basis for every new color TV system adopted throughout the world. In 1955 Jules Herbuveaux, manager of NBC's Chicago station, WNBQ, persuaded Sarnoff to convert the facility to full color broadcasting as a means to promote the sale of color sets. On 15 April 1956 WNBQ (later WMAQ) became the world's first all-color TV station, and Herbuveaux and retailer Sol Polk dramatically increased the number of color sets in operation in Chicago. It was a business model Sarnoff would slowly expand nationwide.

Sarnoff was more supportive of advertising for television than he had initially been for radio. He opposed the concept of fee TV supported by the movie studios. "Pay television violates the American concept of freedom to listen and freedom to look," he said in 1956.

Although not a showman at heart, Sarnoff realized the value of content to promote television. NBC was allowed to pour big sums into star-studded programs that produced a growing market for TV sets. For example, Sarnoff showcased the capabilities of his color TV sets by luring Walt Disney away from ABC for what would become the long-running NBC Sunday evening series *Walt Disney's Wonderful World of Color*.

Sarnoff had built a multibillion-dollar corporation by the time the ailing media mogul retired from RCA in 1970. Sarnoff was succeeded as RCA chairman by his son, Robert. But in following years, RCA suffered from the onslaught of Japanese competition in the manufacturing of TV sets and overdiversification into such far-flung areas as rental cars, greeting cards, and food.

David Sarnoff died in his sleep on 12 December 1971 at the age of 80. Four years later, his son was ousted from RCA by the board. In 1986, in a corporate example of going full circle, a struggling RCA was acquired by General Electric.

DAN LIPPE

Biography

Born in Russia, 27 February 1891; emigrated to the United States, 1900; named general manager, RCA, 1921; helped create the first radio network, NBC, 1926; named president of RCA, 1930; helped launch the first U.S. TV network, NBC, 1940; pushed for new color TV standards that were accepted by the Federal Communications Commission, 1953; retired as chairman of RCA, 1970. Died on 12 December 1971 at age 80.

Further Reading

Auletta, Ken, *Three Blind Mice: How the TV Networks Lost Their Way*, New York: Random House, 1991

"David Sarnoff Gets Ad Council's '65 Award; Predicts Single Medium for Broadcast, Print," *Advertising Age* (20 December 1965)

"David Sarnoff, Radio-TV Pioneer, Is Dead at 80," *Advertising Age* (20 December 1971)

Fox, Stephen R., *The Mirror Makers: A History of American Advertising and Its Creators*, New York: Morrow, 1984

Greenfield, Jeff, *Television: The First Fifty Years*, New York: Abrams, 1977

Mayer, Martin, *Whatever Happened to Madison Avenue? Advertising in the '90s*, Boston: Little Brown, 1991

"RCA Never Tried to Buy Pay TV: Sarnoff," *Advertising Age* (13 June 1955)

"Robert Sarnoff Adds Chairman Title at RCA," *Advertising Age* (12 January 1970)

Smith, Anthony, editor, *Television: An International History*, Oxford and New York: Oxford University Press, 1998

"Tint TV Sales to Zoom, RCA Reports; '64 Sales, Net Rise," *Advertising Age* (8 March 1965)

Scali, McCabe, Sloves

Founded by Sam Scali, Edward A. McCabe, and Marvin Sloves in New York City, 1967; bought by Ogilvy & Mather, 1976, but remained autonomous; purchased majority interests in Martin Agency (Richmond, Virginia) and Fallon McElligott (Minneapolis, Minnesota), 1986; taken over by Lowe Group, 1993; operated as Lowe & Partners/SMS until 1999, when agency was reorganized and SMS dropped from name.

Major Clients

Hebrew National Kosher Foods, Inc.
Mercedes-Benz of North America
Nikon Corporation
Perdue Foods, Inc.
Volvo of North America Corporation

Scali, McCabe, Sloves (SMS) hit some memorable advertising peaks in its 32-year history, as well as a few incredible valleys. It was named *Advertising Age*'s "Agency of the Year" for 1974 and created two of *Advertising Age*'s choices for the top 100 ad campaigns of the 20th century; however, the agency also produced an allegedly deceptive ad for Volvo and lost six major clients—all within a single year, 1990.

AFTER 500 PLAYS OUR HIGH FIDELITY TAPE STILL DELIVERS HIGH FIDELITY.

If your old favorites don't sound as good as they used to, the problem could be your recording tape.

Some tapes show their age more than others. And when a tape ages prematurely, the music on it does too.

What can happen is, the oxide particles that are bound onto tape loosen and fall off, taking some of your music with them.

At Maxell, we've developed a binding process that helps to prevent this. When oxide particles are bound onto our tape, they stay put. And so does your music.

So even after a Maxell recording is 500 plays old, you'll swear it's not a play over five.

maxell

IT'S WORTH IT.

Maxell Corporation of America, 60 Oxford Drive, Moonachie, N.J. 07074

For more information, see reader service card on page 56A.

This 1981 Scali, McCabe, Sloves campaign featuring the "Chair Man" helped Maxell become a leader in the premium audiotape market. *Courtesy of Maxell Corp. of America.*

Sam Scali, Edward A. McCabe, and Marvin Sloves began their agency in New York City in 1967 doing free work for an antipollution lobby. Scali, vice president-creative director for the shop, had been vice president-senior art director at Papert, Koenig, Lois, Inc., in New York City, where Sloves, president of SMS, had been account supervisor for Xerox Corporation. McCabe, the youngest person to be inducted into the Copywriter's Hall of Fame, was vice president-associate copy director at Carl Ally, Inc., before becoming vice president-copy director at the new agency.

The agency's first paying client was the automaker Volvo, which signed on just two months after SMS opened. Its early work for Volvo, a campaign based on the theme of the cars' durability, was ranked 90th on *Advertising Age*'s list of the top 100 campaigns of the 20th century. The Volvo account was good for business for SMS throughout the 1970s and 1980s, but the relationship ended in 1990 with a scandal that cost the agency the $40 million account and a $150,000 settlement with the U.S. Federal Trade Commission (FTC). The problem arose over an ad that showed a "monster" truck driving over the top of a row of cars; a Volvo station wagon was the only one that survived without a crushed roof. An investigation by the Texas attorney general found the ad had been rigged. The Volvo's roof had been reinforced with lumber and steel, while the support pillars of the other cars had been weakened. In the settlement with the FTC, neither Volvo nor SMS admitted violating the law.

Other outstanding early work by SMS included a campaign for Perdue Foods in which the agency succeeded in the challenging task of creating a brand image for a commodity product—fresh chicken. The 1971 slogan, "It takes a tough man to make a tender chicken," was part of a campaign ranked number 67 on *Advertising Age*'s list of the top 100. The agency also was responsible for the slogan, "We answer to a higher authority," created for Hebrew National's kosher hot dogs. The slogan has been used by the marketer for decades.

Advertising Age also named the shop its "Agency of the Year" for 1974. During a year in which the overall economy suffered, the agency reported a 25 percent gain in billings. Its reputation for success was one element that made it an attractive take-over target to Ogilvy & Mather in 1976. Ogilvy agreed to pay SMS stockholders $10 million—a large sum for an agency with $60 million in billings. Three major clients of each agency represented conflicts, but because the two shops would continue to operate independently, the marketers in question did not oppose the deal. The top executives—Sloves, president-chief executive officer; McCabe, vice president-copy director; Scali, vice president-creative director; and two other partners—received their payments over four years, including incentives for performance.

In 1986 SMS acquired a majority interest in the Minneapolis, Minnesota-based Fallon McElligott, which it held until 1992, later establishing McCabe & Company. Also in 1986, McCabe left the company to take a sabbatical from advertising. That same year SMS managers bought back 20 percent of the agency from Ogilvy with options to buy back another 10 percent in two years.

In 1990, however, the agency's New York City office suffered some major reverses. It had already lost the $25 million Hertz

In this 1984 advertisement for poultry purveyor Perdue, from agency Scali, McCabe, Sloves, company spokesman Frank Perdue made a humorous play on a well-known Wendy's tag line.
Courtesy of Perdue, Quality Poultry since 1920.

Corporation account in 1989; in 1990 it lost a $15 million account from Toys "R" Us, another $15 million account from Lotus Development, and the accounts of Nikon Corporation, Maxell Corporate of America, and Chase Manhattan Bank. Some of the decline in business was attributed to agency management being distracted by negotiations to free SMS from Ogilvy; in the meantime, in 1989 Ogilvy had been acquired by the WPP Group, a London, England-based holding company. SMS management had also been busy with its majority interests in Fallon McElligott and another acquisition, the Martin Agency of Richmond, Virginia. At the same time the SMS officers were preoccupied with establishing offices in Canada, Europe, South America, and Australia.

The agency recorded a major rebound in 1992, when it won the $130 million Mercedes-Benz of North America account; the New York City shop won the $90 million Mercedes national advertising account, while $40 million in dealer cooperative spending went to the Martin Agency. The work from SMS gave Mercedes advertising a warmer focus, showing images of a father giving his daughter a Mercedes on her wedding day; a boy's admiring look at a Mercedes classic gull-wing model; and a mother driving a Mercedes—not to impress her neighbors but to protect her children. The agency also helped devise a three-year lease program to make Mercedes autos affordable to a wider range of consumers. As a result of the campaign, leases increased from 40 percent of sales to 55 percent of sales in a single quarter in 1992.

Late in 1993, after an almost two-year-long effort, the Inter-public Group of Companies' Lowe Group bought SMS from WPP for $55.5 million in cash and liabilities. Under the agreement, SMS was merged into Lowe & Partners to form Lowe & Partners/SMS. Included in the deal were the Martin Agency and SMS operations in New York City; Mexico City, Mexico; Paris, France; Madrid, Spain; and in Canada. The latter units claimed combined billings of $550 million in 1992.

At the end of 1998 Sloves retired from Lowe & Partners/SMS to become a consultant to Lee Garfinkel, chairman-chief creative officer of the agency. Scali retired in 1999, the same year Lowe & Partners merged with Ammirati Puris Lintas, and SMS was dropped from the agency name.

NANCY DIETZ

Further Reading

Donath, Bob, "Creativity Does It: AA Picks Scali, McCabe Agency of the Year," *Advertising Age* (24 February 1975)
Dougherty, Philip H., "Scali Avoids Client Woes in Mergers," *New York Times* (8 July 1988)
Levine, Joshua, "Image Maker, Heal Thyself: Arrogance Goeth before a Fall: How Advertising Agency Scali, McCabe, Sloves Spun out of Control," *Forbes* (27 May 1991)
Levine, Joshua, "Mercedes with a Human Face," *Forbes* (14 September 1992)

Scandinavian Countries. *See* Nordic Countries

Schick

Principal Agencies

Briggs & Varley

Arthur Kudner, Inc.

Benton & Bowles, Inc.

J. Walter Thompson Company

The Schick Shaving Products Group was in 2001 a division of Pfizer, a worldwide marketer of consumer and health care products. As one of Pfizer's biggest consumer products groups, it has marketing representation in Asia, Latin America, Australia, Germany, Japan, the United Kingdom, and North America.

Schick was founded by Jacob Schick, an inventive U.S. Army lieutenant colonel, whose first invention was a dry shaver that could be used without water and lather. In 1921, inspired by the army repeating rifle, Schick invented the Magazine Repeating Razor. This razor had replacement blades stored in a clip in the handle and was the forerunner to the famous Schick Injector

Razor, still made in the 21st century. In 1928, convinced that the "wet shave" method would be doomed by the electric razor, Jacob Schick started a separate corporation to manufacture and sell Schick electric shavers. From that date until 1970 there would be two Schick companies.

The Magazine Repeating Razor Company made the injector razor and blades. J.M. Mathes, Inc., was its advertising agency. Jacob Schick sold the company to American Chain and Cable, which was acquired in 1946 by Eversharp, Inc. In the late 1940s Eversharp named the Biow Company, Inc., as its ad agency. Biow created the well-known campaign, "Push, Pull, Click, Click. Change Blades That Quick."

Meanwhile Jacob Schick continued with the Schick Dry Shaver Company, Inc., which used Briggs & Varley as its ad agency in the 1930s, switching to Arthur Kudner, Inc., in about 1940. After World War II the company changed its name to Schick, Inc., and continued making electric shavers exclusively. In 1961 the company moved its manufacturing operations to its present home in Milford, Connecticut. By then Eversharp was using Compton Advertising, while Schick, Inc., was working with Benton & Bowles.

In 1970 both Eversharp and Schick, Inc., were acquired by the Warner-Lambert Company—later part of Pfizer—which continued to produce high-quality shaving products and modern versions of the original injector razor under the Schick brand. In fact, by 1998 Schick and Wilkinson Sword Shaving Products were the third-best-selling brand for the company, with sales of $745 million.

The success of Schick over the years can be traced to the company's ability to spot and capitalize on market trends and its strong advertising and promotions program. Many of its marketing and advertising efforts came to fruition in the 1990s. It should be noted, however, that despite all Schick's efforts, it has always trailed Gillette substantially in market share.

The Schick product lines most responsible for the company's revenue included the Silk Effects and Silk Effects Plus Razors for women and the Tracer and Tracer FX for men. Other Schick products included the Personal Touch Razor for Women, the Schick Protector, and the disposable Slim Twin. Recognizing the increasing importance of women in the razor and shaving markets in the 1990s, Schick introduced the Silk Effects line of razors in 1994, which used low corrosive steel, had rubber safety grips to prevent wet hands from slipping, and wrapped thinner wires around pressure-sensitive twin blades to prevent nicks and cuts. A $12 million print, television, and coupon campaign from J. Walter Thompson USA, New York City (JWT), supported the product.

The Silk Effects Plus version was launched in 1999. This brand extension was positioned to attract younger, active female consumers, and the product came with a suction-cupped shower hanger for the razor and refill cartridge. In a $30 million campaign that broke in May 1999, print ads and television spots from JWT delved into the lifestyle of a time-pressed young woman sharing a messy apartment with two male roommates, showing her struggling to carry her own groceries, shaving her legs in a cluttered bathroom, and going out on the town. The implication of the ads was that independent women would benefit from the ease and safety of the Schick Silk Effects system. In an effort to tap into the younger market (a segment that often drives trends), a print ad for the Silk Effects brand also targeted teens, depicting adolescent girls shopping for back-to-school products in the SoHo district of New York City. The ad announced a Silk Effects contest for a trip to Manhattan and a $1,000 shopping spree at Bloomingdale's.

Schick's products for the men's market included its Tracer and Tracer FX razors, introduced in the early 1990s and 1997, respec-

tively. The Tracer razors, considered revolutionary because the blades bend and flex to conform to the face, were marketed as providing a closer, smoother shave than conventional razors. The TV commercials for the Tracer used a special technology called "morphing," in which a shaver's face is seamlessly transformed, one visage becoming another and then another, to drive home the idea that any man, regardless of the shape of his face, can successfully use the flexible razor. An attention-getting 1995 ad by JWT for the FX razor, part of a $20 million campaign that was specifically designed for sensitive skin and to combat skin irritation, featured a female fashion model shaving her face while cooing into the camera, "Are you the sensitive type? I like that."

One of Schick's major advertising and promotional thrusts in the 1990s was its association with the National Basketball Association (NBA). The Schick Rookie Game was held each year during the NBA All-Star Weekend, and in 1994 Schick began sponsoring a "Picture Yourself at the Schick Rookie Game" sweepstakes campaign, in which entry forms were attached to print ads, freestanding inserts, and displays in more than 20,000 retail outlets. The company also introduced the official NBA Schick Tracer Razor in league colors with the NBA logo, with specially marked boxes of Tracer refills including trading cards showcasing new stars. The promotional program was handled by Marketworks, of Ridgefield, Connecticut. Schick also offered other promotions that tapped into consumer demand for NBA merchandise. For example, consumers who provided proof of purchase of Schick products could send in $39.95 to receive the NBA warm-up suit of their choice. National Media Group, New York City, managed Schick's NBA sponsorship. In addition, Schick has advertised on the NBA Web site and organized a Super Hoops program, in which 600 schools participate in a televised competition affiliated with the NBA.

RAJESH V. MANCHANDA

Further Reading

Bittar, Christine, "High-Tech Effects," *Brandweek* (22 February 1999)

Bittar, Christine, "Silk Effects Ad Depicts Lady's Razor As Solution to Slobby Male Roomies," *Brandweek* (10 May 1999)

Brewer, Geoffrey, "What's in a Name?" *Incentive* (June 1992)

Garfield, Bob, "Magali's a Beauty, But She's No Noxzema Nordic Goddess," *Advertising Age* (27 November 1995)

Jensen, Jeff, "NBA Nets Year-Round Activity," *Advertising Age* (7 November 1994)

Schlitz Brewing Company

Principal Agencies

J.L. Stack
McJunkin Advertising Company
Young & Rubicam, Inc.
Lennen & Newell, Inc.
J. Walter Thompson Company
Leo Burnett Company, Inc.
W.B. Doner & Company

"The beer that made Milwaukee famous" actually had to leave town in order to bring recognition to its Wisconsin home. That was just one of the indirect routes Schlitz followed on its way to becoming one of the world's most famous brewers. In 1848, when August Krug started his brewing business, he hired Joseph Schlitz, a man with no prior experience in the business, as an accountant. After Krug's death in 1856, Schlitz married his widow and took over the Krug brewery, renaming the enterprise the Joseph Schlitz Brewing Company in 1874. He died in a shipwreck the following year, but the company and its name lived on.

Schlitz became recognized as Milwaukee's premium beer after the 1871 fire that devastated Chicago, Illinois. The blaze destroyed Chicago's drink suppliers, including its breweries. Schlitz filled the void by establishing 2,000 taverns, saloons, and other retail locations between Milwaukee and Chicago from 1871 to 1876. It was one of the first breweries to engage in outer-region marketing. "The beer that made Milwaukee famous" slogan began creeping into Schlitz's advertising appeals around 1893, joining the "belted globe" logo, which was unveiled in 1886.

In the early days of beer advertising, the target was not beer drinkers but beer vendors, namely taverns and saloons. Rival breweries each worked to establish networks of saloons selling their products exclusively. The rewards for brand loyalty included an array of furniture, including tables, chairs, and sometimes the bar itself, plus refrigeration equipment. One brewery even underwrote the installation of a bar's new roof. In time the relationship between brewery and vendor would change, as the brewers bought the taverns and then leased them to selected managers, thus ensuring brand loyalty.

The "beer wars" escalated in the late 1880s as brewers took their products on the road to county and state fairs in search of consumer support. The Olympics of beer competition were the world's fairs. In 1893 Pabst won the blue ribbon for its entry at the World's Columbian Exposition in Chicago, but Schlitz walked away with the top prize in the category of beer purity. The purity claim would figure prominently for Schlitz as it appealed to consumers that its brew bore "The highest award for purity." The appeal worked, and Schlitz temporarily claimed the coveted spot of top-selling brewer.

Shortly after the turn of the century, Schlitz hired the J.L. Stack agency of Racine, Wisconsin, to see what it could do about improving Schlitz's bottom line. The years since the World's Columbian Exposition had been challenging for the company, and it was losing market share. Stack put Claude Hopkins on the account, and shortly thereafter he engineered a new national advertising campaign around the purity claim. Hopkins toured the brewery and saw the company's painstaking efforts. He learned from Schlitz executives that the general public had no idea what brewers went through to produce pure beer.

From around 1900 until 1910, Schlitz advertised the purity of its beer in a number of ways. Sometimes the ad copy explained why the beer was healthy to drink; other times the ad let the reader "listen in" on a conversation between two doctors who agreed that beer was a healthful beverage. Frequently the advertising copy was accompanied by the Schlitz maiden, "Purity," in various stages of undress, sometimes holding a white dove, to underscore the company's claim. And always the ads were topped off by the Schlitz Globe and the "Beer that made Milwaukee famous" tag line. Schlitz soon regained its previously lost number-one status.

After 1910, beer sales began to dry up, due in large part to two events: World War I and Prohibition. When the United States entered the war in 1917, Congress restricted the use of the foodstuffs need for the production of alcoholic beverages. This war-born spirit of self-denial helped accelerate the wave of anti-alcohol sentiment that was sweeping the country. Many leading brewers, such as Schlitz, were of German descent, and this taint made the drive against alcohol all the more popular. Between 1920 and 1933, Prohibition laws forced Schlitz to remove nearly all the alcohol from its beverage, then marketed as "FAMO" (derived from the old slogan, 'The Beer that Made Milwaukee Famous") and "Schlitz Special Brew," and to diversify into other areas.

Stack continued to service the Schlitz account until Prohibition was lifted, giving way in 1933 to McJunkin Advertising. Over a 13-year period, McJunkin encouraged beer drinkers to rediscover Schlitz by promoting "that famous flavor" and offering it as an acceptable beverage to upscale audiences by touting it as "a distinguished beer" suitable "for great occasions." It also helped promote Old Milwaukee, a new beer Schlitz produced. World War II, however, forced a curtailment of production, and the company tended to focus its efforts on its flagship product. In 1943 McJunkin premiered the "Kiss of the Hops" campaign.

In 1947 Young & Rubicam took over and serviced the account until 1951, when Schlitz decided to diversify its advertising to take advantage of the growing popularity of television. It gave the television and radio account to Lennen & Newell, which launched *The Schlitz Playhouse of Stars* on CBS. The program ran for eight seasons and showcased the 1955 TV debut of actor James Dean in "The Unlighted Road." Irwin & Vladimir had responsibility for promoting Schlitz overseas, while the Leo Burnett Company drew the job of selling the beer via outdoor advertising.

If the Schlitz plan was to divide and conquer, about the only thing conquered was Schlitz's position as the number-one beer in

A 1957 Schlitz advertisement positioned the beverage as a necessary ingredient for a successful barbecue.
Courtesy of Pabst Brewing Company.

America, which went to Anheuser-Busch in 1957. Some of Schlitz's print ads were criticized for the way they portrayed women, while other ads' use of "Schlitzwords," such as "schlitznic" for picnic, also failed to win favor with beer drinkers. The J. Walter Thompson Company (JWT) handled the account from 1956 until 1961, hyping Old Milwaukee Beer as the "True Milwaukee beer flavor" while at the same time urging consumers to "Move up to quality; move up to Schlitz." Nothing seemed to help Schlitz reclaim number-one status.

Burnett then made a pitch for the account, which it landed in 1962. It was the beginning of a near 17-year relationship between the Milwaukee brewer and the agency, one in which annual ad budgets would rise to more than $50 million, and consumers would be introduced to Schlitz Malt Liquor, Schlitz Lite, and Erlanger in addition to Schlitz and Old Milwaukee. Burnett's warning to consumers in 1966 that "When you're out of Schlitz, you're out of beer" succeeded in getting some beer drinkers to rediscover "The beer that made Milwaukee famous." The agency boosted Schlitz's name recognition with the "Gusto" campaign. Consumers were invited to "Enjoy real gusto," "Reach for the gusto," and "Go for the gusto." They were even reminded that "You only go around once in life: go for all the gusto you can."

But even so, the "Gusto" campaign could not close the gap between Schlitz and Budweiser.

In 1976 Burnett dropped the gusto approach and appealed to drinkers by telling them that "When it's right, you know it," that "Schlitz makes it great," and "There's just one word for beer: Schlitz—and you know it." The campaign produced results, but not the results Schlitz was anticipating. Miller Brewing caught and passed Schlitz, dropping it to number three in sales. Schlitz was soon in the market for another ad agency, returning to JWT in 1978. JWT tried to resurrect the "gusto" strategy, telling consumers that "If you don't have Schlitz, you don't have gusto." But the campaign backfired, and it was scrapped for a series of promotions built around "The Schlitz taste test."

Regardless of the gambit, Schlitz was mired in third place behind Miller and Budweiser. Adding to the company's woes was its inability to produce a beer with a head on it. Chemicals were added to yield the desired results, but they proved to be useless when the beer remained on the shelf for an extended period of time. Schlitz remained in third place until 1981, when the brewery was sold to the Peter Stroh Brewery. The sale marked the end of the trail for Schlitz in Milwaukee, as Stroh relocated the operation to Detroit, Michigan, and gave the advertising account to W.B.

Doner & Company. But the Schlitz odyssey was not over yet. In early 1999 it became part of the Pabst brewing system and moved again, this time to San Antonio, Texas.

JOHN MORELLO

Further Reading
Gunther, John, *Taken at the Flood: The Story of Albert D. Lasker,* New York: Harper, and London: Hamish Hamilton, 1960
Hopkins, Claude, *My Life in Advertising [and] Scientific Advertising,* Lincolnwood, Illinois: NTC Business Books, 1966

Scholz & Friends

Founded by Juergen Scholz and Michael Menzel in Hamburg, West Germany, 1 July 1981; sold a majority stake in agency to Ted Bates & Company, 1985; opened a shop in West Berlin, 1990; Menzel left to start his own small agency, 1991; Scholz retired, 1992; launched an international network, 1995; severed ties to Bates, 1997, with Scholz & Friends becoming its own network within Cordiant; agency wholly owned by Cordiant, 2000.

Major Clients
Chio Chips
FAZ
Lufthansa
Mercedes-Benz (trucks)
Reemtsma
Schwarzkopf & Henkel
Tchibo

The German advertising industry was shocked when word leaked out in the summer of 1981 that Juergen Scholz, one of the four founders of the Hamburg, West Germany, ad agency TEAM (which later became BBDO) was leaving the agency with Michael Menzel to set up his own shop. The new Hamburg agency, Scholz & Friends, took 40 employees from TEAM/BBDO Hamburg. It was the largest such split in German advertising history.

During a festive media conference following the move, Scholz said that he decided to set up his own agency because he was tired of working under all the restrictions implicit in being part of an international network. He also said that he planned to create a local boutique shop that would focus on branding. In an interview with *Advertising Age Europe* a few months later, Scholz discussed at length the building and pampering of brands.

Four longtime clients followed Scholz to the new shop: coffee marketer Tchibo, owned by the Herz brothers; Mars, Inc.'s Whiskas; fashion designer Jil Sander; and Koenig Pilsener brewery. The new agency ended up paying $1 million to TEAM/BBDO to compensate it for the loss of those clients.

Despite the hoopla and media coverage, nobody would have guessed that 20 years later—nearly a decade after its founders had left the shop—the agency's name would appear on doors in more

than a dozen cities in Europe. Despite its anti-network beginnings, Scholz & Friends, a Cordiant subsidiary as of early 2001, was the only German agency with a small international network.

Setting up Scholz & Friends at the age of 52 marked the beginning of Scholz's second career. In 1956 he had been one of the four founders of TEAM in Düsseldorf, West Germany. Scholz had studied graphic design at the Folkwangschule in Essen, West Germany, for two years and decided to go into advertising, then a little known profession in Germany. He had one big advantage: he knew how to sell his ideas to clients. An outspoken, charismatic man, Scholz told *Advertising Age* that while working on Tchibo's coffee account for TEAM, he encouraged the coffee marketer to sell items such as colored boxes in its retail outlets. Tchibo finally gave in to the idea and in 1972 started with a small assortment of goods. Over the years, the agency and Tchibo developed a wide assortment of articles, ranging from custom

Juergen Scholz.

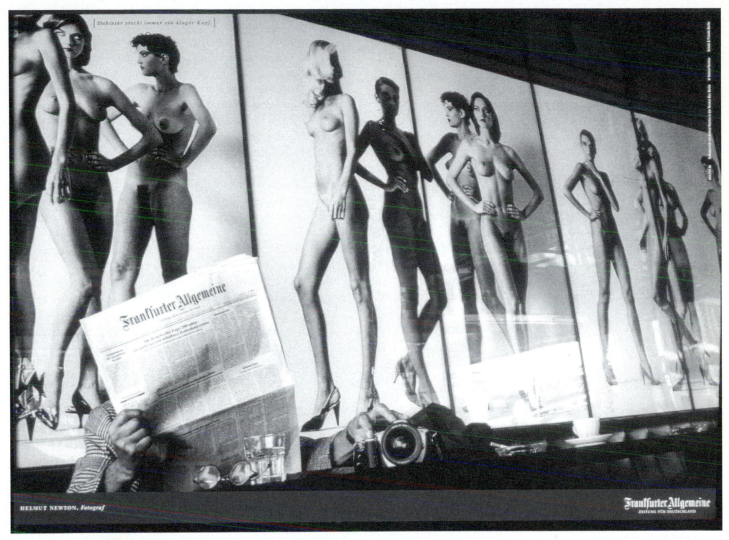

Scholz & Friends created this award-winning campaign for the *Frankfurter Allgemeine Zeitung*, one of Germany's leading daily newspapers.

jewelry to towels, household goods, and underwear, offering new products every week. The agency was not only responsible for the campaign backing the assortment but also for window displays, which were changed weekly. Tchibo's nonfood division's sales grew to $1.35 billion annually, while coffee sales stood at $890 million by 2000.

Tchibo's owners, the Herz brothers, also owned cigarette marketer Reemtsma Cigarettenfabrik, Hamburg, which Scholz & Friends handled. Its West brand, launched in 1981 in Germany and backed by advertising from Scholz & Friends, became the number-two selling cigarette brand in Germany. The brand is sold in 54 countries, mainly in Eastern Europe.

One of Scholz's biggest successes in brand building came with its campaign for the designer Jil Sander. He used a uniform print campaign to launch the fashion line, including fragrances, cosmetics, eyeglasses, and shoes. He convinced the shy, then-37-year-old Jil Sander to use her own photograph in ads for her product lines. After that campaign, the agency's business boomed. In its first full

year, 1982, the agency had billings of $38 million; three years later, its billings had reached $63 million.

Scholz and Menzel sold a majority share in the agency to Ted Bates & Company, New York City, in the fall of 1985. Menzel said he believed the agency would grow much faster with an international link. During the 1980s, international agency networks were striving to boost their presence in the West German market, offering agencies huge sums of money to align with the networks. Despite the majority ownership of Bates, both Scholz and Menzel worked to ensure a degree of independence from headquarters, keeping the Hamburg and Frankfurt, West Germany, offices separate.

By 1989 billings had reached $122 million. Scholz & Friends had won Bayerische Motoren Werke AG's German account in 1986, taking it from Düsseldorf-based Spiess, Ermisch, Abels. While the agency produced well-respected work for BMW, the relationship proved a difficult one, with the car marketer treating the agency as a vendor rather than a partner. Although Scholz lost the account in 1993, BMW returned to the agency in 1995 for three more years.

In the summer of 1990, before German reunification, Scholz met with three German students—Thomas Heilmann, Olaf Schumann, and Sebastian Turner—who planned to start an agency in East Berlin. Instead, they jointly started Scholz & Friends Berlin. Over the years, it became one of the most successful agencies in the city, eventually employing 200 people and working with such clients as *Frankfurter Allgemeine Zeitung*, Mercedes-Benz trucks, and many local companies. Indeed, it was the Berlin office that brought Scholz & Friends its first Lion, a silver, at the International Advertising Festival at Cannes, France.

Meanwhile, his relationship with Scholz deteriorating, Menzel left the agency in 1991 and set up his own shop. By 1992 Scholz, then age 63, felt it was time to retire. Scholz & Friends had grown into a $181 million shop. (As of 2002, Scholz and his wife lived in a farmhouse outside Hamburg. In 1999 he became a board member and adviser to Hamburg-based Jung von Matt, a Scholz & Friends breakaway.)

In 1995 agency Chairman and Chief Executive Officer Peter Schoening, encouraged by client Reemtsma, decided to launch a small Scholz & Friends network in all the markets where the marketer did business. Six offices—Athens, Greece; Budapest, Hungary; Brussels, Belgium; Madrid, Spain; Warsaw, Poland; and Vienna, Austria—were started in 1995. Each outpost consisted of one person with a computer and local media expertise who adapted work for local markets. Prague, Czech Republic, followed in 1997 and Moscow, Russia, and London, England, in 1998. The Scholz & Friends network started with six local people and only one German; two years later the network employed 38. With two acquisitions (Herman Beasley and CKMP), in 2000 the London agency employed 65. In 1999 the agency continued its foreign expansion, opening offices in Kiev, Ukraine; Milan, Italy; and Paris, France.

In 1997 the Bates connection was terminated, and Scholz & Friends became a unit of Cordiant PLC, the parent company of both Scholz and Bates. In 2000 Scholz & Friends employed 850 people and had gross income of $70 million.

DAGMAR MUSSEY

Schweppes

Principal Agencies
Hewitt, Ogilvy, Benson & Mather, Inc. (later Ogilvy & Mather)
Saatchi & Saatchi
Young & Rubicam, Inc.

In 1783 in Geneva, Switzerland, Jacob Schweppes perfected a process for making an artificial mineral water. Nine years later he moved to London, England, where he soon began producing and selling his bottled beverage. By the end of the 20th century, the parent company, Cadbury Schweppes, was the distributor of such well-known soft-drink brands as Dr Pepper, 7 UP, Canada Dry, and Schweppes mineral and tonic waters.

Within the first 70 years of production, Schweppes became such a popular beverage that it was named the official supplier for the 1851 Great Exhibition held in London's Hyde Park. Schweppes adopted as its trademark the celebrated fountain built for the opening of the exhibition. Throughout the 19th century, Schweppes expanded around the globe and, in the 1870s, added tonic water to the range of products bottled under the Schweppes label. Tonic water, flavored with quinine, was marketed as a preventive for malaria.

In 1943 the British beverage industry banded together to form the Soft Drinks Industry (War Time) Association, which, in an attempt to cut costs and support the war effort, eliminated brand labeling of soft drinks. Because of its firm belief in the value of advertising and branding, Schweppes, however, continued advertising its brand. Advertising, according to Sir Frederic Hooper of Schweppes, was the consumer's guarantee of quality.

In 1946 the company launched its "Schweppervescence" campaign, which focused on the carbonation of its soda water. Then in 1951 a campaign titled "Schweppshire" began. In 1957 Schweppes acquired L. Rose and Company, manufacturer of the first concentrated fruit drink, Rose's Lime Juice. At the time, all British ships were required to carry lime or lemon juice, which helped prevent the vitamin C–deficiency condition called scurvy. The nickname "Limey" for British sailors originated from this use. Rose's was the navy's brand of choice.

With the help of British advertising giant David Ogilvy, Schweppes crossed the Atlantic in 1953. Schweppes continued to maintain a relationship with Ogilvy through a succession of agencies, first while he was at Hewitt, Ogilvy, Benson & Mather, Inc., and later at Ogilvy & Mather. In much the same vein as his Hathaway shirt advertisements, featuring a distinguished gentleman wearing an eye-patch, Ogilvy created a campaign for Schweppes centered on Commander Edward Whitehead. With his striking Van Dyke beard and tweed coat, Commander Whitehead even appeared in an official-looking sash at times. In the first "Commander" ad, Ogilvy dubbed him the "Ambassador of Schweppes." The copy began:

Meet Commander Edward Whitehead, Schweppesman Extraordinary from London, England, where the house of Schweppes has been a great institution since 1794. Commander Whitehead has come to these United States to make sure that every drop of Schweppes Quinine Water bottled here has the original flavor which has long made Schweppes the *only* mixer for an *authentic* Gin-and-Tonic.

Dignified yet fun, Commander Whitehead became the personification of "Schweppervescence." This campaign is credited with increasing Schweppes sales 500 percent over nine years. Ogilvy later wrote, "Commander Whitehead of Schweppes started out as a client and became one of my closest companions. We have been shipwrecked together, and our wives solace each other by comparing notes on their husbands' vanities."

In 1965 Schweppes launched the "Schhh You-Know-Who" campaign. This campaign ran until 1973.

Schweppes merged with the confectionery producer Cadbury to form Cadbury Schweppes in 1969. The company then expanded globally and acquired other well-known soft-drink brands such as Dr Pepper, A&W, and Sunkist. It severed its long relationship with Ogilvy in 1972 and moved its American and most of its international advertising to Young & Rubicam (Y&R), which had done the notable "Be a Pepper" campaign for Dr Pepper. For a period in the late 1980s and throughout most of the 1990s, Cadbury Schweppes teamed up with the Coca-Cola Company to distribute Coke products in Britain. At the end of the century, Cadbury Schweppes was the third-largest soft-drink marketer in the United States behind Coke and Pepsi.

During the 1990s Schweppes shuffled its European business from agency to agency. In 1996 the company dropped DDB Needham Worldwide in favor of Saatchi & Saatchi for its European advertising. This came shortly after Schweppes removed Saatchi & Saatchi from the Dr Pepper U.K. business. In 1997 Schweppes launched a major campaign in the United Kingdom with new graphics promoting its line of sparkling drinks.

In 1998 Schweppes, in an effort to establish a more consistent image worldwide, consolidated its international advertising under Young & Rubicam. As a result, Saatchi & Saatchi lost the company's European and Hong Kong accounts and Foote, Cone & Belding relinquished the U.S. business. Y&R, on the other hand, added to its existing Schweppes Australian account.

ANNE CUNNINGHAM

See also color plate in this volume

Further Reading

Cadbury Schweppes <www.cadburyschweppes.com>
Marketing Information Net Directory (MIND) <www.mind-advertising.com>
Ogilvy, David, *Confessions of an Advertising Man*, New York: Atheneum, 1963; revised edition, London: Pan, 1987; New York: Atheneum, 1988
"Saatchi & Saatchi Soaks Up $20m Schweppes Europe," *Advertising Age* (31 October 1996)
"Y&R Appointed to Build Global Schweppes," *Advertising Age* (7 August 1998)

S.C. Johnson & Son, Inc. *See under* Johnson

Scott, Walter Dill 1869–1955

U.S. Research Psychologist

Walter Dill Scott was one of the first psychologists to write in depth about the relation of psychology to advertising. Scott was born in 1869 near Cooksville, Illinois. He graduated from Illinois State Normal University (later Illinois State University) in 1891 and earned a A.B. from Northwestern University in Evanston, Illinois, in 1895. Three years later he earned a B.D. from the McCormick Theological Seminary in Chicago, Illinois. Scott received a Ph.D. in psychology from the University of Leipzig (Germany) in

1900 and, on his return to the United States, became an instructor in psychology at Northwestern University.

In 1901 Scott conducted his first experiments in advertising for the Agate Club of Chicago, an association of area business personnel at whose behest he wrote articles about advertising. Rather than developing a general theory of psychology, he focused on the study of psychology's application to business, especially its relations to advertising and management. In 1902 he started teaching

Walter Dill Scott.
Courtesy Northwestern University Archives.

Advertising in Theory and Practice in 1913. Scott employed findings from his experiments to support certain assertions: that a rectangle was more pleasing to the eye than a square, for example. He believed that many problems in advertising could be solved by analyzing empirical data. He employed surveys to determine why consumers purchased particular products. He calculated the advertising space in certain periodicals to determine which marketers advertised most. He surveyed publishers of magazines to determine their views of advertisements. Scott also recognized that those who worked in advertising would benefit from a better understanding of the basic motivations for human behavior.

Scott took a leave of absence from Northwestern in 1916 in order to teach applied psychology and direct the Bureau of Salesmanship Research at the Carnegie Institute of Technology (today Carnegie Mellon University, Pittsburgh, Pennsylvania). From

courses in advertising and applied psychology. Articles he had published on the subject, including several that had appeared in *Mahin's Magazine,* were the basis for his first book, *The Theory of Advertising* (1903).

Scott explored the subject further in *The Psychology of Advertising* (1908). He was aware that many who worked in the industry did not understand the motivations behind consumer purchases; they also had little knowledge of how to apply psychology to advertising. Scott argued for a scientific approach to advertising that looked beyond the physical characteristics of the ad—typography, color, type of paper—to psychological aspects, which, he noted, were dependent upon the belief system of the target audience. He believed that persuasion was less rational and direct than advocates of "reason-why" theories would have people believe. The process, according to Scott, was more a matter of suggestion than of argument. Eventually, his ideas came to influence many advertising professionals.

Scott was promoted to professor in 1908. A year later he became professor of advertising at Northwestern's new School of Commerce, as well as chair of the Department of Psychology. Although his academic responsibilities occupied much of his time, he continued to write, publishing *The Psychology of*

THE THEORY OF ADVERTISING

A Simple Exposition of The Principles of Psychology In Their Relation to Successful Advertising

By WALTER DILL SCOTT, Ph.D.
Director of the Psychological Laboratory of Northwestern University

SCIRE QVOD SCIENDVM

Boston
Small, Maynard & Company
1903

In 1903 Walter Dill Scott published *The Theory of Advertising,* a pioneering study on the application of psychological principles to advertising techniques.

1917 to 1918 he directed the Committee on the Classification of Personnel, which was sponsored by the U.S. Army. The committee was responsible for classifying and rating the job qualifications of army personnel using tests and rating scales developed by Scott and his associates. In 1919 he became president of the American Psychological Association, as well as director of the Division of Psychology and Anthropology of the National Research Council.

In 1920 Scott was elected president of Northwestern University, after which he rarely lectured or wrote on the topics that had occupied the earlier part of his career. Instead, he wrote several biographies of individuals who had been instrumental in Chicago's growth and development. His last major contribution to his profession was a revised edition of *The Psychology of Advertising* in 1917. He helped to raise more than $70 million for the university and was instrumental in the establishment of a campus in Chicago. He died in Evanston in 1955.

EDD APPLEGATE

Biography
Born 1 May 1869 near Cooksville, Illinois; graduated from Illinois State Normal University (later, Illinois State University), 1891; received A.B. from Northwestern University in Evanston, Illinois, 1895; received B.D. from the McCormick Theological Seminary in Chicago, Illinois, 1898; received Ph.D. in psychology from the University of Leipzig, Germany, 1900; became instructor in psychology at Northwestern University, 1900; appointed director, Bureau of Salesmanship Research at the Carnegie Institute of Technology, 1916, and president, American Psychological Association, 1919; named director of the Division of Psychology and Anthropology of the National Research Council, 1919; elected president of Northwestern University, 1920; awarded Distinguished Service Medal for service in World War I; died in Evanston on 23 September 1955.

Selected Publications
The Theory of Advertising, 1903
The Psychology of Advertising, 1908; revised edition, 1917
Increasing Human Efficiency in Business: A Contribution to the Psychology of Business, 1911; new and enlarged edition, 1923
Influencing Men in Business: The Psychology of Argument and Suggestion, 1911; 2nd edition, 1916
The Psychology of Advertising in Theory and Practice, 1913
Personnel Management: Principles, Practices, and Point of View (with Robert C. Clothier), 1923; 5th edition (with Clothier and William R. Spriegel), 1954

Further Reading
Jacobson, Jacob Z., *Scott of Northwestern: The Life Story of a Pioneer in Psychology and Education*, Chicago: Mariano, 1951

Lynch, Edmund C., *Walter Dill Scott: Pioneer in Personnel Management*, Austin: Bureau of Business Research, University of Texas, 1968

Master, Laurence S., "Scott, Walter Dill," in *Biographical Dictionary of American Educators,* edited by John F. Ohles, vol. 3, Westport, Connecticut: Greenwood, 1978

Sandage, C.H., "Walter Dill Scott: 1869–1955," in *Pioneers in Marketing: A Collection of Twenty-Five Biographies of Men Who Contributed to the Growth of Marketing Thought and Action,* edited by John S. Wright and Parks B. Dimsdale, Jr., Atlanta: Publishing Services Division, School of Business Administration, Georgia State University, 1974

"Scott, Walter Dill," in *The National Cyclopaedia of American Biography,* vol. 42, New York: White, 1958

Sokal, Michael M., "Scott, Walter Dill," in *Dictionary of American Biography: Supplement Five, 1951–1955,* edited by John A. Garraty, New York: Scribner, 1977

Strong, Edward K., Jr., "Walter Dill Scott: 1869–1955," *American Journal of Psychology* 68 (December 1955)

Seagram Company, Ltd.

Principal Agencies
Vickers & Benson
Blackman Agency
Doyle Dane Bernbach, Inc.

Prior to its dissolution in 2001, the Seagram Company, Ltd., a Canadian beverage and entertainment giant, marketed its products in more than 150 countries and territories worldwide. In 2000 it reported $15.7 billion in revenue. Edgar Bronfman, Jr., Seagram's final chief executive officer (CEO), was the grandson of company patriarch Samuel Bronfman, who, with the help of brothers Harry and Allan, had turned a small distillery and liquor wholesaling operation into a leading global marketer of some 200 brands of spirits and wines. Critical to the company's many years of success were its marketing and advertising activities during early forays into the American market in the 1930s and 1940s.

The son of Jewish immigrants who fled Russia in the late 1880s, Bronfman entered the innkeeping and bar business in 1912 with the purchase of the Bell Hotel in Winnipeg, Manitoba, Canada. When the prohibitionist tide forced the closing of all of the province's bars, Sam and his brothers turned to the federally regulated liquor trade between provinces. In 1918 the Canadian federal government halted this trade, but it exempted spirits sold for medicinal purposes. The Bronfman brothers then set up a mail-order business selling liquor to drugstores across Canada. In 1924 they built a distillery in the Montreal suburb of LaSalle, incorporating that year as Distillers Corporation, Ltd. Four years later the company bought Joseph E. Seagram & Sons, an Ontario whiskey distillery that had roots dating to 1857 and was known for its V.O. and 83 brands. The new enterprise adopted the name Distillers Corporation-Seagrams, Ltd. (changed in 1974 to the Seagram Company, Ltd.); its first-year profits were a hefty $2.2 million.

Such lucrative profits were explained largely by Prohibition in the United States and the corresponding demand for bootleg whiskey, much of it shipped from Canada. During the early 1920s the Bronfmans, operating mainly in the prairie provinces, sold whiskey to "export houses" whose agents, in turn, smuggled it into U.S. border states. When, by the late 1920s, enhanced law enforcement had curtailed this traffic, the trade moved eastward to the waters of the Great Lakes, until that too was stymied by stepped-up border patrols. By the early 1930s the base for much of the U.S. whiskey supply had shifted to the French islands of St. Pierre and Miquelon, located off the coast of Newfoundland.

The repeal of Prohibition in the United States in 1933 presented Seagram with a unique marketing opportunity, for unlike most of its American competitors, Seagram had large supplies of aged whiskeys. In 1933 Bronfman bought Rossville Union Distilleries in Indiana and shortly afterward added the Calvert Distilling Company in Maryland. An American subsidiary, Joseph E. Seagram & Sons, Inc., was formed to operate the facilities and to market Canadian whiskey in the United States. Frank Schwengel was hired to oversee the American sales network. The initial marketing strategy stressed the superiority of longer-aged, blended Canadian whiskeys over "straights" and American bourbons. Seagram also campaigned, largely successfully, to overhaul whiskey's lowbrow image, from that of the drink of the hayseed and the bootlegger to one embodying cosmopolitanism, craftsmanship, aristocratic elegance, and social responsibility.

Until it entered the American market, Seagram had limited experience with brand advertising. A strong temperance lobby in Canada meant that liquor advertising was heavily regulated by provincial governments, ranging from a complete ban in Prince Edward Island to the policy in Quebec of allowing both brand and company advertising. Most provinces, including Ontario, the largest marketplace, banned brand advertising in all media. Thus, by necessity Seagram's marketing strategy emphasized promotional tactics such as the sponsorship of boxing matches, foot races, golf tournaments, swimming contests, and snowshoe races. Seagram's principal Canadian ad agency was Vickers & Benson, with which it was associated from 1924 until the 1960s.

In contrast to the policy in Canada, after Prohibition ended, U.S. legislators adopted a more laissez-faire approach to the advertising of alcohol, which allowed Seagram to place high volumes of brand advertising in newspapers and magazines, the latter often color page ads. In 1934 the company launched its Five Crown and Seven Crown labels, which soon afterward became

sales leaders in their categories. Other notable ad campaigns during the 1930s and 1940s included "Say Seagram's and Be Sure"; the "Man of Distinction" series, consisting of endorsements from movie stars, sports heroes, and European royalty; V.O.'s "Exclusively Canadian" series, which featured vignettes from Canada such as ice hockey, the St. Jean Baptiste Festival, and the Calgary Stampede; and "Canada Produces," a V.O. campaign begun in 1949 that highlighted Canada's natural resources industries. For Seagram, selling Canadian whiskey to Americans often entailed linking its brands to Canadian archetypes, traditions, and myths. Seagram's other notable marketing strategies included selling bottled whiskey, rather than barrel consignments, to distributors, thus ensuring greater control over product quality and the design of the bottle and label. The company also advertised and distributed its products nationally, transcending the regional marketing of most bourbon and straight whiskeys.

In 1934 Seagram launched its "Moderation" ad campaign to wide public acclaim. The campaign was proposed by Bronfman and handled by Blackman Advertising, which won the account that same year, and variations of it continued into the 1990s. Combining the themes of gracious living and responsible drinking, the ads sought to alleviate lingering public concerns over the increased accessibility of alcohol. The campaign counseled people to drink moderately and to consider the familial, social, and ethical implications of alcohol consumption. Ads warned against drinking and driving, buying liquor instead of necessities, and appearing drunk before one's children. The campaign formed part of Seagram's general marketing strategy to disassociate whiskey from the saloon and the speakeasy while imbuing Seagram's brands with the themes of social responsibility, urbane sophistication, and male sociability. Fearing public disapproval, Bronfman and other liquor marketers opposed sales appeals directed to women, and until 1958 the U.S. Distilled Spirits Institute's code of ethics banned the appearance of women in liquor ads.

By the early 1950s Seagram had consolidated its position as North America's leading liquor marketer. The company's annual sales, 90 percent of which were outside Canada, reached $700 million, easily eclipsing the $425 million of its main competitor, Schenley Corporation. Seagram expanded into other beverage markets, and in 1942 it bought the Paul Masson vineyards and two years later created the Captain Morgan Rum Company. In 1949 Seagram acquired the Scotch whisky marketer Chivas Brothers, Ltd., and three years later bought the Champagne makers G.H. Mumm and Perrier-Jouët. In 1954 it added the wine company Barton & Guestier to its growing list of acquisitions, which by the 1960s also included the oil company Texas Pacific. By then Seagram's spirits and wine making and marketing operations encompassed Europe, Central and South America, and the West Indies in addition to North America.

Certain consumer trends during the 1950s and 1960s, however, proved disadvantageous to Seagram. The most notable of these were the shift from blended to straight whiskeys and the growing popularity of vodka. In 1946 the consumption of blended whiskey in the United States stood at 160 million gallons, compared to some 20 million gallons for straight whiskeys. By

1957 the gap had disappeared, and sales of each type were in the range of 70 million gallons. Bronfman, a devotee of the art and science of whiskey blending, disparaged straight whiskeys, thus leaving Seagram poorly positioned to capitalize on this growing market. The same held true for vodka, which Bronfman also disdained. In the mid-1950s the sales of vodka were negligible, but by 1972 vodka accounted for 13 percent of the U.S. spirits market. In 1956 Seagram bought Wolfschmidt vodka but gave it minimal promotion, thus allowing Smirnoff to capture the bulk of this market. Similarly, when light Scotch whiskies such as Cutty Sark and J&B gained in popularity, Seagram, with dark, heavy-bodied brands such as Chivas Regal, again found itself poorly positioned.

Seagram's U.S. advertising in the 1960s was handled by Doyle Dane Bernbach, Inc. Bill Bernbach persuaded the reluctant Bronfman to use irony and humor in liquor advertising, which was seen most notably in ads for Chivas Regal ("What idiot changed the Chivas Regal package?") and in the "Soft Whiskey" campaign for Calvert Extra. Bronfman exhibited keen interest in advertising and packaging and distrusted most marketing experts. Consequently, the company did little market research until the early 1960s, when his son Edgar became the president and CEO of Seagram's American operations. During the 1960s and 1970s Seagram commissioned a wide range of market research surveys in the United States and Canada from such firms as Ernest Dichter's Institute of Motivational Research, the Alfred Politz Research Company, Goldfarb Consultants, ORC International, Ben W. Crow & Associates of Canada, and Analytical Research, Ltd.

In the 1980s and 1990s Seagram diversified beyond the spirits and wine sectors. In 1980 it bought 20 percent of E.I. Du Pont de Nemours & Company, becoming its largest shareholder. In 1993 it spent $2.8 billion to acquire 15 percent of Time Warner, Inc. Two years later Seagram sold its Du Pont interest to finance the $5.7 billion takeover of MCA Corporation, the parent of Universal Pictures, later renamed Universal Studios. Seagram capped off its strategy of acquisitions in 1998 with the $10.4 billion purchase of music giant Polygram NV. Soon afterward Seagram combined the music businesses of Polygram and Universal to form Universal Music Group, the world's largest music company.

In June 2000 Vivendi, S.A., and Canal Plus, S.A., entered into a merger agreement with Seagram. The new company was called Vivendi Universal. Vivendi was interested only in the media holdings, however, and sought buyers for the alcohol side of the business. In December 2001 Vivendi closed a deal in which Universal sold Seagram's wine and spirits business to beverage marketers Diageo (itself the product of the 1997 merger of beverage marketers Guinness and GrandMet) and Pernod Ricard. As part of the joint acquisition, certain brands went to each company. With the sale, Seagram ceased to exist as a separate company.

DANIEL J. ROBINSON

Further Reading

Booth, Amy, "The Bronfmans: A Liquid Legacy for the Lineage," *Financial Post* (20 November 1976)

Bronfman, Edgar, *Good Spirits: The Making of a Businessman,* New York: Putnam, 1998

Marrus, Michael R., *Samuel Bronfman: The Life and Times of Seagram's Mr. Sam,* Hanover, New Hampshire: University Press of New England, 1991

Newman, Peter C., *King of the Castle: The Making of a Dynasty: Seagram's and the Bronfman Empire,* New York: Atheneum, 1979

Sears, Roebuck & Company

Principal Agencies
Erwin, Wasey & Company, Inc.
Blackett-Sample-Hummert, Inc.
Roche, Williams & Cunnyngham, Inc. (later Roche, Williams & Cleary, Inc.)
Schwimmer & Scott Advertising Agency
Bisberne Advertising Company
Ogilvy, Benson & Mather (later Ogilvy & Mather)
J. Walter Thompson Company
Foote, Cone & Belding
McCann-Erickson, Inc.
Young & Rubicam, Inc.

Sears, Roebuck & Company grew from a one-man mail-order operation in 1886 to dominate the retailing world for most of the 20th century. The company, for many years the largest advertiser in the United States, got its start supplying farmers with manufactured goods by mail order. By the late 1980s Sears oversaw a vast empire of retailing through stores and catalogs and had subsidiaries in insurance, banking and investments, and real estate. Competition in the marketplace shook Sears in the 1990s, and by 2000 it had dramatically scaled back its operations to consist solely of retail stores. Its ancillary businesses were sold and its catalog business shut down in 1993.

In the early years, however, Sears's timing was perfect. The company's initial growth paralleled the transformation of the

Shop at Sears and save

(their profit is less than 5%)

Sears, Roebuck always charges lower prices than others charge for equal quality. Read how this enlightened policy is made possible by unique know-how in buying, combined with a modest margin of profit.

FIFTY anonymous men and women went shopping yesterday. Across the country.

They bought every imaginable kind of merchandise. Ribbons. Tires. Refrigerators. Bicycles. Skirts. Clocks.

These men and women are Sears *comparison shoppers*. Their purchases, with price attached, are sent to Sears' main office every day.

There, they are checked for quality and price against Sears merchandise.

If Sears cannot offer an equal product for less money or a superior product for the same amount, Sears does not offer you this product at all.

This remarkable policy is possible for two reasons.

First, Sears is content to take a modest profit. Its net profit last year was less than 5%.

Second, the Sears people *know how to buy*.

They buy from thousands of small, efficient factories. These factories are located close to Sears stores and mail-order houses—to cut shipping costs.

The Sears buyers work *intimately* with their suppliers. They will help a manufacturer work out the most economical production system. They will advise him on every aspect of his business.

The results of this policy have been very good for Sears. And for Sears' suppliers. And for you. *Shop at Sears and save.*

◄ *Shop at one of Sears' 740 modern department stores, 944 catalog sales offices, or by phone or mail—and save.*

In the early 1960s Sears, Roebuck & Company focused its advertisements on its policy of offering quality merchandise at low prices. *The ca. 1962 advertisement "Shop at Sears and Save" is reprinted by arrangement with Sears, Roebuck and Co. and is protected under copyright. No duplication in permitted.*

United States from a rural-based society into a fast-growing, urbanized nation demanding diverse merchandise. In the 1920s, when American cities experienced huge growth, Sears responded by building hundreds of stores to meet demand. The economic prosperity and population boom of the 1950s that followed World War II led Sears to open hundreds more full-line department stores in the new suburbs and catalog outlets in nearly every small town in the United States.

Toward the end of the 20th century, the retail industry split into two widely divergent categories: mass-merchant discounters, such as Wal-Mart and Target, and specialty retailers offering niche and upscale products. For the first time in its history, Sears's middle-of-the-market positioning was no longer the ideal place to be, a situation that was reflected in the company's inconsistent sales results.

Early Success

The company owed its early success to the vision and enthusiasm of its founder, Richard Warren Sears, a freight agent in North

Redwood, Minnesota. In 1886 Sears received an order of pocket watches that local jewelers had refused to sell. He began selling the stock to other freight agents, signing them up to distribute more watches and paying each agent a commission on sales.

A year later, the R.W. Sears Watch Company was so busy Sears began making plans to move the enterprise to Chicago, Illinois, to be close to one of the nation's shipping hubs. Shortly afterward he teamed with watch repairman Alvah Curtis Roebuck to form Sears, Roebuck & Company.

Roebuck parted ways with Sears within a few years, and Sears himself retired to Minnesota twice and once sold his share of the business, only to buy it back almost immediately. Operating from Minnesota and driven by his passion for selling, Sears continued his watch-selling business, helped by his skill in writing advertising copy. He relied heavily on newspapers, using florid language and grandiose promises. In 1888 he added a guarantee to his products, an innovation at the time.

By 1891 Sears was publishing a 52-page catalog of watches, and a year later he began adding other merchandise, including

jewelry and revolvers. Customers were required to pay for the catalog and the cost of shipping by rail. By 1893 the catalog had
grown to 322 pages and included such diverse items as sewing
machines, bicycles, organs, and clothing. The guarantee of satisfaction remained, however.

That fall Sears relocated to Chicago, and its catalog adopted
the slogan, "Cheapest supply house on Earth." Catering primarily
to farmers and rural residents who were displeased with limited
merchandise selections at their local general stores, Sears cannily
billed its catalog as the "Consumers Guide for 1894." The timing
was perfect for fueling the dreams of farmers who sought efficiency and entertainment from products that were increasingly
mass-manufactured in cities.

In 1895 Sears bought out Roebuck and added two partners,
one of whom was Julius Rosenwald, a suitmaker who became a
crucial force in Sears's identity over the next several years. Rosenwald attended to operations and toned down the catalog copy's
claims, instituting a new policy of honesty in describing products.
Meanwhile, Sears searched the country for revolutionary gadgets
and new-fangled fashions with which he could excite the population. When he found a new product, such as a cream separator, he
would engage manufacturers to make the item for Sears, undercutting rivals' prices.

With rival catalog retailer Montgomery Ward & Company
making inroads in cities, Sears decided to step up its presence in
the urban centers, while branching out elsewhere. In 1906 Sears
opened a branch distribution office of its mail-order operation in
Dallas, Texas, and another one in Mexico City, Mexico, the first
of several international Sears enterprises.

During the first part of the century Sears sold the widest possible array of merchandise; in 1909 the company began marketing
houses that consumers could order and assemble. Sears resigned
in 1913 and died the following year at the age of 50, leaving
Rosenwald as president.

During World War I, Sears became a supplier to the government, and afterward, U.S. Army Quartermaster Robert E. Wood
joined the company and rose through its ranks. Eventually he
became chairman, serving from 1928 to 1954. He brought mili-
tary-style efficiency to the company's rapidly expanding distribution channels nationwide.

The Retail Business

Sears made its first foray into retail stores in 1925, opening a
storefront operation at its Chicago warehouse. The effort was so
successful that dozens more stores were opened in the Midwest
within a year, and by 1929 there were 319 stores spread across
the United States, primarily along railway shipping routes.

In the late 1920s Sears developed its first in-house brands,
which allowed the company to sidestep the fair trade laws that
prevented chains from undercutting independents by selling popular products at a loss in order to win business. Sears began devis-
ing private-label brands that eventually grew to include Kenmore
appliances, Craftsman tools, and the DieHard battery.

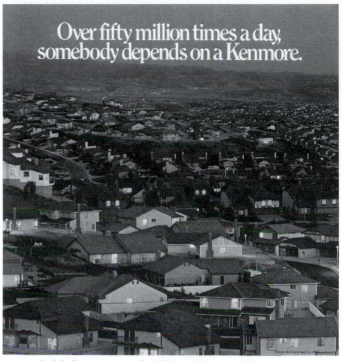

The reliability of Sears's Kenmore brand appliances was the theme of this
1985 print ad.
*The 1985 advertisement "There's More for Your Life at Sears" is
reprinted by arrangement with Sears, Roebuck and Co. and is protected
under copyright. No duplication in permitted.*

The stock market crash in 1929 slowed Sears's growth only
slightly, and the company continued to open new stores during
the Great Depression. In 1931 sales at retail outlets surpassed
mail-order sales. That year, Wood devised the idea of selling automobile insurance to customers through the mail, and the Allstate
Insurance Company was born, named after a brand of Sears automobile tires.

In 1933 Sears began to open Allstate branches inside its stores
to serve walk-in customers, and catalog desks were added inside
the stores, a harbinger of Sears's late-20th-century strategy of selling everything from "socks to stocks" to consumers through the
convenience of one-stop shopping. The growing clout of the retail
side of the business versus mail order also improved Sears's fortunes: whereas mail-order prices were locked in for a year at a
time, stores had the flexibility to raise and lower prices to meet the
ups and downs of the marketplace.

Sears revolutionized department store design in the 1930s by
being the first to design its stores around the merchandise. Store
planners laid out the interior selling space according to principles
of ideal merchandise placement, then built the exterior walls to fit.

For several decades Sears had been experiencing head-to-head competition from crosstown rival Montgomery Ward & Company, which got its start in the mail-order business in 1872. The competition from Ward and other chains, including A&P, F.W. Grand, J.J. Newberry, Walgreen's drugstores, and Western Auto Supply, kept Sears pushing for new innovations and faster expansion to maintain its lead.

Catalog and newspaper advertising was handled by Sears's own ad department. But in the 1930s it began to use Homer McKee to place magazine and radio advertising. By the early 1940s radio was being assigned to Blackett-Sample-Hummert, while Erwin, Wasey & Company handled print. A small Chicago shop, the E.H. Brown Advertising Agency, was assigned the Allstate division.

The Sears Empire

Throughout the 1940s and 1950s Sears continued to expand, including opening its first retail stores in Cuba, Mexico, and Canada. The company added automotive service centers to all its full-line stores and opened direct catalog delivery outlets in small towns across the United States, effectively eliminating consumer shipping costs. The catalogs offered a full range of household and fashion items; farm and specialty merchandise were featured in smaller, targeted catalogs. Sears's consumer credit operation gained ground and became one of the most profitable elements of the company's operation. At one point in the 1970s almost half of all U.S. households had Sears's proprietary credit card.

In 1969 Sears announced it would build a new headquarters facility in Chicago. The 110-story Sears Tower became the world's tallest building, emphasizing the company's role as the dominant retailer on the planet.

Sears's money-back guarantee continued to be a strong element in its print, radio, and catalog advertising, and in the 1970s Sears stepped up its use of television advertising to promote its empire. The company's catalogs helped drive store traffic, and many customers came into the stores to order merchandise available only in its catalogs. In 1977 Sears mailed 15 million copies each of its hefty spring and fall catalogs to U.S. consumers.

Responding to the TV culture, Sears began to offer more licensed merchandise and brand name toys in the 1970s, in addition to its own brands. In 1978 Sears introduced a line of home fashions designed by Diane Von Furstenberg, one of the first in a series of high-profile licensed merchandise arrangements with celebrities, including baseball player Ted Williams, golfer Arnold Palmer, and tennis professional Yvonne Goolagong. Model Cheryl Tiegs was an icon in Sears's catalogs, advertising, and merchandise for several years as the company targeted apparel toward working women.

After Wood retired as chairman in 1954, a series of other leaders served at the company's helm, each for just a few years. Austin T. Cushman was chairman during the high-growth years of 1962 to 1967; Gordon M. Metcalf led the company into an era of heavier advertising between 1967 and 1973; and Arthur M. Wood was chairman for five years, from 1973 to 1978, when Sears's distribution centers became more automated and sophisticated.

Setbacks and Restructurings

Around 1980, however, competition from retailers such as Montgomery Ward, Kmart, J.C. Penney Company, and regional department stores began to take a toll on Sears. That year, Sears's Allstate insurance operation was more profitable than its retail business. Sears's dilemma was that its booming Allstate operation was heavily dependent on the retail stores to generate traffic, and the possibility of setting up an outside network of Allstate offices led to a major strategic change in corporate direction under Chairman Edward R. Telling, who served from 1978 to 1986.

In 1980 Telling oversaw a restructuring and devised the Sears Merchandise Group to separate retailing and catalog sales from the company's other operations. In 1981 he announced plans to create the largest consumer-oriented financial services entity in the world, as Sears acquired brokerage Dean Witter Reynolds and real estate company Coldwell Banker & Company. The idea was to cluster the new real estate and financial services (and eventually mortgage services) inside Sears stores, along with Allstate, to serve consumers' diversified needs. In 1982 Sears formed a world trading company called Sears World Trade and in 1985 introduced Discover, a general consumer credit card that would be accepted at Sears stores.

Throughout the late 1980s Sears struggled to build synergy between its retail and financial services operations, advertising the Sears Financial Network in TV, print, and radio ads. By 1988, though, it was clear Sears's retail sales were losing momentum, and a series of restructurings followed. That year Sears opened its first Brand Central in-store appliance center and began selling more national brands in its stores; soon afterward, it launched HomeLife, its stand-alone furniture stores.

In 1988 Sears also began aggressively pursuing in-store boutiques targeting specific demographic groups and established a relationship with McDonald's Corporation to sell licensed "McKids" branded apparel. Several stand-alone stores offering paint and hardware, appliances, and even McKids merchandise were launched; only the stand-alone Sears Paint & Hardware outlets survived.

"You Can Count on Sears"

Sears relied on a substantial in-house advertising department to handle its heavy newspaper advertising operations over the years. It also sought counsel from a variety of advertising and promotion agencies, including, in the 1930s, Erwin, Wasey & Company, Chicago, for print and Blackett-Sample-Hummert, Chicago, for radio advertising. In the 1940s Sears employed Roche, Williams & Cunnyngham; Schwimmer & Scott Advertising Agency; and Bisberne Advertising Company, all of Chicago. In the 1950s Sears relied on the renamed Roche, Williams & Cleary for advertising concepts; other agencies included Frederick Asher, Chicago; Henry Mayers Advertising, Los Angeles,

WE'D LIKE TO GIVE

YOU TWO FREE GIFTS.

AND YOU DON'T EVEN

HAVE TO INVITE US

TO THE WEDDING.

No additional invitations. No extra place settings. All you have to do for two free wedding gifts is register at Sears Love & wishes Wedding Gift Registry. Our first present? Our wedding Welcome Guide. It's filled with gift ideas from Kenmore, Craftsman, Cuisinart, Canon, Sunbeam, Sony and more, to help you pick out gifts you'll really use. Plus, we'll give you a 5x7 silver-plated wedding frame to preserve your favorite moment. But perhaps best of all? You don't even have to send a thank you note.

SEARS

SEARS.COM

the good life at a great price. guaranteed.

In 1999 Sears introduced "The good life at a great price. Guaranteed," one in a long line of slogans used by the retailer. *The 2000 advertisement "The Good Life at a Great Price. Guaranteed." is reprinted by arrangement with Sears, Roebuck and Co. and is protected under copyright. No duplication in permitted.*

California, and Remsen Advertising Agency, New Haven, Connecticut. In the early 1960s Sears began a long-running relationship with Ogilvy, Benson & Mather, in New York City, which lasted through the 1990s, with other agencies sharing responsibilities and handling promotional and direct mail duties.

Near the height of its power as a catalog and retail merchandising company in 1972, Sears's agency roster included Ogilvy & Mather, successor to Ogilvy, Benson & Mather (which handled home appliances, home fashions, sewing); the J. Walter Thompson Company (JWT), Chicago (lawn mowers, paint, tractors, outdoor equipment); Foote, Cone & Belding (FCB; sports, tires and batteries, hosiery, luggage, diamonds, women's apparel); McCann-Erickson (cosmetics, wigs, men's furnishings); Stern, Walters & Simmons (children's store, detergent); and the Vince Cullers Agency (specialty marketing).

By 1982 Sears had trimmed its roster to Ogilvy (all hard lines); Needham Harper Worldwide (all soft lines); Stern Walters/Earle Ludgin (catalog promotion); Hispania Advertising, New York City (Hispanic); and Stone & Adler (direct response). Sears's agencies in 1987 included Ogilvy (home appliances, home fashions, credit cards); JWT (Craftsman Tools, hardware, paint); and FCB (sporting goods, shoes, women's apparel).

By 1988 Sears had consolidated most of its TV and general advertising with Ogilvy, but in the mid-1990s Sears added Young & Rubicam to its roster, and the two agencies shared core brand duties for several years through 2001, when Sears's total marketing spending totaled $1.5 billion.

Throughout its history Sears's advertising themes consistently touted reliability, the implied guarantee of "satisfaction or your money back," and merchandise diversity. In 1957 its advertising theme was general: "Serving all America's needs for family, home, car and farm." In 1962 Sears introduced a shorter theme line: "Shop at Sears and save." In 1965 the company debuted a long-running theme line: "You can count on Sears." During the 1970s and 1980s major advertising themes included "Solid as Sears" and "Where America shops" (1970s); "There's more for your life at Sears" (1983); "Your money's worth and a whole lot more" (1988); "Come see the softer side of Sears" (1993); "Come see the many sides of Sears" (1996); and "The good life at a great price. Guaranteed" (1999).

Reinventing Sears

In the 1990s Sears expanded its retail operations by acquisition, buying Western Auto Supply, Parts America, National Tire & Battery, and Orchard Hardware Supply stores. Steadily losing market share to deep-discount rivals that offered a narrower assortment of popular merchandise in low-overhead, no-frills formats, Sears attempted to jump-start its sales in its mainline stores in March 1989 by announcing a new commitment to "everyday low pricing." Sears vowed to keep its prices low year-round, eliminating the weekly promotional sales driven by newspaper ads. Instead it planned to move to national, TV-based image advertising that emphasized quality, assortment, and national brands.

Although its proprietary credit card was still a major source of profit, and Discover had become profitable in 1987, Sears's desperation to improve sales was underscored when it announced it would begin accepting Visa and MasterCard. The various schemes to diversify failed. From 1986 to 1994 Chairman Edward A. Brennan presided over continuous restructurings and attempts to streamline operations, finally resulting in mass layoffs and the closing of dozens of underperforming stores in 1992.

In 1993 Sears spun off its Allstate and stock brokerage/credit card operation, Dean Witter, Discover & Company, as separate, nonaffiliated companies. Also sold were the Coldwell Banker real estate operation, the Sears Mortgage Banking Group, and Homard Development Group, Sears's commercial real estate development arm. The Sears Tower corporate headquarters building was sold, and the final blow came in 1993 when the catalog was shut down.

In 1995 Brennan retired and Sears began a renaissance under the leadership of former Saks Fifth Avenue executive Arthur C. Martinez, who served as chairman through 1999. The company moved its headquarters to a 200-acre campus in Hoffman Estates, Illinois, a Chicago suburb. Many of Sears's stand-alone businesses were sold, including HomeLife, Western Auto Supply, and Parts America. The Sears Auto Centers, however, remained. Sales improved steadily through the 1990s, but growth flattened again in 1999.

At the beginning of the 21st century Sears continued to try to redefine its merchandise mix to suit America's changing habits. Primarily locked into enclosed shopping malls, Sears lost market share to deep-discount retailers such as Wal-Mart, Kmart, and Target, which offered competitively priced apparel in "big-box" stand-alone stores and strip malls that allowed consumers easier access in fast-growing areas.

In 2000 Sears ranked as the 12th-largest U.S. advertiser, spending $1.46 billion, down from $1.50 billion in 1999 (when it was ranked 11th). In 1999 the company boasted 860 department stores, roughly the same number it had at its peak, and 2,100 specialty stores. At the turn of the century Sears was continuing its efforts to reinvent retailing. In 2000 it opened four new stores called the Great Indoors, offering one-stop shopping with a wide assortment of products for homeowners, ranging from appliances to home fashions, how-to books, and fixtures.

KATE FITZGERALD

See also color plate in this volume

Further Reading

Hoge, Cecil C., *The First Hundred Years Are the Toughest: What We Can Learn from the Century of Competition between Sears and Wards,* Berkeley, California: Ten Speed Press, 1988

Katz, Donald R., *The Big Store: Inside the Crisis and Revolution at Sears,* New York: Viking, 1987

Weil, Gordon Lee, *Sears, Roebuck, USA: The Great American Catalog Store and How It Grew,* Briarcliff Manor, New York: Stein and Day, 1977

Self-Regulation

In many countries, self-regulation is a major force in the control of advertising. Business groups, working with media associations, heavily influence advertising content in many European countries, including France and the United Kingdom. In New Zealand, ad agencies, advertisers, and media associations work together under a single self-regulatory body. These countries are culturally more homogeneous than the United States, however, and have smaller media systems serving smaller populations. (The entire population of New Zealand, for example, is less than that of many major U.S. cities.) Moreover, because the countries have no constitutional protection for free speech, their governments act more decisively against misleading advertising than does the U.S. government. And because they have no antitrust laws, their trade associations and media are able to work together to restrict many questionable practices. In the United States, on the other hand, the existence of antitrust laws, along with a fragmented and highly diverse media system, means that any effort at self-regulation involves a different set of powers and limitations.

Industry codes merely suggest desired practices, however. Whether advertisers decide to comply depends on other factors. Self-regulation can influence the decisions of many advertisers and can render government intervention unnecessary. But in every country, the threat of government power is the major force compelling advertisers to comply with self-regulatory activities.

While the influence of self-regulation is real and pragmatic, its effectiveness as a consumer protection device is limited. Self-regulation has restricted powers and may address different goals than consumer protection aims to effect. Under U.S. law, a trade group cannot force any of its members to adhere to a code. Any group of competitors that seeks to enforce how its members can sell products is in violation of antitrust laws. Trade associations' powers of enforcement are therefore limited to member cooperation.

First Efforts

In 1911, faced with declining trust in advertising and potential threats of restrictive actions by government, *Printers' Ink,* a major ad industry trade paper in the United States, proposed a model statute for advertising regulation. The model was eventually adopted in some form by all but three states. This action by the trade was seen as a positive and socially aware move. The states also made deceptive advertising a misdemeanor with strong punishments, although they required prosecutors to prove criminal intent. As a result, there are no instances of states using these laws as a cause of action against advertisers.

Over the years, various trade associations have written codes or guidelines for their members. While these actions were often touted as strong forces of consumer protection, critics have found them to be weak in practice; some groups lacked a mechanism for enforcing the code. And even when a trade group could use the code against a business group's leaders, there might be other companies that considered the code irrelevant to their daily operations.

Some closed-shop "guilds" that required members to be licensed had a legal mechanism for the enforcement of advertising practices. These rules restricted physicians, lawyers, optometrists, pharmacists, and many other professionals from advertising. However, starting in the mid-1970s, these bans on advertising were stopped by courts under applications of free speech rights or other laws. Restrictions against pharmacists who advertised prices of prescription drugs were seen as harmful to consumers, who wished to be able to engage in comparison shopping.

Attempts to self-regulate the advertising of consumer goods did not end with the proposals of *Printers' Ink.* The American Association of Advertising Agencies was created in 1917 amid much talk of ethics and self-regulation. Because membership was required if an agency was to be recognized by the media for commission payments, its code had some influence on member practices. But the Justice Department later said that this code violated antitrust laws, thus removing the association's ability to enforce its code by sanction.

New Deal Policies

With the New Deal government of the 1930s, U.S. President Franklin D. Roosevelt helped make the federal government an instrument of consumer interests. A bill to transfer advertising oversight from the powerless Federal Trade Commission (FTC) to the more aggressive Food and Drug Administration (FDA) stirred advertisers to reconsider self-regulation. In 1938 Congress chose to leave advertising oversight with the FTC, but it gave the agency broad new powers to seek court injunctions against deceptive ads, such as the claim by Fleischmann's Yeast that it could straighten crooked teeth.

World War II reduced the availability of consumer goods and therefore the need to advertise; subsequently the threat of regulation declined. After the war, though, there were several high-profile FTC advertising cases. Carter's Little Liver Pills was compelled to admit that its product had no effect on the liver. Geritol ended its claims to awaken "tired blood." And two famous cases of the 1960s addressed questionable television commercials. The first involved a demonstration for Rapid Shave shaving cream that showed a razor supposedly shaving sandpaper. The second concerned a commercial for Campbell's vegetable soup in which marbles were used in the bottom of a soup bowl to push the vegetables to the surface and make the soup appear thicker and more appetizing.

In the late 1960s and early 1970s the growing consumer movement made it hard for advertisers to ignore their misdeeds. A sugar industry campaign, for example, implied that candy and ice cream could "help" control weight. The FTC ordered the sugar industry to print a retraction or run corrective advertising in every publication in which the campaign had appeared. Clearly, self-regulation would not come without the threat of government action.

Enforceable Regulation

In 1969 a handful of industry leaders took up the challenge. Led by Victor Etling, chairman of the American Advertising Federation (AAF) and vice president of advertising at Quaker Oats, and AAF President Howard Bell, they approached the recently formed Council of Better Business Bureaus (CBBB) in search of a partnership.

The basic tone of regulatory concerns had altered, and neither the consumer nor consumer groups would emerge as the most effective monitor of false advertising. Instead, the monitors were themselves advertisers that—with competitors—stood to lose the most from misleading claims. In 1971 this notion became the premise for the National Advertising Review Council (NARC), which was formed in league with the CBBB.

For most of its history the NARC has had three ad review divisions. The National Advertising Division (NAD) was established to receive complaints from consumers, local Better Business Bureaus, and from other advertisers challenging the claims of particular ads. The accused advertiser would then be asked to produce substantiation for the claims, at which point the advertiser could offer evidence, modify the campaign, or withdraw it altogether. If no agreement was reached, the defending advertiser could appeal to a second review unit, the National Advertising Review Board (NARB), which drew its membership from a pool of industry executives. The organization achieved considerable prestige when Charles Yost, former U.S. ambassador to the United Nations, agreed to serve as the NARB's first chairman. The third leg of the NARC was the Children's Advertising Review Unit (CARU), which monitored advertising to young people.

Industry self-regulation was clearly a reaction to the increasingly strong regulatory programs of the FTC, which itself became a major force on advertising practices during the 1970s. Still, many critics asserted that the organization should be more forceful. Some presumed that as the FTC became less active, the NAD/NARB would bring more cases. However, this group was never intended to be a clearinghouse for large numbers of consumer advertising complaints. In addition, it was and continues to be an industry-directed rather than consumer-directed institution, with few consumers even aware of its existence. While its charter states that it should develop standards, the organization decided that an exhaustive code would be "impractical, needlessly restrictive and self-defeating." Instead it decides on a case-by-case basis when and where it will act.

To advertisers, it is an efficient and active body. It is often pointed out that only one firm has ever failed to go along with a final NARB panel decision, and that was in 1997 after many years and thousands of cases. Few advertisers have declined to participate in a NAD inquiry. In fact, cooperation is so complete that fewer than 100 full NARB panels met from 1971 through 1998 to handle appeals from NAD decisions.

This business cooperation is important in that the NAD/NARB is powerless to enforce its will on advertisers. It selects cases involving advertisers most likely to go along with the program. It does not attempt to set codes or go beyond the basic requirements of government, simply because such muscle-flexing would cause cooperation to disintegrate. The only power it possesses is the advertising community's fear of the FTC or of government regulations.

"On Your Side"

The implicit statement from the NAD/NARB to all marketers facing an adverse decision is: "We are fellow members of the business community, people who understand how you operate and how advertising works. We are on 'your side,' yet we still found potential for your advertising to mislead people. Just think what a government agency would say in your case!" An FTC complaint would be more prolonged, more costly, and would probably entail a burden on future claims by the marketer or advertising agency. The NAD is concerned only with questions of deception rather than issues, taste, style, or stereotyping, areas over which the FTC has no jurisdiction.

In Australia the Advertising Standards Association, the main force in advertising regulation, has been increasingly criticized for heavy-handed involvement in cases. In 1997 it examined a faucet manufacturer whose commercial showed a household flood caused by using the wrong faucet. The complaint was that the ad displayed wasting water during a drought. Both the public and business groups responded so strongly to this overreaction that the association was forced to shut down all activities.

In the United States various trade associations boast that their member businesses, because they adhere to self-regulatory codes, are responsible corporate citizens. Such groups often will take credit for desirable business practices, even when such claims are not valid. For several decades the Distilled Spirits Council of the United States claimed (and was generally given) credit for keeping liquor advertising off television through a self-imposed ban. In reality the products continued to be advertised in non-mainstream broadcast realms until 1996. For example, the products were advertised on Spanish-language television up until 1988. If the code kept the products off "mainstream" TV stations and networks, it should have done so for Spanish-language audiences, too.

What really kept distilled products off most television was that few broadcast stations, generally only weak stations in small markets, would accept such commercials. Companies such as Seagram were faced with a simple choice: make commercials for the small audiences that might watch those few stations or design campaigns that depended on print media. Given the potential for strong negative public reactions, coupled with the very limited potential for gain, the decision was to concentrate on print. When Spanish-language stations accepted spots for distilled spirits, the marketers used the broadcast media for those audiences.

In 1996 stations in major markets decided to accept Seagram's commercials. After the commercials aired, and realizing that other stations and advertisers might soon follow suit, the Distilled Spirits Council quickly altered the code to say that television advertising is acceptable, probably to avoid what could otherwise have become a conflict with its major members.

Government leaders, regulators, and some public interest groups have proposed possible regulatory actions, placing all alcoholic beverages under scrutiny and even threatening the broadcasters with possible loss of beer and wine advertising. But actual audience reaction has tended toward apathy, indicating that stations did not err in gauging their audiences' reactions, though the backlash from government has caused potential for concern.

Power of the Media

Existing media might force a group of companies to follow certain practices in deciding how to efficiently reach target audiences. And a trade association might retroactively adopt those practices as part of a code, formally endorsing what has already been put into practice.

No television station, cable or broadcast network, magazine, radio station, or newspaper in the United States is required to accept commercial advertising material it does not wish to carry. There are some limited exceptions for political advertising in the broadcast media. Some media impose strong standards on the types of advertising content they will accept for broadcast or publication.

Every media rejection has the power to influence or alter an advertising campaign. Sometimes the objections or the perceptions of possible deceptions are minor, and the advertiser can make changes to the ad or commercial without harming the message strategy. Of course, the marketer can take the ads to another vehicle, but only if there are others that will accept them and are appropriate to the media strategy.

Two examples of media codes that influenced many business practices are the Comic [Book] Code Authority and the radio and television codes administered by the National Association of Broadcasters. The history of these codes also indicates the limits of trade associations' abilities to restrict their members' actions.

In the mid-1950s public concern of potential harm to children caused by horror comic books resulted in congressional hearings that threatened possible government suppression of the medium. In response, comic book companies agreed to abide by a code of good practice for all aspects of their publications, including advertising. Before distribution, each book was submitted to the Comics Code Authority and, if approved, would be permitted to carry the seal of good practice on the cover. The distributors agreed that they would not carry issues that did not have the seal.

The existence of this code was highly unusual because such codes are usually found to be in violation of antitrust laws. At that time, though, government organizations accepted the Comics Code Authority's limitations on business practices as acceptable. Regardless of potential violations, no publisher attempted to seek legal redress against the Code Authority, nor did the Justice Department attempt to enforce antitrust laws against its activities.

Long after the focus of public attention had drifted away from comics, editorial content in the May 1971 issue of *The Amazing Spider-Man* failed to meet the Code Authority's requirements. The issue depicted the problem of drug abuse, and although it did so in what could be described as a responsible manner—Spider-Man

Fortified with 8 essential vitamins!

Have a good breakfast tomorrow.

Build it around Kellogg's Rice Krispies.

"The best to you each morning." Kellogg's

rescues a self-destructive addict from suicide but laments that his power cannot solve the drug problem—the Code Authority nevertheless forbade any portrayal of drugs whatsoever. The issue was distributed to newsstands without the seal.

The seal has since become irrelevant for distribution; many comic books found on store racks today are not even submitted to the Code Authority, although some comic book publishers still proudly point to the code as evidence of strong and effective consumer protection. While adult comic book fans still criticize the restrictions, they feel the presence of the code diffuses any possible additional regulatory threats. Today the code exists merely as a cautionary note for publishers.

Broadcast Codes

Before 1982 the National Association of Broadcasters (NAB) Radio Code and Television Code exerted significant influence over advertisers' practices. NAB employees interpreted guidelines, reviewed commercials before submission to stations for possible broadcast, and decided which commercials were acceptable. Fewer than two-thirds of television stations and half of radio stations followed their respective voluntary codes, but NAB codes were the basis for acceptance decisions at all three

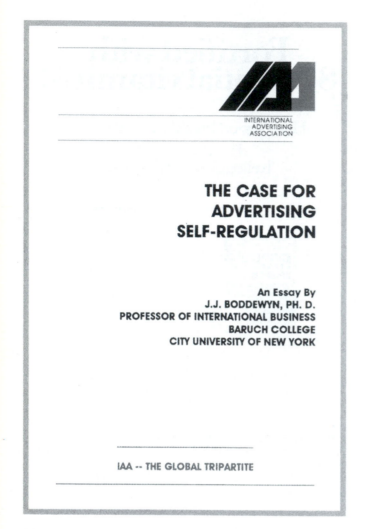

**THE CASE FOR
ADVERTISING
SELF-REGULATION**

An Essay By
J.J. BODDEWYN, PH. D.
PROFESSOR OF INTERNATIONAL BUSINESS
BARUCH COLLEGE
CITY UNIVERSITY OF NEW YORK

IAA -- THE GLOBAL TRIPARTITE

Industry groups such as the International Advertising Association have encouraged self-regulation by their members using various means, including the publication of studies on the topic.
International Advertising Association (IAA), the global partnership of marketing communications professionals.

networks and many major-market stations across the country, accounting for 80 percent of television audiences. While advertisers could always find noncode stations to carry NAB-rejected commercials, advertisers desiring to reach the audiences of the code-subscribing members were forced to abide by the code and meet its requirements.

The radio and television codes served a leadership role. Their pervasive influence led some researchers to incorrectly attribute common business practices based upon the codes to government requirements. Faced with the choice of meeting code requirements or incurring the expense and public relations headaches of producing two sets of commercials for code and noncode stations, many advertisers chose the former. For example, the NAB Code, in effect, stopped lingerie manufacturers from using live models in underwear commercials. And until 1974, when the code dropped its ban on feminine hygiene products (an action viewed by some

as an effort to generate revenue lost when Congress barred cigarette advertising on TV in 1972), advertisers of such products regarded print media as more efficient than limited use of broadcasting via the noncode stations. Unlike the mission of the NAD, which was to police factual content, the NAB codes were equally concerned with issues of taste and style.

The Justice Department sued the NAB under antitrust laws in 1979, claiming that parts of the codes violated antitrust laws by recommending limits on numbers of commercials per hour. After adverse pretrial rulings in 1982, the NAB suspended all code activities, including those related to its guidelines and procedures that reviewed commercials for potentially deceptive or offensive content that were not part of the government's complaint. Many stations report that the now-defunct code guidelines still operate as the basis for current policies. However, claims of adherence to the former code often do not match actual practices.

Member acceptance of a code might be more difficult today. Even if the NAB code were resurrected, it would find its adherents to be a smaller percentage of the broadcast operations, representing a shrinking proportion of the daily audiences. The interests, concerns, and values of broadcasters have become increasingly varied. The number of stations has increased dramatically since the NAB dropped all code activities; there are now more stations and more independent (i.e., non-network affiliate) operations, all fighting for a share of the audience.

Network Policies

The "Big Three" networks—ABC, CBS, and NBC—all follow written codes adopted when the NAB dropped its clearance procedures. While the three often do not agree with each other on actual acceptance decisions for individual commercials, they sometimes influence advertising practices in a manner akin to that previously promoted by the NAB. (The Fox network did not exist when NAB dropped the code, and it makes decisions on an ad hoc, case-by-case basis, with no written guidelines.)

The networks' style and taste concerns for various cologne and perfume commercials set a standard that can direct major changes in presentation. Contemporary practices also illustrate how some networks' acceptance decisions might run counter to public policy goals, such as network decisions to reject condom advertising and related public service announcements designed to disseminate AIDS prevention and "safe sex" messages.

While the networks influence many advertisers' decisions, as network audience shares decline and the number of cable and independent options increase, there are many other outlets for commercials that never undergo review by the networks. There is a wide variation in the willingness of individual television stations to ask advertisers to substantiate claims or reject commercial submissions; many stations accept virtually anything. In the case of radio, research suggests that the technical details of the commercials' production quality are the major priority. Cable TV networks look to a mix of these concerns: the fit between the advertising and programs that might run on the network, followed by technical and aesthetic production quality of the commercial, and then, whether the style of presentation might offend the viewing audience.

On the whole, each broadcast station's general manager and each newspaper or magazine's publisher is responsible for acceptance, and each is free to set guidelines for his or her own vehicle. In general, the "whim" of senior management, more than anything else, sets the tone for clearance standards.

Case studies of advertising acceptance policies and practices point to examples of media managers who forgo revenue to meet audience protection goals. On the other hand, consumer advocates see major gaps in the system, noting that the media are not doing enough and that many audiences are unprotected. Advertisers can avoid strict vehicles altogether.

The FTC would like to encourage vehicle managers to do more to screen ads for potential deceptions, since every deceptive claim caught by attentive media managers represents one less case to occupy the time and attention of the commission. However, the primary concern for most media decisions is how the taste and style of the advertising fits into the overall vehicle image, not whether the claims are true or if the product works. While the vehicle managers probably would not knowingly carry ads that actually harm the audience, for most the primary concern is to avoid offending readers, listeners, or viewers. They focus more closely on deceptions the audience will find on its own than on misleading claims the public might never discover.

Standards and Practices

Because radio commercials came into people's homes in a way advertising never had before, there was some uncertainty as to their welcome. Initially, there was a sense that advertising was an invited "guest" and should behave accordingly. Networks and their affiliates were also aware that the broadcast frequencies they used were licensed at the pleasure of the government in the name of the public. In February 1927, NBC set up an advisory council to consider issues of content regarding advertising and programming, both of which in most cases were created and supplied to the network by advertising agencies. A considerable body of broadcast standards and practices was in place by the end of the 1930s in which the networks reserved for themselves the right to review (and reject) advertising and programming on the basis of taste, content, and other matters. For the most part, this power was exercised for the purpose of avoiding controversies, not restricting advertising claims.

While textbooks and popular wisdom may paint the media as major bulwarks of consumer protection, the acceptance of ads by media was not an endorsement of any claims by either a broadcaster or magazine. Contrary to popular belief, the *Good Housekeeping* Seal of Approval was not an assurance of product testing but rather a promise to stand behind readers who wanted their money back from advertisers whose products did not live up to expectations. The seal was a tool to market the magazine to both readers and advertisers.

With the Internet and other means for the rapid exchange of information, the time and expense involved in verifying advertis-

ing claims is no longer a rationale for ignoring possibly deceptive claims. At the same time, the performance of a radio or TV station manager or a magazine or newspaper publisher is evaluated by profitability. Thus, policy is often driven by a mix of greed and fear—wanting the revenue and not wishing to drive away the audience. And in marketing the vehicle, most managers are concerned with their station's or publication's entertainment value, not its reputation for advertising veracity.

It is difficult to discern what prompts concern for consumer protection or which media organizations are strictest. The influence and power of advertising acceptance policies is tied to a question of point of view. To an advertiser whose primary targets are audiences of restrictive vehicles, the media advertising acceptance policies must form a significant aspect of advertising planning. Similarly, advertisers that wish to reach well-protected audiences only part of the time might see these clearance requirements as an important part of the regulatory landscape. However, a consumer advocate would be interested in how thoroughly the clearance process substitutes for laws and regulations and, accordingly, focuses attention on the quantity of deceptive advertising claims that are not stopped.

There are many valid reasons for deregulation and many examples of government regulations that are contrary to the best interests of consumers. This does not necessarily render government regulation "unnecessary." If greater self-regulation activity is desired, the threat of increased government regulation would be needed to motivate it. Government programs set the framework for self-regulation practices. Without the threat of government action, only the most altruistic of advertisers would be likely to heed self-regulation directives.

HERBERT JACK ROTFELD

Further Reading

Armstrong, Gary M., "An Evaluation of the Children's Advertising Review Unit," *Journal of Public Policy and Marketing* 3 (1984)

Best, Arthur, "Controlling False Advertising: A Comparative Study of Public Regulation, Industry Self-Policing, and Private Litigation," *Georgia Law Review* 20 (Fall 1985)

Garvin, David A., "Can Industry Self-Regulation Work?" *California Management Review* 25, no. 4 (Summer 1983)

Labarbera, Priscilla A., "Analyzing and Advancing the State of the Art of Advertising Self-Regulation," *Journal of Advertising* 9, no. 4 (1980)

McDonough, John, "25 Years of Self-Regulation," *Advertising Age* (2 December 1996)

Rotfeld, Herbert, "Why Don't We See Many Condom Ads? Because We Don't Want To," *Chicago Tribune* (16 December 1991)

Rotfeld, Herbert, "Power and Limitations of Media Clearance Practices and Advertising Self-Regulation," *Journal of Public Policy and Marketing* 11, no. 1 (Spring 1992)

Rotfeld, Herbert Jack, *Adventures in Misplaced Marketing*, Westport, Connecticut: Quorum Books, 2001

Rotfeld, Herbert J., and Patrick R. Parsons, "Self-Regulation and Magazine Advertising," *Journal of Advertising* 18, no. 4 (1989)

Stern, Louis L., "Consumer Self-Protection via Self-Regulation," *Journal of Marketing* 35 (July 1971)

Wyckham, Robert G., "Self-Regulation of Sex-Role Stereotyping in Advertising: The Canadian Experience," *Journal of Public Policy and Marketing* 6 (1987)

Zanot, Eric J., "Unseen but Effective Advertising Regulation: The Clearance Process," *Journal of Advertising* 14, no. 4 (1985)

Senior Citizens Market

It is only in about the past 30 years that senior citizens have became a distinct target market for advertisers. Until the late 1960s, most ad campaigns were aimed at people under 55. Even market researchers tended to ignore older people; in the 1990s, the A.C. Nielsen research company still did not regularly collect viewing data on TV audience members over 65. It did not consistently include those over 55 in its Nielsen Television Index until 1977.

While this emphasis on younger elements of the population was not confined to advertisers and market researchers in the United States, it was particularly pronounced in American culture, where attributes such as youthfulness, vitality, productivity, and independence have long been highly valued. National advertising for products such as the energy supplement Geritol—which was aimed specifically at older consumers and promoted in conjunction with the *Lawrence Welk Show,* a long-running television variety show that attracted older viewers—was the exception. Even cosmetics companies, which recognized that aging people were prime prospects for their products, concentrated on young, attractive, vibrant images and advertising copy that "sold youth."

Another reason older consumers have long been neglected lies in the nature of the products that make up the largest segment of advertising expenditures, specifically branded packaged goods (e.g., toothpaste, cigarettes, soap) that are quickly consumed and repurchased. It has been accepted wisdom in the advertising industry that younger buyers are more easily persuaded by ads, whereas older consumers know what they want and are thus a less profitable target for packaged-goods advertising.

Gaining a Voice

Interest in the seniors market emerged in the 1960s and 1970s, grew in the 1980s, and became quite widespread in the 1990s as advertisers began to understand and respond to several ongoing trends. The first of these, beginning in the 1960s, was the movement by older people in the United States, following the lead of women and various minority groups, to establish themselves as a group with civil rights. The American Association of Retired Persons (AARP), the Gray Panthers, and other groups representing the interests of the elderly were formed and became highly influential. They sought to bring greater political, legal, governmental, and commercial attention to the needs of senior citizens and were vociferous in their efforts to dispel public misperceptions of older people. Among other actions, these groups protested stereotypical portrayals of senior citizens in the media, including such depictions in advertising.

Prompted in part by these civil rights efforts, marketing educators began to conduct research focusing on the preferences of older consumers. However, as George P. Moschis pointed out in *Marketing to Older Consumers* (1992), much of this research merely described how this group of consumers behaved rather than explaining the reasons behind their actions. Some studies focused on the depiction of older people in advertising and other media and its effects. Market researchers largely ignored the knowledge and understanding of aging being gained by researchers in fields such as geriatrics, anthropology, and sociology.

For the most part, advertisers began to pay increased attention to the senior citizens market not because of social movements or improved comprehension of aging, but because older people began to constitute a larger proportion of the population. In the late 1990s, people over age 50 constituted approximately one-third of the U.S. adult population. The baby boomers (i.e., those born between 1946 and 1964), a substantial segment of the American population, were growing older, while at the same time the life expectancy of each succeeding generation was increasing. As a result of these demographic changes, senior citizens were expected to comprise a growing proportion of the overall population in the 21st century. According to one estimate, the under-50 population was expected to increase by 3 percent over the first quarter of the century, while the over-50 population was expected to grow by 73 percent. Similar trends were evident in industrialized countries around the world. Advertisers also came to realize that older consumers possess considerable wealth and discretionary income.

Dispelling Myths and Misconceptions

Still, stereotypes and myths about seniors have persisted, and some authorities say that it is marketers and advertisers that have doggedly held on to them. Among the most typical of these stereotypes is that virtually all older people are in poor health, are senile, crotchety, confined to retirement or nursing homes, inactive, isolated, unproductive, uninterested in sex or romance, indifferent to material possessions, have low incomes, and are rigidly brand loyal. Advertising campaigns based on these assumptions have typically failed. They were created and implemented without heeding classic mistakes such as the one H.J. Heinz made in 1955. The company launched a line of baby food–like meals for adults with chewing problems, only to discover that older consumers were too embarrassed to purchase such a product. Most of all, however, advertisers have mistakenly treated older consumers as a homogeneous market.

Numerous studies over the final three decades of the 20th century showed that these stereotypes were evident in portrayals of older people in a variety of media—prime-time television programming, children's programming, children's and adolescent literature, newspaper stories, magazine cartoons, greeting cards, television commercials, and magazine advertising. Older men tended to be depicted favorably more often than older women, and not surprisingly, portrayals of the elderly tended to be more positive when the publication, program, or product in question was aimed specifically at older consumers. Older models appeared more often in advertising for upscale products. Many scholars and advocates for the elderly have expressed concern about the social effects of these portrayals on individuals, audiences, and society in general. While these effects may be less severe in cultures where elders and tradition are highly respected, in youth-conscious cultures such as that of the United States, these depictions promote, reflect, and reinforce disrespect for senior citizens.

Equally significant, marketing researchers have found that older consumers have been greatly underrepresented in the media and in advertising in the past few decades, although they have become much more visible they once were. Special interest groups representing the elderly have suggested that this lack of representation has caused senior citizens and their unique needs to be undervalued and neglected.

Advertisers and market researchers have found it particularly difficult to define and segment the senior citizens market. Collective labels such as "mature," "elderly," "seniors," and "older" have caused confusion. Definitions of "senior" range from "40 and above" to "over 70" or anywhere in between. Some researchers have focused solely on those senior citizens in retirement homes. Others accept the designation "65 and older," the U.S. Social Security Act mandatory retirement age. The United States census distinguishes four categories: "olders" (55–64), "elders" (65–74), "aged" (75–84), and "very old" (85 and over).

Understanding the Market

Some scholars have concluded that defining older consumers purely in terms of chronological age is ineffective and misleading. Understanding senior citizens and developing promotional efforts on the basis of lifestyles, attitudes, interests, self-perceptions of age and aging, social roles, relative physical health, employment status, and degree of social isolation has been much more fruitful.

Flexagen, a dietary supplement that claims to promote healthy joints, targeted the senior market with an ad featuring a fit, active older woman. *By permission of Whitehall-Robins Healthcare.*

In 1969 the Greyhound Bus Company was credited with being one of the first companies in the United States to advertise extensively to senior citizens. Its consumer research had indicated that many of its passengers were older.

In the years that followed and especially in the 1980s, other advertisers with products or services targeted to seniors began to tailor advertising campaigns to them. For example, advertising for Cadillac automobiles was aimed at older, affluent consumers. In the mid-1980s Eastern Air Lines found success with its "Get-Up-and-Go" campaign (from Lintas Campbell-Ewald) advertising bargain flights. L'Oréal for many years successfully advertised its Grecian Formula hair coloring products to the seniors market, clearly depicting older people in the ads. Other companies developed and advertised new lines of products or services specifically for seniors. Campbell Soup Company led the way in developing and promoting low-calorie products for older consumers. Kellogg Company changed the name of Bran Flakes to 50-Plus Bran Flakes and increased its sales. Many other companies began promoting low-fat and high-fiber food products.

Bristol-Myers and other drug companies offered special products for those over 50 such as Naldecon Senior cough syrups. Metropolitan Life, Aetna, and other financial institutions created investment and retirement services—and correlating advertising campaigns—expressly for senior citizens. For example, a mid-1980s campaign (from Lord, Geller, Federico, Einstein, Inc.) depicted an older couple taking a leisurely walk in the country and discussing how the people at Dean Witter "really listen" and "really care." In 1984 Sears developed Mature Outlook, a discount club for senior citizens that also serves as a market research and product-testing vehicle. Health care institutions, too, have promoted memberships and other services to this market. By the mid-1980s, more than half of the largest corporations in the United States were to some degree targeting products, services, and advertising to the seniors market.

In 1984 Wendy's International, through its national agency, Dancer, Fitzgerald, Sample, unveiled an advertising campaign that featured Clara Peller, an elderly woman eating at a competitor's restaurant and loudly exclaiming, "Where's the beef?" as she examines the skimpy hamburger placed in front of her. The campaign proved to be one of the most successful in advertising history, and Peller became a national icon. The phrase "Where's the beef?" became a part of the language, and Wendy's reaped incredible financial success. Although the Peller character humorously toyed with stereotypes of the elderly and thus even angered some senior citizens, the campaign's popularity drew greater attention to the possible uses of older characters in advertising campaigns for a greater range of products and services and presented an image of older people as outspoken consumers unwilling to be taken advantage of.

The Broader Market

Many successful advertising campaigns of the 1980s and 1990s employed older celebrities as spokespersons in ongoing campaigns for products or services aimed at seniors and other markets. The late baseball star Joe DiMaggio was long featured in campaigns for Mr. Coffee coffeemakers. In his later years, actor Robert Young represented Maxwell House Coffee in its advertising. Another older actor, James Whitmore, served as advertising spokesperson for Miracle Grow fertilizer. Golfer Arnold Palmer pitched Pennzoil; retired baseball pitcher Nolan Ryan served as spokesperson for Advil pain reliever. Actress June Allison was successfully featured in campaigns for Depend, as Kimberly-Clark led the way in developing adult wetness protection into a whole new product category. Actor Art Carney and his grandson appeared in a Coca-Cola campaign, while another older actor, Wilford Brimley, promoted Quaker Oats and other products. As they have aged, James Garner, James Coburn, Ed McMahon, and many other celebrities have served as spokespersons for various products and services targeted to their contemporaries.

In the 1990s advertising campaigns aimed specifically at older consumers grew more common in the United States. For example, Club Med attracted many senior citizen travelers with its "Forever Young" campaign. Levi Strauss and other clothing manufac-turers developed and advertised product lines for more mature figures. The use of older figures in ads targeted to a mass audience also became more evident. For example, a 1995 study entitled "The Representation of Elderly Persons in Primetime Television Advertising" found that advertisers such as Wal-Mart, Sears, Magnavox, RCA, Microsoft, AT&T, and Alpo targeted both older consumers and other market segments while featuring older people in their advertising campaigns. At the same time, elderly characters were not depicted negatively to the extent that was reported in earlier studies, and the characterizations were not confined to advertising for products obviously designed for older people. Compared to their numbers in the overall population, however, seniors continued to be represented in disproportionately low numbers in advertising.

Many market researchers have attempted to characterize the current seniors market. All agree that it is a highly heterogeneous market that will grow more diverse as the number of consumers increases in all age categories over 55.

Reality Check

Astute marketers and advertisers have observed that most people 55–64 and even many of those 65–74 think and act in ways similar to people in their 40s in past generations. Some senior citizens succumb to health problems—although in the United States only about 5 percent of those over 65 are in nursing homes and 15 percent or fewer have a severe health problem—social withdrawal, loneliness, isolation, and depression, particularly in the oldest age categories. However, the great majority of senior citizens tend to be active; independent; learning; growing psychologically, socially, and spiritually; productive; and interested in a wide variety of products and services. They also want advertisers and others to perceive them this way.

More than two-thirds of those over 50 in the United States are married, and many are affluent. An estimated half of all discretionary income and three-fourths of the assets in the United States in the late 1990s were controlled by those over 50. Elderly women outnumber elderly men in most countries, and in the United States, the life expectancy of whites is greater than that of members of minorities. Older consumers tend to be concentrated in specific geographic areas due to migration or permanent relocation. In the United States, Florida and other warm weather areas have a greater number of senior citizens. Seniors also often live near their children, but more often by choice than dependency, as is frequently assumed.

Some market researchers contend that the chronological age of older consumers should be dismissed and that advertisers should concentrate on what various types of people within the senior market want, expect, and need. With the exception of seniors with severe health problems and those who have withdrawn socially, most senior citizens view themselves as much younger than their chronological age. Marketers have an incentive to advertise to them accordingly. An assumption in recent years has been that all senior citizens seek to and actually do retire to a life of leisure. Even among those who retire, however, many find new

In the mid-1980s Eastern Air Lines' "Get-Up-And-Go" promotion offered special discount fares to senior citizens.

full- or part-time work. Others remain busily engaged in volunteer work, traveling, pursuing hobbies, shopping, furthering their education, and tending to grandchildren.

A number of market researchers have segmented the seniors market on the basis of lifestyle. For example, in his article "Life Stages of the Mature Market" (1996) Moschis divided the American senior market into four lifestyle groups: "heavy indulgers" (13 percent—want products and services that will help them get the most out of life and willing to pay for them; desire independence; enjoy shopping); "hearty hermits" (38 percent—value products and services helpful in fulfilling inner goals; not concerned about outward appearance; "self-actualizing" rather than socially driven); "ailing outgoers" (34 percent—will pay for products and services that enable them to maintain a socially active lifestyle); and "frail recluses" (15 percent—interested in health care or other products and services that will simply make life easier).

As older consumers' interests, desires, behavior, and purchasing patterns have become better understood, the seniors market has become particularly attractive to certain industries. The travel industry is a case in point. Tour packages and luxury cruises are often targeted to older consumers, who tend to travel to learn, expand their horizons, and find new friends, while younger travelers primarily seek adventure and escape. Most hotels and motels, responding in part to pressures from AARP and other organizations representing seniors, offer special discounts to them. In the 1990s the restaurant industry took notice of the special eating habits and needs of older consumers, finding that nutrition, speed, and price were important factors in attracting older diners. Some restaurant chains, such as Morrison's (in the Atlantic region and the South), have aimed their products and services toward seniors, although this age group has been found to be an even better prospective market for food products eaten at home.

Market researchers also have discovered that older consumers are not interested solely in life experiences as once thought, but that they often seek material possessions as well. They often desire products and services that will keep them healthy and active. They are prime prospects for such products and services as prescription drugs; over-the-counter health care products and medical supplies; vitamins; new automobiles, especially luxury cars and recreational vehicles; health spas and exercise equipment; beauty salons; hair coloring and other personal care products and services; upscale household furnishings and home remodeling; various types of medical and home-owner insurance products; and financial services. Often occupying the role of doting grandparents, they purchase approximately 25 percent of all toys. In recent years, the cosmetics industry has been preparing for the great increase in older consumers expected in the 21st century. Many senior citizens enjoy in-home shopping services, but most still prefer shopping at stores.

Ads with Senior Appeal

Market researchers and advertisers have discovered a great deal about the types of promotional appeals to which senior citizens tend to respond. Some research suggests that older consumers are more vulnerable to persuasive appeals, misleading advertising, and marketing scams, and are less able to process messages and sort through advertising clutter than younger people. However, a number of studies indicate that the senior market is attracted to appeals that provide information, facts, and brand benefits. Because they are less peer-conscious, older consumers are less responsive to advertising appeals that emphasize status or what is fashionable. Special promotions that include discounts for senior citizens have proven effective in many instances, but marketing and advertising practitioners warn that some age-conscious older consumers actually resist such offers because of the stigma associated with them. Others have pointed out that the common perception that senior citizens are highly price-conscious and parsimonious is false. More important in building brand loyalty in the seniors market are objectivity in advertising, attention to customer service, speed, convenience, and a personal touch. Some have found older consumers particularly responsive to advertising containing testimonials. Lifestyle advertising that includes factual information also has proven effective.

Whether older models need to be included in all advertising content aimed at the seniors market is still uncertain. Some studies have found older consumers prefer this, while some suggest that it may sometimes make little difference. It is clear that many older consumers find stereotypical or negative portrayals of the elderly offensive and that using words in copy that point people directly to the aging process such as "old," "older," "seniors," and "retired" are unlikely to be effective. Because of the heterogeneous nature of the seniors market, some advertisers believe it is effective to depict a variety of healthy, active, older people, often interacting with younger people. Others believe older consumers should not be singled out in advertising that is aimed at general audiences. The fear is that both older and younger audiences may be alienated by it.

Media and Messages

Increasingly, advertisers are also tailoring their media plans to senior citizens. Older people read newspapers more often than their younger counterparts. *Reader's Digest* and *TV Guide* are the publications most widely read by older consumers, but *Good Housekeeping, Better Homes & Gardens, Family Circle, National Geographic,* and *Woman's Day* all have a wide readership among seniors. Niche magazines such as *Modern Maturity* and *Prevention* are increasingly effective in reaching this very pluralistic mar-

ket. Special newspaper sections or supplements aimed at seniors became common in the 1990s. Direct mail advertising is another means that has been successful in reaching this group.

Even in the late 1990s critics of the television industry pointed out that most programming was aimed at younger audiences and seldom contained characters or themes that would interest older people or depicted them in positive, realistic roles and situations, despite their sizeable and increasing numbers. Nonetheless, senior citizens generally have tended to be heavy viewers of television. In the last two decades of the 20th century, older characters in meaningful roles starred in such successful programs as *Maude, In the Heat of Night, Golden Girls, Murder She Wrote, Matlock, Jake and the Fatman,* and *The Love Boat.* These programs attracted large numbers of older viewers, as did such popular programs as *Meet the Press, 60 Minutes, 20/20, Dateline NBC, Oprah,* and game shows such as *Jeopardy!* and *Wheel of Fortune.* The seniors market also preferred the Discovery Channel, the Learning Channel, and PBS to offerings by the "Big Four" broadcast networks (ABC, CBS, NBC, and Fox).

There was some indication in the late 1990s that older viewers were becoming weary of television fare that was overly violent, vulgar, sexual, and/or youth-oriented and that did not meet their interests and needs. They were also becoming exasperated with advertisers that supported such programming. The Prime Life Advisory Network was dedicated to improving the portrayal of mature adults in the media, advertising, and entertainment industries and helped various companies treat the seniors market more sensitively. With the growth of "narrowcasting" and "niche-casting" programming strategies, cable network services aimed at the seniors market were launched with a mixed degree of success. Both the Nostalgia Network and Golden American Network failed, while Prime Life Network, started in 1996, enjoyed some success. Growing interest in the seniors market has also resulted in the development of an industry of consultants, services, and newsletters specializing in this market. One of the more visible of these has been the Senior Network, Inc., a full-service firm.

As the 20th century came to a close, most advertisers and agencies were becoming aware that older consumers comprised a very diverse, greatly expanding, potentially highly profitable market. The seniors of the year 2002 were better educated consumers than their predecessors and were more interested in cultural activities and an active lifestyle. They required products and services geared for them and promotional efforts that were sympathetic and meaningful to them but neither offensive nor patronizing. At the same time, advertisers were trying to figure out ways to tailor products, services, and advertising to the seniors market without disaffecting younger consumers. Responding to the needs of dramatically increasing numbers of healthier, wealthier, and longer-lived senior citizens who probably will be quite different from their counterparts in past generations promises to be one of the greatest challenges facing advertisers in the new millennium.

J.D. KEELER

Further Reading

Burnett, John J., "Examining the Media Habits of the Affluent Elderly," *Journal of Advertising Research* 31 (October/November, 1991)

Cassata, Mary, *Television Looks at Aging,* New York: Television Information Office, 1985

Conaway, Frank, "Television Is Losing Its Largest Viewing Audience," *USA Today* (May 1997)

Day, Ellen, et al., "Reaching the Senior Citizens Market," *Journal of Advertising Research* 27, no. 6 (December 1987/January 1988)

Long, Nick, "Broken Down by Age and Sex: Exploring the Ways We Approach the Elderly Consumer," *Market Research Society* 40 (April 1998)

Milliman, Ronald E., and Robert C. Erffmeyer, "Improving Advertising Aimed at Seniors," *Journal of Advertising Research* 29 (December 1989/January 1990)

Moschis, George P., *Marketing to Older Consumers: A Handbook of Information for Strategy Development,* Westport, Connecticut: Quorum, 1992

Moschis, George P., "Life Stages of the Mature Market," *American Demographics* 18, no. 9 (September 1996)

Peterson, Robin T., and Douglas T. Ross, "A Content Analysis of the Portrayal of Mature Individuals in Television Commercials," *Journal of Business Ethics* 16 (March 1997)

Sagansky, Jeff, "The Representation of Elderly Persons in Primetime Television Advertising," Master's thesis, University of South Florida, 1995

Stephens, Nancy, "Cognitive Age: A Useful Concept for Advertising?" *Journal of Advertising* 20 (December 1991)

Ursic, Anthony C., Michael L. Ursic, and Virginia L. Ursic, "A Longitudinal Study of the Use of the Elderly in Magazine Advertising," *Journal of Consumer Research* 13 (June 1986)

Wolfe, David B., *Serving the Ageless Market: Strategies for Selling to the Fifty-Plus Market,* New York: McGraw-Hill, 1990

Services

Business analysts have been saying for some time that in the advanced economies of the world, such as those of Western Europe, the United States, and Japan, the value of the services produced has come to outstrip the value of manufactured goods. This trend is apparent in the rapid growth of information as a product of modern business. Economies based largely on services rather than goods are considered to be on the cutting edge of postindustrial economic development.

Service as a product is ubiquitous and diverse, ranging from extremely specialized high-tech functions to unskilled, low-wage labor. Regardless of the type of service, however, marketers agree that the services category requires different advertising strategies from those used to sell durable and packaged goods. These different approaches are generally necessary because services and goods are described and understood differently. For example, durable and packaged goods can normally be touched, and they can be evaluated through physical characteristics. Consumers in the market for a particular type of product can shop for the specific item they want and compare the characteristics of competing products. Services, on the other hand, are intangible and cannot be evaluated physically. This is a key problem that service businesses face and need to overcome in their advertising.

Because, unlike many products, services cannot be saved for later use, they are considered to be perishable. In addition, services are produced and delivered or consumed at the same time—a concept known as inseparability. For example, when a person goes for a haircut, he or she is accepting delivery of the haircut at the same time it is produced. The same idea goes for a car wash or a play. The service did not exist prior to the time of delivery and will not exist after that time. Finally, because different people perform services differently, the quality of the service will vary. This property is known as heterogeneity.

One of the most effective approaches in advertising service offerings is to "tangibilize" the product—that is, to make services appear to have physical or tangible characteristics. This technique can help the potential customer visualize the service. The Allstate Insurance Company, for example, tries to tangibilize insurance services by using an image of supportive hands along with the slogan, "You're in good hands with Allstate." The hands provide a concrete, physical presence for Allstate, which otherwise would not have any visual representation of its service. In addition, the hands convey an image of a caring, warm, supportive company. At the same time, the words of the slogan contribute to tangibilization by specifying the thought represented by the hands. Prudential Insurance Company of America and Travelers Insurance, two other well-known insurance companies, use as their trademark icons a rock and an umbrella, respectively, for similar reasons. Yet another example is Orkin Exterminating Company, a company that uses ads that tangibilize pest control by showing the spraying of a house by a man in a science fiction–style robot suit.

It is also possible to tangibilize the service by providing specific facts and details about it. This approach to advertising the service can help considerably because people like to know what they are getting when they purchase a service. Providing specific information about the service can help potential customers reduce risk. For example, because potential customers may be hesitant to visit

What's it like to be the mother of three kids when you're already the father?

There's no one way to describe it because it's different for every man who loses his wife.

But no matter what kind of an emotional adjustment he has to

make, he still has to deal with the economic realities. Somebody's got to take care of the kids and the house. Which may mean hiring a full-time housekeeper.

If his wife had a job, as four out of ten mothers* do these days, that extra money is gone. Money that could have helped later on with the mortgage or the kids' education.

Maybe that's why the traditional idea of insuring the wife with only a token amount doesn't make as much sense anymore.

The Travelers life insurance people have developed a number of plans to meet the needs of today's family.

Since each plan is a little different, you really ought to look up your local Travelers agent in the Yellow Pages to find out which one's right for you.

But do it soon. And do it together.

THE TRAVELERS
Maybe we can help.

*U.S. Department of Labor Statistics

This 1973 ad for Travelers Insurance connected a service with intangible benefits—life insurance—to a concrete life experience.
Reprinted from the 1973 advertisement by Travelers Insurance.

a food establishment with an unknown menu, advertising the specific types of food available can be advantageous to a restaurant. Providing additional information such as prices can further help to reduce the possible risk perceived by the diner. Internet America used both visuals and words in an effort to illustrate its service. In service ads promoting the highly intangible information highway, Internet America portrayed a young woman driving down the highway in an effort to picture visually what the service did—navigate the information highway. Moreover, in an attempt to reduce risk to the potential consumer, the copy that supported the visual emphasized that Internet America required no commitment and no risk.

AAMCO transmissions has attempted yet another approach to tangibilizing the service in its advertisements. The familiar horn honk in its slogan ("Double A [honk, honk] M-C-O") is a sound that makes the automotive service tangible to the audience. Advertisers often call such a tool a "mnemonic device" designed to penetrate a buyer's consciousness. It is commonly used in selling hard goods as well.

Because services and goods are different, service providers must make special efforts when creating their advertisements to ensure that potential customers can fully grasp the service offering, either through physical representations of the service or specific words that provide detailed information. By providing tangible information or cues, services stand to improve their chances of enticing the audience into liking the ad and, better yet, actually trying the service.

MARLA ROYNE STAFFORD

Further Reading

Cutler, Bob D., and Rajshekhar G. Javalgi, "Analysis of Print Ad Features: Services versus Products," *Journal of Advertising Research* 33, no. 2 (March/April 1993)

Hill, Donna J., and Nimish Gandhi, "Services Advertising: A Framework to Its Effectiveness," *Journal of Services Marketing* 6, no. 4 (Fall 1992)

Journal of Advertising 26, no. 4 (Winter 1997) (special issue on services advertising)

Stafford, Marla Royne, "Tangibility in Services Advertising: An Investigation of Verbal versus Visual Cues," *Journal of Advertising* 25, no. 3 (Fall 1996)

Zeithaml, Valarie A., A. Parasuraman, and Leonard L. Berry, "Problems and Strategies in Services Marketing," *Journal of Marketing* 49, no. 2 (Spring 1985)

Seven Up

(Dr Pepper/Seven Up, Inc.)

Principal Agencies

J. Walter Thompson Company
N.W. Ayer ABH International
Leo Burnett Company
Young & Rubicam, Inc.

The soft drink 7 UP was developed by Charles Leiper Grigg in 1929 at the Howdy Company in St. Louis, Missouri. The fizzy beverage that came to be known as the "uncola" originally went by the unwieldy moniker Bib-Label Lithiated Lemon-Lime Soda.

Grigg, a small-town grocer, moved to St. Louis, where he worked first in advertising, then in manufacturing sales while he created an orange drink he called Whistle. At age 51 he struck out on his own, and in 1920 he founded soft-drink marketer Howdy Company with support from investors Edmund G. Ridgway and Frank Y. Gladney. The Howdy Company sold franchised extract to bottlers under strict conditions for consistency in price and packaging. Bottlers shared in the expense of advertising the soft drink.

By 1936, when the Howdy Company changed its name to the Seven-Up Company, Hamblett Charles Grigg, son of the founder, had joined the company as a marketer and designer. H.C. Grigg, who had studied art, produced the product's first logo, the number seven with wings. Three ad campaigns were developed in the 1930s: "7 UP—You Like It. It Likes You"; "7 UP for 7 Hangovers"; and "Fresh Up with 7 UP." In the early years, the ad agencies engaged by the Seven-Up Company produced all ad campaigns and materials, but ad placement was reserved to individual bottlers.

In 1943 the J. Walter Thompson Company (JWT) developed a national advertising effort that linked the drinking of 7 UP with support of the Allied war effort. That campaign marked the beginning of a long-term partnership; JWT continued to work on the 7 UP account for 36 years.

In 1950 the Seven-Up Company emerged from a six-year battle with the U.S. Internal Revenue Service (IRS) when the IRS released the company from any obligation to pay taxes on income from bottlers for advertising. The company began advertising on television, radio, and magazines during the 1950s, and bottlers supported a significant portion of the ad budget. The Seven-Up Company sponsored a radio variety show featuring comedian Bert Lahr (Cowardly Lion in the 1939 movie *Wizard of Oz*) and *The Mark of Zorro* on television.

There's no cola like The Uncola.™

Because The Uncola was made to
go the colas one better.
Fresh, clean taste.
No after taste. Never too sweet.
Gets down to a thirst
like no cola can.
7UP®...The Uncola.
Un in a million.

This 1968 ad was one of the first from Seven-Up's "Uncola" campaign, which continued to run through the 1970s.
7UP is a registered trademark of Dr Pepper/Seven Up, Inc. © 2001.

Also in 1950, the Seven-Up Company initiated "7 UP Floats," a summer promotion that featured 7 UP served with ice cream in a tall glass; the promotion was to become an annual event for the company. In 1961 the company spent $1 million on an advertising campaign to support the "Floats" promotion in newspapers, billboards, television, radio, and magazines such as *American Girl, Boys' Life, Ebony, Life,* and *Reader's Digest.*

In 1961 the Seven-Up Company won a trademark infringement lawsuit against Fizz Up, which marketed one of several carbonated lemon-lime beverages that used the word *Up* as part of their product names. In 1963 the company developed a new product, Like, a diet lemon-lime soft drink that took its name from the company's 1930s theme, created in-house, "You like it. It likes you." The drink was featured in a national print campaign that focused on those watching their weight (1965) and promoted via television and radio spots (1967). Like was reformulated in 1969 and renamed Diet 7 UP, with the theme, "At last, a diet drink that doesn't taste funny." Within months, the account changed agencies twice: JWT's Chicago, Illinois, office lost the Like account to Grey Advertising, New York City, which in turn lost it to Gardner Advertising Company, St. Louis. JWT continued with the 7 UP account.

Beginning in 1935, the Seven-Up Company began moving into other countries, starting with Canada. By 1967 it had franchises in Angola, Mexico, France, Japan, Pakistan, Cyprus, Argentina, British Honduras, Iran, and British Guiana. Foote, Cone & Belding won the company's accounts in Mexico and Argentina in 1967; that year, JWT's offices in Madrid and Barcelona collaborated on a campaign for Spain, with the theme "7 UP changes your thirst for a smile." Also in 1967 Vickers & Benson, Montreal, Canada, began to handle advertising for Montreal's Dominion Seven-Up Company.

Meanwhile, in 1967, JWT replaced 7 UP's "Wet and wild" ads with what was perhaps the soft drink's most memorable campaign—"The Uncola"—which positioned 7 UP directly against rivals Coca-Cola and Pepsi-Cola. The "Uncola" campaign ran through the 1970s, with heavy emphasis in television spots (75 percent of the media budget in 1968) followed by radio and billboards. In the TV spots, a curvy soda-fountain drink glass was filled with the clear beverage, then turned upside down and sipped from. In its first year, the campaign doubled sales of the soft drink.

But the "Uncola" effort, so successful in the United States, did not translate well in other countries. In its place, David McIntyre, advertising manager of Seven-Up International, worked with JWT to create a commercial showing gloved hands that popped out of a little green box demonstrating their preference for 7 UP by dismissing an off-camera antagonist who tried to steal the drink by substituting a cola. Voice-over was kept simple for easy translation into several languages.

Ranked as the third-largest soda marketer in 1972, behind the Coca-Cola Company and PepsiCo, the Seven-Up Company that year acquired several bottling companies. The company had long-range plans to diversify, but in 1977 H.C. Grigg died, and the family-run business was sold the following year to the Philip Morris Companies. N.W. Ayer ABH International replaced JWT in 1979.

In 1982 Ayer's Dominick Rossi and Patrick Cunningham created spots touting the fact that 7 UP contained no caffeine. The ads featured the Calypso-accented voice of actor Geoffrey Holder saying, "Never had it. Never will." The campaign alienated 7 UP bottlers, which also handled caffeinated drinks, leading Philip Morris to sell the international portion of Seven-Up to PepsiCo in 1986 and the U.S. division to Hicks & Haas Investment Group, based in Dallas, Texas, which also owned the Dr Pepper Company. The U.S. company was later renamed Dr Pepper/Seven Up, Inc.

Hicks & Haas introduced new products, Cherry 7UP and Diet Cherry 7 UP, marketed to people ages 13 to 24 with the ad theme, "Isn't it cool in pink?" from the Leo Burnett Company. The campaign sold more than 40 million cases of Cherry 7 UP in the first year. At the same time, Burnett's animated red "Spot" character began to jump off 7 UP bottles and perform antics in TV commercials; the popular "Spot" lasted until 1995, when Cadbury Schweppes PLC, based in London, England, acquired Dr Pepper/Seven-Up, Inc. In 1999 new agency Young & Rubicam featured actor Orlando Jones in a comic role in the "Make 7 UP Yours" campaign. Cadbury Schweppes continued to focus on targeting 7 UP to a younger audience and introduced a Web site for the soft drink.

LINDA BJONE

Further Reading

Cadbury Schweppes <www.cadburyschweppes.com>

Fox, Stephen R., *The Mirror Makers: A History of American Advertising and Its Creators,* New York: Morrow, 1984

Jackall, Robert, and Janice M. Hirota, *Image Makers: Advertising, Public Relations, and the Ethos of Advocacy,* Chicago: University of Chicago Press, 2000

Ries, Al, and Jack Trout, *Positioning: The Battle for Your Mind,* New York: McGraw Hill, 1981; 2nd edition, London and New York: McGraw Hill, 2001

Rodengen, Jeffrey L., *The Legend of Dr Pepper/Seven-Up,* Fort Lauderdale, Florida: Write Stuff Syndicate, 1995

Sex in Advertising

Sex has been, and continues to be, a staple in the daily advertising diet. Ads for jeans, watches, and automobiles—and more recently, ice cream, coffee, and computers—offer the promise that the brand will make the consumer more sexually attractive or sexually fulfilled. Sex has been used as a selling strategy since the early days of advertising. Although early forms may seem mild by present-day standards, the intention was the same: to attract attention, to help position the brand as provocative, and to stimulate purchasing.

Research confirms that sex is a prevalent advertising strategy. Sexual cues are present in 10 percent to 20 percent of mainstream consumer advertising. In *TV Guide,* for instance, 35 percent of network promotional ads contain a reference to sex. More than 40 percent of women in ads in the most widely circulated consumer magazines are suggestively dressed—if they are dressed at all. Depending on how it is defined, sex in advertising is as common—or perhaps more so—as other conventional advertising appeals based on emotions such as humor, fear, and warmth. The trend toward increased explicitness is the combined result of relaxation of cultural norms and the propensity of advertisers to push the boundaries of acceptability in an effort to grab consumers' attention.

Milestones

As with most cultural phenomena, the evolution of sex in advertising has been shaped by historical context. Early forms of sexual imagery, now considered tame, were as provocative in their time as more explicit forms evident today. The origins of sexual appeals in U.S. advertising can be traced to medicinal products advertised before the Civil War. These ads featured wood engravings of women's faces, often the only illustrations on the page, to attract the reader's attention.

During the 1890s ads displaying women's ankles and, later, the backs of their knees, were considered quite provocative. As advertisers continued to push the boundaries of acceptability, subtle forms of nudity began to appear. In 1931 a magazine ad for Listerine deodorant featured a photograph of a nude woman's back and the side of her breast. Woodbury soap featured what is thought to be advertising's first full-figure black-and-white photograph of a naked woman (shot by Edward Steichen) in 1936. Many of the early uses of sex in advertising were in ads for fragrances, beauty products, and undergarments.

In the 1940s ads for Springmaid Fabrics' underwear and sheets marked a turning point. Some authorities claim that these ads were precursors to the sexual appeals used today. The ads used a mixture of double entendre, sexual innuendo, and images of scantily clad women to sell products. Elliott Springs, president of Springs Mills, believed that sex could be used effectively as long as it was used intelligently and subtly masked with double meaning. He also believed that sex attracted attention but that for the ad to be effective the viewer needed to be rewarded by a clever interplay between the copy and the image. These ads were controversial but highly effective in selling Springmaid Fabrics' products.

In 1956 Foote, Cone & Belding launched Miss Clairol, the first one-step home hair color product. Coloring one's hair to look younger was, like sex itself, an activity that combined deception with discretion. Copywriter Shirley Polykoff recognized the relationship and applied the traditional question every man asks about a desirable woman—"Does she or doesn't she?"—to a woman's hair color. In either case it was a woman's secret, one that only her lover—or hairdresser—could answer. The campaign was a landmark in advertising, partially because it sounded more provocative than it was. Ogilvy & Mather had less success with its ad for Ban deodorant, which represented nudity through a montage of classical Greek sculptures (accompanied by copywriter Reva Korda's voice-over copy: "In the mature male and the mature female. . . . "), although neither the intent not the effect was erotic.

The "creative revolution" of the 1960s extended the boundaries of sex in advertising. To the grind of stripper music, a sexy Scandinavian blonde named Gunilla Knutson urged men to "take it all off"—with Noxzema shaving cream. Continental Airlines' stewardesses promised to "move our tail for you" in a campaign that provoked minor controversy, less for reasons of sex than timing: it intersected with the second wave of feminism. One of the most sophisticated uses of sex was in an Ogilvy & Mather ad for Paco Rabanne men's cologne in which a man, portrayed as a bohemian artist in his loft, is pictured lying in bed in the morning chatting on the phone with the woman he had just spent the night with.

A different version of sex in advertising gained attention in 1972 with the publication of the controversial book *Subliminal Seduction.* The author, Wilson Bryan Key, argued that advertisers "seduced" consumers with barely perceptible naked body parts and the word "sex" airbrushed into advertising images. Overt sexual content in ads was also on the rise during the same period, influenced by the sexual revolution and a generally more liberal attitude toward sex in society. This trend continued relatively unabated until the early 1990s, when the Stroh Brewery retracted ads for Old Milwaukee beer featuring the "Swedish Bikini Team." Stroh's employees had filed a sexual harassment suit claiming that the ads fostered a sexist work environment. The ads also prompted protests from feminist groups. Since then beer advertisers have relied less on sex to sell their product and more on appeals that employ humor, animation, and other creative strategies.

Since the early 1980s, however, few advertisers have created as much controversy around the use of sexual imagery as has Calvin Klein. Repeatedly, Klein has been accused of pushing the boundaries of acceptability regarding sexual explicitness in ads. In a controversial 1980 television ad, 15-year-old Brooke Shields, clothed in Calvin Klein (CK) jeans, seductively proclaimed, "Do you know what comes between me and my Calvins? Nothing." Since then its ads for underwear and fragrances have featured naked models in provocative poses. In 1995 Klein cancelled a

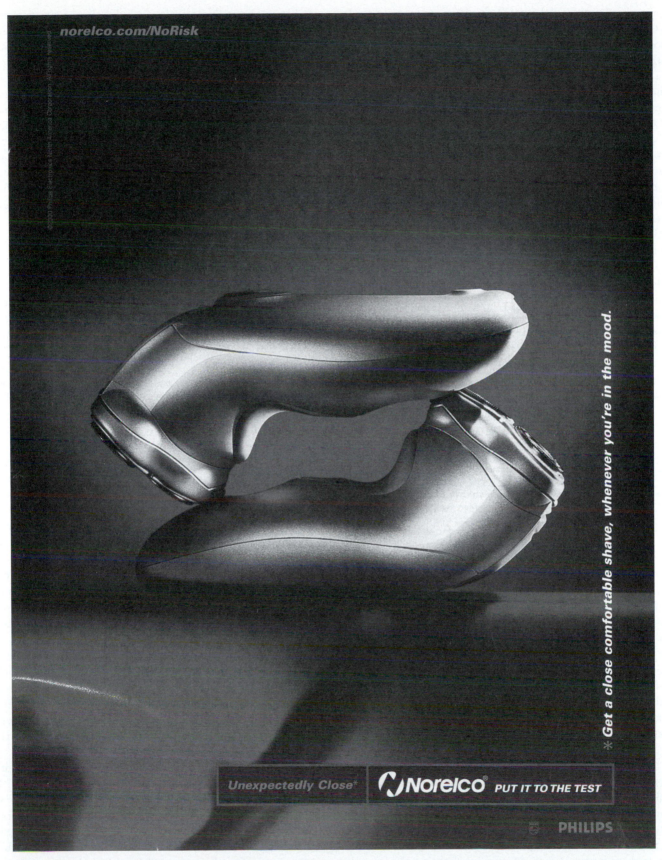

The arrangement of the electric shavers, the tag line ("Unexpectedly close"), and the copy ("whenever you're in the mood") in this 2000 print ad for Norelco, suggested sex without showing it.

campaign that featured adolescent-looking men and women modeling CK Jeans while an older man tells them to "take it off" and "dance around." Although the campaign received much negative attention in the press and protests from parents and professional media critics, sales of CK jeans reportedly increased.

These and other CK campaigns have given the company a reputation for provocative sexuality that sometimes backfires. In 1998 CK ran a double-page ad for children's underwear that featured a group of five-to-ten-year olds wearing only briefs and T-shirts. The ad drew such protest that the company withdrew it and apologized. Yet there was nothing inherently suggestive or in poor taste about the photo, and many observers believed that people saw only CK's reputation for controversy when they viewed the ad. Had the ad been for Fruit of the Loom or Munsingwear, they said, no one would have objected.

In the late 1990s fashion brands such as Guess, Versace, Polo/Ralph Lauren, and Diesel depended heavily on sexual appeals to establish brand identity and stimulate purchases. Underwear and lingerie constitute another product category that uses sex to sell. Provocative ads for Wonderbra were largely responsible for first-year sales of more than $120 million, and in 2000 a television network broadcast the Victoria's Secret fashion show.

By the end of the 20th century it was not uncommon for sex to be employed to sell all sorts of products not traditionally associated with sexuality. For instance, ads for Häagen-Dazs ice cream featured a couple sensuously enjoying dessert. The U.S. sales of Taster's Choice coffee increased 10 percent after it introduced a romantic serial ad campaign involving adult seduction. Celestial Seasonings spent $2 million on "beefcake" advertising to emphasize that its tea had "body." Sex has also been credited with the success of ads for computers, shoes, watches, and pool products. In these cases, sex is linked to the brand as an attribute or made relevant through a creative message strategy.

Cues

Sex in advertising is an all-encompassing term that has come to represent a wide range of stimuli, from ads that feature images of naked models to ads for feminine hygiene and sexually related products such as condoms. Generally, however, sex-based appeals contain information, words, and imagery that viewers perceive as sexual. Reactions to the sexual information in these ads typically take the form of sexual thoughts, feelings, or behaviors.

One research study identified four general characteristics of ads that respondents typically identify with sex in advertising. The most commonly mentioned category included physical characteristics of the models or actors in the ads (e.g., physique or overall attractiveness) and their clothing. The respondents also identified sexually inviting movements by the model (e.g., flirting, dancing) or the model's facial expression as important attributes of a sexy ad. Romance and intimacy displayed between models was also identified as sex in advertising. The fourth category included elements such as music, camera movement, lighting effects, and romantic settings.

Sex in advertising can also include sexual representations or symbols usually not apparent at the conscious level. These images are referred to as sexual "embeds." One type of sexual embed is linked to sexual symbolism and includes representations or objects that connote either genitalia or sexual acts. For example, the image of a key inserted into a lock might represent intercourse in the viewer's subconscious. The second type of sexual embed is usually characterized by hidden images of naked or partially clad humans or words that relate to sex. Examples include explicit words such as "sex" and images of body parts that can be identified under close inspection. The difference between the two cues is that one uses images that register in the mind as sexual while the other is of explicitly sexual images or words, although both are purported to be perceived subconsciously.

Sexual Appeal

The conventional wisdom that "sex sells" is rather simplistic, given what is known about this phenomenon and the advertising communication process. Advertising success can be measured in several ways, depending on the desired objective or goal. For this reason it is necessary to examine the complex effects of sexual appeals. Most research suggests that because sex is linked to survival, sexual appeals are highly effective at attracting and maintaining a viewer's attention. In other words, humans are predisposed by an evolutionary imperative to attend to sexual information. Moreover, findings from medical and psychological research suggest that sexual information evokes an emotional reaction. Depending on variables such as the context and explicitness or intensity of sex in the ad, these reactions are physiologically arousing and favorable. Through repeated pairings of provocative models and the brand in ads, pleasurable feelings can become associated with an advertiser's brand.

This type of association is similar to the concept of classic conditioning. In an environment in which consumers do not have time to process all the marketing communications they are exposed to, images that are evaluated positively can make the difference in purchasing decisions. According to a theory of persuasion known as the Elaboration Likelihood Model, developed by Richard Petty and John Cacioppo, when the opportunity, motivation, or ability to process a persuasive message is low, people are more apt to be persuaded by peripheral cues (e.g., sexual stimuli) in the ad. This theory suggests that sex may be more effective for marketing low-risk products (i.e., products that are inexpensive and routinely purchased and for which little information is required to make a purchase decision).

Sex in advertising is frequently used as either an explicitly mentioned or implicitly inferred benefit of using a brand. Thus, the promise of a sexual encounter is used as an incentive for purchasing the brand. A campaign for Norelco electric razors used the headline, "Give her your closest shave." In other ads the implicit promise is that if viewers wear this clothing, use this fragrance, or drive this automobile, they will be more sexually attractive and, ultimately, fulfilled.

Help or Hindrance?

A frequent criticism of sex in advertising is that women with no discernable link to the product are featured in ads simply to attract attention and adorn the brand. Research suggests that this use of decorative models typically is not effective because viewers either respond negatively to the ad or are so distracted by the model that they do not remember or even read the copy—or both. It is generally believed that a brand or a creative execution must somehow be related or relevant to sex to be effective. Product categories that depend heavily on sexual appeals typically include fragrances, designer clothing and accessories, sport and luxury automobiles, health and beauty products, cigarettes, alcohol, and television promotional ads. In a 2001 survey, however, ad creators said they could create a sexual appeal for almost any brand. They did note that the degree to which sex is "naturally" linked to the product would have an important impact on message effectiveness.

Gender can be an important determinant of the effectiveness of sex in advertising. In many respects, men and women respond similarly to this type of advertising strategy. Both respond favorably to provocative images of the opposite sex. Men and women also respond similarly to images of couples engaged in intimate behavior in ads. It is important to note that the most provocative images of women typically appear in women's magazines. The same is true of male images in men's magazines. These images are not designed to stimulate sexual arousal but rather serve instructional purposes; they teach men and women how to be sexually appealing. Women tend to differ from men in their evaluations of explicit sexual content (e.g., full frontal nudity) in ads, however, responding to such ads less favorably.

What is considered erotic reflects local cultural traditions, symbols, tastes, and norms; therefore, it is not surprising that what is considered sex in advertising differs across cultural boundaries. For instance, although the discussion of sex in Central and South American cultures is discouraged, the sexual content in media and ads is frequently more overt than that in the United States. In some European countries nudity in advertising is more prevalent than would be acceptable in the United States. Some advertising professionals suggest that compared to the West, sex in advertising in Asian cultures is both more "raw" and more symbolic. Research in sociobiology and evolutionary psychology suggests that although sexual drive and motivation are inherent in everyone, cultures shape sexual predilections. Consequently, cultures vary in what they perceive as sexual.

Other Considerations

At one time or another, politicians, religious leaders, feminists, and media critics have condemned the use of sex to sell products. One persistent criticism is that these ads are typically sexist in their representations of women. Most sexual ads portray women as objects of male fantasy and desire. These ads instruct women on how to look attractive to men, or they employ sexy women to represent successful goal attainment for men. Critics argue that these images are harmful because they encourage the perception that the primary purpose of women is to be sexually alluring. Emphasizing this characteristic to the exclusion of others such as intelligence, personality, and ability ultimately affects attitudes toward and treatment of women.

There is some evidence that sexual appeals can be successfully implemented to promote social causes. In the 1990s several health promotion campaigns integrated sexual appeals into the message. Campaigns encouraging safe sex, for example, are particularly suited to sexual appeals. Research suggests that the use of sex in such ads can be attention getting, can evoke favorable response, and most important, can be persuasive. Given that the motivation to be sexually attractive is pervasive and fundamental to humankind, sex will continue to be a feature of advertising.

TOM REICHERT

See also color plate in this volume

Further Reading

Courtney, Alice E., and Thomas W. Whipple, *Sex Stereotyping in Advertising,* Lexington, Massachusetts: Lexington Books, 1983

Gaines, Steven, and Sharon Churcher, *Obsession: The Lives and Times of Calvin Klein,* New York: Carol, 1994

Goodrum, Charles, and Helen Dalrymple, *Advertising in America: The First 200 Years,* New York: Abrams, 1990

Key, Wilson Bryan, *Subliminal Seduction: Ad Media's Manipulation of a Not So Innocent America,* Englewood Cliffs, New Jersey: Prentice-Hall, 1972

LaTour, Michael S., and Tony L. Henthorne, "Female Nudity: Attitudes toward the Ad and the Brand, and Implications for Advertising Strategy," *Journal of Consumer Marketing* 10, no. 3 (1993)

Percy, Larry, and John R. Rossiter, "Advertising Stimulus Effects: A Review," *Journal of Current Issues and Research in Advertising* 14 (1992)

Reichert, Tom, et al., "Beefcake or Cheesecake? No Matter How You Slice It, Sexual Explicitness in Advertising Continues to Increase," *Journalism and Mass Communication Quarterly* 76, no. 1 (1999)

Reichert, Tom, and Jacqueline Lambiase, editors, *Sex in Advertising: Perspectives on the Erotic Appeal,* Mahwah, New Jersey: Erlbaum, 2002

Severn, Jessica, George E. Belch, and Michael A. Belch, "The Effects of Sexual and Non-Sexual Advertising Appeals and Information Level on Cognitive Processing and Communication Effectiveness," *Journal of Advertising* 19, no. 1 (1990)

Soley, Larry, and Leonard Reid, "Taking It Off: Are Models in Magazine Ads Wearing Less?" *Journalism Quarterly* 65 (1988)

Simmons Market Research Bureau

Simmons Market Research Bureau (SMRB) is a New York City–based multimedia research company that provides marketers with information about the products people buy, the brands they prefer, the media they use, and their lifestyles. The company maintains a database on more than 4,000 brands and 800 product categories as well as information on the demographics, self-concept, media habits, and product usage of a national sample of adults, teens, children, Hispanics, Internet users, and computer professionals. This information allows advertising agencies to better target their clients' markets and formulate a plan for media allocation.

SMRB was founded as W.R. Simmons & Associates Research, Inc., in 1952 by Willard R. Simmons. Simmons, who earned his master's degree in economics from Duke University, began his career as assistant director of research for the Virginia State Department of Public Welfare and subsequently worked as an economist and statistician for four federal agencies. He later joined Alfred Politz Research, where much of his work focused on adapting probability-sampling principles to population and marketing research. While head statistician of the Politz organization, Simmons created the Politz-Simmons method of weighting for telephone surveys to take into account people not at home, which minimized the need for expensive questionnaire call-backs on home visitations.

After establishing his own company, Simmons designed the magazine industry's first syndicated audience research study. The first major study using his method was conducted in the fall of 1962. Interviewers went to respondents' homes to ask them a series of questions related to various print media such as magazines and newspapers. A subsample of the respondents completed TV-viewing diaries and provided more specific information on product and brand usage. The surveys provided average issue "through-the-book" measurements (i.e., total audience data) for 36 publications, including *Saturday Evening Post, Better Homes & Gardens, Good Housekeeping, McCall's,* and *Ladies' Home Journal.* For the first time, total audience data were provided for large-circulation magazines such as *Time, Newsweek, U.S. News & World Report, Business Week,* and *National Geographic.* The research study's magazine roster gradually increased from 36 to 80 titles. While the study provided valuable information, one problem with the through-the-book methodology was that the interview kits required constant updating to keep current magazines in hand. In addition, the adoption of year-round interviewing created great strains on the interviewers, and the length of the questionnaires raised issues about respondent fatigue, especially as more titles were added.

With the advent of computers in the 1970s, the company was able to collect and process more information. Computers enabled the researcher to increase substantially both the number of magazines on its roster as well as the size of its respondent base. As of 2001 SMRB reported that approximately 33,000 adults had responded to its National Consumer Survey. In addition, the research company provides data on magazine readership, media mixes, demographic profiles, and budget setting.

Mergers and Acquisitions

In 1973 Simmons left W.R. Simmons & Associates to form Three Sigma Research, where he continued to develop media research studies. That year, Simmons & Associates Research, Inc., came under fire when the 1973 study produced abnormal results and was subsequently canceled. In the wake of the turmoil, the U.K.-based Target Group Index (TGI) won over many of Simmons's customers. In 1975 W.R. Simmons & Associates was bought by National Student Marketing, which in 1976 sold it to a group that included Maxwell Dane and Ned Doyle, of Doyle Dane Bernbach; Paul Chook; and Frank Stanton.

In 1978 the Simmons Market Research Bureau was formed through the merger of W.R. Simmons & Associates and TGI. Frank Stanton, a former chairman of the Simmons organization, was named chairman of SMRB. Later that year SMRB acquired Three Sigma Research, which at the time was conducting surveys on 190 U.S. newspapers. All the major daily newspapers subscribed to the Three Sigma service, which identified each paper's readership and demographics. The acquisition of Three Sigma was significant not only because it meant the return to SMRB of founder Willard R. Simmons, but also because the acquisition gave SMRB a competitive advantage in newspaper research.

In 1998 SMRB was acquired by Symmetrical Resources, Inc., a marketing information company founded in 1992 that specialized in providing consumer purchasing information to media organizations and retailers. Symmetrical offered a range of services from syndicated and custom market research to market segmentation and brand strategies within niche markets of the United States and global markets. As of 2001, Symmetrical Holdings, Inc., was also affiliated with MasterCard International's Transactional Data Solutions (TDS) and Adcom Information Services, Inc. TDS Combines MasterCard transactional data with the Simmons Study of Markets and Media (SMM) to provide transaction-based information products for the retail and media communities; Adcom is a media measurement company.

Simmons

Courtesy of Simmons.

DENISE T. OGDEN

Further Reading

Davis, Joel, *Advertising Research: Theory and Practice*, Upper Saddle River, New Jersey: Prentice Hall, 1997

Gersh, Debra, "The Latest on Simmons, Scarborough," *Editor and Publisher, the Fourth Estate* (2 May 1987)

Honomichl, Jack J., *Honomichl on Marketing Research*, Lincolnwood, Illinois: NTC Business Books, 1986

Kelly, Keith J., "Simmons Shift Opens Door to Research Peace," *Advertising Age* (24 October 1994)

Singapore Airlines

Principal Agency
Batey Ads

The government of Singapore established Singapore Airlines (SIA) in 1972. Previously, the governments of Singapore and Malaysia had jointly operated Malaysia-Singapore Airlines (MSA), but that operating agreement was terminated as part of the process of separation that began in 1965 when Singapore departed from the Federation of Malaysia.

Searching for a way to establish the new airline's identity, SIA executives and its advertising agency, Batey Ads, decided to highlight service, particularly that provided by the airline's flight attendants, the *sarong kebaya*–clad "Singapore Girls." Michael Tan, a senior executive at SIA, explained in 1987 that the new direction was a response to the government's decision to end subsidies to the airline. SIA realized that in order to achieve economic independence, it would have to become customer oriented.

Ian Batey, the founder of Batey Ads, attributed the decision to highlight the Singapore Girl to a 1972 review of advertisements from other airlines, which at that time usually focused on aircraft and pilots. In his view, quality in those areas would soon reach a uniform level across the airline industry; service would therefore become an important feature distinguishing one company from another. The Singapore Girl emerged as a symbol of SIA's superior in-flight service and the focal point of the company's image. One measure of the success of the advertisements was that by 1987 SIA had become the sixth-largest international airline.

In its efforts to present itself as an international carrier, Singapore Airlines decided to pursue a single global advertising strategy. Since 1972 the airline has used Singapore-based Batey Ads to produce all its global advertising in all media. The link between Batey Ads and SIA dates back to the founding of the airline, when Ian Batey, an executive with the Jackson Wain agency who had worked on the MSA account, approached the newly formed SIA and indicated his intention of starting an agency. Batey won the SIA account, and both the airline and the new agency formally opened for business on the same day, 1 October 1972. The first Singapore Girl advertisement in 1972 showed the profile of an SIA flight attendant under the slogan, "This girl's in love with you." The goal was to convey an impression of warmth and charm combined with an agreeable manner that was never too informal. Batey adopted a policy of using as models only genuine SIA flight attendants.

As a commercial symbol, the Singapore Girl proved a huge success, even winning a place in Madam Tussaud's waxworks gallery in London, England. To critics who charged that the Singapore Girl ads are sexist, Batey responded, "We wanted to convey what you really get when you go on board the plane, and the Singapore Girl is a true reflection of the heart of the SIA inflight service."

Perhaps the most memorable of SIA's slogans was that introduced in the mid-1970s: "Singapore Girl, you're a great way to fly." Television advertisement from the late 1970s showed the Singapore Girl seamlessly moving through different cultures, across different continents, completely unfazed by people as diverse as Africans, Inuits, punks, and high-society types. In the 1980s, when SIA advertisements highlighted its acquisition of Boeing 747s and its policy of maintaining a modern fleet with an average age per aircraft of only 30 months, the Singapore Girl remained in focus as a reminder that the company still believed in the "romance of travel." A series of print ads in the 1980s featured lush photographs of the Singapore Girl along with minimal copy reminding travelers, in a paraphrase of the words of the 19th-century Scottish novelist Robert Louis Stevenson, that "the journey is the destination."

In the 1990s SIA's advertising featured the airline's cuisine, its entertainment system (KrisWorld), and even the supply of toothbrushes available on flights from Singapore to Sydney (represented in a drawing in which the latter city's distinctive Opera House is depicted as toothpaste on the brush). In all these ads, the Singapore Girl appeared, even if only minimally, as a symbol of Singapore Airlines. The slogan was changed to suggest that Singapore Airlines is "a great way to fly," but the connection between the Singapore Girl and Singapore Airlines was so firmly

EXPERIENCE AN ORIGINAL.
NON-STOP SERVICE TO AMSTERDAM AND FRANKFURT.

We offer non-stop, non-smoking flights from New York three times weekly to Amsterdam and four times weekly to Frankfurt on our exclusive MEGATOP® 747-400s. Our fleet is known to be the most modern of any major airline in the world. But perhaps the best reason for flying with us is that we also offer inflight service even other airlines talk about. **SINGAPORE AIRLINES** *A great way to fly*

The Singapore Girl, depicted here in a 1995 ad, has been a symbol of Singapore Airlines for more than two decades. *Courtesy of Singapore Airlines.*

established that it was a short cognitive step from the new slogan to the image of the Singapore Girl.

Between 1991 and 1999 Singapore Airlines was consistently voted the best airline by readers of *Business Traveller Asia-Pacific*. The airline also won first place in the *Time* (Asia) image surveys of 1996 and 1999. In the U.S. market, it won the best foreign airline category in *Travel & Leisure* magazine's 1999 survey.

IAN GORDON

Further Reading

Batey, Ian, *Asian Branding: A Great Way to Fly*, Singapore: Addison Wesley, 2001

Batey Ads: The First Twenty-Five Years, 1972–1997, Singapore: Batey Ads, 1998

Tan, Michael, "How SIA Created and Maintains a Successful Global Image," *SIA Perspectives* (April 1988)

Wee, Lea, "Advertising Guru: Flying High with Singapore Girl," *Straits Times* (13 October 1999)

Singleton, John 1941–

Australian Advertising Executive

John Singleton, the chief executive officer of Singleton Group, Ltd., the parent company of advertising agency Singleton Ogilvy & Mather, has spent the majority of his life working in the advertising industry. Born 9 November 1941, Singleton was educated at Fort Street Boys High School, Sydney, Australia, one of the city's leading public selective schools. When he started his first agency, Singleton Palmer Strauss McAllan (SPASM), in 1968, he was reviled by many as showing only the unattractive parts of the Australian national character. His ads were regarded as crass, vulgar, and offensive to anyone who was not a football-playing, beer-drinking Aussie bloke. However, his success has been based on glorifying ordinary Australians. He was the first to use broad Australian accents in advertising, the first to revel in the vernacular, and the first to talk to consumers the way he talked to his mates.

Singleton sold SPASM in 1973 to U.S.-based Doyle Dane Bernbach (DDB) for $1.2 million. He agreed to stay on until 1977 as a salaried managing director but was unhappy with the different corporate culture and approach of DDB. After leaving the agency, Singleton took a nine-year sabbatical. He became a television and radio broadcaster, owned a circus, promoted rodeos, bred race-horses, and bought and sold property. His best single investment

was becoming a member of the consortium that bought the Ten Group television network out of receivership.

In 1993 Singleton owned outright both the Ten investment and a new advertising agency, John Singleton Advertising (JSA), which he founded in 1985. He sold both that year to the public company Singleton Group. In return he received 35 percent of the listed company and $7.7 million in cash. Valued in its prospectus at $11 million, Singleton Group in early 2001 was capitalized at $40 million by the market.

There were plenty of skeptics at the time. Indeed, the prospectus pointed out the potential fragility of client relationships, the paucity of tangible assets, and the company's reliance on its single greatest asset, Singleton himself. Between its first full year of operation in the mid-1980s and the public offering, the amount spent by JSA's clients on advertising grew from $5.5 million to $40 million. In early 2001, it hovered around $80 million.

In a 1993 interview with finance magazine *Business Review Weekly*, Singleton was adamant that he would never again climb into bed with a multinational advertising agency: "I went through the multinational buyout with [his first agency] SPASM. It was a failure. I don't want to do it again."

In November 2000 Singleton revealed his most recent deal: he joined a consortium that had taken a $37 million indirect stake in Indonesia's third-largest television network, SCTV. Singleton said he would invest $22 million on behalf of the publicly listed Singleton Group, which he controlled, plus an undisclosed amount of his personal fortune. Also in on the deal were Singleton Group Chairman Mark Carnegie, his partner John Wylie, their investment fund, and Emtec, a medium-size Indonesian telecommunications and information technologies company. Indonesia was a high-growth advertising market with television advertising revenue in 2000 forecasted to increase by more than 60 percent over the previous year. SCTV posted earnings before interest and tax (EBIT) of $8 million for calendar year 1999 and forecast EBIT of $20 million for calendar year 2000.

Singleton's ability to sell ads is widely acknowledged in Australia. He has a wide range of contacts in Australian politics, sports, and business. Most of all, he is identified with the same rough-diamond image as billionaire media magnate Kerry Packer, former Australian prime ministers Bob Hawke and Paul Keating, former Australian Senator Graham Richardson, and retail giant Gerry Harvey. Singleton's interests include the Macquarie Radio Network, which owns two Sydney radio stations. In 2000 he was president and patron of the Newtown Football Club, patron of the Amateur Boxing Association of Australia, and patron of the North Bondi Surf Club.

Singleton Ogilvy & Mather's clients include KFC Corporation, Pizza Hut, Taco Bell, Qantas Airways, brewery Lion Nathan, and retailer Harvey Norman. It ranked number three among Australian advertising agencies in 2000, with gross income of $50.5 million, up 6.1 percent over 1999, on billings of $380.4 million.

ANDREW HORNERY

Biography
Born in Sydney, Australia, 9 November 1941; educated at Fort Street Boys High School, Sydney; started his first agency, Singleton Palmer Strauss McAllan (SPASM), 1968; sold it to Doyle Dane Bernbach, 1973; founded John Singleton Advertising, 1985; listed company on the Australian Stock Exchange, 1993; merged shop with Ogilvy & Mather to become Singleton Ogilvy & Mather, 1998.

John Singleton.
Courtesy of John Singleton.

However, in July 1998 Singleton presided over the merger of John Singleton Advertising with the Australian arm of Ogilvy & Mather, a subsidiary of the giant U.K.–based holding company WPP Group. Singleton at the time insisted that things would be different. The deal was not a buy-out as the SPASM deal with DDB had been. Singleton's publicly listed Singleton Group would control 66.6 percent of the merged agency, with Ogilvy & Mather holding the rest. Retaining control was "a prerequisite" for Singleton, who had built his business with fierce independence.

Slogan

A slogan is a standard promotional statement used by an advertiser to influence audiences and establish a brand identity. A brief catchword or phrase, a slogan summarizes in a unique and memorable manner the essence of the creative message underlying a marketing and advertising strategy. Over the years, authorities in the field have used various terms to define slogans and describe their functions. Sandra Moriarity (*Creative Advertising: Theory and Practice*), for example, has defined it as "the memorable phrase that is on everyone's lips." George Felton (*Advertising: Concepts & Copy*) calls the slogan "an ad in miniature." Others have described it as a theme line that is repeated throughout an ad campaign and contains the main concept around which all the other elements in the campaign revolve.

Slogans began to emerge late in the 19th century. Chas. H. Fletcher's Castoria castor oil slogan, "Children cry for it," was found in magazines and outdoor advertising during the period. In 2000, 80 percent of magazine advertisements used slogans to create an image or reinforce a brand name. One way to learn how to write and judge slogans is to read and study many of them. The editors of *Advertising Age* have done just that for several decades, and in 1999 they published the following list of their choices for the top ten slogans of the century:

"A diamond is forever" DeBeers/N.W. Ayer & Son (1948)

"Just do it" Nike/Wieden & Kennedy (1988)

"The pause that refreshes" Coca-Cola/D'Arcy Company (1929)

"Tastes great, less filling" Miller Lite Beer/McCann-Erickson Worldwide (1974)

"We try harder" Avis/Doyle Dane Bernbach (1963)

"Good to the last drop" Maxwell House/Ogilvy, Benson & Mather (1959)

"Breakfast of champions" Wheaties/Blackett-Sample-Hummert (1930s)

"Does she . . . or doesn't she?" Clairol/Foote, Cone & Belding (1956)

"When it rains it pours" Morton Salt/N.W. Ayer & Son, Inc. (1912)

"Where's the beef?" Wendy's/Dancer, Fitzgerald, Sample (1984)

Runners-up included Crest toothpaste's "Look, Ma, no cavities!" and General Electric's "We bring good things to life."

Slogans may be divided into four types: product reward, institutional, action, and a combination of both action and reward. Product reward slogans tout the direct benefits derived from the brand and convey to buyers a good reason to purchase the brand (e.g., Morton Salt's "When it rains it pours" and "Finger lickin' good," from Kentucky Fried Chicken, now KFC Corporation). Institutional slogans attempt to create a favorable corporate image. Slogans such as "You can be sure if it's Westinghouse" and "Volkswagen does it again" evoke a corporate image rather than promoting a specific product or service. Action-based slogans, such as "Fly the friendly skies" (United Airlines) and "Come to Marlboro country" (Marlboro cigarettes), command the consumer to do something without explicitly stating direct benefits or the superiority of a brand. Some slogans combine action and reward in a single phrase, such as "Take Sominex tonight and sleep . . . sleep . . . sleep."

Role in Creative Advertising Strategy

Slogans are among the most obvious and influential elements of a creative advertising strategy in both brand and institutional advertising campaigns. A creative advertising strategy specifies a plan for achieving the message-related goals of an advertising campaign. Such a strategy is developed on the basis of a deliberate analysis of the situation facing an advertiser and the vision of that advertiser. It explains the unique approach a campaign should take to register the impression most likely to persuade an audience. Slogans are one of the key executional elements specifically designed to register a special impression. (Other executional elements include the source of the message, medium, logo, art, copy, and colors.)

Slogans are selected with great care for at least two reasons. First, they must align with marketing and advertising strategy. Slogans are developed to reflect such marketing factors as advertising and promotional objectives, product differentiation and augmentation strategies, buyer's needs and motivations, price strategies, quality and value interrelationships, competition, the regulatory environment, and ethical principles. Moreover, advertisers often use slogans to place a brand squarely in one category. Similarly, they may use slogans to convey the situations and conditions in which a brand is particularly useful. In some cases, slogans convey the product's purpose, design form, attributes, functions, and benefits. Since a slogan sets a brand apart from the competition, it reflects the brand's positioning strategy.

Second, slogans are selected in the hope that they will last. Advertisers look for slogans that are likely to remain persuasive over time: in many cases, a slogan will be used across campaigns for a number of years. Rigorous research, detailed planning, and the careful use of syntax and mnemonics underlie the creation and selection of a slogan.

Functions

Slogans perform several important, interrelated functions within an advertising strategy. They are used to repeat the central message communicated in the advertisement. Advertising research indicates that repetition of a message tends to prolong memory of the message and make it easier to access that memory. The repetition of a message also makes it easier for the audience to formulate an attitude toward a brand or firm and use it when making a purchase decision. The repetition of the message through a slogan is likely to set the sponsor favorably apart from competition through competitive positioning.

Persuasion theory suggests that, in some cases, recognition of a brand name alone is sufficient to establish brand preference, as preference may stem from the pleasure of simple recognition of a familiar object rather than from perceptions of the brand's superiority or warm feelings associated with the brand. In other words, simply remembering a product or service may be enough to set it favorably apart from the competition when consumer involvement and interest are low and buyers have little information about brands in the category. Low involvement implies that brand elaboration is "shallow" (in other words, that buyers associate little risk with the purchase decision, view a product category as a convenience good, or sense that the product category is neither personally relevant nor highly gratifying) because the buyers lack the motivation, ability, or opportunity to process brand claims.

Maxwell House coffee's classic "Good to the last drop!"—purportedly first uttered by President Theodore Roosevelt—became a successful ad slogan for the marketer.
MAXWELL HOUSE is a registered trademark of Kraft Foods Holdings, Inc.

The degree of sheer brand familiarity is not necessarily an accurate measure of an advertising campaign's effectiveness. The establishment of familiarity is an important first step in the persuasive process, but advertisers generally seek effects stronger than sheer brand name recognition or recall. They want the audience to identify with the message and their brand. They also want the audience to associate rational benefits and warm feelings with the brand or marketer. Slogans facilitate this process by summarizing and repeating the dominant selling proposition. Learning theory posits that knowledge increases with repetition. On average, three repetitions are required before, in Moriarty's words, a "message crosses the threshold of perception and enters into memory."

Slogans work in two ways to assist an audience in grasping a complex message. As message complexity increases, so must the number of message repetitions for learning to result. Slogans provide the necessary repetition. By simplifying messages and making them easier to comprehend, they facilitate learning.

Moreover, slogans increase learning by placing the brand name and brand information in close proximity to one another in the advertisement, thus helping the audience to connect the two. Learning and attitude theories portray the human mind as housing a system of "nodes." Within an individual's memory, each brand has its own node. Bits of brand information are attached to a brand node much as fingers are joined to a hand. When slogans facilitate the creation of nodes, the audience is more likely to be able to access brand information from memory.

The first advertisers to use slogans believed that a slogan would produce higher levels of brand recognition when constructed using rhyme, alliteration, rhythm, meter, and/or parallel-ism—all devices that supposedly serve as aids in increasing recall. For example, Kellogg's "Leggo my Eggo" and Blue Bonnet margarine's "Everything's better with Blue Bonnet on it" use mnemonics to establish and maintain brand identity. That practice began to change in the early 1970s, soon after a series of articles by Al Ries and Jack Trout, entitled "The Positioning Era," were published in *Advertising Age*. According to the theory of positioning, the main objective of advertising was to establish in buyers' minds the brand name and the distinctive characteristics of the brand that give it a competitive advantage. Positioning stressed unique, positive, important, and memorable difference as the best way to establish a brand as a leader in its category. It assigned relatively less importance to reliance on rhyme, rhythm, and alliteration.

While gimmicks such as mnemonic devices have continued to be regarded as helpful in conveying a message and establishing a brand name, some advertisers have placed less emphasis on mnemonics, electing instead to use a straightforward slogan to associate positive, memorable differences with a brand. With the proliferation of domestic and foreign brands in the 1970s and 1980s, many advertisers, facing increased competition, were quick to embrace Ries's and Trout's argument. Many slogans from this period reflect the straightforward approach—Dove soap's "For the beauty that is already there," for example, dispenses altogether with devices such as rhyme and alliteration.

In the 1990s, however, researchers confirmed earlier notions about slogans, finding that the linguistic devices used in slogans do in fact exert powerful influence on brand recall. Studies have demonstrated that self-reference (i.e., including the brand name in the slogan), alliteration, parallel constructions, metaphors, well-known phrases, and rhyme are found in the most highly memorable slogans. For example, Saturn uses parallel construction and repetition in its slogan, "A different kind of company. A different kind of car." The slogan for Bissell, Inc.'s Multi-Allergen Removal Carpet Powder, "We mean clean," uses rhyme. Carefree Gum's slogan, "Shine your smile with Carefree" is an example of self-reference. Self-reference is also found in the slogan for Cheerios, "The one and only Cheerios." The slogan for Kimberly-Clark Corporation's GoodNites absorbent underpants for children combines parallel construction and self-reference: "Good-Nites mean good morning."

Advertisers rely on slogans to reinforce learning, strengthen memory, and combat the human tendency to forget information over time. Slogans, used over and over, serve as a constant reminder. They act as a continuity device, helping an audience to make associations among the set of ads comprising a campaign and among a message in one campaign and messages received through other campaigns. Slogans combine with other continuity devices such as trade characters, logos, and jingles to increase and sustain memory impact.

Because slogans are brief they often permeate the sponsor's integrated promotional and advertising plans. In addition to being found in advertisements, slogans may be widely displayed in other promotional formats: banners, uniforms, company vehicles and stationery, packages, signage, sales promotions, and corporate reports. The widespread use of such objects serves as a reminder, facilitating brand recognition, learning, and attitude accessibility.

Other functions of the slogan are simplicity and rapid imparting of information. As noted in the examples above, slogans are simple and concise. They may consist of one word or a short phrase. Therefore, they enable advertisers to deal effectively with severe time and space constraints. A brief slogan can be readily tucked into a 15-second television or radio commercial. Nonetheless, some successful slogans have been relatively wordy—for example, David Ogilvy's 1955 slogan for Dove soap: "One-quarter cleansing cream. Dove creams your skin while you wash."

Creative Considerations

A slogan ought to be compelling, short, clearly stated, easily recalled, and readily spoken or sung. The company name should be included in the slogan, if possible. If not, the slogan and company name should appear close to one another in an advertisement. There are many examples of well-known slogans that have been mistakenly associated with a competing brand because the message was equally applicable within the product category. Although "No more ring around the collar" was created by BBDO for Wisk detergent, it did not mention the brand and could easily be associated in the consumer's mind with Tide or Cheer detergents. Conversely, when Leo Burnett Company developed advertising for United Airlines in the 1960s, the slogan "Fly the friendly skies of United," made it impossible to link the slogan to another airline. Foote, Cone & Belding's post–World War II slogan for Dial soap—"Aren't you glad you use Dial? Don't you wish everybody did?"—was still being used more than half a century later, sometimes safely abbreviated to "Aren't you glad?"

Parallelism and contrast are other techniques often employed in slogans. Parallelism implies that identical thoughts should be identical in form, syntax, or sentence structure. The Manwich slogan "A sandwich is a sandwich, but a Manwich is a meal" demonstrates parallelism in that each clause is approximately equal in meter and length. Ore-Ida's slogan "When it says Ore-Ida, it's all-righta" and "The best solution is no solution" slogan for Johnson & Johnson's disposable contact lenses are further examples of this practice. Parallelism often employs wordplay or puns when repeating the first clause. Such tactics create a contrast that holds the audience's attention until they figure out the substitution. Modifying or substituting an aphorism or adage in a slogan increases the power of parallelism. For example, in the General Motors slogan, the adage "when the going gets tough, the tough get going," is transformed into "When the going gets tough, the tough get comfortable."

Copywriters employ mnemonic techniques, substitution effects, jingles, cadence, puns, and wordplay when creating slogans. A slogan should ideally be euphonious; the entire phrase should be pleasant, agreeable, and harmonious. However, the real key to an effective slogan is its ability to reinforce the effective selling strategy without getting sidetracked. Consider the slogan of the *Wall Street Journal*, "The daily diary of the American dream." It is an unexpected way of describing a newspaper, but it holds to the advertising and marketing strategy of the company. The slogan conveys in an interesting way the basic reason why entrepreneurs and business people should read the *Wall Street Journal*: the newspaper conveys insights enabling readers to become more successful in business and capture the American dream.

Challenges

Advertisers face a difficult challenge when attempting to create slogans for international use. Slogans often fail to convey meaning across national and cultural boundaries; consequently, advertisers may have to tailor them so that they conform to local conditions. Differences in views among managers as to the best advertising strategy for their specific country, shifts in competitive positions across regions and countries, and cultural sensitivities can also lead advertisers to use different slogans in different places. Furthermore, in some cultures much has to be explained before the true meaning of a phrase or word is correctly and fully understood. Because of their brevity and propensity to employ wordplay, slogans may not transfer effectively into such contexts.

Copywriters sometimes face legal constraints when constructing slogans. As is the case with any promotional claim, a slogan must be reasonable and must not violate professional ethics or legal standards.

Slogans are factored into the layout and design of advertisements. The effectiveness of a slogan can be increased when it is accompanied by a visual image. When the brand name cannot be included in the slogan, the logo and brand name should be in close proximity to each other. In TV and print advertising, a slogan often appears in display type. Because slogans enrich the company "signature" (the company or brand name, its logo, slogan,

JUST DO IT.

Now you know all about cross-training.

    Now you need to know about cross-training shoes from Nike. Like the Nike Air Trainer SC. It has Nike-Air® cushioning. It's supportive. It's stable.

    Now what all that means: You can run in it. You can walk in it. You can lift weights in it. You can play volleyball in it. You can play tennis in it. You can ride a bike in it. And yes, you can even do aerobics in it.

So, you want to learn more about cross-training and the complete line of Nike cross-training shoes. So call toll-free: 1-800-344-NIKE (7 am to 5 pm Pacific Time). So you don't have a phone, so write: Nike Consumer Relations, 9000 SW Nimbus, Beaverton, OR 97005.

Nike's "Just do it" epitomizes the so-called action-based slogan, which commands the consumer to do something but makes no statement about product benefits or brand superiority.
Courtesy of Nike, Inc.

package design, or any combination of these used to identify the company or brand), they are generally positioned at the point where eyes or ears leave the advertisement (typically at the bottom right corner of a print advertisement or near the end of a broadcast commercial). Accordingly, slogans are also called "tag lines," a name arising from the realization that slogans are normally "tagged onto" the end of a commercial. In some cases, however, especially when the slogan is new, it may be the headline, key visual, or focal point of the advertisement.

When most people think of advertising and its key elements, slogans quickly come to mind. The slogan is not without its detractors, however. Ogilvy, for example, suggested that slogans are often interchangeable and fail to build brand identity. Among the ones he characterized as "self-serving, flatulent pomposity" were "A company worth looking at" (Boise Cascade), "Where science gets down to business" (Rockwell International), "We're involved" (U.S. Steel), and "We know what you're looking for" (J.C. Penney Company). Yet, in the main, leading brands owe their market standing in large measure to slogans.

ALLEN E. SMITH

Further Reading

Bovée, Courtland L., *Contemporary Advertising*, Homewood, Illinois: Irwin, 1982; 7th edition, by William F. Arens, Boston: Irwin/McGraw-Hill, 1999

Cohen, Dorothy, *Advertising*, New York: Wiley, 1972

Felton, George, *Advertising: Concepts and Copy*, Englewood Cliffs, New Jersey: Prentice-Hall, 1994

Kleppner, Otto, *Advertising Procedure*, New York: Prentice-Hall, 1925; 14th edition, as *Kleppner's Advertising Procedure*, by J. Thomas Russell and W. Ronald Lane, Upper Saddle River, New Jersey: Prentice Hall, 1999

Moriarty, Sandra E., *Creative Advertising: Theory and Practice*, Englewood Cliffs, New Jersey: Prentice-Hall, 1986; 2nd edition, 1991

O'Guinn, Thomas C., Chris T. Allen, and Richard J. Semenik, *Advertising*, Cincinnati, Ohio: South-Western College, 1998; 2nd edition, 2000

Reece, Bonnie B., Bruce G. Vanden Berg, and Hairong Li, "What Makes a Slogan Memorable and Who Remembers It," *Journal of Current Issues and Research in Advertising* 16, no. 2 (1994)

Ries, Al, and Jack Trout, *Positioning: The Battle for Your Mind*, New York: McGraw-Hill, 1981

Soap Opera

When the business of advertising met the new medium of radio in the late 1920s, their marriage produced one of the most vital and compelling, yet reviled and misunderstood, cultural offspring of the 20th century. It took on the name "soap opera," a combination of its most typical sponsoring product and a somewhat snide reference to its melodramatic nature. It could more descriptively be called the "daytime serial drama," although why it is restricted to the late morning and early afternoon hours in the United States is not easily understood in other countries. From South America's *telenovela*s to the working-class serials of the British Broadcasting Corporation (BBC) such as *Coronation Street* and *Eastenders*, these programs generally air in the evening hours when the largest possible audience is available. Yet the soap opera form, if not its scheduling or cultural variations, has everything to do with its origins in commercial radio, as does its primary association with women as audiences, main characters, authors, producers, and devotees.

From its first steps to its growing maturity, the soap opera has been a product of the collusion of advertising and drama. Its primary originators were advertisers, its midwives the radio departments of advertising agencies, and its godparents the household product manufacturers who gave it its name. To understand why the form was a natural for commercial broadcasting, it is necessary to go back to the earliest years of radio.

Origin and Development

On American radio—and the United States must take credit for being the home of the soap opera—the origins of the serial drama can be seen in early programs such as *Sam and Henry*, the dialect comedy series that was produced on WGN in Chicago, Illinois, in 1926 by Freeman Gosden and Charles Correll and that was the predecessor of *Amos 'n' Andy*. Although the program would later evolve into something closer to the format of the situation comedy, its focus on recurring characters, a continuing story line, and daily scheduling mark it as a forerunner of current soap operas. A few other, less widely known programs along this line debuted in the late 1920s. One, *Memory Lane*, a historical serial set in the fictional Goshen Center, Indiana, originated in San Francisco, California, at station KPO and later found sponsorship by the General Petroleum Company. Another program illustrates the more typical route of origination that would later dominate. In early 1928 the Chesebrough Manufacturing Company approached NBC with an idea for advertising its product Vaseline, the result being *Real Folks of Thompkins Corners*. It is at this point that one can see why these dramas were such ideal advertising media. The sponsor's message could be seamlessly woven into the drama, hardly interrupting the flow of the story while tying the message to beloved characters. As Irna Phillips, credited with being the originator of the soap opera, described it, "The transition from commercial announcements to the story can be practically painless, and a great deal of actual selling can be done in the story itself."

Another precursor of the soap opera was Gertrude Berg's long-running serial *The Goldbergs.* Begun on NBC in 1929, this five-day-a-week story of the adaptation of a Russian Jewish immigrant family to American life continued throughout the course of network radio and onto television in its early years. Like *Clara, Lu and Em,* sponsored by Super Suds, and *Myrt and Marge,* sponsored by the Wm. Wrigley Jr. Company, *The Goldbergs* started its career on the nighttime network schedule. Not until the mid-1930s did serial dramas, by then directed mainly at women, move to the daytime schedule. By 1935 these early pioneers had been joined by 16 other daytime programs that included some of radio's most beloved characters—Bill Davidson (*Just Plain Bill*), Ma Perkins, Mary Marlin, Betty and Bob, and Vic and Sade. By 1940 their number had risen to 55, and several were aired twice a day, once in the morning and once later in the day, and some on more than one network. All such programs were broadcast, however, in the hours between nine in the morning and five in the afternoon, during what advertisers regarded as women's hours.

In fact, women made up the bulk of the broadcast audience at all times of the day or night. Moreover, more women actually listened to the radio in the evenings than in the daytime (as is also the case with television). By the early 1920s advertisers had noted that women purchased up to 85 percent of most household products sold in the United States. This made women a highly desirable audience, especially for such mass consumer goods as soaps, cosmetics, packaged foods, and health care products. At the same time the major networks had established a policy in the late 1920s of selling airtime during the day at one-half the nighttime rates. It is no wonder, then, that the soap opera thrived on the daytime airwaves.

For half of the cost of evening airtime—and for much less than the production cost of major nighttime shows—advertisers could reach the undistracted ears of precisely that segment of the population they valued most with a form of programming calculated to hold their attention day after day, week after week, year after year. Important sponsors of multiple shows such as Procter & Gamble, General Foods, and Lever Brothers could use their leverage to negotiate favorable rates. And given the less prestigious position of daytime programming—most critics, regulators, and politicians were not listening during the day—advertisers could devote more time per hour to their commercial messages or even work them into the programs, with little scrutiny or criticism of their methods.

This close association with women had both benefits and drawbacks for soap operas. As the evening hours became filled with high-budget, prestigious programs, equally as commercial as the daytime shows but always produced with a primary audience of men in mind—despite the greater numbers of women listeners—the daytime programs became culturally devalued. Perceived as overly commercialized, melodramatic, and feminized, and created according to increasingly rigid formulas, soap operas began

Irna Phillips, known as the "grandmother of soaps," was responsible for some of the most enduring serials in radio and television history, including *Guiding Light, The Right to Happiness,* and *The Brighter Day.* Library of American Broadcasting, University of Maryland.

to attract more than their fair share of criticism in the late 1930s and the 1940s. Even as studies showed that women and men from all economic and educational groups enjoyed following serial dramas, and even as the producers and writers defended their programs for both their dramatic and social functions, the soap opera form became increasingly less respected. Thus network radio and early television actively discouraged serial dramas in the nighttime hours, and television only slowly transferred the form to its daytime schedules. Yet it was during these daytime hours that a generation of female innovators in radio created a uniquely feminine form that addressed the lives and concerns of American women in a way that few other types of programming allowed. Compared to the nighttime hours, where not until the mid-1940s did it become possible for women to headline and produce their own shows, daytime programming provided a type of feminine public sphere never before possible.

The fact that advertisers produced the programs with the primary purpose of selling consumer products in no way detracted from the many and varied uses made of them by the women who listened intently, discussed the characters' ongoing problems, and often found ways to interact with their production. Although relationships and families provided the mainstays of serial dramas, a large percentage also featured women struggling to balance the competing demands of a career and family. Many women in the serials were portrayed as employed outside the home, some with important high-level occupations that supported the entire domestic unit, a situation guaranteed to produce the endless complications endemic to the soap opera.

Innovators of the Form

Early producers of soap operas understood this dual role well. Phillips, often called the "grandmother of soaps," began in 1930 on WGN with *Painted Dreams*, the first daytime serial expressly designed for women. The program evolved into the popular NBC serial *Today's Children*, sponsored by Pillsbury. Phillips went on to create some of the most enduring serials in radio and television history, including *Woman in White* (1938–48), *The Road of Life* (1937–59), *Guiding Light* (1937– present), *Lonely Women* (1942–46), *The Right to Happiness* (1939–60), and *The Brighter Day* (1948–56). Both Agnes Nixon, creator of the television soaps *All My Children* (1970–present) and *One Life to Live* (1968–present), among many others, and William Bell of *The Young and the Restless* (1973–present) were trained as staff writers under Phillips.

Other important innovators included Jane Crusinberry, whose sole dramatic property, the highly popular *Story of Mary Marlin* (1934–52), featured a female lead who became a United States senator, and Elaine Carrington, author of *Pepper Young's Family* (1932–59), *When a Girl Marries* (1939–55), and *Rosemary* (1944–55). Phillips, Crusinberry, and Carrington defied the stereotype of the serial "soap factory" by writing all or most of their own scripts or story lines and closely overseeing production.

Other influential serial creators, especially the prolific team of Frank and Anne Hummert, helped to establish the so-called factory system, employing a stable of writers and editors to carry out their sizable lineup of soap operas. By the late 1930s no more prolific source of soap operas existed than the radio department of Blackett-Sample-Hummert. Historian Raymond Stedman has said that 46 percent of the daytime serials brought to network radio between 1932 and 1937 and 30 percent of those introduced between 1927 and 1942 came from the pens of the Hummerts and their assistants. Their better-known titles included *Just Plain Bill* (1932–55), *The Romance of Helen Trent* (1933–60), *Ma Perkins* (1933–60), *Stella Dallas* (1937–55), and *Backstage Wife* (1935–59). By 1944 more than 40 daily 15-minute serials were being broadcast on the four major radio networks, with many local and regional soap operas adding to the total. When the analyst Rudolph Arnheim conducted his influential study of the soap opera form in that year, his researchers had to contend with more than 60 hours of daytime listening per week.

Transfer to Television

With this kind of success, serial programs would have seemed to be a sure bet for television's yawning schedules as the networks made the transition to the new medium in the late 1940s and the early 1950s. Yet the soap opera was slow to move into television. Not until the fall of 1951 did CBS introduce a midday made-for-television serial lineup, with *The Egg and I* (1951–52), *Love of Life* (1951–80), and, with Nixon as the head writer, *The Search for Tomorrow* (1951–86), all 15 minutes in length and running back to back from 12 noon to 12:45. *Guiding Light* ventured onto TV in the summer of 1952. NBC tentatively dipped its toe into the water in April 1951 with *Hawkins Falls* (1951–55) and then in the summer of 1953 with the short-lived *The Bennetts* (1953–54) and *Follow Your Heart* (1953–54), the latter created by Elaine Carrington. The Hummerts weighed in with *Valiant Lady*

(1953–57) on CBS, and in the winter of 1954 CBS brought Phillips's *The Brighter Day* over from radio and debuted the highly rated *The Secret Storm* (1954–74). NBC once again used the relatively safe summer months to experiment with two more new soap operas, *A Time to Live* (1954, produced in Chicago) and *First Love* (1954–55, produced in Philadelphia, Pennsylvania).

While NBC continued in the mid-1950s to rely mainly on game shows in daytime, CBS countered with the first two half-hour daytime serials on television, both introduced on the same day in the winter of 1956: Phillips's *As the World Turns* (1956–present) and *The Edge of Night* (1956–75). The programs experimented with crime and courtroom themes in the serial context. Both of them, along with *Guiding Light* and *Search for Tomorrow*, were owned and produced by Procter & Gamble, which knew well the value of the daytime serial for attracting its key market. The success of its daytime lineup provided the bulk of CBS's profits throughout the 1950s and 1960s. NBC finally introduced some longer-running soap operas in the summer of 1958, with *From These Roots* (1958–61) and *Today Is Ours*, which, although it lasted only six months, provided the central characters for a bigger hit, *Young Doctor Malone* (1958–63). Not until the fall of 1960 would ABC debut its first soap opera, *The Road to Reality*. This too had only a six-month run, but finally in the winter of 1963 ABC succeeded with *General Hospital* (1963–present).

By the end of the 1960s all television soap operas had shifted to the half-hour or longer format, and such contemporary staples as *Days of Our Lives* (1965–present, a joint production of Phillips and Ted Corday on NBC) and Nixon's *One Life to Live* (1968–present, on ABC) had made their appearances. By the 1980s, led by *Another World* (1964–99, created by Phillips and William Bell for NBC) and *Days of Our Lives* in 1975, all had gone to the hour-long format. The 1970s and 1980s saw the birth and demise of a number of serials, some very popular while they lasted: *Ryan's Hope* (1975–89, on ABC), the vampire drama *Dark Shadows* (1966–71, on ABC), and *Capitol* (1982–87, on CBS). The last serial ended abruptly with one of its main characters facing a firing squad. Later successful debuts included *The Bold and the Beautiful* (1987–present, created by William Bell and his wife, Lee Phillip Bell, on CBS) and *Loving* (1983–97, a half-hour program produced by Nixon for ABC), which changed its title to *The City* in 1995. In line with changes in the industry as a whole, soaps shifted from single to participating sponsorship in the 1960s, taking their production out of the hands of the ad agencies. Procter & Gamble, however, continued to produce its two CBS soaps, *Guiding Light* and *As the World Turns*, into the 21st century, with additional advertising spots sold by CBS. The ABC network produced all its soaps, and a number of independents such as Corday Productions and Bell-Phillip Television provide another model of daytime serial production.

The Form Updated

Daytime soap operas have undergone many changes since the 1960s, but to the continuing gratification of their loyal and con-

PROCTER & GAMBLE BUYS SOAP FROM US.

CADENAS DE AMOR   DOS...PARA UNA MENTIRA   ROBERTA   LA INTRUSA

Since we started broadcasting in January of this year, Procter & Gamble has been
a regular advertiser of Telemundo soap operas, and other Spanish language programs.
And that makes us feel pretty good. After all, with 150 years of experience
behind it, nobody knows soap (or soaps) better than P & G.
Thank you Procter & Gamble.

TELEMUNDO

Serving the U.S. Hispanic community with Spanish-language television from throughout the Hispanic world.

New York	**Miami**	**Los Angeles**	**Chicago**	**San Juan**
WNJU-TV Channel 47	WSCV-TV Channel 51	KVEA-TV Channel 52	Telemundo	WKAQ-TV Channel 2
(212) 935-3480	(305) 854-5151	(818) 502-5700	(312) 642-0894	(809) 758-2222

San Francisco/San Jose *
KSTS Channel 48
(Projected air date: Nov. 1, 1987)

Houston/Galveston *
(Projected air date: Jan. 1, 1988)

TELEMUNDO TELEVISION GROUP The New Era in Spanish Television 1290 Avenue of the Americas New York, NY 10104 (212) 603-5100

*Subject to FCC approval.

With a humorous play on the word *soap,* this 1987 ad for Telemundo Television Group, a broadcaster serving the U.S. Hispanic community, depicted the link between the soap opera and its traditional sponsor.
Courtesy Telemundo Network Group LLC.

stantly replenished audiences, much has remained the same. The late 1970s saw a growing shift to younger characters and adventure-driven plotlines, led by the Luke and Laura phenomenon, a narrative arc on *General Hospital* that went from rape to marriage and became one of the nostalgic highlights of recent soap history. Social issues, though always a source for serial drama, took on a new degree of frankness in the 1980s as soaps introduced story lines involving AIDS, homelessness, racism, and spousal abuse. Nixon is often credited with starting this trend, as well as with the first interracial story line on television. Although many serials over the years had experimented with nonwhite characters, they often played marginal or short-lived roles. By the 1990s, however, most soap operas featured African-American stars in continuing central plotlines, as on *The Young and the Restless, Guiding Light, As the World Turns, All My Children, General Hospital, One Life to Live,* and *Another World,* along with the newcomers *Sunset Beach* (1997–99, produced by Aaron Spelling on NBC) and *Port Charles* (1997–present, on ABC). This development is due at least in part to producers' new understanding of the demographic characteristics of the daytime audience, which includes large numbers of African-Americans and Latinos, as well as more men than ever before (up to 30 percent for some serials).

As more and more women entered the workforce from the 1970s on, however, the overall audience for daytime dramas dropped, a development that was exacerbated by the rise of the daytime talk show in the late 1980s. Yet even as cable TV options increasingly cut into the broadcast networks' audiences in the 1980s and 1990s, daytime serials remained a good investment for advertisers, with relatively low unit costs and a strong cost per thousand. The communities of fans, always an important factor in the popularity of soap operas, found a new outlet on the Internet in the mid-1990s, and not only have producers and networks experimented with ways to attract and hold their audiences via the Internet, fans themselves have produced a burgeoning "cyber-soap" culture of their own.

An era of significant change seems to be at hand, however. First of all, the separation between daytime and evening programming eroded somewhat during the last two decades of the 20th century, beginning with the astounding popularity of prime-time soap operas such as *Dallas, Dynasty, Hotel,* and *Knots Landing.* Although running only one night a week, these dramas had continuing soap opera–like plotlines that entranced audiences and began to change the way networks thought about serial programs. Prime-time series have gradually taken on more and more aspects of soap operas, from police dramas such as *Hill Street Blues* and *NYPD Blue,* to mainstream dramas such as *ER* and *Ally McBeal,* to self-avowed serials such as *Beverly Hills, 90210* and *Melrose Place.* It seems only a matter of time before some network, possibly one of the upstarts such as WB (Warner Brothers) or UPN (United Paramount Network), introduces a daily *telenovela*-style prime-time serial to compete with its rivals.

Cable has introduced a whole new arena for soap operas. In April 1999 ABC announced plans to create a 24-hour soap opera channel, which would not only provide an additional daily outlet for its own soap operas but also give the opportunity for rerunning classics and possibly introducing new ones. ABC was in a particularly strong position to make the move since it, unlike CBS, owned and produced all four of the soap operas on its strong daytime lineup. It was thought that this would allow ABC to recoup some of the audience it had lost to changes in lifestyles and daytime competition, as well as to attract more male viewers. Cable and direct broadcast satellite have also begun to siphon off some Latino viewers, a younger than average segment, as Spanish-language channels such as Telemundo and Univision attract viewers to their *telenovela*s and their more traditional soap operas. Yet soap operas have rebounded from their early 1990s slump, and as long as marketers seek out the 18-to-49-year-old female audience, the romance between advertising and the soap opera remains to be continued.

MICHELE HILMES

Further Reading

Allen, Robert C., *Speaking of Soap Operas,* Chapel Hill: University of North Carolina Press, 1985

Allen, Robert C., editor, *To Be Continued . . . : Soap Operas around the World,* London and New York: Routledge, 1995

Brown, Mary Ellen, *Television and Women's Culture: The Politics of the Popular,* London: Sage, 1989; Newbury Park, California: Sage, 1990

Hilmes, Michele, *Radio Voices: American Broadcasting, 1922–1952,* Minneapolis: University of Minnesota Press, 1997

Lavin, Marilyn, "Creating Consumers in the 1930s: Irna Phillips and the Radio Soap Opera," *Journal of Consumer Research* 22, no. 1 (1995)

Martin, Ed, "Hope for the Soaps," *Inside Media* (25 May 1994)

Mumford, Laura Stempel, *Love and Ideology in the Afternoon: Soap Opera, Women, and Television Genre,* Bloomington: Indiana University Press, 1995

Nochimson, Martha, *No End to Her: Soap Opera and the Female Subject,* Berkeley: University of California Press, 1992

Stedman, Raymond W., *The Serials: Suspense and Drama by Installment,* Norman: University of Oklahoma Press, 1971

Soap Products

Soap has evolved through the centuries from homemade all-purpose bars used for bathing, laundry, and house cleaning to today's myriad of specialized choices, including liquid soap, soap for different skin types, and moisturizing soap. Soap makers are among the oldest American manufacturers, the first to advertise, and some of the biggest corporate names in the United States and Europe.

To advertise soap is to advertise the most fundamental of all packaged goods. When Frederic Wakeman wrote his famous novel about advertising, *The Hucksters* (1946), it was about a soap advertiser, Evan Llewellyn Evans. In one of the novel's most trenchant passages, Evans lectures ad executive Victor Norman on the basics of soap advertising:

> If nobody remembers your brand, then you ain't gonna sell any soap. . . . This company gives your agency $10 million a year to spend on advertising. And do you know why? I'll tell you a secret about the soap business, Mr. Norman. There's no damn difference between soaps. Except for perfume and color, soap is soap. Oh, maybe we have a few manufacturing tricks, but the public doesn't give a damn about that. But the difference, you see, is in the selling and advertising. We sell soap twice as fast as our nearest competitor because we . . . out-advertise 'em. . . .

"Out-advertise 'em" would become the mantra of soap marketing even before the start of the 20th century.

Birth of an Industry

In 1837 William Procter and James Gamble formed a partnership to make and sell soap and candles. The business they started became household products giant Procter & Gamble Company (P&G). P&G was one of the earliest U.S. advertisers, placing text newspaper ads as early as 1838. But those ads did not address a mass audience; rather, they advertised the company's goods to distributors.

At that time, collecting leftover fats and mixing them with ash to create a multipurpose soap was one of the daily chores of women. When soap became a manufactured product, it was seen as a luxury gift item. Like many other products, soap was a generic commodity purchased in bulk at the local store without any packaging or labeling to distinguish among brands.

The U.S. Civil War (1861–65) hastened the introduction of manufactured soaps. When men went to war, women were left to run the farms and households; those responsibilities gave them less time for housekeeping duties, including soap making. That, in turn, led to an increase in purchases of manufactured soap. The majority of soap advertising since that time has been directed at women.

P&G supplied the Union Army with soap during the war, and in 1866 Colgate-Palmolive Company introduced its first soap in the United States. Men who had been soldiers during the Civil War became accustomed to the higher-quality manufactured soap that was available to them, and as they returned home they took their preference with them.

In the 1870s and 1880s soap manufacturers took the lead in advertising to consumers on a large scale, with campaigns for brands such as Sapolio, Ivory, Pears', Lever Brothers, and Kirk. In addition to newspaper ads, fliers were distributed door-to-door, and posters were placed outdoors and on trolley cars.

The period also saw the transition from the selling of goods in bulk to the selling of packaged goods based on brand recognition. In 1882 P&G ran its first consumer ad in a national religious weekly. Five years later the company started its "Ivory babies" campaign with an advertisement that featured an ugly, wrinkled baby; later it commissioned artists to draw rosy-cheeked infants for the Ivory ads. To prove the purity of its Ivory bar, P&G commissioned a chemist to test the product. Results of the tests showed Ivory contained only 0.56 percent impurities, giving birth to Ivory's famous tag line, "99 and 44/100% pure—it floats." Floating Ivory was promoted with the then-unheard-of budget of $11,000. Ivory's 1882 campaign—using the enduring tag line "99 and 44/100% pure"—was ranked 16th on *Advertising Age*'s list of the 100 greatest advertising campaigns.

In the 1890s British-made Pears' Soap ran a similar soft-sell campaign featuring cute babies and the tag line, "Good morning, have you used Pears' Soap?" Another ad featured an infant reaching for the bar of Pears' Soap; the headline read, "He won't be happy till he gets it." Yet another featured a mother asking a child, "How do you spell soap, my dear?" The child answers, "Why, Ma, P-E-A-R-S, of course."

Other major brands from the turn of the century included Pyle's Pearline soap, which used the tag line, "Millions use Pearline," and Frank Siddall's soap, which used the tag line, "Don't be a clam." Improved printing technologies introduced in the 1890s spurred the use of trademarks and portraits in decorative packaging. Among the new products that took advantage of the technologies was John H. Woodbury's facial soap.

Soap and Sex Appeal

As the new century began, soap advertising, led by P&G, moved into new national magazines such as *Good Housekeeping, Harper's Monthly,* and *Ladies' Home Journal.* Ad campaigns from the early 1900s included the Woodbury's facial soap campaign with the slogan, "A skin you love to touch." Written by Helen Lansdowne Resor, a copywriter at the J. Walter Thompson Company (JWT), the ad featured an attractive couple and copy that explained a skincare regimen. The ad was revolutionary because it implied that the soap's benefits included increased sex appeal, which many *Ladies' Home Journal* subscribers found shocking. A 1911 version of the ad was ranked 31st on *Advertising Age*'s list of the 100 greatest campaigns of the 20th century.

This early advertisement featured the memorable "Aren't you glad you use Dial soap?" slogan, which continued to be used by the marketer for more than 40 years.
Courtesy of the Dial Corporation.

This period also coincided with a great rise in the number of ad agencies. In 1900 P&G contracted with its first ad agency, Procter & Collier Company, to produce increasingly sophisticated color ads for Ivory.

With the advent of World War I advertising themes shifted to the patriotic, focusing on companies' contributions to the war effort. P&G's "Ivory Soap follows the flag" told readers the product was "in fact, the very joy of living to Our Boys when they are relieved from the front lines for rest, recreation, clean clothes, and a bath." At the same time Lever Brothers, a company founded in Britain in 1887, entered the United States market with Lux soap; Colgate-Palmolive promoted its Cashmere Bouquet and Palmolive brands.

The Roaring Twenties brought a new affluence to a larger segment of the population, a trend that was accompanied by an underlying anxiety about social acceptance. Etiquette books became popular, and soap advertisers shifted their message to the importance of not giving offense. JWT, which handled ads for Woodbury's and Lux, pioneered this shift by using a psychological appeal to sell products. Whereas references to bodily functions had once been taboo, ads now openly addressed concerns about body odor ("B.O."). Lever Brothers refocused Lifebuoy's posi-

tioning, claiming it would protect wearers from B.O. In the mid-1920s soap manufacturers started a national hygiene campaign to encourage frequent bathing.

At the close of the decade ads were refocused on the beauty benefits of certain brands. A 1927 Lux soap ad featured testimonials from screen stars, while Palmolive adopted the tag line, "That schoolgirl complexion." P&G introduced Camay, positioned to compete directly against one of its own brands. The idea of internecine rivalry and survival of the fittest brand would go on to become a cornerstone of P&G's marketing strategy.

Sponsorships

On radio, soap products were initially promoted in etiquette and beauty chats, but marketers began to move toward sponsorship of individual entertainment programs, including one featuring George, the singing Lava Soap Man, the first P&G-sponsored entertainer created by Compton Advertising. In the 1940s the Biow Company used the percussive masculinity of Sergei Prokofiev's *Classical Symphony* to spell out L-A-V-A untold times.

A full switch-over to entertainment radio shows accelerated in the early 1930s with the advent of what came to be known as the "soap opera." P&G bought the *O'Neills* for Ivory and *Forever Young* for Camay. By the end of the decade, soap commercials had begun appearing on television. In 1939 sports commentator Red Barber pitched Ivory soap during the first-ever telecast of a Major League Baseball game.

During the Great Depression advertisers shifted back to the hard sell. Ruthrauff & Ryan put its experience selling patent medicine via "symptom-and-cure" advertising behind Lifebuoy soap, which was positioned as saving consumers from the disgrace of B.O. Lifebuoy deodorant soap's tag line on radio became a foghorn booming "Beeeeeee . . . Ohhhhhhh."

In 1934 the U.S. Federal Trade Commission (FTC), directed by Congress, began to investigate deceptive ads. Over the next two years the commission issued a number of orders to individual marketers to drop many of the claims they had been making in advertising.

The outbreak of World War II slowed the growth of television, but by the late 1940s TV's popularity was surging. The late 1940s also saw the Dial Corporation's introduction of Dial, the first soap to contain a germicide. Dial was the first true deodorant soap that prevented odors and was introduced with ads from Foote, Cone & Belding (FCB) with the tag line, "Round the clock protection." By 1953 Dial was among the top-selling bars in the United States. Catherine Haynie O'Brien of FCB coined the tag line, "Aren't you glad you use Dial? Don't you wish everyone did?" The marketer continued to use the line into the 1990s, contracting it simply to "Aren't you glad?"

Advertisers moved the soap opera format to television in the 1950s. P&G launched its first TV soap opera, *The First Hundred Years*, in 1950, but the program was short-lived. Subsequent P&G shows were more enduring, including *Search for Tomorrow* and *The Guiding Light*, which started on radio in 1937 and was still running more than 60 years later. By the mid-1950s P&G was sponsoring 13 different soaps on TV.

New Approaches in Advertising

The 1950s saw the advent of motivation research in advertising, which spurred attempts to add psychological value to products to make them more appealing. Ivory soap capitalized on this trend, running soft-sell campaigns again, such as the campaign that featured mothers and children to symbolize the bar's purity.

By the 1960s P&G and Lever Brothers were competing head to head for leadership in the category. P&G's roster listed nine agencies, including Compton Advertising, which handled Ivory soap, and the Leo Burnett Company, which handled Camay. Lever Brothers' account was with 1960s creative powerhouse Doyle Dane Bernbach.

In 1971 Colgate-Palmolive launched Irish Spring soap via Young & Rubicam (Y&R) with a quirky ad campaign that played up the brand's "Irishness." The commercials featured young men playing sports and a narrator with an Irish accent. The campaign, which targeted men with the strongly scented soap, had the tag line, "Clean as a whistle." P&G's Ivory continued to be a strong

seller into the 1970s. By 1979, according to *Advertising Age*, Ivory had sold more than 30 billion bars.

The biggest new-product breakthrough in the category came in 1979 when Minnetonka, Inc., introduced its Softsoap liquid hand soap. The Softsoap brand, purchased by the Colgate-Palmolive Company in 1988, was expanded to include Softsoap antibacterial in 1989, followed by conditioning formulas in 1991 and a sensitive-skin formula in 1992. The success of Softsoap spurred Colgate-Palmolive's rivals to offer liquid versions of their more popular brands.

The 1980s also saw a switch in emphasis to global advertising, led by Unilever, which spent more than $1 billion in 24 countries, and P&G, which spent about $600 million in 19 countries. Global marketing campaigns had to be slightly adjusted to conform to each nation's culture. For example, Lux soap ran an ad in Germany showing a celebrity about to enter a shower, while ads in the United Kingdom pictured the same woman using the soap in a bathtub to reflect differences in bathing preferences.

The 1990s opened with successful campaigns for Irish Spring and the new Lever 2000 deodorant bar. In recognition of the aging of the consumer population, U.S. and European marketers began offering more moisturizing soap products and anti-aging skincare lines. Overall, U.S. sales for bar and liquid soaps reached $2 billion, and the market was facing slow growth of about 3 percent in 1993, according to *Soap Cosmetics Chemical Specialties* magazine.

An early 1990 ad campaign for Irish Spring helped that brand make a comeback after experiencing slow sales in the 1980s. The new spots broadened the brand's appeal from a predominantly male consumer base to include women and children. Irish Spring's 1993 ad campaign was handled by FCB, but in 1994 the account returned to Y&R.

New Products

In the early 1990s Lever edged out its rival P&G, leading the market with its introduction of Lever 2000. But P&G soon regained leadership with the 1993 introduction of its Oil of Olay Bath Bar. Dial responded with few new-product introductions of its own in the bar and liquid soap segments.

The new products from Lever and P&G reflected the soap market in general, appealing to broad target groups. But the 1990s also saw an increase in niche brands, such as fragrance-free and sensitive-skin soaps. Advertising tended to focus on soap's secondary qualities, such as killing germs, moisturizing, and deodorizing. Many cosmetic and bath lines, such as Elizabeth Arden, Revlon, Vitabath, and Neutrogena, also entered the soap market with higher-priced specialty soaps.

The liquid soap market reached $300 million in sales by 1993, according to *Soap Cosmetics Chemical Specialties*. Colgate-Palmolive, the market leader with its Softsoap brand, introduced Kitchen Softsoap Antibacterial with Lemon Juice.

At the beginning of the 21st century, soap marketing exhibited several new trends, including a move away from TV and into

Softsoap™ or bar "soup"?
Now you have a choice at the sink.

It's ironic that the place where you use soap the most is the *one* place where it's always performed the worst.

At the sink.

What with the mess, the glop— there just had to be something better.

And now there is. SOFTSOAP brand liquid soap.

One touch of the pump and out it flows. In neat, metered amounts.

There's no mess, no drip, no soupy puddle at the side of your sink. Plus, there are over 300 wash-ups in each dispenser (the equivalent of 5-8 personal-size soap bars).

Softsoap™
Liquid soap Brand

Soap without the "soupy" mess.

©1979
*SOFTSOAP and design is a registered trademark of MINNETONKA, Inc.
Minnetonka, Minnesota 55343 USA

Softsoap liquid soap, introduced in 1979, was the first entry in what became a major new product category.
Courtesy of Colgate-Palmolive Company.

advertising on the Internet. In 2000 the big household products companies faced the reality of being crowded out of television by advertisers with bigger budgets—marketers of autos, drugs, and telecommunications and financial services and Internet start-ups.

In response P&G cut TV ad spending and moved much of its advertising budget to print. In early 2001 P&G, which spent more than $1 billion on marketing annually, announced that it was establishing a stand-alone marketing management company to coordinate complex and increasingly international marketing campaigns and to get new products to market more quickly. Unilever also cut both print and TV spending, while exploring other marketing avenues, such as partnering with Microsoft Corporation to test new interactive ad styles for its Dove brand on the Internet. Dial Corporation continued to struggle, cutting brands and product lines to reverse declines but promising to consolidate its marketing behind core brands. Colgate-Palmolive also focused on its top brands, including a $100 million relaunch of revamped Softsoap via Y&R.

JENNIFER WHITSON

See also Colgate-Palmolive Company; Household Cleansers; Ivory Soap; Lever Brothers Company/Unilever; Personal Care Products; Procter & Gamble Company; *and color plate in this volume*

Further Reading

Colwell, Shelley M., "Soap Wars: In the Bar and Liquid Soap Markets, the Billion-Dollar Battle for Control Wages On," *Soap Cosmetics Chemical Specialties* (December 1993)

Procter & Gamble: The House That Ivory Built: 150 Years of Successful Marketing, Lincolnwood, Illinois: NTC Business Books, 1988

Riggs, Thomas, editor, *Encyclopedia of Major Marketing Campaigns,* Detroit, Michigan: Gale Group, 2000

Sivulka, Juliann, *Soap, Sex, and Cigarettes: A Cultural History of American Advertising,* Belmont, California: Wadsworth, 1998

Swasy, Alecia, *Soap Opera: The Inside Story of Procter & Gamble,* New York: Times Books, 1993

Tomes, Nancy, *The Gospel of Germs: Men, Women, and the Microbe in American Life,* Cambridge, Massachusetts: Harvard University Press, 1998

Vinikas, Vincent, *Soft Soap, Hard Sell: American Hygiene in an Age of Advertising,* Ames: Iowa State University Press, 1992

Soft-Sell Advertising. *See* Hard-Sell/Soft-Sell Advertising

Sorrell, Martin S. 1945–

British Holding Company Executive

As a student at the University of Cambridge (England) in the 1960s, Martin Sorrell seemed to be on the path to a career in journalism. He wrote for an alternative paper called the *New Cambridge* and covered the 1964 Democratic National Convention in Atlantic City, New Jersey, for that publication. In the late 1970s and early 1980s Sorrell gained considerable experience in corporate acquisitions at advertising agency Saatchi & Saatchi. A brilliant financial statistician, he engineered the brothers Maurice and Charles Saatchi's acquisitions of other advertising agencies, marketing research firms, international management consulting firms, and public relations agencies until Saatchi & Saatchi had become one of the largest agencies in the world. Sorrell also invested in a company called Wire & Plastic Products (WPP), which manufactured wire shopping baskets.

In 1986 he left Saatchi & Saatchi, where he would always have been a junior player, primarily to work at WPP, where, as chief executive, he began to expand the firm's holdings. By the end of the year he had purchased several small firms that specialized in marketing services and renamed the company WPP Group.

In 1987 he proposed to purchase the J. Walter Thompson Company (JWT) and the JWT Group (which owned JWT and other agencies). JWT was one of the oldest and largest advertising agencies in the United States. Although senior executives at JWT disagreed among themselves about the initial proposal, Sorrell offered $566 million, which they eventually accepted. As a result, Sorrell and WPP acquired one of the largest advertising agencies in the world, along with Hill & Knowlton, one of the largest public relations agencies in the world, and MRB Group, one of the largest marketing research firms. But the "takeover" had its repercussions. Sorrell angered Dick Lord, who headed Lord, Geller, Federico, Einstein, Inc., a subsidiary of the JWT Group since 1974. Lord and five other executives resigned and started another agency, Lord Einstein O'Neill & Partners. Within a year, JWT had lost several major accounts, which resulted in more than 100 employees losing their jobs. Some of these accounts and employees went to Lord's new agency, which ultimately prompted Sorrell to file a suit against Lord. Sorrell claimed that Lord had sabotaged Lord, Geller, Federico, Einstein. Lord countersued, claiming that Sorrell was interfering with his new agency.

Sorrell was derailed only temporarily in his efforts to amass more businesses. Although he had purchased several firms before he announced a proposal to acquire the Ogilvy Group in 1989, it was the latter move that captured the attention of the business press. For several months before he announced an offer, Sorrell watched while the media speculated about a bid from him, a strategy that caused the value of the company's stock to increase. The senior executives at the Ogilvy Group reacted similarly to those at the JWT Group. David Ogilvy emerged from retirement to strongly oppose the takeover. Sorrell reacted as he had in the previous situation; he offered more money—$864 million—which was eventually accepted. Once the deal was finalized, many in the industry claimed that Sorrell had paid too much, a criticism that had also been levied earlier about his acquisition of the JWT Group. (When Sorrell purchased the JWT Group, the company's revenue had been $580 million. By the time he purchased the Ogilvy Group, the JWT Group's revenue had increased to $665 million.) The Ogilvy Group included Ogilvy & Mather Worldwide and Research International and made the WPP Group the second-largest advertising, public relations, and marketing conglomerate in the world.

Prior to 1991 Sorrell had witnessed WPP's stock increase in value by 2,000 percent in two years. Like other marketing communications holding companies, however, WPP experienced financial problems in the early 1990s. The conglomerate was in debt. Sorrell had borrowed millions of dollars from numerous banks to acquire other businesses. When advertising agencies experienced a recession in the early 1990s, WPP's ad agencies also felt the pinch. WPP's before-tax profits dropped almost 40 percent in 1991. The company's stock dropped more than 10 percent over a period of a few months during the same year.

Also that year, in an attempt to placate lenders, Sorrell announced the restructuring of WPP's financing, the suspension of some shareholder dividends, and a decrease in other dividends. The conglomerate's agencies acquired more new billings than those of any other global advertising firm in 1991. Fortunately, the creditors postponed the company's repayment on the loans until 1993.

By 1992, however, WPP had not rebounded as Sorrell had thought it would, and he was obliged to renegotiate with WPP's leading bankers and shareholders. He succeeded in heading off two consequences that might have been his downfall, namely, the takeover of a substantial stake in WPP by banks willing to write

Sir Martin Sorrell.
Courtesy of Sir Martin Sorrell, CEO, WPP Group PLC.

off the company's almost $300 million of debt, and a sharp decline in the value of WPP stock.

WPP's mountain of debt had been cut and before-tax profits had increased considerably by 1995. In 1996 the company's debt was down to about $260 million, while profits prior to taxes were up 40 percent, or more than $100 million. WPP continued to expand under Sorrell. In 1997 the firm opened MindShare, the merged media operation of JWT and Ogilvy, in Hong Kong, as well as Savatar, a technology marketing and consulting firm in the United States. WPP also invested in firms in Europe and Asia. In 1998 WPP acquired consulting and marketing firms in the United States, Canada, and England, including Conway/Milliken, a research company, and Goldfarb Consultants, an international marketing research firm.

In 1999 the WPP Group acquired Intelliquest Information Group in the United States as well as other marketing communications firms in England. That same year the conglomerate's pre-tax profits were more than $200 million, and Sorrell revealed the controversial "Leadership Equity Acquisition Plan." This plan would reward up to 15 senior executives, including Sorrell, with a pay-out of $100 million or more at the end of five years. According to the plan, Sorrell and the other 14 senior executives would invest $20 million worth of WPP shares in other ventures. At the end of five years, the stock was to be returned, plus bonuses, depending on how well their investments performed. Sorrell and the WPP Group purchased advertising giant Young & Rubicam for $4.2 billion worth of stock in 2000, then purchased Tempus, a media-buying group, for $491 million in 2001.

EDD APPLEGATE

Biography

Born 14 February 1945 in London, England; earned B.A. degree at University of Cambridge (England) in 1966, M.B.A. degree at Harvard University (United States) in 1968, and M.A. degree at Cambridge, 1970; worked as a consultant at Glendinning Associates, Westport, Connecticut, 1968–70; served as vice president, Martin McCormack Organisation, London, England, 1970–74; held post of director, James Gulliver Associates, London, England, 1975–77, and group finance director, Saatchi & Saatchi, London, England, 1977–86; purchased stake in Wire & Plastic Products (WPP), 1985; became group chief executive of renamed WPP Group, London, 1986; WPP subsequently acquired JWT Group, 1987, and Ogilvy Group, 1989, and purchased Young & Rubicam, 2000, and media-buying group Tempus, 2001. Received numerous awards and honors, including Publicity Club Man of the Year (1996), National Sales and Marketing Hall of Fame (1998), Thomas J. Watson Award (1998); knighted by British Prime Minister Tony Blair, 2000. Served as nonexecutive director, Colefax & Fowler, 1997; member of Advisory Board, IBM, 1997; ambassador for British Business, 1998; member of Dean's Advisory Council, Boston University School of Management, 1998; and member, Board of Directors Association, Harvard Business School, 1998.

Further Reading

"About to Burst? WPP Group," *The Economist* (19 October 1991)

Berss, Marcia, "The Bad Boy of Advertising," *Forbes* (8 July 1991)

"Bowtie versus Calculator," *The Economist* (6 May 1989)

Fallon, Ivan, *The Brothers: The Rise and Rise of Saatchi & Saatchi,* London: Hutchinson, 1988

Fendley, Alison, *Commercial Break: The Inside Story of Saatchi & Saatchi,* London: Hamish Hamilton, 1995; as *Saatchi & Saatchi: The Inside Story,* New York: Arcade, 1996

Goldman, Kevin, *Conflicting Accounts: The Creation and Crash of the Saatchi & Saatchi Advertising Empire,* New York: Simon and Schuster, 1997

Hardigg, Viva, "Madison Avenue Mogul," *U.S. News and World Report* (22 June 1992)

Kleinman, Philip, *The Saatchi & Saatchi Story,* London: Weidenfeld and Nicolson, 1987; as *Saatchi & Saatchi: The Inside Story,* Lincolnwood, Illinois: NTC Business Books, 1989

Machan, Dyan, "I Want 150% of Market Share," *Forbes* (1 November 1999)

Marshall, Caroline, "WPP Executives Set to Profit from Share Plan," *Campaign* (20 August 1995)

"Preferably Not: WPP," *The Economist* (20 June 1992)

Rice, Faye, "Madison Avenue's Bloodiest Brawl," *Fortune* (26 September 1988)

Walmsley, Ann, Larry Black, and Jeremy Hart, "Mediums and Messages," *Maclean's* (29 May 1989)

South America

In his book *Ogilvy on Advertising* (1985), advertising giant David Ogilvy summed up what those who follow global advertising had known for some time: that ad agencies in the United States no longer occupied the top position in the world. Nowhere is that fact more evident than in the story of the growth of advertising in South America.

South America's political history has been an important influence on the development of the region's unique advertising. In general, the countries of South America progressed from rule by colonial monarchies to military dictatorships to the rise of democracies in the 1980s. Along the way there have been some ups and downs. Authoritarianism was supplanted by democracy only to have military coups d'état return countries to dictatorship. However, no such coups succeeded in the region during the last 15 years of the 20th century. U.S. media companies and advertising agencies that came to the region faced rampant inflation and political corruption, but even these seemed to be under control by the 1990s. In Brazil a currency change in 1994 that linked the *real* to the dollar enabled Brazilians for the first time to buy goods on the installment plan. This change opened up Chile and other South American markets to credit-card companies. Administrations such as that of President Fernando Henrique Cardoso in Brazil brought economic stability as well as reduced regulation of the advertising industry and other businesses in an effort to sustain free-market economies by relaxing state controls.

U.S. Influence

Expansion into South America by U.S. advertising agencies was a natural outgrowth of increasing trade and investment in the region. During World War I, U.S. businesses replaced European companies as the major suppliers of manufactured goods for the South American republics. In the 1920s U.S. advertising agencies began handling the accounts of large exporters such as Ford Motor Company, General Motors Corporation (GM), Standard Oil Company, and Quaker Oats Company. By 1935 Latin American radio stations carried ads for more than 50 American products and companies, and several U.S. advertising agencies were established in the region to offer multinationals their services. N.W. Ayer & Son, Inc., the first expatriate advertising agency in Brazil, opened an office there in 1929 to look after the Ford automotive business. The J. Walter Thompson Company (JWT) did the same for GM in 1930. McCann-Erickson followed its client Esso (later Standard Oil) to Brazil in 1935.

U.S. exporters depended on South American media to advertise their products; South American media in turn depended on U.S. advertising dollars as a major source of financial support. Bureau of Foreign and Domestic Commerce reports by the U.S. Department of Commerce show that large newspapers such as *La Nación* of Buenos Aires, Argentina, were establishing offices in New York City in the early 1920s to advise companies on their advertisements and to handle placement of advertising directly.

Mutual Dependency

However, this mutual dependency extended far beyond advertising. By 1920 the United States exercised overwhelming economic and political influence in the region. That influence included dominance of communications and the mass media. As early as 1916 the United States had undertaken a system of radio communications that eventually linked all the nations of the hemisphere. The Pan American Wireless Company controlled radio communication in South America with the support of the United States government. In 1920 the U.S.-based International Telephone & Telegraph Company (ITT) expanded telephone technology on the continent, which by 1930 would help the company acquire principal telephone systems in many South American countries. Companies based in the United States came to dominate wire-service news and the motion picture industry as well.

The South American advertising industry followed a model based upon that of the United States, after U.S. agencies set up shop in the principal cities of South America. As early as the 1930s, U.S.-based agencies were helping foreign multinationals in South America build a culture of consumption using radio and print advertising. The Colgate-Palmolive-Peet Company introduced a radio novella in Brazil to sell its toothpaste as early as 1941. (The choice was fortuitous, as radio remained even in the year 2000 the most popular medium in South America.) By 1940, with the threat of war looming, the U.S. Office of the Coordinator of Inter-American Affairs (OCIAA) drew heavily on the help of advertising executives to implement its "Good Neighbor" policies abroad. These policies included continued purchasing of ads in South American media despite wartime shortages. After the war, advertising agencies continued to carry on Latin American market research for the U.S. government.

The first Latin Americans to come to the United States to be trained in U.S. market research techniques and advertising practices arrived in the mid-1940s. The U.S. agency McCann-Erickson offered important business guidance in advertising to South American colleagues beginning in that decade. It led the way in introducing market research to Brazil and also was instrumental in drawing up the first code of ethics in 1942, which laid the foundation for the Brazilian equivalent of the American Association of Advertising Agencies (AAAA, or the "Four A's," the U.S. advertising industry's professional association), itself established in 1957. Such goodwill allowed U.S. agencies and marketers to continue to expand and develop South American markets.

The Media

In contrast to their counterparts in Europe, the media in South America are mostly privately owned. Over the years, media-baron families developed cozy relationships with authoritarian regimes in order to remain commercially successful. The Marinho family, the dominant factor in Brazilian media, founded in 1926 the newspaper *O Globo,* which became the foundation of the family's media power. Most observers credit multinationals' interest in ventures in the region with spreading democracy and promoting the consumer culture that had taken hold by the end of the 20th century.

Radio developed along the U.S. model of private ownership, as did television, with TV Globo receiving infusions of U.S. aid. This investment allowed the Marinho family to develop by 1965 a private TV empire. The family helped build an important infrastructure in Brazil and South America that enabled the continent to compete in the global new media and technology race. At the turn of the century the $5.4 billion media empire over which the Marinho family held sway included TV, newspapers, magazines, radio, cellular phones, and telecommunications equipment. The Globo TV network was the fourth-largest television network in the world, following ABC, CBS, and NBC in the United States. The media organization Grupo Clarín held a similar position in Argentina.

Such media concentration was common throughout Latin America. The advertising industry was no different: private companies developed their own local advertising agency empires and expanded them through partnerships, mostly with U.S. multinational agencies. Advertising agencies such as McCann-Erickson recognized the power of the local media barons, such as Roberto Marinho, and they moved rapidly to build relationships. In fact McCann's general manager in Brazil, Armando de Moraes Sarmento, became the most famous Brazilian advertising man of his generation. He led McCann-Erickson Brazil from 1935 to 1953, and among his achievements was winning the Coca-Cola account for McCann.

NOS EL DOCTOR DON PEDRO DE VILLAGOMEZ, POR LA

GRACIA DE DIOS, Y DE LA SANTA SEDE APOSTOLICA, ARZOBISPO DE LIMA, del Consejo del Rey nuestro Señor,&c. A vos los Curas, Capellanes, Sacristanes, y personas Eclesiasticas, y Religiosos desta ciudad, y Arçobispado, y a las personas a quien lo contenido en esta carta toca, y atañe, tocar, y atañer puede en qualquier manera, salud y bendicion en nuestro Señor Iesu Christo, que es la verdadera salud. Bien sabeis, y deueis saber, como auiendo precedido las solemnidades, y requisitos que dispone el Santo Concilio de Trento, vuimos dado, y dimos la primera carta general de censuras, por auerse presentado ante Nos la peticion del tenor siguiente. *Illmo señor Juan martel mel garejo marido y conjunta persona de deña Anna manrique Vnica heredera de doña Lorenca de branciuia Sutia difunta declarada portal porel señor Juez mayor de bienes de difuntos: digo que auiendo muerto La dicha doña Lorenca fuera dela ciudad enel pueblo de San Matheo de pilanchor no se quales rnigue personas conpoco temor de Dios nuestro señor. y en perjuicio de sus almas y concienias le cojieron las llaues de su casa y de vn escaparate que tenia en esta ciudad y sacaron y Robaron muchas cantidad de bienes como son cantidad de pesos que tenia en reales, vna sirena de oro con vnas esmeraldas grande, vn hilo de perlas netas, vn cabestrillo de oro, sortijas, perlas, Sarcillos, joyas, plata labrada, y otras muchas piesas de oro, plata y perlas, Ropa blanca, Ropa de Vestir, alfombras, sillas, taburetes, instrumentos de musica y otras muchas alhajas y cosas de adorno de cassa que podian valer mas de seir mill pesos, y entre los dichos bienes an ocultado dos cedulas, o papeles de cantidad de siete mill pesos que auia prestado. o dado los dichos bienes y papeles dela cantidad de siete mill pesos que auia prestado. o dado a guardar la dicha difunta no se a que persona o personas. y aunque tengo hechas muchas diligencias en orden a descubrir los dichos bienes y papeles para cobrarlos en virtud de la dicha herencia no lo he podido conseguir ni para ello tengo prueua plena ni noticia ni otro remedio ni recurso sino es el delas censuras generales que digo por vltimo y subsidiario por tanto = A V S Illmo Pido y suplico mande remedio packen censuras generales hasta la de anathema para que se publiquen en las iglesias que me conuerga para que las personas que ocultan o encubierto dichos bienes y cedulas o papeles y otros qualesquiera de la dicha difunta los manifiesten y le buelban y los que supieren o huieren visto, oydo, o oydo dezir en qualquier manera quien la detiene y cu buen lo declaren en fuerca delas dichas censuras y sea al Dios y a la cruz en forma de derecho ser cierta esta de declaracion y que no es deducido ni deducire juycio criminal contra ninguna persona en esta declaracion de las dichas censuras ni delas declaraciones que en virtud dellas se hizieren ni de los testigos que las depusieren para ninguna accion criminal si no que Vra V.S.I. requiere mi justicia que pido Juan Martel Melgarejo*

2. De la qual, y de su publicacion, y letura consta auerse leydo, y dentro del termino en ella contenido, no se à manifestado, restituido, ni declarado lo referido, porque os mandamos a vos los dichos Curas, y personas Eclesiasticas, y Religiosos, en virtud de santa obediencia, y so pena de excomunion mayor, que si dentro de otros seis dias primeros siguientes de la publicacion, y letura desta carta en adelante, no manifestaren, restituyeren, y declararen, que por publicos excomulgados ayais, y tengais a las dichas personas, y a cada vna dellas: y sabiendo quien son, no las absoluais, ni admitais a las horas, y oficios Diuinós, hasta en tanto que la parte esté satisfecha, y vengan a obediencia de la santa Madre Iglesia, y merezcan beneficio de absolucion en la dicha razon, que Nos por tales los auemos, denunciamos, y declaramos en estos escritos, y por ellos. Y mandamos en virtud de santa obediencia, y so pena de excomunion mayor latæ sententiæ, que esta censura no se notifique en particular a persona alguna. Dada en *la ciudad de los Reyes* firmada de nuestro nombre, sellada con el sello de nuestras armas, y refrendada del infra escripto nuestro Secretario, en *veinte y dos dias del mes de Diziembre de mil y seyscientos y cinquenta y seis años.*

D. Arcobispo de Lima

Domm dee Alspim bre

Melchor de oinnedo

Administrative advertisements such as this 1626 public notice bearing the signature of the Archbishop of Lima, Peru, were common in 17th-century Latin America.
Courtesy of the Rare Book, Manuscript, and Special Collections Library, Duke University.

At the close of the 20th century, Marinho's *Rede Globo* television was a testament to the importance of good media relations with advertising agencies. It handled more than 70 percent of total advertising spending in Brazil and through its television network controlled much of what was broadcast to Brazilians and other South Americans. Marinho early on set the pattern for negotiating media buys through accredited, full-service advertising agencies. This practice helped multinationals with sophisticated brands to flourish. However, Marinho also protected local advertising agencies in pursuit of indigenous business by paying them commissions of 20 percent at a time when by law U.S.-owned agencies received commissions of only 15 percent. It took a federal law in 1965 to change the official commission rate paid to U.S. agencies and level the playing field for overseas players.

Growth of Consumerism

In 1999 *Advertising Age* described the entire Latin American market as having a population of which 65 percent were under the age of 30, with a middle class estimated at 100 million and growing by 10 million people per year. In Brazil and Venezuela, women were moving into the workforce in record numbers, which created a demand for new products.

Julio Ribeiro of the São Paulo advertising agency Talent pinpointed the explosion of consumerism in Brazil to 1994, the year that the "*Real* Plan" tied the Brazilian currency to the U.S. dollar. That action opened access to high-end goods even to those of more modest means. Suddenly, Brazil's 28-million-member middle class could pool family incomes to buy cars, telephones, packaged foods, clothes, and other consumer goods as never before. This consumer progress mirrored the larger economic growth experienced by the country and the region.

By 1994 Brazil had become a significant manufacturer of automobiles, exporting more than 200,000 a year. In 1989 it became a founding member of Mercosur, an economic free-trade group that also included Argentina, Uruguay, and Paraguay.

It seems in South America that as Brazil goes, so goes the region. Indeed, in the last decade of the 20th century, Brazil was home to one-half of the continent's population and dominated its media. In the 1990s Brazil-based multinationals were competing more and more in overseas markets, such as the United States and Japan, and in the local market against brands belonging to foreign multinationals. Although Brazil suffered some setbacks in 1999 owing to the devaluation of currency, it remained among the top-ten global ad markets according to *Advertising Age International*.

Emergence of Local Agencies

Local advertising agencies and their founders, particularly in Brazil and Argentina, helped lead their countries' economic and social developments during the late 20th century. Global accounts of auto, fast-food, and soft-drink marketers began to be won by full-service agencies native to South America. Also, local consumers were buying indigenous products with strong brand images. For example, in Brazil soft-drink giant Coca-Cola Company came

in a distant third behind two Brazilian beverage companies, Antarctica and Cia Cervejaria Brahma, which merged in 1999.

Agency Powers in Brazil

In the 1990s several hot Brazilian ad agencies made a splash worldwide. Among those was DM9, whose president, Nizan Guanaes, was termed a "maestro with a talent for netting awards," by the United Kingdom's *Campaign* magazine. Guanaes himself is one of the most honored advertising men in Brazil. Readers of *Gazeta Mercantil,* the country's daily business newspaper, twice named him Brazil's most effective and creative advertising person. He was the first Brazilian selected as president of a jury at the Cannes (France) International Advertising Festival in 1992.

DM9, founded in 1975 by Duda Mendonca in Salvador, Brazil, has grown to be the sixth-largest ad agency in the country, with gross income of $52.8 million on billings of $278.9 million in 2000, according to *Advertising Age*. Its awards include being named Agency of the Year by the Cannes International Advertising Festival in 1998 and 1999, the first agency not headquartered in New York City or London to receive such an honor; a Cannes Grand Prix in the print and poster competition in 1993 for ads for the soft drink Antarctica Diet Guarana; and numerous U.S. advertising festival honors. The agency, now located in São Paulo, was the creator of the only Brazilian commercial among those chosen as the 40 best of the century by the Cannes festival in 1998. In 1997, in what has been described as the biggest deal in Brazilian advertising, DM9 merged with the DDB Group to form DM9 DDB Publicidade. As a result of the merger, the agency picked up such multinational clients as Texaco, Honda, and Anheuser-Busch Company's Budweiser beer.

Almap/BBDO was founded in 1954 by Caio de Alcantara Machado and his brother José in São Paulo as Alcantara Machado Publicidade. In 1960 the brothers hired Alex Periscinoto, then the ad manager of São Paulo's leading department store, who brought the Volkswagen account to Almap and is credited as the first in Brazil to pair creative directors with copywriters as a team on ad campaigns. In 1993 the shop sold a share to the Omnicom Group's BBDO, gaining access to an international network. In 2000 the shop was named "Agency of the Year" both at the Cannes festival and, for the third consecutive year, by the Advertising Columnists Association of Brazil. In 2000 it had gross income of $42.8 million on billings of $285.4 million, according to *Advertising Age*.

Duailibi Petit Zaragoza Propaganda (DPZ) was founded in São Paulo in 1968 and named for the threesome who founded the agency: Roberto Duailibi, Francesc Petit, and José Zaragoza. One year after its creation, the agency won São Paulo's ad of the year award for a print ad for optical retailer Fotoptica. It created the "Bombril Boy" character in the 1970s for the marketer Bombril, an enduring ad icon that was still being used at the beginning of the 21st century. In 1975 the agency won its first gold Lion at the Cannes festival, for a film that opposed discrimination against older workers. In 1986 Washington Olivetto, the DPZ creative director who often is credited with many of the shop's award-

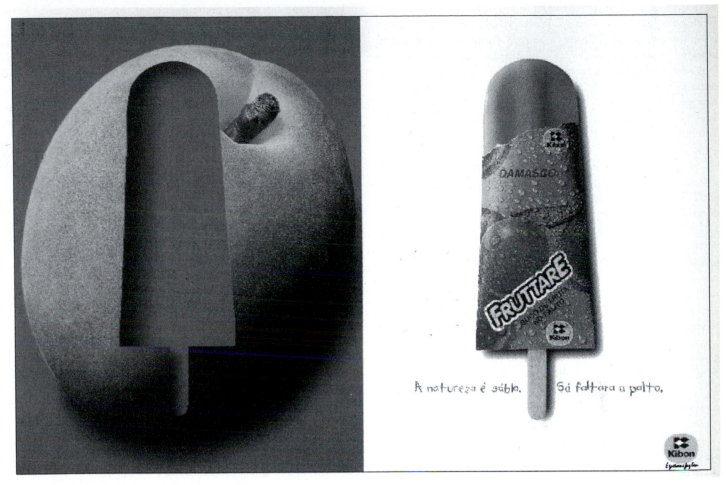

Almap/BBDO's mid-1990s campaign for Kibon Fruttare frozen fruit bars highlighted the product's natural ingredients. The translated headline reads, "Nature is wise, only the stick was missing."

winning campaigns, left the company to set up W/Brasil in cooperation with the Swiss company GGK. In 2000 DPZ had gross income of $48.9 million on billings of $241.4 million, according to *Advertising Age*. But, in a measure of the instability Brazil suffered socially and politically at the turn of the century, Olivetto was kidnapped from his car while en route to his agency on 11 December 2001. After 53 days in captivity he was released unharmed.

A final example of one of Brazil's most successful agencies at the close of the 20th century is W/Brazil, which had gross income of $24.9 million on billings of $144.4 million in 2000. It was founded as W/GGK but renamed W/Brasil in 1988, two years after it opened. At the turn of the century, the shop worked both for large local clients such as Unibanco and Sadia as well as multinational marketers such as Mercedes-Benz and Bombril/Henkel.

Argentine Agencies

Argentina arrived as an ad agency power with the 1994 formation of the Agulla & Baccetti agency. In 1998 *Business Week* recognized its founders, Ramiro Agulla and Carlos Baccetti, as members of Latin America's new business elite. After launching their agency in Buenos Aires, the pair garnered prizes and won accounts ranging from Renault to Italian dairy giant Parmalat. The agency's campaign for Brazil's Banco Itau, which spoofed Argentine banks' notoriously poor service, won the shop considerable attention. In 2000, according to *Advertising Age*, the agency had $14 million in gross income on billings of $70 million, making it the sixth-largest shop in Argentina after the local affiliates of Y&R, Euro RSCG, McCann-Erickson, JWT, and FCB Worldwide, respectively. In 1997 the agency formed a partnership with Britain's Lowe Group, which bought a 20-percent stake. Lowe, part of the Interpublic Group of Companies network, also entered the Chilean market through a partnership with Santiago-based Porta. Raúl Menjibar founded Porta, later Lowe Porta & Partners, in 1981. In 2000 it had gross income of $9.2 million on billings of $54.3 million.

While U.S. advertising agencies predominated in South America in the 1990s, they were not the only foreign multinationals operating in the region. European agencies doing business there included Britain's Saatchi & Saatchi, which had a majority stake both in the Brazilian agency F/Nazca, founded by Fabio

Fernandes, and the Argentinian agency Del Campo Nazca, founded by Pablo Del Campo. French advertising group Publicis bought a controlling interest in Norton Publicidade, a Brazilian agency founded in 1946, which it renamed Publicis Norton. Publicis added 60-percent interest in D&M Comunicação in 1999. In 2000 F/Nazca Saatchi & Saatchi had gross income of $22.7 million on billings of $98.3 million; Del Campo Nazca Saatchi & Saatchi had gross income of $1 million on billings of $6.8 million; and Publicis Norton had gross income of $22.7 million on billings of $136.4 million.

South America has continued to see an entrepreneurial spirit among local advertising agencies, with independents springing up each year in the late 1990s. Many shops were started by talented creative people who had worked at other local agencies such as DM9, DPZ, or W/Brazil but were ready to strike out on their own. One such shop, opened in 1980 in São Paulo, was Talent Comunicação, founded by Julio Ribeiro. (He opened a second agency called Talent Biz in 1995.) Talent had gross income of $59 million on billings of $243 million in 2000. A more recent example is Age (from the Portuguese verb meaning to act), an agency founded in 1999 by three former employees of DM9 DDB: Ana Lucía Serra, Carlos Domingos, and Tomás Lorenti. The French agency Havas bought a minority stake in Age soon after it opened its doors, and the shop became a unit of Havas's Arnold Worldwide Partners, with gross income of $5 million on billings of $28.9 million in 2000.

Contrary to the practice of U.S. and European agencies, South American agencies have been slow to embrace the concept of full-service shops, offering clients more than the creation and placement of ads. Agency principals seem to prefer staying active in the creation of ads rather than moving into the ranks of management.

New Media

South America was already looking to new-media entrepreneurs to expand advertising revenue and sales in the region at the end of the 20th century. One such person was Fernando Espuelas, a Uruguayan-born entrepreneur dubbed the "Bill Gates of Latin America" for his founding of StarMedia with partner Jack Chen. StarMedia is an Internet company started in 1996 to reach Spanish- and Portuguese-speaking consumers with products. Espuelas saw the Internet as a means to enable advertising agencies to bring consumers to a global marketplace where all could share products and ideas across cultures. The Internet offered another venue for advertisers in South America to create consumer demand and to market their wares.

LeAnne Daniels

Further Reading

Akasie, Jay, "The World's Working Rich: The Americas," *Forbes* (6 July 1998)

Fejes, Fred, "The U.S. in Third World Communications: Latin America, 1900–1945," *Journalism Monographs* 86 (1983)

Geier, Philip H., Jr., "Doing Business in Brazil," *Columbia Journal of World Business* 31, no. 2 (1996)

Jones, John Philip, editor, *International Advertising: Realities and Myths*, Thousand Oaks, California: Sage, 2000

McGarvey, Robert, "A Star Is Born (StarMedia Internet and Fernando Espuelas)," *Upside* 11, no. 3 (1999)

Merron, Jeff, "Putting Foreign Consumers on the Map: J. Walter Thompson's Struggle with General Motors' International Advertising Account in the 1920s," *Business History Review* 73, no. 3 (1999)

Smith, Geri, "Marketing in Latin America," *Business Week* (9 February 1998)

Vanden Heuvel, Jon, and Everette E. Dennis, *Changing Patterns: Latin America's Vital Media*, New York: Freedom Forum Media Studies Center, 1995

Wentz, Laurel, "Center Stage: A Band of Passionate, Young Creatives Raise the Latin Nation to the Status of Global Ad Superpower," *Advertising Age* (28 September 1998)

Whitaker-Penteado, J.R., "Hooking up: Some of Brazil's Most Successful Agencies Are Looking for the Right International Connection," *Adweek* (23 October 1995)

South Korea

The advertising industry in South Korea saw tremendous growth in the late 20th century. By the year 2000 the South Korean advertising market was the second largest in Asia, after Japan, in terms of both size and growth rate. The fastest expansion of the South Korean advertising business came with the booming economic growth of the 1970s and 1980s. During this period the country as a whole was transformed from an agricultural to an industrial society. The boom was reflected in the growth in consumer spending, which was accompanied by a tremendous expansion in the number of advertising agencies.

Early History

The history of modern Korean advertising actually goes back more than 100 years. The years between 1886 and 1910 are generally referred to as the early stage of the Korean advertising market. The first modern Korean advertisement, a newspaper ad, appeared in a government gazette in 1886. It was placed by Edward Meyer & Company (known as Sechang Yanghaeng in Korean), a German trading firm active in Korea. This ad, entirely in Chinese characters, appeared in the *Hansung Chubo*, a government weekly, on 22 February 1886 and consisted of a simple list of the goods Edward Meyer & Company imported to and exported from Korea, including animal skins, old coins, clothing, dyes, matches, lamps, and wire. The ad was more like an "announcement" than an advertisement. As for terminology, it would seem that the term "advertisement," as used today, was not generally used then. Following the appearance of the Edward Meyer ad, some Japanese companies also advertised in the same government gazette.

It took another ten years for Korean advertising to really develop. Phillip Jaisohn, a Korean-born medical doctor who had become a U.S. citizen, returned to Korea and established the newspaper called the *Independent* (*Tongnip Shinmun* in Korean) in 1896. This was the first commercial newspaper in Korea. It was published in Korean and English three times a week and carried a few ads in both languages. The *Independent* closed in 1899.

Besides the *Independent*, there were a few other newspapers at the turn of the century. Another bilingual newspaper was the *Korea Daily News*, established in 1904 and published until 1910, when Japan annexed Korea. By that time there were so many ads that more than 50 percent of the total space per issue was taken up by advertisements, predominantly for pharmaceutical products, books, and schools. Advertising had so prospered that an agency handling ads for newspapers and magazines advertised its services in the newspaper, although the agency lasted only a year.

As advertising increased, so did the criticism of the business. But, all in all, the years from 1886 to 1910 saw tremendous development not only in the volume but also in the sophistication of advertising in Korea. The ad industry seemed to have become a part of daily life. Western advertising practices prevailed as far as the rate structure was concerned.

Japanese Annexation

On 29 August 1910, a date that has come to be called National Humiliation Day, Korea was annexed by Japan. A host of Japanese-language dailies and magazines prospered. The introduction of modern printing facilities occurred during this decade, and the size of newspapers was standardized to that of the present day.

Following the nationwide uprising against Japanese colonial rule in 1919, Japan adopted what was called the "cultural policy." Two Korean-language newspapers were given permission to publish in Seoul—*Chosun Ilbo* and *Dong-A Ilbo*—and these became the major media for advertising. From 1920 to 1945 Korea enjoyed a period of growth and expansion.

Classified ads were introduced in 1921. Not only did the rate structure follow Japanese style, but so did all of the advertising practices. Each advertiser had a secretly arranged rate with the media, and this became an accepted practice. During the 1920s Dentsu, the leading Japanese advertising agency, began to emerge as a leader on the Korean media scene. By 1925 Japanese advertisements exceeded 50 percent of the total space of the two vernacular dailies, reaching around 65 percent by 1935. Reliance on Japanese ads became so thorough that the newspapers established branches in both Osaka and Tokyo.

E. MEYER & CO.,

CHEMULPO

Branch office: Whuei Dong, Seoul.

AGENTS FOR

Deutsch Asiatische Bank, Shanghai.
Chartered Bank of India, Australia and China.
Dresdner Bank, Dresden.
Banque de Commerce de St. Petersburg.
Fried Krupp, Grusonwerk
            Magdeburg–Buckan.
A Borsig, Tegel near Berlin, Manufacturer of Locomotives, &c.
Actien Gesellschaft für Feld-und Kleinbahnen–Bedarf,
            vormals Orenstein and Koppel, Berlin.
Siemens & Halske, Berlin.
Felten & Guilleaume, Manufacturers of marine cables, &c
Dynamit–Actien–Gesellschaft
            Vormals Alfred Nobel & Co., Hamburg.
Hamburg Amerika Linie   Steamship Company.
Lloyd's.

Union Insurance Society of Canton, Ltd.
Yangtsze Insurance Association Ltd.
Deutsche Transport–Versicherungs Ges.
Verein Hamburger Assecuradeure.   } Marine
Norddeutsche Versicherungs Ges.
Badische Schiffahrts–Assecuranz Ges.
            Mannheim.
La Fonciere Compagnie D'Assurances.
L'Universo Marine Insurance Co.,
            Milan.

Transatlantic Fire Insurance Co.   } Fire
Imperial Insurance Co. Ltd.
New York Life Insurance Company.
The Stockton Milling Company, San Francisco.
The Vacuum Oil Co., Rochester, N. Y.

Korea's first advertiser in the modern period was Edward Meyer & Company, a German trading company. This newspaper ad listing the company's clients appeared in 1900.

Advertising in Korea reached a peak by the mid-1930s, as evidenced by the increasing number of pages per issue and growth in advertising revenue. However, revenue declined as Japan invaded China in 1937 and attacked Pearl Harbor in 1941. The two Korean-language dailies were forced to close in 1940, leaving only the government organ. A host of Japanese-language dailies were published in Korea during this period.

South Korea in Partition

Korea was liberated in 1945, and the occupying powers (the United States and the Soviet Union) began the work of creating an independent and united Korea under United Nations (UN) supervision. The powers agreed on troop withdrawal, but the Soviet Union opposed UN involvement in elections, believing that north and south should agree on unification on their own. The United States and the UN regarded this as an invitation to civil war.

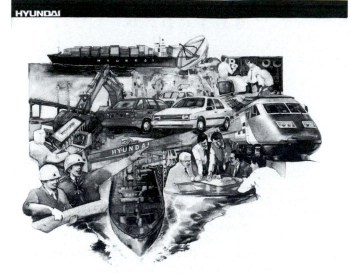

A corporate ad for Hyundai highlighted the diverse line of products
offered by the marketer as well as its important role in the Korean
economy.

United Nations–sponsored elections were held in the south in
1947 and resulted in the formation of the Republic of Korea, with
legal (but not *de facto*) authority over all of Korea. The Russians
then formed the People's Republic of Korea in the north. Thus,
Korea began its long history under two different economic systems, with a controlled economy in the north and a regulated cap-
italistic system in the south.

The Korean War broke out in 1950 and lasted until 1953.
With recovery from the war, what was now South Korea saw the
birth of a commercial television station in 1957 along with the
introduction of television commercials, although these consisted
only of slides. It was not until the mid-1950s that the newspapers
published four pages per issue. Commercial radio came into being
in 1959, but its impact was minimal. The electronic age began in
Korea in the mid-1960s.

Advertising agency service was not widely accepted by Korean
advertisers, which had become used to dealing directly with the
media throughout the Japanese colonial period. In 1958 the
Korea Public Relations Institute was established to perform

agency functions, but agency recognition by the media was slow.
In the mid-1960s, two Americans, Karl L. Bruce and John C.
Stickler, established agencies in Korea. The agencies were Impact
and S/K Associates, respectively, and major clients were foreign
advertisers such as Bank of America, Shell Oil, SAS, Thai Airways, Pepsi-Cola, and Japan Airlines. But their pioneering efforts
did not last long. For all practical purposes there was no viable
agency business until 1968, when Coca-Cola and Pepsi-Cola
entered the Korean market. Before then there had been no real
need for agency service because manufacturers needed only to let
people know what goods were available.

The two soft drink giants, Coke and Pepsi, found their way
into Korea in 1968. With them, Korea saw the arrival of marketing tools such as route sales, advertising campaigns, advertising
agencies, and research. The birth of Manbosa, an advertising
agency established in 1969, was directly related to the market
entry by Coca-Cola. Manbosa Advertising was established with
investments from *Dong-A Ilbo* and Oriental Brewery. Prior to the
establishment of Manbosa, Hapdong News Agency had an advertising bureau that was founded in 1967. It was indeed the first
modern advertising agency in terms of organization, staff, and
billing. Hapdong Advertising established business ties with
Dentsu. Hapdong and Manbosa merged in 1975 and became Ori-
com, a house agency of Oriental Brewery.

Cheil Communications, financed by the Samsung Business
Group, was founded in 1973. In the 1980s Korean conglomerates
(*chaebol*) rushed to form in-house agencies. The dominance of in-
house agencies has been one of the unique characteristics of the
Korean advertising business. The practice, much more prevalent
in the domestic market than in foreign countries, has affected the
neutrality, or lack of it, among agencies, clients, and media; it is
not unusual for the media to provide Korean agencies with financial backing in return for equity.

Internationalization

The period between 1968 and 1987 witnessed the beginning of
the internationalization of the Korean advertising business. A
truly phenomenal growth in the economy and in advertising
marked this period. Korea's total advertising expenditures in
1968 were a meager $32.7 million; however, the figure had risen
to $1.2 billion by 1987. Advertising as a percentage of the gross
national product doubled to around 1 percent. The top advertisers in 1969 included eight pharmaceutical companies and only
two non-pharmaceutical companies. In 1987 all but one (Dae-
woong) were nonpharmaceutical—three household/electrical/
electronic companies (Gold Star, Samsung, Daewoo), two manufacturers of detergents/cosmetics (Lucky, Pacific), and three foods
companies (Lotte, Nhongshim, Haitai).

Two dramatic media changes occurred in 1980 and 1981—the
switch from black-and-white to color TV and the so-called mergers and consolidation. The media as a whole were under tight
government control by 31 December 1980. The Korea Broadcasting Advertising Corporation (KOBACO), a government regulatory agency, was established by the Korea Broadcasting

Advertising Corporation Law and enacted in 1981 after the forced mergers and closures of mass media.

The major activities of KOBACO are advertising sales and agency recognition for broadcast media. KOBACO was a by-product of the political development of the 1980s; as the political system changed, KOBACO gradually adapted to the changes. Meanwhile, the "block" system of airing radio and TV commercials, already successful in Western Europe, was introduced in 1981.

Of the eight agencies fully recognized by KOBACO since 1982, only two were independent. The remaining six were launched either as spin-offs from in-house advertising departments or were previously house agencies. Total billings of the 12 agencies in 1987 were around 60 percent of all advertising expenditures in Korea. Obviously the affiliation with conglomerates made such phenomenal growth possible. There were only seven accredited agencies for broadcast advertising in 1985. This increased rapidly to 121 in 1994.

In 1984 Seoul hosted the 14th Asian Advertising Congress. The congress drew the attention of the West to the Korean market, which had been completely closed to foreign agencies as far as equity investment was concerned.

Liberalization

Political liberalization characterized the flurry of events that took place in Korea after mid-1987. Freedom of the press was reestablished with the abolition of the Basic Press Law. The advertising market was also liberalized, which prompted the entry of multinational advertising agencies into Korea. The trend toward mass media deregulation continued to stimulate the advertising industry.

Seoul hosted the summer Olympics in 1988 and Korean agencies actively participated in the Olympic-related promotions. Imported cigarettes were allowed to advertise, under certain restrictions. Color television sets dominated around 80 percent of the market by 1988 and provided a tremendous boost to the local economy.

In 1988, for the first time, foreign agencies were allowed to establish joint ventures with Korean agencies by acquiring equity shares in existing agencies. Backer Spielvogel Bates Worldwide, Inc., and Ogilvy & Mather entered the Korean market by forming joint ventures with Diamond, owned by the Hyundai Group, and Korad, owned by the Haitai Group.

Liberalization continued in all facets of advertising in the 1990s. Effective 1 January 1991, the Korean advertising market was completely liberalized (i.e., foreign agencies could now do business in the Korean market). The J. Walter Thompson Company, DY&R (a Dentsu-Young & Rubicam joint venture), Bozell, D'Arcy Masius Benton & Bowles, Saatchi & Saatchi, and others established offices in Seoul. Since then multinational agencies have been able to open branch offices or set up wholly owned subsidiaries.

The presidential election of 1992 was another bonanza for the advertising industry. Although the number of ad spots was limited, Korean election law permitted campaign commercials on television for the first time in history.

With increasing liberalization of Korean investment and trade regulations, Korea became one of the fastest growing markets in the world and presented tremendous opportunities to international marketers. The role of international products in the Korean market increased substantially. The 1995 opening of Korea's retail market further boosted the presence of foreign advertisers.

The South Korean economy experienced a foreign currency crisis late in 1997, and, as a result, came under the supervision of the International Monetary Fund. Domestic product growth declined during the recession period of 1997–98, and domestic consumption was sluggish. However, due to the rapid recovery of domestic production, consumer spending was still robust.

Since 1999 South Korea has made substantial progress on its structural reform program. The economy was expected to achieve an average growth rate of 5.1 percent through the year 2010, according to a report by the Korea Development Institute.

Status at Century's End

South Korea ranked as the world's tenth-largest advertising market in 1999, with a total billings base of $5.287 billion, following immediately after Canada ($5.41 billion) and Australia ($5.54 billion). Many of the largest agencies were affiliated with agencies from the United States or other countries. Hakuhodo, the second largest agency in Japan, opened an office in Seoul in July 1999. Diamond Ad, the in-house agency of Hyundai Group, was sold to the U.K.-based Cordiant Communications Group, which also owned Bates Worldwide.

The first agencies focusing exclusively on media services started operation in the 1990s. PDS Media, the first media agency in Korea, was established in July 1999 through joint ventures with Starcom (a unit of the Leo Burnett Company), Phoenix Communications, and Dentsu. McCann-Erickson announced in November 2000 that its worldwide media unit, Universal McCann, under the company name of Universal McCann Korea, would commence operating in Korea the same year.

The right to know is held to be a basic consumer right in South Korea. The Consumer Protection Board reports the results of periodic inspections of consumer goods to help consumers make informed purchase decisions. The Fair Trade Commission has jurisdiction over false and unfair advertising practices, and several industry associations regulate their own activities. There are restrictions on television advertising of tobacco and alcohol products. Also, all television and radio commercials must be previewed by the Korea Broadcast Commission. The government, which formerly prohibited comparative advertising, has allowed comparative ads on condition that the advertiser can provide substantive data for the comparison.

The development of media technology is expanding the alternatives available to advertisers, including the use of outdoor media and the Internet. However, television and newspapers remain the most important advertising media in South Korea. In June 1988 ACNielsen introduced its people meter system to the

Korean advertising and broadcasting industries. Television ratings services are provided by Media Service Korea (owned by AC Nielsen) and Taylor Nelson Sofres, which started its operation in October 1999. The Korea Audit Bureau of Circulations was established in May 1989 to collect statistics on newspaper and magazine circulation. The system was not yet fully established at the turn of the century, but figures were beginning to be available for some of the major newspapers and magazines.

YOUNG SOOK MOON

Further Reading

Advertising Yearbook, Seoul, Korea: Korea Association of Advertising Agencies, 1998

Chang, Won Ho, Teddy Spha Palasthira, and Hung Kyu Kim, *The Rise of Asian Advertising,* Seoul: Nanam Publishing House, 1995

Koranteng, Juliana, "Top Ten Global Markets," *Advertising Age International* (May 1999)

Shin, In Sup, *Advertising in Korea,* Seoul: Shisa Yong-O-Sa, 1989

Spain

The earliest Spanish advertising appeared in the country's newspapers. On 6 April 1825 the *Diario de Avisos* began printing a few advertisements in its daily edition. The newspaper *La Esperanza* (1843–73) had a long life precisely because of its advertising, even though its editorial content was heavily ideological and political, as was the norm in most dailies at that time. The first genuinely commercial newspaper was *La Correspondencia de España,* based on the French model originated by Emile Girardin and introduced into Spain by Manuel María de Santa Ana. As advertising started to become a profitable business, María de Santa Ana founded the Sociedad General de Anuncios de España (SGAE; General Society for Spanish Advertising), the first true Spanish advertising agency. The fourth page of *Correspondencia de España* was sold to SGAE and dedicated entirely to advertising. Other agencies, such as Empresa y Comisión Central de Anuncios and Publicidad-Empresa de Anuncios, were soon established. For the most part, their business involved selling advertising space in newspapers.

The pioneer advertising agencies were subsidiaries of newspapers or other businesses. In 1857 Roldós, named after its founder Ruperto Roldós, was formed. The agency initially worked for newspapers, but it soon started editing brochures and creating some outdoor advertising, such as posted signs. Roldós operated independently through 1929, when it merged with businesses in Madrid and Barcelona, becoming Roldós-Tiroleses. In 1939 it became Roldós, SA.

In the second half of the 19th century, the rates being charged by some newspapers for advertising space were out of proportion to their circulation. In 1880 the Gremio de Anunciantes (Assembly of Advertisers) was established to audit newspaper circulation. The Liga de Prensa (Press League) was founded with the same purpose slightly later. Valeriano Pérez, founder of the agency Los Tiroleses in 1891, was probably the first creative figure in Spanish advertising. He used historic events—such as Spain's war to preserve its territory in North Africa, the Spanish-American War, the quatercentenary of Christopher Columbus's 1492 voyage, and the tricentennial of the birth of dramatist Pedro

Calderón de la Bárca—as the basis for advertising campaigns. He surrounded himself with talented graphic artists and developed a virtual monopoly on outdoor advertising.

Another key figure in early Spanish advertising was Pedro Prat. In 1917 he wrote *Scientific Advertising, a New Technique.* He founded the Fama agency, soon associated with the Swiss agency Publicitas, which had been working in Barcelona since 1898. Prat went to Madrid to found Veritas in 1928 and after the Spanish Civil War (1936–39) founded Oeste (West). He later wrote *Técnica de la Publicidad* (1922) and *Publicidad Racional* (1934).

The advertising multinationals began arriving in Spain in the 1920s, among them Publicitas, Germany's Rudolf Mosse, Britain's Crawford, France's Havas, and, from the United States, the J. Walter Thompson Company (JWT). They came with multinational advertisers such as Shell, Martini, Nestlé, General Electric, Olivetti, Coca-Cola, Renault, Ford, Peugeot, Citröen, and General Motors. JWT came to Spain in 1926 with its client General Motors but left the country a few years later in the wake of the stock market crash of 1929. JWT introduced "reason-why" advertising in Spain (hard-sell advertising appealing to reason, as opposed to soft-sell advertising appealing to the emotions); its ads were different from the then-prevalent poster-art style, having more in common with the modernist aesthetic that was then dominating the Spanish art scene. Spanish advertisers also began to use testimonials. The first National Advertising Conference met in Barcelona; of the 123 participants, 94 were Catalans (i.e, from the northeastern region that includes Barcelona).

Creativity in Spanish Advertising

Art was an important element in early Spanish advertising; from the 19th century to the time of the Spanish Civil War, painters and graphic artists worked together. They used vivid color and were influenced by the Romantic type of illustrations seen in magazines of the day such as *La Moda Elegante* (a fashion magazine founded in 1841) and *La Ilustración Artística* (1889). At the end of the 19th century Catalan artists were heavily influenced by the

French Art Nouveau style. A significant change occurred when modernist and even cubist painters such as Juan Gris began contributing to the popular weekly supplement *Blanco y Negro* (founded in 1891). Cosmetics joined medical remedies as widely advertised items, and to these were soon added new products such as cameras, typewriters, and cars. Women began appearing in ads as something more than decorative figures; they now were actively consuming goods that were fashionable and earned them status. Page ads with spectacular illustrations appeared in the 1920s, and in the 1930s color lithography came into widespread use.

Innovation in the graphic arts was fostered by company-sponsored competitions. The first such contest, held in Barcelona in 1897, drew 172 submissions. Ramón Casas, a modernist painter and friend of Pablo Picasso and Santiago Rusiñol, was the winner. This contest was underwritten by Anís del Mono, a liqueur manufacturer; it was soon followed by other competitions, sponsored by the sparkling wine producer Codorniu and Amatller, a chocolatier.

The modernist style also dominated advertising in Madrid, exemplified particularly in the work of graphic artists such as Rafael Penagos and Federico Ribas. Another graphic artist of note during this period was Josep Renau, who worked in Valencia. Gal cosmetics, the brand that invested the most in advertising in the 1920s, still maintains its own advertising museum in Alcala, a city near Madrid. Its agency was Prat's Veritas. The first advertising billboard was erected by a road near Manresa, in Catalonia, on 2 May 1912.

The 1920s marked the early development of commercial radio advertising in Spain. The broadcaster Unión Radio, established in 1925, initiated an evolution from repetitive and boring messages to a more entertaining radio style. Sponsored programs were rapidly introduced. The beginnings of radio in Spain were wholly commercial; only later were government-owned stations introduced.

Stagnation

The end of the Spanish Civil War inaugurated a less creative era than the one that preceded it. The country was very poor and isolated. Advertising was basically political and served the interests of the regime of Francisco Franco. The advertising industry would not be rebuilt until the economy began to grow and function in a non-subsistence, more prosperous environment.

In the late 1940s agencies such as Oeste, Roldós, Vila, Publicitas, Valeriano Pérez & Sons, Los Tiroleses, Gisbert, and Ruescas started up again. Most advertisers were local, however, and had very small budgets. Only a handful of food, cleanser, toy, medicine, and shaving brands advertised nationally. Newspaper circulation was limited by a scarcity of paper, and the contents continued to be censored. Agencies regressed to becoming mere sellers of advertising space for newspapers. Very little radio, magazine, or outdoor work was done at this time.

After 1952 some multinational corporations such as Nestlé, Coca-Cola, and Firestone returned to the advertising scene, after having left during the Civil War. Radio became the dominant advertising medium, with the Sociedad Española de Radiodifusión (SER) network dominating the market.

Motion pictures offered a new advertising opportunity in the 1950s. Jo Linten found partners in Spain in José Luis Moro and his brother Santiago. In 1955 a commercial agreement between Movierecord and Estudios Moro was reached. Linten imported short films from Britain and short advertising movies from France. For the first time Spanish ads were entered in international contests and won awards. Within the Movierecord group, Linten founded Red for outdoor advertising. Estudios Moro won a number of international awards between 1957 and 1967.

Multinationals Return

Television changed the advertising landscape. The first television station, government-owned Televisión Española, began programming on 28 October 1956. By the end of 1957, the first commercial had been broadcast. The 1960s marked an era of relative prosperity in Spain, with major industrial and economic growth. Consumer spending power increased, and new advertising markets for home technologies were opened. Tourism was becoming a major industry and offered a major new advertising opportunity. A popular ad slogan of the day was "Spain is different." In this new environment, many multinationals that had left Spain during the Civil War returned. The Swedish firm of Günther and Backab returned in 1959, attracted by tourism. Unilever brought its in-house agency, Lintas, with it to Madrid in 1958. The Leo Burnett Company (1964), Ted Bates & Company (1964), and Young & Rubicam, Inc. (1966), opened independent shops. Others formed joint ventures with local businesses: McCann-Erickson absorbed Ruescas in 1963; Grey Advertising took over Publicidad Rasgo in 1965; Arce & Potti beame part of Foote, Cone & Belding in 1968. JWT was associated with Alas between 1964 and 1966 and then worked alone; one of its biggest clients was Nestlé and, in particular, the Nescafé coffee brand. These merged agencies made the finest ads produced in the post–Spanish Civil War period.

Although local shops such as Star, Colón, Cid, Danis, and Carvis continued to dominate the ad industry, Lintas, JWT, and Grey rapidly rose toward the top. JWT, led by Manuel Eléxpuru and Julián Bravo, stood out during the 1970s because of its professionalism and the talent of its personnel. Lintas, under the direction of Manuel Ramiro, was perhaps the leading agency by the beginning of the 1980s. Professionalism was also fostered by two trade magazines, *Control de Publicidad y Ventas* and *IPMark* (both started in 1962), and the Oficina de la Justificación de la Difusión, a nongovernmental auditing body. It was this organization that finally introduced clear parameters for auditing newspaper and magazine circulation. Censorship was abolished by law in 1966. In 1971 Spanish universities began offering degrees in advertising.

Resurgence and Growth

In 1974 Danis united with Benton & Bowles; TBWA opened its Spanish operation in 1975, and Tiempo joined with Batten Barton Durstine & Osborn in 1976. Also in 1976 Luis Bassat founded Bassat y Asociados, a shop in which Ogilvy & Mather

One of the first Spanish companies to advertise using posters was the confectioner Chocolates Matias López. This example dates from 1875.

participated. By the end of the Franco regime in 1975, Spanish advertising was set to enter its contemporary phase. The Spanish agency MMLB would be key in defining the national version of the creative revolution, similar to the U.S. creative revolution of the 1960s. MMLB, a creative boutique rather than a full-service agency, published a manifesto much like those issued by avant-garde artists. Other agencies soon followed suit, including Ricardo Pérez (1978), Tándem Campany Guasch (1978), and RCP (1979), the latter of which counted among its ranks the creative talents Luis Casadevall and Salvador Pedreño. In 1975 multimedia audience measurement was improved by the newly formed Estudio General de Medios (EGM), the result of an industry-wide agreement among agencies, advertisers, and media. In 1977 the AEAP (Spanish Association of Advertising Agencies) gave new consistency to the industry by building a partnership between the largest agency networks in the country. In 1986 the National Cinema and Television Awards were introduced, signaling a golden age of Spanish creativity that probably reached a peak in international recognition in 1993, when Spain tied with

the two major creative countries, the United States and the United Kingdom, in the number of awards won at the Cannes (France) International Advertising Festival.

By the 1990s the Spanish advertising market was the fifth largest in Europe and the eighth largest in the world in terms of spending. In Europe, only Germany, Britain, France, and Italy spent more on advertising. Overall ad spending in Spain did not compare with that of the biggest markets, however. For example, U.S. spending was 24 times that of Spain in 2000.

Advertising expenditures in Spanish media markets have followed the larger pattern of other European Union countries. In the late 20th century the European advertising market was characterized by the growth of television, a medium that developed at a faster rate than any of its predecessors. Digital paid television, through cable or satellite, started in 1999 and promised to reinforce and perhaps accelerate the trend. Television's share of advertising spending grew from 24.4 percent in 1984 to 36.8 percent in 1997. In 1998 media share in Spain (including the Internet) was as follows: TV, 45.7 percent; newspapers, 23.4 percent; magazines, 13.1 percent; radio, 10.9 percent. Advertising spending for television grew more than 90 percent from 1988 to 1993, the early period of commercial television in Spain following deregulation in 1989. During the same period, daily newspapers lost 20 percent, magazines more than 40 percent, and even radio, a powerful medium in Spain, more than 50 percent.

The Spanish market still had room for growth: worldwide it was only 16th in per capita advertising expenditures and 11th in advertising expenditures as a percentage of the gross domestic product (GDP), with 0.83 percent of GDP, well behind the 1.34 percent of GDP in the United States and the 1.23 percent of GDP in the United Kingdom.

Overall growth in ad spending was spectacular in the 1980s, when advertising expenditures were increasing an astonishing 25 percent yearly on average. This boom was followed by an advertising recession in 1992 and 1993, when there was a real decrease in spending, as advertising expenditures were growing at a lower rate than inflation (2 percent and 4 percent, respectively). In the late 1990s the market was again expanding, although more moderately than in the 1980s. By the turn of the century, overall advertising expenditures in Spain had reached approximately $6 billion.

Every medium was different, however. Spain was, above all, a broadcasting market. Per capita advertising expenditures were low for newspapers and magazines—as was readership—compared with those of other European Union countries. The country had low levels of readership, despite audience and circulation growth for dailies in the late 1990s. Magazines were in a process of specialization that was increasing the circulation of monthly issues targeted to specific audiences; at the same time, the circulation figures and market impact of weekly publications were declining. Overall, Spain was the fourth-largest cinema advertising market in the world and the seventh-largest radio and television market. Terrestrial television (i.e., free, transmitter-broadcast television, as opposed to paid, cable, or satellite television) was still drawing huge audiences, and the influence and prestige of radio was higher than in other European markets as a result of earlier deregulation in the 1970s designed to capitalize commercially on radio's large audience. Agencies, media-buying specialists, media companies, and advertisers contributed to the costs of audience research data provided through the Spanish Audit Bureau of Circulations (OJD, established 1964) and were represented on its board. These groups also jointly funded the audience media reports supplied by the EGM and the Association for Research in Communication Media (AIMC), on whose board they were also represented. There was only one audiometer provider in Spain, the French-owned Sofres, which analyzed data from 2,500 households. The reliability and accuracy of these data were matter for debate.

Media and Markets

Even as early as 1980 advertising spending for television represented a little more than 25 percent of total ad spending; by 1999 it was 38.3 percent, thus ranking Spain third behind only Italy and Japan in terms of the percentage so devoted. On the other hand, ad spending for daily newspapers grew slightly, showing a small upward trend from 28.7 percent of total ad spending to 31.3 percent in 1997, far behind the 48.2 percent of Germany and the 43.5 percent of Canada. More important, magazines declined from a 25.4 percent share in 1980 to a mere 15.3 percent in 1997, although only Japan saw an increase of the magazine advertising market during this period. Major magazine publishers included the French publisher Hachette (which published *Elle* and *Car and Driver*) and Germany's Grüner+Jahr (the publisher of *Muy Interesante,* one of Spain's leading monthlies), owned by Bertelsmann. Radio's share of spending also decreased, from 12.5 percent in 1980 to 9.7 percent in 1997. However, Spain was still the European market with the highest radio share. The outdoor advertising market also suffered, declining from 6.4 percent to 4.6 percent between 1980 and 1997.

A number of explanations have been offered for the dominance of television. The 1990s saw the development of commercial broadcast television networks and regional stations. At the turn of the 21st century, the television market in Spain consisted both of national and regional government-owned stations as well as private stations, both national and local. TVE, the most-watched station in the country, depended on the government. The 1990s were also a decade of development for cable systems. The first paid television channel started during these years.

Nontraditional advertising media such as direct marketing (either mail-order marketing or telemarketing), sales promotion, sponsorship (especially in sports programming, which is new in Spain), and the Internet, accounted for half of overall advertising expenditures in 2000. The fragmentation of the television and radio audience, along with the increased ability of TV viewers to avoid or bypass commercials, increased the use of nontraditional media.

U.S. advertising shops dominated the Spanish agency scene by the turn of the century. McCann-Erickson, Bassat Ogilvy, Tiempo BBDO, Grey, and TBWA were the five largest agencies in the country, with billings exceeding 4 billion pesetas ($21 million). Among the top 20 Spanish ad agencies, 18 were owned by non-Spanish advertising agency networks. Besides U.S.-owned agencies, there were French-owned firms, such as Publicis and Euro RSCG, and British- (e.g., Lowe) and Italian-owned (Barro Testa) firms. Spain was not unique in this respect, however. With the exception of France, in fact, every European market was dominated by overseas networks.

In the 1990s there was heated controversy about the way agency billings and income were reported, with accusations of inflated figures circulated among agencies and widespread mistrust over the figures published by trade magazines such as *Anuncios, Control de Publicidad y Ventas,* and *IPMark.* The conflict eased somewhat in the late 1990s following an industry-wide agreement. Agency rankings were thenceforth based on figures audited by Arthur Andersen, Ernst & Young, Pricewaterhouse-Coopers, and KPMG Peat Marwick.

The Spanish advertising agency market was heavily concentrated in the creative hubs of Madrid and Barcelona, where large national and multinational clients were based as of 2001. Local and regional agencies were understaffed and suffered from a lack of strategic knowledge, poor management, and weak local and regional audience research figures.

Because of TV's strong presence in Spain (it had a penetration level of 93 percent) and because the country's biggest advertisers had huge budgets for TV commercials, agencies were more interested in television than in any other medium. Most agencies in the Spanish market were still paid by commission, even though the prevalence of fees and other performance-related payments was slowly increasing. The many well-publicized TV advertising awards provided opportunities for agencies to increase their prestige and for brands to boost their recognition.

Following the French model, large media-buying conglomerates have been established in Spain. They are powerful intermediaries that use their influence to obtain impressive discounts in the media. They have also started to offer medium- and small-sized agencies and advertisers media-planning services and audience research. These services have become all the more necessary as the television audience has become more fragmented. The effects of the 1993 Sapin Law (Loi Sapin) in France—which tried to establish clear-cut, written discount agreements between media-buying conglomerates, advertisers, and media—were felt in Spain, and media-buying specialists encountered some mistrust in the market. Some of these companies were independents, the largest ones being Media Planning and Carat España, a worldwide buying outlet. Others, such as the Media Partnership, were formed by advertising agency buying coalitions (in the case of Media Partnership, by JWT and Ogilvy & Mather).

The largest advertisers had a significant presence in the Spanish market, where local television outlets were not very strong. In fact, the 38 largest advertisers accounted for 45 percent of overall spending, according to Infoadex, the Spanish provider of data on ad spending. El Corte Inglés, a large department store, Procter & Gamble Company (P&G), and the telecommunications company Telefonica were the largest advertisers, with annual budgets of more than 12 billion pesetas ($63 million). Nine automotive advertisers (Renault, Volkswagen-Audi, Opel, Fiat, Peugeot, Ford, Citroën, Nissan, and Seat) were among the top 20 advertisers in the country, even though the highest-ranking was only seventh. Food and beverage advertisers also had impressive figures, with four advertisers among the top 20: Nestlé, Leche Pascual (a dairy producer), Danone (the European counterpart of Groupe Danone), and Coca-Cola. (Pepsi was not among the top 50 advertisers in Spain). P&G and Henkel (a manufacturer of household cleansers, toiletries, and chemicals) were also major advertisers.

Deregulation of the phone system and mobile phone licenses issued in the 1990s attracted advertising expenditures by Telefonica (which also owned one of the major commercial television networks) and its competitors, notably Airtel and Retevision. The development of pay television and digital platforms such as Canal + (51 percent–owned by Canal + France and 49 percent–owned by Spanish media conglomerate PRISA), its digital brand Canal Satelite Digital, and Via Digital, owned by Telefonica, have also contributed to the growth of the advertising market.

Government advertising is a major factor in the Spanish market with $105 million in spending in 2000. The government has developed campaigns to promote safe driving and to inform the public about tax revenues, state treasury funds, the state lottery (17th-largest advertiser in 1996), the Euro currency, and issues such as drug abuse prevention, environmental protection, and AIDS education. Strong advertising figures have also been shown by regional governments, including those of Catalonia, Andalusia, Galicia, Valencia, and the Basque region.

In the 1990s the creativity of Spanish advertising won worldwide recognition and prestige thanks to superb performances by Spanish agencies in the major advertising awards programs, especially the Cannes festival. In 1997 Delvico Bates, Tandem DDB, SCPF, Casadevall Pedreño & PRG, Tiempo BBDO, BDDP Mancebo Kaye, and FCB Tapsa led the pack in national and international advertising awards. In 1997 Delvico took six Clio awards and four prizes in Cannes; Tandem DDB won four in New York and six Clio awards; Casadevall Pedreño & PRG also took four prizes in New York and two in Cannes; and BDDP Mancebo Kaye, two in New York and four in Cannes. *Advertising Age* estimated that in 2000, Spanish agencies overall had gross income of $638.1 million on billings of $5.24 billion.

FRANCISCO J. PÉREZ-LATRE

See also color plate in this volume

Further Reading

Albarran, Alan B., and Sylvia M. Chan-Olmsted, *Global Media Economics: Commercialization, Concentration, and Integration of World Media Markets*, Ames: Iowa State University Press, 1998

Cabello, Fernando, *El mercado de revistas en España*, Barcelona: Ariel, 1999

Díaz Nosty, Bernardo, *Informe anual de la comunicación, 1997–1998: Estado y tendencias de los medios en España*, Spain: Grupo Z, 1998

Eguizábal, Raúl, *Historia de la Publicidad*, Madrid: Editorial Eresma y Celeste Ediciones, 1998

García Ruescas, Francisco, *Historia de la Publicidad en España*, Madrid: Editora Nacional, 1971

Gustafsson, Karl-Erik, and Lennart Weibull, "European Newspaper Readership: Structure and Development," *The European Journal of Communication Research* 22, no. 3, 1997

Pérez-Latre, Francisco J., *Centrales de compra de Medios*, Pamplona: Ediciones Universidad de Navarra, 1995

Pérez-Latre, Francisco J., *Curso de medios publicitarios*, Pamplona: Ariel, 1997

Sánchez-Tabernero, Alfonso, *Estrategias de marketing de las empresas de televisión en España*, Pamplona: Ediciones Universidad de Navarra, 1997

Spokes-Character

A "spokes-character," or trade character, is an animate being or animated object used to promote a product, service, or idea. A spokes-character does not have to be a legal trademark or appear on the package, but to be successful it must be used consistently in conjunction with a product over time. Traditionally, such characters have been associated with low-involvement products such as food, cleaning supplies, and children's items. More recently, characters have been used to promote high-involvement adult products—for example, the appearance of the Peanuts characters in ads for Metropolitan Life Insurance. Spokes-characters are an important and highly effective tool in modern advertising practice, appearing in almost 8 percent of all ad campaigns.

Spokes-characters can be classified on the basis of their physical form, the medium in which they appear, their origin, and their role in the promotion of the product. In terms of form, characters may range from human (for example, Mr. Clean, Ronald McDonald) to animal (Morris the Cat) to mythical (the Jolly Green Giant, the Keebler Elves). Yet another category called product personification includes such figures as the California Raisins and the Dow Scrubbing Bubbles. Characters often appear in more than one medium. Some appear in print ads, in TV commercials, on package labels, and on promotional merchandise.

Many spokes-characters have been created as live-action people portrayed by actors. Among the most enduring has been the laconic Marlboro Man created in 1955 by the Leo Burnett Company for Marlboro cigarettes. Other long-running live-action presenter/symbols include the lonely repairman from Maytag (also from Burnett), portrayed for 22 years by actor Jesse White and for 11 years by Gordon Jump; Parker Fennelly as the New England farmer for Pepperidge Farm (Ogilvy & Mather); Mr. Whipple for Charmin Tissue (Benton and Bowles, Inc.); and actress Nancy Walker as Rosie the waitress demonstrating Bounty paper towels, "the quicker picker upper" (Benton & Bowles).

Characters also can be categorized according to origin. Advertisers can license characters that have nonadvertising origins—for example, those from comic strips, TV programs, and books—to promote their products. Such characters are called celebrities and include Dilbert for Office Depot and the Pink Panther for Owens Corning. Noncelebrity characters are created specifically for advertising purposes, such as the Pillsbury Doughboy, a creation of Burnett. In fact, few agencies have developed more imaginary presenters than Burnett, starting in the early 1940s with "Chico" for the Santa Fe Railroad. Burnett developed a particular reputation for its "critters," a collection of animated animals and cartoon creatures that covered product categories from cereals (Tony the Tiger for Kellogg's Frosted Flakes) to banks (Hubert the Lion for the Harris Bank). Many were overseen by creative director Robert Noel, the agency's unofficial "vice president of elves and gnomes," who ran the department that produced the Keebler Elves, Morris the Cat (for 9-Lives Cat Food), and Charlie the Tuna (for Star-Kist).

Finally, spokes-characters are categorized according to their role in product promotion as active or passive. Active promotion includes speaking for the product or demonstrating it; active characters usually are featured in the ads themselves. Passive characters do not act or speak; often, they appear only on the product packaging. Characters may change from active to passive and back again over time based on advertiser needs and consumer response. For example, Elsie the Cow first appeared in ads speaking for Borden milk, then became a figurehead on the package, and in the late 1990s returned to an active role once again.

There are three major reasons why advertisers choose trade characters over other advertising appeals: characters create product identification, characters give a product personality, and characters provide continuity over time. Spokes-characters create product identification by forging links among the product, the packaging, and the advertising in the minds of consumers. A successful character connects the advertising message to the brand so that consumers recall the message when they see the product package. The Jolly Green Giant is one example of a character who appears on product labels, in television and print advertising, and on sales promotions such as coupons and premiums. The character ties these marketing activities into a cohesive unit that communicates a consistent message of product quality.

Beyond product identification, spokes-characters add personality and emotional appeal to a product. Characters can give a product personality by symbolizing the product's attributes or benefits. For example, Betty Crocker has come to stand for reliability, while the Energizer Bunny symbolizes endurance. Spokes-characters add emotional appeal to an impersonal brand by lending the warmth of a recognizable personality to the product. Thus, Smokey Bear provides an emotional link between consumers and the seemingly remote problem of forest fires. Some characters, such as the Campbell Kids, become so beloved that they become objects of nostalgia and spawn premiums and collectibles.

Spokes-characters also appeal to advertisers because they provide continuity over time. One of the longest-lived spokes-characters is the RCA dog, Nipper, who was created in 1901. Many of today's most popular characters, such as Kellogg's Snap, Crackle, and Pop; Borden's Elsie; and Planter's Mr. Peanut, have been used consistently by the advertisers for more than 60 years. These characters build invaluable brand equity over time because their role in creating product identification and personality is constantly reinforced.

Trade characters are ideal for long-term use because, unlike their human counterparts, they do not age, change, demand more money, or engage in scandalous behavior. In addition, characters are flexible, appearing on everything from billboards to the Internet to video games. Longevity is limited only if the advertising message changes. For example, the Exxon tiger was discontinued for a time in the United States during the 1970s when its message of smooth, silent power appeared wasteful during the oil crisis, and Smokey Bear's soft, fuzzy image was deemed unsuitable for

TONY THE TIGER SAYS:

"You bet your life they're Gr-r-reat!"

No wonder Groucho's speechless. What if a tiger stole your microphone and your favorite line. But that's Tony for you. And he's all for you when he tells you to try these big, crackly flakes of corn. Because they're the ones with the secret Kellogg's sugar coating all over. Gr-r-reat? You bet your life.

 SUGAR FROSTED FLAKES

During the 1950s Kellogg's Tony the Tiger spokes-character was a featured guest on many popular television shows, such as this appearance with Groucho Marx.
Courtesy of Groucho Marx Productions. Kellogg's®, the Kellogg's® logo, and Frosted Flakes® are registered trademarks of Kellogg Company. All rights reserved. Used with permission.

A logo from a 1919 ad featured Buster Brown and his dog, Tige, fictional characters created in 1902 by Richard Outcault for the Brown Shoe Company.
Brown Shoe Co.

hard-hitting ads reporting strict jail terms for setting fires. Other characters are occasionally updated to continue to appeal to consumers year after year. The Kool-Aid pitcherman, which first appeared on the package in 1955, was modified in 1985 to appeal to older children. Betty Crocker's hair and wardrobe have been modernized many times since her creation in 1921. In 1950 General Mills took the unprecedented step of extending its Betty Crocker trademark to a fully dimensional live-action personification. Actress Adelaide Hawley Cumming assumed the complete identity of Betty Crocker, not only in commercial messages but also as host of the weekly *Betty Crocker Television Show* and *The Betty Crocker Star Matinee*. Cumming played Betty Crocker in thousands of public appearances as well, never stepping out of the persona for nearly a decade. General Mills claimed to have made her the second-most-recognizable woman in the United States after Eleanor Roosevelt, which explains why during the 1950s millions believed the trademark to be a real person.

BARBARA J. PHILLIPS

See also color plate in this volume

Further Reading

Callcott, Margaret F., and Wei-Na Lee, "Establishing the Spokes-Character in Academic Inquiry: Historical Overview and Framework for Definition," *Advances in Consumer Research* 22 (1995)

Callcott, Margaret F., and Barbara J. Phillips, "Observations: Elves Make Good Cookies: Creating Likable Spokes-Character Advertising," *Journal of Advertising Research* 36, no. 5 (September/October 1996)

Dotz, Warren, and Jim Morton, *What a Character! 20th-Century American Advertising Icons*, San Francisco: Chronicle, 1996

Phillips, Barbara J., "Defining Trade Characters and Their Role in American Popular Culture," *Journal of Popular Culture* 29, no. 4 (Spring 1996)

Phillips, Barbara J., and Barbara Gyoerick, "The Cow, the Cook, and the Quaker: Fifty Years of Spokes-Character Advertising," *Journalism and Mass Communication Quarterly* 76 (Winter 1999)

Sacharow, Stanley, *Symbols of Trade: Your Favorite Trademarks and the Companies They Represent*, New York: Art Direction, 1982

Sports

Sports have the ability to create dramatic tension and winners. For marketers seeking to differentiate their products from those of the competition or to position their products in the best possible way, connection with a winner is a valuable asset. Moreover, sports are generally seen as driven by competition, hard work, discipline, and the will to win—all qualities that are valued by society at large and that confer benefits by association.

Early Sports Advertising

One of the earliest examples of sports advertising, however, did not speak of winning. Rather, it spoke of adventure and hardship. Placed by the polar explorer Ernest Shackleton in 1900, the 26-word classified ad that appeared in London, England, newspapers read as follows:

> Men Wanted for Hazardous Journey. Small wages, bitter cold, long months of complete darkness, constant danger, safe return doubtful. Honor and recognition in case of success.

The advertisement was hugely successful, and Shackleton later commented, "It seemed as though all the men in Great Britain were determined to accompany me, the response was so overwhelming."

The growth of sports in modern society has been similarly overwhelming. From the late 1790s in England (when horseracing publications first appeared) until the onset of the 21st century (when a 30-second television ad during the Super Bowl cost up to $2 million), sports have provided both events and heroes for the advertising industry. In the United States the sale of the first sports publications—among them, John Stuart Skinner's *American Turf Register* and William Trotter Porter's *Spirit of the Times*—can be traced to the 1820s. By 1893 the Pulitzer newspapers were featuring the first sports departments, and in 1895 the Hearst newspapers offered the first sports sections. With these developments the visibility of sports increased until they gradually became a daily feature of American life. At the same time, sports imagery came to be used by advertisers, particularly in targeting males age 12 to 54.

By the 1920s broadcasts of sports events such as championship boxing matches were regularly used to help sell radios. The symbiotic relationship between sports and the media continued with the introduction of television in the 1940s. It was with television that advertisers began to realize they could place ads in sports programming to talk directly to men in order to sell products such as automobiles, razors, and beer.

One of the earliest advertisers to understand this strategy was the Boston, Massachusetts-based Gillette Company. In 1952 its ad agency, Maxon, Inc., of Detroit, Michigan, introduced an animated parrot named Sharpie. Originally drawn as a white-line silhouette on a black background, Sharpie was superimposed on the screen over the live telecast of a baseball game or over a boxing ring. The character appeared on a World Series telecast in 1952, advising viewers that they could "Look sharp! Feel sharp! Be sharp!" The squawking parrot was later fully animated, and a catchy score (the "To Look Sharp and Be on the Ball . . ." jingle) was added that promised the "quickest, slickest shave of all." Gillette's discovery of sports as an advertising vehicle would lead to the company's sponsorship of the *Cavalcade of Sports,* one of the earliest sponsorships of sports on television and one of the earliest sports anthology shows.

Another company to recognize the power of sports early on was General Mills. In 1933 Blackett, Sample & Hummert created the fictional character of Jack Armstrong for General Mills' Wheaties brand, which had first appeared on the market in 1928. Armstrong was a sports hero of Hudson High who became involved in crime-fighting adventures on the side. The radio program *Jack Armstrong, All-American Boy* ran from 1933 to 1950, always sponsored by Wheaties. The company also signed real-life heroes to personify the brand, choosing sports idols who would appeal to young people. The first was Babe Ruth in the 1930s.

Twenty years later the medium of television was growing dramatically, and the agency for Wheaties, by then Fitzgerald Advertising, signed baseball stars Duke Snider of the Brooklyn Dodgers and Stan Musial of the St. Louis Cardinals, as spokesmen. In one 1953 spot the two sluggers sat at a table, each eating a bowl of Wheaties while glaring at the camera. The message was that real men do not talk much—they let their home runs or stolen bases do the talking. Within ten years Wheaties was putting athletes on its packaging, thus visually reinforcing its product as the "Breakfast of Champions." Over the years many sports heroes, including

Olympic decathlon gold medalist Bruce Jenner, Olympic gymnast Mary Lou Retton, basketball great Michael Jordan, golf champion Tiger Woods, and football player Brett Favre, have appeared on the orange Wheaties box.

Sports Advertising Comes of Age

One of the most famous uses of a sports celebrity was Coca-Cola's 1979 spot, created by McCann-Erickson, that featured the Pittsburgh Steeler defensive lineman "Mean" Joe Greene. In the commercial, revered for its use of football realism, Greene was shown limping down the players' tunnel on his way to the locker room. It was apparent that the Steelers were losing and that Greene was finished for the day. He was met in the tunnel by a young boy holding a large bottle of Coke. The boy asked Greene if he wanted his soda, but Greene declined. The boy persisted, stammering that Greene was one of his heroes ("I just want you to know that—that you're the greatest"). Obviously nervous, the boy again tried to give his Coke to the giant player towering over him. At this point Greene reconsidered and accepted the humble gift. Grabbing the bottle, he chugged the soda down in one swig. The commercial could perhaps have ended there, but McCann-Erickson's script called for the dejected boy to start walking away. He had failed to impress his hero. But as the camera pulled back, the viewer saw Greene yell, "Hey kid . . ." and toss the boy his jersey. The boy's response was "Thanks, Mean Joe!" and his huge, broad grin perfectly embodied Coke's slogan at the time, "A Coke and a smile."

While Coca-Cola generated huge awareness from its commercial, the Miller Brewing Company's Miller Lite brand was already six years into a long-running campaign that almost always featured retired sports heroes. Miller used ex-jocks because of restrictions imposed by the Bureau of Alcohol, Tobacco, and Firearms, which interpreted the appearance of active athletes in commercials for alcoholic beverages as potentially implying that drinking alcohol could improve athletic performance. Further, the company did not want to use active players because of the young audiences that watched televised sports.

The Miller Lite campaign, with its tag lines "Less filling; tastes great" and "Everything you always wanted in a beer . . . and less," was also created by McCann-Erickson. The campaign began in July 1973 with a commercial in which ex–New York Jets running back Matt Snell was shown talking into the camera about the many empty beer bottles at his bar table. Snell's monologue included the comment that he had not consumed all of the beers himself but had, in fact, had help. The message was clear, however. Miller's new low-calorie beer ("a third less calories than their regular beer") allowed people to drink more without feeling full. Over the next 17 years, in what came to be considered one of the greatest sports-connected campaigns of all time, Miller featured former sports stars including football legends Dick Butkus (Chicago Bears), Ray Nitschke (Green Bay Packers), Bubba Smith (Baltimore Colts), and Deacon Jones (Los Angeles Rams).

Miller was also comfortable poking fun at itself and at the whole idea of sports advertising, and some of Miller Lite's best-known spots (created by ad agency Backer & Spielvogel, formed in 1979 after principals Bill Backer and Carl Spielvogel left McCann-Erickson) featured baseball players such as Bob Uecker and Marv Throneberry, who had been less than great on the field. As antiheroes, they helped push the Miller Lite campaign to national prominence and helped the brand become the second-largest-selling beer in the United States. In many ways Miller Lite's recurring use of sports celebrities paved the way for the next phase of advertising using sports heroes, which was epitomized by the ad campaigns of a brash new footwear company called Nike.

About the time the Miller Lite campaign had become overly familiar and formulaic, Nike began making product commercials that revolutionized sports-themed advertising. In the period from 1982 to 2002, with the agencies Chiat/Day and, more prominently, Wieden & Kennedy, the company created numerous award-winning spots that featured sports professionals as product endorsers. The best-remembered television commercials for Nike generally featured basketball legend Michael Jordan (Chicago Bulls), multisport star Bo Jackson (Oakland Raiders/Kansas City Royals), basketball player Charles Barkley (Philadelphia 76ers, Phoenix Suns, and Houston Rockets), and tennis great John McEnroe. The spots were made even more powerful with terse catchphrases such as "Just do it" or "Must be the shoes."

Nike's first notable advertising efforts, however, were built around posters that consumers could hang on the wall. Company executives realized early on that Nike was seen as a marketing-focused company rather than a technology or production company and that marketing its products through the use of sports heroes—as individuals rather than as a part of a team—was the most effective way to connect with mainstream America. Posters had the advantage of being cheap, and they were easy to distribute to retailers and customers.

Nike was also the first company to create commercials using an athlete who was HIV-positive (marathoner Ric Muñoz), a disabled athlete, and a senior citizen who was an active athlete. Nike's 1995 commercial by Wieden & Kennedy entitled "If You Let Me Play" featured girls and young women describing the benefits of encouraging girls to get involved in sports, among them reducing the number of teen pregnancies, gaining the confidence to leave a physically abusive partner, and increasing the likelihood of completing high school.

In 1993 McDonald's and the Leo Burnett Company raised the sports hero as pitchman to a new level in a commercial for Quarter Pounders that centered on competition between Michael Jordan and on-court rival Larry Bird. The ad featured Jordan and Bird challenging each other to make impossible shots ("off the billboard, through the tunnel, nothing but net"). It mixed traditional playground bravado with references to the product in such a comfortable way that fans could relate to the dueling stars. McDonald's unveiled the spot during Super Bowl XXVII and followed it with a football-themed spot using the same challenge concept but involving kickers Pete Stoyanovich of the Miami Dolphins and Chip Lohmiller of the Washington Redskins.

Keeps the logical side of the brain pinned to the back of your skull.

Press the accelerator of the 911 Turbo, and what happens next is astonishing. The raw surge of power. The incredibly honed balance. Yes, it's crazy to take automotive achievement to such an extreme. That may be the best reason of all. Contact us at 1-800-PORSCHE or porsche.com.

PORSCHE

Like other marketers of luxury goods, Porsche found a target market among enthusiasts of sports such as golf, tennis, and skiing. This ad appeared in *Tennis* magazine in April 2001.
PORSCHE, the PORSCHE CREST and 911 are registered trademarks and the distinctive shapes of PORSCHE automobiles are trade dress of Dr. Ing. h.c. F. Porsche AG. Photograph and trademarks used with permission of Porsche Cars North America, Inc., and Dr. Ing. h.c. F Porsche AG. Copyrighted by Porsche Cars North America, Inc.

The Super Bowl Stakes

It was Super Bowl XVII that saw the debut of what was perhaps the greatest single new piece of advertising. Chiat/Day wanted to put Apple Computer on the map, and to do so it enlisted movie director Ridley Scott, known for his futuristic films *Alien* and *Blade Runner*, and created a script that borrowed heavily from George Orwell's 1949 novel *1984*. The brash California agency wanted to create the kind of commercial that would make people talk about Apple and its new product, the Macintosh computer.

According to Lee Clow, Chiat/Day's executive creative director at the time, it had originally been planned that the commercial, called "1984," would run on January 1 during a college bowl game. If it had, the spot might simply have been another commercial buried under the weight of more than 300 ads on telecasts of football games on New Year's Day. Because the Apple Macintosh was not ready, however, the commercial was moved to the Super Bowl, where a minute's worth of time cost what then seemed to be the outlandish sum of $400,000. Having spent $500,000 to produce the commercial, Chiat/Day embarked on an aggressive public relations campaign to suggest that viewers tune in to the Super Bowl to see a special commercial.

What the audience saw was a parable based on Orwell's novel about a totalitarian regime's control over the individual will of its citizens. In the commercial, a female athlete wielding a giant hammer ran toward a giant television screen that showed a representation of Big Brother, a dig at competitor IBM Corporation. The woman then launched the hammer toward the screen. When the screen exploded, a blinding flash of light swept over the stunned audience watching the screen, and an announcer solemnly intoned, "On January 24, Apple Computer will introduce Macintosh. And you'll see why 1984 won't be like '1984.'"

Since that time advertisers have used the Super Bowl, the only championship in professional sports that is resolved in a single game, to debut their newest and frequently their most expensive work. There are two principal reasons for this. The first is that the Super Bowl traditionally reaches close to 50 percent of all U.S. homes, something rare among the increasingly segmented TV audience, and more than 700 million viewers worldwide. And the second reason is that advertising on the Super Bowl appears to work. In fact, on the day after Super Bowl XVII, Apple executives said that 200,000 people went into stores to look at the Macintosh and that within 100 days 72,000 people had bought the $2,495 computer. This kind of success breeds imitation, and perhaps for that reason alone Super Bowl advertising is traditionally sold out well in advance of the game. Of course, the price of Super Bowl advertising has skyrocketed, with the 60-second unit that cost $400,000 in 1984 going for $3.8 million in 2002.

Other Prominent Venues

The Super Bowl is not the only sports programming to offer broad consumer appeal. The Olympic Games, soccer's World Cup, and, to a lesser degree, the World Series and the National Basketball Association (NBA) finals are all notably successful in attracting large, diverse audiences. All of these events warrant telecasts in prime-time schedules, and all receive extensive attention from the media. In fact, in the case of the Super Bowl, *USA Today* regularly covers not only the game but also the advertising.

Some sports, however, appeal to more narrow segments of the public. For example, tennis, golf, and horseracing (particularly the Kentucky Derby, Preakness, and Belmont Stakes) have been used effectively by the television networks and advertisers to reach more upscale audiences. Companies such as financial service institutions (Visa, American Express), high-end automakers (Mercedes, BMW), and insurance firms (Prudential, John Hancock) have used the appeals of particular sports to advertise to selected groups. Likewise, auto racing, particularly NASCAR

(National Association for Stock Car Auto Racing) events, has been particularly successful in reaching middle- and lower-income families. In fact, of all sports NASCAR may be the most effective at suggesting to its fans that there is a connection between the support of sponsors and the very existence of events. To that end NASCAR fans are thought to be the most emotionally connected and loyal to the products of the advertisers and sponsors of the racing teams they follow.

NASCAR's practice of putting the names of sponsors on race-cars and drivers' uniforms is relatively unusual in the United States. With the exception of professional soccer, golf, and tennis, which do allow advertising to appear on the clothing worn in competitive events, the practice is not permitted in U.S. professional sports.

In the case of the National Football League (NFL), NBA, National Hockey League (NHL), and Major League Baseball, advertising has traditionally been reserved for those areas of the stadium where the games are actually played. In hockey, ads are used on the dasher boards and have increasingly come to be painted under the ice. Basketball and baseball use rotating Dorna boards (in the case of the latter behind home plate) that contain several ad messages that are changed during the course of a game. All four of these sports use wall and scoreboard signs, some of them illuminated, for advertising messages.

The situation is different for college sports in the United States and for the Olympic Games, where the intent is that the games are played in a largely commercial-free setting. In Europe, Japan, Australia, and other parts of the world, however, signs on soccer fields and on professional players' uniforms are quite common.

The Effect of Television

The televising of sports has had an enormous effect on advertising. In their book *Sport Marketing* (2000), Bernard Mullin, Stephen Hardy, and William Sutton point out that in 1960 the three principal U.S. broadcast networks (ABC, CBS, and NBC) produced about 300 hours of sports programming per year. By 1982 the amount had grown more than fivefold—to 1,600 hours. Estimates for the late 1990s suggested that more than 20,000 hours of sports were being telecast each year. This level of programming requires a huge amount of advertising.

Cable television networks such as ESPN and Fox Sports, which provide either national or regional cable coverage of sports, have made it possible for people to view sporting events and sports news 24 hours a day, 365 days a year. Because of the enormous costs associated with purchasing the rights to premier sporting events, however, both the broadcast and cable networks must advertise their own sports programming in order to hold existing viewers and to attract new ones. Perhaps the best example of this is the relationship of the NFL with its four broadcast partners (ABC, ESPN, CBS, and Fox). The NFL was able to sell the television rights to its games for eight years (1998–2006) for $17.6 billion. In turn, the four networks that bought the rights must regularly run promotional advertising to get viewers to watch pregame shows, the games themselves, and play-offs.

Since the early days of advertising, marketers have recognized the benefits of linking their products with sports events and heroes. This 2001 print ad for Planters nuts featured a promotion for a Super Bowl weekend.
Courtesy of Kraft Foods Holdings, Inc.

ESPN has been one of the most successful networks in advertising its own programming. It grew from humble beginnings in Bristol, Connecticut, in 1979, broadcasting Australian football; by 2002, it was broadcasting U.S. professional football, basketball, hockey, baseball, and soccer games, as well as college football and basketball games. What ESPN did in 1995 was to give viewers a glimpse, frequently a fictitious glimpse, behind the scenes at its headquarters. Using Wieden & Kennedy, already known for its work for Nike, ESPN asked for a campaign that would promote its nightly recap show, *SportsCenter,* as well as its primary news anchors, Dan Patrick and Keith Olbermann. What made the spots stand out was the number of athletes who contributed bits to the antics of the ESPN anchors. Baseball player Roger Clemons, driver Michael Andretti, gymnasts Kerri Strug and Mary Lou Retton, basketball player Jason Kidd, and then–home run record holder Mark McGwire all made appearances that suggested that a person never knew what he might see on *SportsCenter.*

The Antihero and the Cutting Edge

At their heart, sporting events have an unpredictability that endears them to advertisers. New heroes and villains, whether individuals or teams, are created almost daily. In fact, one trend in advertising has been to employ the "bad boys" of sports to help sell products. Examples have included basketball players Charles Barkley (Nike), Dennis Rodman (Chicago Bulls; Pizza Hut, Converse, Kodak), and Allen Iverson (Philadelphia 76ers; Reebok), all of whom brought with them a certain street credibility as a result of their recurring antisocial behavior. Rodman, for example, a classic product of the rock music culture of antiheroes, was frequently under the scrutiny of the sports media for various acts that included kicking a courtside cameraman and removing his own shoes on the bench during a game. Despite such behavior, Rodman had endorsement agreements with Converse, Victoria's Secret, Kodak, Pizza Hut, and Carl's Jr., a regional hamburger chain.

A similar phenomenon occurred outside the United States. In The Netherlands, Wieden & Kennedy used former Manchester United soccer player Eric Cantona in a Nike commercial that was titled "Good vs. Evil." The advertisement, which was ultimately banned in some areas and panned by soccer purists, featured an all-star team of Nike endorsers playing a game against the "forces of evil." The mock contest was decided when Cantona, who had previously been suspended for entering the stands and attacking a heckler, scored the game's only goal. His curt "Au revoir," spoken before blasting a goal through the belly of the demonic goalkeeper, became a popular saying among European teenagers.

The extraordinary popularity of Manchester United, possibly the world's most closely followed team, illustrates another tie-in between advertising and sports. One reason for Manchester United's appeal has been the team's use of Web sites and other communications technology, which have made it possible to advertise the team globally. Such efforts have included on-line shopping for Manchester United licensed apparel and team updates via club news.

The Internet, including the use of various forms of banner advertising, has begun to change the face of sports again. Sports fans have a reputation for being hungry for information, and in this respect the Internet has made television obsolete in terms of providing certain services. It is thus not surprising that Internet advertising connected to sports has grown rapidly. In fact, the Internet may represent the next great frontier for sports advertising. Nike, for example, was the first to create a commercial that began on television but concluded on the Internet. In fact, in its "whatever.NIKE.com" campaign, viewers who went to the Internet to finish the commercial were rewarded with multiple choices. Nike also provided the first commercial to be streamed via ESPN.com.

Another method of sports advertising that has developed is known as "virtual signage." With virtual signage, which is created electronically, television viewers, for example, see advertising on an arena's floor or a stadium's pitch that spectators in the actual venue do not see. (Another example of this technology—absent commercial support—is the use of the virtual first down line in American football or the appearance of country flags in speed-skating or swimming lanes at the Olympics.) This form of advertising allows marketers to show commercials without interfering with the play of the game. It is particularly useful in sports that do not have frequent built-in breaks, as, for example, American football and baseball do.

New developments simply prove that, wherever sporting events or games are played, advertisers are interested in determining who is watching and how they can be reached with compelling advertising.

RICK BURTON

See also color plate in this volume

Further Reading

Burton, Rick, "Sports Marketing and the Super Bowl," in *The Advertising Business: Operations, Creativity, Media Planning, Integrated Communications,* edited by John Philip Jones, Thousand Oaks, California, and London: Sage, 1999

Burton, Rick, Francis Farrelly, and Pascale Quester, "Exploring the Curious Demand for Athletes with Controversial Images: A Review of Anti-Hero Product Endorsement Advertising," *International Journal of Sports Marketing and Sponsorship* 2, no. 4 (December/January 2001)

Deford, Frank, *Lite Reading,* New York and London: Penguin, 1984

Enrico, Dottie, "The Fifty Greatest TV Commercials of All Time," *TV Guide* (3 July 1999)

Hall, Jim, *Mighty Minutes: An Illustrated History of Television's Best Commercials,* New York: Harmony, 1984

Jacobs, A.J., and Ken Tucker, "The Pauses That Refreshed: The 50 Greatest Commercials of All Time!" *Entertainment Weekly* (28 March 1997)

Kanner, Bernice, *The 100 Best TV Commercials—And Why They Worked,* New York: Times Business, 1999

Katz, Donald, *Just Do It: The Nike Spirit in the Corporate World,* Holbrook, Massachusetts: Adams, 1994

McChesney, Robert, "Media Made Sport: A History of Sports Coverage in the United States," in *Media, Sports, and Society,* edited by Lawrence Wenner, Newbury Park, California: Sage, 1989

Mullin, Bernard, *Sport Marketing,* Amherst: University of Massachusetts Press, 1980; 2nd edition, by Mullin, Stephen Hardy, and William Sutton, Champaign, Illinois: Human Kinetics, 2000

Rothenberg, Randall, *Where the Suckers Moon: An Advertising Story,* New York: Knopf, 1994

Strasser, J.B., and Laurie Becklund, *Swoosh: The Unauthorized Story of Nike and the Men Who Played There,* San Diego, California: Harcourt Brace Jovanovich, 1991

Walker, Sam, "Show Me the Money," *Wall Street Journal* (17 May 1999)

Watkins, Julian Lewis, *The 100 Greatest Advertisements: Who Wrote Them and What They Did,* New York: Moore, 1949; 2nd edition, New York: Dover, 1959

Springer & Jacoby

Started as Springer in Hamburg, West Germany, by Reinhard Springer, 1979; renamed Springer & Jacoby with the addition of Konstantin Jacoby, 1983; landed its biggest and most prominent account, Mercedes-Benz Germany, 1989; 50 percent of principals' shares given to top agency employees, 1994; launched multimedia agency Elephant Seven, 1996; created Springer & Jacoby International with a London, England, office, 1999; sold 35.5 percent of its shares to True North, Chicago, Illinois, in 2000 with options to buy additional shares in the future; True North acquired by the Interpublic Group of Companies, 2001.

Major Clients

DaimlerChrysler (Mercedes-Benz and SMART)
Deutsche Bank 24
Deutsche Telekom
Mercedes-Benz

Reinhard Springer and Konstantin Jacoby were young, talented advertising men when they met in 1977 at GGK Düsseldorf, a now-defunct agency that at the time was known for its high creative standards. Within a few years the two would leave to create what would become the hottest agency in Germany.

Springer, born in 1948, began his career with an apprenticeship at Gilde Agency, in Hamburg. In 1970 he moved to Ted Bates Frankfurt and in 1975 became an account director at GGK Düsseldorf, a Swiss agency. In October 1979 Springer decided to leave GGK Düsseldorf to start his own shop in Hamburg. The agency, called Springer, got off to a slow start; Springer operated the shop from two rooms rented at the Poststrasse, which still houses the agency's main office, and lived in the office for a few months to save money. He signed his first client, footwear retailer Schuhhaus Goertz, six months later.

Business remained slow until 1983, when Konstantin Jacoby joined him. Jacoby, born in 1953, had studied art at Berlin University before starting his career as a copywriter at Univas

Düsseldorf; from there he moved in 1977 to GGK Düsseldorf, where he became creative director in 1979. The two renamed the agency Springer & Jacoby, and it began to grow. In just a few months, the agency had added more clients, including the newsweekly *Der Spiegel,* Panasonic, Carlsberg Beer, Neckermann Mail Order, and Nixdorf Computers.

Within about a year Springer & Jacoby had became the hottest agency in Germany, a reputation it maintained into the 21st century. Contributing to the agency's new image was the bronze Lion it won at the 1984 Cannes (France) International Advertising Festival, for a commercial for *Der Spiegel.* At the same time it was adding more clients: Bacardi Rum, Reemtsma Cigaretten, and household appliance marketer Miele. The agency grew steadily through the 1980s; by 1991 it ranked number 14 in Germany, with a gross income of $24.6 million and 246 employees, according to the German newsletter *Der Kontakter.*

In 1989 Springer & Jacoby landed a coup when it won the German Mercedes-Benz account. The Stuttgart automaker had invited six agencies to participate in its account review because it wanted more creative work for its premium-priced vehicles. While Mercedes-Benz subsidiaries are independent and can choose their own ads, Springer & Jacoby commercials featuring tennis star Boris Becker and racecar driver Mika Häkkinen were aired in many markets. Rival automakers have been said to request "ads like Mercedes-Benz" from their agencies. Business continued to grow in the 1990s, with the agency adding new clients such as Deutsche Post subsidiary Postbank and IBM Corporation.

In 1994 Springer and Jacoby decided to step down from full-time operations at the agency and give younger managers a chance to head the agency. The partners gave 50 percent of their shares to leading employees, a decision that was unheard of in German agency history. Top management was split among five employees.

In 1995 Deutsche Telekom appointed Springer & Jacoby to handle its $10 million "product sales" budget. But with the privatization of Deutsche Telekom and new rivals entering the market,

Konstantin Jacoby.
Courtesy of Springer & Jacoby.

the budget grew to $85 million, making it the agency's biggest account in 2001.

Not all account wins proved successful. In 1997 Deutsche Lufthansa appointed Springer & Jacoby as its global agency. The relationship deteriorated, but some critics said the campaign was Springer & Jacoby's best work. Early in 2000 the global account moved to McCann-Erickson Worldwide, Frankfurt.

During the 1990s Springer & Jacoby began to expand beyond its local origins within Germany and soon thereafter expanded internationally. In 1995 the agency opened its first brochure and catalog agency, e-fact, in London, England. That shop, which worked entirely online, handled all Mercedes-Benz's sales literature worldwide in 11 languages. In February 1996 Springer & Jacoby started multimedia agency Elephant Seven in Hamburg, which grew into a highly creative multimedia shop with gross income of $8.6 million in 2000.

Springer & Jacoby believed that in a time of globalization the lack of an international network, or even a European one, meant it would not be invited to international presentations, which limited the shop's growth potential. Both Springer and Jacoby had enormous fears about giving up their independence, but they lacked the financial means to set up an international network on their own.

In 1999 the agency opened Springer & Jacoby International with a small London office. With a staff of 23 it handled projects for Mercedes-Benz and some small local accounts. At the same time Springer & Jacoby knew it would eventually need a partner, and DaimlerChrysler assured the agency that international

Mercedes-Benz budgets would follow if it set up an international network.

In September 2000 Springer & Jacoby sold 35.5 percent of its shares to True North, Chicago, Illinois. (True North had an option to acquire up to 51 percent of the shop by 2003.) With True North's financial backing, the agency planned to set up offices in Europe, the United States, and Japan. In 2001 True North was acquired by the Interpublic Group of Companies.

Despite the Lufthansa account loss, 2000 proved to be an excellent year for the agency. Springer & Jacoby won its first gold Lion at the Cannes International Advertising Festival for work it did for Hamburg's police force. DaimlerChrysler moved its $45 million European SMART budget to the agency. And the Coca-Cola Company, with its new strategy of employing local agencies instead of relying on worldwide campaigns, tapped Springer & Jacoby to handle its branding account in Germany.

In September the agency opened S&J España Barcelona; Mercedes-Benz awarded the agency its Spanish budget for cars and commercial vans, with SMART expected to follow. The agency planned to open an Italian office in 2001. In February 2001 the agency acquired the minority of Milan-based Colnaghi & Manciani, a small Italian agency. The partners had handled the Mercedes-Benz brand in Italy for the previous ten years. In October Springer & Jacoby Paris was opened, with DaimlerChrysler France's Mercedes-Benz account.

For almost two decades no other agency in Germany has influenced the German advertising world as much as Springer & Jacoby. At the same time, both founding fathers backed off from

Reinhard Springer.
Courtesy of Springer & Jacoby.

400 CDI. Der bulligste PKW-Diesel der Welt.

▶ auto motor und sport war beein-
druckt: „ein neuer Maßstab" schrieb sie
über den 400 CDI. Recht hat sie. Das

Achtzylinder-Aggregat für S-Klasse und
G-Modell ist der momentan stärkste
Serien-Diesel der Welt. In Zahlen: 560

Nm Drehmoment ab 1.700 Umdrehun-
gen und 250 PS. Aber der Motor kann
noch mehr. Durch Common Rail Direct

Injection, Biturbo mit variabler Turbi-
nengeometrie und Aluminium-Leicht-
bauweise ist er auch sparsam, sauber

und leise. Pure Kraft ist schließlich
nicht alles. Mehr Informationen fin-
den Sie unter www.mercedes-benz.de.

Mercedes-Benz
Die Zukunft des Automobils.

Translated into English, the headline of this ad for Mercedes-Benz from Springer & Jacoby reads, "The beefiest diesel passenger car in the world."
Courtesy of DaimlerChrysler AG.

the agency in two steps. First, they handed the operative business to their successors in 1994; since 1997 they have worked as board members only. Jacoby divides his time between Hamburg and Palma, on the island of Mallorca, Spain; Springer & Jacoby has set up a Creative Center there, where Jacoby gives courses in copywriting. At the same time, he is very involved with Daimler-Chrysler's Mercedes-Benz overseas project. Springer set up his own counseling group in Hamburg. For 2000 Springer & Jacoby had gross income of $58.9 million, down 13.2 percent from the year earlier, on billings of $382.9 million, ranking it at number nine in Germany for that year, according to *Advertising Age* figures.

DAGMAR MUSSEY

Further Reading
Mussey, Dagmar, "Interview with Konstantin Jacoby," *Advertising Age* (11 July 1985)

Standard Brands

Principal Agencies
J. Walter Thompson Company
Ted Bates & Company
Lee King & Partners, Inc.

Standard Brands traces its roots to the entrepreneurial late 1800s and its demise to the megamerger 1980s. What began as a yeast company would eventually encompass a product line ranging from beer to nuts, including such well-known American brands as Baby Ruth candy bars, Fleischmann's margarine, Chase & Sanborn coffee, and Planters peanuts, as well as imports such as Moosehead beer. The New York City–based company was in the vanguard of several major advances in advertising, including making health claims for its products and using radio and television as ad media. Leaders of the company ranged from a 19th-century immigrant brewer and an Indiana pharmacist to a poster boy for 1980s corporate excess.

In 1868 Charles Fleischmann, trained in Austria as a brewer, and his brother, Maximillian, developed Fleischmann's yeast, the first compressed yeast to be sold in North America. The Fleischmann's brand name would remain a major force in the company the brothers founded, eventually expanding to alcoholic beverages such as Fleischmann's gin and the only national brand of corn oil margarine in the United States. Fleischmann's Yeast Company grew and prospered as the brothers established an extensive distribution system and made good use of advertising and promotion.

Buying up Brands

In June 1929 the Fleischmanns acquired four smaller companies—Royal Baking Powder Company, Chase & Sanborn Company, E.W. Gillette Company, Ltd., of Canada, and Widlar Food Products Company—to form Standard Brands. Many of Standard Brands' best-known products came to the company via acquisition rather than through its own development efforts. Royal Baking Powder had been the creation of Fort Wayne, Indiana, druggist Joseph C. Hoagland, who in 1865 mixed up some baking powder and sold it as a substitute for yeast. He advertised the product in religious and women's magazines, and in the 1870s Royal was one of the first major advertisers to feature a picture of the product in its ads. By the early 1890s, Royal was spending $600,000 a year on newspaper ads and was among the first advertisers to reject bombast in favor of more sedate, believable approaches. Under Standard Brands, Royal expanded to include an entire dessert line.

Standard Brands acquired another famous brand in 1961— Planters. Planters Nut & Chocolate Company, the longtime leader in the peanut industry, was founded in 1906 by Italian immigrant Amedeo Obici and his future brother-in-law, Mario Peruzzi. Early on, the partners emphasized quality and their brand name, and

understood the value of advertising. The enduring Mr. Peanut icon was not conceived by an ad agency but via a 1916 contest to come up with the best sketch for a Planters trademark. A 14-year-old Virginia schoolboy won with his drawing of Mr. Peanut, a nut sprouting arms and legs. A commercial artist later added the top hat, cane, and monocle. In 1918 Planters began advertising on a national scale with an ad in the *Saturday Evening Post*. Planters were the first peanuts to be advertised.

In 1964 Standard Brands bought the Curtiss Candy Company, a Chicago, Illinois, confectioner. Curtiss, founded by entrepreneur Otto Schnering in 1921, was known for its Baby Ruth bar, which, in a masterstroke of marketing, was named after President Grover Cleveland's daughter. Butterfinger debuted in 1923. In one promotional stunt for Butterfinger, candy bars were dropped from an airplane on cities in 40 states. Decades later, stunts were part of the marketing of Standard Brands' ill-fated Reggie! candy bar.

Julius Wile Sons & Company, marketer of imported liqueurs, wines, and specialties—at that time among the fastest-growing segments in the alcoholic beverage industry—was acquired in 1972. Other Standard Brands products included Chase & Sanborn coffee; Tender Leaf tea; Moosehead beer, a Canadian import marketed via its All Brand Importers subsidiary; Fleischmann's Egg Beaters; Blue Bonnet margarine, which started in 1943 as a regional brand in Texas named after the state's flower; Dry Sack sherry; and Pernod liqueur. Standard Brands' other major line of business was selling food ingredients, including corn-based products, vinegar, and baking ingredients, to industrial customers. In 1980 Standard Brands' last year of business before merging into Nabisco in 1981, consumer products would represent 78 percent of net sales; the remainder came from food ingredient product sales.

Pioneering Forays into Advertising

Despite its reputation as a staid, conservative company, Standard Brands made pioneering forays in several areas of advertising. A 1969 ad for Fleischmann's, the top-selling premium-priced margarine in the United States, can be seen as an emblem for the brand's long-standing pitch. The ad from Ted Bates & Company, New York City, asks, "Is swimming as good for you as Fleischmann's margarine?" and goes on to proclaim Fleischmann's as "The premium margarine doctors name most" and "made from 100% corn oil."

Standard Brands had used health claims and physician testimonials for decades, sometimes with dubious underpinnings. The J. Walter Thompson Company (JWT) applied testimonials to Fleischmann's yeast in the 1920s, advertising the product as a cure for ills ranging from acne to constipation, and even the common cold. When the American Medical Association cracked down on members who engaged in such testimonials, JWT account executive William L. Day found European physicians who would cooperate for a fee. Standard Brands was hardly the

Standard Brands recognized Americans' growing interest in the benefits of a low-fat diet when promoting Fleischmann's Margarine in this 1969 advertisement.
Courtesy of ConAgra Foods.

1936 Chase & Sanborn sponsored the *Major Bowes Original Amateur Hour* on which 19-year-old Frank Sinatra made his radio debut with the Hoboken Four. Between the *Fleischmann's Yeast Hour* and the *Chase & Sanborn Hour*, Standard Brands had at its disposal two of the biggest variety shows in radio out of which would come even bigger stars. Bob Hope and Jack Benny made some of their earliest radio appearances on the Fleischmann show. But the comic that JWT would discover through the show and build into a national sensation on behalf of Standard Brands was perhaps the most unlikely for radio, ventriloquist Edgar Bergen and his dummy Charlie McCarthy. Bergen appeared with Vallee in December 1936 and by the following May had taken over the *Chase & Sanborn Hour*. Bergen and McCarthy would represent Chase & Sanborn, and then Royal Pudding, for the next 12 years on radio.

The company's agency roster expanded in the 1940s; McCann-Erickson took on Royal Baking Powder and Sherman K. Ellis & Company handled Royal gelatins and puddings. After World War II, Ted Bates & Company was added for Blue Bonnet and some Royal products.

Standard Brands ventured into television in 1946 with *Hour Glass*. Although less widely known than *The Texaco Star Theater* or *Your Show of Shows* and on the air for less than a year (May 1946–March 1947), it was the first big-time variety program produced for television. JWT produced the show for Chase & Sanborn and Tender Leaf. Standard Brands put an estimated

only marketer to make such claims, and in 1938 the Wheeler-Lea amendments to the Federal Trade Commission (FTC) Act added injunctive power to cease-and-desist orders from the FTC. In the next two years, the government forced Fleischmann's to stop making its outrageous claims.

JWT, one of the most active ad agencies in the early days of radio, also helped make Standard Brands a pioneer in that medium and later in television. The agency produced two Standard Brands–sponsored radio programs that helped create the template for future variety shows. The *Fleischmann's Yeast Hour,* a Thursday night musical variety show that debuted in September 1929, featured Rudy Vallee and his Connecticut Yankees. It was one of the first musical variety hits, and became the first really big-time variety program. In 1932 the show began emphasizing guest stars, featuring vaudeville and Broadway performers. JWT and Standard Brands followed up with the *Chase & Sanborn Hour*. The show began in 1929 with Maurice Chevalier, then switched to Eddie Cantor in 1931. Cantor would set the general style for many major radio comic-variety hosts to come. From 1935 to

In 1978 Standard Brands introduced the short-lived Reggie candy bar, named after the Most Valuable Player of the 1977 World Series, Reggie Jackson.

Look! There's something for everyone in Planters Mixed Nuts! The most famous peanuts in the world plus the most delicious tree nuts in the world: mellow cashews, crunchy almonds, tangy filberts and crisp Brazil nuts or buttery pecans—that's what's in mixed nuts the way Planters makes them! PLANTERS—THE QUALITY NAME FOR NUTS

Standard Brands acquired Planters—and its Mr. Peanut spokes-character—in 1961, the year this ad appeared. *Courtesy of Kraft Foods Holdings, Inc.*

$200,000 into the nine-month run, by far the largest amount that had ever been devoted to a sponsored show at that time. Prospects of continued heavy spending on *Hour Glass* led to its cancellation, though Standard Brands was satisfied with its ability to push its products. The experience would prove valuable for JWT, which went on to produce the long-running *Kraft Television Theatre.*

Consigned to History

Standard Brands' desire for acquisition would eventually erase the Standard Brands name, thanks to the machinations of F. Ross Johnson. In 1971 Johnson, a former accountant and General Electric lightbulb salesman, was named to head Standard Brands' Canadian operation. His flamboyant style shook up the Canadian operation with firings but got results, and he was promoted to the New York City headquarters. In May 1976 Johnson was named chief executive officer (CEO) of the company, succeeding Chairman and CEO Henry Weigl. The following year, Johnson added the chairman title. The staid days of Standard Brands were over. The high-living, celebrity-loving Johnson was committed to more aggressive new-product activity to take full advantage of the company's distribution strengths. The results, however, would be less than impressive.

One product perhaps more than any other combined Johnson's desire for new products and his penchant for hobnobbing with celebrity athletes. In 1978 Standard Brands introduced the Reggie! candy bar, named after New York Yankees baseball star Reggie Jackson. The chocolate-and-peanut cluster, though simply a renamed national version of a product that was already on the market regionally, was part of an intensified effort to reduce dependence on commodity-oriented businesses and expand the company's branded consumer goods business. The pairing of the athlete and candy bar garnered a lot of press. Stunts accompanied the introduction: fans entering Yankee Stadium on opening day that year got a Reggie! bar; whenever Jackson hit a home run, Reggie! bars rained onto the field. Lee King & Partners, Inc., handled advertising for Reggie!, as well as the other Curtiss candy brands. Despite these promotions, the Reggie! bar sold sluggishly, though the candy division posted record earnings in 1980 on the strength of the venerable Baby Ruth and Butterfinger brands. Reggie! was dropped in 1980.

While building a spotty record in new products (another doomed idea was Smooth 'N Easy, an instant gravy sold in stick form, like margarine) and failing to energize profits, Johnson remained ardent about acquisitions. Standard Brands was outbid by Grand Metropolitan in 1980 in a move to acquire Liggett Group, which marketed cigarettes. But a year later, he spearheaded the deal that would erase the Standard Brands name: the $2 billion merger with Nabisco. The number-one marketer of margarine and branded nuts and the country's top purveyor of cookies and crackers merged to create the fourth-largest food company in the United States, with a combined $6 billion in sales. Individually, both companies had been struggling for growth opportunities and neither was known as an innovator in marketing, but Nabisco had an extensive sales force that observers surmised would be used to sell Standard Brands products. For years Nabisco had tried to diversify into salty snacks, and now it had snatched Planters. Standard Brands brought international strength, especially in Latin America, to the marriage, and the deal would reduce Standard Brands' dependency on its cyclical corn sweetener business.

Johnson became president and chief operating officer of the new food giant. At the time of the merger in April 1981, the plan was to keep the two operations separate, but in July the company made the surprise announcement of a unified restructuring plan under the new moniker Nabisco Brands. The Standard Brands name was history.

In 1985 R.J. Reynolds Tobacco Company acquired Nabisco for $4.9 billion, forming RJR Nabisco. Johnson became chairman and was named chief executive officer in 1987. In 1986 he sold off the Fleischmann's yeast business, the original foundation of Standard Brands. But Johnson's biggest gamble came in 1988, when he made a bold bid to take RJR Nabisco private through a leveraged buyout. Johnson, and the buyout battle, became symbols of 1980s merger mania and corporate greed. An investor group led by Kohlberg Kravis Roberts & Company eventually won, snapping up RJR Nabisco for $25 billion. By the year 2000, the only former Standard Brands products left at Nabisco were Planters and Royal. Nestlé Food Corporation by that time had acquired Butterfinger and Baby Ruth, and ConAgra Foods had Fleischmann's and Blue Bonnet margarines, as well as Egg Beaters.

DAN LIPPE

Further Reading

Burrough, Bryan, and John Helyar, *Barbarians at the Gate: The Fall of RJR Nabisco,* New York: Harper and Row, and London: Cape, 1990

Canada's Digital Collections <collections.ic.gc.ca>

Essential Information <www.essential.org>

Fading Ad Campaign <www.frankjump.com>

Fox, Stephen, *The Mirror Makers: A History of American Advertising and Its Creators,* New York: Morrow, 1984

Giges, Nancy, "Nabisco, SB Seek Spark," *Advertising Age* (27 April 1981)

"Leading National Advertisers: Nabisco Inc., Standard Brands," *Advertising Age* (10 September 1981)

"Leading National Advertisers: Standard Brands," *Advertising Age* (28 August 1961)

"Leading National Advertisers: Standard Brands," *Advertising Age* (29 August 1977)

Museum of Broadcast Communications <www.mbcnet.org>

"Nabisco Brands Sets Its Sights for Overseas," *Business Week* (11 May 1981)

"Nabisco Lands on Top in the Brands Merger," *Business Week* (24 Aug 1981)

Sherrid, Pamela, "Cookies, Peanuts . . . and Life Savers?" *Forbes* (7 December 1981)

Smith, Roy C., *The Money Wars: The Rise and Fall of the Great Buyout Boom of the 1980s,* New York: Dutton, 1990

Winston-Salem Journal <www.journalnow.com>

"Yanks' Reggie Jackson Goes to Bat for Standard Brands' Youth Promos," *Advertising Age* (9 May 1977)

Starch, Inc.

Starch Advertising and Media Research was a division of Roper Starch Worldwide in 2000. But the company existed as an independent enterprise for many years until the death of its founder, Daniel Starch, in 1979. During its formative years, it developed important new ways in which advertisers could gauge and analyze the impact of their ads on readers.

Daniel Starch was born on 8 March 1883. The Starch family operated a 420-acre farm in La Crosse, Wisconsin. After completing elementary school at a one-room schoolhouse in Wisconsin, Starch attended the Charles City Preparatory School in Iowa and graduated in 1899. He then attended Morningside College in Sioux City, Iowa. A double major in psychology and mathematics, he was the youngest graduate in his class, receiving a bachelor of arts degree in 1903. Through his undergraduate studies, Starch became interested in the new field of experimental psychology, and he enrolled at the University of Iowa, where he earned a master's degree in psychology and education in 1904. He received a doctoral degree from the University of Wisconsin in 1906.

He returned to the University of Wisconsin in 1908, and over the next 12 years he published numerous articles and books, including *Principles of Advertising: A Systematic Syllabus of the Fundamental Principles of Advertising* (1910) and *Advertising: Its Principles, Practice, and Technique* (1914). Starch left the University of Wisconsin in 1919 to take a lecturer position at Harvard Business School.

Advertising research at the turn of the 20th century was best exemplified by the theoretical research of Northwestern University professor Walter Dill Scott, who conducted controlled experiments using fake ads to assess consumer reactions to advertising. Starch, however, was interested in studying how consumers reacted to advertisements they encountered in real magazines under ordinary (not controlled) circumstances. The concept of trying to measure readership was disparaged by many advertising practitioners, but Starch developed a magazine readership measurement method that for the first time applied recognition measures to advertising research. He later wrote of his method, "the definite purpose of the recognition was to maintain normal conditions of observing and reading. The purpose of the technique is to ascertain the extent to which certain advertisements are seen and read." His findings were published in 1923 in *Principles of Advertising*, a tremendously successful book, which garnered more income for Starch than did his salary at Harvard. On the basis of this success, Starch created the Daniel Starch and Staff Research Company in 1923.

Principles of Advertising was a landmark book in advertising. Its popularity sprang from its comprehensive, pragmatic approach. The text addressed five fundamental questions advertisers face: To whom may the commodity be sold? By what appeals may it be sold? How may the appeals be presented most effectively? By what media may the appeals or advertisements be presented? and What is a reasonable expenditure for advertising the commodity? The text also offered coverage of such topics as market research and advertising ethics. *Principles of Advertising* influenced the structure of advertising textbooks for decades.

As Starch continued to teach at Harvard Business School and worked in his newly established market research company, he

Now you can get something you've always wanted in a performance car. Your family.

Call 1-800-NISSAN-6 for more information. *M.S.R.P. excluding taxes, title, license, destination charges and options. Optional equipment shown.

What's the last thing you expect when you press the accelerator in a typical mid-size sedan?

Acceleration.

But perform that simple act in the all-new Nissan® Stanza® and you're in for a mind-altering experience.

Because along with the things that make the Stanza such a great family car— comfort, reliability, economy, practicality—you get all the best parts of a very impressive performance car.

The major one being the 2.4-liter,

138-horsepower, 12-valve, multi-port, sequentially fuel-injected engine, the most powerful standard engine in its class.

Our exclusive Advanced Traction Control,™ standard on the GXE, provides optimum traction to the drive wheels on unstable surfaces like ice, dirt and gravel.

Anti-lock brakes, available on the GXE model, deliver straight, controlled stops on wet or icy roads.

And on all surfaces, few sedans offer the stability and handling response of the Stanza, thanks to 4-wheel independent suspension and both front and rear

stabilizer bars as standard. As a carrier of family stuff, the Stanza p equally well. It ha 90.7 cu. ft. of space in the passenger compartment. Plus a grocery-bag gobbling 14 cu. ft. of trunk space.

There really isn't much more you could ask for in a mid-size sedan. Except for this one, last, very impressive feature.

The price.

B   Human Race.

The New Stanza. $11,450.

This 1989 print ad for the Nissan Stanza was analyzed for reader recall using the Starch method. Labels applied to the ad show Starch scores on various measures.
Copyright, Nissan (1989). Nissan and the Nissan logo are registered trademarks of Nissan.

became a leading name in the advertising industry. In 1924 the American Association of Advertising Agencies (AAAA) asked Starch to be the director of its new research department. He agreed to work for the association two days a week, while still teaching at Harvard and working for his own company.

While research director at the AAAA, Starch moved into the study of media beyond magazine advertising. He studied magazine and newspaper circulation and undertook pioneering research in radio. The National Broadcasting Company (NBC) commissioned Starch to undertake the first project to estimate the size of the national radio audience in 1928. Using probability sampling techniques, he estimated the number of households with radios to within four percentage points of the figure determined by the 1930 federal government census. Starch's research in print media provided some of the first estimates of duplicate readership, a measure of the number of people that may read more than one medium or specific media vehicle. At a macro level, duplicate readership is an estimate of the number of people who would read both newspapers and magazines, or listen to the radio and read magazines. At a more specific level, it estimates which magazines a person reads and which radio formats he or she listens to. For example, if a woman reads *Cosmopolitan* magazine, researchers could see what other magazines she reads or radio formats she listens to. Beyond the specific findings of his AAAA studies, Starch's greatest contributions to the field of advertising were his methodological innovations.

It was not until 1932 that Starch formally started collecting data for his ad files. At first, a small number of advertisers and magazines commissioned Starch to study their readership. Top national magazines, including *Cosmopolitan, Ladies' Home Journal, McCall's,* and *Saturday Evening Post* subscribed to Starch's Continuing Readership Program, and these magazines soon found that the data provided a wealth of information about how to attract magazine readers' attention to advertising. Given the overwhelming success of this program, it is hard to believe that a top ad executive told Starch in 1930 that readership could not be measured satisfactorily. Daniel Starch and Staff went on to employ hundreds of interviewers across the United States, using the information gathered to measure readership for thousands of advertisements.

The Methodology

Although technology has brought about changes in the techniques used to collect data, the Starch methodology is basically the same as it was when Starch created it in 1923. The process begins with field interviewers identifying a statistical sample of those persons who have read a particular issue of a magazine. Starch tested samples with sizes ranging from less than 100 to 10,000, and he found that stability of results was obtained with sample sizes of approximately 200. For a particular issue of a magazine, 100 to 200 men or women are interviewed. The gender of the respondents is determined by the gender of the target audience for the particular magazine; each sample is collected from 20 to 30 different areas of the United States.

Once a respondent has been identified, the interviewer then turns the pages of the magazine, waiting for the respondent to indicate if he or she had read or seen a particular ad. To guard against boredom and order effects, each interview starts at a random page location within the magazine. If a respondent indicates that she or he has seen an advertisement, the interviewer probes the depth with which the respondent read the advertisement. For each advertisement of one-half page or more, the following Ad-as-a-Whole statistics are reported:

Noted: The percentage of magazine readers who say they had previously seen the advertisement in a specific magazine.

Associated: The percentage of magazine readers who say they had seen or read any part of the advertisement that clearly indicates the name of the product or advertiser.

Read Most: The percentage of readers who looked at the advertisement and indicated that they read more than half of the written ad copy.

Additional scores are also recorded for the major visuals and the advertisement signature. (See illustration on page 1484.)

When examining Starch scores, it is important to have a benchmark for comparison purposes. To this end, Starch calculates Adnorms, which are the average noted, associated, and read-most scores for the previous year for all advertisements. Adnorms are calculated for each product class, and within each product class they are measured separately for men and women for each magazine. Adnorms are also calculated separately for specific types of advertisements, such as half-page, page, black and white, and color.

During the 1930s, a rival researcher from Iowa, George Gallup, also began assessing print advertising effectiveness. Gallup first undertook experimental studies, similar to those conducted by Walter Dill Scott, in which he worked to perfect his aided recall measure. A basic assumption underlying the recall measure is that the advertisement leaves a memory trace after a person has been exposed to it. To assess aided recall, respondents were asked a series of questions beginning with a product-class prompt and ending with inquiries about ad copy. Gallup worked for a time as the research director for Young & Rubicam, where he extended his aided recall measure to radio, and then established the Gallup and Robinson Research Company, where he and Claude Robinson further refined the aided recall methodology. Gallup's aided recall approach gained popularity over Starch's recognition method, primarily due to the easy adaptation of recall assessments to broadcast media and the prevailing assumption among advertising analysts that recognition measures resulted in an over-reporting of ad readership.

As recall gained in popularity, especially with the advent of new broadcast media, interest in recognition measurements waned somewhat, but that did not mean that Daniel Starch and Staff was without research projects. It was busier than ever, for magazines still found value in the Continuing Readership Study. In fact, Starch published a series of research reports beginning in

A 2001 promotional brochure highlighted Roper-Starch's wide range of print media and advertising research services. *Reprinted with permission from Roper Starch Worldwide Inc.*

1934 that discussed factors of ad design that could make advertising more effective and capable of gaining readers' attention. The results of Starch's research have stood the test of time and been validated through repeated analysis.

In 1966 Starch published *Measuring Advertising Readership and Results,* which provided an update on Starch Continuing Readership research. In addition to providing a brief history of recognition research, Starch addressed the debate over recognition versus recall methods, contending that recognition was a superior measure to the more popular aided recall. He wrote, "The recognition method undoubtedly comes the closest to measuring the total number of readers of an advertisement. Recall methods, particularly unaided recall procedures, do not uncover all advertisements originally seen or read by a particular reader."

Starch died 5 February 1979, at the age of 95. The company he established has evolved through several mergers with other research companies to continue the research legacy established by its founder. Daniel Starch and Staff acquired the C.E. Hooper Company in 1969 and expanded its international presence with the acquisition of International Research Associates in 1974. In the early 1980s the company, then known as Starch/INRA/ Hooper, Inc., acquired the Roper Organization, a public-opinion research firm founded by pioneer pollster Elmo Roper, which continued as a subsidiary of Starch under its own name until 1993, when the name of the company was changed to Roper Starch Worldwide, Inc.

Roper Starch Worldwide currently consists of four divisions: Starch Advertising and Media Research, Roper Marketing and Opinion Research, Friedman Data Collection, and INRA, which conducts international research. The company has affiliates in more than 35 countries.

In 1923 Starch wrote, "All advertising problems are subsidiary, in the last analysis, to the one main question, namely: by what means and in what manner may the mind of the potential customer be influenced most effectively." This question continues to perplex many advertisers in the quest to persuade consumers to purchase products, services, and ideas.

HARLAN E. SPOTTS

Further Reading

Borden, Neil, "Daniel Starch," *Journal of Marketing* 21 (3 January 1957)

"Daniel Starch," in *The Ad Men and Women: A Biographical Dictionary of Advertising,* edited by Edd Applegate, Westport, Connecticut: Greenwood Press, 1994

Graham, Irvin, *Encyclopedia of Advertising,* New York: Fairchild, 1952; 2nd edition, 1969

McElwain, Max, "Daniel Starch," in *Profiles in Communication: The Hall of Fame of the University of Iowa School of Journalism and Mass Communication,* edited by McElwain, Iowa City: University of Iowa, 1991

Presbrey, Frank, *The History and Development of Advertising,* New York: Doubleday, 1929; reprint, New York: Greenwood Press, 1968

"Starch: The Man Behind the Name," *Printers' Ink* 278, no. 7 (February 1962)

Wier, Walter, *How to Create Interest-Evoking, Sales-Inducing, Non-Irritating Advertising,* New York: Haworth Press, 1994

Stereotype. *See* Archetype/Stereotype

Studebaker

Principal Agencies
Burke Dowling Adams, Inc.
Roche, Williams & Cunnyngham, Inc. (later Roche, Williams & Cleary, Inc.)
Benton & Bowles, Inc.
D'Arcy Advertising Company, Inc.
W.B. Doner & Company

In 1852 Clement and Henry Studebaker started a blacksmith and wagon shop in South Bend, Indiana. Over the next 18 years, three of their brothers joined the company, as it attained prominence by supplying wagons to the booming midwestern agricultural market. In 1870 the company was incorporated as Studebaker Brothers Manufacturing Company and established its first branch office in St. Joseph, Missouri, to outfit settlers moving west. The company produced more than 750,000 wagons during its history, employing the motto, "Always give more than you promise."

In 1897 the Studebakers began to experiment with automobiles. By 1902 the company was building electric cars, and two years later, gasoline-powered automobiles. A leader in styling and engineering, Studebaker was also ahead of its time in its recognition of the importance of advertising. As early as 1858, company president John Studebaker proclaimed, "We must advertise and never cease to advertise." Studebaker was one of the first corporations to make a commitment to spending money on advertising and research in order to inspire consumer confidence and attract new customers.

Studebaker's advertisements always began with a declaration of an ideal, typically one that focused on the importance of family ties, quality of workmanship, or economy of operation. One of the most famous campaigns was the long-lived "father and son" series, which featured fathers and sons who worked in Studebaker plants and emphasized a common family interest in the building of cars. During World War I the ads depicted a father working in the factory to turn out war goods needed by his son fighting overseas.

In the early history of the company, Studebaker advertising was created in-house by nonspecialists. Eventually the company began hiring advertising professionals to design and create its ads. After significant corporate reorganization in 1935, Studebaker no longer maintained an in-house advertising department. Instead, in an effort to economize, company executives dealt directly with representatives of the company's advertising agency. This and other operations changes enabled Studebaker to survive in the era of horseless carriages—the only major wagon and buggy maker to do so.

Burke Dowling Adams, Inc. (BDA), of South Bend was the early agency of record. Just as Studebaker's image was that of a company rooted in tradition, BDA executives referred to their operation as a "shirt-sleeve" agency, rather than a large Madison Avenue shop. Account executives were expected to spend a good deal of their time with the client's sales force to become completely familiar with the sales effort.

Studebaker switched agencies in the mid-1930s to Roche, Williams & Cunnyngham, Inc. (RW&C, later called Roche, Williams & Cleary, Inc.). It also hired specialized agencies to handle special projects and promotions. For example, Studebaker contracted with the public relations firm Hill & Knowlton, Inc., to handle publicity for the company's centennial in 1952. In 1955, when Studebaker hired Benton & Bowles, Inc., the advertising budget was increased by 30 percent to $8 million (unprecedented for Studebaker), which was spent on a multimedia advertising campaign.

In an effort to serve the post–World War II market and tap into pent-up consumer demand for cars, Studebaker merged with Packard in 1954. Although Studebaker's coffers were full after its success with defense contracts (it produced trucks and tractors that were shipped as far as Siberia), rapidly declining sales, escalating labor costs, and shrinking market share threatened the company. Merging with Packard provided an expanded cash pool and larger market share. In 1959 the D'Arcy Advertising Company, Inc., was hired to handle the marketing program for the 1959 Studebaker-Packard models.

Despite a softening automobile market after the 1950s, Studebaker's sales continued to rise. Studebaker explored the compact market while the larger companies held back. The company enjoyed some success with this approach, particularly with the 1959 Lark, the 1961 Lark, and the 1961 Hawk. The company credited its success to the following formula: (1) offer cars with strikingly new designs, priced slightly above the cheapest models sold by the Big Three (Chrysler Corporation, Ford Motor Company, and General Motors Corporation) and just below cars from the other independents (Hudson, Nash, Willys, and Kaiser-Frazer); (2) get new models on the street first; (3) advertise heavily, with copy much like that of the preceding year; and (4) supply plenty of advertising and promotional materials to dealers. When asked why the agency stuck to this formula for Studebaker, RW&C President J.P. Roche said, "Advertising should not be produced to have people admire it or comment on its cleverness. It is a sales tool, not entertainment."

The company's media planning strategy was based upon a mix of magazine, newspaper, radio, and, later, television ads. Typically, a barrage of magazine ads appeared approximately one month after newspapers ran announcements about the new models, so the cars reached the dealerships before the ad campaigns began. Color ads were then used to pick up and sustain introductions made at dealer showrooms. Headlines such as "Now here! The 'next look' in cars" appeared in cooperative newspaper ads, while color spreads appeared in magazines such as *Life, Newsweek, Better Homes & Gardens, Business Week,* and *Farm Journal.* The magazine ads were similar to those that ran in newspapers, although the former had a slicker look. Just as the company pared down the styling of its vehicles to achieve a lean and distinctive look—employing innovative features such as fenders that gave its Champion model a bullet-nosed appearance—the ads were equally spare and unusual. Ads described the styling in futuristic terms as "the next look."

There was some tension, however, between the way Studebaker's ad copy adhered to the same look while maintaining an emphasis on innovative car designs. Consistent with a respect for tradition and a reputation for reliability, the company resisted the temptation to change advertising copy simply for the sake of change. Studebaker ads featured photographs, instead of illustrations, to convey a feeling of realism, believability, and glamour. Magazine ads were almost always color, and layouts followed the top-to-bottom sequence of picture, headline, copy, and logo. Studebaker was known for slogans and headlines in its ads. For example, compact cars were advertised with the slogan, "The common sense cars." Studebaker's innovative design and advanced engineering were reflected in headlines such as, "From the speedway comes their stamina . . . from the skyway comes their style," "You're out of date without an eight," and "Smart to be seen in . . . smarter to buy." The tradition of reliability and affordability were located in headlines such as, "Your thrifty one in '51," and "Studebaker—the great independent." (All of the above slogans were created by RW&C.)

Studebaker had a presence not only in the United States but also in world markets. In countries such as France, Spain, and Portugal, Studebaker took care to create advertising that was culturally and linguistically appropriate. After World War I, Studebaker Vice President D.C. Gaskin launched the largest foreign advertising campaign in the automobile industry, buying page newspaper ads in South Africa, Australia, South America, Europe,

Craftsmanship

with a flair!

Here's the look of luxury—and it's in the *low price field!* It's the big new Studebaker—and never before has there been such a difference in low price cars. Here's why:

You get the longest wheelbase—120½ inches—and the biggest power—210 hp.—in its class. You get a fabulous floating ride, along with silky bursts of speed that only the costliest cars can rival.

And from its massive new grille to its high-falutin' dual exhausts, you get beauty. Inside, surrounded by lovely color-keyed interiors, soothed by a sound-conditioned ceiling, you get luxury beyond compare.

Yes, only Studebaker brings you new style, new power, new beauty—*Craftsmanship with a Flair* in the low price field! There are 16 new and different models for you to choose from: beautiful passenger cars, *big* station wagons, exciting family sports cars. See them at your Studebaker Dealer's soon!

Studebaker

THE BIG NEW CHOICE
IN THE LOW PRICE FIELD

STUDEBAKER DIVISION, STUDEBAKER-PACKARD CORPORATION—WHERE PRIDE OF WORKMANSHIP STILL COMES FIRST!
Tune in TV Reader's Digest every week.

A 1956 advertisement for Studebaker focused on both engineering features and styling of the automobile with the slogan "Craftsmanship with a flair!"
Studebaker National Museum, Inc., South Bend, Indiana.

and Asia. The Canadian portion of the campaign was handled by Export Vice President P.A. Hutchinson.

Despite Studebaker's reputation for reliable, innovative products and its commitment to advertising, the Studebaker brothers' dream of becoming the fourth player in the Big Three roster came to an end in the late 1960s. In 1950, Studebaker's best year, the company held 4.2 percent of the automotive market. By the end of 1960, it had dropped to 1.3 percent. Throughout its history, the company had managed several notable comebacks. Studebaker had been the only automobile manufacturer to file for bankruptcy during the Great Depression and survive. Each time the company appeared to be going under, another innovative automobile turned things around: in the 1930s it was the Champion, in 1959 the Lark, in 1961 the Lark and the Hawk, and in 1962 the Avanti. There was to be no comeback now, however. Several factors contributed to the demise of the company. Known as "the friendliest plant," Studebaker was a company built on tradition. For many years, Studebaker paid the highest wages in the automotive industry and hired the most experienced and most highly skilled workers. Furthermore, the company had not modernized its outdated U.S. production plant in South Bend. The only car company in history that had made the transition from wagon to modern car, Studebaker relied on the idea that a well-engineered car was what it took to survive and compete. How-

ever, changing management ideas and, in the 1960s, desperate efforts to diversify holdings moved Studebaker-Packard's focus from its core business. The autonomous family operation fell victim to the realities of a marketplace that quashed all competitors to the Big Three. Studebaker closed its South Bend plant on 9 December 1963. It shuttered its Canadian operation in 1966.

DEBRA MERSKIN

Further Reading

Corle, Edwin, *John Studebaker: An American Dream*, New York: Dutton, 1948

Critchlow, Donald T., *Studebaker: The Life and Death of an American Corporation*, Bloomington: Indiana University Press, 1996

Hall, Asa E., and Richard M. Langworth, *The Studebaker Century: A National Heritage*, Contoocook, New Hampshire: Dragonwyck, 1983

Sackheim, Maxwell, *My First Sixty Years in Advertising*, Englewood Cliffs, New Jersey: Prentice-Hall, 1970

Smallzried, Kathleen Ann, and Dorothy James Roberts, *More Than You Promise: A Business at Work in Society*, New York and London: Harper and Brothers, 1942

"Studebaker: A Case Study," *Time* (2 September 1949)

Subliminal Advertising

The term *subliminal* was first used in 1824 by the German philosopher and psychologist Johann Friedrich Herbart to describe perception "beneath the threshold" (Latin *sub limen*) of consciousness. Reports of subconscious perception began to appear in the professional literature around 1900, and the word was first used in English in the *Journal of Psychology* in 1938.

The phrase *subliminal advertising*, which first appeared in American mass media in September 1957, means advertising messages intended not to be consciously perceived. It has been applied incorrectly to techniques such as the depiction in ads of scantily clad women and the use of single-frame cuts (a single frame of motion-picture film or single video image spliced into a film sequence or reel, a process that has been legally banned from use in commercials in several countries). The phrase *subliminal advertising* has also been used to describe the supposed depiction in ads of sexual organs, vulgar words, and death's-heads, as well as the use of dominant trade colors in advertising illustrations (e.g., the use of "Newport blue" as the color of the ocean that appears in a beach scene in an ad for Newport cigarettes)—all of which can readily be perceived consciously. Only images or sounds that cannot be consciously recognized are literally subliminal, however, and despite extensive testing, no significant effects on brand awareness or buying behavior have been proved for such messages.

In 1956 the British Broadcasting Corporation tested subthreshold awareness by flashing a four-word news item for 1/25th of a second during a TV program and deemed the results inconclusive. The only on-air tests in the United States reported to the Federal Communications Commission (FCC) were conducted by two TV stations, WTWO in Bangor, Maine, and WTTV in Bloomington, Indiana, in 1958. Neither had any significant effect. A test the same year by the Canadian Broadcasting Corporation that involved flashing the words "Telephone now" during a half-hour program resulted in no calls being made and not a single report even of a desire to telephone among 500 viewers surveyed.

Despite the failure of these efforts to show any effect, the association of advertisers in Britain banned use of such techniques by members, and the National Association of Radio and Television Broadcasters amended its code of ethical practices to discourage subliminal ads. The three major U.S. television networks—the American Broadcasting Company, the Columbia Broadcasting System, and the National Broadcasting Company—and the Canadian Broadcasting System assured viewers that they had not and would not expose their audiences to subliminal messages. Since the 1950s numerous legislative provisions have been initiated in the United States to prohibit a practice that has neither been

PEOPLE HAVE BEEN TRYING TO FIND THE BREASTS IN THESE ICE CUBES SINCE 1957.

The advertising industry is sometimes charged with sneaking seductive little pictures into ads.

Supposedly, these pictures can get you to buy a product without your even seeing them.

Consider the photograph above. According to some people, there's a pair of female breasts hidden in the patterns of light refracted by the ice cubes.

Well, if you really searched you probably *could* see the breasts. For that matter, you could also see Millard Fillmore, a stuffed pork chop and a 1946 Dodge.

The point is that so-called "subliminal advertising" simply doesn't exist. Overactive imaginations, however, most certainly do.

So if anyone claims to see breasts in that drink up there, they aren't in the ice cubes.

They're in the eye of the beholder.

ADVERTISING
ANOTHER WORD FOR FREEDOM OF CHOICE.
American Association of Advertising Agencies

In the mid-1980s, in the wake of allegations that marketers were attempting to influence consumers with subliminal messages, the American Association of Advertising Agencies countered with its own ad campaign debunking the concept of subliminal advertising.

Used by permission, American Association of Advertising Agencies.

proved to be possible nor to have any effect on attitudes, opinions, or behavior. No cases have been prosecuted.

There have been several fictitious examples of subliminal advertising, most notably the famous "Popcorn Experiment" reported in 1957, which proved to be a fraud perpetrated to boost the consulting business of a self-employed market researcher named James McDonald Vicary. In September 1957 *Printers' Ink* magazine published a short piece reporting that Vicary had demonstrated his purported subliminal technique in a film studio in New York City to some 50 reporters. The article also described a purportedly scientific test in a motion picture theater in which, Vicary claimed, 45,699 persons unknowingly had been exposed to two advertising messages projected subliminally on alternate nights. One message, he said, advised the movie-goers to "Eat popcorn," the other to "Drink Coca-Cola." According to Vicary, the invisible advertising increased popcorn sales an average of 57.5 percent and sales of Coca-Cola an average of 18.1 percent.

But Vicary's entire operation was a fabrication aimed at bamboozling advertisers, supported by intensive publicity, and abetted by journalists eager for an intriguing story. Vicary seems to have disappeared from the advertising scene in June 1958, although an article in *Advertising Age* on 17 September 1962, the fifth anniversary of Vicary's original announcement, quoted him as admitting his "Popcorn Experiment" was a gimmick intended to save his failing business and that it had no scientific or practical validity. All efforts to locate Vicary since seem to have failed.

Perhaps the fiction of subliminal advertising was accepted so readily in the late 1950s in part because U.S. military propaganda after the Korean War (1950–53) attributed the defection of some American troops to a mysterious new tactic called "brainwashing." Another factor might have been the 1953 activities of Senator Joseph McCarthy of Wisconsin, who shocked the nation by alleging that there were traitors, spies, and subversive plots among some of the United States' most trusted citizens.

The idea that devious and perhaps evil conspiracies abounded and were secretly influencing the American people was further enhanced by the 1957 publication of Vance Packard's *The Hidden Persuaders*. An immediate best-seller, it revealed manipulation of American consumers consciously through the mass media and became required reading for journalists and academics in the fields of psychology and communications.

The only official test of subliminal advertising was ordered by the FCC and was conducted in Washington, D.C., in January 1958. There Vicary reportedly flashed an "Eat popcorn" message for members of the FCC, Congress, and the media. The only response recorded was that of Senator Charles E. Potter of Michigan who said, "I think I want a hot dog." *Printers' Ink* wrote of the test, "Having gone to see something that is not supposed to be seen, and having not seen it, as forecast, [the FCC and congressmen] seemed satisfied."

In the early 1970s Canadian sociologist Wilson Bryan Key gave subliminal advertising a new twist. Key's thesis was that obscene words and images were secretly "embedded" in advertisements to make people buy things they did not want or need. Key wrote four books on the topic, *Subliminal Seduction* (1973), *Media Sexploitation* (1976), *The Clam-Plate Orgy* (1980), and *The Age of Manipulation* (1989). Most of the illustrations in his books were retouched to emphasize the words and images he envisioned. The books contained no footnotes or quotations from advertising practitioners, and they were not particularly influential.

Advertising executives have observed that if subliminal advertising were actually practiced, there would be subliminal boutique agencies and many technical books offering detailed analyses of how to do it. In fact, there are neither. Furthermore, if subliminal messages were truly effective, government agencies would by now have successfully used the technique to eliminate child abuse, drug addiction, drunk driving, and tax evasion. Despite sensationalistic and paranoid accusations of marketing "mind control," there is no evidence of such practices in contemporary advertising.

STUART C. ROGERS

Further Reading

"Devilish?" *Newsweek* (14 October 1957)

Haberstroh, Jack, *Ice Cube Sex: The Truth about Subliminal Advertising*, Notre Dame, Indiana: Cross Cultural Publications, 1994

"Invisible Ads Tested," *Printers' Ink* (20 September 1957)

Kalis, William H., "The Phantom of the Soap Opera," *Public Relations Journal* 14 (March 1958)

Moore, Timothy E., "Subliminal Perception: Facts and Fallacies," *Skeptical Inquirer* 16 (Spring 1992)

Pratkanis, Anthony R., "The Cargo-Cult Science of Subliminal Persuasion," *Skeptical Inquirer* 16 (Spring 1992)

Rogers, Stuart, "How a Publicity Blitz Created the Myth of Subliminal Advertising," *Public Relations Quarterly* 37, no. 4 (Winter 1992–93)

"Subliminal Has a Test; Can't See if It Works," *Printers' Ink* (17 January 1958)

"Subliminal Projection," *Information Bulletin* (Federal Communications Commission) (November 1977)

Weir, Walter, *How to Create Interest-Evoking, Sales-Inducing, Non-Irritating Advertising*, New York: Haworth, 1993

Supermarket. *See* Grocery and Supermarket

T

Targeting

Targeting is a fundamental marketing activity that involves identifying and approaching groups that have similar purchasing patterns. The target segment is the subgroup chosen as the focal point in the marketing program and advertising campaign. Marketers decide whom to advertise to and what to say in their ads. The groups are chosen on the basis of specific characteristics and potential for profitability.

In deciding the appropriate target markets, advertisers divide, or segment, the total market into a variety of categories. The four major bases of segmenting markets are: geographic, demographic, behavioristic, and psychographic. Using geographic segmentation the market is divided on the basis of such different geographical units as nations, states, regions, counties, cities, or neighborhoods. The company can operate in one or a few geographic areas, or it can operate in all areas while paying attention to local variations. In demographic segmentation the market is divided on the basis of the population's numerical characteristics using such quantifiable factors as age, sex, ethnicity, religion, occupation, and income. Behavioral segments are determined by such variables as purchase occasion, benefits sought, user status, user rate, loyalty status, readiness stage, and attitude toward the product. Finally, in psychographic segmentation, target markets are chosen on the basis of lifestyle or personality and values. Most advertisers use a combination of the above criteria in targeting prospective customers.

To be meaningful, target segments should have four characteristics. First, they should be measurable—that is, characteristics such as purchasing power and size of the target markets can be estimated. Second, the target segments should be significantly large and profitable enough to warrant serving. Third, the target markets should be effectively accessed and served. Reaching the members of the target market through appropriate programming or editorial content should not be difficult. And finally, the markets should be distinguishable—they should be conceptually differentiable and respond differently to various marketing mix elements and programs.

In evaluating assorted target markets, a company must consider two critical factors—the market's overall attractiveness and the marketer's objectives and resources. There are four basic targeting strategy patterns of target market selection:

(1) A marketer may advertise a single undifferentiated product to a single market segment.

(2) A marketer may choose to specialize in a particular product, which it advertises to several market segments. For example, companies that enjoy monopolies or operate in developing countries where demand far exceeds supply may offer a single, undifferentiated product or service for a number of market segments.

(3) A marketer may focus on meeting the needs of a particular market segment with a differentiated offering, the objective being to increase the overall share of the target market with several differentiated offerings.

(4) A marketer may select all market segments to target. It could offer the same product to all segments, or it could choose to differentiate its product offering by examining the needs of each target market and offering it only those services that the target market needs.

After selecting the target market, advertisers have to consider who should receive and interpret messages sent through the mass media. Though several forms of target audiences are possible, five broad classes exist:

(1) Household consumers. In the United States, where there were more than 100 million households and approximately 270 million household consumers in 2000, this group accounts for more than $3 trillion in annual spending. It is primarily targeted through advertising and other forms of consumer-oriented sales promotions.

(2) Members of business organizations. This group consists of producers of business and industrial goods and services as diverse as airplane engines and janitorial services and sell to a very limited number of key decision makers. While personal selling happens to be the anchor promotional tool in reaching this audience, advertising plays an equally

In this 2000 print ad, marketing services company Bounty SCA Worldwide used an image of a target to make the point about its ability to identify receptive audiences.
Courtesy of Bounty SCA Worldwide.

critical role in creating awareness as well as favorable attitudes.

(3) Members of trade channels. Intermediaries and retailers are an audience for both household and business goods. Unless a producer is able to garner adequate support from these channels, it will be unable to reach its ultimate customers. Since this target audience is easily identifiable, personal selling is the most widely used tool. However advertising can serve as a useful supplementary form of promotion.

(4) Professionals. Doctors, lawyers, accountants, teachers, or any other individuals who have received special training or certification are considered professionals. Advertising directed at this group is primarily for products targeted at them or their clients and is carried out through trade publications.

(5) Government officials, employees, and organizations. Government representatives purchase goods and services to support the internal operations of their agencies and municipalities and provide products such as highways, education, water, energy, and national defense to their constituencies. Advertising to this group is dominated by direct mail.

Target marketing strategies can be tailored to meet the needs of local customer groups (trading areas, neighborhoods, even individual stores). Citibank, for example, offers customized banking services in its branches based on neighborhood demographics. The retailer Target Stores tailors its stores' merchandise based on similar characteristics. Kraft Foods assists supermarkets in determining which cheeses to carry and where to position them on the shelf to maximize sales in low-, middle-, and high-income stores, as well as in various ethnic neighborhoods. Mass advertising is less effective and wasteful in such cases, as it fails to distinguish variances in local needs.

Local marketing is likely to have potential pitfalls as well. Due to reduced economies of scale, the manufacturing and marketing costs are likely to be higher. In trying to meet varying local needs, the logistical problems may be accentuated. In addition the equity and image of the brand has the potential of being diluted as a result of inconsistencies in product and promotions.

In contrast to the mass form of communications, direct response marketing communicates directly with prospects or customers and they in turn respond directly to the offer. The message is delivered at the individual level and is highly measurable. Response rates vary considerably, although a response rate of 2 percent is often used as a benchmark in calculating profitability. It is estimated that various forms of direct marketing communication generate 10 percent of all consumer sales and 5 percent of all business-to-business sales.

Direct marketing is generally done in one of three ways: by mail, by telephone, or in person. Technology has contributed greatly to direct marketing, offering such tools as advanced database marketing and the World Wide Web. Direct mail usually consists of catalogs or other written material sent via the postal service. The key to success is acquiring a list of good prospects. Telemarketing, the sale of products and services over the telephone, may be "outbound" (a company calls potential customers to encourage purchase) or "inbound" (a customer calls to get information about or purchase products). A variety of toll-free numbers (using the prefixes 800 or 888) make inbound calling fast and economical. Database marketing is used to develop, maintain, and utilize computer records to target customers with relevant information and pertinent offers. This requires long-term strategic thinking since the process of building the database is time consuming.

The major advantages of direct marketing are individualized communications, measurable response, database formation, and customer feedback. Direct response marketing can be highly targeted and designed specifically for an individualized customer. The total number of responses can be tallied easily and monitored at the individual level. The relevant customers can then be placed in a database with critical, pertinent information that can be used in future direct marketing efforts. The feedback provided by the customer can be used to make useful changes and improvements. Drawbacks exist with direct marketing as well— high cost, customer avoidance, and small reach. Due to its highly individualized approach, it tends to be costly. If potential customers are not interested, they can ignore the message either by throwing away the mail or hanging up the phone. Only a small group of people can be reached due to highly targeted efforts and high costs.

The ultimate direct targeting strategy considers "segments of one"—also called "one-to-one marketing" or "mass customization"—in which companies deliver a customized product or service on a mass basis. Advancements in technology have enabled more companies to capture more information about their customers and target them individually so as to win their loyalty. Although this targeting practice is common in business-to-business marketing, it is also becoming prevalent among advertisers of consumer products. Hallmark Cards, for example, uses technology to offer custom-made cards. Mattel Corporation allows youngsters to log on to its Web site at barbie.com and design their own Barbie Pal. Levi Strauss & Company's customers can purchase jeans made to their measurements via the Internet.

The orientation of promotion is an important strategic decision that involves targeting. A "push" strategy is used if the advertiser's goal is to convince the wholesaler or retailer to carry and sell the particular merchandise. The manufacturer starts with trade advertising and other promotional tools to convince the wholesaler to carry and sell the merchandise. The wholesaler, in turn, has the responsibility of pushing the merchandise forward by persuading the retailer to handle the goods. Finally, the retailer uses advertising, displays, and other forms of promotion to convince the consumer to buy the "pushed" products.

The "pull" strategy, on the other hand, stimulates consumer demand by focusing the advertising and other promotional efforts on end consumers or opinion leaders. As consumers begin demanding the product, the retailer orders the merchandise from the wholesaler. The wholesaler, faced with the rising demand, then

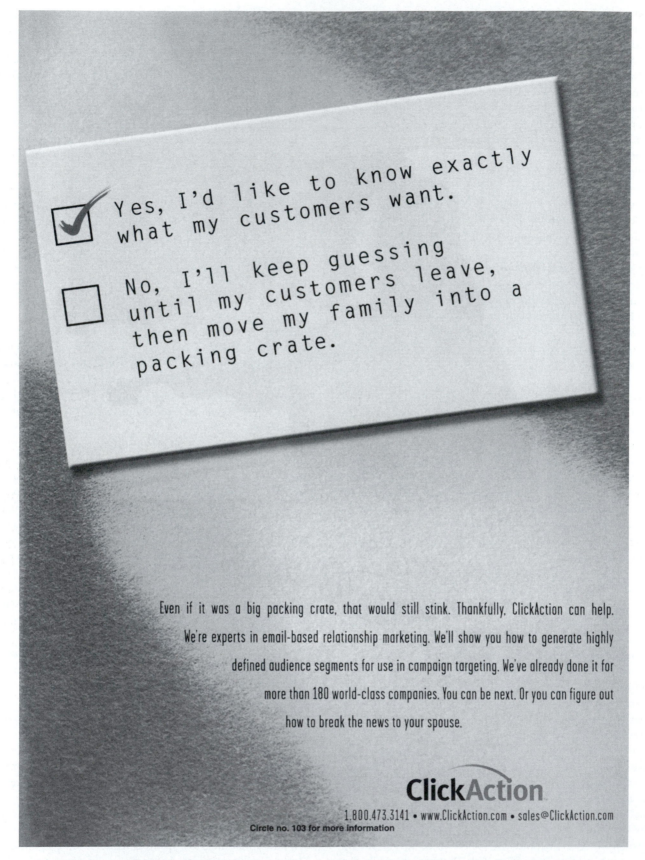

ClickAction used the image of a direct-response card to advertise its targeted marketing services in this 2000 print ad.
ClickAction, Inc., and New & Improved Advertising.

purchases the merchandise from the manufacturer. Consumer demand "pulls" the product through the channel of distribution.

A push strategy is especially appropriate when there is low brand loyalty in a category, brand choice is made in the store, the product is an impulse item, and product benefits are well understood. A pull strategy works best when both brand loyalty and involvement are high, consumers perceive differences in brands, and purchases are planned before entering the store. Rivals within the same industry may differ in their emphasis on push or pull. For example, Lever Brothers relies more on push, whereas Procter & Gamble Company relies more on pull. Push and pull policies are not mutually exclusive; marketers can use both policies simultaneously.

Targeting policies have often generated public controversy. Although marketers argue the importance of successfully identifying, understanding, and reaching specific groups, such practices have generated immense controversy when the groups being targeted were considered vulnerable. Sensitive or vulnerable groups are those whose members have limited chance of making informed choices. The elderly, the disabled, young children, and racial and ethnic minorities are examples of such groups (although, as discussed below, some have questioned whether categorizing some of these groups as "vulnerable" is itself problematic).

The cereal industry has been criticized for targeting high-powered appeals at children, using engaging characters to encourage kids to eat sugary products of dubious nutritional value. R.J. Reynolds Tobacco Company was criticized for targeting Uptown, a menthol cigarette, to low-income African-Americans. G. Heileman Brewing Company was faulted for targeting the same group with its Colt 45 and Powermaster malt liquors. Some activist groups questioned Smith and Wesson's targeting of handguns to women.

In defense of targeted promotions, businesses have questioned the ethics of labeling certain groups incompetent to make sound decisions in the marketplace. Businesses point to their constitutional guarantee of free speech, asserting that promoting a product should be legal if the sale of the product is legal in the marketplace. They assert, moreover, that customers make the ultimate decision by choosing not to consume something that they dislike. Critics of targeting argue that *legal* is not synonymous with *ethical*, claiming that companies must be socially responsible and must try to refrain from irresponsible targeting efforts that might have the potential to do harm.

ABHIJIT ROY

See also Demographics; Psychographics

Further Reading
Freeman, Laurie, "Fits Like a Glove," *Advertising Age* (18 October 1999)
Macchiette, Bart, and Abhijit Roy, "Sensitive Groups and Social Issues: Are You Marketing Correct?" *Journal of Consumer Marketing* 11, no. 4 (1994)
Orr, Alicia, "Offers That Are Way Off," *Target Marketing* (October 1999)
Peppers, Don, and Martha Rogers, *Enterprise One to One: Tools for Competing in the Interactive Age,* New York: Currency Doubleday, 1997
Pine, B. Joseph, *Mass Customization: The New Frontier in Business Competition,* Boston: Harvard Business School Press, 1993
Pinson, Linda, and Jerry Jinnett, *Marketing: Researching and Reaching Your Target Market,* Fullerton, California: Out of Your Mind . . . and into the Marketplace, 1988; 3rd edition, as *Target Marketing: Researching, Reaching, and Retaining Your Target Market,* Chicago: Upstart, 1996
Schonfeld, Erick, "The Customized, Digitized, Have-It-Your-Way Economy," *Fortune* (28 September 1998)
Webber, Harry, *Divide and Conquer: Target Your Customers through Market Segmentation,* New York: Wiley, 1998
Weinstein, Art, *Market Segmentation: Using Demographics, Psychographics, and Other Segmentation Techniques to Uncover and Exploit New Markets,* Chicago: Probus, 1987; revised edition, as *Market Segmentation: Using Demographics, Psychographics, and Other Niche Marketing Techniques to Predict and Model Customer Behavior,* 1994

Tatham-Laird, Inc.

(Tatham-Laird & Kudner, Inc.; Euro RSCG Tatham; Euro RSCG McConnaughy Tatham)

Formed in 1946; merged with the Kudner Agency to become Tatham-Laird & Kudner, Inc., 1965; restructured as a partnership, 1974; acquired by RSCG (later Euro/RSCG), 1988; name changed to Euro RSCG Tatham (a unit of the Havas holding company), 1999; merged with McConnaughy Stein Schmidt to become Euro RSCG McConnaughy Tatham, 2001.

Major Clients
Admiral
Bayer Corporation
Bendix Home Appliances, Inc.
Goodyear Tire and Rubber Company
Libby, McNeill & Libby

Miles Laboratories (Bactine)
Pan American World Airways
Procter & Gamble Company (Fluffo, Head & Shoulders, Bold,
    Mr. Clean, Pringles)
RCA Record Club
C.A. Swanson & Sons
Toni Company (White Rain)

Tatham-Laird & Kudner, as it was known during its prime years in the 1960s and 1970s, was formed in Chicago, Illinois, in 1946 as Tatham-Laird, Inc., by Arthur E. Tatham and John Kenneth Laird. Although their careers were in Chicago, they first met in October 1933 in Washington, D.C., at an advertisers convention. The two men, both in their twenties, went for a stroll around the Capitol and chatted about business.

Back in Chicago, the conversation continued as they came to know each other better. In 1938 Ray Rubicam persuaded Tatham to take over the languishing business of Young & Rubicam (Y&R) in Chicago, and Tatham asked Laird to join him. The fortunes of Y&R, then at 333 N. Michigan Ave., soon began to turn around; the agency won the accounts of Good Luck margarine, 7 UP and, above all, Bendix.

Increasingly, Tatham and Laird began to ask the question that eventually occurs to all successful advertising executives: Why are we making all this money for someone else when we could be doing it for ourselves? In 1943 Tatham was transferred to Y&R in New York City, and Laird left for Dancer, Fitzgerald, Sample, where he first encountered the Procter & Gamble Company (P&G). Tatham joined the Navy in 1943, worked in the Pentagon under Navy Secretary James Forrestal, and frequently represented the Navy before congressional committees. By 1944 Rubicam was ready to make him heir apparent to all of Y&R.

But the correspondence between Tatham and Laird hinted at other objectives, and Chicago agency people swapped rumors about a Tatham-Laird shop, which Laird fueled with nondenial denials. In an unpublished memoir, Laird tracked the endless detail the two men weighed as they plotted their future together: capital estimates, business plans, monthly payroll estimates, operational minutiae, personnel, presumptions, predictions, projections. What they needed was one client worth at least $250,000.

Driving home to Chicago from his summer retreat in South Bend, Indiana, one weekend in 1945, Laird stopped for dinner and ran into Judson Sayre, the founder of Bendix and a gruff, irascible man who made every agency he had ever hired miserable and neurotic. But he had become so enamored of Tatham and Laird when they handled his account at Y&R that when they departed, so did Bendix. If they started an agency, Sayre said, they could count on his business. Tatham-Laird, Inc. (T-L), was founded that August evening. Only the formalities remained. Tatham became president, Laird took the title of vice president and treasurer. Mary Kyak, Tatham's former secretary, became the company's third staff person. Total start-up capital was $45,000.

Bendix agreed to pay a monthly advance on commissions of $3,750, and the founders took no salary until the agency could pay its way. A kind of one-room shadow office opened in Chicago on 1 February 1946, while more permanent quarters were prepared. A month later T-L opened for business at 111 West Washington Street with 11 employees, two clients, and several beaverboard offices. Bendix was joined by the Munising Paper Company, another relationship built during the Y&R days. The Bear Brand Hosiery and Majestic Radio accounts were smaller dividends of old friendships.

In September, T-L moved into the Civic Opera Building, where it would remain for the next five years and the first $5 million in agency growth. By the end of 1946, T-L was billing more than $500,000. At the end of its first full fiscal year, 31 January 1947, it boasted net profits of $815.60.

In 1947 Majestic Radio went into bankruptcy. With parts and cabinetry in short supply and demand exploding, the company had taken on orders it could not meet. T-L had bought $100,000 in media and then found that its client had a warehouse full of half-finished radios, no parts to finish them, and no money to pay its bills. Before Majestic finally went under, T-L managed to recover more than 90 percent of its money. The agency would never again take on a client whose accounts were not insurable.

The trickle of payments squeezed from Majestic was more than covered by the deluge that poured from Bendix and drove 1947 billings to nearly $2.7 million. The addition of General Mills' Kix cereal, Trane Company, and Admiral Corporation's kitchen appliances by 1950 continued the success. By the time T-L celebrated its fifth anniversary in 1951, billings had grown to $5 million.

Television was stalled in a license freeze that would halt its growth until 1953, but T-L edged its way into the new medium. Bendix went on the air with a panel show called *The Name's the Same*. TV commercials for Toni Company's White Rain product line featured girls in white rain coats. And C.A. Swanson & Sons became a major TV presence, first with pot pies and then in 1954 with the first "TV dinner." All this helped push billings to $9.5 million.

Originally the founders had promised themselves that $10 million would be the limit of their growth. But by 1954 that figure looked far less distant or final than it had in 1946. Growth did not divert T-L from frugality or resourcefulness. As offices in the Civic Opera Building grew cramped, there was no rush to pricey Michigan Avenue quarters. Instead, in 1951, T-L found space in the south Loop alongside the elevated transit ("El") line. The first three floors of the building were occupied by Lyon & Healy, a well-known music store. The space above was not pretty, but it was cheap and plentiful. During the next 19 years the company became known as "the little agency over the music shop."

The sobriquet was a rare example of understatement in the advertising business. T-L was not little. Campbell Soup Company bought Swanson for $26 million in 1955 and retained T-L into the 1960s. In 1955 billings hit $20 million, better than a quarter the size of the already venerable Leo Burnett Company. Not surprisingly, the two agencies would soon share a formidable client.

Among the telegrams of congratulations the founders had received in 1946 was one from Howard Morgens of P&G:

"When two men such as you start an agency, this is an event we will watch with considerable interest." The chief watcher would be Bill Batterberry, who kept detailed dossiers on various agencies considered to have P&G potential. Every year Batterberry phoned Laird or Tatham when he was in Chicago and asked them to drop by for an update, always with the caveat that there was nothing specific in the wind. In 1956, however, something was.

"Fluffo" was a cooking fat with a cartoonish name that sounded as if it belonged to one of the Marx Brothers, not to a P&G product complementing its 45-year-old sibling brand, Crisco, which was handled by Burnett. (Crisco was a vegetable shortening; Fluffo combined vegetable and animal fats in a formula that could be adjusted with changes in the market prices of the components.) After a presentation, the $1.5 million account went to T-L in April 1956. Fluffo never put serious pressure on Crisco, the market leader, but it tied T-L's fortunes to those of the leading package goods advertiser.

Every agency wants to enrich its clients. Few aspire to confer real immortality, an achievement that comes only when an ad campaign yields a phrase or idea that transcends its origins and enters into the language itself, becoming a cultural reference point. T-L's first contribution to the vernacular was "Mr. Clean."

The name, coined by Harry Barnhart, who had come to T-L from Y&R in 1954, originated from the custom of honoring contemporary icons as "Mr. Television" (Milton Berle), "Mr. Baseball" (Stan Musial), and "Mr. Republican" (Robert Taft). "Mr. Clean" combined art director Ernie Allen's image of a bald strongman in a T-shirt with a catchy kindergarten jingle. The product would ultimately outsell rivals Lestoil and Spic & Span. More than that, the phrase would spill into broader usage, often with a sarcastic edge when applied to politicians of unimpeachable but lackluster character.

Despite the P&G factor, the Clark Oil account, and some American Home Products business, T-L billings dropped by nearly 20 percent in 1957 and 1958. This situation changed in 1960, as Mr. Clean went national and American Home Products assigned T-L its Easy-Off and Dristan brands. In one year, billings nearly doubled. But other weaknesses cut deeply into the agency's strength between 1961 and 1963. Fully one-third of its billings disappeared, and the New York City office, opened in 1954, lost nearly half its client base by 1964.

T-L was not the only New York City shop facing tough times. Back in the days when T-L handled Admiral Dual Temp Refrigerators, the agency had looked longingly at Admiral's TV set business, which accounted for 90 percent of the company's profits and was handled by the Kudner Agency, Inc. By 1964 the two agencies' New York City positions had weakened to the point where merger negotiations began. In May 1965 a deal was consummated. In his memoir, Laird gave a detailed account of the cuckoo's nest of power politics T-L proposed to digest. It was a stock-for-stock exchange, with incentives built in to ensure that Kudner held onto its major accounts: General Telephone & Electronics Corporation (GT&E), Goodyear Tire & Rubber Company, General Motors Corporation, and Pan American Cargo.

it works! this dandruff shampoo doesn't kid around

Tatham-Laird & Kudner prospered in the late 1960s, in part owing to its work for Procter & Gamble Company and brands such as its Head & Shoulders, featured in this 1966 ad.
Courtesy of The Procter & Gamble Company.

Thus in 1965 was born a new $58 million agency, Tatham-Laird & Kudner, Inc. (TLK), with a revitalized New York City presence. P&G emerged as the largest account at $14 million and was soon to grow on the strength of Head & Shoulders shampoo and Bold detergent. Next were GT&E ($11 million) and Goodyear ($3.8 million). About six months later, General Motors, relieved of any guilt it might have had cutting Kudner off when it was down, withdrew its remaining business from a revitalized agency.

The decade ended with the retirement of Laird in February 1969. Both he and Tatham had retreated to board positions in 1964 to make way for a second generation of management. Charles Standen, who had joined T-L in 1947 at 31, became president and then chief executive officer (CEO). In 1969 with Laird retiring, Standen became chairman to make room for Paul Schlesinger, who had joined T-L in 1949, to assume the title of CEO. In March 1971, on the agency's 25th anniversary, Tatham went into semi-retirement to head the strategy review board and passed the last shares of original stock back to the company. He cut his final ties with the agency early in 1973 and died in 1985.

Laird died in 1973 at age 70. Two months after the shop's 25th anniversary, the era of "the little agency over the music shop" ended, too, as TLK moved to the top five floors of 625 North Michigan Avenue.

Along Michigan Avenue, the big agencies and their bosses were discovering the virtues of going public. TLK had special reason to pay attention because its stock, all privately held, was valued according to an almost philanthropic formula that delighted retiring managers but was increasingly out of register with the agency's actual book worth. By the time the second generation reached retirement and cashed in, the coffers were likely to be cleaned out. The first instinct of agency executives was to follow the flow and go public. But TLK was not yet in a financial league with Foote, Cone & Belding, and experience suggested that Wall Street was not bullish on mid-size agency equities. Also, as early as 1961 Laird had blasted public ownership as potentially disastrous. "Capital is no substitute for talent," he cautioned.

Then one day a savvy lawyer named Richard Murphy asked Standen if he had ever wondered why law and accounting firms were partnerships and not corporations. The answer was buried in federal tax codes, which taxed earned income at a maximum of 50 percent and levied no corporate tax. On 31 July 1974, TLK became the only legal partnership of its size in the industry, wiping out the usual hierarchy of agency titles and replacing them with a lineup of uniformly empowered "managing partners." Over the next five years, billings grew by 35 percent to more than $90 million. How much of this increase could be attributed to the restructuring cannot be measured, although the fact that each of the charter partners was now personally liable for agency debts and losses down to his house and car made for a strong incentive. It surely steadied the long-term future of the firm's equity, and this in turn made it possible for TLK to go shopping in the open market for the best talent.

In January 1979 TLK recruited Charlotte Beers from the J. Walter Thompson Company (JWT), where she had etched a high profile in 1973 as the agency's first woman senior vice president. She became TLK's first woman managing partner. But more was involved than mere tokenism. Starting at JWT as an account executive in 1968 on the Alberto-Culver business, Beers had penetrated glass ceilings with ease to become director of client services. When she was passed over for a key promotion, she did not wait for explanations before jumping to TLK.

Beers was the first of three top TLK managers to come over from JWT in the next nine years. The second was JWT's international chief, William Ross, whom Beers brought over in 1981 to boost creative strength. Ross agreed to serve for five years. He brought Coors beer to TLK in 1983 and became chairman in 1985. The following February he pronounced his mission completed and retired. The third fugitive from JWT was Ralph Rydholm, who had been bypassed for a top job at JWT Chicago and resigned his creative post after 19 years with the agency. After 14 months with Ted Bates in New York City, Rydholm joined TLK

But the 1980s at TLK were dominated by Beers, who became CEO in 1982, then chairman in 1986 and set out, in her words, to "cultivate the star system—deliberately." As she explained it, "We

put a great premium on very elite, talented sophisticated people who are stars." Billings tripled during her first six years to nearly $250 million, and the glow of such growth brought many corporate suitors to her door. There was talk of a Bozell & Jacobs takeover in 1982. TLK turned up on the Saatchis' shopping list in the mid-1980s. Interpublic denied reports it was eyeing TLK, but few believed it. Independents such as Chiat/Day and Hill, Holliday, Connors, Cosmopulos came calling. There was even a story that P&G, impatient with the agency merger epidemic, might buy its own agency and take everything in-house, although TLK was mentioned only as one of P&G's top ten agencies. Some complained privately that Beers, while insisting her purpose was "building, not selling," was quietly preparing TLK for a sale. What rankled others was watching middle management bypassed in favor of JWT imports Ross and Rydholm.

Signs of a merger appeared late in 1987 when TLK fired 16 percent of its staff. In the spring of 1988, TLK was acquired by the huge Paris, France, shop RSCG (Roux, Seguela, Cayzac & Goudard), a unit of Havas, in which Beers would become the fifth owner and other TLK partners would receive shares. The senior partner of the combo was clearly RSCG, with billings exceeding $1 billion. Together the two private agencies became the world's 19th-largest network. TLK now had a parent company with a 70 percent holding, but with its own partnership structure, management, and autonomy intact.

Merger was not enough to spare TLK rough going, however. The 1987 cutbacks and more that followed were prompted by the loss of NutraSweet, R.J. Reynolds Tobacco Company, part of the Coors beer business, and a streak of bad luck on new business. The losses were replaced by 1989, and in 1991 Tatham acquired Peter Rogers Associates, which had long been one of P&G's smaller agencies.

The Beers era ended in 1992. By the time she retired, the phrase "the first woman" seemed to have become part of her legal name. Rydholm finally won the triple crown denied him by JWT: chairman, CEO, and chief creative officer. After several no-growth years, the agency captured Hardee's and later another P&G brand, Clearasil.

But in November 1995 the $6.2 billion parent company brought in an intermediate management layer, former N.W. Ayer partner Steve Dworin. His mandate, according to *Advertising Age,* was to make Euro RSCG "less Euro and more global." For Tatham and Rydholm, Dworin had the appearance of a hands-on boss, if not an heir apparent.

In June 1991 TLK was renamed Tatham/RSCG. A year later, after RCSG and Eurocom wed, yet another press release heralded the arrival of Tatham Euro RSCG. In 1999 the name became Euro RSCG Tatham. In June of that year the agency was dropped from P&G's roster, costing it such brands as Mr. Clean, Coast deodorant, Head & Shoulders, Old Spice, Vidal Sassoon, and Metamucil, and leaving the agency without P&G business for the first time since 1956. In 2001 the agency merged with McConnaughy Stein Schmidt Brown, Chicago, to become Euro RSCG McConnaughy Tatham. The new partner, Tom McConnaughy, had been a creative director with Ogilvy & Mather, Chicago, before going into business for himself in the late 1980s. Bill Stein had headed the Chicago office of Campbell Mithun Esty before it closed in the early 1990s. The merger brought with it several prominent retail accounts, including Circuit City, Crate & Barrel, Wickes, Inc. (building materials), and the Walgreen Company.

JOHN MCDONOUGH

See also color plate in this volume

Further Reading
Bernstein, Sid, "Tatham-Laird Simultaneously Hit 5th Birthday, $5,000,000 Billing," *Advertising Age* (12 March 1951)

"40 Years on a Goodyear 'Diet,' Owens Anticipates No 'Menu' Change," *Advertising Age* (2 July 1956)
"Frigidaire Switches from FC&B to Kudner," *Advertising Age* (22 August 1955)
Llewellyn, Bob, "The Too-Good Idea," *Advertising Age* (30 October 1989)
Meyers, William, "Charlotte Beers: Lean Machinist," *Adweek* (July 1985)
McDonough, John, "Tatham's Half Century: A Commemorative," *Advertising Age* (13 May 1996)
"TV Boot May Have Led Buick to Fire Kudner," *Advertising Age* (23 December 1957)

TBWA/Chiat/Day. *See* Chiat/Day, Inc.

TBWA Hunt Lascaris. *See* Hunt Lascaris

TBWA/Paris. *See* BDDP Group

Technology, Introduction of

Advertising plays a vital role in introducing new technologies to consumers. When a new technology is launched, the primary function of the early advertising campaign is to establish a certain comfort level with unfamiliar products. A successful ad campaign creates awareness of, interest in, and positive feelings about the new products. Such a campaign also encourages trials of the newly introduced items and ultimately develops and supports their regular use.

One of the most noted, innovative campaigns that launched a new technology was Apple Computer's "1984" ad campaign to introduce the Macintosh personal computer, via agency Chiat/Day. The new product was innovative and expensive, and most consumers were unaware of its potential advantages. The 60-second "1984" TV commercial was planned and implemented on the basis of an assessment of Apple's products and of the personal computer industry. Its purpose was to make the public aware of the product and to arouse curiosity about it prior to its formal introduction into the marketplace. The communication objective was to inform consumers that although small in size, the Macintosh was tremendously powerful. The commercial attracted an enormous amount of attention and generated $100 million in Macintosh sales during the ten days after its only airing, on the 1984 Super Bowl.

Other less famous, though still noteworthy, examples of creative campaigns include the introduction of such products as television, color television, microwave ovens, fax machines, printers, and cellular phones. To launch these and similar products, marketers often use advertising that encourages consumers to feel discontented with the status quo—a technique known as marketer-induced problem recognition. In many cases, marketers repeatedly

Natural selection at work.

The challenge of digital imaging is not to show greener grass, a bluer sky or brighter carrots than we see on earth. Canon's approach is different. We believe a natural-looking image is best. Natural textures. Natural lines. Natural colours. From capture to connection to output, Canon's digital imaging technology shows you the world as you see it.

http://www.canon.com

CAPTURE　**CONNECT**　**OUTPUT**

Digital Cameras　Bubble Jet Printers　Color Laser Copiers

Canon

Ads for innovative technology products seek to show consumers how the new technology is different from—and superior to—that already available. This 1999 print ad from Canon, Inc., suggested that its digital images were as good as the original subjects.
Copyright 1999 Canon, Inc. All rights reserved. Used by Permission.

identify for consumers the obstacles they face as a result of the limitations of their current technology and explain how the advertised product will make their lives easier. Once consumers perceive a problem and are motivated to seek alternative solutions, they proceed through the recognized stages of the decision-making process: information gathering, alternative evaluation, purchase decision, and post-purchase evaluation. During these steps, advertising can continue to play an important role in providing relevant purchase information, influencing the consumer's perception of alternative products, shaping attitudes toward products and brands, and providing post-purchasing satisfaction. In the late 1990s, for example, the ads for Canon copying machines and related products showed a rabbit trying to eat a lifelike picture of carrots—thereby demonstrating both the ability of Canon's digital cameras to create a natural-looking image and the quality of its color copying machines. The ad suggested that existing office equipment could not produce comparable images and sought to motivate the purchase of the entire line of Canon digital imaging products.

The success of any advertising campaign for new technology is dependent on the following factors:

- Communicating how the new technology is different from that already available.
- Positioning the brand difference by which new technology will be marketed. In particular, differentiation must be based on a specific product category to which the new technology belongs.
- Linking product differences with the benefits consumers are seeking in their purchase.
- Providing supporting evidence of the compatibility of the new technology with existing products and demonstrating its simplicity of operation. This goal can be accomplished by demonstrations showing how the new product works, endorsements and testimonials from others who have used it, and information about the unique qualities of the new technology.

In addition to the fact that new technology is often expensive and requires a significant amount of investment on the part of early adopters and innovators, it also demands that users acquire new knowledge and learn new techniques of operation. In a 1967 article in the *Journal of Marketing,* Thomas S. Robertson defined three types of technological innovations, distinguished by the extent to which they represent novel products calling for marked changes in consumer behavior: 1) discontinuous innovation, 2) dynamically continuous innovation, and 3) continuous innovation. A clear understanding of what position the new technology occupies in the innovation spectrum helps marketers to implement effective campaigns.

A discontinuous innovation is a major technological advance that involves the introduction of a new product and the formation of new behavior patterns. Some examples include the automobile, television, air conditioner, personal computer, fax machine, and cellular phone. In the case of the automobile, for example, consumers had to learn basic mechanics, driving skills, traffic regulations, and insurance requirements. Riding a bicycle, on the other hand, required less knowledge on the consumer's part.

A dynamically continuous innovation is a new product representing a major technological advance but one that does not fundamentally change current consumer behavior patterns. Examples include color copiers, electric toothbrushes, compact disc players, and touch-tone telephones.

A continuous innovation is a minor technological advance that involves extension or modification of current products—for example, liquid soap dispensers, nonalcoholic beer, and the self-focusing camera. Consumers are not required to drastically change their behavioral and cognitive patterns in order to make use of such products.

New technology is often characterized by complexity, rapidity of arrival on the scene, and discontinuity with the past. These characteristics tend to significantly increase the risks perceived by consumers when deciding to purchase a new, largely unknown item. In consumer behavior research, this perceived risk has been found to significantly influence the following stages of the decision-making process: information searching, quality evaluation, and criteria selection. To launch new technological products successfully, advertising needs to reduce the perceived risk by providing consumers with relevant product information, emphasizing product quality within the specific category, and establishing criteria of product selection. When Philips introduced its Flat TV in 1998, the TV spots by Messner Vetere Berger McNamee Schmetterer/Euro RSCG emphasized the product's specifications, excellence, and its resemblance to fine art. Ads for Sega's Dreamcast video game console characterized the product as a "thinking machine," a reference to its capacity for "learning" how an individual plays and responding to those actions. The campaign by Foote, Cone & Belding, which included three 30-second TV spots, emphasized that this feature not only makes a game more challenging with each play but also differentiates it from other, similar products.

Some new technologies require basic education before distinctions can be made among brands. In the late 1950s and early 1960s when the first jet aircraft replaced the DC-7 in commercial aviation, various airlines created commercials designed to reassure the consumer of the safety, smoothness, and comfort of the new Boeing 707s. One airline demonstrated smoothness by balancing a nickel on end during flight. This and other advertising sold the concept of jet air travel by emphasizing selling points common to all carriers. At that early stage when the market was being created, competing companies decided it was in their interest to sell the category first and the brand second. As jet travel became the standard, brand differentiation became the main goal of advertising. Similarly, in the 1970s competing makers of microwave ovens spent several years educating consumers about the advantages of this new form of cooking. When consumers had become familiar with the technology and the market was established, advertisers then turned to competing for shares of that market.

In many cases, advertising needs to do more than promote the product; it must change how a company or a brand is perceived. Ogilvy & Mather's 1998 campaign for IBM's ViaVoice 98, a speech dictation software, tried to teach consumers to view "Big Blue" as a technologically savvy enterprise that would enable many companies to capitalize on opportunities of e-commerce. The campaign won an Edison Award in 1999.

To conceptualize the different stages through which consumers pass in the process of adopting new technology, the innovation adoption model was derived from past studies of the diffusion of innovation. The steps preceding adoption include: 1) the creation of awareness and interest among consumers; 2) the formation of favorable attitudes about the technology after actual use; and 3) the acceptance and long-term adoption of the technology.

The likelihood of adoption and future diffusion of a new technology are also dependent on certain product characteristics. Five characteristics are likely to increase the rate of consumer acceptance of a new technology. These include relative advantage, compatibility, simplicity, observability, and trialability Studies have found that relative advantage and compatibility are the most critical factors affecting the adoption of a new technological product.

The introduction of new technology requires marketers to employ every possible promotional technique to facilitate the consumer's adoption process. In the late 1990s the growing interest in integrated marketing communication encouraged California-based Apple Computer to use public relations as its lead marketing tool. The award-winning campaign, "Think Different," was created by TWBA/Chiat/Day, New York City. Public relations figured prominently in the advertising of Apple's iMac products. Massive media coverage preceded the appearance of the iMac in stores. The successful campaign quickly made iMac the country's top-selling computer in 1999. Other techniques that emerged at the turn of the 20th century—such as Internet marketing and relationship marketing—are also likely to have an impact on the way new technologies are introduced into the marketplace.

KENNETH C.C. YANG

Further Reading

Assael, Henry, *Consumer Behavior and Marketing Action,* Boston: Kent, 1981; 6th edition, Cincinnati, Ohio: South-Western College, 1998

Belch, George Eugene, and Michael A. Belch, *Introduction to Advertising and Promotion Management,* Homewood, Illinois: Irwin, 1990; 5th edition, as *Advertising and Promotion: An Integrated Marketing Communications Perspective,* Boston: Irwin/McGraw Hill, 2001

Curry, Sheree R., "Innovation Is Only Half The Battle; O&M's Challenge Is Getting The Word Out," *Marketing News* (29 March 1999)

Engel, James F., Roger D. Blackwell, and David Kollat, *Consumer Behavior,* New York: Holt, Rinehart, and Winston, 1968; 8th edition, by Engel, Blackwell, and Paul W. Miniard, Forth Worth, Texas: Dryden, 1995

Kelly, Jane Irene, "FCB Unveils Sega's Dreamcast," *Adweek* (Western edition) (30 August 1999)

Kurtz, David, and Louis Boone, *Contemporary Marketing,* Hinsdale, Illinois: Dryden, 1974; 4th edition, London: Dryden, 1983; 8th edition, Fort Worth, Texas: Dryden, 1995

Ostlund, Lyman, "Perceived Innovation Attributes as Predictors of Innovativeness," *Journal of Consumer Research* 1, no. 2 (September 1974)

Robertson, Thomas S., "The Process of Innovation and the Diffusion of Innovation," *Journal of Marketing* 31 (January 1967)

Rogers, Everett M., *Diffusion of Innovations,* New York: Free Press of Glencoe, 1962; 4th edition, New York: Free Press, 1995

Thorson, Esther, *The Principles of Advertising at Work,* Lincolnwood, Illinois: NTC Publishing Group, 1989

Ted Bates & Company. *See* Bates Worldwide

Telecommunications

Until the mid-1980s virtually all telephone service in the United States was provided by American Telephone & Telegraph Corporation (AT&T). AT&T monopolized long-distance service, while the Bell System provided local service to all but a few communities served by independents. Despite the fact that AT&T had no need to defend its share of the market against competition, it still was one of the best known of all advertisers. The purpose of its advertising was public relations—the creation of a favorable atmosphere of public opinion for AT&T's monopoly status. And this it achieved through campaigns such as "Reach Out and Touch Someone," which N.W. Ayer ABH International introduced in 1979 and which became a part of the national consciousness within five years.

It was in the early to mid-1980s that AT&T's position began to change. Alternative long-distance providers such as MCI appeared, offering service at prices substantially below those of AT&T. For decades the ritual of the long-distance telephone call had been a special occasion for most people, reserved for family holidays and lifetime milestones. Callers spoke loudly and clearly so as not to waste a word and tended to avoid idle conversations. But communications satellites were changing the way the world used long distance, and increasingly, casual long-distance calling was being put in the hands of the middle-class mass market. The first challenge to AT&T came in the form of long-distance service at greatly reduced rates but which provided access to only a few selected major U.S. cities. Over a period of 12 to 18 months, however, the coverage expanded rapidly until low-priced long-distance calls could be made to anywhere in the United States.

The telecommunications battle was joined in 1984 with the court-ordered breakup of AT&T, which established eight companies where there had been one: AT&T and seven regional "Baby Bell" companies to handle local service. It also opened the way for other companies to compete with AT&T for long-distance customers. Through the 1990s, the telecommunications market exploded, thanks to rapid technological advances that opened the way for the growth of the Internet, the advent of wireless service, and the entrance of new players in all telephone markets. By the 21st century, the marketing and advertising strategies had expanded to include highly specialized offerings and packages that included long-distance, high-speed Internet access, digital service, and wireless. But the efforts still included the more traditional marketing ploys of low-cost long-distance pitches and, especially important as companies assumed new names to match their new services, corporate identity campaigns.

Competition among the "Big Three" long-distance providers—AT&T, MCI Corporation, and U.S. Sprint—resulted in an escalating battle of ad campaigns. One particularly sharp jab was AT&T's "Put It in Writing" effort (from Ayer), which appeared to be a veiled attack on MCI's telemarketers and implied that most of its rival's claims were false. The confrontations hit an unprecedented level of absurdity in 1991, when the National Advertising Review Board (NARB), responding to a complaint by Sprint against AT&T, determined that, while AT&T may have been quicker at connecting long-distance phone calls, it was wrong to assert that the extra time it took its competitors to do the same was "wasted." The NARB agreed with Sprint that some callers, while waiting to be connected, would engage in such productive pursuits as planning what they would say. AT&T agreed to take such consideration into account in future advertising.

Meanwhile, MCI boosted its marketing spending from $12 million in 1989 to $100 million in 1992 to launch its "Friends and Family" 20 percent discount calling program in a major TV campaign supported by heavy direct mail. Under pressure from shareholders to perform, MCI in 1990 had hired Messner Vetere Berger McNamee Schmetterer/Euro RSCG, New York City, to replace Wells, Rich, Greene, Inc., after having tried a long list of agencies, including D'Arcy Masius Benton & Bowles and Ally & Gargano. In offering "Friends and Family," MCI improved its share of the core long-distance telephone business by two points to 15 percent. It countered rivals' special offers with deals such as an hour of free long-distance telephone time for consumers who traded in calling cards from other phone companies for one of MCI's own cards. The campaign took a more warm-and-fuzzy approach at one point, touting "MCI. Newer. Different. Better . . . Let us show you." In what became the first in a long line of sentimental ads from all the telephone companies, MCI featured grandchildren giving their grandparents personal 800-service as a gift, while members of an Irish-American family indulged in a New Year's Eve telephone conference call with relatives scattered across the globe.

As the services being offered grew more complicated and diverse, and the number of companies offering those services multiplied, it became increasingly difficult for advertisers to differentiate themselves. Celebrity spokespersons went a long way in distinguishing one company from another during the 1990s as the marketplace became cluttered and chaotic. Among the first—and perhaps most memorable—was actress Candice Bergen's long-running successful relationship with Sprint. Starting in 1990, Bergen, the star of the then-popular CBS TV series *Murphy Brown*, appeared in dozens of commercials from J. Walter Thompson USA (JWT), of San Francisco, California, Sprint's agency since 1981. With her deadpan wit and classy brand of sarcasm, she humanized Sprint, which until then had largely relied on technical pitches about fiber optics, punctuated by the claim that its connections were so noiseless, one could "hear a pin drop." In one TV spot, Bergen explained that by using Sprint and pocketing the savings "you can get to be one of those rich companies that everybody resents," an obvious reference to AT&T.

The ads also offered a welcome respite from what had up until then been hard-core mudslinging. Instead, working with Grey Advertising in 1994, Sprint established itself as a company that cut technological clutter with "Real Solutions" for its business customers. AT&T countered with a rebuttal campaign in which customers were warned not to trust rivals' claims about low prices and good service.

Meanwhile, in 1993, MCI and Sprint unveiled new calling programs backed by heavy TV and print campaigns and promotions. AT&T scrambled to follow their lead, which at the time included MCI's 1-800-COLLECT discount calling card service, "Christmas in July" offering, and "Friends and Family," as well as Sprint's "The Most Worldwide" international discount calling program. AT&T responded with a corporate campaign (from Ayer) themed "You Will," which promoted the company's new wireless and broadband technology. AT&T simultaneously rolled out its $100 million campaign for the "I" plan, a residential discount calling program.

By 1994 telecommunications advertising and marketing spending had risen 8 percent to $3.5 billion, 75 percent of which was comprised of the "Big Three" long-distance companies (then AT&T, MCI, and Sprint) and the so-called Baby Bells. By comparison, cellular phone advertising budgets totaled about $153 million. At the time the stakes were high. AT&T claimed approximately 60 percent of the $77 billion long-distance market, while MCI trailed with about 20 percent and Sprint had 10 percent, with hundreds of smaller companies making up the difference. AT&T was outspending its rivals two to one with a record $461 million in measured media in 1993—a figure it surpassed in the first nine months of 1994.

By 1995 AT&T turned to "True"-themed ad campaigns. While it was by far the leader, it had seen a drop in customers. With the new campaign, this situation changed; for the first time in a decade, the company began to regain customers. AT&T's broadly integrated "True" effort, which touted a variety of well-targeted long-distance calling products—such as True USA discount and True Voice—was created by lead agency FCB/Leber Katz. It echoed a "True" campaign that AT&T had first used in 1993. Some of the spots featured celebrities—for instance, actress Joanne Woodward with her daughter, vocalist Lissy Newman. The True Voice spots were accompanied by a second series of 30-second spots with the voice-over provided by actor Spaulding Gray, touting AT&T's frequent-caller rewards program. The final spot in the series was a competitive ad claiming that four out of every five MCI and Sprint users preferred the quality of AT&T's

MCI Telecommunications Corporation launched its "Proof Positive" campaign in 1993 to win back customers who had switched to rival AT&T Corporation.
Courtesy of MCI and Messner Vetere Berger McNamee Schmetterer/Euro RSCG.

True Voice technology. A year after launching the "True" campaign, backed by a $500 million budget, AT&T told analysts that it had attracted an estimated 200,000 new customers, most of them defectors from MCI.

It was no surprise that MCI responded to AT&T's "True" campaign, dropping its coolly humorous advertising attitude in favor of newspaper page ads declaring, "Shame on you, AT&T," accusing its rival of telling half-truths. The campaign turned out to be one of the more expensive such efforts in advertising history.

Meanwhile, MCI set out to differentiate itself with the first full-blown ad campaign in the category to include both traditional media and a Web site. It was a breakthrough effort by a major advertiser. MCI used a new area it created on the Internet to offer free information and even the trial use of the business services it was advertising on television and in print. The new Web site included the stories behind the characters featured in the advertisements, which focused on a fictitious publishing company called Gramercy Press. The 12-spot series, from Messner Vetere, touted networkMCI Business, a software package for businesses of all sizes. Visitors to the site saw graphic color displays of the TV spots, a blueprint of the Gramercy offices, plus a virtual visit to the characters' offices.

Boosting MCI was its spokeswoman, actress Whoopi Goldberg, who by 1996 had emerged as the most recognized of the phone company presenters. She helped to give a new identity to MCI in advertisements created by Messner Vetere at a time when the services and even advertisements of the three largest long-distance providers appeared painfully similar.

By the mid-1990s many companies, including the local phone companies, had entered the fledgling wireless market, with Bell Atlantic Mobile and US West Cellular joining companies such as Cellular One in the race to build regional and national networks. The key marketing tactic for these companies was the giving away of free phones. By 1995 companies were spending as much as $700, largely on advertising and promotion, to acquire one customer, according to GTE Telecommunications Services, Inc.

With the passage of the Telecommunications Reform Act of 1996, the telecommunications industry was opened to a range of new participants, and the established companies were allowed into other areas as well. Telecommunications providers of all kinds and sizes faced having to educate consumers before they could sell complex service and pricing packages to them amid fierce price competition. For consumers, choosing a telephone company became a complex process, as mystifying to many as reading a legal document.

In 1996 Sprint entered into a wireless, long-distance, and cable joint venture with Comcast Corporation, Cox Communications, and Tele-Communications, Inc., that was called Sprint Spectrum. Later renamed Sprint PCS, the venture originally was supported by its own $30 million ad budget. At the time it was lauded as the wave of the future, but it fell short in all areas but wireless.

Also in 1996, WorldCom, which at the time was the nation's number-four long-distance company after being formed by a merger only a year earlier, leaped to number two after buying MCI. Within a year, WorldCom had nearly doubled the size of its ad budget, beginning with an $8 million ad campaign featuring TV spots with WorldCom spokesman and basketball superstar Michael Jordan, under the tag line, "One company, a world of solutions," created by Earle Palmer Brown, Bethesda, Maryland. The humorous spots (directed by veteran commercial director Bob Giraldi) showed Jordan in business situations selling WorldCom products or servicing them.

Although their ad budgets had grown to many times their previous size by 1999, the telecom companies remained as engrossed as ever in undercutting each other's market share through heavy-handed marketing and aggressive pricing. The complex offerings bombarding consumers came to include 5-cent Sundays, 10-10-321, 10-10-220, and 1-800-COLLECT products. By 1998 AT&T was battling a declining consumer long-distance business with a grassroots marketing blitz aimed at derailing MCI's 10-10-321 plan and other such so-called dial-around offerings that were severely eroding AT&T's consumer market. AT&T said MCI's plan did not save consumers money on most calls because they were still paying the same or nearly as much as AT&T's

basic rates. AT&T, whose basic rates were the highest in the industry at the time, said it wanted to give consumers the facts so they could make an informed decision. But these were the facts: MCI's 10-10-321 offered a penny a minute off AT&T's basic or highest rate; for calls of more than 20 minutes, consumers were given 50 percent off the AT&T rate. While AT&T argued that most long-distance calls were less than 10 minutes, MCI insisted that nearly three-quarters of its 10-10-321 traffic was made up of calls of 20 minutes or longer.

While the dominant telephone service players wrestled with their own internal problems and each other, the Baby Bells encountered their own challenges as they merged and repositioned themselves. SBC Communications Corporation, parent of Southwestern Bell, acquired Pacific Telesis Group, parent of Pacific Bell, in 1996 and Ameritech Corporation in 1999. Bell Atlantic Corporation acquired Nynex Corporation in 1996 and in June 2000 merged with GTE Corporation, in the process forming Verizon Communications. Bell Atlantic became the first Baby Bell to go head to head with AT&T, MCI, and Sprint in the long-distance area with ads in 1996 created by Saatchi & Saatchi. In one TV spot, actor James Earl Jones doing voice-over said, "For your life that lives in other places."

About the same time, Pacific Bell filed a complaint against MCI and its ad campaigns that claimed the local phone companies were overcharging customers on access charges. MCI countered with a warning to consumers, "Big Bell monopolies see you as big fat cash cows." The U.S. Telephone Association, a group representing the regional Bells, GTE Corporation, and about 1,000 smaller phone service providers at the time, countered with an ad campaign and Web site themed "Call them on it." Ironically, in 1997, the local phone market, valued at about $90 billion, was larger than the $75 billion long-distance market.

As the Baby Bells began spending more, AT&T and MCI each curtailed ad spending in 1997 and in 1998, relying more on promotions, contests, and sweepstakes to build their brand images. In 1997, for instance, AT&T had reduced its advertising spending more than 9 percent to $547 million, while MCI scaled back 5 percent to $300 million. However, total ad commitment was up owing to increased advertising by newcomers such as WinStar and MFS WorldCom and the Baby Bells in their bid for a larger national customer base.

By 1998 the telephone companies had moved some of their ad dollars to the Internet, where telephone companies were spurred on not only by each other but by America Online, which was rapidly converting Internet surfers into long-distance phone customers. Working with long-distance reseller Tel-Save Holdings, America Online (AOL) signed up 200,000 subscribers in just two months. Thus it was no surprise when Sprint launched Sprint Sense AnyTime, a new long-distance calling plan on www.sprint.com, and AT&T unveiled One Rate Online—a flat dime-a-minute calling plan billed directly over the Internet to customers' credit cards—and the Internet telephony plan WorldNet Voice.

In what was perhaps the ultimate diversification move for any telecommunications company, AT&T in the mid-1990s began transforming itself into the largest cable television operator in the United States. Its efforts were anchored by its acquisition of TCI Communications in 1999 and by its acquisition of MediaOne Group in 2000. Concurrently, AT&T developed a wireless business that eventually became a dependable high-growth business.

Seen as a risky and expensive means of rolling out cable telephony, which had yet to materialize as a major market segment even in 2001, AT&T found itself burdened by debt and the problem of upgrading cable systems. From the time it stepped into the cable business, it fought the battle of rapidly expanding costs before new services and their revenue streams could be launched. Constant across-the-board streamlining gnawed at AT&T's marketing and advertising budget. The company used the 2000 Sydney (Australia) Olympic Games as a platform for combating its image as a stodgy, old telephone company and to launch a new image-building campaign as a cutting-edge provider of digital broadband services. It was part of a critical two-year effort to reposition AT&T for the digital age.

Meanwhile, by 2000, Sprint pulled its consumer account from Grey, which continued to handle its corporate ads when Sprint shifted its marketing focus from mass advertising to more customer-focused advertising. Two years earlier, Sprint had fired JWT, its longtime agency of record, following conflicts over creative strategy. It moved its $150 million account to AT&T's former ad agency, McCann-Erickson Worldwide, reflecting the company's determination to build its image as a service provider rather than as a long-distance telephone company. At the time, it was countering competition from MCI WorldCom, AT&T, the regional Bells, new carriers such as Quest and Excel, and even Internet service providers.

At the same time, MCI WorldCom unveiled an elaborate push aimed at business decision makers that positioned the company more prominently in the digital world. Underscoring its vast Internet assets, the TV spots and print ads used only the WorldCom name. After the U.S. Justice Department blocked WorldCom's plans to acquire Sprint, WorldCom in mid-2000 began gearing up for a bigger marketing push after having slashed its estimated $600 million ad budget by almost half in 1999. Its shift in focus was to business-to-business, emphasizing that WorldCom was no conventional telephone company but a reflection of the new economy. The approach was personally initiated by WorldCom Chairman and Chief Executive Officer Bernard "Bernie" Ebber.

With telecommunications mergers and acquisitions expected to slow in 2001, companies were laying plans to refine their competitive positions and new services by building off existing operations rather than continually integrating new ones. However, they found themselves competing against more unfamiliar players in an increasingly wireless, global, and bundled marketplace. At a time of declining stock prices and massive restructurings, the telecommunications industry was also looking over its shoulder at a new hybrid player—AOL Time Warner—that could change things yet again. Even before the $104 billion merger closed in mid-January 2001, AOL had premiered a new wireless telephone service and started testing cable telephony. Time Warner was contemplating,

but not committed to, digital cable telephony for its nearly 13 million cable subscribers.

That was just the tip of the iceberg that would continue to transform the telecommunications industry. A slew of megamergers and the creation of dozens of upstart companies became driving forces for change. The United States Telecom Association—on behalf of the 1,000 companies it represented, including local exchange carriers, Internet service providers, wireless and cable companies, and more conventional long-distance and local telephone companies—in 2000 called on the U.S. Congress to adopt a uniform policy allowing broadband and other telecommunications-related technologies to compete on an equal, deregulated footing.

In preparation for this change, telecommunications companies by 2001 had already started to shift their marketing and sales emphasis to the more profitable and growing new areas of communications such as wireless, broadband, data, and networking services. For example, WorldCom launched the "Generation D" campaign (from Messner Vetere), to symbolize the company's evolution from a voice carrier to a data and Internet-centric service provider. SBC Communications, which absorbed Ameritech in 2000, was developing a $250 million effort for its U.S. wireless operations, ranking second domestically. And Verizon, the product of a Bell Atlantic-GTE merger, using a variety of agencies, built a wireless brand that made its Bell Atlantic parent the first Baby Bell with a national wireless offering, with service in 96 of the top 100 markets. The campaign was supported by a $400 million-plus advertising and promotion budget.

After more than a year of tumultuous change, AT&T secured the ad agency veteran Cathy Constable in the fall of 1999 to design a brand campaign and coordinate the company's various agencies while assuring consistency throughout. In the fall of 2000, it launched the new corporate image campaign, "Boundless," with Y&R Advertising producing the television spots and FCB Worldwide the print ads. At the same time, AT&T shifted its emphasis from direct-response TV and direct marketing to TV advertising of wireless, high-speed, digital cable, and other such products.

But the company also stunned the telecommunications industry in October 2000 by announcing its second break-up, this one self-imposed. The $1.95 billion in advertising and marketing AT&T spent annually as of 1999 on its businesses would be divided among what would within a year become four separate businesses—broadband, business, consumer, and wireless—serviced by even more ad agencies. It would immediately face what it took years to encounter and wrestle with after its initial, government-ordered 1984 break-up.

In an October 1997 review of telecommunications companies, *Advertising Age* observed that the mergers, acquisitions, and management shake-ups created by deregulation of telecommunications industry would cause major shifts in marketing and advertising strategies. The impact on related industries such as ad agencies was swift and certain. But ad spending rose along with the competitive stakes, with the competition not limited to AT&T, MCI, and Sprint at the top or the Baby Bells in the center, but also including a number of other nontelephone company marketers offering local, Internet, and other kinds of communications services. As ad agencies bid for the "transitional kitty," as telephone companies' transition image-building ad spending was called, it was clear that the ad industry, if not telecommunications, stood to benefit from the changes.

But things would change in a big way yet again in 2001, for AT&T in particular. By December of that year, AT&T agreed to merge its broadband unit with Comcast Corporation to create the dominant cable service provider in the United States and advance its three-pronged digital video, high-speed data, and telephony offerings. Its wireless business pushed forward as a separately traded public entity, while its long-distance business, like those of some competitors, came under pressure on the stock market and in regulatory circles.

DIANE MERMIGAS

See also AT&T Corporation; British Telecom; Ericsson (China) Company, Ltd.; Ericsson, Inc.; Motorola, Inc.; Nokia Corporation; *and color plate in this volume*

Further Reading

Beatty, Sally, "Adam and Eve, and Other Pitches for a New AT&T," *Wall Street Journal* (27 July 1998)

"The Calls of the Wild," *Adweek* (15 November 1993)

Carnevale, Mary Lu, "MCI, in New Phone War Skirmish, Files Suit over AT&T Ad Claims," *Wall Street Journal* (11 October 1989)

Cleland, Kim, "WorldCom Doubles Budget to Seize '97 Opportunities," *Advertising Age* (7 April 1997)

Cleland, Kim, "Baby Bells Lash at MCI for Its Local Ad Efforts," *Advertising Age* (14 April 1997)

Cleland, Kim, "Sprint Moving beyond Product Ads," *Advertising Age* (12 May 1997)

Crain, Rance, "Telcos to Unleash Ad Bonanza," *Advertising Age* (8 January 1996)

Dunlap, Bill, "The Big Three: Agency Players for AT&T, Sprint, and MCI Discuss Points of Distinction in a Crowded Category," *Shout* (3 March 1997)

Egolf, Karen, "Cellular Carriers Confront Churn," *Telephony* (17 July 1995)

Elkin, Tobi, "AT&T Breakup Plan Will Spur Marketing Landgrab," *Advertising Age* (30 October 2000)

Elliott, Stuart, "The Media Business: Advertising: The Marketing Implications of the Bidding War of Sprint Are the Buzz of Madison Avenue," *New York Times Abstracts* (5 October 1999)

Farrell, Greg, and Michael McCarthy, "AT&T's 'True Voice' Takes on MCI 'Family,'" *Adweek* (20 December 1993)

Fitzgerald, Kate, "Actress Candice Bergen Is Funny, Effective in Keeping Sprint Nipping at AT&T, MCI," *Advertising Age* (3 May 1993)

Fitzgerald, Kate, "AT&T Shifts Budget to Lure Customers," *Advertising Age* (26 July 1993)

Fitzgerald, Kate, "Sprint Ads Aim at Businesses," *Advertising Age* (1 April 1994)

Fitzgerald, Kate, "MCI Dips Gramercy Press in Cyberspace: Fictional Publishing Company Hits the Internet," *Advertising Age* (14 November 1994)

Fitzgerald, Kate, "AT&T's 'True'-ly Effective Campaign," *Advertising Age* (2 January 1995)

Fitzgerald, Kate, "Telcos Take a Twist: Telecommunications: Wireless, Networking, Data Services Take Center Stage in Massive Ad Blitz," *Advertising Age* (9 October 2000)

Friedman, Wayne, "MCI Scales Back on Its 'Wild West' and Tie-Ins," *Advertising Age* (3 May 1999)

Garcia, Shelley, "Signing Jordan, WorldCom Seeks Shop," *Adweek* (22 January 1996)

Goldman, Kevin, "Long-Distance Phone Companies Try Long-Winded Ads for Savings," *Wall Street Journal* (3 June 1994)

Goldman, Kevin, "MCI Ad Rebukes AT&T Tactics in Move to Regain Market Share," *Wall Street Journal* (20 December 1994)

Keller, John J., "AT&T Prepared Advertising Campaign to Battle MCI's 'Dial-Around' Plan," *Wall Street Journal* (7 April 1998)

King, Thomas R., "Sprint Counts on Candice Bergen to Lend Appeal to Its New Ad," *Wall Street Journal* (8 October 1990)

Koprowski, Gene, "Theories of Negativity: When Is the Right Time to Lash Out against the Competition?" *Adweek* (20 February 1995)

Lipman, Joanne, "US Sprint Tries to Reach Out and Thump AT&T over Snafu," *Wall Street Journal* (17 January 1990)

McCarthy, Michael, "Next Up for AT&T: Consolidating Direct Marketing," *Adweek* (29 November 1993)

McCormack, Kevin, "Ruling Nixes AT&T 'Wasted' Tie Claim," *Adweek* (1 January 1991

Petrecca, Laura, and Tobi Elkin, "AT&T Shootout: Agencies Seek Olympic Gold," *Advertising Age* (7 August 2000)

Pringle, Rodney, "Telecom Industry Mostly Shrugs Off Impact of AOL-Time Warner Deal," *Communications Today* (17 January 2001)

Sloan, Pat, and Kim Cleland, "Post-Breakup AT&T Stays $1 Billion Advertiser," *Advertising Age* (25 September 1995)

Snyder, Beth, "Power 50: As Telcos Spread Webs, Ad Dollars Can Only Go Up," *Advertising Age* (20 October 1997)

Snyder, Beth, "Strategies Focus on Products, Services Telecommunications: Pitch to Nitches a Priority over Image Ads," *Advertising Age* (5 October 1998)

Snyder, Beth, "Sprint's Kelly Tackles NFL, and Challenges Facing Brand," *Advertising Age* (2 November 1998)

"Sprint Awards Contracts," *The Wall Street Journal* (16 March 1998)

"Sprint Lets Customers Tell Its Tale," *Adweek* (11 July 1994)

Taylor, Cathy, "Grey Answers Sprint's Call, Ending Intensive Review," *Adweek* (28 March 1994)

Vadehra, Dave, "Transactions: Campaign Clout: Whoopi's MCI Role Poses Risk of Look-Alike Ads in Long-Distance," *Advertising Age* (22 January 1996)

Warner, Bernhard, "Sprint Drops Dimes to Bolster 'Sense' beyond Advertising," *Adweek* (31 March 1997)

Warner, Bernhard, "Telco Lobby Evolving into Marketing Assn.," *Adweek* (21 April 1997)

Warner, Bernhard, "Telecommunications," *Adweek* (12 May 1997)

Warner, Bernhard, "Phone Wars II: Coming to a Web Site near You," *Adweek* (2 March 1998)

"Yahoo! Inc.: Venture with MCI Is Set to Launch Rival to AOL," *Wall Street Journal* (16 March 1998)

Telemarketing: Overview

The telephone was first used as a sales tool in the early 1900s, when industries such as steel and financial services began to employ the then-new device to contact current and potential customers. Calls, which tended to consist of hyperbole-filled scripts, originated in so-called boiler rooms of calling operations that lacked knowledge of business or sales. In addition to inexperienced but legitimate participants, numerous con artists used the technique.

It was not until the late 1970s that telephone technology became sophisticated enough for centralized call centers to make sense economically. Telemarketing, as it has come to be known, came into being during the early 1980s. In 1981 total business expenditures for telemarketing exceeded the dollars spent on direct-mail advertising for the first time; by 1987 spending on telemarketing was more than double that for direct mail ($41.2 billion vs. $17.2 billion), according to the American Telemarketing Association (ATA). The average telemarketing sale to a consumer was $61, while the average to a business was $1,500.

Several trends contributed to the growth of telemarketing during the 1980s. These included the ever-higher cost of personal sales calls, which made telemarketing more attractive, especially in a business-to-business environment; advances in telecommunications, computers, and database management, which decreased costs and increased efficiency; consumer acceptance of 800 numbers, which led to a rise in inbound telemarketing; and a growing body of successful inbound and outbound telemarketing campaigns, which led more companies to try the phone as a sales tool.

By 1985 there were 50 telemarketing service agencies in the United States—some companies used these third-party calling centers while others set up in-house operations—that employed a half-million people. A decade later, the number of agencies had grown to 900, with 60 percent having staffs of 50 or more; total agency employment was 4.5 million. The number of telemarketing operations, in-house and outsourced, in the United States rose from fewer than 80,000 in the early 1980s to 240,000 in 1985 and 565,000 in 1995.

By the mid-1990s, U.S. businesses, including financial service, technology, automotive, insurance, and telephone companies, spent nearly $90 billion a year on telephone marketing. The ATA estimated that the telephone generated more than $280 billion in sales of goods and services to 81 million Americans.

By the beginning of the 21st century, virtually all consumer marketers had set up 800 numbers for inbound telemarketing purposes. This toll-free service allowed consumers to call in with questions, an occasion that often provided the marketer additional sales opportunities. Meanwhile, outbound telemarketing also remained strong for both business-to-business and business-to-consumer purposes. As of 2000 there were approximately 69,500 in-house and third-party call centers in the United States, according to Datamonitor, an international market research company; the Direct Marketing Association (DMA) estimated industry employment at 5.6 million Americans and sales of goods via telephone marketing at approximately $585 billion.

The top-ten telemarketing companies together had the capacity to make more than 1 million calls per hour in 2000. That capacity is continually enhanced by new technologies such as predictive dialing, an automated system that allows sales representatives to spend their time only on calls that are answered rather than on dialing and waiting for the phone to ring, and computer-telephone integration, which allows sales representatives to access information about the customers with whom they are speaking.

Telemarketing is increasingly entwined with both database marketing and Internet-related sales efforts, which allows a closer match between the corporate message and the consumer's desires, translating to higher sales. The Internet has boosted the number of inbound telemarketing calls, as consumers turn to the Web for customer service and information on purchases and then use the telephone to order. Correlating the Internet and the telephone increases efficiency by enabling salespeople to handle multiple queries simultaneously.

Despite this progress, the industry has not been able to shake the disreputable image that has persisted since its earliest days. In the late 1990s, the U.S. Justice Department estimated that telemarketing fraud cost consumers $40 billion to $50 billion each year, or about 10 percent of the legitimate sales over the telephone at the time. As of 2000, annual fraud costs had increased to an estimated $60 billion.

Con artists tend to target older Americans for phone fraud. In 1999 the American Association of Retired Persons (now known simply by the acronym AARP) estimated 56 percent of telemarketing fraud victims were age 50 or older; this group accounted for 36 percent of the population. AARP began a campaign in the late 1990s to fight fraud. The U.S. Postal Inspection Service, the Federal Trade Commission, the Department of Justice and other organizations joined in with a campaign called Project Know Fraud. A postcard warning consumers about telemarketing fraud and how to protect themselves from it was sent to 118.8 million addresses and was promoted by President Bill Clinton in his weekly radio address.

Aside from outright fraud, telemarketing also endures a bad reputation because many people simply do not like to have their lives interrupted by sales calls. A 2000 Shopper Report survey found that 93 percent of U.S. households polled wanted to stop receiving telemarketing calls entirely (not just at inconvenient times such as dinnertime) and that 85 percent felt strongly about their opinion.

The DMA telephone name removal list grew from 900,000 to 2.5 million names in less than a year in 1999, nearly as many as the 3 million on the DMA's mail preference service file, which is intended to reduce the amount of "junk mail" received by consumers. By 2000 the telephone removal service was up to 3.2 million names. The DMA attributed the growth to the use of predictive dialers, which may cause panic in call recipients because, if no operator is available, the line goes dead when answered, leading recipients to assume that they are the target of prank callers or thieves.

In 2000 several states set up their own do-not-call lists, each with significant penalties. New York, for example, required all telemarketers to purchase a copy of its list and fined them $2,000 for each listed name they call. More than 180,000 New Yorkers had signed up within a few months of the law's passage in October 2000. Tennessee has a similar list with the same penalty, for which 380,000 residents, or 20 percent of the 1.9 million residential telephone service subscribers in the state, signed up soon

thereafter. Eleven other states had similar laws and more were considering instituting such prohibitions.

The telemarketing industry is cognizant of its reputation, and many organizations involved in the business have changed their names in response: the American Telemarketing Association rechristened itself the American Teleservices Association, *Telemarketing* magazine became *Call Center Solutions,* and APAC Teleservices, one of the largest call-center service organizations, renamed itself APAC Customer Services.

Despite the negative connotations—which center primarily on outbound consumer efforts and not on inbound or business-to-business calling—telemarketing continues to drive significant sales, especially in industries such as financial services and telecommunications. That fact, along with technological advancements that allow in- and outbound telephone sales to become more effective and less costly, will allow telemarketing to maintain its place as a key marketing strategy in the United States and throughout the world.

KAREN RAUGUST

Further Reading

Fitzgerald, Kate, "Putting Tech into Telemarketing," *Credit Card Management* 12, no. 4 (July 1999)

Kaplan, Fred, "Demands for Privacy Curb Telemarketers," *Boston Globe* (26 December 2000)

Martin, Zack, "State Bans Some Telemarketing Calls," *Card Marketing* 4, no. 11 (December 2000)

Miller, Paul, "Outbound Explosion," *Catalog Age* 15, no. 8 (July 1998)

Sisk, Kathy, *Successful Telemarketing: The Complete Handbook on Managing a Profitable Telemarketing Call Center,* New York: McGraw-Hill, 1995

Telemarketing: 800 Numbers

Toll-free telephone numbers that begin with one of several specially designated dialing prefixes (frequently 800, 888, or 877) are generally referred to as "800 numbers." A caller using a toll-free number is not charged for the call. Toll-free numbers are used heavily in business-to-business as well as business-to-consumer programs, primarily in direct-response advertising and direct-mail campaigns. The first 800 number service was introduced by the American Telephone & Telegraph Corporation (AT&T) in 1967. These phone numbers are available in many formats. Subscribers can choose geographical areas they want to cover: intrastate (within a state), interstate (groups of states), international, or a combination of all three.

The pioneering users of the service were the astute marketers at the Sheraton Corporation, who envisioned serving the needs of travelers who might be stranded without coins to make a phone call and who might need to make emergency hotel reservations. Their toll-free service drew many new customers, and before long the entire travel-and-leisure industry started jumping on the toll-free bandwagon. Hotels, airlines, travel agents, and limousine services were some of the major industries that started using this service profitably.

Most other industries, however, were slow to capitalize on this new technology. It was not until 1980, when AT&T started aggressively marketing its 800 service, that this phenomenon began to catch on with other businesses. Since then, the use of toll-free numbers has grown dramatically. In 2000 Dial-A-Mattress, for example, was generating more than $65 million in revenue annually with nothing more in the way of a place of business than a toll-free designation—no "bricks-and-mortar" locations.

At the outset of the 21st century, there were more than 800,000 toll-free numbers in use in the United States. In 1996 the "888" prefix was approved by the Federal Trade Commission (FTC) to expand the dwindling supply of 800 number designations and was followed by the addition of the "877" toll-free prefix. The new prefixes provided more flexibility for companies and individuals who wanted to establish a "vanity" phone number, spelling out a company's name, catchy slogan, or acronym in the actual telephone number (e.g., "1-888-get-thin").

Toll-free numbers are portable and can be moved to another office, home, or even across state lines. A number may be used for any working business or residential telephone, voice mail, pager, cellular phone, fax, or modem line. Toll-free numbers appear in various media. They are equally likely to be seen in print media (magazines and newspapers) as on television, in the phone book, or in brochures or pamphlets, and increasingly on the Internet.

Internationally, the systems and names for toll-free numbers vary. Designations include, for example, 0800 in the United Kingdom; 050 in Norway; 020 in Sweden; 0600 in The Netherlands; and "numero vert," or "green number," in France. Transnational telemarketers have to be very attentive to language and legislative issues pertaining to the various countries.

The applications for toll-free calling are becoming more numerous, varied, and sophisticated. The original and most common use for 800 numbers is to generate orders. Retailers, catalog companies, periodical subscription businesses, gift delivery order companies, and others entice customers to buy by phone. Toll-free numbers are also invaluable for building databases and generating leads. Most ads in the business sections of major newspapers carry toll-free numbers. The service can be useful in locating the nearest dealer that might carry a particular product, providing information to prospective customers before they buy the product, and enabling readers to call and request copies of catalogs.

The inclusion of 800 numbers in print ads has been shown to increase response by as much as 20 percent. Almost three-fourths of the people who use 800 numbers do so to obtain information, and more than half use them to order goods or make a purchase. A study of 21 major newspapers in the United States revealed that more than 5 percent of the national ads they carried displayed 800 numbers. The usage is heavier in general news magazines (15 percent of the ads in *Time* and *Newsweek* carry an 800 number), while the figure rises to more than 20 percent for business magazines such as *Fortune* and *Business Week*.

Research has also shown that 800 numbers provide a powerful business advantage over comparable tools. When advertised together with a mail-back form, 65 percent of respondents used the toll-free number to contact the business, compared to 35 percent using the mail-in form. Studies have also shown that customers are more likely to do business with a company offering a toll-free contact number. In addition to increasing customer loyalty,

Bell can show you how to do more with less.

A single, toll-free 800 number can take the place of the two or more you have now. Your advertising can become less complicated. More effective. You can increase sales while reducing costs.

You do it by choosing Expanded 800, an innovation of the Bell network, the world's largest and most advanced information management system. It's one of the latest developments in the mix of technology and management systems called Telemarketing, and it can give you better control and greater flexibility in running your business.

With Expanded 800, your customers call the same toll-free number whether they're calling from out of state or within. Since a single number is easier to remember, you're likely to get more calls, write more orders, make more sales.

The network can also route customer calls the way you want them handled. When it's quitting time for your East Coast office, calls can shift to your offices still open further west. You pick up added sales and provide nonstop customer service while saving on overtime expenses.

Expanded 800 can also help your telephone sales become a mirror of your field sales operation. If you know that certain areas demand special attention, calls from those areas can go to your people best equipped to handle them.

Bell can demonstrate to you right now the effectiveness of Telemarketing with Expanded 800. We use it ourselves.

All you have to do is call 1 800 821-2121. Put our knowledge to work for your business. **Bell System.**

1 800 821-2121

The knowledge business

A 1982 ad explained the benefits of the Bell System's Expanded 800 service to business customers.
Courtesy of BellSouth Intellectual Property Marketing Corporation.

800 numbers also have been shown to increase the number of orders, increase the size of orders, and allow companies to expand into new markets, along with achieving a much quicker reaction time.

Although there are distinct benefits to using 800 numbers, there are a few caveats. At the outset, it is important to train service communicators handling these calls in order to gain maximum effectiveness. Companies should also ensure that there are enough lines to handle incoming calls. They should anticipate peaks and valleys in calling times so that customers do not experience constant busy signals. Finally, to achieve optimum benefit it is very important that toll-free calling be integrated into a firm's overall marketing program.

ABHIJIT ROY

Further Reading

Barragan, Napoleon, Maxine Brady, and Frank Brady, *How to Get Rich with a 1-800 Number,* New York: Regan, 1997

Gable, Robert A., *Toll-Free Services: A Complete Guide to Design, Implementation, and Management,* Boston: Artech House, 1995

Kordahl, Eugene B., "Inbound Telemarketing," in *The Direct Marketing Handbook,* edited by Edward L. Nash, 2nd edition, New York: McGraw-Hill, 1995

Lefton, Terry, "Toll-Free Turf Wars," *Adweek's Marketing Week*

(27 January 1992)

McKean, Aldyn, "Inbound Telemarketing," in *Encyclopedia of Telemarketing,* edited by Richard Bencin and Donald Jonovic, Englewood Cliffs, New Jersey: Prentice Hall, 1989

Telemarketing: 900 Numbers

Telephone numbers beginning with the 900 prefix are also referred to as "Dial-it" telemedia. They differ from toll-free numbers (prefixed 800, 888, and 877) in that to use a 900 number, the caller must pay a set minimum fee, usually an initial charge followed by per-minute rates far exceeding regular long-distance or local charges. Moreover, unlike toll-free numbers, 900 numbers do not have portability. Each carrier (e.g., AT&T Corporation, WorldCom, Sprint Corporation) is assigned specific numbers for 900 service that are used exclusively by it.

AT&T introduced the first 900 number service in September 1980. It was an extension of the existing Public Announcement Service, which had previously been offered by local telephone companies under such names as Dow Jones Report, Sportsphone, Time, and Weather. The advantage of the 900 service was that it enabled callers to voice their opinions in addition to merely receiving information.

The first major use of the Dial-it service was during the 1980 U.S. presidential debate between Jimmy Carter and Ronald Reagan, when about 750 million people called a 900 number to register their opinion about who had won the debate. Since then, 900 number activity has increased substantially. Interactive pay-per-call was introduced in 1987, and innovative and aggressive marketers soon started using this medium for a variety of purposes. AT&T, quickly followed by MCI and Sprint and a new player, Telesphere, began to offer the interactive service. At the turn of the century it was one of the fastest growing segments of the telecommunications industry.

Most people associate 900 numbers with telephone sex services and psychic advisors or with contest scams and other unscrupulous businesses. But according to the *Direct Marketing Association 1996 Factbook,* the greatest use for 900 numbers was actually for medical referrals, financial advice, restaurant and movie recommendations, sports scores, and computer information. The service provides an opportunity for mass-market response to sales promotions and has been successfully used for everything from Dial-a-Prayer to political polling. In 1998, 900 numbers brought in more than $1 billion in revenues, compared with $752 million in 1995.

As a more diverse range of legitimate businesses adopt this telemedium, its tarnished image is likely to brighten. And as more consumers make use of interactive lines and the demand grows for quicker and more accurate information, increasing numbers of

businesses will switch from 800 to 900 services. Kaiser Permanente, Hewlett-Packard Company, and Microsoft Corporation are just a few of the many established companies that have had success with this tool. The companies benefit in two ways: they do not have to bear the cost of the toll call, and at the same time they are able to charge consumers a fair rate for the service they are providing.

The success of a 900 number hinges on several factors. First, there must be a demand for the information to be marketed. Sec-

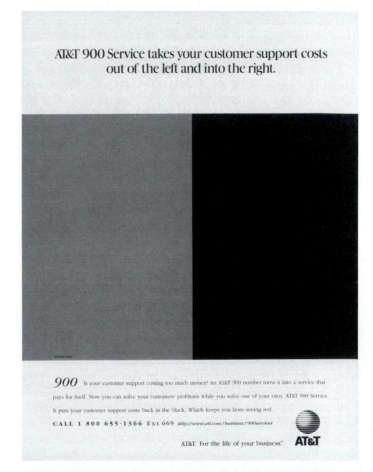

In 1996 AT&T ran a campaign to show business customers how they could save money with AT&T 900 service.
Courtesy of AT&T.

ond, this information must be marketable, and callers must find it to be useful and worth the price. Another key element in a successful program is to present the service in a unique way so as to capture the user's interest. Frequent updating and changing of the message help to sustain interest, ultimately converting callers into loyal customers. Integrating the 900 number with other forms of promotion is also critical. Finally, the number must be aggressively marketed to the appropriate target audience.

There are several restrictions on the use of 900 numbers. Programs that target children under 12 years old, specifically those with slogans such as "Call and talk to Santa Claus," are prohibited by law. Educational information may be provided, however, with parents' permission. (When the child calls the 900 number, a parent must be with him or her to give consent.) The dissemination of information about criminal activities such as gambling and illegal drug sales is not allowed. Credit card fraud involving 900 numbers has attracted the attention of both state and federal regulators. Credit plans that promise to erase bad credit records and offer cards with guaranteed acceptance are forbidden, although legitimate techniques for creative financing are acceptable.

Customers have the option of blocking 900 numbers from their phones. The FCC mandates that local phone companies make blocking available where technically feasible, for a "reasonable" fee. However, subscribers with new phone numbers can request this service for free if they call within 60 days of getting their connection. Businesses in the United States and Canada have been the primary users of 900 numbers, although they are available in most countries.

ABHIJIT ROY

Further Reading

Bohner, Kate, "Hewlett Does 1-900," *Forbes* 158, no. 1 (1 July 1996)

Goldstein, Linda A., "New 900 Regulations Final," *Telemarketing* 12, no. 5 (November 1993)

Hume, Scott, "900 Numbers: The Struggle for Respect," *Advertising Age* (18 February 1991)

Mastin, Robert, and Carol Morse Ginsburg, *Money-Making 900 Numbers: How Entrepreneurs Use the Telephone to Sell Information*, Newport, Rhode Island: Aegis, 1995

Stark, Jerrold L., "The New Direct Marketing Channel: A Baseline Descriptive Study of 1-900 Telephone Users," *Journal of Direct Marketing* 8, no. 3 (Summer 1994)

Television

Television advertising is one of the astounding success stories of the past 50 years. As an ad medium, TV first registered on the annual (since 1935) McCann-Erickson survey of U.S. ad spending in 1949, when advertisers placed some $58 million into the hands of the networks and stations. While this must have seemed a huge number at the time, it is minuscule compared with the amounts that were regularly being spent by the end of the century. In 2000, according to a survey prepared for *Advertising Age*, television accounted for $59.2 billion of U.S. advertising expenditures—nearly one quarter of the total.

Television's triumph as an ad medium is now global, although nowhere else does business lavish so much money on TV advertising as in the United States. According to 2000 estimates of ad spending on media (except for direct mail), 35 percent of all monies ($11.1 billion) went to television in France, 39 percent in Canada ($5.3 billion), 41 percent in Spain ($5.4 billion), 45 percent in both Japan ($33.2 billion) and Italy ($8.3 billion), and a whopping 60 percent in Brazil ($6.9 billion). In the United Kingdom television, at 34 percent, ranked just behind newspapers at 39 percent (of a total spending of $15.8 billion) as the major advertising medium. Only in one market, Germany ($21.6 billion), was television third, at 23 percent, behind magazines, at 24 percent, and newspapers, at 45 percent.

Commercials and Commercialism

The triumph of television advertising would have seemed unlikely in 1950. In the beginning, many governments were sufficiently worried about commercialism to ban or limit advertising on their new television systems, as they had in the case of radio. Initially, the British Broadcasting Corporation, funded through an annual listeners' fee, was granted a monopoly on transmissions. France (1948), Switzerland and Belgium (1953), and Holland and Scandinavia (mid-1950s) all started public, noncommercial TV systems.

The costs of producing and delivering television were so high, however, that other governments decided to allow some forms of commercial system. In 1949 Canada granted its Canadian Broadcasting Corporation a monopoly of network telecasts (service began in 1952), funded by tax monies; even so, the government required the corporation to work with privately owned affiliates and carry a certain amount of television advertising, both to generate extra revenue and to give Canadian business a new voice. Mixed systems of one kind or another were launched in Italy and West Germany (1953), Spain (1956), Finland (1958), and Austria (1959). Both Italy and Germany, though, confined advertisements to particular blocks of time. A third group of governments,

The

J. WALTER THOMPSON COMPANY

Television Workshop

A unique proving ground to insure the quality of television commercials

A 1955 booklet described one of the first workshops given by the J. Walter Thompson Company on the production of television commercials.
Courtesy of the J. Walter Thompson Company.

including those of Japan and Australia in the mid-1950s, authorized competing public and private systems. In 1954 the British authorities established a heavily regulated commercial service, ITV. In 1960 the Canadian government allowed the creation of an independent, ad-supported service, made up of new private stations in major markets plus a new network, CTV, to meet the consumer demand for choice.

By contrast, in the United States advertising revenues alone fueled the rapid development of mass television. Companies such as Lever Brothers, Bulova Watch (purportedly the sponsor of the first spot in 1941, at a cost of $9, on NBC's New York City station), Gillette Razors, Pan American Airways, Firestone Tire, and Esso all took to television in 1945. By the end of 1948, 933 sponsors had bought time. In 1949 actress Betty Furness began to appear as spokesperson for Westinghouse, a job that ultimately made her one of the most familiar faces on television. Soon, enthusiasts could recount stories of the astounding impact of all this advertising; according to one of the most repeated such tales, sales of Hazel Bishop lipsticks went from a mere $50,000 a year in 1950 to $4.5 million two years later, solely because of TV. A 1952 survey found that Borden's Elsie the Cow was more readily recognized than Senator Robert Taft, a then-prominent Republican. Ad revenues had topped $1 billion by 1955, and television had become the leading medium of national advertising in the country, surpassing radio and magazines. By 1960 three networks—ABC, CBS, and NBC—plus more than 500 mostly affiliated stations distributed programs throughout most of the day and night to 87 percent of U.S. homes (45.7 million households).

The near-total reliance on ad revenues had significant aesthetic consequences. Much entertainment throughout the 1950s was controlled by advertising agencies, which bought program time on the networks and supervised the production of each show, a pattern inherited from network radio. These agencies were hired by clients that sponsored a program, sometimes attaching their names to individual shows (e.g., *Goodyear Television Playhouse*), expecting not only to advance sales but also to enhance their corporate images. This practice produced censorship; in 1955 Batten Barton Durstine & Osborn (BBDO) ordered the script of Rod Serling's "Noon on Doomsday" for the *U.S. Steel Hour* altered to avoid offending Southern sensibilities about race relations. More important, advertiser sponsorship also worked to favor the shows that captured the largest audience, since these offered advertisers the maximum number of viewers. The drive to capture a mass audience had the effect of eliminating specialty television shows, such as the various playhouses, and replacing them with action drama, notably the cowboy sagas that filled the evening schedules of all three networks at the end of the 1950s. The priority given to commercials even organized the shows themselves; the action of the story was built around the commercial inserts to ensure that viewers would be in an appropriate frame of mind to watch the ads.

Network executives were not happy with agency control. Sylvester L. ("Pat") Weaver, Jr., president of NBC (1953–55), proposed instead the "magazine format," whereby the networks would direct production and sponsors would buy inserts. That approach won little support at the time, although two fringe programs, *Today* and *The Tonight Show*, did employ a "magazine" format. In 1959, however, Charles Van Doren, a big winner on the quiz show *Twenty-One*, admitted that he had been coached to ensure that the agency got what it wanted, namely drama and heroes. Further disclosures revealed that rigging had infected many of the popular quiz shows, including the infamous $64,000 *Question*, where Charles Revson (of Revlon Cosmetics) had determined the fate of contestants. The scandal, which originated in a minor NBC summer quiz show called *Dotto* in August 1958, and the uproar that followed led to congressional hearings and a Federal Communications Commission (FCC) probe. The networks sought to gain control of their schedules and to adopt Weaver's "magazine" concept. Indeed sponsorship gave way, in practice if not always in theory, when multiple advertisers began to buy spot time on hit shows.

Most commodities could be promoted on television, except for a restricted list enshrined in the Television Code (since 1952), notably liquor, birth control devices, and feminine-hygiene products, although such prohibitions would slowly pass in later decades. How these commodities might be advertised depended in part on the standards and practices departments of each network, censors who vetted storyboards or commercials before they were aired to ensure the absence of offensive material. At first the commercial was little more than radio with pictures, a talking head or two who acted as salesmen, extolling the virtues of the product, in 60 seconds, usually with a few props, and the product always prominent. The announcer employed a form of direct address; he—and with few exceptions it was a man—looked the viewer straight in the eye and spoke of "you" or "your" needs, all to establish a connection.

Many spots, especially in the early 1950s, were done live, by program personalities, which was supposed to enhance their appeal by capitalizing on the rapport already established with viewers. Live spots had their perils. In one infamous case in 1954, the door of a Westinghouse refrigerator stubbornly refused to yield to June Graham's tug until forced by an unseen assistant. Film enabled ad makers to edit out any mistakes. It also encouraged tricks. In 1961 the Canadian magazine *Marketing* reported how producers added ink to ketchup to make it look richer, shot a car from floor level to make it look longer, and used double-strength ingredients to ensure a pudding did not collapse under studio conditions. No trick could get around the limitations imposed by black-and-white telecasts; it was very difficult to convey the sensual qualities of nail polish without color. Nonetheless, TV advertising swiftly established itself as one of the most expensive and advanced forms of the audiovisual art. By 1960 it even boasted its own awards festival, the Clios, given to the best spots and campaigns of the year.

Commercials came in many different styles. There were testimonials (baseball stars Pee Wee Reese and Roy Campanella sold Gillette razors to teen fans in one 1955 ad), jingles ("Winston tastes good like a cigarette should," 1956), some sexual innuendo (Clairol's "Does she . . . or doesn't she?" 1957), cartoon

A 1959 print ad for Telesistema Mexicano emphasized the potential of television as an advertising medium in Mexico.

characters (Mr. Clean arrived in 1958), and so on. Some campaigns—the Anacin ads from Ted Bates & Company, for example—used a particularly irritating form of hard sell that hammered home the message with sharp sounds and much repetition. Yet, in retrospect, what characterized the overall message of the commercials, even those that used humor, was a tone of earnest enthusiasm. Ads often used the "reason-why" technique introduced by advertising pioneers John E. Kennedy and Albert Lasker to tell viewers how marvelous or unique a product was. Altogether, they conveyed the impression that Americans lived in a utopia of goods that could solve every conceivable problem of ordinary life. Irony was largely absent in this common chant of affluence. These styles and this tone were exported to other parts of the world, so that ads for Gibbs toothpaste in Britain (in 1955, purportedly the first British commercial), Anacin in Canada ("Silent Sufferer," 1963 winner of the first Bessie, an award modeled on the Clios), and Shiseido ads in Japan during the 1960s conformed to the common American mode of persuasion.

In a typical week in May 1957, according to *Variety* magazine, an American viewer might be cajoled by more than five hours of commercials. That barrage had an impact. A rueful Vance Packard lamented that his eight-year-old daughter was singing the jingle, "Don't Miss the Fun of Smoking!"—this while he was writing the chapter on television ads in his industry exposé *The Hidden Persuaders* (1957). Slogans such as "The cleanest clean under the sun" (Tide), "You'll wonder where the yellow went" (Pepsodent), and "How are you fixed for blades?" (Gillette) were ingrained in the memories of people of all ages. During the 1950s the demand for nationally branded foods and drinks exploded because of their exposure on television. Put another way, television advertising had taken over the main task of constructing the consumer, a desiring (and fearing) creature, always a bit dissatisfied, always in the marketplace, convinced that receiving pleasure and avoiding pain required the purchasing of goods.

There was a series of alarms over this apparent brainwashing of the American public. In the late 1950s a report by James Vicary, a champion of motivational research, claimed that he had been able to program people's buying behavior via the practice of "subliminal" advertising. The report led to prohibitions against hidden messages (i.e., not consciously noticed but nonetheless supposedly registered on the mind) in ads in the United States, Canada, and Britain. In 1962, Newton Minow, the newly appointed FCC chairman, blasted television as a "vast wasteland," partly because of the incessant advertising but also because of the kinds of programming that advertising sponsored. Yet one extensive survey, Gary Steiner's *The People Look at Television*, published in 1963, suggested that the mass audience accepted both this programming and its advertising. People might be irritated by the timing of commercial breaks and the content of the ads, but some found particular kinds of commercials very amusing—beer and wine commercials, in particular, were singled out. Many claimed that advertising did provide information, and fully three-quarters (of nearly 2,500 respondents) agreed that commercials were "a fair price to pay for the entertainment you get."

TV and the "Creative Revolution"

Television advertising was reinvented in the 1960s. That was the most important aspect of the "creative revolution," a brief, explosive moment when innovation and experimentation seemed to dominate New York City's Madison Avenue. The revolution amounted to a resurgence of the "carnivalesque," a spirit of fun and excess, a fascination with the erotic and the exotic, an emphasis upon indulgence, rebellion, and self-transformation, which had always been a part of the advertising tradition in the United States. In short, advertising became entertaining.

The upheaval was rooted in the general prosperity of the times, and in the resulting advertising boom, as business rushed to capture the affluent. The amounts spent on television in the United States more than doubled, from $1.5 billion in 1959 to $3.5 billion in 1969. By 1964 CBS, the ratings leader among the three networks, was asking $50,000 for a 60-second ad in prime time. The networks were soon ranked among the most profitable corporations in America. A similar situation prevailed overseas. In 1960, one of Britain's television program companies, Associated-Rediffusion, earned a pretax profit of £7.9 million, which amounted to more than 100 percent of issued share capital. By 1972 in Canada, roughly half the dollars spent on national advertising went to television stations.

Super profits did not necessarily mean enriched programming, rather the opposite. Independents working under contract now produced most network fare (71 percent in 1965) in the United States. Entertainment was designed to satisfy the mass taste, however artificial that might be. According to Paul Klein, a former director of NBC research, viewers (he wrote in 1971) searched through the channels to find the "least objectionable program." Shows that did not get the right demographics—that is attract those viewers who were thought to be big spenders—were doomed. In 1970 CBS dropped such popular favorites as *The Jackie Gleason Show, Petticoat Junction,* and *The Red Skelton Show* because they were reaching an audience too old and too rural for the tastes of advertisers. Cynicism aside, the commercial priority crafted a type of show, usually a filmed drama, that the ratings indicated was consistently popular. The American style of drama proved popular abroad and less expensive than home-grown shows, especially those fashioned to meet some ideal of public service. By 1965, for example, the major CTV stations in Canada's top markets were earning huge sums on ad revenue generated simply by showing American imports.

Prosperity was only one factor behind the revolution, however. Technology and economics changed the very look of television advertising. Color telecasts became commonplace in the mid-1960s; by the end of 1965, NBC's evening offerings were almost completely in color. Leading advertisers took to color even more quickly than consumers because black-and-white ads on color sets might appear tawdry. A bit later, the costs of television time encouraged a move toward the more-compact, 30-second format. That shift escalated in 1971; the networks had recently lost a lucrative revenue stream, when cigarette advertising (valued at roughly $150 million in business in 1970) was banned from television. They recovered by offering cheaper 30-second slots, although at more than half the cost of the regular 60-second spot. These changes worked against the principles of "reason-why" advertising: color heightened sensation, brevity fostered stereotype, and both favored an appeal to the emotions rather than the intellect.

By far the most important agent of reinvention was the arrival of new people in the ad business: Jewish copywriters, Italian art directors, young men attuned to the "youthquake" that rocked the cultural life of America, and even a few women. Their leader and their example was Bill Bernbach of Doyle Dane Bernbach (DDB), one of the few so-called Jewish agencies of the 1950s in a profession dominated by white Anglo-Saxon Protestant men. Bernbach preached a gospel of art; wit, humor, clever imagery, a bit of subversion were the effective techniques of persuasion. DDB's most famous campaign promoted the Volkswagen Beetle in a series of magazine and television ads that positioned the homely car as a cute, utilitarian, and very inexpensive alternative to Detroit's behemoths. The agency also won kudos for efforts on behalf of Avis (turning its number-two ranking behind Hertz into an advantage in the "We Try Harder" campaign) and Alka-Seltzer. Altogether DDB won 51 Clios (out of a possible 401) between 1963 and 1971. That total was surpassed by another agency noted for its creativity: Young & Rubicam (Y&R) under Stephen Frankfurt, which captured 56, including campaign awards for Goodyear Tires (1963, 1965), Union Carbide (1968), and Excedrin (1968). Overall, DDB increased its billings from $130 million in 1965 to almost $250 million five years later, while Y&R reached $356.4 million, making it the second-ranked agency in the United States.

In fact, creativity had become a watchword throughout the advertising industry. The Leo Burnett Company, Chicago, masterminded the "Marlboro Country" campaign that featured rugged, modern cowboys living the free life in the wide-open spaces of a mythical West. Sales of the cigarette doubled between 1965 and 1970, up to 51.4 billion units, making it number three in the land, just before television advertising of cigarettes was cut off. BBDO launched the "Pepsi Generation" campaign, which positioned Pepsi-Cola as the drink of youth—or at least the young at heart—an excellent example of what would later be called a psychographic approach to persuasion. On behalf of Coca-Cola McCann-Erickson retaliated with "It's the Real Thing" late in 1969, out of which came one of the most famous spots of all time, "Buy the World a Coke" or "Hilltop," in which a group of clean-cut youngsters of many cultures (actually embassy children stationed in Rome, Italy) mouthed the words to the song "I'd Like to Teach the World to Sing." People phoned television stations requesting more airtime for the spot, and their passion turned a slightly altered version of the song into a major hit. The twin campaigns set off the never-ending "cola wars" that boosted sales of both Pepsi and Coke at the expense of other brands of soft drinks.

Meanwhile, the reinvention of advertising had spread beyond the boundaries of the United States. In Canada, Jerry Goodis of Goodis Goldberg Soren, also a "Jewish" agency, won fame and fortune by replicating the style of Bernbach and others during the 1960s. A bit later Charles and Maurice Saatchi, the sons of an Iraqi Jewish businessman and thus also outsiders, played a similar role in the United Kingdom. During the 1970s, though, world advertising broke away from its dependence upon the American lead; in country after country, ad makers fashioned appeals that suited their particular milieu. Goodis himself became one of the founders of a distinctly Canadian style that employed a soft sell to tout everything from shoes to mufflers to insurance: mild humor, sometimes wit or satire, gentle music, pastel colors, a pleasant manner. Japanese ad makers developed a flair for visual extravaganza. In France ad makers explored the surreal look. The British shaped their own creative breakthrough, particularly in the realm of humorous ads. One of the most famous was the "Refreshes" campaign for Heineken beer (handled by Lowe Howard-Spink), begun in the mid-1970s, which spoofed classics of literature, such as *Frankenstein*, and television icons, such as *Star Trek*.

Ironically, the emphasis upon creativity was on the wane in the United States. Perhaps the sharp recession of the early 1970s and the emergence of "stagflation" undermined advertisers' eagerness to finance artsy campaigns. Keynote speakers at the annual Clio dinners lectured the ad makers on the need to emphasize commerce over art. In 1976 *Newsweek* suggested the trend was "toward an older, simpler style," citing the infamous Charmin campaign featuring grocer George Whipple furtively squeezing a role of toilet paper. Some advertisers returned to the hard sell. Pepsi-Cola employed a product-oriented approach in its "Pepsi Challenge," commencing in the mid-1970s, where consumers showed they preferred the taste of Pepsi to that of Coke. The sentimental or heart-warming commercial found new favor; Coca-Cola won notice for its "'Mean' Joe Greene" advertisement (1979) in which a rugged black football star shared a moment of affection (and a big Coke) with a white kid, a devout fan. A survey of the creative community in the early 1980s found a widespread sense of malaise: "I'd say right now we're rife with mediocrity," complained Martin Puris of Ammirati & Puris.

No such depression afflicted the network executives. It was still a seller's market, since the networks controlled the lion's share of the television audience (roughly 90 percent of that audience in the evenings). The normal brands of entertainment were situation comedies and crime dramas, both of which used jolts—of humor or violence—to stimulate a general audience. After all, an extra rating point for a network could translate into earnings of $75 million. The cost of a 60-second spot on an evening hit program had risen to $200,000 by the end of the 1970s. One estimate had network profits growing from $1 billion to $3 billion during the decade. The 1970s would prove the last decade of such clear-cut network hegemony financed by lush advertising revenues.

The Expanding Empire of Advertising

After 1980 the status quo in the United States and elsewhere was transformed by the rapid expansion of television advertising into new territories and new domains. First came the arrival of new private networks. Canadian authorities had licensed a third English-language service, grandly called Global Communications, in the richest province, Ontario, in 1972. Italy had broken away from the tradition of public broadcasting dramatically in the mid-1970s. Most important, however, was the wave of privatization in France after 1984, especially the appearance of new commercial channels, which set off an explosion in television advertising (up 77 percent in the 1980s) and forecast a change throughout Western Europe. Germany, Spain, Denmark, Greece, and Portugal all adopted commercial television in the 1980s. In the United States, the Public Broadcasting System (PBS) accepted more and more corporate monies to finance programming, sometimes defended as an extension of corporate support for the arts; but in fact that practice marked the commercialization of the service, as corporations sought to win the hearts and minds of the upscale audience that typically viewed PBS. Norway and Sweden moved to adopt commercial TV in the next decade, by which time Eastern Europe and Russia had also licensed commercial services. In Hungary, in 1992, the commercials that would be shown during the TV day were actually listed in the newspaper program schedule alongside the names of the programs themselves.

The new channels offered not only more choice but what seemed to be innovative programming, from sports to imported American shows to homegrown mysteries and drama. The contrast between commercial and noncommercial broadcasting was especially clear in countries such as Spain, where an often-dull public television had once reigned supreme. Even in the United States a change was evident; to attract the younger viewers so highly valued by advertisers, the Fox network, which had debuted late in 1986 and gradually expanded to a prime-time schedule, featured edgy—some said tasteless—youth-oriented shows such as *The Simpsons* and *Married . . . with Children*.

The second shock was the parallel expansion of cable and satellite broadcasting. Cable had spread very rapidly in Canada after the late 1960s to ensure better reception and more choice—and, in particular, more U.S. broadcasts—which cut into the market shares of existing networks. By the end of the 1980s the onslaught of cable and satellite channels such as HBO, Showtime, and ESPN had reduced the U.S. networks' share of the audience to around 70 percent; it would continue to drop in the 1990s. Of course, many of the new cable channels of the 1980s in North America were funded through viewer subscriptions, meaning that they competed for viewers but not ad dollars. CNN (also launched in 1980) was ad-supported, however, and this all-news network became a major force with its massive coverage of the Gulf War in 1991. In Europe, a series of new satellite services such as Eurosport and Sky aired commercials, usually in English, to Western European audiences. The next decade saw a move to similar kinds of satellite services into Asia. By 2000 the cable networks in the United States had captured nearly $11 billion of advertising revenue, compared to a little less than $16 billion for the four television networks.

In a different vein was the arrival of new modes of selling on television. The enormously successful MTV (launched in 1980) displayed a succession of music videos, which employed the styles

ON TELEVISION
Thursday, July 7th*

General
EISENHOWER'S
"CRUSADE in
EUROPE"

Chapter No. 10
"Rise and Fall
of a Dictator"

March on Rome . . . Duce in his glory . . . His empire extended . . . France stabbed . . . Debacle in Greece . . . Fascism bursts . . . Nazis rescue Duce . . . Dead Duce mobbed . . . Allies victorious.

Showing on ABC network
in the following cities . . .

ATLANTA	MIAMI
BALTIMORE	MILWAUKEE
BOSTON	MINNEAPOLIS
BUFFALO	NEW HAVEN
CHICAGO	NEW ORLEANS
CINCINNATI	NEW YORK
CLEVELAND	PHILADELPHIA
COLUMBUS	PITTSBURGH
DAYTON	RICHMOND
DETROIT	ST. LOUIS
ERIE	SALT LAKE CITY
FORT WORTH	SAN FRANCISCO
HOUSTON	SCHENECTADY
LOS ANGELES	SEATTLE
LOUISVILLE	SYRACUSE
MEMPHIS	TOLEDO
WASHINGTON	

*On different evenings in some cities.
See your newspaper for evening and time.

LIFE & TIME
The Weekly Newsmagazine
TELEVISION PRESENTATION

Much of the programming in the early years of television consisted of documentary newsreels similar to those shown in movie houses. A 1949 print ad informed viewers of an upcoming episode in a series on General Dwight D. Eisenhower's World War II military campaigns.

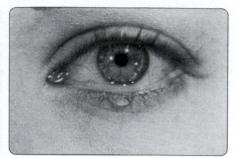

WOMAN: Flavor?
MAN: Just like fresh.
WOMAN: Durkees Instant Minced Onion?
MAN: No work.
WOMAN: Durkees Instant Onion.

MAN: No tears.
WOMAN: Durkees Instant Minced Onion. What'll they think of next?

[MUSIC]
MAN: If you don't see it in the store, ask your grocer.

This television spot for Tone Brothers' Durkee's Instant Minced Onion won the first Clio Award in 1960.

and the imagery of television commercials. Such exposure contributed much to the sudden rise of singer Michael Jackson to superstardom with his *Thriller* album. MTV and its imitators everywhere became one of the major engines of record sales in the popular music field. The United States' annual Super Bowl broadcast emerged as a special showcase for commercials, particularly after the success of Apple's "1984" commercial (in 1984), which resulted in skyrocketing sales of the new Macintosh computer. Advertisers were willing to pay top dollar to reach what was one of the largest audiences that television assembled each year.

Then there were the video news releases, or VNRs, noticeable toward the end of the 1980s, first in the United States. The VNR marked a return to the sponsored program, except the sponsor was not mentioned. It usually constituted a brief feature on some issue of general concern that pushed the agenda of a particular company or group. The feature was then sent, often via satellite, to TV stations across the country to fill their news slots. The result was free publicity for the company and free programming for the station. One variant was product placement, or plugs, where advertisers supplied money, goods, or services in exchange for favorable notice in an entertainment program. Health Canada, a government agency, actually worked with producers to embed the messages of good living in one episode of a popular homegrown drama.

But the most intriguing hybrid of advertising and programming was the infomercial, usually a half-hour-long, syndicated program that employed the style of the talk or interview show. In fact, the program was put together solely to sell a product. Individual stations scheduled these in the late evening time slot; they received a couple of thousand dollars, which was usually more profitable than running an old movie and trying to sell ad time. By 1992 infomercials had proven their value, generating an estimated $750 million in sales, and spreading well beyond North America, even into Eastern Europe.

Perhaps the most startling development was the use of television advertising to spread democratic ideals across the globe. Public service ads of all kinds—and in Canada often funded by the regional governments—promoted the virtues of healthy living, increased productivity, and tolerance, trying always to make good citizens. The television ad became an increasingly important component in American election campaigns, particularly after 1964. DDB's infamous "Daisy" ad for the Democratic Party featured the apparent obliteration of a cute little girl by a nuclear explosion, leaving the impression this was the world's fate if the bellicose Republican Barry Goldwater was elected. The ad caused a wave of excitement among viewers and demonstrated the potential of advertising to shock.

It was not until after the mid-1970s, however, that governments, nonprofits, and, eventually, political parties around the world began to employ TV advertising consistently as the most-common form of ordinary propaganda. Such ads constituted a major weapon in the battle the Canadian and Quebec governments waged around 1980 over the issue of Quebec's sovereignty. Soon the campaigns against smoking, drugs, drinking and driving, and, especially, AIDS inspired a host of television spots across the globe. Many of these commercials employed scare tactics, trying to inspire sufficient fear or revulsion to make the public change its attitudes or behavior. During the 1990s, the U.S. style of election advertising also spread into Western Europe and Israel.

In the United States, political ads became increasingly negative after the furious 1988 contest between George Bush and Michael Dukakis and the "Willie Horton" spot in which Dukakis's criminal rehabilitation policies were blamed for a murder committed by a Massachusetts prisoner while on furlough. The political spots were joined by an assortment of advocacy ads, once banned by the networks but now welcomed as a source of new dollars and allowed because the FCC had ceased to apply the Fairness Doctrine to telecasts. The "Harry & Louise" campaign of 1993–1994 was credited with undermining media, and eventually public, support for President Bill Clinton's health care initiative. However effective, the general use of the attack ad demobilized large numbers of people who came to regard politics as fundamentally dirty.

Less than half of the American electorate voted in the 1996 presidential contest, only slightly more (51 percent) in 2000.

Humor, Shock, and Titillation

The expansion of television advertising exacerbated the problem of clutter, especially after 1982, when the Television Code was eliminated and the 15-second commercial introduced. At the beginning of the 1990s, the four American television networks purportedly aired more than 6,000 commercials a week. The public's ability to recall ads just viewed fell from 18 percent in 1965 to 4 percent in 1990. While the problem of saturation was not so obvious outside the United States, the habit, common in Western Europe, of clustering many spots, often more than a dozen, in one lengthy segment had a similar effect. In 1991 Winston Fletcher, an English advertising man, claimed that the "average" Briton watched between two and a half and three hours of commercials a week.

Ad makers met the challenge of clutter by using celebrities, popular music, humor, and sex, often spiced with special effects, to jolt the audience. Hit tunes from earlier years were revived in ads: Levi's used American rock-and-roll classics to sell its 501 jeans in Britain and Europe during the 1980s and early 1990s. The 1983 launch of Pepsi's "New Generation" campaign, designed by BBDO, featured the rising superstar Michael Jackson, at a cost of $5.5 million. It was an event in its own right. Stars from the worlds of sports and entertainment became commonplace in television ads. This trend was evident overseas as well—the Hollywood action hero Arnold Schwarzenegger appeared in ads in Japan. In the 1990s movie stars and sports figures were joined by the occasional retired politician, perhaps the most notable example being presidential candidate Bob Dole's role as pitchman for the drug Viagra.

Humor and irony gained favor among national advertisers because they entertained viewers. Using a spokesman who told obvious lies about the performance of its cars, for example, won Isuzu loads of publicity in a U.S. campaign of the late 1980s. More than others, however, the British ad makers excelled at the comedy of manners, character, and ideas to sell goods ranging from Volkswagens to Hamlet Cigars, the Barclay Card to Creda appliances, and Radio Rentals to British Caledonia (an airline). Their approach capitalized on a British taste for wit and satire, a desire to see the promotion masked by humor.

Ad makers also adopted bizarre or surreal imagery—mock violence, references to bodily functions once deemed vulgar, and ugly and occasionally frightening sights—to overcome indifference. In the mid-1990s, for example, Superga ran a famous ad in Italy entitled "The Challenge," which showed graphic scenes of an animal rights demonstration, complete with tear gas and beatings, to sell its shoes. But the most startling kinds of imagery during the decade of the 1990s were sexual. First in Europe, but also in America and Asia by the 1990s, the sexual sell was used to promote not only jeans and perfumes but also potato chips, diet drinks, telephone service, just about anything. Diesel Jeans made a name for itself throughout the decade with its "For Successful Living" campaign, which flirted with all manner of so-called perversions. In Australia, Hot Bods employed sadomasochistic imagery—of bondage, torture, and dominance—in twin 1997 ads touting its underwear. In France a spot aired in 2000 focused on a beautiful and elegant woman who, watched closely by some handsome men, ripped open her dress, thus to free her legs so that she could slither through the back of her Alfa Romeo Sportwagon into the front seat. Here was advertising as erotica.

At times the results were confounding. A 1991 British survey found that English youngsters preferred beer commercials to ads for toys. In the United States, Calvin Klein's "August Campaign" (1995) for a line of jeans shocked sensibilities with images that suggested the sexual exploitation of young teenagers, hardly likely to please many consumers. For advertisers, however, the successful marketing via television of such diverse products as Budweiser beer, Diet Pepsi, Nike footwear, Ikea furniture, Chanel perfume, and the Jeep Cherokee made the risk of offending the audience with startling or sexual or bizarre images worthwhile.

A Curious Communication

The television commercial is a peculiar type of communicative device—neither entirely truthful nor entirely false. It breaks down the distinction between fact and fiction, news and entertainment, image and substance. At times, to employ the typology of Jean Baudrillard, the French theorist of postmodernity, it "masks and denatures a profound reality" about the advertiser, the use of the product, the consequences of ownership. At others, it bears "no relation to any reality whatsoever; it is its own pure simulacrum"—the fantasy is complete, all is simulation. Yet television advertising has become the most compelling discourse about objects, about private and public goods, present in the affluent world. Which is why the commercial was and is so important as both a symptom and an agent of that postmodern moment of unending images that dominated the culture in the opening years of the 21st century.

PAUL RUTHERFORD

See also MTV, Influence of

Further Reading

Ansolabehere, Stephen, and Shanto Iyengar, *Going Negative: How Attack Ads Shrink and Polarize the Electorate*, New York: Free Press, 1995

Arlen, Michael, *Thirty Seconds*, New York: Farrar Straus and Giroux, 1980; London: Penguin, 1984

Barnouw, Erik, *The Sponsor: Notes on a Modern Potentate*, New York: Oxford University Press, 1978

Baudrillard, Jean, *Simulacres et simulation*, Paris: Galilée, 1981; as *Simulacra and Simulation*, translated by Sheila Faria Glaser, Ann Arbor: University of Michigan Press, 1994

Bogart, Leo, *Commercial Culture: The Media System and the Public Interest*, New York: Oxford University Press, 1995

Diamant, Lincoln, *Television's Classic Commercials: The Golden Years, 1948–1958*, New York: Hastings House, 1971

Diamond, Edwin, and Stephen Bates, *The Spot: The Rise of Political Advertising on Television*, Cambridge, Massachusetts: MIT Press, 1984; 3rd edition, 1992

Frank, Thomas, *The Conquest of Cool: Business Culture, Counterculture, and the Rise of Hip Consumerism*, Chicago: University of Chicago Press, 1997

Kurtz, Bruce, *Spots: The Popular Art of American Television Commercials*, New York: Arts Communications, 1977

Mattelart, Armand, *L'internationale publicitaire*, Paris: La Découverte, 1989; as *Advertising International: The Privatisation of Public Space*, translated by Michael Chanan, London and New York: Routledge, 1991

Paletz, David, Roberta Pearson, and Donald Willis, *Politics in Public Service Advertising on Television*, New York: Praeger, 1977

Poster, Mark, "Baudrillard and TV Ads: The Language of the Economy," in *The Mode of Information: Poststructuralism and Social Context*, by Poster, Chicago: University of Chicago Press, and Cambridge: Polity, 1990

Pratkanis, Anthony, and Elliot Aronson, *Age of Propaganda: The Everyday Use and Abuse of Persuasion*, New York: Freeman, 1992; revised edition, 1997

Riordan, Steve, editor, *Clio Awards: A Tribute to 30 Years of Advertising Excellence, 1960–1989*, Glen Cove, New York: PBC International, 1989

Rutherford, Paul, *The New Icons? The Art of Television Advertising*, Toronto, Ontario, and Buffalo, New York: University of Toronto Press, 1994

Rutherford, Paul, *Endless Propaganda: The Selling of Public Goods*, Toronto: University of Toronto Press, 2000

Television, Representations of Advertising in. *See* Motion Pictures, Television, and Literature, Representations of Advertising in

Armando Testa

Established in Turin, Italy, by Armando Testa, 1946; gave rise ten years later to Studio Testa, founded by Testa along with his wife, Lidia, and associate Franco de Barberis; became joint-stock company under the firm Armando Testa S.P.A., 1978; became Italy's largest advertising agency by the late 1980s.

Major Clients
Barilla
Benckiser
Esselunga
Lavazza
Lines
Nestlé
Telecom Italia

The Armando Testa agency actually has many dates of genesis. The agency's roots date to 1937, when Testa won his first competition with a poster for ICI, a company that manufactured printing inks and paints. Abandoning his work as a printer, Testa began to dedicate himself to graphic art in 1946. Working in

Turin, Italy, he began to create labels, logos, packaging, brochures, covers, and posters. Although he began working for small clients, he later gained accounts for larger, more well-known firms such as Martini and Rossi, Carpano (liqueur), and Borsalino (hats).

In the 1950s Testa found himself confronting a new concept in advertising: marketing. On a creative level he faced the challenge of two revolutionary new communication tools, television and color photography. In 1956, together with his wife, Lidia, and an associate, Franco de Barberis, he founded Studio Testa as a full-service advertising agency providing its clients with specific marketing strategies, media planning, and research, as well as creative functions.

In 1959 Testa visited the United States for the first time, acquainting himself with the U.S. advertising industry and the U.S. art world. The 1960s were boom years for the agency, as several of its clients—Carpano, Lavazza (coffee), Olio Sasso (oil), and Simmenthal (canned meats)—became market leaders.

Television advertising first began to gain a strong foothold in Italy around this time. *Carosello*, launched in 1957, was a nightly block of advertising that featured a variety of live and animated characters promoting products in comic sketches and short films. The format combined entertainment with advertising and became a true social phenomenon. Many commercials from these early television years still evoke fond memories for Italians, from Caballero and Carmencita (cartoon characters appearing in *Carosello* and created in 1964 by Armando Testa to promote Lavazza's Paulista, the first Italian coffee distributed nationally) to Punt e Mes; from Pippo to "your tummy's gone"; from the blonde Peroni to the Antonetto digestive tablets and to Papalla.

Testa's creativity stood out in the Italian market. The agency's originality also attracted American giants such as Procter & Gamble Company and S.C. Johnson & Sons, Inc., companies that realized how much more effective a detailed, precise marketing approach could be when it was supported by a decidedly unconventional creative approach.

In the 1970s an indisputably more rational kind of advertising came to the forefront in Italy. The *Carosello* advertising format was replaced by shorter, faster-paced, message-intensive advertising spots. In this new context the Testa agency reinvented itself, although humor and warmth remained its trademarks. It was in this atmosphere that the Lavazza campaign with Nino Manfredi was developed; first appearing in 1977, it would become one of the longest-running and most successful Italian campaigns. With Alitalia, the Italian airline, the agency acquired its first major corporate account. In November 1978 Testa became a joint-stock company.

The 1980s were years of great expansion and marked another turning point for the company. With an ever-expanding roster of clients, the agency began to expand its operations throughout Italy, opening a branch in Rome in 1980, followed by another in Milan in 1992. Dynamic creativity and bold experimentation were at their peak. At the Cannes (France) International Advertising Festival, the Testa agency won its first Lion awards, for its Lavazza, Sole Bianco detergent, and Bistefani biscuit campaigns.

In 1985 Testa's son Marco took over the leadership of the agency. Along with traditional product campaigns, the first integrated communication campaign was launched—promoting sugar—as well as corporate campaigns, such as that for Ferruzzi. Unconventional language and unknown territories, such as the area of fashion advertising, were explored. The consulting relationship with Gianfranco Ferrè dates to these years. Under Marco Testa, the agency became a creative powerhouse. Highly original campaigns such as those for BMW and Elah toffee candies were produced. These years saw other leading multinational corporations—among them Benckiser, H.J. Heinz Company, and Nestlé—bringing their accounts to the agency. By 1989 it had become the market leader.

In the meantime, the agency had become Gruppo Testa, formed by a merger of three independent companies: Arte Film, Media Italia, and In Testa. Arte Film had been founded by Armando Testa in 1961 as an experimental film production boutique. Media Italia had been launched as the country's first media buying firm in 1982 under the chairmanship of Eugenio Bona, Testa's son-in-law. In 1993 it integrated its services, becoming a full-service media agency particularly active in the field of media

Among Armando Testa's best-remembered works was this 1994 campaign for Telecom Italia featuring the Italian actor Massimo Lopez. *Courtesy of Telecom Italia.*

research. The originator of a set of exclusive media analysis tools, it was invited in 1995 by the American Research Foundation to present an original study on the TV audience in New York City. In Testa, established in 1989 by Antonella Testa,

Testa's daughter, was a specialized agency that focused on the corporate image of its clients, as well as the design and packaging of their products.

After a life devoted to his agency, Testa occupied himself in the years following his retirement in 1985 with painting and the design of posters and other publicity pieces for cultural and social organizations such as Amnesty International; the Red Cross; the Festival of the Two Worlds at Spoleto, Italy; the Royal Theatre in Turin; and the Car Museum of Turin. In 1985 Testa was appointed an honor laureate during the sixth International Poster Biennial in Fort Collins, Colorado. He died in 1992 just prior to his 75th birthday.

Marco Testa and his associates reacted to the loss of the agency's founder by committing themselves to continued growth, assuring constant creative innovation, and expanding the agency into the rest of Europe. In 1999 the company had operations in Brussels, Belgium; Frankfurt, Germany; London, England; Paris, France; and Madrid, Spain.

The agency retained its characteristic humor, the roots of which may be traced to the comedy of *Carosello,* while utilizing state-of-the-art technology and special effects to produce remarkable, eye-catching brand images. Memorable campaigns included the creative serial for Telecom with the well-known actor Massimo Lopez as the prisoner sentenced to death (winner of Testa's first Cannes gold Lion award); the Parmacotto ham campaign with actor Christian De Sica as a delicatessen owner; and the ad campaign for Sisal lotteries, in which Nancy Brilli portrayed Lady Luck. Of particular note is the Lavazza coffee ad campaign with actor Tullio Solenghi in heaven, which started in 1995; the campaign featured the slogan, "Only when it's good, coffee goes to heaven." The campaign conveyed feelings of warmth and closeness to consumers, emotions that Lavazza traditionally sought to attach to its brand.

The Lancia campaigns introduced sophisticated special effects to Italy for the first time. Commercials for the Mulino Bianco line of pasta utilized symbolic natural imagery, while noted film director Wim Wenders animated works of art in the Ariston campaign. Testa took on the Mulino Bianco line of baked goods for Barilla in 1990, creating three different campaigns.

In outdoor advertising as well, the agency maintained the standards of creativity of its early days. The Esselunga supermarkets campaign, in particular, featured creative work worthy of Armando Testa himself. This campaign boasted exhibition space in the Louvre Museum in Paris.

The agency continued to broaden its field of operations, tackling new ventures and sectors. Its campaigns for Mediaset (commercial television) and Sanpaolo bank attracted hundreds of thousands of investors. Testa International has begun exporting campaigns throughout Europe. A Gatorade campaign featuring a lion and gazelle on the African savannah (in an attempt to evoke a healthy, pure life) impressed top U.S. management of the Quaker Oats Company, which owned the brand.

By the 1990s Gruppo Testa was in a position to act in a wide range of communications activities, offering integrated services from advertising to sales promotion, from TV sponsorship to audiovisual production, and from design to packaging. In 2000, with Marco Testa as chairman–chief executive officer, the agency had gross income of $67 million on billings of $732 million, up 19.1 percent from 1999.

EDOARDO T. BRIOSCHI

Testing Methods

Each year testing is conducted on tens of thousands of advertisements at an estimated cost of $125 million. The importance of testing has long been recognized. In 1879 N.W. Ayer & Son used ad testing to land a major account. By 1920 ad testing had become one of the standard services offered by advertising agencies and researchers.

Testing can delay a campaign's launch by weeks or months. It can also be expensive, but it is easily justified by the need to make the most of media time and ad production costs. In the development and planning stages, advertising research can help in deciding the type of appeal to use. Pretest results (e.g., physiological or persuasion tests) focus advertisers on the appropriate issues, giving ads better chances of success. After a campaign, posttesting (e.g., recognition, recall, or behavioral measures) can determine the reasons for success or failure, which may help in creating the next campaign.

In times of great competition for consumers, marketers rely more heavily on ad testing. During the Great Depression, for example, U.S. and Canadian manufacturers, advertising agencies, and advertising research firms developed new testing methods and expanded existing techniques. Canadian Facts Registered, Canada's first advertising research firm, was formed in response to a request by advertising agency executives in 1933. In Britain and Western Europe, ad testing would not become common until the 1950s. In the increasingly competitive media environment of the late 1990s, testing became important in creating effective advertising worldwide.

The earliest testing methods were behavioral measures. The ad agency Lord & Thomas began an ongoing testing operation in the United States in 1900. It requested that its clients provide mail-order and sales-fluctuation records for all advertised products. By 1906 its Record of Results Department was analyzing data from more than 600 clients for ads appearing in more than 4,000 magazines and newspapers.

Sales response continues to be an important test of ad effectiveness. In 1933 A.C. Nielsen Company (later ACNielsen Corporation) began to audit product sales in food and drugstores, providing the first widely available measure of share of sales. Packaged-goods manufacturers subscribing to this service were able to analyze sales response versus the geographical coverage of the media vehicles in which their ads appeared. Later store audits used scanner data to record sales. By 2002, ACNielsen's Scantrack was auditing the sales of more than 4,800 stores. Subscribers could monitor sales trends and evaluate the effect of price and promotion changes by looking at fluctuations in sales.

Panel data combine television viewing and purchase behavior. For example, ScanAmercia, a joint venture of Control Data's Arbitron Ratings Company and Selling Areas-Marketing, Inc. (SAMI), began collecting panel data in Denver in 1985. Participants record purchases at home by passing a penlike wand over bar codes. The information is transmitted daily through Arbitron's people meter device attached to the participants' television sets; telephone lines carry people meter data to Arbitron's electronic data centers for compilation and analysis.

With split viewing, households in a community are divided into equivalent demographic groups, their purchase behavior is monitored, and test ads are inserted into the television or cable signal of only a subset of households. Split viewing has been found to produce reliable and valid results because advertising is the only manipulated variable and the tests have external validity: rather than artificial laboratory responses, the tests involve actual commercial viewing and product purchase decisions of a sample of households representative of the general population. The method requires at least six months and is very costly ($200,000 to $300,000 per test). Scanner and panel data are less expensive because the subscribers share costs. Information Resources, Inc. (IRI), and ACNielsen have services that combine split viewing and scanner data. IRI monitors television viewing in more than 3,000 households and can test commercials over cable systems. Before household supermarket purchases, an identification card is swiped, and all sales data are sent to IRI. ACNielsen's system has the advantage of testing on-air commercials; thus, its sample is not skewed toward higher-income cable subscribers.

In the 1920s the primary ad testing method was ad inquiry testing, using coupons that were incorporated into advertisements. The coupons could be cut out and returned for product samples, information booklets, or special premiums. Coupons were keyed by the post-office box or room number to which they were addressed. To let the advertiser know which magazines or newspapers produced which responses, researchers tabulated the returned coupons to evaluate the effectiveness of the ad. This allowed comparisons of identical ads in different magazines or newspapers and comparisons of ads with different copy or art work in the same vehicle. While the ad inquiry method provides a rough indication of effectiveness and continues to be used, questions have been raised about whether those who return coupons are representative of a publication's readers and whether coupon returns are related to sales. Research has found that not everyone is equally likely to redeem coupons, although they may still buy the advertised brand, and those who do redeem coupons are more likely to switch brands when a competitor offers a coupon.

Recognition and Recall

Recognition tests show an advertisement to people and ask if they remember having seen it. Recognition measures memory traces left under typical low-involvement processing. Recognition tests produce results somewhat similar to other measures of advertising effectiveness (e.g., ad inquiries). Problems include the expense of individual interviews and the yea-saying bias, in which people report seeing ads they did not see.

A well-known print-ad recognition test was developed by pioneering advertising researcher Daniel Starch in 1922, and it has been used by his organization, Starch Continuing Readership Research Program, since February 1932 in the United States and since 1949 in Canada. In 2002 its successor, Roper Starch Worldwide, continued to gather data on approximately 30,000 advertisements in almost 1,000 consumer and farm magazines, business publications, and newspapers by personally interviewing subjects who have previously read any part of the latest issue. In the subject's home, the interviewer goes through the issue page by page, asking the subject about each advertisement being studied. To determine whether the subject noted the ad while reading, the interviewer asks, "Did you see any part of this advertisement?" If the answer is yes, the subject is asked to indicate which parts of the ad were processed. For each ad, three scores are calculated: (1) noted (the percentage of readers who recognize the advertisement as one they previously saw in that magazine issue), which measures an ad's attention-getting ability; (2) associated (the percentage of readers who saw or read any part of the advertisement that clearly indicated the brand advertised), which indicates the level of brand processing; and (3) read most (the percentage of readers who read half or more of the ad's written material), which indicates reader involvement.

In the 1960s Starch demonstrated the external validity of "read most" scores by showing strong correlations with eye-tracking data (described below). Starch scores have been found to correlate with brand attitude and purchase probability. Also, Roper Starch Worldwide has examined ads nominated by the Magazine Publishers of America for Kelly Awards and found higher-than-average Starch scores for all the Kelly nominees.

Academic research has identified several variables that influence one or more of the Starch scores. Recognition scores are influenced by the periodical's thickness, the ad's position in the periodical, ad color, ad size, ad shape, product category advertised, ad layout, the type of visual, the appearance of attractive models or celebrities, humor, premiums or special offers, headline font, type of headline, puffery, appeals in the copy, and copy length.

Despite the expense of personal interviews, the cost of Starch's recognition test (as well as similar tests, such as Chilton Research Service's Ad-Chart and Readex, Inc.'s Readex, the latter a mail survey method developed by ad agency owner Bob Pendergrast, who went on to found Readex, Inc., in 1947) is kept down by syndicating results to many corporate and advertising agency subscribers. Often, publishers pay for their periodicals to be studied, while subscribers receive periodicals with their ads' scores and scores for all other ads. Subscribers may also purchase specialized questions about the sales points, impact, message believability and acceptance, behavioral intentions, and associated attitude changes of particular ads. Starch also provides similar syndicated recognition tests of outdoor advertising.

The Bruzzone Research Company conducts a television-commercial recognition test. Mall shoppers complete questionnaires with scripts showing scenes from commercials minus the brand names. If they remember having seen a commercial before, they are asked to identify the brand and to rate the commercial on likability and relevance to their needs. Bruzzone tests share many of Starch's advantages: reliable scores, relatively low cost (about $1,500 per commercial), and norms to help interpret scores.

The TLK (Tatham-Laird & Kudner) Picture Sort task has been used to study the effectiveness of specific portions of commercials by asking consumers if they recognize photographs of different frames (e.g., the opening and closing shots) 15 to 20 minutes after viewing. It found strong relationships between the nature of opening and closing shots and brand linkages in the other shots to overall effectiveness.

Unlike Roper Starch, which focuses on the extent to which an ad is noticed, the other most commonly used ad posttesting service, Gallup & Robinson, measures recall. When Raymond Rubicam asked George Gallup to set up a copy research department for Young & Rubicam in 1932, his staff also used recognition measures. But during the late 1930s and early 1940s, Gallup switched to recall measures. Recall requires mental reproduction of the ad, while recognition is awareness of having previously seen it. Recall tests can be expensive (e.g., $9,000 to $17,000 per commercial and $7,000 to $13,000 per print ad). Recall measures advertising message penetration and the correctness of the impressions communicated. However, studies have repeatedly failed to link recall with measures of persuasion or sales.

Day-after-recall (DAR) is a measure of the percentage of the people who recall something specific about the ad (e.g., sales message or a visual) the day following exposure. DAR was developed by George Gallup in the early 1940s. Gallup & Robinson Magazine Impact Research Service measures the depth of impression (i.e., DAR, main copy points recall, and intention to buy or learn about the brand) left by magazine advertisements. ASI Print Plus, using a method similar to its pretesting service, also conducts DAR posttests of print ads, with the distinct feature of a pre-exposure brand attitude measure.

In a television-commercial DAR test, the Burke Day-After-Recall Test, the evening after a commercial appears on a prime-time network program, interviewers make thousands of random phone calls until they have contacted about 200 people who were watching the program when the commercial appeared. Interviewers ask the subjects if they remember any commercials for the product category in question (i.e., unaided recall). If they remem-

ber the category but do not identify the brand in question, the interviewers ask if they remember seeing a commercial for that brand (i.e., aided recall). They are then asked what the commercial said about the brand, what it showed, what it looked like, and what the main ideas were. DAR is an on-air test of commercial exposure in a natural, realistic in-home setting. DAR usually ranges from 0 to 70 percent with an average of 20 percent.

DAR tests have also been developed for radio commercials. Shoppers at a mall are asked to complete a questionnaire. They perform the task in a room with a radio playing in the background. The next day, they are telephoned and asked to recall radio commercials they heard while completing their questionnaires.

An aided-recall measure that taps general audience awareness of commercials currently running, rather than the recall of a sample known to have been exposed to the commercial, is in use in South Africa. In 1984 Impact Information, Ltd. (PTY), began conducting weekly measures of the aided recall of television commercials a few weeks after they first aired, using random samples of 200 people.

Physiological Measures

Physiological pretest measures record consumers' physical reactions to ad messages. One primary benefit of these measures is their ongoing record of responses to determine which components of an ad attract attention. This information is used to insert important message points at these attention-attracting times or to change components that fail to attract attention. Since the reactions are involuntary, they are unlikely to be biased by subjects attempting to behave or answer in socially acceptable ways. Third, since most actual ad processing is under conditions of low involvement, researchers use physiological measures to determine consumer response without requiring their mental effort. One disadvantage is that physiological measures can neither determine if a response was positive or negative nor if the consumer learned any brand information. Another disadvantage is the unnatural environment of ad exposure; many tests involve the attachment of instruments to subjects in a laboratory. This requirement reduces the sample's representativeness, as many consumers will not agree to participate in such tests.

Eye-tracking systems can be used to monitor eye movements across commercials or print ads. This is done either with a beam of infrared light that reflects off the subject's eye or with goggles connected to a computer that records the wearer's eye movements, pupil dilation, and the amount of time spent viewing different parts of an ad. Eye cameras have also been used to photograph subjects' eye movements while they read an ad or watch a commercial. The resulting data indicate whether a subject is processing the elements of the ad in the order the advertiser intended. The data can be misleading, however, as a subject's eye may linger because of comprehension difficulty, on the one hand, or rapt attention, on the other.

Galvanic skin response (GSR) is a tool that was in vogue during the 1940s and 1950s. GSR measures minute changes in per-

Identification

12.00 % of the 400 respondents correctly identified the masked advertisement.
29.75 % remembered seeing it.

Readership

When shown the complete unmasked advertisement 34.75 % of the 400 respondents stated unequivocally they remembered seeing it.

All scores are based on a sample of 200 men and 200 women.

Correct Identification

	MEN	WOMEN	AVERAGE
Correct Identification	13.5 %	10.5 %	12.00 %
Masked Remembrance	31.0 %	28.5 %	29.75 %

Readership

	MEN	WOMEN	AVERAGE
Unmasked Remembrance	36.0 %	33.5 %	34.75 %

Misidentifications

AMONG MEN	AMONG WOMEN
5.5 %	7.0 %

Total Resident Readership
Persons 15 Years or Over.

Males	97,232
Females	103,142
Total	200,374

PLUS
Resident Children Under 15
Non-resident transients

METRO MARKET   **New Orleans**

POSTING DATE   **November 1, 1963**   FOR **60** DAYS

TOTAL PANELS IN METRO AREA FOR THIS DESIGN   **14***

SHOWING SIZE INDEX   **29.16**

TYPE OF COVERAGE — GENERAL ☐   SPECIAL ☒   ROTARY ☐

ADVERTISER   **Browne Vintners Company, Inc.**

PRODUCT   **White Horse Whiskey**

SURVEY # **2**   DATE   **December 15, 1963**

*Major arterial coverage and locations near key outlets.

24   27   30   M

A recall test using a "masked" advertisement—in this case, a billboard—is one method for measuring an ad's effectiveness.

spiration or electrical resistance of the skin, which indicate arousal when viewing advertisements.

Pupil dilation response (PDR), a method that was popular in the 1960s, tracks changes in pupil size, an indication of the amount of information processed while viewing an ad or commercial. Subjects' heads are placed in fixed positions and pupil dilation is continuously tracked. More recent research has discounted the notion that PDR measures emotional response (i.e., the greater the dilation, the more positive the response). Ohio State University GSR and PDR studies found consistent relationships between memory and high levels of GSR and PDR in response to advertisements.

Voice response analysis measures vocal inflections when discussing an ad. Subjects are asked to respond to a set of ads. Responses are recorded and computer analyzed. Deviations from a flat response indicate arousal or excitement.

With conjugately programmed analysis of advertising (CONPAAD), subjects operate a foot or hand device controlling audio and video television-signal intensity. Subjects must exert effort to sustain the signals, which decay in a preprogrammed pattern. Exertion indicates attention and interest.

Electroencephalographic (EEG) data can be collected at several electrical frequencies up to 1,000 times per second. Consumers have electrodes placed on the front, back, left, and right of their scalps. During ad exposure, EEG data from each location are recorded. Analysis of the frequency and amplitude of the recorded impulses is used to determine the ability of the whole ad and its components to attract attention. Ad recognition is related to increased left-hemisphere processing. Because occipital alpha activity (alpha brain waves—those in the frequency range of 8 to 13 cycles per second—measured near the rear of the skull) is strongest when people rest, a sudden drop in the alpha signal indicates attention; furthermore, the length of time it takes the alpha signal to return to resting levels is directly related to the subject's interest in the stimulus.

The tachistoscope, basically a slide projector with controlled presentation time and illumination, assesses an advertisement's communication speed. Faster ad recognition is correlated with higher readership. About 20,000 persons per year are tested with the tachistoscope at the Leo Burnett Company, Inc., and other shops use the test as well.

Binocular rivalry tests competing advertising stimuli (e.g., adjacent billboards, packages, or ads) presented simultaneously, one to each eye. Illumination and presentation time can be controlled. When two stimuli are given an equal chance to dominate awareness, the one with more impact should predominate. Binocular rivalry has been used by the HRB-Singer Corporation to measure the visual efficiency of advertisements.

Persuasion Tests

Persuasion tests typically use before/after designs. People from the target market are recruited, and their preexposure brand attitudes are measured. They are then exposed to the test ad. Following exposure, their attitudes are measured again to gauge the effect of the ad on brand attitudes.

On-air persuasion tests are also conducted. For example, Mapes & Ross airs test commercials in prime time on UHF stations in three major markets. Up to 200 viewers are telephoned and asked to participate in a survey and cash drawing that requires viewing the test program. Subjects provide unaided brand-name preferences for various products. The day after exposure, subjects provide DAR of brands advertised and their postexposure brand preferences, from which brand-preference change is calculated. Validation studies have found purchases of the test brand to be 3.3 times higher among those who changed their brand preference. Another on-air persuasion test is Gallup & Robinson In-View, which measures the test spots' DAR, idea communication, and persuasion.

ASI Recall Plus and Persuasion Plus use cable transmission to test ads on a recruited audience. Recall Plus subjects are called the day of the test and asked to preview a new television program. The program includes four tests and one dummy commercial. Subjects are recontacted to measure DAR and spot effectiveness. Persuasion Plus adds brand-change measures within two hours of viewing.

Similar persuasion tests have been developed for print ads (e.g., Gallup & Robinson Rapid Ad Measurement and ASI Print Plus). Test ads are embedded in magazines, which are given to subjects. Subjects are told that the researcher will interview them tomorrow, and, as compensation, they need to indicate their brand preferences for prizes to be given away in a drawing. The next day, subjects are told that their original questionnaires were misplaced, so they need to complete another. This measures postexposure attitudes. In some tests, subjects review test ads and evaluate ad features or brand interest.

Video Storyboard Tests evaluate rough or finished print ads in a mock magazine, *Looking at Us*. Subjects are asked to preview a pilot issue of this new magazine. Individual interviews are conducted in shopping malls. Subjects rate ads on persuasion, product uniqueness, believability, competitive strength, and likability.

Persuasion measures have been linked to sales, making persuasion tests desirable. For example, a 1994 study by John R. Rossiter and Geoff Eagleson found that persuasion measures predict in 82 percent of cases which of two commercials would lead to better sales. However, persuasion tests for well-known brands typically lead to minimal changes in brand attitude after one ad exposure. Since small changes can be unreliable, the advertiser cannot tell whether they represent actual attitude change or some random error.

Persuasion tests are fairly expensive, averaging $11,000 to $15,000. Hard-to-find samples and more realistic exposure increase costs. To control costs, subjects are usually asked to evaluate four to six ads in different product categories during the same test.

Off-air persuasion tests, such as theater tests, are often disguised as pretests of new television programs. Theater testing was pioneered by Horace Schwerin and Paul Lazarsfeld in the 1940s. Theater tests are becoming a worldwide advertisement pretest method. For example, the ASI In-Theater Test analyzes approxi-

Portrait of Craftsmanship in Action

The all new *Packard Hawk*

THE MOST ORIGINAL CAR ON THE AMERICAN ROAD

You will find no other car like the Packard Hawk. It is the most original and distinctive automobile crafted in America, styled to match the tempo of our times. Its unique flowing lines are aerodynamic. Its fins: functional. It is designed with that imaginative flair you only expect to find in Europe's most fashionable automobiles. Faithful to its thoroughbred breeding, the Packard Hawk is a *luxury* automobile with smooth, soft leather seats and elegant, tasteful interior appointments. Its appearance is complemented by power from a highly efficient supercharged V-8 engine, capable of instantaneous acceleration, or smooth performance under the most trying conditions of stop-and-go traffic. The Packard Hawk is *the* new car with a regal air that immediately distinguishes its owner as a man of position. Put yourself in that position . . . behind the wheel of a Packard Hawk, soon.

Coming soon . . . watch for the other luxurious new '58 Packards: The 4-Door Town Sedan (above) . . . the Country Sedan . . . and the elegant Packard Hardtop.

Studebaker-Packard offers the most varied line of cars in America. See them all . . . economy cars . . . sports cars . . . station wagons . . . luxury sedans and hardtops.

Visit your Studebaker-Packard dealer today!

 Studebaker-Packard
CORPORATION
Where pride of Workmanship comes first!

Packard Motor Car Company.
Quality craftsmanship and originality of design, two themes prominent in this print ad for Studebaker-Packard Corporation's 1958 Hawk, were longstanding elements in Packard's advertising. The 1958 model year was the company's last.
Used with permission of Studebaker National Museum Archives.

Pepperidge Farm, Inc.
For more than three decades Pepperidge Farm's advertising, such as this 1991 ad for Goldfish crackers, developed the theme of nostalgia, using the slogan "Pepperidge Farm remembers."
Provided courtesy of Campbell Soup Company.

Close-up
gave me whiter teeth, fresh breath ...and a fresh start with Stan.

Things with Stan had just about fizzled out and I couldn't understand why. Then I discovered Close-up® that marvelous red gel toothpaste. Close-up got my teeth as white as they always should have been, and that tingly Close-up mouthwash really freshened my breath.

Well, Close-up did the trick and we're getting to know each other all over again. And since he just gave me his "heart," I'd say we're headed in the right direction.

Whiter teeth, fresh breath, and Stan. Not bad for a toothpaste.

Personal Care Products.
A 1977 advertisement for Close-up, a clear-gel toothpaste combined with mouthwash, was part of a campaign that focused on the social benefits of whiter teeth and fresh breath.
The CLOSE-UP print ad was reproduced courtesy of Chesebrough-Pond's USA Co.

Pharmaceuticals.
Like other prescription-only drugs for common conditions such as arthritis and anxiety, Schering Corporation's Claritin allergy medication became a household word thanks to an aggressive direct-to-consumer ad campaign. This 1999 print ad included an endorsement by television personality Joan Lunden.

backpack $17.99

lampshade $11.99

fashion and housewares.

TARGET

Photography and Photographers.
Matthew Rolston's arresting photographs for Target Corporation helped the retailer produce award-winning advertisements in the 1990s.
Copyright © 1997 Matthew Rolston Photographer, Inc. Courtesy Target Corporation.

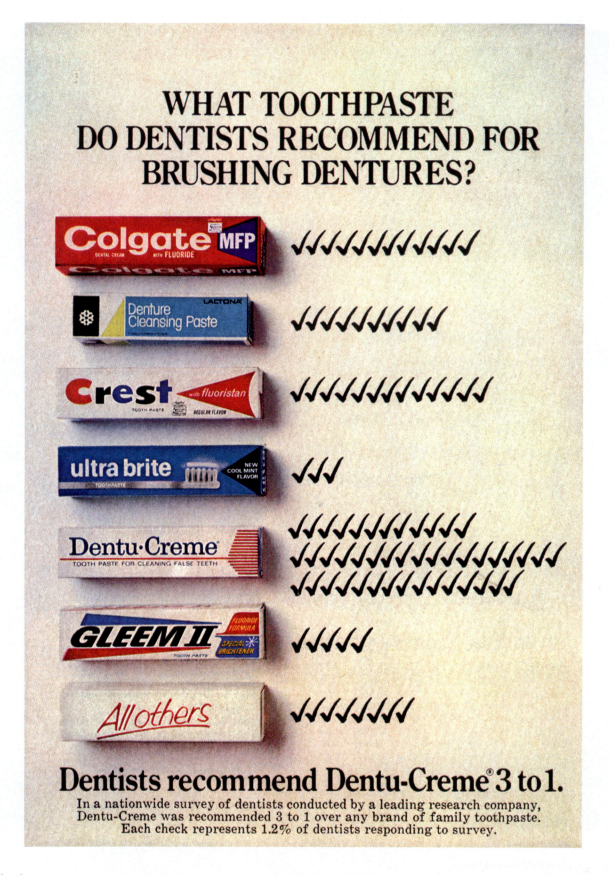

Positioning.
This 1972 ad used survey data to position Dentu-Creme as the toothpaste dentists recommended for cleaning dentures.
Courtesy Block Drug Company, Inc.

For healthy, shiny Pantene hair, just add water.

Pantene® Pro-V® Shampoo and Treatment Conditioner contain pro-vitamins. They penetrate deeply, to improve hair. For healthy, shiny hair, all you need is Pantene Pro-V... and water.

Damaged hair...

treated with Pro-V

PANTENE PRO-V. FOR HAIR SO HEALTHY IT SHINES.

Procter & Gamble Company.
In 1992 Procter & Gamble Company launched a campaign to transform its Pantene shampoo into a global leader.
Courtesy of The Procter & Gamble Company.

AMERICA ON ITS KNEES:

A PUBLIC SERVICE MESSAGE BY CONRAD N. HILTON,
PRESIDENT, HILTON HOTELS CORPORATION

☆ ☆ ☆ *not beaten there by the hammer & sickle, but* FREELY, INTELLIGENTLY, RESPONSIBLY, CONFIDENTLY, POWERFULLY. *America now knows it can destroy* communism *& win the battle for peace. We need fear nothing or no one...* ...except GOD.

OUR FATHER IN HEAVEN:

WE PRAY that YOU save us from *ourselves.*

The world that YOU have made for us, to live in peace,
    we have made into an armed camp.
    We live in fear of war to come.

We are afraid of "the terror that flies by
    night, and the arrow that flies by day
    the pestilence that walks in darkness
    and the destruction that wastes at noon-day."

We have turned from YOU to go our selfish way
    We have broken YOUR commandments
    and denied YOUR truth. We have left YOUR altars
    to serve the false gods of money and pleasure and power.

FORGIVE US AND HELP US

Now, darkness gathers around us and we are confused
    in all our counsels. Losing faith in YOU,
    we lose faith in ourselves.

Inspire us with wisdom, all of us of every color, race and creed,
    to use our wealth, our strength to help our brother,
    instead of destroying him.

Help us to do YOUR will as it is done in heaven
    and to be worthy of YOUR promise of peace on earth.

Fill us with new faith, new strength and new courage,
    that we may win the Battle for Peace.

Be swift to save us,   *dear God,*
    before the darkness falls ★ ☆ ★

PAINTED BY TEXANA

COPIES OF THE ADDRESS AND COLOR REPRINTS OF
"AMERICA ON ITS KNEES" MAY BE OBTAINED BY WRITING

★ ☆ ★ FROM "THE BATTLE FOR PEACE," an address by CONRAD N. HILTON

Conrad N Hilton
PRESIDENT HILTON HOTELS CORPORATION

9970 SANTA MONICA BOULEVARD
BEVERLY HILLS, CALIFORNIA

Propaganda.
At the height of the Korean War in 1952, this public service message from Hilton Hotels President Conrad N. Hilton used an emotional appeal to stir Americans' patriotism.
Courtesy of the Hospitality Industry Archives and Library, University of Houston.

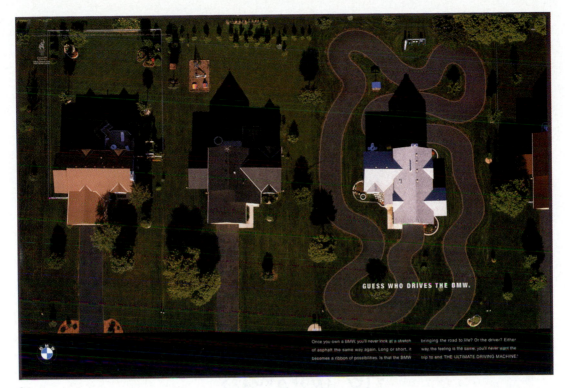

Psychographics.
Marketers use psychographics to develop an image or profile of consumers who buy their products, then create advertising designed to appeal to that group. In this ad from 2001, BMW portrayed the BMW owner as a person who relishes the experience of driving.

Ratto Agency.
With little text and a minimum of images, this award-winning 1997 campaign from Ratto/BBDO sent the message that the VW Golf GTI was a "hot" car.

He worships
the ground you walk on.
So let him walk
on the ground where
you worship.

Invite a friend to your house of worship.

RELIGION IN AMERICAN LIFE

©1995

Religion, Advertising of.
This poster encouraging religious practice is from a 1990s campaign by Religion in American Life, the oldest U.S. interfaith organization.
Developed by RIAL in conjunction with Foote, Cone and Belding, Inc.

The man from Schweppes is here

MEET Commander Edward Whitehead, Schweppesman Extraordinary from London, England, where the house of Schweppes has been a great institution since 1794.

Commander Whitehead has come to these United States to make sure that every drop of Schweppes Quinine Water bottled here has the original flavor which has long made Schweppes

the *only* mixer for an *authentic* Gin-and-Tonic.

He imports the original Schweppes elixir, and the secret of Schweppes unique carbonation is locked in his brief case. "Schweppervescence," says the Commander, *"lasts the whole drink through."*

It took Schweppes almost a hundred years to bring the flavor of their Quinine Water to its

present bittersweet perfection. But it will take you only thirty seconds to mix it with ice and gin in a highball glass. *Then,* gentle reader, you will bless the day you read these words.

P.S. If your favorite store or bar doesn't yet have Schweppes, drop a card to us and we'll make the proper arrangements. Address Schweppes, 30 East 60th Street, New York City.

FLEECE GLOVES
SALE PRICE $3.75*

KRUPS

2 SLICE TOASTER
SALE PRICE $29.99 **

Whatever Makes You Merry.

Find it at the Merry Side of SEARS℠

Sears, Roebuck & Company.
Sears, Roebuck & Company put a holiday twist on its "Come see the softer side of Sears" slogan in this 1998 print ad.
The 1998 advertisement "Find it at the Merry Side of Sears" is reprinted by arrangement with Sears, Roebuck and Co. and is protected under copyright. No duplication in permitted.

Your Chances... Are Better...

When You Use
MENNEN SKIN BRACER
Its He-Man Aroma
WOWS *the Ladies!*

A SMART TRICK — after every shave dash Mennen Skin Bracer on your face, neck, and chin. Discover why Mennen Skin Bracer is America's favorite after-shave lotion.

HELPS HEAL RAZOR NICKS — and you'll really enjoy Skin Bracer's "wake-up" tingle. Get it today! Regular size only 50¢ — big 12-ounce bottle only $1.00

MENNEN SKIN BRACER

• Special ingredients wilt whiskers faster. Get MENNEN LATHER SHAVE — Plain or Menthol-Iced.

Sex in Advertising.
The promise of increased sex appeal has a long history in advertising. This ad for Mennen Skin Bracer appeared in 1947.

How a Spring day in Ireland inspired a new long lasting deodorant soap.

In Ireland, a Spring day is a long day, where the sun stays up past ten at night. And so the idea for Irish Spring® was born.

Irish Spring, a soap that gives you long, long deodorant protection.

Double Deodorant System

Cut open a bar. You'll see why. In those green and white stripes is a Double Deodorant System. Two deodorants, not just one. That's what gives a man the long lasting protection he wants.

New fresh scent

Sniff a bar of Irish Spring. It has a scent that's fresh as its name. So fresh, it's like taking a shower in Ireland.

New rich lather

Feel that Double Deodorant lather on your skin. Thick. Rich. Clean. Irish Spring gives you a truly luxurious experience.

New manly shape

Look at the bar. That slightly curved shape fits a man's hand better. Makes it easier to hold when wet.

Ladies like it too

Discover a new kind of long lasting deodorant protection. It's powerful enough to protect a man. Yet mild enough to please a lady. Try new Irish Spring.

New Irish Spring
Manly protection that lasts.

®1971 Colgate-Palmolive Co.

Soap Products.
In 1971 Colgate-Palmolive Company launched Irish Spring, one of the first major soap brands to target men.
Courtesy of Colgate-Palmolive Company.

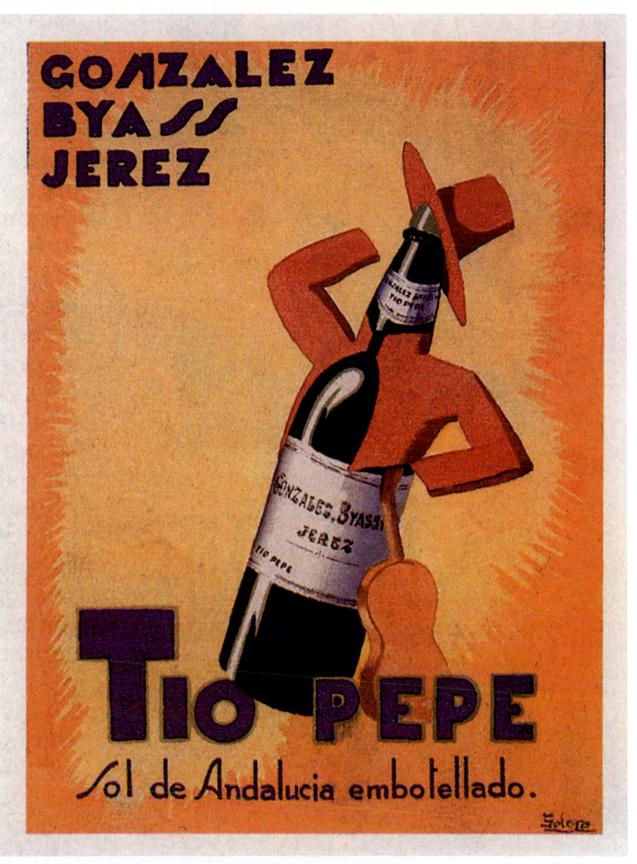

Spain.
This ad for Tio Pepe dry sherry, one of Spain's best-known exports, appeared in 1934. The enduring icon, a stylized bottle wearing the costume of a flamenco guitarist, was still in use in the 21st century.
Courtesy of Gonzalez Byass.

Spokes-Character.
In a humorous play on the advertising tradition of the spokes-character, M&M's introduced its "spokes-candy," seen here in an ad from 2000.

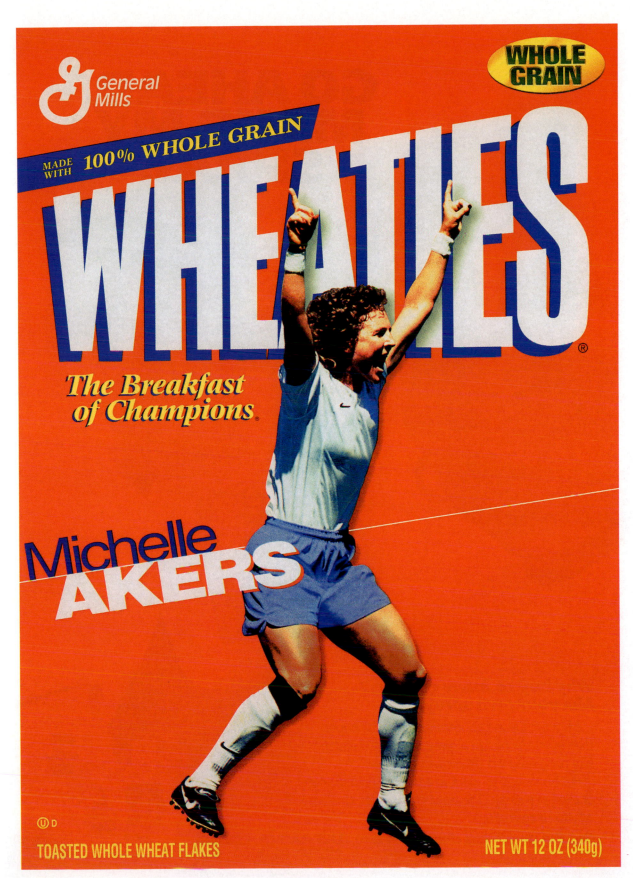

Sports.
Having one's picture appear on the Wheaties box has become a measure of achievement for U.S. athletes. Women's soccer star Michelle Akers was so honored in 1999.
Courtesy of Michelle Akers and the General Mills Archives.

GO AHEAD. MAKE MY SPRAY.

MR. CLEAN SPRAY

Why buy so many cleaners? Mix your own spray!

Ultra Mr. Clean's concentrated, and stronger than ever. Mix him in a spray bottle, and watch him cut greasy dirt on contact!

Put his muscle to work in a bucket, on a sponge or even in a spray. One powerful cleaner. One easy way to clean it all!

Get the whole job done with one...ULTRA MR. CLEAN

SPRAY RECIPE:
1 PART MR. CLEAN
2 PARTS WATER

Tatham-Laird, Inc.
Created by Tatham-Laird in the 1950s, Mr. Clean remains a widely recognized advertising icon in the United States.
Courtesy of The Procter & Gamble Company.

Have you ever installed a phone on your wrist?

YOU WILL®

In the near future, no matter where you are, the nearest phone will be close at hand.

Miniature. Wireless. Small enough to wear on your wrist. Yet powerful enough to reach anyone. Anywhere in the world.

The strap-on telephone.

The company that will bring it to you is AT&T.

AT&T
Your True Choice

©1994 AT&T. ©1995 AT&T

Telecommunications.
AT&T's "You Will" campaign from the 1990s focused on telecommunications possibilities of the future.
Courtesy AT&T.

Tires.
Michelin's ad icon Bibendum, also known simply as the Michelin Man, originated in 1898 and has undergone several makeovers. The Bibendum shown here dates from 1917.
Reprinted by permission of Michelin & Cie.

Toys and Games.
The technological advances of the second half of the 20th century revolutionized electronic games, making them smaller and faster. This ad for Nintendo of America's Game Boy Pocket appeared in 1996.
© 1996 Nintendo of America, Inc. All rights reserved.

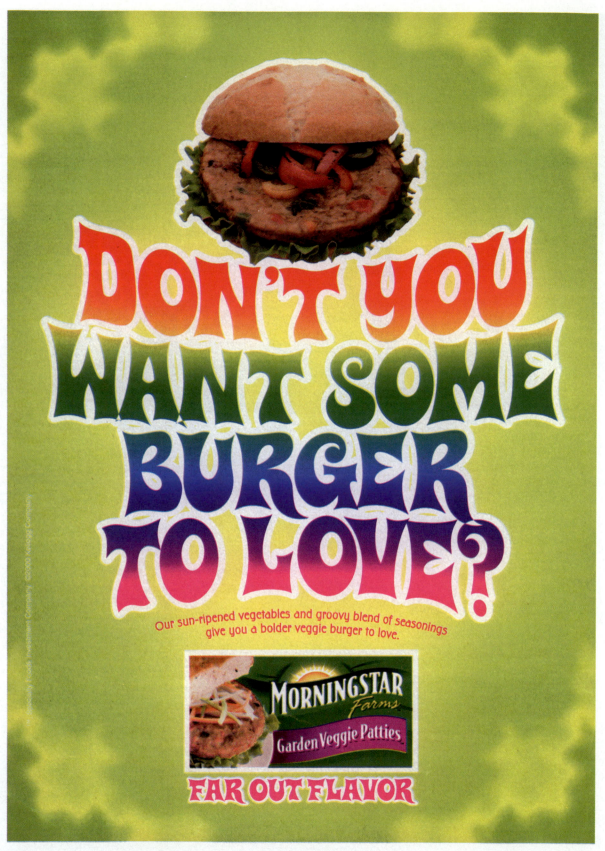

Typography.
The psychedelic colors and stylized typography of this 2000 ad for Morningstar Farms Garden Veggie Patties evoked the counterculture movement of the 1960s. A hit song of the era—"Somebody to Love"—was adapted for the tag line. MORNINGSTAR FARMS™ is a trademark of Kellogg Company. All rights reserved. Used with permission. Parody lyrics of the song "Somebody to Love" originally written by Darby Slick used by permission of Irving Music, Inc.

SHE'S VERY CHARLIE.

Women: Representations in Advertising.
Revlon's Charlie perfume updated its 1973 campaign showing confident, aggressive working women in this 1988 ad, which illustrated liberation of another kind.
Courtesy of Revlon.

Big night... snapshot night !

Good friends never part . . . in the pictures they take. Now it's easy to get them indoors at night . . . in gorgeous full color or crisp black-and-white.

Just use a flash camera, or most *any* camera plus an inexpensive Kodak Photo Flasher. For full color, load with the new Kodacolor Film, Type A—designed for indoor pictures . . . Remember, the snapshots you'll want tomorrow, you must take today.

EASTMAN KODAK COMPANY. ROCHESTER 4, N. Y.

Kodak Duaflex Camera makes wonderful snapshots —easily. Negatives, 2¼ x 2¼. With Kodet Lens, $12.75. With Kodar f/8 Lens, $19.85. Flasholder, $3.33. Prices include Federal Tax.

Only Eastman makes Kodak Cameras and Kodak Film

Youth Market.
In the years following World War II, advertisers such as Eastman Kodak Company recognized a potential new market in the growing teenage and young adult segment and began to target that age group.
Courtesy Eastman Kodak Company.

mately 1,500 spots per year. Viewers list the brands they would prefer if they win the end-of-the-session drawing. On the movie screen, they view a cartoon, a half-hour program, five commercials, another half-hour program, and another cartoon. Before the final cartoon, subjects are told that the first questionnaire contained an error, and they are asked to complete another brand-choice questionnaire. After the final cartoon, subjects complete a recall questionnaire. While viewing, one subsample operates handheld dials to indicate viewing interest. A GSR device records physiological responses for a second subsample. A third subsample answers a questionnaire after viewing. Advertisers can also recruit audience members for focus groups or in-depth discussions afterwards.

Another theater test is Research Systems Corporation's Advertising Research Services (ARS). Unlike the ASI method, which is recall-based, ARS is recognition-based; subjects choose the brands that they would prefer to win from pictures of the packages. Another difference is a recall test given over the telephone after 72 hours to a subsample. The ARS score has successfully predicted which of two commercials would achieve higher test-market sales.

In a third example of an off-air persuasion test, McCollum/Spielman recruits a 450-person sample from four geographically dispersed locations. Groups of 25 subjects at a time report to the viewing location in their area to preview television programming. Some differences from the other tests are the use of television instead of movie screens, a measure of unaided brand-name recall, repeat exposure, and an attitude-shift measure after repeat exposure to the test commercials embedded in programming. Many advertisers contend that fewer than two exposures represents an artificial and invalid test, because emotional advertisements gain in response more slowly with repetition than rational ones. Also, one exposure does not accurately represent the exposure frequency in the marketplace.

Gallup & Robinson's InTeleTest adapts theater tests to in-home viewing with videotaped programming containing six test and six actual commercials. The day after the viewing, a researcher conducts a telephone interview and takes DAR measures related to the advertising in the program. Later, subjects view a tape containing only test ads and complete recognition, likability, and overall-reaction measures.

The Future

With the dawn of the 21st century, advertising researchers are finding ways to adapt their testing methods to emerging ad media such as the Internet. In 1999, for example, ACNielsen announced a joint venture with NetRatings, Inc., to form a global service that would track audiences, advertising, and user activity on the World Wide Web. In 2001, DoubleClick introduced its Diameter division, which conducts Internet audience measurement and advertising effectiveness research to compete with Nielsen NetRatings.

The challenge of creating advertising that has the power to persuade continues to grow as media vehicles proliferate and target increasingly smaller, more specialized audiences. Adding to the challenge are the growing problem of ad clutter, increasing intensity of global competition, and tendency of consumers to become more savvy. These changes will inevitably lead to increased testing and, undoubtedly, to improved testing methods.

BRUCE A. HUHMANN

See also ACNielsen Corporation; Starch, Inc.

Further Reading

Clark, Eddie M., Timothy C. Brock, and David W. Stewart, editors, *Attention, Attitude, and Affect in Response to Advertising,* Hillsdale, New Jersey: Erlbaum, 1994

Davis, Joel J., *Advertising Research: Theory and Practice,* Upper Saddle River, New Jersey: Prentice Hall, 1997

Du Plessis, Erik, "Recognition versus Recall," *Journal of Advertising Research* 34, no. 3 (1994)

Haskins, Jack, and Alice Kendrick, *Successful Advertising Research Methods,* Lincolnwood, Illinois: NTC Business Books, 1993

Jones, John Philip, *When Ads Work: New Proof That Advertising Triggers Sales,* New York: Lexington Books, 1995

King, Karen W., John D. Pehrson, and Leonard N. Reid, "Pretesting TV Commercials: Methods, Measures, and Changing Agency Roles," *Journal of Advertising* 22, no. 3 (1993)

Lipstein, Benjamin, "An Historical Perspective of Copy Research," *Journal of Advertising Research* 24, no. 6 (1984)

Rossiter, John R., and Geoff Eagleson, "Conclusions from ARF's Copy Research Validity Project," *Journal of Advertising Research* 34, no. 3 (1994)

Rotenberg, Ronald H., *Advertising: A Canadian Perspective,* Toronto, Ontario: Allyn and Bacon, 1986

Stapel, Jan, "Recall and Recognition: A Very Close Relationship," *Journal of Advertising Research* 38, no. 4 (1998)

Starch, Daniel, *Measuring Advertising Readership and Results,* New York: McGraw-Hill, 1966

Swan, Carroll J., *Tested Advertising Copy: 201 Tests of 480 Ads, with Factual Results in Readership, Inquiries, or Sales, and Analyses of Basic Success Factors for Ad Copy As Viewed by Gallup, Politz, Shepard, and Schwerin,* Pleasantville, New York: Printers' Ink Books, 1955

J. Walter Thompson Company

Founded as Carlton & Smith, New York City, by William James Carlton, 1864; renamed J. Walter Thompson Company when James Walter Thompson bought out Carlton for $500, 1878; incorporated, 1896; sold by Thompson to his partners, Stanley Resor and Charles E. Raymond, for $500,000, 1916; merged into the WPP Group, 1987.

Major Clients

DeBeers Consolidated Mines
Ford Motor Company
Kraft Foods
Pfizer/Warner-Lambert Company
Qwest Communications
Shell Oil Company
Standard Brands (Chase & Sanborn, Royal, Fleischmann's)
Unilever

The J. Walter Thompson Company (JWT) was born out of the U.S. Civil War, with a trademark spirit to challenge conventions about what advertising should and could be and to advance the roles of women and research in this ever-changing field. The company, originally called Carlton & Smith, was founded on 5 December 1864 by Union Army Captain William James Carlton, a wholesaler of space in religious periodicals. He teamed up with James Walter Thompson, who, at age 20 and fresh out of the Marine Corps, was convinced that the future of the advertising business was in women's magazines such as *Godey's Lady's Book* and Peterson's *Ladies' National Magazine*. Thompson, with a unique appreciation for the power of magazine advertising, "prospered not by cutting down competitors but by inventing his own domain," Stephen Fox observed in his book *The Mirror Makers*.

"It Pays to Advertise"

In 1878 Thompson bought the business from Carlton for $500, which was $300 less than he paid for the furniture in their shared New York City office. A year later he gave the agency his own name. The company's early symbol was the owl and the lamp. Its mission statement read: "To create the most effective, distinctive advertising in the marketplace." He coined the phrase "It pays to advertise" and devised the concept of the account executive.

Thompson's initial challenge was to convince magazines, some of which reluctantly ran only several pages of advertising in each issue, to sell him more space. Thompson organized the first national media buy with a "List of Thirty Select Magazines," which he sold as a group on a select basis to advertisers. By 1895 Thompson was providing a wide range of advertising services, including copy, layout, package design, trademark development, and rudimentary market research. In 1899 he opened a London, England, office, making JWT the first U.S. agency to open for business abroad.

In 1911 Thompson produced the white paper, "Things to Know about Trade-Marks," which displayed a basic knowledge of branding that prevails today. His early branding efforts included establishing the Rock of Gibraltar as the trademark for Prudential Insurance.

Thompson's regularly published *Blue Book* reviewed the full range of services and examples of its best-known branding efforts for clients, led in the early years by Cream of Wheat, Libby's Food Products, and Swift and Company. Thompson's Achilles' heel proved to be allowing his account executives to control the company's creative efforts, which by 1900 resulted in JWT lagging behind its rivals.

Still, Thompson surrounded himself with some of the most notable early contributors to the world of advertising, such as James Webb Young, Helen Lansdowne, and Stanley Resor. Resor eventually partnered with Charles E. Raymond, founder of JWT's Chicago, Illinois, office, to buy the company from Thompson.

Thompson sought to expand his firm internationally and traveled abroad every summer to land new accounts. His 1889 book, *Advertising in America*, was a 440-page French and English text designed to explain the U.S. market and publications to European manufacturers. Such intellectual, straightforward efforts went a long way in reversing advertising's sullen image, which was a product of the flimflam and casual corruption of the Gilded Age. In his memoirs Raymond wrote that Thompson "found advertising a thing despised by the cultured" as a way "for the unscrupulous to sell wares of doubtful value." He lived to see advertising occupy a place of honor, and to know that he had contributed largely to this result," Raymond observed. As *Advertising Age* said in 1982, Thompson "personally set the pattern for the whole agency business."

The Resor Era

From the time he bought the company from Thompson in 1916 for $500,000 until his retirement in 1961, Resor and his wife, copywriter Helen Lansdowne Resor, built it from a $3 million agency with 117 people to a $368.7 million agency with 6,587 people doing business on six continents. Like Thompson, the Resors did not just build a business, they influenced the form, methods, and practices of the modern advertising agency.

A Yale graduate who studied the classics, Resor first made his mark creating advertising for Procter & Collier, agency for the giant soap manufacturer Procter & Gamble Company (P&G), which was one of the biggest of the early advertisers. Resor strove to make advertising scientific and predictable. As the first major advertising agency leader to boast a college degree, Resor fashioned campaigns and brand names after lifestyles of the well-to-do. He helped make JWT the first major agency used by P&G, and he led JWT to become the first agency shop to break $100 million in billings.

His wife, a gifted copywriter and ardent feminist, instilled the agency's work with the emotion and magic that brought advertis-

There's a *Ford* in your future!

FORD HAS BUILT MORE THAN 30,000,000 CARS AND TRUCKS

In 1945, even before Ford's assembly lines had fully shifted over from wartime production, the J. Walter Thompson Company coined the slogan "There's a Ford in your future" to alert consumers that new cars would soon be available.
Courtesy of Ford Motor Company.

J. Walter Thompson.
Courtesy of the J. Walter Thompson Company.

ing to life. She created the first international ad campaign for Pond's skin cream with one of the first uses of testimonial advertising, soliciting such names as Vanderbilt, Astor, and du Pont. The testimonial approach hit its stride when JWT began parading Hollywood personalities for its 1927 campaign that declared, "Nine out of ten screen stars care for their skin with Lux toilet soap." But it was Helen Resor's tag line for Woodbury facial soap—"A skin you love to touch"—that made the most impact by introducing the notion of marketing through sex appeal.

Helen Resor was responsible for developing JWT's reputation as an agency in which bright young women could succeed by best meeting the needs and interests of female consumers. JWT became the first agency to promote women into major executive positions. These female executives controlled most of JWT's prestigious soap, food, drug, and toiletry accounts, which led JWT to advertise itself as the "Woman's Agency." In her own time, Helen Resor was followed by a generation of skilled, ambitious women that included Ruth Waldo, JWT's first female vice president, and

Nancy Stephenson, JWT's first female director. In the late 1990s, after she had served in several key posts, Charlotte Beers, a brilliant strategic thinker, became the world's highest-ranked woman in advertising as JWT chairman; in 2001 she took her advertising skills to the federal government with her appointment as undersecretary of state for public diplomacy under President George W. Bush.

Meanwhile, Stanley Resor created a business evaluation formula called the "Thompson T-Square," which posed a series of fundamental questions: "What are we selling?" "To whom are we selling?" "Where are we selling?" Its aim was to prompt everyone involved in the planning, production, and placement of advertising to contemplate its final effect on the ad's target reader.

In his book *Madison Avenue, U.S.A.,* Martin Mayer observed, "Resor's original and continuing contribution to his agency and to the advertising industry as a whole has been his conviction that advertising is neither a circus sideshow nor a business, but an independent force in the community—and a profession that should have a status comparable to that of law or medicine." Resor used the force of advertising to promote social and charitable causes and resisted using it for such purposes as to promote the sale of hard liquor and cigarettes (a policy changed under later leadership). He rejected the chance to create slogans to win the giant Camel cigarette account, because to do so "would be prostituting my profession," Mayer recounted.

Resor was not much interested in the tables of organization, flow charts, or scientific management that prevailed at other major ad agencies. Instead he built a talent pool that included artists, writers, sociologists, scientists, lawyers, photographers, dress designers, and technicians, all headquartered in elaborate New York City offices in the Graybar Building next to Grand Central Station on Lexington Avenue. This team of free thinkers was headed by James Webb Young and Sam Meek.

Young is described in JWT company history as a born entrepreneur who went to work at age 12 and did not return to school until he became a professor at the University of Chicago. In and out of JWT for more than 50 years, Young brought his own brand of intellectual influence to the agency as the chief "pattern maker" for some of JWT's greatest ad campaigns. In 1919 he created the ad headline, "Within the curve of a woman's arm," to sell Odorono deodorant to proper and shocked consumers. The campaign yielded a 112 percent increase in sales. His 1930s textbooks, *How to Become an Advertising Man* and *A Technique for Producing Ideas,* remain classics in the field.

Expansion Overseas

Young's influence reached far beyond the ads themselves. In 1927 he expanded JWT's reach abroad by taking seven staff members, three of their wives, one child, and a cat to Europe to open offices in Germany, Belgium, Denmark, Spain, and later Egypt. Young served on a committee of leading advertisers, publishers, and ad agency executives to study compensation methods. The result was what today remains the definitive written work on the subject. Young also was actively involved in creating the forerunner to today's Advertising Council and lectured widely on one of the council's founding tenets: the need to do advertising in the public interest, in support of causes that could affect the public good and improve public perception of the business.

Meanwhile, Sam Meek concentrated on growing JWT's interests abroad from its London, England, office. When Meek joined the company in 1925, the London office boasted the whole of the agency's international staff of 18 and $500,000 in annual billings from such accounts as Libby's Food Products and Sun-Maid raisins. JWT's London office had briefly closed during Resor's tenure as a cost-cutting move. But the manufacture of Ford cars on European assembly lines refocused JWT and other agencies on international business.

Meek's do-or-die attitude led to a string of new, influential British clients that gave JWT much needed international credibility as "an American agency," creating witty, upscale advertising for companies such as Guinness and Campari. Other hard-won accounts included Horlick's, Rowntree, and Unilever, which, at the turn of the century, was JWT's and the advertising industry's longest-running corporate account. When he retired in 1965, Meek had expanded JWT's foreign operation to 135 offices, with billings of more than $150 million annually.

A Pioneer in Marketing Research

During the Depression years, JWT overtook longtime competitors such as Lord & Thomas and N.W. Ayer & Son to become the largest ad agency in the United States and one of the largest in the world, using consumer demographic and other research data that were established as a priority by Thompson in 1915.

Thompson focused intensely on pioneering marketing, research, and behavior studies methods. He drew on the best minds from the world of academia, including Yale history professor Stewart Mims and controversial Johns Hopkins professor John Broadus, who was known as the father of behaviorism, a field of psychology that Resor applied to mass marketing. JWT also consulted with famed behavioral psychologist John B. Watson. Paul Cherington, a Harvard marketing professor, pioneered consumer sampling techniques, and economist Arno Johnson headed JWT's developing research efforts. In an effort to better understand consumers, Virgil Reed, a one-time acting census director, edited the 1951 and 1961 editions of *The Population and Its Distribution*, a marketing analysis distinguished as the first analysis of raw U.S. Census data, itself a landmark demographic study.

It was from JWT's early research work that Resor emerged with a clear proposition: the most efficient use of the advertising dollar targeted the most concentrated viewers. In 1920 he led JWT to be the first advertising agency to write copy based on scientifically researched information. In an effort to keep advertising respectable and honest, he helped found the American Association of Advertising Agencies.

JWT also did the first qualitative analysis of magazine readership in 1924 and a revolutionary reclassification in 1935 of urban and rural markets by buying-power concentrations rather than by geography. The agency that earned a reputation as the "University of Advertising" by assembling a community of scholars and experts to set new business practices and standards also came to produce the white paper, "Interurbia Study," compiled at Yale University, as well as Brookings Institute studies on economics. These efforts were the forerunners to modern marketing research.

At the same time, JWT continued to be home to notable creative people. The poet Hart Crane briefly worked as a copywriter at JWT, as did John P. Marquand, who, when fired from the agency, wrote about the world of advertising in some of his award-winning novels. Walter Lord, author of a book on the Titanic, *A Night to Remember*, had previously written house ads for JWT. Even in politics, the ad agency business made for strange bedfellows. Long before Watergate, H.R. Haldemann, later a key staff member in the Nixon administration, worked as an account executive for JWT in New York City and Los Angeles, California.

Radio and Television

The company's early creative juices were revitalized in the broadcasting era. JWT's radio department was headed by John Reber, who was frequently referred to as the "Ziegfeld of radio." He played a major role in establishing JWT's media dominance, beginning with the *Chase & Sanborn Coffee Hour* in 1929, an all-musical review that built the little-known coffee into a national brand. JWT's *Fleischmann's Yeast Hour* with Rudy Vallee, an early musical variety hits show, drew on the agency's Hollywood contracts for guest star power. Both were for Standard Brands, a major JWT client. Al Jolson starred in the first JWT-produced *Kraft Music Hall* radio broadcasts, followed by Paul Whiteman and, from 1936–46, Bing Crosby.

It was Reber and, in particular, JWT writer Carroll Carroll who virtually created Bing Crosby's droll radio persona when Crosby took over as host of the *Kraft Music Hall*. The agency brought Edgar Bergen and Charlie McCarthy to radio in 1937, first in the *Chase & Sanborn Show* and later for Royal pudding, both for Standard Brands. In the 1940s JWT produced the *Fred Allen Show* for Tenderleaf Tea (also Standard Brands) and later Ford Motor Company. One of the longest running of all JWT programs was *Lux Radio Theatre* for Lever Brothers, which from 1934 to 1955 presented weekly one-hour versions of popular motion pictures, often with original cast members, and made Lux soap synonymous with Hollywood. The agency also produced *One Man's Family* for various Standard Brands products from 1935 to 1949. In 1936 Standard Brands was the largest network radio advertiser after P&G, spending $2.73 million, all through JWT.

JWT approached television with the same vigor, staging the first commercial TV program in 1930 for Chicago client Libby, McNeill & Libby. After World War II, with only about 1.5 million television receivers in use in the United States, JWT created the first variety series for Standard Brands (which was later folded into Nabisco) and soon lured other major clients to the tube, including Ford, Kraft, RCA, Elgin Watch, and Ballantine Beer. It

The J. Walter Thompson Company was the first advertising agency to operate a radio production unit in Hollywood, California, the site of the major U.S. film studios. This 1934 ad for the *Lux Radio Theatre* showed some of the motion picture stars who appeared in radio plays produced by the agency.
Courtesy of Unilever HPC.

also produced the first hour-long television entertainment series, *The Hour Glass,* in 1946.

Kraft Television Theatre was a live, hour-long anthology drama that produced a new play 39 weeks of the year. Its specially commissioned scripts were a testing ground for young directors such as George Roy Hill and David Susskind.

By 1947 JWT had 60 vice presidents, nine U.S. offices, and 18 foreign branches. Together they made the agency the first shop in history to break $100 million in billings. The next biggest agency was Young & Rubicam (Y&R), with $65 million. By 1958 JWT was the industry leader in TV billings.

JWT was among the large domestic agencies that led Madison Avenue into television to represent packaged goods and durable goods giants such as P&G. But JWT never lost sight of the underlying purpose of such production: to connect advertising clients with a target audience and then to use that audience to study their response to products and marketing approaches. For instance, JWT maintained a 5,000-person consumer panel it monitored every other week to find out consumers' product, service, and entertainment preferences. The data were provided to JWT's advertising clients. "Innovative in both copy styles and the variety of services offered to clients, JWT swept past the competition into first place in total billings, a position that it would keep for five decades," Fox wrote in *The Mirror Makers.* The achievement was attributed primarily to Stanley and Helen Resor.

The Post-Resor Era

When JWT became too unwieldy to be run by one man alone, Resor gave up the reins of power in 1955 to Norman Strouse. Strouse was another self-taught ad man who brought a sense of organization and more business discipline to what continued to be an agency that placed creativity and intellect first.

Strouse was succeeded in 1964 by Dan Seymour, a former CBS radio personality who became JWT's fourth president. He had been master of ceremonies, editor, producer of television programs such as *We, the People,* and part of the cast of Orson Welles's famous "War of the Worlds" radio broadcast. In 1949 Seymour joined Y&R, where he oversaw the agency's programming and production. Strouse then lured Seymour to JWT to organize its radio and television activities. Broadcast billings accounted for more than half the company's total domestic billings, or about $153 million, in 1964, and more than 100 of JWT's clients were in broadcast advertising. Major JWT clients involved in television at the time included Ford, Chesebrough-Pond's, Liggett & Myers, Quaker Oats, Lever Brothers, Standard Brands, RCA, Kodak, and Kraft.

Seymour attracted name talent. George Roy Hill, who would later direct the film *Butch Cassidy and the Sundance Kid,* was a television director at JWT. Authors Ernest Hemingway and John Steinbeck appeared in Ballantine Beer testimonials in the early 1950s. Some of the famous photographers JWT used included Edward Steichen, Cecil Beaton, Irving Penn, and Richard Avedon.

Not surprisingly, Seymour was responsible for such sponsored television "events" as the first TV showing of the theatrical *The Wizard of Oz* and the first single sponsorship of a film, Ford's "Startime" broadcast of *The Bridge on the River Kwai.* Seymour signed singer Perry Como at the height of his career to host *Kraft Music Hall* and brought together Pete Rozelle and Lee Iacocca to make Ford an inaugural sponsor of *Monday Night Football.*

In 1969 during Seymour's tenure, JWT went from a private to a publicly traded company. Seymour retired from JWT in 1974 and was succeeded as chief executive officer (CEO) by Don Johnston. Johnston took over a company weakened by business losses and by a lack of stable top management that drove JWT stock to less than a fifth of its 1969 price, or seven dollars a share. Unlike his predecessors, Johnston had a masters of arts degree in international economics from Johns Hopkins University. He had overseen JWT's continental European operations and worked as a protégé to JWT's Tom Sutton. While the agency grew into an international giant under his leadership, most of its regional offices came under the call of managers and account people. In the 1970s JWT creative types—not formerly considered interested in administrative posts—began pushing into the upper management ranks. The move coincided with heightened client concerns about creative effectiveness of their advertising and marketing efforts.

In 1980 Johnston founded the JWT Group, in which J. Walter Thompson Company was the largest subsidiary. Other subsidiaries included the recently acquired Hill and Knowlton, MRB Group, Inc., and Lord, Geller, Federico, Einstein, Inc. Johnston presided over both companies as chairman and chief executive officer.

Rapid Growth

The 1980s were a time of rapid growth, despite problems involving overbillings to clients for spot media buys by the agency's syndication department. Income and profits rose sharply during the early 1980s. Then in 1986 the agency's advances seemed to stall. Because it came at a time of increasing merger and takeover activity in the business, JWT's weakened position made it a desirable takeover prospect. Toward the end of May 1987, JWT shares were being acquired by a secret bidder, which turned out to be a small British company called WWP Group, headed by Martin Sorrell, who had engineered much of the recent expansion of Saatchi & Saatchi through acquisition. Sorrell's group had bought nearly 5 percent of JWT's stock and announced in June that it intended take control of the company. It seemed hard at first to think that WPP could take over a company 18 times its size against its will. But leveraged buyouts had proved a powerful force in the restructuring of the American corporate establishment in the 1980s. The JWT Group said at first it would not be acquired, a stand that caused the share price to jump to $50.50. Finally, after two weeks of negotiations, an agreement was reached in which WPP would buy JWT for $566 million, or $55.50 a share.

The merger marked the return to JWT of Burt Manning, who was CEO of J. Walter Thompson USA when he left in August 1986 to open his own advertising agency. Manning was the first CEO of JWT to come up through the creative ranks in his native Chicago and in New York City. He unleashed the agency's creative talent, resulting in memorable campaigns for such clients as Kodak, Ford trucks, Gerber baby food, Goodyear Tires, Bally Health and Tennis, Kellogg's Corn Flakes cereal, Oscar Mayer hot dogs, British Telecom, Pepsi-Cola, the U.S. Marine Corps, Rolex watches, McDonnell Douglas aerospace, and Southland's 7-Eleven. The turnaround in product and reputation translated into double the agency's billings between 1980 and 1985, and double the revenues, double the profits, and improved margins at J. Walter Thompson USA.

During its history, JWT claimed a good many firsts. It introduced the first paper towel for Scott; RCA's 45-rpm record in 1949; the first home pregnancy test; the Ford Mustang in 1964 and the Taurus in 1986; the Kodak Instamatic camera; the first modern cartoon sequence comic strip in 1919 for an Aunt Jemima ad; the first beauty soap, Lux; Kraft's Miracle Whip in 1932; Pan Am's first passenger jet flight to Paris, France, in 1958; 7 UP's "Uncola" campaign; and the first color television commercial in 1957. Among JWT's most memorable slogan creations were Kodak's "Do you remember the times of your life?" Kellogg's "Snap, crackle, pop!" and Ford's "There's a Ford in your future."

Positioned for the New Century

Under CEO Christopher Jones, the agency instituted the use of a proprietary protocol, Thompson Total Branding, to assist clients in adopting new forms of content-related advertising, entertainment and digital communications, and interactive communications (Digital@JWT); direct response and database marketing (ThompsonConnect); and recruitment communications (JWT Specialized Communications). Jones, who at age 45 was the seventh and youngest CEO in the agency's history, led JWT to $1 billion in new business gains in 1999—the largest in its history. After joining JWT in London in 1984, the University of Cambridge graduate and former Saatchi board director was named CEO in 1989. In 1999 JWT became the first agency-owned subsidiary designed to integrate advertising, entertainment properties, and digital communications into new forms of content in a multimedia marketplace.

By the year 2000 JWT, an agency within the WPP Group, was the fourth-largest advertising agency brand in the world and the second largest in the United States. JWT's consolidated worldwide gross income exceeded $8 billion and its billings passed $10.87 billion, with new clients such as Sun Microsystems, KPMG, iPlanet, Spencer-Stuart, Foster's Beer, Avon, and Telecom Italia and established blue-chip clients that included Ford, Unilever, Kraft, Pfizer, and Shell. The company had broadened its international reach to 311 offices in 155 cities in 90 countries. In a single year it had made 20 key global acquisitions and investments in areas of digital branding, direct, database, and promotional marketing. Additions included Tonic 360, Imagio/JWT in Seattle, Washington; New York City–based Coolfire; Interactive Marketing concepts of Toronto, Canada; and Thompson Digital of Korea. JWT acquired major stakes in TMI, a full-service agency operating in Middle Eastern countries, and in APCU Thompson Asociados, a general agency operating in six Central American countries. It also increased its stake in Israel's Tamir Cohen in Tel Aviv.

Notable business initiatives included the launch of @JWT to integrate advertising, entertainment properties, and digital communications into new forms of brand-centric content for the convergence space. The initiative provided JWT clients with access to Basic/Brillstein-Grey, a Hollywood, California-based producer and distributor of television and films. The agency's newly established Worldwide Creative Council, comprised of a core group of 12 creative leaders from across JWT, developed a plan to sharpen the way in which the agency articulated and executed on its creative philosophy.

DIANE MERMIGAS

SOME HOME RUNS CLEAR THE BENCHES, OURS CLEAR THE SHELVES. From a pin drop heard round the world for Sprint® to six words that taught consumers to butter their bread with Philly® instead. From the Few, the Proud, the Marines to a question asked by our consumer research that helped make Ford Escort the best-selling small car and Ford Taurus the best-selling wagon in the U.S.A. From candid testimonials that helped Jenny Craig™ grow from 200,000 clients to over a million to a slogan that became a battle cry, "Nupe It.™" We hit home runs–we're J.Walter Thompson. Winning 50 EFFIES for effective advertising, 1987-1991. More EFFIES, for more clients, than any other agency. Need a home run? Call Ron Burns or Jim Patterson at (212) 210-7000. Give us the chance to go to bat for you.

JWT
NORTH AMERICA

This 1992 house ad featured some of the classic slogans created by the J. Walter Thompson Company.
Courtesy of the J. Walter Thompson Company.

Further Reading

"Creating the First Powerful Medium," *Advertising Age* (27 November 1989)

Earle, Richard, *The Art of Cause Marketing: How to Use Advertising to Change Personal Behavior and Public Policy*, Lincolnwood, Illinois: NTC Business Books, 2000

Fox, Stephen R., *The Mirror Makers: A History of American Advertising and Its Creators*, New York: Morrow, 1984

Goldsborough, Robert, "Great Names Get Start in New York Shops," *Advertising Age* (27 January 1997)

Goodrum, Charles, and Helen Dalrymple, *Advertising in America: The First 200 Years*, New York: Abrams, 1990

Manning, Burt, *J. Walter Thompson: Advertising Leadership, 1864–1989*, New York: Thompson, 1989

Mayer, Martin, *Madison Avenue, U.S.A.*, New York: Harper, 1958

Mayer, Martin, *Whatever Happened to Madison Avenue? Advertising in the '90s*, Boston: Little Brown, 1991

Packard, Vance Oakley, *The Hidden Persuaders*, New York: McKay, 1957; revised edition, New York: Pocket Books, 1980

Stabiner, Karen, *Inventing Desire: Inside Chiat/Day: The Hottest Shop, the Coolest Players, the Big Business of Advertising*, New York: Simon and Schuster, 1993

Wells, Melanie, "Agencies: Heady Days We Had the Money to Do Unbelievable Things," *Advertising Age* (28 February 1995)

Timex Corporation

Principal Agencies

Hirshon-Garfield, Inc.

Warwick & Legler, Inc.

W. B. Doner & Company

Grey Advertising

Fallon McElligott

The Timex Corporation traces its origins to 1857, the year that Benedict & Burnham Manufacturing Company, a brass-making enterprise located in Waterbury, Connecticut, established an independent Waterbury Clock Company. The company successfully integrated brass movements into a mass-produced line of spring or weight-driven clocks in rosewood cases, thereby contributing to the obsolescence of wooden clock parts and the demise of clock making as a craft. The company's extensive and expanding product line was promoted primarily through catalogs in the 1860s and 1870s and through "sales depots" established in New York City, Chicago, Illinois, San Francisco, California, and other key American cities.

When the pocket watch industry began to develop in the United States, Benedict & Burnham established another corporation, the Waterbury Watch Company, in 1880. Its first offering, the Long Wind pocket watch, featured a nine-foot-long, punched brass mainspring. Because it could be produced less expensively than was typical at the time, the company was able to sell it at a relatively low ($2.50 to $4.00) retail price. Sales of the Long Wind were brisk, as consumers were attracted to its reasonable price and reliability. The establishment of uniform time and time zones in the United States in 1883 also enhanced sales. Another version of the Long Wind, called the Jumbo after showman P.T. Barnum's elephant, was introduced in 1887.

Unfortunately, the Waterbury Watch Company deviated from the formula that had led to its original success. Its ladies' Elfin watch, introduced in 1894, was hailed in advertising as "the smallest made in this country." But it contained substantially more moving parts that necessitated a complicated, costly manufacturing process. By 1898 the financially troubled company again was compelled to sell watches to wholesalers to be used as premiums and was reorganized as the New England Watch Company. Efforts to sell ornate, jeweled pocket watches and a ladies' jeweled pendant watch failed. Although the company went bankrupt in 1912, it did not go out of business.

During this time an innovative, consumer-oriented marketer, Robert H. Ingersoll, entered the watch industry. In 1892 he bought 1,000 Jumbo watches from the Waterbury Clock Company (parent of the Waterbury Watch Company) and resold them through his own company catalog. In 1893 he contracted with the same company to produce two models of a much smaller watch. In 1894, 225,000 of these were sold; the following year, 485,000 were sold. The Ingersoll Yankee, an even smaller, less costly watch, was produced in 1896 and retailed at the unheard-of price of $1.00. Ingersoll backed it with a simple free-repair-or-exchange guarantee and advertised the Yankee as the "cheapest guaranteed watch in the world." Consumer demand forced dealers to carry the Yankee, and heavy price-oriented advertising obligated them to maintain the $1.00 retail price. By 1900 annual sales reached 6 million watches.

Just prior to World War I, French and Swiss watch designers introduced the wristwatch, initially as a piece of jewelry. Ingersoll, who had bought the New England Watch Company, advertised his own new wristwatch to the "cavalryman, farmer, motorist and above all, the woman who has no pockets." The popularity of the wristwatch with men soared after the U.S. Army made it standard military equipment during the war. Ingersoll and the Waterbury Clock Company cooperatively produced watches for the war effort and created a zinc/radium compound formula labeled "Radiolite" that enabled watch hands to

A suspicious
package was delivered to
a southern county courthouse
addressed simply "To Lisa." With
tensions high over the Gulf war,
a bomb squad set off a deliberate
blast to destroy it. Inside was Boomer,
a kitten. "This is a very sweet kitty,"
said a vet called to the scene. "It was
trusting, not angry or snippy."
Boomer's watch is quartz, so
it doesn't tick loudly. It
costs about $55.

TIMEX

For the retailer nearest you call 1-800-367-8463.

In the early 1990s Timex updated its celebrated "It takes a licking and keeps on ticking" slogan, using vignettes of individuals—and, in the case of this 1992 ad, animals—that survived harrowing experiences.

be illuminated at night, a feature highlighted in the company's ads.

In the 1920s Swiss companies developed smaller watches that were equal in precision to their larger U.S. counterparts. They produced fashionable wristwatches in many shapes and styles that appealed to a growing American interest in fashion. American watch companies were unable to compete. Ingersoll, already hurt by the rising cost of raw materials, quickly fell into financial insolvency, allowing the Waterbury Clock Company to gain complete control of his business in 1921.

Waterbury Clock promptly established a new company division, Ingersoll-Waterbury Company, to manufacture Ingersoll watches and alarm clocks. Despite heavy national advertising in a variety of newspapers and magazines that emphasized the strong Ingersoll brand name, sales lagged through the 1920s as Swiss imports flooded the market. By the early 1930s, the company that had been promoted as "the largest timepiece manufacturer in the world" was nearly out of business.

The company was rescued by an exclusive arrangement with Walt Disney Enterprises to produce character watches and clocks. The Mickey Mouse watch was introduced in 1933 under the Ingersoll name and initially sold directly off a miniature assembly line at the Chicago World's Fair. It became immensely popular with children and was followed by a variety of other Mickey Mouse watches and clocks, as well as Big Bad Wolf and Three Little Pigs watches, Tom Mix pocket watches, and Girl Scout and Boy Scout watches that displayed the scout honor code. A Donald Duck watch was launched in 1939.

Plagued by outdated machinery, poor quality, and return problems in the late 1930s and early 1940s, the company managed to survive and sold an average of 1.6 million watches per year. The "Ingersoll sweep second hand," a "new all-purpose watch," was introduced in 1940. New Kelton line models and a lower-priced Ingersoll line still addressed a market segment interested in inexpensive watches. In 1941 Thomas Olsen purchased control of the Waterbury Clock Company, and fellow Norwegian immigrant Joakim Lehmkuhl was placed in charge of daily operations. Under Lehmkuhl's leadership, the company excelled in its fulfillment of government-mandated wartime contracts for clocks and bomb fuses and the sophisticated mechanization of manufacturing processes. National advertising was built around war support themes. However, Swiss watches dominated the American jeweled watch market the entire decade.

Inspired by its advertising campaign for "the new Ingersoll clocks with the Timex heart," Waterbury Clock changed its name to United States Time Corporation and began using the Timex trademark in 1945. Overall sales grew in the years immediately following the war, but the company suffered losses in 1949.

In 1950 the company introduced its Timex line, containing an innovative yet simple design that allowed it to compete with other jeweled watchmakers. The watch was offered at a low price ($6.95 and $7.95, depending upon the model) that was highlighted in advertising along with its durable, "shock-resistant" quality and a one-year guarantee. At first it was sold primarily through drug, variety, and tobacco stores. Point-of-purchase pro-

motions were designed to demonstrate how well the watches were made: watches were submerged in water or beaten repeatedly on anvils to show their durability. Salesmen even threw watches against the wall and used other imaginative tactics to impress distributors. But although Timex captured 18 percent of the low-priced watch market by 1952, sales stalled.

In 1952, working with ad agency Hirshon-Garfield, Inc., the company developed the preliminary version of an advertising campaign that eventually became one of the most successful and memorable in advertising history. Ads in popular magazines such as *Life, Look,* and the *Saturday Evening Post* featured golfers Ben Hogan and Babe Didrikson Zaharias, as well as boxer Rocky Marciano describing how perfectly the durable Timex watch suited their athletic lifestyles. Other ads attempted to conclusively demonstrate that Timex watches were shockproof, waterproof, and dustproof. "Amazing test by Mickey Mantle proves Timex watches are really rugged" announced one advertisement that went on to describe how the baseball star had hit 50 home runs with a Timex strapped to the middle of his bat. "Turtles test Timex," another headline declared. Ten turtles with watches strapped to their backs had swum about in a tank of water for a day to prove the Timex "waterproof, shock-resistant guarantee." Other ads reported that the watches had survived such tests as being strapped to the leg of a racehorse, taped to a lobster's claw, thrown into New York Harbor tied to a boat anchor, and spending a week inside a running vacuum cleaner. The campaign was so successful that within a year the company could not meet consumer demand for the watches. By 1955, 15 percent of all watches sold in the United States were Timex watches.

In 1956 U.S. Time turned to television as its principal advertising medium in order to boost disappointing sales in metropolitan areas and to provide visibility that would encourage the federal government and others to support high tariff protection against Swiss and other imports. John Cameron Swayze, former anchor of NBC's *Camel News Caravan,* was hired as spokesperson for live, dramatic Timex commercials based on the torture-test theme that appeared first on the Steve Allen variety show and then on a series of TV jazz specials featuring Louis Armstrong, Duke Ellington, and others. Timex watches eventually survived tests that involved paint mixers, jackhammers, washing machines, dishwashers, water-skiers, a porpoise, and an 87-foot dive off the cliffs at Acapulco, Mexico. Swayze's popularity, credibility, and flair for the dramatic enhanced the effectiveness of this continuing campaign. The slogan "It takes a licking and keeps on ticking" became an integral part of American culture.

In 1958 Warwick & Legler, Inc., replaced Hirshon-Garfield as U.S. Time's principal ad agency, but the torture-test campaigns continued. To ensure that audiences believed the demonstrations involved no camera or editing tricks, Marshall Stone, who directed many of the commercials, was instructed to avoid "cutaways," the use of additional cameras or shots. When a 1958 commercial featuring a Timex attached to a boat propeller failed because the watch was lost when its watchband had broken or the watch had simply fallen off the propeller, the company repeated the demonstration the following week. This generated positive publicity, increased the credibility of the commercials, and stimulated sales. Consumers wrote to the company with suggestions for torture tests or testimonials about the durability of their Timex. The torture-test commercials were supplemented by endorsement advertising featuring Bob Hope, Bing Crosby, Jerry Lewis, Dean Martin, Mae West, and other celebrities.

In 1958 the company introduced the Swing-A-Ling, a new line of well-built but stylishly thin "Swiss-looking" watches with tiny movements. The Timex brand had captured nearly 25 percent of the watch market by 1960. Advertising efforts were highlighted by sponsorship of special prime-time television variety programs featuring such celebrities as Hope, Crosby, Martin, Frank Sinatra, and Elvis Presley. A 1962 holiday special, "Mr. Magoo's Christmas Carol," was rerun every year for a decade. The company also sponsored special programs such as the Academy Awards and Grammy Awards and acclaimed documentaries such as the *NBC White Paper* and "The Making of the President." By the end of the decade it was spending approximately $10 million annually on television advertising. To take advantage of the tremendous name recognition of the Timex brand, the company officially changed its name to the Timex Corporation in 1964.

During this period the company also was innovative in promoting watches as a fashion item. Advertising for its Cavatina, a women's model that sold for $9.95 to $17.95, depicted how women could have "a whole wardrobe of watches" to wear for any occasion at a price comparable to that of one expensive competitor's watch. One print ad displayed nine different watches and noted that "more smart women wear Timex than any other watch in the world." The company was able to garner more than one-third of the women's watch market within three years. In 1961 the company also introduced its first Electric Timex, a men's model manufactured at a newly acquired facility in Pforzheim, Germany, and sold at a price ($39.95) that undercut its nearest competitor by one-half. The company also began to compete with Swiss companies in the jeweled mechanical watch category. Hattori, Japan's largest watchmaker (Seiko brand), was contracted to provide discounted 17-jewel movements that were cased by U.S. Time Corporation and sold under the Timex name. (Jeweled watches have bearings made from gemstones, which improve the accuracy of the movement.) Beginning with this arrangement and using the same basic design, it sold 500 million men's jeweled, automatic, and self-winding Timex watches into the mid-1970s. The line between jeweled and nonjeweled watch market segments was blurred.

The company's sales success and strong emphasis on television advertising prompted jewelers and department stores to join grocery, drug, and tobacco stores as distribution channels for some of the Timex line. Rival companies found it difficult to compete with Timex's lower prices. By the end of the decade, the company was selling watches in 30 countries and had one-third of the market in England and about one-half of the U.S. market alone.

The 1970s were a time of turbulence for Timex and most traditional watch companies generally. Lehmkuhl and the small, loyal top management team that had guided Timex for many years retired, and Fred Olsen, son of the company's original Norwegian investor, gained control in 1973. He installed Martin Siem as president and later chairman. Siem and his successor, Robert Weltzien, implemented a new management philosophy, reorganized the company around product lines, and quickly doubled the number of employees worldwide.

The strains caused by these changes were exacerbated by dramatically changing conditions in the watch industry. Digital technology was being applied to watches, which could now be driven by integrated circuits instead of moving parts. At the same time, expensive quartz-technology watches were being introduced by American, Japanese, and Swiss companies. Everyone underestimated the great popularity that digital watches would soon enjoy, particularly after LED (light-emitting diode) technology, which made digital displays easy to read, was refined, and watches became multifunctional, providing calendars, calculators, and other features. Traditional watchmaking companies such as Timex were not only slow to develop digital products but also were unsure about which digital technologies to concentrate on. The high quality and low cost of integrated circuits allowed hundreds of other companies to enter the watchmaking field and sell digital watches at increasingly lower prices. Texas Instruments led the way, offering a digital watch for $20.00 in 1976 and $10.00 in 1977. Timex was offering its own digital watches by 1977, but priced between $24.95 and $34.95. This eroded the high-quality, low-cost image Timex had worked for years to establish and the market segment it had cornered. In addition, the influx of low-cost watches into the marketplace caused Timex to lose many of the drugstores, variety stores, and other traditional distribution outlets it had cultivated. In the meantime a longstanding contractual relationship with the Polaroid Corporation was phasing out and finally ended in 1978. (Timex had produced Polaroid cameras at its Little Rock, Arkansas, plant and at other U.S. plants since 1950.)

Sales of Timex watches continued to be strong, reaching a high point in 1978. By this time digital watches produced with low-cost labor in Hong Kong and other parts of Asia were flooding the U.S. market. Their $5-and-under price tags drove all American companies other than Texas Instruments out of the category. Working with Grey Advertising, which had been its primary agency since 1975, Timex tried to counter these trends by changing the image of its products. Campaigns built around the torture-test theme were retired in 1977. National print and TV ad campaigns that depicted strong associations with jewelers across the country sought to deal with distribution problems. A new spokesperson for Timex television advertising was Jim McKay, host of the popular weekly TV show *Wide World of Sports* on ABC.

Struggling in the late 1970s and early 1980s, Timex attempted to diversify its product line. Olsen replaced Robert Weltzien as head of Timex in 1980. The company bought General Electric's clock and timer division in 1979 and successfully marketed the products under the Timex name. In 1980 the company introduced its Nimlo 3-D camera. In 1982, backed by an advertising campaign created by J. Walter Thompson USA, Timex introduced its $99 Sinclair 1000 personal computer. In the same year, it started a HealthCheck product line that included digital scales, thermome-

TAKE TWO
They're small!

And so petitely priced from $9.95 to $15.00! Why spend money needlessly when you can buy one, two, three . . . a bowlful of Timex watches without being extravagant. Each deliciously styled . . . each carefree, contemporary, chic as you are. Beautiful reasons why more smart women wear **TIMEX** than any other watch in the world.

PRICES PLUS 10% FED. TAX

With the campaign theme "More smart women wear Timex than any other watch in the world," Timex captured one-third of the women's watch market in the early 1960s.

ters, and electronic blood pressure monitors. By 1984, all these businesses had failed or been sold and the company had been pared down considerably worldwide. Ending its mechanical watch business was part of this process.

Timex executives decided to concentrate on the watch industry again beginning in 1984. They manufactured a new line of quartz-analog watches that used a technology that reduced production costs. Campaigns from Grey Advertising focused on technological innovation and style. In response to the new Swiss Swatches, colorful, low-priced plastic watches designed for the young and stylish consumer, Timex introduced and promoted a Watercolors watch line. However, the company's first serious inroad into the marketplace in the postmechanical watch era took advantage of Americans' increasing interest in physical fitness and Timex's previous sponsorship of runners and the Hawaiian triathlon. The Ironman watch, introduced in 1984, was the forerunner of the 1986-launched Triathlon watch, which became the world's best-selling sports watch and one of the best-selling watches overall in the United States for the next ten years. Although it was initially sold to athletes involved in professional or highly competitive amateur sports, its popularity was expanded through promotional efforts that appealed to a broader market of aspiring amateur athletes or focused on special models of the watch designed for race car fans, skiers, and other sports enthusiasts. Timex spent approximately half of its approximately $10 million advertising budget on its sports watch line. Its top model, the Atlantis 100, was unveiled in a dramatic, $1 million underwater commercial produced by Grey Advertising for Superbowl XX.

In 1987 Fallon McElligott replaced Grey Advertising as Timex's principal advertising agency. When research indicated that American baby boomers were immersed in a wave of nostalgia, Timex joined other advertisers in a trend of reviving old advertising campaigns. In 1988, under Fallon McElligott's direction, the company brought back "It takes a licking and keeps on ticking" for television-dominated advertising campaigns, with new twists on the old theme: Timex watches were strapped to the stomachs of sumo wrestlers, the voice of an opera star broke everything but a Timex watch, and a heavy-metal guitarist used a Timex watch as a pick. One spot, which won a Clio award in the personal items category, featured a psychic who was able to bend a fork and curl a key but could not stop a Timex watch from ticking. Old audio recordings of John Cameron Swayze saying the classic slogan were inserted in some commercials. In 1990 advertising emphasis shifted to print and was more image-oriented. One print ad revealed an attractive Timex watch placed in dirty tire tracks. The headline read, "Grace under pressure." A two-month print campaign that year portrayed people who had survived serious accidents while wearing a Timex watch that "takes a licking and keeps on ticking." With all its watches priced below $75, Timex's share in the U.S. watch market was close to 50 percent by the end of the 1980s. However, competition in this market was intense, and this share eroded in the early 1990s.

In 1991 Timex purchased the Norwalk, Connecticut-based Callanen Watch Company. Timex watches were already being distributed effectively to mass-market stores such as J.C. Penney

Company and Wal-Mart Stores. The purchase gave the company penetration into upscale department stores that often carried Callanen's popular Guess line of watches. A breakthrough year for Timex was 1992. The company introduced four new watch brands, including Callanen's Guess and Monet brands, into the United Kingdom to compete successfully with the Swiss Swatch in that country. It also entered into an exclusive agreement with Paramount Pictures to produce futuristic-looking *Star Trek* watches. In addition, the company followed a watch industry trend of experimenting with company-owned retail watch outlets.

The company was revitalized most, however, when it equipped many of its digital and analog quartz watches with its new, patented Indiglo electroluminescent watch face. A print and television ad campaign revolving around the Indiglo night-light feature and incorporating humor supported the introduction of these watches and was repeated in modified form in subsequent years. An initial Fallon McElligott commercial depicted a firefly falling in love with the watch's blue glow to the strains of Frank Sinatra singing "Strangers in the Night." When the wearer's hand smacked the bug, the classic tag "Takes a licking and keeps on ticking" was heard via voice-over. The same tag line was used in print advertisements such as one that featured an Indiglo watch on green satin sheets with the accompanying headline, "Make your husband really shine in bed." Another declared, "You can tell your husband exactly when he started snoring last night." Advertising of this type was supported by a newsletter, *Perpetual Times,* that presented stories about ways consumers were making use of their Indiglo watches. Videotapes on the matter were distributed to stores, and a "Bright Idea Contest" was held in which consumers entered their best tales of Indiglo heroics. In response to market pressures and a declining market share, the company achieved some success in promoting its Indiglo line. This led to a 30 percent increase in sales and one-third of the U.S. watch market in 1992. By 1994 Indiglo technology had been fitted into more than 200 Timex styles, including women's watches, in response to consumer demand. Timex was spending all of its record-high $18 million advertising budget on promoting Indiglo.

Timex continued to produce novelty watches for the Walt Disney Company and others into the 1990s. At the same time, the company was making an effort to become more of a fashion brand. In 1994 it became the official timekeeper for the Seventh on Sixth fashion show in New York City. It also obtained a license to produce Nautica designer watches for the New York City-based Nautica Apparel Company. The company introduced the Data Link watch in 1995, at an initial price of $130. The watch was equipped with a wireless optical scanner that facilitated the collection and storage of appointment locations, telephone numbers, and other data taken from personal computers, using Windows-based software that came with the watch.

As the century drew to a close, Timex still occupied its position as the most prominent seller of watches in the United States, a status it had maintained for decades despite various business ups and downs. Timex was consistently rated highly among fashion brands. The company also was exploring ways to merge new technologies with its primary watchmaking and marketing activities. It entered into agreements with other companies, including a deal with Austin Innovations, Inc., to produce and market night-lights, an arrangement with Texas Instruments to integrate Indiglo technology into various tools, and a contract with Colonial Data Technologies Corporation to apply Indiglo technology to its caller identification products. The company joined with Motorola Corporation to produce a wrist pager in 1998. Timex also introduced an extremely shock- and water-resistant watch called the Humvee after the all-terrain vehicle whose name Timex secured through a licensing agreement.

In 1998 Timex also introduced the Turn and Pull alarm watch, touted as the first analog watch with an accurate alarm. The product introduction was backed by a Fallon McElligott campaign that spoofed 1950s television demonstration commercials and print ads with the tag line "More convenient than any excuses." In 1999 Timex added six versions of a Barbie doll analog wristwatch to its novelty line. It also developed a TMX line of analog and digital watches, aimed at preteens, in a variety of colors and straps and featuring a screen-saver mode and randomly chosen "mystery answers" that could be given to questions asked. Applying cutting-edge technology and novel ideas to its product lines, the company seemed determined to remain primarily focused on the watchmaking business and faithful to its long legacy of providing innovative products at affordable prices.

J.D. KEELER

Further Reading

Brown, Christie, "Sweat Chic," *Forbes* (5 September 1988)

DeSilvo, Kathy, "Fallon McElligott Goes Back in Time," *Shoot* (4 June 1999)

Fahey, Alison, "Another 'Lickin,'" *Advertising Age* (7 November 1988)

Ginsberg, Michael, "Digital Watches Bringing Watchmaking Back to the U.S.," *Business Week* (27 October 1975)

"The Great Digital Watch Shake-Out," *Business Week* (2 May 1977)

"Japanese Heat on the Watch Industry: Timex and TI Wilt under the Far East Challenge," *Business Week* (5 May 1980)

Lewis, Scott, "Timex Corporation," in *International Directory of Company Histories*, vol. 25, edited by Laura E. Whitley, Chicago: St. James Press, 1999

Magnet, Myron, "Timex Takes the Torture Test," *Fortune* (27 June 1983)

McDermott, Kathleen, *Timex: A Company and Its Community, 1854–1998*, Middlebury, Connecticut: Timex Corporation, 1998

Morgenstern, Steve, "Watch Out! New High-Tech Wristwatches Do Everything but Phone Home," *Home Office Computing* (December 1995)

Underwood, Elaine, "Indiglo Watch Lights Up Better Times for Timex," *Brandweek* (25 April 1994)

Jack Tinker & Partners

Founded by McCann-Erickson, Inc., 1960; attracted attention because of its experimental workshop structure, but adopted a more traditional agency structure, early 1960s; merged with various Interpublic agencies, early 1970s; disappeared after its merger with Campbell-Ewald International, 1976.

Major Clients

Braniff International Airways
Bulova Watch Company, Inc.
Carling Brewing Company
Coca-Cola Company
General Motors Corporation (Buick Motor Division)
Miles Laboratories, Inc. (Alka-Seltzer)

Jack Tinker & Partners (JT&P) was an experiment in advertising-agency structure, set up and built with the resources of McCann-Erickson and its parent company, Interpublic, Inc. It sought to isolate and nurture the purely creative function apart from the day-to-day aspects of normal agency activity, particularly administrative duties, which were seen as a drain on time and creative freedom. This approach was inspired in part by Doyle Dane Bernbach (DDB) and the then-recent advertising phenomenon that was being called the "creative revolution" and in part by an effort to look for what Jack Tinker called "a third way." The agency briefly became a major creative influence in the 1960s and home to Mary Wells, Gene Case, and other luminaries of the period before self-destructing in the 1970s.

Tinker arrived late at the most innovative stage of his career. He was a graduate of the Philadelphia (Pennsylvania) Academy of Fine Arts when he began his professional life at the age of 20 in 1926 at N.W. Ayer & Son. In 1933 he moved to J. M. Mathes, Inc., where he remained for six years before arriving at McCann-Erickson in 1939. Except for a six-month period at the J. Walter Thompson Company (JWT), he remained associated with McCann for the rest of his career. After becoming a creative director at McCann in 1951, he grew increasingly involved in noncreative business and administrative functions, a pattern he resented and one that led him at one point to consider leaving the agency. When he discussed this possibility with Marion Harper, president of McCann, Harper responded with a suggestion for an alternative workshop arrangement, which soon developed into a McCann affiliate able to devote its full time to seeking new ways to use creativity and media and other communication tools without the pressure of immediate deadlines and short-term goals. It was exactly what Tinker wanted.

The Tinker "Laboratory"

Finally on 1 May 1960 John H. Tinker & Partners (soon to be called simply Jack Tinker & Partners) opened in temporary space in the Waldorf-Astoria Hotel in New York City and moved a short time later to more permanent quarters in the Dorset Hotel on West 54th Street. The key personnel included Tinker and three McCann vice presidents: Donald Calhoun, the creative director, who had joined McCann in 1948; Myron McDonald, account supervisor, who had been with the agency since 1945; and Herta Herzog, a psychologist and authority on behavioral and motivational research, with McCann since 1943. The parent agency would make assignments on a special-project basis from among its regular clients (Buick and Coca-Cola were among the first) to the Tinker "laboratory" and sometimes detach selected people on a temporary basis from the main agency. The purpose was to move certain "experimental" work outside normal agency channels. The trade press began referring to the new company as "Tinker's thinkers." Among the projects it worked on was the introduction of the Bulova Accutron watch. Several McCann clients, including Standard Oil of New Jersey and National Cash Register, paid $40,000 a month for Tinker's services.

In November 1961 Tinker ran a full-page want ad over his signature in *Advertising Age* announcing four new positions. This action represented an unprecedented openness in personnel matters, always notoriously secretive in advertising, and was intended to demonstrate the agency's willingness to ignore precedent. "What we offer you," he wrote in the ad, "is a unique creative atmosphere, considerable freedom from deadlines and telephones, and four permissive, experienced minds to bang against. . . ." The notice was also specific about salary: $21,000, which was a considerable sum in 1961 when $10,000 was considered respectable for a middle-management executive. Some blamed Tinker for setting off a spiral of salary inflation. The ad attracted about 350 responses. Tinker ultimately chose three advertising people and a former comedy writer for Steve Allen and Andy Griffith.

In the early and middle 1960s, JT&P was the most exciting place to work in the ad industry. With the exception of its ads for the Buick Riviera, a model that JT&P named and launched, the agency was extremely discreet about both its work and its clients. The high level of security emphasized that this was a special agency set up to handle special problems on an ad hoc basis. An advertiser could therefore approach Tinker without the knowledge of its current agency and be sure the agency would never find out. Routine maintenance work was avoided. Each of the firm's selected projects received maximum effort. Shortly after JT&P was established, McCann-Erickson underwent a major reorgani-

A 1961 house ad for Jack Tinker & Partners demonstrated the company's unique approach to hiring, as well as an inclination not to take itself too seriously.

zation that resulted in the formation of Interpublic, Inc. (later renamed the Interpublic Group of Companies), a holding company consisting of three agency networks with Harper as chairman. Though JT&P remained a unit of McCann, it reported directly to Harper and Interpublic.

Tinker began to look more like a conventional agency when it announced in May 1964 that it had been appointed agency for Miles Laboratories, makers of Alka-Seltzer, after the company dismissed its long-time agency, Wade Advertising, which had handled the brand since its introduction in the 1930s. It was the first business to be handled by Tinker in the manner of a traditional account and was valued in the $11 million–$12 million range. Behind the account switch, however, lay a three-year effort by Harper to get the Alka-Seltzer business by acquiring the Wade agency. In 1964, when Miles was reviewing its agency relationships, Harper proposed a merger of Wade into Interpublic's Compton agency, a plan that failed to materialize. That was when Harper brought Tinker into the picture. Miles's management was said by *Advertising Age* to be "deeply impressed" by its presentation—so impressed, in fact, that Harper made the decision to set Tinker up as an independent agency capable of handling account administration on a day-to-day basis. Thus in the spring of 1964, Jack Tinker & Partners became a bona fide advertising agency, statements by Tinker to the contrary notwithstanding.

In October 1965 Harper tried to hire the Miles account team at Wade, which continued to handle several Miles brands, and install it into the Tinker group. Jeff Wade, chairman of the Wade agency, proposed that Interpublic buy the whole agency, a plan Harper rejected. Finally, in January 1966 Wade liquidated the agency; the Miles account group went to JT&P, which also took on One-A-Day Vitamins, Chocks, and Nervine from Miles and the Toni Company, a unit of Gillette.

About the time the Wade people came to Tinker, the agency's star creative personality, Mary Wells, left to form her own agency. Wells had been hired by Harper at $60,000 in 1963 and not only became a major presence on the Alka-Seltzer account but also brought $2.5 million worth of Braniff airline business into the agency ("The end of the plain plane"). Tinker had a heart attack in 1966 and decided it was time to reduce his workload. There were reports that both he and Harper were eager to make Wells the next president of JT&P. An announcement was close to being made when partners McDonald and Herzog threatened to resign if Wells was elevated to the top job. With the presidency blocked, Wells departed with Stewart Greene, Richard Rich, and the Braniff account to found Wells, Rich, Greene, Inc. (WRG). Another loss was partner Donald Calhoun, who that same year published a novel called *Dando Shaft*. The story concerned the advertising business, and Tinker saw the characters as a thinly disguised portrayal of himself and several associates.

Through it all, Tinker insisted his firm was not becoming an "agency," merely an expanded version of the "think tank" it had been, despite the fact that JT&P joined the American Association of Advertising Agencies and undertook normal media-buying functions. During this period, the agency introduced the Tech-matic razor for Gillette and won the Carling Brewing Company account. JT&P also entered into political advertising in 1968, managing the preconvention campaign for Nelson Rockefeller in his fight for the Republican nomination against Richard M. Nixon (whose ad agency was Fuller & Smith & Ross). At the time, it was considered to be the most expensive advertising effort ever mounted to win a nomination, costing an estimated $5 million. Nixon won five important primary elections, however, and was nominated on the first ballot.

The Alka-Seltzer Effort

JT&P's best-remembered work was for Alka-Seltzer. "No matter what shape your stomach's in," created by Rich and Greene, was done in several variations and featured a montage of images of people's abdomens. In a celebrated 1969 commercial filmed by N. Lee Lacy Associates production company, actor George Raft, known for his portrayal of gangsters, was seen in a prison dining hall banging a tin cup on the table and starting a riot for Alka-Seltzer (a parody of similar scenes from such prison movies as *The Big House* and *White Heat*). By the end of the 1960s, Miles Labs had grown into a $20 million account for JT&P. But the failure of the agency to win and hold other accounts of similar size made it increasingly dependent on a single piece of business. The first weakness came in 1967, when Miles moved its vitamin brands to JWT. Then in September 1968 William Weilbacher, the key account person on Miles at Tinker, also went to JWT. The situation was aggravated by a general weakening of Interpublic's profitability and the need for significant retrenchment. These developments culminated in 1967 when Interpublic bought out Harper's contract and ousted him as chairman in November. By this time, Tinker himself was in semiretirement.

In an effort to strengthen the position of the agency, which billed $25 million to $30 million by decade's end, the parent company merged Tinker into Erwin, Wasey & Company, Inc., another Interpublic shop, in July 1969. But some observers felt the move might have the opposite effect, and indeed it did. Many in the industry believed that by merging JT&P with Erwin, Wasey, Interpublic made it easier for Miles to feel that the future of the agency was no longer dependent on its continued business. In any case, two weeks later Tinker lost the account to DDB, and JT&P ended the decade in the "$3 million agency" class, according to the *New York Times*, down from a peak of $47 million two years before. (DDB had the account only a year before it went to WRG, where Wells and her partners, who had worked on the business from 1964 to 1966, were reunited with the brand.)

During the five years JT&P handled Alka-Seltzer, the agency brought about a fundamental change in the way antacid medicines were advertised. Tinker did away with the diagrams of acid dripping on stomach linings and hammers pounding on silhouettes of skulls. In their place, the agency brought wit, parody, irony, and a new level of believability to their messages through innovative and creative advertising. It was a tradition Alka-Seltzer would continue in its future associations with DDB and WRG.

Without Tinker and Harper, the agency began to drift within the Interpublic family. Four months after the Erwin, Wasey merger, JT&P was reestablished as an independent shop, only to be merged again in November 1970 with Pritchard Wood Associates, founded in London, England, in 1922 and acquired by Interpublic in 1961. JT&P became Tinker-Pritchard Wood Associates. Less than a year later, in September 1971, Interpublic bought Dodge & Delano, which had been founded in 1923 as Lawrence C. Gumbinner Advertising. In 1963 it joined briefly with North Advertising to become Gumbinner-North, then ended the relationship in 1969 to become Dodge & Delano. When it became Tinker, Dodge & Delano (TD&D) in 1971, Bruce Dodge and Lester Delano became chairman and president, respectively, and Pritchard Wood was dropped from the name.

The 1970s passed with little growth, as the agency held its billings in the $20 million–$25 million range. In March 1976 Interpublic merged TD&D with Campbell-Ewald International (C-E), a separate unit from the domestic Campbell-Ewald agency, headquartered in Warren, Michigan, and serving General Motors. Now it was Tinker, Campbell-Ewald, Inc., housed in C-E's New York City offices.

By the end of the decade, the Tinker name had been merged out of existence by the same parent company that had established it as one of the most innovative creative forces in advertising in the 1960s. Jack Tinker died in 1985 at the age of 79.

JOHN MCDONOUGH

Further Reading

Grant, Don, "New Tinker Generation Works to Make Billings Live Up to Its Billing," *Advertising Age* (7 April 1969)

Higgins, Denis, "Ending 3-Year 'Test,' Tinker Looks to Future," *Advertising Age* (2 September 1963)

Johnston, Russ, *Marion Harper: An Unauthorized Biography,* Chicago: Crain Books, 1982

"McCann Set Up Creative Unit Free of Administrative Details, Worries," *Advertising Age* (20 June 1960)\

Tires

The tire industry is considered by many to be a rather pedestrian business, turning out products barely distinguishable from one another. Yet despite this lackluster image, the industry boasts two of the most recognizable and enduring corporate icons ever created— Bibendum (the roly-poly "Michelin Man") and the Goodyear blimp—as well as an advertising slogan ("Where the rubber meets the road") that has taken on a life of its own.

Michelin's First Hundred Years

Created in 1898 during Michelin's infancy, Bibendum has been used consistently ever since, giving the company a "comfortable" identity with consumers. The name *Bibendum,* taken from the Latin phrase *Nunc est bibendum* (Now is the time to drink), was adopted by the Michelin brothers, Andre and Edouard, to underscore the ability of their products to "swallow" obstacles and keep going. The character has become so widely recognized that in 2000 it was voted the top corporate logo of all time by an international jury of business and marketing professionals. One of the judges, the British graphic designer Peter Saville, pronounced Bibendum "a fabulous piece of corporate iconography" and probably the foremost example of "liquid identity." John Hegarty, chairman of the ad agency Bartle Bogle Hegarty, described it as "a simple, easily recognizable, but very powerful design that communicates so much."

The first incarnations of Bibendum reflected the tires of the day, which were very narrow; the early Bibendum was thus comprised of dozens of tires stacked on top of one another, making the figure appear somewhat mummylike. Later, as tires became wider, Bibendum's appearance was modified, becoming more and more the roly-poly character familiar worldwide today. (Today's Bibendum is typically drawn 12 tire widths tall, whereas in the early days he stood as many as 32 tire widths tall.) He was originally drawn with a cigar—the 1908 French copyright includes a description of it—and he continued to be an avid smoker until the 1930s, when tuberculosis reached near-epidemic levels.

Through the years designers have refined Bibendum's image, making the figure softer and gentler. Bibendum was even cited by Harvard zoologist Stephen Jay Gould in a 1982 study of evolution. Gould showed how representations of the tire man (and Mickey Mouse, as well) over time illustrate the biological phenomenon of neotony (retention of childhood characteristics by a mature individual).

The original idea for Bibendum is reported to have come from Edouard Michelin, who, at an 1894 exhibition in Lyons, France, saw a stack of tires arranged in such a way as to resemble a human torso and head. By coincidence, a French artist, Marius Rossillon—alias "O'Galop"—called on the Michelins shortly after the trade show to try to interest them in his caricatures and advertising sketches. Among them was a poster depicting a portly King Gambrinus—reputed to have discovered the art of brewing—lifting a glass of beer and offering the toast, *"Nunc est bibendum."*

A Munich, Germany, brewery had rejected the image, but Andre Michelin reportedly saw a resemblance between King Gambrinus and his brother's idea for a man of tires. O'Galop was commissioned to transform King Gambrinus into the Michelin Man; the stein of beer was replaced with a cocktail glass full of nails and broken glass, and the phrase *"Nunc est bibendum"* was supplemented with "The Michelin tire swallows obstacles" in the revised posters, first issued in June 1898. The Michelin Man's white color reflected the hue of tires of that time; the rubber industry had not yet discovered that carbon black (essentially, soot produced under controlled burning of oil) was an ideal strengthening ingredient; so early automobile tires were white rather than black.

The character came to be called Bibendum as a result of an incident that occurred a few months after its creation. A competitor in that year's Paris-Amsterdam motor race shouted out, "Here comes Bibendum," when he saw Andre Michelin approaching the starting line. The name stuck, and the brothers began in earnest to employ the character as the company's image in the marketplace. Bibendum first appeared in print advertisements in 1899 and remained a mainstay of the company's advertising and promotional efforts for decades.

The Michelin brothers proved adept at a range of promotional efforts. "Our sole purpose was to combine business with pleasure," Andre Michelin once said, describing his concept of advertising. Early on, competition played a key role in convincing first the cycling and later the motoring public that pneumatic tires were superior to solid or semi-solid tires. More than a century later, motor sports continued to play an important role in the company's promotional efforts—evidenced by Michelin's decision to re-enter Formula One racing in 2001, after a 15-year hiatus, as a tire supplier.

The Michelin brothers, however, saw considerable promotional opportunity in the nascent motoring industry itself, and in 1900 the company issued the first *Guide Michelin*—a simple red-covered, pocket-sized book containing information vital to the motorist's safe and enjoyable journey: maps, and locations of gasoline and repair stations, inns, restaurants, and hotels. The *Guide Michelin* eventually developed into a business of its own and continues to turn out millions of guides for tourists around the world. The practice of rating hotels began with the first edition, and the practice of awarding restaurants stars—a highly prestigious honor today—began soon thereafter. Michelin also undertook the task of helping to map France's network of roads—there were fewer than 3,000 cars there in 1900—and later led a petition drive to force the French government to come up with a logical system of numbering roads.

Andre Michelin is also credited with one of the earliest examples of the "advertorial." In 1901 he used advertising space in daily newspapers to publish what appeared to the reader to be an editorial column, addressing topics of interest to both the cycling and motoring public. Known as *Les Lundis de Michelin* (Michelin Mondays), the columns ran weekly for more than 13 years, ending upon the outbreak of World War I. Andre Michelin sought out another market segment by buying the back cover of an illustrated magazine *(L'illustration Theatrale)* and creating *Le Theatre Illustre du Pneu* (The Illustrated Tire Theater). The posterlike illustrations portrayed a scene drawn from that issue's contents, casting Bibendum in a starring role.

Bibendum nearly went out of favor in the post–World War II period as Michelin, like other rebuilding companies, struggled with its own identity amidst the postwar chaos. Michelin also was hampered by the deaths of its founders—Andre in 1931 and Edouard in 1940—and the lack of a clear-cut successor. In addition, the company was shifting enormous resources to converting its growing production capacity to steel-belted radial construction—a design that was developed and patented by Michelin in 1937 but that only came to the fore after World War II. During the 1950s, advertising and promotion took a backseat to manufacturing investments as demand outstripped supply.

As the company's creative minds struggled over whether to update Bibendum or replace him, an event occurred in July 1969 that was beyond the company's control and breathed new life into the Michelin Man. Many viewers who witnessed U.S. astronauts take their first walks on the moon could not help but be struck by

Bibendum, the Michelin Man, made his debut in 1898 and, with occasional updating, has maintained a presence in Michelin's advertising ever since. This version of the spokes-character dates from 1987. *Reprinted by permission of Michelin North America, Inc.*

a resemblance between the space-suited heroes and Bibendum. Global attention to the moon landing coincided with the build-up of the Michelin brand in North America. Michelin had sold tires in the United States for decades; it even operated a plant in New Jersey in the 1920s. But it was not until the early 1970s that the company made a full-scale assault on the world's largest automotive market, opening three plants in the United States and Canada between 1971 and 1975. Its first U.S. ad agency was George P. Clarke Advertising.

Coinciding with a heightened public interest in automotive safety—fueled by consumer advocate Ralph Nader's condemnations of the vehicle industry—Michelin's quality orientation found favor with the American consumer. In the late 1970s and early 1980s, the creative director for Michelin North America's advertising department, Walter Storozuk, gave Bibendum a fresh, more dynamic appearance for use at a national sales conference. The new Bibendum was a hit with American dealers and consumers and forced Michelin designers in France to rethink the figure from top to bottom. In 1985 Michelin decided to give Bibendum a fresh look globally. It cost the company more than $300 million to phase in the new image, putting the character's likeness on company stationery, vehicles, and more.

Besides its century-old Tire Man icon, the French tire maker's U.S. subsidiary lays claim to an advertising campaign whose message remained virtually unaltered for more than 18 years—the infant safety campaign highlighting the company's safety-oriented tag line: "Because so much is riding on your tires."

The campaign debuted in the United States in 1983 in point-of-purchase promotional materials. The ads—featuring images of cute babies sitting inside tires—were so well received that Michelin asked the agency, DDB Needham, to transform the message into the company's primary image advertising campaign in 1984. The effort was so successful that it continued as Michelin North America's signature campaign for 17 years. The concept proved versatile, allowing the company to adapt it to wet driving conditions, winter driving, and off-road adventuring. In 1998, Bibendum's

For nearly 80 years Goodyear has used its blimps and dirigibles, as featured on this 1929 billboard, as an integral part of its marketing in North America.

centennial year, Michelin blended its two highly recognizable symbols into one, with a commercial from DDB Needham Worldwide that showed a baby crawling up to the Bibendum character, who then lifted the baby and cradled it—once again driving home the safety message.

For 2000, the campaign got a fresh twist. The infant disappeared from the ad, but its presence was implied as friends of a pregnant woman give her a set of Michelin tires at a baby shower. The DDB Needham–created campaign developed a cult following of sorts. The company claimed it frequently receives requests to have a child or grandchild considered for a future shoot. The baby campaign was largely a North American franchise. Although other Michelin companies internationally used the concept sporadically, none adopted the campaign on a widespread basis.

Michelin North America retired the baby campaign in mid-2001 and turned over its account to Detroit-based Campbell-Ewald for 2002 and beyond. Campbell-Ewald retained the tag line, "Because so much is riding on your tires," but replaced the baby with images of Bibendum caressing tires in a factory before their release for sale or of Bibendum flying into space aboard the Space Shuttle (Michelin makes the Space Shuttle's tires).

Goodyear: Triumph of the Blimp

The Goodyear Tire & Rubber Company's use of the blimp as an advertising and promotional vehicle—and later as a corporate symbol—has developed over time, beginning in 1917, when the company received contracts to build airships for the U.S. Navy. Goodyear built both rigid dirigibles and nonrigid blimps; the former were phased out following a series of high-profile accidents that culminated with the Hindenberg disaster; the latter

were used fairly regularly by the Navy throughout the 1930s and 1940s.

After the close of World War II, Goodyear bought back five Navy blimps to use for advertising and promotional purposes. It was not until 1958 that the company began to use the blimps for promotion. That year Goodyear hired Robert H. Lane as director of public relations. At that time, the company had only one blimp in service, and management was on the verge of decommissioning it.

Lane saw the promotional possibilities and convinced the management to give him a year to work with the blimp. A publicity tour of the eastern U.S. seaboard exposed millions to the Goodyear blimp and convinced the company to put more funding behind the effort. When the Navy scrapped its remaining blimps in 1962, Goodyear's "Skytacular" was the only blimp flying in North America. An array of programmable lights on each flank of the blimp allowed Goodyear to broadcast both corporate and civic messages at night.

By the mid-1960s the company had commissioned two more blimps; they were in constant demand as aerial TV platforms for sporting events and other outdoor spectacles. As Lane frequently pointed out to management: "Nobody else has a blimp. It's like having the only ad in *Life* magazine, the only sign in Times Square, or the only billboard along the Los Angeles freeway."

Despite the obvious popularity of the blimp, it has not been a focal point of company advertising except on one occasion. In 1982 Goodyear television ads featured the blimp flying at treetop level following cars as they drove along. The message: "Put the blimp behind you." Goodyear had a monopoly on the skies for more than two decades before other companies took to the air with their own, albeit smaller, blimps. Young & Rubicam (Y&R)

was Goodyear's agency for passenger tires, replacing the Kudner Agency in the 1940s. N.W. Ayer handled corporate and institutional for a period also. Y&R remained with the company until it was replaced by the J. Walter Thompson Company (JWT) in 1985. The blimp played a starring role in the 1977 thriller *Black Sunday,* in which terrorists hijacked it and tried to use it to wreak havoc on the Super Bowl. In the late 1970s, rival tire maker B.F. Goodrich—playing off the confusion between the Goodyear and Goodrich names—and its ad agency, BBDO, created a "We're the Other Guys" campaign that used comic situations to point out the fact that "Goodrich doesn't have a blimp." In early 2001 Goodyear split with its agency of 15 years, JWT, and switched its advertising to Goodby, Silverstein & Partners in San Francisco, which created a campaign called, "On the Wings of Goodyear." This campaign focused on the human element—scenes of carpooling, the morning commute, and family vacations, for example—instead of the firm's technological accomplishments. It replaced the "Serious Freedom" campaign Goodyear had used from the mid-1990s and into 2001.

Expanding Field

Over the course of the 20th century the tire business became progressively more competitive. By the 1930s several major U.S. brands were actively advertising, including Goodyear (ads by the Kudner Agency; Y&R; JWT), Firestone (Sweeney & James Company), General Tire (D'Arcy Advertising), B.F. Goodrich (Ruthrauff & Ryan, Inc.; BBDO after 1940), Kelly-Springfield (J. Stirling Getchell, Inc.; Compton Advertising, Inc., after 1942), United States Rubber (Campbell-Ewald Company), and about a dozen smaller companies.

Firestone was among the first to aggressively enter network radio when Sweeney & James launched *The Voice of Firestone* on NBC in 1928, a year after the founding of the network. The program of concert music was intended to distinguish the company with a reputation for quality and would remain on the air in the same time period (Monday at 8:30 P.M.) until 1954. Firestone also entered television early, simulcasting the radio show starting in 1949. The TV show continued under Firestone's sole sponsorship until 1963. Goodrich Tires also came to radio early, sponsoring the *Goodrich Silvertown Orchestra Program* between 1925 and 1935.

In the mid-1950s Firestone coined a phrase in-house that has withstood the test of time: "Where the rubber meets the road." Featured in numerous ad campaigns since its introduction, the slogan and its jingle (which debuted in the 1960s) still are heard often today; oddly, Bridgestone/Firestone does not use the coinage in its promotional materials. Instead, the phrase "rubber meets the road" has taken on a meaning all its own in the public domain—as a rough equivalent to "the buck stops here"—and is uttered frequently by politicians. Firestone founder Harvey S. Firestone understood the value of a good slogan and coined a few of his own through the years. In the company's early days, for example, he told his engineers to use the letters from the word "non-skid" to make a tread pattern; this led to the slogan that a Firestone tire "left its name wherever it went."

By the 1990s still more companies had entered the field, but the familiar names still dominated, although they were somewhat reconfigured and consolidated. Firestone merged with Bridgestone to become Bridgestone/Firestone, with advertising handled by TBWA Chiat/Day. Goodrich merged in 1987 with the tire division of chemical giant Uniroyal, Inc., to become Uniroyal-Goodrich Tire Company, which subsequently was bought by Michelin in 1989. As of the year 2000, however, all of these continued as active brands with their own advertising efforts. Michelin's ads were handled by DDB, while W.B. Doner & Company handled Goodrich, and Trone Advertising represented Uniroyal. Dunlop Tires had been marketed in the United States since the 1930s, first as the U.S. subsidiary of Dunlop Rubber/Dunlop Holdings, then as an independent in the mid-1980s. Sumitomo Rubber Industry, Ltd., of Kobe, Japan, bought Dunlop in 1986, and Goodyear acquired Dunlop in 1999.

BRUCE DAVIS

See also color plate in this volume

Further Reading

Darmon, Olivier, *Le grand siècle de Bibendum,* Paris: Hoëbeke, 1997; *The Michelin Man's First Hundred Years,* translated by Jeffrey C. Rian and Isabelle Taudière, Paris: Hoëbeke, 1997
O'Reilly, Maurice, *The Goodyear Story,* edited by James T. Keating, Elmsford, New York: Benjamin, 1983

Tobacco. *See* Cigarettes

Tourism. *See* Travel and Tourism

Toyota Motor Corporation

Principal Agencies
Clinton E. Frank, Inc.
Dancer, Fitzgerald, Sample, Inc. (later DFS Dorland)
Saatchi & Saatchi Los Angeles

Although now it may be difficult to believe, Toyota was not always a household name in the United States. When the company's vehicles first arrived in the American market, public awareness of the brand was nil. Toyota turned to advertising to build its brand name. For the past several decades, the company has been a leader in brand and marketing campaigns, and among import automakers, it frequently ranks among the highest in brand awareness.

Toyota advertising has evolved slowly over the years. Proud of its image for reliability and quality, the company aimed to reinforce those values while inducing consumers to associate additional positive traits with its cars. Modifying rather than replacing its ad campaigns has allowed Toyota to continually enhance and refine its overall message, communicating the company's values to consumers.

Toyota's basic early advertising message, "Toyota outperforms other imports," has prevailed through the years. Like other imports, it has typically stuck with its themes longer than its U.S. rivals. For example, the carmaker changed its ad theme only three times in 14 years from 1975 to 1989, a period in which U.S. auto marketers often changed themes with each model year.

The Toyota Motor Company began operations in Japan in 1937. It was the world's fourth-largest producer of motor vehicles, after General Motors, Ford, and Volkswagen, when it entered the U.S. market in 1957. Toyota Motor Sales Company (later renamed Toyota Motor Sales, U.S.A., Inc.) was formed on 31 October 1957 following the lifting of restrictions on Japanese auto production imposed after World War II. The creation of the sales company reversed Toyota's orientation to the marketplace, subordinating production to marketing goals.

Toyota's first foray into the American market was the Toyopet, an unattractive, slow-moving vehicle that never sold more than 1,000 units. Toyota withdrew the Toyopet in 1961 but returned to the U.S. market in 1965 with the Corona. The car was marketed first via a network of 65 dealers, all in the Los Angeles, California, market. The launch was accompanied by extensive TV advertising. The advertising allowance per Toyota vehicle in the United States at the time was $70, paid half by the dealer and half by Toyota. Toyota's portion included an estimated $5 for production of commercials. The company had an additional U.S. advertising budget set by Toyota in Japan, which was estimated at $4 million. Consumer print ads were paid for out of this account.

Toyota's first U.S. campaign debuted on the West Coast in regional editions of national magazines. Most national magazines—such as *Time, Life,* and *Newsweek*—had begun to publish regional editions with lower advertising rates than their national editions. By purchasing ad space in these local publications, Toyota achieved just as much prominence as its U.S.-based rivals while paying only a fraction of the price.

While print ads heightened Toyota's exposure, the company used the medium of television to showcase the new Corona. Because of financial constraints, Toyota formed its first dealer advertising association in 1965, with the company and dealerships splitting media costs. Toyota spent the bulk of its $5,000 TV production budget on one commercial from Clinton E. Frank, Inc., which ran for eight months in both 30- and 60-second versions.

Since no other Japanese automaker was advertising on TV at the time, the Toyota name quickly gained recognition among Americans in the key California markets of Los Angeles, San Diego, and San Francisco and in Portland, Oregon, another major market. Toyota's first national spot, taken from a 1967 customer testimonial, was "Get your hands on a Toyota . . . you'll never let go." The Clinton E. Frank agency handled the Corolla spot. Some dealerships held promotions in which a person who kept his or her hands on a displayed Toyota for the longest time would win the vehicle.

In 1965, the first year the company advertised on television, 6,500 Corollas were sold; in the following two years, Corolla sales reached 21,000 and 38,000, respectively. By 1969 Toyota Motor Sales, U.S.A., Inc., in Torrance, California, was the nation's 114th-largest advertiser with a $12 million budget, nearly triple its 1968 total.

In 1968 the Clinton E. Frank agency achieved a first in import advertising in the United States when it went after the Detroit automakers in two new commercials, "Helicopter" and "Ferryboat." These were seen as a major departure for import car advertising. (Table 1 lists several of the prominent campaigns that would propel Toyota to leadership of the import market over the decades.)

When Toyota introduced "Who could ask for anything more?"—a tag line created by Dancer, Fitzgerald, Sample (DFS) at

Table 1. Major Toyota U.S. Advertising Campaigns.

Date	Campaign (Agency)
1967	"Get your hands on a Toyota . . . you'll never let go (Clinton E. Frank)
1974	"Small car specialists for 40 years" (Clinton E. Frank)
1975	"Oh what a feeling" (Dancer, Fitzgerald, Sample)
1976	"Who could ask for anything more?" "You asked for it, you got it!" (Dancer, Fitzgerald, Sample)
1987	"Toyota quality. . . . Who could ask for anything more?" (Dancer, Fitzgerald, Sample)
1990	"I love what you do for me" (Dancer, Fitzgerald, Sample)
1997	"Toyota! Every day" (Saatchi & Saatchi)

a time when Toyota wanted to build more emotional appeal—the company said its previous slogan ("Small car specialists for 40 years") was the best-recalled ad theme of any importer. Toyota made the change to broaden its image from that of a strictly small car manufacturer to that of a full-line marketer. In 1985, the company retained the image of the jumping man that had punctuated "Oh what a feeling," believing it was too valuable an icon to discard. The jump itself eventually gained more renown than any of the company's other ad themes. The 2 February 1981 edition of *Sports Illustrated* celebrating the Oakland Raiders' Super Bowl victory featured the headline, "Oh what a feeling," and a photo showed a Raiders player jumping for joy. In 1985 a group of 4,000 Ball State University students set a *Guinness Book of World Records* record for a "group Toyota jump."

After two years "Who could ask for anything more?" had not succeeded in translating a high level of emotion about Toyota ownership into increased sales. The automaker considered dropping the theme but feared that doing so might have a negative impact on its image of reliability. So, in typical Toyota fashion, the campaign was modified. In 1987 the company added "Toyota quality" to the slogan as it sought to emphasize what had made Toyota successful. A year later, the company revised the campaign again, adding the sub-theme, "My Toyota—I love it."

Toyota faced its first U.S. crisis in 1971, when the government added a 10 percent surcharge to the price of imported products. For five years, Toyota had been positioned as a low-priced economy car that offered American style and additional features at no

Toyota's first national ad campaign in 1967 used the slogan "Get your hands on a Toyota . . . you'll never let go."
Courtesy of Toyota.

The "Oh what a feeling!" campaign debuted in 1975 and sometimes depicted owners of new Toyotas jumping for joy.
Courtesy of Toyota.

extra cost. Now the company had to reestablish itself as a low-priced, high-value option for the U.S. consumer at a time when Ford's Pinto and Chevrolet's Vega could be had for hundreds of dollars less than the price of imported cars. Canceling holiday vacations, Toyota and its ad agency, Clinton E. Frank, began an intensive program to solve the problem. The company prepared emergency magazine, newspaper, television, radio, and outdoor advertising. All of the ads emphasized that buyers could once again purchase a Toyota for less than $2,000. Toyota's dealers decided against making head-on comparison claims against the competition. Instead, they continued to advertise Toyota as a quality product and an outstanding value.

Toyota provides a national umbrella of advertising in the United States through the use of national magazines covering the general consumer market for passenger cars. The company has used special-interest publications for such models as its Land Cruiser and pick-up trucks.

Toyota spent approximately $14 million in various media in 1970, including co-op funds (local advertising whose cost is shared by the company and local dealerships). It spent approximately $2.8 million in magazines, and the bulk of the remainder

went into TV commercials. Dealer and distributor associations, however, placed nearly all of their ad dollars—more than $10 million—into TV spots. Neither spent much on newspaper advertising, traditionally a large category for automakers.

Toyota added newspapers to its mix in 1971 when it needed to communicate an important piece of news to the public: a new price. Toyota's top 45 markets were the recipients of large newspaper ads in big-circulation publications. The markets accounted for 75 percent of Toyota's overall sales. In nine weeks in 1971, Toyota spent $1.8 million on newspaper ads via agency Clinton E. Frank.

From January through March 1972 Toyota launched an ad campaign to assure U.S. consumers that Toyotas could still be purchased at the same market price. By this time, the company had 910 dealers selling the Corolla, Corona, and Corona Mark II marques, plus Crown model sedans, station wagons, and trucks.

In 1973 a TV commercial for Corona (from Clinton E. Frank) leaped 2,000 years into the future to show the wisdom of purchasing a Toyota. Set in a stark 41st-century museum, it featured a museum guide escorting a group through an exhibit of artifacts from the 20th century. The central exhibit: a Toyota Corona four-door sedan apparently floating on a circle of light. The guide explained that 20th-century humans spent large amounts of something called "money" to worship their giant idol "car." However, he added, some people spent only small amounts since they believed they could get all the room they needed from a Toyota Corona. The guide called the Toyota worshipers "the most intelligent classes and probably the aristocracy."

Another spot, run in the same markets a few months later, showed a Toyota truck pulling a procession of competitors—Chevrolet Luv, Datsun, Mazda, and a Ford Courier—up an incline. The tag line: "Of course we don't expect you to try this."

In 1974 the automaker extended the "price and value" theme that had carried it to record car sales the year before and featured it as part of a summer campaign. Advertising advised prospective buyers to "See how much car your money can buy from Toyota." That phrase preceded the basic theme adopted company-wide for 1974, "Small car specialists for 40 years" (a neat mathematical trick considering the company was founded in 1937). The new theme was the basis for a multimillion-dollar campaign that emphasized Toyota's experience in the small-car field at a time when small cars were a popular item. The 13-week campaign (from Clinton E. Frank) was the largest summer ad campaign in Toyota's 16 years in the U.S. market and the longest such sustained TV campaign ever scheduled by the company. Toyota sponsorships included such shows as *Kojak, Sanford and Son,* and *The Tonight Show.*

In 1975 Toyota's advertising, now at DFS, continued to revolve around a consumer-oriented message: Toyota owners get special satisfaction from their vehicles. Toyota continued to use its "Oh what a feeling" tag. That feeling remained alive and well in 1984 thanks to what has been described as the strongest ad campaign in Toyota history. It was fueled by the largest Toyota ad budget, a substantial portion of which went to truck ads. A 200

CAMRY V6

PASS THE ENTRANCE EXAM.

Going from zero to traffic speed in the length of an on-ramp can be a real test of nerve for the average sedan owner. Luckily, the Camry V6 is not at all average.

Thanks to a Four-Cam, 24-valve, electronically fuel-injected engine, the Camry V6 develops 156 horsepower and 160 ft.-lbs. of torque. So even with its generous passenger space filled, the Camry has plenty of power for on-ramps, traffic, or hills.

Of course, power isn't the only reason the Camry V6 is so special. For three years in a row, Camry has been the most trouble-free compact car sold in America.*

So whether the hills are mild or steep, the Camry V6 can be counted on to move to the head of its class. Further proof that with the Camry V6, you have just about the perfect car.

"I love what you do for me."

TOYOTA

Call 1-800-GO-TOYOTA for a brochure and location of your nearest dealer. *JD Power and Associates 1988, 1989, 1990 Initial Quality Surveys.℠ Based on owner-reported problems during the first 90 days of ownership. Get More From Life…Buckle Up! © 1990 Toyota Motor Sales, U.S.A., Inc.

Toyota's "I love what you do for me" campaign debuted in 1990.
Courtesy of Toyota.

percent ad budget increase over the previous four years helped keep Toyota trucks in the media.

TV advertising continued Toyota's consumer-oriented stories, including a spot from DFS showing Old Saint Nick, who shed his sleigh for a Tercel four-wheel-drive wagon to get around in snowy weather. The Tercel, originally introduced in late 1979, was termed the "Official car of Santa Claus." One-word headline copy for print ads saw "Hot" describe Supra, "Reborn" for Corolla, and "Lots" for Camry. A 1988 TV spot from DFS Dorland (a later incarnation of DFS following a merger) for Corolla showed the car on a screen in a movie theater, then driving through the screen and down the aisle of the theater while the audience gasped. The voice-over said, "Toyota Corolla—new for 1988. Dramatic new looks that will stun you. Performance that will surprise you. And value that is legendary."

In October 1994 Toyota unveiled new TV spots and print ads for the redesigned Celica that showed parts of the car at first, followed by the Celica bursting onto the screen in a surreal environment created on Utah's Bonneville Salt Flats. The spots were introduced during the World Series. Follow-up spots appeared after the car reached showrooms. The Camry was also the recipient of a new tango-themed TV campaign from Saatchi using catchy phrases such as "Table for two" and "Two to tango" to emphasize its new two-door car. The commercials featured actor Martin Sheen.

In 1997, in an effort to boost Toyota's overall brand image and establish an emotional bond with consumers, the company unveiled a new slogan, "Every day." It featured the song, "Everyday People" by Sly and the Family Stone. "Every day" was Toyota's first major ad theme change since the debut of "I love what you do for me" in 1990.

In 2000 Toyota was the second-largest advertiser among all companies headquartered in the western United States. Slow and steady characterized the Toyota advertising strategy over the years. By sticking to variations on a basic theme, Toyota managed to make its name one of the world's best-known auto brands.

ALAN SALOMON

Further Reading

Toyota Motor Corporation, *Toyota: A History of The First Fifty Years,* Toyota City, Aichi Prefecture, Japan: Toyota Motor Corporation, 1988

Toyota Motor Sales, U.S.A., Inc., *The Toyota Marketing Story,* Torrance, California: Toyota Motor Sales, 1972

Toyota Motor Sales, U.S.A., Inc., *Toyota U.S.A.: The First Fifteen Years,* Torrance, California: Toyota Motor Sales, 1973

Toyota Motor Sales, U.S.A., Inc., *Toyota: The First Twenty Years in the U.S.A.,* Torrance, California: Toyota Motor Sales, U.S.A., 1977

Toys and Games

In many ways, the toy industry and the promotion and advertising of its products are different from those of nearly every other industry. The toy industry, for instance, has created some of the most enduring brands in any category: Barbie, Slinky, Etch-a-Sketch, Monopoly. And it has done so in some cases with very little advertising; Monopoly, for example, was introduced in 1935 but did not launch another major ad campaign until 1982.

At the same time, the toy industry is a sector that, until the 1950s, did not depend heavily on brand identification—children wanted a doll, not a Barbie doll. Moreover, instead of following the straight marketing line of progression of many industries—from print to radio, television, and finally the Internet—toy companies and their advertising agencies have relied heavily on word of mouth, demonstrations, celebrity association, and promotional tie-ins with movies and fast-food restaurants. Finally, few other industries' advertising has been as carefully overseen and regulated as the toy industry's.

Some of the earliest mass-produced toys were dolls and trains, starting in the 1800s, but the U.S. toy industry did not see huge growth until the mid-1900s. Toy sales (excluding video games) reached some $24 billion in 2001, compared with $8.3 million in 1899. Factors such as mass production, the rise of enormous merchants such as Toys "R" Us, and the advent of huge marketing campaigns and, especially, television advertising had much to do with this increase.

But something else happened in the 20th century: the nature of children's play changed dramatically. In the early 1900s, children wanted to emulate adults—not to escape into fantasy—and played with miniature versions of household products and farm or factory machines as well as with dolls and children's tools. But at the end of the century, toy makers were forced to compete with the Internet, video games, and television—which shortened the number of years that children remain interested in more traditional toys and nonelectronic games. They had to contend with a shrinking population of children as well.

The 1950s: Realizing the Value of Advertising

In 1951 toy makers sold $500 million worth of toys but spent just a fraction of that—$5 million—on advertising. Marketers selling to children were cereal and beverage makers that offered small trinkets as incentives to buy the principal product but did not sell them as toys. At the time, the toy industry claimed that the major difficulty with advertising toys was that toys were primarily Christmas sellers. Critics in the industry wanted a 12-month merchandising plan instead of a season-oriented one. Toy makers did little to accommodate this notion, despite the fact that in the early 1950s toys were becoming a year-round business. More toys were sold in the first ten months of 1950 than in all of 1941.

In 1952 the toy business broke its record with more than $800 million in retail sales. One reason for the spike in sales was the advent of television. The popularity of Hopalong Cassidy movies on early TV generated huge sales of Hopalong Cassidy gun and holster sets and other related items. And in 1954 when *Disneyland* telecast a three-part story about Davy Crockett, the coonskin cap became an essential item for every child under 14. But another factor was increased ad spending. Toy advertising in 1952 exceeded the previous year by one-fourth to one-third. The advertising rise indicated an increasing realization by toy manufacturers that the business could be a year-round enterprise.

If there was any doubt that advertising expenditures meant increased sales, one only had to consider American Metal Specialties. In 1951 American Metal experimented with a small ad that brought the company a 35 percent hike in sales. The company placed a black-and-white ad in *Life* magazine in November 1951

for Amsco Doll-E-Toys. The next year, American Metal launched its first full-scale consumer advertising campaign through its agency, Lavenson Bureau of Advertising, Philadelphia, Pennsylvania. The campaign consisted of a color strip in the Metropolitan Sunday Comics Group and 30 other Sunday supplements. Page ads ran in *Life* and *Parents* magazines. The ads were designed to make the toys as realistic as possible. The dolls in the ads were doing things children see adults doing all the time, such as washing and drying dishes. Coupons accompanied the ads.

Among those who agreed that toy manufacturers were investing too little in advertising was R.G. Meythaler, president of the Playskool Manufacturing Company. Playskool's more aggressive advertising approach was an exception to that of other toy companies of that time, and its emphasis on the Playskool name paid dividends. In 1951 the company boosted its ad budget to more than $100,000 for its educational toys and Lincoln Logs.

In 1954 the toy industry introduced an industrywide promotion program with a budget of $1.3 million earmarked for local TV. It tied in all segments of the toy industry and promoted 104 individual toys. The program included a 13-week TV series in the 40 top TV markets, with buys in half-hour programs, a publicity and merchandising program, and the creation of a new toy catalog called the *Toy Yearbook*. Commercials created by Friend-Reiss-McGlone, the toy industry council's agency, showed children using various toys.

Throughout the 1950s ad budgets continued to increase, ad campaigns expanded, and sales soared. In 1953 toy sales and advertising surpassed all previous records, with advertising increasing 15 percent. Transogram Company launched the biggest fall ad campaign in its history in 1955 with TV and magazines as the principal media. The TV drive used commercials and participation on children's shows in Cincinnati and Cleveland, Ohio, and New Haven, Connecticut. Featured toys were Little Country Doctor kits, Play Nurse kits, Walt Disney's Steps 'n' Slides, and Disneyland Games. In shows where it was possible, commercials included audience participation; otherwise there was simply a product demonstration. *Child Life, Life, Parents,* and *American Weekly* were the principal print media. Lester Harrison, Inc., was the agency.

But the largest single-medium advertising expenditure in toy history to that point was a $375,000 fall television campaign from the Ideal Toy Company in 1955. Commercials aired on CBS's *Winky Dink* and *Romper Room*. Ideal—which would later merge with Sawyer's ViewMaster, taken over by Tyco, which itself would be consumed by Mattel—also sponsored the Macy's Thanksgiving Day parade on NBC.

That year, Mattel finally became convinced of the need to try to end the cycle of seasonal selling and signed on to sponsor ABC's *Mickey Mouse Club*. Its 52-week contract called for two commercials every other week and one in alternate weeks. One product it promoted on the show was the "burp gun," which Mattel's agency, Carson/Roberts, Los Angeles, California, tried to sell without provoking controversy. The agency's solution: a "dream" commercial technique designed to avoid offending. In the commercials, the burp gun is shown as a lead-in to a child's

How To Give Your Family A Wonderful Time!

For a solid investment in family fun, give MONOPOLY for Christmas. Everybody's a financier, in this fascinating, world-famous game! Players can make fortunes — or go bankrupt. They run railroads, buy waterworks ... mortgage property, build hotels. Monopoly is famous for keeping the young folks home at night ... Like all Parker Games, it's fascinating entertainment for one and all.

MONOPOLY White Box Edition (illustrated). Complete equipment for 3 to 10 players: removable Bank Tray, double supply of "Money", 10 attractive tokens, 32 houses, 12 Grand Hotels stamped in gold, 2 sets of cards, pair of dice, unique playing field on folding board, complete rules ... all, in one handsome box. $4.00

Monopoly, De Luxe Edition — $10.00

Monopoly, Popular Edition — $3.00

CLUE The "whodunit" game that makes every player feel like a real detective. A houseful of clues helps you solve the mystery! $3.00

KEYWORD Best Crossword Board Game. Pile up bonus points with three exclusive crossword features! Fast play, easy scoring! $2, $3, $5

BING CROSBY'S GAME Call Me Lucky. Bing's own game is unusual and exciting. Wonderful family entertainment! $3.00

CHILDREN'S HOUR Very young children are amused for hours with these three games, all packed in one box. $2.00

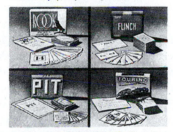

ROOK, PIT, FLINCH, TOURING These four wonderful games are perfect Christmas gifts. Rook, $1; Pit, $1; Flinch, $1.50; Touring, $1.25

SORRY Parker Brothers' trade-mark name for its slide pursuit game. Skill and chance are equally combined in this famous board game! $2.50

DIXIE-POLLYANNA
STAR REPORTER
HOLLYWOOD "GO"
BOOM OR BUST
RICH UNCLE
PEGITY
WINNIE THE POOH
ROPES & LADDERS
DIG
VAN LOON
ACROSS THE CONTINENT
THEY'RE OFF
PIGSKIN
PARKER BASEBALL
TIT TAT TOE
5 WISE BIRDS
MAGIC DOLL
EDDIE CANTOR'S JUDGE
FUN CARDS
U. S. MAP
PING PONG
CAMELOT
BONUS 20
ROL-IT
HICKETY PICKETY
LONE RANGER
FINANCE

FAMOUS PARKER GAMES
at all leading stores

Send for this fascinating booklet!
How to have family fun, popular parties, with Parker Games. 28 illustrated pages. Mail 10¢ today, with name and address, to: Parker Brothers, Inc., Dept. 128, Salem, Mass.

fantasy that he is hunting wild game in Africa or is a member of the French Foreign Legion. The gun is shown as a playmate, not as a deadly weapon. Mattel's burp gun flew off the shelves, and at the height of the Christmas buying season there were none to be found. But as Mattel and other toy companies would soon find out, it was wise to be concerned about the reaction to ads.

As the decade ended, the Toy Manufacturers of the United States advertised on 13 pages in the 23 November 1959 issue of *Life,* making it the biggest Christmas promotion in the country. Grey Advertising handled the account. Ninety-eight toys were promoted on 12 black-and-white pages and one color page. That year's Christmas push was made via 27 television stations in 24 markets.

The 1960s: Birth of Branding

The beginning of the 1960s saw the emergence of strong brand identification in the toy industry. Suddenly little girls did not write to Santa Claus for just any doll. They wrote for a Chatty Cathy doll, a Barbie doll, or Miss Ideal. Boys did not sit on Santa's lap in department stores and ask for a toy train or truck. They wanted a Lionel Satellite Train or a Tonka Truck or a Robot Commando.

Toy makers spent nearly $25 million in advertising in 1961, up nearly 50 percent from 1960, and etched specific brand names into the minds of youngsters who could barely spell. In the next five years, toy makers added $8 million to their TV ad budgets—finally hitting $10 million in spending—and the gross jumped by more than $650 million, from $1.3 billion to $2 billion.

In 1961 Mattel spent $2.5 million to advertise its products, which at this point included the classic Hot Wheels and Barbie doll lines, both of which had been introduced in 1959. It signed on for a yearlong sponsorship on ABC's *Matty's Funday Funnies* and ran ads in *Playthings* and *Toys & Novelties* magazines. Carson/Roberts continued as the Mattel agency.

That Christmas season, Lionel purchased pre-Christmas TV spots on at least 75 stations in 38 markets in the United States and Canada. In addition to a heavy schedule of 20-, 30-, or 60-second commercials in those markets, the electric train maker ran one-minute ads around a 27-minute color feature film it produced called *The Wonderful World of Trains.* The film starred the Suzari puppets and child actor Paul O'Keefe. Lionel made the film available free to department stores, schools, and Parent-Teacher Association (PTA) groups.

Using celebrities also became a popular way to sell toys. In 1962 the industry jumped on the bandwagon of an American phenomenon: Roger Maris's successful 1961 surpassing of Babe Ruth's single-season home-run record. Transogram Company, with its agency Mogul, Williams & Saylor, based a $2 million spring ad campaign on Maris. The campaign ran through June and featured the new Roger Maris Home Run Trainer, a batting device. In the commercial, Maris appeared in a newsreel clip, and Mel Allen, the voice of the Yankees, delivered the message. The 33-week TV campaign replaced the company's usual 13-week Christmas campaign. Later, the company used sponsorship in a

network show to promote its brand identity as a leader in creating items of entertainment for the entire family.

Milton Bradley placed ads for its game lines, including running a national ad program for games and teaching aids. Page ads were scheduled for *Good Housekeeping, Ladies' Home Journal,* and *Life,* plus TV coverage in more than 15 major markets.

In 1963 Ideal also moved into year-round TV sponsorship, backing two 30-minute cartoon shows on 157 stations. The $30 million package, including a custom-made series of four animated cartoon programs over a five-year run, was the largest sponsorship for television ever undertaken by a toy manufacturer at that time.

By 1968 the leading toy advertisers and their major agencies were Mattel, represented by Carson/Roberts/Inc.; Ideal, represented by Grey Advertising; Marx, represented by Ted Bates & Company, Inc.; Hasbro, represented by Bruns Advertising Agency, Inc.; Aurora, represented by Adams Dana Silverstein, Inc.; Wham-O, represented by Marlin Advertising; Remco, represented by J.M. Webb & Associates; Deluxe Topper, represented by Dancer, Fitzgerald, Sample; and Kenner, represented by Leonard M. Sive & Associates. In the game field, the leading companies were Milton Bradley, represented by Harvey & Carlson, Inc., and Parker Bros., with Badger and Browning & Parcher. Mattel was by far the biggest advertiser, spending $11 million, more than all its competitors combined.

This was a time of explosive growth in the industry. In 1969 toy industry sales topped the $2 billion mark for the first time, up 11 percent from 1968's $1.8 billion. Mattel added weekday afternoon network TV to snare more mothers and include school-age children. Television accounted for 90 percent of Mattel's media spending; the rest went to magazines.

Meanwhile, more toys were being introduced. Mattel, the creator of Barbie and the first to exploit the potential of TV salesmanship, put its money behind 40 to 50 products a year, more than half of them new. A civilian version of the military G.I. Joe line—Action Joe—was introduced and came with a racing car and an Action Joe trooper with a motorcycle. Mattel introduced its Baby's Hungry, a doll that chewed and drank liquid, plus Talking Tiles, a learning machine.

Milton Bradley, the nation's largest marketer of games, said that year it would spend $3.5 million in TV and magazines, up $1 million from the year before. Pressman Toy Corporation hit the $1 million mark for the first time, and Parker Bros. spent more than $2 million to advertise games other than Monopoly. It was estimated that in this television age, it took $250,000 to launch a new and important toy. But the rewards spoke for themselves.

Regulation

It is perhaps no surprise that around the time branding and advertising took off in the industry, so, too, did scrutiny of the targeting of ads to children. In 1961, fearing outside regulation, the National Association of Broadcasters (NAB) developed a TV code of ethics. Toy manufacturers conceded that the TV code would cause few ad changes, but did not embrace the guidelines and fought to make them temporary.

"I've never seen a purple cow
But my sister used up my brown
And I don't think a yellow cow looks
Too good."

Give them a fresh box and see how they grow.

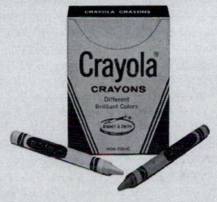

Crayola crayons have been popular playthings for nearly 100 years.
Crayola, chevron and serpentine designs are registered trademarks of Binney & Smith, used with permission.

The proposed code asked that advertisers avoid the following: demonstrations or dramatizations that show a toy in use in a manner that is not authentic; the use of language such as "only" and "just" applied to the price of a toy exceeding a few dollars; implying that a toy requiring a material investment can be had for the asking; presumptions that every boy and girl wants, or should have, a toy, especially when it is highly priced; and hammering the sales message. It asked advertisers to reflect the toy in the framework of a play environment, performing in a way that actually represented the toy; present a toy on its actual merits as a plaything; make clear the special nature of a toy of above average cost; and try to appeal to children's imaginations.

But many critics believed that self-regulation was not enough. In 1970 Peggy Charren, by then a well-known children's advocate, wrote a one-page petition to the Federal Communications Commission (FCC) asking the federal agency to eliminate commercials on children's television. Although Charren and her group, Action for Children's Television (ACT), did not succeed in getting rid of commercials, she did gain much ground. She was successful in banning commercials that showed vitamins as "candy"; reducing the total amount of commercial time to nine minutes and 30 seconds per hour on weekends and 12 minutes per hour weekdays; banning program hosts from endorsing or selling products; and getting "bumpers," or five-second separator devices, inserted before and after commercials to help children better distinguish between a commercial and programming.

In 1978 the Federal Trade Commission (FTC) proposed a rule that could regulate or even ban television advertising to children, citing it as "unfair." But in 1980, after many proceedings, Congress barred the FTC from using "unfairness" as a legal point for making sweeping rules to regulate an entire industry. It said that the FTC could only regulate or ban advertising on a case-by-case basis. In 1981 Congress restricted the focus of the inquiry into children's programming. This action was a response to intense lobbying efforts by networks and advertisers, themselves responding to the requests for a banning of advertising and a study of deceptive practices in children's ads. Sensing a change in the political winds under the new administration of President Ronald Reagan, in 1982 NAB abandoned its children's advertising guidelines. In the months and years to follow, the major television networks adopted their own children's guidelines using the NAB code as a base. These voluntary guidelines, still in use by the networks, their affiliates, and some independent broadcasters, state that commercials must:

- represent the toy accurately in appearance;
- show the toy in a safe play situation;
- demonstrate the actual product solely on its merits as a toy;
- disclose the exact method of the toy's operation;
- disclose any assembly requirements;
- disclose what is inside a toy package;
- disclose any battery requirements.

By 1983 the FCC had eliminated children's policy guidelines that had been in effect since 1974; it then dispensed with limits on the number of commercials that could be aired in a given time period. Things looked dark indeed for those who supported limits on children's advertising.

In 1990, however, after congressional hearings and expert testimony from Charren, the Democrat-controlled Congress passed the Children's Television Act of 1990. Stations were not allowed to air more than 10 1/2 minutes of commercials per 30 minutes of programming on the weekends and 12 minutes per 30 minutes on weekdays.

The 1970s: Toys Reflect Changes in the World

The toys of the 1970s began to reflect changes in the real world. Astronauts shared the spotlight with aquanauts, and parents got ready to listen to the patter of extra little feet around the home, thanks to robot dolls. Space toys in 1970 were more popular than in 1969, when a U.S. astronaut first walked on the Moon. Toy makers saw the Apollo flight boosting sales by $2.7 billion with new entries such as Zeroids, Astrolites, Billy Blastoff, and Tri-Module. Earthlings followed the adventures of the Apollo astronauts on TV, and the leading toy companies, for the most part, used the same vehicle to set their space-age toy wares into their sales trajectory. The *Star Wars* fad in the late 1970s produced characters such as R2-D2, C-3PO, Chewbacca, and Luke Skywalker. Ads tied into the blockbuster movie were launched.

The number of TV series–related dolls and toys increased. The stars of *The Bionic Woman, Six Million Dollar Man,* and *The Waltons* appeared in TV commercials for Kenner Products to promote toys based on their characters. This cleared the way for more celebrity dolls, such as Fonzie, Mr. Kotter, and Wonder Woman. But unlike in the past, spots were aired on non-children's programming, such as *Charlie's Angels, Sonny and Cher,* and *Barney Miller.*

In 1970 Transogram Company made a brief stab at a computerized basketball game and used pros Walt Frazier and Billy Cunningham in a 30-second TV spot, with Smith/Greenland Company, Inc., as the agency. Dodeca invented a baseball game using dice. It was put to the test by Little Leaguers, adult baseball fans, and members of the armed forces. The game was promoted via mail-order ads in *Sports Illustrated* and the *New York Times Magazine,* plus a number of sports and armed forces publications.

In 1975 Milton Bradley became one of the first toy makers to terminate its ad agency relationship, this one with Young & Rubicam, in favor of its new in-house ad agency, MB Communications. Its aim was to keep its staff lean, so the game maker drew largely on outside creative work to handle its $8 million account. The decision was based on predicted cost savings and a drive to get the highest-quality creative work possible.

Another toy manufacturer discovered it had greater success with promotions and premiums than with media advertising. Schaper Toys, handled by Bozell & Jacobs, Minneapolis, Minnesota, determined that its Playmobil action sets were hard to present in a 30-second TV spot. So it developed a 12-page color brochure describing Playmobil and packed it into the company's other games and toys. The brochure included a premium offer,

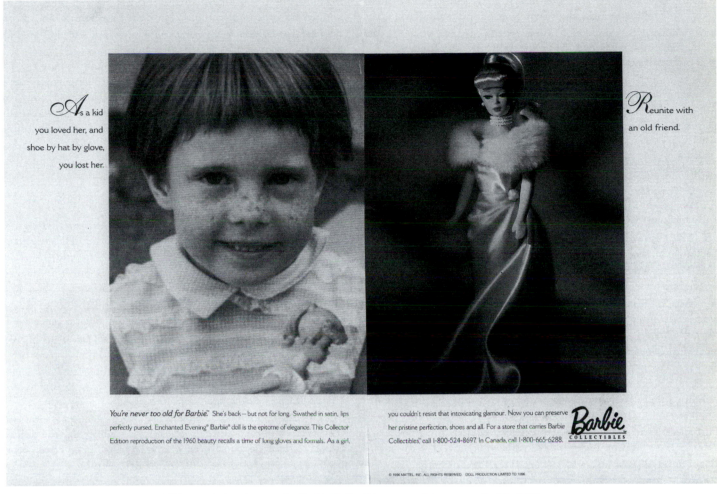

This 1996 advertisement for Barbie Collectibles targeted the mature Barbie doll fan.
Barbie® doll ad courtesy of Mattel, Inc.

such as a sample of any of the Playmobil family for 50 cents. Tens of thousands of consumers responded. The promotion also featured a coupon for a 10 percent discount on a Playmobil set.

While many companies touted everything as "new" in the 1970s, Fisher-Price went the other direction in its ads, reminding that "not such a very long time ago, toys weren't novelties. They were sensible and sturdy. That's the kind of toys Fisher-Price still makes. They aren't designed just for a season but to last through a whole childhood, and another childhood and a childhood after that." *McCall's, Redbook, Family Circle, Ladies' Home Journal,* and *Parents* received the bulk of the marketer's print ad spending. Also, a concentrated push hit TV on ABC and CBS plus spot markets.

The 1980s: Hula Hoops and Video Games

In the 1980s and into the 1990s, toys and games began to take a new and different route to the pocketbooks of America. Print media gained more ground in toy advertising, with the Internet catching on in the late 1990s. TV was used primarily as a quick

hit to promote line extensions, such as new Barbie outfits and supplements to already established dolls of both genders. Department store ads, trade books, newspaper supplements, and direct mail garnered most of the media dollars during these decades.

As the nation's economy slowed in 1981, toy marketers lowered prices and marketed lower-priced items such as Rubik's Cube, board games, dolls, and the hula hoop. Schaper Toys promoted "inflation fighter" toys priced lower than $5. Except for toys based on *Star Wars*, the market for space toys lost steam, and many companies promoted playthings with medieval or mythological motifs, such as the "Dungeons and Dragons" electronic game.

The early 1980s also brought a new, hot product category: video and electronic games. At the Toy Fair in February 1983, these were the biggest areas, along with crafts and toys based on military themes, and licensing (such as a Benji dog tied to the movie of the same name and a Brooke Shields doll modeled after the actress). In 1982 one-third of the total toy volume of $9 billion was attributable to video games. The next year Cabbage Patch dolls appeared on the market near Christmastime, with consumers rushing to stores to empty shelves of them. Parker Bros., still selling board games such as Monopoly and Risk, got into video games with a game called Q-Bert.

But old-line toys continued to sell well, too. An estimated 8.5 million G.I. Joes sold in 1982, and Mattel's Barbie was coming back, with an $11 million ad budget. Tonka Corporation, looking to revamp its marketing efforts, hired two former Mattel executives, Liz Hanrahan and Ray McDonald, among other Mattel alums, to step up marketing efforts.

The 1990s: Licensed Toys and Changing Demographics

The biggest trends to hit the world of toys in the 1990s were probably the "Mighty Morphin' Power Rangers" and "The Lion King." Playing off the power of the blockbuster animated theatrical, Walt Disney Company's *Lion King*–licensed toys were backed by a huge and well-executed merchandising push by Toys "R" Us, J. C. Penney Company, and Kmart Corporation. Mattel, the largest vendor of *Lion King* merchandise, scored heavily with the property, as did fast-food tie-in partner Burger King, which sold 30 million *Lion King* collectible figures with kids' meals in less than five weeks. It represented the maturing of the toy industry's relationship to Hollywood, which had been revolutionized with the release of *Star Wars* in 1974.

Bandai America's Power Rangers, with a TV series, national mall tour, and upcoming movie, achieved cult status, selling some 6 million units. Other companies rushed in to try to duplicate Bandai's success with Power Rangers, searching markets for properties with universal appeal. Later in the decade, another such phenomenon, imported from Japan, would take its place: Pokemon.

Meanwhile, video game sales continued to rally, with sales rising 5.3 percent to $17.5 billion in 1993 with Sega and Nintendo the major players. Sega's inroads into the field—it had snagged half of the $6 billion market—forced Nintendo to spend $10 million on an image campaign in the second half of 1994.

Among the traditional-toy sellers, Mattel was on its way to surpass leader Hasbro in 1994 on the strength of *The Lion King* movie and the summer's other big box-office draw, MCA/Universal's *The Flintstones*. Mattel sales hit $1.1 billion through the first six months of the year compared with Hasbro's $933 million. Mattel's merger with Fisher-Price had given it a stronghold in the preschool category. Mattel and Hasbro fought for the overseas marketing rights to the popular game Scrabble; Mattel won.

Mattel's Barbie celebrated her 35th anniversary and continued selling $1 billion worth of merchandise a year. The original 1959 doll was reissued with fashions and accessories aimed at collectors. The company's Hot Wheels, Nickelodeon, Disney, and Polly Pocket lines also were selling well.

Hasbro had a harder time during this period. The popularity of Barney and *Jurassic Park* toys was fading, and even G.I. Joe, who celebrated his 30th birthday, could not help. Most little boys wanted only one thing: Power Rangers toys.

Lego, the venerable toy created in Denmark, increased its media budgets for four years in a row in the early 1990s. In 1993 it was spending about $22 million, making it a heavily advertised brand in the toy segment. Lego also announced plans for an amusement park that would build on the Lego brand. The efforts paid off: the company saw two consecutive years of double-digit growth.

Retail sales of licensed toys hit $7.85 billion in 1996, up 5 percent from 1995 for a 45 percent share of toy and video game sales. Gross margins on licensed toys ran high. But as many toy companies were to discover, it is the rare licensed toy that really takes off. Even 1995's popular "Goosebumps" was disappointing over the Christmas season in all but apparel, books, and a Parker Bros. board game.

Future Directions

By the late 1990s the U.S. toy industry's major marketers and their agencies were: Mattel (Ogilvy & Mather and FCB Advertising, Los Angeles), spending $245.2 million; Nintendo (Leo Burnett USA, Chicago, Illinois), spending $90.6 million; Hasbro (Grey Worldwide, New York City) spending $264.2 million; and Sony, (TBWA/Chiat/Day, Playa del Rey, California) spending $89.8 million. But the industry was facing a new problem. Children, growing up faster than ever, were losing interest in traditional toys much earlier than their older siblings had. Comfortable with technology, they forsook dolls, toy trucks, and board games and took instead to the Internet, video games, and CD-ROMs at a young age.

Sales of Mattel's stalwart Barbie decreased 14 percent, though it still took in nearly $2 billion. Trying to modernize the doll to appeal to this new generation, Mattel launched interactive Barbie products and updated the doll, creating Generation Girl, a Barbie line with an international twist and some 1990s features (skateboards, urban fashion; one doll even had a pierced nose). A group of Ogilvy & Mather offices gave Barbie an image makeover, launching a new campaign with the theme, "Be anything." Billboards and posters featured girls in sporty settings, including one as a hockey player. The tag line: "Be your own hero." Thirty- and 60-second television spots also emphasized the new "empowerment" brand image for the doll. At the same time, Mattel brought two interactive players into its fold, acquiring both the Learning Company, a software maker, and niche player Purple Moon.

Nor was Barbie's decline in popularity the company's only problem. Mattel wanted to turn Power Wheels, a traditional holiday gift, into a year-round staple. So Mattel's preschool unit, Fisher-Price, increased marketing efforts for its motorized vehicles in 1999, with an expanded product line, sales promotions, and a 25 percent boost in advertising. It spent more than $8 million directed at parents and kids, including the brand's first foray into movie theaters. A 60-second spot created by agency Gardner, Geary, Coll & Young, San Francisco, California, was directed at parents and ran in 1,500 theaters with G- and PG-rated movies. The tag line: "Don't you wish you had one when you were a kid?" The tag line and theme carried over to 30-second parent-targeted ads on television, along with promotional messages. Ads directed at kids highlighted specific models, such as X-treme Machine and The Wild Thing.

In the second half of the 1990s, network television ads for toys lost ground to cable TV; spot TV declined steadily from $231 million in 1995 to $53 million in 1999, newspaper ad expenditures declined drastically from 1998 ($7.1 million) to 1999 ($4 million), and outdoor advertising saw a dramatic rise from $83,000 in 1995 to a bit more than $1 million in 1999.

Wherever they are spending their ad dollars, toy companies will continue to grapple with shifting demographics and children's increasing sophistication. Thus analysts believe that the key to success is to move to overseas markets. Estimates are that toy manufacturers that have entered or will enter the global market in the years to come will get nearly half their revenues from overseas sales.

ALAN SALOMON

See also Charren, Peggy; Children: Targets of Advertising; *and color plate in this volume*

Further Reading

Inge, M. Thomas, editor, *Handbook of American Popular Culture*, 3 vols., Westport, Connecticut, and London: Greenwood Press, 1978–81; 2nd edition, revised and enlarged, New York and London: Greenwood Press, 1989

Robie, Joan Hake, *Turmoil in the Toy Box II*, Lancaster, Pennsylvania: Starburst, 1989

Schroeder, Joseph J., and Barbara C. Cohen, editors, *The Wonderful World of Toys, Games, and Dolls, 1860–1930*, Northfield, Illinois: Digest Books, 1971

Tracy-Locke Company, Inc.

Founded as Southwestern Advertising Company in Oklahoma City, Oklahoma, by Shelley Tracy and Raymond Locke, 1913; reincorporated as Tracy-Locke-Dawson Advertising, Inc., 1923; reorganized as Tracy-Locke Company, Inc., 1943; merged with BBDO International, Inc., to form Tracy-Locke/BBDO, 1982; merged with DDB Needham Worldwide, assuming the name Tracy-Locke, a DDB Needham Agency, 1992; Tracy-Locke dropped, with agency retaining the name DDB Needham, Dallas, 1996.

Major Clients

Borden Company
Dr Pepper Company
Frito-Lay
Haggar Company
Imperial Sugar Company

From the beginning Tracy-Locke was known for its service. Founders Shelley Tracy and Raymond Locke had two simple goals: to do effective work and to serve each client well. It was the enduring nature of its client relationships that set Tracy-Locke apart: Borden for 75 years; Imperial Sugar, 70 years; Mrs. Baird's Bread, 67 years; Haggar, 54 years; Frito-Lay, 42 years. Tracy-Locke established remarkably close partnerships with its clients, and some stayed until there was no longer a Tracy-Locke.

Tracy-Locke's predecessor shop, Southwestern Advertising Company, was formed in 1913 with Tracy as president and Locke as first vice president. It was the first agency in the Southwest to be admitted to the American Association of Advertising Agencies. Joe Dawson joined the agency in 1919, and he eventually became second vice president. The agency was reincorporated as Tracy-Locke-Dawson Advertising in 1923, with Tracy the salesman and Locke and Dawson the idea men.

In 1915 Southwestern opened a Dallas, Texas, branch, which became the agency's home office two years later. Over the years there were many different offices, including one opened in 1933 in New York City when Continental Oil Company (Conoco) moved its headquarters there from Denver, Colorado. The success of Tracy-Locke-Dawson in New York City caused friction with the Dallas office, which eventually led to the resignations of both Tracy and Dawson. Tracy left the New York office in 1939. Because differences with Dawson were so severe, Locke reorganized the agency in 1943 and cut Dawson from its name. Dawson stayed in New York and took several clients, including Conoco, to Geyer, Cornell & Newell. Locke retained the Tracy name out of respect for his first partner, and Tracy-Locke once again became a Dallas agency.

One of the agency's early accounts was the small Dallas-based Dr Pepper Company. Acquired in 1926, the account was personally nurtured by Locke for 23 years, and he built its brand image. The slogan "Drink a bite to eat at 10, 2 and 4 [o'clock]" was coined under his leadership. When Dr Pepper, then under new management, severed the relationship in 1949, Locke—who was known as "the dean of southwestern advertising men"—retired, leaving the agency in the hands of Morris Hite, now president and principal shareholder.

Like the founders, Hite believed that service—including the account executive—was paramount. He joined Tracy-Locke in 1937 on a 90-day trial basis for $300 a month. By the early 1940s he had leapfrogged to the number-two position. With Locke's retirement he took over the company, heading it for more than 20 years. He inherited an agency of about 35 employees and annual billings of slightly more than $1 million.

Tracy-Locke Company, Inc., of Dallas, Texas, created this 1947 campaign for Dr Pepper.
DR PEPPER is a registered trademark of Dr Pepper/Seven Up, Inc.
©2001.

Hite's confidence in the agency brought a flood of new business, including Maryland Coffee Club, Tex Sun Citrus Exchange, Frito Company, and Chance-Vought. His frank style also yielded an assortment of memorable sayings: "This is a simple business. Just make sure the coming in is more than the going out"; "Here's what we ought to do. Now get me some research to prove it"; "A pat on the fanny gets you further than a kick in the butt."

The 1960s was a decade of remarkable growth for Tracy-Locke. From 40 employees and $10 million in billings in 1960, the agency grew to nearly 200 employees and $27 million in billings by 1969. Tracy-Locke introduced Doritos in 1966, but it was the 1968 campaign for the product that put the agency on the map nationally. Within two years Doritos topped $100 million in sales, and the product was hailed as one of the best brand introductions of the 1960s. Copywriter Jim Albright, who along with art director Ron McQuien created the "Taste as Good as They Crunch" campaign, later recalled its impact: "That single campaign lasted 12 years. It was one of the Top 100 campaigns of 1968, and the 'Crunch' theme is still being used for Doritos 30 years later."

The mid-1960s also saw a push by Tracy-Locke to become a total communications company through diversification into allied fields such as research, public relations, broadcasting, film production, and photography. The first subsidiary, M/A/R/C (Marketing and Research Counselors, Inc.), was a result of the spin-off of the research department in 1965. Point Communications began in 1970 as a Tracy-Locke graphics design subsidiary. Both M/A/R/C and Point Communications separated from Tracy-Locke when it merged with Batten Barton Durstine & Osborn (BBDO) to become Tracy-Locke/BBDO in 1982.

By the early 1970s, Hite realized a need for a line of succession. The three obvious choices were the three most accomplished account people: Bob Brown, Norm Campbell, and Stewart Mitchell. The three spent a weekend at what became known at Tracy-Locke as the "Summit in Santa Fe," mapping out their responsibilities and the agency's future. The three assumed titles of executive vice president and managed as a triumvirate: Campbell oversaw corporate development, Mitchell oversaw account services, and Brown oversaw creative and administrative services. They recommended that Campbell be groomed to succeed Hite as president.

In 1971 Tracy-Locke lost three major accounts—Pearl Beer, Southwest Volkswagen, and Frontier Airlines—within 90 days. The losses shook the agency and triggered the long-awaited change as Campbell took over as president, with Hite continuing as chairman. By the time Tracy-Locke turned 60 in 1973, the lost business had more than been replaced with a variety of clients that ranged from Texas International Airlines, Inc., and Phillips Petroleum Company to Korbel wines and meat marketer Wilson & Company, Inc. In 1971 the agency ranked 43rd among U.S. agencies, with billings of $32.7 million. That September Tracy-Locke went public.

While new business was good, there were fewer lucrative regional accounts to pursue. To make the leap to even larger national and global accounts, Tracy-Locke needed an affiliation with a national or international agency. In 1982 Campbell, who had begun his advertising career with BBDO, facilitated the merger of the two agencies into Tracy-Locke/BBDO. With its new worldwide capabilities, the agency acquired Pepsi Light, Taco Bell, and Labatt Importers of Canada. After the merger, Hite focused his attention on community service until his death in an automobile accident the following year. Hite was inducted into the American Advertising Federation's Advertising Hall of Fame in 1996. He received the Horatio Alger Award given to those who overcame humble beginnings to become leaders in their fields. He also received, among many others, the Linz Award, which is Dallas's highest individual recognition for public service.

In 1981 Campbell became chairman, and Senior Vice President Howard Davis became president. Ten years later Senior Vice President Mike Rawlings, who had been groomed by Davis, took his place as president. In 1992 Tracy-Locke was acquired by DDB Needham, a good match because of two clients the agencies shared—Frito-Lay and GTE. The merger with DDB Needham created the Southwest's largest advertising agency, with billings of almost half a billion dollars. Both agencies were part of Omnicom Group, based in New York City. The Tracy-Locke name was initially retained, but on 19 March 1996 the Southwest's oldest advertising name was retired, and the shop began to do business as the Dallas office of DDB Needham.

SHERI J. BROYLES

Further Reading

Brown, Richard, *Eighty-Three Years and No Longer Counting: An Informal History of Tracy-Locke Advertising, 1913–1996,* Dallas, Texas: Brown, 1997

Pate, Russ, *Adman: Morris Hite's Methods for Winning the Ad Game,* Dallas, Texas: E-Heart Press, 1988

Trade Publication

A trade publication is a narrowly targeted magazine, tabloid, or newspaper that serves a business or business-related audience. Trade publications, once commonly known as trade papers, fall under the general category of business-to-business media.

Readers of trade publications share a common work function, are affiliated with a specific industry, or are deeply engaged in a specialized segment of a particular industry. For example, the broader construction industry is served by *Construction Equipment,* while *Masonry Repair Digest,* a niche publication, mainly serves masons. Some trade publications focus on geographical areas, ranging in scope from city coverage (e.g., the *Chicago Purchasor*) to global reach (such as *International Business Magazine*).

Trade publications earn revenue from several streams of income. Revenue is earned by providing advertisers access to markets (i.e., income from advertising and other promotional programs offered to businesses), intelligence (e.g., marketing research, database information, etc.) and future employees (e.g., recruitment advertising and other special recruiting services). Trade publications also earn money through subscriptions and sales.

As a special class of print media, trade publications perform at least two major functions. First, they carry advertisements to audiences comprising the business-to-business segment of the economy. Business-to-business advertisers emphasize trade and general business publications over other media. According to a 1999 article in *Business Marketing,* IBM was the leading spender in business-to-business advertising in 1999, with $293 million, followed by AT&T Corporation, with $289 million. Other heavy spenders were financial services and insurance companies, high-technology companies, and telecommunication providers.

Second, readers consult trade publications for editorial information they need to develop business or technology strategies or to further their careers. They seek insight into such areas as historical accounts, environmental landscapes, and industry developments, as well as accounts of competitive practices, innovations, executive viewpoints, industry challenges, and contemporary issues.

The advertising industry is served by a host of trade publications. *Advertising Age,* according to the *Standard Periodicals Directory,* is the industry leader for advertising news and information. Among the other publications that now cover or have covered various areas of marketing are *Promo, Broadcasting, Marketing News, Ad Agency Insider, Radio & Media, Advertising Age's B2B, Ad Age Global, Creativity, Adweek, Brandweek, Hispanic Media and Market Source, Database Marketer, Exhibit Review, MC, Mediaweek,* and *Printers' Ink.*

Classification Systems

There are several taxonomies used to classify business-to-business print media. Beginning around 1915 business publications were divided into three general categories: retail, industrial, and class. Retail publications were aimed at retailers that sell goods directly to consumers. Industrial publications were aimed at specific industries, such as railroads, construction, and steel. Class publications were aimed at specific segments sharing the same general function regardless of their businesses or occupations. A more recent classification system uses four categories: industrial, trade, professional, and agricultural publications. However, this system restricts trade publications to those that serve only wholesalers, distributors, and retailers.

Another, more inclusive approach divides general business and trade publications into horizontal and vertical categories while recognizing special cases that target more narrowly defined audiences. Horizontal publications target people who hold similar jobs or perform a specific set of related functions in different companies across various industries, a select set of related business tasks, or a particular class of technology. *Purchasing Magazine,* for example, is a specialized trade publication that targets purchasing agents. Conversely, vertical publications are aimed at people who hold different jobs within a specifically defined industry. For example, *Mediaweek, Folio,* and *Chain Store Age Magazine* are understood by almost anyone familiar with the industries that they serve, regardless of their occupations or titles.

Acceptance of horizontal and vertical trade publications varies from one country to another. In the United Kingdom, vertical trade publications have captured a strong position among business publications. With the exception of *The Economist* and *Management Today,* general business publications have been unpopular in the United Kingdom. However, in most other countries, horizontal publications are better received than vertical trade titles.

Similar to trade publications, general business publications cut across vertical and horizontal categories. They include such magazines and newspapers as *Business Week, Fortune, Forbes, The Economist,* and the *Wall Street Journal.* Since they contain editorial content that is broad and inclusive, they are read by diversified audiences that cross standard industry lines. Their readers include investors, government officials, public policy makers, financial analysts, scientists, technicians, professionals, and students. While general business publications began to enjoy larger shares of business-to-business media budgets at the end of the 20th century, trade publications generally receive the bulk of a company's business media allocation.

Trade publications compete for business-to-business marketers' budgets with such rivals as directories, direct mail, outward-bound telemarketing, publicity, product research, catalogs, e-commerce, trade shows, trade promotions, and consumer media. In industrial marketing, personal selling is often the dominant promotional tool.

Spending and Revenue

Business-to-business communication spending estimates, while controversial, provide important insights into trade publications. An estimated $73 billion was spent on business marketing communications in 1997. Nearly one in four of those dollars was spent on advertising, making it the most popular promotional tool in business-to-business marketing, according to the Outfront II study published in 1999 by *Advertising Age's Business Marketing.* Companies with $50 million or more in annual revenue spent $17.7 billion on advertising. Trade publications received an esti-

mated $5.7 billion of that. In contrast, on-line advertising, although the fastest-growing category at the time, garnered an estimated $174 million, placing it 11th among 13 media categories studied. Spending in business publications by the top 100 business-to-business advertisers rose 4.2 percent in 1998, from about $1.17 billion in 1997 to $1.21 billion a year later, according to *Advertising Age's Business Marketing.* During the period, however, business advertisers increased their spending in consumer media at an even greater pace.

Editorial Profile

Intense pressure exists to improve the efficiency and effectiveness of both business-to-business advertising efforts and procurement practices as advertisers seek improved, measurable results through increasingly cost-efficient programs. Against this background, innovative trade publishers continue to offer more integrated communication programs while improving the quality and usefulness of their editorial content, the non-advertising part of a magazine. The fit between an audience and its editorial content is described in the publisher's "editorial profile," which profiles prime readers, identifies the type of trade publication, and provides a written overview of the magazine, its key contents, and special sections. A media planner uses the publisher's editorial profile to evaluate a publication, determining how close it comes to matching a target audience and enhancing the image of the advertiser or its brand. If the fit is good, other aspects of the publication are then evaluated in light of specific media objectives and strategies.

Editorial profiles are found in advertising directories, such as Standard Rate and Data Service's *SRDS Business Publication Advertising Source.* The publisher's editorial profile of *Advertising Age,* for example, as taken from the October 2001 *SRDS Business Publication Advertising Source* reads:

> *Advertising Age* provides complete and timely coverage of the entire world of marketing, with special reports, information, and analysis written for advertising, marketing, and media executives. News journalism covers brand marketing and advertising issues affecting marketers from the top 100 megabrands to new product launches. Regular news features and departments report the latest in marketing techniques such as advertising, research, sales promotions, and events. Category reports provide industry analysis and brand information on packaged goods, technology, automotive, health & beauty, etc. The weekly Interactive Media & Marketing section reviews new technology applications. Plus, special reports throughout the year feature subjects such as the 100 Leading National Advertisers, the Marketing 100, the top 200 Megabrands, the top 500 Agency Report, and Media Mavens.

Trade publications typically offer advertisers carefully controlled circulations. In lieu of charging a subscription fee, some trade publications "qualify" individuals or companies that fit a unique buyer profile based on occupation, job title, responsibilities, type of industry, specialized functions, company size, number of employees, and past sales.

Since many competing trade publications exist, advertisers need to know which are more likely to achieve their media objectives at the lowest possible cost. In the early days of advertising, little information about trade publications was made available; circulation figures, ideas about editorial content, audience profiles, and circulation data were unverified and often incorrect. Often circulation figures were purposely inflated, eventually leading advertisers to demand more accurate information. Advertisers and publishers have voluntarily come together in a process called "comparability" to jointly develop the publisher's editorial profile. Comparability signifies that both publishers and advertisers jointly define each of the major audiences served by a publication. It is completed market by market on a voluntary basis during open meetings.

Circulation

Publishers use the publisher's editorial profile to verify circulations and calculate advertising rates. Once each target reader segment is profiled, the descriptions are used to quantify the trade publication's "qualified circulation." This is the circulation—paid or nonpaid—sent to the markets served, along with recipient qualification and the correct business or occupational classifications verified by auditable, documentary evidence that is dated within 36 months. Qualified recipients must receive each issue of the trade publication, subject to normal removals and edition variations.

Audits of circulations are used to verify and adjust a trade publication's circulation. An audit is a formal, third-party check of a magazine's or newspaper's circulation. An "audit unit" is an audited report attesting to the validity of the number of units, plants, or establishments a publication serves. A "breakdown," a customary component of an audit, is the division of circulation as to the types of businesses or industries that a trade publication reaches, the functions or titles of recipients, and their geographic locations.

The Audit Bureau of Circulations (ABC) in Schaumburg, Illinois, is an independent, nonprofit organization of advertisers, advertising agencies, and publishers that provides verified audits of the circulation of newspapers and magazines, including trade publications. Audits also can be obtained from other companies, such as Business Publications Audit of Circulation, Inc. (BPA), in New York City, and Verified Audit Circulation of San Rafael, California. Some trade publications, given their small, specialized circulation, are not audited but instead offer "nonqualified distribution" circulation figures—a circulation estimate that does not conform to the information found in audited circulations reports. Often publishers of nonaudited trade publications provide circulation data as a "statement," which alerts media planners and advertisers to the fact that the data have not been verified.

Media planners and advertisers also glean information describing trade publications from various magazine directories. For

Crain Communications, Inc.'s Ad Age Group publishes several trade publications for the advertising and marketing communities. *Reprinted with permission of Advertising Age. Copyright, Crain Communications, Inc.*

example, *Benn's Media Directory,* a directory of print media that is published in the United Kingdom, identifies magazines, periodicals, and newspapers for all countries. Its data on some countries are incomplete, reflecting the diversity of kinds of media information available. The *Standard Periodicals Directory* provides comprehensive information on U.S. and Canadian periodicals, described along such category lines as automotive, demography, electronics and electrical engineering, exhibitions, and machinery. Trade publications are indexed alphabetically and are classified as association or business publications; editorial content is described in terms of scope, purpose, and content.

Challenges

As competition for business-to-business advertisers continues to intensify, the one-size-fits-all, print-only approach to business advertising has become passé. Advertisers seeking to develop powerful communication strategies for domestic and world markets have begun to look beyond the practice of simply buying advertising space. Trade publishers, in response, have begun to expand the set of support services they have traditionally provided to advertisers, going beyond reader service numbers, the combining of editorial and advertising material, special issues, and trade shows.

To make their editorial content more alluring, aggressive trade publishers around the globe provide advertisers with a menu of integrated promotional tools such as customized niche publications, run-of-magazine sponsorships, free publicity in one or more of the publisher's other magazines, database direct-marketing promotions, special supplements, fast faxes, and Web marketing opportunities. The publisher's toolbox also includes special events, seminars, and conferences, as well as annual events specifically designed for key markets. The acquisition of major conferences or expositions by trade magazine publishers, for example, grew from 38 percent in 1997 to 75 percent in 1999.

Some of the strongest names in business-to-business marketing declined in power at the end of the 20th century. This development—along with the increasing importance of relational marketing, the growing need for integrated communications, and the emergence of e-commerce—has challenged advertisers to rethink their creative message strategies. Many have found it necessary to reevaluate their commitment to qualitative and quantitative research as integral to creation of ad messages.

Trade magazines have traditionally been regarded as tools for conveying the features, attributes, functions, specifications, and benefits of a product or service. The development of a brand image, on the other hand, a process that requires establishing an emotional relationship between the reader and a company or a brand, has been regarded as the forte of consumer marketers. For business-to-business marketers to compete in the 21st century, traditional notions of how to use trade publications to create and solidify brand image will need sharp adjustments, and creative concepts will have to become more original and compelling.

International Picture

Successful trade publications are by no means limited to businesses in the United States. One directory of British media listed more than 5,150 business and trade magazines published in the United Kingdom alone in 1999. Among the trade publications advertisers can make use of in international advertising campaigns are *Exhibit Mexico, Business Latin America, Business India Intelligence, Business Japan,* and *Business Middle East.* Directories such as *BRAD, Canadian Advertising Rates and Data,* and *European Marketing & Data Statistics* also supply useful information. Nonetheless, trade advertisers have lamented both the lack of global and pan-regional trade publications and the inaccuracy of the circulation data available for many countries. The International Advertising Association, headquartered in New York City, is one group that works to remedy such inaccurate data.

Growth: A Case in Point

Trade publications have in many instances come a long way from their humble roots. *Advertising Age's B2B* mirrors the historical growth of trade publications. The predecessor to *Advertising Age's B2B,* a horizontal trade publication serving business-to-business advertisers, was called *Class* when it was launched in 1916. It was 32 pages, with 18 devoted to advertising, and G.D. Crain, Jr., the publisher, charged charter advertisers $15 a page for the digest-size monthly. By 1923 the publication had a circulation of 5,300, and some issues reached 200 pages in size. In 1927 its name and format were changed, and *Class & Industrial Marketing* emerged in magazine format. In 1930 Crain introduced *Advertising Age,* a weekly horizontal publication primarily serving the consumer advertising industry, partly as a vehicle in which to promote *Class.* As an austerity measure during the Great Depression, the two publications were merged, with *Class & Industrial Marketing* folded into the first issue of the month of *Advertising Age.* As the economy improved, *Class and Industrial Marketing* reemerged in 1935 under a new, abbreviated title, *Industrial Marketing.*

As business-to-business advertising and trade shows proliferated during the years following World War II, *Industrial Marketing* and other trade publications thrived. In 1983 the magazine changed its name to *Business Marketing* to reflect a broadened scope. In 1994 its name and format were again changed; it was renamed *Advertising Age's Business Marketing* and shed its magazine format to become a tabloid. Its Web Price Index feature is the only long-running national benchmark of World Wide Web development prices. Daily news is added to its Web site (http://netb2b.com), where readers can communicate electronically with the editors. Interested subscribers receive e-mail notices of breaking news. The name was shortened again in March 2000 to *B2B.*

The Future

The early years of the 21st century are widely regarded as a golden time for trade publications and other forms of business-to-business media, which are growing in size and influence. Debate has begun as to whether advertising agencies or trade publications are better positioned to plan integrated communication programs for business-to-business marketers.

In 2001 Veronis Suhler, a media investment banking company, released an industry forecast that suggested business-to-business media would continue to grow through 2005, although the estimated compound growth rate of 4.0 percent would be considerably less than the 6.0 percent seen from 1996 to 2000. Spending in trade publications and on trade shows in 2005 was expected to reach $10.9 billion and $11.3 billion, respectively.

ALLEN E. SMITH

Further Reading

Barnes, Beth E., "Business-to-Business Advertising," in *The Advertising Business: Operations, Creativity, Media Planning, Integrated Communications,* edited by John Philip Jones, Thousand Oaks, California: Sage, 1999

Bovée, Courtland L., and William F. Arens, *Contemporary Advertising*, Homewood, Illinois: Irwin, 1982

Callahan, Sean, "Veronis: B-to-B Ad Growth to Continue: But Study Finds Rate of Increase Will Slow over Next 5 Years to 6.2%," *Advertising Age's Business Marketing* 84, no. 12 (1 December 1999)

De Mooij, Marieke K., and Warren J. Keegan, *Advertising Worldwide: Concepts, Theories, and Practice of International, Multinational, and Global Advertising*, New York: Prentice Hall, 1991

Dunn, Samuel Watson, *Advertising: Its Role in Modern Marketing*, New York: Holt Rinehart and Winston, 1961; 8th edition, by Dean M. Krugman et al., Fort Worth, Texas: Dryden Press, 1994

Egolf, Karen, "Dawn of the B-to-B Millennium: Things Just Keep Getting Better all the Time," *Business Marketing* 84, no. 12 (1 December 1999)

Goldsborough, Robert, "Our 80-Year Mission," *Advertising Age's Business Marketing* 82, no. 1 (2 February 1997)

Kleppner, Otto, *Advertising Procedure*, New York: Prentice-Hall, 1925; 14th edition, as *Kleppner's Advertising Procedure*, by J. Thomas Russell and W. Ronald Lane, Upper Saddle River, New Jersey: Prentice Hall, 1999

Mahin, Philip William, *Business-to-Business Marketing*, Boston: Allyn and Bacon, 1991

McGann, Anthony F., and J. Thomas Russell, *Advertising Media: A Managerial Approach*, Homewood, Illinois: Irwin, 1981

O'Guinn, Thomas C., Chris T. Allen, and Richard J. Semenik, *Advertising*, Cincinnati, Ohio: South-Western College, 1998; 2nd edition, 2000

SRDS Business Publication Advertising Source (1995–)

SRDS Consumer Magazine Advertising Source (1995–)

The Standard Periodical Directory (annual; 1989–)

Wells, William, John Burnett, and Sandra E. Moriarty, *Advertising: Principles and Practice*, London: Prentice-Hall International, and Englewood Cliffs, New Jersey: Prentice Hall, 1989; 5th edition, Upper Saddle River, New Jersey: Prentice Hall, 1999

Trahey, Jane 1923–2000

U.S. Advertising Copywriter

Jane Trahey, the first woman in advertising to earn $1 million a year, set the standard for fashion copywriting, creating such campaigns as the long-running "What becomes a legend most?" for Blackglama mink and Danskin, Inc.'s "Danskins are not just for dancing." Trahey was born 19 November 1923 in Chicago, Illinois, the daughter of David and Margaret Hennessy Trahey. She graduated from Mundelein College, in Chicago, in 1943 and studied for two years at the University of Wisconsin, in Madison. (In 1975 Trahey received an M.F.A. from Columbia University, New York City.) Her first job was in the news morgue of the *Chicago Tribune*, followed by a position in the survey research department of the *Chicago Daily News*.

From there, Trahey moved to a receptionist job with Carson, Pirie, Scott & Company, a Chicago department store, and worked her way into her first advertising job as a copywriter for the retailer. Her work brought her to the attention of the upscale department store Neiman-Marcus, which in 1947 lured her to Dallas, Texas, with an advertising copywriting position that paid $600 a month. While she originally planned to stay only two years in Texas, she instead remained with the retailer for almost nine years, earning promotions to eventually become advertising and sales director, which paid $28,000 a year. During her years at Neiman-Marcus, Trahey forged a reputation for innovative fashion copywriting, setting a standard for others to

follow. She experimented with color in retail ads and also with scented inks.

In 1956 she moved to New York City to open 425 Advertising Associates as the in-house agency for Julius Kayser, Inc., a lingerie and hosiery manufacturer. In 1958 she opened her own agency, Jane Trahey Associates, Inc., specializing in fashion and cosmetics advertising. In 1962 the name of the agency changed to Trahey/Cadwell, reflecting the addition of partner Franchellie Cadwell.

That partnership lasted only until June 1964, when Cadwell and Trahey dissolved the business arrangement. Operating as Trahey Associates/Advertising and then in 1965 as Trahey Advertising, Inc., the agency's clients included Charles of the Ritz, Elizabeth Arden, Pauline Trigere, Rob Roy Shirts for Boys, and the textile division of Union Carbide Corporation. By 1966 the agency was billing about $2.5 million and had 18 employees, whom Trahey often referred to as "my kids."

In 1967 Trahey again changed the name of the agency, this time to Trahey/Wolf Advertising, Inc., with the addition of Art Director Henry Wolf as a partner; that arrangement lasted until 1972, when Wolf left and Trahey returned to doing business as Trahey Advertising, Inc. In 1976 Peter Rogers, an executive vice president at the agency, became a partner as well, and the shop was renamed Trahey/Rogers Advertising. Trahey herself left to become a consultant in 1978, selling the shop to Rogers.

Jane Trahey.
Jerry Schatzberg/Courtesy Staley-Wise Gallery, New York.

Over the course of her advertising career, Trahey received more than 200 awards, including the American Advertising Federation's 1969 Advertising Woman of the Year honor. Her chief campaigns included those for Bill Blass, Calvin Klein, Elizabeth Arden, and Olivetti typewriters. Among the well-remembered slogans she created were "Foot-loose and Famolare!" for Famolare footwear and "It's not fake anything, it's real Dynel" for Union Carbide's synthetic hair.

Perhaps Trahey's best-known campaign was that for Black-glama mink, which she created in 1968 with Peter Rogers for the Great Lakes Mink Association. The effort featured women so well known they did not need to be identified by name in the ads to be recognized. In each ad a single celebrity, wearing a mink coat and shot by top photographer Richard Avedon, was featured along with the line, "What becomes a legend most?" The celebrities, who received a mink coat and the portrait by Avedon as payment, included Lauren Bacall, Marlene Dietrich, Judy Garland, Rita Hayworth, Leontyne Price, and Barbra Streisand. The ads continued after Trahey left the agency; the last one, in 1996, featured dancer Tommy Tune, the first male in the campaign.

But running an ad agency was not enough to keep Trahey's creative juices flowing. By 1966 she was writing a weekly column for the *Chicago Tribune* and, by the late 1960s, was a regular colum-nist for *Advertising Age* as well. She was listed as a fairly regular contributor in such publications as *Cosmopolitan, Harper's Bazaar, McCall's,* and *Ladies' Home Journal.* She also wrote a number of books and plays and spent three years editing *Harper's Bazaar: 100 Years of the American Female,* published in 1967. Her 1962 novel, *Life with Mother Superior,* a humorous portrayal of Trahey's own experiences at a Catholic high school, was made into the 1966 movie *The Trouble with Angels* by Columbia Pictures.

She was also active in the feminist movement, creating public-service advertising for the National Organization for Women (NOW) Legal Defense and Education Fund, and serving as vice president and a member of the board for that branch of the organization. She credited her mother, who raised Trahey and her sister, Anita, on her own after the death of her husband, with instilling in her a strong drive and sense of ambition.

Still, Trahey, with her infectious laugh and her love of humor, complained that advertising was too serious. Articles about her often described how her statements would "spark a chuckle"; her humorous delivery prompted one interviewer to describe her as "a Phyllis Diller with neat hair."

Trahey never married. In an *Advertising Age* interview in 1966, she acknowledged the difficulty women in advertising faced in getting ahead:

> To get to the top in the advertising business, a woman has to have almost a neurotic devotion to her career, and this almost excludes marriage. Sooner or later, the adwoman who is married and has children is going to have to make a decision in favor of home, and this decision, even though it is the right one, will hurt her career.

After leaving the agency, Trahey continued working as a consultant while writing and lecturing. She died at her home in Kent, Connecticut, on 22 April 2000 at the age of 76.

LAURIE FREEMAN

Biography
Born in Chicago, Illinois, 19 November 1923; graduated from Mundelein College, Chicago, 1943; became a copywriter for Neiman-Marcus, Dallas, Texas, 1947; opened 425 Advertising Associates, New York City, an in-house agency for Julius Kayser, Inc., a women's fashion marketer, 1956; opened Jane Trahey Associates, New York City, 1958; agency name changed to Trahey/Cadwell, 1962; agency name changed to Trahey Associates/Advertising, 1964, then Trahey Advertising, 1965; renamed Trahey/Wolf, 1967; renamed Trahey Advertising, Inc., 1972; renamed Trahey/Rogers, 1976; received M.F.A., Columbia University, 1975; sold agency to Peter Rogers, 1978; died in Kent, Connecticut, 22 April 2000.

Selected Publications
The Magic Yarn, 1960
Life with Mother Superior, 1962
editor, *Harper's Bazaar: 100 Years of the American Female,* 1967

Ring around the Bathtub (play), 1968
Pecked to Death by Goslings, 1969
Life with Mother Superior (play), 1974
Jane Trahey on Women and Power: Who's Got It? How to Get It? 1977
Thursdays 'til 9, 1980
The Clovis Caper, 1990

Further Reading

"Adwoman Trahey Finds Agency Life Totally Non-Boring," *Advertising Age* (7 July 1969)

"Jane Trahey; Created Blackglama Fur Ads," *Los Angeles Times* (14 May 2000)

Keding, Ann Maxwell, "Jane Trahey," in *The Ad Men and Women: A Biographical Dictionary of Advertising*, edited by Edd Applegate, Westport, Connecticut: Greenwood Press, 1994

Schiro, Anne-Marie, "Jane Trahey, Advertising Woman in 1960s, also Wrote Novels and a Play," *New York Times* (25 April 2000)

Wood, Ray, "Busy Jane Trahey Finds That Creating Ads Helps Sharpen Writing Talents," *Advertising Age* (3 January 1966)

Travel and Tourism

Since the late 1800s, tourism has grown to be big business—and the advertising and marketing of the industry is big business as well, one with a rich history. From railroads to automobiles to hotels and resorts, each segment of the industry has developed strategies to lure people away from home.

Travel opened up largely with the advent of mass transportation. The introduction and rapid growth of railroads, followed closely by the development of the oceangoing steamship, created new opportunities for travel and tourism. While the wealthy had long enjoyed annual trips to summer homes or spas, the new ships and railroads opened up even more possibilities.

The South Carolina Railroad launched the first steam-powered passenger train in the United States, touted in large ads as "The best friend of Charleston," carrying 141 passengers on a six-mile strip of track for its inaugural run in 1830. By the start of the U.S. Civil War in 1860, 30,000 miles of track had been laid; by 1869 the first transcontinental railroad was completed when tracks of the Union Pacific met those of the Central Pacific.

Attracting the Elite

By the late 1870s, the railroads were advertising themselves as a way for the wealthy traveler to see the wonders of Yosemite and Yellowstone in style and comfort, thanks in large part to George Pullman's revolutionary development, the sleeping car, in the 1860s. One Northern Pacific railroad ad that ran in *Harper's Weekly* explained that the expense of the trip was a guarantee that travelers would not be subjected to "undesirable company"—only the wealthy could afford such a journey. Following through on the same theme, the railroads marketed the national parks as elite destinations with amenities designed exclusively for the enjoyment of the upper classes and advertised luxurious accommodations both on and off the train. In 1880 Northern Pacific announced its Yellowstone Park Line, and Southern Pacific began to advertise its Sunset Limited line (from Los Angeles to New Orleans). Advertising for Yosemite, on the western slopes of the Sierra Nevada Mountains in central California, was designed to make it seem less like the remote area it was and more like a gentrified wilderness civilized by the presence of the railroad.

The railroads handled the marketing challenge skillfully, producing ads that resembled scenes painted by the landscape artist Albert Bierstadt and thus making Yosemite seem safe and familiar to residents of the eastern states. Southern Pacific's ads in the 1880s played on the dramatic sense of scale showcased in western images of the 1860s and recalled the rapturous praises of past visitors to the area. Once advertising had established Yosemite as the "civilized wilderness," the railroads began to sponsor hotels in the area and advertise them in the same manner. Railway advertising through the years continued to emphasize the luxury amenities of trains: fine dining, sunroof tops, and the Pullman berth.

Meanwhile, hotels were also beginning to advertise. The great hotel names of the late 19th century included Willard, St. Charles, Palmer House, Brown Palace, Chalfonte, and Haddon House. Superlatives flowed freely in the ad copy. Ads for the Haddon House, in Boston, Massachusetts, proclaimed that the hotel possessed a "perfect system of sewerage and ventilation" and a location that offered guests "every possible facility and convenience of rapid and commercial transfer from all points." In the 1890s, an ad for the Union Hotel in New York City posed the question, "What good hotel is near the depot?"—the answer, of course, itself.

The evolution of print media also affected hotel ads. In 1890, for example, the *New York Times* carried ads for hotels and resorts comparable in appearance to today's classified advertising. Hotel ads of that era usually consisted of a routine description of the facilities set in a distinct typeface and occasionally supplemented with a line illustration of the building exterior. All the ads for hotel accommodations appeared on a single page; as

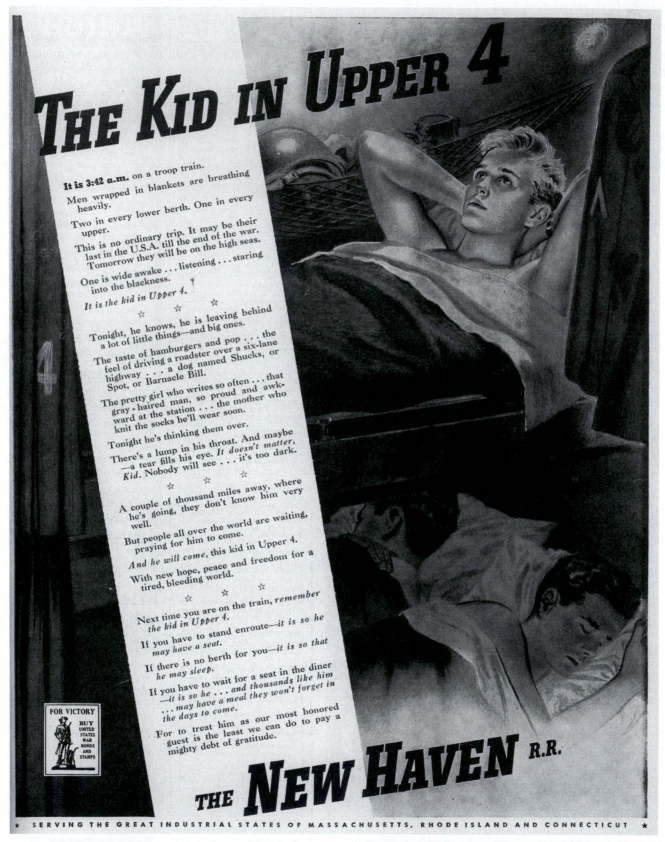

In 1942 the New Haven Railroad responded to complaints about its service during wartime with this sentimental advertisement appealing to its riders' patriotism.
American Financial Enterprises, Inc.

hotels proliferated and newspapers grew, however, the hotel ads became larger and were distributed throughout the paper.

Middle-Class Tourism

In 1907 Ellsworth Statler opened the Buffalo Statler in Buffalo, New York, offering "a room and a bath at a dollar and a half." The hotel, which became the first in a chain of middle-class Statler hotels, was the first to have telephones, radios, and built-in closets in every guest room. Statler also standardized restaurant offerings as well as amenities for all his hotels. His success spurred others to copy his formula. In 1954 Conrad Hilton bought the Statler chain.

By the 1930s hotels were starting to advertise, and epithets referring to a hotel's uncommon qualities were frequent: "ideal," "famous," "superb," "magnificent," and "best" often appeared in ad copy. Still, most hotels of the 1930s were independent, which meant that mass advertising had limited value; because each hotel had but one point of sale, in one city, national advertising was of little value. In fact, only about one hotel in 100 ran national ads.

Through the 1930s, the railroads were starting to feel increasing pressure from the automobile industry, which was opening up tourism to the middle class. With the accompanying growth of the national highway system, resorts and hotels were no longer dependent on a nearby city or railroad depot for their clientele. With post–World War II prosperity, this trend continued, despite the railroads' efforts to lure passengers back for a postwar vacation. A campaign from the Great Northern railway told Americans it was the "right year and this is the right train" for a great vacation.

Still, automobiles were fast replacing trains as the preferred mode of travel, and by the 1950s, a new form of lodging was springing up along with the U.S. interstate highway system: the motel. In 1952, the first Holiday Inn opened in Memphis, Tennessee, targeting middle-income families. The founder, Kemmons Wilson, built several more Holiday Inns and then began franchising the name to others to meet the growing demand. Travelers came to expect each Holiday Inn to offer free parking, ice, and telephones, along with a swimming pool, air-conditioning, and an on-premises restaurant; in addition, children could accompany parents at no extra charge. By the end of the 1950s, there were 100 Holiday Inns around the country; by 1964, there were 500; and by 1968, 1,000. Holiday Inns' ad agencies have included D.P. Brother & Company (named in 1960), the John Cleghorn Agency (which became Beard, Lawson & Potter in 1966), Cosmopolitan Agency (Holiday Inn's in-house agency), Boyce Advertising, Bozell & Jacobs, the J. Walter Thompson Company (JWT), Young & Rubicam (which succeeded JWT in 1976), and more recently Fallon McElligott.

At the same time, resorts were growing in areas that had previously been hard to reach. With the introduction of jet travel in 1958, domestic and overseas locations once considered inaccessible were drawing the interest of developers. By 1965 the resort business had become the largest-spending of all hotel advertising categories and warranted a special section in most newspapers.

Distinguishing the Destination

By the late 1970s, generic advertising of destinations was on the decline. Travel marketers were discovering that they had to communicate clearly how one destination was different from all others. A case in point was the Caribbean islands. Ads for St. Kitts/Nevis were designed to take business away from other islands. A typical ad read: "Frankly, only 250 Americans a week come to Nevis and St. Kitts to do practically nothing. Isn't that wonderful." Agencies were beginning to realize that people who chose such a distinct destination were part of a sophisticated market—travelers who had been to the Caribbean several times and had outgrown the popular Virgin Islands and Bahamas. An ad for Eden II, a couples-only resort in Jamaica, pictured the bare feet of a twosome sitting on the beach, thus positioning the resort for romance. Club Med ads from Ammirati & Puris, Inc., were aimed at vacationers who wanted to shed the trappings of the city and promised "the antidote for civilization."

The market for luxury properties held up during the recession of the 1970s, while the fringe markets did not. Savvy travel advertisers moved beyond traditional marketing techniques. A campaign for Bahamas tourism in the late 1970s, from Nardelli Tamen, changed the emphasis of the islands' ads. The agency had discovered that only 6 percent of vacationers visited the outer islands, yet half the Bahamas' print budget was spent promoting them. The islands began spending more money on themselves, leaving the others to go it alone. The fragmented marketing among all Caribbean islands continued into the 21st century.

Recognizing that generic ads were losing their effectiveness, the travel and tourism bureaus of many states and countries also began adopting innovative approaches to marketing their destinations as unique and distinct. Virginia's wildly successful slogan, "Virginia is for lovers," created by the advertising agency Martin & Woltz, Inc., in 1969, attracted visitors to the state's plantations, Civil War battlefields, mountains, beaches, and theme parks. Tourist spending in Virginia in the 1990s topped $11 billion, up from the $809 million spent 30 years before.

In the 1980s Texas tourism officials turned to a local agency, GSD&M, in Austin, to help the state erase its image as a hot, dry, dusty place known for its collapsed savings-and-loan industry and plunging oil prices. In 1988 the state was not even in the top-ten list of preferred travel destinations. A new campaign, with the theme, "Texas. It's like a whole other country," was launched in TV commercials and on postcard inserts in magazines, featuring the red rock canyons, San Antonio's canals, and the Gulf Coast beaches. By 1997 Texas was the fourth-most-popular state to visit in terms of tourist spending, with travel revenue jumping to $29.3 billion from $18 billion in 1989. Later in the 1990s, McCann-Erickson Worldwide, Dallas, took over the account, keeping the essential concept but creating a campaign with the theme, "Texas. It's more than you think."

The same nongeneric approach was also taken by countries trying to boost their tourism income. Australia, playing up its image as a friendly place, enlisted D'Arcy Masius Benton & Bowles, which created a series of TV spots, including one called

JAMAICA

© JAMAICA TOURIST BOARD

Meet Mallica Reynolds: wood sculptor, painter, family man, Bible scholar. And Pocomaniac.

Mallica Reynolds burns myrrh for inspiration and writes mystical explanations in Biblical Aramaic for his dark, sensuous works.

He's also a gentle father.

He's also a little mad.

On Sundays, he leads the services of a hand-clapping revivalist religion called Pocomania (literally, "little madness").

In Jamaica, we have a lot of swinging hymn-singing.

Sunday morning to Sunday night, drive up and down the North Coast and hear heavenly voices floating over cane fields. (We sing loud, too.)

Stop. Come into our country churches, our cathedrals, our reading rooms, our temples.

Yes, temples.

We have the oldest Jewish community in the Western world.

Plus Anglican, Buddhist, Salvation Army, you name it.

Our religions come from the whole world.

Same as our people—descended and blended from every national ancestry.

Same as our food—a mixture of fried wonton, fettucine, boeuf fondue, scones, and Typhoo tea.

Same as our language—a gar-

ble of English, African, Spanish, Scottish and Welsh that winds up calling a married woman "mistress," calling men *and* women "mon," and using the words "bare" and "pure" to mean "only."

(As in what a man said after visiting a Moravian church: "Mon, on one side they have bare women; and on the other, pure men.")

For more about our mixed-up country, see your local travel agent or Jamaica Tourist Board in New York, San Francisco, Chicago, Los Angeles, Miami, Toronto.

DDB's work for the Jamaica Tourist Board was the first campaign to effectively use culture to promote vacation travel. The logo DDB designed was still in use by the tourist board in 2002.

"Dining al Fresco," where a couple eating fresh oysters at a sea-side restaurant watches as a fisherman wading into the waters looks back and says, "Be right back with your main course." New Zealand, meanwhile, with its ad agency M&C Saatchi, came up with "100% pure New Zealand." The three-year campaign in the 1990s committed $30 million worldwide to print and cable TV ads that tied in to pure adventure, pure nature, and pure culture. Tourism increased only slightly.

One sector that got an unexpected marketing boost in the early 1980s was the cruise industry. Until that point, only 5 percent of Americans had ever taken a cruise. Then in 1977, ABC premiered *The Love Boat,* a weekly series about romantic entanglements aboard a cruise ship. The series ran until 1986, and the cruise market faced a shortage of available berths. The ship featured on the show belonged to Princess Cruises, which played on the tie-in with "Love Boat"-themed ads—some starring actor Gavin MacLeod, the captain on the series—from Tracy-Locke, Los Angeles, California, and later Lintas:Campbell-Ewald, Los Angeles. With ship capacity increasing faster than passenger loads, cruise lines stepped up advertising in 1988—some by as much as 100 percent, according to *Advertising Age.* Still, by 1996, only 8 percent of Americans had taken a cruise.

Advertising Advantages of Chains

Throughout the 1970s and 1980s, the hotel industry continued to expand, finding huge benefits in forming chains and franchising. Marketing expenses, for example, could be shared and, with a name known nationally or even internationally, hotel chains had a marked advantage over their independent brethren. Television reigned as the primary advertising medium of the 14 leading hotel chains in 1979. Of the $59 million spent on ads by these chains, television accounted for $21 million. Magazines and newspapers followed in ad expenditures with $15 million and $14 million, respectively, accounting, in combination, for half the total. Radio trailed all other media, accounting for only 6 percent. Network television was highly favored over spot television in the chains' advertising decisions, receiving 81 percent of the total expenditures in this medium. The hotel chains divided their newspaper advertising dollars almost evenly among retail advertisements placed in various papers within 50 miles of the hotel, spending $18 million. Only two chains, Sheraton Corporation and Hilton Hotels Corporation, spent more than $5 million on advertising in 1979.

In the early 1980s leading hotel chains targeted business travelers with ads that promoted both overall image and individual properties. Hotel chains worked on the premise that two issues were important in developing lodging advertising. The first was whether and how strongly to relate the parent company's overall image to the appeals of an individual hotel or resort. The second hinged on a debate between two ad strategies—whether to create a fantasy or simply to show the product. Merely showing a guest room may not seem like very creative advertising, yet at least one major chain's research indicated that this was what consumers wanted to see and what they remembered.

Hotels also advertised upgraded services, while holding the line on rates. The Ramada Inn chain, which spent $20 million in 1981, a 33 percent increase over 1980, produced a TV spot showing the transformation of a room in process via a time-lapse photo process. Foote, Cone & Belding was the chain's agency.

Hyatt called attention to itself with a new campaign headlined, "Other hotels try to give you a touch of Hyatt. Only Hyatt gives you them all." The ad, from the J. Walter Thompson Company, combined hard-sell copy with an ambience of tasteful luxury. Noting that times were tough and costs were skyrocketing, it emphasized Hyatt's luxury and services as being "standards, not options."

Marriott Hotels opted for a print ad to business travelers and used its president, Bill Marriott, to deliver the message. The ad showed the executive next to the front door of a Marriott, dressed as the quintessential business traveler. He tells the reader that he travels more than 100,000 miles per year. The idea is that during his inspections of the hotels, he draws from personal experience. The hotel chain handled advertising in-house and at Ogilvy & Mather, Inc., during the period.

Westin Hotels, which was Western International until January 1981, suffered an identity crisis. Travelers were not aware of its corporate identity and did not associate the Plaza Hotel in New

In the 1980s airlines and hotels targeted the growing number of business travelers. A 1983 campaign by Marriott depicted company President Bill Marriott as the quintessential business traveler.
Marriott International, Inc.

York City with Western International. The individual hotels were better known than the Western International name. Holiday Inn faced this same problem almost ten years later, in 1990, when it was purchased by Bass, PLC, London, England. The Holiday Inn name always overshadowed the Bass name and Choice Hotels. There were no "Bass" or "Choice" properties, so customers did not know with whom they were actually staying. There was no way to know that Holiday Inn Express was owned by Bass Hotels. Bass burned the marketing midnight oil wondering if anyone actually cared.

Some hotel chains, such as Holiday Inn, began advertising their brands separately; others grouped brands together under a corporate umbrella. The print ad announcing the Western change made the statement that "Our great name had one small problem"—run under a towel rack showing two towels, side by side. One had "Western Internati" on it and the other "onal Hotels." The subhead read "Westin Hotels." The ad ran in business, news, and travel agent publications in the United States and abroad. Cole & Weber, Inc., was the chain's agency in 1981.

Hotel operators in the 1980s had to do far more than earlier hoteliers who simply waited for customers to find them. To capture business, operators developed advertising that spoke to the benefits consumers considered important in a hotel, identified what the hotel uniquely offered guests, and followed up with an effective, well-orchestrated campaign.

Motel 6: A Success Story

The budget chain Motel 6 is often used as a case history for lodging advertising. Its agency usually did not go along with the trendy messages of the larger, more expensive chains, but it created memorable advertising and the chain grew. One of these efforts was the Tom Bodett radio campaign, one of the best-known ad campaigns of the 1980s and 1990s. The Richards Group was hired by Motel 6 in 1986. Its objectives were simple: Richards was to reverse the 25-year-old chain's several-year decline in occupancy; broaden the customer base by attracting new guests; and critique the product from the guest's perspective. In 1986 advertisers from all lodging industry segments spent $107 million on media advertising, mostly to buy TV and print ads. Very little was being spent on radio. Bucking trends, Richards decided that radio made the most sense for Motel 6; the decision was to make an end run around the competition by using a medium the other lodging chains rarely touched.

At the time, phones were not included in guest rooms. That changed following focus-group studies that indicated guests wanted them, and the chain soon ordered 50,000 telephones. Richards designed a radio campaign to announce this new amenity and trumpeted the fact that Motel 6 was "moving into the fast lane." Motel 6 bought airtime on a spot basis, one market at a time. By the fourth quarter of 1987, all the phones were in and Motel 6 advertised its entire system on national radio.

As always, the choice of a spokesman was critical. Bodett, a resident of Homer, Alaska, and a homebuilder turned writer, intrigued the agency. He was largely unknown by the public, and the advertiser feared that his lack of celebrity might result in too little notice among the target audience to build awareness of the brand. On the other hand, would a bona fide star ever stay at a Motel 6? The first radio spots featuring Bodett ran in late 1986. He did about 100 more over the next five years. Motel 6 saw a turnaround in its six-year occupancy slide in the first full year of the campaign. Occupancy rose 6 percent while revenue grew from $256 million to $297 million and continued to rise.

Few campaigns succeeded like this one. No other lodging campaign had such a long run. The lesson of the campaign was not to use radio, a witty spokesman, or even appeal to consumers' desire to make a smart choice. It was to use a disciplined process that begins with research to learn about consumers' behavior, respond to those insights, and then follow through.

Discounting and Other Enticements

In the late 1980s, hotels began to borrow a page from airlines' marketing textbooks. Fighting an industrywide oversupply of rooms, Holiday Inn was the first to resort to discounting programs rivaling those offered by major airlines while hoping to avoid airline-style price wars. It introduced the Great Rates supersaver program, which was the first step in a pricing strategy aimed at winning customers not ordinarily drawn to Holiday Inn's mid-price properties. A $2 million campaign from Bozell, Jacobs, Kenyon & Eckhardt (later Bozell Worldwide) supported the program. At the same time, Days Inn introduced a room discount program similar to Great Rates. Many other national chains offered supersaver type discounts good mainly for weekend stays.

Hotels also have long used alliances to promote stays in their properties. Pan American World Airways opened properties in San Juan and Brazil in 1947. The next year it announced plans for its Inter-Continental Hotels subsidiary to build 11 more properties in Latin America. In 1967 there was an upswing in airline-hotels alliances that compared to the railway-owned hotel chains of yesteryear. By the late 1960s, 25 airlines had ties to hotels, including SAS, Pan Am, Trans-World Airlines, Inc. (with Hilton), and Westin (which merged with United Air Lines' parent in 1970).

Through the year 2001, PricewaterhouseCoopers predicted pretax profits in the travel industry would hit $29 billion, a 14 percent increase over the previous year. Lodging industry analyst firm Smith Travel Research, of Nashville, Tennessee, said that the average daily rate for hotels rose from $81.61 in 1999 to $84.87 in 2000 and revenue per available room increased about 4 percent to $53.72 in 2000. In addition, the average profit margin for U.S. hotels declined slightly, from 29.8 percent in 1998 to 29.3 percent in 2000.

Hotel companies have seen an increase in tourists from overseas, according to PKF Consulting. Overall, international travelers to the United States through 2003 were expected to reach nearly 55 million, an 18 percent increase over the 1998 number. And in the 21st century, more than at any other time, those travelers have hotels designed to meet their particular needs. From budget to luxury, from no service to limited service to full service, new hotel products are introduced each year. Travelers are expected to continue to rely on two of the biggest names in travel, American Express Corporation and Carlson Wagonlit Travel, both of which have been heavy marketers, using both destination and image advertising to get out their message.

To lure those travelers, advertisers have also increased spending. In 1999 advertisers in the airline and ship travel and hotels and resorts category spent $3.37 billion to draw customers, an increase of 11.2 percent over 1998. Of that total, $1.12 billion was spent in local newspapers, followed by $694.7 million in consumer magazines, and $446.9 million in spot TV.

The events of 11 September 2001 brought the industry to a standstill for several months. Hotel occupancies dropped, airlines cut employees and flights, and tight security reigned at airports. Traveling was no longer fun, a fact reflected in the reduced number of passengers. For the time being, at least, people had stopped taking that "extra" trip.

ALAN SALOMON

Further Reading

Amtrak, *Background on Amtrak,* Washington, D.C.: National Railroad Passenger Corporation, 1974

Charleston Chapter, National Railway Historical Society: "The Best Friend of Charleston" <www.charleston.net/org/railroad>

Explorations in Entrepreneurial History 7 (1955)

Gonzales, Monica, "Let's Cruise," *American Demographics* (February 1988)

Itzkoff, Donald M., *Off the Track: The Decline of the Intercity Passenger Train in the United States,* Westport, Connecticut: Greenwood Press, 1985

Lodging Magazine (1990–)

Robbins, Michael, *The Railway Age,* London: Routledge and Paul, 1962; 3rd edition, Manchester, Greater Manchester: Mandolin, and New York: Manchester University Press, 1998

Travel Agent (1988–)

Wilson, Neill Crompton, and Frank J. Taylor, *Southern Pacific: The Roaring Story of a Fighting Railroad,* New York: McGraw Hill, 1952

True North Communications, Inc.

True North Communications, Inc., was established in January 1995, succeeding Foote, Cone, and Belding Communications, Inc., as the holding company for Foote, Cone & Belding (FCB), one of the largest advertising agencies in the United States. True North's roots date back to the pioneering years of modern advertising and an operating tradition that has always emphasized strategic acquisitions.

FCB originated when Emerson Foote, Fairfax Cone, and Don Belding took over leadership of the Chicago, Illinois, agency Lord & Thomas when Albert Lasker, often cited as the father of modern advertising, retired in 1942. In 1943, with $22.5 million in billings, the agency—with Foote heading up the New York City operations, Cone in Chicago, and Belding in Los Angeles, California—already seemed intent on offering diversified communications services in an expanding marketplace.

In 1963 FCB became the third agency to become a public company, following Albert Frank–Guenther Law (1929) and Papert, Koenig, Lois (1962). In 1968 it reached more than $250 million in billings, and in 1980 it surpassed the $1 billion mark. Innovative creative talent as well as the company's range of offerings were primarily responsible for ever-expanding revenues, though industry deals also served to raise net worth. In 1986 FCB acquired Leber Katz, New York City. In 1992 the Australia-Pacific-based Mojo network came under its umbrella, and in 1993 it bought a stake in Borders, Perrin, and Norrander, Portland, Oregon. In 1992 FCB ranked number one among U.S. agencies in billings.

The most important expansion deal would be FCB's formal alliance with Publicis, the largest agency in France. The arrangement, announced in May 1989, created a joint company called Publicis-FCB, with Publicis holding an equity share of 51 percent and FCB, 26 percent. It would prove to be a profitable combination, contributing an 80 percent share of True North earnings in the mid-1990s.

Taking advantage of synergies between its independent communications concerns and leveraging its size to court top advertising clients had already become standard operating procedure for FCB. The impetus to actually create the holding company was largely spurred by opportunities presented by new network technologies, the desire to develop new markets for communications services, and the rise of globalization.

In December 1994, along with its announcement to operate as True North Communications, Inc., a global communications holding company, FCB and digital communications company R/GA Media Group established a strategic joint venture called TN Technologies. The charter of this new enterprise was the development of digital and interactive technologies, an arena that company leaders envisioned as the key to future expansion.

With the establishment of the True North holding company, True North Communications and FCB as its flagship agency continued to make strategic acquisitions and focus on global opportunities. In 1995 FCB acquired Megacom, China (renaming it FCB Megacom); in 1997 FCB acquired the Bosman Johnson agency as part of the Lindsay Smithers/FCB South Africa network; in 1998 FCB Worldwide acquired Giovanni Communicaçoes, one of the top five independent agencies in Brazil. Smaller but strategic additions for FCB came in 1999 with the acquisition of McElroy Communications, a youth-oriented marketing organization from southern California, and Hacker Group, a direct marketing agency based in Seattle, Washington. In 2000 the company added Ad Fabrika, a strong creative shop, to its existing operations in Poland.

This strategy for growth was played out on a much larger scale by the holding company itself. Between 1995 and the end of 2000, True North acquired, among others: Bayer, Bess Vanderwarker (in January 1996, it merged with FCB); Harrod & Mirlin, Ltd., Toronto, Ontario (1996); Wilkens International European Network (1997); Bozell, Jacobs, Kenyon & Eckhardt, (BJK&E, 1997); Don Coleman Advertising (1999), then the United States' third-largest African-American-owned advertising/marketing agency; KSL Media (1999), the second-largest independent media management company in the United States; Imada Wong Communications Group (2000), a leading Asian-American marketing communications company; and Genus Media (2000), parent to MBS Media in the United Kingdom. It ended 2000 with the announcement that it would be adding Springer & Jacoby, Germany's largest independent advertising group and a Daimler-Chrysler agency, to its operations.

In its first two and a half years of existence, True North acquired 24 separate businesses, virtually all of which were international or technology companies. With its acquisition of BJK&E in 1997, True North became the sixth-largest holding company in the world, according to *Advertising Age*, with $11.5 billion in billings, $1.2 billion in revenue, and more than 11,000 employees in approximately 300 locations worldwide.

Innovative collaborations and strategic moves on the technology side of the business did not overshadow acquisition fever during this period. In 1996 True North acquired Modem Media, a digital marketing services company, to operate under the TN Technologies banner. This enterprise changed composition in 1998 when it merged with Poppe Tyson (part of the BJK&E package), to form one of the top three interactive marketing communications companies in the world. Reflecting its high stature in this new market, Modem Media Poppe Tyson and R/GA Interactive, a leader in broadband technology and also a unit of True North, represented two of the six agencies chosen by IBM Corporation to support its global interactive marketing program.

In the interim, however, the partnership with Publicis had become a mutually bitter relationship. By the time True North was formed late in 1994, problems had already developed. A year earlier Publicis had bought a French company that owned a U.S. agency called Bloom Advertising, an FCB rival. This purchase angered Bruce Mason, by then FCB chairman and the only member of the FCB board to have voted against the partnership with Publicis in 1989. When Mason announced early in 1995 that True North would seek a majority interest in Publicis-FCB and that the company would set out to build its own European network, Publicis Chairman Maurice Levy decided to end the partnership.

More than a year of bitter negotiations followed before the parties agreed in principle on terms of separation in March 1996; however, the company created by the original agreement continued to function.

Finally in January 1997 the partnership ended with True North divesting itself of Publicis-FCB, which became Publicis Europe. Publicis continued to hold an 18.5 percent stake in True North. With the True North acquisition of BJK&E, the relative size of that stake would drop to 11 percent. In July 1997 Publicis announced a hostile takeover of True North, a strategy whose intent many believed was to undermine the BJK&E merger. In December 1997 True North sued in federal court, which quickly put a stop to the Publicis bid, and the merger of BJK&E was consummated.

True North's portfolio of companies at the beginning of the 21st century may best be viewed according to the markets it serves. With this perspective, potential synergies between companies are easily seen. A partial list follows:

Global advertising:
- FCB Worldwide, a full service advertising agency, whose accounts included Chase Manhattan Corporation, Nabisco Biscuit Company, Northwest Airlines, Quaker Oats Company, and Coors Brewing Company.
- FCB Direct Worldwide, the fastest-growing segment of FCB, which, through over 29 offices in 23 countries, has managed campaigns for Amazon.com and the U.S. Postal Service.
- FCB Healthcare, an industry-specific advertising enterprise that has flourished as more pharmaceutical companies focus on direct to consumer advertising.
- Bozell Worldwide, a full-service advertising agency, whose accounts included DaimlerChrysler, Sara Lee Corporation, and Unisys.
- Marketing Drive Direct, an integrated marketing organization, offering marketing consulting services (such as brand positioning, target segmentation); promotions marketing; marketing services (such as event marketing, co-marketing); relationship and interactive marketing (such as creative development, Web site design, tracking, and analysis); and branding and design.
- BSMG Worldwide, sibling company to FCB Worldwide (focusing on integrated marketing and marketing communications campaigns).

U.S. advertising and public relations:
- Temerlin McClain, the largest advertising agency headquartered in the southwestern United States, focusing on service and retail clients, including American Airlines and J.C. Penney Company.
- Tierney and Partners, a 70-year-old advertising and public relations agency, serving clients such as Bell Atlantic.

Media buying:
- TN Media, a leading independent media services company, providing media planning, buying, optimization modeling, and other services.

Promotions:
- Market Growth Resources, a leading promotion company, specializing in developing national plans for retail location and customer-focused activities.
- McCracken Brooks, a specialist in behavior marketing, creating changes in employee and consumer behavior through promotions, communications, and event marketing.
- The Petersen Group, providing strategic design and marketing communications focusing on identity development.

Multicultural marketing:
- New America Strategies Group, the leading U.S. company in multicultural marketing, focusing largely on programs for three growing consumer groups—U.S. Hispanics, African-Americans, and Asian-Americans.

Marketing analysis:
- Skunkworks, a consultancy focusing on financial return on marketing communications expenditures.

Yellow Pages advertising:
- Bozell Yellow Pages, which handled creative work specifically geared for this medium.
- Wahlstrom & Company, a Yellow Pages advertising program design utilizing computer analysis to maximize budget allocations.

Interactive design and digital production:
- R/GA, consisting of two arms: R/GA Interactive, specializing in Web site design, generally using interactive technology, and R/GA Studios, a leader in linear digital broadcast production, creating special effects for film and commercials.

True North's current growth strategy emphasizes promoting "organic growth" (increased billings from new accounts); building FCB's global position; encouraging greater development of global brands in the high-growth areas of marketing communications; and optimizing collaboration between different operating units. However, the loss of the $240 million DaimlerChrysler account in 2000 was a major setback for FCB and one that made True North a vulnerable takeover target. In June 2001 Interpublic Group of Companies bought True North for $2.1 billion in stock to create the world's largest advertising company, based on its combined $7.1 billion in 2000 revenue.

DEBORAH HAWKINS

See also Foote, Cone & Belding; Kenyon & Eckhardt, Inc.

Further Reading
BSMG Worldwide <www.bsmg.com>
True North <www.truenorth.com>

Turner, Robert Edward (Ted) 1938–

U.S. Media Entrepreneur

Robert Edward (Ted) Turner is one of the most colorful, controversial, and influential media entrepreneurs of the 21st century. He helped shape modern media by creating 24-hour cable news and transforming an over-the-air broadcast station into a cable "superstation." In the 1990s he helped the maturing cable industry reposition itself with advertisers, demanding placement consideration and pricing comparable to that offered to TV broadcasters with similar audience reach.

Turner has acknowledged that he had the advantage of being "the right man in the right place at the right time." Over two decades, he transformed his father's fledgling outdoor billboard-advertising company into a cable TV and entertainment empire that he sold in 1996 to Time Warner for $7.5 billion. After a frustrated career-long bid to acquire a major broadcast network, Turner parlayed his stake as the largest single shareholder in Time Warner (comprised of $2.5 billion in Time Warner stock) into a pivotal position in what was eventually to become the first significant hybrid of old and new media, America Online Time Warner. Always outspoken, in his heyday the maverick media baron was frequently known by such epithets as "The Mouth of the South" and "Terrible Ted." But no nickname seemed more appropriate than "Captain Courageous," which he earned winning the 1977 America's Cup race at the helm of his yacht, *Courageous.*

He was born Robert Edward Turner III on 19 November 1938, in Cincinnati, Ohio, to Ed and Florence Turner. His early education included the military-type McCallie School in Chattanooga, Tennessee. He attended Brown University in Providence, Rhode Island, and following a brief stint in the U.S. Coast Guard, he took over his family's ailing business at age 24 after his father's suicide in 1963.

In 1970 he bought the struggling independent UHF TV station WJRJ-TV in Atlanta, Georgia. At the time, the station was losing half a million dollars annually. Turner changed the company's name to Turner Broadcasting System, Inc., and the station's call letters to WTBS and quickly beefed up its programming. His acquisition of local sports franchises, such as Major League Baseball's Atlanta Braves in 1976 and the

Ted Turner.
2001 TBS, Inc. An AOL Time Warner Company.

major cable operators that were his primary customers. Still, he continued to expand and build on his program holdings with the creation of the Cartoon Network in 1992. His key acquisitions included Hanna-Barbera animation, and the motion picture production companies Castle Rock Entertainment and New Line Cinema.

The essence of his cable success was the repackaging of common content into many forms to create a family of cable channels, each aimed at different audiences and advertisers. The Turner cable networks complemented content from Warner and Time, just as the Warner and Time distribution platforms enhanced Turner content.

But not every business venture was a success. A failed takeover of Columbia Broadcasting System (CBS) in the mid-1980s cost him $20 million; subsequent efforts to launch a women's network and a cable channel serving southern lifestyles, art, and sports were later abandoned.

With the sale of TBS, Inc., to Time Warner in 1996, Turner became vice chairman of Time Warner, allowing him to make a freewheeling mark on parts of the company's vast business empire, such as program syndication, news, and sports coverage. Turner promised to play a more subdued role in the combined AOL Time Warner after the merger of the two in January 2001.

However, Ted Turner found himself in the center of new controversy in late 2001, when chief executive officer and long-time Time Warner boss Gerald Levin suddenly announced plans to retire by May 2002. Turner's public feud with Levin, over Turner's suppressed role at the combined company, prompted Chief Operating Officer–Elect Richard Parsons, AOL Time Warner's diplomatic co-chief operating officer, to publicly woo Turner into signing up again as the company's vice chairman, which Turner did.

Still, his obsession with owning a major broadcast network lingered. According to a book by CNN founding president Reese Schoenfeld (whom Turner fired), Turner told a gathering of bureau chiefs that he would pay for the General Electric–owned NBC network out of pocket after the AOL-Time Warner merger.

In 1997 Turner pledged $1 billion, nearly half his fortune at the time, to the United Nations over time for good works, the largest philanthropic donation in history. His Turner Foundation, established in 1990, has contributed millions of dollars to environmental causes.

DIANE MERMIGAS

Biography

Born in Cincinnati, Ohio, on 19 November 1938; took over his family's ailing billboard business following his father's suicide, 1963; bought UHF independent TV station WJRJ-TV, which later became superstation WTBS, 1970; bought the Atlanta Braves baseball team, 1976; purchased the Atlanta Hawks basketball team, 1977; launched Cable News Network, 1980; paid $1.6 billion for MGM/UA Entertainment Company, 1986; launched the Goodwill Games, 1986; sold his cable television and entertainment empire to Time Warner for $7.5 billion, 1996; pledged $1 billion to the United Nations, 1997.

National Basketball Association's Atlanta Hawks in 1977, brought their televised games to WTBS, along with a mix of vintage TV series and films. With satellite communications extending the station's early cable base, Turner used WTBS as the foundation for an empire that grew from 2 million to more than 34 million national viewers and more than $70 million in profits by 1986. His love of sports led to the origination of the now defunct Olympics-style international Goodwill Games, which he began in Moscow, U.S.S.R., in 1986.

Turner launched the 24-hour Cable News Network (CNN) in 1980, setting in motion a rigorous competition in television news between cable operators and traditional broadcasters and thriving on major breaking news such as the 1986 *Challenger* space shuttle disaster and the 1991 Persian Gulf War. His creation of CNN and the first national "superstation," TBS Superstation, made cable TV a more competitive, interesting venue than it had been before.

After paying $1.6 billion—or what many observers described as half a billion dollars too much—for MGM/UA Entertainment Company in 1986, Turner began colorizing many of the 4,000 classic black-and-white films in the studio's library. Turner Network Television (TNT) was launched in 1988 as a major showcase for the films. Under the strain of debt, Turner eventually was forced to sell the film library to retain control of TBS, Inc. He made the unusual move of selling large stakes in his company to

Selected Publication
Ted Turner Speaks: Insight from the World's Greatest Maverick, compiled by Janet Lowe, 1999

Further Reading
"Company Town: Ted Turner's Broader Role Defined," *Los Angeles Times* (2 June 2000)
Goldberg, Robert, and Gerald Jay Goldberg, *Citizen Turner: The Wild Rise of an American Tycoon,* New York: Harcourt Brace, 1995
Roberts, Johnnie L., "As Ted's World Turners: Will Ted Turner

Muck Up the AOL Time Warner Merger?" *Newsweek* (12 June 2000)
Schonfeld, Reese, *Me and Ted against the World: The Unauthorized Story of the Founding of CNN,* New York: Cliff Street, 2001
Stasi, Linda, and Don Kaplan, "Turner Aims to Buy NBC after AOL Merger: Book," *New York Post* (9 May 2000)
Vaughan, Roger, *Ted Turner: The Man behind the Mouth,* Boston: Sail Books, 1978
Williams, Christian, *Lead, Follow, or Get out of the Way: The Story of Ted Turner,* New York: Times Books, 1981

Typography

From the earliest scribbles, humans have used writing to communicate ideas. Whether by means of a pictographic language such as Chinese or an alphabet in which characters represent distinct sounds, people have sought to express abstract, intangible thoughts in concrete, objective form. Written typographic expression has been called "thoughts made visible" and "frozen sounds."

From the wedge-shaped markings of Sumerian writing to the digitally composed fonts of the late 20th century, the evolution of typography has been guided by several important inventions, the earliest being the creation of the first alphabet between 1700 and 1500 B.C. by a Semitic-speaking civilization near ancient Mesopotamia. Other significant inventions are listed below (see Table 1, Milestones in the History of Typography).

Form and Function

A cursory examination of fonts used on magazine covers and in advertisements clearly demonstrates the effectiveness of certain typefaces for projecting certain kinds of images. News magazines, for example, select solid, upright fonts that convey credibility; fashion and beauty publications seek elegant typefaces that evoke style and glamour; and health magazines choose vibrant, energetic designs that suggest well-being and fitness. In *New York Magazine*'s masthead, the type selected for the N, Y, and K suggests the stylish sophistication of New York City, while the alternating use of upper and lower cases echoes the city's rhythmic pulse. *Vogue* magazine's logo, with its contrasting thick and thin strokes, suggests chic elegance.

Advertisers, too, use type to create an impression and project an image. The legendary ad executive David Ogilvy of Ogilvy & Mather perfected a kind of classic "Ogilvy & Mather look" in ad typography, characterized by traditional serif type, always in upper and lower case; Ogilvy eschewed such practices as over-printing on illustrations and reversing white type out of black backgrounds. The very successful "Man in the Hathaway Shirt" campaign is a prime example of this classic Ogilvy style.

Type can be used in a number of different ways to enhance communication and promote viewer comprehension. In the technique called visual correspondence, type is selected to create a word or phrase that appears the same whether one reads it from left to right or from right to left, or to create a word or phrase that looks the same rightside up or upside down. For example, in *Vista* magazine's all-cap logo, the "A" is an upside-down "V" and the "I" is an upside-down "T"; thus, the logo can be recognized when seen upside down. Substitution is the technique in which a picture replaces a letter or vice versa, as, for example, in the use of an apple in place of the letter "a" in the word *apple*.

Other widely used typographic techniques include:

- simultaneity: a word or letter functions in two ways at the same time—for example, replacing the letter "g" with the number eight in the word *eight* (ei8ht);
- exaggeration: meaning is exaggerated through the selection of type—for example, depicting the words *ice skating* as a three-dimensional ice sculpture;
- visual transformation: the size of the letters is manipulated to create a specific image, such as resizing the two "i's and the "l" in the word *families* to resemble a mother, father, and baby;
- spatial interaction: the type is manipulated so as to relate to its space, as, for example, in a multiline logo set in a box (e.g., Margo Chase's 1992 E! Entertainment Television logo with the words "EXTREME CLOSE UP" vertically boxed).

Through such techniques, typography can create a variety of visual equivalents to abstract ideas or concepts such as "hot" or "chic." A designer of an advertisement for an early-evening event might decide to use the color orange for the letter "o," hoping

Table 1. Milestones in the History of Typography.

105 A.D.	Paper invented by Ts'ai Lun, a Chinese government official.
8th century	Caroline minuscules, the precursor to lowercase letters, created.
1045	First movable type apparatus invented by Chinese alchemist Pi Sheng.
1276	Chinese papermaking techniques spread westward; first paper mill opens in Fabriano, Italy.
1455	Invention of first European system of movable type by Johannes Gutenberg.
1470	First Gothic font, Jenson, with even kerning, created by Nicolas Jenson.
1490s	Old Style bracketed serifs (with tapered, curved lines) invented by punchcutter Francesco Griffo, an employee of Manutius.
1702	First transitional type, Roman du Roi, created by Philippe Granjean.
Early 1700s	Creation of typographic point system by French typographer Pierre-Simon Fournier.
1784	Modern Style type created by François Ambroise Didot.
1815	First Egyptian font (slab serif, with thick square or rectangular serifs) created by English type designer Vincent Figgins.
1827	Invention of mechanical router by Darius Wells allows for printing of large, handcarved wooden display type.
1886	First Linotype machine invented by German-born American Ottmar Mergenthaler, making possible the setting of type one line, not one letter, at a time.
1887	First Monotype machine invented by American Tolbert Lanston, which cast individual characters from hot metal and assembled them using a typewriter-like keyboard.
1980s	Development of digital typography and computer technology, enabling electronic page design.

that this orange circle will conjure up the image of the setting sun. Consider the concepts evoked by manipulating type in the following examples: $_u$P, depar t, SHRINKING.

Typography has been used to serve many different artistic and ideological objectives. The early 20th-century futurist movement led by the Italian poet Filippo Marinetti understood typographical innovation as one way to express individuality in the age of machine-made uniformity. In posters and advertisements, the Italian futurist designer Fortunato Depero blended sans serif type with fonts inspired by ancient Roman stone inscriptions to suggest how modernity, in his view, blended elements of old and new and to convey a sense of the rapid-fire tempo of his newly mechanized world. Artists associated with the constructivist movement in Russia manipulated type to express revolutionary fervor, designing posters that creatively used bold display fonts to proclaim their support for the Bolshevik uprising, whereas the

dadaists in western Europe envisioned typography as a means of spreading the movement's anarchistic spirit of artistic expression.

Type has long been used as a persuasive element in military propaganda—for example in the German *Plakatstil* (a flat-color minimalistic design style) used in World War I posters, the post-Bauhaus posters of the German Weimar Republic promoting National Socialism, and Leo Lionni's World War II version of the U.S. army recruiting poster featuring the finger-pointing Uncle Sam declaring, "I Want You." Type also has been an effective voice for advocacy campaigns. Two examples come from the 1960s movement to emphasize the importance of pure drinking water: the "Water is Life" poster by Hirokatsu Hijikata and Stanlislaw Podelko's "H$_2$OMO," with the letters written in the sand and the ocean as a backdrop.

Type and the Commercial Message

While many designers have used typography as a means to artistic and/or political ends, others have regarded the choice of a typeface as serving a social purpose. In a celebrated 1927 *Frankfurter Zeitung* article ("Was ist neue Typographie?" or "What Is New Typography?"), typographer Walter Dexel argued that the wants of the audience, not the designer's particular philosophy or vision, should be the most important factor when designing type. Typography should be "an objective and impersonal presentation, free of individuality," he wrote, adding, "Messages must appeal to the audience's different interests." Advertisers, given that their primary objective is to anticipate the "different interests" of their individual audiences—that is to target specific groups of consumers—find themselves in agreement with Dexel.

One remarkable example of the important role that type can play in conveying a commercial message is seen in a three-panel French poster series for Dubonnet designed in 1932 by Adolphe Mouron Cassandre, the creator of some unique Art Deco fonts. In this poster, the product name, the visual, and the creative use of type interact to communicate the advertiser's message. In the first panel, an outline illustration of a man poised in anticipation of his first sip of the liquor is only partly filled in, his right arm extended and holding a full glass. Design and typography reinforce each other, as Cassandre has placed the extended arm above the first four letters of the brand name. The type starts to tell the story, with the D, U, B and O of the brand name filled in like the character's arm and the other letters shown in outline type. In the second panel, the man is shown drinking the beverage, with part of the outline at the top filled in. The type beneath now shows the product name with an additional letter filled in as well, DUBON—suggesting "bon," French for "good." In the third panel, the entire outline of the figure (now shown replenishing his glass) is completely filled in as are the letters that spell Dubonnet, suggesting that the imbiber is now fully satisfied.

Typography is often used by designers of advertising to transcend what are conventionally assumed to be limits of print as a medium—its static quality, for example, or its flatness. Fluorescent paint, three-dimensional letters, and moving type have all been used to transform ordinary billboards into captivating new

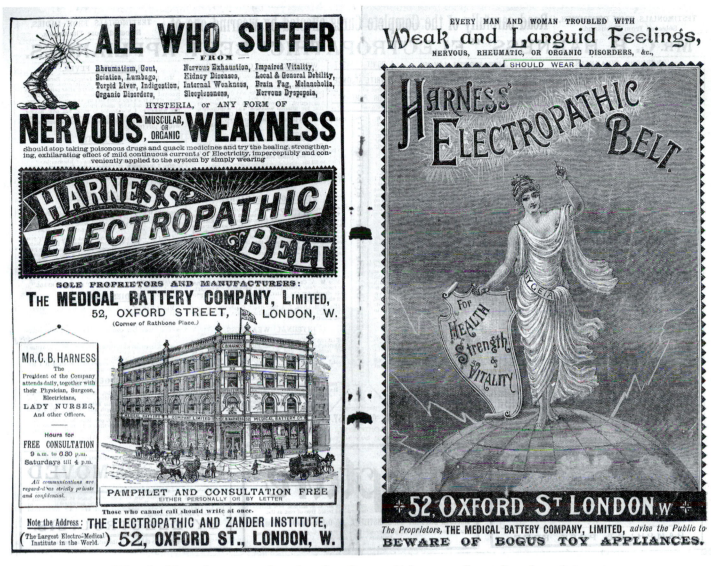

Print ads of the 19th century used a variety of typefaces to add drama as well as to direct the reader's eye.

forums for advertisements; dramatic type appears on entertainment posters to entice consumers to buy records or to attend films and concerts; and designers enliven the ordinarily low-key type on annual report covers through various graphic techniques such as blind emboss, spot varnish, or color on color. In a 1959 poster for an Igor Stravinsky concert, the designer Kohei Sugiura integrated calligraphic type and mixed fonts. In a poster for the 1968 Olympic Games, by Eduardo Terrazas and Lance Wyman, the words "Mexico City" are highlighted by concentric circles, extending outward in waves, echoing the letters' shapes.

Often a certain typestyle becomes the prevailing fashion, such as the typographic collages that were so popular in the late 1950s and early 1960s. Robert Brownjohn's 1959 album cover for a recording of Latin music graphically depicts the words "Sí, sí, no, no" in a bright, multicolored repeat pattern. Ivan Chermayeff's 1957 record cover for the Boston Symphony's recordings of

Beethoven's *Eroica* used type to create the menacing appearance of a cut-and-paste ransom note.

During the same era, some U.S. advertising designers chose "modern" fonts such as Futura, Akzidenz Grotesk, Beton, and Stymie, while others harked back to centuries-old typefaces such as Baskerville and Garamond. Visual images and type merged into a single unified communication: advertising's "big idea." Entire campaigns were built around a single "big" concept, using a consistent layout, visual approach, and font in TV commercials and print ads. In both media, the visual components were positioned and presented in the same manner. For example, in the Marlboro "Western" campaign, the use of the same font, reverse type (light type on a dark background), and western visuals of a cowboy on horseback are common elements throughout the campaign, regardless of media. Other, more recent examples are the Absolut "Bottle" and the "Got Milk?" milk mustache.

In the 1950s a New York City design shop called the Composing Room introduced "talking type" to advertising, making the font itself a pun, giving the type its own "voice." Also during that decade, Gene Federico created persuasive images through his manipulation of type—for example, in a 1953 ad for *Woman's Day*, in which the words "go out" (in the headline "She's got to go out to get Woman's Day") were connected to form a bicycle. Lou Dorfsman expressively used type and image, employing blank space as a graphic element. His typography for CBS in the 1960s defined the company's character and image. Herb Lubalin, who created the three-dimensional sculpted Ice Capades logo, among others, mastered the art of trademark and typeface design.

Other renowned U.S. logo designers of the 1950s included Thomas H. Geismar, who designed logos for Mobil Oil and Xerox, and Paul Rand, who created some of the most readily identifiable logos for ABC, IBM, Cummins Engine Company, and Westinghouse Electric. Rand's Westinghouse trademark, the "Circle-W" logo, incorporated three dots at the top of the "w" to suggest electric plugs and circuitry. The red "o" in *Mobil* in Geismar's sans serif Mobil Oil logo served to draw the viewer's eye inward. Viewers could interpret the "o" as they pleased: it might represent a tire, an oilcan, or an odometer. Regardless, the simple typographic differentiation of this single letter demanded instant attention.

In the 1960s, during an era known as the "eclectic modern" period, type designers reacted against the restrictiveness of the 1950s. In New York City Push Pin Studios blended Victorian, Art Nouveau, and Art Deco styles with novelty fonts. Typography was being stretched as never before. It became distorted and focused on negative space; it incorporated exaggerated versions of so-called Egyptian fonts (a kind of type introduced in the early 1800s). The 1960s was a decade of cultural experimentation and rebellion, and, as in other aspects of life, all the established rules concerning type were challenged. This period of innovation led to the invention of psychedelic type, which seemed to capture the spirit of the time. The late 1960s psychedelic posters of Victor Moscoso, which used tightly kerned (i.e., horizontally compressed, tightly spaced) semicircular type that expanded concentrically, suggested the perceptual effects of the mind-altering drugs associated with this era. What had once been taboo in typography now became the norm: designers enthusiastically embraced illegible type, fluorescent inks, and vibrating colors.

From Hot Metal to the Digital Revolution

In 1886 Ottmar Mergenthaler, who came to the United States from Germany, developed a type composing machine, the Linotype, that used small brass matrixes with impressions of the letterforms, numbers, and symbols. Ninety keys, similar to typewriter keys, controlled vertical tubes that released a matrix when the corresponding key was struck. The matrix slid down a chute and was aligned with the other characters set on the same line. Melted lead was poured into the line of matrixes, creating a slug of an entire line of raised type. Mergenthaler's system was replaced by

the Monotype machine, invented by American Tolbert Lanston, which cast single characters from hot metal. Although it was developed in 1887, it took a decade until it became efficient enough to be included in production. In 1925 the Thothmic photographic composing machine was invented by two Londoners, E.K Hunter and J.R.C. August. It was not until the 1960s, almost a half-century later, that phototypography finally revolutionized typesetting. The major advantage was its cost effectiveness when introducing new typestyles. Type now could be set by exposing film negatives of type characters onto photopaper.

Phototypography marked the greatest change in type production since Johannes Gutenberg's invention of movable type in the 15th century. The new technique made type more flexible, allowing the leading (vertical space between lines of type) to be compressed and letters to overlap without compromising readability. Using phototype, designers could mix different kinds of type and vary the spatial relationships of type and images—for example, as Otto Storch did in a 1961 ad in *McCall's,* where a block of type stands in for a mattress and follows the curves of the image of a reclining woman.

The introduction of Apple Computer's Macintosh machines in 1984 revolutionized typography yet again, fully establishing the age of digital type design. As the digital revolution promoted novel display fonts, a number of digital foundries emerged in the United States and elsewhere. On the U.S. West Coast, April Greiman combined photography, odd geometric shapes, psychedelic colors, a mixture of light and heavy fonts, bold rules, open leading, and wide kerning; she layered type with colorful images and color-on-color design. Examples of her unique use of type include the 1978 masthead for the monthly men's catalog *Luxe* and a 1980 ad for the Los Angeles restaurant and bar China Club. By the 1980s a new Muscovite style had emerged in Russia, based on a Polish poster style and avant-garde typography of the 1920s and 1930s, which employed a wide range of typographic faces that were energetic and bursting with excitement. Two proponents of this style were Latvian artist Laimonis Chenberg and Zelmanovitz, an art director who designed a 1990 table of contents for *Reklame,* a magazine whose focus was the analysis of Russian design groups' graphic works. The style has been referred to as new wave typography, one movement under the umbrella of the Postmodern era. At the same time, the retro movement emerged in New York and soon spread globally. In England an experimental movement took type to the brink of illegibility with unusual cropping, exaggerated compression, and liberal use of superimposition.

As in the psychedelic decade of the 1960s, San Francisco, California, in the 1980s was a center for innovative design. Designers Michael Vanderbyl and Michael Cronin fostered the Bay Area postmodern style, which combined a free, unrestricted use of space and form with an integration of cheerful pastel colors. Vanderbyl's distinctive use of type and color are evident in his 1979 poster for California Public Radio and his 1985 promotional mailer for the Simpson Paper company. Cronin and his codesigner Shannon Terry used type horizontally and vertically; a signature Cronin design was his 1983 poster for the San Francisco

Symphony Beethoven Festival, in which he employed flames as a visual metaphor for the composer's unruly mane.

Emigré, a design publication created in 1983 by Rudy VanderLans and Zuzana Licko, showcased new, unconventional fonts. Together, VanderLans and Licko established their own type business, Emigré Graphics (later renamed Emigré Fonts) and became leaders in nontraditional type design. Expounding on her own design philosophy, Licko has said: "Typefaces are not intrinsically legible. Rather it is the reader's familiarity with faces that accounts for their legibility. Studies have shown that readers' habits are everchanging. . . . Type styles that we perceive as illegible today may well become tomorrow's classic choices."

Recent Trends

In the 1980s and 1990s, designers throughout the United States were interested in the use of type to create corporate symbols that would appeal to international audiences. A vernacular style of design evolved, characterized by the use of sans serif fonts (fonts such as Helvetica and Arial that have no "tails," as at the top and bottom of the capital letter "I"), textured backgrounds, and silhouetted photos. Vernacular design borrows earlier graphic forms, such as old baseball cards and matchbook covers, as well as less sophisticated illustrations and printing from earlier periods.

Other new styles also emerged in the 1980s and 1990s. One of these was "retro," created by such designers as Paula Scher and Louise Fili, who drew inspiration from the Vienna secessionist school and post–Art Deco styles while integrating mixed fonts and extreme kerning into their typefaces. Scher's 1985 Swatch Watch poster is a clear example of the retro design movement of the 1980s. Here Scher brazenly parodied a famous 1934 Herbert Matte poster promoting Swiss tourism. Scher also developed posters and record covers for CBS Records. She viewed typography as one of many essential parts of an ad's design, arguing that type should be used to make a point, complement an idea, create an ambiance, or evoke nostalgia. Scher's work is an eclectic solution to design problems, blending the gravity-free Russian constructivism with the weight and power of the woodcut. Her often humorous work places typography at center stage.

Fili's subtle and polished work using eccentric and long-ignored fonts is known through her many book covers and corporate trademarks, including those for Crawford Doyle Booksellers, Hyperion books, and Flatiron, a baking company. Like Scher, Fili engaged in an unorthodox use of color, space, and texture, experimenting with fonts, kerning, and color-on-color layering. Returning to the United States after her annual overseas vacations, Scher applied to her work some traditional European approaches to type, incorporating textured backgrounds and silhouetted photographs into her book jacket designs.

Grunge type was another popular form developed in the 1990s, taking its name from the post-punk music that started in Seattle, Washington, and its style from the eclectic fashions associated with that musical scene. Grunge type seemed to be in

Table 2.   Chronology of Type Development.

1450	First Textura-style type by Johann Gutenberg
1467	First Roman style type by Conrad Sweyndeym and Arnold Pannartz
1470	Jenson by Nicolas Jenson
1501	First italics by printer and scholar Aldus Manutius
1532	Garamond by Claude Garamond
1702	First transitional-style type, Roman du Roi, by Philippe Grandjean
1722	Caslon Old Style by William Caslon
1757	Baskerville by John Baskerville
1780	Bodoni by Giambattista Bodoni
1815	2-Line Pica Antique (first Egyptian font) by Vincent Figgins
1816	2-Line English Egyptian (first sans serif font) by William Caslon IV
1890	Golden by William Morris
1892	Troy by William Morris
1893	Chaucer by William Morris
1898–1906	Akzidenz Grotesk by the Berthold Foundry
1915–16	Goudy Old Style by Frederic W. Goudy
1927–29	Futura by Paul Renner
1928–30	Gill Sans by Eric Gill
1929	Broadway by Morris Benton
1929	Bifur by Adolphe Mouron Cassandre
1931	Times New Roman by Stanley Morison
1936	Acier Noir by Adolphe Mouron Cassandre
1950	Brush by Harold Brodersen
1950	Palatino by Hermann Zapf
1957	Univers by Adrian Frutiger
ca. 1957	Helvetica by Max Miedinger
1965	Fritz Quadrata by Ernest Fritz
1974	Korinna by Edward Benguiat and Vic Caruso
1975	ITC Bookman by Edward Benguiat
1977	Benguiat by Edward Benguiat
1979	Zapf Chancery by Hermann Zapf
1983	Weidemann by Kurt Weidemann and Kurt Strecker
1990	Journal by Zuzana Licko
1990	Tekton by David Siegel

motion—shaking, quivering, trembling—and it struck a chord with nonconformists.

David Carson, one of the most celebrated grunge designers, broke new ground commercially as art director of several influential publications, including *Beach Culture* and *Ray Gun.* Although many designers denounced his type as illegible, others discovered that difficult-to-read type may actually engage the reader's curiosity.

Design in the 1990s often took a deconstructionist turn, flouting conventional rules and restrictions in ways that asked the reader to decipher multi-font images, multi-layering, bits of type mixed with distortion, and obscure visuals. These texturally complex messages invited individual interpretations.

Adobe Systems—inventor of the Postscript programming language, which was the foundation of digital page design and computer-generated type—became an important and influential digital type foundry. Two of Adobe's main designers were Carol Twombly (designer of Charlemagne, Lithos, and Trajan) and Robert Slimbach (designer of Adobe Garamond, Minion, Caflisch Script, Poetica, Adobe Jenson, Cronos, and Myriad, on the last of which Twombly and Slimbach collaborated).

In the late 1980s designers such as Neville Brody, who started the highly influential type foundry known as the FontShop, borrowed techno type fonts (e.g., Modula) from nightclub flyers and applied them to advertising. Brody also served as art director for English magazines such as *The Face* and *Arena,* in addition to designing graphics and album covers for rock music. Brody and another English designer, Jonathan Barnbrook, blurred the line between legibility and readability. The T-26 Type Foundry, started by Carlos Segura in the 1990s, had a profound impact on fontography (the design and development of new fonts). Using anti-alias type (blocklike fonts often found in designs for the Internet), the foundry's cutting-edge fonts reflected the rave and techno movements sweeping fashion and popular culture. (The term *techno* was coined to describe a musical sound that combined elements of industrial music by groups such as Kraftwerk with elements of disco. Raves began as underground parties but soon grew into massive electronic music festivals, sometimes with corporate sponsorship, with as many as 60,000 young people attending.)

In designing the "Just do it" slogan for Nike, Brody revived an earlier mode of manipulating type by juggling the size, weight, and position of the letters. Using a stacked design, he made the word *just* small, the word *do* larger and bolder; *it* was printed at an angle. His typographic ingenuity was also seen in such magazines as *Vogue* and *Interview* from the mid-1980s through the early 1990s. Brody explored ways to completely redesign letters, producing a totally new alphabetic form. He has proposed that a given letter may be transformed through usage—for instance, in words using "ph" a new letter may emerge to represent the "ph" sound.

In the late 1990s the U.S. type designer Charles Anderson, known as Chank, was selling his innovative fonts on his Web site. His work was so widely acclaimed that it was included in a typography exhibit at the prestigious Cooper-Hewitt National Design Museum in New York City in 1997. His fonts could be found everywhere, from the Cartoon Network on cable TV to coupons for Nestlé Toll House Morsels. One of his popular fonts, known as Mister Frisky, appeared on Taco Bell wrappers and Welch's Grape Soda cans.

At the start of the 21st century type was continuing to evolve, becoming increasingly imaginative and playful. Many innovative fonts were a difficult-to-label amalgamation of existing typefaces—proof of the continuing adaptability of typography and ingenuity of type designers.

MARGO BERMAN

See also color plate in this volume

Further Reading

Blackwell, Lewis, *Twentieth-Century Type,* Munich: Bangert, and New York: Rizzoli, 1992

Booth-Clibborn, Edward, and Daniele Baroni, *Il linguaggio della grafica,* Milan: Mondadori, 1979; as *The Language of Graphics,* translated by Anna Harper, New York: Abrams, 1979; London: Thames and Hudson, 1980

Carter, Rob, *American Typography Today,* New York: Van Nostrand Reinhold, 1989

Carter, Rob, Ben Day, and Philip B. Meggs, *Typographic Design: Form and Communication,* New York: Van Nostrand Reinhold and Wiley, 1985; 2nd edition, New York: Wiley, 1993

Dexel, Walter, "What is New Typography?" in *Functional Graphic Design in the 20's,* edited by Eckhard Neumann, New York: Reinhold, 1967

Dexel, Walter, *Der Bauhausstil-ein Mythos: Texte 1921–1965,* Starnberg: Keller, 1976

Drucker, Johanna, *The Alphabetic Labyrinth: The Letters in History and Imagination,* London: Thames and Hudson, 1995

Heller, Steven, and Louise Fili, *Typology: Type Design from the Victorian Era to the Digital Age,* San Francisco: Chronicle, 1999

Jeavons, Terry, and Michael Beaumont, *An Introduction to Typography,* Secaucus, New Jersey: Chartwell, and London: Apple Press, 1990

Lewis, John, *Typography: Basic Principles: Influences and Trends since the 19th Century,* New York: Reinhold, 1964; London: Studio Vista, 1967

Meggs, Philip B., *A History of Graphic Design,* New York: Van Nostrand Reinhold, and London: Allen Lane, 1983; 3rd edition, New York: Wiley, 1998

Petzinger, Thomas, Jr., "For a Designer Known as Chank, Letters Are Art," *Wall Street Journal* (7 November 1999)

U

Unilever. *See* Lever Brothers Company/Unilever

United Kingdom

The rise of advertising in the United Kingdom coincides with the development over several centuries of a modern consumer market. By the 13th century, the need for advertising was apparent, given the size of the population and the range of goods available, and town criers, pictorial shop signs, and written announcements served the purpose. The spread of printing in the late 1400s enabled printed announcements, and later posters, to supplant written notices. More significantly, newspapers began to develop as an advertising medium of great importance.

The earliest known English newspaper advertisement appeared in *Weekly Relations of Newes* on 23 August 1622; it announced to the public that back issues of the paper were for sale. As the 17th century progressed, advertisements for books, coffeehouses, and patent medicines spread slowly as the population and business expanded, especially around London. Shopkeepers continued to rely largely on signs, although poster advertising was used as well.

Newspaper advertising, while not widespread, allowed sellers to reach businesses and affluent, literate households. Recognizing advertising's potential, publishers such as John Houghton began to refine advertising copy and displays for books, shoe blacking, ink, foods, and apparel. By the 1740s ads commonly employed headlines to attract readers' attention.

Dawn of Modern Advertising

The Industrial Revolution fueled the growth of advertising in the late 18th century. Innovations in agricultural production reduced the demand for farm laborers. Workers in turn shifted to newly mechanized industries. Improvements in transportation enabled efficient distribution of factory-produced goods. Shopbills (or trade cards), printed in varying sizes with a decorative design and brief text, became the primary medium as advertising gained acceptance as a business tool.

Centered in London, the British ad industry expanded along with the burgeoning of newspapers, despite the burdensome stamp taxes levied on each. The affluent read newspapers and, notwithstanding high rates of illiteracy, so did some members of the working class. Lotteries and auctioneers such as Christie's were among the heaviest advertisers in the early days of newspapers. Some newspapers appealed to the upper class and ran advertisements for country estates and books. Others featured announcements for soap, tobacco, and patent medicines. Country papers, written and read outside London, provided advertisers with a means to reach remote markets.

By the end of the 18th century marketers were using advertising to make consumers aware of their products and where they could be bought. They also offered advertising as an incentive to retailers to carry their brands. Marketers of ink powders, polishes, and sauces started to "brand" their products to gain leverage with consumers and retailers.

By the 19th century advertising was recognized by manufacturers as a good investment. By the early 1800s Schweppes, Crosse & Blackwell, and Lea & Perrins each were running ad campaigns that covered large geographic areas. Warren's Shoe Blacking was one of the first consumer products advertised on a large scale in the United Kingdom; its advertising appeared on the walls of city buildings, on fences along country roads, and in newspapers throughout England, Scotland, and Ireland. One particular Warren's Shoe Blacking ad, depicting a cat spitting at its

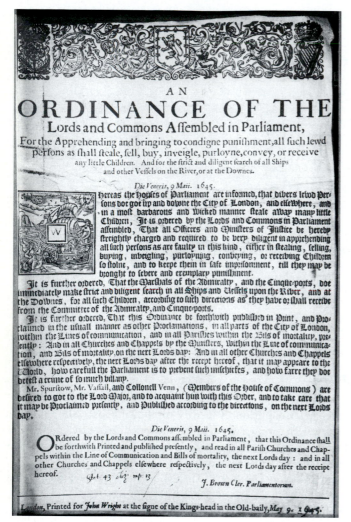

A public notice dating from 1645 announced an English law condemning those who would "steale, sell, buy, inveigle, purloyne, convey, or receive any little children."
Courtesy of the Rare Book, Manuscript, and Special Collections Library, Duke University.

reflection in a shiny boot, was the first instance of "idea" illustration in U.K. print advertising.

Use of poster advertising grew, as did the number of newspaper advertisements, which jumped from about 500,000 in 1800 to 1.9 million per year in 1850. National advertising expenditures were approximately £161,000 in 1800 and reached £1 million in 1850. Medical advertisers and retailers spent aggressively. By midcentury, Holloway's pills, Rowland & Company's Kalydor skin oil, and tailors Moses & Son and Heal & Son were among the United Kingdom's biggest advertisers. Small retailers commonly limited their efforts to posters, trade cards, or manufacturer-sponsored advertising.

The burdensome stamp taxes on newspapers and advertising gave rise to new forms of out-of-home advertising. Sandwich boards and horse-drawn advertising carts filled the streets of London and other cities. Railway advertising in station buildings, on platforms, and in passenger cars also became available around midcentury. Handbills were distributed to pedestrians and placed under the doors of residents. Posters for inns, taverns, local tradesmen, official announcements, and entertainment were plastered indiscriminately on walls, lampposts, and even the doors of private homes. By the 1840s such abuse of posters was rampant, but in the 1850s powerful bill-posting companies imposed some order by creating authorized advertising sites called "hoardings." Even so, "oversticking" reduced the effectiveness of poster advertising.

Rise of the Agency

The earliest advertising agents emerged from newspaper agencies and coffeehouse reading rooms, making recommendations, extending credit, and sometimes writing copy. Marketers that wanted to reach a wider geographic market for their brands needed to become familiar with local newspapers and their advertising rates and schedules, and so they sought assistance with the process of placing ads. William Tayler was one of the earliest London advertising agents to channel advertising toward country newspapers. Tayler found a partner (Sir William Newton, a painter of miniatures and, later, court miniature painter to William IV), and his company was named Tayler & Newton, then Newton & Company. James White, another important early agent, entered advertising when buying newspaper space for his employer, Christ's Hospital School. By 1800 White had begun to place advertisements for other businesses as well.

After White's death in 1820 the agency continued and was run by his widow. Later, under the direction of her second husband, Richard Barker, it was renamed Barker & Company. Barker & Company and its predecessor were recognized as leaders in handling London and provincial newspaper placements. Samuel Deacon, a contemporary who first accepted advertising placements in the coffeehouse he opened with his brother, was by 1838 also a full-fledged agent. The success of these early agents encouraged others outside London—such as publisher David Robertson of Edinburgh, Scotland—to become advertising agents.

Not all the first agents were representatives of newspapers. Some represented advertisers, placing advertising, negotiating rates, and offering opinions on which newspapers to use. By the mid-1800s agents were publishing directories of British and foreign newspapers, indicating papers' publication schedules, political affinities, and in some cases average circulation and per-copy ad volume. In the second half of the century agents began to introduce other innovative practices. Charles Mitchell generated additional publicity for his book publishing clients by sending review copies of books to country newspaper editors along with ads to promote them. In 1856 Mitchell supplemented his newspaper directory with an essay, "The Philosophy of Advertising." It was the first English treatise on advertising theory that dealt with copywriting techniques, circulation, and market analysis.

The abolition of the newspaper and advertising taxes in the 1850s led to the growth of newspapers, and consequently an increase in the amount of advertising space they could offer marketers. Magazines flourished, too, especially women's magazines, whose number increased from four in 1846 to 50 by 1900. Meanwhile, consumer product choice began to expand, even for the working class. Advertising was used to introduce new products, and the practice of branding spread to basic household items. Newspaper ads chased rising incomes, offering furniture on credit, men's ready-to-wear clothes, and sewing machines for women.

As the 19th century closed, the advertising industry blossomed. Companies such as Beecham, the marketer of the patent medicine Beecham's pills, significantly increased its advertising budget. The tobacco companies W.D. & H.O. Wills and John Player and the department stores Robinson and Cleaver and Selfridges also became major advertisers. But soap manufacturers led the way. A.&F. Pears, Ltd., a high-profile advertiser, was one of the first to introduce pictorial art to its poster advertising. Posters evolved from simple displays of text into a visually based sales medium, often simply adding brand names to academic paintings. Pears acquired Sir John Millais's painting *Bubbles,* from which the company's agency, T.B. Browne, Ltd., produced a celebrated poster in 1888. The poster became the best-known work of art of its time throughout the British Empire and placed Pears among the most famous names in the history of British advertising. Pears extended its reach to the United States in 1883 and subsequently introduced pictorial art to magazine advertising there. Lever Brothers first used paintings to advertise its Sunlight soap in 1889 and followed Pears's lead by advertising Sunlight in U.S. magazines in the late 1880s.

The late 19th century also witnessed the evolution of some novel advertising media: matchboxes, balloons, paving stones, and sidewalk stenciling were pressed into service. Advertisers placed enamel signs near railway stations and on fences, and used direct mail to target the homes of likely prospects. Some even sent multiple-address telegrams, essentially mass mailings of telegrams to thousands of target households, sometimes scheduled to arrive at the same, high-impact time, such as during dinner; owing to their intrusiveness, such methods tended to get the public's attention and annoy recipients.

The number of advertising agents continued to grow through the late 1880s, especially in London. As competition among agents in London increased, many went farther afield in pursuit of new clients in cities such as Glasgow, Scotland, and Liverpool, England. By the turn of the century T.B. Browne was the largest agency in the United Kingdom, employing more than 200 people. Browne's client list included Pears, and the agency had offices in London; Glasgow; Manchester, England; and Paris, France.

Large agencies handled most of the leading consumer products companies. S.H. Benson, Ltd.'s clients included Bovril Company's Bovril meat extract, Rowntree's Elect Cocoa, and Procter & Gamble Company's (P&G's) Ivory soap. Thomas Dixon's client list included Crosse & Blackwell and W.D. & H.O. Wills and John Player. Mather & Crowther, Ltd.'s list included Bond's Soap, Bushmill's Irish Pure Malt Whiskey, and Royal Worcester American Corsets.

The advertising industry was becoming more international in scope. Paul E. Derrick, who opened an agency in London in 1894 to service the Quaker Oats Company when that company decided to enter the British market, is credited with introducing innovative American methods into British advertising.

Agencies began to offer more services to clients. Some became "service agents" that kept the full media commission of 15 percent of the cost of media purchased on behalf of advertisers and, in addition to placing ads, provided creative and technical expertise. Mather & Crowther offered print production, art, and editorial departments; S.H. Benson advised marketers on media selection, copy, and design. Most of the smaller agencies functioned solely as space buyers, retaining a small part of the commission and rebating the remainder to the advertiser. By 1900 most large agencies employed copywriters, who used common approaches such as extended anecdotes, testimonials, and endorsements—real or fabricated—from satisfied users, especially British royalty.

Abuse and Regulation

While relations with clients were generally sound, advertising agencies often engaged in controversial business practices such as "farming," wherein the agency bought print space in bulk at reduced rates then resold space to clients at the full rate. In some cases agencies held financial interests in publications in which they bought space, raising suspicion that their recommendations to clients were less than objective.

Advertising methods during the 19th century evolved through trial and error. While most advertising was practiced responsibly, abuses were inevitable—as was a backlash by consumers and critics, who attacked advertisements for "obscene" publications and products, such as books and photographs offered in newspaper advertisements and circulars sent through the mail. Patent medicines promoted with false claims were a prime target of critics in the second half of the century; although self-regulatory and legal controls were slowly put in place, mechanisms to closely police the industry were absent.

Concerns about particular media grew in the late 1800s and early 1900s. Plans by the Bovril Company to place signs on prime property in Edinburgh, Scotland, for example, met with public outcry, as did signs erected on the cliffs at Dover by Quaker Oats. Sentiment against outdoor advertising was so strong that the National Society for Controlling the Abuses of Public Advertising was formed in 1893, with membership consisting of academics, physicians, lawyers, religious leaders, and members of Parliament. Multiple-address telegrams, which had been a bane earlier, continued to be popular with marketers even during World War I, despite complaints from anxious consumers whose friends and relatives were at war.

In response, the advertising industry took steps to regulate itself. As early as 1824, the book *Periodical Press of Great Britain and Ireland* noted that many newspapers refused advertisements that contained exaggerated claims. Later in the century, some publishers responded by blaming agencies or claiming that they could not screen all advertising. Others hired representatives to inspect the products offered by mail-order companies and guaranteed consumers a refund for misrepresented articles advertised in

Thomas Barratt, a partner in A.&F. Pears, Ltd., bought the rights to the 1886 painting *Bubbles* by Sir John Millais and used it in this 1905 print ad.
Courtesy of Unilever HPC.

their newspapers and magazines. To defuse public outcry and to avert regulatory legislation, owners of bill-posting sites in 1890 established a committee to evaluate and screen poster content.

Legal controls on advertising gradually increased over the 19th century. Parliament's Vagrancy Act of 1824 addressed obscene advertisements, subjecting violators to imprisonment. London's Metropolitan Paving Act of 1817 and the Metropolitan Police Act of 1839 required licenses for the placement of posters and regulated projecting signs and sandwich-board men. The London Hackney Carriage Act of 1853 dealt with advertising cart obstructions by permitting advertising only on vehicles that carried goods or passengers. Parliament's Indecent Advertisements Act of 1889 attempted to curb the activities of medical quacks. And Parliament's Advertisements Regulation Act of 1907 empowered local authorities throughout the United Kingdom to regulate hoardings and signs.

The courts also got involved in advertising issues, with decisions that found comparative advertising to be legal provided the advertising did not misrepresent a rival product. One significant case, *Carlill v. The Carbolic Smoke Ball Company* (1892), served as a warning to advertisers and agencies to exercise care making claims about products or services. The marketer advertised that its smoke ball prevented influenza and offered a payment to any consumer who contracted the flu after using its product. The plaintiff, one Mrs. Carlill, did fall ill with influenza after using the product and applied to the marketer for payment. The company refused to pay, and the courts ruled in favor of the plaintiff, finding that an advertisement could constitute part of a contract.

War and Peace

World War I marked a turning point for the advertising industry in the United Kingdom. Suffering from strained production capacity during the war, marketers virtually ceased advertising, shuttered their advertising departments and terminating agreements with advertising agencies, bill-posters, and printers. Some smaller agencies went out of business. National newspapers suffered a newsprint shortage, and advertising volume dropped. Yet opportunity arose for some. Women found employment in agencies as men left to join the armed forces. Local and provincial newspapers gained the advertising that national newspapers were unable to accommodate owing to the newsprint shortage.

The sort of companies that bought advertising changed during the war, as did the tone and scope of their creative appeals. Advertising for luxury items and travel all but disappeared, while military outfitters, department stores, and cigarette marketers continued to advertise. New, discount cigarette brands challenged established ones; American car advertising filled the gap left by British manufacturers, and theaters in London's West End promoted themselves as diversions from the war.

The government became a major advertiser, using a wide array of war-related appeals. In 1917 the Association of British Advertising Agents was formed to assist with the war effort. Its keynote slogan "Wake up, England!" appeared in all media to rally the nation. Advertisements encouraged men to volunteer for the army and small investors to buy war bonds; campaigns in Scotland and Ireland called for farmers to increase the acreage they cultivated.

Marketers of consumer products also made patriotic appeals in their advertising. The Maypole Dairy Company claimed its margarine was made from nuts captured on German ships. Sunlight soap used an illustration of the trenches and a carton of soap with the headline, "The cleanest fighter in the world—the British Tommy." As the war progressed, advertising for food and clothing emphasized product performance and value rather than patriotic themes.

The period between the world wars was in some ways a golden age for British advertising. Advertising expenditures grew from roughly £31 million in 1920 to about £57 million in 1928. The Association of British Advertising Agents was renamed the Institute of (Incorporated) Practitioners in Advertising in 1929 in part to represent advertising agents as professionals. The Newspaper Proprietors Association, established in 1906 and later renamed the Newspaper Publishers Association, finally rid the industry of shady agencies' rate-cutting practices by requiring all new agencies to sign, as a condition of recognition, an agreement that banned the rebating of commissions. And the Advertising Association, which represented British advertising interests and raised standards of practice, emerged from one district of a worldwide association of advertising clubs in 1925.

Two agency heads—Charles Higham of Charles F. Higham, Ltd., and William Crawford of W.S. Crawford, Ltd.—dominated advertising in the 1920s. Higham, who got his start in the business selling advertising space on theater curtains, advanced his career by assisting the government in its advertising efforts during World War I. He carved a niche in the business through skillful salesmanship and by sometimes guaranteeing, to especially troubled clients, sales increases of 33 percent or the advertising was free. Crawford, Higham's rival, also sold advertising space before starting his own agency in 1914. He built his reputation on his inter-war government service, and his agency was among the leaders in London. Higham and Crawford apparently thought highly of each other; once when Crawford was unable to agree with a client on a campaign proposal, he took the client to Higham for arbitration on the matter.

In the 1920s and 1930s advertising campaigns became more advanced, typically guided by careful research and planning rather than hunch and instinct. The British ad industry began using census data and research analyzing print media readership to segment consumers into groups of prospective buyers. The use of market research became widely accepted in the 1930s.

The media, however, were entering a period of transition. While radio was becoming widely popular, commercial broadcasts were prohibited in the United Kingdom. Advertisers, however, placed messages on overseas stations, such as Radio Normandy and Radio Luxembourg, that could be received in England and which were popular with local audiences. The cinema's role as an advertising medium grew as once-skeptical theater owners came to accept humorous and entertaining advertising cartoons. Other media also began to appear, including airplane banners, sponsored dirigibles, and skywriting. Neon signs and loudspeakers were affixed to aircraft, and vans bearing company emblems drove the streets.

As advertising became more pervasive, many social critics denounced it as an effort to sell people products they neither wanted nor needed. But more often their complaints were directed at advertising claims. Wright's Coal Tar soap, for example, was promoted as a cure for "skin constipation," a condition that didn't exist, and advertising for Ephazone claimed it cured asthma.

To address these problems, the Advertising Association drove unethical advertisers out of newspapers, largely by investigating claims and revealing to agencies clear examples of fraudulent advertising. Individual media outlets imposed their own standards. The newspaper the *Daily Mail,* for example, rejected 634 advertisements over a five-year period, from 1932 to 1936.

But such actions did not eliminate concerns over fraudulent claims made by advertisers. In 1934 the Royal College of Surgeons reported that marketers of patent medicines were still making exaggerated and dishonest claims. To avoid the possibility of more government oversight, the Proprietary Association of Great Britain, a body of reputable medical marketers, in 1936 introduced voluntary advertising standards that were adhered to by its members. These rules were extended to all medical advertisers in the 1948 British Code of Standards Relating to the Advertising of Medicines and Treatments.

During World War II the Advertising Association encouraged major advertisers whose products were unavailable due to war shortages to maintain brand awareness and build consumer goodwill. Campaigns for biscuits, soap flakes, and soft drinks urged customers to use those products sparingly and offered tips on how to make them last. Patriotic symbolism was widely used, ranging from idealized images of the armed forces and brave British housewives to caricatures of Hitler.

The government dominated advertising between 1940 and 1945, spending nearly £10 million. Government advertising communicated essential information to the public about ration books, gas masks, identity cards, and air-raid shelters. People were admonished to walk, eat, and spend less—and to say nothing. An animated character, "Squanderbug," reminded the public to save money.

The planned, systematic approach to advertising adopted in the 1930s was largely forgotten during the war. Access to the media was limited, and advertisers bought what was available rather than what was strategically appropriate. Paper shortages limited the use of direct mail, catalogs, and brochures; the German occupation of several countries on the European continent put an end to radio advertising; and newspapers remained the chief advertising medium, although wartime newspaper ad rates soared. Larger ad agencies with little work in the consumer goods sector turned their attention to technical and industrial journals, and advertising in these publications increased.

Rivalry with U.S. Agencies

The loss of staff and expertise during wartime had a serious effect on British agencies. In the United States, advertising was being widely integrated into marketing, while British companies developed no comparable marketing programs. Because of this, and the fact that British agencies were rarely held accountable for advertising effectiveness, British marketers and their agencies were unprepared for American competition after the war.

Advertising did not expand significantly immediately after the end of the war. Many goods were still rationed, and wartime controls were only slowly dismantled. But as the transition began to a peacetime economy, the industry began to thrive again. Advertising expenditures, estimated at £76 million in 1947, grew to roughly £120 million in 1952. After 1952, as controls were lifted on coffee, tea, biscuits, sugar, eggs, and gasoline, ad spending increased by more than 10 percent a year for the remainder of the decade. Demand for televisions, refrigerators, and washing machines grew along lines that paralleled the demand for construction of new homes.

The most significant change in British advertising after World War II was the advent of commercial television, which began broadcasting in 1955. Although early commercials were awkward adaptations of print executions, television advertising grew quickly. A novelty, it produced some significant sales increases, leading many retailers to prefer to offer consumers products that were advertised on television. Agencies championed television's creative versatility and the incipient audience-measurement techniques. Television Audience Measurement, Ltd., and A.C. Nielsen Company offered systems that relied on viewing diaries and meters attached to a sample of household television sets.

Between the 1950s and 1980s U.S. companies that used sophisticated marketing techniques—P&G, Colgate-Palmolive Company, and General Foods Corporation, among others—expanded into Britain, using it as a beachhead for further expansion into Europe. American agencies followed their international clients, sometimes establishing their own operations in London, such as BBDO in 1959, but more often buying existing agencies, such as Compton Advertising's 1960 purchase of S.T. Garland Advertising Service, Ltd., and Leo Burnett Company, Inc.'s 1962 acquisition of an interest in Legget Nicholson and Partners. This trend continued into the early 1980s, when only four of the top 20 agencies were British-owned.

To compete with American rivals, British companies went to their advertising agencies for guidance on marketing policy, research, and planning. British agencies by and large lacked expertise in marketing, however, and so British companies eventually began to hire American agencies. In response, British agencies offered clients services for no charge, including marketing, public relations, and research, and hired American advertising professionals who already had this much-needed expertise. Consequently, early British television advertising was dominated by American-style 60-second live commercials and sponsored programs. In this highly competitive environment, more new consumer brands were introduced than ever before, most offering few discernible advantages for the consumer. British agencies struggled to distinguish these brands from established ones, and in their efforts to do so many were influenced by American advertising concepts, such as advertising practitioner Rosser Reeves's

This 1931 poster for Schweppes Table Waters targeted discriminating consumers with the tag line "Standard of good taste."
Schweppes is a registered trademark of Schweppes International, Ltd. © 2001 Schweppes International, Ltd.

unique selling proposition, or USP, a promise to consumers that states a specific, unique benefit gained from using the product.

Upheaval and Self-regulation

By the early 1960s, as ad expenditures climbed (reaching £371 million in 1963), social trends led advertisers and their agencies to specialized magazines targeting more affluent consumers with resources to pursue their hobbies and interests. Amid the general economic uncertainty of the mid-1960s, advertising expenditures declined, causing the industry to cut costs: Some agencies merged to slash overhead, many reduced their staff, and others, even well-established ones, disappeared altogether. Some British agencies sold out to bigger, better financed American agencies. Most prominently, Mather & Crowther, Ltd., of London merged with Ogilvy, Benson & Mather, Inc., of New York in 1964. Others chose to take their companies public, but that did not guarantee independence. The publicly traded agency Dorland Advertising, Ltd., bought W.S. Crawford, Ltd., only to be acquired itself in 1971 by John Bentley, an investor in prestigious office buildings, whose goal in part was to gain the valuable real estate holdings Dorland had acquired with Crawford.

Adding to a variety of emerging advertising media in the United Kingdom, such as taxi and bus exteriors as well as stadium and arena signage, was the advent of independent commercial radio, finally approved by Parliament in 1971. Commercial radio franchises were available in 1972, but the first stations went on the air only in 1973. Commercial radio had little effect on the practice of advertising, as U.K. national advertisers and their agencies were slow to embrace the new medium. In the mid-1970s British agencies saw further competition emerge in the form of media-buying consultants and in-house advertising departments that were developed by marketers. Creatively, agencies developed an indigenous style of British television advertising based on aspects of the national culture such as class divisions, affection for eccentricity, and understated humor.

Television advertising was first closely monitored by the Independent Television Authority (ITA), whose powers were derived from the Television Act of 1954. With the advent of commercial radio the ITA was renamed the Independent Broadcasting Authority and made responsible for all broadcast advertising. The Broadcast Act of 1990 revised this structure, creating a separate Radio Authority and Independent Television Committee. Each is empowered to regulate advertising through its own code of standards and practices. The Independent Television Committee works to ensure that television advertising is not misleading, does not encourage harmful behavior, and does not cause widespread offense. Television advertising directed at children and claims made by advertisers in certain product categories, such as medicines and weight-loss aids, are closely scrutinized. The Radio Authority seeks to ensure that radio advertising is legal, decent, honest, and truthful. Both organizations have systems in place to vet commercials for code compliance prior to transmission.

In 1961 the Advertising Association introduced the British Code of Advertising Practice to prevent statutory oversight from being applied to non-broadcast advertising media. The code's basic principles stated that all advertisements should be legal, honest, decent, and truthful; be responsible to the consumer and society; and follow the principles of fair business competition. Specific aspects of advertising were also addressed, such as claims for health care products and advertising aimed at children. Critics, however, complained that the association's code was biased in favor of advertising industry interests, and in 1962 critics created the independent Advertising Standards Authority (ASA). The code and ASA were strengthened in 1974 by a revision to the code itself, mounting a widespread campaign urging the public to complain about advertising that violated its codes and implementing a system to monitor advertising of potentially troublesome product categories such as cigarettes and "roll your own" tobacco. Both of these tobacco products were banned from television in 1965 by an agreement between the tobacco industry and the Independent Television Authority.

Britain's Creative Counterrevolution

In the 1980s British agencies centered in London—such as Saatchi & Saatchi, Bartle Bogle Hegarty, Boase Massimi Pollitt, and Abbott Mead Vickers—gained international acclaim for their creativity and as pioneers of "account planning." The London office of J. Walter Thompson Company and Boase Massimi Pollitt were the first to develop account planning. Account planners work from the perspective of the consumer in the advertising planning process, focusing the creative team on objectives and strategy. They combine intuition, observation, lateral thinking (i.e., the application of different perceptions, concepts, and approaches to solve problems by unorthodox, even illogical methods), and formal research to understand consumer wants and needs. U.S. agencies became interested in account planning after their clients began to hire British account planning specialists. But since account planning was an imported specialty, it took time for U.S. shops to develop or hire enough planners to meet the needs of their marketer clients.

While account planning slowly caught on in the United States, the Saatchi brothers and Martin Sorrell spearheaded a more significant British invasion that changed the face of advertising on both sides of the Atlantic. Charles and Maurice Saatchi founded Saatchi & Saatchi Company in 1970, led the agency to renown as London's creative hot shop, and reached the top ranks of the world's advertising networks. The agency attracted early notice with its campaign for the Health Education Council featuring a sulking man with a bulging belly over the caption, "Would you be more careful if it was you that got pregnant?" Its 1979 ads for the Conservative Party, depicting a long line of unemployed Britons with the headline, "Labour's not working," won international acclaim, as did the agency's work for British Airways, tagged, "The world's favourite airline," which won a Clio award for its "Manhattan Landing" spot. With the agency's success, the brothers looked overseas beginning in 1977 to build an international agency network.

Saatchi & Saatchi shook the U.S. advertising industry with its acquisitions of Compton Advertising, Inc., in 1982; McCaffrey & McCall, Inc., in 1983; and Dancer Fitzgerald Sample, Backer & Spielvogel, and Ted Bates Worldwide, Inc., in 1986. Difficult economic times in the early 1990s hit Saatchi & Saatchi hard. New financial management and pressure from shareholders forced the Saatchi brothers out of their agency in December 1994. They subsequently formed M&C Saatchi and were followed out of Saatchi & Saatchi by major clients British Airways and Mars, Inc.

Similarly, WPP Group PLC, since 1986 run by the Saatchis's former lieutenant Sorrell, who had been the financial officer who kept Saatchi & Saatchi afloat despite its run of cash-draining acquisitions, stunned the ad world in 1987 with a hostile takeover of the much larger JWT Group, including the venerable 123-year-old J. Walter Thompson Company, for $566 million. Then WPP Group bought Ogilvy Group, owner of Ogilvy & Mather, for $864 million in 1989. At the end of 2000 WPP Group consisted of four agency groups: J. Walter Thompson Company, Ogilvy & Mather Worldwide, Red Cell, and Young & Rubicam, which it acquired late in 2000. The holding company had gross income of $7.97 billion on billings of $67.22 billion in 2000.

In the 1980s Britain was seized by a media mania that continued into the 21st century. A long-standing distaste for commercialism became appreciation, even reverence, for advertising as culture. Copywriters became celebrities, and BBC television broadcast the advertising industry's award ceremonies. American advertising professionals began looking to Britain for creative inspiration, emulating its humor and cinematic quality.

As part of Britain's creative resurgence, other London agencies attained prominence. One of the first to do so was Collett Dickenson Pearce, which emulated the creative revival in New York City of the late 1960s and early 1970s, creating English versions of American advertising. Under the creative guidance of John Webster, Boase Massimi Pollitt (BMP) made a significant creative imprint on British advertising in the 1970s and 1980s. BMP's reputation was launched on its long-running "Martians" campaign for Cadbury's Smash potatoes. Other award-winning work included campaigns for John Smith's Bitter, NatWest, and the Health Education Authority's AIDS campaign.

Bartle Bogle Hegarty (BBH), founded in 1982, built a reputation for creative excellence under John Hegarty's direction; its defining 1985 work increased European sales of Levi's 501 jeans from 80,000 to 600,000 units. The agency's work ran internationally for clients such as Coca-Cola Company and Haagen-Dazs Company, Inc. BBH became famous in the ad industry for refusing to produce speculative creative work; i.e, unlike most agencies, which seek new business by providing sample ads on speculation, it did not do work for a marketer until after it had won the account.

The Gulf War and economic recession in Britain in the early 1990s hurt the British advertising industry as big advertisers cut their budgets. Layoffs, mergers, and a general malaise were the rule. Advertising expenditures in Britain reached £10.14 billion in 1994. By the mid-1990s the industry's vitality returned and other agencies stepped forward as creative trendsetters.

This television commercial for Hovis breads, created in the 1970s by Collett Dickenson Pearce and directed by Ridley Scott, evoked the warmth and comfort of an earlier era.

Abbott Mead Vickers PLC, formed in 1977, was named agency of the year in 1996 and 1997 by trade publication *Campaign*. AMV, perceived as lackluster in the 1980s, sold a minority stake to BBDO in 1991 and served as the U.S. agency's London outpost, creating advertising for such well-known brands as British Telecom, *The Economist,* and the cereal marketer Weetabix Company. Top multinational clients included Pepsi-Cola Company, Gillette Company, and Pizza Hut.

Rainey Kelly Campbell Roalfe, founded in 1993 and acquired by Young & Rubicam, Inc., in 1999, has emerged as one of the fastest growing and most creatively respected agencies in Britain, handling accounts for Virgin Group, *The Times,* and Miller Brewing Company's Miller Genuine Draft.

Issues of criticism and control continued in the 1990s. Perhaps the highest profile case found the ASA confronting Benetton and its agency, JWT. Benetton sought ASA clearance for a poster campaign depicting a newborn baby covered in blood, umbilical cord still attached. The ASA judged it to be offensive, but Benetton proceeded with the campaign. Within days the ASA received more than 800 complaints. Though Benetton voluntarily withdrew the campaign, that cast some doubts on the effectiveness of self-regulation.

The ASA also focused its efforts on misleading advertisements for health, beauty, and weight-loss products by imposing a pre-publication copy clearance procedure with the agreement of the Newspaper Publishers' Association. Following a European Union Directive on tobacco advertising, the government announced in 1999 it would introduce the Tobacco Advertising and Promotion Bill to limit remaining tobacco promotion opportunities, including a ban on billboard, magazine, and newspaper advertising. The bill, however, had been blocked in Parliament.

In 1998 one of the most recognizable, successful, and long-running British advertising campaigns drew to a close. McCann-

Erickson Worldwide's "soap opera" about the love affair between Tony Head and Sharon Maughan for Nescafe's Gold Blend garnered a unique place in British popular culture. Although maligned by the creative community, the campaign drove sales up 70 percent over the 11 years it aired and regularly topped consumer polls of favorite advertising. It was so popular that 30 million viewers watched when Tony told Sharon he loved her, and a novel based on the ads and a branded CD of love songs became best-sellers in the United Kingdom.

In 2000 ad spending in the United Kingdom was about $16.5 billion, according to *Ad Age Global*, driven by top advertisers Unilever, P&G, British Telecom, Mars, Dixons Stores, General Motors Corporation, and Nestlé, and spread primarily across newspapers (39 percent), television (33 percent), magazines (17 percent), outdoor (5 percent), radio (4 percent), and cinema (1 percent).

RANDY JACOBS

Further Reading

Goldman, Kevin, "Maurice and Charles Saatchi Rode High on the Hog in the '80s As They Built the Biggest Advertising Company in the World," *Advertising Age* (29 March 1999)

Heal, Ambrose, *London Tradesmen's Cards of the XVIII Century: An Account of Their Origin and Use*, New York: Scribner, and London: Batsford, 1925; reprint, New York: Dover, 1968

"Heroes: Webster," *Creative Review* (1 November 1999)

Hindley, Diana, and Geoffrey Hindley, *Advertising in Victorian England, 1837–1901*, London: Wayland, 1972

Martin, Michele, "A Drama to the Last Drop," *Guardian* (15 June 1998)

Messinger, Gary, *British Propaganda and the State in the First World War*, Manchester and New York: Manchester University Press, 1992

Nevett, Terence R., *Advertising in Britain: A History*, London: Heinemann, 1982

O'Leary, Noreen, "AMV's Quiet Rise," *Adweek* (22 September 1997)

Presbrey, Frank, *The History and Development of Advertising*, Garden City, New York: Doubleday, 1929; reprint, New York: Greenwood Press, 1968

Richards, Thomas, *The Commodity Culture of Victorian England: Advertising and Spectacle, 1851–1914*, Stanford, California: Stanford University Press, 1990; London: Verso, 1991

Rickards, Maurice, *The Rise and Fall of the Poster*, New York: McGraw-Hill, and Newton Abbot, Devon: David and Charles, 1971

Rothenberg, Randall, "Brits Buy Up the Ad Business," *New York Times* (2 July 1989)

Turner, Ernest Sackville, *The Shocking History of Advertising!* London: Joseph, 1952; New York: Dutton, 1953; revised edition, London: Penguin, 1965

Vickers, Graham, "Heroes: Hegarty," *Creative Review* (1 June 1999)

United States

The territory that was to become the United States of America was colonized in the late 1600s and 1700s by advertising—the same medium that, as a full-fledged industry, later fueled the growth of the country's economy. As a far-off colony of England, America was settled largely as a result of an effort by major trading companies that hoped to profit from the riches of the New World's natural resources. Advertisements—mostly printed broadsides—urged the poor, weary, downtrodden classes of London and other overcrowded ports to venture across the sea to the "land of opportunity."

Once the flow of immigrants had begun, promoters found success with a method of advertising still in use in the 21st century: the endorsement. William Penn, the founder of Pennsylvania, instructed his associates to publicize life in the colony using firsthand accounts of the benefits and bounty of the new land. One such testimonial from 1693 reads, "Here there are no beggars. . . . Jealousies among Men here are rare." To the poor of crowded England, this was a persuasive message. Between 1630 and 1800,

more than 5 million people came to the colonies. But, as is true today, the glowing promises of the advertisements were not always kept. Whereas many worked and prospered in America, some who made the voyage did so in exchange for a life of servitude, and their living conditions were often as poor as those they had emigrated to escape. In fact, one well-documented use of advertising in colonial times was the notice of reward for the return of indentured workers who had fled.

Early Days

The predominant use of advertising, however, was to sell goods such as tobacco and timber throughout the eastern coastal colonies. The primary medium of advertising in those days—one that still thrives—was the newspaper. The first regularly published newspaper, the *Boston News-Letter*, was started in April 1704. One of its first advertisements was for a house for sale in Long Island, New York. Benjamin Franklin had in the mid-1700s founded one of the most significant newspapers, the *Philadelphia Gazette*. Located in the Pennsylvania city that was then the economic center of the American colonies, the *Gazette* is of note because it was the first quality publication from the printer (and inventor) Franklin, who not only wrote the ads but also brought illustration into the advertising process. In 1744 he advertised his own invention, a home fireplace.

As Philadelphia thrived as a business center, advertising flourished in the signage and placards plastered throughout the town. It was also the site where artistic talent made its entry into advertising, with one notable practitioner being artist Matthew Pratt. Before and during the American Revolution, ads were used to urge the boycott of British goods and to recruit men for armed service. Samuel Adams is credited with using advertisements to foment the rebellion.

With American independence came a greater need for industry, as the new nation now competed with Britain to sell goods to other countries. The first U.S. president, George Washington, promoted the use of homegrown and manufactured textiles in his inaugural address, and inventions such as the cotton gin (invented by Eli Whitney in 1793) soon spurred manufacturing, industry, and overall economic growth.

Advertising burst upon the 1800s as the nation cut and cleared more land and expanded westward. So-called Yankee peddlers, with their painted displays and wagons, soon were promoting goods from the East to people living on the frontier. Salesmanship was honed to a fine art, and its practice helped feed, clothe, and build towns farther and farther from the Atlantic Ocean. The towns prospered; virtually every one had a newspaper, and advertising flowed into their pages. By about 1830 there were approximately 1,000 newspapers carrying advertising in the United States. Some of that advertising promoted the sale of land for further expansion and development, and thus more towns sprang up, largely with a big push from the new railroading industry.

At about this time, the thriving eastern cities saw the birth of the "penny press," inexpensive newspapers whose low price was made possible by advertising revenues; the *New York Sun* was among the first of these. Print advertising was becoming a big business. Immigrants poured into the United States in the early 1800s, fueling the mass production of goods, while the railroads provided the mass distribution. Advertising was the means for selling from a distance, and the ads soon trumpeted their message much as the peddler or "drummer" had done in person.

Invention of the Ad Campaign

Showman P.T. Barnum is widely credited as being the first to employ the "modern" technique of planning and producing an advertising campaign. He promoted his carnivals and shows well in advance with a program of posters, parades, and decorative ads in newspapers, all using the flamboyant language now associated with his name. In an autobiography published in 1835, Barnum said he "thoroughly understood the art of advertising." He later said that "every dollar sown in advertising would return to me in tens, and perhaps hundreds, in a future harvest." From this exam-

To be Sold,

ONE Moiety or half Part of the Island of *Roanoak* scituate and being in the County of *Albemarle* and Province of *North Carolina*, containing about six Thousand Acres of Land and Marsh, as it was surveyed in the Year 1718, by *William Maule*, Surveyor General of said Province : Any Person inclining to purchase the same, may apply themselves to *Samuel Swann*, Esq; of the Precinct of *Pequimmans* in the County of *Albemarle*, and Province aforesaid, where they may receive all reasonable Satisfaction as to said Title ; or to Doct. *Belcher Noyes*, of *Boston* in the Province of the *Massachusetts Bay* in *New England*, who is the rightful Owner thereof.

Boston, May 26th. 1740.

A notice printed in 1740 advertised the sale of "about 6,000 acres of land and marsh" on Roanoke Island, North Carolina.
Courtesy of the Rare Book, Manuscript, and Special Collections Library, Duke University.

ple was born an industry, as manufacturers rushed to advertise their products by any means possible, making extravagant claims and exciting the imaginations of the masses.

Makers of patent medicines were the most prominent users of the orchestrated national advertising campaign. Following in the footsteps of Barnum, they produced ads for every available space—including the sides of barns and even outcrops of rock in the countryside—with persuasive messages touting the restorative powers of their products. The active ingredient in these remedies was most often alcohol, but some even contained opium, morphine, or cocaine. The advertising message for the tonic called Scott's Emulsion was typical:

As a flesh producer there can be no question but that Scott's Emulsion of Pure Cod Liver Oil and Hypophosphites of Lime and Soda is without rival. Many have gained a pound a day by the use of it. It cures Consumption, scrofula, bronchitis, coughs and colds, and all forms of wasting diseases.

One product of that day called Carter's Little Liver Pills lasted into modern times under the moniker Carter's Little Pills.

The makers and marketers of patent medicines became the major U.S. advertisers in the years immediately following the American Civil War, going from sales of about $3.5 million before the war to $75 million annually afterward. In the 1880s St. Jacob's Oil was the top advertiser, having gone so far as to paint the hull of a Mississippi River steamer with its name. This particular product is noteworthy because it has gone down in advertising history as having "proved" the power of advertising. Flush with success, the Baltimore, Maryland, druggist who produced St. Jacob's Oil decided to stop spending money for ads; his sales halted. Another product often given equal credit in serving as an example of what not to do in advertising is Lydia E. Pinkham's Vegetable Compound, made by a family in Massachusetts. The "positive cure for female complaints" was an early example of "branding," with an image of Mrs. Pinkham "burned" onto its label (imagery that was to remain long after her death) and sales messages inspired by her. The Pinkhams employed an advertising "agent" based in New Haven, Connecticut, to place the wide-ranging ads for the product but ceased the practice when they discovered the sizable commissions the agent was earning. Sales dropped precipitously. They switched to a new agent, started advertising again, and sales once again soared.

Major Milestones

The first advertising agent hung up his shingle in 1843 in booming Philadelphia. Volney Palmer was not a creator of advertising; he served merely as an agent for the newspapers he represented, soliciting the advertisers to fill the publishers' available ad space and, in the end, collecting the money for them. A man from his staff moved to New York City, opened up shop there, and slightly changed this way of doing business—he was an independent space broker, taking his pay out of the money the advertisers remitted to the ad medium. As the marketing of manufactured goods grew, this process led to underhanded dealing, and, in turn, to the reputation of advertising as a not entirely reputable business.

The individual who played a major role in cleaning up the ad business and giving it respectability was George P. Rowell. In 1865, the year the Civil War ended, Rowell set up a new business in Boston, Massachusetts. He had been serving as a newspaper agent, but with the expansion of advertising beyond patent medicines to all U.S. industry, he managed to "list" the ad rates of widespread publications (thus helping legitimize their business). He also bought print space on a mass basis, guaranteeing payment, then filled the space by placing ads on behalf of manufacturers. By 1867 he had moved to New York City and become the largest advertising "agency."

Still, he worked primarily for the media, not the advertiser. It was Francis Wayland Ayer who changed the ad industry to serve the latter. Ayer opened his office in Philadelphia in 1869 to represent the advertiser and establish an "open contract" between the company and the publication to carry advertising. The financial terms (including the set agency commission of 15 percent) were established "above board," and advertising was on its way to becoming a business of its own, a force in expanding U.S. industry.

That agency, named N.W. Ayer & Son (he used his father's name rather than his own), still exists more than 130 years later, albeit as a smaller part of a larger worldwide advertising company.

Other milestones in the industry's growth can be traced to Rowell. His business representing publications evolved into *Rowell's American Newspaper Directory,* a guide to more than 5,000 newspapers in North America that printed all of their ad rates, as well as he could determine them. Not necessarily popular with publishers, this development was another factor in legitimizing the advertising business. By about 1888, Rowell was producing a trade magazine called *Printers' Ink,* placing a further stamp on advertising as an industry.

The profession received further contributions from other early practitioners. As an agent in Chicago, Illinois, in the 1870s, Daniel M. Lord offered to help advertisers improve their ads, thus expanding his role to more than that of an agent and "placer" of ads supplied by the advertiser. His agency, Lord & Thomas, was one day to employ Albert Lasker, one of the greatest copywriters in the formative years of advertising. But the birth of the "creative" role within advertising—the early example for others—occurred in 1880, when Philadelphia retailer John Wanamaker hired copywriter John E. Powers, who is accorded the distinction of being the first person to work solely on the crafting of advertising messages.

In addition to his job, Powers worked other wonders for advertising. He was quoted in *Printers' Ink* near the turn of the century as saying that his success had come from writing "the truth." He said it had been his practice to work to correct "whatever's wrong in the merchant's business. If the truth isn't tellable, fix it so it is." He used plain language in his ads, what he called his "talking style of writing." Early on, he persuaded Wanamaker to change the name of his department store from Grand Depot—too French sounding, he said—to Wanamaker's. Powers went on to write ads on a freelance basis, creating work for Carter's Little Liver Pills and Murphy's Varnish, among other products. Powers's example of truthful, exaggeration-free advertising produced some needed change and helped pave the way for "reason-why" advertising, a fact-based approach that sought to persuade consumers that there were solid reasons to chose a specific product. It was to dominate the business in the late 1800s and continue into the early 1900s.

Growth of Print

As advertising was growing, so too were the media. Although newspapers were the primary medium of this period, they were all published locally. To reach a national audience, advertisers also put their sales messages onto postcard-sized "trade" cards. They were often slipped into the product packaging or supplied to grocers, who passed them along to their customers. The printing industry then moved into consumer magazines, which eventually took the large manufacturers' advertising business away from newspapers. E.C. Allen started a magazine in Maine called the *People's Literary Companion,* and its profits came from advertising rather than subscription costs borne by readers.

Prominent in this development was Cyrus H.K. Curtis, who in the 1880s expanded an idea from his farm magazine to produce a magazine for women, the *Ladies' Home Journal*. Until this point, most magazine publishers balked at advertising, ignoring Allen's example. But Curtis, too, charged readers less and based the publication's profits on revenue from advertisers. His success changed the business forever. The *Ladies' Home Journal*, started in 1883, was the first magazine to surpass 1 million readers, one possible reason being that Curtis ran an advertising campaign promoting the magazine via the N.W. Ayer & Son agency. He put his sights on a magazine for men and bought an existing one that traced its roots to Benjamin Franklin, the *Saturday Evening Post*; it had 2 million readers ten years later, up from approximately 2,000 at the time of purchase.

A Massachusetts native named J. Walter Thompson entered the advertising agency business in New York City and earned his reputation promoting magazines as a national ad medium. He worked to develop a so-called standard list of publications that he represented, many of them highbrow magazines such as *The Atlantic* and *Harper's*. Among the advertisers that gained entry into the "better" magazines as the result of Thompson's work was Lydia E. Pinkham's Vegetable Compound. The advertising industry grew another notch. As Thompson's business developed, the agency moved beyond magazine exclusivity and became one of the first examples of a full-fledged, modern advertising agency. Alongside Ayer and the Lord & Thomas agency in Chicago, the J. Walter Thompson Company (JWT) lays claim to being a pivotal player in the industry's growth as it segued from the late 1880s to the 20th century.

Growth of Branding

Advertising expenditures in the years following the Civil War are estimated to have been around $40 million; for 1900, they were the equivalent of $450 million, a full 3 percent of the country's gross national product (GNP) at the time. The railroads had spanned the country; in fact, they helped support a thriving group of business magazines. Among the groundbreaking advertising as the new century dawned was that for the National Biscuit Company's Uneeda biscuit, the first food product previously sold in bulk to be individually packaged and branded. Henry N. McKinney of the Ayer agency came up with the brand name—Uneeda biscuit—and the product soon was supported with the first $1 million advertising campaign. As Lydia Pinkham had shown earlier, branding and advertising worked.

Even before the success of Uneeda, such brand names as Ivory soap, Campbell's soup, Quaker Oats, and Coca-Cola—destined to be the most ubiquitous in the world—had been launched. The manufacturer of Ivory, the Procter & Gamble Company (P&G), had found its first big advertising success almost by accident. In the late 1870s the Cincinnati, Ohio, company had produced a white bar soap (other soaps on the market were gray or brown, including one of the most popular and most advertised of the period, Sapolio) that had more air inside because a batch inadvertently had been whipped by the machines longer than necessary.

When customers wrote to P&G to order more of the soap that "floated" on water, Harley T. Procter set to work to take advantage of the fluke of production. He renamed the soap Ivory and, after much effort, persuaded the company to advertise the product widely. In 1882 Ivory was advertised as "99 and 44-100ths per cent pure" and as the soap that "floats." The company's growth and success were set for generations to come; exactly 100 years later, P&G was the largest advertiser in the world, a position it had held during much of the 1900s. Other advertising successes of the late 19th century included Kodak cameras, Kellogg and Post cereals, and Prudential Insurance and its "strength of Gibraltar" slogan. Eastman Kodak was reported to be the largest U.S. advertiser in 1899, spending $750,000.

Emerging Professionalism

Although the agency business was firmly established as advertising entered the 1900s, the creation of the actual ads still remained the province of the manufacturers, even though increasingly the work had been hired out to freelance writers. Some of the more famous at the turn of the century, men who helped make the practice of creating advertising a worthy occupation, were Nathaniel Fowler, Charles Austin Bates, and Earnest Elmo Calkins. Calkins soon concentrated his attention on the use of art to enhance the messages, and eventually he formed an agency called Calkins & Holden. By now, ad agencies increasingly were rounding themselves into full businesses. Calkins presided over artists at his shop, and his agency was prominent in the creation of ad jingles as well. J. Walter Thompson pioneered the use of so-called account executives to manage the expanding internal work of the agency on behalf of the client and, when necessary, to explain the process to the client. But the man who was to take the agency business itself to new heights was Albert D. Lasker, a Texan who joined the Lord & Thomas agency in 1898.

Initially, Lasker traveled the Midwest to sell the agency to potential clients. As he sought to secure clients, he studied advertising, starting with the mail-order business, pioneered in the late 1800s by Montgomery Ward and then Richard Sears (who wrote all of his own catalog ad copy) to serve rural America. Then Lasker studied copywriting; he struggled with the question of what made some advertising work and some not. He brought in tremendous business for the agency and by 1903 became one of its owners by buying out Lord—at the age of 23. One of his important actions as a partner was to hire John E. Kennedy as a copywriter. Few agencies had full-time writers as yet, but the trend would soon complete the circle for the business. N.W. Ayer & Son established a copy department at about this time.

Kennedy had secured the job by telling Lasker, who still sought the key to what made sound advertising, that advertising was nothing more than "salesmanship in print" (also reported as "salesmanship on paper"). That phrase brought the business back to its roots in the Yankee peddler and patent medicines and somewhat satisfied Lasker in his quest. By 1906 Lasker had acquired Thomas's share of the agency, and two years later he hired a copywriter who would go on to even greater fame as the most prolific

Printers' Ink was one of the earliest journals covering the American advertising industry. The cover of the 5 September 1900 issue featured an ad celebrating the venerable medium of the sandwich board.

practitioner of "reason-why" advertising—Claude Hopkins. It was Hopkins who thought of advertising Schlitz beer as "steam cleaned," an attribute of the production process for all beer; it was Hopkins who toured a Quaker cereal plant to see grains "shoot" upward in the processing to increase their size and came up with the ad slogan "Shot from guns" for Puffed Wheat and Puffed Rice. Lord & Thomas's billings—the amount of money spent on advertising by the agency's clients—went from $800,000 in 1898, when Lasker joined, to $6 million in 1912, when Lasker finally bought out the remaining partners. It was the largest advertising agency in the United States.

Some of the firsts in advertising during this period were the use of coupons (by Lord & Thomas) and the introduction of ad appeals keyed to beauty (by Lord & Thomas for Palmolive soap). Out of New York City, the J. Walter Thompson Company is cred-

ited as being the first to use sex appeal, with the legendary slogan for Woodbury's soap, "The skin you love to touch." Lasker himself considered this a breakthrough.

Business in general—and advertising in particular—was booming in the United States at the start of the 20th century. A modern consumer society was being created, and advertising was a powerful force in shaping both the economy and popular culture. Ad expenditures were estimated at $1 billion in 1910. Increasing government regulation cleaned up some of the longtime abuses (the Pure Food and Drug Act of 1906 targeted patent medicines), although many such products remained active. Self-regulation of the advertising industry also surfaced, without great success, first with a national confederation of ad clubs, then a breakaway Association of National Advertisers (1910) and the American Association of Advertising Agencies (1917).

Advertising and the Auto Industry

The U.S. boom also was being fueled by the new automobile industry. Autos were a novelty at the turn of the century, but by 1907 Henry Ford had produced a car—the Model T—priced for the masses and worked over the next six or seven years to improve the manufacturing process to one of mass production. In 1913 Ford reduced the man-hours needed to make a Model T from 12.5 to 1.5. General Motors (GM) was created through the merger of several independent automakers in 1908 and, under the later direction of Alfred Sloan, competed with Ford by developing more appealing cars and more appealing advertising. Ford, on the other hand, was a reluctant advertiser, striving instead for free publicity. The auto industry would produce ads and individuals to rank as ad industry milestones and leaders. A copywriter at GM, Theodore MacManus, believed in creating an "atmosphere" with his advertising. An ad headlined "The penalty of leadership" for Cadillac ran only once, in 1915, and is still considered one of the greatest ads of all time. Requests for reprints flooded into GM, and salesman carried the reprints around the country. Its soft-sell, intellectual approach was in sharp contrast to the pretested, nothing-left-to-chance, reason-why buying appeals made by Lord & Thomas's Hopkins and other ad practitioners of the day.

With the advent of automobiles, U.S. advertising also took to the roads, highways, and byways of America. Posters and signs spread across the country at an enormous clip. Barns carried product names, such as Mail Pouch tobacco. Lighted signs earned New York City's Broadway the nickname "The Great White Way." Neon signs came in the 1920s. Back out on the highways, 1925 saw another first—the amusing verse signs created by a Minnesota company called Burma-Vita for a new product dubbed Burma-Shave. They were to dot U.S. highways into the early 1960s. Advertising also took to the air; the Goodyear blimp made its appearance in 1925.

Advertising did not even slow its pace in wartime; in fact, as much as $1.5 million in donated ad space supported the government's efforts in World War I, with private companies also featuring war themes and pushing Liberty Loans. Ads for the Red Cross earned widespread fame; a poster illustration of Uncle Sam by art-

A view of a New York City street in 1905 showed the ubiquity of advertising even at that early date.

ist James Montgomery Flagg that declared, "I Want YOU for U.S. Army," enjoyed enduring fame. In 1918 armistice brought a return to the consumer economy and increased ad budgets by industry. Expenditures went from $1.24 billion in 1918 to $2.48 billion in 1920.

Radio

Money aside, monumental change hit the ad business in 1920, when the first radio station—KDKA in Pittsburgh, Pennsylvania—went on the air. Although commercial messages were resisted initially, within two years a ten-minute commercial for a real estate development in Jackson Heights, New York, aired on New York City station WEAF with tremendous success. The new broadcasting industry went on to carry entire programs that were sponsored by advertisers. Among the earlier advertisers was the American Tobacco Company, maker of Lucky Strike cigarettes and run by the dynamic, autocratic George Washington Hill. Through Lord & Thomas, the "Lucky Strike Dance Orchestra" was heard nationwide on NBC. The medium's power was tested when Hill temporarily stopped all of his advertising in newspa-

pers and magazines. In those two months, the brand's sales rose 47 percent. Memorable tag lines for Lucky Strike cigarettes include, "Be happy—Go Lucky" and "LS/MFT, Lucky Strike Means Fine Tobacco." Lever Bros.' Pepsodent toothpaste went on to sponsor the most popular radio program ever, the *Amos 'n' Andy* show. Jingles for such products as Rinso detergent could be heard throughout the land.

Lord & Thomas and JWT—the latter then being run by Stanley Resor and under the creative direction of his wife, Helen Lansdowne Resor, one of the most influential copywriters of the 1920s—were the agencies that dominated the new medium in the early days. But other major agencies, including Young & Rubicam (Y&R) and Batten Barton Durstine & Osborn (BBDO), were being formed in the 1920s. A new agency, Benton & Bowles, Inc., also became important in radio advertising. Blackett-Sample-Hummert (B-S-H), an offshoot of Lord & Thomas, came to the medium with its adopted reason-why approach and created the soap opera, a daytime drama with continuing characters and plot lines, designed exclusively for American homemakers and the soap makers' products. From Procter & Gamble, for Oxydol laundry detergent, came the serial *Ma Perkins* (its first radio show, for Crisco, was on cooking). In the 1930s, B-S-H handled more radio shows than any other agency, and Frank Hummert was the highest-paid man in the ad business. Not all radio shows were soap operas, of course; generations of young boys grew up to the strains of a jingle for Wheaties cereal on the popular, long-running *Jack Armstrong, All-American Boy*.

Those developments continued despite the Great Depression. P&G, for one, believed strongly that it should continue advertising its household goods during hard times. Between 1935 and 1937, it more than doubled advertising expenditures on radio alone. Generally, however, the industry witnessed a drop in spending, from near $3 billion in 1929 to about $1.3 billion in 1933. During this period, ad pitches focused not on glamour or atmosphere but on necessities. Lever had to invent "B.O." (body odor) to sell its soap, and Gillette pitched razor blades by showing facial stubble as the reason for a man's failure to get a job. The industry encountered new criticism in these years; in a movie, the popular humorist Will Rogers characterized advertising as something that "makes you spend money you don't have for something you don't want."

There were threats of a government takeover of the business. It was Y&R's Raymond Rubicam who worked tirelessly to maintain ethical standards for advertising in tough times. His agency grew to be ranked number two behind JWT during these years. Notably, it was Rubicam who brought opinion research into the business when he hired George Gallup to work in advertising.

Government Regulation

But 1938 did bring greater regulation of the business, when Congress gave increased powers to the Federal Trade Commission (FTC) and the Food and Drug Administration (FDA). FTC injunctions were soon putting a halt to some advertising claims. This was also the year that radio replaced magazines as the number-one medium for advertising. But as the United States emerged from its economic woes, a world war broke out once again. The industry offered its services to the government, and the War Advertising Council was formed, a predecessor to the ongoing Advertising Council, which continues to administer public service messages. And, unlike the World War I period, advertisers did not reduce their consumer-product ad support; expenditures approached $3 billion by 1945, up from around $2.2 billion in 1941. Also during the war years, Albert Lasker retired from the advertising business, handing over the reins of his agency to three associates—Emerson Foote, Fairfax Cone, and Don Belding.

The postwar years witnessed a tremendous boom for the United States. Such ad agencies as JWT, BBDO, Y&R, and McCann-Erickson surpassed $100 million in billings each by the early 1950s. The $2.84 billion in ad spending registered in 1945 was dwarfed by the 1950 figure: $5.7 billion (2.9 percent of the GNP). The baby boom years saw rampant home construction in newly developed suburbs. Automobile advertising soon surpassed that of everyday household products, and GM became the leading national advertiser.

Television

The biggest impact on advertising following World War II was to come from television. While TV was invented in the late 1920s, and the first TV commercial, for Bulova watches, actually aired in 1940, significant broadcasting did not begin until late 1944 with the first successful network TV program, *The Gillette Cavalcade of Sports*. The next year, the Federal Communications Commission (FCC) approved commercial TV, and retailer Sears, Roebuck & Company began selling TV sets to Americans on a broad basis. As with the first show, by and large it was the major advertisers that sponsored and produced the programming. American Tobacco moved right into the medium with its radio show, a new *Your Hit Parade*. Soap operas made their way to daytime TV. Although NBC altered the pattern when it produced *Your Show of Shows* and sold time to multiple sponsors, it would be many years before the TV industry itself supplanted advertisers as owners and agencies as producers of the programming. That change came in the late 1950s, when it was revealed that many of the popular TV quiz shows were being rigged to keep audiences large. In 1959 the networks took complete control of their airtime.

The New Consumerism

The post–World War II era can be seen as the second boom period for U.S. advertising, the first being the latter part of the 1800s and the early 1900s, when it became an industry, organized by businessmen specializing in the field. From 1949 to 1951 advertisers are said to have boosted their TV spending from $12 million to $128 million. BBDO, under the leadership of Ben Duffy, moved swiftly; by 1949 his agency was spending 80 percent of its clients' money in TV.

The reason for the boom was that television was a visual medium, perfect for the live demonstration of products. Stars personally endorsed their brand sponsors—"See the USA in your Chevrolet," sang performer Dinah Shore. Cartoon characters such as Speedy Alka-Seltzer were created to strut the praises of products, virtually becoming the symbols for the brand (much like the initial wave of trademarking at the turn of the century, when registrations of distinguishing symbols for products jumped from just over 100 in 1870 to more than 10,000 by 1906). Ad agencies, too, multiplied in the early 1950s, with startups, mergers, and great growth the result of the demand for advertising services.

New names gaining fame in the agency field included that of the Leo Burnett Company, a prewar startup in Chicago that created many of the animated characters associated with its clients' brands—the Green Giant for the popular vegetable line; Snap, Crackle, and Pop for Rice Krispies cereal; and Charlie the Tuna for Star-Kist. In New York City, Rosser Reeves of the Ted Bates agency strove much as Albert Lasker had done earlier to understand what made good advertising. His hard-sell theory of a product's "unique selling proposition," or USP, is illustrated by the animated pounding head and repeated "Fast, fast, fast relief" slogan for Anacin headache remedies. Another was "melts in your mouth, not in your hand" for M&M's candies. Reeves's style flew in the face of another widely used tool of the 1950s: motivational research. The practice of studying consumer behavior became a subject of a best-selling book in 1957, *The Hidden Persuaders* by Vance Packard, which had a negative effect on the industry during this Cold War–inspired, Big Brother–fearing era.

Another visionary who would have a far-reaching effect on the ad agency side of the industry was Marion Harper, Jr., who built McCann-Erickson into Interpublic, a large, multiservice conglomerate. Interpublic was the first to include virtually all disciplines of mass marketing. Harper was not only an empire builder but a ruthless seeker after ever-bigger clients in every field. His ideas, somewhat notorious in the late 1950s and the 1960s, became the norm in later decades, and his dream of a mega-agency was dwarfed by the worldwide ad conglomerates of the late 20th century. Whereas Harper concentrated on the business aspects of advertising, Leo Burnett and others—most notably William Bernbach, of Doyle Dane Bernbach, and David Ogilvy, of Ogilvy & Mather, both in New York City—were starting to lead advertising into a new era of creativity. In their individual styles, each was to show the true depth of power of good advertising.

For the Philip Morris Company, Burnett in 1955 repositioned a low-selling women's cigarette brand called Marlboro to one targeting men. It was a drastic change for a filtered cigarette, but the Chicago agency built an image around the cowboy, the West, and the wide-open spaces of "Marlboro Country . . . where the flavor is." Sales went up 3,000 percent in one year, and the new brand image made Marlboro the top-selling cigarette worldwide. Bernbach in 1959 broke a campaign for a German import into the U.S. car market, the Volkswagen Beetle. Not only had the vehicle been a project of Adolf Hitler, it was also terribly small for a U.S. auto market dominated by large cars. But Bernbach, leading a team of writers and artists, took his style of clean, uncluttered, understated advertising to its zenith with such print ads as "Think Small" and "Lemon." David Ogilvy took his philosophy of well-researched ideas, intelligently executed, to become the other key driving force in advertising during the 1960s—a period now known as the "creative revolution." Mary Wells, the first woman to head a major ad agency, was reportedly the person who made the most money from this period of creative flowering. Advertising became high art, and expenditures soared. From 1959 to 1971, ad spending in the United States climbed from $11 billion to $20.7 billion.

Amid this exuberance, consumerism and government regulation were having an impact on the industry as well. The last half of the 1960s, following a report by the U.S. Surgeon General on the health hazards of smoking, was filled with attacks on cigarette advertising. In 1971 Congress banned broadcast advertising of tobacco products—a loss of about $220 million annually for TV and radio. The wave of reform also brought about the development of real self-regulation by the industry, which established a National Advertising Review Board in a monumental alliance among the major ad associations—the American Advertising Federation, the Association of National Advertisers, the American Association of Advertising Agencies—and the Council of Better Business Bureaus. This did not keep the federal government away completely, however, as new regulations were directed at advertising to children, and for the first time a major product manufacturer was ordered to advertise the fact that its previous advertising had been deceptive to consumers. The product was Listerine, the ads for which in the early 1920s had coined the term *halitosis,* for bad breath, to great effect.

During the 1970s advertising once again became more serious, in line with the period's tougher economic times and more stringent controls. Previously, ads never mentioned a competitor— "Brand X" was born in the early 1950s as a stand-in; two decades earlier, a groundbreaking ad from the J. Stirling Getchell agency had used comparison indirectly when it urged prospective car buyers to "Look at all three" low-priced car brands and choose Plymouth. In the 1970s, though, direct comparisons in advertising were encouraged by consumerists, and from this time forward brand names were named. As the business of creativity had ruled advertising in the 1960s, the business of business ruled in the 1970s, as a wave of ad agency mergers changed the Madison Avenue landscape. With multiplying layers of shops, billings at the top agencies grew faster than the gross national product (GNP). Ad spending soared to $53.7 billion in 1980.

Advertising as Entertainment

The 1980s brought a return to more "showy" advertising, as color TV sets by then dominated in U.S. households. Increasingly, advertising became a form of entertainment in addition to a selling showcase. New techniques in commercial production made for an extravaganza effect in television "spots" (so-called because the networks sold ad time in 15- and 30-second bursts rather than in the full one-minute slots of the early 1970s). A 30-second commercial on the highly rated telecast of the National Football League's annual Super Bowl game in January was going for $500,000 in 1984, when Apple Computer advertised the introduction of its Macintosh personal computer with the now-legendary spot called "1984." The commercial, built around George Orwell's novel *1984,* was by the Los Angeles, California, agency Chiat/Day, which brought a strong West Coast creative influence; the spot, directed by Ridley Scott, famous for his work on such movies as *Alien* and *Blade Runner,* cost almost as much to produce as the cost of the airtime. The Pepsi-Cola Company enlisted the aid of pop music superstar Michael Jackson to sing and perform feats of derring-do in a series of commercials; it paid $5 million to sign him and spent $2 million just to produce the spots. Entertainment as advertising was the craze. Advertising was, as never before, an integral part of the cultural fabric of the country.

With ad expenditures exceeding $100 billion and single companies—such as GM and P&G, the perennial leaders—spending more than $1 billion each year from 1985 onward, acquisitions and mergers among ad agencies increased to a degree never seen before in an industry known for combinations of names on the door. And it was a global trend. An upstart agency in London, England, called Saatchi & Saatchi had used its public ownership status to generate enough money to buy such old-line U.S. agencies as Compton Advertising, which had worked for P&G since it became that advertiser's first full-time outside agency in 1922, and Dancer, Fitzgerald, Sample, the latter name going back to the birth of soap operas in the early days of radio. Largely as a result of this new climate on Madison Avenue, the most monumental merger ever was engineered in 1986. Three sizable agencies—BBDO; Needham, Harper & Steers; and Doyle Dane Bernbach—were combined to form Omnicom Group. Possibly more important to the industry, an offshoot of Saatchi & Saatchi in London pulled off the first hostile takeover of a U.S. agency, the venerable J. Walter Thompson Company. The price of the takeover, completed in 1987, was $566 million. Two years later, the same British company made another such raid on the public stock market in the United States, acquiring Ogilvy & Mather for $864 million. Thus, the WPP Group became the largest advertising organization in the world.

Although there were recession and cutbacks in the ad industry itself—ad expenditures in 1991 were $2 billion less than they had been the previous year—the U.S. economy and marketplace were gearing up for a tremendous boom in the late 1990s, and advertising again was playing a role in the greatest consumer growth ever. In 1998 ad spending topped $200 billion; a single 30-second spot on the Super Bowl telecast sold for $1.3 million. In 2000 the WPP Group acquired Young & Rubicam for $4.7 billion.

Industry Rankings

For the year 2000, U.S. agencies had worldwide billings of $295.28 billion, including $150.64 billion in U.S. billings, according to *Advertising Age*. In the publication's ranking of U.S. agencies by gross income, Grey Worldwide topped the list, followed by the J. Walter Thompson Company, McCann-Erickson Worldwide, FCB Worldwide, and Y&R Advertising. The top ad spender, according to 1999 figures, was the General Motors Corporation, followed by the Procter & Gamble Company, the Philip Morris Companies, Pfizer, and AT&T Corporation. In spending by media, network TV drew 17.4 percent; magazines, 9.3 percent; spot TV, 8.2 percent; newspapers, 6.8 percent; cable TV, 6.2 percent; syndicated TV, 2.9 percent; national newspapers, 1.2 percent; spot radio, 1.1 percent; outdoor advertising, 0.7 percent; Sunday magazines and the Internet, 0.5 percent; network radio and the Yellow Pages, 0.2 percent; unmeasured spending made up the remaining 44.9 percent.

At the outset of the 21st century, advertising's practitioners were participating in every form of communications possible, even in obtaining for their clients free publicity—as Henry Ford had a century earlier—in an exploding array of media formats, including the Internet and wireless devices. The interactivity of the new computer world, and of the advertising and selling it is producing, may one day provide an answer to a problem that has plagued advertisers since it was first articulated by Wanamaker, the man who hired the first full-time ad copywriter. "I know I waste half the money I spend on advertising," Wanamaker was quoted as saying, "The problem is, I don't know which half."

LARRY EDWARDS

Further Reading

Applegate, Edd, *Personalities and Products: A Historical Perspective on Advertising in America*, Westport, Connecticut: Greenwood, 1998

Boorstin, Daniel G., "Advertising and American Civilization," in *Advertising and Society*, edited by Yale Brozen, New York: New York University Press, 1974

Dobrow, Larry, *When Advertising Tried Harder: The Sixties, the Golden Age of American Advertising*, New York: Friendly Press, 1984

Fox, Stephen, *The Mirror Makers: A History of American Advertising and Its Creators*, New York: Morrow, 1984

Goodrum, Charles, and Helen Dalrymple, *Advertising in America: The First 200 Years*, New York: Abrams, 1990

Lears, T.J. Jackson, *Fables of Abundance: A Cultural History of Advertising in America*, New York: Basic Books, 1994

Marchand, Roland, *Advertising the American Dream: Making Way for Modernity, 1920–1940*, Berkeley: University of California Press, 1985

Schudson, Michael, *Advertising, the Uneasy Persuasion: Its Dubious Impact on American Society*, New York: Basic Books, 1984; London: Routledge, 1993

Sivulka, Juliann, *Soap, Sex, and Cigarettes: A Cultural History of American Advertising*, Belmont, California: Wadsworth, 1998

Strasser, Susan, *Satisfaction Guaranteed: The Making of the American Mass Market*, New York: Pantheon, 1989

Tedlow, Richard, *New and Improved: The Story of Mass Marketing in America*, New York: Basic Books, 1990

USWeb. See CKS Group

USWeb. *See* CKS Group

V

Vegemite

Principal Agencies
J. Walter Thompson Company
Mojo

Sold almost exclusively in Australia, Vegemite is a concentrated yeast-extract spread made from brewer's yeast. Its advertising history illustrates both the power of nonadvertising promotions (such as label tie-ins, coupons, contests, and samples) and the influence of World War II in creating household brands.

In 1922 Fred Walker & Company Pty., Ltd., a food marketer in Melbourne, Australia, was looking for a new product to launch. Cyril Percy Callister, the chief chemist at Fred Walker, supplied it when he created a vitamin B-rich spread made from brewer's yeast, a product similar to the English product Marmite. In what was to be the first of many innovative promotions, the company ran a contest to name the spread. The winning entry was "Vegemite," and the product was launched in Australia in 1923.

Despite a high level of public awareness of the product, initial sales were slow. The lack of customers was attributed primarily to the spread's intensely strong taste. Because most people were accustomed to the relatively weak flavors of mayonnaise and a ketchup-like substance called brown sauce, many likened the taste of Vegemite to that of "rusty salt" or "highly concentrated soy paste" before learning to spread it thinly on bread. A little Vegemite—or "A mere smear"—they found, went a long way. In 1926 Fred Walker joined with James L. Kraft of Chicago, Illinois, to form the Kraft Walker Cheese Company, which began manufacturing processed cheese in Australia. In 1928 Walker, still controlling the Vegemite brand, changed the product's name to Parwill, parodying the popular Marmite slogan ("My Mate—Marmite") with the slogan, "If Ma might, then Pa will!" The new name failed to increase sales, and it was soon changed back to Vegemite. The Walker-Kraft partnership continued until 1935, when Kraft acquired controlling interest in the company after Walker's death.

The first truly successful campaign for Vegemite came in a 1935 promotion; a coupon included with Kraft-Walker Blue Packet Cheddar Cheese dramatically increased sales of the spread.

The campaign that launched Vegemite across Australia, however, came two years later in the form of a contest in which consumers submitted limericks with a Vegemite theme to win prizes such as imported cars. The contest generated tremendous national awareness of Vegemite, and sales grew dramatically. These two promotions accomplished more for the brand than the previous ten years of advertising. Following this boost in awareness, Vegemite received a nutritional endorsement from the British Medical Association in 1939. Soon doctors across Australia, acting almost as an unofficial sales force, began to recommend it to patients as a balanced and nutrient-rich food. The perceived health benefits of Vegemite were also essential in what was to prove a key turning point in the brand's history: World War II.

When Australia entered the war, Vegemite was in every Australian soldier's ration kit. The demand for Vegemite among soldiers suddenly became so strong (the intense taste made the rest of the meal ration more palatable) that domestic shortages were common. Making Vegemite an indispensable part of every soldier's meal also made it indispensable when they returned home. Most were hooked on the spread, and domestic sales soared. As the postwar baby boom began, an entire generation of children grew up with Vegemite in the cupboard. In 1946 label tie-ins with Walt Disney Company characters further cemented the product's image as the healthy spread for parents to feed their children. This "family image" led to the 1954 launch of the product's only famous ad campaign, "We're Happy Little Vegemites"—"We all enjoy our Vegemite / For breakfast, lunch, and tea"—created by Allan Weeks of J. Walter Thompson Company (JWT).

What began as a radio jingle soon became a national craze (as had happened in the United States with the Oscar Mayer Wiener jingle), and sales continued to rise. The jingle was copyrighted and Vegemite received international exposure when the 1956 Olympics were held in Melbourne. The "Happy Little Vegemites" campaign lasted until it was replaced with the less memorable "Three Stages of Man" campaign in the mid-1960s. The "Three Stages" campaign emphasized the health benefits of Vegemite to all age groups. Sales soon leveled, and the "Pass the Vegemite, Mum" campaign was created, which ran until the 1980s.

"Thanks Wally!"

Young Wally is giving his Vegemite to the troops

It may seem strange, but by depriving yourself and your family of Vegemite, you are actually helping the War Effort. Every jar of Vegemite we can make is needed for our fighting men. As you know, Vegemite is a concentrated extract of yeast, which contains three vital vitamins — B^1, B^2, and P.P. (the anti-pellagric factor). These three vitamins are essential to physical fitness — that is why Vegemite is so necessary to our fighting men at home and overseas. So, if you notice a lack of Vegemite in your local shop, just remember that until we have won this war, a lot of Vegemite will be going to the troops. And in helping them, you're helping Australia along the road to victory.

VEGEMITE

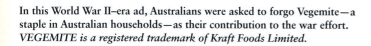

In this World War II–era ad, Australians were asked to forgo Vegemite—a staple in Australian households—as their contribution to the war effort. *VEGEMITE is a registered trademark of Kraft Foods Limited.*

Vegemite by now had been transformed from a mere product into an Australian cultural icon. The Australian band Men at Work gave the brand international exposure in the song "Down Under," with the lyric "he just smiled and gave me a Vegemite sandwich." Recognizing a trend, Kraft brought back the "Happy Little Vegemites" campaign with a retro twist, using the same jingle but matching it with nostalgic 8mm film. In 1992 an exhibit at Sydney's Powerhouse Museum paid tribute to the history and cultural impact of Vegemite, with displays of advertising campaigns and of World War II soldiers in exotic locations. This exhibit generated positive publicity, which Kraft capitalized on by launching the "Toaster Bus" campaign, a promotion featuring a bus that was converted into a huge toaster, capable of toasting hundreds of slices at a time. The vehicle cruised the streets of Australia's cities dispensing complimentary Vegemite sandwiches.

Vegemite celebrated its 75th anniversary in 1997. At that time, Australians were consuming 22 million jars of Vegemite a year, and more than 90 percent of Australian homes had Vegemite in the cupboard. Kraft celebrated by sponsoring a competition in which more than 900 schools sang the "Happy Little Vegemites" jingle for a chance to win a US$75,000 award.

The brand's advertising has always been developed in Australia. The Vegemite account was handled by JWT for the majority of the brand's history until the late 1980s, when it was shifted to Mojo, Melbourne. With the exception of the "Happy Little Vegemites" jingle, very few of the Vegemite ad campaigns have been memorable. Instead, good fortune and clever promotional work brought the brand from minimal sales in the 1920s to the status of a national food by the millennium. The naming and limerick contests got the brand off the ground; the inclusion of Vegemite in soldier's rations allowed it to grow with the baby boom. With recent promotions such as the museum exhibit in Sydney, Vegemite has demonstrated the power of nontraditional promotional methods to break through advertising clutter.

BRIAN WANSINK AND S. ADAM BRASEL

Vegemite is a registered trademark of Kraft Foods Limited.

Further Reading

Wansink, Brian, "Changing Habits on the Home Front: Lost Lessons from World War II Research," *Journal of Public Policy and Marketing* 20, no. 4 (Spring 2002)

Wansink, Brian, and Cynthia Huffman, "A Framework for Revitalizing Mature Brands," *Journal of Brand and Product Management* 10, no. 4 (2001)

Vickers & Benson

(Vickers & Benson Arnold, Inc.)

Founded in Montreal, Canada, by Rex Vickers and Don Benson, 1924; spun off Carder Gray, 1980; opened Chicago, Illinois, branch, 1998; became a founding member of Arnold Worldwide Partners, 2000; changed name to Vickers & Benson Arnold, Inc., 2001.

Major Clients
Bank of Montreal
British Airways
Canadian Tourism Commission
Evergreen Foundation
Human Resources Development Canada
M&M Meat Shops, Ltd.
mbanx
Playtex, Ltd.
Royal Doulton

The establishment of Vickers & Benson (V&B) in Montreal, Quebec, Canada, in 1924 was financed by a $400 loan from the Bank of Montreal, a financial institution that would later become one of the advertising agency's largest and most loyal clients. As of 2001 V&B was the oldest totally Canadian-controlled agency, with a reputation for strategy-grounded creativity, a strong commitment to public service, and an unbroken tradition of employee involvement in ownership. It is one of the most dedicated account-planning shops in Canada, with the highest ratio of planning to billings in the country. For most of its existence, V&B has consistently ranked among Canada's top ten agencies in revenues and billings.

Founder Rex Vickers was the business mind behind the venture, while Don Benson was the creative force. Benson had family ties to the owners of Canada Starch, a national brand that became the new agency's first account. But it was Seagram's that proved the most important piece of business for the young agency and helped anchor billings during its formative years. In the mid-1930s Benson moved to Toronto, Ontario, to set up what would become V&B's main office. Vickers stayed behind to supervise affairs in Montreal.

V&B was an early and enthusiastic proponent of television advertising. In 1952 the agency created and placed the first TV spot in Canada—a commercial for a Montreal General Motors automobile dealership. This interest in video was a natural extension of the shop's radio involvement as creator-producer of alternating twin musical programs on behalf of Imperial Tobacco's Du Maurier cigarettes. On one night the Denny Vaughan big band was broadcast live from Montreal's Queen Elizabeth Hotel. On the next night, a young agency-discovered singer laid the groundwork for his future stardom by crooning "The Trend Today Is to Du Maurier." The vocalist was Robert Goulet.

By this time, an employee group led by account executives George Disher and Blake Dennis and Seagram's account creative director Mac Shoub was well on the way to purchasing the agency from its founders. When Benson became ill, however, he surprised his colleagues by naming an outsider, public relations executive J. Bryan Vaughan, as his interim replacement. (Coincidentally, Vaughan was the brother of the bandleader featured in the agency's Du Maurier broadcasts.) After Benson's recuperation, he named Vaughan agency president. Vaughan subsequently became chairman and assembled a new ownership group that included art director-designer A. Stanley Furnival, who rose to head all creative operations and stimulated V&B's 1960s creative renaissance. The third key player was Maurice Brisebois, an executive in the Montreal office.

This ownership group upheld V&B's strong reputation in broadcast production by hiring Gabor Apor from Dancer, Fitzgerald, Sample in New York City to set up an in-house production facility christened "Projections." In addition to V&B client work, the unit shot projects for outside agencies in other cities. Breakthrough successes of the 1960s included the Canadian Breweries' "Carling Red Cap Forever" campaign—complete with its own anthem and the Red Cap Forever Association for the loyal imbibers of Red Cap brew—which relaunched the label and brought unprecedented awareness, sales, and market share to a brand that had been in steep decline. At about the same time, V&B recruited Canadian comedy duo Wayne and Shuster to the only commercial campaign in which they ever participated: "At Gulf, We Hurry." This theme spawned more than 200 television and radio spots and became one of the most noticed campaigns in Canadian history. In 1967 Canadian history itself was promoted by V&B as agency of record for the country's centennial celebration. The shop used musician Bobby Gimby and his song "Ca-Na-Da" in a carefully managed, two-year, coast-to-coast campaign. On behalf of the Department of National Defence's recruiting efforts, V&B capped a decade of broadcast involvement by constructing the first Canadian intercollegiate television package in 1968. Ever since, it has showcased Canadian college football, basketball, and other sports via Saturday afternoon sports broadcasts over superstation Channel 11 (Hamilton, Ontario).

In 1971 a group of employees, including Terry O'Malley and Bill Bremner, committed to purchasing the agency. O'Malley had joined V&B in 1964 as its copy chief. The following year, he recruited account services executive Bremner to join him. The two had previously worked together at the Foster and MacLaren agencies. Gradually, the ownership group was reduced to these two executives. With O'Malley on the creative side and Bremner concentrating more on the business aspect, the duo dominated the agency for more than two decades. O'Malley became the principal shareholder upon Bremner's death in 1993.

As a writer, O'Malley won hundreds of domestic and international awards and honed V&B's creative edge from the 1970s through the mid-1990s. The agency's work for the Dairy Bureau of Canada took the Canadian Cheddar brand to massive sales increases with the "Show your cheddar more warmth, take it out of the fridge more often" theme, which evolved into the landmark "Cheese Please" campaign. Also in the 1970s, Weston Food asked V&B to take on its struggling Loblaw supermarket chain. With *Star Trek*'s William Shatner as spokesman and the theme "More than the price is right, but by gosh the price is right," the campaign moved Loblaw's from a grocery also-ran to category dominance with more than 50 percent of the national market. From 1965 to 1985 the agency built on its heritage as a broadcast programmer through its work for the Insurance Bureau of Canada. V&B helped create the National Driving Test and the National Home Safety Test that dovetailed *TV Guide*–distributed home questionnaires with the programs so that viewers could calculate their own liability and insurance risks. Both projects generated substantial ratings and long-term awareness.

The agency also became particularly active in sports, public service, and political advertising. In 1972 it initiated the Soviet Union–Canada hockey series and created the Team Canada name, the design for its sweaters, and the positioning of this phenomenon as an icon of Canadian culture. From that point on V&B handled all promotional and public relations work for the Canada (later World) Cup competition, bringing together all the hockey nations of the world. The agency's travel work for Canada ("Canada borders on the magnificent"), Ontario ("It's incredible"), and Toronto ("Couldn't you use a little Toronto?") garnered substantial increases in tourism and created related souvenirs and collateral that have remained prominent. Beginning with Pierre Elliott Trudeau's ascendancy to prime minister in 1968, V&B began its long-standing political advertising relationship with the Liberal Party, including work on the successful 1990s campaigns of Prime Minister Jean Chretien and for Ontario provincial and Toronto municipal candidates.

Organizationally, the agency undertook many innovations during the 1970s and 1980s, but it also experienced some setbacks. In 1973 it created March Chait Advertising, the first direct marketing agency affiliate in Canada—a unit later known as Vickers & Benson Direct. At the same time, in a move to further integrate client services, it partnered with Joe Warwick to set up Warwick & Associates as its promotional and public relations unit. In the late 1970s V&B helped establish the Home Shop, a direct-marketing company that soon moved beyond direct mail into shopping by television. After a decade's involvement, V&B sold its stake in the Home Shop back to its founding partners.

A much more substantial spin-off occurred in 1980. Bill Bremner initiated a deal with Paul Carder, a V&B account director, and Carder's creative counterpart Gary Gray, to shift the agency's major packaged goods clients to a new agency, Carder Gray. Although Carder Gray's gradual purchase of its independence was initially profitable for V&B, it also directed the parent agency away from a strategy that would have made it the largest Canadian-owned shop in the country, poised to create its own network. (Carder Gray was subsequently sold by its principals to Doyle Dane Bernbach and has vanished as an independent Canadian entity.) In the mid-1980s, any remaining possibility of a V&B national network evaporated when the manager of its Montreal office, Yves Gougoux, declined the V&B presidency to accept a similar post at BCP Agency, the leading French-Canadian firm. (V&B ultimately closed its Montreal office in 1990 as Quebec provincial ownership regulations made it more prudent to partner with Francophone shops.)

In 1985 Terry O'Malley became V&B chairman and assumed the task of refocusing the agency. Among the shop's most notable subsequent successes were its work for McDonald's Corporation and Bank of Montreal. For McDonald's, it was V&B account executive John Alexander who created the "News to the crews" concept that gives the franchise's employees throughout Canada advance notice of upcoming campaigns and promotions. The plan won a special award from McDonald's Oak Brook, Illinois, headquarters, which adopted it for use throughout its international network. Ending a period of limited advertising by its client, V&B brought the Bank of Montreal back to center stage in the 1990s with its "We're paying attention" campaign. This approach, which evolved into the "It is possible" statement, resulted in Canada's third-largest bank becoming the best known bank in the minds of consumers. Pro bono endeavors have remained a V&B cornerstone. Its work for Toronto's United Way campaign was judged this charity's best in all of North America, and the agency was active on a dozen additional public service accounts, ranging from the Canadian Cancer Society to the Toronto Rape Crisis Centre.

By 1998 the O'Malley group was in the final stages of selling V&B to a new ownership team. This team was headed by Toronto native John Hayter, who returned to the city after serving as worldwide marketer for Alberto Culver and general manager of Young & Rubicam, Chicago, Illinois. The other two principals were Terry Bell, head of creative services, and Jim Satterthwaite, chief operating officer. Bell started his career as a projectionist in the V&B screening room and, after stints both inside and outside the agency, returned to direct all of its creative work. He won the Bessie Award three years in a row for the best TV commercial in Canada, continuing the agency's long-standing record of broadcast success. Hayter had assumed operational leadership of the agency in the mid-1990s, first as president and then as chairman. He put further emphasis on developing the technological capabilities essential to bolstering the firm's direct marketing and Web site design activities as well as those of maxxmedia, V&B's independent media-buying entity.

In 1998 Hayter established a Chicago office to service the growing needs of such U.S. clients as Harris Bank and Enesco Corporation. Two years later V&B became a founding member of Arnold Worldwide Partners, a division of global Havas Advertising. On 22 February 2001, the agency officially changed its name to Vickers & Benson Arnold, Inc., and announced the formation of wideframe, a new Internet professional services firm. At the beginning of 2002 Vickers & Benson Arnold encompassed its namesake agency, that agency's Chicago branch, Vickers & Benson Direct and Interactive, Arnold Brand Promotions, Warwick Public Relations, massmedia, and wideframe.

PETER B. ORLIK

Further Reading
Caragata, Warren, "Adapting to a New Climate: Changes at an Advertising Agency Illustrate the Art of Political Survival," *Maclean's* (2 May 1994)

Hume, Scott, "V&B Sets Aggressive Growth Plan," *Adweek* (Midwest Edition) (20 July 1998)
McDowell, Edwin, "Canada Is Coaxing Americans to Go North and Help Reduce or Eliminate Its Travel Imbalance," *New York Times* (4 June 1996)
Medcalf, Laura, "One Face of a Big Idea," *Marketing* (Maclean Hunter) 99 (August 1994)
Menzies, David, "How to Launch a Bank," *Marketing* (Maclean Hunter) 102 (December 1997)

Vince Cullers Advertising, Inc. *See under* Cullers

Virgin

Principal Agencies
Still Price Court Twivy DeSouza
Simons Palmer
Rainey, Kelly, Campbell, Roalfe/Young & Rubicam

When the 20-year-old British entrepreneur Richard Branson started a small record business as a moneymaking extension of his *Student* magazine in 1970, he set in motion the development of a worldwide company that would eventually encompass a recording label, an airline, alcoholic beverages, a cola, mobile phones, health clubs, condoms, banking, vacations, investment services, the Internet, and much more. The now world-famous Virgin brand he founded long ago left behind the sniggers that once accompanied the mere mention of the name. Virgin has established itself as a powerful brand that has been successfully parlayed across business sectors and international borders—in no small part because of the active involvement and marketing prowess of its charismatic founder and chairman.

Branson, born in 1950, is one of the world's most colorful high-profile entrepreneurs, carefully cultivating a hip, charming image. He holds the world record for fastest crossing of the Atlantic in a boat. He has crossed the Atlantic in a balloon and has said that he hopes to circle the globe in one. For the launch of his Virgin Cola, he drove a tank into New York City's Times Square and fired at the prominent Coca-Cola sign. He donned a wedding dress to help launch publicity for a wedding division, a business suggested by a Virgin flight attendant. Branson's fondness for aviation history led him to set up Vintage Airlines, which carried passengers between Orlando, Florida, and Key West, Florida, on DC-3 planes.

Virgin used a variety of advertising agencies and media buyers around the world as it developed its businesses. However, it came to focus much of its main creative work through WPP Group subsidiary Rainey, Kelly, Campbell, Roalfe/Young & Rubicam, of London, England. The agency was particularly involved in the company's Virgin Atlantic, Virgin Mobile (telephones), and Virgin Trains campaigns.

Virgin's corporate structure is akin to that of a venture capital organization, with a number of operating companies that are joint ventures. Each Virgin company has its own marketing and public relations unit, and each is responsible for its own advertising and marketing budget. However, cross-group media buying is coordinated in the United Kingdom, where Omnicom subsidiary Manning Gottlieb Media channels some 90 percent of Virgin's U.K. ad spending.

Branson established the mail-order record company in 1970. By 1972 his Virgin Records music label had released its first album, Mike Oldfield's "Tubular Bells." The record's release resulted in the company's first pan-U.K. advertising campaign, created by Branson and Virgin cofounder Simon Draper. The result was a massive commercial hit. Oldfield's music was used as the theme and in the advertising for the film *The Exorcist*. As the decade progressed, Virgin forged a major music business. The introduction of the company's mega-store format in London in 1978 was accompanied by an irreverent style of advertising—produced in-house—used to promote the new entertainment/lifestyle retail outlets.

It was another six years before the company started mainstream global advertising, with the launch of Virgin Atlantic airlines. The business was inspired by Freddie Laker's Skytrain, which a cartel of airlines had put out of business in 1982. Virgin

A 1999 poster illustrated the gentleness with which Virgin Atlantic Airways handled passengers' luggage.
Virgin Atlantic Airways/Agency: BBDO Net#Work.

was a different sort of airline—boasting reasonable fares on transatlantic flights with extras such as in-flight massages, ice cream, and movies—and its ad campaign, too, was different. Based on parodying competitors whose advertising tags included Air Canada's "A flight so good you won't want to get off" and British Airways' "World's favourite airline," Virgin aimed to shake up the industry.

Irreverence has been the company's advertising mantra. One Virgin advertisement featured a steward holding an airsick bag with a tag line that read: "If you believe their flights are so good that you won't want to get off, you'll want to take one of these with you." Another memorable outdoor campaign in 1989 featured an image of Panamanian General Manuel Noriega, who was about to be extradited to the United States on drug charges. The copy read: "The only man who can get to Miami for less than Virgin's £99."

Much of the early Virgin Atlantic advertising was created by Virgin's then in-house marketing director, Chris Moss. While Virgin's corporate advertising work went to advertising agencies such as Still Price Court Twivy DeSouza and Simons Palmer, the decision to put virtually all of its advertising in the hands of Rainey, Kelly, Campbell, Roalfe in 1992 represented a more focused corporate approach.

In 1999 Virgin Atlantic joined with the producer of the movie *Austin Powers: The Spy Who Shagged Me* to launch a U.S. advertising and promotion campaign, including a Web site that featured a slot machine–style competition to win transatlantic tickets. It was backed by a number of regional newspapers and a billboard campaign in major U.S. cities and attracted more than 25 million hits on the site.

In 2000 Virgin Atlantic's advertising deliberately sought to use celebrities who did not normally appear in advertising. Actors Terence Stamp, Helen Mirren, Anna Friel, and Simon Callow as well as singer Marianne Faithful were used in a number of separate ads by Rainey, Kelly.

For years Virgin Atlantic claimed the lion's share of ad spending among Virgin units in the United States, the United Kingdom, and Japan. However, by the mid-1990s, Virgin had launched several consumer-advertising intensive new businesses that went on to eclipse the airline in spending. Virgin Mobile, which has interests in the Far East, Australia, and the United Kingdom (the latter with close to 1 million customers) was launched in November 1999 with an ad budget that year of about $19.4 million. Virgin Direct, the financial services business, was launched in the United Kingdom in 1995; its 1999 U.K. advertising budget was $16.2 million. (Virgin Atlantic spent about $14.5 million for advertising that year.)

Virgin's advertising—even when supported by Branson's astute marketing magic—has not always been successful. The company's Virgin Clothing venture folded in April 2000 after a two-year effort backed by extensive print advertising to establish the brand in British stores. Neither the campaign, which Virgin says was limited, nor the products seemed to appeal to British shoppers.

Another Virgin product line, Virgin Cola, had been heavily advertised in the United Kingdom since its launch in 1995 but had captured only about 3 percent of the country's cola market by 2001. The campaign to launch the brand in the United States in the summer of 1998 immediately ran into trouble when TV stations declined to air nearly all of the controversial advertising, including a commercial featuring a lesbian wedding. In January 2001 Virgin's U.S. market share of the cola sector was less than 1 percent.

In June 2000 Virgin Net, the on-line leisure and entertainment service, launched a $3.7 million cinema, radio, and Internet advertising campaign. The campaign, "Make the most of your free time," centered on a monk having to decide between a life in the monastery or outside.

The Virgin Group planned to increase its consumer spending even more in the first few years of the new century. Virgin Mobile planned a U.S. launch, while Virgin Active, which claimed to have become the world's third-largest health and leisure center operator by membership, with outlets in the United Kingdom and South Africa, also had U.S. market intentions. The company's frequently maligned Virgin Trains operation in the United Kingdom planned a major ad campaign highlighting its efforts to upgrade its equipment.

Branson, who was knighted in March 2000, was directly involved in all Virgin advertising until the early 1990s. By the 21st century he had limited his participation to major strategic cam-

Among other innovations to attract customers, Virgin Atlantic Airways introduced onboard massages, advertised on this 1999 billboard.
Virgin Atlantic Airways/Agency: BBDO Net#Work.

paigns and those campaigns where his name or image is used, leaving key executives responsible for major decisions and brand management worldwide. But Branson's standing edict and, no doubt, lasting legacy is that ads should be irreverent, witty, fun, and different from those of major competitors. Early in the new millennium Sir Richard sold a 55 percent stake in Virgin Active as well as his share in premiere hotel Le Manior aux Quat' Saisons, raising an estimated £68.5 million. He has indicated a desire to purchase a second island in the Caribbean on which to create an island paradise to rival his home at Necker in the Virgin Islands.

SEAN KELLY

Further Reading

Branson, Richard, *Losing My Virginity: The Autobiography,* London: Virgin, 1998; as *Losing My Virginity: How I've Survived, Had Fun, and Made A Fortune Doing Business My Way,* New York: Times Business, 1999

Clifton, Rita, and Esther Maughan, editors, *The Future of Brands: Twenty-Five Visions,* London: Macmillan, Interbrand Group, and New York: New York University Press, 2000

Stewart, Catherine, *Superbrands: An Insight into 50 of the World's Superbrands,* edited by Marcel Knobil, Horsham, West Sussex: Special Event Books, 1995

Volkswagen

Principal Agencies

Doyle Dane Bernbach, Inc. (later, DDB Needham Worldwide)
Arnold Communications, Inc.

It was perhaps the least likely partnership in marketing history: the utilitarian car created under the Nazi regime to provide cheap transportation to German citizens and the heavily Jewish New York City advertising agency Doyle Dane Bernbach, Inc. (DDB). But they combined during the 1960s to change the face of advertising. In 1999 *Advertising Age* named DDB's work for Volkswagen the number-one campaign of the century.

The origins of Volkswagenwerk AG, generally known simply as Volkswagen, go back to 1927 when designer Ferdinand Porsche, who had created a number of expensive state-of-the-art cars, turned his attention to a simpler low-end vehicle. In 1933 Adolf Hitler, the new German chancellor, took an interest in Porsche's ideas. Four years later, in 1937, a company was set up by the German government, with the headquarters in Wolfsburg, to achieve a single purpose: create a cheap automobile, easily mass-produced and with nothing more than the most basic amenities, that every German citizen could afford. Thus, the Volkswagen was born. By 1938 Porsche had perfected the essential design of what was then called the KdF-Wagen but would soon take the name of "people's car," or Volkswagen (VW). It had a small, rounded body powered by a noisy four-cylinder, air-cooled engine that generated about 23 horsepower. The Nazi German Labor Front financed and operated the company from its beginnings, but already Germany was gearing up for war. A small quantity of cars was produced and each sold for 990 marks, about $396 in 1938 currency. By the start of World War II, however, all German production shifted to military hardware, and the VW never reached a serious level of manufacture.

After the war the Wolfsburg plant lay in rubble. It might have remained that way had it not been located in West Germany, which the three Western Allies decided had to be revitalized as a bulwark against what was seen as a growing Soviet threat. Production resumed by the end of 1945, and growth was brisk. About 10,000 cars had been made by the fall of 1946. The British, in whose sector of occupation the plant was located, attempted to sell it to private interests, but no one was interested. By the turn of the decade the Volkswagen operation had become the principal force driving the reconstruction of the German auto industry, and a slightly updated version of the basic car Porsche had designed was finding its way into the export market. In September 1949 the Allies turned the company over to the Federal Republic of Germany.

The Beetle in the States

The Volkswagen reached the United States that same year, when two vehicles were reportedly sold. In the context of a market dominated by flashy Detroit automobiles, however, the Volkswagen was embarrassingly austere. Without any advertising and only a tiny dealer network, sales slowly climbed to 2,000 by 1953 and 150,000 by 1959. The price of the car averaged about $1,295. The VW bus also arrived in the early 1950s, and a sporty two-seater called the Karmann Ghia was introduced in 1956. In 1955, with annual sales reaching nearly 30,000, the company set up a U.S. headquarters and established Volkswagen of America. Industry observers expected serious marketing efforts to begin soon. In March 1958 Volkswagen retained its first American ad agency, J.M. Mathes, Inc., then billing about $17.5 million. But the relationship lasted only one year.

Meanwhile in Germany Volkswagen, which had been operated as a ward of the occupying Allies and then the West German state since the end of the war, announced that the government would be cutting its ties to the company and selling 60 percent of the equity in an initial public offering (IPO). On 16 January 1961, Volkswagen went public. The company had also selected a new ad agency by then. In the spring of 1959 Volkswagen of America, under the leadership of Carl Hahn, began its long and precedent-breaking partnership with Doyle Dane Bernbach (DDB). Initial VW billings amounted to $1 million, not including dealer and distributor expenditures, which soon followed the corporate business to DDB. The truck division was assigned to another agency, Fuller, Smith & Ross, but went to DDB within a year.

In October 1961 Doyle Dane Bernbach entered into a 50-50 partnership with von Holzschuher & Bauer of Düsseldorf, West Germany. The arrangement was unique in two respects. Whereas most American agencies went abroad to serve American clients expanding into foreign markets, DDB went abroad to serve a foreign client expanding in the United States. Moreover, many in the industry noted that an agency heavily staffed by Jewish personnel and associated with such advertisers as Orhbach's, Levi's Rye Bread, El Al Airlines, and other clients with predominantly Jewish management was taking on a German brand with deep roots in the country's Nazi past.

This was of little concern to Doyle Dane Bernbach. Since the rebuilding of Volkswagen after the war, all domestic advertising had been created and placed by the company's large in-house ad department headed by Herbert Hahn. Finally, in September 1962, after running the department for 14 years, Hahn retired, and the company awarded its $2 million domestic advertising to the DDB Düsseldorf office.

By then the advertising for Volkswagen coming out of Doyle Dane Bernbach's New York office was attracting attention and winning awards. The print ads were unlike any that had ever been created to sell an automobile, a procession of small masterpieces. Designed by art director Helmut Krone and written by Julian Koenig, they turned deficiencies into virtues by emphasizing, not concealing, the characteristics that set the basic VW model 1200 apart from the conventional wisdom of Detroit. Great white landscapes of limbo underlined the car's tiny size, and the black-and-white layouts and plain sans serif type conformed to the product's austerity. The ads were witty and self-deprecating and invited readers to reconsider all of the established assumptions concerning cars.

The force behind the campaign, in addition to Krone and Koenig, was William Bernbach, a cofounder and the creative director of DDB. A colleague once said that Bernbach hated being Jewish, not because it provoked prejudice in others but because it encouraged parochialism in other Jews. Some have suggested that the Volkswagen personality was Bernbach's own, and the VW, a Jewish car. Neither the ads nor the car ever stepped out of character, a wily combination of the good-hearted bumbler who is also a marginalized outcast. VWs were the little guys, wrote historian Stephen Fox, "plucky, struggling newcomers standing up to the bigger, privileged competition; using their wits and humor to avoid being squashed." VW became the perfect down-to-earth outsider in a marketplace in which veneers of jet styling had made common sense look doughty.

Both Volkswagen and Doyle Dane Bernbach recognized the impossibility of competing on Detroit's terms with such a product. But by stressing the negatives in the ads, DDB turned them into a witty positive. A car that never changed also never grew obsolete. A 1970 ad with the headline "Practice makes perfect" showed a year-by-year progression of VWs from 1945 to the present—all identical. A car that did not have a lot of power also used very little gas. A commercial for the Karmann Ghia lampooning American auto advertising showed the car poised to rip triumphantly through a large tissue barrier in the manner of a Detroit introduction—but the vehicle is unable to break through the paper. The ads allowed readers to draw the final conclusions, often while mocking masculine Detroit values. They broke the so-called fourth wall in advertising. Readers were not lectured; they were included.

In the 1960s the Volkswagen Beetle became the best-selling imported car in America, and its advertising became the most influential in the industry. For all the praise the campaign has received, however, it should be noted that the product offered Doyle Dane Bernbach a creative luxury: it was not the sort of "parity" product agencies typically struggle to separate from the competition. The VW was a unique product that virtually forced its uniqueness upon the advertising.

By the late 1960s Japanese car companies had joined Volkswagen and other European manufacturers to create a market segment for small cars in America that Detroit could not ignore. VW, on the other hand, introduced various extensions with a view toward encouraging its maturing customers to trade up within the brand. Square-back and fastback models reached the American market in 1966, and microbuses arrived in 1968. But as the traditional VW matured, the first Middle East oil embargo—which, as it suddenly raised gasoline prices, produced a memorable VW ad of a man holding a gas pump nozzle to his head as if it were a pistol—set off a wide-scale downsizing of the American car. It also presented VW, which was still standing by a flagship product that had not changed significantly in 20 years, with heavy competition that severely affected sales. Ford had met the VW challenge with

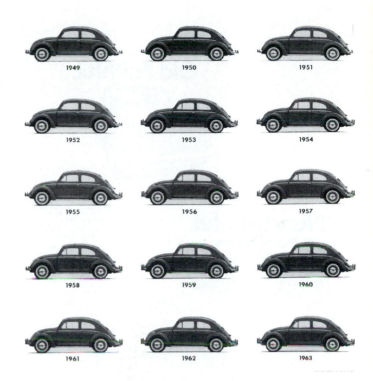

The Volkswagen Theory of Evolution.

A 1962 ad emphasized the enduring nature of Volkswagen styling. *Courtesy Volkswagen of America.*

the Pinto and Chevrolet with the Vega, the first of the American subcompacts. Then VW introduced the Super Beetle in 1971, which offered improved suspension, a curved windshield, and more trunk space while staying within the same familiar shape. But the novelty of making a statement by owning a Beetle was over, and the car had begun a decline that would last nearly a decade. Features such as sunroofs ("Let a little sunshine into your life"), rosewood dashboards, and special editions such as the Ultimate Bug were marketing stopgaps that only bought time and perhaps made denial of the decline easier.

Later Volkswagen Cars

A replacement came in 1975 with the Rabbit, a front-wheel-drive car with a water-cooled engine. It was soon joined by the Golf and Jetta. Although they never reached the levels of sensation the Beetle had achieved, these models kept Volkswagen a force in the American market as the Beetle began to be phased out. But DDB produced one final commercial masterpiece. The 1979 spot, called "1949 Auto Show," started with a period announcer in front of a microphone saying, "And now the star of the 1949 Auto Show, the car the public wants, the all-new DeSoto." The camera

This 1976 ad portrayed the Volkswagen Rabbit, introduced the year before, as the successor to the original Beetle.
Courtesy Volkswagen of America.

panned to an exhibit presided over by an engineer in a white coat who explained the air-induction ports of another Detroit behemoth. It then showed an announcer in front of a Packard and next a trio of girl singers proclaiming, "Longer, lower, wider; the 1949 Hudson is the car for you." The camera finally found a lonely man in a bow tie no one seemed to be paying attention to, the personification of the "little man." "So Volkswagen will constantly be changing," he said, "improving and refining their car. Not necessarily to keep in style with the times but to make a better car. Which means to all of you better mileage." As the camera drew back, a voice-over noted, "Of all the promises made at the 1949 auto show, we at Volkswagen kept ours."

The ad was as much about what had happened in advertising since 1949 as it was about Volkswagen. The viewer looked back on a series of ads within the ad. The DeSoto, Packard, and Hudson were carefully chosen, since they no longer existed. But Doyle Dane Bernbach also seemed to be implying that the advertising styles that surrounded these cars no longer existed either. The commercial was a prime early example of postmodern advertising, the start of the pseudosubversion the industry would recognize in the 1990s as Generation X advertising, full of self-effacing irony.

But the character of the company as well as the prices of its products (about $8,000 for a 1983 Rabbit) had outgrown the "Think small" days of the early 1960s, and this was reflected in its advertising. By the early 1980s whimsy began to vanish from Volkswagen advertising and was replaced by hard-selling information intended to position the company on the basis of "technological leadership." But the old Beetle legacy hung on, as too many middle-age buyers remembered it as the car they drove in college. Between 1970 and 1992 Volkswagen of America watched its sales drop 87 percent.

Second Coming of the Beetle

Among its other problems, Volkswagen was perceived by some in much the same way the Japanese carmakers were—as a foreign company siphoning sales from the American auto industry and causing thousands of U.S. laborers to be thrown out of work. In 1992 DDB Needham Worldwide (DDB and Needham Harper Worldwide had merged in 1986) noted the perception and mounted a campaign that promised to cover the car payments of any buyers who lost their jobs.

One of the most bewildering ad campaigns ever to come from DDB Needham was one based on the German word *fahrvergnugen,* meaning driving pleasure or enjoyment. But both the word and the campaign were puzzling to American car buyers, who associated the brand with some of the most memorable advertising ever created. This was soon replaced by another campaign: "Drivers Wanted."

But what drew the most attention in the second half of the 1990s was the introduction of a new, streamlined Beetle. Unveiled in 1994 for auto show audiences in Detroit, the car created a storm of publicity and a warm sense of nostalgia, though the company avoided any official references to it as a Beetle. Volkswagen wanted to "return to its roots," it said, but this was a whole new car full of the most modern technology. The company made the rounds of world auto shows over the next two years building market interest. By 1996 the car was officially recognized by Volkswagen as the New Beetle, and it was successfully introduced in April 1999.

Actually, the traditional Beetle continued to be produced outside the United States in such countries as Mexico and for the huge Brazilian market. Volkswagen de Mexico S.A. was set up in 1964 for importation and assembly but grew into a full-scale production operation three years later, exporting some of its output back to Germany. By May 1981, 20 million Beetles had been built in the factory at Puebla. Even larger production facilities were established in São Paulo, Brazil, in 1953, operations that eventually became the largest outside Germany. The original Volkswagen Beetle (called Fusca, "folk" in Portuguese) arrived in Brazil in 1950. Production ceased in 1986 but resumed in 1993, allegedly under polite pressure from President Itamar Franco.

But as the company prepared to relaunch the Beetle in the United States, Volkswagen's talk about returning to its roots did not included returning to DDB. In 1995 the company turned to Arnold Communications, Inc., a midsize Boston, Massachusetts,

A car like this comes around only twice in a lifetime.

Drivers wanted.

In 1999 Volkswagen promoted the new Beetle with a humorous reference to the car's popular predecessor model.
Courtesy Volkswagen of America and Arnold Communications.

agency founded in 1946 and now a unit of Havas Advertising. Introduced amidst much publicity, the New Beetle was supported by a campaign that acknowledged the equally famous DDB advertising that was as much a part of its heritage as the car's shape. The early ads built on the traditional off-beat image that had made the original Beetle stand out. They were humorously self-deprecating of standard car advertising and evoked a kind of 1960s nostalgia, though the $20,000-plus sticker price was anything but nostalgic. Nevertheless, sales exceeded all expectations during the first year, surpassing 55,000 by December. In 1999 more than 83,000 New Beetles were sold on ad spending of only $33.5 million, according to figures from Competitive Media Reporting (now known as Taylor Nelson Sofres' CMR).

By 2000, however, the honeymoon was over. As total VW sales grew by 12.6 percent, New Beetle sales decreased 2.8 percent. VW tripled the ad budget to $218.6 million, according to CMR, but the sales decline continued in 2001. Consumer perceptions were that the car was cramped inside. So in the spring of 2001 Arnold launched a new campaign based on the theme "Round for a reason." Without sacrificing the dry wit of previous work, the advertising emphasized the New Beetle's interior spaciousness. One ad showed the car's dashboard adorned with a chorus line of 13 plastic hula dancers swaying their hips. Another calculated the number of coffee cups, laundry bags, and dachshunds that could fit inside a New Beetle, an ad reminiscent of an early Joe Sedelmaier commercial for Van Brunt Advertising, ca. 1970, that showed a Pontiac filled with ping-pong balls. "The first campaigns were about the shape from the outside," a senior art director at Arnold told Stuart Elliott of the *New York Times*. "This campaign is about the shape from the inside."

Although Volkswagen sales remained sluggish in the United States, the company continued to be the number-one car enterprise in Europe. It also had assembly plants in Canada, South Africa, Argentina, China, Taiwan, Nigeria, and Indonesia.

JOHN MCDONOUGH

Further Reading

Fox, Stephen, *The Mirror Makers: A History of American Advertising and Its Creators*, New York: Morrow, 1984

Frank, Thomas, *The Conquest of Cool: Business Culture, Counterculture, and the Rise of Hip Consumerism*, Chicago: University of Chicago Press, 1997

Hixon, Carl, "The Bernbach Fantasies," *Advertising Age* (11 August 1986)

Levenson, Bob, *Bill Bernbach's Book: A History of the Advertising That Changed the History of Advertising*, New York: Villard, 1987

Rothenberg, Randall, *Where the Suckers Moon: An Advertising Story*, New York: Knopf, 1994

Schudson, Michael, *Advertising, the Uneasy Persuasion: Its Dubious Impact on American Society*, New York: Basic Books, 1984; London: Routledge, 1993

Twitchell, James B., *Twenty Ads That Shook the World,* New York: Columbia University Press, 1999

Vanden Bergh, Bruce G., "The Bug with Chutzpah," *WorldPaper* (April 1993)

Volvo

Principal Agencies
Carl Ally, Inc.
Scali, McCabe, Sloves, Inc.
Messner Vetere Berger McNamee Schmetterer (later Messner Vetere Berger McNamee Schmetterer/Euro RSCG)

Assar Gabrielsson and Gustaf Larson wanted to build a car that could navigate Sweden's hills, snow, and mud. They incorporated Volvo in 1926, choosing a name that originated as a trademark for ball bearings but soon stood for automobile safety and durability. In Latin *volvo* means "I roll," and that is exactly what Volvo has done.

Volvo's culture, engineering, and advertising grew out of the convictions of its founders. Early on they wrote, "Cars are driven by people. For this reason safety is, and must remain, the guiding principle behind everything we do." Gabrielsson and Larson are even believed to have written many of Volvo's first ads.

Volvo launched its first car in 1927 and its first truck in 1928; truck sales financed the company for the next 20 years. During the first decade the company focused on trucks, buses, even taxis. The business grew, and Volvo was soon exporting vehicles, particularly to South America.

Volvo faced a challenge from General Motors Corporation (GM) during the tough times of the Great Depression. In 1931 GM positioned Chevrolet as "Swedish made" in an industry magazine. Volvo quickly countered, claiming its car was "the *Swedish* car." In 1935, after five consecutive years of profitability, Volvo shares were listed on the Stockholm exchange.

During World War II, Volvo's development activities were funded by the Swedish government. The period produced strong product innovation, laying the foundations for postwar expansion. In 1944 Volvo installed laminated windshields as standard equipment in all cars; the U.S. government did not make this a requirement until a quarter of a century later.

Volvo's reputation and image were dominated by the founders through the 1950s. Volvo cars won endurance races around the world, and its reputation soared—but Gabrielsson and Larson harbored a strong distaste for races and refused to sponsor them, a policy that did not change until the 1960s.

In the mid-1950s Volvo, confident of the durability of its car, introduced a five-year warranty for the PV444. The company was promptly sued by the Swedish insurance industry. The suit was dismissed, and Volvo featured the warranty prominently in its advertising.

In 1955 Volvo entered the U.S. market on a test basis on the West Coast. The United States was a tempting market for many reasons, including the fact that it was the only nation with an auto industry that did not have any protective tariff. Volvo had become Sweden's second-largest car manufacturer by then, with annual sales of $150 million. Within the first year, its U.S. network had expanded to 27 dealers with combined sales of about 500 units a month.

By the end of 1956 franchises were being opened in Chicago, Illinois, and Milwaukee, Wisconsin. The launch was accomplished without advertising, which did not begin until the end of that year. The Ed Belford Agency of Studio City, California, handled all advertising and public relations during the company's early period in the United States. The initial strategy had been to position the car as a second vehicle. But with a price of $2,000, Volvo found that many owners bought a Volvo as their only car.

In August 1959 Volvo Import, Inc., now based in Englewood Cliffs, New Jersey, appointed Anderson & Cairns, Inc. (subsequently Chirurg & Cairns, Inc.), as its ad agency, with a budget of about $1 million, none of which was allocated to television. The campaign emphasized the quality of the vehicle, with price a subtheme. "Volvo economy does not mean compromise," the headline promised.

In the early 1960s, however, Volvo, along with every import car brand, faced the onslaught of Volkswagen (VW). In January 1961 Volvo dismissed Chirurg & Cairns and moved its advertising to Sind & Sullivan, Inc. Robert Sind had run the Volvo account at the previous agency. Volvo's advertising continued to focus on quality, with the ultimate benefit of durability and long life.

A pattern began to develop in Volvo's rapidly changing agency relationships. Six months after the Sind appointment, it switched once again, becoming the first account of Carl Ally, Inc., effective 1 July 1961. Ally would move Volvo into television and sharpen the durability theme with the promise that "9 out of every 10 [Volvos] registered here [i.e., in Sweden] in the last 11 years are still on the road." The 11-year average life of the car became the basis of the advertising for years to come. The agency also took on VW directly, even though Volvo was not competitive with the German car. One headline read, "If you'd like a good used Volkswagen, see your Volvo dealer." The copy explained that more VWs were traded in for Volvos than any other brand. The relationship with Ally lasted until June 1967, when the account moved for the fifth time since coming to the United States, once again becoming the first client of another new agency, Scali, McCabe, Sloves, Inc. (SMS), whose founding partners had supervised the Volvo business at the Ally agency. Ally was understandably bitter over the loss, which by 1967 amounted to $3.75 million; Carl Ally said publicly that he would have preferred to resign the business.

SMS continued the basic durability/longevity theme, comparing the Volvo's strength to that of a tank, while pointing out its comfort, space, and gas mileage. Other ads took aim at the quick obsolescence of U.S. cars. The advertising never sought, however, to make Volvo one of the "foreign economy models," in the manner of VW and its clones. By 1970, 50,000 Volvos were sold in the United States. In a useful product placement coup, the Volvo P1800 sports coupe became the car driven by Roger Moore in the 1967 to 1969 TV spy series *The Saint*. The Ally agency promoted the car as "a souped-down Ferrari."

As Volvo increasingly relied on exports, marketing and advertising responsibilities were decentralized and managed locally. Many different agencies were involved. While ads often looked different, the strong Volvo culture and products ensured that the core brand equities remained the same: solidity, durability, and safety. In 1959 Volvo became the first car with a three-point safety belt, which later became standard on all cars.

During the 1960s Volvo was also marketing the 122S, a less sporty model, with the slogan, "Stronger than dirt." Volvo was adding to a growing reputation for cars that lasted forever from a company that did not introduce one new model after another. It emphasized this theme in an ad that read, "Your car is obsolete. Again." In 1970 Volvo established the Volvo Technical Centre, funded with 4 percent to 5 percent of sales. At the same time key ad campaigns by SMS in the United States and in the United Kingdom solidified Volvo's reputation as the owner of automotive safety with statements such as SMS's "It shouldn't take an act of Congress to make cars safe." In fact, in 1976 the U.S. government bought 24 Volvos and used them in the crash tests that formed the basis for all auto safety standards.

By the end of the 1970s Volvo made the decision to split its car and truck businesses into separate subsidiaries. In the 1980s Volvo introduced the 769 sedan with an ad that read, "The car that took 10 years to build." The message was consistent with its image of dedicated fine engineering and disdain for continual stylistic changes.

Volvo's relationship with SMS ended when the agency resigned in a dispute over a commercial. "Bear Foot," filmed in 1990, showed a monster truck crushing every car in a row, save the Volvo. While based on a true story, the footage used in the ad was a re-creation; all of the cars used in the ad had been doctored. As a result of this incident, both Scali and Volvo entered into voluntary agreements with the Federal Trade Commission (FTC) and paid fines.

In 1991 Volvo hired Messner Vetere Berger McNamee Schmetterer (later Messner Vetere Berger McNamee Schmetterer/Euro RSCG), which began with a complete reassessment of the brand.

CAPITOL TOWER
Hollywood, Calif.

Outstanding...
VOLVO

VOLVO ... a brilliant achievement of superb Swedish engineering and craftsmanship ... is now available to American motorists. Bumper to bumper, Volvo is every inch "an automobile" ... easy to handle ... amazingly roadable ... with all the controlled-power of a sports car in action.

Here is *the* imported family sports car that has Speed, Economy, Safety and Comfort ... room for a family of five.

AN INDESCRIBABLE THRILL...

awaits you and your family the first time you drive the Volvo. Here is everything desirable in an imported family sports car, yet priced with the lowest. Volvo offers more ... for less.

Parts and service throughout the world.

DRIVE THE **VOLVO** TODAY
CALL WESTERN UNION OPERATOR 25
FOR YOUR NEAREST VOLVO DEALER

AUTO IMPORTS, INC. 11689 VENTURA BOULEVARD STUDIO CITY, CALIFORNIA

34 DD   *Call Esquire's Shopping Service in any of the cities listed on page 8 to learn where you can buy this merchandise.*   ESQUIRE

The Volvo PV444 was introduced in the United States in 1957. *Courtesy of Volvo Cars.*

This Volvo definitely has a bug in it.

97% of a Volkswagen fits inside a Volvo.

The 3% got squished in the squeeze.

Of course, the act of squeezing a VW into a Volvo was a small achievement when compared to the final result.

The world's first car with a trunk in its engine compartment. And an engine compartment in its trunk.

Obviously, this incredible automotive breakthrough has a purpose.

And it's not to belittle the beetle.

It's to correct a misconception people have about Volvo.

Many people think that a Volvo is a tiny little car.

The full absurdity of this thinking becomes apparent when you consider that Volvo is built in Sweden, the land of the vikings. Did you ever hear of a four-foot viking?

Actually, Volvo is built to accommodate six-footers.

In the front, Volvo has only three-tenths of an inch less legroom than a Buick Riviera. In the back, it has two-tenths of an inch *more* legroom than a

Chrysler. In headroom, Volvo has more than an inch on the Rolls-Royce Silver Shadow.

But, as everyone knows, quality matters more than quantity.

So we'll tell you about something Volvo has in common with the Rolls-Royce. Both have been voted among the seven best-made cars in the world by Road & Track Magazine.

Which means the Volvo you buy should definitely not have a bug in it.

VOLVO

This 1969 ad parodied Bill Bernbach's celebrated ad for Volkswagen, positioning Volvo as a "big" car.
Courtesy of Volvo Cars.

The late 1980s and early 1990s saw dramatic change in the global car industry. Consolidation was rampant. Demographics changed, and the baby boomer generation was aging. Other auto companies had begun emphasizing their own safety features. Volvo car sales had plummeted.

Messner found that Volvo was strongly identified with safety but also with being boxy, boring, and tanklike. It was time for Volvo to establish itself as stylish and fun to drive but still, above all, safe. Having been primarily a print advertiser, in 1991 Volvo shifted its focus to television. In 1994 Volvo was recognized as having the best advertisement in all categories for an effort called "Survivors." It featured real people who had survived car accidents and credited Volvo with saving their lives.

Volvo also enlarged its product line to cater to people in all stages of life, not just the young families it had previously targeted. Volvo worked to solidify this redefinition through striking new advertising campaigns, including Messner's positioning of the 850 GLT, the first front-wheel-drive Volvo in the United States, as a fun lifestyle choice. In 1996 it ran an ad showing an 850 Turbo Wagon outracing a BMW 328i. BMW protested the ad, and the case went before the National Advertising Review Board.

The Volvo Car Corporation unleashed its first global ad campaign in 1998 to launch the C70 coupe and convertible. Messner created the campaign as a symbol of change for Volvo. The new approach featured an emotional television and print campaign with a tag line stating, "It will move you in ways Volvo never has." This new image was closely tied to the release of *The Saint,* a Paramount Pictures film reprising the Roger Moore television character. Volvo sponsored the film, starring Val Kilmer and Elisabeth Shue; Kilmer's character drove a C70.

Volvo continued to redefine its image and its product line in a second global campaign. This campaign was created by British agency Abbott Mead Vickers BBDO and launched the S80, Volvo's first foray into the luxury car segment.

In 1999 the Ford Motor Company announced it would purchase Volvo cars, while trucks would remain with AB Volvo. Ford broke new ground running a single television commercial in numerous countries around the world. The ad, which had no dialogue but featured 13-year-old Welsh soprano Charlotte Church, highlighted Volvo and Ford's six other brands.

In the same year, "Volvo for life" was introduced as a global tag line. This new slogan, created by Messner and Forsman & Bodenfors of Sweden, incorporated both the theme of respect for life for which Volvo was already famous as well as the zest for life that was becoming a hallmark of Volvo's advertising.

KAREN WEIGERT AND JOHN MCDONOUGH

Further Reading

Chadwick, Kathleen, editor, *40 Years: The Story of Volvo's First Forty Years in America,* Rockleigh, New Jersey: Olle Alexson/ Volvo Cars of North America, Inc., 1995

Lindh, Björn-Eric, *Volvo: The Cars—From the '20s to the '90s,* Malmö, Sweden: Förlagshuset Norden AB; 3rd revised and enlarged edition, 1988

Olsson, Christer, and Henrik Moberger, *Volvo: Gothenburg, Sweden,* St. Gallen, Sweden: Norden, 1995

Volvo North America Corporation, *Forty Years of Selling Volvo,* Cobham, Surrey: Brooklands Books, 1995

W

Wade Advertising Agency

Founded by Albert G. Wade, 1909; took on business of Miles Laboratories, 1917, and was instrumental in success of Miles's Alka-Seltzer brand; lost Alka-Seltzer account to Jack Tinker & Partners, 1964; closed, 1966.

Major Clients
Alberto-Culver Company
Martin Marietta (Construction Materials Division)
Miles Laboratories (Alka-Seltzer)
Toni Company (division of the Gillette Company)

Albert G. Wade founded the Wade Advertising Agency in 1909 in Chicago, Illinois. The Wade family retained ownership of the advertising agency until it closed in 1966, with the stewardship of the company passing from Albert to his son Walter in 1932, then to his grandson A.G. (Jeff) Wade III. During its 57 years, the agency grew to more than 150 employees in four offices and succeeded in attracting some of the top talent in the business. (During the 1960s, Thomas J. Burrell worked at Wade as a copywriter prior to starting his own agency, and Hal H. Thurber served as a company officer for several years before becoming a senior vice president at Lennen & Newell, for which he established a Chicago office in 1965.)

The agency built a stable of accounts in both industrial and consumer marketing and, over its history, made several significant contributions to the advertising business. One such innovation was the introduction of the Bon Ami "little chick" icon. This endearing symbol, used to support Bon Ami's claim that its gentle cleanser was nonabrasive ("Hasn't scratched yet"), was part of a successful campaign that lasted more than 50 years and is generally recognized as the first animal character used in mass advertising.

Wade Advertising's biggest claim to fame, however, was its relationship with Miles Laboratories and its Alka-Seltzer brand. Wade's fortunes seemed to rise and fall based on its relationship with this account. Alka-Seltzer got its start when Franklin Miles, a physician in Elkhart, Indiana, took some of the formulas he used successfully in his practice and began to produce and merchandise them for the home health market. Among the products was a bromine sedative syrup, a product he called Restorative Nervine, which he started marketing in 1884; other remedies followed, including an analgesic and a laxative. From 1928 to 1930, under the direction of Charles and Hub Beardsley, the original Nervine was reformulated in effervescent tablet form, and Alka-Seltzer was born.

The brand was launched with a print campaign inviting people to get a free sample of Alka-Seltzer at their local drugstore; in 1932 radio spots began airing on WLS in Chicago on a popular program called *The Songs of Home Sweet Home.* In 1933 Alka-Seltzer became the sponsor of one of the station's most highly rated shows, *Saturday Night Barn Dance,* personally produced by Walter Wade. The show featured the characters of Fibber McGee and Molly, along with stars such as Gene Autry and the duo of Roy Rogers and Dale Evans. The print advertising for Alka-Seltzer touted both the benefits of the product and Miles's sponsorship of *Barn Dance.* The tag line, "For prompt, pleasant relief," appeared along with information about the NBC radio network broadcast.

In 1940 Alka-Seltzer began to sponsor *The Quiz Kids,* another entertainment mainstay on radio and television through the 1950s. The show was created by Louis G. Cowan, who would later develop *The $64,000 Question* for Revlon. *Quiz Kids* was hosted by Joe Kelly, with whom Wade had worked as emcee of *Saturday Night Barn Dance* since 1933. Sponsorships became a staple of Miles's advertising strategy, and it barely missed a beat as radio's popularity was gradually eclipsed by that of TV. Alka-Seltzer commercials, as well as spots for other Miles products, were associated with most major radio shows (*Lum 'n' Abner, Hilltop House, Just Plain Bill, Herb Shriner*), and sponsorship continued on such early television favorites as *The Rifleman, Bonanza, Combat, Hootenanny, The Flintstones,* and the shows of Andy Williams and Jack Paar.

Wade Advertising signed Miles in 1917 and was instrumental in the early success of Alka-Seltzer and Miles's other brands. Some of that success can be attributed to Wade's aggressive approach to media buying. The agency's philosophy—that it was necessary to spend money to make money—led to a nearly $5 million ad budget in the years preceding World War II, a very high figure for the

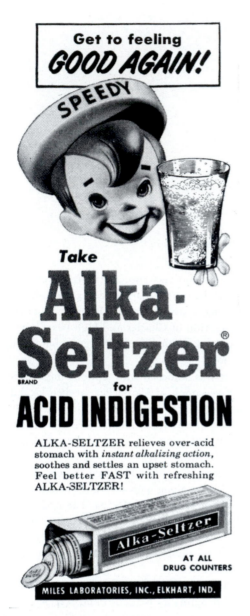

Get to feeling
GOOD AGAIN!

Take

Alka-Seltzer®
for
ACID INDIGESTION

ALKA-SELTZER relieves over-acid stomach with *instant alkalizing action*, soothes and settles an upset stomach. Feel better FAST with refreshing ALKA-SELTZER!

AT ALL
DRUG COUNTERS

MILES LABORATORIES, INC., ELKHART, IND.

Alka-Seltzer's enduring Speedy spokes-character, seen in this 1955 ad, was created three years earlier by the Wade Advertising Agency. *Courtesy of Bayer Corporation.*

time. Miles was the 16th-largest network radio advertiser in 1939, billing $1.2 million in that medium alone. Wade also introduced some creative and catchy slogans, such as, "Be wise—Alkalize with Alka-Seltzer!"

During radio broadcasts, tablets of the product would be dropped into a glass of water and held next to a microphone while the announcer extolled the virtues of effervescence with the words, "Listen to it fizz!" Rhymes and slogans continued for years as a mainstay of Wade's program for the product. In 1952 the pitch "Alka-Seltzer—for that feel better feeling" was first unveiled; it was used for the next nine years. In the mid-1950s the agency coined the tag lines "Action in a glass" and "Relief is just a swallow away."

In 1951, under the direction of Jeff Wade, the agency worked to develop a cartoon character to represent the product. Robert Watkins, a commercial artist, helped the Miles team develop "Speedy," a red-haired, rosy-cheeked boy with a toothy grin and a magic wand. The character, originally a painted wooden figure, wore an Alka-Seltzer tablet on his head emblazoned with his name; another tablet comprised his torso. In radio and TV spots Speedy's voice was provided by actor Richard Beals. For ten years Speedy was featured as the line's chief advertising symbol, appearing in more than 100 television spots and returning for comeback appearances during 1976 (the U.S. Bicentennial) and briefly in 1980 for the Olympic Games, before the United States withdrew. An internationally recognized icon, in Mexico and South America he was known as "Pron-tito." Speedy won numerous advertising awards, including one for top commercial of the 1950s.

Whether Speedy's prolonged tenure as Alka-Seltzer's key advertising element was the primary reason for the breakup is unclear, but in 1964 Miles withdrew the business from Wade, saying it wanted to seek wider creative options for the Alka-Seltzer line. It awarded the account to Jack Tinker & Partners (a division of New York City's Interpublic Group). This bold move shook the advertising world and marked the beginning of the end for the Wade agency, which seemed untouched by the "creative revolution" that shook Madison Avenue in the 1960s.

While Miles and Alka-Seltzer did not constitute the agency's total business, they represented a high percentage of annual billings and accounted for much of its reputation. In work for clients other than Miles, Wade had proved to be an aggressive shop. As a media buyer, it focused on acquiring prime slots for clients with popular television and radio shows. (In 1951 more than 75 percent of its overall billings were for radio and television.) It used acquisition as a growth strategy, buying up smaller agencies, such as H.W. Kastor & Sons in 1960. Major accounts followed when it opened new offices and took personnel from other agencies. In addition, Wade picked up the Alberto-Culver account in 1956 and Martin Marietta's construction materials business in 1961. Total billings grew from $9 million in 1950 to more than $26 million in 1960.

In October 1963 the agency tried a new tactic for increasing its local visibility and influence by sponsoring a TV panel show, *Mid-America Marketing on the March* on Chicago's primary independent station, WGN. This weekly show, which aired no commercials, featured interviews with top executives and major midwestern companies.

It was its role with Miles, however, that determined the agency's success. While Forrest Owen, president of Wade, tried to hold the business together after the departure of Alka-Seltzer, everything started to unravel. Accounts left, including Falstaff Brewing and Seven-Up Bottling of Los Angeles, California; the loss of key executives followed. Then, slowly, the other Miles lines departed; in 1965 Bactine went to Tinker, leaving only the Miles One-A-Day and Chocks vitamins accounts at Wade. Wade came close to merging with the Compton Agency, a unit of Interpublic, in 1964, but account conflicts and the desire of many employees to remain independent prevented it.

In January 1966, after a solid client presentation to Miles for its vitamin lines, Wade Advertising realized it had a losing battle on its hands. Miles was taking away the rest of its business. Jeff Wade made a deal with Interpublic conceding the remaining Miles business to Tinker, while retaining a position on Tinker's account team. Whether the deal would have gone through regardless of Wade's interest in this role was a subject of some debate. The Toni Company, another key account, switched to Tinker just days later. Within two weeks of the Miles decision, the historic Wade agency closed its doors.

DEBORAH HAWKINS

Further Reading

Cray, William C., *Miles, 1884–1984: A Centennial History,* Englewood Cliffs, New Jersey: Prentice Hall, 1984

McGeehan, Pat, "The Burrell Style Building a Solid Base on Michigan Avenue," *Advertising Age* (19 December 1985)

"Miles Okay Key to Compton-Wade Merger Proposal," *Advertising Age* (27 April 1964)

"Thurber Leaves Wade to Set Up Chicago Lennen and Newell Unit," *Advertising Age* (14 June 1965)

Vobrecht, John L., "A Writer's Account of Wade's Last 12 Days," *Advertising Age* (31 January 1968)

Wal-Mart Stores, Inc.

Principal Agencies

Bernstein-Rein

GSD&M

E. Morris Communications

Lopez Negrete Communications

Sam Walton started Wal-Mart Stores, Inc., in 1962 with a single 16,000-square-foot outlet in Rogers, Arkansas—a humble beginning for a company that by the end of the 20th century was the largest and most powerful retailer in the United States, with almost 2,000 Wal-Mart stores, close to 500 supercenters, 450 Sam's Club stores, and yearly sales exceeding $165 billion. As part of its effort to maintain low, competitive prices, its advertising spending-to-sales ratio has always been low. Wal-Mart ranked as the 63rd-largest spender in the United States in 2000, according to *Advertising Age;* spending totaled $497.8 million, with most of the dollars allocated to network and spot TV. By comparison, Sears, Roebuck & Company spent $1.4 billion that same year. Wal-Mart is highly effective in its advertising, generating more than $250 in sales per ad dollar versus less than $60 by Kmart Corporation and less than $40 by Sears.

Walton was 44 and already a successful businessman when he started the business. In his travels he began to see the potential of the then-fledgling discount store, such as Kmart. Walton decided to go into business, targeting rural markets. The first store communicated Walton's message with signs on the front of the store that said, "We sell for less" and "Satisfaction guaranteed." Those words continue to adorn Wal-Mart stores and became the inspiration for subsequent advertising campaigns.

Although some retailers had reservations about his early stores, Walton pressed on, keeping costs low and his enthusiasm for the business high. By early 1969 he had opened 13 Wal-Mart stores and was planning a 70,000-square-foot warehouse and headquarters. Stores expanded in size to add such new merchandise as men's and women's apparel. By year-end Wal-Mart mushroomed to 31 stores. One year later Wal-Mart completed a public offering. That was the start of a rapid growth period that propelled Wal-Mart to the forefront of U.S. retailing.

In the 1970s the success stories of the Bentonville, Arkansas–based retailer began to circulate. Although the initial public offering in 1970 was small—300,000 shares priced at $16.50 per share—it gave Walton the money he needed to expand his chain.

Until 1974 Wal-Mart handled all its advertising in-house, keeping expenditures low. While most major mass merchants typically put 52 circulars into the hands of customers each year, Wal-Mart only published 11. Instead of touting sales on certain items, the advertising was institutional to convey the retailer's "always-low-price" strategy, a philosophy that remained in place at the beginning of the 21st century. Wal-Mart also built a reputation for customer service through such touches as a greeter who welcomes customers as they enter the store and directs them to what they need.

In 1974 Walton contacted Kansas City, Missouri–based Bernstein-Rein to handle its advertising. Walton had seen spots the agency did for a local supermarket and thought it would fit with Wal-Mart's corporate culture. Working with Wal-Mart executives, Bernstein-Rein created advertising that educated shoppers about Wal-Mart's "everyday-low-pricing" strategy. The agency remained part of Wal-Mart's advertising strategy into the 21st century, under the direction of Paul Higham, senior vice president of marketing for Wal-Mart, and Rusty Scholtes, senior vice president of Bernstein-Rein. The ads have often featured Wal-Mart shoppers talking about their feelings about the retailer.

One notable campaign, "Watch for falling prices," introduced around 1993, showed price signs falling and crashing to reveal lower prices as Patsy Cline's song "I Fall to Pieces" played in the

"Versa always comes into the garden shop to see what's growing. But our warm friendship is, by far, what's growing best."

Verna
Assistant Manager
Jacksonville, FL

Friendly Service and Low Prices...

WAL★MART
Always.

Wal-Mart's "Always" campaign, seen in a 1997 ad, depicted the marketer's competitive prices and helpful employees.
Courtesy of Wal-Mart Stores, Inc., and E. Morris Communications.

background. That effort led to further campaigns featuring the price rollback theme. Bernstein-Rein also handled some category advertising, such as photo and paint, and spots highlighting Wal-Mart's corporate charitable missions.

Analysis of what did and did not sell helped Wal-Mart grow to 276 stores by the end of 1979 with sales of $1.25 billion and earnings of $41.2 million. As the 1980s unfolded Wal-Mart's reputation flourished. It added food to its retail mix and expanded into international markets. There were concerns, however. The ability of Wal-Mart's regional, homegrown philosophy to work on a larger scale was questioned, as well as whether a succession plan could be instituted to keep management as fresh as it had been under Walton. Wal-Mart proved it was ahead of the technology game, and that outweighed any negative aspects of its grassroots form of management. In 1980 Wal-Mart was one of the first chains to test universal price code scanners (UPC). The net benefits were improved cashier productivity and greater distribution efficiencies. From fiscal year 1980 to fiscal year 1990, Wal-Mart soared from sales of $1.25 billion and 276 stores to 1,500 stores with sales of $25.8 billion.

The 1980s also saw Wal-Mart delve into other retailing formats. In 1983 Wal-Mart opened its first Sam's Club, a wholesale club. Wal-Mart flirted unsuccessfully with a hypermarket format

in the mid-1980s, but the company eventually used the knowledge it gained from this experiment to open supercenters.

In 1988 Wal-Mart added more layers to its advertising, hiring San Antonio, Texas–based GSD&M, which further helped it grow from a regional power to a national presence. The agency continued creating advertisements centered on the retailer's price image, while establishing Wal-Mart's reputation for offering brands consumers trust.

In the 1990s Wal-Mart reached the $100 billion sales mark and surpassed Kmart Corporation as the nation's largest discount retailer. In 1990 it acquired McLane Company, a wholesale distributor familiar with the food distribution business that Wal-Mart needed for its superstores. Wal-Mart also began expanding into Puerto Rico in 1990.

Sam Walton died in April 1992, shortly after President George H. Bush awarded him the Medal of Freedom, the nation's highest civilian award. Rob Walton replaced his father as chairman of the company. Sam Walton's ideas and thoughts continue to echo throughout the chain's headquarters. The "post-Sam" era has been highlighted by international growth as well as by such new strategies as a small-store format that can fit into established neighborhoods.

In the mid-1990s chains found that price specials alone were no longer enough to draw customers. Wal-Mart initiated its "Always" campaign, emphasizing that its prices were always low. At the end of 1993 Wal-Mart recorded measured media spending of $104.2 million. In the late 1990s Bernstein-Rein introduced a smiley face in its advertising to represent its philosophy of rolling back prices. Despite its "everyday-low-price" strategy, Wal-Mart found the rollback theme more successful in drawing customers. The ubiquitous smiley face was repeated in its monthly circulars and in-store signage.

Recognizing the importance of taking its message to all customers, Wal-Mart in 1993 tapped E. Morris Communications, of Chicago, Illinois, to help introduce African-Americans to Wal-Mart. Morris helped add a visible African-American presence to the company's advertising. In 1997 Wal-Mart added Lopez Negrete Communications, Houston, Texas, to its roster to aid in courting Latino shoppers.

Wal-Mart's pricing strategy has not been without some problems. A predatory pricing lawsuit in Arkansas resulted in Wal-Mart's admittance that it sold merchandise below cost; however, it did not admit to predatory pricing practices. Shortly after the case, Wal-Mart changed its slogan from "Always the low price" to "Always low prices." The National Advertising Review Board ruled the old slogan communicated that its low prices were always the lowest rather than just competitive. Wal-Mart also experienced trouble with a "Buy American" advertising program. The chain was faulted for saying that it bought mostly U.S.-based products, when many items on its shelves were imported. Subsequently, the "Buy American" statement was dropped from promotional materials.

Wal-Mart's size and power have also made it the target of many lawsuits ranging from those brought by towns that did not want the gigantic stores to those brought by married couples who were told they could not work in the same store. A particular public relations headache occurred in June 2001, when Wal-Mart was charged with discriminating against women in promotions, pay, and job assignments.

In 1998 Wal-Mart entered the United Kingdom with the purchase of Asda, that country's third-largest supermarket chain. Asda was already mimicking many of Wal-Mart's strategies, including its "everyday low pricing." As Wal-Mart continued to expand abroad, the company hired local advertising agencies to market its brand. For example, Wal-Mart tapped Uilot Media of Hamburg for its German campaign. In the United States Wal-Mart launched its Neighborhood Stores, combining a discount store and a drug chain. As of 2001 Wal-Mart was edging toward $200 billion in annual sales.

FAYE BROOKMAN

Further Reading

Huey, John, "100 Builders and Titans," *Time* (7 December 1998)

Ortega, Bob, *In Sam We Trust: The Untold Story of Sam Walton, and How Wal-Mart Is Devouring America*, New York: Times Business, 1998; London: Kogan Page, 1999

"Power Retailer: Wal-Mart," *Discount Store News* (7 June 1999) (special annual issue)

"Retailer of the Century: Wal-Mart," *Chain Store Age* 75, no. 13 (December 1999)

Thompson, Molly, producer and director, *Sam Walton: Bargain Billionaire* (videorecording), New York: A and E Home Video, 1997

Walton, Sam, and John Huey, *Sam Walton, Made in America: My Story*, New York: Doubleday, 1992

Wanamaker, John 1838–1922

U.S. Retail Advertising Pioneer

John Wanamaker set the standard for retail advertising at the beginning of the 20th century when he helped pioneer such revolutionary ideas as fixed prices and money-back guarantees at his department stores in Philadelphia, Pennsylvania, and in New York City. Wanamaker was a religious man who refused to advertise on Sundays and never sold playing cards in his stores. His desire for honesty, openness, and fair dealing served him well throughout his career, standing him in good stead with his customers.

As a boy, Wanamaker edited a small periodical, *Everybody's Journal*. This experience taught him the benefits of publicity. At the age of 14, Wanamaker began working as an errand boy for a bookstore in Philadelphia. He later became secretary of the city's Young Men's Christian Association (YMCA), a position he held from 1857 to 1861.

A temperate Presbyterian, Wanamaker considered entering the ministry but instead decided to go into business. Still, he had an evangelical purpose: "The idea clung to my mind that I could accomplish more in the same domain if I became a merchant and acquired means and influence with fellow merchants."

Wanamaker entered into a business partnership with his brother-in-law, Nathan Brown. With $3,500 in capital, they opened Wanamaker and Brown (W&B) in the Oak Hall Building in Philadelphia, with "one price" as the store's policy and men's tailor-made clothes as its merchandise. The U.S. Civil War was just beginning as the store opened for business in 1861.

Unfortunately, most people walked right past those open doors. The capital was rapidly being depleted when Wanamaker learned of a clothing manufacturer anxious to dispose of surplus stock during the troubled times. W&B bought the stock and touted the "Oak Hall Clothing Bazaar" as selling ready-made men's clothing in six separate ads, each with a different headline, on the front page of the *Philadelphia Public Ledger*. The ads were a success, and the business began to prosper. Throughout the next few years, when uniforms for Union Army officers were the mainstay of the business, W&B put every available dollar into advertising in order to continue to build the enterprise.

Not only did W&B use newspaper advertising, it also used stunt publicity: 20-foot balloons were sent up, and a suit of clothes was given to each person who brought one back to the store. When "tally-ho coaching" became popular, Oak Hall employees, dressed in the most fashionable coaching clothes, traveled the country scattering advertisements to the sound of the horn. The advertising paid off. By 1869 W&B had become the largest retailer of men's clothing in the United States, with Wanamaker continuing to expand the business after his partner's death in 1868. He formed John Wanamaker & Company in 1869 as a separate entity from W&B. While W&B's advertising continued to emphasize low prices, the new company appealed to customers who desired quality and elegance.

Wanamaker astonished his rivals in 1865 when he announced a new policy guaranteeing a full refund if the purchaser was not

John Wanamaker.

satisfied for any reason, so long as the item was returned within ten days. A quick foray into bankruptcy was predicted for the entrepreneur. However, Wanamaker's trust in the quality of his goods paid off, and his business continued to grow.

Wanamaker's next expansion targeted Philadelphia's Grand Depot. The Pennsylvania Railroad had built a large temporary depot in the city for the nation's centennial celebrations. After the centennial exposition closed, Wanamaker purchased the station to house his third store. The depot included two acres of aisles and showcases—more room than Wanamaker could use for men's clothing displays. When he could not convince other merchants to open shop under his roof, he added women's wear and household goods to his inventory, thus creating the first department store.

The Grand Depot became the first large general store in the United States. Hailing it as the "new kind of store," advance advertising lured 70,000 people to the opening day—when nothing was yet for sale. The following day, Wanamaker was dubbed the "Merchant Prince."

The opening of this third store marked a more widespread influence in advertising for Wanamaker. Until this point, he had advertised extensively, increasing his advertising in response to any problem. However, he now began several innovations that were to become commonplace.

Wanamaker's primary contribution to the development of advertising was his use of large space ads. He began to buy full-page ads for his businesses; while expensive, these pages also resulted in a large volume of sales for the retailer. Wanamaker was the first to use such advertising, showing others that money spent in this manner paid off. He ran the first page ad for a U.S. store in 1879; he often ran ads of two to four columns. In 1888 he began to use page ads regularly, and in 1909, this became a daily practice.

In 1880 Wanamaker hired John E. Powers as a full-time department store copywriter, another advertising innovation. While their personal relationship was troubled, their professional relationship was strong, as Powers adhered to Wanamaker's philosophy of honesty and truth in advertising. Powers's style—stressing common sense, direct and factual copy, and content over style—through time was widely emulated among advertisers.

Other merchants began to study, and then to copy, Wanamaker's style in advertising, as it became clear that he owed much of his success to his ads. Along with Powers, Robert C. Ogden and Manly M. Gillam produced Wanamaker's advertising of the era. Wanamaker insisted on sincerity and honesty in copy, layout, and type, and considered other aspects of format secondary. Merchants throughout the nation subscribed to the Philadelphia papers so they could read Wanamaker's ads; it was not unusual to see the department store's ads—merchandise and copy—used throughout the nation after the ads appeared in Philadelphia. One adman made it his business to supply ideas from the ads to other merchants, while an ad journal published in Philadelphia is said to have been established specifically to supply suggestions gleaned from Wanamaker's copy.

In 1896 Wanamaker purchased A.T. Stewart and Company, a waning, well-known dry goods store that occupied a six-story building covering a full city block in New York City. After the acquisition, it was remarked that "John Wanamaker does more advertising in a week than A.T. Stewart and Company did in a year."

Wanamaker frequently is credited with the now famous saying, "I know half the money I spend on advertising is wasted, but I can never find out which half." (He was probably aware that this was also uttered by the English Lord Leverhulme.)

Wanamaker also supported political and religious causes. He founded the Bethany Sunday School of Philadelphia in 1858; he ran for several political offices; he offered his employees time off for military service. He also provided business classes and benefits for his employees, practices uncommon at the time.

Wanamaker served as postmaster general of the United States from 1889 to 1893. He is credited with making several improvements in the post office, including the establishment of the parcel post system.

BARBARA KNOLL

Biography

Born 13 November 1838; opened Wanamaker and Brown (W&B) men's clothing store in Philadelphia, Pennsylvania, 1861; through creative use of advertising, W&B became the country's largest men's clothing retailer, 1869; opened John Wanamaker & Company, which became the country's first department store with the addition of women's wear and housewares, 1869; hired John E. Powers as a full-time copywriter for Wanamaker, the first retail store to hire its own copywriter, 1880; served as United States postmaster general, 1889–93; died 12 December 1922.

Further Reading

Fox, Stephen R., *The Mirror Makers: A History of American Advertising and Its Creators*, New York: Morrow, 1984

Presbrey, Frank, *The History and Development of Advertising*, Garden City, New York: Doubleday, Doran, 1929; reprint, New York: Greenwood Press, 1968

War, Impact on Advertising of

When a country goes to war, many of its essential resources, goods, and services either become unavailable or are severely limited. Mass-production facilities are converted to military production, thereby eliminating or curtailing the manufacture of most consumer goods. Ad budgets supporting durable consumer goods such as automobiles and refrigerators are diverted, as sales of such goods decrease. Business slows and strategies are changed. As noted by *Advertising & Selling* magazine in March 1942, "With nothing to sell the public, advertising must concern itself with intangibles."

The U.S. advertising industry's activities during both world wars offer insight into the development of new trends in the industry as well as paralleling advertising's professional ascendancy. During the major conflicts of the 20th century, the American ad industry managed to grow despite a dearth of new consumer goods to market. Ad industry executives were able to shift their emphasis from selling immediate gratification to promoting patriotism and faith in the industry as one voice of democracy.

World War I

In 1916 President Woodrow Wilson was reelected by a narrow margin with the slogan, "He kept us out of war." But after Germany sank several American ships at sea, the United States in February 1917 cut diplomatic ties with Germany, and Wilson had to quickly establish a policy on how to deal with the negative public opinion that would surround the country's entry into the war. Rather than clamping down on news and introducing censorship, President Wilson decided to flood the media with pro-war publicity to enlist support from a diverse population whose members held widely differing opinions as to what his actions should be. Laborers perceived the conflict as a rich man's war; immigrant groups with cultural links to Europe were accused of being security risks; Irish-Americans' hostilities toward England, an ally of the United States, raised concern; and even white, Protestant, middle-class Americans championed isolationism. On 6 April 1917 the United States declared war against Germany, and a week later, on 13 April, President Wilson by executive order created the Committee on Public Information (CPI) to handle that effort, with the progressive journalist George Creel as its chairman.

The CPI's job was to organize the flow of information that connected the average citizen with the federal government through media already familiar to Americans. The CPI maintained that the United States' participation in the war was a struggle to preserve democracy. Implicit in this message was the argument that no "real" American would allow democracy to falter. Yet, the CPI's mandate was not intended to coerce patriotism, but rather to allow citizens to arrive at "correct" assumptions made through logical arguments. By disciplining the course and content of information, a form of truth could be manufactured and the public mind effectively managed.

The CPI was divided into departments that oversaw different media channels, such as the Division of Syndicated Features, the Film Division and the Bureau of Cartoons, the Division of News, the Division of Advertising, and the Division of Pictorial Publicity. William H. Johns, president of the American Association of Advertising Agencies, led the Division of Advertising, formed in 1918. Johns's division acted as a clearinghouse to organize the volunteer efforts of the country's ad agencies and ad people. It was also supposed to make war advertising more efficient by managing all ad copy preparations and designs. This management involved improving coordination among advertisers, agencies, government organizations, and media channels; preparing copy and artwork; and providing any advertising planning and design service except for dealing with printing costs, editorials, and securing ad space. While brokering space was not one of the division's responsibilities, each company that donated space had its name printed beneath the CPI and Division of Advertising's seal: "This space contributed to the winning of the war by. . . ." Johns encouraged businesses to link their names and brands with war information dispatched by the agency. Under the Division of Advertising's direction, $2.25 million in ad space ultimately was donated, $1.6 million of which was directly used by the division.

According to Creel's estimates, in peacetime the Division of Advertising's services would have cost $5 million—all of which the government received gratis. Such largesse in the donation of ad space and time set an important precedent for the advertising

There's Something About a Uniform . . .

...and something more behind it— a national change of mind. Today Compton fact-finding continues to help the advertising of our clients keep pace with America's beliefs, hopes and fears.

Have the recent changes in America's thinking suggested a change in your advertising thinking? A change, perhaps, in what you're saying in your advertising? A new and closer look at down-the-scale media? Consideration of newly prosperous marketing areas?

Compton clients are getting facts that answer these questions as part of normal adver-

tising practice. Compton research into minds, markets and media is always carried out *before* an advertising campaign runs. We use a wide variety of methods—many of which we have developed ourselves. And the advertising that results is based not on last year's practice or this year's guess—*but on today's cold facts.*

Compton fact-finding has played an important part in the sales curve we reprint here. It represents the sales of all Compton-advertised products in both good years and bad.

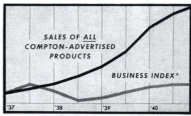

Federal Reserve Board Index of Non-Durable Manufactures

COMPTON ADVERTISING, INC.
630 FIFTH AVENUE, NEW YORK

The copy in this 1941 ad alluded to the changes in Americans' thinking as a result of the war and promoted Compton Advertising's ability to meet marketers' wartime advertising needs.

industry, which continues to produce pro bono advertising for public service today.

The Division of Pictorial Publicity was led by the illustrator Charles Dana Gibson, the creator of the popular feminine icons known as "Gibson Girls." Gibson's approach made emotional appeals to the American public rather than logical arguments. While Creel envisioned the CPI as "a vast enterprise in salesmanship, the world's greatest adventure in advertising," under Gibson, the Division of Pictorial Publicity actually undermined Creel's progressive notion of a public prepared to be convinced by rational arguments. It operated instead on the assumption that the public psyche was largely illogical and could more effectively be led to embrace a cause through emotional appeals.

Gibson's division used traditional techniques of illustration rather than the modernist graphics that characterized war posters produced by the Germans and Austrians. Following avant-garde design trends, European posters produced by the Central Powers wove slogans and images together in bold, two-dimensional patterns. The pictorial aspects of Allied posters and ads tended toward the literal, and thus communicated through complex narrative scenarios or allegories. In James Montgomery Flagg's famous 1917 "I Want You" poster, a scowling Uncle Sam leans toward potential recruits with a finger aimed at the viewer.

One of the best-remembered ads from World War I featured the headline, "The greatest mother in the world," and depicted a nurse cradling in her arms a wounded soldier who lies on a stretcher. The triangular composition and the woman's monumental image draped in layers of flowing cloth recall Michelangelo's *Pietà*—an appropriate pictorial metaphor for the mother mourning a son. The ad, written by the Alley & Richards agency's Court Smith and illustrated by A.E. Foringer, was done for the American Red Cross. Its tag line was, "Every dollar of a Red Cross War Fund goes to war relief."

In 1917 overall advertising spending reached $1.6 billion. While that dropped to $1.5 billion in 1918, the final year of the war, spending rebounded to $2.3 billion in 1919.

World War II

The U.S. ad industry's role during World War II went beyond selling bonds and promoting rationing. Marketers were wary of the possible negative impact that converting their manufacturing operations to producing military equipment—such as bombs, tanks, and guns—might have on their brands and services. Some observers, however, contended that the threat to trademarks, brand names, and market niches—all of which consumers could begin to forget if they were no longer supported by advertising—should be a strong argument to businesses to continue their advertising during the conflict. In 1941 *Advertising & Selling* wrote: "Public morale . . . will suffer more . . . if consumers are forgotten by the corporations that have been in the pattern of their lives for years. . . . Once a corporation or its products become forgotten, then they are well on the way to becoming non-existent."

Rejecting government-backed organizations such as the CPI, President Franklin Roosevelt wanted his administration to remain only tacitly engaged in advertising the war. Roosevelt, who rose to power in an age when public relations and advertising had attained great persuasive authority, recognized that advertising was better suited to engineering consent than was the government. Furthermore, allowing ad makers to sell war bonds and to promote recruitment, salvage drives, and rationing programs not only freed the government from charges that it might be using the media to promote negative propaganda but also lifted from it the burden and the cost of advertising its programs.

The WAC

Leaders in the ad industry offered their expertise to the government, forming the War Advertising Council (WAC) in February 1942, a public message service run and financed by the advertising industry.

The WAC, first chaired by Young & Rubicam's Chester J. La-Roche and staffed by volunteers from agencies and the media, was organized to help manage government campaigns to engage civilian support for the war. WAC leaders wanted the organization to exemplify the positive aspects of advertising, serving as an ethical model for the rest of the industry. The council set out to locate sponsors that would cover costs and to distribute to advertisers guides on how to incorporate official war messages into their ad copy and images, including public service announcements about buying war bonds, abstaining from luxuries, preventing venereal disease, and recruiting women into war service and production.

The OWI

Despite the WAC's efforts, bureaucratic problems of government agency overlap and lack of consolidation arose. In an attempt to alleviate those problems, President Roosevelt created the Office of War Information (OWI) in June 1942. The OWI, which, unlike the WAC, was a government-run agency, functioned as a central clearinghouse for disseminating information and news about the war to the public and the media. In September 1942, OWI Director Elmer Davis, a journalist and broadcaster, appointed former NBC marketing director Ken R. Dyke as head of the OWI's Bureau of Campaigns, and Gardner Cowles, Jr., a midwestern newspaper publisher, as director of the agency's domestic branch. Cowles in turn selected Price Gilbert, a former advertising manager of Coca-Cola Company, to head the Bureau of Graphics and Printing, and he gave key positions in other OWI units to media executives from radio and Hollywood.

The OWI had retained members of the Office of Facts and Figures (OFF), the agency that the OWI supplanted in 1942. OFF had been headed by Librarian of Congress Archibald MacLeish and had included a number of liberal writers who wanted to infuse war information with social idealism. These writers clashed with their counterparts from the advertising industry and grew increasingly disdainful of the commercialism they perceived

This 1955 Revlon advertisement urged women to declare war on chapped hands with its Aquamarine Lotion, newly fortified with an ingredient developed during World War II.
Courtesy Revlon Consumer Products Corporation.

as infiltrating their moral efforts. The liberal-minded members of the OWI embraced campaigns such as Ben Shahn's poster of 1943, "This is Nazi brutality," in which the socialist-oriented idioms of modern art were used to define the war effort in moralistic terms—not commercial ones. The battle ended with the demise in 1943 of the domestic branch of the OWI. Despite excess-profits taxes (which cut into advertising budgets), hostile criticism, and a lack of consumer products to sell, advertisers championed the war effort, associating victory with the "American Way" and the free-enterprise system.

Wartime Advertising

Nash/Kelvinator wartime ads by the Geyer, Cornell & Newell agency were typical of the campaigns that linked patriotism and free enterprise. The Nash/Kelvinator ads, placed in both women's and trade magazines, put the viewer in the mind of an infantry soldier as he entered battle:

I'm not outguessing madmen with machine guns in their hands for the privilege of being told what to say and when to say it. I'm fighting for freedom! I'm fighting for the things that made America the greatest place in the world to

live in. . . . So don't anybody tell me I'll find America changed. . . . Don't anybody tell me there's a ceiling on my opportunity to make a million or be president. . . . That's what took the humanity out of the men I'm up against now. . . . I want to come back to the same America I left behind me . . . where our way of living has always brought us new and better things . . . That's what I'm fighting for.

War-bond advertisements, such as those for the General Electric Company from N.W. Ayer & Son, Inc., and Maxon, Inc., used similar tactics: "And this shall be our victory: In a free nation . . . each home shall be a shrine of freedom." Democracy was linked in war-bond ads with the freedom to make consumer choices. Bond campaigns equated patriotism with capitalism through "the world of tomorrow" theme, in which tantalizing displays of "revolutionary" consumer products were paraded before an American public. An ad from Armco Sheet Metals, published in *American Home* magazine (May 1942), pictured the war as a battle to achieve a higher standard of living. Images of a future filled with streamlined kitchens and houses in the suburbs attracted would-be bond buyers with the notion that they could enter the middle class. Hotpoint's ads from Maxon, such as one that ran in *Life* magazine, promoted the war effort through promises of a "new and improved" domestic life after victory:

Buy War Bonds today—electric kitchens tomorrow. . . . Every dollar I spend for War Bonds gives me a great big thrill of satisfaction! I figure I'm not only helping win the war but hastening the day when I'll be able to own the kitchen I've always dreamed about.

The "world of tomorrow" theme conveyed to consumers the idea that advertisers intended to work for progress in peacetime just as they were helping to win the war. In reinforcing public confidence in American business' abilities, the advertising industry also reinforced its role promoting marketers' products and services, which would once again become available to consumers as American business converted to peacetime production. While corporate patriotism promoted the unselfish side of business and built consumer goodwill, ads envisioning the postwar world cemented the relationship between marketers and the average consumer with the promise of a better America.

Perhaps the most well-known campaign to come out of World War II was the 1943–44 Libbey-Owens-Ford (L-O-F) "Kitchen of Tomorrow," designed by H. Creston Doner, which was featured not only in magazines and newspapers across the country, but also mass-marketed in a Paramount film short. In addition, three models of the "Kitchen of Tomorrow" traveled around the country, to be experienced in person by more than 1.6 million visitors. The L-O-F kitchen was based on several postwar kitchen prototypes advertised throughout the war years in women's and business magazines by architects, designers, and manufacturers such as Revere Copper and Brass, Bundy Tubing, and Superior Steel. Manufacturers of almost every sort of product, including plastics and electronics, advertised their version of the "kitchen of tomorrow," and like Libbey-Owens-Ford, showed how their wartime contributions would revolutionize domesticity after victory. The L-O-F kitchen, similar to its counterparts, had a built-in, glass-covered oven, glass-front storage cabinets, a built-in drawer refrigerator as well as vertical, glass refrigerator space. Appliances such as a waffle iron and an electric mixer were built into the countertops. The main argument behind such utopian images of the postwar world, as epitomized by the popular L-O-F kitchen, was that when American manufacturers applied their war-won knowledge to civilian production once again, they could easily liberate domesticity as they had Asia and Europe.

According to *Advertising Age,* the number of ad agencies in the United States grew from 1,628 in 1939 to 5,986 in 1948. Advertising spending dipped slightly after the United States entered the war, from $2.23 billion in 1941 to $2.16 billion in 1942, but total advertising spending increased steadily throughout the war years, reaching $2.88 billion at the end of 1945. Overall, the WAC claimed it allocated $1 billion in donated advertising media space and work time toward war-themed ads from 1942 to 1945. After the end of World War II the War Advertising Council became the Advertising Council, composed of advertisers, agencies, and the media, which continues to provide ad campaigns to public service organizations.

CYNTHIA LEE HENTHORN

Further Reading

Brandes, Stuart D., *Warhogs: A History of War Profits in America,* Lexington: University Press of Kentucky, 1997

Buitenhuis, Peter, *The Great War of Words: British, American, and Canadian Propaganda and Fiction, 1914–1933,* Vancouver: University of British Columbia Press, 1987

Census Bureau and Social Science Research Council, *Historical Statistics of the United States: Colonial Times to 1957,* Washington, D.C.: U.S. Department of Commerce and Bureau of the Census, 1960

Ewen, Stuart, *PR! A Social History of Spin,* New York: Basic Books, 1996

Fox, Frank W., *Madison Avenue Goes to War: The Strange Military Career of American Advertising, 1941–1945,* Provo, Utah: Brigham Young University, 1975

Frank, Thomas C., *The Conquest of Cool: Business Culture, Counterculture, and the Rise of Hip Consumerism,* Chicago: University of Chicago Press, 1997

Griffith, Robert, "The Selling of America: The Advertising Council and American Politics, 1942–1960," *Business History Review* 57 (Autumn 1983)

Haddow, Robert H., *Pavilions of Plenty: Exhibiting American Culture Abroad in the 1950s,* Washington, D.C., and London: Smithsonian Institution Press, 1997

Henthorn, Cynthia Lee, "Commercial Fallout: The Image of Progress, the Culture of War, and the Feminine Consumer from World War II to the Atomic Age," in *The Writing on the Cloud: American Culture Confronts the Atomic Bomb,* edited by Christopher G. Geist and Alison Scott, Lanham, Maryland: University of America Press, 1997

Henthorn, Cynthia Lee, "The Emblematic Kitchen: Household Technology as National Propaganda, U.S.A., 1939–1959," *Journal of Knowledge and Society* 12 (2000)

"The Impact of War on Advertising" (32 articles in the series), *Advertising and Selling* (January 1942–July 1944)

Martin, Susan, *Decade of Protest: Political Posters from the United States, Viet Nam, Cuba, 1965–1975,* Santa Monica: Smart Art Press, 1996

Oakes, Guy, *The Imaginary War: Civil Defense and American Cold War Culture,* New York and Oxford: Oxford University Press, 1994

Sentman, Mary Alice, and Patrick S. Washburn, "How Excess Profits Tax Brought Ads to Black Newspapers in World War II," *Journalism Quarterly* 64 (1987)

Vaughn, Stephen, *Holding Fast the Inner Lines: Democracy, Nationalism, and the Committee on Public Information,* Chapel Hill: University of North Carolina Press, 1980

Winkler, Allan M., *The Politics of Propaganda: The Office of War Information, 1942–1945,* New Haven, Connecticut: Yale University Press, 1978

War Bonds

Modern warfare is expensive, and governments, in seeking to raise necessary funds, must take care to avoid triggering inflation by increasing the demand for goods. One way to avoid inflation is to raise taxes, but this is a method that risks making a war unpopular. Selling bonds, on the other hand, is a method of financing war that reduces the demand for goods and services by taking money out of circulation and redirecting it toward the war effort. War bonds thus reduce the need for tax increases; instead, citizens invest in the government just as they might invest in the private sector.

During World War I the U.S. government raised $5 billion through the sale of Liberty Bonds, enlisting the aid of celebrities such as actor Douglas Fairbanks. But in general, when people use

During World War II ads that graphically depicted the harsh realities of war made an emotional appeal to the American public to buy war bonds.
Courtesy of Honeywell Consumer Products Group.

the term *war bonds*, they are referring to those sold during World War II. In part this is because both the number of bonds sold and the scale of the media campaign to promote them were considerably greater than during World War I. World War II was also the last U.S. war to be financed by the sale of bonds.

From 1 May 1941 to 3 January 1946 the Defense (later War) Savings Program, a division in the U.S. Department of the Treasury, sold $185.7 billion worth of war bonds through a series of radio and print advertisements, posters, sales drives, and mailings. Among the factors that contributed to the success of the effort was the assembling of a huge sales force made up of some 500,000 committee volunteers and another 5 million to 6 million volunteers who were known as "minute men." The treasury had full access to the media, which provided free space and time estimated to be worth more than a quarter of a billion dollars. Through the offices of the War Advertising Council, led by Young & Rubicam's Chester J. LaRoche, it also had the use of the staffs of leading agencies. Among those who donated their services was Edward Dexter, also of Young & Rubicam. Thomas Hart Benton and Norman Rockwell were among the artists who produced war bond posters. Mailing lists, along with certain information on income supplied by the Internal Revenue Service, were additional marketing tools.

Various segments of the population were targeted with specific appeals. New parents, for example, were sent certificates designed by the Walt Disney Studios urging them to buy bonds for their babies. The Inter-Racial Section of the War Savings Program, headed by William Pickens, the field director of the National Association for the Advancement of Colored People, targeted the African-American population; specific ethnic groups were addressed via radio and the foreign-language press. The youth market was also included. Comic book publishers carried advertisements and columns urging readers to tell their parents to buy bonds and exhorting the youngsters themselves to purchase ten-cent defense stamps. The covers of *Batman* and *Superman* comics appealed to readers to buy war bonds with slogans such as "Keep Those Bullets Flying" and "Slap a Jap."

Henry Morgenthau, secretary of the treasury at the time, said that he wanted "to use bonds to sell the war, rather than vice versa." He believed that there were quicker and easier ways for the government to raise money but that getting people to buy bonds would increase their stake in the war effort. The advertising and sale of war bonds went hand in hand with the broader strategy of the advertising industry known as "A war message in every ad." Many businesses, such as the California department stores May Company and Foreman & Clark, promoted the purchase of war bonds as part of their regular advertising.

Bond drives featuring celebrities were another sales tool. In a single day in 1943, for example, singer Kate Smith sold $40 million in bonds in a 16-hour radio session. Actress Loretta Young sold bonds at a Kiwanis meeting, and Hollywood star Betty Grable auctioned off her stockings at a fund-raising event.

Bonds are, of course, only one of the means at a government's disposal for regulating a wartime economy and financing a war. During World War II the cost of living in the United States increased by 33 percent. Most of the increase occurred before 1943, when the government put strict price controls in place through the Office of Price Administration. The Revenue Act of 1942 established a new U.S. tax structure, which saw the country's tax base increase fourfold and which introduced tax withholding. Through these measures the government raised about 50 percent of its war expenses. This was a considerable increase over the 30 percent generated by taxes during World War I and the 23 percent derived from taxes during the Civil War. Thus, bonds accounted for only about a quarter of the government's costs of waging World War II—although they sparked some of the most colorful advertising efforts of the day.

IAN GORDON

See also Military Advertising

Further Reading

Blum, John Morton, *V Was for Victory: Politics and American Culture during World War II*, New York: Harcourt Brace Jovanovich, 1976

Fox, Frank W., *Madison Avenue Goes to War: The Strange Military Career of American Advertising, 1941–45*, Provo, Utah: Brigham Young University Press, 1975

Marchand, Roland, *Creating the Corporate Soul: The Rise of Public Relations and Corporate Imagery in American Big Business*, Berkeley: University of California Press, 1998

Polenberg, Richard, *War and Society: The United States, 1941–1945*, Philadelphia, Pennsylvania: Lippincott, 1972

Samuel, Lawrence R., *Pledging Allegiance: American Identity and the Bond Drive of World War II*, Washington, D.C.: Smithsonian Institution Press, 1997

Warner-Lambert

Principal Agencies

J. Walter Thompson Company

Ted Bates & Company (later Bates USA)

William R. Warner & Company, a pharmaceuticals and cosmetics marketer, was founded in 1920. For the next three decades, the company and its successor, Warner-Hudnut, Inc., acquired dozens of businesses in the consumer health care and pharmaceuticals industries, including prescription drug maker New Jersey Chilcott Laboratories. Warner-Hudnut merged with the Lambert Pharmacal Company, best known as the marketer of Listerine, and on 31 March 1955 Warner-Lambert was born.

Warner-Lambert's aggressive acquisition strategy continued through the next two decades and into the 1980s. Among the companies it purchased were Emerson Drug, the marketer of Bromo-Seltzer; American Optical; Schick Electric, Inc.; Schick Safety Razor Division of Eversharp, Inc.; pharmaceuticals company Parke, Davis; and American Chicle, the marketer of Chiclets. (Analysts criticized the latter acquisition because they thought the purchase price of $200 million in stock was too high, but by 1983 American Chicle's sales were nearing $1 billion.)

Despite ongoing acquisitions, the 1970s were turbulent for Warner-Lambert. The U.S. Securities and Exchange Commission accused it of making illegal international payments; its American Chicle plant in Queens, New York, was the site of an explosion that killed or injured 55, resulting in several company executives being indicted for negligence (charges were later dropped); its Benylin cough syrup lost its over-the-counter status for a time after the Food and Drug Administration (FDA) raised questions about it. But in 1978 the company purchased Entenmann's Bakery, which became its most profitable division. The unit suffered from rumors of alleged links to the Reverend Sun Myung Moon's Unification Church, and eventually it was sold to General Foods Corporation.

Financial instability led the company to restructure in 1979. It sold off several subsidiaries, including American Optical; closed plants; and cut its staff nearly in half. While these efforts helped the company's financial status, a combination of events including consumer trends toward herbals and away from traditional medications, the health-care-reform movement, a recession in the late 1980s, and falling consumer goods prices proved deleterious to the company, and in 1991 it once more was forced to restructure. It again laid off staff and consolidated its operations into two units—pharmaceuticals and consumer products.

Warner-Lambert entered the controversial transdermal nicotine patch market in 1992 with its Nicotrol brand. Nicotrol had early but short-lived success in an already-crowded sector. The company was the first to market in 1993 with Cognex, an FDA-approved drug that slowed the development of Alzheimer's disease, and it created an alliance with rivals Glaxo and Wellcome to help all three quickly move their products from prescription to over-the-counter to generic status.

During the late 1980s and early 1990s Warner-Lambert's profit margins were low compared to others in the industry, but sales grew, especially internationally. The company invested $1.3 billion in advertising and promotion and $473 million in research and development in 1992, when consumer goods accounted for 60 percent of annual sales.

One prominent example of Warner-Lambert's advertising is that for Listerine. Lambert Pharmacal had first marketed Listerine in 1895 to doctors and dentists as a surgical antiseptic; in 1914 it was sold over the counter. It generated fairly steady sales for the company through the 1920s, during Prohibition, when its 25 percent alcohol content created demand for it as a beverage.

Listerine came of age in the 1920s when the company came up with the idea of marketing it as a cure for "halitosis," or bad breath. The brand's advertising emphasized the term halitosis, believing that its medical-sounding, somewhat scary connotation would drive sales. Lambert & Feasley, Inc., a new New York City ad agency, created a campaign that featured the headline, "Often a bridesmaid but never a bride." The campaign appeared in women's magazines such as *Ladies' Home Journal* through the 1930s and 1940s and highlighted the plight of Edna, who would never be married because of her halitosis.

By 1954 sales of Listerine reached $35 million a year, enough to attract the attention of Warner-Hudnut. In the 1960s, Listerine competed with Colgate-Palmolive Company's Colgate 100 and Scope, a product of the Procter & Gamble Company (P&G), but it remained the market leader. Warner-Lambert extended the brand into toothpaste, breath freshener tablets, and throat lozenges, and expanded its profile overseas. By 1967 the brand's advertising budget was $80 million, about half of that devoted to television.

Some of the 1960s marketing tactics supporting Listerine were unusual. In 1964 a hefty percentage of promotional dollars went toward an educational film, *The Story of Dr. Lister*, which was shown in U.S. schools. In 1965 Warner-Lambert spent $8,000 on supporting Listerine with a mailing of first-day-issue stamps to 120,000 stockholders and frequent customers.

In the 1970s some of Listerine's competitors started to point to the product's taste, which was bitter compared to other, mostly minty brands. In 1971 Warner-Lambert took that accusation and used it to its advantage with the tag line, "The taste you hate, twice a day." In 1974 P&G took the battle a step further by alleging that Listerine caused "medicine breath," a claim that was supported by research from the Council of Better Business Bureaus, which had concluded that Listerine tasted "mediciney."

Meanwhile, a long-running Federal Trade Commission investigation into the brand's claims—starting as early as the 1930s and continuing through the 1950s—that it could cure colds, sore throats, and even the Asian flu, was finally resolved against the company. Warner-Lambert had to spend $10 million for two years of revised statements countering those claims on all Listerine advertising.

During the 1970s the company continued to offer Listerine line extensions, but not all were successful. Throughout the 1970s and 1980s Listerine maintained its lead in the mouthwash category. In 1984 it claimed the product could prevent plaque buildup and gingivitis and spent $16 million three years later to publicize this attribute. These pronouncements, as well as its claim that it could cure halitosis, were investigated by the American Dental Association, the FDA, and *Consumer Reports* magazine during the late 1980s and early 1990s. Although some of these probes found the claims to be untrue, consumers stuck with the brand. In fiscal 1992 Warner-Lambert spent $221.1 million a year (33 percent of all mouthwash sales) on Listerine and an additional $80.1 million on the new extension, Cool Mint Listerine, introduced that year.

In 1998 Warner-Lambert introduced Tartar Control Listerine with a $27 million advertising budget; total marketing expenditures for the whole brand in 1999 were $114 million, of which $54 million was spent on consumer media advertising. Nine million samples of Tartar Control Listerine were sent to consumers in 1999, supported by freestanding inserts (FSIs) in newspapers, featuring Rosie O'Donnell. (Talk show host O'Donnell became a Listerine spokesperson after competitor Procter & Gamble Company's Scope named her one of the ten least-kissable celebrities.) By 1999 Listerine held a 41 percent share of the mouthwash market, with private label brands its closest competitor.

In 2000 Listerine introduced PocketPacks, breath-freshening strips that dissolve on the tongue and deliver the same ingredients found in Listerine mouthwash. The introduction was supported with $39 million in advertising over 12 months, plus the distribution of 50 million samples. Many of the samples were attached to other Warner-Lambert products. Direct mail and professional sampling through dental offices were also part of the campaign. As of 2000, the J. Walter Thompson Company (JWT), of New York City, was the agency for the Listerine brand.

Another Warner-Lambert consumer brand that has been heavily advertised is Sugarless Trident gum, the second-best-selling gum of any type, after the Wm. Wrigley Jr. Company's Sugar-Free Extra. When it was introduced in 1962 by the American Chicle Company, which was acquired by Warner-Lambert the same year, it was the first sugarless chewing gum and transformed the industry. In 1964 the National Aeronautics and Space Administration (NASA) selected the product as the official gum for the Gemini space flights.

From the beginning, Trident's cavity-fighting properties and good taste were the foundation of its advertising message. Its first tag line was "4 out of 5 dentists surveyed recommend sugarless gum for their patients who chew gum," which emphasized that no other gum could make the same health claims. As time went by, Trident's advertising focused more on its breath-freshening power and new flavors, but all ads delivered the anti-cavity message.

In the mid-1980s Warner-Lambert began to publicize research showing that Trident gum could prevent cavities if chewed after eating sugary snacks, spending $15 million to promote the message. It marked the first time a gum was able to make such a claim to dentists and consumers.

In 1971 Listerine countered rivals promoting pleasant-tasting mouthwashes in ads for its own brand with the line "Anything that tastes that bad has gotta work."
LISTERINE is a registered trademark of Warner-Lambert, a Pfizer company.

Meanwhile, the market was becoming more competitive, with 21 new gum products, many of them sugarless, debuting in 1991 alone. At the same time, other products from toothpastes to fluoridated water also were able to prevent cavities. Consumers thus not only demanded cavity protection, they also wanted long-lasting flavor and fresh breath. Trident began to focus on those properties, for example with the tag line, "All that good stuff and great taste, too." In 1998 Warner-Lambert introduced Trident Advantage Gum, spending $20 million to support the extension. This was the first gum to make clinical whitening claims. Its tag line: "As exciting as oral hygiene gets." JWT was the ad agency.

Sampling has been a cornerstone of Trident marketing. In 1998 Warner-Lambert promoted Sugarless Cherry Trident by including five-stick sample packs on 3 million 1-liter bottles of Clearly Canadian's cherry-flavored sparkling water. That was backed by $22 million in national television and radio advertising and in-store marketing support, including point-of-sale displays with the tag line "Chew on this!"

Trident had traditionally been an adult brand but expanded into the children's market in 1999 with Trident for Kids.

After research showed that Trident gum could help prevent cavities, Warner-Lambert spent $15 million to promote this added benefit to consumers.
TRIDENT is a registered trademark of Warner-Lambert, a Pfizer company.

McDonald's Corporation distributed 5 million samples in the chain's Happy Meals for two months and highlighted the product on 26 million tray liners, while elementary schools gave away an additional 4 million in conjunction with an educational package for teachers about dental care. Toys "R" Us distributed another 2 million samples. The brand was marketed to parents in a $5 million print campaign, emphasizing the product's clinically proven teeth-strengthening abilities, in 17 magazines, including *Woman's Day, Parenting, Family Fun,* and *People,* as well as in 24 million FSIs offering a buy-one-get-one deal. Radio Disney spots targeted children.

In 2001 Warner-Lambert extended the Trident Advantage brand into mints, supported with a $15 million ad campaign and sampling. The message promoted the ingredient Recaldent, which strengthens teeth. Warner-Lambert encouraged retailers to set up oral-care displays at the checkout counter to cross-merchandise the new mints, Trident Advantage gum, and Trident for Kids. JWT handled advertising for the brand.

Another leading Warner-Lambert consumer brand is Certs, a breath-freshening mint supported by TV and sampling. When it was introduced in 1956 by American Chicle, it was the first product to both provide good taste and freshen breath. At the turn of the century it continued as the best-selling brand of hard-candy breath mints in the United States. It contained Retsyn, a homogenized vegetable oil and one of the components of chlorophyll, the latter an ingredient used in previous breath mints. (It combated bad breath but stained the tongue green.)

Warner-Lambert priced Certs slightly higher than Lifesavers, its main competitor on the candy side, and slightly lower than Clorets, a breath-freshening gum. At first, the brand did not do well, despite several new flavor introductions and heavy TV advertising. Finally, when Ted Bates & Company, Inc., hit on the tag line "Two, two, two mints in one," which pointed to both the great taste and fresh breath attributes of the product, sales started to rise. That was in 1960, after which Certs expanded nationally.

The company introduced several line extensions, each supported by advertising and promotions and sometimes new packaging. In 1982 Sugarfree Certs was introduced, aimed at women looking for fewer calories. New Sugarfree Certs, with NutraSweet, debuted in 1987. In the late 1980s and early 1990s, Warner-Lambert launched Sugarfree Mini-Mints to compete with Tic Tacs; Certs Fresh Fruit; and Certs Blizzards Mints, for older consumers who wanted stronger breath protection. Extra Flavor Certs, which were 10 percent larger than regular Certs, debuted in 1993.

The "Two, two, two mints in one" tag line was retired in 1978 after 18 years. (It was reintroduced in 1989.) During the late 1970s and 1980s, several other tag lines were used, including, "Be certain with Certs," which focused on romance; "Get Certs. Get closer," a more humorous romantic theme; and "The Certs encounter," which ran from 1982 to 1985. The launch campaign for Sugarfree Certs in 1982 featured for the first time graphics of a drop of Retsyn hitting the mint and splashing up as a gold-colored liquid.

Certs has experimented with entertainment marketing as well as traditional advertising. As of 2001, it was the lead sponsor of *All Access,* a behind-the-scenes concert movie for Imax theaters. It was the first tie-in by Imax with a packaged-goods maker; the five-year deal, handled by Kobin Enterprises, New York City, gave Certs North American sponsorship rights that included the right to promote the tie-in via advertising, point-of-purchase displays, and promotional overlays.

Another Warner-Lambert brand, Schick, is a key product for the company in the consumer-targeted personal care market. The company also spends heavily in measured media to support this brand, to a total of $40 million in 2000. Schick's brands, which include Tracer, Protector, Silk Effects, and Personal Touch, have about a 20 percent share of the razor market, far behind number-one marketer Gillette. New-product introductions generate higher spending, such as a $30 million TV campaign from Bates USA in support of Schick's Silk Effects+ brand extension in 1999.

Warner-Lambert also is a significant player in the over-the-counter remedy market. Its Neosporin brand is the best-selling first aid ointment/antiseptic product, exhibiting a 10.9 percent sales increase in 1999 in what was otherwise a flat category. The company positioned the product to emphasize its scar-reducing properties and began a print and TV campaign to promote this feature. Neosporin and Neosporin Plus collectively have about 25 percent of the ointment/antiseptic category. Bates USA was the agency.

Warner-Lambert's Zantac brand ranks fourth in the acid-blocker category, supported by media expenditure of $43.3 million under JWT, its lead agency. The company has the fourth- and fifth-ranked cough and cold medications with Benadryl and Sudafed, both at Bates USA in New York City, and supported by $25.3 million and $29.5 million in spending, respectively, as of 1999.

Warner-Lambert extended its Sudafed brand into the children's market in 1998, introducing a character called "Blockhead" to advertise the new brand. The "Blockhead" campaign borrowed from Sudafed's "Medicine Head" effort, launched in 1997 to support its adult brand.

Warner-Lambert's Rolaids antacid advertising is best known for its "R-O-L-A-I-D-S spells relief" campaign, a long-running effort created by Bates that featured endorsers such as Tommy Lasorda, then-manager of the Los Angeles Dodgers baseball team. A tongue-in-cheek version of the campaign, highlighting fans of pro sports, was launched in 1998.

The company's Halls Defense line of supplements introduced a vitamin C product in 1999 with a marketing campaign that included radio, TV, and billboards, as well as FSIs. Part of the focus of the new effort was to reach consumers who were being lured away by herbal products and substances touted as cold preventives. The campaign highlighted the fact that Halls contained 100 percent of the recommended daily requirement of vitamin C. It starred two new ad icons—a computer-generated Old Man Winter and an animated football player called the Halls Defense linebacker—who battled it out in commercials, with Halls victorious. In 1999 Warner-Lambert spent $20 million on the Halls brand, via JWT, according to *Brandweek* magazine, including $9.5 million on the vitamin C drops. Halls had a 35 percent share of the cough drop segment as of 2000.

Warner-Lambert is a player in the $4 billion-and-growing herbal remedy market with its Quanterra brand. It has adopted the industry-wide trend of specifying uses for its herbal supplements, such as its Quanterra Sinus Defense product introduced in 2000. Herbal remedies are not regulated by the FDA. But Quanterra became the first brand to tout clinical proof of its claims in a 1998 campaign from Bates USA with the tag line, "If it's not clinically proven, it's not Quanterra."

In addition to the consumer side of its business, Warner-Lambert also has been active in the prescription drug market throughout its history. When it acquired New Jersey Chilcott Laboratories in 1952, it received Peritrate, a blood vessel enlarger and one of Chilcott's flagship brands. By 1966 more than half of those with heart disease used the drug. Warner-Lambert supported the product with a controversial ad campaign in medical journals that claimed it worked not only for the treatment of angina but also as a preventative product for all cardiac patients, even those who had not developed angina. The claim was based on a single study and ran into opposition from the FDA.

Zantac 75 is one of Warner-Lambert's most heavily promoted brands. ZANTAC is a registered trademark of Warner-Lambert, a Pfizer company.

By the late 1990s, sales of prescription drugs were at a historic high owing to a faster FDA approval process. Sales of prescription drugs in the United States reached $94 billion in 1998, up 16 percent from the previous year, excluding mail-order sales, according to the National Institute for Healthcare Management.

During the 1990s, drug marketers upped their consumer advertising campaigns, spending 35 cents of every revenue dollar on marketing, versus 15 cents to 18 cents on research and development. New FDA rules went into effect in 1997 that allowed direct-to-consumer advertising of prescription products for the first time. That led direct-to-consumer advertising to grow at a double-digit pace throughout the late 1990s. Total promotional spending directed at consumers and physicians collectively reached more than $13.9 billion in 1999, with consumer TV advertising for prescription drugs accounting for $1.1 billion of that. All told, advertising expenditures to consumers reached $1.8 billion in 1999. The top-ten products accounted for 41 percent of total direct-to-consumer spending.

Increased consumer advertising led to increased sales for prescription drugs. The sector accounted for $111.1 billion in retail sales in 1999. Several Warner-Lambert brands benefited from this trend. Sales of the company's cholesterol-lowering drug, Lipitor, increased 56 percent in 1999 over 1998, reaching $2.6 billion in

—————— men ——————
ARE LIKE MOISTURIZERS.
IT'S THE ONES THAT HANG
ALL OVER YOU
THAT YOU
DON'T WANT.

Thank goodness there's a clean moisture lotion like Lubriderm.

Lubriderm's clean moisture formula is the perfect relationship. That's because it's a hardworking moisturizer that doesn't act clingy or greasy. Clean moisture gives dry skin everything it needs, but feels almost weightless. So it's recommended by dermatologists even more than before.

Visit our Internet website at http://www.skinhelp.com ©1997 Warner-Lambert Co.

See you later, alligator.

This 1997 ad for Lubriderm was created by the J. Walter Thompson Company, Warner-Lambert's lead advertising agency. *LUBRIDERM is a registered trademark of Warner-Lambert, a Pfizer company.*

sales by 1999. The company's consumer advertising expenditures for Lipitor increased from $7.8 million in 1998 to $55.4 million in 1999, ranking it among the top-ten pharmaceutical brands in spending.

Another drug industry trend in the late 1990s was consolidation, as major worldwide companies merged. Warner-Lambert was no exception, being purchased by Pfizer, Inc., in 1999. Just prior to the merger, Warner-Lambert had ranked number ten among the top 30 drug companies in consumer advertising, spending $63.6 million (up 134.5 percent from 1998), while Pfizer ranked number five with $151.5 million. The Pfizer/Warner-Lambert merger marked the first time a single company controlled more than 10 percent of the prescription medicine market; the combined company claimed an 11.1 percent share of the pharmaceutical market worldwide.

As in its early days in the drug industry, some of Warner-Lambert's advertising continues to attract controversy. In 2000 the first U.S. nationwide class-action suit against the company alleged that Warner-Lambert had produced deceptive advertising and had influenced the FDA to gain approval of its diabetes drug Rezulin. The suit said that, after approval, the drug had been linked to health and safety concerns and that Warner-Lambert concealed facts from the FDA. The company had spent $25 million in 1999 to advertise Rezulin, which had become a billion-dollar brand by 2000.

Warner-Lambert ranked number 11 in ad spending among all national advertisers in 1999 (pre-merger), according to *Advertising Age,* devoting a total of $1.1 billion to media, $386.5 million of that measured. The company spent $186.2 million on network TV, $39.5 million on network radio, $38.7 million on magazine advertising, and $38 million on cable. Listerine was its top brand in terms of spending with $45.9 million, followed by Zantac 75 ($43.3 million), Sudafed ($37.3 million), Benadryl ($35.7 million), Schick ($31.8 million), Trident ($24.4 million), Lubriderm ($20.8 million), Certs ($20.3 million), Rolaids ($20.1 million), Rezulin ($19.3 million), Halls ($19.2 million), Dentyne ($17.9 million), and Neosporin ($13.3 million).

The merged Pfizer/Warner-Lambert was a $5 billion concern with more than 20,000 employees. It was expected that, under its new ownership, most of Warner-Lambert's brands would continue to be among the most-advertised names in the consumer health and personal care industries and in the pharmaceutical market.

KAREN RAUGUST

Further Reading

Beirne, Mike, "Trident Goes Sample Mad for Kids," *Brandweek* (10 May 1999)

Bittar, Christine, "Silk Effects Ad Depicts Lady's Razor As Solution to Slobby Male Roomies," *Brandweek* (10 May 1999)

Bittar, Christine, "Halls Defense Tackles Ol' Man Winter As It Seeks Cure for Herbal Incursion," *Brandweek* (9 October 2000)

Cardona, Mercedes M., "Listerine Breath Strips Break Oral Care Boundaries," *Advertising Age* (28 February 2000)

Darby, Rose, "On a Roll! Baby Boomers, Advertising, and Science Fuel a Pharmaceuticals Boom, but for How Long?" *Investment Dealers' Digest* (8 November 1999)

Fitzgerald, Kate, "Icast Site, Listerine Explore Campus Comedic Capabilities," *Advertising Age* (16 October 2000)

Goetzl, David, "DTC Execs Quick to Learn Upfront Value," *Advertising Age* (15 May 2000)

Pollack, Judann, "Warner-Lambert to Roll Listerine Line Extension: New Tartar Control Mouthwash Supported by $27 Million Ad Budget," *Advertising Age* (28 September 1998)

Snyder, Beth, "Warner-Lambert Gives Trident $20 Million Advantage," *Advertising Age* (7 December 1998)

Snyder, Beth, "Schick: Diamonds Are Everyone's Best Friends," *Advertising Age* (8 November 1999)

Wilke, Michael, "Rolaids Seeks Boost with $20 Million Drive," *Advertising Age* (6 July 1998)

Wilke, Michael, "Quanterra Ads to Cite Proof of Herbal's Claims," *Advertising Age* (30 November 1998)

Warwick & Legler, Inc.

Established in New York City in 1939, although its principals had been part of Cecil, Warwick & Cecil; created Pabst beer campaign, 1940s; sued Schick, Inc., in precedent-setting intellectual property case, 1957–58; became Warwick, Welsh & Miller, 1973; became Warwick Advertising, 1982; became Warwick, Baker & Fiore, 1989; renamed Warwick, Baker & O'Neill, 1996; closed its doors after 62 years, 3 August 2001.

Major Clients

Equitable Life Assurance Society
Pabst Brewing Company (Pabst Blue Ribbon beer)
Revlon, Inc.
Jacob Ruppert, Inc.
Schick, Inc.
Seagram Distillers Corporation
Sherwin-Williams Company

The agency known widely as Warwick & Legler through the 1940s to the 1960s was also known in its early years as Cecil, Warwick & Cecil, and then, after 1 January 1973, as Warwick, Welsh & Miller. In 1982 it became known simply as Warwick Advertising and in 1989, Warwick, Baker & Fiore. In 1996 it became Warwick, Baker & O'Neill, a midsize, independent agency with a solid network of global affiliations. Many in the industry were surprised in 2001 when, after several client losses, the agency suddenly went out of business after 62 years.

Although the agency gave 1939 as the year of its founding, substantially the same company that emerged in 1939 as Warwick & Legler had existed under several predecessor names, mostly in offices at 230 Park Avenue in New York City. The agency was founded by J.R. Warwick and H.P. (Paul) Warwick around 1919 with the Seagram Distillers business, an account that would remain with the company for 46 years. With the arrival of James and John Cecil in 1923, it was renamed Cecil, Warwick & Cecil; then in 1937, with the absorption of Henry Legler, who came over as creative director from the J. Walter Thompson Company, it was renamed Cecil, Warwick & Legler. During this period, the agency handled two film studios (Selznick International Pictures and Samuel Goldwyn Studios), the Sherwin-Williams Company, and the George Washington Coffee Refining Company, for which the agency produced network broadcasting's first weekly quiz program, *Professor Quiz*, in 1936. During the 1930s, the agency also produced *Twenty Thousand Years in Sing Sing* for the William R. Warner Company, maker of Sloan's Liniment.

Then in September 1938, Paul Warwick and Henry Legler resigned to form Warwick & Legler (W&L). They took with them all but six clients, including Seagram and Sloan's. Cecil, Warwick & Legler ceased to exist as an entity (James Cecil took over the Frank Presbrey Company in January 1939), although its lineal descendent became Warwick & Legler, operating out of the same offices as its now-defunct predecessor, at 230 Park Avenue. Its dozen clients included the Hearst *Comic Weekly* Sunday funnies section, the *New York Evening Post,* and the Julius Kessler Distilling Company (a unit of Seagram). In 1940 the agency moved Sloan's advertising into what would become a classic radio crime show, *Gang Busters,* and kept it there until the account moved in 1944. The agency grew steadily during World War II, moving from less than $6 million in billings in 1943 to more than $7 million in 1945. With offices in New York City and Hollywood, California, the agency remained active in network radio, producing *This Is Your FBI* from 1945 to 1953 for the Equitable Life Assurance Society.

But its most sustained radio efforts were for Pabst Brewing Company and its Pabst Blue Ribbon beer brand, which the agency won in 1941 from Lord & Thomas and which soon became its dominant account, billing $2.5 million by 1945. Legler is credited with inventing one of the most famous slogans/jingles in advertising history for the client: "What'll you have? Pabst Blue Ribbon." W&L supervised the production of such Pabst shows as *Blue Ribbon Town* with Groucho Marx (1943–44), *The Danny Kaye Show* with prominent comedy writer and performer Goodman

Ace as chief writer (1945–46), *The Eddie Cantor Show* (1948–49), and two seasons of *The Life of Riley* (1949–51). The agency served a small but active list of not more than ten clients generating billings of more than $8 million by 1948, most of it from Pabst, Equitable, and Seagram. In 1948 W&L was chosen as the ad agency for the Democratic National Committee, to oversee the reelection campaign of U.S. President Harry Truman.

In 1950 W&L graduated to the top agency ranks, which *Advertising Age* then defined as any shop billing $10 million or more. The loss of Pabst Blue Ribbon in 1955, which had been driving much of the agency's growth, was a setback. But a year later W&L was back in the beer business, winning Jacob Ruppert, Inc., in February 1956. It would be an unstable relationship, however, foreshadowed by the fact that Ruppert had on a Friday sent a telegram informing Compton Advertising that Compton had won its advertising business; then on Monday Ruppert sent a second telegram saying that Warwick & Legler had won the account. In February 1957 the account did move to Compton, and then, after a brief period at Norman, Craig & Kummel, back to Warwick & Legler in January 1961. Exactly two years later, it was reassigned again and never came back to Warwick & Legler.

During 1957 and 1958 the agency became involved in a precedent-setting and bitter legal dispute with Schick, Inc., involving ownership of ideas. The agency had won the Schick account in October 1955 and then lost it in June 1957. The dispute centered on an idea for a television commercial developed by W&L and presented to Schick in December 1956, in which a cotton ball was rubbed across facial skin shaved with a Schick electric razor. The closeness of the shave was demonstrated by the absence of cotton fibers adhering to the skin. Schick rejected the idea, offered no reimbursement to the agency for its work, and left Warwick & Legler soon after. The agency held onto the film and the rejected idea, an action consistent with "usual trade practice" in similar cases. But when Schick's next ad agency, Benton & Bowles (B&B), presented a similar "cotton test" idea, allegedly devised independently of any work W&L had done, W&L insisted on compensation if the idea was used. Schick declined, authorized B&B to produce the commercial, and ran it on *Dragnet* on 19 September 1957. A single ad using the theme also ran in *Look* magazine.

Meanwhile, W&L presented the cotton test idea to a new client prospect, Remington Rand, which had been shaving peaches to demonstrate its razor's close shave. Remington agreed to buy the cotton test on the condition that Schick was not permitted to run it after the single *Dragnet* and *Look* exposures. In October 1957 W&L won a temporary injunction against Schick and B&B, stopping any further use of the idea for the moment. Schick in turn filed a $1 million suit against W&L for breach of fiduciary relationship.

The case was tried in the spring of 1958 by Judge J. Cullen Ganey in Philadelphia, Pennsylvania. There were two questions. First, did B&B have any information on W&L's idea when it presented its own cotton test; and second and more important, who owned the unpublished ideas generated by an agency on behalf of a client, the agency or the advertiser? Judge Ganey found no evidence that B&B had devised its cotton test independently. He also affirmed that unused ideas presented to Schick by W&L during their relationship remained the property of the agency and not the client. The decision established a firm legal precedent on a major issue of intellectual property affecting the agency-client relationship.

About the time W&L lost Schick, it won significant business from Revlon, Inc. But the agency's relationship with the client did not involve it in the production of *The $64,000 Question,* which became the center of the famous television quiz show scandals of 1958 to 1960. It lost the $5 million Revlon account in 1963, but added U.S. Time Corporation about the same time, giving it another major piece of consumer business. Henry Legler retired in 1959.

In 1964 the agency moved into the ranks of the $25 million-plus agencies as Paul Warwick moved to chairman and his son John P. Warwick became president. John Warwick reorganized the creative department and set up a creative strategy execution committee. In the early 1970s, after some healthy growth to the $40 million level, the agency acquired stakes in ad agencies in London, England; Frankfurt, Germany; and Paris, France. In 1974 it created Warwick International Partners to coordinate European activities. John Welsh became vice chairman and Robert Miller, vice president and creative director in 1972, and the agency changed its name to Warwick, Welsh & Miller on 1 January 1973.

By the mid-1980s, Warwick's relative ranking among other agencies was starting to drop. From a rank of 30 in 1973, according to *Advertising Age,* and with billings of $60 million, Warwick continued to grow but not at the pace of other larger agencies. By 1982 it had slipped to a rank of 47, and by 1984 to 53, by which point the name had changed to Warwick Advertising. In 1985 Seagram trimmed its agency roster from seven to three, and Warwick did not make the cut. For the first time since 1919, Seagram was not a Warwick client. Late in the 1980s, the agency's name

changed again, to Warwick, Baker & Fiore, as Chairman Wilder D. Baker and Executive Creative Director Robert J. Fiore put their names on the door. By 1991 billings were a healthy $160 million. But the era of agency consolidation was under way. With only modest growth, the agency's ranking among major agencies dropped to 82 by 1994. Kevin O' Neill was hired as president and chief creative officer, and once again the name was changed, to Warwick, Baker & O'Neill. At the beginning of the new century, the agency continued as a midsize and still independent shop with a network of European partnerships from London, England, to Warsaw, Poland.

Warwick, Baker & O'Neill had 2000 income of nearly $24 million on billings of $158 million, substantially the same as 1994, according to *Advertising Age.* While the agency was not growing, it took pride in remaining independent in an era of acquisitions. Then in 2000 it agreed to be acquired by EPB Communications, a unit of Panoramic Communications, but the deal collapsed early the next year. Subsequently, several major client departures, including Panasonic shavers and the East Coast Energy Council, made the agency's financial position untenable. At the same time Fruit of the Loom filed for bankruptcy protection, and Bestfoods was acquired by a new parent. Both were important clients. Suddenly on 3 August 2001, in an unexpected move, Warwick, Baker & O'Neill closed its doors for good, ending the story of a significant company in advertising history. The company had 55 employees when it shut down.

JOHN MCDONOUGH

Further Reading
"Cotton Test Idea Is W & L's, Court Decides," *Advertising Age* (12 May 1958)
"Warwick & Legler's Schick Suit May Set Precedent on Ownership of Ideas," *Advertising Age* (28 October 1957)
"'We'll Take Account, Let Commission Go,' Warwick & Legler Told Schick," *Advertising Age* (4 November 1957)

W.B. Doner & Company. *See* Doner

W/Brasil Publicidade

Founded by Washington Olivetto, in partnership with the Swiss group GGK under the name W/GGK, 1986; renamed W/Brasil Publicidade, 1988; became part of Prax Holding, Ltda., 1996.

Major Clients
Bombril/Henkel
Cirio (food products)

Cofap (car parts)
Credicard
Chocolates Garoto
Editora Globo
Folha de São Paulo (newspaper and Internet site)
Grendene (footwear)
Hering (textiles)
Luigi Bertolli
Mercedes-Benz
Unibanco

The story of W/Brasil Publicidade is largely the biography of Washington Olivetto, who has one of the largest collections of Lion awards won for creativity at the Cannes (France) International Advertising Festival. Olivetto founded W/Brasil Publicidade in 1986 in partnership with the Swiss group GGK under the name W/GGK. Olivetto had been the creative director of Duailibi Petit Zaragoza (DPZ) for many years, where he played a large role in winning many domestic and international prizes and attracted significant attention, both in Brazil and abroad. In 1988 Olivetto bought out his Swiss partners and invited Gabriel Zellmeister and Javier Llussá Ciuret, who were already working at W/GGK, to join him as partners in the advertising agency, which he renamed W/Brasil.

From the start, the agency was very successful and made a point of using modern, Brazilian styles and images. A celebrated Brazilian pop singer and composer, Jorge Ben Jor, named one of his songs after W/Brasil, which did not prevent it from selling close to 2 million records in 1990. W/Brasil views itself as an agency that creates "pop advertising." One of its core tenets is the belief that all of its campaigns are products of the cultural industry, competing for space in the media and in consumers' minds, not only with other advertising campaigns but also with news, popular songs, hit films, and the soap operas Brazilians adore. As a result, many of its campaigns are incorporated into the popular culture much more frequently than are other campaigns and employ both memorable characters and situations. Notable W/Brasil ad campaign characters include *Folha de São Paulo*'s mouse, Cofap's Spare Parts' dachshund, and the Bombril Boy.

W/Brasil's concepts are consistent and its campaigns long-lived. Olivetto has said that the purpose of W/Brasil's advertising is to turn its customers into stars. Many of the original ideas conceived at the agency, if not copied outright, have been the objects of adaptations and parodies.

The agency endeavors to enjoy great visibility and cultivates a highly creative profile, thanks to the personality of Olivetto. In a professional poll in 1999, Olivetto was chosen as adman of the century in Brazil; the honor was repeated when he was chosen adman of the century in Ibero-America by the Iberian American Association of Advertising Agencies.

Olivetto was born in São Paulo in 1951. At age 18, as he was beginning his advertising career, he won his first Lion at the Cannes Festival. Counting gold, silver, and bronze awards, he has amassed 48 Lion statuettes, exclusively in electronic media.

Olivetto won the first Professional of the Year Award, sponsored by Brazil's TV Globo Network, in 1978. He is the most awarded professional in the *Year Book of the Creative Club of São Paulo.* Besides Cannes Lion awards, he has won Clios, Andys, awards at the Festival Ibero-Americano de Publicidade (FIAP), and many others. Olivetto is also responsible for the two Brazilian ads cited in the book *The 100 Best TV Commercials,* by Bernice Kanner (i.e., "Valisere," for First Bra, and "Hitler," for the newspaper *Folha de São Paulo*). The awards, plus his many public appearances around the world and his high-quality work developed over 30 years, have conferred on Olivetto a kind of "pop star" status in Brazil—an image that has helped to attract clients.

W/Brasil describes itself as "a totally independent company working exclusively for private companies." The agency does not accept work for the government or for political candidates. Practically since its inception, W/Brasil has ranked among the five largest ad agencies in Brazil in billings. In April 2000 *Advertising Age* estimated W/Brasil's annual gross income for 1999 at $25,105,000, a decline of 34.5 percent over the previous year. (The decline was mostly owing to the Brazilian currency devaluation between 1999 and 2000; the agency's revenues remained steady.)

W/Brasil's large local clients include Unibanco, Sadia, Grendene, *Folha de São Paulo,* and Chocolates Garoto. But it also handles significant international accounts such as Mercedes-Benz, Bombril/Henkel, and AIG Insurance. One of the campaigns run by the agency in 2000 (but created for Bombril cleansing products while Olivetto was still at DPZ) has been included in the *Guinness*

Washington Olivetto.
Courtesy of Washington Olivetto.

Book of World Records since 1995 as the campaign with the largest number of ads in the world that feature the same creator and the same character.

In 1996 W/Brasil decided it preferred to maintain its independence rather than link up with a multinational group, but it also wanted to grow. Olivetto and his partners, Gabriel Zellmeister and Javier Llussá Ciuret, formed Prax Holding, Ltda. The holding company eventually oversaw another trio of successful ad agencies, Propaganda Registrada, Guimares Profissionais, and Lew, Lara. It also oversees Thimus, a strategic-planning firm; Made in Brasil, a design agency; Pop Com, an Internet agency; and Parra e

Associados, a promotional agency. These companies work independently and appoint their own managers, while Olivetto, Zellmeister, and Llussá Ciuret devote their time and effort to running W/Brasil.

On 11 December 2001 Olivetto was kidnapped in São Paulo, taken from his car while on his way to the office from his home. He was the 200th person kidnapped in 2001 in São Paulo alone and the fourth owner of an agency. After 53 days in captivity he was released unharmed. He has since gone back to work for the agency.

J. ROBERTO WHITAKER-PENTEADO

Weaver, Sylvester L. (Pat), Jr., 1908–2002

U.S. Television Network Executive

As vice president, president, and chairman of NBC from 1949 to 1956, Sylvester L. (Pat) Weaver, an advertising executive-turned-programmer, changed the way broadcast networks sold and positioned airtime for advertisers. Weaver was born in Los Angeles, California, on 21 December 1908. He attended Dartmouth College, from which he graduated in 1930 with a bachelor's degree. After college, he worked for two California radio stations—Los Angeles's KHJ beginning in 1932, and KFRC, San Francisco, beginning in 1934—before moving on to a post as ad manager at the American Tobacco Company. From 1942 to 1945, he served in the U.S. Navy during World War II. Having served two stints as a producer and executive at Young & Rubicam (Y&R), and having learned the production ropes at CBS-affiliated KHJ, he understood the strategic and creative needs of advertisers while leading broadcast networks at a pivotal point to reclaim their own airtime and content. In the process, he revolutionized the entire broadcasting industry.

Weaver's hallmark was the development of the "magazine" format, which set a new precedent for buying and selling ad time and scheduling program content. By instituting what Weaver called the new "program service," NBC worked around advertising agencies that were accustomed to creating and controlling their clients' programming. Ironically, Weaver left NBC in 1956 to return to the agency world he had upset, becoming chairman of the McCann-Erickson ad agency and eventually going on to pioneer a subscription TV venture.

Weaver's first stint at Y&R was from 1935 to 1938 as the producer of NBC radio's *Town Hall Tonight*. The show starred comedian Fred Allen, who loved to make ad men the butt of jokes. In Weaver's autobiography, *The Best Seat in the House,* he recalled the time he evicted NBC President Deke Aylesworth and sponsor Bristol-Myers President Lee Bristol (neither of whom Weaver rec-

ognized) from the control booth when he first took command of the show's production for Y&R. When he recounted the incident to Allen, the comedian declared Weaver his new hero, thanking him for providing him with fodder for his routine.

Little did Allen or agencies such as Y&R realize that the joke eventually would be on them. Weaver was astonished that the networks in radio and later in TV were little more than technical facilities for the advertisers and agencies that controlled and produced the entire product, even news, from the on-camera talent to the content.

Weaver jumped to NBC, vowing to wrest control of production and programming from the ad agencies by getting inside the broadcast system to change it. In the 1940s his first target was "time franchises"—slots sponsors refused to surrender.

When Weaver came to NBC in 1949 as vice president and head of NBC-TV, Y&R and other major agencies were losing ground to network packagers and independent production on the outside, as well as the network's own media department. His immediate problem was controlling rising production costs that resulted, for instance, in Frigidaire paying $100,000 for each hour-long Bob Hope special on NBC.

Weaver responded to trepidation from both agencies and the network with a history-making memo that outlined his new program service. He advocated signing up multiple sponsors within a show to help amortize rising production costs.

These were the seeds for a revolution in the selling of network time—participating sponsorship. Cutting the basic unit of time to one minute eliminated sponsor and agency control of programming, as the networks and program producers sold "spots" of time from an inventory of programming created under network control. Major advertising agency executives vowed to fight the proposal, shocked that one of their own would propose such an arrangement. Though large advertisers felt betrayed, smaller ones hailed Weaver for offering them affordable access to network broadcasting for the first time.

Weaver set vehicles in motion at NBC to demonstrate the concept, creating *Today* with Dave Garroway (complete with monkey J. Fred Muggs), *Home* with Arlene Francis, and *The Tonight Show* with Steve Allen. All were successful. In prime time, he launched *Saturday Night Revue* and *Your Show of Shows,* which showcased Sid Caesar and Imogene Coca.

NBC's new production and schedule tactics led to major confrontations with sponsors such as Firestone, which saw its *Voice of Firestone* canceled over a time slot tug-of-war in 1954, ending a reign that began in 1928 on NBC radio.

By the late 1950s independent packagers, major talent agencies, film studios, producers, and even the networks' in-house production operations rushed to fill the void created by the increasing agency exodus from program production.

The quiz show scandal, in which advertisers were caught rigging big-money game shows by giving favored contestants answers in advance, gave the networks the opportunity to assume even greater control of programming from agencies. The networks charged agencies with failure to properly monitor contestants and the answers to questions posed on the air. "It is time for advertisers to get out of show business," *Advertising Age* declared in 1958, echoing Weaver's sentiments and agenda.

The mass-appeal programming Weaver and contemporaries such as CBS President Frank Stanton and Program Director Hubbell Robinson instituted was predicated on a different set of ratings and profits measurements. These measurements left little room for the small, targeted audiences of the past that were sought after by sponsors willing to pay a premium to broadcasters for the time. Programs that attracted large audiences became the strategic objective, primarily in 30-minute and 60-minute series blocks, and in two-hour time slots for movies and specials.

Weaver's goal was to create "a great television service that meets its obligations and duties, not a fragmented service that solves the problems of some elements on the periphery of the industry," he told colleagues at the 1957 National Association of Radio and Television Broadcasters' annual convention in Chicago, Illinois. Weaver said he believed television should be "the real intercontinental missile that will wake people up." Indeed, that's what he delivered.

Weaver was named chairman of the board of NBC in 1955, relinquishing daily administrative duties to Robert Sarnoff in order to spend more time on the broad implementation of his program service plan. He ran his own TV company for several years before returning to Madison Avenue. As chairman of McCann-Erickson International, Weaver took control of M-E Productions, the radio and television division of Interpublic, Inc.

He resigned from McCann-Erickson in 1963 to become president–chief executive officer of the California-based, early pay-TV venture Subscription Television, Inc. Weaver continued to publicly blast those who controlled network television for failing to break out of their "program rut," and he forecast the dual-stream strength that would come from subscription revenue. He was named to the Television Hall of Fame in 1985, an honor followed up in 1999, when *Advertising Age* named him one of the top 100 advertising people of the 20th century. Weaver died at the age of 93 on 15 March 2002 in Santa Barbara, California.

DIANE MERMIGAS

Biography

Born in Los Angeles, California, 21 December 1908; B.A., Dartmouth College, 1930; worked for Young and MacCallister, an advertising and printing company; writer/producer/director at Los Angeles radio station KHJ, starting 1932; program manager, San Francisco's KFRC, starting 1934; moved to Young & Rubicam, 1935; became supervisor of programs at the radio division, 1937; became advertising manager, American Tobacco Company, 1938; served in the U.S. Navy, 1942–45; vice president for radio and television at Y&R, 1947–49; vice chairman, president, then chairman of NBC, 1949–56; chairman of McCann-Erickson, 1958–63; president of Subscription TV, Inc., Los Angeles, California, 1963–66; named to Television Hall of Fame, 1985; named one of the top 100 advertising people by *Advertising Age*, 1999; died 15 March 2002 in Santa Barbara, California.

Selected Publication

The Best Seat in the House: The Golden Years of Radio and Television (with Thomas Coffey), 1994

Further Reading

"It's Sarnoff to Weaver to Sarnoff at NBC," *Advertising Age* (12 December 1955)

McDonough, John, "TV's Seismic Shift: In the Beginning, There Were Sponsors; "Weaver Heads Interpublic's TV Unit," *Advertising Age* (17 July 1961)

Weaver's Seminal Plan Moves Power to the Back Seats," *Advertising Age* (28 February 1995)

"Weaver to Head Pay TV Venture on West Coast," *Advertising Age* (16 October 1963)

"Y&R at 75" *Advertising Age* (2 November 1998)

Weight-Loss Products and Plans

The history of weight-loss advertising reflects the history of society's view of beauty and standards of appropriate body size and shape. As a consequence, most products that make weight-loss claims have been aimed at women rather than men. At the same time, the methods for losing weight have reflected the values and relative technological sophistication of different eras.

Diet teas, creams, ointments, and over-the-counter diet pills represented early products of choice. Weight-loss "systems"—a combination of counseling, meal-planning, weight monitoring, and calorie-controlled prepackaged meals—as provided by companies such as Weight Watchers International, Jenny Craig International, and Nutri-System, grew in popularity in the 1960s as "support groups" became an accepted cultural phenomenon. Food products touted as meal replacements, such as Slim-Fast drinks and snack bars, became popular in the late 1970s and early 1980s as "convenience" assumed increasing importance to dieters. In 2000, as quick-result remedies again were returning to popularity, the pharmaceutical and dietary supplement side of the industry was growing, and the major weight-loss "systems" companies were retooling their images to focus less on thinness and more on health and fitness, two other mantras of the era.

The value of being thin, especially for women, seemed to start as a largely American preoccupation. In the 1890s, as society women began taking up sports, the trendier fashion magazines began featuring "Gibson Girls" as the image of an ideal woman. Charles Dana Gibson's *Life* magazine illustrations were the source of these images. While Gibson portrayed women with different faces and in different moods, they were always youthful, slim, and athletic. This ideal of thinness, born in the 1890s, has to a great extent remained in fashion, although full-figured women made a brief comeback during World War II.

Several factors served to keep "thin" the ideal body type through the decades. One theme equated thinness with health. Images repeated in the advertising and entertainment media linked thinness with happiness and success.

In 1901 insurance companies, in an attempt to demonstrate a connection between obesity and shortened life expectancy, began charting ideal weights for men and women. This development helped make the bathroom scale a standard household item and led to the creation of a variety of weight-loss products. Most of these were available in drugstores, but direct-mail advertising was typically used to supplement drugstore sales. About 1910 Rengo, a company that manufactured corsets as well as a weight-loss product, promoted its remedy to women with the promise, "You can eat it like fruit or candy and easily reduce your fat a pound a day." In the 1930s Silph chewing gum and Elfin fat-reducing gumdrops, containing laxative, sugar, and wintergreen, were actively marketed weight-loss products.

Ironically, one of the first major pitches promising weight loss to women was not for a weight-loss product but for a cigarette, and its positioning as a diet aid served as an example of the power of this claim. During the 1920s, ads for Lucky Strike cigarettes advised, "To keep a slender figure, reach for a Lucky instead of a sweet." These ads helped the American Tobacco Company spring from third to first in sales from 1926 to 1930.

Versions of "diet miracle" ads from the 1930s often featured a photograph of a svelte society woman accompanied by a personal narrative about how she lost a substantial amount of weight in a short time. For example, a company called Wallace ran personal story ads with a headline that read, "It's so easy to do! No starving. No punishment." These ads often included a "free trial" offer.

In 1939 the Carlay Company and its ad agency, Presba-Fellers-Presba, Inc., began marketing a product called Ayds Candies, adding a new twist to the industry's most common advertising strategy. Its success with this approach lasted for decades and greatly influenced later entrants to the market. (Carlay was acquired by the Campana Corporation in the 1950s.) Instead of merely featuring a single photograph showing a successful dieter, the company's testimonial ads included "before" and "after" shots. Instead of celebrities or socialites, it found that actual named women and their personal diet stories generated the best response. Headlines such as "I got stuck in a church pew before I lost 70 pounds" or "When I was fat, I had to 'act' happy. But at 128 pounds, I can be myself" propelled Ayds Candies to the status of a well-known brand name. The stories themselves were largely based on letters from customers, rewritten or reformatted for different magazines by Campana's ad agency, Hartford, Connecticut–based Wilson, Haight & Welch. After polling consumers, the company changed its format slightly. To accentuate the positive, it began using a larger "after" photo instead of running same-size before and after shots side by side. Though Ayds used some television advertising, testimonial print ads remained the core of its advertising efforts.

After a short hiatus during World War II, the proliferation of diet products continued. Supported by fashion trends and remaining a common editorial focus in women's magazines such as *Ladies' Home Journal*, diet information could be found everywhere. From 1951 to 1953, the number of articles on dieting listed in the *Reader's Guide to Periodical Literature* increased fivefold.

The extravagance of the claims also increased and, in one case, helped bring down the fortunes of an ad agency. In the 1950s and early 1960s Drug Research Corporation marketed a weight-reducing product called Regimen. The advertising produced by Kastor Hilton Chesley Clifford & Atherton claimed that buyers could lose weight with "no diet." In June 1960 the government indicted Drug Research for fraudulent advertising and, in a surprise move, made Kastor Hilton, then billing about $20 million, a co-conspirator in the case. Several years passed while the parties awaited trial, during which agency volume shrank to $12 million. In May 1965, in a controversial decision, both advertiser and agency were found guilty. Kastor Hilton paid a fine of $50,000 but argued strenuously that the decision would set a dangerous precedent. It was normal business practice, it said, for agencies to accept a client's research and facts on faith.

When I was fat, I had to "act" happy. But at 128 pounds, I can be myself.

By Lorraine Marks—as told to Ruth L. McCarthy

Here I am, mimicking Sophie Tucker. In one way, I had a lot more to offer my audience: 260 pounds.

IT'S a kind of self-defense, laughing at your own fat. Like the water ballet I once took part in at the Country Club. At 260 pounds, it was impossible for me to sink or swim. If I dove under water, I bounced right back up again. So I finally rolled over on my back, stuck a rose in my mouth, a tray of drinks in my hand and floated to stardom amid a bevy of slender beauties.

Believe it or not, I weighed 110 pounds at my wedding. But in less than a year after the birth of my daughter, I gained 50 pounds. And it was up, up and away after that.

As the years rolled on, my family could see what was happening to me, but not how it happened. That's because I was a secret eater. I'd buy a chocolate cake for dinner but never take a piece in front of anyone. Then, when everyone was in bed, I'd get up and, if half the cake was left, I'd eat it. Next day, before my family got home, I'd buy another cake just like it, eat half and they'd all think I hadn't touched a crumb.

My husband never insulted me about my weight. Once, however, he did proposition me. "Lose some weight and I'll buy you a mink stole." I took him up on it and took off 50 pounds. But no sooner did I have the stole than I started to sneak eat again. I knew better, too, because I'm a Registered Nurse. I just continued to lie to myself and cover up with funny acts.

I finally learned my lesson on the golf course. Because I was so heavy, I had to wear men's golf shorts and I wanted to wear a skirt on the green.

Thank heavens I'd seen those Ayds® ads. Since everything else had failed, I thought maybe those reducing-plan candies might help kill my craving for sweets. When I bought my first box at the drugstore—the chocolate fudge kind—I learned from the list of ingredients on the package that Ayds contains vitamins and minerals, but no "filler" substances, like cellulose, and no drugs.

I started taking Ayds as directed: one or two before breakfast, then juice and an egg. Mid-morning, I'd have Ayds and bouillon. That was my own idea. At lunch, Ayds, soup and salad. And at dinner, Ayds, then probably chicken, salad and milk. And Ayds anytime I woke up hungry in the middle of the night.

It took a lot of losing before people began to notice. But the Ayds plan worked, and I went down and down on the scale. The first 50 pounds actually took me six months to lose. After that, it came off faster because I think my stomach had shrunk.

Incidentally, I'm not a new loser. My weight's been off a few years, but I still remember Ayds in case my scale and I have a showdown. After all, I don't want to have to go back to "acting" happy when it's so much nicer to simply be myself.

For my 25th anniversary, the best gift I could give my husband was my new figure.

BEFORE AND AFTER MEASUREMENTS		
	Before	After
Height	5'4½"	5'4½"
Weight	260 lbs.	128 lbs.
Bust	46"	37"
Waist	44"	26"
Hips	app. 46"	34"
Dress	24½	8-10

This text-heavy 1971 ad in the form of a personal narrative was typical of the testimonial advertising used by the marketer of the weight-loss product Ayds.

In light of the conviction, the argument went, Kastor Hilton and all other agencies would have to set up their own research departments or retain outside research services to double check client product claims. The *Wall Street Journal* ran a detailed article supporting the Kastor Hilton argument. But the government pointed out that the agency had ignored repeated warnings about the Regimen "no diet" claims, yet continued to conspire with Drug Research in a fraudulent campaign. Within two years after the conviction, Kastor Hilton billings were reduced to $2 million. To rescue its fortunes, in 1965 it brought in Emerson Foote of Foote, Cone & Belding as partner and 33 percent owner. But not even Foote's reputation for integrity (he had resigned from McCann-Erickson when the agency took on a cigarette account) could save the agency. Its remnants were acquired by Bozell & Jacobs in 1967, and Kastor Hilton ceased to exist.

In 1963 a new approach was introduced to the market, when Weight Watchers founder Jean Nidetch began inviting friends to her home to discuss effective strategies for losing weight. Adding the dimension of group support, these gatherings launched what became a large, international business. Weight Watchers' approach has always included providing guidelines for meal planning and lifestyle changes. Since its inception, it has also sponsored camps for overweight adolescents; marketed its own line of food products, including frozen meals, available at most major grocery chains; and in 1968 launched its own magazine. Much of Weight Watchers' success, however, can be attributed to treating its dieters as members of a club. (One of the benefits it often touts is that customers who successfully reach their weight goals and maintain them earn "lifetime membership.")

Like Ayds Candies, Weight Watchers used testimonial stories and before-and-after images in its advertising. While largely placing advertising in women's magazines and buying commercial time on television programs popular with women, in 1969 Weight Watchers ran print ads in *Business Week, Newsweek,* and *Time* using a photograph of an overweight business executive stuck in his chair. The caption "An executive should carry extra weight on his shoulders but not on his hips," from ad agency Ted Barash & Company, sought to expand the appeal to the men's market. In later campaigns, while still pitching membership, the advertising turned more of its focus toward retail food products.

During the 1970s, still with Barash, Weight Watchers launched its "Great American Shape Up" campaign. With print ads in *Woman's Day* and spots on NBC's *Tonight Show,* the organization positioned itself as a supporter of fitness with its "portion-controlled" packaged foods, products that would appeal to dieters and fitness-conscious nondieters. A 1976 campaign, "Stay in the Pink. Reach for a Pink," was aimed at building brand identification based on the color featured in Weight Watchers packaging.

In the 1990s Weight Watchers advertising adopted the use of celebrity spokespersons. In 1994 the company launched a large television campaign using former CBS News anchorwoman Kathleen Sullivan and later, under the direction of the New York City–based Selden Group, hired Sarah Ferguson, the Duchess of York, as spokeswoman for its "points" system. Aiming at women ages 35 to 49, spots aired in 2000 used the tag line, "We all have our winning points. Let Weight Watchers show you yours."

The celebrity spokesperson has been a staple in industry advertising since its early days. When Lillian Russell, a well-known actress in the 1890s, lost a significant amount of weight, she became a spokeswoman for a wide range of weight-loss products. Jenny Craig, another modern-day diet system marketer in a group that also includes Nutri-System, Physician's Weight Loss Centers of America, and Diet Center, has used celebrities along with "everyman" testimonials in many campaigns. Spokespersons for Jenny Craig, since it came on the scene in 1983, have included Regis Philbin, Elliott Gould, television's Susan Ruttan of *L.A. Law,* Cyndi Williams of *Laverne and Shirley,* Jerry Mathers of *Leave It to Beaver,* and Jenny Craig herself. For a short time, a few television spots featured Monica Lewinsky, following disclosure of her association with then-President Bill Clinton. The company's choice of celebrities, according to corporate marketing, is based on its goal of appealing to baby boomers.

Jenny Craig's major positioning, according to the company's Web site, is as a "weight-loss management services company."

"WEIGHT WATCHERS
HAS MORE
DELICIOUSNESS
THAN ANYBODY ELSE."

LYNN REDGRAVE

"Weight Watchers has 23 entrees. That's more than those others have. With Weight Watchers I can have pizza, divine Chicken Parmagiana or a pasta. Sweet and Sour Chicken. Creamy Chicken a la King. Or crispy Southern Fried Chicken. Or any one of 17 more. I don't repeat a dish in over 3 weeks of delicious dining—unless I get stuck on a favorite. Weight Watchers, this is living!"

WEIGHT WATCHERS® FROZEN FOODS

A 1985 ad for Weight Watchers frozen foods featured a testimonial from English actress Lynn Redgrave.
Weight Watchers is a registered trademark of H.J. Heinz Company and is used with permission.

Founded in 1983 in Australia, the company, by the end of 1999, had more than 660 owned and franchised outlets throughout Australia, New Zealand, the United States, and Canada. Although it did not adopt the group meeting approach used by Weight Watchers, Jenny Craig attempts to satisfy the "support" issue by promoting one-on-one consulting.

During the 1980s the company focused on information-oriented advertising explaining why its programs work. During the 1990s its messages instead concentrated on lifestyle issues. While customers include both men and women, advertising has been aimed at professional women ages 35 to 55 and, in particular, those who failed at previous diets. Jenny Craig named Doner, Southfield, Michigan, as its ad agency in 2000, after six years with Los Angeles, California–based Suissa Miller. Effective campaigns from Suissa Miller included "We Change Lives" and "The New Jenny Craig: It's Your Choice," which promoted the company's health and lifestyle approach to permanent weight loss. A campaign launched in 2001 featured the tag line, "You've always had the will. Let us show you the way."

The history of Nutri-System, a company founded in 1973, exemplifies many of the ups and downs of the industry. During the 1970s its ads featured a lot of before-and-after type testimonials; media spending was heavy. In the wake of financial troubles, it closed its outlets and began restructuring, using direct-response advertising and a Web site to sell consumables such as foods and supplements directly to customers.

Slim-Fast Foods Company represents a different branch of the weight-loss industry, emphasizing its products as calorie-controlled meal replacements. (Other entrants in this segment include Nestlé's Sweet Success, whose sales equaled about one-quarter of Slim-Fast's.) Slim-Fast and Ultra Slim-Fast drinks, along with powders and snack bars, are distributed through major grocery chains.

In 1997 the company launched a program called "Jump Start," aimed at people interested in quick weight loss. Possibly setting out to compete with pharmaceutical products just coming into the market, this campaign from Grey Advertising, New York City, used consumer testimonials based on customer letters. Sales were strong, as were advertising expenditures; the latter were estimated at $45 million for 1996.

In 1993 the Federal Trade Commission (FTC) investigated the weight-loss industry and issued consent orders requiring increased disclosure in advertising and marketing. These orders required that a personal weight-loss claim be accompanied by a disclaimer indicating that results might vary and that weight loss could be temporary. The orders also required that companies choosing to use comparative charts in their advertising materials improve their methods for qualifying the data they used as well as their research methods. While these orders did not eliminate the industry, they put constraints on some types of advertising and kept the issue of appropriate advertising claims in the spotlight.

In 1997 a national conference on the subject of weight-loss products and programs was sponsored by members of the FTC, the American Society for Clinical Nutrition, the National Institute of Diabetes and Digestive and Kidney Diseases, and the Centers for Disease Control and Prevention. Program attendees included representatives from academia, public advocacy groups, and the industry. One result of the conference was the formation of a panel that would do continuing work in the area of appropriate disclosure. All parties recognized the importance of creating guidelines and standards for collecting and disseminating weight-loss data that consumers use in making decisions.

A new wave of weight-loss products hit the market during the 1990s. Very much reflecting a culture amenable to taking drugs for virtually any ailment, companies began introducing newly approved prescription drugs designed to help people lose weight. In 1996 American Home Products began to market Redux; in 1998 Knoll Pharmaceuticals introduced Meridia; and in 1999 Hoffman-La Roche brought out Xenical. All three were introduced with large budgets, thanks to relaxed restrictions on the advertising of prescription drugs directly to consumers (a development that also brought pitches for allergy and hypertension remedies to prime-time television). Redux, among others, relied on fenfluramine, an ingredient common in many herbal and over-the-counter supplements, and was taken off the market in 1997 owing to concerns about side effects. Meridia, which acts as an appetite suppressant, met with less than overwhelming success when commercials first hit the airwaves, while Xenical, a lipase inhibitor, which blocks the absorption of dietary fat, tallied higher early sales.

The relative success of each product seemed to be directly related to its advertising spending and approach. Knoll spent about $5 million per month on Meridia's launch, then slowed spending to $3 million per month for the next nine months. Hoffman-La Roche spent more than $11 million in its product's second month, leveled off at $7.5 million per month through the sixth month, then shot up to a $30 million per month for a consumer campaign over the next three months. The largest portion of Hoffman-La Roche's advertising budget went to direct-to-consumer marketing. According to Dow Jones Reports, in late 2000 Xenical ranked number five in consumer recall; Meridia ranked number 42, despite the fact that the campaign for Xenical operated under a much shorter time frame.

In view of the findings of the 1997 conference, weight-loss ads of the 21st century are likely to emphasize health and lifestyle choices, focusing especially on the promotion of realistic weight goals and an increased level of physical activity. Direct-to-consumer advertising is likely to grow, as are sales via the Internet, a medium that proved particularly suitable for providing data and making disclosures in a discreet way.

Traditionally, the strong period for advertising spending in the industry has been January through April. Weight-loss marketers often spend up to 50 percent of their year's budget after Christmas and before the bathing-suit season. According to auditing company Competitive Media Reporting, Weight Watchers, which was sold by H.J. Heinz Company to Artal Luxembourg in June 1999, spent $26 million on advertising in 1999. Other industry leaders were Hoffman-La Roche ($145 million in ad spending), Slim-Fast ($102 million), Knoll ($64 million), Jenny Craig ($22 million), and Nutri-System ($729,000).

DEBORAH HAWKINS

Further Reading

Fitzgerald, Kate, "Weight Loss Business May Get Crash Diet," *Advertising Age* (10 May 1993)

Fraser, Laura, *Losing It: America's Obsession with Weight and Weight Loss and the Industry That Feeds on It*, New York: Dutton, 1997

Liebman, Milton, "Head to Head Marketing . . . May the Best-Promoted Drug Win" <www.djinteractive.com>

Poulton, Terry, *No Fat Chicks: How Big Business Profits by Making Women Hate Their Bodies—And How to Fight Back,* Secaucus, New Jersey: Carol, 1997

Stearns, Peter N., *Fat History: Bodies and Beauty in the Modern West,* New York: New York University Press, 1997

Thompson, Stephanie, "Two Ad Pitches for Weight Loss Gain More Heft: Weight Watchers and Jenny Craig Stress Personalized Diet Programs," *Advertising Age* (4 December 2000)

United States Federal Trade Commission Bureau of Consumer Protection, "Commercial Weight Loss Products and Programs: What Consumers Stand to Gain and Lose: A Public Conference on the Information Consumers Need to Evaluate Weight Loss Products and Programs," <www.ftc.gov/os/1998/9803/weightlo.rpt.htm>

Wells, Rich, Greene, Inc.

Opened in 1966; achieved success for several decades under leadership of Mary Wells Lawrence; issued initial public offering, 1968; returned to private control through a bonds-for-stock exchange, 1974; Wells Lawrence resigned as CEO, replaced by Ken Olshan, 1990; sold to French company BDDP and renamed Wells Rich Greene BDDP, 1991; sold to GGT PLC of London, England, 1996; renamed Wells BDDP, 1997, and subsequently acquired by Omnicom Group; went out of business, May 1998.

Major Clients

American Motors Corporation
Braniff Airlines
Bristol-Myers Corporation
Hertz Corporation
IBM Corporation
Miles Laboratories (Alka-Seltzer)
Philip Morris Companies (Benson & Hedges)
Procter & Gamble Company (Pringles, Oil of Olay)

In the 1960s and 1970s Wells, Rich, Greene, Inc. (WRG), and particularly the ambitious, smart, and stylish Mary Wells, personified everything glamorous and exciting about advertising at the height of the "creative revolution." Born in Youngstown, Ohio, as Mary Georgene Berg, she acquired her better-known surname when she married her first husband, Bert Wells, while studying at Carnegie Tech. Trained as an actress in her teens, she believed that advertising was not marketing but show business. She began her advertising career at Macy's in New York City and then joined McCann-Erickson as a copy chief at age 24. In 1957, at age 28, she joined Doyle Dane Bernbach (DDB) just when its creative work was making it one of the most influential postwar agencies; she remained there for seven years. In January 1964 Wells moved to Jack Tinker & Partners, a unique boutique

agency set up by the Interpublic Group of Companies to experiment with a more daring, creative kind of advertising than the holding company's other shops were producing. Her primary responsibility there was the $6 million Braniff Airlines account. A little over two years later Wells decided to start her own agency. Originally announced as Mary Wells & Associates the day she resigned from Tinker, the new agency opened in early April 1966 in four rooms of the Hotel Gotham in New York City as Wells, Rich, Greene, Inc., when two other Tinker employees joined her as partners.

Copy director Richard Rich had a background similar to Wells's. He had also started at DDB in 1961 and then moved to Papert, Koenig, Lois, Inc., for a year before rejoining Wells at Tinker in 1964. There he worked closely with art director Stewart Greene on the Alka-Seltzer account, creating a series of commercials based on the theme "the shape your stomach's in." Prior to Tinker, Greene had been with Daniel & Charles for six years and before that with the Gumbinner Agency for six years.

But it was Wells who would draw the attention of the media and give the agency the force of a celebrity brand. In the first months of WRG, the glow of publicity included profiles on Wells in publications ranging from *Cosmopolitan* to *Fortune* to *L'Express.* "Girl wonder," "the gray flannel gal," and "the Madison Avenue bombshell" were among the phrases she inspired. In 1986 *Adweek* called her "Mary, queen of spots." She understood the value of being an attractive, young, and supremely self-assured woman in a profession still dominated by aging legends such as Leo Burnett and Fairfax Cone. She leveraged those assets smartly. "I can say things a bit forward if I'm a girl that would seem out of line if said by a man," she told *Advertising Age* in 1966. She was right.

By 1968 potential clients were begging to get into WRG's new quarters in the General Motors Building between 58th and 59th streets. In addition to Braniff, the agency took on the Philip Morris

The New American Car.

This is the American Motors Gremlin. It is the kind of car this country has needed for a long, long time.

It is designed to give the American motorist a car that is easy to buy, easy to handle, easy to take care of, and, at the same time, fun to drive.

The Gremlin is the smallest production car made in America.

It is 161 inches long, just 2½ inches longer than the Volkswagen.

Yet its turning circle, at 32 feet, 8 inches, is about 3 feet less than VW's.

Which makes the Gremlin about the easiest car in the world to park and handle.

The Gremlin gets the best gas mileage of any car made in America. It goes about 500 miles without stopping for gas.

This is great gas mileage, when you consider that the Gremlin has a bigger standard engine than any car near its size and price, 128 hp to VW's 57.

This engine gets from 0 to 60 in 15.3 seconds, the pickup you need on expressways.

And nobody's going to push you around in a Gremlin. It is 10 inches wider, 7 inches lower and 765 pounds heavier than a VW.

Which gives you about the smoothest, most stable ride possible in a car this size.

The Gremlin is remarkably easy to service and maintain.

Its normal oil change interval is 6 months or 6,000 miles; lubrication is normally needed only every 24,000 miles.

There are two basic Gremlin models.

A two-passenger, with storage area in the rear.

A four-passenger with fold-down rear seats for extra storage and flip-up rear window for easy access.

Both models cost about what you'd pay for an imported economy car.

The four-passenger lists for $1,959.

The lowest list price of any car made in America.

Except for the two-passenger Gremlin. It lists for $1,879.

Which is quite a bargain, when you consider what you get for your money.

The new American car.

American Motors Gremlin
$1,879 **$1,959**
2-Passenger 4-Passenger

Be sure to see the Gremlin and all the other fine American Motors cars at the auto show.

Wells, Rich, Greene, Inc., in 1970 launched American Motors' Gremlin, the automaker's most popular model of the decade.

Companies' Benson & Hedges, Burma Shave, and other hand-picked accounts that took billings to the $30 million level within a year. In September WRG launched its Benson & Hedges campaign centering on the advantages and disadvantages of smoking a 100 mm cigarette ("You won't light your nose"). The agency became famous for redesigning the color schemes of Braniff aircraft and uniforms in an array of pastels—"the Easter egg airline," one critic called it.

By its second birthday in April 1968, WRG was billing $59 million (notwithstanding published reports of $85 million) and was one of America's top-15 agencies. Wells boasted that she could attract the best creative talent to WRG and paid salaries so lavish she upset the prevailing wage schedules among the top agencies. In August 1968 the agency gave up its charter client, Braniff, which had been taken over in January by conglomerate Ling-Temco-Vought, and took on the much larger TWA business, worth nearly $15 million. WRG briefly inherited the famous "Up, up, and away" theme that Foote, Cone & Belding, TWA's agency

since 1956, had developed for the airline only a year before but quickly discarded it. The most remarkable aspect of the account shift, however, was that it came within nine months of Mary Wells's marriage to Braniff Chief Executive Officer (CEO) Harding Lawrence in Paris, France, in November 1967.

It was widely noted in the trade press that the brash, often ironic humor of WRG might work with advertisers that had little to lose but would be inappropriate for a market leader. And indeed many clients were second-tier brands looking for attention. One was Royal Crown, which had inaugurated the diet cola category with its Diet-Rite brand. Another was the American Motors Corporation (AMC), which WRG won in June 1967 from Benton & Bowles and helped return to profitability after two years in the red with advertising for the AMC Javelin and later the Gremlin. One commercial showed a small street gang of punks considering stealing a Gremlin while the leader (played by a young, pre-Hollywood Richard Dreyfuss) pointed out the car's main selling points. They were created by Charlie Moss, the first employee hired by Wells Lawrence in 1966, and Stan Dragoti, who would soon leave WRG and go on to a successful directing career in Hollywood (*Love at First Bite, Mr. Mom*) before returning to advertising in the 1990s.

But WRG also had its share of blue-chip clients. In 1967 it won business from General Mills, Hunt-Wesson, and Bristol-Myers. The next year it took its first Procter & Gamble (P&G) business, Gleem toothpaste, from Compton Advertising. And in 1971 it became agency of record for P&G, overseeing the TV program *The Jimmy Stewart Show* in a rare throwback to radio in which a single advertiser undertook sponsorship of an entire show.

In October 1968 WRG became the ninth American agency to become a public company. As billings approached $90 million, the initial offering on the over-the-counter market started at $17.50, but by the end of the first day the price had shot to $25. The move provided the company with more than $1.3 billion in cash. Such demand attested to the heat WRG was generating within the industry. The move also made Mary Wells Lawrence the highest paid woman executive in history. According to *Advertising Age,* her salary and deferred payments totaled $250,000 a year, not only higher than any other executive in advertising, including Dan Seymour, CEO of the J. Walter Thompson Company, but also more than her husband. Shortly afterward, at age 40, she became the youngest person ever inducted into the Copywriters Hall of Fame.

Among the most defining of the WRG campaigns of the 1970s were those it created for Alka-Seltzer. WRG had snatched this account from DDB in 1970 in a coup that astonished not only DDB, which had won the account only a year before and produced the well-known "Spicy meatball" campaign, but the entire advertising world. Wells Lawrence had worked on the brand during her years at Tinker and intended to make it a signature landmark for WRG. By all accounts she succeeded, certainly matching and perhaps topping DDB with the "Plop, Plop, Fizz, Fizz" campaign as well as with memorable one-shot vignettes such as "Try it, you'll like it" and "I can't believe I ate the whole thing."

The spectacular growth of the agency proved too rapid for Richard Rich, who was uneasy with Wells Lawrence's plan to diversify into film production. Rich was "dismissed" from the agency by the board in April 1969, leaving on a cordial basis with about 225,000 shares of WRG stock. Greene left the agency in 1974, but growth seemed to be reaching certain limits by then. Although billings remained healthy, the stock price leveled off and then retreated. In 1974 Wells Lawrence announced that WRG would "go private." Share price, which reached a high of $28 in 1972, was running as low as half the value per share prior to the announcement.

After WRG lost AMC in 1972 because, by some accounts, it took too much credit for the company's rebound and gave too little to its dealer network, the agency began to keep a lower profile and to build its research and account management strengths. By the end of the 1970s, WRG ranked 18th among U.S. agencies with billings of $378 million and offices in Chicago, Illinois; Detroit, Michigan; Dallas, Texas; St. Louis, Missouri; Seattle, Washington; Phoenix, Arizona; Newport Beach, California; and one office in London, England. (The St. Louis office was known as Gardner Advertising, a $60 million agency rich in Ralston-Purina business, which WRG acquired in December 1972 in an exchange of stock, although Gardner continued to operate under its own name.)

Wells Lawrence's daring continued to make news and amaze the industry. When Kenyon & Eckhardt dropped Ford for Chrysler in 1979, several pieces of important Ford business became available, one of which had narrowed its choice to a short list of three major contenders. Wells Lawrence, whose agency was not under consideration, flew to Detroit at the 11th hour and after a personal meeting with Henry Ford walked away with the $12 million Ford corporate account. In 1982 she pulled off the remarkable act of holding two accounts in the same category. Once again, her coup involved the airline business. In January WRG, already the agency for Continental Airlines, won the $35 million Pan American World Airways business without an agency review and without notifying Continental of its plan. It kept both clients; a WRG subsidiary was promptly set up to accommodate Continental, which, though angered, did not withdraw its business.

By 1986 WRG was 20 years old, billing a comfortable $650 million, and settling into a long period of interesting but more often routine creative work for established clients. The desire to be on the creative edge was ebbing among agencies and particularly advertisers. Although agency mergers were the trend, WRG was determined to remain independent. Yet, it was not averse to making an opportunistic acquisition. There had been talks with DDB, and Wells Lawrence had even made a play for Saatchi & Saatchi before it became a major buyer itself. But by the late 1980s, she was spending more time in France than New York and was beginning her withdrawal from active agency management. She did not participate in the agency's pitch for the IBM Corporation account in 1988.

The agency was also slipping increasingly behind in the race for global position, a fact that attracted the attention of the

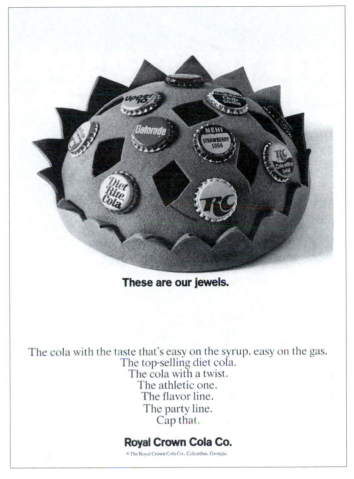

These are our jewels.

The cola with the taste that's easy on the syrup, easy on the gas.
The top-selling diet cola.
The cola with a twist.
The athletic one.
The flavor line.
The party line.
Cap that.

Royal Crown Cola Co.

The Royal Crown Cola Co., Columbus, Georgia.

Wells, Rich, Greene helped popularize the brands of the Royal Crown Cola Company with ads such as this example from 1971.
RC, Diet RC, Cherry RC and ROYAL CROWN are registered trademarks of The Royal Crown Company © 2001 Dr Pepper/Seven Up, Inc.

French agency Boulet Dru Depuy Petit (BDDP). As Wells Lawrence officially stepped down as CEO in favor of Ken Olshan, who had come to the agency when it acquired Doherty, Mann & Olshan in 1975, she sold a minority interest of 40 percent of WRG to BDDP in April 1990. Prior to that she had owned 100 percent of the agency. Fourteen months later BDDP raised its stake to 70 percent and changed the name to Wells, Rich, Greene BDDP Communications, Inc. After the withdrawal of the charismatic Wells Lawrence, Olshan watched $150 million in billings leave the agency—IBM, Mobil Corrporation (Hefty Bags), Alka-Seltzer, Continental, and Midas Muffler. Then in the spring of 1995 an embezzlement scandal involving WRG President David Sklaver and its chief financial officer, Tom Fagen, further tarnished the agency's reputation, despite a profitable new business record and a rank of 15th among American agencies. The following September, after months of negotiations with BDDP over management restructuring, Olshan was summarily fired a month after winning the $20 million Heineken beer account. The reason given was "disappointing results" (widely interpreted as insufficient growth) during his five-year tenure.

'TIS THE SEASON TO PLOP PLOP FIZZ FIZZ FAST FAST

ALKA-SELTZER

Alka-Seltzer for upset stomach with headache the plop plop fizz fizz is fast fast.
Read the label, use only as directed. Miles Laboratories, Inc. c1977.

A holiday season ad from 1977 featured a version of the memorable "Plop plop, fizz fizz" slogan created by Wells, Rich, Greene, Inc., for Alka-Seltzer.
Courtesy of Bayer Corporation.

After Olshan's ouster, morale in New York declined. Meanwhile, in Paris rumors about the future of BDDP were making the rounds. In May 1996 a management group within the agency was reported to be preparing a takeover bid. Another possible buyer was Martin Sorrell of the WPP Group. That September, however, BDDP was sold to a relatively small upstart, GGT PLC (Gold Greenless Trott), which suddenly became the world's 13th-largest advertising company. In July 1997 the official name of WRG was changed once again to Wells BDDP.

A series of account losses in New York caused management to panic: first Bristol-Myers, then Tag Heuer, and in early January 1998 Liberty Mutual Insurance. Combined with high turnover and the unexpected resignation of several key executives, major clients such as Procter & Gamble, which placed a high value on stability, began to review their positions. That in turn caused the situation to unravel with alarming speed. Late in January P&G finally decided that Wells BDDP was no longer viable and pulled

its combined $125 million accounts for Oil of Olay and Pringles potato chips. As a result, GGT's stock plunged so steeply that it became an instant takeover target. At that point the Omnicom Group began to quietly inquire among Wells's clients whether they might stay within the Omnicom group of agencies if Omnicom should make a bid. Hertz, the History Channel, and Georgia Pacific agreed; Toys "R" Us had already chosen a small agency set up by a departing Wells creative director, Linda Kaplan Thaler, several months before.

Among employees, the run was on. Sixty resigned (many moving to Saatchi & Saatchi and Grey Advertising along with the P&G business) and another 40 were scheduled for layoff. By the end of February only a handful of accounts remained.

On 13 March 1998 Wells became part of Omnicom, which promptly "put it out of its misery," according to the *Wall Street Journal*. The new parent waited 60 days before closing Wells's doors for good on May 13. Although WRG, which had once enjoyed nearly $1 billion in billings and was one of the industry's most glamorous shops during its most glamorous era, ceased to exist, Omnicom nevertheless acquired valuable assets that included some of Europe's best agencies. BDDP was merged with TBWA, creating a combination that would rank among the world's top-ten agency networks.

JOHN MCDONOUGH

Further Reading

Danzig, Fred, "After 10 Years Wells Rich Greene Says It's Time to Get Its Act Together," *Advertising* Age (3 May 1976)

Dickstein, George, "Mary Wells' Dream," *Advertising Age* (18 April 1966)

Elliott, Stuart, "Advertising: Seeking Stability," *New York Times* (10 February 1995)

Elliott, Stuart, "Advertising: Two High Level Executives Leave Wells Rich," *New York Times* (13 April 1995)

Fox, Stephen R., *The Mirror Makers: A History of American Advertising and Its Creators*, New York: Morrow, 1984

Kanner, Bernice, "An Agency Comes of Age," *New York Magazine* (1 December 1986)

Kim, Hank, "After 32 Years, Wells Has Run Dry," *Adweek* (16 March 1998)

King, Thomas R., "Wells Rich Links with France's BDDP," *Wall Street Journal* (16 April 1990)

Lafayette, Jon, "Mary Wells: On the Record," *Advertising Age* (1 August 1988)

Lipman, Joanne, "BDDP Takes Majority Control of Wells," *Wall Street Journal* (12 June 1991)

"Madison Avenue: See Mary Run," *Newsweek* (3 October 1966)

"Mary Wells Interview," *Adweek* (9 November 1998)

Myers, Bill, "Mary Wells Lawrence: Dedicated Pro, or Gifted Opportunist?" *Adweek* (Eastern edition) (25 January 1982)

Siekman, Philip, "Wells, Rich, Greene," *Fortune* (August 1966)

Wendy's International, Inc.

Principal Agencies

Dancer, Fitzgerald, Sample, Inc.
Backer, Spielvogel, Bates, Inc. (later Bates USA)

Founder Dave Thomas opened the first Wendy's Old-Fashioned Hamburgers outlet in downtown Columbus, Ohio, in November 1969. The business, named for Thomas's daughter, expanded quickly, and by 1976 there were 500 outlets, including locations in Canada. The restaurant chain built itself on a reputation for being both "homespun" and "hip."

From Wendy's earliest days, its management considered advertising fundamental to growth. Early regional efforts included the 1972 "Eat 'em up" effort from Munger, Reithmiller & Associates and the 1973 "C'mon to Wendy's" from Stockton, West, Burkhart, Inc. The chain's differences from its rivals were always a major focus of the advertising.

Wendy's first national campaign, a $3 million effort from the Dick Rich agency in 1977, took aim at McDonald's and Burger King. The effort, themed "Hot 'n' Juicy" told consumers, "If you ever had a dry, chewy hamburger, you're going to love Wendy's hot and juicy hamburgers."

Over the next decade, Wendy's grew dramatically in sales and in the number of outlets, both domestic and foreign. As the chain grew, its advertising strategy continued to revolve around promoting old-fashioned values and being "different" as being synonymous with being "good." A key aspect of promoting Wendy's differences involved targeted advertising around its ever-changing range of menu items, a strategy specifically aimed at setting the franchise apart from "burgers only" establishments. By 1981, after regional rollouts, the salad bar had become a staple on its national menu, making it the first quick-service restaurant with this type of offering. In 1983 Wendy's was the first hamburger chain to offer baked potatoes, a niche market trend that began in the late 1970s. Other major product introductions included "The Big Classic" bacon cheeseburger in 1986; the Super Value Meal, nine items listed for 99 cents each, 1989; the grilled chicken sandwich, designed to satisfy the demand for more healthful fast-food options, 1990; and five salads that could be ordered to go, 1992. Later menu additions included spicy chicken-and-pita sandwiches (1997) geared to appeal to calorie-conscious women customers and to further satisfy U.S. consumers' desire to eat a healthy, low-fat diet.

In addition to its menu choices, the creative aspect of Wendy's advertising was always seen as another arena for innovation. While Wendy's has historically spent only a fraction of McDonald's or Burger King's budgets for advertising, its commercials have consistently scored high in memorability and artistry. Early work from Dancer, Fitzgerald, Sample, Inc. (DFS), included a 1982 campaign that suggested that "discriminating" consumers were "Wendy's Kind of People," and "Burger Wars," a 1983 blast at the competition that portrayed fast-food customers as victims of "those other hamburger places," having to settle for inferior products; the ads pictured competitors using patties taken from large cartons labeled "Frozen."

One of its most memorable campaigns came in 1984 with "Where's the Beef?" Four ads, created by DFS and directed by Joe Sedelmaier, featured a trio of senior citizens, played by Clara Peller and sidekicks Mildred Lane and Elizbeth Shaw, eyeing the inadequacies of "typical" fast-food burgers—all bun, no beef. This campaign captured the public with its tongue-in-cheek cleverness, and its tag line quickly became part of the lexicon as a metaphor for something lacking in substance.

While "Where's the Beef?" was a difficult act to follow, Wendy's managed a good follow-up with its "Parts is Parts" campaign, which lampooned the competition's use of generic "chicken meat" versus the top-grade chicken breast Wendy's used in sandwiches. While not as popular as the "Where's the Beef?" campaign, it still caught consumers' attention.

This 1992 Wendy's ad featured the chain's founder, Dave Thomas, whose affable personality made him an ideal spokesperson to promote the company in its advertising.
Courtesy of Wendy's.

Its next big effort, from new shop Backer Spielvogel Bates, Inc., was "Hamburger A, hamburger B," which ran from 1987 to 1989. This taste-test campaign resulted in the largest testimonial advertising campaign in television history.

Beginning in the early 1990s, however, Wendy's found its best spokesman to be its founder, Dave Thomas, who gave consumers a face and a personality to associate with Wendy's image. Before his death on 7 January 2002, Thomas starred in more than 700 Wendy's spots over the years, during which time he moved from the realm of credible spokesperson to a bit of an American cultural hero. In 1991 he published his autobiography, *Dave's Way*, followed in 1994 by his second book, *Well Done*, which featured inspirational stories about successful people.

At the end of the 20th century Wendy's ad budget continued to be small relative to those of its competitors. It surpassed $200 million for the first time in 1999 to reach $217.8 million. This figure was dwarfed in comparison to those of McDonald's ($627.2 million) and Burger King ($403.6 million). As of 2001, the company had 5,600 Wendy's Old-Fashioned Hamburgers outlets worldwide and 2,000 Tim Horton's in the United States and Canada.

DEBORAH HAWKINS

Further Reading

"An Appetite for Wendy's," *Advertising Age* (14 August 2000)

Garfield, Bob, "Olympian Dave Thomas? That's Tough Sledding," *Advertising Age* (7 February 1994)

Garfield, Bob, "Top 100 Advertising Campaigns," *Advertising Age* (29 March 1999)

Howard, Niles, "Wendy's Aims to Take Big Bite of Fast Food," *Advertising Age* (28 March 1977)

Hume, Scott, "Wendy's: Charlie Rath," *Advertising Age* (6 July 1992)

Kramer, Louise, "Wendy's to Greet New Year with Beefed-Up Budget," *Advertising Age* (19 October 1998)

Pollack, Judann, and Mark Gleason, "The Struggle for the Next Helping," *Advertising Age* (7 October 1996)

Sutherland, Max, *Advertising and the Mind of the Consumer: What Works, What Doesn't, and Why*, St. Leonards, New South Wales: Allen and Unwin, 1993; 2nd edition, by Sutherland and Alice K. Sylvester, St. Leonards, New South Wales: Allen and Unwin, and London: Kogan Page, 2000

Wendy's Restaurant <www.wendys.com>

Whalen, Jeanne, "KFC, Wendy's Go National with Wraps: Fast-Feeders Join Trend for Lighter Sandwiches," *Advertising Age* (21 April 1997)

Wieden & Kennedy, Inc.

Founded by Dan Wieden and David Kennedy in Portland, Oregon, 1982; opened offices in Amsterdam, 1992; New York, 1995; London, 1998; and Tokyo, 1998.

Major Clients

Coca-Cola Company
Microsoft Corporation
Miller Brewing Company
Nike, Inc.
Subaru of America, Inc.

One of the largest independently owned advertising companies in the world by the turn of the 21st century, the Portland, Oregon–based Wieden & Kennedy (W&K) began in 1982 with a single client, Nike, for which the agency created the now internationally known slogan, "Just do it!" W&K has made its reputation with hip and quirky advertising that borrows from the ironic sensibility of the younger generation. Conceived in an era of public cynicism toward the claims of advertisers, W&K styles itself as a "rebel shop" that openly disdains traditional advertising.

Founders Dan Wieden and David Kennedy started out in traditional advertising venues. Wieden was the son of Duke Wieden, a big name in the small world of Portland advertising. Despite some reservations, Dan followed his father into the business, writing copy for local wood products companies. Kennedy began his career in Chicago, Illinois, eventually working as an art director for Leo Burnett Company. Wieden and Kennedy discovered one another in the Portland outpost of the McCann-Erickson agency, where they shared work on the Louisiana-Pacific Corporation account. They also shared a common discontent with advertising-as-usual. When the William Cain, Inc., agency snagged the Louisiana-Pacific Corporation account in 1980, both Wieden and Kennedy left with it. Shortly afterwards, Nike came into their lives.

A company begun in 1964 by former University of Oregon track star Phil Knight, who sold running shoes out of the back of his car at track meets, Nike had grown to a point where it needed to think seriously about brand positioning. In 1979 Nike fired John Brown & Partners and turned in 1980 to local talent Cain. With only $300,000 in billings, Nike was a minor account, so Cain gave the job to his youthful creative team of Wieden and Kennedy. Within two years, Wieden and Kennedy jumped ship again, this time to form their own agency, bringing with them Cain's media specialist Jane Kirby and production manager Dennis Fraser, and most important, Nike. On 1 April 1982 Wieden &

WHICH SPORTSCENTER DO YOU WATCH?
5 AM – 12 PM, 6 PM, 11 PM, 1 AM, 2 AM ET

TIM DUNCAN WATCHES THE 11 PM SPORTSCENTER.

ESPN

Wieden & Kennedy's "Which Sportscenter Do You Watch?" campaign for ESPN, launched in 1999, promoted the network's sportcasts as the choice of professional athletes.
Courtesy of Wieden & Kennedy New York.

Kennedy was born—with only one client, but one that would help the agency make its name.

Wieden & Kennedy was not the first to create an image campaign for Nike; that achievement belongs to Brown, which in 1977 had eschewed the more traditional sneaker ad for a full-page picture on the back of *Runners World* magazine of a lone runner on a country road, with the sparse copy, "There is no finish line." But W&K ran with this image of athletic existentialism, crafting the slogan "Just do it!" (implying a similarly simplistic view of life to that expressed in the antidrug "Just say no" campaign, but one considerably more successful) in 1988 and creating quirky advertisements that equated individuality and rebellion with a sneaker.

In 1987 W&K rolled out its now well-known "Revolution" TV spot for Nike, using the Beatles' 1968 anthem "Revolution" as the sound track. This launched a series of W&K ads for Nike that used improbable subcultural references—such as a song by proto-punk rocker Iggy Pop or pitchmen such as Beat author William Borroughs—to push the product of what was now a multinational corporation. W&K even imitated subcultural media itself, quietly promoting Nike sneakers by publishing a low-key "fan-zine," a medium that had been created by bohemians in explicit reaction against commercial culture. In 1997 W&K went so far as to ask media artists Negativeland, a group whose raison d'être is criticizing advertisements, for permission to use one of its songs for a Miller beer ad. Negativeland declined.

Working on the Nike account, W&K further developed a style of "anti-advertising" pioneered a generation earlier by Doyle Dane Bernbach for Volkswagen. One W&K TV ad, featuring basketball great Michael Jordan and shot by independent filmmaker Spike Lee, deconstructs the traditional celebrity star spot. In it Lee tells the audience that they are welcome to buy Nike sneakers but that wearing them will not make them able to do the tricks Jordan can do. Lee then confesses that his ad is just an ad, yelling out his window at his noisy neighbors, "Shut up! I'm doing a Nike commercial here." By acknowledging the false promises of advertising, W&K was playing to what *Business Week* in 1992 called "savvy—and cynical—consumers." W&K, with an ironic wink, let the TV audience know that it, too, disliked advertising. In fact, the mantra of W&K, often repeated by staff, is "We hate advertising."

Despite this disdain, the ad business has been good to Wieden and Kennedy. Kennedy retired in 1993 to pursue studies in art,

Dan Wieden.
© 2001 *Steven Bloch.*

worth more than $9 billion by 2000. The agency itself had gross income of $60 million on billings of $601.3 million in 2000, ranking it 50th among U.S. agencies.

If Nike symbolizes the promise of the W&K style, then the Subaru campaign highlights the problems. Hired in 1991 by Subaru America to re-create the brand image of the well-engineered but dowdy all-wheel-drive auto, W&K opened an office in Philadelphia, Pennsylvania, and channeled some of its best creative talent into the job. The work they created was classic W&K: ads more about advertising than about the product. In one, a man ridicules the overwrought claims of typical automobile advertisements, claiming that a car "won't make you more handsome. Or prettier. Or younger." Instead, he states, "A car is a car." These ads were a hit with the ad industry, but they failed with consumers and the Subaru sales force. Even W&K's tried and true tactic of appropriating subcultural style failed. One advertisement that promised that Subaru was like "punk rock" became a running joke among the Gen-Xers it aimed to attract. W&K was fired by Subaru in 1993, leading to layoffs of 60 employees and the closing of its Philadelphia office. The account went to Temerlin McClain, which promptly took Subaru's image back to its dull but profitable engineering roots, showcasing "The beauty of all-wheel drive."

Wieden & Kennedy sells its services with the claim that it "specializes in understanding cultural trends." In reaction to an environment increasingly awash in advertisements, one cultural trend to arise at the end of the 20th century was public disgust with advertising, marketing, and commercialism in general. It remains to be seen whether contempt for advertising is a viable advertising strategy for the long run, but if it is, W&K is in the lead.

STEPHEN DUNCOMBE

including creative collaborations with his daughter, but W&K has continued to grow, with more than 430 employees in 2000 and branch offices in Amsterdam, The Netherlands (opened 1992); New York City (opened 1995); London, England (opened 1998); and Tokyo, Japan (opened 1998). It has garnered numerous awards, including being named "Agency of the Year" by both *Advertising Age* and *Adweek* in the same year (1991). During W&K's tenure Nike grew from a $270 million company to one

Further Reading

Berger, Warren, "They Know Bo," *New York Times Magazine* (11 November 1990)

Feit, Josh, "It's Still Your Father's Beer, But These Sure as Hell Aren't Your Old Man's Beer Ads," *Willamette Week* (9 July 1997)

Rothenberg, Randall, *Where the Suckers Moon: An Advertising Story,* New York: Knopf, 1994

William Esty & Company, Inc. *See under* Esty

Wine. *See* Beverages, Alcoholic

Wm. Wrigley Jr. Company. *See under* Wrigley

Women: Careers in Advertising

In 1926 some of the guests arriving at a gala dinner of the New York Council of the American Association of Advertising Agencies (AAAA) presented a problem. Six women who worked in positions of responsibility at six of the 50 agencies represented at the event were kept waiting at the door while it was decided whether or not they would be allowed to attend. Aminta Casseres, a group head in the copy department of J. Walter Thompson Company (JWT) at the time, wrote, "If it had been an association dinner of magazine or newspaper people, of book publishers or, strangely, of the advertising staffs of department stores (all kindred fields), the proportion of men and women would have been considerably otherwise. Certainly fifty-fifty. Possibly thirty-seventy."

Persisting Disparities

Women working in advertising in the early decades of the 20th century most often found employment as copywriters or researchers and, occasionally, as space buyers. Women account representatives and art directors were unknown at the time. It was not until 1926 that Nedda McGrath became the first woman art director of the century, when she was hired by Blackman Advertising.

According to Stephen Fox, a noted historian of advertising, a 1924 survey of more than 600 women employed in New York advertising agencies found only five media space buyers; 22 of the women worked as copywriters. The rest were in lower-level, mostly clerical jobs. A similar gender disparity was evident in salaries—women space buyers, for example, earned 50 percent less than men. In the 19th century, women had enjoyed considerably more opportunities in advertising. With the professionalization of the industry, however, men took control. Nonetheless, over the course of the 20th century, conditions for women in the advertising industry improved steadily.

In 1994 *Campaign* magazine reported that women were still excluded from two London advertising dining clubs (Solus and the 30 Club). The results of a 1993 U.S. survey sponsored by Advertising Women of New York (AWNY) were more optimistic, however. In the survey 2,000 men and women working in various communications industries were questioned about gender dis-

crimination and sexual harassment. Both sexes agreed that gender discrimination was of greater concern than sexual harassment. Women perceived a "glass ceiling" that effectively barred them from advancement to higher levels of management, while the majority of men believed that there was no such barrier. Even so, men did acknowledge that women had fewer opportunities at top management levels—only 28 percent of the women surveyed were in top management positions, compared with 68 percent of the men.

While women gained more access to positions in media and account management during the 1980s and 1990s, they lost ground in creative departments. A telephone survey conducted by *Advertising Age*'s *Creativity* magazine in 1997 revealed that there were no women in the creative department of one small agency and an average of 26 percent in the other small agencies contacted. All of the larger agencies had women represented in their creative departments, but the average was only 24 percent.

The AWNY study also reported that women in advertising earned less than men, especially in their early career years. The differences in salary were as great as 54 percent. Women who worked in the industry from 10 to 19 years might earn only 70 percent of the salaries of their male counterparts.

The 1998 annual report from the United Kingdom's Institute of Practitioners in Advertising showed that men and women were employed in roughly equal numbers as account handlers (managers) and account planners. Men exceeded women in media six to four. Men reigned supreme in creative departments in the positions of art director and copywriter by about eight to two, while women more frequently held positions in television production, finance, media buying, and on secretarial staffs. A woman who wanted to become a member of the board of directors of an agency was wise to consider a career in account planning. In 1998 a woman with this particular career specialization had an almost equal chance as her male counterpart of being appointed to a directorship. Otherwise, the chances of such an occurrence were as slim as one in ten.

During the 1960s some agencies made efforts to correct the underrepresentation of African-Americans in advertising. The efforts, however, did not receive sufficient support to have a lasting

A photograph from the J. Walter Thompson Company's 1958 recruiting publication *Advertising as a Career for Women* gave the impression that the number of male and female employees was equal—which was not the prevailing situation in the ad industry at that time. *Courtesy of the J. Walter Thompson Company.*

effect. By the close of the 20th century, 8 percent of employees in advertising agencies and related media services companies were African-American women. The percentages were even lower for Hispanic women (5 percent) and Asian/Pacific Islander women (3 percent). Thus, regardless of her ethnic origins, a woman who is a member of a minority group had even less opportunity than a white woman of working as a professional in advertising or in a related industry.

According to Fox, men on New York City's Madison Avenue have long held that advertising treats women better than other businesses or professions do. While the facts do not support this claim, it is nonetheless true that some women have risen to positions of prominence within the industry. Among them are Mary Wells, Reva Korda, Rochelle Lazarus, and Charlotte Beers.

Organization and Advancement

Several organizations have helped smooth the way for women who enter the highly competitive field of advertising. When J. George Frederick, editor of *Printers' Ink,* told his wife, Christine, who worked alongside him, that she could attend a meeting of the Advertising Men's League of New York only if she sat in the balcony behind a curtain, she took matters into her own hands. Forming the League of Advertising Women in 1912, she created an organization that inspired similar groups in Philadelphia, Pennsylvania, and Chicago, Illinois. In 1934 the League of Advertising Women took the name Advertising Women of New York.

From the beginning the mission of the league was to "promote the profession of advertising and to open new opportunities for women in the field." In 1935 AWNY was given airtime on radio station WNYC to host a half-hour show. As its membership grew and its members became known as effective speakers, the league developed a speakers bureau. It also bestowed an annual Advertising Woman of the Year Award. Recipients of this award were in high demand as guest speakers and maintained a rigorous public appearance schedule.

AWNY thus developed a reputation as an outstanding organization because of the prestigious speakers it attracted and because of its ambitious philanthropic goals. Speakers at AWNY meetings over the years included first lady Eleanor Roosevelt, photographer Edward Steichen, media mogul Ted Turner, and television personality Barbara Walters. Philanthropic work has included a health and social services center for homeless women and an independent elementary school for inner-city children in New York City's East Harlem.

AWNY also provides members opportunities for mentoring, networking, and staying abreast of industry trends. Both men and women are invited to join and participate in all events. The group hosts the annual Advertising Career Conference for female college students. It also cosponsors the Cannes International Festival Gala, held at Lincoln Center in New York City.

The Women's Advertising Club of Chicago was established in 1917 and by the end of the century had more than 300 members. The organization, which places a strong emphasis on education, gives its members high visibility and provides a chance to network. Copywriting was the predominant specialization among the 35 charter members of the club, but by the late 1990s one-third of the membership worked in advertising sales. Other groups that help women network or stay abreast of developments in the field include Women in Advertising and Marketing, in Washington, D.C., and the Network for Professional Women, which originated in 1979.

Other organizations acknowledge individuals—women among them—who have made their mark on the industry. The American Advertising Federation, founded in 1967 with the merger of the Advertising Federation of America and the Advertising Association of the West, operates the Advertising Hall of Fame. Since its inception in 1949, eight women and 136 men have been inducted. The first woman to be admitted was Erma Perham Proetz, a copywriter at Gardner Advertising in St. Louis, Missouri, who won three of the early Harvard-Bok awards for creativity for her campaigns for Pet condensed milk.

The Art Directors Club of New York maintains its own Hall of Fame. Among the 102 inductees, six women were granted the prestigious honor between 1975 and 1997. Perhaps because women have more often held positions as copywriters, the One Club, which recognizes achievements in art direction and copywriting, has a slightly higher proportion of women among its honorees. By 2001 four women had been inducted. The first to be acknowledged was Bernice Fitz-Gibbon, in 1967, followed by Phyllis K. Robinson (1968), Mary Wells Lawrence (1969), and Shirley Polykoff (1974).

Changing Roles

Across the 20th century the role of women in advertising has been affected by a variety of social and cultural events outside the profession itself. Early in the century, Helen Resor, one-half of the famous JWT husband-and-wife team, organized a group of JWT women to march in the 1915 suffragette parade in New York City. In 1926, when Aminta Casseres spoke out about women being barred from a men's advertising club, women banded together to form their own.

When men went off to fight during World War II, women went to work. Helen Resor, along with James Webb Young and Bill Berchtold, formed the War Manpower Commission and created the slogan "Women must work to win this war." In 1944 Jean Wade Rindlaub, a copywriter at Batten Barton Durstine & Osborn (BBDO), became the agency's first female vice president.

During the 1960s, women inside and outside the advertising industry began to speak out for equal rights and equal pay. At Doyle Dane Bernbach, Phyllis Robinson supervised a creative staff that included Mary Wells, Paula Green, Judith Protas, Lore Parker, and Rita Selden. And by the 1990s Ilon Specht, who had launched her career working on the L'Oréal account ("I'm worth it") at McCann-Erickson in 1973, was the creative director at Jordan, McGrath, Case & Partners.

Many women started their own agencies around this time. Adrienne Hall and Joan Levine launched Hall and Levine in Los Angeles, California, in 1959. Janet Marie Carlson also started her own agency. In 1958 Jane Trahey launched the New York agency Jane Trahey & Associates. Mary Wells Lawrence founded Wells, Rich, Greene in 1966, and Jo Foxworth founded her agency in 1968. In 1973 JWT awarded Charlotte Beers the rank of senior vice president. She was the first woman to achieve the rank at the agency—even Helen Resor had only attained the status of vice president.

Prominent Advertising Women

It may not be immediately clear what it was that enabled certain women to elevate themselves to positions of recognition and authority in the profession. A look at the career paths of some notable examples, however, may help to explain why they achieved success in this largely male-dominated industry.

Helen Lansdowne Resor. Helen Lansdowne (1886–1964) graduated as the valedictorian of her high school class in Covington, Kentucky. Shortly after graduation she found her way into copywriting. Stanley Resor, then the account manager at Procter & Gamble Company's house agency, Procter and Collier, noticed her work and went to the trouble of calling on her at her home to offer her a job. She accepted his offer in 1907. A year later Resor, his brother Walter, and Lansdowne opened the JWT office in Cincinnati, Ohio. Lansdowne, who worked on major accounts for products such as Woodbury's facial soap and Pond's cold cream, was widely recognized for her innovative ideas. Her prolific stream of new ideas helped lift her to a position of authority. She was also the first woman invited to attend a Procter & Gamble board meeting, in 1911.

Lansdowne and Resor married in 1917. While Stanley Resor ran the business, Helen Resor managed the creative department at JWT, and during her tenure the firm became known as an agency with a favorable attitude toward women. She mentored the women who worked for her and saw that they had opportunities that would allow them to grow. It was widely known among JWT employees and in the industry that her husband discussed serious business matters with her before making a decision. They were equally revered and respected, and over their more than four decades running the agency, they built JWT into a multimillion-dollar multinational business.

Anne Ashenhurst. Anne Ashenhurst (1905–1996) and Frank Hummert were another legendary team. They built an empire in advertising through radio soap operas. Ashenhurst was Hummert's assistant when he created the concept of the soap opera at Blackett-Sample-Hummert (BSH). Hummert created the characters and plotlines for a radio show and then gave them to Ashenhurst to execute. Among the programs they developed were *Just Plain Bill,* sponsored by Kolynos toothpaste; *Betty and Bob,* sponsored by Gold Medal Flour; and *Ma Perkins,* sponsored by Oxydol detergent. These were the first radio dramas targeted to housewives, and they became wildly successful, making Hummert the richest man in advertising. BSH earned its payment according to a percentage of billings, while Hummert maintained the ownership of the shows.

In the early 1930s Hummert was widowed, and in 1935 he and Ashenhurst were married. They set up an efficient operation to churn out soap operas, paying writers $25 per script. When under a deadline, a writer might be confined to a hotel room and given provisions until the script was done. As the protector of the private and reclusive Frank Hummert, Anne Hummert essentially managed the business. She spoke for her husband and directed the work of the writers, directors, actors, and musicians. By the late 1930s their shows were receiving a million fan letters a week, while 14 writers delivered 50 scripts weekly. By the end of the decade the Hummerts had become the wealthiest and most powerful people in radio.

Shirley Polykoff. Shirley Polykoff (1908–1998), the daughter of Russian Jewish immigrants, grew up in Brooklyn. She claimed that she had learned to be an American from magazine advertisements. Flamboyant and somewhat eccentric, she was also brilliant. A colleague once affectionately described her by saying, "Shirley would wear three outfits, all at once, and each one of them would look great." Convinced that brown hair did not go with the personal qualities she most admired, she began dyeing her hair blond when she was a teenager. This was a bold move for the time, as dyeing one's hair was something done only by actresses, the very wealthy, or women with questionable morals. After meeting her stern Orthodox Jewish mother-in-law-to-be, Polykoff learned that her future in-law had disapprovingly asked, "Does she color her hair or doesn't she?" According to Polykoff's daughter, Alix Neson Frick, Polykoff was fascinated by the American dream and wanted nothing more than to be an attractive blond housewife with blond children living in the suburbs. Although she became an attractive blond, in reality she was only a housewife for two weeks of her life, after which her lawyer-husband encouraged her to return to work.

In 1956, when she was a copywriter, Polykoff was assigned to the Clairol account at Foote, Cone & Belding (FCB). The company was introducing Miss Clairol, the first product that made it possible for women to lighten, tint, and condition their hair at home. The product represented a significant breakthrough and helped redefine the hair color category, and the advertising helped change the way women felt about dyeing their hair. Polykoff had made the decision to color her own hair long before she faced the challenge of advertising Miss Clairol. She fully appreciated how changing the color of one's hair gave a woman an opportunity to redefine herself, and this understanding led her to write the famous line, "Does she or doesn't she? Only her hairdresser knows for sure." This slogan was later followed by "Is it true blondes have more fun?"; "The closer he gets the better you look"; "If I've only one life, let me live it as a blonde"; and "Every woman should be a redhead at least once in her life." When the campaign was launched, only 7 percent of U.S. women admitted to coloring their hair. Six years later more than half of all adult women said that they used some form of hair color.

When Polykoff retired from FCB in 1973, she had been the agency's highest paid salaried employee for many years. It was said that she had had her salary held at $25,000 so as not to exceed her husband's but that, when he died in 1961, the agency doubled her salary twice in less than a decade. Polykoff was inducted into the One Club Hall of Fame in 1974 and into the American Advertising Hall of Fame in 1980. The only other woman to be inducted into both was Bernice Fitz-Gibbon.

Herta Herzog. In 1943 Marion Harper, then the head of copy research at McCann-Erickson, hired Herta Herzog (born 1910). Her job was to implement motivational research and to direct qualitative research on radio programming and commercials.

Herzog, born and raised in Austria, studied at the Institute of Psychology at the University of Vienna. Her mentors included Paul Lazarsfeld, a statistical social psychologist whom she later married, and Charlotte and Karl Buhler, both experimental psychologists. Influenced by Lazarsfeld, she did the first large field experiment in Austria for her doctoral dissertation, replicating a study done by T.H. Pear in England that had examined the effects of the human voice and personality as they came over the radio.

For this project Herzog developed what was called the "one-questioning method," which became the open-ended, or depth, interview. She used the method throughout her career in both individual interviews and with focus groups. At McCann-Erickson she used this as well as other techniques that were based upon physiological measures. She used the Lazarsfeld-Stanton Program Analyzer, a device that recorded listeners' emotional responses to music, and she introduced the use of the Eye Camera, a device that measured a reader's pupil dilation and tracked eye movements.

Herzog also initiated the use of projective methods with focus groups, asking participants to draw pictures of products and to tell stories about them. She used the material gathered from these groups to develop insights about the relationships people formed with products and brands. Herzog designated the information she gleaned from this process a product's "image."

As Harper developed McCann-Erickson and established the multinational Interpublic Group holding company, Herzog's responsibilities grew as well. She became head of Marplan when the research functions at McCann-Erickson were spun off into a separate company. Her duties there were to implement marketing research programs abroad by training employees. Later, at Harper's request, she moved to Jack Tinker & Partners, a creative think tank formed to handle issues related to clients, including new product introductions and changes in marketing strategy. Of the four partners, Herzog was the one in charge of research. She had influence on well-known products and campaigns, such as the one created by Mary Wells for Alka-Seltzer. Herzog left Jack Tinker & Partners in 1970 to spend time with her family, and she later returned to Europe.

Charlotte Beers. Sometimes referred to as the most powerful woman in advertising, Charlotte Beers (born 1935) graduated in 1957 from Baylor University with a degree in mathematics. Her first job was teaching engineering algebra to petroleum managers in southeastern Texas. Born in Beaumont, Texas, the daughter of a cowboy who worked as an engineer for Standard Oil, Beers grew up in the company of men. Her extroverted personality and strong ambition have led people to romanticize her, but it has been her ability to make strategic decisions that has allowed her to gain the trust of demanding clients such as Procter & Gamble and to succeed.

After college Beers married and had a daughter, but she eventually went back to work full-time. She was hired by Uncle Ben's, Inc., where she became one of the first female brand managers. An affinity for the people she met at JWT, Uncle Ben's agency, moti-vated her to move into advertising. At JWT she became a senior vice president and director of client services. When she had the opportunity in January 1979 to become the operating chief executive officer of Tatham-Laird & Kudner (TLK) in Chicago, Beers moved on. She merged TLK with the European agency RSCG and quadrupled the billings over the following ten years. In 1982 she became chief executive officer at TLK, and in 1988 she became the first female chairman of the American Association of Advertising Agencies.

Beers attempted to take time off after leaving TLK in 1991, but she was wooed into taking the top management position with Ogilvy & Mather Worldwide the next year. She thus went from running a one-office advertising agency in Chicago to the task of turning around a New York company with 270 offices worldwide. She retired in 1996 but came out of retirement to accept the chairmanship of JWT in 1999. In 2001 JWT and parent WPP did not renew her contracts. In September 2001 she became undersecretary of state for public diplomacy in the administration of President George W. Bush.

Marie Theresa Rainey. Marie Theresa Rainey shared Herzog's interest in psychology and cognitive processes. Rainey's dissertation for a master of science degree at Aston University, Birmingham, England, on the subject of signal-detection theory, was published by the North Atlantic Treaty Organization.

Rainey began her career in marketing sales for a yachting magazine. She soon set her sights on the advertising industry, however, and she was hired as an account planner by TBWA/London. She made her mark quickly and moved to Gold Greenlees Trott, where she was a contemporary of other account planning pioneers, included Damian O'Malley, Charlie Robertson, and Simon Clemmow.

Rainey became known for her ability to solve advertising problems, a reputation that led Jay Chiat, a principal of Chiat/Day Advertising, to her door. She moved to the United States in 1980 to introduce account planning. She worked on the Apple Computer advertisement "1984," which ran during the telecast of the Super Bowl that year and made advertising history. After a decade in the United States she returned to England and opened the Chiat/Day/TBWA office in London. In 1993 she and three partners opened Rainey Kelly Campbell Roalfe.

Caroline Jones. Caroline Jones (1942–2001) majored in English and science at the University of Michigan, where she graduated in 1963. She landed her first job in advertising as a secretary at JWT before moving on to become a copywriter. She was the first female African-American copywriter in the agency's history. After Jones left JWT, she worked for a number of other agencies, including Kenyon & Eckhardt and BBDO. While with BBDO, she became the first female African-American vice president of a major advertising agency.

It was during this period that Jones also helped found Zebra, an early African-American advertising agency. In 1977 she joined with Frank Mingo to form Mingo-Jones. The agency's billings quickly increased from $500,000 to $25 million; its clients included Miller High Life Beer, Kentucky Fried Chicken, and Westinghouse Electric.

Jones struck out on her own in New York City in 1987 and formed Caroline Jones Advertising, Inc. Because of Jones's strong belief in target marketing, her agency was approached by R.J. Reynolds Tobacco Company with a request to launch Uptown, a new brand of cigarettes targeted specifically to blacks. Fierce public disapproval forced R.J. Reynolds to withdraw the offer, however, and to abandon its strategy. The agency suffered from this incident, but its fortunes improved soon afterward when it became the agency of record for Trump City, a Manhattan housing development owned by real estate magnate Donald Trump. Jones produced and moderated the WNYC radio show *Focus on the Black Woman,* and for ten years she hosted WWOR-TV's show *In the Black: Keys to Success.*

Overcoming Inequities

While the advertising industry has increasingly opened its doors to women, inequities persist. Even at the beginning of the 21st century, there were few women at high levels of management. A common characteristic of those women who have achieved acclaim and recognition in this highly competitive field is that each has had a strong sense of personal identity and an unwavering commitment to her career.

ANN MAXWELL

See also Beers, Charlotte; Lawrence, Mary Wells; Lazarus, Rochelle (Shelly); Polykoff, Shirley; Resor, Helen Lansdowne; Robinson, Phyllis K.; Trahey, Jane

Further Reading

Advertising Women of New York, "The History of AWNY from 1912 on . . . over 86 Years of ONWARD and UPWARD," *White Paper* (9 September 1999)

Casseres, Aminta, "But Masculine Timidity Is Wearing Off before the Real Services That Women Are Performing," *Printers' Ink* 136, no. 2 (1926)

Fleming, Robert, *The Success of Caroline Jones Advertising, Inc.: An Advertising Success Story,* New York: Walker, 1996

Fox, Stephen, *The Mirror Makers: A History of American Advertising and Its Creators,* New York: Morrow, 1984

Gladwell, Malcolm, "True Colors: Why Did America Go Blond?" *New Yorker* (22 March 1999)

Gooding, Tessa, "Latest Advertising Agency Employment Figures Released," <www.ipa.com>

Kazenoff, Ivy, and Anthony Vagnoni, "Babes in Boyland," *Creativity* (18 October 1997)

Love, Barbara J., editor, *Foremost Women in Communications: A Biographical Reference Work on Accomplished Women in Broadcasting, Publishing, Advertising, Public Relations, and Allied Professions,* New York: Bowker, 1970

Maxwell-Keding, Ann, "Helen Lansdowne Resor," in *The Ad Men and Women: A Biographical Dictionary of Advertising,* edited by Edd Applegate, Westport, Connecticut: Greenwood, 1994

Miles, Laureen, "Women in Advertising Still Earn Less Than Men and Struggle to Reach Top Levels: Industry Survey," *Mediaweek* (10 May 1993)

Mitchell, Alan, "MT Rainey: 'A West of Scotland Person,'" *Marketing* (30 September 1993)

O'Leary, Noreen, "Charlotte's Web," *Adweek* (Eastern edition) (6 April 1992)

Perse, Elizabeth M., "Herta Herzog (1910–)," in *Women in Communication: A Biographical Sourcebook,* edited by Nancy Signorielli, Westport, Connecticut: Greenwood, 1996

Richmond, Susannah, "The Secret World of Advertising Clubs," *Campaign* (27 May 1994)

"Tapping Talent Pipeline Still a Tough Challenge," *Advertising Age* (15 February 1999)

"Women's Ad Club Ages with Dignity, Enters 70th Year," *Back Stage* 28, no. 4 (1987)

Women: Representations in Advertising

The goal of advertising has always been the sale of goods and services, and the primary decision-makers regarding the purchase of those goods and services have overwhelmingly been women. Over the years, researchers have estimated that women have made 75 percent to 95 percent of all consumer purchases. Thus, from the point of view of advertisers, women—as the ones who control the major share of household spending—have been the most important customers. When a large segment of the population shifted from farms to cities and the packaging of goods became more widespread, advertisers began to direct their copy toward the women who lived and worked in cities and who had the resources to purchase the advertised goods and services.

Although women are depicted in various roles and statuses in advertising—ranging from homemaker to business executive and from sex object to superwoman—it is only since the mid–20th century that women have been shown in roles other than purchaser of domestic products. And because U.S. women did not enter the workplace in significant numbers until World War II, their images in ads up to that time were almost exclusively conceived and executed by men.

Since the 1950s, however, a large number of educated career women have entered the ad industry, both on the creative and account management sides as well as in senior management positions. The manner in which women have been represented in ads has not always reflected the values and lifestyles of these professionals, many of whom might wish to create representations modeled more closely on their own lives. This discrepancy, combined with the general evolution of women's roles in Western society over the last several decades of the 20th century, has made the female image in advertising a topic of acute political sensitivity. But the process by which advertising is created does not easily accommodate agendas of political correctness. Increasingly, ad development has become a research-driven procedure in which concrete data are used to determine who is most likely to buy a given product and what images and appeals will motivate the purchase. While some observers may be impatient with the traditional images of women that dominate the advertising of major packaged-goods marketers, the fact is that these depictions reflect careful research, often meticulously calibrated to detect the subtlest element of potential offense in the target group. This market research–based advertising may not always show trend-setting women the images they want to see. But when properly conducted, market research seldom leads advertisers far astray. In short, the roles of wife and mother continue to be performed by large numbers of women whom advertisers seek to address.

Targeting Women: Early Days

U.S. newspaper publishers Joseph Pulitzer and William Randolph Hearst can be credited with emphasizing the interests of females during the 1890s, when women began buying more newspapers. Also at this time, publishers were beginning to recognize the importance of securing a larger female audience for department store advertising. Increases in the number of women readers and circulation promotions for the *Ladies' Home Journal, Woman's Home Companion, Delineator,* and *McCall's* were factors in the growth of advertising geared toward women. Advertisements in the new women's magazines tutored women in the rituals of self-transformation and educated them in the art of selecting merchandise from competing marketers.

One of the most pervasive and enduring female characters in advertising is Aunt Jemima, a trademark that had its beginnings in 1889. The product was important for three reasons: first, the product was the first ready-made pancake mix; second, the mix was the first convenience food product; and third, it was the first to give away a free product to stimulate sales. Invited to breakfast with millions of families all over the world for more than a century, the character of Aunt Jemima was woven into mainstream American culture and eventually became a national icon. By the end of the 20th century, the logo had undergone several face-lifts to meet the demands of the evolving African-American consumer market.

As times changed, so did the desires and aspirations of the women being portrayed in ads. Some wanted to engage in activities previously regarded as reserved for men. One 1912 advertisement for Velvet Tobacco showed a "respectable" woman sitting with a man who was smoking. "I wish I were a man," she muses, implying that she would gladly trade places with a man if only she were given permission to smoke. Another cigarette brand that wooed women was the American Tobacco Company's Lucky Strike. George Washington Hill, the head of American Tobacco, made several changes in the brand's approach to advertising to entice women to take up the habit. First, he was concerned that women were rejecting the cigarettes' green packaging because it clashed with their clothes. To solve this problem, Hill hired Edward L. Bernays, a public relations pioneer, who used Lucky Strikes to promote the color green in fashion shows so that the dark green Lucky packages would complement women's attire. It was during this time that women endorsed the product and popularized the image of the up-to-date lady, who, while she did smoke cigarettes, still embodied style and class. Aviator Amelia Earhart endorsed Lucky Strike cigarettes in 1928 at the behest of her flight crew, even though she was not a smoker.

Some products—Miss America brand canned vegetables (1929) and Martha Washington Powdered Sugar (1922)—were named to entice women to buy them. But none of these enjoyed the success of Gold Medal flour and its Betty Crocker trade character. As a result of a successful promotional campaign for a pincushion, the Washburn Crosby Company, miller of Gold Medal flour (and forerunner of General Mills), found itself besieged with requests for the premium—along with more than 30,000 letters asking questions about baking. Sam Gale, head of the company's advertising department, made sure each of the letters was answered. He decided that a single fictional spokesperson should sign the letters, and the name Betty Crocker was suggested. The last name came from a recently deceased company officer; the first name was selected simply because of its popularity. Florence Lindeberg, an employee at Washburn Crosby, provided the signature in 1921; Blanche Ingersoll, another Washburn Crosby employee, became the voice on the radio in 1924; and the trademark received a face in 1936. Since that time there have been at least seven different images of Betty Crocker. The last one, introduced in 1996, was a multicultural Betty—a composite of the features of 75 women of varying ethnicities.

The 1920s saw an increase in the frequency of the appearance of women in advertising. At the time, women were the "shoppers of the world . . . buying 80 to 90 percent of the things in general use," according to Carl A. Naether, the author of *Advertising to Women* (1928). Naether suggested, however, that advertising was disrespectful of women's intelligence and individuality and insinuated that they were concerned solely with a "desire to look young and be sexually appealing." Yet some advertising historians have held that during the 1920s advertisers presented a "new woman" who embodied the promise of modernity—youthfulness, sexual freedom, style, and conspicuous consumption.

During the 1920s, the color and design of products achieved a new importance and became a feature to be advertised. The

For him... and him... and him...

"I pledge myself to guard every bit of Beauty that he cherishes in me"

To help you in keeping this pledge, trust the _one_ leading beauty soap that's made with Olive and Palm Oils!

Today, those moments with him are fleeting, rare, and . . . infinitely precious. For his sake, and yours, be at your lovely best, whenever you're together.

Turn now, as so many charming women are doing, to Palmolive for your beauty care. For, since the dawn of history, Olive and Palm Oils have been treasured as Nature's finest aids to feminine loveliness. And Palmolive _alone_, among all leading soaps, is made with Olive and Palm Oils!

No wonder Palmolive is the largest selling beauty soap in all the world! You can truly feel the difference in its silk-and-cream lather. You can truly trust its gentle help in keeping your skin soft and fresh and radiant as the dawn.

Palmolive costs _so_ little! Why not let it do the nice things for your body that it does for your face? Keep your pledge of beauty with Palmolive. Guard your loveliness . . . 'til he comes marching home!

REMEMBER PALMOLIVE'S BEAUTY OILS...

olive and palm oils – no others – go into the making of Palmolive. Look for the olive color.

PALMOLIVE

Despite the increased number of women in the workforce during World War II, ads often focused on their roles as wives and sweethearts, in this case counseling them that it was their duty to remain beautiful for their men in uniform. *Courtesy of Colgate-Palmolive Company.*

purchase of a new dress now also entailed acquiring matching accessories and complementary makeup. Before long, this desire to coordinate, promoted by advertising strategies, extended to household appliances as well.

Depression and War: Changing Roles

The Great Depression and World War II left an indelible mark on American society, and Rosie the Riveter and other notable ad icons and personalities left their marks on advertising. The period spawned a carnival culture as Americans sought refuge from harsh realities through the escapism provided by the mass media. Advertising relied heavily on curvaceous celebrities offering borrowed glamour and comic strip–style narratives with confessional copy. Through the 1930s ad copy continued to portray women primarily as homemakers or objects of sexual desire. It was during this period that advertisers became more daring. In 1931 a magazine ad for Listerine deodorant featured a photograph of a nude woman's back and the side of her breast. A color advertisement for Cannon Towels depicting the back of a woman's body appeared in 1933. Woodbury soap featured what is thought to be advertising's first full-figure black-and-white photograph of a naked woman (shot by Edward Steichen) in 1936.

The conflict between women's actual role in society and the ways in which advertisers portrayed that role came to the forefront during World War II. From 1940 to 1944, the number of women in the workforce increased 30 percent, to about 19 million. While wartime propaganda encouraged women to labor for country and family, advertisers at the same time urged female factory workers to remain glamorous and keep the home running smoothly. Many advertisers portrayed women in their newly expanded roles. For instance, Eureka showed three women in its vacuum cleaner ads—one in a military uniform, one in pants, and another in typical housewifely garb, complete with apron. Throughout the war years, women were portrayed in advertising as effective, efficient employees, taking care of the homeland while the men were at war.

But these same advertisements sometimes reminded women that their new roles were only temporary. By late 1944 women were being prepared, often through strategically placed advertising, to give up their jobs when the soldiers returned home. At the end of the war, advertisers began once again to show women at home, sometimes going so far as to suggest that a working mother was not a good mother. In an advertisement by Adel Precision Products Corporation, a young child asks, "Mother, when will you stay home again?" At the end of the war, many women did indeed leave their jobs and dutifully return home to clean, bake, and nurture. In essence, advertising's portrayal of women from the 1930s again became the norm.

As more women found themselves in the workplace during the war and postwar years than ever before, ad industry professionals pondered the vital question "How can we target this new group of consumers?" Articles on this topic abounded in popular advertising trade journals such as *Printers' Ink* and *Advertising and Selling*.

1950s: Return to the Home

Ads of the 1950s were set primarily in the home, and the housewife often played the starring role. Thus, during the 1950s most advertisers portrayed women as wives and mothers, despite the fact that by 1951 the number of women in the workplace had grown to more than 19 million.

As more women entered the workforce, another kind of advertising made use of them as a means for selling goods and services. These ads, showing women as clerks, telephone operators, and secretaries using the latest office equipment and office furniture, were generally placed in such publications as *Fortune*, *Saturday Evening Post*, *Time*, and *Life*. These advertisements provide a historical documentation of women's roles at the office and reveal the attitudes held by both men and women about women's role in the workplace during this era. Women in the ads are generally employees not the boss, followers rather than leaders; ultimately, the ads reminded readers that a woman's job was a means for finding a man, and that the primary purpose for women at work was to help men succeed.

Traditional images associated with women prior to World War II began to reappear in the 1950s. Such images included scenes of women pampering their husbands, chauffeuring their children, baking, scrubbing, washing, ironing, shopping, and, most importantly, teaching their daughters the art of doing the same. In these ads women are shown reacting ecstatically as their husbands and children present them with a host of household appliances essential to having clean, all-American homes and robust, healthy families. Although some have suggested that these advertisements were stereotypical in nature, they did represent that segment of female consumers who were homemakers and mothers.

Another approach to the portrayal of women in advertising—and one many women dubbed stereotypical and vehemently resented—involved scantily clad females in alluring poses and compromising positions; these images most often appeared in advertisements for products used by men. Sexual explicitness in ads featuring women expanded with the proliferation of male-oriented magazines favoring advertising that mirrored their editorial content.

One of the major technological advances of the mid–20th century was the introduction of television. Compared with radio, television offered the illusion of greater personal interaction with the characters who regularly entered Americans' living rooms. The 1950s saw society's passion for mass consumption shift into high gear. Coupled with a national commercialized television system, U.S. advertising experienced a tremendous growth spurt—advertising spending went from $5.7 billion in 1950 to almost $12 billion in 1960.

1960s: Era of Feminism

One of the chief targets of the women's movement was the representation of women in advertising and all mass media forms. Advertising, although a target, also became an ally as the industry provided a larger variety of venues and activities for the single, self-supporting woman. Myriad images of women were presented, some flattering, some stereotypical, and some simply reflective of the era. Because many women remained at home, women were portrayed quite often as housewives. Another revolution, the Civil Rights movement, also changed the image of women in advertising: the first black female model, Beverly Johnson, graced the cover of *Vogue* in 1964.

The women's movement, revitalized in the 1960s, gained momentum in the years that followed. The National Organization for Women (NOW), founded in 1966, sought to eliminate gender-based stereotypes in the mass media, and the debate over women's images in advertising intensified. Advertisers came under severe scrutiny from feminist groups, women's organizations, and students of mass communications.

Despite the progress made by some ad agencies in hiring women and the focus on women in the industry by feminist advocacy groups, through much of the 1960s women continued to be depicted in the roles of housewife and mother. In an era that emphasized convenience and labor-saving devices, advertising was used to promote products that would ease the lot of women who chose to stay at home rather than enter the entrepreneurial or corporate arenas. Other depictions and archetypes of this era included the shy but attractive single girl, the triumphant bride, and the nosy next-door neighbor.

It was during the 1960s that emphasis began to be placed on the independent woman who, although married, drove her own car, had a fulfilling job, and participated in or made major purchasing decisions. These successful middle-class women usually appeared in ads for more expensive items in sophisticated magazines such as *The New Yorker* and *Harper's Bazaar*. Subsequently, the first organized expressions of dissatisfaction with advertising came from educated middle-class women, who, armed with college degrees and the birth control pill, identified more with the image of the career woman than with that of the housewife. This era culminated in a December 1969 protest outside Macy's Department Store in New York City. The protest, which may have been the first organized demonstration against the image of women in advertising, was staged against Mattel Toys in reaction to an advertisement the company had placed in *Life* magazine to promote its Christmas toy line.

1970s: Criticism and Change

Women's liberation, Americans' growing interest in their ethnic heritage, criticism of capitalism, and a compelling attraction to the "natural look" all served as vanguards of the 1970s, and advertising drew upon these symbols and times to identify new consumer niches. In March 1970 NOW held a national convention and created the Barefoot and Pregnant Awards of the Week; the group distributed thousands of stickers that proclaimed: "This ad insults women." (More than 30 years later, in September 2001, GraceNet, a San Francisco area women's technology organization, began giving monthly "awards" to companies that produced the ads most offensive to women.) Fully 43 percent of U.S. women were working by the early 1970s; by the end of the

decade, that number had risen to 50 percent. During this time, advertising executives were reevaluating their portrayals of women's roles in society. A 1974 edition of Grey Advertising's newsletter, *Grey Matter,* quoted William A. Yoell of the Behavior Research Institute as saying, "Until it is recognized that women are not irrational creatures in their behavior, advertising cannot be totally effective." A classic advertisement from that period came from the Polaroid camera campaign featuring actors James Garner and Mariette Hartley. Hartley was shown in a distinctly nontraditional role for a woman of the time—fixing a car.

The sentiment expressed in the Polaroid ad signaled a change in the depiction of women in advertising, but it did not silence advertising's critics, who demanded a more comprehensive and diverse representation of women. Advertising research was used to make the case. A 1971 study by Alice and Lockeretz Courtney of ads appearing in general periodicals and established women's magazines and television commercials concluded that the image of women in advertising had changed very little over the years. The study analyzed the roles portrayed by women in thousands of magazine advertisements. It found that the ads suggested the following: "A woman's place is in the home, women do not make important decisions or do important things, women are dependent and need men's protection, and men regard women primarily as sex objects who are not interesting as people."

In 1974 another study, "Sex Stereotyping in Advertising," published in the *Journal of Communication,* concluded, "There's little evidence in the world of television commercials to show that the family structure may be changing or that women are capable of performing responsible tasks other than those associated with the family and home." Other studies documented evidence supporting the assertion that television commercials were dominated by males: there were more male characters in commercials than female characters, and there were significantly more male voice-overs than female voice-overs. Previous research had shown that the general public found male voices to be more believable than those of females. This research, conducted by Alice Courtney and Thomas Whipple, also confirmed the notion that most working women wanted to be represented in advertising but were still "virtually ignored."

Another area of criticism of advertising focused on depictions that reinforced the notion that women were inept and depended on men to solve their problems. In his book *Gender Advertisements* (1976), sociologist Erving Goffman provided these critics with a scientific gauge for analyzing the image of women in advertising. Goffman noted that in a great number of ads women appeared to be helpless, were often shown as being much smaller than men, and were cast most often in family scenes rather than workplace settings. He also found that women were depicted in such a way as to imply that they were subordinate to men, were shown being instructed by men, and had their hands positioned differently from men's (e.g., not firmly grasping objects).

One of the turning points in advertising's portrayal of women came with a landmark campaign from Revlon in 1973. The Charlie perfume campaign featured confident young women in tailored pantsuits pursuing traditionally male-oriented activities.

This 1968 ad for Suzy Homemaker toys encouraged girls to shun the hippie counterculture and instead pursue more traditional female roles.

In 1975 a new agency, Advertising to Women, Inc., was founded. Its intent was to reach the contemporary, confident, career-oriented woman who was not inhibited by her sexuality. Market research conducted by the agency showed that women were responsible for most household purchases, 60 percent of all vacation destination choices, and nearly 30 percent of new car selections.

The depiction of women as dependent and subordinate was not limited to the American advertising industry. During the 1970s the United Nations Commission on the Status of Women studied the images of women in advertising in 28 countries. It reported:

> Women are shown primarily as housewives in commercials, although they comprise from 35 to 55 percent of the labor force of the different countries. . . . Women are offered basically two roles, that of the beautiful but passive glamour girl and that of the housewife caring for the home and children. Both are shown as dependent on men and receiving

their social identity not in themselves but through men. Women seem to be obsessed with cleanliness.

For many years, mainstream advertisers in the United States had been reluctant to use black models, particularly in ads for cosmetics or health and beauty aids. As a result of the Civil Rights movement, however, during the 1970s black female models became more prominent in advertising. No longer was the Aunt Jemima stereotype the sole image of the African-American woman.

By the end of the decade, marketers had also begun to recognize that growing numbers of women were earning higher salaries than ever before. Therefore, advertisements not only depicted the professional woman at work but also increasingly featured women selling cars, homes, and insurance to other women.

1980s: The Superwoman

The 1980s advertising attempted to portray career-minded women as "superwomen," and the industry often grappled with the ambiguity inherent in the attempt to integrate the traditional and contemporary roles of women. A classic advertisement of the period that perpetuated the superwoman stereotype was one for Enjoli perfume, which depicted a sexy but capable woman who could "bring home the bacon, fry it up in a pan, and never let you forget you're a man." The Enjoli advertisement was designed to show that a woman could do it all: she could earn a salary, care for her family, and cater to the needs of her man.

Some critics objected to the theme of women catering to men and to ads that portrayed women as subservient to men. In an ad for Singapore Airlines, the youthful Asian air hostess is pictured reading a poem sent to her by an infatuated passenger:

> Gentle hostess in your sarong kebaya,
> You care for me as only you know how.
> Singapore girl,
> You're a great way to fly.

Women Against Pornography, a U.S. lobbying group, was concerned about the sexual images of women portrayed in advertising and the influence of such images on sexual violence against women. The group founded an annual awards program to applaud and censure ads on the basis of presence or absence of sexist overtones.

In 1983 Jockey, a company known primarily for its line of men's underwear, introduced the "Jockey for Her" campaign (from Minneapolis, Minnesota–based Campbell-Mithun), which featured real women representing a range of professions, ages, and body types. The brand became an instant success; within five years, it was the most popular U.S. brand of women's underwear, commanding an astounding 40 percent share of the market.

Overall, advertising's view of women was fairly slow to change. A sample of prime-time television commercials over a three-week period in October 1986 was conducted by Carol Ferrante, Andrew

Haynes, and Sarah Kingsley and appeared in the spring 1988 issue of *Journal of Broadcasting and Electronic Media;* the study concluded that women were most often portrayed in the role of wives and mothers. Still, the range of professions portrayed by women increased from 18 in 1972 to 47 in 1986. Women were predominantly pictured in the home, while men were more frequently shown in the business world.

As the scale of feminine beauty and success broadened to include women of all ages, colors, and social classes, advertising's female consumers were splintered into myriad categories no longer confined by the barriers of past stereotypes. Rena Bartos's *Marketing to Women around the World* (1989) highlighted some of the views of advertising held by women from various countries. Bartos found that women in Italy had quite negative attitudes toward advertising overall. Japanese women for the most part were tolerant and accepting of advertising and primarily used it as a source of consumer information. Their major criticism, which was also voiced by women in Mexico and Venezuela, was that there was simply too much advertising. Women in Great Britain had positive reactions to as well as disdain for advertising. They were most likely to object to advertising that made them feel that the advertiser considered women to be unintelligent, indecisive, or inefficient They particularly resented commercials in which the advertiser preached to women, pictured one housewife trying to explain a product to another, showed an idealized and unrealistic picture of women, or made exaggerated claims regarding women.

1990s and Beyond: Emerging Images

By the 1990s some dramatic changes had occurred in the treatment of women in advertising. One of the most groundbreaking advertisements was a print ad for Maidenform, which pictured some of the objects representing slang terms for *woman*—a fox, a tomato, a doll, and a chick. The text accompanying the advertisement read, "While images used to describe women are simple and obvious, women themselves rarely are. Just something we like to keep in mind when designing our lingerie." Nike and Equal followed suit with advertisements that showed women to be men's equals in working environments (occupations) and performing athletic activities.

A study of general circulation magazines in the 1990s found a disproportionately high number of advertisements that portrayed women in "traditional" roles as compared to ads that showed women and men together as equals. The researchers also found that traditional presentations of women in advertising had decreased since the 1980s and that "equality portrayals" were on the rise.

A 1995 *Self* magazine survey of more than 1,000 American women aged 18 to 49 revealed the arrival of an "era of self-acceptance" and suggested that advertisers needed to understand that women were increasingly looking for resources, images, and careers that would allow them to fulfill their own needs while balancing work and family obligations.

In 1998 the American Advertising Museum designed a multimedia traveling exhibit, *Dream Girls: Images of Women in Advertising,* which had its premiere in New York City at the Art Directors Club during its 75th anniversary celebration. The exhibit explored the history of the feminine image in advertising. The *New York Times* wrote, "For more than 100 years, Madison Avenue has been placing women in the center ring of the cacophonous circus known as the American consumerist society. . . . [This] exhibit seeks to place sales pitches in their cultural, historical and social contexts."

During the 1990s, some advertisers abandoned the traditional strategies that had typically been used to depict women in advertising. It was during this decade that advertisers of traditionally male-targeted products such as athletic shoes, cars, and beer began to focus on female consumers. With this newfound level of consciousness, some ads that would once have been considered acceptable were shelved. For instance, an Old Milwaukee beer commercial featuring a provocatively clad "Swedish Bikini Team" was retired in 1991 because of negative publicity. Another factor that caused some advertisers to abandon their usual practices was the establishment of the Dangerous Promise Coalition, whose purpose was to put an end to alcohol advertisements that denigrated women and encouraged violence against them by dehumanizing them. A national billboard campaign begun by the group in 1994 requested, "Quit using our cans to sell your cans."

A new genre of advertisements came to the forefront during the 1990s. These ads signaled a new attitude of "reverse sexism." Advertisers used the liberated women's "I don't need a man" mind-set to create an entirely new reservoir of ads portraying women. One of these parodies used images of headlights, door knockers, and melons—objects men have commonly associated with women's breasts—accompanied by the tag line: "Bamboo Lingerie, a company owned by two women. Put that in your pipe and smoke it." Some of the ads were not quite so tame. Bodyslimmer Lingerie showed a woman from the neck down wearing a one-piece undergarment with copy that read, "While you don't necessarily dress for men, it doesn't hurt, on occasion, to see one drool like the pathetic dog that he is." Ads for Campbell Soup, Nike, Equal, and Pepsi-Cola emphasized women as being equally as sexual, competitive, cunning, and career-driven as their male counterparts.

The 1990s also presented tremendous challenges. As some advertisers were striving to move beyond the older stereotypical images of woman, others were still presenting her as the dim-witted sex object or the one-dimensional homemaker eager to please her man. Other advertisements creatively addressed such women's issues as maintaining control without being a superwoman, combating fatigue, and balancing family and work, while also promoting health and beauty products to make women feel better about themselves.

A breakthrough occurred in 1992 when the first nonwhite model signed a contract to represent a major cosmetics company in its ads. The company was Cover Girl; the model was a young African-American woman, Tyra Banks. Research that showed a definitive correlation between eating disorders and advertising gained prominence in the 1990s. Because many female models were extremely thin—often two to three sizes smaller than the

In this 1996 Nike print ad, basketball star Sheryl Swoopes took on a male competitor in a play for gender equality on the court.
Courtesy of Nike, Inc.

average American woman—psychologists, nutritionists, and activists focused on advertising as contributing to the growing numbers of girls and women being diagnosed with bulimia and anorexia nervosa. Omega Watches temporarily withdrew its ads from British *Vogue* in 1996 in protest against the use of the waif-like models.

Historically, the image of the housewife has been the most commonly used archetype of women in advertising, but through the years other stereotypes have been promulgated. Prior to the sexual revolution, women were frequently pictured in scanty costumes and sexually provocative poses. There have been decades when these images were rare, and it seemed certain that they had all but disappeared from the scene. Yet a 1998 study heralded the resurgence of such images, concluding, "Without question, randomly selected television ads, presented during prime-time sports and entertainment television, communicate an abundance of negative stereotypic images regarding females."

Some advertisers have retired or redesigned campaigns targeted toward women out of a sense of social responsibility; others have done so purely because of the effect of such campaigns on their profits. Some advertisers have been persuaded by consumer research that indicated women exerted more influence than men over most household purchases for products such as groceries, children's clothing, and toys, as well as influencing 80 percent of car purchases. In Japan, for example, the housewife makes most of the major purchases for the family and buys the family's food, household supplies, and clothing. She usually receives her husband's paycheck and decides how the money should be spent. Therefore, she is the person to whom advertisers must target their campaigns. Regardless of the rationale for changes in ad strategies and images, they have been touted as evidence of the emergence of a new society that is attuned to the roles of women in a progressive and consumer-centered world.

By the turn of the 21st century many key positions in advertising were occupied by women, enabling them to exert a major influence on ad campaigns. Critics of the portrayal of women in advertising were hopeful that this situation would help to eliminate some of the pejorative ads of earlier eras and would give rise to more positive images of women.

MARILYN KERN-FOXWORTH

See also color plate in this volume

Further Reading

Atwan, Robert, Donald McQuade, and John Wright, *Edsels, Luckies, and Frigidaires: Advertising the American Way,* New York: Dell, 1979

Bartos, Rena, *Marketing to Women around the World,* Boston: Harvard Business School Press, 1989

Biagi, Shirley, and Marilyn Kern-Foxworth, *Facing Difference: Race, Gender, and Mass Media,* Thousand Oaks, California: Pine Forge, 1997

Cortese, Anthony J., *Provocateur: Images of Women and Minorities in Advertising,* Lanham, Maryland: Rowman and Littlefield, 1999

Courtney, Alice, and Lockeretz Courtney, "A Woman's Place: An Analysis of the Roles Portrayed by Women in Magazine Advertisements," *Journal of Marketing Research* 8 (February 1971)

Courtney, Alice, and Thomas Whipple, *Sex Stereotyping in Advertising,* Lexington, Massachusetts: Lexington Books, 1983

Fox, Stephen, *The Mirror Makers: A History of American Advertising and Its Creators,* New York: Morrow, 1984

Goffman, Erving, *Gender Advertisements,* Washington, D.C.: Society for the Anthropology of Visual Communications, 1976

Kern-Foxworth, Marilyn, *Aunt Jemima, Uncle Ben, and Rastus: Blacks in Advertising, Yesterday, Today and Tomorrow,* Westport, Connecticut: Greenwood Press, 1994

Kilbourne, Jean, "Beauty and the Beast of Advertising," *Media and Values* (Winter 1989)

Lont, Cynthia M., *Women and Media: Content, Careers, Criticism,* Belmont, California: Wadsworth, 1995

Millum, Trevor, *Images of Woman: Advertising in Women's Magazines,* Totowa, New Jersey: Rowman and Littlefield, and London: Chatto and Windus, 1975

Moog, Carol, *"Are They Selling Her Lips?" Advertising and Identity,* New York: Morrow, 1994

Scanlon, Jennifer, *Inarticulate Longings: The Ladies' Home Journal, Gender, and the Promises of Consumer Culture,* New York: Routledge, 1995

Sivulka, Juliann, *Soap, Sex, and Cigarettes: A Cultural History of American Advertising,* Belmont, California: Wadsworth, 1998

World Wide Web. *See* Internet/World Wide Web

WPP Group

The WPP Group PLC, headquartered in London, England, is among the world's largest advertising holding companies, with $67.22 billion in billings, $7.97 billion in gross income, and 40,000 employees globally. In terms of sheer size, the company is rivaled only by the Omnicom Group and the Interpublic Group of Companies, which briefly moved ahead of WPP with its 2001 purchase of True North Communications.

The giant conglomerate became a holding company in 1985, when British businessman Martin Sorrell and a partner, Preston Rabl, spent $750,000 to purchase a 30 percent stake in a shopping cart manufacturer called Wire Plastic & Products Ltd. and renamed it WPP Group. For Sorrell, the chief executive of WPP, the company was a platform on which to build an empire. British-born and educated at Cambridge University and Harvard Business School, he had made a name for himself by taking over companies long before purchasing WPP. As finance director at London's Saatchi & Saatchi, he helped shepherd that agency's transformation from a 12-person business in 1970 into the largest ad agency in Europe by 1984.

After acquiring WPP, Sorrell promptly spent the next few years buying more than a dozen small communications companies in Britain and the United States. Early members of the group included the marketing companies Sidjakov, Berman, Gomez & Partners, San Francisco, California, and Walker Group/CNI, New York City and Los Angeles, California.

Then, in 1987, the ambitious Sorrell pulled off a coup that stunned Madison Avenue. He took over the JWT Group, parent company of the New York City–based J. Walter Thompson Company (JWT), in the first hostile takeover in advertising history—a move that industry observers had previously believed impossible.

Although JWT executives rejected WPP's initial bid of $45 per share, or $434.6 million, and even initiated a lawsuit to stop the takeover, Sorrell could not be derailed in his quest to make JWT the cornerstone of his nascent empire. Two weeks of frenzied activity in June 1987 culminated in Sorrell increasing his offer to $55.50 a share, for a total of $566 million, and the agency reluctantly agreed. Along with JWT, WPP acquired Hill & Knowlton, one of the world's largest public relations companies.

During the negotiations, three of JWT's most significant clients—Ford Motor Company, Goodyear Tire & Rubber Company, and Eastman-Kodak Company—threatened to put their accounts into review if the takeover happened. Goodyear carried through immediately with a review, and Ford pulled an estimated $90 million in billings from the agency. Other major clients that left after the takeover included Burger King Corporation and Sears, Roebuck & Company's Discover Card. After the takeover, Sorrell also lost his business partner, Rabl, who disagreed with the aggressive expansion strategy.

Just two years later, in 1989, Sorrell once again astonished the advertising world with another hostile takeover, this time of the Ogilvy Group, parent of New York City–based ad agency Ogilvy & Mather Worldwide. The purchase price was $54 a share, or approximately $864 million. As with JWT, some top executives at Ogilvy were adamantly opposed to the agency being bought by Sorrell, whose penchant for hostile takeovers earned him the name "the ogre of Madison Avenue." Ogilvy Chairman Kenneth Roman, who opposed the deal, resigned.

In gaining Ogilvy, WPP also gained powerhouse clients IBM Corporation and American Express Company and strengthened its relationship with Ford Motor Company and Unilever, since those marketers had accounts with both Ogilvy and JWT. However, notwithstanding the strong client base, the costly Ogilvy deal threatened to derail Sorrell's empire. WPP had to borrow heavily to buy Ogilvy, and when recession hit the advertising world, the takeover looked unwise.

In 1990 a WPP profits warning caused shares to plummet 66 percent in just four days. The total stock market value of the company decreased from $498 million to $32 million during the recession, and in 1992 the company barely escaped receivership by restructuring its $1 billion debt. One result of the downturn was that in 1993 WPP divested itself of the Ogilvy-owned agency Scali, McCabe, Sloves, selling it to the Interpublic Group of Companies' Lowe Group. WPP also agreed to allow Fallon McElligott, of Minneapolis, Minnesota, one of Scali's agencies, to purchase its independence for $14.6 million.

Although business was rough until about 1994, the booming economy of the latter half of the decade helped WPP climb back from the brink of financial disaster. In a testament to his contributions, Sorrell was knighted in 2000. In fact, WPP had regained so much of its power by then that it was able to complete the largest takeover in the history of advertising, purchasing Young & Rubicam (Y&R), parent company of New York City agency powerhouse Y&R Advertising, for $4.7 billion in stock. Sorrell had set his sights on Y&R as early as 1997 but was rebuffed by Peter Georgescu, its chairman and chief executive officer. Since Y&R had not yet gone public, Sorrell had no choice but to accept rejection. In 1998, however, Y&R did become a publicly traded company, setting the stage for its acquisition in 2000. Talks broke off in April 2000 as Y&R explored whether another holding company, Publicis Groupe, would become its white knight, buying the agency in WPP's stead.

But that May, after several weeks of negotiations, Y&R agreed to be purchased by WPP Group in an all-stock transaction valued at $4.7 billion. The transaction also gave WPP additional public relations agencies—Y&R's Burson-Marsteller and Cohn & Wolfe, as well as Impiric, formerly known as Wunderman Cato Johnson. With this deal, WPP became the world's leading advertising communications company until Interpublic bought True North in June 2001; by year's end, however, WPP was again on top.

For Y&R, the merger was a significant distraction during a particularly rocky year. The agency, with worldwide billings of $13.8 billion, lost nearly $800 million in accounts in 2000, including such blue-chip clients as KFC Corporation, Ericsson, Citicorp's U.S. Citibank, H&R Block, the U.S. Army, and Kraft Foods' Jell-O account, Y&R's oldest client.

WENDY DAVIS

Further Reading

"Ad Man on Fire," *Fortune* (10 July 2000)

"An Englishman in New York," *Adage Global* (December 2000)

"Sorrell Touts His Latest Effort, WPP, and This Time They Aren't Laughing," *Wall Street Journal* (17 March 1987)

Waller, Martin, "Brickbats Fly As WPP Escapes Receiver," *London Times* (6 August 1992)

"WPP Frees Fallon, Scali Sale Coming," *Advertising Age* (25 October 1993)

Wm. Wrigley Jr. Company

Principal Agencies

Neisser-Meyerhoff, Inc. (later BBDO Worldwide)

J. Walter Thompson Company

William Wrigley, Jr., was a 29-year-old soap and baking powder salesman when he decided to enter the already-competitive chewing gum business in the 1890s. His commitment to quality products and costly advertising proved to be justified. At the start of the 21st century, the Wm. Wrigley Jr. Company sold its products in more than 140 countries and commanded 50 percent of the domestic and global markets.

Wrigley came to Chicago, Illinois, from Philadelphia, Pennsylvania, in 1891 and soon switched from selling soap to selling

This Wrigley's billboard earned honorable mention for its graphic design in the 1932 Hundred Best Posters of the Year competition.
Copyright Wm. Wrigley Jr. Company, used by permission.

baking powder. He changed products again a year later after he found that the premium he included with a box of baking powder—two packages of chewing gum—proved more popular than the baking powder itself. The first two brands marketed under the Wrigley name were Lotta and Vassar; a year later, in 1893, the product line found what would become its core products with the introduction of first Juicy Fruit and then Wrigley's Spearmint gum.

Six large competitors joined forces to create what was known as a "chewing gum trust" in 1899; Wrigley was invited to join but declined and remained independent. Wrigley himself went on the road to sell his gum, using premiums to encourage merchants to carry his products alongside the other, more-established brands. He eventually printed catalogs with premiums ranging from lamps to razors; the strategy proved effective. He also experimented early with advertising, first in 1906 by talking up the benefits of Wrigley's Spearmint in newspapers and magazines and on outdoor boards. Whenever the cost of advertising was questioned, Wrigley's standard response was, "Anybody can make chewing gum. The trick is to sell it." And sell it he did: by 1908 sales of Wrigley's Spearmint topped $1 million a year.

One of its first advertising icons was "Spearman," introduced in 1915. The impish creature, which played on the Art Nouveau movement's penchant for pixies and fairies, was first used in a book of children's rhymes given away to promote the product. The words to the children's game "Pat-a-cake" were changed to "Pat-a-cake, pat-a-cake, candy man, buy Wrigley's Spearmint as fast as you can." Spearman, who at first resembled an arrow with a face, grew to resemble a piece of gum and continued to be used in the company's ads until 1970.

Wrigley began building its goodwill with the public early. During World War I company ads encouraged Americans to buy Liberty Bonds and War Savings Bonds, contribute to the Red Cross, and comply with food and fuel regulations. After the war, despite the rising cost of materials, Wrigley opted to keep the price of a pack of gum at a nickel, with the 1919–20 campaign theme: "Five cents before the war, five cents during the war, five cents now." Indirectly, the war greatly benefited Wrigley; U.S. servicemen acted as unofficial ambassadors for the company, showing Europeans how to chew gum. Sales rose from $15.4 million in 1917 to $27 million only two years later.

By the mid-1920s Wrigley's ad program had grown to include comic strips that promoted its gum and featured different characters from the King Features Syndicate. Wrigley's son, Philip, who was elected company president in 1925, convinced his father to add radio advertising to the company's media portfolio, and in December 1927 *The Wrigley Review* aired. It was one of the first coast-to-coast radio network programs, aired on 27 stations affiliated with the National Broadcasting Company (NBC) network. Satisfied with the results, a year later Wrigley sponsored a broadcast featuring Guy Lombardo and his band on 26 stations affiliated with the Columbia Broadcasting System (CBS). Commercials during the broadcasts were direct and to the point, highlighting the benefits of chewing gum. Still, most of the ad budget at the conservatively run company was dedicated to posters and public transportation car cards. When one car-card provider went bankrupt, Wrigley formed the New York Subways Advertising Company, which it retained until 1949.

Like his father, Philip Wrigley firmly believed that the key to success was to sell the gum. In March 1936 the company unveiled a ten-story-by-one-city-block-long sign on New York City's Broadway, between 44th and 45th streets. The ad was a pitch for Wrigley's Spearmint. The price tag for this display was a then-outrageous $1 million. The grand sums being spent on advertising caused even the *Wall Street Journal* in 1936 to question the effectiveness of ad dollars, but Wrigley did not flinch.

By this time Wrigley had a reputation for dealing directly with the creative forces at his advertising agency rather than with just the account executives. Neisser-Meyerhoff, Inc., took the account in 1933 and held onto it for years. By 1940 the agency had become Arthur Meyerhoff & Company, always with offices in the Wrigley Building on Michigan Avenue in Chicago. Describing his close involvement in the company's advertising in an interview in *Printers' Ink* in 1938, Wrigley said, "I know where every advertising dollar goes and why it is being spent. I select media, copy and art work. I even write copy and select whatever materials we may use. Nothing is initiated or changed without my knowledge and approval."

Also started during the late 1930s was what proved to be the popular "Twins" campaign for Doublemint gum, a product introduced in 1914. Radio programs featured pairs of piano players and double-talking comedians. The print ads featured identical twins. In 1940 Doublemint was assigned to the J. Walter Thompson Company, which put the brand into radio sponsoring *Gene Autry's Melody Ranch*. It was a relationship that lasted for more than 15 years and survived until Autry left TV in 1956. In 1959 television spots featuring Wrigley twins were introduced, along with the "Double Your Pleasure, Double Your Fun" jingle, which was written by a CBS radio staff musician in Chicago.

World War II provided another test of the company's mettle, and it hit a public-relations home run. By 1940 Wrigley's sales were the highest in its history, but Europe was at war, and the United States was soon to follow. As its supply of raw materials dwindled and large amounts of Wrigley's Spearmint, Juicy Fruit, and Doublemint were shipped to the armed forces overseas, Wrigley found it could not meet demand at the retail level. It opted to remove the brands from store shelves and devote its entire output to the war effort rather than use what it deemed to be inferior ingredients for its flagship brands. For the civilian market, it developed a brand called Orbit, which, Philip Wrigley freely admitted, did not have the same high-caliber ingredients as Wrigley's other brands.

By early 1945 Wrigley had entirely ceased production of its three signature brands. Competitors blasted Wrigley for the move—Alan F. Clark, president of Clark Brothers Chewing Gum Company of Pittsburgh, Pennsylvania, called Wrigley's move the "greatest mistake in their entire history"—but servicemen and even some other companies publicly praised it. Calvert Distillers Company ran ads in 60 leading newspapers saluting Wrigley's policy and its honesty.

Wrigley's brands may have been dormant, but its advertising was not. To keep its product in the consumer's mind, a campaign was created that showed an empty Wrigley's Spearmint wrapper. The text read: "Remember this wrapper—it means chewing gum of the finest quality and flavor. It will be empty until gum of Wrig-

The long-running "Double Your Pleasure" campaign for Doublemint gum always featured a set of twins. This ad appeared in 1989.
Copyright Wm. Wrigley Jr. Company, used by permission.

ley Spearmint's quality can again be made." Wrigley also maintained its use of transit car cards, posters, newspaper ads, and radio sponsorships, which included three CBS network radio programs devoted to the war effort.

Wrigley's Spearmint and Juicy Fruit went back on store shelves in 1946 and Doublemint followed in 1947. The end of the war allowed Wrigley to greatly expand its global market, although the first non-U.S. operations started with factories the company already had established in Toronto, Canada, and Melbourne, Australia, before 1920.

The marketing pitches had to be tailored to the local populations; in some cases this was successful, in others it was not. In England chewing gum was considered an inappropriate activity despite the company's presence there since 1911. Initially, ads promoted the use of gum as an aid to relaxation, but the real marketing push came in the 1950s. Wrigley took out ads in upscale publications promoting the use of chewing gum at polo matches and at Buckingham Palace. The flamboyant nature of the campaign was deemed a winner and sales improved.

Product introductions were next. From the mid-1970s through the mid-1990s, Wrigley introduced sugar-free Orbit and launched Freedent, Big Red, Hubba Bubba, Anurol, Extra, and Winterfresh gums. The conservative, family-run company had deviated little from what it knew best, in terms of both packaging and pricing. In 1978 Batten Barton Durstine & Osborn (BBDO) acquired Wrigley's longtime agency, Meyerhoff, and began to handle Wrigley's advertising.

By the mid-1990s, however, the Wrigley company realized it needed an advertising overhaul. The company was still on top, but competitors such as Warner-Lambert Company's Chiclets and Beechnut were encroaching on its turf. A campaign for Wrigley's Spearmint touted the gum's use as a cigarette substitute in non-smoking venues. The pitch for the Winterfresh brand joked about bad breath. Juicy Fruit was positioned as a ten-calorie alternative to fattening desserts, and Doublemint moved away from its use of twins, instead adopting the tag line, "Fresh taste. Fresh breath." "We're sort of trying to give everything a visual breath of fresh air," said Phillip Gant, executive vice president and chief creative officer of BBDO Worldwide, Chicago, in an interview with *Advertising Age*.

Just three years later, Wrigley found that its oldest product, Juicy Fruit, had fallen out of favor with teens, and its tag line, "Taste is gonna move you," was moving no one. The company and BBDO surveyed the core teen market, which said it liked Juicy Fruit's sweetness, and came up with the "Gotta have sweet" campaign in summer 1998.

The campaign tinkering continued, as Wrigley restored TV advertising for some of its key brands after hiatuses and experimented with marketing on the World Wide Web. But some still considered Wrigley stodgy, particularly because new competitors were around the corner in the form of "curiously strong mints." The Philip Morris Companies' Altoids, a 200-year-old British breath mint whose sales skyrocketed in 1995 following hip ads from the Leo Burnett Company, quickly became Wrigley's nemesis. Its quirky ads dared consumers to try the product and featured a bodybuilder holding a tin, with the text, "Nice altoids." Another ad showed an Altoids tin with the text, "Mints so strong, they come in a metal box." Other companies raced to the sector to share in the sales wealth of a product that some consumers found more acceptable than chewing gum. Mint sales skyrocketed 50 percent between 1995 and 2000.

Still sticking with gum, Wrigley responded in 1999 by introducing Eclipse, a premium sugarless pellet gum. It was Wrigley's first new product introduction since 1994. The $15 million ad pitch, aimed at baby boomers, was that Eclipse would eliminate rather than mask bad breath. "Die, bad breath" was the slogan, and it was well received. In just over a year, Eclipse rose to claim the number-six spot in the sugarless gum category. Another high-intensity gum, Everest, was introduced by Amurol Products Company, a Wrigley subsidiary since 1958. Like Altoids, Everest was packed in tins.

As the end of the century approached, it remained unclear how much Wrigley was willing to step outside the box. At the 2000 annual meeting, President and Chief Executive Officer Bill Wrigley, Jr., the fourth generation of the family to run the company, said Wrigley was actively promoting innovation and new product development. While Wrigley said executives reviewed the impact of breath mints regularly, he noted it was not that large a business compared with the chewing gum market.

MARY ELLEN PODMOLIK

Further Reading

Angle, Paul, *Philip K. Wrigley: A Memoir of a Modest Man*, Chicago: Rand McNally, 1975

Dotz, Warren, and Jim Morton, *What a Character! 20th-Century American Advertising Icons*, San Francisco: Chronicle Books, 1996

Naughton, Keith, "Chewed Out by Mints," *Newsweek* (1 November 1999)

Podmolik, Mary Ellen, "Marketing 100: Juicy Fruit," *Advertising Age* (26 June 2000)

Thompson, Stephanie, "Wrigley Readies New Ads to Freshen Sales: Big Red, Doublemint, Spearmint Campaigns Under Way," *Advertising Age* (25 October 1999)

Thompson, Stephanie, "Die, Bad Breath, Eclipse Proclaims in $15 Million Ad Push," *Advertising Age* (9 October 2000)

Whalen, Jeanne, "Wrigley Pumps Up Visual Freshness," *Advertising Age* (21 November 1994)

"Wrigley Chews on Ways to Revive Stale Sales," *Associated Press* (11 September 2000)

Wunderman

(Wunderman Cato Johnson)

Founded by Lester Wunderman, Irving Wunderman, Harry Kline, and Ed Ricotta as Wunderman, Ricotta & Kline, 1958; purchased by Young & Rubicam (Y&R), 1973; merged with Y&R subsidiary Cato Johnson Associates to become Wunderman Cato Johnson, 1992; combined with Y&R Advertising into a single profit center, 1997; became part of WPP Group when WPP acquired Y&R, 2000; briefly adopted new name, Impiric, but changed to Wunderman, 2001.

Major Clients
AT&T Corporation
Citigroup
Ericsson, Inc.
Ford Motor Company
IBM Corporation
Sony Corporation
Star Alliance
Xerox Corporation

The advertising agency of Wunderman, Ricotta & Kline (WRK), later Wunderman Cato Johnson, was launched in 1958 and quickly grew to become one of the largest direct-marketing agencies in the world. In 2000 it adopted the name Impiric (quickly changed to Wunderman). Yet approximately three-quarters of its billings continued to come from direct marketing. In fact, the agency and its founder, Lester Wunderman, are credited with coining the term *direct marketing* as well as with inventing several techniques of the trade, including magazine response cards, free-standing newspaper inserts, and direct-response television spots that feature toll-free numbers.

Prior to founding WRK, Wunderman and his brother, Irving, had owned their own agency, Coronet Advertising Service, in New York City; they subsequently joined forces with a direct-mail specialist, Cap Pinkster. Pinkster and Lester Wunderman were key figures in the early use of comic books as an advertising medium; thanks largely to their work, comics became one of the most important ad media during World War II, especially for army recruiting.

After leaving Pinkster, the two brothers joined the advertising agency Maxwell Sakheim & Company in New York City in 1947. There they made many of the contacts that would follow them to WRK, which they founded in 1958 with two other Sakheim employees, Harry Kline, an account supervisor, and Ed Ricotta, an art director. The previous year, Lester Wunderman had helped found the groundbreaking Columbia LP Record Club, and that company became one of the new agency's first four clients, along with Facts on File, Jackson & Perkins, and the Alexander Hamilton Training Institute.

WRK was one of the first agencies to focus on mail-order advertising. The practice was a success from the start, turning WRK into the largest mail-order agency in the country within a year of its founding. In 1961 it became the first direct-mail agency to be invited to join the American Association of Advertising Agencies (AAAA, or "Four A's"), symbolizing the industry's acceptance of mail order—which had long suffered from a lack of respect—as a viable advertising technique.

WRK often won accounts because its clients' agencies of record, the large general advertising companies, did not understand the principles of direct mail. By the 1960s WRK's roster included Consumers Union, Dow Jones, Time-Life, and the Advertising Council, the last for a campaign encouraging use of the Postal Service's zip code, introduced in 1967.

Wunderman continued to be perplexed by direct mail's reputation as a second-class advertising technique and the failure of leading advertisers to embrace it as an integral part of the marketing mix. He also believed that mail order had to evolve into a new concept he called "direct marketing." He first used the term in public in 1961, forecasting that mail order would be replaced by direct marketing, which he described as "a new and more efficient method of selling, based on scientific advertising principles and serviced by increasingly more automated warehousing, shipping, and collection techniques." He later wrote, "In my mind, direct marketing was a system of interactive transactions that would restore a measure of dialogue and human scale to the way we made, sold, and bought things."

His ideas did not attract much notice until 1967, when he made a speech outlining his vision of direct marketing to a group of professors at the Massachusetts Institute of Technology. His tenets made their way into the trade press, and within a year, change was in the air. The *Reporter of Direct Mail*, a trade publication, renamed itself *Direct Marketing*; AAAA started a direct marketing committee; and Direct Mail Day became Direct Marketing Day.

Meanwhile, WRK continued as one of the world's largest agencies in the field now known as direct marketing. Well before merger mania hit the advertising industry, WRK's partners began to seek a buyer that would provide the agency with more resources and give it access to the largest advertisers, while allowing it to remain autonomous. Wunderman ultimately decided on Young & Rubicam (Y&R), which purchased it in 1973 and remained the agency's parent into the 21st century.

From then through the 1990s, WRK continued as a major direct-marketing specialist, sharing with Y&R accounts such as Ford Motor Company, DuPont, Philip Morris Companies, Swissair, Xerox Corporation, AT&T Corporation, and Taco Bell. One key moment in the evolution of direct marketing was when General Foods Corporation, a large mass-market advertiser, introduced Sweden's leading coffee brand, Gevalia Kaffe, to U.S.

consumers through an upscale direct-mail subscription service developed by WRK.

In the late 1980s WRK changed its name to Wunderman Worldwide to reflect its international capabilities; one of its first global accounts was American Express's Optima Card. In 1992 Y&R merged Wunderman with Cato Johnson Associates, a sales-promotion agency that Y&R had taken over in 1976 and built into one of the leading organizations of its type. The new entity, Wunderman Cato Johnson (WCJ), specialized in both direct marketing and sales promotion. In 1997 WCJ merged with a sibling unit, Y&R Advertising. The move eliminated competition between the two while allowing them to remain operationally separate. About 80 percent of Y&R's clients at the time used both agencies, which together accounted for 65 percent of the parent company's revenue.

By 1998—the year Wunderman retired from the agency at age 77—WCJ was offering what it called "integrated solutions" to its advertising clients, providing database marketing and Internet-based services as well as traditional direct-response advertising. Direct marketing still represented 75 percent of WCJ's $2.14 billion in revenue, however, and the agency maintained a vibrant business in infomercials, telemarketing, and mail order.

WCJ continued to diversify. Y&R acquired Capital Consulting and Research in 1998 and folded it into WCJ, bringing the agency additional consulting services, branding capabilities, and database marketing expertise. In 1999 WCJ underwent a restructuring, closing some of its international offices and laying off employees. The intent was to transform WCJ from a direct-marketing and sales-promotion agency into a full-service customer relationship company.

The reorganization culminated in the merger of WCJ with Knowledge Base Marketing, an e-commerce and database company acquired by Y&R in 1999. The new company also received a new name, Impiric, and tag line, "The art and science of customer relationships." The new moniker was deemed necessary because the WCJ name was closely associated with direct marketing, and the company viewed such a tie as detrimental to its quest to establish itself as the leading customer relationship–management agency.

As part of its repositioning, Impiric launched a worldwide research and development unit called Marketing Lab and entered into strategic alliances with Digital Impact, an e-marketing services provider; EchoMail, an e-mail management service; and Value-Flash.com, an Internet direct marketer, among others. The agency offers its integrated marketing solutions through 80 offices with 4,000 employees in 40 countries, building on the direct-marketing foundation established by Wunderman, Ricotta & Kline and later Wunderman Cato Johnson. The Impiric name was dropped in 2001, and the company renamed itself simply Wunderman.

KAREN RAUGUST

Further Reading

Gleason, Mark, "Y&R Formally Links Ad Unit with Wunderman," *Advertising Age* (3 March 1997)

Levin, Gary, "'Personalized' Marketing Will Gain Dominance," *Advertising Age* (25 October 1993)

McDonough, John, "Wunderman Cato Johnson: A Direct Marketer—Plus," *Advertising Age* (2 November 1998)

"WCJ Expands Integrated Service Offerings, Changes Name to Impiric," *Direct Marketing* (May 2000)

Wunderman, Lester, *Being Direct: Making Advertising Pay*, New York: Random House, 1996

X

Xerox Corporation

Principal Agencies

Doyle Dane Bernbach, Inc.

Papert, Koenig, Lois

Needham, Harper & Steers Advertising, Inc. (later Needham Harper Worldwide)

Ted Bates & Company

Young & Rubicam, Inc.

The Xerox Corporation got its official name at a shareholders meeting on 18 April 1961, but its antecedents can be traced to the Haloid Company, founded in 1906 to make and sell photographic paper. Haloid expanded its line to photocopiers in 1935 with its acquisition of the Rectigraph Company.

Haloid's big break came in 1947 when it obtained a license for an invention called "electrophotography" under development at Battelle Memorial Institute in Columbus, Ohio. Battelle in 1944 had taken up the challenge of refining the process whereby electrostatic images are transferred to paper from a photoconductive surface. The invention was the work of patent attorney and part-time inventor Chester Carlson, who developed the technology in 1938 and presented it for development to more than 20 companies, including IBM Corporation, General Electric Company, and Eastman-Kodak Company, before contracting with Battelle. Haloid introduced the Model A copier in 1949, and changed the name of the process to "xerography," believing the term "electrophotography" unwieldy; the new word had been coined for Haloid by a classical languages professor from Greek words for "dry" and "writing."

Haloid added Xerox to its name in 1958 and in April 1959 introduced the Xerox 914, the first simplified office copier. Within three years Xerox held a skimpy 2 percent share of the 400,000 office copiers in the United States, but its high-volume Xerox 914 was producing more than 25 percent of the market's 3 billion copies of documents. The machine was aimed at the 2,000-and-more-copies-per-month market, a gamble at that time when low-to-medium volume machines were the norm. Xerox also had very little competition for copying materials used to supply its own equipment.

In 1961 the company dropped Doyle Dane Bernbach, Inc. (DDB), as its lead creative agency when DDB pursued and won Polaroid Corporation as a client; Polaroid said at the time it planned to enter the copier business, and it ultimately developed a small copier for IBM Corporation. Papert, Koenig, Lois (PKL) succeeded DDB on the $500,000 consumer account, nearly all in print and for the Xerox 914.

The market for copiers in Europe and Japan at that time trailed the U.S. market by two years, but Xerox wanted to be prepared for emerging growth. It struck a deal for a 50-50 joint venture with Fuji Photo Film Company in Japan, forming Fuji-Xerox in 1961 and, with the Rank Organization, formed Rank-Xerox in Europe, taking two-thirds equity.

The ad budget rose to $1.75 million in 1962, about 75 percent media, and in 1963 it reached $4 million, with much of the hike going into the introduction of Xerox's first desktop unit, the Xerox 813. The desktop unit brought an ad shift from half print–half TV to 40-60 in favor of TV. When the first decade of copiers on the market closed in 1963, sales were $500 million, divided by eight large manufacturers, 30 smaller producers, and 70 suppliers of copier equipment materials. The Xerox 914 accounted for $100 million in sales. Ironically, Xerox had asked another company to market the Xerox 914, and a research company hired by this potential host company turned thumbs down, saying the market was too restrictive. The growing dominance of the Xerox 914 encouraged Xerox to consolidate its four separate sales staffs handling the Xerox 914, xerography equipment, high-speed Copyflo printers, and photographic products.

By the mid-1960s, Xerox was counted among a select group of single-program network TV sponsors, at times even funding the cost of production. This type of sponsorship, dubbed "entertainment-with-a-purpose," led Xerox to underwrite six public-service TV specials about the United Nations (UN) shot on location around the world at a cost of $4 million. Xerox created the Telsun Foundation, a nonprofit organization to produce the special TV films. All profits were turned over to the UN or to groups working to further its causes. The programs ran without commercials, with only a single credit line showing Xerox as the sponsor. Xerox continued into the 1970s to use sole-sponsor documentaries, musicals, and theatrical events as marketing vehicles, creating its own "spot network" of 100 stations (which later grew to 120) to get a bigger audience than just a single network. Stockholders were skeptical as to whether it was in Xerox's best interest to produce programming without commercials. They were also concerned that the company might be duped by the propaganda agendas of special-interest groups (such as supporters of the UN). But corporate executives were proud when the John Birch Society urged followers to boycott Xerox for its "lack of wisdom" in aiding and abetting the UN. By the late 1960s Xerox wielded such spending power that network executives scheduled press conferences to announce deals with the company.

In 1968 PKL lost the $4 million corporate, business products and systems, and information systems division account to Needham Harper & Steers (NH&S), as Scali, McCabe Sloves (two of its principals were PKL alums) got the emerging Xerox education division account valued at $1 million. Acquisitions subsequently fueled the Xerox education division, centered on the 1968 purchase of R.R. Bowker Company, a New York City–based publisher of business papers, reference books, and library materials. The division grew to include Ginn & Company, Xerox microfilm, educational publications (*Weekly Reader*), and family education services. The unit was sold in 1985.

Diversification, a corporate modus among America's leading companies in the 1960s, left its mark on Xerox. After its purchase of Bowker in 1968, Xerox in 1970 bought the computer hardware producer Scientific Data Systems, of Santa Monica, California, and changed its name to Xerox Data Systems. It introduced the portable Xerox 400 Telecopier that year, its second move in the facsimile business. Two years earlier Xerox had agreed to market, install, and handle field service for Magnavox Company's Magnafax 840, which became the Xerox Magnafax Telecopier. The company's ad budget by the end of the 1960s hit $10 million, split equally among TV, print, and marketing services.

In the 1970s Xerox began its long courtship of public television, introduced an electronic typewriter–word processor, bailed out of the computer market following feeble efforts to build that line of business, found its copier market dominance vulnerable at the low end, and fostered award-winning TV commercials highlighted by the "Miracle Monks" spots from NH&S.

The company sponsored the *Civilisation* series on the Public Broadcasting Service (PBS), presented by British journalist Kenneth Clark, and promoted it by developing the one-hour program "Civilisation: A Preview" that aired on NBC during prime time. The special carried six commercial minutes, all devoted to Xerox copiers. Typical of Xerox's ancillary advertising supporting its minimally advertised TV fare was the integrated marketing effort behind a heralded new TV series, *America: A Personal History*, that ran on NBC in 1972. On the program it slotted 90-second commercials to promote its office equipment, educational programs, and corporate objectives. It encouraged NBC to "hold down" station break messages so that continuity would not be too sharply interrupted. Xerox sent 500,000 leaflets to schools to promote the series and ran tune-in ads in magazines and newspapers.

Xerox entered the electronic typewriter market in 1974 with its 800 electronic typing system (a typewriter–word processor that was billed in ads as 100 percent faster than IBM's popular market leader, the Selectric). The intro could be read as a shot across the bow at IBM, which had entered the copier business in 1972. In 1975 Xerox settled an antitrust suit with the U.S. Federal Trade Commission (FTC) that barred it from promoting or taking orders for new copier models more than three months before availability. The FTC said the action stemmed from new-model announcements that indicated early availability and caused copier buyers to hold off on purchases—possibly from competitors—until Xerox came out with its product much later. Indeed, in 1964 Xerox had introduced the Xerox 2400 copier in an $800,000 pre-launch campaign featuring the actor-comedian George Goebel a year before the machine was available. The act of a dominant marketer running a campaign, even with no product available, encouraged potential customers to defer purchasing an office copier until the latest Xerox model arrived.

Xerox got out of the computer business in July 1975. Its little-advertised computer unit was capital intensive and would have required huge investments to make Xerox a major player, the company said at the time. It was a costly venture: Xerox had paid almost $1 billion for Scientific Data Systems just six years earlier. The flight from the market dominated by IBM followed a similar exodus by General Electric and RCA Corporation. Xerox never got more than 2 percent of the business, while IBM held 67 percent of the market when Xerox bailed out.

Xerox can lay claim to one of the most popular TV commercials in the 1970s, the 1975 "Miracle monks" ad by NH&S that introduced Brother Dominic, the cherubic monk who used a Xerox 9200 duplicating system to produce 500 copies of a hand-illuminated manuscript, thus saving decades of work in the scriptorium. Brother Dominic's abbot called this apparent laboring by the scribes a "miracle" as the roly-poly friar looked heavenward, thanking Xerox for the 9200. The ad aired on Major League Baseball's All-Star game, two years after Xerox began favoring championship sports events on TV by advertising during the Super Bowl. The Xerox 9200 captured 15 percent of the market by 1985, noted Frost & Sullivan, a research company. Meanwhile, Xerox's overall market share had fallen from 60 percent at the beginning of the decade to just less than 50 percent by its end as Canon and Savin, a Ricoh Corporation brand, pummeled it with new products on the low end. In fact, during the late 1970s Xerox took measures to stem share erosion by introducing three rounds of price cuts in 14 months. One round of cuts was announced in a *Wall Street Journal* page ad headlined, "Good news."

Diversification continued in the 1980s as Xerox bought companies involved in optical character recognition, faxing, desktop publishing, and scanning. It also made numerous missteps in developing its computer potential. Xerox bought Crum & Forster, an insurer. It opened a chain of retail stores in 1980 to pursue

makes copies on ordinary paper

The new XeroX 914 Office Copier does not require expensive sensitized paper, or intermediate film negative, or liquid chemicals. It copies directly onto standard office paper (plain or colored), your own letterhead, or card stock. Up to six copies per minute!

There are no exposure adjustments to make with the XeroX 914 Office Copier and, therefore, no waste of materials (the biggest cost item in conventional office copying). Each copy, *every* copy of the original is a *perfect* copy. The last copy is as good as the first.

Copies everything—never misses a color! A letter, invoice, statement, contract—anything written, typed, printed, stamped or drawn can be copied on the new XeroX 914...even pages in a thick bound book. Copies all colors, even reds and blues, with sharp black-on-white fidelity.

Easiest of all office copiers to operate for multiple copies or just one. Simply place original document face down on the scanning glass, select the number of copies you want, and push "Print" button. Anyone can make perfect copies every time on the XeroX 914 Copier.

About 1¢ per copy for supplies. If you now spend $50 to $100 per month for copying supplies, you can't afford to be without the new XeroX 914 Copier. Supplies cost about 1¢ per copy, the machine is available without capital investment on a unique pay-as-you-use plan starting at $95 a month.

For complete information about this remarkably fast, inexpensive method of copying, write HALOID XEROX INC., 9X-14 Haloid Street, Rochester 3, New York. Offices in principal U.S. and Canadian cities. *Overseas:* Rank-Xerox Ltd., London.

HALOID XEROX®

NEW XEROX® 914
OFFICE COPIER

This 1960 print ad for the Xerox 914, the first plain-paper office copier, featured two recurring themes in Xerox's advertising: reliability and simplicity of operation.
XEROX® is a registered trademark of Xerox Corporation.

In the 1990s Xerox repositioned itself as "The document company." XEROX® and The Document Company® are registered trademarks of Xerox Corporation.

low-end users of its office equipment. The outlets were sold in December 1983 to Genra Group, a Dallas, Texas, computer chain. The stores were meant to complement Xerox's direct sales force, but the company found it more profitable to let other retailers assume the overhead and marketing expenses.

Xerox revisited the computer business in 1981, introducing its eight-bit 820 computer for business computing. It beat IBM's Personal Computer (PC) to the market by six months and had strong distribution via its sales force and retailers. But fortune quickly faded when IBM's PC brought 16-bit technology to the desktop market. Xerox's machine was further crippled by its lack of compatibility with IBM's PC operating system. Xerox also failed to react when software developers scurried to write programs for IBM. It never regained its momentum. In 1984 lack of market support caused Xerox to scrap its laptop battery-powered computer a year after it introduced the machine.

In May 1985 Xerox introduced its first desktop computer compatible with IBM's PC, although the product, developed by Xerox, was produced by Olivetti & Company. Xerox's marketing strategy to revive its fortunes in computers relied on employing photocopier salespeople to sell computers. Xerox spent more than $20 million to train its sales force, according to market analysts

interviewed by *Advertising Age*. Xerox scuttled its personal computer business for good in 1987, selling PCs only as part of its desktop publishing system. Profit margins on the PC business had been little to none. Xerox's conservative marketing approach ultimately stalled the company, killing its chances of being a player in the market.

Xerox continued to staunch erosion in its other business lines. Once a leader in the fax industry, it had steadily lost market share since the 1970s when rivals started introducing lower-price products. Sharp Electronics Corporation, Canon, and Ricoh (Savin) had all surpassed Xerox. The company repositioned its fax machine business in 1988 from up-market to down-market. It introduced a line of thermal paper fax machines, priced at $2,000, to attack the upstarts on pricing—deemed more important at the time than the quality and convenience embodied in its standard $3,500 cut-sheet, plain-paper machines. Direct mail and print ads vowed Xerox would give customers $5 for every fax transmission that failed to arrive.

The Japanese invasion in both the fax and copier market had taken a toll on Xerox. Internal company research in the mid-1980s found that the public no longer perceived Xerox as the apotheosis of efficiency and high-tech knowledge. In 1985 Xerox sought to revive those perceptions with a massive $70 million corporate and product ad campaign by Needham Harper Worldwide called "Directions." Past introductions included one or two new products at a time, but Directions introduced 14 new office systems products at once, serving notice that Xerox was serious about its leadership in office automation. The campaign spent $30 million on network TV, $25 million on business-to-business, and $15 million on lifestyle magazines. By this time, 80 percent of the company's U.S. sales were from copiers and electronic typewriters, and in the larger copier market, Xerox's share had dropped to 36 percent.

Xerox, arguing that it needed to seek new ideas and approaches to advertising, moved its account to Ted Bates & Company in 1986. Needham Harper Worldwide, as it was then called, claimed at the time that it was caught between two corporate systems, the Rochester, New York–based business systems group and the corporate offices, located since 1969 in Stamford, Connecticut. Needham had to weather bureaucratic overlay with its work for the business-systems group (65 percent of the account). Each campaign had to be approved in Stamford. The Rochester group, on the other hand, chaffed at the ease at which Needham-created corporate campaigns got quick approval.

Xerox began shifting its emphasis from reprographics, which it had been working to reestablish for several years, to computer output businesses, particularly laser printers, copier products, and computer communications (it developed the Ethernet for linking computers on local networks).

In 1990 Xerox shifted its ad account to Young & Rubicam, Inc. (Y&R), whose task it became to change the company's image from that of a copier company to that of a marketer offering a diverse document line. As part of that shift, Xerox introduced an Olympic-themed commercial focusing on the company's role as the "official document processing company" of the 1992 Summer

Olympics. Xerox also served as exclusive copier sponsor in NBC-TV's coverage of the Games in Barcelona, Spain.

By 1992 Xerox held 60 percent of the high-end document processing market (*Fortune* 1,000 companies and governments), but only 15 percent of the low end, leading the company in 1993 to target small businesses and in-home users for its copiers, printers, and facsimile products. Its U.S. media spending in 1992 and 1993 was about $30 million a year, heaviest in print and marketing services. Alliances with computer manufacturers took the place of production as the company supplied Compaq Computers and Apple Computer with print engines in 1992 and 1993, the latter a snub to Canon, which had been Apple's sole supplier for eight years. Other alliances followed with Adobe Systems, Cisco Systems, Dell Computer Corporation, IBM, Intel Corporation, Microsoft Corporation, Novell, Oracle Corporation, and Sun Microsystems. In 1993 Xerox also brought out network color laser printers and software for printing Web documents.

Xerox toyed with retail once again, founding Xerox Document Centers in 1994 in supermarket chains to sell copier and fax paper, self-stick notes, and computer diskettes. Xerox sold its struggling insurance units from 1996 to 1998, and bought out Rank's ownership in its European venture in 1997. Its first product for home use, a $500 PC printer, copier, and scanner, was introduced in 1997, and ex-IBM Chief Financial Officer Richard Thoman was hired as president and chief operating officer to move Xerox into network and digital products.

Xerox underwent restructuring in 1998 at a cost of $1 billion and pared 10 percent of its workforce. It bought XLConnect (renamed Xerox Connect) and parent Intelligence Electronics, and in 1999 purchased SET Electronique, a French company that made high-speed digital printers. Xerox moved on-line to sell its products and reorganized its sales force by shifting from a geographic- to a customer-industry base. The company laid off 14,000 workers in 1998 and 1999 under the restructuring plan, but critics of the company claimed the restructuring was botched. Cuts were so severe that customer bills went uncollected and many of Xerox's top account executives left. By 2000 its worldwide ad budget had grown to $130 million—$80 million in the United States, $40 million in Europe, and $10 million in Latin America.

Xerox bought Tektronix's struggling color printing and imaging division in early 2000, and linked with Fuji and Sharp in a joint venture to produce low-cost inkjet printers. Profits had slumped, however, abetted by fears of the so-called Y2K bug, a strong dollar, and economic pressures in several world markets. The company was on the verge of using up a $7 billion line of credit. Its credit rating was lowered. Xerox eliminated 2,000 more jobs in 2000. Xerox predicted it would turn itself around by building cash reserves, selling up to $4 billion in assets, and cutting $1 billion in costs.

By 2002 the company had become more focused and much more nimble. Under the leadership of Anne M. Mulcahy, the new chairman-CEO who negotiated the $925 million purchase of now very profitable Tektronix, Xerox losses in 2001 were pared 80 percent from the prior year to only $8 million on revenue of $16.6 billion, down 13 percent. Front-office actions, including a reduction in the workforce by 13,600 employees in 2001, were producing $1.1 billion in annualized savings by year-end, strengthening Xerox's position in refinancing and extending the maturity of its $7 billion revolving line of credit. The company also launched a multimillion-dollar global ad campaign from Y&R, focusing on services—a sign of things to come at a company whose culture has emphasized selling copiers.

CRAIG ENDICOTT

Further Reading

Abelson, Reed, et al., "The Fading Copier King," *New York Times* (19 October 2000)

"All-Out Assault on Big Blue Turf: Xerox, Compaq PCs Bow," *Advertising Age* (6 May 1985)

Bianco, Anthony, and Pamela L. Moore, "Downfall: The Inside Story of the Management Fiasco at Xerox," *Business Week* (5 March 2001)

Moran, Brian, "Needham Is Xerox's Ex-Agency," *Advertising Age* (31 March 1986)

Moran, Brian, "Needham Fell to Xerox Tug-of-War," *Advertising Age* (7 April 1986)

Moore, Pamela L., "She's Here to Fix the Xerox," *Business Week* (6 August 2001)

Trout, Jack, and Al Ries, "How to Position Your Product," *Advertising Age* (8 May 1972)

"Xerox Goes Retail," *Advertising Age* (14 April 1980)

"Xerox Shift from PKL May Signal TV Idea Revamp," *Advertising Age* (8 March 1968)

Y

Yahoo!

Principal Agency
Black Rocket

In the year 2001 the Internet service provider Yahoo! entered the new millennium as the only significant, profitable, solely advertising-supported company of its kind. Ninety percent of its $316 million in revenue in 2000 came from the type of traditional advertiser spending that has supported more traditional media. But, unlike broadcast, cable, and print, Yahoo! could account in detail for its audience, having data on who, when, and what was being viewed in addition to interactively linking the advertiser with the consumer.

Who uses Yahoo! is just as important as its advertising backbone. In 2001 it reached 60 percent of all Internet users worldwide and 70 percent of the workers at the 500 biggest companies in the United States. It also tracked the on-line moves of its 166 million users, one-third of whom offered detailed information about their identities and personal preferences. While the cost of Internet banner advertising fell as much as 75 percent, Yahoo!'s targeted ads were selling for as much as nine times the cost of a 30-second spot during the Super Bowl. Tailored e-mails to targeted groups were priced as high as page ads in major business magazines. With 40 percent of its users outside the United States and half overall accessing the service from broadband devices, Yahoo! also emerged as the first global interactive advertising vehicle at a time when the very nature of advertising was in flux.

Yahoo! was created in the spring of 1994 when Stanford University students Jerry Yang and David Filo began maintaining an eccentric list of trendy Web sites. "Through most of 1994, even though we were playing with Yahoo! as a hobby, we were looking for another start-up idea. . . . We really didn't think Yahoo! could possibly be it. There was no possible business model that fit it," Yang told *Fortune* magazine in March 2000. Originally the company had been called Jerry's & Dave's Guide to the World Wide Web. But Yang and Filo later felt they needed to formalize the name and decided on the Yahoo! moniker—an acronym for Yet Another Hierarchical Officious Oracle!

Less than a year later, Sequoia Capital backed the venture with $2 million. In May 1995 Young and Filo were joined by Timothy A. Koogle, a mechanical engineer and former Motorola employee who was president of a bar code scanner division of Litton Industries when he was lured to Yahoo! to be the business brains behind the on-line operation. Shortly afterward, Netscape Communications Corporation gave Yahoo! distribution on its popular Web site and access to millions of users.

A year later in April 1996, Koogle took Yahoo! public, issuing 2.6 million shares at $13 each. The price jumped to $33 a share on the first day of trading, eventually climbing to more than $300 a share. Yahoo! used its stock to buy into some Internet service and content companies. The acquisitions included $5.7 billion in stock for the video service Broadcast.com, which would be used to create a broadband version of Yahoo!, and $4 billion for Geocities, which aided in the building of personal Web sites. In 1998 Yahoo! was one of the first dot-com companies to turn profitable, reporting $15 million in profits on $245 million in mostly advertising revenue. By 2000 profits topped $280 million on more than $1 billion in revenue. Yahoo!'s business model was based on more than 3,565 advertisers paying about $25 for every 1,000 Yahoo! page views, with more than 10,500 e-merchants giving Yahoo! a cut of their sales, and 575 content partners.

Yahoo! made many successful moves in forging a major Internet brand. It was the first major Internet company to turn to television to build consumer and advertiser awareness of its brand with commercials that began airing in 1996. It began with a $5 million series of irreverent TV commercials, handled by Black Rocket, a San Francisco, California, agency. The spots showed regular people using Yahoo! to improve their everyday lives; Yahoo! radio ads ended with a signature yodel. The revolutionary marketing strategy positioned Yahoo! as vivacious and approachable, cultivating a loyalty that was reinforced by the "myYahoo!" personalization features and consumer support services.

In addition to its zany marketing programs, the company struck deals with content providers and distributors to extend its reach. It offered consumers free access to its service and free e-mail, paging, and other personal features, unlike rival America Online (AOL). Conveying a sense of utility, access, and irreverence

Free fantasy sports. Live the dream.

Yahoo! Sports

Ever wish you could be down there with the best of them?

Well, now you can.

Yahoo! has free fantasy games

for just about every major sport.

So you can live the glory days all over again.

In your mind.

sports.yahoo.com

A 2000 print ad highlighted Yahoo! Sports, one of the Internet service's growing range of information and entertainment services.

network provides maximum choice to consumers. He vowed to protect consumer privacy by cautiously using the data Yahoo! compiles on its more than 100 million registered users. In fact at a meeting in 1998, Koogle was among the major Internet service provider chief executives who widely condemned traditional media companies for paying lip service to an on-line future that they said eventually would overshadow them. Still, a weak stock market and advertising market in 2000 drove Yahoo! to begin emphasizing the value of services it offered advertisers rather than focusing primarily on targeted reach. The turmoil set off speculation about Yahoo!'s future, ranging from a broad marketing and cross-promotion deal with a traditional media company such as Viacom/CBS, a partnership with News Corporation in its proposed Sky Global satellite roll-up, or acquisition by the likes of software giant Microsoft Corporation.

In 2001 Koogle turned over day-to-day management of Yahoo! to Terry Semel, a longtime Hollywood studio mogul and Warner Brothers chief whose connection to the world of mainstream entertainment and media would be used to reshape Yahoo!'s competitive and strategic positioning. However, those plans were stalled early in 2002 when Yahoo! and other new and old media concerns suffered from a volatile stock market and one of the worst advertising slumps in history.

DIANE MERMIGAS

Further Reading

Carpenter, Phil, *Ebrands: Building an Internet Business at Breakneck Speed,* Boston: Harvard Business School Press, 2000

Hardy, Quentin, "The Killer Ad Machine," *Forbes* (11 December 2000)

Hwang, Suein, and Mylene Mangalindan, "Watch This Space: Yahoo!'s Grand Vision for Web Advertising Takes Some Hard Hits," *The Wall Street Journal* (1 September 2000)

Keeton, Ann, "Yahoo CEO Doesn't See Deal Like AOL's Buy of Time Warner," *Dow Jones News Service* (18 December 2000)

Mermigas, Diane, "New Media Takes on the Old," *Electronic Media* (11 May 1998)

Mermigas, Diane, "Yahoo! Streams Ahead: Broadcast.com Deal Boosts Both Web Powers," *Electronic Media* (5 April 1999)

Pulliam, Suan, and Mylene Mangalindan, "Investors Wonder If the Tide Has Finally Turned for Yahoo!" *The Wall Street Journal* (1 September 2000)

Roth, Daniel, "Surprise! Yahoo! Goes Broadband," *Fortune* (29 May 2000)

Schiender, Brent, "The Customer Is the Decision-Maker," *Fortune* (6 March 2000)

Sutherland, Max, *Advertising and the Mind of the Consumer: What Works, What Doesn't, and Why,* St. Leonards, New South Wales: Allen and Unwin, 1993; 2nd edition, by Sutherland and Alice K. Sylvester, St. Leonards, New South Wales: Allen and Unwin, and London: Kogan Page, 2000

Swisher, Kara, "Boom Town: Grumpy Won't Say What's Next for Yahoo!" *The Wall Street Journal* (6 March 2000)

CELEBRATE THE EVOLUTION OF MEDIA IN THE **20TH CENTURY BY SPENDING ALL YOUR BUDGET ON THE DOMINANT MEDIUM OF THE 21ST.**

What is media in the 21st century? It's Fusion Marketing Online. No, it's not toxic. It's like this: talk to us, then target, direct market and sell your product. All at once. From the same place. We call it our 'online media toolkit.' Enjoy. adkit.yahoo.com.

YAHOO!
The world's largest online audience.

By 1999 Yahoo! was able to turn its Internet customer base and online expertise into Fusion Marketing Online, a market research and targeting service for advertisers.

became the company's hallmark. Yahoo! became loosely known as the common person's home in cyberspace. As the company matured, so did its approach to marketing, press relations, and dealing with investors, who generally were pleased with the triple-digit price of Yahoo! stock until the bottom fell out of Internet stocks in the year 2000.

The biggest blows to Yahoo! were the weakening of the overall advertising marketplace and the collapse of what was loosely referred to as dot-com advertising, i.e., marketing by Internet-related companies, which was the dominant source of Yahoo! ad revenue. Leading Internet analysts called on Yahoo! to devise a new business model if it was to survive. Yahoo!'s bubble had finally burst.

Even as AOL was merging with Time-Warner, however, Yahoo! was stalwartly independent. It resisted a deal estimated at $20 billion to align with the Walt Disney Company. Though its stock price was at a fraction of its all-time high, like most Internet companies, Yahoo! maintained a market capitalization of $30 billion, making it a rich buy for nearly any company.

Speaking to a group of executives late in 2000, Koogle said that Yahoo! would resist such a mega-merger because its open

Yellow Pages

Many consumers familiar with the Yellow Pages and its "walking fingers" icon do not realize its power as a major advertising medium. In 2001 marketers spent $13.6 billion on Yellow Pages advertising in the United States and almost $25 billion globally. In the United States, the medium outpaced cable television (at $10.4 billion) and trailed spot TV ($14.9 billion) and magazines ($16.5 billion), according to Taylor Nelson Sofres's CMR, a provider of U.S. marketing and advertising expenditure data.

The Yellow Pages often is the primary form of advertising for thousands of local businesses. Their ads account for 86 percent of Yellow Pages advertising revenue. National advertisers such as General Motors Corporation; Sears, Roebuck & Company; State Farm Insurance; U-Haul International; and Roto-Rooter, Inc., account for the balance.

The first phone books in the United States appeared in the late 1800s as simple lists of residential and business names published and distributed by the telephone company to its local customers. Separate classified listings, or "headings" such as florists, restaurants, and furniture, did not appear until the early 1900s. The listings first appeared on yellow paper when a Cheyenne, Wyoming, printer ran out of white paper stock and made a substitution. As towns and cities grew, consumers became increasingly dependent on these classified yellow sections to help them keep track of new and existing businesses. The phone company also saw a potential source of revenue in these "Yellow Pages" and began enhancing classified sections for that reason as well as to meet the needs of advertisers and consumers.

Yellow Pages directories are found throughout the world today, although the United States and Canada are the most highly developed markets. By 2002 almost 250 companies throughout North America were publishing Yellow Pages directories. Yellow Pages publishing companies fall into two distinct types: utility-related publishers (i.e., those that publish directories for telephone service providers) and independent publishers (those not associated with a phone company). Utility publishers create directories for the service areas of each of their clients, and both utility and independent publishers also produce a variety of other directories—such as neighborhood, areawide, business to business, and specialty—often within the same market area. In an effort to woo consumers, publishers add user-friendly features to their books, including indexes, maps, zip code listings, stadium seating charts, and restaurant guides. In addition to print directories, many publishers also offer an electronic or Internet version. Most directory publishers give each business a free alphabetical listing in the Yellow Pages under the heading of their choice. Marketers then can purchase additional advertising in two major categories: in-column ads and display ads. In-column ads are an extension of the advertiser's business listing and are one column wide. The length of the ad varies based on the amount of information included. In-column ads, created by the publisher's sales teams or certified marketing representatives, can include trademark names, logos, color, and a variety of type fonts. Display ads are arranged around the in-column ads and can be as small as one column wide or as large as an entire page. Display ads allow advertisers to include larger amounts of text, artwork, photographs, and eye-catching features such as unique borders. Because printed directories generally are published only once a year, advertisers need to ensure that the information in their ads will remain relevant for 12 months. Prices, sale dates, and other kinds of variable information usually are not included. Because it is possible for listings in Internet Yellow Pages to be updated more frequently, these can include more time-sensitive information.

The Yellow Pages works differently from other advertising media. For example, when a person turns on the television set, it is to view a program not a commercial spot. But when a consumer goes to the Yellow Pages, it is normally to look at the ads and listings. Thus, a Yellow Pages ad—whether in print, online, or on a wireless device such as a personal digital assistant or a cell phone—captures consumers when they are most ready to buy. According to a January 2002 study by CRM Associates, an independent market research company based in Boulder, Colorado, a Yellow Pages ad extended the reach of other media, and the Yellow Pages ad returned $14 in revenue for every $1 invested.

The Yellow Pages is called a "directional medium" because it points willing consumers in the proper direction to make their purchase and helps close the sale. The Yellow Pages does not create awareness of or demand for products or services. People do not pick up the Yellow Pages and come to the realization that they need a car. But having made the decision to shop for a new vehicle—a choice that can be influenced by print ads and commercial spots—consumers often consult the Yellow Pages to find a car dealer or even to consider a brand. According to a study conducted in 2000 by Statistical Research, Inc. (SRI), later renamed Knowledge Networks/SRI, adults typically turn to the directory an average of 1.4 times per week. It tends to be used equally by men and women, generally in the 25-to-49-year-old age group, who are employed in professional, clerical, or sales positions; have relatively high household incomes ($60,000 or more); and are well-educated (attended or graduated from college).

SRI also found that more than 90 percent of consumers believe the Yellow Pages is an easy and effective shopping resource and were able to find the product they were looking for there. Consumers use the Yellow Pages to identify businesses and to determine their locations, the brands they carry, their hours of operation, and the services they provide. Unlike other media in which sellers seek buyers, a Yellow Pages directory is a place where buyers seek sellers. A study of consumers over two years, 1999 and 2000, by the Yellow Pages Publishers Association in conjunction with SRI found that 84 percent of consumer trips to the Yellow Pages resulted in a store or business being contacted and almost 90 percent of these references resulted in an intended purchase or a purchase. As a medium that brings buyers and sellers together, the Yellow Pages is often the final link in the buying cycle.

JOEL RAPHAEL, CHRISTOPHER BACEY, AND KEN CLARK

Nynex used a play on words to distinguish its Yellow Pages in this award-winning 1993 billboard campaign.
Courtesy of Nynex.

Further Reading

Coen, Robert, "Robert Coen Presentation on Advertising Expenditures," *The Insiders' Report: McCann-Erickson Worldwide* (December 1997)

Davis, Joel J., *Understanding Yellow Pages*, Troy, Michigan: Yellow Pages Publishers Association, 1995; 2nd edition, 1998

Davis, Tom, *The Truth about Yellow Pages: Making Them Work for You*, Delray Beach, Florida: St. Lucie, 1997

Young & Rubicam, Inc.

Founded in Philadelphia, Pennsylvania, 1923; headquarters moved to New York City, 1926; grew rapidly during era of network radio to become the second-largest U.S. agency by 1944; issued first initial public offering, 1998; acquired by WPP Group, 2000.

Major Clients

American Airlines
American Home Products Corporation
AT&T Corporation
Bristol-Myers Company
Chrysler Corporation
Dr Pepper
General Electric Company
General Foods Corporation
International Harvester
Lever Brothers
Packard Motor Car Company
Procter & Gamble Company
Time-Life, Inc.

For an agency that has been at one address for all but the first three years of its history, Young & Rubicam, Inc. (Y&R), has proved remarkably willing to reinvent itself as the occasion warrants. By the end of the 20th century the agency claimed to have created a "new and unique marketing communications model," not a holding company of different agencies but a "wired network" of communications services under the Y&R banner.

Many observers believed that a new model was needed for the venerable blue-chip agency. In 1996 net losses for the company totaled nearly $240 million, and the following year they were $24 million. Much of the information about Y&R was industry speculation, of course, since it was a closely held private company at the time. But in March 1998 the agency opened its books to the Securities and Exchange Commission when, in the year of its 75th birthday, it made a $350 million initial public offering. Few people were startled at the poor numbers, but with new business back on track, investors fought one another to buy up the shares.

Although Y&R was ranked as the world's fifth-largest ad company in 1998, its revenues were still less than half those of the next biggest global group, the WPP Group. But Y&R had one thing such holding companies did not: an illustrious name that connected the 1990s trend toward one-to-one databased marketing to a time when advertising was only a marginal function in American business.

Origins and Early History

The founders, John Orr Young and Raymond Rubicam, first met sometime around 1918. Rubicam joined the F. Wallace Armstrong agency, in Philadelphia, Pennsylvania, in 1916 after working as a bellboy, usher, projectionist, salesman, and a reporter for the *Philadelphia Inquirer*. He remained at the agency for three years. Young was by far the more seasoned advertising man. After graduating from Lake Forest College near Chicago, Illinois, in 1908, he spent five years at Lord & Thomas as a writer and another two at the Procter & Gamble Company overseeing its advertising for Crisco. He then made a couple of tries at running his own business: Young, Henri & Hurst (1914–1915) in Chicago and the John Orr Young Company (1916–1918) in New York City. In 1918 he went to Philadelphia, Pennsylvania, to work at the Armstrong agency, where he shared an office with Rubicam and brought in the Fels soap account, which would later follow him to Y&R.

Within a year Rubicam became involved in a dispute with Armstrong, and in 1919 he moved to N.W. Ayer & Son, then the country's largest agency. There he began building a reputation by producing what would become two of his most famous ads: "The Instrument of the Immortals" for Steinway (ranked number 71 on *Advertising Age*'s list of the top 100 advertising campaigns) and a long-copy piece for Squibb under the headline "The Priceless Ingredient." More than 20 years later, when a hugely successful Rubicam remarried and promptly had a son, Y&R Executive Vice President Louis Brockway tendered congratulations with a telegram that read: "Glad to learn that the Instrument of the Immortals still contains the Priceless Ingredient."

Young went to Ayer in 1921, where he and Rubicam became close associates. Each was becoming impatient with the pyramid of power in agency structures. They talked about a new kind of agency in which writers, artists, media experts, and account people would share both power and profits, an agency in which a collection of specialists would replace the custom of one-man rule. On 23 May 1923 Young & Rubicam opened its doors in the Atlantic Building at Broad and Spruce streets in Philadelphia with capital of $5,000 and a weekly payroll of $30.

With his experience and contacts, Young set out to administer and attract new business, while Rubicam devised the ads. Years after they retired, each man would dispute the early contributions of the other, with Rubicam often sounding especially resentful toward his former partner. It is likely that there was little love lost between the two even from the start. Rubicam, for example, claimed to have landed Postum in 1924, a popular coffee substitute that would be the key to Y&R's future growth and glory, a claim Young disputed. But there is no dispute over the importance of the brand to Y&R's history. A year before the agency was established, cereal maker C.W. Post had reincorporated as the Postum Company, with ambitious plans for diversification into other grocery products. The first acquisition came in 1925 when Postum bought the Jell-O Company. The next year it was Swans Down flour and Minute Tapioca and then Log Cabin, La France, and Maxwell House Coffee. By the time Birdseye came into the fold in 1929, the company had become an empire, and it took a new name—General Foods Corporation.

Rubicam thus found himself in on the beginning of one of the great packaged-goods conglomerates. To the extent that an agency is defined by the profile of its clients, Y&R could not have been luckier. It had linked up with a company that produced inexpensive household brands for the mass market. The agency and the client would grow up together, even to the point where Rubicam would negotiate the purchase of Gaines dog food and La France bleach for General Foods. Robert Work's original 1924 ads for Postum ("Why men crack," "When the iron man begins to rust"), written with Rubicam, promised relaxation and sound sleep to coffee drinkers, as well as prosperity to the 19 employees Y&R had taken on by the end of the year. On Christmas Eve of 1924 they split a $1,500 bonus fund.

The late 1920s were busy but unglamorous years as Y&R assembled its basic personnel and structure. In 1928 Tony Geoghegan took over media work. His instincts were uncanny; in 1936 he told Time, Inc., publisher Henry Luce to forget the mountain of research telling him that his idea for a picture magazine, to be called *Life*, was a loser. To back his conviction, Geoghegan bought a schedule of ads for each of Y&R's eight most important clients at a guaranteed circulation rate of 250,000. Within four weeks the circulation of *Life* magazine would hit 1.25 million. "It nearly busted Time, Inc.," Geoghegan's protégé Warren Bahr later said, "but Luce never complained." Nor did the eight fortunate clients Geoghegan had favored. *Life* would be a Y&R client for the next 32 years.

In 1928 Rubicam hired Sam Cherr from the *New York American* to set up a merchandising department. He paid Cherr more than he paid himself to add the "cats and dogs" (ad jargon then for collateral such as brochures, promotional materials, and other nonmedia materials) to his own elegant headlines. For example, "The key to the Postum campaign," Rubicam wrote in 1977, "was the so-called 'Thirty Day Test,' a coupon offer for a week's sample free." Postum's success led to Grape Nuts in 1926 and the promise of Jell-O just ahead. But there was a difficult condition attached to the Postum account. The company badly wanted the flagship office of its agency in New York City, not Philadelphia.

It was not an easy choice. Rubicam resented coercion of any kind from clients. He would later turn down Eastman Kodak rather than hire someone Kodak insisted the agency take on. And he would claim that he resigned $2.5 million in Pall Mall business rather than put up with the demands of the American Tobacco Company. In 1926, however, Young & Rubicam did not have that much influence. Rubicam reluctantly complied, left behind a small office in Philadelphia, and moved Y&R to the ninth floor of 285 Madison Avenue in New York City, the oldest address in the history of American advertising in 2001. The Jell-O business followed.

Few partnerships are ever temperamentally equal, and Y&R was no exception. Young believed that getting rich was no excuse to "prostrate yourself at the idol of success." But the fierce work tempo at the agency as set by his partner made Young look unambitious at best. In 1927, the same year Y&R took over an entire floor at the Madison Avenue address, Rubicam became president and took the controlling interest. Young took a vice presidency and then left the agency late in 1934 under the cover of failing health, although the real ailment was boredom with an agency he no longer felt in touch with. He died 1 May 1976 at the age of 89, after a long behind-the-scenes career as an executive headhunter and merger engineer. He tried to recruit Dwight D. Eisenhower for the 1948 Republican presidential nomination, and he refereed the merger of D'Arcy Advertising with the Federal Agency; of Cowan & Dengler with Donahue & Coe; and of Ivan Hill with Cunningham & Walsh. In 1949 he published a memoir, *Adventures in Advertising.* But his ultimate immortality hangs over the doors at 285 Madison Avenue—his name.

In 1930 Young & Rubicam had three vice presidents, 250 employees, and about $10 million in billings. Its clients included Black Flag, Borden, Budd railroad cars, Columbia Phonograph, Fels, General Foods, International Silver, Johnson & Johnson, Norwich, Quaker State, Reo and Rolls-Royce, and Spalding. To give Y&R a competitive edge, Rubicam, like other ad executives before him, looked to research. At the J. Walter Thompson Company (JWT), John Watson had been applying a form of behavioral psychology to purchasing behavior since the early 1920s. But the results never seemed to influence the ads and confused Watson even more than his bosses. Rubicam wanted to offer his clients measurements based on science but without the confusion. In July 1932 he recruited George Gallup from the campus of Northwestern University, in Evanston, Illinois, to set up a copy research department. Gallup combined the scholarship of an academic with the legwork of a cop and made research a practical reality in advertising. A network of interviewers blanketed the country, dug

The only captive audience
that counts is the one that's
captured by the sheer excellence
of your commercials.

YOUNG & RUBICAM, INC.

Advertising: New York · Chicago · Detroit · San Francisco · Los Angeles · Hollywood · Montreal · Toronto · Mexico City · London

Y&R was among the charter advertisers in *Fortune* magazine in 1930 and continued its advertising in every issue until the late 1960s. This ad dates from 1955.
Courtesy of Young & Rubicam New York.

out real data, and used them to get Y&R ads read by more people. Rubicam had found his edge.

While well known in the ad world, the agency was not as familiar to the presidents and chief executive officers the ads served. Thus when Luce debuted a sumptuous new business magazine called *Fortune* in 1930, Y&R was among six agencies to become charter advertisers. Y&R's ad said a lot about the agency. Whereas the other agencies saluted themselves and their trade, Y&R toasted *Fortune* and its readers. More importantly, the agency continued advertising in *Fortune* year after year, in good times and bad, never missing a month. Y&R's persistence pointed up a subtle hypocrisy afflicting many other agencies, which were forever urging clients to pour more money into advertising yet never spent a nickel advertising their own services. Y&R thus made itself the foremost example of advertising's effectiveness.

If the elegance and substance of the prose in the first *Fortune* ad was intended to suggest that it came from an agency where copy was king, it worked. "It was the place everyone wanted to be," recalled Bill Colihan, who started as a copywriter in May 1936. By then the agency had taken over two and a half floors, was billing $20 million, and had added General Foods' Sanka, Cluett, Peabody & Company (Arrow shirts), Parke-Davis, Northern Paper Mills, and the Packard Motor Car Company to its roster. It had closed its office in Philadelphia but had opened offices in Chicago and in Detroit, Michigan; operations in Toronto and Montreal in Canada and Hollywood, California, were just ahead. It had also developed something of a "Rubicam school" of advertising. "Advertising's first job was to intrigue people into reading something," Colihan remembered in the company's oral history. "The Rubicam school could be defined as a curiosity headline."

On the Radio

The so-called Rubicam school had little to say, however, about where every big advertiser was going in the 1930s, which was to radio. By 1935 network radio was drawing Y&R into the fastest and headiest times of its history and into the vortex of show business. Fortunately, Young's desire to retire created space for two key Y&R executives who would carry the agency into its glory days of growth and glamour. When Chester J. (Chet) LaRoche became president and Sigurd Larmon took over new business, Y&R rushed into broadcasting, a medium Rubicam had been reluctant to enter. "Look," he told LaRoche in 1934, "this [radio] doesn't interest me. You'd better take it over." With that, Y&R began taking broadcasting seriously. Johnson & Johnson and General Foods had been the first Y&R clients to go into radio, in 1929 and 1930, respectively, but the agency itself had no feel for the new medium. It threw together a small radio department in 1930 to broker daytime slots, but the agency did not know how to produce a program.

By the mid-1930s there were four radio networks whose only product was time. Aside from political conventions and coverage of special events, they provided little original programming, filling only the slots they could not sell. The time that was sold was bought exclusively by ad agencies on behalf of their clients. The networks provided the studios and equipment plus oversight of the content. It was up to the agencies to put on a show.

By 1934 Jell-O's advertising was being eclipsed by that of rival Royal Puddings, and General Foods was getting impatient with the lack of radio skills at Y&R. At that point the agency might gladly have traded half its account management department for one good showman. LaRoche, however, quickly found two: Bill Stuhler, who had staged "Triangle" shows at Princeton University before going to Batten Barton Durstine & Osborn (BBDO), and Don Stauffer, who was working in a bookstore. They, in turn, quickly employed a young staff of talent buyers and producers that included such future executives such as Sylvester L. (Pat) Weaver and Hubble Robinson. Within 20 years Weaver would be president of NBC and Robinson head of programming at CBS.

A vast agency bureaucracy grew up to hire gag writers, dramatists, musicians, singers, directors, announcers, actors, and stars, all of whom reported to Y&R. By 1938 the radio staff outnumbered the copy department 80 to 58. It was the power center of the agency because the programs it created had become the power behind the advertising. Account executives and producers enjoyed a charmed life. While the copywriters worked at their typewriters, the executives and producers were negotiating with agents, attending script readings, overseeing rehearsals, lunching with celebrities, and watching live broadcasts from the exclusive "sponsor's booth." There was a broadcast in the evening for the eastern United States and the Midwest and then a repeat performance closer to midnight for the West Coast. "Even today," Weaver wrote in 1993, "I must say [Young & Rubicam] was the best place I ever worked."

Much of the aura that surrounded Young & Rubicam at the end of the 20th century was rooted in the glory of two of the most remarkable performers in broadcasting, Jack Benny and Fred Allen, whose shows the agency produced every week for General Foods and Bristol-Myers, respectively. Y&R did not have high hopes for Benny, who had had two years and three sponsors on NBC's second-tier network, NBC Blue. "He was not our first, second, or third choice," Brockway later recalled in an interview for the company's oral history. "But he was available and was the best we could get." On 14 October 1934 *The Jack Benny Show* went on the air for Jell-O, and suddenly Benny's career clicked. By January Jell-O had pulled out of its rut and was posting record sales. More importantly, the Benny program established Y&R as a top radio agency alongside JWT (Bing Crosby and Edger Bergen/Charlie McCarthy) and Lord & Thomas (Bob Hope). Y&R moved the program to NBC Red in 1936 and stayed with it for the next eight years. When Benny went to Hollywood in 1936, Y&R went with him, opening its first West Coast office, under Tom Lewis, a block away from NBC.

Y&R hired Allen, also in 1934, to fill the second half of a one-hour time slot in which Bristol-Myers wanted to sell two products, Ipana toothpaste and a laxative called Sal Hepatica. It was a rule of advertising at the time that each sponsor needed consistent identification with a single program. Accordingly, Y&R created two programs: a music format for Ipana and the Allen show for Sal Hepatica. When the music program failed and Allen took off, Bristol-Myers complained that Ipana was being shortchanged. Y&R responded with a revolutionary nugget of common sense: expand Allen to a full hour under a dual sponsorship. The result was *Town Hall Tonight* and the first provisional steps toward participating sponsorship in broadcasting. Another dividend was stardom for Allen. His sharp intelligence and brittle cynicism made him uneasy with the pretensions and petty hypocrisies of radio as an advertising platform. There was in his voice a distinctly postmodern attitude of mocking self-awareness toward the illusions he both sustained and subverted.

Allen's wit found many targets, but none more ripe than Y&R itself. Ad agencies then were virtually invisible to the public, and Allen "outed" the agency to his audiences. He saw a simple pecking order in the power politics of radio: the talent feared the agency; the agency feared the client; and the client feared the consumer. It was a satirist's dream.

"An advertising agency," Allen said, "is 85 percent confusion and 15 percent commission." The more Y&R and Bristol-Myers tried to edit his jibes, the more entrapping they grew. The agency became his adversary as well as his patron; its vice presidents, mindless "molehill men." An agency vice president, Allen said, "comes to work at 9 A.M. and finds a molehill on his desk. He has until 5 P.M. to make his molehill into a mountain. An accom-

Young & Rubicam owns the building at 285 Madison Avenue, New York City, where the agency has been located since 1926.
Courtesy of Young & Rubicam New York.

plished molehill man will often have his mountain finished before lunch."

Allen's stereotype of the Madison Avenue adman with his attendant figures of speech ("pick up the ball," "send it up the flagpole," and, of course, "mother hen" as a verb) would prove more compelling and persistent than any reality. Brilliantly amplified by Stan Freberg later on, the caricature of the ad agency survives today largely unchanged from Allen's original creation, despite the fact that it has been more than 40 years since Young & Rubicam—or any agency—has produced a network program.

Following Y&R's success on radio in the 1930s, the agency continued to build its reputation in the 1940s with the *Kate Smith Show.* From that show the agency spun off comedians Bud Abbott and Lou Costello and *The Aldrich Family.* In 1944 it produced one of broadcasting's most enduring family sitcoms for the International Silver Company, *Ozzie and Harriet.* When the agency won Lipton Tea in 1945, it developed the suspense classic *Inner Sanctum.* Two years later it moved Lipton to Arthur Godfrey's show just before he went on to become the most talked-about star of television's first decade. For General Foods alone the agency would produce *Burns and Allen, Mr. District Attorney,* the Eddie Cantor and Dinah Shore shows, *Baby Snooks,* the original *Father Knows Best,* and the daytime soap operas *The Second Mrs. Bur-*

ton and *When a Girl Marries.* Many Y&R radio productions would later move so easily onto television that in the 1949–50 season literally half of the top ten TV shows were in-house Young & Rubicam productions.

Y&R was not only helping to shape American popular culture but was dabbling in politics as well. When the Republican convention seemed to turn spontaneously toward Wendell Willkie for the U.S. presidential nomination in 1940, a number of well-connected Y&R men were working behind the scenes to help plan the spontaneity. Among them were LaRoche and Larmon, both moderate Republicans and heirs apparent in an agency whose billings were approaching $40 million at about the same time Rubicam himself was approaching 50. He had weaned Y&R from the cult of his personality to assure its survival and growth as an institution. Rubicam might have retired then if it had not been for World War II.

In New York, General Foods asked Y&R to release LaRoche for six months to start the War Advertising Council (WAC), the predecessor to the Advertising Council. When LaRoche returned to Y&R in 1942, he remained involved in the WAC, a diversion that made Rubicam uneasy. Rubicam had other worries as well. He believed that LaRoche was needlessly in debt, and the thought of such a man running Y&R concerned him. For these and other reasons, Rubicam fired LaRoche. LaRoche started his own agency, the C.J. LaRoche Company, which later became McCaffrey & McCall.

Larmon succeeded LaRoche as president of Y&R. Two years later, in 1944, Rubicam retired without ceremony just after the opening of the Y&R office in London, England, during the buildup to D-Day. Rubicam had become impatient with the lumbering organization he had created. It was nearly 30 years before he would be coaxed back for a final bow during the company's 50th anniversary celebration. He died five years later, at age 86.

After Rubicam

With Rubicam's retirement, Y&R became Larmon's shop, and it remained so for nearly two decades. As president, he left the post of chief executive officer (CEO) vacant for 14 years. Finally, in October 1958, he appointed George Gribbin, who had come to Y&R as a copywriter in 1935, as president, and Larmon became chairman and CEO. He retired in 1963 at age 71.

During his incumbency Larmon had taken the agency from the heights of radio into the early triumphs of television, largely on the strength of General Foods (Bob Hope, *Captain Video, December Bride, Twilight Zone*), Bristol-Myers (*Tele-Varieties, Playhouse 90*), General Electric (Ray Milland, *Cheyenne*), the long-running *Goodyear Playhouse,* and many other programs. It was also Y&R that opened the door to television production for MCA, then the largest talent agency in show business, and its subsidiary, Revue, with the *General Electric Theater* and *Alfred Hitchcock Presents* for Bristol-Myers. In the 1950s Y&R and General Foods became involved in two incidents of political blacklisting centering on *The Aldrich Family* and *The Goldbergs,* both of which featured actors suspected of unfashionable political affiliations.

Meanwhile, production costs in television were driving a revolution both within Young & Rubicam and across network broadcasting. Weaver, who had started at Y&R in 1935, was now running NBC and was determined to take control of production and programming away from the agencies. Within Y&R the radio and television departments, which had once overseen all production and negotiated all of the buying of time, were losing ground to network packagers and to independent production on the outside and Y&R's own media department on the inside. The question of whether to accept network packages had come up in the last days of the Rubicam era. By the time Larmon retired, Y&R had ceased virtually all program production. Live programming had shifted to film, and the agencies owned no film studios. By the 1960s the term "a shoot" had come to refer to the production of a TV commercial not a show, and media buyers were shopping the networks for participating minutes rather than one-hour blocks. The art and copy departments evolved into the modern Y&R creative department. It was no longer the agency's job to gather an audience. The networks did that. Y&R's job was harder—to make sure that viewers did not leave the room during the commercials.

Y&R also played a major role in bringing *Life* magazine to television as the first company to sponsor coverage of the Republican and Democratic national conventions, both held in Philadelphia in 1948. Y&R and NBC had discussed the proposition, along with a budget of between $150,000 and $250,000. But radio was still the prestige venue for broadcast news, and few of its leading lights—men such as Robert Trout, Edward R. Murrow, and Eric Sevaried—were interested in television. Even to NBC, television coverage was considered a nuisance. When *Life* publisher Andrew Heiskell and a dozen Y&R account people arrived three days before the Republican convention, they found that NBC had neglected to put anyone in charge. So by default *Life* magazine and Y&R took over editorial control of the convention coverage. David Levy, Y&R's television producer, became the frontline convention news director, arranging countless cutaways and interviews to fill the dull periods on the convention floor, essentially creating the matrix for the basic gavel-to-gavel coverage that would mark convention telecasts for the next 25 years. He even thought to mount an "NBC-LIFE" sign on the microphone, thus ensuring that the client's name would be on camera constantly.

Advertising campaign lines have a way of lingering in television memory. Among Y&R's lasting contributions to the advertising of the TV era, and particularly to the period of the so-called creative revolution of the 1960s and 1970s, were "Number one to the sun" and "The wings of man" (Eastern Airlines), "Bet you can't eat just one" (Lay's potato chips), "The dog kids love to bite" (Armour), and "Be a Pepper" (Dr Pepper). As the structure of Y&R changed, its size soared. By the time Larmon stepped down in 1963, billings were at $280 million, and the agency headed into a race with JWT for the number one position that would last through the 1970s.

Foreign revenues were growing, too. In 1956 the agency's tiny network of six international offices (in Canada, Mexico, Puerto Rico, Venezuela, West Germany, and the United Kingdom) earned about $16 million. In the Larmon era Y&R did not want to move too fast. But Gribbin and Ed Bond, who succeeded him in 1965, worried that it might already be too late, and they rushed to catch up. By the end of the 1960s, Ed Ney, as head of Y&R International, had built overseas revenues to $113 million, and he was on a fast track to the top.

Ney had joined Young & Rubicam in 1951 after four years at BBDO and had been mentored by Gribbin, who seemed to have no great desire to prolong his own incumbency. Ney became CEO in November 1970, fired a third of the agency, and appointed former football star Alex Kroll to tame what Chief Financial Officer Jim Mortensen later called the creative department's "arrogant, here it is, folks" attitude. Ney then launched a campaign of domestic and international expansion that would not slow down until Kroll succeeded him in 1986. It began in earnest in 1971 when the executive committee decided that Y&R should be a "total communications" company. "We literally put these little boxes on the wall," Kroll told *Advertising Age* in 1998, "and labeled them: promotion, direct marketing, PR, medical design. These were the businesses we needed to get into fast. It would have taken us 50 years to learn them. So we decided we'd better just buy them."

In February 1973 Ney and Matthew Hennessey agreed to an exchange of stock that brought Sudler & Hennessey, with its $30 million in medical advertising, into Y&R. In November a similar merger was worked out with Lester Wunderman, whose Wunderman, Ricotta & Kline direct response shop brought in $30 million or more, putting Y&R ahead of JWT for the first time. Cato Johnson came soon afterward, followed by Landor Associates, a corporate identity design firm. In October 1979, after eight years of pursuit by Ney, Y&R acquired Marsteller, Inc., and Burson-Marsteller, a Chicago-based advertising and public relations combination that added revenues of $306 million. According to Kroll, the agency was eager for better national coverage as well. In seeking to acquire the best company in each geographical area, Y&R also got some good specialties, but it remained something of a patchwork network, falling short of the total communications strategy.

Y&R also built agencies from scratch. In 1973 Chrysler Corporation's Chrysler-Plymouth Division introduced the Trailblazer, a vehicle that competed directly with the Scout made by International Harvester, a key account at Y&R's Chicago office. To save both, the agency induced Ralph Ammirati and Martin Puris to leave Carl Ally, Inc., and establish a new agency with Julian AvRutick. Fifty percent of the financing for the new agency came from Y&R. In August, Ammirati Puris AvRutick was launched with the Trailblazer business. (It did not save the International Harvester business, however, and the Chicago office died a slow death over the next few years, until New York finally decided to pull the plug and start over. In 1980 a rising account man named Peter Georgescu was sent out with instructions to build a new Chicago operation.) By the mid-1970s Y&R began orchestrating its new assets in what it called "the Whole Egg," a nickname for integrated communications. The *Wall Street Journal* wrote about the idea in 1972, and it became something of a brand name for Y&R.

Young & Rubicam's 1999–2000 "The Walkman Has Landed" campaign for Sony revolved around the adventures of a fuzzy blue alien.
Courtesy of Sony Electronics, Inc.

Japan had loomed hazily in Y&R's plans since since the Larmon days, when the first informal contacts with Dentsu were made. It came to be understood that, if the time ever came for a joint venture, it would be between the two agencies. This issue was pressed in many meetings during the 1960s; Dentsu clients were beginning to sell around the world, and Y&R was eager to have an office in Tokyo. But Dentsu management was elderly by U.S. advertising standards and shaped by wartime experiences, and Ney never pressed very hard. In 1972 Y&R opened an office in Tokyo with a staff of 40. The intent was to demonstrate to Dentsu that Y&R was serious about Japan without presenting itself as a threat. Finally, in 1981 a Dentsu-Y&R joint venture was announced, essentially no different from what had been proposed 15 years before. Today Dentsu, Young & Rubicam is active throughout Asia.

By the time Kroll took over Young & Rubicam in 1985, the agency was moving on five separate tracks at once. The Whole Egg notion was still expanding. The agency was still trying to catch up in the race for global presence behind competitors JWT and McCann-Erickson. It had about 160 offices in 1985 and nearly 340 nine years later. It had three agencies in Latin America and four in Asia. The agency attempted to leapfrog into the developing markets and went into China in 1985 as the first non-Chinese agency based there. Y&R arrived in Moscow in 1988, a year before the collapse of the Soviet Union. Expansion into other Soviet bloc countries followed. The Dentsu relationship continued to expand as well.

By the beginning of 1990, after opening an average of one and a half offices a month for eight years, management decided that Y&R was in every place it needed to be. "One hundred years after the American frontier closed," Kroll said, "our frontier closed." Y&R after Kroll, who retired in 1994, continued to interconnect its many capabilities. This was the proclaimed mission of Georgescu, who became chairman of Y&R in 1995.

In the 1990s there was a strong effort to lift the agency's profits from a slump. In 1997 Y&R restructured its media operations by buying the Media Edge, a unit originally formed in 1994 with Ayer as a quasi-independent profit center free to solicit business from companies outside the Ayer client roster. It became a unit of Y&R in mid-1997. A separate global division was launched in September 1998. In May, with annual billings in excess of $12 billion and the book value of the company's stock rising at about 4 percent a year, Y&R became among the last of the agency giants to go public with an initial public offering. In September Thomas Bell, whose actual advertising background was limited to electing conservative Republicans such as Dan Quayle and John Tower in the 1970s, came over from the Burson-Marsteller division to become worldwide chairman and CEO of Y&R Advertising.

In April 2000 reports began to circulate that Y&R was a take-over target of Martin Sorrell's WPP Group, which already owned JWT and Ogilvy & Mather. As talks between Tom Bell, who had succeeded Georgescu in 1999, and Sorrell were being confirmed, two other possible buyers stood in the wings: Anderson Consulting, itself a Y&R client, and Publicis, a large French ad company. With three bidders in the picture, speculation was that the agency could go for much more than the $2.8 billion suggested by 1998 revenue figures. When WPP talks stalled briefly, attention shifted to Publicis, and selling price estimates passed $6 billion. Behind the timing of the talks was the fact that a Y&R management voting trust, established in 1996 so that a committee of five top Y&R executives could control a majority of the voting stock, was due to lapse in May.

On 5 May WPP and Y&R resumed talks and by 12 May 2000 reached terms: $53 per share for a total price of $4.7 billion. Some analysts believed the price was low, well below the $5.7 billion initially announced on 9 May. Indeed the company's stock was 25 points higher earlier in the year. But *Advertising Age* estimated that Georgescu and Bell could receive about $62 million each from the

deal, with about another $1 billion being divided among former employees and retirees. The deal was the largest in advertising history to that time and briefly made the WPP Group the world's largest advertising company, surpassing Omnicom. The following year Interpublic briefly became the largest when it bought True North. According to figures for 2000, Y&R ranked fifth among U.S. agencies in gross income and third in worldwide billings.

JOHN MCDONOUGH

Further Reading

Barnouw, Erik, *The Golden Web: A History of Broadcasting in the United States, 1933–53*, New York: Oxford University Press, 1968

Fox, Stephen, *The Mirror Makers: A History of American Advertising and Its Creators*, New York: Morrow, 1984

Grant, Don, "Y & R Celebrates 50th with Upswing in Revenues," *Advertising Age* (14 January 1974)

Gribbin, George, "George Gribbin Talks about How He Writes Copy," *Advertising Age* (22 March 1965)

Linnett, Richard, "WPP Sits at the Top," *Advertising Age* (15 May 2000)

Rubicam, Raymond, "Rubicam Calls for Return to Higher Code of Ethics," *Advertising Age* (5 January 1976)

"Tributes and Memories for Raymond Rubicam," *Advertising Age* (1 August 1977)

Voight, John, "The Market Years," *Adweek* (9 March 1998)

Weaver, Pat, *The Best Seat in the House: The Golden Years of Radio and Television*, New York: Knopf, 1994

Y & R and Broadcasting: Radio and Television Growing Up Together, New York: Museum of Broadcasting, 1988

"Y & R's Parade of 'Firsts' in Media Buying," *Advertising Age* (16 September 1965)

Youth Market

Youth marketing developed during the course of the 20th century from small-scale advertising campaigns to its current position as a lucrative marketing enterprise. The American youth market of the late 1990s alone was estimated to be worth $200 billion a year. The selling of goods and services to youngsters is a trend that reflects the significant economic and social changes that took place during the 20th century as Western societies attenuated the period of adolescence and created the "teenager," a term not coined until the early 1940s. Traditionally, most young people went to work in their early teens, although they remained the legal responsibility of their parents until their early 20s. Their wages were absorbed into the family budget. Paradoxically, the extension of high school and college education since World War I

and the enactment of child labor laws reduced the age at which youngsters became independent of their parents but delayed their entry into the adult world of full-time employment.

Broadly, the term "youth market" covers the marketing of products to children, teenagers, and young adults. The term has also meant the selling of "youthfulness" as a product attribute, most notably with the long-running "Pepsi Generation" advertising campaigns, and repositioning adult consumer goods to appeal to youngsters. The concept also includes purchases by adults for youngsters, such as the back-to-school market, and the ability of youngsters to influence family or household purchases. The youth market frequently re-emerges as the potential "next big thing" for advertisers as demographic change is tracked. Nonetheless, young consumers have been a difficult target market for advertisers and agencies to exploit fully. The youth culture is often insular and one step ahead of marketers' abilities to follow fads and fashions. Teenagers are adept at subverting and filtering out advertising messages. Finally, youngsters' spending, while largely discretionary, is far smaller than that of adults.

The Pepsi Generation

Advertising alone did not create the preoccupation with youth, but it has greatly influenced its development by enshrining youthful images in the cultural consciousness. Cultural and business historians have noted the increasing prevalence of youthful images in Western advertising from the 1920s onward. The Roaring Twenties is associated with images of flappers and flaming youth, and the 1930s and 1940s are inseparable from the images of teens dancing to the music of Benny Goodman and swooning over Frank Sinatra. From the beginning of the 20th century, working-class youngsters enjoyed commercialized leisure in establishments such as dance halls, amusement parks, and movie theaters. Dating moved from the chaperoned environs of the family home to the secluded corners of dance halls and, eventually, into the even more secluded confines of the automobile. The extension of secondary education meant that more children continued their schooling into their mid- to late teens, delaying entry into the labor force. Yet since World War II, the gradual shift in Western society to service-based economies has created numerous part-time employment opportunities for teenagers. Youngsters' financial power in the marketplace has been a combination of parental allowances and part-time earnings. This money is generally accepted as the teenager's personal income rather than being handed over to the family.

Marketing historians have debated exactly when the "youth market" came into existence. Stanley Hollander and Richard Germain's 1992 book *Was There a Pepsi Generation before Pepsi Invented It?* advanced the argument that advertising campaigns to various sectors of the youth market can be found in the early part of the 20th century. In his 1990 book *New and Improved: The Story of Mass Marketing in America,* Richard Tedlow dates the beginning of a concerted attempt to tap into the youth market to the 1960s and the decision by Pepsi-Cola and its ad agency, Batten Barton Durstine & Osborn, to launch the "Pepsi Generation" (although the concept represented a youthful attitude and enthusiasm characteristic of young adults—"those who think young"—not a specific age group and definitely not teenagers exclusively). Both views have merit. Businesses certainly became interested in youngsters as consumers in the wake of the explosion of consumer goods into industrial nations, notably Britain and the United States, but this early conceptualization of a youth market focused on college students, an affluent but narrow sector of the population. In the years following World War II, the mass youth market began to appear as a natural consequence of the baby boom. It came to the fore as a consumer force in the late 1950s and early 1960s as pop music led advertisers to youth. Products such as Noxzema's Cover Girl medicated make-up and Pepsi-Cola were specifically marketed as youth brands at this time.

A definite youth-market business was established following World War II, first in the United States and later in Europe, Australia, and Asia. The dominant influences were both demographic and economic. The postwar baby boom began in 1946 and continued for well over a decade, with almost 4 million births in the United States each year. Other Western countries lagged slightly behind as economic growth returned after the end of hostilities.

Two innovators stand out from the late 1940s and early 1950s as champions of the youth market: the editorial team of *Seventeen* magazine, launched by Triangle Publications in September 1944, and Eugene Gilbert, who established the first specialist youth-marketing agency the following year. *Seventeen* provided a new medium for advertisers seeking to target affluent teenage girls. The publishers successfully sold *Seventeen* to hesitant advertisers. Its editorial content, fashion pages, and special features, combined with a rapid circulation growth, created a perfect vehicle for advertisers to reach young consumers. The magazine quickly established itself as the "Bobby-Soxers' *Vogue.*" The magazine showcased American teenage consumerism to eager readers on the other side of the Atlantic in the late 1940s and 1950s.

Market researcher Eugene Gilbert provided businesses with data on the spending habits of teenagers during this period. His main innovation was employing youthful researchers able to "feel the pulse" of America's youth. Gilbert also publicized the youth market to a wide audience with his weekly column distributed by the Associated Press, "What Young People Think," and his "how-to" guide, *Advertising and Marketing to Young People,* published in 1957. Starting out as a single entrepreneur with a novel idea, Gilbert's youth-marketing company had annual turnover of $1 million, employing 15 full-time staff by the mid-1950s. His company's clients included Exxon, Borden's milk, Mars candy, Van Heusen, Wide World Photos, Royal typewriters, and the U.S. Army. A decade before the launch of the "Pepsi Generation" in 1964, Gilbert persuaded Charles E. Hires and its agency, N.W. Ayer & Son, Inc., to concentrate its $1.25 million advertising budget for "root beer" directly on teenagers.

Much of the groundwork establishing the youth-market business was in place before the arrival of Elvis Presley in the mid-1950s. *Seventeen* and Gilbert acted as intermediaries between the target audience and advertisers. Rather than selling directly to teenagers, they sold the idea of the youth market to businesses. For example, Gilbert estimated that the "average" American teenager had $10 per week of disposable income, creating an annual market worth $10 billion. These figures were certainly exaggerated but presented an attractive new market opportunity. Gilbert visited Europe in the mid-1950s, hoping to establish an overseas operation, but his field research convinced him that the time was not right. European teens did not have the necessary disposable income to support his new venture.

The phenomenal success of Elvis Presley around the world in 1956, however, opened the eyes of skeptics to the potential of the youth market. At a time when U.S. network radio was losing advertising revenue to television, local radio stations were able to deliver a teenage audience to advertisers' rotations of top-selling records. During the 1960s pirate radio stations supported by advertising revenues, such as Radio Caroline and Radio Luxembourg, broadcast pop music to European teenagers while state-owned radio systems ignored rock and roll. Teenage magazines and music radio provided the perfect conduits to sell to youngsters. Advertising rates were low compared with television, and the delivery mechanism was one sought after by youngsters themselves.

Enthusiasm for the youth market peaked in the 1960s with the arrival of the "teeming teens." It was widely claimed (inaccurately as it turned out) that half of America's population was younger than 25. Yet the cult of youth, from U.S. President John F. Kennedy's Peace Corps volunteers to the historic gathering at Woodstock in 1969, gave youngsters a prominent place in American society. Likewise, the British pop explosion of the mid-1960s, associated with the music of the Beatles and the Rolling Stones and the fashions of London's Carnaby Street, led to the export of English youth culture to the rest of the Western world, influencing advertising styles and fashions. Advertising agencies, notably Doyle Dane Bernbach, influenced by the nonconformity of the counterculture, heralded the industry's creative revolution of the 1960s. The more prominent and aggressive a distinct youth market became, the more it assumed an openly adversarial position against traditional adult consumer groups and their values. Conservative advertisers sometimes found it increasingly difficult to speak to both in the same voice, providing a double incentive for careful targeting: first, to reach one's desired youth market; second, not to be overheard doing it. Youth marketing embraced more than soft drinks, clothes, make-up, and music; in a culture increasingly segmented by generation, it also influenced the styling and marketing of automobiles. Thomas Hine wrote in the book *Populuxe* that in 1964 "the Mustang was perhaps the last thing that Americans of all generations really liked." Articles in the business press celebrated the arrival of affluent young consumers in the mid-1960s with headlines such as "Look out: teenagers are here."

Backlash

The late 1960s and early 1970s marked a watershed in youth marketing. Despite the euphoria over the demographic tidal wave of young consumers and the spread of youthful lifestyles into mainstream advertising, it became apparent that advertising was not terribly successful in influencing the buying habits of young people. Expectations were not necessarily realized at the cash registers. Numerous specialized youth-marketing agencies were launched, some dealing with young children and others with minority youth groups, although until the late 1960s youth advertising assumed an all-white, predominately suburban, middle-class audience. Despite the proliferation of youth-marketing experts and advisers, skeptics wondered if the youth market was all it was claimed to be. One commentator described the youth market as a "psychedelic maze." Members of the counterculture questioned the "plastic civilization" celebrated by advertising agencies. The young people portrayed in advertisements did not resemble protesting students across the Western world.

In the 1970s, as the Western demographic wave petered out, the youth market became an important but not a dominant factor in retailing. The spending power of adults was rediscovered, along with new segments, for example, the "gray" and "gay" markets. In the 1980s young urban professionals (so-called yuppies) became the new marketing phenomenon. By the 1990s a second wave of teenagers, named after Douglas Coupland's 1991 novel *Generation X*, was the latest group to excite youth marketers.

Youth marketing has received criticism from social critics and concerned parents. On a philosophical level, commentators have questioned the morality of putting commercial pressure on youngsters, who are more vulnerable than adults to advertising and marketing campaigns. Some critics have viewed the encouraging of youngsters to acquire material possessions as making them old before their time. A sociologist in the early 1960s described the baby boomers as a leisured class of unemployed consumers. Childhood, according to these observers, was meant to be a time of discovery and learning, not a time for shopping. Pressure groups such as Action for Children's Television, formed in the late 1960s, were especially concerned about what they saw as the poor quality of children's broadcasting. More recently the use of cartoons and movies to generate "spin-off" licensed products has raised the ire of frustrated parents. On one side of the issue, critics have argued that youth marketing conditions youngsters for a lifetime of consumption. On the other side are those who note that since youngsters will soon face the marketplace as grown-ups, it is unreasonable to expect a barrier to be placed between childhood and adult consumption. However, most Western countries have accepted the basic premise that some children's entertainment should have a noncommercial basis.

Virtually all Western nations have put limitations on the marketing of cigarettes and alcohol to youngsters, albeit with limited success. Tobacco companies have a long record of seeking young smokers, from sponsoring pop music radio shows in the 1930s, such as *The Camel Caravan* with Glen Gray, Benny Goodman, and Bob Crosby; *The Chesterfield Show* with Glenn Miller; and *The Lucky Strike Hit Parade*, to the "Joe Camel" cartoon character for R.J. Reynolds Tobacco Company's Camel cigarettes. During the 1960s most Western governments placed strict limits on the use of youthful and attractive images in cigarette advertisements in an attempt to reduce the number of teenagers taking up the habit. The tobacco industry has argued that it only promotes cigarette smoking as an "adult" pastime and that advertisers seek to maintain a brand's market share, not recruit new smokers. Similar arguments have been used to defend alcohol advertising. To circumvent restrictions, tobacco and liquor advertisers have promoted sporting events and rock concerts to maintain their presence among younger smokers and drinkers.

New—and Narrower—Market

The launch of Music Television (MTV) in 1981 and its subsequent global expansion provided new opportunities for advertisers to reach an ultradefined market. Like the rock 'n' roll radio stations in the 1950s and 1960s and Dick Clark's *American Bandstand,* MTV provided an advertising environment that targeted only the youth market.

The fragmentation of communications media since the 1960s—with the development of such technologies as transistor radios, portable cassette and compact disc (CD) players, and the Internet—means that a new advertising environment has emerged. Youth culture, popular culture, and advertising have become closely interlinked. The concept of "family" listening or viewing has fallen by the wayside. With it has fallen one of the most venerable formats of network broadcasting, the variety show, which once ensured that everyone had at least some working knowledge of what everyone else was watching or listening to. Young viewers tuning into Elvis Presley's first network TV appearances on the *Dorsey Brothers' Stage Show* in January 1956 would also have to watch comic Joe E. Brown and singer Ella Fitzgerald. And when Beatles fans in the United States saw the group for the first time on *The Ed Sullivan Show* in February 1964, they were also obliged to see singer Mitzi Gaynor and comedian Myron Cohen. "Narrowcasting" now allows the delivery of new music videos, advertising campaigns, and teenage fashions directly to youngsters without the mediating influence of alien performers or parental disapproval.

Youth marketers in the 1960s argued that a unitary youth market was a fiction, that there actually were numerous submarkets, ranging from "moppets" through "teeny-boppers" to college-age students. Broad concepts, such as "Generation X," embracing those born between 1965 and 1977, are not particularly helpful in describing millions of young people from diverse backgrounds. Whether today's young consumers are more cynical and "savvy" than their baby boomer predecessors is open to question. Lifestyles in industrialized countries continue to be underpinned by economic and social criteria: the provision of formal education, family and kinship structures, financial independence, distinctive youth media, and local youth cultures.

On the front lines of the youth market are those retailers that sell exclusively to it. "A handful of retailers make it their business to spot trends early and shift gears fast," according to a 1998 *Wall Street Journal* survey of youth marketing. These mass retailers were paying attention to "underground tastemakers" such as apparel and accessory marketers Gadzooks, Hot Topic, Wet Seal, Arden B., Diesel, and Contempo Casual; they watched youth-oriented television programs such as the WB Network's *Dawson's Creek,* and if they heard an unfamiliar music group, they bought up every CD they could find. All of these cultural manifestations contain within them the codes by which youth markets communicate.

But in the 1990s, with so many avenues of delivery and so much diversification, exploiting these codes became increasingly challenging. Youthful trendsetters tended to define themselves in opposition to the establishment: what the establishment embraced, they rejected. Therefore, the moment the establishment unraveled a code, the trendsetters abandoned it. The act of discovery by an outsider was, by definition, fatal. This situation was the subject of a Public Broadcasting System *Frontline* program in

This 1961 ad from the *New York Times* emphasized *Seventeen* magazine's attractiveness to marketers seeking to target teenage girls. *Courtesy of* Seventeen *Magazine www.seventeen.com.*

2001 called "Marketing Cool," which probed the ways marketers have learned to address the youth market covertly, hiding their intentions and often concealing their identities.

The ad campaigns of Sprite, a brand of the Coca-Cola Company, are a textbook case. In 1990 Sprite was a minor product in a competitive soft drink marketplace. But that status began to change with a tongue-in-cheek commercial featuring basketball player Grant Hill parodying the typical sports-hero-as-salesman holding up a product. Hill was used just as any celebrity presenter would be. The difference was in the use of an ironic visual subtext that undermined the primary message by speaking directly to the skepticism of young viewers toward profit-driven marketing. By acknowledging the inherent falsity of advertising, the commercial positioned Sprite as a brand that youth could relate to. But that was only the beginning. As the irony began to wear thin, Sprite began developing a network of relationships within the hip-hop and rap music culture, which many young people regarded as cool and cutting edge. Using a marketing consultancy called Cornerstone run by two former record company executives, Sprite embraced a kind of "under the radar" marketing strategy to sneak the brand message into the youth market through Internet chat rooms, concerts, and parties that were covertly sponsored or underwritten by the company. In launching a Web site, Sprite.com, for example, the company staged a party-dance built around trendy "urban authenticity" with stars from the hip-hop world. The entire event was videotaped by Sprite as if it were a news event. The videotape of the launch party, with all its music acts, became paid programming on MTV. By 2000 Sprite was the leading soft drink brand among youth.

By the 1990s youth trends, whether rap, rave, or rage rock, were being fabricated and marketed by a cultural power structure consisting of five huge U.S. companies: NewsCorp, which owned the teen-oriented Fox Network; Disney, parent to ABC; Viacom, which owned CBS, MTV, Comedy Central, and the Infinity network of radio stations; Vivendi Universal, which owned Universal Pictures, record companies, and the Havas advertising network; and AOL Time Warner, which owned vast motion picture, recording, and media interests, including the youth-oriented WB Network. Marketers that wished to speak to youth in 2000 had to know their way through this maze of conglomerates that controlled virtually every important media outlet to young people in the major U.S. markets, along with recordings, books, theme parks, television production, and Internet channels. Robert McChesney, a professor of communications at the University of Illinois, has compared them to the 19th-century colonial European powers. In their hands, teenagers, he has said, are "like Africa"—passive objects of exploitation.

In the 1960s marketers reached youth essentially through mainstream channels, which provided occasional supervised accommodations to teen taste such as *American Bandstand* or *Hulabaloo*. By 2000 the media that reached youth had become highly targeted. They had little incentive to accommodate their offerings to mainstream taste, and their content was often intentionally outrageous, anti-establishment, often violent (wrestling became hugely popular with teen males), raunchy, and purposely offensive. In the 1960s a prominent advertiser would have been reluctant to associate a major brand with the kind of content being targeted toward youth in the 1990s for fear that it might sully the brand image in the larger core market. But the precision with which messages could be delivered by 2000 largely removed that problem, because the risk of a message being seen by an unintended audience was minimal.

The worldwide consumption of youth culture seems to be accelerating. Much has been written about the domination of U.S. popular culture. Yet there are examples of successful foreign penetration of the U.S. youth market. In the 1960s the Volkswagen Beetle became the vehicle of choice for the counterculture. The Japanese Sony Walkman, Swiss Swatch watch, and Doc Martins shoes from Great Britain have found a place in U.S. youth culture, while other cultures and societies adopt and adapt U.S. youth culture to suit their particular environment. With the teen population expected to grow by 10 percent in the United States alone during the first decade of the 21st century, there is ample incentive for advertisers to continue to seek new ways to connect with and capitalize on this distinctive market.

IAN BRAILSFORD

See also color plate in this volume

Further Reading

Acuff, Dan, *What Kids Buy and Why: The Psychology of Marketing to Kids,* New York: Free Press, 1997

Douglas, Susan, *Where the Girls Are: Growing up Female with the Mass Media,* New York: Times, 1994; London: Penguin, 1995

Frank, Thomas, *The Conquest of Cool: Business Culture, Counterculture, and the Rise of Hip Consumerism,* Chicago: University of Chicago Press, 1997

Gilbert, Eugene, *Advertising and Marketing to Young People,* Pleasantville, New York: Printers' Ink, 1957

Graham, Lawrence, and Lawrence Hamdan, *Youthtrends: Capturing the $200 Billion Youth Market,* New York: St. Martin's Press, 1987

Hollander, Stanley, and Richard Germain, *Was There a Pepsi Generation before Pepsi Discovered It? Youth-Based Segmentation in Marketing,* Lincolnwood, Illinois: NTC Business Books, 1992

Hornblower, Margot, "Great Xpectations," *Time* (9 June 1997)

Palladino, Grace, *Teenagers: An American History,* New York: Basic Books, 1996

Pollay, Richard, "Targeting Tactics in Selling Smoke: Youthful Aspects of 20th-Century Cigarette Advertising," *Journal of Marketing Theory and Practice* 3, no. 1 (Winter 1995)

Tedlow, Richard, *New and Improved: The Story of Mass Marketing in America,* New York: Basic Books, 1990

Z

Zip Code

The five-digit numbering code and sorting system known as zip code—for "zone improvement plan"—was implemented by the United States Postal Service in 1967 to streamline mail delivery and speed customer service and to improve the sorting of third-class bulk-rate mail. The number sequence arranges addresses against a numerical list, beginning with 00000 and progressing through 99999. Each zip code refers to a specific geographic mail delivery area. A single unique zip code can cover an area within a state or can represent a single company or building that receives a high volume of mail. In rare instances, a zip code area can cross state borders. A nine-digit numbering system, referred to as zip+4, was introduced in 1983, adding the extra numbers to designate carrier route to further improve delivery services to businesses.

Direct marketers and advertisers, however, have reaped far greater benefits from the zip code system than has the postal service. The system encouraged a host of strategies that enabled marketers to profile, evaluate, target, reach, influence, and service selected geographic market segments. At the beginning of the 21st century, 85 percent of marketing database information was organized around geographic files, such as telephone numbers, addresses, census tracts, and zip codes. In fact, almost four decades after the zip code plan was introduced, e-commerce marketers were still designing new ways to tap the rich commercial opportunities found in zip codes and similar postal code systems around the world.

Janathan Robbin, a U.S. marketing researcher, developed a system based on zip codes that segmented markets and ushered in the era of "geodemographics." Selling products and services using market segmentation produced greater profitability than did mass marketing, its forerunner. Mass marketing entails the selling of one standardized offering to all consumers, without consideration for the special characteristics that define subgroups, or market segments, which have unique needs or desires for special products and services.

Market segmentation seeks to understand and fulfill the needs of individuals who compose unique market "clusters" within a mass market and thereby to achieve higher margins by offering an item carefully aligned with the unique preferences of a specific market cluster. Segmentation groups individuals into a set of clusters by uncovering similarities and differences in characteristics such as demographics or desired benefits sought in a product or service. Each cluster is composed of individuals who share similar characteristics that generate homogeneous needs. Conversely, each cluster is heterogeneous with respect to other clusters: different characteristics and purchasing behaviors separate one segment from another.

Target marketers identify one or more attractive segments, then plan and implement a particular marketing mix (i.e., product, price, promotion, and distribution strategies) to satisfy each target market. In the early 1970s it was standard marketing practice to delineate the mass market into segments using such variables as demographics, direct benefits sought, usage rates of the product or service in question, lifestyle, emotions, and previous commitments to other products and purchases (e.g., home ownership). Demographic variables include such factors as age, income, religion, occupation, education, sex, and ethnicity. The category of direct benefits sought includes desirable outcomes derived from a product's features or performance (e.g., aluminum ladders are lighter and longer-lasting than their wooden counterparts). Another system attempts to segment markets and better allocate resources by classifying consumers as heavy, moderate, or light users of products or services. The heavy-user profile of Dove bath soap, for example, consists of females between 35 and 57 years of age who are concerned about the appearance of their skin.

Segments also can be distinguished on the basis of lifestyle. People who have common lifestyles tend to share particular motivations, emotions, and activities. These, in turn, produce a similarity in purchasing behavior among members of the lifestyle group. The importance of lifestyle segmentation to modern marketing and advertising is reflected by the growing number of special-interest magazines catering to people who share well-defined interests, such as politics, physical fitness, photography, or fishing.

Finally, mass markets can also be divided according to consumers' prior commitments. For example, people typically purchase homeowner's insurance after they have purchased a house. Likewise, they become interested in products such as disposable diapers after the birth of a baby.

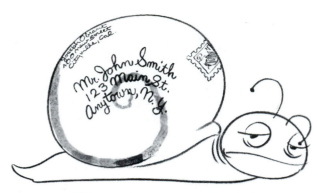

Snail Mail

Without ZIP CODE
the growing U.S. Mail load
would move at a snail's pace—

if it moved at all!

Like you, the people at the Post Office hate sluggish mail. That's why they created Zip Code! With it, mail is sorted up to *15 times faster*—and makes fewer stops along the way to its destination. To get the Zip Codes you need—see the information pages of your phone book for local Zips, and your Post Office's Zip Code directory for all others, or just call the Post Office. Put a rabbit in your mail—use Zip Code and mail early in the day. Then the Post Office can actually *guarantee* you the fastest possible mail delivery.

Mail moves the country—
ZIP CODE moves the mail!

 advertising contributed
for the public good

In the 1960s the U.S. Post Office promoted the use of zip codes with a series of humorous ads. Few would have predicted that by the 1990s the phrase *snail mail* would enter into popular use with a radically different meaning from that seen here.

In heralding zip codes as a powerful segmentation variable, Robbin noted that neighbors tend to share similar needs owing to like sociodemographic and lifestyle characteristics. Moreover, he sensed that commonality tends to decrease as geographical boundaries increase. Consequently, Robbin was successful in mapping proprietary survey results onto zip code demographics and then targeting only the small neighborhood clusters thought to want a particular offering.

Robbin's method was widely embraced by direct-mail strategists, who realized that not all zip code areas responded uniformly to direct-mail offerings. Some neighborhoods produced more responses to direct-mail campaigns than others did. Working with this "clustering" of zip codes proved an efficient means of increasing direct-mail productivity while reducing waste, the cost of sending offers to nonusers. Thus, zip codes provided the initial infrastructure necessary for the field of geodemographics.

Geodemographic segmentation identifies local neighborhoods that share common demographic profiles, financial standing, lifestyle characteristics, and similar purchasing behaviors. Geodemo-

graphic market characteristics can be profiled around zip codes, zip+4 codes, census tracts, census block groups, and postal carrier routes. Geodemographic data help researchers discriminate among the relative attractiveness of market segments in terms of a set of statistical calculations applied to U.S. census, zip code, or other, proprietary, data.

Statistical methods used to produce geodemographic profiles differ depending on whether the data under examination are categorical or continuous variables. Continuous variables, such as income, financial status, and age, can have any value. They are transformed into averages, ranges, and so forth. Categorical data concern single-dimensional conditions such as sex, full-time occupation, level of education, stage in the family life cycle, and main residence. Categorical data are assigned nominal values (e.g., 1=female and 2=male; 1=blue-collar worker, 2=teacher, 3=professional, 4=supervisor). After descriptive statistical procedures are completed for the geographic areas of interest, factor analysis and cluster analysis produce cluster profiles. A resulting cluster contains neighborhoods that have similar profiles in terms of such dimensions as average income, lifestyle, family size, type of home, average home value, and occupation.

Geodemographics based on zip codes came into question in the mid-1980s as marketers more aggressively sought to increase responses and cut waste. Zip code areas frequently included diverse market segments rather than one tight group as had been hoped. The early 1980s showed zip code clusters, which averaged 6,000 households, being replaced first by census-tract clusters, which offered more precisely defined groupings of 1,500 members on average. Seeking the best prospects and greater reduction of waste, many marketers purchased mailing lists from database providers and shifted to subcensus-tract classifications, which typically consist of only 300 households.

At the turn of the century, all these methods were being used, with one method selected over others depending on the task at hand, established campaign objectives, and the perceived situation facing the planner. For example, if a narrow market, such as very wealthy, upscale consumers, is targeted, then planners are most likely to select the postal route level over census-tract or zip code levels to target more precisely and reduce waste.

Geocoding software integrates the census block group or zip code area of each customer with other fields of information. Among the most common fields used in creating domestic geodemographic profiles are categories such as age, city, credit limit, earliest purchase date, geographic location, highest single purchase amount, and home value. Additional files commonly included in the database include marital status, most recent purchase amount, most recent purchase date, name, sex, state, telephone number, total purchase since inception, and zip code.

A number of companies provide marketers with information related to geodemographic segmentation, such as CACI Marketing Systems; Claritas, Inc.; and SRI International. CACI Marketing Systems publishes the *Sourcebook of Zip Code Demographics,* which contains statistics on all residential zip codes in the United States. It provides information on population, gender, age distributions, ethnicity, households, and families.

CACI's Acorn Clustering System provides geodemographic information as small as block groups (i.e., 250–550 households), blocks (i.e., 25–59 households), and ZIP+4s (i.e., 6–25 households). Claritas, Inc.'s Prizm system and Strategic Mapping's Cluster Plus 2000 segment U.S. neighborhoods into 62 and 60 clusters, respectively. SRI International publishes Values and Lifestyles Segmentation 2 (VALS 2), which uses lifestyles to segment adult markets.

The Direct Marketing Association estimated that U.S. companies spent $42 billion on direct mail in 1999. As of 1998 expenditures on direct sales were growing at 8.7 percent, nearly twice the rate of growth realized by the traditional retailer, according to economic information researcher WEFA Group. However, the future role of zip codes in traditional direct-mail advertising is a concern to marketers. Consumers increasingly are bombarded with direct mail, making clutter a factor, and more shoppers are turning to electronic shopping. Some of the most successful advertising agencies—such as Starcom USA; J. Walter Thompson Company; Ogilvy & Mather Worldwide, Inc.; BBDO Worldwide, Inc.; and Foote, Cone & Belding—use mapping technology to uncover and highlight new marketing opportunities and improve media strategy and selection for clients. Many use zip codes in tracking, controlling, and feedback tools that allow them to assess the effectiveness of outdoor and direct-advertising campaigns.

E-commerce retailers are finding meaningful ways to increase sales, refine targeting efforts, and improve customer service satisfaction through zip code–based programs. Amazon.com's "Purchase Circle" sorts on-line book purchases by city, university, or company using zip codes and the domain names on members' e-mail addresses.

As e-commerce grows, consumers also are benefiting from advances in geodemographics practices. New e-commerce solutions, many based on zip codes, help customers meet a wide variety of needs. Homeradar.com, for example, asks consumers to enter their street address, zip code, and e-mail address to get lists of recent home sales in their neighborhoods. Easy Connect, a directory assistance provider, enables cellular telephone users to identify businesses within their zip code areas. Clients of some insurance agencies use the Internet to file claims with nearby insurance agents located via zip code. Using the shoppinglist.com site, consumers can get coupons by entering their zip codes.

Zip codes, geodemographics, and e-commerce can also be used to harm consumers. A great deal of consumers' personal information is readily accessible via databases, and customer profiles are constantly being sharpened and databases upgraded by the addition of new descriptive information that profiles individuals. Individual privacy thus becomes a concern as mailing lists are openly rented, traded, and sold, and personal information becomes public. As profiles reveal more about individuals, unscrupulous people are using geodemographic information to the detriment of countless consumers. As a result, a grassroots consumer movement is pressing for legislation to restrict database marketers under the banner of "right to privacy." Many consumers believe direct marketers unjustly invade their privacy and may compromise an individual's security through their tracking and profiling activities. A person could be denied medical insurance or employment, for example, because of a piece of personal information gleaned from a database initially created for an unrelated purpose.

ALLEN E. SMITH

Further Reading

Baines, Adam, editor, *The Handbook of International Direct Marketing,* London: Kogan Page, 1992

David Shepard Associates, Inc., *The New Direct Marketing: How to Implement a Profit-Driven Database Marketing Strategy,* New York: McGraw Hill, 1999

Emerick, Donald, Kimberlee Round, and Susan Joyce, *Exploring Web Marketing and Project Management,* Upper Saddle River, New Jersey: Prentice Hall, 2000

Hughes, Arthur M., *The Complete Database Marketer: Second-Generation Strategies and Techniques for Tapping the Power of Your Customer Database,* Chicago: Irwin, 1991

Jones, Susan K., *Creative Strategy in Direct Marketing,* Lincolnwood, Illinois: NTC Business Books, 1998

Mooij, Marieke K. de, *Advertising Worldwide: Concepts, Theories, and Practice of International, Multinational, and Global Advertising,* New York: Prentice Hall, 1991

Shaver, Dick, *The Next Step in Database Marketing,* New York: Wiley, 1996

Wedel, Michael, and Wagner A. Kamakura, *Market Segmentation: Conceptual and Methodological Foundations,* Boston: Kluwer, 1998

APPENDIXES

APPENDIXES

Advertising Hall of Fame

1949
Rollin C. Ayres
Cyrus H.K. Cardiss
Alfred W. Erickson
William H. Johns
Lewis B. Jones
Theodore F. MacManus
Edwin T. Meredith
John Irving Romer
Walter A. Strong
John Wanamaker

1950
F. Wayland Ayer
Stanley Clague
Benjamin Franklin
James H. McGraw
Merle Sidener

1951
William Cheever D'Arcy
E. St. Elmo Lewis

1952
J. Earle Pearson
Erma Perham Proetz

1953
Samuel C. Dobbs
James O'Shaughnessy
Charles Coolidge Parlin

1954
John E. Powers
Frank Presbrey

1955
Henry T. Ewald
George Burton Hotchkiss

1956
(None elected)

1957
Claude Clarence Hopkins
Herbert S. Houston

1958
Orlando Clinton Harn
Albert D. Lasker

1959
Merlin Hall Aylesworth
Kerwin Holmes Fulton

1960
James Randolph Adams
Allen Loren Billingsly

1961
Barney Link
Harley Procter

1962
Donald W. Davis
Mac Martin

1963
Gilbert T. Hodges
Paul B. West

1964
Homer J. Buckley
Edgar Kobak
Jesse H. Neal

1965
Robert M. Feemster
Samuel C. Gale
Harrison King McCann

1966
Lee Hastings Bristol
Walter Dill Scott

1967
Earnest Elmo Calkins
Helen Lansdowne Resor
Stanley B. Resor
George P. Rowell

1968
Russell T. Gray
Charles W. Mears
Alex F. Osborn

1969
Bruce Barton
Thomas D'Arcy Brophy

1970
Don Belding

Laurence W. Lane
Graham C. Patterson

1971
(None elected)

1972
Leo Burnett
Ralph Starr Butler
Philip Livingston Thomson

1973
John P. Cunningham
Bernard C. Duffy

1974
Raymond Rubicam
James Webb Young

1975
Fairfax M. Cone
G.D. Crain, Jr.
Artemus Ward

1976
William Bernbach
Victor Elting, Jr.
David Ogilvy

1977
John Caples
George Gallup

1978
John H. Crichton
Barton A. Cummings
William A. Marsteller
J. Walter Thompson

1979
Atherton Wells Hobler
Neil Hosler McElroy

1980
Tom Dillon
Roy Larsen
Shirley Polykoff

1981
Ted Bates
Charlie Brower
Bernice Fitz-Gibbon

1982
Paul Foley
Alfred Seaman

1983
Clarence Eldridge
John Elliott, Jr.

Howard J. Morgens
Owen Burtch Winters

1984
Thomas B. Adams
James S. Fish
Charles H. Sandage

1985
Donald A. Macdonald
Samuel W. Meek
Arthur Harrison Motley

1986
Carl W. Nichols
Arthur C. Nielsen, Sr.
Raymond J. Petersen
Robert W. Woodruff

1987
Eugene H. Kummel
Edward N. Ney
Vance L. Stickell

1988
Sidney R. Bernstein
Robert V. Goldstein
Ray A. Kroc

1989
James E. Burke
Raymond O. Mithun
Jean Wade Rindlaub

1990
Carl J. Ally
Sam R. Bloom
John S. Bowen
Philip H. Dougherty

1991
Neil H. Borden
Richard C. Christian
Theodore S. Repplier

1992
John S. Bowen

1993
Ralph Carson
Charles T. Coiner
Rosser Reeves

1994
Ira C. Herbert
John E. O'Toole
Michael J. Roarty

1995
Edwin L. Artzt

William M. Backer
Howard H. Bell
Thomas S. Murphy

1996
Jo Foxworth
Morris L. Hite
William E. LaMothe
Frank L. Mingo

1997
Gertrude Crain
Alex Kroll
Paul Schrage

1998
Jay Chiat
O. Milton Gossett
Joyce C. Hall

Marion Harper, Jr.
John E. Kennedy
Burt Manning
Leonard Matthews
Frank Stanton
Janet L. Wolff
Lester Wunderman

1999
Bernard Flanagan
Mary Wells Lawrence
Stanley Marcus

2000
Reginald Brack
Peter A. Georgescu
Patricia Martin
William S. Paley

Source: American Advertising Federation

Notable U.S. Advertising Degree Programs

(as of 2001; listed alphabetically by state)

University of Alabama, Tuscaloosa
California State University at Fullerton
San Jose State University, San Jose, California
University of Colorado at Boulder
University of Florida, Gainesville
University of Georgia, Athens
Northwestern University, Evanston, Illinois
Southern Illinois University, Carbondale
University of Illinois, Urbana-Champaign
University of Kansas, Lawrence
Louisiana State University, Baton Rouge
Boston University, Boston, Massachusetts

Michigan State University, East Lansing
University of Missouri, Columbia
University of Nebraska, Lincoln
Syracuse University, Syracuse, New York
University of North Carolina, Chapel Hill
Ohio University, Athens
University of Oregon, Eugene
University of South Carolina, Columbia
University of Tennessee, Knoxville
Texas Tech University, Lubbock
University of Texas at Austin
Virginia Commonwealth University, Richmond

Source: Billy I. Ross

Top U.S. Advertising Agencies
(ranked by billings)

Year	Rank	Name	Billings *(millions of U.S. dollars)*
1945	1	J. Walter Thompson Company	63.0
	2	Young & Rubicam, Inc.	51.8
	3	Batten Barton Durstine & Osborn, Inc.	40.0
	4	N.W. Ayer & Son, Inc.	39.0
	5	McCann-Erickson, Inc.	36.5
	6	Foote, Cone & Belding	31.0
	7	Ruthrauff & Ryan, Inc.	30.5
	8	Dancer, Fitzgerald, Sample	25.0
	9	Biow Company, Inc.	22.0
	10	Compton Advertising	21.0
1950	1	J. Walter Thompson Company	130.0
	2	Young & Rubicam, Inc.	92.0
	3	Batten Barton Durstine & Osborn, Inc.	87.0
	4	N.W. Ayer & Son, Inc.	79.0
	5	McCann-Erickson, Inc.	67.0
	6	Foote, Cone & Belding	61.0
	7	Ruthrauff & Ryan, Inc.	45.0
	8	Benton & Bowles, Inc.	44.0
	9	Grant Advertising, Inc.	40.0
	10	Kenyon & Eckhardt, Inc.	38.0
1955	1	J. Walter Thompson Company	172.0
	2	Young & Rubicam, Inc.	166.0
	3	Batten Barton Durstine & Osborn, Inc.	162.5
	4	McCann-Erickson, Inc.	132.0
	5	N.W. Ayer & Son, Inc.	92.0
	6	Leo Burnett Company	69.2
	7	Benton & Bowles, Inc.	68.0
	8	Foote, Cone & Belding	68.0
	9	Kenyon & Eckhardt, Inc.	68.0
	10	J. Kudner Agency	60.0
1960	1	J. Walter Thompson Company	250.0
	2	Batten Barton Durstine & Osborn, Inc.	232.5
	3	McCann-Erickson, Inc.	216.0
	4	Young & Rubicam, Inc.	212.0
	5	Ted Bates & Company	119.3
	6	Leo Burnett Company	116.7
	7	Benton & Bowles, Inc.	114.0
	8	N.W. Ayer & Son, Inc.	110.0
	9	Dancer, Fitzgerald, Sample	100.7
	10	Foote, Cone & Belding	99.6
1965	1	J. Walter Thompson Company	351.5
	2	Young & Rubicam, Inc.	306.1
	3	Batten Barton Durstine & Osborn, Inc.	292.7
	4	McCann-Erickson, Inc.	270.0
	5	Foote, Cone & Belding	186.0
	6	Leo Burnett Company	184.7
	7	Ted Bates & Company	180.4
	8	Dancer, Fitzgerald, Sample	139.1
	9	Doyle Dane Bernbach, Inc.	139.1
	10	Benton & Bowles, Inc.	130.2

Year	Rank	Name	Billings (millions of U.S. dollars)
1970	1	J. Walter Thompson Company	436.0
	2	Young & Rubicam, Inc.	356.4
	3	Batten Barton Durstine & Osborn, Inc.	324.4
	4	Leo Burnett Company	283.0
	5	Ted Bates & Company	254.0
	6	Doyle Dane Bernbach, Inc.	249.7
	7	McCann-Erickson, Inc.	246.5
	8	Grey Advertising, Inc.	201.0
	9	Ogilvy & Mather, Inc.	179.0
	10	Foote, Cone & Belding	159.0
1975	1	Young & Rubicam International, Inc.	476.6
	2	J. Walter Thompson Company	432.8
	3	Leo Burnett Company	400.0
	4	Batten Barton Durstine & Osborn, Inc.	369.8
	5	Grey Advertising, Inc.	287.0
	6	Ted Bates & Company	280.2
	7	Foote, Cone & Belding Communications	275.3
	8	Ogilvy & Mather International, Inc.	266.1
	9	D'Arcy-MacManus & Masius, Inc.	234.0
	10	McCann-Erickson, Inc.	230.8

Year	Rank	Name	Gross Income*
1980	1	Young & Rubicam, Inc.	200.0
	2	J. Walter Thompson Company	137.8
	3	Ogilvy & Mather International, Inc.	125.5
	4	Foote, Cone & Belding Communications	109.1
	5	Leo Burnett Company	108.2
	6	Ted Bates & Company	108.0
	7	BBDO, Inc.	105.8
	8	Doyle Dane Bernbach, Inc.	98.1
	9	Grey Advertising, Inc.	78.7
	10	Benton & Bowles, Inc	73.8
1985	1	Young & Rubicam, Inc.	340.6
	2	Ogilvy Group	307.2
	3	Ted Bates Worldwide	287.5
	4	BBDO International, Inc.	274.0
	5	J. Walter Thompson Company	251.2
	6	Foote, Cone & Belding Communications	213.7
	7	D'Arcy Masius Benton & Bowles	197.5
	8	Grey Advertising, Inc.	183.2
	9	Leo Burnett Company	179.7
	10	SSC&B Worldwide	170.0
1990	1	Leo Burnett Company	299.3
	2	Saatchi & Saatchi Advertising	270.7
	3	Foote, Cone & Belding Communications	262.7
	4	Grey Advertising, Inc.	256.3
	5	J. Walter Thompson Company	251.7
	6	Ogilvy & Mather Worldwide	228.7
	7	Young & Rubicam, Inc.	216.6
	8	McCann-Erickson Worldwide	210.1
	9	BBDO Worldwide	207.1
	10	D'Arcy Masius Benton & Bowles	204.4

Year	Rank	Name	Gross Income (millions of U.S. dollars)
1995	1	Leo Burnett Company	370.6
	2	J. Walter Thompson Company	347.0
	3	Grey Advertising, Inc.	326.7
	4	DDB Needham Worldwide	284.7
	5	McCann-Erickson Worldwide	279.6
	6	Saatchi & Saatchi Advertising	275.5
	7	BBDO Worldwide	259.5
	8	Foote, Cone & Belding Communications	244.2
	9	Ogilvy & Mather Worldwide	209.5
	10	Young & Rubicam, Inc.	205.8
2000	1	Grey Worldwide	610.0
	2	J. Walter Thompson Company	574.5
	3	McCann-Erickson Worldwide	507.1
	4	FCB Worldwide	502.2
	5	Y&R Advertising	452.8
	6	Leo Burnett Worldwide	428.1
	7	Euro RSCG Worldwide	399.0
	8	BBDO Worldwide	398.5
	9	Ogilvy & Mather Worldwide	397.6
	10	DDB Worldwide Communications	390.9

* In 1976, *Advertising Age* began ranking agencies in terms of gross income rather than billings.

Source: Advertising Age

Top U.S. Advertisers
(ranked by advertising expenditures)

Year	Rank	Name	Ad Spending (millions of U.S. dollars)*
1955	1	General Motors Corporation	170.4
	2	Procter & Gamble Company	85.0
	3	General Foods Corporation	75.0
	4	Ford Motor Company	72.9
	5	Chrysler Corporation	68.6
	6	Colgate-Palmolive Company	62.0
	7	General Electric Company	60.7
	8	Lever Brothers Company	55.0
	9	National Dairy Products Corporation	35.0
	10	Distillers Corporation Seagram's, Ltd.	30.4
1960	1	General Motors Corporation	168.5
	2	Procter & Gamble Company	127.0
	3	General Foods Corporation	110.0
	4	Ford Motor Company	90.5
	5	Lever Brothers Company	80.5
	6	General Electric Company	73.0
	7	American Home Products Corporation	65.0
	8	Colgate-Palmolive Company	59.0
	9	Chrysler Corporation	56.9
	10	R.J. Reynolds Tobacco Company	50.0
1965	1	Procter & Gamble Company	245.0
	2	General Motors Corporation	173.0
	3	General Foods Corporation	120.0
	4	Ford Motor Company	116.0
	5	Bristol-Myers Company	108.0
	6	Colgate-Palmolive Company	95.0
	7	Lever Brothers Company	90.0
	8	Sears, Roebuck & Company	86.0
	9	Chrysler Corporation	80.0
	10	American Tobacco Company	71.0
1970	1	Procter & Gamble Company	265.0
	2	General Foods Corporation	170.0
	3	Sears, Roebuck & Company	130.0
	4	General Motors Corporation	129.8
	5	Warner-Lambert Pharmaceutical Company	126.0
	6	Colgate-Palmolive Company	121.0
	7	Bristol-Myers Company	117.0
	8	American Home Products Corporation	100.0
	9	Ford Motor Company	90.2
	10	AT&T Corporation	86.6
1975	1	Procter & Gamble Company	360.0
	2	General Motors Corporation	225.0**
	3	Sears, Roebuck & Company	225.0**
	4	General Foods Corporation	203.0
	5	Bristol-Myers Company	170.0
	6	Warner-Lambert Company	169.0
	7	American Home Products Corporation	138.0
	8	Mobil Corporation	135.9
	9	R.J. Reynolds Industries	113.6
	10	U.S. government	113.4

Year	Rank	Name	Ad Spending (millions of U.S. dollars)*
1980	1	Procter & Gamble Company	649.6
	2	Sears, Roebuck & Company	599.6
	3	General Foods Corporation	410.0
	4	Philip Morris Companies	364.6
	5	K-Mart Corporation	319.3
	6	General Motors Corporation	316.0
	7	R.J. Reynolds Industries	298.5
	8	Ford Motor Company	280.0
	9	AT&T Corporation	259.2
	10	Warner-Lambert Company	235.2
1985	1	Procter & Gamble Company	1,600.0
	2	Philip Morris Companies	1,400.0
	3	RJR Nabisco	1,090.0
	4	Sears, Roebuck & Company	800.0
	5	General Motors Corporation	779.0
	6	Beatrice Companies	684.0
	7	Ford Motor Company	614.7
	8	K-Mart Corporation	567.0
	9	McDonald's Corporation	550.0
	10	Anheuser-Busch Companies	522.9
1990	1	Procter & Gamble Company	2,280.0
	2	Philip Morris Companies	2,210.0
	3	Sears, Roebuck & Company	1,510.0
	4	General Motors Corporation	1,500.0
	5	Grand Metropolitan	882.6
	6	PepsiCo	849.1
	7	AT&T Corporation	796.5
	8	McDonald's Corporation	764.1
	9	K-Mart Corporation	693.2
	10	Time Warner	676.9
1995	1	Procter & Gamble Company	2,780.0
	2	Philip Morris Companies	2,580.0
	3	General Motors Corporation	2,050.0
	4	Time Warner	1,310.0
	5	Walt Disney Company	1,300.0
	6	Sears, Roebuck & Company	1,220.0†
	7	Chrysler Corporation	1,220.0†
	8	PepsiCo	1,200.0
	9	Johnson & Johnson	1,170.0
	10	Ford Motor Company	1,150.0
2000	1	General Motors Corporation	3,940.0
	2	Philip Morris Companies	2,600.0
	3	Procter & Gamble Company	2,360.0
	4	Ford Motor Company	2,340.0
	5	Pfizer, Inc.	2,260.0
	6	PepsiCo	2,100.0
	7	DaimlerChrysler	1,980.0
	8	AOL Time Warner	1,770.0
	9	Walt Disney Company	1,760.0
	10	Verizon Communications	1,610.0

*Figures in the billions are rounded to the nearest $10 million.
**Spending was virtually identical.
†Rounding makes figures appear to be equal.

Source: Advertising Age

Top Worldwide Advertising Agencies
(ranked by billings)

Year	Rank	Name	Billings (millions of U.S. dollars)*
1965	1	J. Walter Thompson Company	530.1
	2	McCann-Erickson, Inc.	420.0
	3	Young & Rubicam, Inc.	372.7
	4	Batten Barton Durstine & Osborn	304.4
	5	Ted Bates & Company	237.5
	6	Dentsu Advertising	234.4
	7	Foote, Cone & Belding	233.0
	8	Leo Burnett Company	188.6
	9	Ogilvy & Mather International	156.4
	10	Doyle Dane Bernbach, Inc.	148.9
1970	1	J. Walter Thompson Company	764.0
	2	McCann-Erickson, Inc.	546.9
	3	Dentsu Advertising	522.3
	4	Young & Rubicam, Inc.	520.2
	5	Ted Bates & Company	414.2
	6	Leo Burnett International	389.0
	7	Batten Barton Durstine & Osborn	350.4
	8	Doyle Dane Bernbach, Inc.	291.4
	9	Grey Advertising, Inc.	251.4
	10	Ogilvy & Mather, Inc.	250.2
1975	1	Dentsu Advertising	945.8
	2	J. Walter Thompson Company	900.1
	3	Young & Rubicam International	800.9
	4	McCann-Erickson, Inc.	775.1
	5	Leo Burnett Company	623.0
	6	Ted Bates & Company	604.0
	7	Ogilvy & Mather International, Inc.	581.6
	8	BBDO International, Inc.	525.0
	9	Foote, Cone & Belding	396.4
	10	D'Arcy-MacManus & Masius, Inc.	329.5

*Gross Income***

Year	Rank	Name	Gross Income**
1980	1	Dentsu, Inc.	394.4
	2	Young & Rubicam, Inc.	340.8
	3	J. Walter Thompson Company	322.5
	4	McCann-Erickson, Inc.	268.7
	5	Ogilvy & Mather, Inc.	245.9
	6	Ted Bates & Company	210.6
	7	BBDO International, Inc.	175.6
	8	Leo Burnett Company	169.7
	9	SSC&B	166.7
	10	Foote, Cone & Belding Communications	164.3
1985	1	Young & Rubicam, Inc.	536.0
	2	Ogilvy Group	481.1
	3	Dentsu, Inc.	473.1
	4	Ted Bates Worldwide	466.0
	5	J. Walter Thompson Company	450.9
	6	Saatchi & Saatchi Compton Worldwide	440.9
	7	BBDO International, Inc.	377.0

Year	Rank	Name	Gross Income (millions of U.S. dollars)*
	8	McCann-Erickson Worldwide	345.2
	9	D'Arcy Masius Benton & Bowles	319.5
	10	Foote, Cone & Belding Communications	284.2
1990	1	WPP Group	2,710.0
	2	Saatchi & Saatchi Advertising Worldwide	1,730.0
	3	Interpublic Group of Companies	1,650.0
	4	Omnicom Group	1,340.0
	5	Dentsu, Inc.	1,250.0
	6	Young & Rubicam, Inc.	1,070.0
	7	Eurocom Group	748.0
	8	Hakuhodo, Inc.	586.0
	9	Grey Advertising, Inc.	583.0
	10	Foote, Cone & Belding Communications	536.0
1995	1	WPP Group	3,130.0
	2	Omnicom Group	2,570.0
	3	Interpublic Group of Companies	2,330.0
	4	Dentsu, Inc.	1,990.0
	5	Cordiant	1,380.0
	6	Young & Rubicam, Inc.	1,200.0
	7	Hakuhodo, Inc.	958.6
	8	Havas Advertising	909.4
	9	Grey Advertising, Inc.	896.5
	10	Leo Burnett Company	803.9
2000	1	WPP Group	7,970.0
	2	Omnicom Group	6,990.0
	3	Interpublic Group of Companies	6,600.0
	4	Dentsu, Inc.	3,090.0
	5	Havas Advertising	2,760.0
	6	Publicis Group	2,480.0
	7	Bcom3 Group	2,220.0
	8	Grey Global Group	1,860.0
	9	True North Communications	1,540.0
	10	Cordiant Communications Group	1,250.0

*Figures in the billions are rounded to the nearest $10 million.

**In 1976, *Advertising Age* began ranking agencies in terms of gross income rather than billings.

Source: Advertising Age

Top Worldwide Advertisers

(ranked by advertising expenditures)

Year	Rank	Name	Ad Spending (millions of U.S. dollars)*
1990	1	Procter & Gamble Company	3,420.0
	2	Philip Morris Companies	2,720.0
	3	Unilever NV	1,930.0
	4	General Motors Corporation	1,910.0
	5	Nestlé SA	1,240.0
	6	Toyota Motor Corporation	1,040.0
	7	Ford Motor Corporation	1,000.0
	8	McDonald's Corporation	947.9
	9	Nissan Motor Company	740.9
	10	Matsushita Electric Industrial Company	729.0
1995	1	Procter & Gamble Company	5,340.0
	2	Philip Morris Companies	3,410.0
	3	Unilever NV	3,270.0
	4	General Motors Corporation	2,860.0
	5	Nestlé SA	1,900.0
	6	Ford Motor Company	1,870.0
	7	Toyota Motor Corporation	1,820.0
	8	PepsiCo	1,580.0
	9	Johnson & Johnson	1,480.0
	10	McDonald's Corporation	1,350.0
2000	1	Procter & Gamble Company	4,150.0
	2	General Motors Corporation	3,980.0
	3	Unilever NV	3,660.0
	4	Ford Motor Company	2,320.0
	5	Philip Morris Companies	2,310.0
	6	Toyota Motor Corporation	2,140.0
	7	DaimlerChrysler	2,110.0
	8	Nestlé SA	1,880.0
	9	AOL Time Warner	1,840.0
	10	Volkswagen	1,710.0

*Figures in the billions are rounded to the nearest $10 million.

Source: Advertising Age

NOTES ON ADVISERS
AND CONTRIBUTORS

Aikat, Debashis ("Deb"). Associate Professor and Media Futurist, School of Journalism and Mass Communication, University of North Carolina, Chapel Hill. Contributor to *Convergence: The Journal of Research into New Media Technologies* (2001) and *Popular Music and Society* (2001). **Essay:** E-Commerce.

Alan, Stuart. Ph.D. candidate, Department of Marketing, Florida International University, Boca Raton. Contributor to *Proceedings of the Seventh Conference on Marketing History and Thought* (1995). **Essay:** Cigarettes.

Alozie, Emmanuel C. Professor, Department of Communications and Training, Governors State University, University Park, IL. **Essay:** History: 1990s.

Alvaro, Eusebio. Essay: Mass Communications Theory.

Amin, Hussein Youssry. Full Professor, Department of Journalism and Mass Communication, Cairo, Egypt. Coauthor with Leo Gher of *Civic Discourse in the Middle East and the Digital Age of Communications* (2000). Contributor to *Gazette: The International Journal for Communication Studies* (1998) and *Global News: Perspective on the Information Age* (2001), edited by Tony Silvia. Member of editorial board for *Journal of International Communication* (2001). Senior editor of *Journal of Transnational Broadcasting Studies.* **Essay:** Middle East.

Appel, Marsha C. (Adviser). Senior Vice President, Member Information Service, American Association of Advertising Agencies, New York, NY. Author of *Illustration Index VII* (1993) and *Illustration Index VIII* (1998). **Essays:** American Association of Advertising Agencies; Duane Jones Company, Inc.; Lennen & Newell, Inc.

Applegate, Edd. Full Professor, School of Journalism, Middle Tennessee State University, Murfreesboro. Author of *Personalities and Products: A Historical Perspective on Advertising in America* (1998). Contributor to *Journalism Educator* (1995) and *Journalism Studies* (2000). Editor of *The Ad Men and Women: A Biographical Dictionary of Advertising* (1994). **Essays:** Consumers' Research; Consumers Union; Lasker, Albert D.; Scott, Walter Dill; Sorrell, Martin S.

Ariga, Masaru. Senior Marketing Planner, Dentsu, Inc., Tokyo, Japan. **Essay:** Dentsu, Inc.

Arrigo, Jan. Author of *New Orleans: A CitiGuide* (2002). **Essays:** Age: Representations in Advertising; Photography and Photographers.

Ashdown, Paul. Professor, School of Journalism, University of Tennessee, Knoxville. Editor of *James Agee: Selected Journalism* (1985). Contributor to *Dictionary of Literary Biography* (1997, 1998), *American National Biography* (1999), *Dictionary of Political Communications* (1999), and *Soundings: An Interdisciplinary Journal* (1999). Member of editorial board for *Soundings: An Interdisciplinary Journal* (1998–2000). **Essay:** Prudential Insurance Company.

Bacey, Christopher. Director of Communications, Yellow Pages Integrated Media Association, Berkeley Heights, NJ. **Essay:** Yellow Pages.

Baker, Michael. Equity Analyst (telecommunications and media), Dongwon Securities, Seoul, South Korea. Contributor to *Science Magazine* (1998–2001) and *Ad Age Global* (1999–2001). Seoul-based correspondent for *Christian Science Monitor,* CBS News (radio), *Advertising Age, The Deal,* and *Science Magazine* (1996–2001). **Essay:** Cheil Communications, Inc.

Balasubramanian, Siva K. Professor, Department of Marketing, Southern Illinois University, Carbondale. Contributor to *Journal of Advertising* (1994, 2000). Member of editorial board for *Journal of Services Marketing* (1995–). **Essay:** Endorsement.

Barnes, Beth E. (Adviser). Chair, Department of Advertising, S.I. Newhouse School of Public Communication, Syracuse University, Syracuse, NY.

Barr, Paul. Freelance journalist, Chicago, IL. Contributor to the *Chicago Tribune, Crain's Chicago Business,* and *Access Magazine.* **Essay:** Consumer Electronics.

Barry, Thomas E. Vice President for Executive Affairs and Professor of Marketing, Southern Methodist University, Dallas, TX. Author of *Marketing: An Integrated Approach* (1986). Coauthor of *Advertising Management: Text and Cases* (1979). Contributor to *Journal of Advertising Research.* Member of editorial board for *Journal of Advertising.* Recipient of Outstanding Contribution to Advertising Research, American Academy of Advertising (1995). **Essay:** Comparative Advertising.

Basso, Joe. Assistant Professor, Department of Communication, Villanova University, Villanova, PA. Contributor to *IEEE Transactions on Professional Communication* (March 1997) and *The Journal of Leadership Studies* (1998). **Essay:** Consumer Movement.

Battema, Doug. Ph.D. candidate, Department of Communication Arts, University of Wisconsin, Madison. Coeditor of *The Velvet Light Trap* (2000–02). Contributor to *The Journal of African-American Men* (1998), *The Cooperstown Symposium on Baseball and American Culture, 1997 (Jackie Robinson)* (2000), edited by Peter M. Rutkoff, and *The Cooperstown Symposium on Baseball and American Culture, 1999* (2000), edited by Peter M. Rutkoff. **Essays:** Gillette Company; Pepperidge Farm, Inc.

Beardi, Cara. Reporter, *Advertising Age,* Chicago, IL. **Essays:** Eastman Kodak Company; Rapp Collins Worldwide.

Beckman, Kristen. Copy editor, *RCR Wireless News,* Denver, CO. **Essays:** Ericsson, Inc.; Nokia Corporation.

Berman, Margo. Associate Professor, Department of Public Relations and Advertising, School of Journalism and Mass Communication, Florida International University, North Miami. Creator of tactikPAK, a patented audiocassette learning system covering such disciplines as marketing, creativity, design, presentation, promotion, and public relations. Contributor to *Journal of Advertising*

Education (1997, 2000), *American Society of Business and Behavioral Sciences* (1998), and *Business Research Yearbook* (1998). **Essays:** Music and Jingles; Typography.

Bernt, Joseph P. Professor, Journalism, Ohio University, Athens. Author of *The History of Magazine Publishing Companies in the 20th Century* (forthcoming). Coeditor with Marilyn Greenwald of *The Big Chill: Investigative Reporting in the Current Media Environment* (2000). Contributor to *Newspaper Research Journal* (1991, 2000), *History of the Mass Media in the United States* (1998), edited by Margaret A. Blanchard, and *Journalism and Mass Communication Quarterly* (1999–2001). **Essay:** Ballyhoo Magazine.

Bjone, Linda. Graduate student, Medill School of Journalism, Northwestern University, Evanston, IL. **Essays:** Burger King Corporation; Seven Up.

Blankenhorn, Dana. Editor, a-clue.com, Atlanta, GA. Author of *Bulletin Board System for Business* (1991) and *Web Commerce: Building a Digital Bussiness* (1998). **Essays:** America Online, Inc.; Computers.

Bolen, William H. Business Alumni Professor, Department of Management and Marketing, Georgia Southern University, Statesboro. Author of *Contemporary Retailing* (1978, 1982, 1988) and *Advertising* (1981, 1984). Contributor to *World Book Encyclopedia*, *Journal of Advertising Research*, and *American Business Review*. Member of editorial board for *Journal of Consumer Marketing* (1982–) and *Journal of Services Marketing* (1987–). **Essay:** Newspapers.

Bowman, Nancy. Teacher, History Department, The Bishop's School, La Jolla, CA. Contributor to *Women of the Commonwealth: Work, Family, and Social Change in 19th-Century Massachusetts* (1996), edited by Susan Porter, and *Beauty and Business: Commerce, Gender, and Culture* (2000), edited by Philip Scranton. **Essays:** American Tobacco Company; Liggett & Myers Tobacco Company; Philip Morris Companies; R.J. Reynolds Tobacco Company.

Brailsford, Ian. Department of History, University of Auckland, New Zealand. Contributor to *International Journal of Advertising* (1998) and *Australasian Journal of American Studies* (1999). **Essay:** Youth Market.

Brasel, S. Adam. Ph.D. candidate, Graduate School of Business, Stanford University, Stanford, CA. Contributor to *Journal of Family and Consumer Sciences* (2000). **Essay:** Vegemite.

Bratten, L. Clare. Ph.D. candidate, Department of Communication Arts, University of Wisconsin, Madison. Contributor to *Children's Literature Association Quarterly* (1997) and *Small Screens, Big Visions: Television in the 1950s* (2001), edited by Janet Thumim. **Essays:** Feminine Hygiene and Intimacy Products; Microsoft Corporation.

Brikell, Pia Grahn. Freelance journalist, Stockholm, Sweden. **Essay:** Nordic Countries.

Brioschi, Edoardo T. Professor, Institute of Business Economics, Catholic University of the Sacred Heart, Milan, Italy. Author of *Introduction to Advertising* (1971), *Advertising and Sales Promotion Policies* (1980), and *Advertising Economics and Technique*, 2 vols. (1984, 1985). Editor of *Business Communications in the Nineties* (1990), *Bank Communications: Strategies and Techniques* (1996), and *The Effectiveness of Communication: Profiles and Experiences in an International Environment* (1996). Contributor to *Comunicazioni sociali* (1981), *Problemi di gestione dell' impresa* (1986, 1997), *Giornale di marketing* (1995), *Handbook of Bank Marketing* (1995), edited by Walter G. Scott, *Aggiornamenti sociali* (1998), and *Working across Cultures* (1998), edited by A. Löhr and H. Steinmann. Member of editorial advisory board for *Comunicazioni sociali* (1981–), *Giornale di marketing* (1994–96), and *Problemi di gestione dell' impresa* (1996–). **Essays:** Barilla Pasta; Fiat Panda; Italy; Pirella Göttsche Lowe; Armando Testa.

Brookman, Faye. Freelance journalist, Skillman, NJ. Contributor to *Crain's New York Business*, *Drug Store News*, *Stores Magazine*, and *Women's Wear Daily*. **Essays:** Deutsch, Inc.; Hair Care Products; Nast, Condé; Perfume; Wal-Mart Stores, Inc.

Broyles, Sheri J. Assistant Professor of Advertising, Department of Journalism, University of North Texas, Denton. Contributor to *Journalism and Mass Communication Educator* (1996, 1998), *Southwestern Mass Communication Journal* (1999, 2001), *Advertising: Principles and Practice* (2000), and *Journal of Advertising Education* (2001). **Essay:** Tracy-Locke Company, Inc.

Bullington, Michael R. Assistant Archives Manager, Kraft Foods, Inc., Northfield, IL. **Essay:** Kraft Foods, Inc.

Bunish, Christine. Writer and editor, Cedar Grove, NJ. Contributor to *Business Marketing* (1996–99) and *Advertising Age* (1999–2000). **Essays:** Backer & Spielvogel, Inc.; Benton and Bowles, Inc.; Borden, Inc.; Goodby, Berlin & Silverstein; H.J. Heinz Company; Hertz Corporation; Nabisco, Inc.

Burgoon, Michael. **Essay:** Mass Communications Theory.

Burns, Neal M. Professor, Department of Advertising, University of Texas, Austin. Coeditor of *Unusual Environments and Human Behavior* (1963). Member of editorial board for *Journal of Interactive Advertising* (2000–). **Essay:** Modernity.

Burton, Rick. Director, James H. Warsaw Sports Marketing Center, University of Oregon, Eugene. Coeditor of *When Ads Work: New Proof that Advertising Triggers Sales* (1995) by John Philip Jones. Contributor to *The Advertising Business* (1999), edited by John Philip Jones, and *International Journal of Sports Marketing and Sponsorship* (2001). Member of editorial board for *Marketing Management* (2001). **Essays:** Nike, Inc.; Sports.

Cappo, Joe (Adviser). Senior Vice President–International, Crain Communications, Inc., Chicago, IL. Author of *FutureScope: Success Strategies for the 1990s and Beyond* (1990). Contributor to *Advertising Age* (1990–). Publisher of *Advertising Age* (1989–92). President of the International Advertising Association

(1998–2000). Advertising columnist for the *Chicago Daily News* (1969–78).

Cardona, Mercedes M. Financial Editor, *Advertising Age*, New York, NY. **Essays:** Fashion and Apparel; Intimate Apparel.

Carmichael, Matthew. Freelance writer and photographer, Chicago, IL. Founder of rocknroll.net. **Essay:** Apple Computer.

Cassada, Megan. Freelance writer, Corpus Christi, TX. **Essays:** Alka-Seltzer; D.L. Blair, Inc.; CKS Group; Coffee; Doremus & Company; Freeman, Cliff; IBM Corporation; Military Advertising.

Catanese, Lynn Ann. Archivist, Manuscripts and Archives Department, Hagley Museum and Library, Wilmington, DE. Author of *Guide to Records of the Court of Common Pleas, Chester County, Pennsylvania, 1681–1900* (1987) and *Women's History: A Guide to Sources at Hagley Museum and Library* (1997). **Essay:** Avon Products, Inc.

Chan, Kara. Department of Communication Studies, Hong Kong Baptist University, China. Contributor to *International Journal of Advertising* (1995–2000). **Essay:** Kowloon-Canton Railway Corporation.

Chapman, Roger. Ph.D candidate, American Culture Studies Program, Bowling Green State University, OH. Author of *It Started with Doctors on Horseback* (2001). Coeditor of *Northwest Ohio Quarterly* (1999–2000). Contributor to *Columbia Journal of American Studies* (2001). **Essay:** Propaganda.

Chura, Hillary. Reporter, *Advertising Age*, Boston, MA. **Essay:** Miller Brewing Company.

Clark, Claudia. Assistant Professor, School of Management, University of Alaska, Fairbanks. **Essay:** House Agency.

Clark, Eric. Author and journalist. Author of *The Want Makers* (1989). Writer and commentator on advertising and marketing in various newspapers and magazines throughout the world. Adviser to graduates and groups of new professionals in former Eastern bloc countries on Western marketing practices. **Essays:** Dichter, Ernest; Reeves, Rosser.

Clark, Ken. Vice President, Business Development, Yellow Pages Integrated Media Association, Berkeley Heights, NJ. **Essay:** Yellow Pages.

Clark, Philip B. MBA candidate, Fordham University, New York, NY. Formerly Senior Reporter, *BtoB Magazine*, Crain Communications, Inc., New York, NY. Managing Editor of *Institutional Investor* (1996–99). Contributor to *Wired Magazine* (1999). **Essay:** Insurance.

Clark, Randall. Visiting Professor, Division of Electric Media and Film, Southern Methodist University, Dallas, TX. Author of *At a Theatre or Drive-In Near You* (1995). Contributor to *Cineaction* (2000). Editor of *Dictionary of Literary Biography: American Screenwriters, Second Series* (1986). **Essay:** Campbell Soup Company.

Clover, Steve. Advertising Coordinator, Allied Advertising, Philadelphia, PA. Formerly Special Projects Researcher, *Advertising Age*. **Essays:** Animation; Cadbury; Polaroid.

Cooper, Ann. Freelance writer, London, England. Contributor to *London Sunday Times* (1982), *Campaign* (1983–85), *LCB Radio* (1983), *Scotland on Sunday* (1983), *The Scotsman* (1983), and *Media World* (1984). Media Editor of *Marketing* (1979–82), Creative Editor of *Adweek* (1992–96), and Contributing Editor to *Owe Magazine* (1997–). **Essays:** Director, Commercials; Production: Commercials.

Cooper, Caryl A. Advertising and Public Relations Department, University of Alabama, Tuscaloosa. Contributor to *Media Management Review* (1997), *The Age of Mass Communication* (1998), edited by William David Sloan, *The Western Journal of Black Studies* (1999), and *The Press and Race: Mississippi Journalists Confront the Movement* (2001), edited by David R. Davies. **Essay:** Audit Bureau of Circulations.

Cote, Kevin. Emeritus Editor-in-Chief of *Zitty Magazine*, Berlin, Germany. Contributor to *Coca-Cola, Jazz and AFN: Berlin und die Amerikaner* (1995), edited by Tamara Domentat, and *Time Out Guide to Berlin* (2000), edited by Dave Rimmer. **Essay:** Michael Conrad & Leo Burnett.

Crawford, Anne-Marie. Europe Editor of *adageglobal*, Editor of *Media and Marketing Europe* (January 2000–July 2000). Contributor to *Campaign* (1995–97). **Essay:** Pouzilhac, Alain de.

Cunningham, Anne. Assistant Professor, Manship School of Mass Communication, Louisiana State University, Baton Rouge. Contributor to *Journal of Mass Media Ethics* (1999), *Journal of Current Issues and Research in Advertising* (2000), and *Religion and Popular Culture: Studies on the Interaction of Worldviews* (2001), edited by Daniel A. Stout and Judith M. Buddenbaum. **Essays:** Saatchi, Charles and Maurice; Schweppes.

Cunningham, Peggy. Associate Professor, Marketing, Queen's University, Kingston, Ontario, Canada. Coauthor with Philip Kotler and Gary Armstrong of *Principles of Marketing*, 3rd, 4th, and 5th Canadian editions (1997, 1999, 2001). Coauthor with Philip Kotler and Ron Turner of *Marketing Management*, 10th Canadian edition (July 2000). Contributor to *Journal of the Academy of Marketing Science* (1995, 1999, 2000) and *Journal of International Marketing* (1997). **Essays:** Air Canada; Canadian Tourism Commission; Fruit of the Loom; Labatt Brewing Company; Molson, Inc.

Curtin, Patricia A. Associate Professor, School of Journalism and Mass Communication, University of North Carolina, Chapel Hill. Contributor to *Handbook of Public Relations, Communication Yearbook*, vol. 20, and *Journalism and Mass Communication Quarterly, Public Relations Review, Newspaper Research Journal, Journalism and Mass Communication Educator, American Journalism, Teaching Public Relations, Proceedings of the American Academy of Advertising* (1998–99), and *Proceedings of the Conference on Communication and Our Environment*. Member of editorial board for *Journal of Public Relations Research*. **Essay:** Environmental Movement.

Daniels, LeAnne. Associate Professor, W. Page Pitt School of Journalism and Mass Communications, Huntington, WV. Contributor to *Journalism Quarterly* (1992), *International Academy of Business Disciplines Business Research Yearbook* (1997), *Contemporary Media Issues* (1998), edited by David Sloan, *Historical Dictionary of Political Communication in the United States* (1999), edited by Guido H. Stempel III, and *Southwestern Mass Communication Journal* (1999). **Essay:** South America.

Danna, Sammy R. Full Professor, Department of Communication, Loyola University, Chicago, IL. Contributor to *Communication Arts Books* (1975), *Guide to United States Popular Culture* (2001), and *American Broadcasting*. **Essays:** Classified Advertising; Coca-Cola Company; McDonald's Corporation.

Dattner, Amy I.S. Freelance writer and editor, Chicago, IL. Associate Editor of Thomson Financial's *IPO Reporter* (1996–98) and *Mergers & Acquisitions Report* (1996–98). **Essays:** Carl Ally, Inc.; British Airways; Ford Motor Company; Grant Advertising, Inc.; Johnson & Johnson; Post-Keyes-Gardner, Inc.

Dattner, Derek. Freelance writer and editor, Chicago, IL. Associate Editor and Managing Editor of Institutional Investor's *Bank Investment Product News* (1995–97) and Managing Editor of Institutional Investor's *Fund Action* (1997–98). **Essays:** Carl Ally, Inc.; British Airways; Ford Motor Company; Grant Advertising, Inc.; Johnson & Johnson; Post-Keyes-Gardner, Inc.

Davis, Bruce. Special Projects Editor, *Rubber and Plastics News* and *Tire Business*, Akron, OH. Member of editorial board for *Rubber and Plastics News* (1980–2001) and *Tire Business* (1983–2001). **Essay:** Tires.

Davis, Judy Foster. Associate Professor, Marketing, Eastern Michigan University, Ypsilanti. Contributor to *Journal of Direct Marketing* (1996, 1997), *Mid-American Journal of Business* (1997), and *Advertising and the World Wide Web* (1999). **Essay:** Burrell Communications Group, Inc.

Davis, Wendy. Reporter, *Advertising Age*, New York, NY. **Essays:** Bcom3 Group; Cordiant Communications Group; WPP Group.

DeLinda, Destiny. Freelance writer, Louisville, KY. **Essay:** Bristol-Myers Squibb Company.

Dietz, Nancy. Freelance writer, Ankeny, IA. Emeritus copy editor for Crain Communications, McGraw-Hill Company, and Meredith Corporation. **Essays:** Della Femina, Jerry; Freberg, Stan; Marschalk Company; McCaffrey and McCall, Inc.; Omnicom Group; Hal Riney & Partners, Inc.; Scali, McCabe, Sloves.

Dover, Caitlin. Author of *PRINT's Best Letterheads and Business Cards 6* (2000). Author of *PRINT's Best Logos and Symbols 6* (2000). Member of editorial board for *PRINT Magazine* (February 2000–). **Essay:** Illustration.

Drewniany, Bonnie. Director, Advertising and Public Relations Sequence, College of Journalism, University of South Carolina, Columbia. Coauthor with William Ryan of *Advertising to the Mature Market* (1990). Coauthor with A. Jerome Jewler of *Cre-*

ative Strategy in Advertising (1997, 2001). Contributor to *Images that Injure* (1996). **Essays:** Kirshenbaum Bond & Partners; Ohrbach's.

Duncombe, Stephen. Assistant Professor, Gallatin School, New York University. Author of *Notes from Underground: Zines and the Politics of Alternative Culture* (1997). Editor of *Cultural Resistance: A Reader* (2002). **Essay:** Wieden & Kennedy, Inc.

Edwards, Larry (Adviser). Emeritus Managing Editor, *Advertising Age,* Chicago, IL. **Essays:** Campbell Mithun; Ketchum, MacLeod & Grove, Inc.; United States.

Egolf, Karen (Editor). Project Development Editor, *Advertising Age,* Chicago, IL. Editor of *Telephony Magazine* (1995–96) and *Advertising Age's Business Marketing* (1996–2000). **Essays:** Polykoff, Shirley; Resor, Helen Lansdowne; Robinson, Phyllis K.

Ellis, Sandra L. Associate Professor, Journalism, University of Wisconsin, River Falls. Contributor to *Encyclopedia of Television News* (1999) and *Historical Dictionary of American Radio* (1999). **Essays:** Firestone Tire & Rubber Company; Hallmark Cards, Inc.

Endicott, Craig. DataCenter Editor, *Advertising Age,* Chicago, IL. **Essays:** Cunningham & Walsh; Holding Company; Xerox Corporation.

Engelhardt, Nancy. Ph.D. candidate, Department of Communication, University of Southern Mississippi, Hattiesburg. **Essays:** Mediamark Research, Inc.; Museums and Archives.

Erevelles, Sunil. Assistant Professor of Marketing, University of California, Riverside. Contributor to *Journal of Business Research* (1993, 1998, 2000), *Journal of Consumer Research* (1994), *Journal of Marketing Management* (1998, 2000), *Journal of Database Marketing* (1999), *Journal of International Consumer Marketing* (1999), and *The Use of GIS in Marketing* (1998). Editor of *Journal of Business Research*, Special Issue. **Essay:** Logo.

Farnall, Olan. Assistant Professor, Department of Communication, California State University, Fullerton. Coeditor of *Disabilities Studies Quarterly* (2001). Contributor to *Journalism and Mass Communication Quarterly* (1999). **Essay:** C.F. Hathaway Shirt Company.

Fikri, Hanzada. Lecturer, Journalism and Mass Communication Department, American University, Cairo, Egypt. Worked for 16 years in the international media covering the Middle East for ABC News, United Press International, *The Times* (London), and *U.S. News & World Report.* **Essay:** Middle East.

Fisher, James. Theater Department, Wabash College, Crawfordsville, IN. **Essay:** Blacklisting.

Fitzgerald, Kate. Business journalist, Scottsdale, AZ. Contributor to *Advertising Age* (1988–). **Essays:** Integrated Marketing; Sears, Roebuck & Company.

Fonseca, Vanessa. Assistant Professor, Department of Communications, College of Social Sciences, University of Costa Rica, San Pedro de Montes de Oca, San Jose. Coauthor of *Agustin Lara, Poeta del Modernismo* (forthcoming). Contributor to *Revista de Ciencias Sociales: Universidad de Costa Rica* (1992–98), *Revista Reflexiones: Facultad de Ciencias Sociales: Universidad de Costa Rica* (1994–97), and *Identidades y producciones culturales en America Latina* (1996). **Essay:** Modernity.

Fox, Stephen (Adviser). Historian, Boston, MA. Author of *John Muir and His Legacy* (1981) and *The Mirror Makers: A History of American Advertising and Its Creators* (1984). Contributor to *Civilization* (1996) and *Smithsonian* (1996, 2000).

Freeman, Laurie. Freelance business writer, Edina, MN. Contributor to *Advertising Age, Business Week, BtoB, Electronic Media, License,* and *Marketing News.* **Essays:** Association of National Advertisers, Inc.; Beers, Charlotte; Interpublic Group of Companies; Lawrence, Mary Wells; Lazarus, Rochelle ("Shelly"); McCann-Erickson Worldwide Advertising; Trahey, Jane.

Fries, Gary R. (Adviser). President and Chief Executive Officer, Radio Advertising Bureau, New York, NY.

Fullerton, Jami A. School of Journalism and Broadcasting, Oklahoma State University, Stillwater. **Essays:** Coupon; Retail Advertising.

Gartrell, Ellen (Adviser). Director, Hartman Center for Sales, Advertising, and Marketing, Duke University, Durham, NC.

Goetzl, David. Reporter, *Advertising Age,* New York, NY. **Essays:** Pfizer, Inc.; Pharmaceuticals.

Goldsborough, Robert (Adviser). Special Projects Director, *Advertising Age,* Chicago, IL. **Essays:** Avis Rent A Car, Inc.; Crain, G.D., Jr.; General Foods Corporation; Grocery and Supermarket; Hearst, William Randolph; S.C. Johnson & Son, Inc.; Ross Roy, Inc.

Goldsmith, Elizabeth. Professor, Textile and Consumer Sciences, Florida State University, Tallahassee. Author of *Family Resource Management* (2000) and *Personal Finance* (2001). Member of editorial board for *Journal of Family and Consumer Sciences* (1993–96) and *Journal of Family and Economic Issues* (2001–03). **Essays:** Colgate-Palmolive Company; Good Housekeeping Seal.

Gordon, Ian. Associate Professor and Convenor, American Studies Program, Department of History, National University of Singapore. Author of *Comic Strips and Consumer Culture, 1890–1945* (1998). Editor of *Comics and Ideology* (2001). Contributor to *American Quarterly* (1991, 2000). Member of editorial board for *Australasian Journal of American Studies* (1998–). **Essays:** Batey Ads; Consumption, Culture of; Cultural Symbols; Singapore Airlines; War Bonds.

Gordon, Sandra (Adviser). Group Managing Director, AdVantage, Sandown, South Africa.

Gould, Stephen J. Full Professor, Department of Marketing, Baruch College, CUNY, New York, NY. Contributor to *Values, Lifestyles and Psychographics* (1997), edited by L.R. Kahle and L. Chiagouris, *Psychological Review* (1999), *The Elgar Companion to Consumer Research and Economic Psychology* (1999), edited by P.E. Earl and S. Kemp, and *Journal of Consumer Research* (1991, 1995). **Essay:** Quantitative/Qualitative Research.

Gudis, Catherine. Assistant Professor, Honors College, University of Oklahoma, Norman. Author of *The Road to Consumption: Automobility, Outdoor Advertising, and the American Cultural Landscape* (forthcoming). Coeditor with Elspeth Brown and Marina Moskowitz of *From Babbitt to Rabbit: Representations of Business Culture in America* (forthcoming). **Essay:** Burma-Shave.

Gulas, Charles S. Associate Professor, Department of Marketing, Wright State University, Dayton, OH. Contributor to *Journal of Advertising* (1992, 1995, 2000) and *Journal of Business Ethics* (1999). **Essay:** Humor.

Gunn, Donald (Adviser). Leo Burnett, Ltd., London, England.

Ha, Louisa. Research Director, the Gallup Organization. Author of *Essentials of Media Planning* (1991). Contributor to *Journal of Current Issues and Research in Advertising* (1995), *Journal of Advertising* (1996), *Journal of Advertising Research* (1996), *Journal of Broadcasting and Electronic Media* (1998), and *Journal of Advertising Education* (1999). **Essay:** Market Research.

Halliday, Jean. Detroit Bureau Chief, *Advertising Age,* Detroit, MI. **Essay:** Automobiles.

Hamilton, Carl. Writer, television host, and political commentator, Stockholm, Sweden. Author of *Absolut: Biography of a Bottle* (2002). **Essay:** Absolut Vodka.

Harris, Thomas L. Emeritus Adjunct Professor, Medill School of Journalism, Northwestern University, Evanston, IL. Author of *The Marketer's Guide to Public Relations* (1991) and *Value-Added Public Relations* (1998). Contributor to *Reputation Management* (1995–2000) and *Front-Line* (2000–01). Winner of the 2000 Gold Anvil Award. Named one of the 100 Most Influential Public Relations People of the 20th Century by *PR Week.* **Essay:** Public Relations.

Hawkins, Deborah. Freelance writer, Chicago, IL. Contributor to *Success 2000: Moving into the Millennium with Purpose, Power and Prosperity* (1997), *The Presenter's Journal* (1998), and *Angel First Aid: Rx for Miracles* (1999). **Essays:** Motorola, Inc.; Oil Companies; True North Communications, Inc.; Wade Advertising Agency; Weight-Loss Products and Plans; Wendy's International, Inc.

Hendriks, Alexandra. Ph.D. candidate, Department of Communication, University of Arizona, Tucson. Contributor to *Canadian Journal of Communication* (1999) and *Critical Studies in Media Communication* (2002). **Essay:** Beverages, Alcoholic.

Henthorn, Cynthia Lee. Visual culture historian, New York, NY. Contributor to *American Institute of Graphic Arts Journal* (1992), *The Writing on the Cloud: American Culture Confronts the Atomic Bomb* (1997), edited by Alison Scott and Chris Geist, *Knowledge and Society* (2000), and *PS1 Contemporary Art Center, Greater New York Exhibition* (2000). **Essay:** War, Impact on Advertising of.

Hilinski, Wayne. Senior Lecturer, Advertising and Public Relations, Penn State University, University Park, PA. **Essays:** Canada; Kellogg Company; MacLaren McCann Canada, Inc.

Hill, Julianne. Freelance writer/producer, Chicago, IL. Consulting editor/columnist for *Writers' Digest* (1999–). Contributor to *Advertising Age* and PBS, NPR, and A&E networks. **Essay:** Multinational Campaign.

Hilmes, Michele (Adviser). Professor, Department of Communication Arts, University of Wisconsin, Madison. Author of *Hollywood and Broadcasting: From Radio to Cable* (1990), *Radio Voices: American Broadcasting 1922–1952* (1997), and *Only Connect: A Cultural History of Broadcasting in the United States* (2001). Coeditor with Jason Loviglio of *Radio Reader: Essays in the Cultural History of Radio* (2001). Member of editorial board for *The Velvet Light Trap* (1995–) and *Television and New Media* (2000–). **Essays:** Radio; Soap Opera.

Hines, Randall. Associate Professor, Department of Communications, Susquehanna University, Selinsgrove, PA. Coeditor with Jerry Hilliard of *A History of Tennessee Newspapers* (1996), edited by Jack Mooney. Contributor to *Journalism and Mass Communication Quarterly* (1996), *Encyclopedia of Propaganda* (1998), and *Encyclopedia of the 1960s* (1998). Member of editorial board for *Journal of Ministry Marketing and Management* (1995–). **Essays:** Bull Durham; Religion, Advertising of.

Holmes, John H. Emeritus Professor, Department of Marketing, Bowling Green State University, OH. Editor of *Managing the Advertising Effort: Experience in Campaign Development* (1984, 1986). Contributor to *Journal of the Academy of Marketing Science* (1987) and *Journal of International Consumer Marketing* (1990). Coeditor of *International Advertising Association World Education Conference Proceedings* (1996, Kuala Lumpur, Malaysia; 1998, Zagreb, Croatia; 2000, Miami, FL). Director of Professional Development (1995–2001) and recipient of the Honorary Life Member Award (2001) of the International Advertising Association. **Essay:** International Advertising Association.

Hornery, Andrew. Reporter, Sydney, Australia. **Essays:** Australia and New Zealand; Campaign Palace; Colenso; Singleton, John.

Hoyt, Frederick B. Associate Professor, Department of Business Administration, Illinois Wesleyan University, Bloomington, IL. Editor of *Marketing Insights* (1997–2000). Contributor to *Journal of Midwest Marketing* (various). **Essay:** Bayer Bess Vanderwarker.

Huhmann, Bruce A. Assistant Professor, Department of Marketing, New Mexico State University, Las Cruces. Author of *Rhetoric and Advertising Readership* (Doctoral Dissertation, University of Alabama, 1999). Contributor to *Journal of Health Care Market-*

ing (1995), *Journal of Advertising* (1997), *Asia Pacific Journal of Management* (1999), and *Journal of Consumer Research* (2002). **Essay:** Testing Methods.

Hultquist, Clark. Assistant Professor, Department of History, University of Montevallo, Alabama. **Essays:** Bleustein-Blanchet, Marcel; Eurocom; Euro RSCG; France; Publicis Group.

Hunter, Kara. Graduate student, Mass Communication Department, California State University, Northridge. **Essay:** Saatchi & Saatchi Advertising.

Jacobs, Randy. Associate Professor, School of Communication, University of Hartford, West Hartford, CT. Contributor to *Journal of Media Economics* (1996), *Cable Marketing and Promotion* (1999), and *Communication Research Reports* (1999). **Essays:** Catalogs; Compton Advertising, Inc.; Intel Corporation; United Kingdom.

Johnston, Russell. Assistant Professor, Communications, Brock University, St. Catharines, Ontario. Author of *Selling Themselves* (2001). Contributor to *Canadian Historical Review* (1994) and *Historical Journal of Film, Radio, and Television* (1997). **Essay:** Cossette Communication-Marketing.

Jones, Heather. Freelance writer and journalist, Middlewich, Cheshire, England. **Essay:** John Smith's Bitter.

Junger, Richard. Professor, Departments of Communication and English, Western Michigan University, Kalamazoo. Author of *The Journalist as Reformer: Henry Demarest Lloyd and Wealth against Commonwealth* (1996). Contributor to *American Journalism* and *Howard Journal of Communication*. **Essays:** Cosmetics; E.I. Du Pont de Nemours & Company; Government Regulation; Maytag Corporation.

Katz, Helen. Vice President, Media Research Manager, Optimum Media/DDB Needham Worldwide, Chicago, IL. Author of *Towards a Normative Theory of Advertising Media Planning: A Case Study of the Cable Television Industry* (Ph.D. dissertation, University of Illinois at Urbana-Champaign, 1988) and *The Media Handbook* (1995). Coauthor with Kent M. Lancaster of *Strategic Media Planning* (1998) and with Bruce Vanden Bergh of *Advertising Principles: Choices, Challenges and Change* (1999). Contributor to *Journal of Current Issues and Research in Advertising* (1992), *Journal of Advertising Research* (1993), *Proceedings, ARF Interactive Media Research Day* (1995, 1996), and *Integrated Communication: Synergy of Persuasive Voices* (1995), edited by Esther Thorson and Jeri Moore. **Essay:** Events.

Keeler, J.D. Full Professor/Director of Doctoral Studies, College of Communication and the Arts, Regent University, Virginia Beach, VA. **Essays:** Lever Brothers Company/Unilever; Senior Citizens Market; Timex Corporation.

Keenan, Kevin L. Associate Professor, Department of Journalism and Mass Communication, the American University in Cairo, Egypt. Contributor to *Journalism and Mass Communication Quarterly* (1986–2001), *Handbook on Mass Media in the United*

States (1994), *Encyclopedia of Propaganda* (1997), and *International Journal of Advertising* (2000). **Essay:** Africa, Northern.

Kelly, Sean. Freelance journalist, London, England. **Essays:** Boase, Martin; Boase Massimi Pollit; Collett Dickenson Pearce; HHCL and Partners; Leagas Delaney Partnership, Ltd.; St. Luke's; Virgin.

Kern-Foxworth, Marilyn. Full Professor, Mass Media and Educational Consultant, Silver Spring, MD. Author of *Aunt Jemima, Uncle Ben and Rastus: Blacks in Advertising, Yesterday, Today and Tomorrow* (1994). Coeditor with Shirley Biagi of *Facing Difference: Race, Gender and Mass Media* (1997). Member of editorial board for *The Howard Journal of Communication* (1995–2001) and *Public Relations Research Journal* (1999–2001). First African-American in the nation to receive a Ph.D. with a concentration in advertising. First African-American female president of the Association for Education in Journalism and Mass Communication in its 88-year history. **Essays:** African-Americans: Representations in Advertising; Vince Cullers Advertising, Inc.; Minorities: Representations in Advertising; Women: Representations in Advertising.

Kerr, Gayle. M.S., Communication, Queensland University of Technology, Brisbane, Australia. **Essay:** Mojo Partners.

Kinney, Lance. Assistant Professor, Advertising and Public Relations, University of Alabama, Tuscaloosa. **Essay:** Product Placement.

Kishii, Tamotsu (Adviser). Tokai University, Japan.

Kissane, Sharon. President, Kissane Communications, Barrington, IL. **Essays:** General Motors Corporation; Ipana Toothpaste/Sal Hepatica.

Knoll, Barbara. Freelance writer, Shippensburg, PA. Author of *A Time to Dance* (1991), *Mommy, Are You Afraid of Monsters?* (1995), and *Mommy, Is God as Strong as Daddy?* (1995). **Essays:** Anacin; Calkins, Earnest Elmo; Caples, John; J. Stirling Getchell, Inc.; Gossage, Howard Luck; Marsteller, Inc.; Packard, Vance; Pytka, Joe; Wanamaker, John.

Koenderman, Tony. Editor-at-Large, *Financial Mail*, Johannesburg, South Africa. Author of *Sanctions: The Threat to South Africa* (1977) and *South African Industry* (1979). Editor of *AdFocus* (1991–2001). Contributor to *Financial Mail* (1990–2001). **Essays:** Africa, Sub-Saharan; Hunt Lascaris; Ogilvy & Mather Rightford.

Lawler, Edmund. Instructor, Department of Communication, DePaul University, Chicago, IL. Author of *Underdog Marketing* (1996) and *Lessons in Service from Charlie Trotter* (2001). **Essay:** Business-to-Business Advertising.

Lepkowska-White, Elzbieta. Assistant Professor, Department of Management and Business, Skidmore College, Saratoga Springs, NY. Contributor to *New Directions in Electronic Commerce* (2001), edited by Charles Steinfield. Contributor to *Journal of Marketing Management* (2000) and *Journal of Consumer Affairs* (2001). **Essay:** Argentina.

Levy, Sheree R. Curry. Business journalist, CurryMedia.com. Contributor to *A Guide to Jewish Student Leadership* (1988) and *Chicago: Rising from the Prairie* (2000), edited by Richard Cahan. Society of Professional Journalists Peter Lisagor Award for Exemplary Journalism recipient for best magazine feature, "Surviving Breast Cancer," *People Magazine* (1998). **Essay:** Luce, Henry R.

Li, Hairong. Assistant Professor, Department of Advertising, Michigan State University, East Lansing. Contributor to *Mass Media Effects across Cultures* (1992), edited by Felipe Korzenny, Stella Ting-Toomey, and Elizabeth Schiff, *Desert Storm and the Mass Media* (1993), edited Bradley S. Greenberg and Walter Gantz, *Journal of Direct Marketing* (1993), *International Journal of Public Opinion Research* (1994), *Journal of Current Issues and Research in Advertising* (1994), *Journalism and Mass Communication Quarterly* (1999), and *Journal of Interactive Marketing* (2001). Editor of *International Advertising Magazine* (1996–), *Modern Advertising Magazine* (1997–), and *Journal of Interactive Advertising* (1999–). **Essay:** Media.

Lincecum, Jerry B. Shoap Professor of English, Department of English, Austin College, Sherman, TX. Coeditor with Edward Hake Phillips of *Adventures of a Frontier Naturalist* (1994) and with Edward Hake Phillips and Peggy A. Redshaw of *Gideon Lincecum's Sword: Civil War Letters from the Texas Home Front* (2001). Contributor to *Texas Books in Review* (1990–) and *Notes in Modern Irish Literature* (1995–2001). **Essay:** Medicine Show.

Lippe, Dan. Managing Editor, *Advertising Age* Special Reports, Chicago, IL. **Essays:** Sarnoff, David; Standard Brands.

Liu, Yuping. Ph.D. candidate, Department of Marketing, Rutgers University, Newark, NJ. Editor of *Directory of Chinese Advertising Agencies* (1997). **Essay:** Ericsson (China) Company, Ltd.

Loeffler, Jaromir (Adviser). Marketing and Kommunikation, Zurich, Switzerland.

Luthy, Michael R. Associate Professor of Marketing, Department of Business Administration, Bellarmine University, Louisville, KY. Contributor to *Industrial Marketing Management* (2000) and *International Research in the Business Disciplines* (2001). **Essay:** Outdoor Advertising.

MacDonald, Scott. Research Coordinator, *Advertising Age,* Chicago, IL. **Essays:** Chrysler Corporation; Honda Motor Company; Packard Motor Car Company.

Macklin, M. Carole. Former Professor, College of Business Administration, University of Cincinnati, Ohio. Contributor to *Journal of Advertising Research* (1992), *Journal of Consumer Research* (1994, 1996), *Psychology and Marketing* (1994), *Marketing Letters* (1998). Editor of *Proceedings of the 1997 Conference of the American Academy of Advertising* (1997). Coeditor with Les Carlson of *Advertising to Children: Concepts and Controversies (1999)*. **Essay:** Children: Targets of Advertising.

Madden, Normandy. Asia Editor, *Advertising Age,* Hong Kong. **Essay:** Results Advertising.

Maloney, John C. (Adviser). John C. Maloney and Associates, Inc., Chicago, IL.

Manchanda, Rajesh V. Assistant Professor, Department of Marketing, University of Manitoba, Winnipeg, Canada. Contributor to *Psychology and Marketing* and *Journal of Consumer Research.* **Essays:** Ralston Purina Company; Schick.

Mandle, Mark. Librarian, Crain Communications, Inc., Chicago, IL. Contributor to *Chicago Jewish History* (1978–88) and *Synagogue History of K.A.M. Isaiah Israel 1847–1997.* **Essay:** American Home Products Corporation.

Martin, Brett. Senior Lecturer, Marketing, University of Auckland, New Zealand. Contributor to *Journal of Advertising Research* (2001) and *Journal of Consumer Marketing* (2001). **Essays:** MTV, Influence of; Recall.

Maxwell, Ann. Associate Professor, School of Journalism and Communication, University of Oregon, Eugene. Contributor to *American Academy of Advertising Conference Proceedings* (1991–99), *The Ad Men and Women* (1994), edited by Edd Applegate, *Advertising: The Business of Brands* (2000), edited by Jim Avery and Jim Marra, and *Newspaper Research Journal* (2001). **Essay:** Women: Careers in Advertising.

Mazzarella, William. Graduate student, Department of Anthropology, University of California, Berkeley. **Essays:** Cliché; Critics of Advertising.

McBride, Michael H. Full Professor, Department of Mass Communication, Southwest Texas State University, San Marcos, TX. Member of editorial board for *Journal of Consumer Marketing* (1993–2001) and *Journal of Services Marketing* (1994–2001). **Essay:** Europe, Eastern.

McCracken, Allison. Ph.D. candidate, Program in American Studies, University of Iowa, Iowa City. **Essay:** Feminism, Impact of.

McDonough, John (Editor). Freelance writer and cultural historian, Chicago, IL. Contributor to *The Wall Street Journal* (1986–), *Advertising Age* (1987–), *World War II: The Best of American Heritage* (1991), edited by Stephen W. Sears, *American Scholar* (1994), and *Oxford Companion to Jazz* (2001). Contributing Editor for *Down Beat Magazine* (1968–). Three-time Grammy Award nominee for best album notes; participated with author Benny Green in the Grammy-winning *Complete Ella Fitzgerald Song Books* (1995). **Essays:** Ammirati Puris Lintas; Archetype/Stereotype; Bates Worldwide; BBDO Worldwide, Inc.; Biow Company, Inc.; Blacklisting; Bozell Group; Burnett, Leo; Leo Burnett Company, Inc.; Cecil & Presbrey; Cramer-Krasselt; Dancer, Fitzgerald, Sample; DDB Worldwide, Inc.; Donahue & Coe, Inc.; Doner; Dorfsman, Louis; Draft Worldwide; Erwin, Wasey & Company; William Esty & Company, Inc.; Foote, Cone & Belding; Fuller & Smith & Ross, Inc.; Geyer, Cornell & Newell, Inc.; Hill, Holliday, Connors, Cosmopulos, Inc.; History: 1930s; History: 1940s; Kenyon & Eckhardt, Inc.; Lasker, Albert D.; Lintas:

Worldwide; Lord & Thomas; Lord, Geller, Federico, Einstein, Inc.; Maxon, Inc.; Media Agency; Mediamark Research, Inc.; Motion Pictures, Television, and Literature, Representations of Advertising in; Needham, Harper & Steers Advertising, Inc.; Ogilvy, David; Ogilvy & Mather Worldwide, Inc.; Package Design; Papert, Koenig, Lois, Inc.; PepsiCo, Inc.; Production: Programming; Ruthrauff & Ryan, Inc.; Tatham-Laird, Inc.; Jack Tinker & Partners; Volkswagen; Volvo; Warwick & Legler, Inc.; Wells, Rich, Greene, Inc.; Young & Rubicam, Inc.

Mendoza, Norma A. Assistant Professor, Department of Marketing and Transportation, Sam M. Walton College of Business, University of Arkansas, Fayetteville. Contributor to *Advances in Consumer Research* (1996) and *Journal of Applied Social Psychology* (2000). **Essay:** Corrective Advertising.

Mermigas, Diane. Editor-at-Large, *Electronic Media,* Chicago, IL. Contributor to *21st Century News Project (Radio and Television News Directors Association.)* (1998) and *Financial Manager* (1998–). **Essays:** Arledge, Roone; Murdoch, Rupert; Paley, William; Presenters; Telecommunications; J. Walter Thompson Company; Turner, Robert Edward ("Ted"); Weaver, Sylvester L. ("Pat"), Jr.; Yahoo!

Merskin, Debra. Associate Professor, School of Journalism and Communication, University of Oregon, Eugene. Guest editor of *Mass Media and Society* (2000). Contributor to *Growing Up Girls* (2000). Member of editorial board for *Mass Media and Society* (currently). **Essays:** History: 1920s; Studebaker.

Michels, Tara Anne. Assistant Professor, Department of Journalism and Communications, Elon College, Elon, NC. **Essay:** Minorities: Targets of Advertising.

Middlebrook, Sallie. Marketing Consultant, Houston, TX. **Essay:** Awards.

Minnick, Mimi. Archivist, Archives Center, National Museum of American History, Washington, D.C. **Essay:** N.W. Ayer & Son, Inc.

Mizuno, Yutaka. Senior Manager, Lifestyle Studies Department, Dentsu, Inc., Tokyo, Japan. Coauthor with Sadafumi Nishina and Hiroshi Tanaka of *Advertising Effectviness* (2001), edited by Sadafumi Nishina; coauthor with Ichiro Furukawa, Yuko Yamashita, and Tuyoshi Matsui of *Digital Life Revolution* (2001), edited by Ichiro Furukawa and the study group of Dentsu Digital Lifestyle. Trustee of Japan Academy of Advertising. Awarded "Best Article of the Year" by the Japanese Academy of Advertising (2000). **Essay:** Hakuhodo, Inc.

Montgomery, Sara Teasdale. Online Editor, *Advertising Age,* Chicago, IL. **Essay:** Norman, Craig & Kummel, Inc.

Moon, Young Sook. Associate Professor, Department of Advertising and Public Relations, Hanyang University, Seoul, South Korea. Contributor to *The Korean Journal of Advertising, Journalism Quarterly* (1990), *Journal of Public Policy and Marketing* (1991), *Advances in International Marketing* (1996), and *Journal of Advertising* (2000). Translator for *Integrated Marketing Com-*

munication (1993) and *Consumer Insight Workbook* (1999). **Essay:** South Korea.

Morello, John. Professor, Department of General Education, DeVry Institute of Technology, Addison, IL. Author of *Selling the President, 1920: Albert D. Lasker, Advertising, and the Election of Warren G. Harding* (2001). **Essay:** Schlitz Brewing Company.

Morris, Bourne. Full Professor, Reynolds School of Journalism, University of Nevada, Reno. Contributor to *Nevada Public Affairs Review* (1993) and *The Journal of the Association of Schools of Journalism and Mass Communication* (2001). **Essay:** Ethics.

Morrison, Deborah K. Associate Professor, Department of Advertising, University of Texas, Austin. Contributor to *American Academy of Advertising Conference Proceedings* (1993–1994, 1996), *Voices from the Industry* (1997), edited by Anne Hart, and *The Ad Men and Women: A Biographical Dictionary of Advertising* (1997), edited by Edd Applegate. **Essays:** Bernbach, William ("Bill"); Charren, Peggy.

Morrison, Margaret A. Assistant Professor, Department of Advertising, University of Tennessee, Knoxville. Contributor to *Journal of Advertising* (1997) and *Journal of Broadcasting and Electronic Media* (2001). **Essay:** Account Planning.

Mueller, Barbara. Full Professor, Department of Communication, San Diego State University, CA. Author of *International Advertising: Communicating across Cultures* (1996). Coauthor with Katherine Toland Frith of *Advertising and Societies* (2002). Contributor to *Journalism Quarterly* (1992) and *Journal of Advertising* (1996). **Essays:** Global Advertising; Russia and the Commonwealth of Independent States.

Mussey, Dagmar. *Advertising Age* correspondent, Düsseldorf, Germany. Contributor to *Advertising Age* and *Advertising Age Global*. Editor of *Ist die Werbung noch retten* (1989), by Howard Luck Gossage. **Essays:** Scholz & Friends; Springer & Jacoby.

Neff, Jack. Freelance journalist, Cincinnati, OH. Contributing editor for *Advertising Age* and contributor to various business and trade publications covering food and graphic design industries. **Essays:** Household Cleansers; Ivory Soap; Procter & Gamble Company.

Noel, Noel Mark. Associate Professor, Marketing Department, University of South Florida, Sarasota. Coauthor of *The PDMA Handbook of New Product Development* (1997), edited by Milton D. Rosenau. Contributor to *Psychology and Marketing* (1996) and *Design Management Journal* (2000). **Essay:** Planned Obsolescence.

O'Connor, William F. Professor, Department of Business, Asia University, Tokyo, Japan. Coauthor with Fumio Takemae of *Cover to Cover* (1989). Coeditor of *Kenkyusha's Dictionary of English Collocations* (1995). Contributor to *Human Communication Education*, vol. 2 (1998), and *St. James Encyclopedia of Popular Culture* (2000). **Essay:** Hill and Knowlton, Inc.

O'Dwyer, Gerard. Journalist and author, Stockholm Business School, Sweden, and University of Helsinki, Finland. Author of *The Meaning of Fenno-Soviet Relations* (1987). Editor of *NordBalt Investment Report* (1990–) and *NordBalt M&A Report* (1990–). **Essays:** Forsman & Bodenfors; Paradiset.

Ogden, Denise T. Ph.D. candidate, Marketing Department, Temple University, Philadelphia, PA. Coauthor with J.E. Finch and J.R. Ogden of *The Best Test Preparation for the CLEP Principles of Marketing* (1996). Contributor to *Journal of Food Products Marketing* (1993) and *Significant Marketing Contributions in the New Millennium (AMA Summer Conference Proceedings)* (2000). **Essays:** Census; Simmons Market Research Bureau.

Ogden, James R. Full Professor and Chair, Marketing Department, Kutztown University of Pennsylvania, Kutztown. Author of *The Essentials of Advertising* (1992, 1994) and *Developing a Creative and Innovative Integrated Marketing Communications Plan* (1998). Contributor to *Great Ideas for Teaching Marketing* (1994) and *American Business Review* (1998). **Essays:** Grey Advertising Agency, Inc.; Perrier.

Ogud, Atilla M. (Adviser). Publisher, *Marketing Turkiye Magazine*, AVC Marketing Publications, Istanbul, Turkey.

Ohlemeyer, Ken, Jr. Account Director, Glennon Company, St. Louis, MO. **Essay:** History: 1950s.

Ohmer, Susan. Assistant Professor, Department of American Studies, University of Notre Dame, Notre Dame, IN. Author of *George Gallup in Hollywood* (2002). Contributor to *The Velvet Light Trap* (1993) and *Identifying Hollywood's Audiences* (2000). Member of editorial board for *Cinema Journal* (1997–). **Essay:** Gallup Research.

Olson, Kathleen K. Assistant Professor, Department of Journalism and Communication, Lehigh University, Bethlehem, PA. **Essay:** Legal Issues.

O'Neil, Patrick. Ph.D. candidate, Park Fellow, School of Journalism and Mass Communication, University of North Carolina, Chapel Hill. **Essays:** Corporate Advertising; Financial Services; Hostile Takeover.

Orlik, Peter B. Professor and Chair, Department of Broadcast and Cinematic Arts, Central Michigan University, Mt. Pleasant. Author of *The Electronic Media: An Introduction to the Profession*, 2nd edition (1997), *Broadcast/Cable Copywriting*, 6th edition (1998) and *Electronic Media Criticism: Applied Perspectives*, 2nd edition (2001). Contributor to Fitzroy Dearborn *Encyclopedia of Television* (1997). Contributor to and member of editorial board for Fitzroy Dearborn *Encyclopedia of Radio* (2002). **Essay:** Vickers & Benson.

Otnes, Cele C. Associate Professor, Department of Business Administration, University of Illinois at Urbana-Champaign. Coauthor with Elizabeth Pleck of *The Cinderella Dream: The White Wedding in Contemporary Consumer Culture* (forthcoming), edited by Ron Grimes and Robbie David-Floyd. Coeditor with Richard F. Beltramini of *Gift Giving: A Research Anthology*

(1994). Contributor to *Journal of Consumer Research* (1993, 1997, 1999) and *Journal of Advertising* (1996, 1999). **Essays:** DDB Worldwide, Inc.; DeBeers Consolidated Mines, Inc.; Fallon Worldwide; Resor, Stanley B.

Pappas, Charles. Huntsville, AL. Writer for *Yahoo! Internet Life.* **Essay:** Clutter/Ad Ubiquity.

Pardun, Carol J. Associate Professor, School of Journalism and Mass Communication, University of North Carolina, Chapel Hill. Editor of *Mass Communication and Society* (2001–03). Member of editorial board for *Journal of Advertising Education* (2000–). **Essay:** General Electric Company.

Pashupati, Kartik. Assistant Professor, Department of Communication, Florida State University, Tallahassee. Contributor to *Advertising in Asia* (1996), edited by Katherine Toland Frith, and *Media Psychology* (forthcoming). Member of editorial board for *Journal of Interactive Advertising* (2000–). **Essays:** Advocacy Advertising; India.

Pendleton, Jennifer. Freelance journalist, Los Angeles, CA. Contributor to *Entertainment Weekly, Fortune, Fortune Small Business, Los Angeles Times, Variety,* and *Working Woman.* **Essay:** Motion Pictures.

Pérez-Latre, Francisco J. Full Professor, Department of Advertising, University of Navarra, School of Communication, Pamplona, Navarra, Spain. Author of *Centrales de Compra de Medios* (1995) and *Planificación y gestión de medios publicitarios* (2000). Contributor to *Media Ethics* (2000). Member of editorial board for *Comunicación y Sociedad* (2000). **Essay:** Spain.

Phillips, Barbara J. Associate Professor, Department of Management and Marketing, University of Saskatchewan, Saskatoon, Canada. Contributor to *Advertising to Children: Concepts and Controversies* (1999), edited by M. Carole Macklin and Les Carlson. Contributor to *Journal of Advertising Research* (1996), *Journal of Advertising* (1997, 2000), and *Journalism and Mass Communication Quarterly* (1999). **Essay:** Spokes-Character.

Podmolik, Mary Ellen. Freelance writer, Chicago, IL. **Essays:** Airlines, U.S.; Batteries; Beverages, Nonalcoholic; Heineken; Kimberly-Clark Corporation; Lowe, Frank; Oscar Mayer Foods Corporation; Quaker Oats Company; Wm. Wrigley Jr. Company.

Pokrywczynski, James V. Associate Professor, Department of Advertising and Public Relations, Marquette University, Milwaukee, WI. Contributor to *Advertising: Its Role in Modern Marketing* (1990, 1994), *Journal of Newspaper Research* (1997), and *Journal of Advertising Research* (2001). **Essays:** Campbell-Ewald; Cramer-Krasselt; Henderson Advertising, Inc.

Prince, Melvin. Associate Professor, Department of Marketing, Southern Connecticut State University, New Haven. Author of *Social Crisis and Deviance* (1969) and *Consumer Research for Management Decisions* (1982). Editor of *Journal of Business Research.* Contributor to *Journal of Advertising* (2000), *Journal of Advertising Research,* and *International Quarterly Journal of*

Marketing. Member of editorial board for *Journal of Marketing Research.* **Essay:** Mexico.

Qassim, Ali. News Editor, *adageglobal,* London, England. **Essays:** Agulla & Baccetti; Ratto Agency.

Quicke, Andrew. Full Professor, School of Cinema Television, Regent University, Virginia Beach, VA. Coauthor with Andrew Laszlo of *Every Frame a Rembrandt* (2000). Coauthor with Juliet Quicke of *Hidden Agendas: the Politics of Religious Broadcasting in Britain, 1987–1991.* Contributor to *Journal of Popular Film and Television* (1999) and *Journal of Film and Video* (2000). Winner of 6 CINE awards, 2 Academy of Television Arts awards, and another 22 prizes in international competitions. **Essay:** Gevalia Kaffe.

Raphael, Joel. Acting Director, Yellow Pages Research Institute, Berkeley Heights, NJ. **Essay:** Yellow Pages.

Raphaelson, Joel (Adviser). Former Senior Vice President, International Creative Services, Ogilvy & Mather, Chicago, IL. Coauthor with Kenneth Roman of *Writing that Works,* 3rd edition (2000). Editor of *The Unpublished David Ogilvy* (1987) and *Viewpoint* (1983–94). Contributor to *Harvard Business Review* (1983).

Raugust, Karen. Freelance writer, Minneapolis, MN. Author of *Merchandise Licensing in the Television Industry* (1995), *The Licensing Business Handbook* (1995, 1997, 1999), *International Licensing: A Status Report* (1996, 1998), *The EPM Fad Study* (1999), and *The EPM Licensing Benchmark Study* (2001). Contributor to *American Artist* (1996–), *Animation Magazine* (1996–), *E-Commerce Business* (1996–), *Educational Marketer* (1996–), *Publishers Weekly* (1996–), *Supermarket News* (1996–). Editor of *The Licensing Letter* (1990–96). **Essays:** ACNielsen Corporation; Collectibles; Design and Designers; FHV; General Mills; Netherlands, The; Pet Care Products; Pillsbury Company; Restaurants/Fast Food; Telemarketing: Overview; Warner-Lambert; Wunderman.

Ravalo, Bethel Ann. College of Journalism and Communications, University of Florida, Gainesville. Contributor to *Proceedings of the American Academy of Advertising* (1998). **Essays:** AT&T Corporation; Chesebrough-Pond's, Inc.

Reichert, Tom. Ph.D., Assistant Professor, Department of Advertising and Public Relations, University of Alabama, Tuscaloosa. Contributor to *Journal of Advertising* (2001). Member of editorial board for *Sexuality and Culture* (2000). **Essay:** Sex in Advertising.

Riedman, Patricia. Senior Editor, *Advertising Age,* Chicago, IL. **Essay:** Modem Media Poppe Tyson.

Robinson, Daniel J. Assistant Professor, Faculty of Information and Media Studies, University of Western Ontario, London, Ontario, Canada. Author of *The Measure of Democracy: Polling, Market Research, and Public Life, 1930–1945* (1999). **Essays:** Cockfield, Brown & Company, Ltd.; Seagram Company, Ltd.

Rogers, Stuart C. Clinical Professor, Marketing, Daniels College of Business, University of Denver, CO. Author of *Marketing Strat-*

egies, Tactics and Techniques: A Handbook for Practitioners (2001). Coauthor of *How to Market Your Accounting Services* (1994). Contributor to *Public Relations Quarterly* (1992–93) and *Journal of Business and Industrial Marketing* (1995). **Essay:** Subliminal Advertising.

Rose, Patricia B. Professor and Chair, Department of Advertising and Public Relations, Florida International University, North Miami. Contributor to *Journalism Educator* (with Brett Robbs, 2001) and *Public Relations Quarterly* (2002). Member of editorial board for *Journal of Advertising Education,* (1999–). **Essay:** Direct Marketing/Direct Mail.

Ross, Billy I. Distinguished Professor, Manship School of Mass Communication, Louisiana State University, Baton Rouge. Author of *Status of Advertising Education* (1989). Coauthor with Ralph L. Sellmeyer of *School Publications; The Business Side* (1989). Contributor to *Journalism/Mass Communication Journal* (2000) and *Journal of Advertising Education* (2001). **Essay:** Education.

Rotfeld, Herbert Jack. Professor, Department of Marketing, Auburn University, Alabama. Author of *Adventures in Misplaced Marketing* (2001). Editor of *Marketing Educator* (1996–97) and *Journal of Consumer Affairs* (2001–). Member of editorial board for *Journal of Consumer Marketing, Journal of Current Issues and Research in Advertising,* and *Health Marketing Quarterly.* **Essays:** Infomercial; Self-Regulation.

Roy, Abhijit. Assistant Professor, Department of Marketing, Sellinger School of Business, Loyola College in Maryland, Baltimore. Coeditor with Bart Macchiette of *Taking Sides: Clashing Views on Controversial Issues in Marketing* (August 2000). Contributor to *Journal of Direct Marketing* (1991) and *Journal of Services Marketing* (1992). **Essays:** American Advertising Federation; Targeting; Telemarketing: 800 Numbers; Telemarketing: 900 Numbers.

Rutherford, Paul. Full Professor, Department of History, University of Toronto, Ontario, Canada. Author of *The New Icons? The Art of Television Advertising* (1994) and *Endless Propaganda: The Advertising of Public Goods* (2000). **Essay:** Television.

Ryan, Michael. Special Reports Editor, *Advertising Age,* Chicago, IL. **Essay:** Political Advertising.

Rydholm, Ralph W. (Adviser). Former Chief Executive Officer, Euro RSCG Tatham Advertising, Chicago, IL.

Salomon, Alan. Journalist, Memphis, TN. Contributor to *Hotel and Motel Management* (1987–2001) and *Advertising Age* (1984–2001). **Essays:** Lorillard Tobacco Company; Luxury Goods; Miles Laboratories, Inc.; Toyota Motor Corporation; Toys and Games; Travel and Tourism.

Sapolsky, Barry S. Full Professor, Communication, Florida State University, Tallahassee. Member of editorial board for *Journal of Broadcasting and Electronic Media* (1992–). **Essay:** Product Placement.

Saunders, Dave. Author of *Professional Advertising Photography* (1988), *The World's Best Advertising Photography* (1994), *Shock in Advertising* (1996), *Humour in Advertising* (1997), and *Twentieth-Century Advertising* (1999). **Essays:** Bartle Bogle Hegarty; Hamlet Cigars.

Schultz, Don E. (Adviser). President, Agora, Inc., Evanston, IL.

Schumann, Mark. Research Coordinator, *Advertising Age,* Chicago, IL. **Essays:** Crest; Geritol; Sara Lee Corporation.

Schwarz, Angela. Assistant Professor, Department of History, Gerhard-Mercator-Universitaet Duisburg, Germany. Author of *Die Reise ins Dritte Reich: Britische Augenzeugen im nationalsozialistischen Deutschland (1933–39)* (1993) and *Der Schluessel zur modernen Welt: Wissenschaftspopularisierung in Grossbritannien und Deutschland* (1999). Contributor to *Journal of Contemporary History* (1993) and *Archiv fuer Kulturgeschichte* (1991, 2001). **Essay:** Germany.

Secrist, Mark Matthews. Associate Professor of Advertising, School of Communication, University of Idaho, Moscow. Contributor to *American Journalism* (1986) and *American Nurseryman* (1993). **Essays:** Demographics; Ratings.

Sego, Trina. Assistant Professor, Lally School of Management and Technology, Rensselaer Polytechnic Institute, Hartford, CT. **Essay:** Public Service Advertising.

Seymour, Susan. Associate Professor, Department of Communications and Journalism, Webster University, St. Louis, MO. **Essays:** Ad Council; Anheuser-Busch, Inc.; D'Arcy Advertising Company, Inc.; D'Arcy Masius Benton & Bowles.

Shaluta, Cliff. Associate Professor of Advertising, Western Kentucky University, Bowling Green. Author of *C-Store Combat* (1994). Editor with Courtland L. Bovée of *Advertising Excellence* (1995). **Essay:** Levi Strauss & Company.

Shaw, Eric H. Professor, Department of Marketing, Florida Atlantic University, Boca Raton. Author of *How to Write a Marketing Plan* (1993) and *Marketing to Win* (1997). Editor of *Journal of Macromarketing* (1991–) and *Selected Cases in Strategic Marketing* (1995). Coeditor of *Proceedings of the World Marketing Congress* (1989). Contributor to *Journal of the Academy of Marketing Science* (1990), *Marketing* (1993), edited by Stanley C. Hollander and Kathleen M. Rassuli, *Research in Marketing* (1994), edited by Ronald Fullerton, *Journal of Macromarketing* (1995), and *Journal of Marketing Theory and Practice* (1997). **Essays:** Cigarettes; A. Eicoff & Company.

Sher, Hanan. Senior Editor, *The Jerusalem Report,* Israel. **Essay:** Israel.

Shinkman, Ron. Writer, Los Angeles, CA. Author of the novel *Black Projects* (2000). Contributor to *Autoweek, Healthleaders, Los Angeles Business Journal,* and *NurseWeek.* **Essay:** Nissan Motor Company.

Siegel, Jason. Ph.D. candidate, Health Communication Research Office, University of Arizona, Tucson. Coauthor with Dan Weaver of *Breaking into Television* (1998). **Essay:** Mass Communications Theory.

Sivulka, Juliann (Adviser). Assistant Professor, College of Journalism and Mass Communications, University of South Carolina, Columbia. Author of *Soap, Sex, and Cigarettes: A Cultural History of Advertising in America* (1998) and *Stronger than Dirt: A Cultural History of Advertising Personal Hygiene in America, 1890–1940* (2001). Commentary on the History Channel's *Sell and Spin* (1999) and *American Classics* (2001). Contributor to *Journal of American Culture* and *Sex in Advertising* (2002). Fulbright Lecturer, University of Tokyo, Japan (2001–02), and Margaret Storrs Grierson Fellow at Smith College (2001). **Essays:** History: Pre–19th Century; History: 19th Century; History: 1900–1920.

Smith, Allen E. Associate Professor, Department of Marketing, Florida Atlantic University, Boca Raton. Coauthor with James MacLachlan, William Lazer, and Priscilla La Barbera of *Marketing 2000: Future Perspectives on Marketing* (1989) and with William Lazer, Priscilla La Barbera, and James MacLachlan of *Marketing 2000 and Beyond* (1990). Contributor to *Industrial Marketing Management* (1986) and *Journal of Business Research* (1988). **Essays:** Demonstration; Executional Variable; Magazine Advertising; Persuasion Theory; Promotions and Merchandising; Psychographics; Slogan; Trade Publication; Zip Code.

Smith, Tommy V. **Essays:** Brown & Williamson Tobacco Corporation; Carter's Little Liver Pills; Mars, Inc.

Smoot, Carrie. Freelance writer, Falls Church, VA. Contributor to *Encyclopedia of Major Marketing Campaigns* (1998–99). Her two-part series "Kids and Guns: Keeping Children Safe" (*Virginia Parent News,* April 2000) received 2001 Silver Award in reporting from Parenting Publications of America, Los Angeles, CA. **Essays:** American Red Cross; FedEx Corporation.

Snyder, Wallace S. (Adviser). President and Chief Executive Officer, American Advertising Federation, Washington, DC.

Speer, Lawrence J. Correspondent, *Advertising Age,* Paris, France. **Essays:** BDDP Group; Citroën; CLM/BBDO; Havas Advertising.

Spotts, Harlan E. Associate Professor of Marketing, Department of Marketing, Western New England College, Springfield, MA. Coeditor with H. Lee Meadow and Scott Smith of *Proceedings: Global Marketing Issues at the Turn of the Millennium* (2001). Coeditor with H. Lee Meadow of *Proceedings: Developments in Marketing Science,* vol. 23 (2000). Contributor to *Journal of Advertising Research* (1995) and *Journal of Marketing Education* (1998). **Essays:** Hard-Sell/Soft-Sell Advertising; Starch, Inc.

Stafford, Marla Royne. Associate Professor, Department of Marketing, University of North Texas, Denton. Coeditor of *Journal of Advertising,* Special Issue on Services Advertising (1997). Contributor to *Journal of Advertising* (1995, 1996, 1998), *Journal of Retailing* (1997). **Essay:** Services.

Stringer, Carolyn. Associate Professor, Department of Journalism, Western Kentucky University, Bowling Green. Contributor to *The Admen and Women,* edited by Edd Applegate (1994). **Essay:** Harper, Marion.

Tarpley, J. Douglas. Full Professor, Director of Washington Graduate Journalism Center, School of Journalism, Regent University, Northern Virginia, Alexandria. Contributor to *Journalism Quarterly* (1994), *Contemporary Media Issues* (1998), edited by David Sloan, and *Journalism and Mass Communicatin Quarterly* (July 2001). **Essays:** History: 1970s; History: 1980s.

Taylor, Catharine. Freelance writer, Pelham, NY. Contributor to *Advertising Age* (2001–02) and *Adweek* (1989–2000). **Essay:** Internet/World Wide Web.

Till, Brian D. Associate Professor, Marketing, Saint Louis University, MO. Contributor to *Journal of Advertising* (1998, 2000) and *Psychology and Marketing* (2000). **Essay:** Positioning.

Turow, Joseph (Adviser). Professor, Annenberg School for Communication, University of Pennsylvania, Philadelphia.

Twitchell, James B. Professor, Department of English, University of Florida, Gainesville. Author of *Adcult USA: The Triumph of Advertising in America* (1995) and *Twenty Ads that Shook the World: The Century's Most Groundbreaking Advertising* (2000). Contributor to *Wilson Quarterly* (1999) and *Advertising Age* (1999). **Essay:** Lambert Pharmaceutical.

Umberger, Daryl. Freelance writer, St. Petersburg, FL. Contributor to *Journal of Midwestern Folklore* (1997), *Encyclopedia of Popular Culture* (2000), and *Encyclopedia of American Studies* (2001). **Essay:** Hershey Foods Corporation.

Vagnoni, Anthony. Creative Editor, *Advertising Age,* New York, NY. **Essay:** French, Neil.

Verdera, Francisco. Lecturer, Department of Public Communication, University of Navarra, School of Communication, Pamplona, Navarra, Spain. Author of *Conflictos entre la Iglesia y el Estado en España: La revista "Ecclesia" entre 1941 y 1945* (1995). Contributor to *Del gacetero al profesional del periodismo* (1999), edited by Carlos Barrera del Barrio. General secretary (1991–97) and deputy director (1997–2000) of the journal *Comunicación y Sociedad.* **Essays:** Bravo Navalpotro, Julián; Casadevall Pedreño; Contrapunto.

Vinikas, Vincent. Professor, Department of History, University of Arkansas, Little Rock. Author of *Soft Soap Hard Sell: American Hygiene in an Age of Advertisement* (1992). Contributor to *Journal of Social History* (1989) and *Journal of Southern History* (1999). **Essay:** Personal Care Products.

Walley, Wayne. Freelance writer, Darien, IL. Contributor to *Australian Consolidated Press* (1978–85), *Advertising Age* (1985–91), *Electronic Media Magazine* (1991–96), and *The World Book Annual Science Supplement* (1991). Editor of *Global Telephony* (1996–2001). **Essay:** British Telecom.

Wang, Jian. Communications Specialist, McKinsey and Company, Shanghai, China. Author of *Foreign Advertising in China: Becoming Global and Becoming Local* (2000). **Essay:** China.

Wang, Linda. Ph.D. candidate, Murrow School of Communication, Washington State University. **Essays:** Negative Advertising.

Wansink, Brian. Professor, Department of Marketing and Department of Advertising, University of Illinois at Urbana-Champaign. Author of *Fifty Years from the Front: The American Soldier in World War II* (2002). Coauthor with Seymour Sudman of *Consumer Panels* (2002). Member of editorial board for *Journal of Marketing* (1996–) and *Journal of Advertising Research* (1992–). **Essays:** Point-of-Purchase Advertising; Vegemite.

Warlaumont, Hazel G. Associate Professor, Communications, California State University, Fullerton. Author of *Advertising in the '60s: Turncoats, Traditionalists, and Waste Makers in America's Turbulent Decade* (2000). Contributor to *Journal of Current Issues and Research in Advertising* (1995, 1998) and *Journalism and Mass Communication Quarterly* (1997). **Essay:** History: 1960s.

Webster, Nancy Coltun. Senior Editor, Special Reports/Multicultural Media and Marketing Editor, *Advertising Age*, Chicago, IL. **Essays:** Minorities: Employment in the Advertising Industry.

Weigert, Karen. Consultant, Chicago, IL. **Essay:** Volvo.

Weilbacher, William M. (Adviser). President, Bismark Corporation, Dennis, MA. Author of *Choosing and Working with your Advertising Agency* (1991), *Managing Agency Relationships* (1991), *Brand Marketing* (1993), and *Current Advertiser Practices in Compensating Their Advertising Agencies* (1995). Contributor to *Journal of Advertising Research* (1962), *Journal of Marketing* (1967), *Public Opinion Quarterly* (1970), *International Journal of Advertising* (1988), and *The Advertiser* (1995). **Essays:** Brand; Commission System; Fee System.

Weinberger, Marc G. Full Professor, University of Massachusetts, Amherst. Coauthor with Leland Campbell and Beth Brody of *Effective Radio Advertising*. Contributor to *Journal of Advertising* (1982, 1989, 1992, 1997) and *Journal of Marketing* (1990). Member of editorial board for *Journal of Advertising, Journal of Business Research, Journal of Marketing Education*, and *Marketing Intelligence and Planning*. **Essay:** Humor.

Wentz, Laurel. International Editor, *Advertising Age*, New York, NY. Formerly editor of *Ad Age International*. **Essay:** Abbott Mead Vickers/BBDO.

Whitaker-Penteado, J. Roberto. Freelance journalist and marketing/communications consultant, Rio de Janeiro, Brazil. He has been associated with the Brazilian School of Marketing and Advertising for 30 years. **Essays:** Almap/BBDO; DM9/DDB; DPZ; W/Brasil Publicidade.

Whitson, Jennifer. M.A. candidate, Medill School of Journalism, Northwestern University, Chicago, IL. **Essays:** Nestlé S.A.; Soap Products.

Wildermuth, Kurt. Associate Professor, School of Communication, Northern Arizona University, Flagstaff. **Essays:** Censorship of Advertisers; Popular Culture.

Wilkerson, Kristen. Ph.D. candidate, Advertising, University of Texas, Austin. **Essay:** Benetton.

Wiloch, Thomas. Freelance writer and editor, Canton, MI. **Essay:** Chiat/Day, Inc.

Wolburg, Joyce M. Assistant Professor, Department of Advertising and Public Relations, Marquette University, Milwaukee, WI. Contributor to *Journal of Advertising Research* (2001), *Journal of Communication* (2001), *Journal of Advertising, Journalism and Mass Communication Quarterly*, and *World Communication*. **Essays:** Censorship by Advertisers; Cultural Imperialism.

Wong, Wendy Siuyi. Assistant Professor, Professional and Technical Communication, SUNY Institute of Technology, Utica, NY. Author of *Advertising, Culture and Everyday Life I: Hong Kong Newspaper Advertisements, 1945–1970* (in Chinese) (1999). Contributor to *Civic Discourse, Civil Society and the Chinese Communities* (1999), *Journal of Design History* (2000), and *Mass Communication and Society* (2000). **Essay:** HongkongBank.

Woodard, James P. Ph.D. candidate, Department of History, Brown University, Providence, RI. **Essay:** Brazil.

Yamaki, Toshio. Professor of Advertising, Faculty of Communication Studies, Tokyo Keizai University, Japan. Author of *Advertising and the Media Industry* (1991), *Science of Advertising Creativity* (1991), *History of Japanese Advertising* (1992), *Comparison of World TVCM* (1994), and *The New Practical Advertising Strategy* (1995). Editor of *Advertising Note* (1955–84), *Modern Public Relations* (1979), *Human Science of Advertising* (1981), *Reading Advertising* (1983), *Nikkei Advertising Research Bulletin* (1984–97), and *Dictionary of Advertising Words* (1994). Contributor to *Brains* (1962–88), *Nikkei Advertising Research Bulletin* (1967–98), *Commercial Photo* (1971–76), *Advertising Science* (1976–98), *Measurement of Advertising Effects Handbook* (1984), *The Image Change Society* (1986), *IMIDAS (Innovative Multi-Information Dictionary, 1987–98)*, *Britannica International Chronicle* (Japanese Edition, 1989–94), and *International Commerce* (1996–97). **Essay:** Japan.

Yang, Kenneth C.C. Fellow, Information and Communications Management Program, National University of Singapore. Contributor to *Journal of Marketing Communications* (1997), *Cyberimperialism: Global Relations in the New Electronic Frontier* (2000), edited by Ebo Bosah, and *International Journal of Information, Communication, and Society* (2000). **Essays:** Asia, Southeast; Merger; Technology, Introduction of.

INDEX

INDEX

Page numbers in boldface indicate article titles; page numbers in *italics* indicate illustrations.